[Everyone's an Author]

Everyone's an Author
WITH READINGS
FIFTH EDITION

BEVERLY J. MOSS
THE OHIO STATE UNIVERSITY

ANDREA LUNSFORD
STANFORD UNIVERSITY

MICHAL BRODY

JESSICA ENOCH
UNIVERSITY OF MARYLAND

CAROLE CLARK PAPPER

with
ANNETTE VEE
UNIVERSITY OF PITTSBURGH

W. W. Norton & Company

W. W. NORTON & COMPANY has been independent since its founding in 1923, when William Warder Norton and Mary D. Herter Norton first published lectures delivered at the People's Institute, the adult education division of New York City's Cooper Union. The firm soon expanded its program beyond the Institute, publishing books by celebrated academics from America and abroad. By midcentury, the two major pillars of Norton's publishing program—trade books and college texts—were firmly established. In the 1950s, the Norton family transferred control of the company to its employees, and today—with a staff of five hundred and hundreds of trade, college, and professional titles published each year—W. W. Norton & Company stands as the largest and oldest publishing house owned wholly by its employees.

Copyright © 2026, 2023, 2021, 2020, 2017, 2013 by W. W. Norton & Company, Inc.

All rights reserved
Printed in Canada

Editor: Erica Wnek
Project Editor: Christine D'Antonio
Assistant Editor: Ailyn Del Rio
Managing Editors, College: Kim Yi and Carla Talmadge
Production Manager: Jane Searle
Media Editor: Joy Cranshaw
Senior Associate Media Editor: Jessica Awad
Media Editorial Assistant: Felicia Jarrin
Ebook Producer: Jay Barrett
Junior Media Producer: Daria Turner
Marketing Manager, Composition: Michele Dobbins
Design Director: Rubina Yeh
Designer: Jo Anne Metsch and Jennifer Montgomery
Director of College Permissions: Megan Schindel
Permissions Associate: Patricia Wong
Photo Editor: Ted Szczepanski
Photo Research: Fay Torresyap
Manuscript Editor: Jude Grant
Indexer: Eric Chernov
Composition: MPS Limited
Manufacturing: Transcontinental—Beauceville

Permission to use copyrighted material is included in the credits section of this book, which begins on p. 1019.

Library of Congress Control Number: 2025940103

ISBN: **978-1-324-10069-0** (pbk)

W. W. Norton & Company, Inc., 500 Fifth Avenue, New York, NY 10110
   wwnorton.com
W. W. Norton & Company Ltd., 15 Carlisle Street, London W1D 3BS

1 2 3 4 5 6 7 8 9 0

For our students, authors all.

Preface

elcome to the Fifth Edition of *Everyone's an Author*! As always, this revision has been a labor of love, and like earlier editions, this one has been guided by our commitment to helping students recognize and take on their roles as authors—as rhetors who use a range of strategies and technologies to communicate with audiences near and far, face-to-face and online, about everything from music, TV, and fashion to politics, work, social issues, and more. And when we look around us, despite serious challenges and tumultuous times, we are happy to see so many students who are indeed practicing what it means to be an author: listening, thinking critically, and communicating—with passion and with ethics.

As we planned and wrote this new edition, we have looked to students as our guides. Specifically, we have worked to build on and around what our students bring into our classrooms: what they care about, what they can do, and what they already know. We see students as deeply engaged in varied and sophisticated ways of communicating. And in this Fifth Edition, as with previous editions, we strive to respect and acknowledge students' strengths, while expanding their communicative and rhetorical skills.

But we also know that our students face serious challenges today. Many are dealing with post-pandemic isolation and disengagement. They're feeling the impact of deep political and social divisions. As they embark on their journeys in higher education, the value of a college education is being questioned, even though data show that those with a college degree will earn more over their lifetime than those without. And we, their teachers, find ourselves constantly having to justify our practices, our theories, our very existence.

While the challenges are many, our students are still in our writing classes, and they are resilient. They are engaged in the world around them. They read and they write—text messages, social media posts, rap and song lyrics, podcasts, opinion pieces, speeches. They testify at state and local hearings. They grapple with artificial intelligence. They question, they challenge, they inquire. Our students use their rhetorical skills as active participants in unique, interesting, and meaningful ways.

And we, as writing teachers, support our students' goals to be activists, influencers, lyricists, speakers, and writers. We, too, are resilient, as we navigate the political and social climates in which we teach, the new technologies our students are exploring, and, for some of us, the uncertainty about our positions. We do so by always keeping our students and their well-being in mind as we strive to adapt to new and varied teaching environments. We are here—for and with our students.

We have had these contexts front and center in our minds as we worked on the Fifth Edition. We've also had in mind our continued goal to make spaces for every student to see themselves in this book—and to make connections with fellow students, community members, and teachers through reading and writing. Once again, we assert that *everyone* is an author. Our author team celebrates the commitment of students and teachers to build ethical, caring, collaborative learning environments that welcome and respect the voices of the many.

To support students and writing teachers in building such a collaborative learning environment, this Fifth Edition includes three new chapters. The first, "**Collaborating with Others: Peer Review and Group Work**," invites students into a community of writers who support each other by providing feedback on each other's writing. Students will find practical suggestions for giving and getting helpful feedback during peer review, as well as a model of peer review comments on a student essay. Recognizing the value of collaborative work in many writing classes, this chapter also provides strategies on how to work effectively in small groups.

A second new chapter, "**Navigating AI as an Author**," written by writing and technology scholar/teacher Annette Vee, addresses the growing prominence of generative artificial intelligence (AI) in almost every aspect of today's society. What's a writing student to do? Our goal is to support teachers and students as they wade through massive amounts of information about generative AI and its evolving impact on our lives, including our classrooms. This chapter offers guidance for making good, rhetorical decisions about AI by weighing the benefits of its use and the drawbacks—biases, environmental concerns, and short-changing your own learning, for example. We also offer ideas for how to use AI ethically and responsibly, when it is permitted. Throughout, we advise students to consult with their instructor and to follow class policies on using AI (or not).

A third new chapter, "**Recognizing Arguments**," shows students that arguments are everywhere in their everyday lives and offers advice for spotting them and understanding how they work. Through vivid new examples, students are introduced to the ways that arguments are multimodal, purpose-driven, and contextual—all to help prepare for crafting their own effective positions.

But we've added more than new chapters to this edition. You will find **a new model student essay in every genre chapter**, ranging from a position essay on copyright laws in the hip-hop industry to a proposal for AI uses in the criminal justice system. These six new full student essays, along with additional new briefer student examples throughout, highlight the creative and ethical use of rhetoric employed by students from an assortment of colleges and universities.

And that's not all! **All model essays now include annotations** highlighting the author's rhetorical choices. With this change, we engage and support students in close reading and make the relationship between reading and writing even more visible. And the Norton Illumine Ebook includes **new assignable "Reflect & Write" prompts**, which encourage active reading and get students to practice low-stakes writing as they complete their assigned reading. Prompts help students connect what they're reading to their own lives and writing—all to help build up confidence. And "Check Your Understanding" questions following each embedded video hold students accountable for the multimodal content in the ebook as well.

To help make room for all that's new, we've shortened the part openers of each section and moved the chapter "Writing for a Public Audience" into the ebook, still available for easy reference.

So, you may well ask, with all these new chapters and features, what still remains? First and foremost is our commitment to *all* students, to making sure they see themselves in the pages of this book, to recognizing their unique strengths as users of language, and to making their voices and ideas heard. That's why we've retained the chapter "Language, Power, and Rhetoric," which invites students to think about how rhetorical choices about language may create a welcoming space for some while creating barriers for others. That chapter asks students to think deeply about and act on the power of language to bridge divides, to create community—something needed more than ever as this book goes to press.

Preface

As teachers, we have been privileged to work with generations of students, to engage technological changes to literacy and to rhetoric unimaginable to us when we entered the field, and to act and react critically in terms of the changing ways that information is created and distributed. We've continued to learn from and with students about how best to meet such challenges. As scholars, we've read widely in debates surrounding AI, social media, and threats to privacy, as well as in work that reveals how languages and images can be manipulated more easily than ever before and the ongoing effects of linguistic bias. As researchers, we have studied the changing scenes of writing with a mixture of consternation and excitement. And as always, our goal in writing this book has been to take some of the best ideas animating the field of writing and rhetoric and make them accessible to and usable by students and teachers—and to invite *everyone* to become authors, whose words—spoken, written, digital—will help shape the world we live in for the better. Wishing you and your students all the best—and happy writing!

Highlights

- ***The genres students need to write:*** You'll find guidelines for writing arguments, narratives, analyses, reports, summary / responses, reviews, proposals, reflections, visual analysis, literacy narratives, profiles, and literature reviews. Chapter 39, "Composing and Remixing across Media," gives students advice for transforming writing into a new genre or making use of multiple modes.

- ***The power of rhetoric:*** From Chapter 1, "Thinking Rhetorically," to Chapter 4, "Language, Power, and Rhetoric," to the many prompts throughout the book that help students think about their own rhetorical situations and choices, this book helps them understand and harness the power of rhetoric.

- ***Reflection:*** When students pause to examine their writing choices and processes, their knowledge and skills are more likely to transfer to new situations. Chapter 12, "Reflecting on Your Writing," helps students do just that, as do "Reflect" prompts throughout the book and the new assignable "Reflect & Write" prompts in the ebook.

- **Argument:** All facets of argument are covered in Chapter 14, "Arguing a Position"; Chapter 21, "Analyzing and Constructing Arguments"; Chapter 22, "Strategies for Supporting an Argument"; and **NEW** Chapter 20, "Recognizing Arguments"—which provides guidance on unpacking how the arguments that surround us work.

- **Research:** The challenge today's students face is making sense of massive amounts of information and using it effectively in support of their own arguments. Chapters 23 to 33 cover all stages of research, from finding and evaluating sources to citing and documenting them. Research advice has been updated for navigating AI tools, including guidance on composing AI acknowledgment statements and citing AI tools.

- **Easy to use:** Roadmaps for writing, menus, directories, color-coded documentation templates, and a glossary / index make the book easy to use—and understand. Animated videos in the ebook also reinforce challenging concepts and skills with models designed to support student learning in a variety of modalities.

- **Reading support:** Chapter 6, "Reading Rhetorically," instructs students on how to become engaged readers of all kinds of written and visual texts; Chapter 7, "Annotating, Summarizing, Responding," addresses strategies—with examples—for high-stakes reading; and Chapter 8, "Distinguishing Facts from Misinformation," gives advice on reading with a critical eye. **NEW** annotations on all model essays help students see critical reading strategies in action, and **NEW** "Reflect & Write" prompts in the ebook give them practice applying what they've learned.

- *Examples and readings students will relate to—many NEW:* From an argument for warning labels on social media platforms and a student review of a popular video game, to an analysis of *Barbie* and a *YouTube* explainer video of the *World Happiness Report*, we hope that all students will find examples across media that will make them smile—and inspire them to read and write and think.

Everyone's an Author is available in two versions, with and without an anthology of twenty-seven readings at the back, fifteen new to this edition. Readings are arranged alphabetically by author, with menus indexing the readings by genre and theme.

Resources

The Norton Illumine Ebook, available standalone and free with all new print copies of the text, includes assignable "Reflect & Write" activities that get students reading actively, thinking rhetorically, and practicing writing as they read. Short prompts encourage students to reflect on what they've read and apply it to their own writing while providing an opportunity for low-stakes practice to build confidence. And "Check Your Understanding" questions with rich answer-specific feedback hold them accountable for watching embedded videos on key topics. The active reading experience includes the ability to highlight, take notes, search, read offline, and more. Instructors can embed their own content into the text and promote student accountability through easy-to-use assignment tools in their learning management system (LMS).

InQuizitive for Writers activities get students thinking like writers, researchers, and editors through an interactive, low-stakes learning tool. After practicing with InQuizitive, students will be better prepared to start drafting their writing assignments, approach research projects with more focus and confidence, and edit their writing. The activities are adaptive, so students receive additional practice in the areas where they need more help, and explanatory feedback with links to *The Little Seagull Handbook* ebook offers advice precisely when it's needed. A robust activity report helps students identify challenging concepts and focus on where they can improve. The Fifth Edition features thoroughly revised activities with updated advice and many new examples, as well as a **NEW** activity on using inclusive language. InQuizitive for Writers is included with all new copies of *Everyone's an Author* and can be integrated directly into the LMS of most campuses.

Animated videos. Expanded for the Fifth Edition, a collection of thirty short, animated videos is embedded in the ebook and cross-referenced at relevant points in the print book. New topics include understanding academic arguments, responding to the views of others, using AI as a resource in your writing process, strategies for revision (with special attention to peer review), understanding plagiarism, and much more. All videos are followed by "Check Your Understanding" questions in the ebook, making them easily assignable.

Preface

Everyonesanauthor.tumblr.com hosts a dynamic collection of additional readings, providing a rich source of online media—including articles, speeches, advertisements, and more—for inspiration, analysis, and response. Readings are sortable by theme, genre, and medium, and each reading is accompanied by a headnote and prompts that guide students to evaluate, reflect, and develop arguments. You can also find a chapter-by-chapter menu of the online examples in this book by clicking "Links from the Book."

Quizzes on topics not covered in InQuizitive for Writers—within the broad categories of sentences, language, punctuation / mechanics, and paragraph editing—as well as pre- and post-diagnostics for InQuizitive, can be easily imported into your LMS.

Norton Teaching Tools. The Norton Teaching Tools site is your first stop when looking for creative, engaging resources to refresh your syllabus or design a new one. The Norton Teaching Tools site is searchable and can be filtered by chapter or by resource type, making it easy to find exactly what you need, download and customize it, and import it into your LMS course. Contents for the Fifth Edition include:

- A comprehensive guide to teaching first-year writing, with chapters on developing a syllabus, responding to student writing, teaching research and information literacy skills, and more

- Access to *The Norton Guide to Equity-Minded Teaching*, written by renowned teaching and learning experts, to help any instructor striving to ensure that all students—and, in particular, historically underserved students—have an equal chance for success

- A robust collection of sample writing assignments, peer review templates, and rubrics

- Thoroughly revised tips for teaching every chapter and reading in the book

- Class-activity *PowerPoint*s for most of the chapters in the book

- A collection of sample student essays organized by genre, rhetorical mode, and field, including some that are documented and annotated

Resources for your LMS. All of Norton's digital resources can be easily added to online, hybrid, or lecture courses right within your campus's existing LMS. Integration links allow for single sign-on, and graded activities can be configured to report to the LMS course gradebook.

Access all of the resources for *Everyone's an Author* at **digital.wwnorton.com/everyone5** and for *Everyone's an Author with Readings* at **digital.wwnorton.com/everyone5r**.

Acknowledgments

e are profoundly grateful to the many people who have helped bring *Everyone's an Author* into existence. In addition to the brilliant guidance of Marilyn Moller, we have been graced with the editorial skills and organizational acumen—not to mention the generosity and good humor—of our editor, Erica Wnek, who has herded this particular group of cats through a long and difficult process. We are similarly grateful to many others who contributed their talents to this book, especially Christine D'Antonio and Jane Searle, for all they did to produce this book (no small undertaking). Thanks as well to Patricia Wong for her work clearing the many text permissions and to Ted Szczepanski and Fay Torresyap for their work finding and clearing permissions for the many images. Last but certainly not least, we thank Ailyn Del Rio for undertaking countless tasks large and small with efficiency, conscientiousness, smarts, and good cheer.

Everyone's an Author is much more than a printed book, and we thank Joy Cranshaw for her guidance, inspiration, and encouragement leading the development of the many resources that contribute to this text. We're grateful to Felicia Jarrin, Jessica Awad, Jay Barrett, José Ortiz, Lindsey Heale, Allen Cooper, Sophia Purut, Daria Turner, and Alice Garrard for helping bring to life the ebook, InQuizitive, LMS resources, Norton Teaching Tools, companion website, and more.

The design of this book is something we are particularly proud of, and for that we offer our special thanks to several amazing designers. Stephen Doyle created the spectacular covers for this—and every—edition of our book. Carin Berger created the illuminated alphabet, made of text, that opens every part and chapter. Jo Anne Metsch and Jen Montgomery did the lovely interior design. And Debra Morton-Hoyt, Rubina Yeh, and Michael Wood oversaw the whole thing as well as adding their own elegant—and whimsical!—touches inside and out. Best thanks to all of them.

Special thanks also to the fabled Norton Travelers, who have worked tirelessly to spread the word to instructors across the country about what this text and resources can offer them. And a big thank-you to Michele Dobbins, Ryan Schwab, Heidi Balas, Emily Frankenberger, Mia Steinmetz, Sarah Purnell, Erin Brown, and Annie Stewart for helping us keep our eye on our audience: teachers and students at colleges where rhetorics of this kind are assigned. Finally, we are grateful to Julia Reidhead, Mike Wright, Ann Shin, Erik Fahlgren, and Steve Dunn, who have given their unwavering support to this project for more than a decade now. We are fortunate indeed to have had the talent and hard work of this distinguished Norton team.

We are also deeply grateful to a small group of teachers who helped us understand how the textbook works in their courses, who provided invaluable response to drafts of new chapters and materials, and who shaped improvements in the ebook: Christa Albrecht-Crane, Utah Valley University; Ashley Burchett, University of Wyoming; Karen Sutter Doheney, Northern Virginia Community College; Kimberly Harrison, Florida International University–Biscayne Bay Campus; Heather Hill, Northwest Missouri State University; Megan McIntyre, University of Arkansas; Keely Mohon-Doyle, Austin Peay State University; Seth Muller, Northern Arizona University–Flagstaff Campus; Shannon Stimpson, Brigham Young University–Idaho; Kristen Weinzapfel, North Central Texas College–Gainesville; and Lydia Wilkes, Auburn University.

We owe a special debt of gratitude to Professor Annette Vee, a leading scholar in computers and writing studies, who guided our author team in thinking about how we should approach generative AI in this new edition. Most importantly, she composed our new chapter, "Navigating AI as an Author." Her deep knowledge about all things AI were invaluable.

A larger and extremely helpful group of reviewers has also helped us more than we can say. In particular, we have depended on their good pedagogical sense and advice in revising every chapter of this book. Special thanks to Logan Bearden, Nova Southeastern University; Beth Boswell, University of Alabama in Huntsville; Erin Breaux, South Louisiana Community College; Megan Busch, Charleston Southern University; Cheryl Cardoza, Truckee Meadows Community College; Scott Challener, Hampton University; Jennifer Coenen, University of Florida–Gainesville Campus; Katheryn Crane, Eastern Washington University; Daryl Lynn Dance, Hampton University; Christina Davidson, University of Louisville; Eric d'Evegnée, Brigham Young University–Idaho; Karen Doheney, Northern Virginia Community College; Elizabeth Donley, Clark College; Africa Fine, Palm Beach

Acknowledgments [xvii]

State College; Paul Formisano, University of South Dakota; Charlene Marie Green, Collin County Community College District; Rima Gulshan, Northern Virginia Community College; Lyra Hilliard, University of Maryland; Andrea Holliger, Lone Star College–CyFair; Cody Hunter, University of Nevada, Reno; Derek Jones, Navarro College; Sara Kelm, University of Wisconsin–Madison; Keri Lamb, Chattanooga State Community College; Kerry J. Lane, Joliet Junior College; Alyson Muenzer Lynn, Middle Tennessee State University; Ruenchuan Ma, Utah Valley University; Anna Maheshwari, Schoolcraft College; Joanne Mallari, University of Nevada, Reno; Christine Martorana, Florida International University; Mary Elizabeth Rogers, Florida Gateway College; Jordan Sanderson, Mississippi Gulf Coast College; Kelly Ann Shea, Seton Hall University; Joshua Weiss, University of Maryland; Margo Williams, Cape Fear Community College; and Cheryl Windham, Jones County Junior College.

We'd also like to thank the instructors who have contributed to authoring the digital resources for *Everyone's an Author*, including Troy Appling, Florida Gateway College; Deborah Bertsch, Columbus State Community College; Megan Busch, Charleston Southern University; Paige Huskey, Clark State College; Katharine Ings, Manchester University; Tanya Rodrigue, Salem State University; Mary Elizabeth Rogers, Florida Gateway College; Christopher Smith, Columbus State Community College; Jason Snart, College of DuPage; and Kyle Stedman, Rockford University.

Collectively, we have taught for over 150 years: that's a lot of classes, a lot of students—and we are grateful for every single one of them. We owe some of the best moments of our lives to them, and in our most challenging moments—including some working on this edition—they have inspired us to carry on. In *Everyone's an Author*, we are particularly grateful to the student writers whose work speaks so eloquently in this text: Yazmin Carbajal, Sonoma State University; Maggie Carson, Dickinson College; Elena Castrence, Northern Virginia Community College; Katherine Evers, Framingham State University; Paloma Garcia, Santa Clara University; Glavee Glavee, San Diego State University; Kennedi L. Goode-Bey, North Carolina Agricultural and Technical State University; McCade Gowdy, Drake University; Sierra Jaquez, San Jose State University; Aleksander Lam, Chapman University; Angelina X. Ng, Harvard University; Kristin Perry, University of Maryland; Melissa Rubin, Hofstra University; Sydney Sallman, DePaul University; Tarika Sankar, University of Maryland; Katherine Spriggs, Stanford University; Emi Vaughan, Endicott College; Yuliya Vayner, Hunter College; and Shauna Vert. We'd also like to thank the 111 students who completed a survey about their experience using this book in the Spring of 2024; your responses about what motivates you, what challenges you, and what you recommend we do to make this book better for future writers inspired our work on this edition.

Each of us also has special debts of gratitude. Beverly Moss thanks her mother, Sarah Moss, for her love, encouragement, and confidence in her when her own wavered. In addition, she thanks her Ohio State students and Bread Loaf Teacher Network Fellows, who inspire her and teach her so much about teaching. She especially thanks Melissa Guadrón, who worked tirelessly to support her work on this edition. Beverly also wants to express gratitude to her colleagues in the Writing, Rhetoric, and Literacy program at Ohio State for their support. Finally, she thanks two of her own former English teachers, Dorothy Bratton and Jacqueline Royster, for the way they modeled excellence inside and outside the classroom.

Andrea Lunsford thanks her students and colleagues in the Program in Writing and Rhetoric at Stanford University and at the Bread Loaf School of English, along with sisters Ellen Ashdown and Liz Middleton; friends for life Marilyn Moller, Shirley Heath, Betty Bailey, Cheryl Glenn, Beverly Moss, Marvin Diogenes, Adam Banks, and William McCurdy; and beloved grand-nieces Audrey and Lila. Most especially, Andrea gives thanks for her late coauthor and friend of fifty years, Lisa Ede, whose presence she will always miss—and treasure.

Michal Brody would like to thank her partner, Mucuy Moó; may her memory be a blessing. She thanks her two wonderful families in the United States and Yucatán who so graciously support (and endure) her restless and crazy transnational life. Her conversations—both the actual and the imagined—with each and all of those loved ones provide the constant impetus to reach for deep understanding and clarity of expression. She is also grateful to her students in both countries, who continue to remind her every day that we are all teachers, all learners.

Jessica Enoch would like to thank her partner, Scott Wible, and her children, Jack, Nancy, and Teddy, for their support (and necessary distractions!). She offers her deepest appreciation for her administrative team at the University of Maryland's Academic Writing Program—Joshua Weiss, Lyra Hilliard, Erin Green, Lexi Walston, and Scott Eklund—who have helped her think through all the wonderful opportunities and complexities of teaching writing. Jess is also deeply grateful for the English 101 students at the University of Maryland who remind her of the great importance of what it means to be an author.

Acknowledgments

Carole Clark Papper would like to thank her husband, Bob, and wonderful children—Dana, Matt, Zack, and Kate—without whose loving support little would happen and nothing would matter. In addition, she is grateful for the inspiration and support over the years of teachers, colleagues, and students at Ohio State, Ball State, and Hofstra, but especially for Beverly Moss and Andrea Lunsford for launching her on this journey.

Everyone's an Author would not be in its Fifth Edition without two important contributors to the earlier editions, Keith Walters and Lisa Ede. Keith, we thank you for all that you've contributed. Lisa, we miss you terribly.

Finally, we thank those who have taught us—who first helped us learn to hold a pencil and print our names, who inspired a love of language and of reading and writing, who encouraged us to take chances in writing our lives as best we could, who prodded and pushed when we needed it, and who most of all set brilliant examples for us to follow. Indeed, where we have been able to succeed, it has been because we could stand on the shoulders of giants. We thank them all.

—Beverly J. Moss, Andrea Lunsford, Michal Brody,
Jessica Enoch, Carole Clark Papper

Contents

Preface   *vii*

Introduction: Is Everyone an Author?   *xxxiii*

PART I   The Need for Rhetoric and Writing   2

1   Thinking Rhetorically   4
First, Listen   7
Hear What Others Are Saying—and Think about Why   9
What Do You Think—and Why?   10
Do Your Homework   11
Give Credit   12
Be Imaginative   13
Put In Your Oar   14

2   Engaging Productively with Others   18
Get to Know People Different from You   19
Practice Empathy   21
Listen to People's Stories   23
Demonstrate Respect   24
Search for Common Ground   25
Examine Your Own Positions   27
Be Open to Challenging Conversations   28
Join the Conversation: Collaborate! Engage! Participate!   29

3 Rhetorical Situations *31*
   Purpose *34*
   Genre *34*
   Audience *35*
   Stance *36*
   Context *36*
   Language *37*
   Medium and Design *37*

4 Language, Power, and Rhetoric *39*
   How Does Language Relate to Power—and Privilege? *41*
   Look into Your Own Attitudes about Language *42*
   What Is Standardized English? *45*
   What's an Author to Do? *47*

5 Joining Academic Communities / Habits for Success in College *51*
   Why Participate? *52*
   Habits for Success *53*

   CHARACTERISTIC FEATURES *55*
   Use clear and recognizable patterns of organization / Mark logical relationships between ideas / State claims explicitly and provide suitable support / Present your ideas as a response to others / Express your ideas directly / Be aware of how genres and conventions vary across disciplines / Document sources using the appropriate citation style

PART II Reading Processes *62*

6 Reading Rhetorically *64*
   Thinking about Your Rhetorical Situation *66*
   Becoming an Active, Engaged Reader *67*
   Fast—and Slow—Reading *68*
   Unfamiliar or Difficult Texts *69*
   On-Screen and Off *70*
   Across Genres *74*
   Across Academic Disciplines *74*

Contents [xxiii]

7 Annotating, Summarizing, Responding 76
Annotating 77
Summarizing 83
Responding 86
Summary / Response Essays 90
YULIYA VAYNER, *The Higher Price of Buying Local* 93

8 Distinguishing Facts from Misinformation 97
Defining Facts and Misinformation 97
Think about Your Own Beliefs 100
Read Defensively—and Laterally—to Find the Good Stuff 101
Fact-Check Photos and Videos 104

PART III Writing Processes 108

9 Navigating the Writing Process / From Generating Ideas to Drafting and Revising 110
Generate Ideas 115
A ROADMAP 117
Approach Your Writing Pragmatically 123

10 Collaborating with Others / Peer Review and Group Work 124
What Collaboration Means for You as a Student 124
Collaborating in Small Groups 126
Collaborating through Peer Review 128
Collaborating at the Writing Center 131
A Sample Peer-Reviewed Essay 132

11 Navigating AI as an Author 137
What Is Generative AI? 138
Authorship, Agency, and AI 140
Questions to Consider before Using Generative AI 140
Some Ways AI Can Help 143
Proceed with Caution 148
The Future of AI 150

12 Reflecting on Your Writing 151
Reflecting as a Writer 153
Make Reflecting a Habit 155
A ROADMAP 157
ANNAYA BAYNES, *Becoming the Writer I Am* 164

PART IV Genres of Writing 168

13 Choosing Genres 170
What You Need to Know about Genres of Writing 170
Deciding Which Genres to Use 173

14 Arguing a Position / "This Is Where I Stand" 177
Across Academic Disciplines / Media / Cultures and Communities / Genres

CHARACTERISTIC FEATURES 181
An explicit position / A response to what others have said or done / Useful background information / A clear indication of why the topic matters / Good reasons and evidence / Attention to more than one point of view / An authoritative tone and stance / An appeal to readers' values

A ROADMAP 195

READINGS
RUSSEL HONORÉ, *Work Is a Blessing* 203
VIVEK H. MURTHY, *Social Media Platforms Need Warning Labels* 205
ALEKSANDER LAM, *Sampling or Stealing? Copyright Infringement and Hip-Hop* 209

15 Writing a Narrative / "Here's What Happened" 215
Across Academic Disciplines / Media / Cultures and Communities / Genres

CHARACTERISTIC FEATURES 221
A clearly identified event / A clearly described setting / Vivid, descriptive details / A consistent point of view / A clear point

LITERACY NARRATIVES 230
A well-told story / A firsthand account / An indication of the narrative's significance

A ROADMAP 232

READINGS
RAYA ELFADEL KHEIRBEK, *Healing the Doctor-Patient Relationship* 238
ANGELINA X. NG, *It'll Grow Back. It Always Does.* 244
PALOMA GARCIA, *First Day of School* 249

Contents

16 Writing Analytically / "Let's Take a Closer Look" 252

Across Academic Disciplines / Media / Cultures and Communities / Genres

CHARACTERISTIC FEATURES 257

A question that prompts a closer look / Some description of the subject / Evidence drawn from close examination of the subject / Insight gained from your analysis / Clear, precise language

VISUAL ANALYSIS 272

A description of the visual / Some contextual information / Attention to any words / Close analysis of the message / Insight into what the visual "says" / Precise language

A ROADMAP 276

READINGS

SYDNEY SALLMAN, *What Is the Invisible Problem with TikTok?* 286
SHAAN SACHDEV, *The Key to Beyoncé's Lasting Success* 292
MELISSA RUBIN, *Advertisements R Us* 297

17 Reporting Information / "Just the Facts" 303

Across Academic Disciplines / Media / Cultures and Communities / Genres

CHARACTERISTIC FEATURES 310

A topic carefully focused for a specific audience / Definitions of key terms / Trustworthy information / Effective organization and design / A confident, informative tone

PROFILES 316

A firsthand account / Detailed information about the subject / An interesting angle

A ROADMAP 320

READINGS

TATE RYAN-MOSLEY, *How Digital Beauty Filters Perpetuate Colorism* 327
MCCADE GOWDY, *The Future of the American City: Omaha's Hope* 334
BILL LAITNER, *Heart and Sole: Detroit Walks 21 Miles in Work Commute* 341

18 Writing a Review / "Two Thumbs Up" 348

Across Academic Disciplines / Media / Cultures and Communities / Genres

CHARACTERISTIC FEATURES 352

Relevant background information about the subject / Criteria for the evaluation / A well-supported evaluation / Attention to the audience's needs and expectations / An authoritative tone / Awareness of the ethics of reviewing

A ROADMAP *364*

READINGS

SWAPNA KRISHNA, Thirsty Suitors: *I Feel Seen by This Game* *370*
KENNEDI L. GOODE-BEY, Guts (spilled) *by Olivia Rodrigo: An Album for the Ages* *374*

19 Making a Proposal / "Here's What I Recommend" *378*

Across Academic Disciplines / Media / Cultures and Communities / Genres

CHARACTERISTIC FEATURES *381*

A precise description of the problem / A clear and compelling solution / Evidence that your solution will address the problem / Acknowledgment of other possible solutions / A statement of what your proposal will accomplish

PROJECT PROPOSALS *388*

An indication of your topic and focus / An explanation of why you're interested in the topic / A plan / A schedule

A ROADMAP *390*

READINGS

EMI VAUGHAN, *Uses for AI in the Criminal Justice System* *396*
JONATHAN HOLLOWAY, *To Unite America, Make People Work for It* *403*
DAVID PASINI, *The Economic Impact of Investing in Sports Franchises* *407*

PART V The Centrality of Argument *410*

20 Recognizing Arguments *412*

Arguments Are Multimodal *412*
Arguments Have a Purpose *413*
Arguments Are Contextual *415*

21 Analyzing and Constructing Arguments *419*

Where's the Argument Coming From? *421*
What's the Claim? *423*
What's at Stake? *427*
Means of Persuasion: Emotional, Ethical, and Logical Appeals *429*
Are There Any Problems with the Reasoning? Fallacies *441*

What about Other Perspectives? *444*
Ways of Structuring Arguments *447*
Classical / Toulmin / Rogerian / Invitational
Matters of Style *459*

22 Strategies for Supporting an Argument *461*
Analogy *461*
Cause / Effect *463*
Classification *465*
Comparison / Contrast *466*
Definition *469*
Description *471*
Examples *473*
Humor, Sarcasm, and Exaggeration *474*
Narration and Narrative Sequencing *475*
Problem / Solution *478*
Repetition, Reiteration, and Call and Response *479*
Signifying *482*

PART VI Research *484*

23 Starting Your Research / Joining the Conversation *486*
Find a Topic That Fascinates You *487*
Consider Your Rhetorical Situation *488*
Narrow Your Topic *489*
Do Some Background Research *491*
Articulate a Question Your Research Will Answer *491*
Plot Out a Working Thesis *493*
Establish a Schedule *493*

24 Finding Sources / Online and at the Library *495*
Starting with *Wikipedia* or Social Media *496*
What Kind of Sources Do You Need? *497*
Determining If a Source Is Scholarly *498*
Types of Sources—and Where to Find Them *501*
Research Sites: On the Internet, in the Library *505*
Running Searches, Narrowing Results *511*

25 Conducting Research in the Field 513
Observations *514*
Interviews *515*
Surveys and Questionnaires *518*

26 Keeping Track / Managing Information Overload 523
Keep Track of Your Sources *523*
Take Notes *524*
Maintain a Working Bibliography *526*

27 Evaluating Sources 528
Is the Source Credible and Useful? *529*
Practice Lateral Reading *529*
Fact-Check and Triangulate *531*
Check for Your Own Biases *532*
Consider Alternative Perspectives *532*
Read Your Sources with a Critical Eye *533*

28 Annotating a Bibliography 536
CHARACTERISTIC FEATURES *536*
Complete bibliographic information / A brief summary or description of each work / Evaluative comments / Some indication of how each source will inform your research / A consistent and concise presentation
MAGGIE CARSON, *Nonresistance in the Battle for Freedom* *538*

29 Synthesizing Ideas 541
Synthesizing the Ideas in Your Sources *542*
Moving from What Your Sources Say to What You Say *543*
Entering the Conversation You've Been Researching *545*

LITERATURE REVIEWS *547*
Survey of relevant research on a focused topic / Fair-minded synthesis and summary of the literature / An evaluation of the literature / Clear organization / Complete, accurate documentation
KRISTIN PERRY, *Exploring the Hardships and Stigma Students With Invisible Disabilities Face* *549*

30 Quoting, Paraphrasing, Summarizing 554
Deciding Whether to Quote, Paraphrase, or Summarize 555
Quoting 556
Paraphrasing 560
Summarizing 561
Incorporating Source Material 563
Incorporating Visual and Audio Sources 566

31 Giving Credit, Avoiding Plagiarism 568
Knowing What You Must Acknowledge 569
Fair Use and the Internet 571
Avoiding Plagiarism 571
Documenting Sources 575
What about Generative AI? 576

32 MLA Style 578
A Directory to MLA Style 578
In-Text Documentation 581
Notes 587
List of Works Cited 588
Formatting a Research Essay 617
WALTER PRZYBYLOWSKI, *Holding Up the Hollywood Stagecoach* 620

33 APA Style 635
A Directory to APA Style 635
In-Text Documentation 637
Notes 642
Reference List 643
Formatting a Research Essay 665
GABRIELA A. URIBE, "¿Por qué no sabes español?" 668

PART VII Style 686

34 What's Your Style? 688
Suitability and Correctness 689
Connecting with Audiences 692
Levels of Formality 694
Stance 695

Tone 697
Across Media 698
Across Disciplines 700
Thinking about Your Own Style 701

35 Mixing Languages and Dialects 703
Using Standardized English and Other Dialects 705
Connecting with Audiences 706
Providing Translation 707
Illustrating a Point 709
Drawing Attention 711
Quoting People Directly and Respectfully 711
Evoking a Particular Person, Place, or Community 712

36 How to Craft Powerful Sentences 715
Four Common Sentence Patterns 717
Ways of Emphasizing the Main Idea in a Sentence 722
Opening Sentences 725
Closing Sentences 727
Varying Your Sentences 729

37 Polishing and Editing Your Writing 734
Editing for Inclusion 736
Sentences 736
Pronouns 747
Verbs 756
Quotations 763
Commas 768
Words That Are Often Confused 773

PART VIII Design and Delivery 778

38 Designing What You Write 780
Thinking Rhetorically about Design 781
Choosing Typefaces and Fonts 784
Adding Headings 785
Using Color 786
Using Visuals 787
Putting It All Together 795
Getting Responses to Your Design 798

39 Composing and Remixing across Media   800
    Defining Multimodal Writing   800
    Considering Your Rhetorical Situation   802
    Illustrated Essays   804
    Websites   805
    Audio Essays and Podcasts   807
    Video Essays and Digital Storytelling   809
    Posters and Infographics   812
    Social Media Posts and Campaigns   815
    Remix Projects   817
    Managing Multimodal and Remix Projects   820

40 Making Presentations   822
    Across Disciplines   823
        HALLE EDWARDS, *The Rise of Female Heroes in Shoujo Manga*   825

    A ROADMAP   831

Readings   837

    *CÉSAR ALBARRÁN-TORRES, *Why Multilingual TV Is Good for Everyone*   838
    *KATE ARONOFF, *Carbon Offsets (Taylor's Version)*   843
    LINDA BARRY, *The Sanctuary of School*   849
    *CHRISTOPHER BASGIER, *AI Is Like Cake*   855
    ALISON BECHDEL, *Fun Home*   859
    *JENNA BLOOM, *I Quit Social Media in College. This Is How My Life Changed.*   870
    *DANIELLE K. BROWN, *Media Coverage of Campus Protests Focuses on Spectacle*   876
    DANA CANEDY, *The Talk: After Ferguson...*   883
    CHARLOTTE CLYMER, *They Called Me a Girl*   888
    *ADAM CLARK ESTES, *Your TV Is Watching You*   893
    *JEFF GAGE, *How Country Music Is Addressing the Opioid Crisis*   899
    GLAVEE GLAVEE, *Black Enough*   905
    ANNETTE GORDON-REED, *Origin Stories*   915
    *LING LING HUANG, *How I Escaped the Tyranny of the Prophets of Beauty*   923
    *KEVIN M. KEARNEY, *One Star*   927
    *ROBIN WALL KIMMERER, *Strawberries*   932
    *KEREN LANDMAN, *Why Are Whole-Body Deodorants Suddenly Everywhere?*   938

*New to the Fifth Edition

*KIESE LAYMON, *My Favorite Restaurant Served Gas* 946
JUDITH NEWMAN, *To Siri, with Love* 952
*DAN NOTT / SCOTT CAMBO, *Our Labor Built AI* 960
*MEGHAN O'GIEBLYN, *I Failed Two Captcha Tests. Am I Still Human?* 967
MIKE ROSE, *Blue-Collar Brilliance* 972
*ALLY SHWED, *Cracking the Color Code* 982
ZEYNEP TUFEKCI, *Why the Post Office Makes America Great* 989
JOSE ANTONIO VARGAS, *My Life as an Undocumented Immigrant* 993
TATÉ WALKER, *The (Native) American Dream* 1003
MISSY WATSON, *Contesting Standardized English* 1010

Credits *1019*

Author / Title Index *1027*

Glossary / Index *1040*

About the Authors *1074*

About the Alphabet *1076*

The Norton Writer's Prize *1079*

MLA and APA Directories *1080*

Bonus Ebook Chapters

digital.wwnorton.com/everyone5r

A. Writing and Rhetoric in the Workplace
B. Assembling a Portfolio
C. Publishing Your Writing
D. Writing for a Public Audience

*New to the Fifth Edition

INTRODUCTION

Is Everyone an Author?

E'VE CHOSEN A PROVOCATIVE TITLE for this book, so it's fair to ask if we've gotten it right, if everyone is an author. Let's take just a few examples that can help make the point:

- You post your review of *Wicked* on *Reddit* and are surprised by the lengthy debate it sparks in the comments.

- Parents of a second grader take a photo of their child's handwritten letter to her favorite gymnast and share it in the family group chat, where aunts and uncles share reactions.

- The CEO of United Airlines writes an open letter to customers explaining the decision to cancel several daily flights out of one of the busiest airports in the country. Published in a variety of online platforms, it reaches millions—and generates lots of response.

- A technical writer, using *ChatGPT* for assistance, drafts instructions for a new product their company is about to test with focus groups.

- Students in a college writing class interview a group of activist alumni, and their write-ups of those conversations become part of the university's archives, available to the public.

- A group of Navajo students submit their Kneel Down Bread recipe to *foodgawker* and are thrilled at the response from other cooks.

- You get your next assignment in your college writing class and set out to do the research necessary to complete it. When you're finished, you turn in your twelve-page argument to your instructor and classmates for their responses—and you also share an excerpt from it in your *Substack* newsletter.

All these examples represent important messages written by people who might not call themselves authors. Yet they illustrate what we mean when we say that today "everyone's an author." Once upon a time, the ability to compose a message that reached wide and varied audiences was restricted to a small group; now, however, this opportunity is available to anyone with access to the internet.

The word "author" has a long history, but it is most associated with the rise of print and the ability of writers to claim what they have written as property. The first copyright act, in the early eighteenth century, ruled that authors held the primary rights to their work. And while anyone could potentially be a writer, an author was someone whose work had been published. That rough definition worked pretty well until a few decades ago, when traditional copyright laws began to show the strain of their 300-year history, most notably because the internet makes it so simple and easy to share content.

In fact, the web has blurred the distinction between writers and authors, offering anyone with access to the internet the opportunity to publish what they write. If you have access to the internet, you can publish what you write and thus make what you say available to readers around the world. And those readers can often publish their responses to what you write, too.

Think for a minute about the impact of blogs, which first appeared in 1997 and allowed people to publish their writing on their own personal website. When this book was first published, there were more than 156 million public blogs, and as this new edition goes to press, there are more than 800 million personal websites and blogs on *WordPress* alone. Add to blogs the rise of *TikTok*, *Reddit*, *YouTube*, *Instagram*, *X*, *Bluesky*, and other social networking sites for even more evidence to support our claim: today, everyone's an author. Moreover, twenty-first-century authors just don't fit the image of the Romantic writer, alone in a garret, struggling to bring forth something unique. Rather, today's authors are part of a huge, often global, conversation; they build on what others have thought and written, they create mashups and remixes, and they practice teamwork at almost every turn. They are authoring for the digital age.

Introduction

Redefining Writing

If the definition of "author" has changed in recent years, so has our understanding of the definition, nature, and scope of "writing."

Writing today, for example, includes much more than words, as images and graphics play an important role in conveying meaning. In addition, writing now includes sound, video, and other media. Perhaps more important, writing now often contains many voices, as information from the internet is incorporated with ease into the texts we write. Finally, as we noted earlier, writing today is almost always part of a larger conversation. Rather than rising mysteriously from the depths of a writer's original thoughts, a stereotype made popular during the Romantic period, writing almost always responds to some other public text (written, visual, or audio) or to other ideas. If, to quote John Donne, "No [person] is an island / Entire of itself," then the same holds true for writing.

Writing today is also often highly collaborative—both with people and with technologies like generative AI. You might work with a team to produce an illustrated report, the basis of which is used by members of the team to make a key presentation to management. You and a group of classmates might research a community problem that requires consulting with experts and reading credible sources, coming to consensus on proposing a solution, writing a script, and presenting your findings to the class in a ten-minute documentary. A business class project may call on you and others in your group to divide up the work along the lines of expertise and then to pool your efforts in meeting the assignment. You may even turn to *ChatGPT* to help you organize and refine your script notes for a new podcast you're launching with a friend. In all these cases, writing is also performative—it performs an action or, in the words of many students we have talked with, it "makes something happen in the world."

Authors whose messages can be instantly transported around the world need to consider those who will receive those messages. Writers can't assume today that they write only to a specified audience or that they can easily control the dissemination of their messages. We live not only in a city, a state, and a country but in a global community as well—and we write, intentionally or not, to speakers of many languages, to members of many cultures, to believers of many creeds. And with the growing prominence of generative AI tools and large language models, what we write can become part of someone else's text without attribution or proper context. Therefore, we must write with care and precision.

Introduction

Everyone's a Researcher

Since almost all writing responds to the ideas and words of others, it usually draws on some kind of research. Think for a moment about how often you carry out research. We're guessing that a little reflection will turn up lots of examples: you may find yourself digging up information on the pricing of books for classes, searching *LinkedIn* or sites like *Indeed* for a good job, comparing two new smartphones, looking up statistics on a favorite sports figure, or searching for a recipe for tabbouleh. All these everyday activities involve research. In addition, many of your most important life decisions involve research—what colleges to apply to, what careers to pursue, where to live, how trade wars might impact your plan to buy a new car, and more. Once you begin to think about research in this broad way—as a form of inquiry related to important decisions—you'll probably find that research is something you do almost every day. Moreover, you'll see the ways in which the research you do adds to your credibility—giving you the authority that goes along with being an author.

But research today is very different from the research of only a few decades ago. Take the example of the concordance, an alphabetized listing of every instance of all topics and words in a work. Before the computer age, concordances were done by hand: the first full concordance to the works of Shakespeare took decades of eye-straining, painstaking research, counting, and sorting. Some scholars spent years, even whole careers, developing concordances that then served as major resources for other scholars. As soon as Shakespeare's plays and poems were in digital form—voilà!—a concordance could be produced automatically and accessed by writers with the click of a mouse.

Just think of how easy it is now to check temperatures around the world, track a news story, or keep up to the minute on stock prices. These are items that you can google, but you may also have many expensive subscription databases available to you through your school's library. You can even connect via *Zoom* with a scholar who lives thousands of miles away. It's not too much of an exaggeration to say that the world is literally at your fingertips.

What has *not* changed is the need to carry out research with great care, to read all sources with a critical eye, and to evaluate information (especially from generative AI tools) before depending on it for an important decision or using it in your own work. What also has not changed is the sheer thrill research can bring: while much research work can seem plodding and even repetitious, the excitement of discovering materials you didn't know existed, of analyzing information in a new way, or of tracing a question through one particular historical period brings its own rewards. Moreover, your research adds to what philosopher Kenneth Burke calls "the conversation of humankind" as you build on what others have done and begin to make significant contributions of your own to the world's accumulated knowledge.

Everyone's a Student

More than 2,000 years ago, the Roman writer Quintilian set out a plan for education, beginning with birth and ending only with old age and death. Surprisingly enough, Quintilian's recommendation for a lifelong education has never been more relevant than it is in the twenty-first century, as knowledge is increasing and changing so fast that most people must continue to be active learners long after they graduate from college. This explosion of knowledge also puts great demands on communication. As a result, one of your biggest challenges will be learning how to learn and how to communicate what you have learned across wider distances, to larger and increasingly diverse sets of audiences, and using an expanding range of media and genres. Another challenge is how to navigate the vast amount of information at your fingertips. While the internet makes connecting with a global audience possible, it also facilitates the travel of misinformation. More than ever, you will need to be an astute critical reader and writer.

In fact, reading and writing with a critical eye are part of the lifelong learning that we should all engage in, whether we began college right out of high school or after experience in the working world. Maybe you returned to college for new training when your job changed, or perhaps you are attending college while working part-time or full-time. College is just one part of a process of lifelong learning. You are likely to hold a number of positions during and after your college career—and in each new position, you'll spend time learning and engaging in a range of new writing experiences and technologies.

Citizens today need more years of education and more advanced skills than ever before, whether you obtain an associate's degree, a bachelor's degree, or a certification in specialized training. But what you'll need isn't just a college education. Instead, you'll need an education that puts you in a position to take responsibility for your own learning and to take a direct, hands-on approach to that learning. Most of us learn best by *doing* what we're trying to learn rather than just being told about it. What does this mean in practice? First, it means you will be doing much more writing, speaking, and researching than ever before. You may, for instance, conduct research on an economic trend and then use that research to create a theory capable of accounting for the trend; you may join a research group in an electrical engineering class that designs, tests, and implements a new system; you may be a member of a writing class that works to build a website for the local fire department, writes brochures for a nonprofit agency, or makes presentations before municipal boards. In each case, you will be doing what you are studying, whether it is economics, engineering, or writing.

Without a doubt, the challenges and opportunities for students today are immense. The chapters that follow try to keep these challenges and opportunities in the foreground, offering you concrete ways to think about yourself as a writer—and yes, as an author; to think carefully about the rhetorical situations you face, about the many and varied audiences for your work, and about the choices you will make and the consequences those choices will have as you expand your writing repertoire to include new genres, new media, and new ways of producing and communicating knowledge.

[Everyone's an Author]

PART I

The Need for Rhetoric and Writing

We didn't burn down buildings....You can do a lot with a pen and pad.

—ICE CUBE

CLOSE YOUR EYES and imagine a world without any form of language—no written or spoken words, no drawings, no numbers, no music—no way, that is, to express yourself. It's pretty hard to imagine, and with good reason. We seem to be hard-wired to express ourselves. As languages and other forms of communication have evolved over thousands of years, so has a need for effective ways to use, interpret, and organize these forms of expression. And from this need emerges rhetoric—the art, theory, and practice of communication. In discussing rhetoric, Aristotle says we need to understand this art for two main reasons: first, in order to express our own ideas and thoughts and, second, to protect ourselves from those who would try to manipulate or harm us.

We think there's one more main reason: rhetoric can be used to create community as we learn from—and about—others.

We believe the need for understanding rhetoric may be greater today than at any time in our history, since technologies allow us to communicate across time zones, cultural differences, and language boundaries, reaching people in all parts of the world with ease. We can broadcast our thoughts, hopes, and dreams—and invectives—in *YouTube* videos, text messages, and a plethora of other ways. The means for communication continue to proliferate, bringing with them the potential for miscommunication, a major challenge, but this proliferation also presents an opportunity to embrace difference, to learn new ways of communicating, to value all languages and all cultures.

At its best and most ethical, rhetoric provides us the means to communicate our messages to a wider range of people and to understand and value a wider range of messages from a more diverse group of people. Rhetoric creates pathways for listening, learning, and sharing. Rhetoric offers you solid ground on which to build both your education and your communicative ability and style. The chapters that follow will introduce you more fully to rhetoric and writing—and guide you in acquiring and using their powers.

 **REFLECT**

Think about a time when you've needed to communicate with someone you didn't know well. What language strategies did you use? What strategies worked well? Which ones didn't?

ONE

Thinking Rhetorically

The only real alternative to war is rhetoric.

—WAYNE BOOTH

**ROFESSOR WAYNE BOOTH** made this statement at a conference of writing scholars and teachers held only months after the 9/11 terrorist attacks on the United States, and it quickly drew a range of responses. Just what did Booth mean by this stark statement? How could rhetoric— the art, theory, and practice of ethical communication—act as a counter to war?

A noted critic and scholar, Booth explored these questions throughout his career, identifying rhetoric as an ethical art that begins with intense listening and searches for mutual understanding and common ground as alternatives to violence and war. Put another way, two of the most potent tools we have for persuasion are language and violence: when words fail us, violence often wins the day. It is language and rhetoric that provide the basis of negotiation, debate, and compromise—acts that de-escalate the kinds of confrontations that lead to divisiveness, separation, and, yes, violence. Booth sees the careful and ethical use of language as our best approach to keeping violence and war at bay.

Rhetoric can play an important role in how individuals, groups, and countries see and hear each other—and it provides pathways for audiences to receive and understand our messages (or not). While the words used to define "rhetoric" differ across fields—"the available means of persuasion," says ancient Greek philosopher Aristotle; a tool "for building and connecting communities" say Young and Robinson, experts on African American rhetoric—the common thread is that rhetoric relates to effective communication. We believe in the need and power of rhetoric to work for good—and that it's no understatement to see rhetoric, as Booth does, as a counter to war.

Consider how Booth's words resonate in light of the Israeli-Hamas conflict or the Russian war on Ukraine—both of which have led to the destruction of entire cities, and to the deaths and harm of thousands of people on both sides. How could the careful and ethical use of rhetoric by all stakeholders have affected these events?

In many countries, including the United States, protests are effective ways of making our views known to a wider audience. Organized marchers raise their voices for or against changes in voting rights legislation, controversial topics taught in schools, and the results of an election. Concerned citizens post on message boards, paint murals, and create signs about a variety of issues, everything from climate change to abortion bans. People on social media use hashtags to amplify causes—from #prolife and #plasticfree to #metoo and #blacklivesmatter. All of these are examples of rhetoric in action.

Note that while Booth speaks of rhetoric as an "ethical art," rhetoric can also be used for unethical purposes, as Hitler and other dictators have done; in fact, rhetoric used in unethical ways can itself lead to violence. That's why Aristotle cautioned that people need to understand rhetoric—both

A public mural in Glasgow, Scotland, highlights losses due to climate change (left). Pro-life supporters at a rally carry a banner making their position clear (right).

to get their own ethical messages across *and* to be able to recognize and resist unethical messages that others attempt to use against them. We take Aristotle's point and focus in this book on how to think rhetorically both as readers and as writers. When we define rhetoric as the art, theory, and practice of ethical communication, we mean *how* and *why* you use language and other means of conveying a message as much as *what* you communicate.

So how can you go about developing your own careful, ethical use of language? Our short answer: by learning to think and act rhetorically—that is, by developing habits of mind that begin with listening and searching for understanding before you decide what you yourself think, and by thinking hard about your own beliefs before trying to persuade others to listen to and act on what you say.

Learning to think rhetorically can serve you well as you negotiate the complexities of life today. For example, many of us have engaged with classmates or colleagues who hold different opinions about vaccines. In spite of such disagreements, we aim to communicate well enough to get things done in a responsible and ethical way. In other words, we need to come to some consensus that moves us forward toward completing a project—and maybe even saving a relationship—despite differing views.

When students in some communities disagreed with their school districts' decisions to ban books or close libraries, they came together to voice

Teachers, students, and community members use signs and conversation to protest book bans.

their opposition in responsible yet powerful ways, like the members of the Panther Anti-Racist Union in Pennsylvania, who organized parents, teachers, and other concerned community members to protest the bans. Others have run banned-book clubs to get around school mandates. And still others have designed flyers and posters, spoken up at school board meetings, and written essays published in local newspapers—in other words, they've used a variety of strategies to invite others to join them and to present their argument to the audiences who can make a change. They've collaborated to take action together, and they've had to think about how to communicate with people who may not share their values. Some of these actions have, indeed, led to the reversal of book bans. These students were thinking and acting rhetorically, and doing so responsibly and ethically. In other words, none of us can manage such actions all by ourselves; we need to engage in conversation with others and listen hard to what they say. Perhaps that's what philosopher Kenneth Burke had in mind when he created his famous "parlor" metaphor:

> Imagine that you enter a parlor. You come late. When you arrive, others have long preceded you, and they are engaged in a heated discussion, a discussion too heated for them to pause and tell you exactly what it is about.... You listen for a while, until you decide that you have caught the tenor of the argument; then you put in your oar.
>
> —KENNETH BURKE, *The Philosophy of Literary Form*

In this parable, each of us is the person arriving late to a room full of animated conversation; we don't understand what is going on. Yet instead of butting in or trying to take over, we listen closely until we catch on to what people are saying. Then we join in, using language and rhetorical strategies to engage with others as we add our own voices to the conversation.

This book aims to teach you to *think and act rhetorically*—to listen carefully and respectfully and then to "put in your oar," join conversations about important issues, and develop strong critical and ethical habits of mind that will help you engage with others in responsible ways.

See the ebook for a video on understanding rhetorical situations.

First, Listen

Thinking rhetorically begins with listening, with being willing to hear the words of others in an open and understanding way. It means paying attention to what others say before—and even as a way of—making your own contributions to a conversation. Think of the times you are grateful to others for listening closely to you: when you're talking through a conflict with a family member, for instance, or even when you're trying to explain to your doctor what's bothering you. On those occasions, you want the person you're addressing to really listen to what you say.

This is a kind of listening that rhetorician Krista Ratcliffe dubs "rhetorical listening," opening yourself to the thoughts of others and making the effort not only to hear their words but also to take those words in and fully understand what people are saying. It means paying attention to what others say as a way of establishing goodwill and acknowledging the importance of their views. And yes, it means taking seriously and engaging with views that differ, sometimes radically, from your own.

Rhetorical listening is what activist Ciaran O'Connor demonstrates when he discusses his quest to bring together those on opposite sides of the gun control debate. O'Connor, who works with Braver Angels, a nonprofit organization seeking to "bridge the partisan divide," knows that he needs to talk with those whose views differ from his:

> [A]s a leader at Braver Angels, . . . I'm committed to talking with—rather than simply at or about—those whose views, experiences, and politics differ from mine. And in the wake of the recent mass shootings in Buffalo, New York, Uvalde, Texas, and, most recently, Highland Park, Illinois, I've been working to cross America's gun divide to see if I can learn anything that might be helpful to other Americans mired in fear, anger, and despair.
> —CIARAN O'CONNOR, "Can We Bridge Our Differences over Gun Laws?"

After facilitating conversations between staunch gun rights advocates and strict gun control proponents, O'Connor concludes:

> Acknowledging each other's fears and pain is hardest when it feels like it legitimizes a perspective we find false and harmful. But "seeing" someone in this way is not a zero-sum game, and acknowledging an opponent's fears does not invalidate our own. Over time, it enables us to find the true empathy needed to transcend the fears that blind us to one another's humanity and prevent us from working together for the common good.

Hear What Others Are Saying—and Think about Why

When you enter any conversation, whether academic, professional, or personal, take the time to understand what is being said rather than rushing to a conclusion. Listen carefully to what others are saying and consider what motivates them: where are they coming from?

Developing such habits of mind will be useful to you almost every day, whether you are participating in a class discussion, negotiating with friends over what movie is most worth watching, or studying a local ballot issue to decide how you'll vote. In each case, thinking rhetorically means being flexible and fair, able to hear and consider varying—and sometimes conflicting—points of view.

In ancient Rome, Cicero argued that considering alternative points of view was key to making a successful argument, and it is just as important today. As O'Connor suggests, even when you disagree with a point of view—perhaps especially when you disagree with it—allow yourself to see the issue from the viewpoint of its advocates before you reject their positions. Don't dismiss their views out of hand. Listen to their concerns, try to understand their fears. Think about their perspective and how you might carefully respond.

Thinking hard about others' views also includes considering the larger context and how it shapes what they are saying. When you think rhetorically, you look at the larger context—historical, political, or cultural, for example—to recognize and consider where a certain point of view is "coming from."

In analyzing the issue of gun control, for instance, you would not merely consider your own thinking or do a close reading of texts that address the issue. In addition to these strategies, you would look at the whole debate in context by considering its historical development over time, thinking about the broader political agendas of both those who advocate for and those who oppose stricter gun control, asking what economic ramifications adopting—or rejecting—new gun restrictions might have, examining the role of constitutional rights in the debate, and so on. In short, you would try to see the issue from as many different perspectives and in as broad a context as possible before you formulate your own stance. When you write, you draw on these sources—what others have said about the issue—to support your own position and to help you consider counterarguments to it.

> **REFLECT**
>
> Find an online space where readers post comments—a social media feed, a conversation site like *Reddit*, or even your class discussion boards. Read a few conversation threads and then describe how and where you see rhetorical listening in action—or note ways the contributors could have better connected and engaged with others.

What Do You Think—and Why?

Examining all points of view on any issue will engage you in some tough thinking about your own stance—literally, where you are coming from on an issue—and why you think as you do. Such self-scrutiny can eventually clarify your stance or perhaps even change your mind; in either case, you stand to gain. Just as you need to think hard about the motivations of others, it's important to examine your own motivations, asking yourself what influences in your life lead you to take certain positions. Then you can reconsider your positions and reflect on how they relate to those of others, including your audience—those you wish to engage respectfully in conversation or debate.

In your college assignments, you probably have multiple motivations and purposes, one of which is to convince your instructor that you are a hardworking student. But think about additional purposes as well: What could you learn from doing the assignment? How can doing it help you achieve your goals?

Examining your own stance and motivation is equally important outside the classroom. Suppose you are urging fellow members of a campus group to lobby for a rigorous set of procedures to deal with accusations of sexual harassment. On one level, you're alarmed by the statistics showing a steep increase in cases of rape on college campuses and you want to do something about it. But when you think a bit more, you might find that you have additional motivations. Perhaps you've long wanted to become a leader of this group. You may have seen *The Hunting Ground*, a documentary about rape on US college campuses, and found it deeply upsetting—and persuasive. These realizations shouldn't necessarily change your mind about what action you want your group to take, but examining what you think and why will help you to challenge your own position—and to make sure that it is fair.

Do Your Homework

Rhetorical thinking calls on you to do some homework, to find out everything you can about what's been said about your topic, to **ANALYZE** what you find, and then to **SYNTHESIZE** that information to inform your own ideas. To put it another way, you want your own thinking to be aware and deeply informed, to reflect more than just your own opinion.

Maybe you've seen politicians arguing about the role of diversity, equity, and inclusion (DEI) policies and programming on college campuses. You've read headlines about teachers and adminstrators being fired. Rather than immediately taking a position on whether DEI results in inclusivity or discrimination, rhetorical thinking moves you to do some careful research to find out more about the topic—and about why you want to know more. Is your own campus affected? Are you thinking about becoming a teacher? Maybe you are simply concerned about the nastiness of the debate in your community or state.

So you get to work to find out just what DEI means. What are the historical, social, academic, and political contexts surrounding it? As you research this topic, you'll examine definitions of the three key terms—"diversity," "equity," "inclusion"—and how those terms have been used in higher education. You'll examine the history of DEI policies and programs on your campus and other colleges, public and private, in your state. You'll read arguments for and against DEI efforts and consult research about the impact of such policies. You might even interview experts as well as those who have been personally affected by DEI programming and policies. Only after exploring such questions and understanding the rhetorical situation can you responsibly engage with the arguments on opposing sides of the issue. Who are the stakeholders on each side? How do stakeholders' arguments hold up when fact-checked? Are there stakeholders who have not been heard?

This kind of rhetorical thinking prompts you to pay attention to the rhetorical strategies and appeals writers and speakers use to persuade. What kind of tone are they using? Are they using inclusive language? Are their examples factual? Are they relying on credible sources or unsubstantiated claims? Once you've read, synthesized, and analyzed all the material you've gathered, you may even talk with a classmate or friend, someone

THINK BEYOND WORDS

↗ TAKE A LOOK at the Salesforce ad "The March" featuring Matthew McConaughey on everyonesanauthor.tumblr.com. You see McConaughey first in a laundromat contemplating the state of the world and then "marching" through a city; a growing group of followers joins him as he suggests solutions to thorny problems. "Let's have less cancellation and more conversation," he states. At the end, he leaves viewers with one final proposal: "[I]t's not 'goodbye world,' it's 'hello team Earth.' " What is the message of this ad? Who is the target audience? How do the writers and film director get their message across? What evidence do you see of rhetorical thinking? What makes this ad successful or not—what does it do for Salesforce, a company selling software and services to businesses for connecting with customers?

who will be a sounding board and ask tough but fair questions, as you figure out what you think. Then you will be ready to offer a well-informed opinion and to judge others' perspectives. Doing this kind of research is an example of rhetorical thinking.

Rhetorical thinking is not meant just for such weighty topics as gun regulations and DEI programs. In your everyday life, you make decisions that require rhetorical thinking: buying a new computer, making a decision about a job, choosing a major, considering graduate school. Each of these decisions calls on you to do your homework, to do research, to be open-minded, and to engage in careful and ethical thinking. You want to be well-informed to make the best decisions and to take thoughtful positions.

Give Credit

As part of engaging with what others have thought and said, you'll want to give credit where credit is due. Acknowledging the work of others will help build your own ethos, or character, showing that you have not only done your homework but also that you want to credit those who have influenced you. The great physicist Isaac Newton famously and graciously gave credit when he wrote to his rival Robert Hooke in 1676, saying:

> What Descartes did was a good step. You have added much in several ways, and especially in taking the colours of thin plates into philosophical consideration. If I have seen a little further, it is by standing on the shoulders of giants. —ISAAC NEWTON, letter to Robert Hooke

In this letter, Newton acknowledges the work of Descartes as well as of Hooke before saying, with a fair amount of modesty, that his own advancements were made possible by their work. In doing so, he is thinking—and acting—rhetorically.

You can give credit informally, as Newton did in this letter, or you can do so formally with a full citation. The method you choose will depend on your purpose and context. Academic writing, for instance, usually calls for formal citations, but if you are writing post for social media or an entry on a personal website, you might embed a link that connects to another's work—or tag a friend who contributed to your thinking. In each case, you'll want to be specific about what ideas or words you've drawn from others, as Newton does in referring to Hooke's consideration of the colors of thin plates. Such care in crediting your sources contributes to your credibility—and is an important part of ethical, careful rhetorical thinking.

Be Imaginative

Remember that intuition and imagination can often lead to great insights. While you want to think carefully and analytically, don't be afraid to take chances. A little imagination can lead you to new ideas about a topic you're studying and suggest how to approach it in a way that will interest others. Such insights and intuitions can often pay off big-time. Nova Thrasher, a writing tutor in training, opened their final project on gender inclusivity in college writing centers with this personal reflection:

> I wait for introductions with bated breath, hoping for and dreading what comes in the split second after "Tell everyone your name—" . . . Time drags on, suspense building in the space between exhale and inhale . . . "—and pronouns. We'll go around the room . . ." and exhale. The question has been asked, and I am theoretically safe in this room.
> —NOVA THRASHER, "Gender-Inclusivity and the Onus of Progress on the Writing Center"

It was rhetorical thinking that led Annette Gordon-Reed to question what she had learned in school about the history of slavery in the United States, and her thinking led to new insights about things she had always taken for granted. Read her essay on p. 915.

This personal experience led Nova to examine writing center websites for statements on using inclusive pronouns. Before they knew it, Nova had a full-fledged research project that analyzed thirty college writing center websites, discussed writing center scholarship, and covered current debates about gender. Nova found that less than half of the thirty writing center websites addressed gender inclusive pronouns. Interested in becoming a tutor who wants to make the writing center safe and inviting for all, Nova conducted valuable research. Like this student, you can benefit by using your imagination, reflecting on your own experiences, and listening to your intuition. You may discover something exciting and meaningful.

Put In Your Oar

So rhetorical thinking offers a way of entering any situation with a tool kit of strategies that will help you understand it and "put in your oar." When you think rhetorically, you ask yourself certain questions:

- How do you want to come across to your audience?
- What can you do to represent yourself as knowledgeable and credible?
- What can you do to show respect both for your audience and for those whose work and thinking you engage with?
- How can you show that you have your audience's best interests at heart?

This kind of rhetorical thinking will help ensure that your words will be listened to and taken seriously.

We can find examples of such a rhetorical approach in all fields of study. Take, for instance, the landmark essay by James Watson and Francis Crick deciphering the structure of DNA, published in *Nature* in 1953. This essay shows Watson and Crick to be thinking rhetorically throughout, acutely aware of their audience (major scientists throughout the world), including competitors who were simultaneously working on the same issue.

Here is Wayne Booth's analysis of Watson and Crick's use of rhetoric:

> In [Watson and Crick's] report, what do we find? Actually scores of *rhetorical* choices that they made to strengthen the appeal of their scientific claim. (Biographies and autobiographies have by now revealed

that they did a lot of conscientious revising, not of the data but of the mode of presentation; and their lives were filled, before and after the triumph, with a great deal of rhetoric-charged conflict.) We could easily compose a dozen different versions of their report, all proclaiming the same scientific results. But most alternatives would prove less engaging to the intended audience. They open, for example, with

> "*We wish to suggest* a structure" that has "*novel* features which are of *considerable* biological *interest*." (My italics, of course)

Why didn't they say, instead: "We shall here demonstrate a *startling, totally new structure* that will *shatter* everyone's conception of the biological world"? Well, obviously their rhetorical choice presents an ethos much more attractive to most cautious readers than does my exaggerated alternative. A bit later they say

> "We have made the *usual chemical assumptions,* namely . . ."

Why didn't they say, "*As we all know*"? Both expressions acknowledge reliance on warrants, commonplaces within a given rhetorical domain. But their version sounds more thoughtful and authoritative, especially with the word "chemical." Referring to Pauling and Corey, they say

> "They *kindly* have made their manuscript available."

Okay, guys, drop the rhetoric and just cut that word "kindly." What has that got to do with your scientific case? Well, it obviously strengthens the authors' ethos: we are nice guys dealing trustfully with other nice guys, in a rhetorical community.

And on they go, with "*In our opinion*" (rather than "We proclaim" or "We insist" or "We have miraculously discovered": again ethos—we're not dogmatic); and Fraser's "*suggested*" structure is "*rather ill-defined*" (rather than "his structure is stupid" or "obviously faulty"—we *are* nice guys, right?).

And on to scores of other such choices.

—WAYNE BOOTH, *The Rhetoric of Rhetoric*

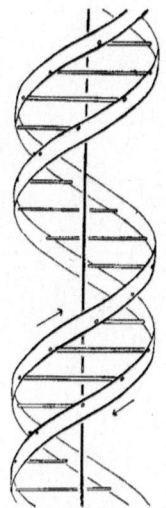

The original sketch showing the structure of DNA that appeared in Watson and Crick's article.

Booth shows in each instance that Watson and Crick's exquisite understanding of their rhetorical situation—especially of their audience and of the stakes involved in making their claim—had a great deal to do with how that claim was received. (They won the Nobel Prize!) However, Watson and Crick could have done better when it came to giving credit: scholars have pointed out that the work of Rosalind Franklin, a contemporary scientist, greatly influenced Watson and Crick's discovery, though they did not sufficiently acknowledge or credit her.

As the example of Watson and Crick illustrates, rhetorical thinking involves certain habits of mind that can and should lead to something—often to an action, to making something happen. And when it comes to taking action, those who think rhetorically are in a very strong position. They have listened attentively, engaged with the words and ideas of others, viewed their topic from many alternate perspectives, and done their homework. This kind of rhetorical thinking will set you up to contribute to conversations—and will increase the likelihood that your ideas will be heard and will inspire real action.

The need to think rhetorically has never been more important than in today's global world. Rhetorician Jacqueline Jones Royster provides a clear guide to engaging in rhetorical thinking and acting:

> My experiences tell me that we need to do more than just talk and talk back. I believe that in this model we miss a critical moment. We need to talk, yes, and to talk back, yes, but when do we listen? How do we listen? How do we demonstrate that we honor and respect the person talking and what that person is saying, or what the person might say if we valued someone other than ourselves having a turn to speak? How do we translate listening into language and action, into the creation of an appropriate response? How do we really "talk back" rather than talk also? The goal is not, "You talk, I talk." The goal is better practices so that we can exchange perspectives, negotiate meaning, and create understanding with the intent of being in a good position to cooperate, when, like now, cooperation is absolutely necessary.
>
> —JACQUELINE JONES ROYSTER, "When the First Voice You Hear Is Not Your Own"

In the long run, if enough of us learn to think rhetorically, we just might achieve Royster's goals "to exchange perspectives, negotiate meaning, and create understanding" and avoid the violence and war, literal and figurative, that Booth speaks of.

> **N**ever doubt that a small group of thoughtful committed citizens can change the world; indeed, it's the only thing that ever has.
>
> —MARGARET MEAD

 **REFLECT**

Identify an effective changemaker, someone (or maybe an organization, local or global), who's been effective bringing together people with diverse perspectives to make change. How did they model thinking and acting rhetorically to achieve success? Then think about your own life and the ways in which you have worked with others to bring about some kind of change. In what ways were you called on to think and act rhetorically in order to do so?

TWO

Engaging Productively with Others

Re we living in a unique moment in history—a prolonged moment, at that—when we struggle to engage with those with whom we disagree? It certainly feels that way when we see daily news headlines about a "divided America." Can we turn things around? How can we work through what feel like unsolvable disagreements? This division set journalist Judy Woodruff on a mission to investigate the divide. In an essay for *PBS NewsHour,* Woodruff opens:

> America is as divided today as it's been in a very long time. I want to know why. I grew up believing there was something special—our history, our democratic system—that holds Americans together. While the country has experienced deep divisions before—and in fact, split in two over slavery—we have always found a way to come back together, through a civil war, or a century later, the protests of the 1960s or the war in Vietnam. That again seems to be fraying. I want to understand what is driving the American people further and further apart. . . .
>
> [F]or the past decade and more, it's become clear politics has been generating deeper divides—not only over issues, but over culture and character. We hear leaders of one party calling the other not

just wrong, but anti-American. Surveys show that more than two-thirds of Americans today view members of the other party as immoral and dishonest. What used to be seen as a tolerable set of policy differences has become profoundly personal.

—JUDY WOODRUFF, "Listening to a Divided America"

Woodruff's concerns led her to embark on a research project, gathering data and stories from Americans of all walks of life and locations about why they think this divide exists and what they think we can do to fix it. Her work shines a light on how communities are negotiating their differences. Woodruff practices **RHETORICAL LISTENING** and along the way discovers strategies for engaging productively with others. She states:

> I hope at the end to have a better understanding of what's driving our political divide. . . . I don't presume we'll have found the formula that makes our differences melt away: The fact that we can have differences out in the open is what makes our democracy strong. But listening to each other and illuminating the views of others might bring us a step closer to understanding this moment in the American story.

The goal of this chapter is to encourage and guide you as you engage with others: listening to their stories and contributing to a process that may make some positive change or at least unearth some common ground. Here are some steps you can take to realize this goal.

Get to Know People Different from You

It's a commonplace today to point out that we often live and act in "silos" where we encounter only people who think like we do, who hold the same values. We increasingly choose to interact with like-minded people—online and in person. We are in what some call "filter bubbles" or "echo chambers," where we hear our views echoed back to us from every direction. In such an atmosphere, it can be easy—and comforting—to think this is the real world, but it's not! Beyond your own bubble of posts and conversations lie countless other people with different views and values.

So one of the big challenges we face today is finding ways to get out of our own echo chambers and get to know people who take different positions, hold different values. But simply encountering people who think

differently is just the start. Breaking out of our bubbles calls for making the effort to understand those different perspectives, to listen with openness and empathy, and to hear where others are coming from. All of these are habits that take practice—especially using empathy, the ability to share the feelings of someone else.

Dylan Marron is someone who shows how this can be done. As the creator and host of several popular video series on controversial social issues, Marron has gained quite a bit of attention and, he says, "a lot of hate." Early on, he tried to ignore hateful comments, but then he got interested and began visiting commenter profiles to learn about the people behind them. Doing so, he said, led him to realize "there was a human on the other side of the screen"—and prompted him to call some of these people on the phone, conversations he shares on his podcast *Conversations with People Who Hate Me*—and in his book by the same name.

Dylan Marron, creator and host of *Conversations with People Who Hate Me*, a podcast featuring conversations between people who disagree.

In one of these talks, Marron learned that Josh, who in a comment had said that being gay was a sin, had recently graduated from high school. When Marron asked him, "How was high school for you?" Josh replied that "it was hell" because he'd been bullied by kids who made fun of him for being "bigger." Marron shared his own experiences of being bullied, too, and as the conversation progressed, listening laid the groundwork that helped them relate to each other.

Marron's work demonstrates the power of practicing empathy and how it can help us to see one another as human, even in the most negative and nasty places. In his TED talk, Marron again stressed the importance of empathy, noting, however, that "empathy is not endorsement" and doesn't require us to compromise our deeply held values but rather to acknowledge the views of "someone raised to think very differently" than we do.

Watch Marron's TED talk and listen to his podcast by visiting everyonesanauthor.tumblr.com.

Practice Empathy

So how can you practice empathy? First comes curiosity, an interest in learning why someone feels what they feel or sees the world as they do. One way to practice empathy when talking about controversial topics, especially with someone who holds a different opinion, is to ask questions:

- Why do you think so? What has led you to that conclusion?
- How have your experiences influenced the position you're taking?

- Why do you think others see the situation differently? Might there be value in some of their views?
- What would need to happen for you to rethink your position?
- Are there things that leave you uncomfortable or fearful about the issue we're discussing? about other positions?
- What do you want those who disagree with you to know about you and your position? How do you think that information will help them understand you?

At the Center for Creative Leadership (CCL), a nonprofit organization aiming to "make the world a better place through more effective leadership," researchers identify another important reason to practice empathy: it's a quality of good leaders. By analyzing data from thirty-eight countries, the CCL concluded that "demonstrating empathy in the workplace—a key part of emotional intelligence and leadership effectiveness—improves human interaction in general and can lead to more effective communication and positive outcomes, in both work and home settings." So practicing empathy isn't just for productive conversations with friends and family, but it also has the power to enhance your leadership skills beyond the classroom—and to help you grow as a professional.

Ted Olson, a conservative attorney who argued before the Supreme Court sixty-five times, made a similar claim in an interview with CBS News, noting that "trying to understand both sides of an issue and being persuasive on this side, and then being persuasive on the other side" helped him improve his professional skills. He added, "In today's world, people are so polarized ... there's not a lot of time spent trying to think the way the other side thinks, or try[ing] to express what the other side is expressing and believing," a situation he saw as unfortunate. Olson argued all kinds of positions before the Court. For example, he represented Republican presidential candidate George W. Bush in *Bush v. Gore*, the case deliberating the results of the 2000 election. But he also argued for "Dreamers," undocumented immigrants brought to the United States as children, in the case upholding DACA (Deferred Action for Childhood Arrivals), a program that has provided some protection from deportation. Olson reported that he agreed to take on the Dreamers case, a stance many wouldn't expect of a conservative attorney, after meeting with people impacted by the policy and hearing their stories. That's the power and the promise of practicing empathy.

> ### REFLECT
>
> Think back to a conversation you've had with someone whose position you disagreed with and didn't understand. What did you ask that person to try to understand their position? Which of the questions above do you wish you had asked? Why? How might those unasked questions have changed the conversation?

Listen to People's Stories

Practicing empathy is about more than asking questions; it also requires listening. By listening, you learn a lot about not only a person's experiences but also the worlds they have inhabited and the events and situations that shape their positions. Good listening means withholding judgment and avoiding interrupting. Part of your task as a listener is to consider your knee-jerk responses. In this way, listening gives you a chance to learn something about yourself, too.

That's certainly what one Canadian student found when she spent a semester in Washington, DC. Shauna Vert had expected the highlights to be visiting places like the museums of the Smithsonian Institution or the Library of Congress, but her greatest experience, as she describes it on her website, turned out to be an "unexpected gift: While in DC, I became close, close friends with people I disagree with on almost everything." As she listened to these people's experiences, she found that they were

> funny, smart, and kind. We all really liked music, . . . We even lived together. We ate dinner together, every single night. So I couldn't look down on them. I couldn't even consider it. And when you can't look down on someone who fundamentally disagrees with you, when you're busy breaking bread, sharing your days, laughing about the weather . . . well.
> —SHAUNA VERT, "Making Friends Who Disagree with You (Is the Healthiest Thing in the World)"

During a conversation with one of her housemates, a conservative Christian from Mississippi, Vert mentioned that she was "pro-choice," realizing as she did so that this was "dangerous territory." To her surprise, she met not resistance or rebuke but curiosity:

> She wanted to know more. Her curiosity fueled my curiosity, and we talked. We didn't argue—we debated gently, very gently. . . . We laughed at nuance, we self-deprecated, we trusted each other. And we liked each other. Before the conversation, and after the conversation. To recap: Left-wing Canadian meets Bible Belt Republican. Discusses controversial political issues for over an hour. Walks away with a new friend.

This kind of careful, responsible, respectful exchange requires listening with an open mind. The point is that it's worth making the time to try to find and engage with those who hold different ideas and values than you do. And this means listening to other people's stories. It's time to shut down the echo chambers, seek out people outside of our silos, and listen with empathy.

Demonstrate Respect

"R-E-S-P-E-C-T." That spells respect. If you've never heard Aretha Franklin belt out these lyrics, take time to look her up on *YouTube*. Franklin added this now-famous line to her 1967 rendition of Otis Redding's original song, inspiring millions to expect and to demand R-E-S-P-E-C-T.

Franklin's message is still a timely one today, and the strategies in this chapter will lead you to demonstrate respect. Yet respecting others with whom we disagree has sometimes been interpreted as a call to "just be nice." While we support being civil and tolerant, we are not suggesting that you hold back your dissent when you oppose something or that you sit by silently when you see or hear injustice.

We recognize that, many times, those in subordinate positions or marginalized groups are expected to demonstrate respect while receiving little respect in return. Respect should be reciprocal. Anyone who demands respect should also give it. Black Lives Matter cofounder Alicia Garza reminds us, "You don't get far being mealy-mouthed about what you want. You just don't." If you don't receive the respect that you are owed, think and act rhetorically to demand what you deserve.

Aretha Franklin performs onstage in 1968.

Search for Common Ground

Even children learn early on that digging in to opposing positions doesn't usually get them far: "No, you can't!" "Yes, I can!" can go on forever, without going anywhere. Rhetoricians in the ancient world understood this very well and thus argued that for conversations to progress, it's necessary to establish some **COMMON GROUND**, no matter how small. If "No, you can't!" moves on to "Well, you can't do that in this particular situation," then maybe a conversation can begin.

Searching for and building on common ground has helped Jewish Americans and Muslim Americans engage across difference. Writing for the *Baltimore Sun* in 2021, coauthors Sabeeha Rehman, a Muslim woman, and Walter Ruby, a Jewish man, explain how their communities are finding a way forward:

> What is different this time is that dialogue once avoided is now taking place in some communities. The ties of mutual affection we have built and the sense of solidarity and common purpose we have achieved has

Visit everyonesanauthor.tumblr.com for tips on having difficult conversations provided by "Living Room Conversations," a group that aims to connect "people across divides."

given us increasing confidence that we *can* have that difficult conversation about Israel-Palestine . . . and come out of that dialogue with our friendships intact. . . . Despite our very real differences over the rights and wrongs of Israel-Palestine and what is the optimum solution to the conflict, we are determined not to allow what is happening over there to imperil our success in strengthening Muslim-Jewish relations where we live. . . . Making common cause will have the effect of further buttressing our relationship on this side of the ocean and thwart the efforts by forces who would use our differences over Israel-Palestine as a wedge to pull us apart here in the U.S.

—SABEEHA REHMAN & WALTER RUBY, "Jews and Muslims Must Stand Together and Refuse to Be Enemies"

Rehman and Ruby discuss how they personally overcame biases about the other's faith in their book *We Refuse to Be Enemies: How Muslims and Jews Can Make Peace, One Friendship at a Time.* Rehman had never met a Jewish person while growing up in Pakistan, and Ruby, growing up in the United States, had never met a Muslim until he was a young man. However, when the two met, they listened carefully to each other, asked questions, reconsidered their assumptions, and ultimately built a friendship and collaboration as writers. And they continued to listen to each

Coauthors Sabeeha Rehman and Walter Ruby discuss their writing and their friendship in a virtual interview. Watch their talk by visiting everyonesanauthor.tumblr.com.

other and share their example of relationship-building as the conflicts in the Israeli-Hamas war raged. They are finding common ground where it is least expected.

>  **REFLECT**
>
> Some would say it's pointless or even wrong to try to find common ground with people whose views you find problematic. Based on your own experiences, what do you think—and why? What do you think the writers featured in this chapter would say?

Examine Your Own Positions

If your goal is to interact with others in ways that might move them—or you—to look at things differently, then you'll need to think deeply about how who you are and what you've experienced influence your views. Consider these questions in order to build that awareness:

- Why is this issue important to me? What's my stake in it?
- What emotions, memories, or experiences come up for me when this topic is raised? when someone disagrees with my stance? What experiences have shaped my understanding?
- Do I identify with a "side" on this issue?
- What information am I relying on to support my position? Is it reliable?
- When it comes to this topic, what am I certain about? What am I unsure about?
- What is my biggest fear about what could happen in a conversation about this topic?
- How can I respond with curiosity, rather than judgment, to positions different from my own?

These questions invite you to investigate ideas and reactions that you may have taken for granted. The examples in this chapter all show people open and curious about their own views, which helped them engage more deeply with others. Building self-awareness won't always be comfortable, but it is sure to be productive.

When you examine the sources of information you rely on, it's not just accuracy that matters; the way information is presented makes a difference, too. See how Danielle K. Brown presents information and sources on p. 876.

Be Open to Challenging Conversations

> Visit everyonesanauthor.tumblr.com to see all episodes of Woodruff's series, "America at a Crossroads."

By engaging with those who see the world differently than we do, all of us can build shared understandings that will benefit us as individuals and as a society. That's exactly what journalist Judy Woodruff found when she spent time in Alamance County, North Carolina, talking to residents about the issues that divide them. There she met Republican county commissioner Craig Turner, who explains, "In addition to being divided, we're anxious. The county is anxious. People in the country are anxious. And so what that does is, it has a tendency to make us huddle in the groups that we already exist in and it requires us to be intentional to come outside of those groups and to listen to one another and to trust one another."

Difficult conversations like these are never entered lightly, and many groups have developed techniques to increase the likelihood that everyone involved can be safe. A common practice for such conversations is to begin by reviewing a set of principles like the ones below that all have agreed to work toward:

- Stay engaged.
- Listen to understand, rather than thinking of what you'll say next.
- Allow time between speakers.
- Disagree with someone's *ideas* but avoid criticizing the speaker.
- Let others speak if you have already spoken.
- Be willing to do things differently.
- Be open to some discomfort.
- Expect no clean resolution; listening and thinking is a good start.

Many issues are messy and different groups and cultures have different preferred ways of interacting. Some cultures may invite vigorous public debate while others prefer engaging through questions. Working to respect what everyone brings to the table, and being open to following their lead and doing things differently, helps put everyone on equal footing.

Communicating across differences about hot-button topics is often going to leave all involved a little uncomfortable. After all, you're listening to others whose experiences and views are different from, even contradictory

Journalist Judy Woodruff and retired US Navy commander Theodore Johnson discuss the ideas and actions that divide Americans.

to, your own. As Dylan Marron reminds us, practicing empathy in those moments doesn't mean you agree with the opinions you hear but that you acknowledge others see the world differently for reasons that, at least to them, seem sound. It is an acknowledgment that our society—and the world—is bigger and more diverse than you had realized it was.

Join the Conversation: Collaborate! Engage! Participate!

Especially in times of deep societal divisions, it may be tempting to retreat, to put our heads in the sand and hope that, somehow, things will get better. But don't give in to that temptation. Your voice is important, your thoughts are important, and you can best make them heard if you engage and join with other people. That may mean working with groups of like-minded people to speak out—for or against—on issues you care about. That kind of civic engagement and participation is important in a democracy. But there are smaller ways, too, like looking beyond those who think as you do, seeking to collaborate with them, listening with empathy, understanding their reasons for thinking as they do—and then looking hard for a shared goal that you can work toward together.

As a country, as a world, we have a lot riding on our willingness to reach across barriers, work together for the common good, and keep on trying even in the most difficult circumstances. As writers, readers, and thinkers, we all have much to offer in this endeavor. And the writing you do in your college courses is good way to get started. So let's get going!

◈ REFLECT

Look back through the examples in this chapter of people working out disagreements or finding ways to empathize with one another. Pick one of the examples and analyze how the participants are practicing empathy (or not). What does practicing empathy look like in the example you chose?

THREE

Rhetorical Situations

URING HER SECOND SEMESTER in college, Lucia gave a virtual presentation, complete with slides, to seniors in her former high school about differences between high school and college—and then fielded questions from the audience. The same week, Lucia and two friends designed a flyer to advertise a dance-a-thon their Spanish club was sponsoring to raise funds for the club's tutoring program. The flyer, posted around campus and on social media, attracted 150 students to the event, raising enough money to fund the program for another year.

Lucia's projects required that she negotiate multiple, diverse contexts—or rhetorical situations—as an author and speaker. She moved from one to another, each with a different purpose and audience and each calling for different genres, media, languages, and so on. Shifting from one rhetorical situation to another is common; we do it all the time, especially as college students. For Lucia's virtual presentation, she speaks to an audience in a different location—an important part of her rhetorical situation. The geographical location, audience, topic, and technology, as well as Lucia's status as a college student, are all part of the rhetorical situation. In a different rhetorical situation, Lucia collaborates with others, using a visual medium (a flyer), presented on social media and in print, to communicate with a large group of college classmates about

Six different rhetorical situations (clockwise from top left): a lone writer texting, students hang and distribute flyers, a gamer live streams their performance, a group works on an in-class project, a panel gives a talk on climate change to college students, and a group collaborates online.

their club's fundraising event. Think about how this situation—creating a flyer—is different from the first one—giving a presentation. The flyer needs to attract attention with bright colors and bold, catchy headlines in Spanish and English to reach the broadest audience and persuade them to attend while also providing information about the event. The high school presentation requires a computer with a camera, a quiet setting, and informative, well-designed slides to present at a *Zoom* meeting.

In each scenario, an author is writing (or speaking) in a different set of specific circumstances—addressing certain audiences for a particular purpose, using different technologies. So it is whenever we write. Whether we're texting a friend, outlining an oral presentation, or writing an essay, we do so within a specific rhetorical situation. We have a purpose, an audience, a stance, a genre, a medium, a design—all of which exist in some larger context. This chapter covers each of these elements and provides prompts to help you think about some of the choices you have as you negotiate your own rhetorical situations.

Every rhetorical situation presents its own unique constraints and opportunities, and as authors, we need to think strategically about our own situation. Adding to a class discussion thread presents a different challenge from writing an in-class essay exam, putting together a résumé and cover letter for a job, or working with fellow members of a campus choir to draft a grant proposal to the student government requesting funding to go on tour. A group of neighbors developing a proposal to present at a virtual community meeting will need to attend to both the written text they will submit and the oral arguments they will make.

The workplace creates still other kinds of rhetorical situations with their own distinctive features. Reporters, for instance, must always consider their deadlines as well as their ethical obligations—to the public, to the persons or institutions they write about, and to the story they are reporting. A reporter working for six months to investigate corporate wrongdoing faces different challenges from one who covers local sports day to day. The medium—print, video, radio, podcast, social media feed, or some combination of these—also influences how reporters write their stories.

REFLECT

Take a look at the images on the previous page and think about the rhetorical situation each presents. Pick one image. What does that image suggest about what the speakers / writers needed to keep in mind about their rhetorical situations?

Think about Your Own Rhetorical Situation

It is important to start thinking about your rhetorical situation early in your writing process. As a student, you'll often be given assignments with very specific guidelines—to follow the conventions of a particular genre, in a certain medium, by a specific date. Nevertheless, even the most fully developed assignment cannot specify every aspect of any particular rhetorical situation.

Effective writers—whether students, teachers, or journalists—know how to analyze their rhetorical situations. They may conduct this analysis unconsciously, drawing on the rhetorical common sense they have developed as writers, readers, speakers, and listeners. Particularly when you are writing in a new genre or discipline—a situation that you'll surely face in college—it can help to analyze your rhetorical situation more systematically.

> Jose Antonio Vargas risked everything by revealing his status as an undocumented immigrant. See how he navigated that rhetorical situation on p. 993.

THINK ABOUT YOUR PURPOSE

- *How would you describe your own motivation for writing?* To fulfill a course assignment? To meet a personal or professional commitment? To express your ideas to someone?
- *What is your primary goal?* To inform your audience about something? To persuade them to think a certain way? To call them to action? To entertain them? Something else?
- *How do your goals influence your choice of genre, language, medium, and design?* For example, if you want to persuade neighbors to recycle, you may choose to make colorful posters for display in public places. If you want to inform a corporation about what recycling programs accomplish, you may want to write a report using charts and data.

THINK ABOUT YOUR GENRE

- *Have you been assigned a specific genre?* If not, do any words in the assignment imply a certain genre? "Evaluate" may signal a review, for example, and "explain why" could indicate a causal analysis.
- *If you get to choose your genre,* consider your **PURPOSE**. If you want to convince readers to recycle their trash, you would probably write an

argument. If, however, you want to explain how to recycle food waste into compost, your purpose would call for a process analysis.

- **Does your genre require a certain organization?** A process analysis, for instance, is often organized CHRONOLOGICALLY, whereas a visual analysis may be organized SPATIALLY —and an annotated bibliography is almost always organized alphabetically by author's last name.
- **How does your genre affect your TONE?** A lab report, for example, generally calls for a more matter-of-fact tone than a film review.
- **Are certain DESIGN features expected in your genre?** You would likely need to include images in a review of an art show, for instance, or be required to use a standard typeface for a research paper.

THINK ABOUT YOUR AUDIENCE

- **Who is your intended audience?** An instructor? A supervisor? Classmates? Members of a particular organization? Visitors to a website? Who else might see or hear what you say?
- **How are members of your audience like and unlike you?** Consider demographics such as age, gender, religion, income, education, occupation, and political attitudes.
- **What's your relationship with your audience?** An instructor or supervisor, for example, holds considerable authority over you. Other audiences may be friends, coworkers, or even strangers. What expectations about the text might they have because of your relationship?
- **If you have a choice of MEDIUM**, which one(s) would best reach your intended audience?
- **What do you want your audience to think or do** as a result of what you say? Take your ideas seriously? Reflect on their beliefs? Respond to you? Take some kind of action? How will you signal to them what you want?
- **Can you assume your audience will be interested** in what you say, or will you need to get them interested? Are they likely to resist any of your ideas?
- **How much does your audience know about your topic?** How much background information do they need? Will they expect—or be put off by—the use of technical jargon? Will you need to define any terms?

- *Will your audience expect a particular* GENRE*?* If you're writing about Mozart for a music class, you might analyze a piece he composed; if, however, you're commenting on a music video posted on *YouTube*, you'd be more likely to write some kind of review.

- *What about audience members you don't or can't know?* It goes without saying that you won't always know who could potentially read your writing, especially if you're writing online. The ability to reach hundreds, even thousands, of readers is part of the internet's power, but you will want to take special care when your writing might reach unknown audiences. Remember as well that anything posted on the internet may easily be shared and read out of context.

> In his report about TV technology, Adam Clark Estes describes innovations in a factual, straightforward manner, but he still reveals his own stance of skepticism. See how he does it on p. 893.

THINK ABOUT YOUR STANCE

- *What's your attitude toward your topic?* Objective? Strongly supportive? Mildly skeptical? Amused? Angry?

- *What's your relationship with your* AUDIENCE*?* Do they know you, and if so, how? Are you a student? a friend? a mentor? an interested community member? How do they see you, and how do you want to be seen?

- *How can you best convey your stance in your writing?* What TONE do you want it to have? How will your stance and tone be received by your audience? Will they be drawn in by both?

THINK ABOUT THE LARGER CONTEXT

- *What else has been said about your topic,* and how does that affect what you will say? What would be the most effective way for you to add your voice to the conversation?

- *Do you have any constraints?* When is this writing due and how much time and energy can you put into it? How many pages (or minutes) do you have to deliver your message?

- *How much independence do you have as a writer* in this situation? To what extent do you need to meet the expectations of others, such as an instructor or a supervisor? If this writing is an assignment, how can you approach it in a way that makes it matter to you?

THINK ABOUT YOUR LANGUAGE

- *What language does the rhetorical situation invite?* If Lucia's presentation to high school seniors included students from diverse language backgrounds, she probably spoke English. However, if all the students were bilingual, Spanish-speaking students, she could have given the presentation in Spanish or some combination of English and Spanish. Choose the language that best fits your situation.

- *What DIALECT does the rhetorical situation encourage / require?* Does the assignment specify a dialect? If you get to choose, it can be tricky. Most people think of standardized English as the default choice—or what's expected—in American classrooms and workplaces. But this assumption isn't always correct, and another dialect may be more effective or necessary to connect with your audience and achieve your purpose.

- *What level of formality and tone does your rhetorical situation call for?* Does it suggest a serious tone and formal stance? Something more lighthearted and informal? What will your audience expect in terms of tone and formality?

THINK ABOUT YOUR MEDIUM AND DESIGN

- *If you get to choose your medium,* which one will work best for your audience and purpose? Print? Spoken? Digital? Some combination?

- *How will the medium determine what you can and cannot do?* For example, if you're submitting an essay online, you could include video, but if you were writing the same essay in print, you'd only be able to include a still shot from the video.

- *Does your medium favor certain conventions?* Paragraphs work well in print, but presentation slides usually rely on images or bulleted phrases instead. If you are writing online, you can include links to sources and background information.

- *What's the best look for your writing given your rhetorical situation?* Plain and serious? Warm and inviting? What design elements will help you project that look?

- *Should you include visuals?* Would any part of your text benefit from them? Will your audience expect them? What kind would be suitable—photographs? videos? maps? Is there any statistical data that would be easier to understand as a table, chart, or graph?

- *If you're writing a spoken or digital text,* should you include sound? still images? moving images?

>  **REFLECT**
>
> Because you're using this textbook, we can assume you're taking a writing class—you're probably also taking courses in other disciplines and fields of study at the same time. Think about an assignment you recently completed for your writing class, and then think of a written assignment you completed for a different class (physics, business, biology, psychology, art, etc.). Describe the rhetorical situation you faced for each one, using the guidelines in this chapter. Conclude with a bit of analysis: which piece do you think is more successful at addressing the rhetorical situation, and why?

FOUR

Language, Power, and Rhetoric

So, if you really want to hurt me, talk badly about my language. Ethnic identity is twin skin to linguistic identity—I am my language. Until I can take pride in my language, I cannot take pride in myself.

—GLORIA ANZALDÚA

YOU MIGHT REMEMBER being told when you were a child that words do not matter, that "sticks and stones may break your bones, but words will never hurt you." But even as we heard those words, most of us knew they weren't true. Words matter. We can all point to instances when words have been so powerful that they have changed what we think, angered or hurt us, or moved us to action—or when we have used words in the same ways ourselves, for good or for ill.

That was the case for Chicana scholar and author Gloria Anzaldúa, who recalled that when she was growing up in southern Texas in the 1950s, she got slapped on the knuckles with a sharp ruler if she was caught speaking Spanish. When she tried to tell the teacher how to pronounce her name, she was sent to the corner for "talking back." Years later, Anzaldúa and all the Chicana/Chicano students at University of

Texas–Pan American at that time were required to take two speech classes in order to "get rid of [their] accents."

Anzaldúa's experiences were not unusual. Even today, interactions like this happen in the United States, not only for speakers of languages besides English but also for speakers of the many dialects that differ from "standardized English," the variety of language generally used in US schools, newspapers, mainstream media broadcasts, and most textbooks, including this one. African American studies professor Vershawn Ashanti Young refers to these varieties as "undervalued dialects," which include Black English, the Chicano English mentioned by Anzaldúa, signed language, and many other social and regional dialects. And it's not just the dialects that are undervalued; their speakers are often subjected to acts of intolerance, as Anzaldúa recounts. In short, the words we choose can sometimes do harm.

This chapter invites you to reflect on your attitudes about language (including your own ways of communicating) and to consider how to use your full repertoire of languages and dialects in ways that are effective and also fair and just for everyone concerned, including yourself. Thinking rhetorically will be a key tool for achieving these goals.

Gloria Anzaldúa, who asserted, "I am my language."

> ### REFLECT
>
> Have you had experiences of being "corrected" for something you said or the way you said it? Was it about your pronunciation? word choice? grammar? Who made the comment? Why did they do so? On the other hand, can you think of any times when you were praised or rewarded for your language use? How do you think those experiences have contributed to the ways you use language today?

How Does Language Relate to Power—and Privilege?

It's our job as ethical authors to understand how our language choices are connected to power and privilege. "Power" is the ability to control or influence, while "privilege" refers to advantages or benefits available to some but not to others. Language is one engine through which power and privilege operate. Think for a moment about whether you've ever witnessed someone mocked for the way they speak or write—or maybe you have experienced this yourself.

This is exactly what talk show host and South Carolina native Stephen Colbert experienced when he decided at a young age that he didn't want to have a Southern accent. In an interview on *60 Minutes*, Colbert explained, "When I was a kid watching TV, if you wanted to use a shorthand that someone was stupid, you gave them a Southern accent. And that's not true. Southern people are not stupid." What Colbert says shows how self-conscious people can become when the way they speak is considered in some way inferior, and how entire groups of people may be ostracized for the way they use language. And it's about more than just feelings: a 2018 study by urban policy professor Jeffrey Grogger found that people with identifiable Southern accents earned lower wages than those without the same accent. In other words, Colbert wasn't imagining things; research shows evidence of discrimination.

As these examples suggest, language plays a key role in establishing—and maintaining—power and privilege. With so many languages and dialects spoken in the United States (the Census Bureau reports one in five Americans use a language other than English at home!), it's important to

THE NEED FOR RHETORIC AND WRITING

Stephen Colbert, on the set of his late-night TV show.

understand how words and language grant privileges to some, hinder others, and offer opportunities for us all. Doing so is an important step in understanding the **CONTEXT** for our language choices. Whatever else language is all about, it is certainly about power and privilege.

Look into Your Own Attitudes about Language

> Glavee Glavee describes some language attitudes—including their own—that have affected their life and identity. Read about it on p. 905.

Attitudes—how we think and feel about something—affect our lives at every turn. But what do attitudes have to do with language? We all have attitudes toward particular languages or dialects, pronunciations, and other ways of using words. If a certain accent strikes you as comforting, snooty, or unsophisticated, those reactions are based on feelings, even unconscious ones, that can affect how you relate to people—or even to yourself. So our attitudes about languages can have consequences. For example, linguists John Rickford and Sharese King analyze how, in the George Zimmerman trial for the murder of Trayvon Martin, the testimony of key prosecution witness Rachel Jeantel was largely dismissed by jurors because of her use of African American Vernacular English:

Not only was Jeantel's vernacular pivotal in the disregard of her critically important testimony in this case, but in numerous other cases in the United States and around the world in which witnesses and defendants use a vernacular rather than the mainstream variety, they tend to be misunderstood or discredited, and encounter dialect unfamiliarity or prejudice in courtrooms and potentially unfair judicial outcomes.
—JOHN RICKFORD & SHARESE KING, "Language and Linguistics on Trial: Hearing Rachel Jeantel (and Other Vernacular Speakers) in the Courtroom and Beyond"

Research confirms that the linguistic discrimination pointed out by Rickford and King plays a role in the judicial system as well as in housing, education, and employment opportunities.

So how can you go about examining your own language attitudes? Changing how we think and feel can be a long process. What you can do right now, though, is be more aware of your responses to language—stop to think through your automatic reactions and examine your beliefs and assumptions. You can also consider how language, power, and privilege are at work around you, which is called practicing **CRITICAL LANGUAGE AWARENESS**. Developing the habit of checking your own language attitudes will prepare you to make better-informed choices as an author.

Let's take a look at how such language awareness works—or doesn't work! In 2021, sports commentator Stephen A. Smith caused quite a stir when he made on-air comments about Major League Baseball (MLB) star and Japanese native Shohei Ohtani, who uses an interpreter during media interviews. Smith said:

> The fact that you've got a foreign player that doesn't speak English . . . contributes to harming the game to some degree. . . , I don't think it helps that the number one face [of baseball today] is a dude that needs an interpreter so you can understand what the hell he's saying.
> —STEPHEN A. SMITH, *First Take*

After a backlash in response to his comments, Smith offered apologies. First, on *Instagram*, he acknowledged his comments were "insensitive and regrettable" and went on to say that "Ohtani is one of the brightest stars in all of sports . . . making a difference as it pertains to inclusiveness and leadership." He also apologized on air, admitting, "I messed up and I hurt people with my words." Smith's original comments showed a

ESPN commentator Stephen A. Smith (left) and billboard of baseball superstar Shohei Ohtani (right).

big lack of critical language awareness, while his apologies suggest that awareness is growing. Ironically, Smith's claim that Ohtani's language harms the MLB were inaccurate. In fact, Ohtani signed a $700 million contract, the largest in US sports history, not too long after Smith made these remarks. The face of the MLB and also a global icon, Ohtani has landed enormous endorsement deals that feature him on billboards in New York City's Times Square and around the world. We can do better than Smith and go beyond apologies to ask where our assumptions about language come from and to intentionally practice language awareness rather than language discrimination.

> ### REFLECT
>
> Are there any ways of speaking that you really like? How about ones that you find irritating? Where do your own ways of speaking fall on this spectrum? Do you have any general opinions about the users of the languages that came to mind? Examine those reactions to check if any stereotypes slipped in. Would the speakers or users of that variety agree with your assessments? Upon reflection, do you think your judgments are accurate and fair?

4 ⌘ Language, Power, and Rhetoric

What Is Standardized English?

We can't discuss language, power, and rhetoric without considering the variety of English widely used in US schools, government, businesses, and industries: the variety we call standardized English. It's the variety we use in this textbook and one your rhetorical situation will likely point you toward during your college and professional careers. Understanding some of the controversy and debate about standardized English is important as you consider your own language choices. There is no single, universally accepted name for this variety; it also goes by "academic English," "White mainstream English," and "dominant English." The authors and editors of this book have chosen "standardized English" because it emphasizes the fact that this isn't a naturally occurring, organic variety. Further, "standardized" signals that this variety of English is always (slowly) shifting and changing rather than being a fixed "standard."

Some form of standardization exists for every language that has an active writing and publishing tradition. And some standardization is useful, for example, by allowing published works to reach the broadest possible audiences. Some argue that using standardized English in certain contexts can open doors—especially in professional worlds. As high school English teacher Jasmine Lane puts it, she would never "discount the impact that my command of Standard English has had on my success."

But you might wonder why the standardized English we know today is the way it is. Why, for example, is it so close to how many upper- and upper-middle-class people in the United States speak? In almost all languages, the dialect chosen to be the "standard" has been the one generally used by social elites. Over time, the standardized variety comes to be used in most public contexts—like in government and education. Many come to see it as the "best," "most proper," or "correct" form of the language, which can result in all other dialects being viewed as "less than."

At the same time, resistance to standardization has always existed, not only among those who speak other dialects in the United States but also among artists, activists, and educators—people who use a variety of resources to champion linguistic justice. And today, there are many examples of "standards" being up for intepretation. As rhetoric and composition professor Asao Inoue points out, we can see such variation at work in the standards guiding highway speed limits, which dictate 65 mph in Arizona, 70 in Michigan and Mississippi, and 80 in South Dakota. Is it really safer to go 80 in South Dakota just over the border from Iowa, where the standard is 70? Inoue goes on to consider how such standards apply to language:

> Standards are decisions made by people for particular reasons, but they are not universal, nor are they infallible. This goes for language standards too. They may very well be capricious and cause some people undue harm. They are just the rules we have inherited today, made by people who had the power to do so yesterday.
>
> —ASAO INOUE, *Above the Well: An Antiracist Literacy Argument from a Boy of Color*

Inoue's example points out what scholars of language have argued for a long time: considering one "standard" variety of a language better than all others is a mistake. Or as the University of Michigan's Linguistics Department puts it, "no language is superior or inferior to another." In other words, every language, and every variety of language, is vital, valid, and can be used effectively—including standardized English and all the many varieties and languages beyond it. And you can judge what will be most effective by analyzing your **RHETORICAL SITUATION**.

We know, however, that not every variety is welcome in every setting. An academic setting like the college classroom is one place where a standardized version is often still expected. Many scholars and instructors of writing have worked for change around language standards in American English classes. One notable attempt occurred in 1974.

Students' Right to Their Own Language. In 1974, the Conference on College Composition and Communication, a professional organization for teachers of college writing, adopted a statement called "Students' Right to Their Own Language." It began: "We affirm the students' right to their own patterns and varieties of language—the dialects of their nurture or whatever dialects in which they find their own identity and style." This statement sounded a call for teachers of writing to be more critically aware of language, and to recognize that the dominant "standard" being taught was just one variety of English—one that had too often left out or suppressed many student voices. The Students' Right statement urged teachers to recognize this discrepancy and to honor linguistic diversity in their classrooms.

Demand for Black Linguistic Justice. Since issuing the 1974 statement, that same professional organization has issued more than a dozen statements and resolutions on topics related to linguistic diversity, awareness, and justice. In 2020, a special committee released a position statement titled "This Ain't Another Statement! This is a demand for Black Linguistic Justice!," which demands, among other things, that "teachers stop using standard English as the accepted norm, which reflects White Mainstream English." In 2021, the organization issued another statement, with the resolution: "We reaffirm our commitments to linguistic diversity and to the multiple languages and linguistic histories of our students and communities."

Although the organization's statements are clear and strong, many still seek practical guidance for how to ensure that the rights these statements recognize can be met. In the past, teaching standardized English was a tidy way to approach a wide range of languages and dialects in one course. But as you've seen, this approach can also present barriers. What if standardized English were instead expanded and enlarged, making space within it so that many varieties could be recognized and appreciated?

 **REFLECT**

Did you ever consider that the language you use is something you have "rights" about? Would those rights include only what you say, sign, and write, or could they also include what you hear, see, or read? How might you describe or explain your language rights?

What's an Author to Do?

Today, debates about standardized English and other powerful ways of communicating are a hot topic. In such a time, what's a college student to do? How can you navigate language expectations? How can you make careful language choices in all the writing, speaking, and listening that you do? How can you make the most of all your language abilities while negotiating any risks? In short, how can you become a just, effective, and responsible communicator?

Answering these questions is a tall and complex order. There are no easy solutions, but we can offer some guiding thoughts and questions to

Missy Watson, a composition instructor, has a lot more to say about standardized English. Read her essay on p. 1010.

consider, which all begin with practicing language awareness—keeping in mind the social and political contexts of all language choices.

- *Understand your* RHETORICAL SITUATION. What are your AUDIENCES' expectations? What is your PURPOSE and how can your language choices help you achieve it? Does your CONTEXT or GENRE come with certain language expectations? How will your STANCE be most clearly stated? What's at stake for you when making decisions about how to respond to your specific rhetorical situation?

- *Navigate language expectations.* You might be thinking, "No one language or dialect is better than another, but there is still this thing called standardized English and expectations or requirements to use it." You're right, there is and there are. So, what if you're most comfortable communicating in a dialect that's not standardized English? How do you, as a writer, create a space for yourself, and set yourself up for success, in a setting that values or requires standardized English? Believing that standardized English is not superior to other dialects doesn't eliminate the power that standardized English has, particularly in classrooms or boardrooms. And using it is neither "bad" nor "good"; it's all about assessing which language choices will best help you achieve your goals.

    For example, it's no coincidence that this textbook is written in standardized English. We could use a different dialect to communicate our writing advice effectively; however, the rhetorical situation we've assessed—a writing textbook for a broad audience of college writers across the United States, multiple coauthors from diverse language and cultural backgrounds, and the expectations of an American textbook publisher, to name a few factors—figured in our decision. You, too, will need to make decisions by analyzing your RHETORICAL SITUATION, what's expected, and your own values and goals.

- *Explore all the language resources you bring with you* from your community, your family, and your life experience (multiple languages, several dialects). Consider how power and privilege may be at play in the choices you make but remember also that your resources are strengths you can consider drawing on. (See Chapter 35 for suggestions on mixing languages and dialects in your writing.)

- REFLECT *on the language choices you're making,* why you're making them, and how those choices help you take control of your writing.

▶ See Ch. 35 in the ebook for a video about writing how you speak.

Reflect, too, on the times you may want to resist expectations—of a particular genre or rhetorical situation—and when you may choose to accept and conform to them.

- **REFLECT** *on your own attitudes about language.* What beliefs do you have about English and its relationship to other languages and dialects? Where do these beliefs come from?
- *Consider how you use different varieties of language* to communicate and/or to position yourself inside or outside of a group. Have you been in a situation where someone has used language to position you as an outsider? Have you used language in order to position yourself as an insider?
- *Think carefully before using AI to speak for you* because those tools don't have the unique, individual voice that only you possess. What's more, the writing they produce tends to use standardized English, which may not always be the best choice for your writing situation.
- *Observe how others act on their attitudes toward language.* What do you notice about how individuals and groups use language to establish bonds with others? to create or reinforce identity? to support others? to put others down?
- *Listen and read carefully* to understand and engage with speakers and writers from diverse language backgrounds. Use social media as a resource for getting acquainted with people who use language differently than you do. Be open-minded and pay attention to check any knee-jerk reactions you have to someone's language or dialect. Examine what assumptions or biases are behind any immediate reactions to see if you're being fair.

We've all read writers, listened to songs, and viewed advertisements in which a dialect of English different from the standardized version was used. We've probably all admired writers who push the boundaries of language expectations. Take a look, for example, at this passage from Gloria Anzaldúa's essay, "How to Tame a Wild Tongue": "Even our own people, other Spanish speakers *nos quieren poner candados en la boca* [they want to put padlocks on our mouths]. They would hold us back with their bag of *reglas de academia* [academic rules]." Anzaldúa, a widely celebrated writer and often-cited scholar, included many Spanish words and phrases in her academic writing; some editions of her work, but not all, include translations (as we've done here). The linguistic risks she took certainly contributed to her effectiveness and success as a writer.

If no one pushes back against established power structures, what chance is there to challenge the privileges that lead to inequity? Yet, we recognize that you, as college students, are in precarious positions and that pushing back against language expectations may threaten your academic success. We invite you to understand the challenges, risks, and benefits of using standardized English and other varieties in college classrooms and then make informed choices. If you're interested in doing more, consider these further steps:

- *Ask* your instructor if your class can have discussions about language expectations, linguistic diversity, and rhetoric. These kinds of discussions are sure to benefit everyone.
- *Explore and learn* about research on the history of specific language practices in your home and community.
- *Develop,* as best you can, proficiency in a variety of dialects and languages, appreciating the power and value of all your language tools.
- *Think* about how you as a writer can effect changes toward a more just world through your writing. This is, perhaps, the most important step you can take.

REFLECT

Professor of anthropology and African American studies H. Samy Alim poses two questions that prompt language awareness: "How can language be used to maintain, reinforce, and perpetuate existing power relations?" and "Conversely, how can language be used to resist, redefine, and possibly reverse these relations?" How would you answer these questions based on your own experiences? Write a brief description of a time when you used language either to maintain or to resist existing power relations. Reflect on why you made the choices you did.

FIVE

Joining Academic Communities
Habits for Success in College

LLEN MACNAMARA ARRIVED at college excited but anxious. She had grown up in a small rural town with an almost all-White population and attended a school that offered few options in terms of learning languages or taking Advanced Placement classes, where most students sought employment right after high school. The first person in her family to go to college, she wondered what she was in for.

Luis Garcia arrived at college from his home in Brownsville, Texas, where his grandparents emigrated from Mexico in the 1960s. With family on both sides of the border, Luis grew up speaking Spanish and a Tex-Mex dialect, using English only in school. A strong student throughout high school, Luis received a local scholarship—and he, too, was excited but nervous about what he could contribute to the college community he was entering.

Like Ellen and Luis, millions of students enter college wondering about college expectations, especially about how they'll "fit in" to the big group of students and teachers that make up the community on their campus—and more specifically, what steps they can take to become an active participant of that community. One student we know described arriving at college and getting to know what's expected by saying, "It's almost like learning a new language!" This chapter aims to help you successfully join in the conversations and communities you'll be a part of in college.

Why Participate?

A vibrant academic community is built on students and teachers engaging, listening, and working together. You'll find yourself invited into a great many conversations on campus, and you'll want to think about how and what it means to contribute meaningfully. The images below show some examples: talking in small groups, presenting ideas to captivated listeners, pairing up to share writing with classmates, and so on.

Thoughtful and consistent participation is key for learning to happen in any class, but especially in your writing classes. As a writing student, you'll likely be invited to investigate issues you care about; you'll dig into research and deliberate viewpoints; you'll produce your own arguments, trying out different strategies to get your point across; and you'll work through a process for writing, reflecting on what works for you—or not—along the way. Each of these steps depends on sharing your ideas and work with others—people who listen, read, and help you refine your thinking. Meaningful participation—showing up, listening, thinking, and sharing—is at the heart

Writers on campus engage, contribute, and participate in a variety of ways.

of strong academic conversations and communities; your and your peers' learning depends on it. So strive to find ways to engage, contribute, and participate in all your college classes.

Participation can take many forms. Review your syllabus or talk with your instructor about what's expected (and if or how it counts toward your grade). In writing classes, participation means speaking up during class meetings and small-group work, posting and responding to online discussion boards, crafting feedback on your peers' writing, and unpacking assigned readings (like the chapters in this textbook!) with classmates. You might worry about sharing your ideas and writing in these ways, with some activities feeling more comfortable than others. That's normal—sharing your thoughts takes courage! Push yourself to take the risk because vibrant academic conversations depend on students building trust with one another. Remember that everyone is working out ideas in progress. Your and your peers' collective and frequent participation is what makes a class successful—and fun! In fact, in a survey of writing students at University of Maryland, respondents identified "interactions with and feedback from peers" as *the key elements* of their academic success.

 **REFLECT**

Think about the ways you tend to contribute in class meetings. Which strategies do you get the most out of? Which do you avoid? "Participation" isn't one-size-fits-all, and many instructors and campuses offer accommodations to ensure all students are able to contribute. Take a minute to reflect on your own participation style and consider talking to your instructor or looking up campus resources on accommodations if you could use support to participate in class.

Habits for Success

While every college campus has its own unique culture, its own ways of doing things, there are some general expectations that hold across campuses. Your ability to evaluate the expectations at your own school will also be of major importance. Practicing these habits in your coursework will put you on a path toward success as you work to become an active writer and an engaged participant in your classes.

- **Be curious.** Inquire, investigate, poke, and pry until you discover or create something new. Ask a lot of questions: Why are the parking lots or dorms on campus so far away from the academic buildings? How does the distance affect students who don't have bikes, for instance, or those with physical disabilities? Who makes these decisions, and why?

- **Be creative.** Take a risk investigating an idea or topic outside your comfort zone. Try methods, approaches, or styles that are new to you. Try looking at your topic from different points of view. Perhaps use a different medium for representing an idea or mix languages and/or dialects in making your point. If you think about your favorite school endeavors, you may find that creativity played an important role.

> Would it ever occur to you to compare AI to cake? Christopher Basgier wrote a whole essay doing exactly that (p. 855), and surprisingly, it works. The creative risk paid off!

- **Be open and flexible.** Work hard at looking at all sides of any issue, especially those that seem strange or incorrect to you. Listen carefully to opposing views. In a discussion about campus safety, for example, try to put yourself in the position of people with different perspectives—perhaps an older faculty member or someone who identifies with a different gender category than you do.

- **Be engaged.** Grapple with the ideas of others, responding to them and looking for connections between them. Seek out something in every course or assignment that really interests you, even if the course is not your favorite. A student we know was taking a course on ancient religious texts, primarily to fulfill a requirement, but when they read the Samson and Delilah story in different traditions, they used a passion for comics to create a graphic narrative of one version. A seemingly boring topic became exciting!

- **Be persistent.** Keep at it. Take advantage of opportunities to redo and improve. Keep track of what's challenging or hard for you—and talk with your instructor or a writing center consultant (or a good friend!) to look for ways to overcome those obstacles. Or keep asking why these obstacles exist: Where do they come from? What about them is in your power to change? A student searching for information on a distant relative who had played a role in the civil rights movement kept coming up empty-handed and was tempted to give up. Persistence paid off, though, when she decided to call her grandmother's cousin, who remembered a name she was able to trace to an ancestry website—one more try led to a big breakthrough.

- **Be responsible.** Hold yourself responsible for making the most of your education—own it. And be a responsible participant in academic conversations by acknowledging the words and ideas of others and engaging with them thoughtfully and fairly. At the same time, take responsibility for holding others accountable. You may see major unfairness at work, for example, in the process of inviting students into honor societies, or the way financial aid is awarded. When you note such inequities, work with others to confront them.

- **Think about the way you think.** Take time to reflect on how you learn and think. Such purposeful REFLECTION provides a snapshot of you as a thinker, a snapshot you can learn from as you identify obstacles to your learning and create ways to overcome them.

- **Be true to yourself.** While you, like almost all students, will change during college, developing intellectually and emotionally, acquiring a great deal of new knowledge, and growing more surely into the person you want to become, that definitely does not mean leaving behind core values or cultures or languages. You may come to question some of your earlier values or revise them; you may add an understanding of other cultures and languages—but you have the right, and perhaps the responsibility, to do so while also honoring your own.

CHARACTERISTIC FEATURES

Of course, one major way you'll contribute to academic conversations is through the texts you compose. And writing assignments often specify certain features that those in the academic community expect to find. No list of features can describe all the kinds of texts you'll be assigned to write, particularly given the differences among disciplines. But there are some things you're generally expected to do in college writing:

- Use clear and recognizable patterns of organization (p. 56)
- Mark logical relationships between ideas (p. 57)
- State claims explicitly and provide suitable support (p. 57)
- Present your ideas as a response to others (p. 58)

See Ch. 20 in the ebook for a video on understanding academic arguments.

- Express your ideas directly (p. 58)
- Be aware of how genres and conventions vary across disciplines (p. 59)
- Document sources using the appropriate citation style (p. 60)

Use Clear and Recognizable Patterns of Organization

Academic writing is often organized in a way that's clear and easy for readers to recognize. In fact, writers generally describe the pattern explicitly early in a text by including a **THESIS** statement that states the main point and says how the text is structured.

At the paragraph level, the opening sentence generally serves as a **TOPIC SENTENCE**, which announces what the paragraph is about. Readers of academic writing expect such signals for the text as a whole and within each paragraph, even in shorter texts like essay exams. Sometimes you'll want to include headings to make it easy for readers to locate sections of text.

Readers of academic writing look for organization not only to be clear but also to follow some kind of logical progression. For example:

- Beginning with the simplest ideas and then moving step by step to the most complex ideas
- Starting with the weakest claims or evidence and progressing to the strongest ones
- Treating some topics early in the text because readers must have them as background to understand ideas introduced later
- Arranging the text chronologically, starting with the earliest events and ending with the latest ones

Some academic documents in the sciences and social sciences require a specific organization known as **IMRAD** for its specific headings: introduction, methods, results, analysis, and discussion. Although there are many possible logical patterns to use, readers will expect to be able to see that pattern with little or no difficulty. Likewise, they generally expect the **TRANSITIONS** between sections and ideas to be indicated in some way, whether with words like "first," "next," or "finally," or even with full sentences like "Having considered three reasons to support this position, I will now present some alternative positions."

Finally, remember that you need to conclude your text by somehow reminding your readers of the main point(s) you want them to take away.

See the ebook for a video on topic sentences.

Often, these reminders explicitly link the conclusion back to the thesis statement or introduction.

Mark Logical Relationships between Ideas

Academic writers usually strive to make clear how the ideas they present relate to one another. Thus, in addition to marking the structure of the text, you'll want to mark the links between ideas. If you say in casual conversation, "It was raining, and we didn't go on the picnic," listeners will interpret "and" to mean "so" or "therefore." In academic writing, however, you have to help readers understand how your ideas are related to one another. For this reason, you'll want to use **TRANSITIONS** like "therefore," "however," or "in addition." Marking the relationships among your ideas clearly and explicitly helps readers recognize and appreciate the logic of your arguments.

State Claims Explicitly and Provide Suitable Support

One of the most important conventions of academic writing is to present **CLAIMS** explicitly and support them with **EVIDENCE**, such as examples or statistics, or by citing authorities. Notice the two distinct parts: presenting claims clearly and supporting them suitably. In academic writing, authors don't generally give hints; instead, they state what is on their minds, often in a **THESIS** statement. If you are from a culture that communicates by hinting or by repeating proverbs or telling stories to make a point, check to be sure that you have stated your claims explicitly in your academic writing.

Qualify your statements. Note that being clear and explicit doesn't mean being closed minded. You'll generally want to moderate your claims by using qualifying words like "frequently," "often," "generally," "sometimes," or "rarely" to indicate how strong a claim you are making. Note as well that it is much easier to provide adequate support for a qualified claim than it is to provide support for a broad unqualified claim.

Choose evidence your audience will trust. Whatever your claim, you'll need to use **EVIDENCE** that will be considered trustworthy and persuasive by your audience. And keep in mind that what counts as acceptable and suitable evidence in academic writing often differs from what works in other contexts. Generally, for example, you probably wouldn't cite from uncorroborated social media posts for academic arguments. In addition, writers today need more than ever to act as fact-checkers, making certain that their sources are accurate and credible. And keep in mind that generative AI tools can "hallucinate," or cite sources that seem real, but in fact don't exist at all.

Consider multiple perspectives. You should be aware that your readers may have a range of opinions on any topic, and you should write accordingly. Thus, citing only sources that reflect one perspective won't be sufficient. Be sure to consider and acknowledge COUNTERARGUMENTS and viewpoints other than your own.

In considering what kind of evidence to use in supporting your claims, remember that the goal is not to amass and present large quantities of evidence but instead to sift through all the available evidence, choose the evidence that will be most persuasive to your audience, and arrange and present it all strategically. Resist the temptation to include information that does not contribute to your argument.

Present Your Ideas as a Response to Others

Academic writing is a way of entering a conversation—of engaging with the ideas of others. That means that strong academic writers do more than just make well-supported claims. They present their ideas as a response to what else has been said (or what might be said) about their topic. English professors Gerald Graff and Cathy Birkenstein identify one strategy for introducing readers to this conversation: start with what others are saying and then introduce your own ideas, showing how you're engaging those you're in conversation with.

Providing support for your claims will often involve SYNTHESIS : weaving the ideas and even the words of others into the argument you are making. And since academic arguments are part of a larger conversation, all of us are always responding to others, even as we are developing our own individual ideas.

Express Your Ideas Directly

Be specific in your language. DEFINE terms you use, both to be sure readers will not be confused and to clarify your own positions. Clarity of expression in academic writing also means being direct and concise. Academic writers in the United States tend to avoid elaborate sentence structures or flowery language, and they don't let the metaphors and similes they use get the best of them either, as this author did:

> Cheryl's mind turned like the vanes of a wind-powered turbine, chopping her sparrowlike thoughts into bloody pieces that fell onto a growing pile of forgotten memories.

In fact, this sentence was the winner of an annual "bad writing" contest in which writers try to write the worst sentence they can. It's easy to see why this one was a winner: it has way too much figurative language, and the metaphors get in the way of one another. Use metaphors carefully in academic writing, making sure they add to what you're trying to say. Here's one way the prize-winning sentence might be revised to be clearer and more direct: "Cheryl's mind worked incessantly, thought after thought piling up until she couldn't keep track of them all."

Be Aware of How Genres and Conventions Vary across Disciplines

As you are no doubt discovering, academic disciplines have their own sets of conventions: the use of first person is "conventional" in some humanities courses, for instance, but in the sciences—not so much. Passive voice verbs are preferred in the sciences, while writers in the humanities often go for active verbs. The social sciences generally use the conventions of the documentation system endorsed by the American Psychological Association (APA); those in the humanities use the systems endorsed by the Modern Language Association (MLA) or *The Chicago Manual of Style* (Chicago); those in the sciences use the system endorsed by the Council of Science Editors (CSE). As you choose a major and enter a discipline, reading articles and books in the field and composing assignments, you will learn more and more about the particular conventions expected of you.

Despite the significant differences in genres across academic disciplines, you'll also find that there are some common rhetorical moves you'll likely make in much of the academic writing you do. You'll find that academic essays and research articles generally open with three such moves:

- First, you give the **CONTEXT** or general topic of whatever you are writing. Frequently, you will do this by discussing the existing research or commentary on the topic you are writing about.

- Second, you point out some aspect of this topic that merits additional attention, often because it is poorly understood or because there is a problem that needs to be solved—that is, you'll show there is a gap of some kind in our understanding.
- Finally, you'll explain how your text addresses that problem or fills that gap. This explanation often comes in the first paragraph or two.

Document Sources Using the Appropriate Citation Style

Finally, academic writers credit and **DOCUMENT** all sources carefully. Understanding how Western academic culture defines intellectual property and **PLAGIARISM** is complicated. Although you never need to provide a source for common knowledge that no one disputes (for example, that the US Declaration of Independence was approved by Congress on July 4, 1776, in Philadelphia), you will need to document words, information, or ideas that you get from others, including, of course, any content (words or images) you find on the internet. Think of documentation as another way to show your readers the academic conversation you're entering. Your **WORKS-CITED** or **REFERENCES** page is like a list of the people you've been talking with. And when you cite sources, you're letting readers know more about the conversation you're contributing to and providing the information they need to learn more or join in themselves. You're also thinking and acting rhetorically.

What else do you need to know about academic writing? It's important to note that the academic expectations, moves, and conventions discussed in this chapter are solidly set in Western traditions of language and thought, ways of knowing and of persuading that have long been associated with the dominant, often elite, culture in the United States as well as with the dialect of standardized English. Throughout our history, this dialect—along with Western academic conventions—have been thought to provide a common ground for communication, something everyone could learn and use. But "everyone" has turned out to leave a lot of people out. Thus, as noted in Chapter 4, resistance to such "standard" practices has a long history in the United States, and today many aspects of Western academic conventions, including standardized English, are under scrutiny as writers push the envelope of academic discourse to make room for more expansive methods of research, means of organization, languages and dialects, and styles. As professor of literacy studies Elaine Richardson says, learning to use academic styles today needs to allow for experimentation and inclusivity and must not "lock us into evaluating students' cultures. Curricula must be conceived in such a way that students are trained to discern, appreciate, and master diverse styles."

Taking such a flexible approach recognizes that there's usually more than one effective way to say or write something. And while the use of Western forms of academic discourse and standardized English is one way (and still the dominant way in most academic writing), it's not better or worse than other ways. As you enter the academic conversations of your choosing, your audience and purpose should ultimately guide the choices you make.

REFLECT

Think about a time when you've practiced one of the habits of success discussed in this chapter. How did it make you feel? What motivated you to take this approach and what was the outcome? What's one habit of success you *haven't* tried that you plan to work on this term? Jot down one or two ways you'll put this new habit into practice.

PART II

Reading Processes

*I don't read such small things as letters;
I read men and nations.*

—SOJOURNER TRUTH

O YOU REMEMBER the first word you learned to read? For many, that first word was their own name: you printed it over and over again and—suddenly, as if by magic—you could read it! Those first reading moments open up entire new worlds to us; "Oh, the places you'll go!" as Dr. Seuss says, once you can read. As this example shows, reading and writing are reciprocal processes: writing leads to reading and reading leads to writing, like two sides of the same coin.

You probably spend so much time reading, on your phone and other devices, that you don't even notice it: you take it for granted, like breathing. But reading turns out to be a complicated process. The aim of the following chapters is to call attention to the complex processes and practices of reading and to get you to think carefully as you do them. Another aim of these chapters is to do what ethnographers recommend to spark new ideas: make the familiar strange. We want to make the processes and practices of everyday, commonplace reading "strange" in order to get you to look at them with fresh and creative eyes and to think carefully—about what you are doing when you read, about different ways of reading, and about the processes that reading demands of you.

 **REFLECT**

Think about the reading you do regularly. Is it most often for fun? to find information? for school? And what kind of a reader do you think you are? Impatient and speedy? Anxious? Curious? What else? Finally, what kind of reading do you enjoy most—and why?

SIX

Reading Rhetorically

**HANCES ARE, YOU READ MORE** than you think you do. You read print texts, and you probably also read regularly on a phone, tablet, or computer. Reading is now, as perhaps never before, a basic necessity. In fact, if you think that reading is something you learned once and for all in childhood, think again.

"But wait," you say. "Can't I just ask AI to read and make a summary for me?" While AI might produce misinformation and even make things up, when used carefully, AI tools might help unpack dense, difficult texts; define unfamiliar terms; and more. But AI cannot *read* for you. That is, AI cannot fire the complex processes in your brain that lead to comprehension and deep understanding. Only you and your brain and your emotions can engage and analyze what you are reading and then draw your own conclusions from it.

We call the kind of reading we're advocating for "rhetorical reading," and while such reading uses tools of all kinds, including AI, it also calls for strategic effort and attention. In his book *The Economics of Attention*, rhetorician Richard Lanham explains: "We're drowning in information. What we lack is the human attention needed to make sense of it all."

When so many texts are vying for our attention, which ones do we choose? In order to decide what to pay attention to, we need to practice what media critic Howard Rheingold calls "infotention," a word he came up with to describe a "mind-machine combination of brain-powered attention skills and computer-powered information filters." Rheingold is writing before AI chatbots appeared, but in describing the "mind-machine combination" he was ahead of his time. And his concept of "infotention" is important for reading any kind of text because it calls for synthesizing and thinking rhetorically about the enormous amount of information available to us in both print and digital sources. And while some of us can multitask, most of us are not good at it and must learn to focus our attention when we read.

In other words, we need to learn to read rhetorically. Reading rhetorically means attending carefully and intentionally to a text. It means being open-minded to that text. And it means being an active participant in understanding and thinking about and responding to what is in the text. As Nobel laureate Toni Morrison says, "The words on the page are only half the story. The rest is what you bring to the party."

So how do you learn to read rhetorically and to practice infotention? Some steps seem obvious: especially for high-stakes reading, like much of what you do for school, you need to find space and time in which you can really focus—turn off social media and put your phone out of sight. Beyond such obvious steps, though, you can improve your reading by approaching texts systematically. This chapter and the chapters that follow will guide you in doing so.

So many texts vying for our attention!

 **REFLECT**

Think about how and when you multitask while reading. Do you take breaks to do something else, and if so, what? How long do you read at one stretch and maintain full concentration? Write a brief response to these questions and reflect on how well the reading processes you describe have worked for you. How satisfied are you with the way you read?

THINKING ABOUT YOUR RHETORICAL SITUATION

Before jumping into a text, consider your RHETORICAL SITUATION; doing so will help you get straight where the author—and you—are coming from. Following are some questions to consider when approaching a text:

- What's the PURPOSE for your reading? To learn something new? To fulfill an assignment? To prepare for a test?

- Who's the intended AUDIENCE? What words or images in the text make you think so? Are you a member of this group? If not, there may be unfamiliar terms or references that you'll need to look up.

- What's the GENRE? An argument? Report? Review? Proposal? Knowing the genre will tell you something about what to expect.

- How might the MEDIUM affect how you will read the text? Is it a written print text? an oral text? a visual or multimedia text, such as an infographic? How will you go about attending carefully to different media elements?

- How do LANGUAGE choices affect your reading of the text? Are languages other than English used, and if so, why? Is the REGISTER formal? informal? friendly? something else? How does the register affect your reading of the text?

- What do you know about the larger CONTEXT of the text? What do you know about the topic? What do you need to find out? What resources can you draw on for the information you will need?

- What is your own STANCE on the topic? Are you an advocate? a critic? an impartial observer?

Setting your rhetorical bearings prepares you for your first job as a reader: making sure you understand what you read. Chapter 7 offers guidance on other essential strategies for understanding texts: previewing, annotating, and summarizing. The rest of this chapter focuses on how to be a motivated, engaged, and persistent reader.

BECOMING AN ACTIVE, ENGAGED READER

It's the weekend, and as you look at assignments and due dates for the week ahead, you're wondering how you'll get all that required reading done. True, you've procrastinated. What to do? Skim the readings, jot down some notes, and hope for the best? Ask AI to summarize for you and hope that will be good enough? Ignore the reading altogether and do the assignments without it? There are times when you might be forced to make one of these choices, but we hope they are few and very far between. Maybe it's time to stop and ask yourself: What's all that reading for anyhow? And what's in it for you? Contemporary cognitive research shows that the kind of engaged, active reading this chapter encourages leads to better learning, deeper understanding, and more meaningful connections between you and the ideas in the text, which is more than any kind of skimming or AI-generated summaries can provide.

What this means is that you need to pay close attention to when it's fine to skim—trying to determine whether a source is worth pursuing further, for example, or locating just one piece of information—and when the stakes are high and you need to be an active, engaged reader who is in it to learn and to understand.

This kind of engaged reading is easy to do when you are really interested in the text at hand. But just how can you get yourself "invested" in something you've been assigned to read, especially if it's a text you wouldn't choose to read otherwise? There's no magic wand you can wave to make this happen, but we can offer some advice:

- **Find your comfort zone,** someplace where you'll be able to concentrate. A comfy lounge chair? A desk chair with back support? Some students tell us they like to be a little *uncomfortable* because it keeps them on their mental toes.

- **Choose a device that helps you focus.** Some students like print texts best for taking notes, while others like reading on a device without internet distractions.
- **Make it social.** In the case of difficult texts, two heads are usually better than one—and discussing a text with someone else will help you both engage with it. Try to explain something in the text to a friend; if you can get across the major points, you've surely understood it!
- **Start with what's easy, then tackle what's difficult.** The introduction may be easy to read, so begin there and make sure you understand it before moving on to more difficult material. If the text is short, read it all the way through once, marking the hard parts. Then return to the tricky parts; you'll probably find they are easier to understand once you've read through the entire text once.
- **Annotate as you read.** Chapter 7 will give you guidelines for using annotation to understand and respond to what you read.

FAST—AND SLOW—READING

Sometimes there are good reasons to read fast or skim texts, particularly when you are looking for specific information. You can skim across passages looking for keywords that signal information you need, or you can read the first sentence of a paragraph to get the gist. Reading expert Louise Rosenblatt calls this kind of reading "efferent," reading that's aimed at getting into a text and extracting key information in the swiftest and most effective way possible. She uses the example of a parent whose child has swallowed a dangerous substance: the parent is looking for the antidote and needs only one piece of information—fast!

The opposite of such fast reading is, logically enough, slow reading. There are lots of "slow" movements with loyal participants today: slow travel, slow food, slow fashion, and even slow reading. In his book *The Art of Slow Reading*, English professor Thomas Newkirk describes some "slow" practices that can help you be an active engaged reader, and we've added a couple of our own:

- **Make a mark.** Annotate what you notice as key parts of a text, what stands out to you as central or important to remember.

- *Find problems.* Stop to note a problem or confusion in the text and try to come up with a strategy for solving it. Such problem finding can work especially well if you are reading with someone else, someone you can talk with about the problem or confusion.
- *Read like a writer,* asking yourself about the decisions or moves the writer is making: Why shift topics here? Why introduce a particular piece of evidence at this point? Why choose this word?
- *Elaborate,* going beyond the text by comparing and contrasting it with other texts or drawing out unstated implications from the text.
- *Read aloud,* ideally with one or two friends who are reading the same text. Reading aloud lets you hear as well as see the text, and that auditory input can help lock in the meaning of what you're reading.
- *Stop occasionally* to let what you are reading "sink in" and to paraphrase what you just read. Doing so also helps lock in the meaning.

Slow reading, then, doesn't refer simply to speed. Rather, it's about attending carefully to the text, taking responsibility for your reading practices.

READING UNFAMILIAR OR DIFFICULT TEXTS

You are sure to encounter subject matter and texts that are difficult but important for you to understand. You'll want to slow down with such texts. Some students tell us they find this kind of slowing down easier to do with print rather than digital texts because they can move back and forth in the text to find and mark key information. Here are some other tips for making your way through difficult texts.

See the ebook for a video on reading scholarly articles.

- On your first reading, read for what you can understand, and simply mark places that are confusing or where you don't understand.
- Then choose a modest amount of material to read—a chapter, say, or even part of a chapter. Look it over to figure out how it is organized and see its main points—look at headings, for example, as well as any THESIS and TOPIC SENTENCES.
- Check to see if there's a summary at the beginning or end of the text. If so, read it very carefully.

- Reread the hard parts. Slow down, and focus. Better yet, read slowly with a friend, and stop to talk about what you do and do not understand.
- Try to make sense of the parts: "this part offers evidence," "that paragraph summarizes an alternative view," "here's a signal about what's coming next."
- If the text includes visuals, what do they contribute to the message?
- Resist highlighting: better to take notes in the margins that briefly state what you're reacting to and why.
- If your instructor's policies allow you to use AI, try asking it to help you prepare for a particularly difficult text by giving it prompts, such as "Ask me questions to help me figure out the major claim or argument in this text" or "Help me identify the three or four key ideas this text discusses by posing questions for me to answer about the text."

READING ON-SCREEN AND OFF

Once upon a time "reading" meant attending to words on paper. But today we often encounter texts that convey information in images and in sound as well—and they may be on- or off-screen. When you approach such texts, think carefully about how the medium of delivery may affect your understanding, engagement, and response.

Researchers have found that we often take shortcuts when we read on-screen, searching and scanning and jumping around in a text or leaping from link to link. This kind of reading is very helpful for finding answers and information quickly, but it can blur our focus and make it difficult to attend to the text carefully and purposefully. Here are a few tips to help you when you're reading on-screen:

- Be clear about your purpose for reading. If you need to understand and remember the text, remind yourself to read carefully and avoid skimming or skipping around.
- Close pages or tabs that may distract you from reading.
- Learn how to take notes in PDFs, *Word* documents, and *Google Docs*. Then you can make notes as you read on-screen, just as you would when reading a print text. Or take notes on paper.

- Look up unfamiliar terms as you read, making a note of definitions you may need later.
- If it increases your focus, consider printing out the text to read.

We are spending so much time today reading on screens that you may think everyone prefers to read this way. But current research suggests that many students still prefer print for high-stakes reading that needs to be thoroughly understood and remembered. Print texts, it's worth remembering, are easy to navigate—you can tell at a glance how much you've read and how much you still have to go, and you can easily move back and forth in the text to find something important.

In addition, researchers have found that students reading on-screen are less likely to reflect on what they read or to make connections and synthesize in ways that bind learning to memory. It's important to note, however, that studies like these almost always end with a caveat: reading practices are changing and technology is making it easier to read on-screen.

Online texts often blend written words with audio, video, links, charts and graphs, and other elements that you can attend to in any order you choose. In reading such texts, you'll need to make decisions carefully. When exactly should you click on a link, for example? The first moment it comes up? Or should you open it in a separate tab to check it out later since doing so now may break your concentration—and you might not be able to get back easily to what you were reading? In addition, scrolling seems to encourage skimming and to make us read more rapidly. In short, reading on-screen can make it harder to stay on task. So you may well need to make a special effort with digital texts—to read them attentively and to pay close attention to what you're reading.

We are clearly in a time of flux where reading is concerned, so the best advice is for you to think very carefully about why you are reading. If you need to find background information quickly, reading on-screen is often the way to go. But if you need to fully comprehend and retain the information in a text, you may want to stick with print.

Reading Visual Texts

Take a look at the Thistle advertisement on the following page. You may know that Thistle is a subscription-based meal delivery service for "plant forward" foods; if not, a quick look at the company's website will fill in

Thistle's post makes a visual argument.

this part of the ad's CONTEXT . This ad, which appeared on a social media platform, might be bite-size, but there's a lot going on in terms of its rhetorical situation. It combines several elements—all very spare and minimal—in order to capture the attention of this specific audience, who tend to scroll quickly through content.

Thinking through the rhetorical situation tells you something about the ad's purpose and audience. Of course its major PURPOSE is to sell as many meals as possible, but you can tell right away that Thistle isn't trying to compete with McDonald's, say, or Burger King. Its appeal is to a much more exclusive AUDIENCE . What clues can you gather about who the intended audience really is? What might that audience want?

Reading a visual begins, then, with studying the purpose, audience, message, and context. We need to examine all the elements and how they each contribute to a coherent whole. This visual combines a color photo with just a few brief sentences. The short, snappy TONE conveys information quickly, and the message hits three important values of many

See Ch. 16 in the ebook for a video on examining a visual text closely.

young adults: nutrition, time management, and health. Three more important bits of information appear: plant-forward, gluten-free, and delivered—all there in one tidy package. In addition to the company's social media handle (@ThistleCo), the ad also includes Thistle's URL.

Then there's the photo. What you see is a viewed-from-above image of a square container holding some kind of colorful salad. The salad is held in someone's lap, with their frayed jeans visible. We can also see this person's hand, seemingly holding the device that snapped the photo. It resembles the kind of quick photo anyone might take and post to show off their own healthy lunch, if only they had the perfect food to show. Is this food meant to be savored, combined with delightful conversation in a glamorous setting? Not likely. This is a meal eaten alone and quickly by a busy person, a person who can pay for premium-priced, high-nutrition meals that require zero effort to prepare.

In short, this Thistle ad is skillfully designed and placed in a strategic **CONTEXT** where its intended audience of high-income, career-driven, and probably single people will encounter it and absorb its message in the second or two that it takes to scroll across the screen.

"Reading" Spoken Texts

Today, lots of reading takes place via listening—especially to podcasts or digital newsletters that feature the author speaking or reading the "news" aloud. Working out in the gym, biking across campus, commuting to class—all offer good opportunities to "read" with our ears. Students tell us that this kind of listening/reading is great while they are on the go, but it requires focus. So if a podcast or other spoken text is one that you need to understand and be able to paraphrase, you'll need to think twice about doing it while multitasking. That's why we save audiobooks or entertaining podcasts for "low stakes" or fun reading. If we need to have a really firm grasp on the information we are listening to, we opt for doing so somewhere we can concentrate and even take notes.

You will also have many opportunities to "read" spoken texts in the form of presentations or lectures, as you view images displayed on a screen or provided in a handout. If the presentation is a really good one, these elements will complement each other, joining together to get their message across. Still, you may need to learn to split your attention, making sure you are not focusing so much on any slides or handouts that you're missing what

> Take a look at the excerpt from Alison Bechdel's graphic memoir on p. 859. You could read only the words in the narrative boxes and get a good sense of the story she tells, but how much more deeply do you understand her narrative from viewing the drawings?

the speaker is saying—or vice versa. Remember, too, that you'll be a better audience member if you look at the speaker and any visuals rather than staring at your laptop or looking down at the desk.

READING ACROSS GENRES

Genres affect how we read and can help guide our reading. Knowing the characteristic features of a GENRE, therefore, can help you read more attentively and more purposefully. When you read a NARRATIVE, for example, you expect to follow a story told from a particular point of view and with a clearly described setting and lots of vivid details. When you read a REVIEW, you expect to find some judgment, along with reasons and evidence to support that judgment. And you know to question any ARGUMENT that fails to acknowledge likely counterarguments. In other words, what you know about common genres can help you as a reader. Knowing what features to expect will help you read with a critical eye, and just recognizing a genre can help you adjust your reading as need be (reading directions more slowly, for example).

READING ACROSS ACADEMIC DISCIPLINES

Differences in disciplines can make for some very difficult reading tasks, as you encounter texts that seem almost to be written in foreign languages. As with most new things, however, new disciplines and their texts will become familiar the more you work with them until, eventually, you will be able to "talk the talk" of that discipline yourself.

Pay attention to terminology. It's especially important to read rhetorically when you encounter texts in different academic fields. Take the word "analysis," for instance. That little word has a wide range of definitions across fields. In philosophy, analysis has traditionally meant breaking down a topic into its parts in order to understand them—and the whole—more completely. In the sciences, analysis often involves the scientific method of observing a phenomenon, formulating a hypothesis, and experimenting to see whether the hypothesis holds up. And in business, analysis usually refers to assessing needs and finding ways to meet them. When you're assigned to carry out an analysis, then, it's important to know what the particular field of study requires you to do and to ask your instructors if you aren't sure.

Know what counts as evidence. Beyond attending to what particular words mean from field to field, you should note that what counts as effective EVIDENCE can differ across disciplines. In literature and other fields in the humanities, textual evidence is often the most important: your job as a reader is to focus on the text itself. For the sciences, you'll most often focus on evidence gathered through experimentation, on facts and figures. Some of the social sciences also favor the use of "hard" evidence or data, while others are more likely to use evidence drawn from interviews, oral histories, or even anecdotes. As a strong reader, you'll need to be aware of what counts as credible evidence in the fields you study.

Be aware of how information is presented. Finally, pay attention to the way disciplines format and present information. You'll probably find that articles and books in the fields of literature and history present their information in paragraphs, sometimes with illustrations. Physics texts present much important information in equations, while those in psychology and political science rely more on charts and graphs of quantitative data. In art history, you see extensive use of images, while much of the work in music relies on notation and sound.

So reading calls for some real effort. Whether you're reading words or images or bar graphs, literary analysis or musical notation, in a print book or on a screen, you need to read rhetorically—attentively and intentionally and with an open mind. And on top of all that, you need to be an active participant with what you read. After all, good writing is about the unique perspective you bring to what you read.

 **REFLECT**

Look back through this chapter at the strategies suggested for becoming an active and engaged reader. Are you already using some of these strategies, and if so, which ones? How well are they working for you? Are there others you'd like to try working with—and why?

SEVEN

Annotating, Summarizing, Responding

OW DO YOU READ when the stakes are high, when you really need to understand and remember what you're reading? One student we know, who chooses to read hard copy, keeps a highlighter and a stack of sticky notes on hand in order to talk back to the text. Another student makes comments using a note-taking app. And still another takes photos of lecture slides and annotates them in a *Google Doc* while in class. These students are all using strategies they've developed for reading purposely and attentively, strategies that suit their own needs.

Like these students, you've likely already developed reading strategies that work for you, and you'll surely be developing new strategies as you encounter new kinds of texts and disciplines. This chapter offers guidance on three key strategies that will help you engage actively and productively with all kinds of texts. **ANNOTATING** —the process of taking notes, underlining important information, and marking passages of a text that strike you as important—helps you focus and attend carefully to what you read. **SUMMARIZING** helps you synthesize the ideas in what you are reading, consolidate your understanding, and remember important points. And responding gives you an opportunity to engage the text directly, talking back and joining the conversation.

Each of these strategies marks a point where reading and writing intersect: reading leads to writing (annotating, summarizing, responding), and writing about what you've read often leads you to reread.

ANNOTATING

Annotating might sound simple: you just mark up the text as you read, right? Keep in mind, however, that what you annotate should be driven by your purpose for reading. Whatever that purpose, annotating will help you read actively—thinking, questioning, and responding as you go. Like Hansel and Gretel sprinkling bread crumbs in the forest, it's also a way of leaving a trail you can revisit later if you need to review concepts for an exam or find a quote for an essay. Taking the following steps will help you annotate purposefully and productively.

Think about your purpose for reading. If you're reading a biology textbook to prepare for an exam, you might highlight key concepts, summarize theories to be sure you understand them, and respond to the chapter's review questions. When reading a treatise by Aristotle to prepare for discussion in a philosophy class, however, you may mark passages that are hard to understand, write out questions to ask in class, and highlight statements to remember. Consider the following questions:

- *Why are you reading this text?* As a model for writing you'll be expected to do? So that you'll learn about a certain topic?
- *What do you need to be able to do with this text?* Apply concepts? Respond to the author's argument? Cite it in something you're writing?

Preview the text. Rather than plunging right in, skim the text first to get a sense of what it's about and how it's organized. Jot down what you notice.

- *What do you already know (and think) about the topic?* Do you have any personal experience with the subject? What do you want or expect to learn?
- *Who are the authors or sponsors?* Where do you think they're coming from? Might they have a particular agenda or purpose?
- *Who published the text,* and what does that tell you about its intended audience and purpose?
- *What does the title tell you?* If there's a subtitle, does it indicate the author's argument or stance?

- ***If there's an abstract,*** read it. If not, read the introduction. What new information do you learn?
- ***Scan any headings*** to see what's covered, and look at any text that's highlighted. How will the design help you read the text?
- ***How is the text organized?*** Chronologically? One point at a time, most important first? As a series of questions? Using flashbacks? What does the organization suggest about the author's purpose?
- ***What is your initial response*** to the text based on your preview of it?

> Why not try your hand at annotating now? The report by Kate Aronoff on p. 843 is a good one to practice with.

Annotate as you read. Annotate the text as a way of talking back to it—marking what the author is saying, how the author is getting their message across, and how you are reacting to what you're reading.

WHAT'S THE TEXT SAYING?

- What claims does the text make? Underline the THESIS statement. If there's no explicit thesis, what key questions and issues does the text address?
- What REASONS and EVIDENCE does the author provide? Are they sufficient?
- Does anything surprise you or make you feel skeptical? Mark any facts or statements that seem questionable.
- Note any COUNTERARGUMENTS. Does the author represent and respond to them fairly? Are any other perspectives missing?
- Identify key terms (and look them up if necessary). AI can help provide definitions and examples, but remember that AI can make things up, so keep a trusted online dictionary close at hand.
- Do you understand graphs, charts, or other visual elements? These often play an important role in the sciences and social sciences.

WHO'S THE INTENDED AUDIENCE?

- Who do you think the author is addressing? Students like you? Other scholars? The general public? Mark words that make you think so. Are you included in that group? If not, does that affect your response?
- What do you know about the audience's values? Highlight words that suggest what the author thinks the audience cares about.

WHAT DO YOU KNOW ABOUT THE AUTHOR?

- Who wrote the text? Is the author credible and reliable? What makes you believe that this is the case? Note places in the text where the author demonstrates **AUTHORITY** to write on the topic. Is the author a scholar? a popular commentator? To learn more about the author, search their name in sources you trust.
- What is the author's **STANCE**? Objective? Passionate? Something else? Mark words that indicate the author's stance.
- How would you describe the author's **STYLE** and **TONE**? Formal? Casual? Serious? Humorous? Mark any words or passages that establish that style and tone.
- What kinds of **LANGUAGE** choices does the author make? Do they use language their audience likely expects? Do they use language in surprising or especially effective ways? Mark language choices that you find interesting.

HOW IS THE TEXT DESIGNED?

- How do the format, layout, typefaces, and use of white space affect the clarity and accessibility of the text?
- Note headings, sidebars, or other design features that add emphasis.
- If the text includes visuals, what do they contribute to the message?

WHAT ARE *YOUR* REACTIONS?

- Mark places in the text where you agree, disagree, or both. Note why.
- Note any claims, facts, or other things you find surprising—and why.
- Note any passages you find confusing or difficult to understand. What questions do you have?
- Jot down any possible counterarguments or conflicting evidence that you need to check out.
- If a passage reminds you of a past experience, memory, or strong emotion, take note of it, which may be useful in your own response to the text.
- While noting your reactions, consider what experiences, beliefs, or biases inform your responses. Do you need to check any of your gut reactions to be sure you're staying fair and open-minded?

> We bet you'll have a lot to say when you annotate Jenna Bloom's narrative on quitting social media for a year (p. 870).

[80]   READING PROCESSES

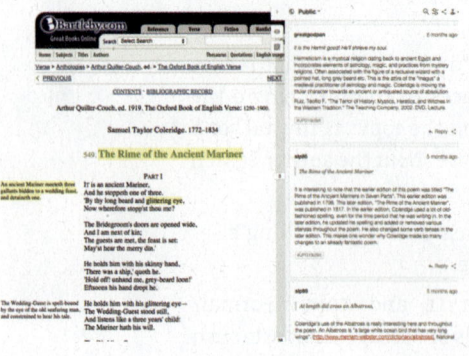 

Online or on a printed page, there are many methods and tools for annotating as you read. Try a few to find the ones that work best for you.

If you're reading a particularly important text, read it more than once, paying attention to different elements each time. For example, to prepare for a class discussion you might first focus on the argument and then reread focusing on how the writer supports that argument. With long or dense texts, you may want to annotate by summarizing paragraphs or sections as you go.

↪ To read—and annotate—a digital version of this book, visit digital.wwnorton.com/everyone5r.

Since you likely read on-screen often, take the time to learn one of the many free programs that make it easy to annotate digital texts. *Hypothesis* and *Adobe Acrobat Reader* are two programs that allow you to add notes, highlight, insert URLs and images, and more. In fact, the ebook version of this book includes annotation tools to mark up what you're reading right now!

So annotating keeps you active and helps you engage more deeply with what you read. Annotating also helps you approach reading as a social activity, bringing you into conversation with writers, engaging them and their ideas actively. Sometimes, especially for a research project, you'll be assigned to write formal annotations in the form of an ANNOTATED BIBLIOGRAPHY. That's a reading (and writing) situation with its own characteristic features. For now, focus on making annotating a habit—especially when you read academic texts.

A SAMPLE ANNOTATED TEXT

↪ To read Sprigg's full essay, visit everyonesanauthor.tumblr.com.

On the following pages, you'll find the opening of an essay by Katherine Spriggs on shopping locally, along with annotations by Yuliya Vayner, a former Hunter College student who read and annotated this piece for a summary/response essay assignment.

A Sample Annotated Text

Americans today can eat pears in the spring in Minnesota, oranges in the summer in Montana, asparagus in the fall in Maine, and cranberries in the winter in Florida. In fact, we can eat pretty much any kind of produce anywhere at any time of the year. But what is the cost of this convenience? In this essay, I will explore some answers to this question and argue that we should give up a little bit of convenience in favor of buying local.   *Thesis statement*

"Buying local" means that consumers choose to buy food that has been grown, raised, or produced as close to their homes as possible ("Buy Local"). Buying local is an important part of the response to many environmental issues we face today (fig. 1). It encourages the development of small farms, which are often more environmentally sustainable than large farms, and thus   *This paragraph states her stance: strongly in favor of sustainable farming and buying local.*

Farmers' markets are expensive. Many people—including me!—can't afford to shop at them.

Fig. 1. Shopping at a farmers' market is one good way to support small farms and strengthen the local economy. Timothy Mulholland. *Dane County Farmers' Market on the Square Madison Wisconsin.* 2008, *Alamy*.

But what about people who don't have access to locally produced food or who can't afford to buy it?

Here comes some evidence. Looks like she's done research to inform her argument.

I want to check out this source; I'm a little suspicious of what she says here.

She's serious about this issue and is making a strong case. Including these researched facts lends credibility, but I'm waiting to see if she acknowledges the fact that many people can't afford or easily get to locally grown food.

strengthens local markets and supports small rural economies. By demonstrating a commitment to buying local, Americans could set an example for global environmentalism.

In 2010, the international community is facing many environmental challenges, including global warming, pollution, and dwindling fossil fuel resources. Global warming is attributed to the release of greenhouse gases such as carbon dioxide and methane, most commonly emitted in the burning of fossil fuels. It is such a pressing problem that scientists estimate that in the year 2030, there will be no glaciers left in Glacier National Park ("Global Warming Statistics"). The United States is especially guilty of contributing to the problem, producing about a quarter of all global greenhouse gas emissions, and playing a large part in pollution and shrinking world oil supplies as well ("Record Increase"). According to a CNN article published in 2000, the United States manufactures more than 1.5 billion pounds of chemical pesticides a year that can pollute our water, soil, and air (Baum). Agriculture is particularly interconnected with all of these issues. Almost three-fourths of the pesticides produced in the United States are used in agriculture (Baum). Most produce is shipped many miles before it is sold to consumers, and shipping our food long distances is costly in both the amount of fossil fuel it uses and the greenhouse gases it produces.

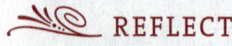 **REFLECT**

Take a look at any annotations or notes you've made so far in this chapter. Did you call out keywords, ideas, or claims? Did you mark passages that confused you or that were unclear? Looking back, are there annotations you didn't make but that might have proven useful? If so, try adding them now!

SUMMARIZING

Summarizing a text helps you understand and engage with it—and internalize and remember what you read. When you summarize, you're boiling a text down to its central ideas, claims, and theories in your own words. Besides helping you understand what you read, summarizing is also essential for weaving the viewpoints of others into your own writing. Both at work and at school, you'll be expected to summarize something—the plot of a short story, the results of a scientific study, takeaways from a meeting. The following advice will help you craft strong summaries in academic and professional writing.

See the ebook for a video on summarizing for reading comprehension.

Read the text carefully—and annotate. Read the text to figure out its main message, idea, or argument. Annotate as you read, marking key ideas and claims as well as supporting points such as anecdotes, supporting evidence, and counterarguments. When you identify a sentence or paragraph that states a main point, try restating it in your own words. A pair of highlighters can help; try using different colors to distinguish the main ideas from the supporting points.

When you summarize something other than a printed text—a music video, a printed advertisement, a speech—practice the same careful reading. Observe your subject and take note of the main message as well as the supporting details that lead you to draw this conclusion.

Be brief, stating the main points while leaving out minor supporting details. Summaries are generally brief, stating the main ideas while leaving out the supporting evidence and anecdotes that aren't necessary for understanding. A summary serves as a stand-in for readers who aren't familiar with the full text, so your aim is to get readers up to speed on the main points without getting lost in the details.

Be fair and accurate, using neutral language. Think of a summary as stating the facts, not sharing your opinion. Use neutral language to present the author's main ideas with evenhandedness and respect, not judgment or criticism. Imagine the author reading your summary of their work. Would they find it accurate? Have you left out an important point? Would the writer find it fair? Have your opinions snuck in?

Use SIGNAL PHRASES to present what the author says as distinct from what you say—and use quotations in moderation. Summarizing calls for boiling down information and presenting it in your own words and sentence structure. Use signal phrases such as "she concludes" or "the report states" to indicate that you're summarizing someone else's ideas and claims, not your own. At the start of a summary, state the author's name, credentials, and the title of the work so it's clear what you're referring to. While you may quote notable phrases or key terms, your summary should be made up of mostly your own unique language and sentence structure. And any text you summarize should be documented in a list of works cited or references.

Consider visuals. Not all summaries are written text: summaries can also be presented visually. In scientific, technical, or social science writing, charts, graphs, or maps often summarize key information and data from other sources. For example, the following map from the US Census Bureau shows the most-used language other than English or Spanish in each of the fifty states. The colorful visual presents the information in a way that's easier to understand (and more compact) than if the same data were presented using only words or lists.

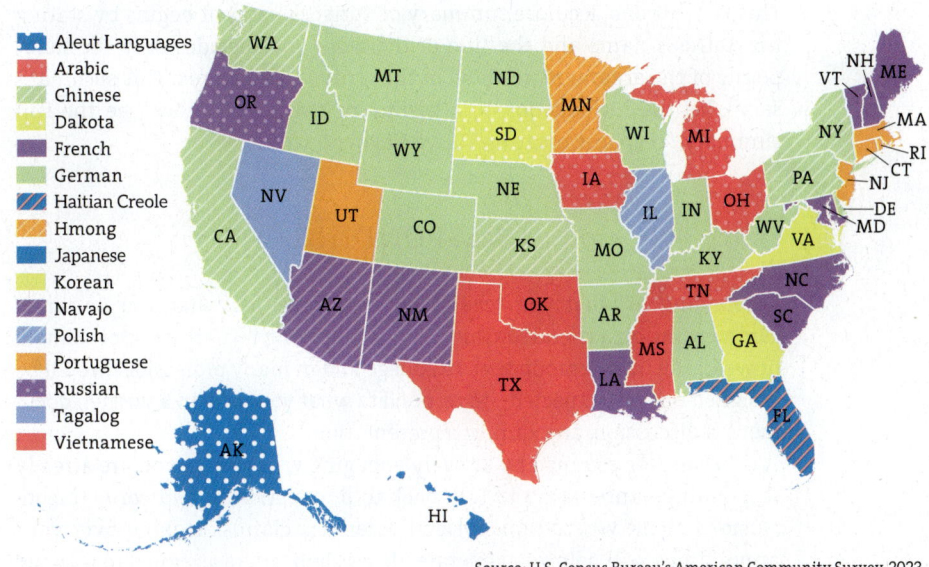

Source: U.S. Census Bureau's American Community Survey, 2023.

A colorful US map shows each state's most commonly spoken language beyond English or Spanish, helping readers see regional trends and main takeaways at a glance.

A Sample Summary

Here is a summary of Katherine Spriggs's essay "On Buying Local":

> In her essay "On Buying Local," college student Katherine Spriggs argues that consumers should purchase food grown locally whenever possible. After demonstrating the environmental and practical reasons for doing so, Spriggs shows that buying local can offer an alternative to destructive mass farming, help small farmers and their families, build sustainable agricultural models, reduce the cost of shipping food from faraway places, and avoid the exploitation of workers, especially in third-world countries. In spite of a few drawbacks (local food may be more expensive, and seasonal variation may reduce the number of choices available), she concludes that shopping local is an easy lifestyle change that will make a big difference to our environment.

Read Spriggs's complete essay at everyonesanauthor.tumblr.com.

This is a fair and accurate summary of Spriggs's essay. It begins by stating the author's name and the title of the work and includes only the main points of the argument, restated in the writer's own words. This summary serves as the introduction to a summary / response essay (see the full summary / response essay by Yuliya Vayner on p. 93).

RESPONDING

Responding to what you read is nothing new—it's what you do when commenting on a friend's *Instagram* post, replying to an instructor's email, or weighing in on a group text. In college and in many professions, you'll be assigned—or just expected—to respond to what you read, in a written document, a discussion, an exam, or a presentation.

Whenever you read by actively engaging with a text, you are already responding—annotating to talk back to it, question it, and come to conclusions about whether or not you accept its claims. Looking over your annotations will help you generate ideas when you're assigned to respond formally. Do your annotations reveal any patterns? Maybe you disagreed with many of the author's claims, jotted down a related experience, or noted the author's use of emotional appeals. As you take stock of your annotations, consider which of the following ways you'll respond to what you've read: argue with what the text says, analyze the way it says it, or reflect on its ideas.

Respond to what a text says, agreeing or disagreeing with its position—or both. However you respond, you'll be making an ARGUMENT for what you say. Before you come to any final conclusions, keep an open mind by saying "yes," "no," and "maybe" to the text. First say "yes" by making an effort to understand the way the author sees the topic and where they're coming from. Doing so can be especially important if you find yourself strongly disagreeing with the author's position. Then say "maybe" to any passages that seem confusing or poorly supported—and consider why. Finally, look for anything to which you feel obligated to say "no," and think about why it seems unacceptable or just plain wrong. Here are some questions to consider when you're responding to what a text says:

- What does the text CLAIM, and what REASONS and EVIDENCE does the author provide?

- Do you agree or disagree with the author's position? Why?
- Does the author acknowledge any other positions? If so, are they treated fairly? What other perspectives should be addressed?
- Has the author overlooked anything?
- Is it clear why the topic matters, why anyone should care?
- What's the larger CONTEXT? How does the text fit into the larger conversation on the topic? Is the author's point corroborated by what others have said, or is it a claim that hardly anyone else agrees with?

See how Yazmin Carbajal, a student at Sonoma State University, responds to a passage from Georgina Kleege's essay "Call It Blindness" (you can read the passage on p. 225), focusing on what the text says:

> Georgina Kleege describes the reaction her college students have when she introduces herself by saying she is "legally blind." Since she isn't using a cane or a guide dog and she has just entered the class like anyone else, the students are uncertain, a little nervous, and unsure of what's going on. Kleege defuses the situation by making a joke, saying that maybe she should have said she is "visually challenged." That gets a relieved laugh as Kleege muses about how people seem to insist on slapping "a verbal smiley-face" on anything that's a little different. In the end, she gives the students an easy out, saying the "challenged" joke is just one way to say she "doesn't see very well." This passage makes an implicit claim that people's reaction to difference—like to somebody who is legally blind—suggests that they are the ones who can't see very well! The students are uneasy and uncertain about what they "see," while the legally blind Kleege sees every detail of the scene clearly.

Analyze the way a text is written to figure out how it works, what makes it tick. Here are some questions to consider when you're analyzing how a text is written:

- What does the text CLAIM? Is it stated explicitly—and if not, should it be? Has it been carefully qualified—and if not, does it need to be?
- Look for and assess the REASONS and EVIDENCE provided in support of the claim. Are you persuaded? If not, what other kinds of evidence would help?

- Does the author use emotional, ethical, or logical appeals? Do you notice any logical FALLACIES ?
- Has the writer mentioned any COUNTERARGUMENTS or alternative points of view? If so, are they described respectfully and fairly? And how does the writer respond—by acknowledging that other writers have a point? Refuting what they say?
- How does the author use LANGUAGE ? Do they meet or challenge their audience's expectations? Do they take risks with language? How effective are their language choices?
- Does the author use vivid images, metaphors, sentence fragments, one-word sentences, or other special effects to help make or underscore a particular point?
- How has the author established AUTHORITY to write on this topic? Do you think the text is trustworthy and fair?
- What design elements help convey the text's main message?

See how Katherine Evers, a student at Framingham State University, responds to how Georgina Kleege's text is written:

> Kleege's writing style and use of language help convey her main claim that our culture's obsession with euphemizing disabilities leads to discomfort around people who are disabled. She establishes a casual, almost conversational tone with the reader, walking them through her thought process as she speaks to her students. "I am legally blind," she tells them, rather than "stick[ing] a verbal smiley-face on any human condition which deviates from the status quo." Since the essay is about a serious topic—disability—this tone subverts the reader's expectations, challenging the tendency to ignore or look away from disabilities in everyday conversations. While a less confident writer might end up undermining their point by approaching it in such a seemingly casual way, Kleege's message is strengthened by her style and tone, which maintain her clarity of purpose.

Reflect on a text's ideas by drawing connections to your own personal experiences, beliefs, or ways of thinking. Maybe the text leads you to see a topic in a new light, question your assumptions and biases, or wonder about how your beliefs influenced your reaction. Here are some questions to consider when you're reflecting on a text's ideas:

- What impact has the reading had on you—as a student, scholar, citizen, and researcher? What are the big takeaways for you personally?
- Did any parts of the text make you feel uneasy, laugh, or cry? Investigate why.
- Which past experiences or memories did you recall while reading the text? Can you relate to anything in the text? Why or why not?
- How does the text uphold or challenge any of your values or beliefs?
- What other texts, images, videos, etc., does the text remind you of?
- What lessons, insights, or ideas has the text taught you? How might you apply those lessons in your own writing or thinking?

Here is a paragraph Elena Castrence, a student at Northern Virginia Community College, wrote reflecting on Kleege's essay and its connection to her own experiences:

> Georgina Kleege's point, in "Call It Blindness," about the different ways other people define and disregard her blindness resonated with me. I'm half Filipino on my dad's side and half white on my mom's, so I have never fully felt like I belonged to either side. Growing up, I got to know my mom's side of the family, often visiting them in Colorado for Thanksgiving and Christmas. I can't say the same about my dad's side, unfortunately. This isn't to say that I don't feel any connection to my heritage. I remember when Dad took my sister and me to Pinoy markets, house parties, and festivals where we could experience Filipino culture. Still, people think those things don't qualify me to call myself Filipino. After all, I don't speak Tagalog, I don't have any Filipino friends, and, until recently, I hadn't been to the Philippines. Yet I have done my best to learn about my heritage. Taking back her identity, Kleege prefers "the simplicity of a single, unmodified adjective" and chooses the word "blind" to describe herself. I, too, prefer simple words. Learning about my Filipino heritage, despite not being surrounded by that community, has shaped me. I don't have to constantly explain or deny who I am. I am proud to be Filipino.

SUMMARY / RESPONSE ESSAYS

A summary / response essay demonstrates that you have engaged with a text, understand its main message, and have something to say as a result. This assignment is common in first-year writing classes because of the focus on critical reading and supporting a position with evidence. Unless the assignment names other requirements, your summary / response should cover the following ground.

A Fair, Accurate, and Concise Summary

A fair and objective summary of the text to which you are responding is essential. To make your subject crystal clear, begin by stating the author, title, and author's credentials. And keep the following points in mind:

- Include the main claims and primary supporting points of the text, and exclude examples or supporting ideas that aren't essential to the text's main message.
- Use an even and objective TONE. Would the author of the text find your summary fair and accurate?
- Be concise. Most summaries of full texts are 100 to 125 words, giving readers enough information to understand what you're responding to without unnecessary details.
- Make it clear that you are summarizing someone else's text by using SIGNAL PHRASES like "according to X." Words such as "asserts," "argues," and "examines" are also good signals—just be sure they are neutral. Include quotations only when keywords and phrases are central to the overall argument.

A Clear Response, Supported by Evidence

Your response is the meat of a summary / response essay. There's more than one way to respond to a text. See if you're being asked to respond in a particular way—for example, to "assess the author's argument and take a stance" or "analyze how effectively the text addresses its intended audience." If the assignment isn't specific, think about what you're most interested in doing: responding to what the text says, analyzing how the text works, reflecting on the text's ideas, or some combination. No matter how you respond, support your position with evidence.

- If you're responding to what the text says, take a position—agreeing, disagreeing, or both. State your position explicitly in a **THESIS** statement. Support your position with evidence from the text and from outside sources, if necessary. Facts, statistics, anecdotal evidence, and textual evidence can serve as support. Think about and address any **COUNTERARGUMENTS** to your position.
- If you're analyzing how the text works, you'll describe both what the text is saying and the strategies used to convey the message. You might analyze a text's organization, **DICTION**, language choices, use of appeals, design, or other elements. Include evidence from the text to demonstrate the features or strategies you're analyzing. Be sure you state your main takeaway in an explicit thesis statement. Why did you choose to analyze what you did and why does it matter?
- If you're reflecting on the text's ideas, you'll likely explain some way in which the text impacted you personally or evoked a particular emotion, memory, or idea. Passages from the text that prompted your response should be cited as evidence. And your own beliefs, experiences, or emotions might serve to support and explain your personal response. Boil down your main point in a thesis statement—even a reflection should tell readers what you're saying and why it matters.

A Logical Organization

A summary / response can be organized in different ways, and your assignment may ask for a specific structure. Here are some general ways of structuring a summary / response to help you get started:

- Summarize first, and then respond: introduce and summarize the text, then state your thesis (this might all fall in the first paragraph). Then respond to the text, providing supporting points for your thesis. End by summing up your response and its implications.

- Summarize and respond point-by-point: introduce the text and state your thesis. Then summarize a claim or strategy from the text and respond to it. Do this for as many supporting points as you have to develop and defend your thesis. End by summing up your response and its implications.

SUMMARY / RESPONSE / An Annotated Example

The Higher Price of Buying Local

YULIYA VAYNER

In her essay "On Buying Local," Katherine Spriggs argues that consumers should purchase food grown locally whenever possible. After demonstrating the environmental and practical reasons for doing so, Spriggs shows that buying local can offer an alternative to destructive mass farming, help small farmers and their families, build sustainable agricultural models, reduce the cost of shipping food from faraway places, and avoid the exploitation of workers, especially in third-world countries. Though Spriggs acknowledges that buying local can be inconvenient, she argues that the benefit outweighs the inconvenience and concludes that shopping local is an easy lifestyle change that will make a big difference to our environment.

But is buying local truly an "easy step" that "everyone can take"? Is inconvenience the only drawback? There are at least two additional challenges to buying local that Spriggs doesn't acknowledge in her analysis: cost and access.

YULIYA VAYNER, a former Hunter College student, summarizes and responds to Katherine Spriggs's essay "On Buying Local" in the example included here. You can read Spriggs's full essay by visiting everyonesanauthor.tumblr.com. Vayner primarily responds to what the text says—taking a position that both agrees and disagrees with Spriggs's argument. This essay is organized around several counterarguments that Vayner says Spriggs does not address.

Presents THESIS: *buying local is good for the environment but not all people can participate.*	It's clear that buying locally grown food benefits the environment, but because cost and access limit some people from being able to buy local, it is not a habit everyone is equally able to practice.
Agrees with part of Spriggs's ARGUMENT *and explains why in her first major point.*	Spriggs makes a convincing argument that giving up a bit of convenience in return for a healthier environment is a worthy trade. In discussing polyculture farming (producing a variety of crops from the same land—an approach small farms tend to prefer), Spriggs juxtaposes personal convenience and environmental benefits. She concedes that being unable to buy whatever produce we want whenever we want is less convenient than most consumers are used to but suggests this sacrifice would allow farmers to harvest from healthier
SUMMARIZES *Spriggs's argument in her own words.*	soil and foster a healthier environment. Spriggs explains that while monoculture farms (producing a small number of single crops—the approach large mass-production farms use) provide the convenience of year-round access to
QUOTES *specific details from Spriggs's essay.*	produce, they do so by resorting to "modern fertilizers, herbicides, and pesticides [that] allow farmers to harvest crops from even unhealthy land" (190). By giving up the convenience of eating strawberries at any time of year, Americans could begin to rely less on chemical treatments that damage the environment and more on natural resources.
Notes COUNTER-ARGUMENT *that Spriggs does not address: how will people who live in food deserts access locally produced foods?*	However, Spriggs doesn't acknowledge that some people would be giving up more than just evergreen strawberries in an attempt to buy local. For many, lack of access to any fresh produce at all is an issue, making the sacrifice of buying produce that's locally sourced unaffordable. According to a recent report by the US Department of Agriculture's Economic Research Service, an estimated 1 in 8 Americans or 40 million people experienced food insecurity, which is defined as "a lack of consistent access to enough food for an active, healthy life" in 2017 ("What Is Food Insecurity?"). So when Spriggs argues that
Quotes a trustworthy, credible source as EVIDENCE.	there's little reason to ship strawberries from California all over the United States when they can easily be grown closer to the customers who want to eat them, she fails to acknowledge that there are areas that can't readily access or grow fresh produce (190). These areas are sometimes called food deserts: areas that have limited access to affordable and nutritious food, forcing residents to rely on food sold at convenience stores or fast-food chains, which is often highly processed and of limited nutritional value
CITES *more credible sources to support the point: some places aren't able to grow fresh produce.*	("Why Low-Income and Food-Insecure People"). These food deserts exist

overwhelmingly in low-income areas, and studies have shown that "both poverty and race matter when it comes to having healthy food options" (Brooks). So, although Spriggs does not mention these issues, buying local is also a question of access—which is impacted by race and income level rather than being purely one about convenience and ease.

Time becomes an issue of access as well: for some, there is no time to make a long trip for fresh, local produce. People living below the poverty line tend to work multiple jobs (Sherman); in addition, they may be responsible for household errands and family care. Lower-income families are not only less likely to have places nearby that sell locally grown food, they are also less likely to have the time and the means to visit them ("Why Low-Income and Food-Insecure People").

This adds yet another aspect to the challenge of buying local that Spriggs doesn't address: low-income individuals are significantly less likely to be able to afford the extra expense of locally sourced food, which Spriggs explains as only slightly pricier. Yet, "slightly more expensive than 'industrially grown' food" (Spriggs 192) is subjective. Not only would buying local strain the budgets of the poor, it could also make it harder to use government assistance programs like SNAP (Andrews). So for many, buying local is not just an inconvenience, it's not a financial possibility. Furthermore, the price gap seems wider than Spriggs admits; a journalist for *The Washington Post* reports that in 2016 "cage-free eggs, cheese, mushrooms, salad mix and both organic and conventional strawberries" came to be $64.62 at the local market in Richmond, Virginia—"I could have bought them all from Kroger for $31.37" (Hise). At nearly double the price, this difference is far from Spriggs's claim that buying local is only "slightly more expensive" (192). The price increase that comes with buying local is not a mere inconvenience but rather a question of affordability for many.

While Spriggs succeeds in showing that buying local can contribute to a healthier environment, in addressing the obvious drawback of inconvenience she considers only one aspect of a complex issue involving race, income level, and access. The inconvenience of buying local comes at a much higher price for some people, a fact Spriggs leaves out. To many, industrially grown food is a necessity rather than, as Spriggs suggests, a convenience.

Presents another ARGUMENT *Spriggs doesn't cover: how time issues affect whether people can buy local.*

A third COUNTER-ARGUMENT *Spriggs doesn't cover: the expense of buying local.*

EVIDENCE *to support the claim in the first sentence of this paragraph.*

Appeals to AUDIENCE'S EMOTIONS *by providing a concrete example of higher food prices from a trustworthy source.*

Concludes by SUMMARIZING *her own argument in response to Spriggs.*

Leaves readers with something to think about: is locally grown food a necessity or a convenience?

Works Cited

Citing sources accurately builds CREDIBILITY.

Andrews, Michelle. "Technical Difficulties May Jeopardize Food Stamps at Farmers Markets." *NPR*, 5 Nov. 2018, www.npr.org/sections/thesalt/2018/11/05/662322655/technical-difficulties-may-jeopardize-food-stamps-at-farmers-markets.

Brooks, Kelly. "Research Shows Food Deserts More Abundant in Minority Neighborhoods." *Johns Hopkins Magazine*, 10 Mar. 2014. *The Hub*, Johns Hopkins U, hub.jhu.edu/magazine/2014/spring/racial-food-deserts/.

Hise, Phaedra. "Why Does a Strawberry Grown Down the Road Cost More than One Grown in California?" *The Washington Post*, 21 June 2016, www.washingtonpost.com/lifestyle/food/why-local-food-costs-more-a-strawberry-case-study/2016/06/20/c7177c56-331f-11e6-8ff7-7b6c1998b7a0_story.html.

Sherman, Erik. "More People Probably Work Multiple Jobs than the Government Realizes." *Forbes*, 22 July 2018, www.forbes.com/sites/eriksherman/2018/07/22/more-people-probably-work-multiple-jobs-than-the-government-realizes.

Spriggs, Katherine. "On Buying Local." *Everyone's an Author*, by Andrea A. Lunsford et al., 4th ed., W. W. Norton, 2022, pp. 186–94.

"What Is Food Insecurity in America?" *Hunger and Health*, Feeding America, hungerandhealth.feedingamerica.org/understand-food-insecurity/. Accessed 1 June 2021.

"Why Low-Income and Food-Insecure People Are Vulnerable to Poor Nutrition and Obesity." *Food Research & Action Center*, www.opportunityhome.org/wp-content/uploads/2018/04/frac_org.pdf. Accessed 1 June 2021.

REFLECT & WRITE

Vayner analyzes Spriggs's essay, noting what in the argument works for her and what doesn't. Conduct your own analysis of Vayner's essay, identifying what points are more—and less—effective. Explain your evaluation and provide evidence from Vayner's essay to support your conclusions.

EIGHT

Distinguishing Facts from Misinformation

EET PRINCESS DIANA'S Secret Daughter!" "NASA Decodes Lost Gospels." "Pope Francis Says God 'Has Instructed Me to Revise the Ten Commandments.'" "Taylor Swift Banned from All Future NFL Games for Being a Distraction." Really? Well, actually, no. While these are actual headlines, not one is anywhere near true. But being false hasn't kept them from being widely shared—and not as jokes but as facts. With people spreading misinformation, unsubstantiated claims, and even outright lies, it can be hard to know whom and what to trust or whether to trust anything at all. The good news is that you don't have to be taken in by such misinformation. This chapter provides strategies for navigating the choppy waters of news and information so that you can make confident decisions about what to trust—and what not to.

Defining Facts and Misinformation

Some say we are living in a "post-truth" era, when the loudest voices take up so much airtime that they can sometimes be seen as telling the truth no matter what they say. A 2018 study by MIT scholars examined posts about every major contested news story in English across the ten years of *Twitter*'s existence and came to the conclusion that satirist Jonathan Swift was right: "the truth simply can't compete with hoax and rumor." In fact, the study says, "fake news and false rumors reach more people, penetrate deeper into the social network, and spread much faster than accurate stories."

Try these tips to help you distinguish fact from fake.

8   Distinguishing Facts from Misinformation

The prominence of "hoax and rumor" remain sky-high in the years since that study. In fact, advances in technology, from AI chatbots to video generators, have made it even easier to spread false information—so much so that a 2024 World Economic Forum study concluded that false information from AI posed the greatest global risk in the coming years, greater even than "famine or war."

It's worth asking why misinformation and disinformation garner so much attention—and so many believers. While it is notoriously difficult to establish airtight cause-and-effect relationships, MIT researchers suspect that several reasons account for the "success" of false stories. First, they're often outlandish in a way that attracts attention. Second, the content of such stories is often negative and tends to arouse strong emotions. Third, they use language that evokes surprise or disgust, as compared to accurate stories, which, the researchers found, use words associated with trust or sadness rather than surprise or disgust: as they note, "the truth simply does not compete." For all these reasons, misinformation tends to attract attention and spread quickly.

Lies and misinformation are nothing new. What's new is that anyone with an internet connection can post whatever they think (or want others to think) online, where it can easily reach a wide audience. In addition, AI chatbots and trolls can crank out false information at an alarming rate, which then can get passed on by people who do not recognize it as false or fake. And unlike traditional newspapers and other publications, all this information goes out without being vetted by editors or fact-checkers.

Perhaps it's time to step back, take a deep breath, and attend to some basic definitions. Just what is a "fact"? What's "misinformation"? And what about "disinformation"? Both misinformation and disinformation are untrue statements; what makes them different is the motive behind each. Misinformation is factually incorrect, but the error may not be intentional; disinformation, on the other hand, is purposely misleading and designed to cause harm. The person who spreads disinformation intends to deceive the audience; it's not an innocent mistake. And "fake news," a form of disinformation, is fabricated information presented as authentic news. It's a common method for spreading conspiracy theories or deliberate hoaxes, and the more bizarre the better: "Billionaire withheld water from those fighting massive LA wildfires," "Post Malone Elected Mayor of Ohio Town!" While some people may dismiss anything they don't like or agree with as fake, we know that facts can be independently verified and supported by reliable evidence.

Think about Your Own Beliefs

It's one thing to be able to spot unsubstantiated claims and exaggerations in the words of others, but it's another thing entirely to spot them in your own thinking and writing. So you need to take a good look at your own assumptions and biases (we all have them!).

ATTRIBUTION BIAS is the tendency to think that your motives for believing, say, that the Environmental Protection Agency (EPA) is crucially important for keeping our air and water clean are objective or good while the motives of those who believe the EPA is not at all necessary are dubious or bad. We all have this kind of bias naturally, tending to believe that what we think must be right. When you're thinking about an argument you strongly disagree with, then, it's a good idea to ask yourself why you disagree—and

why you believe you're right. What is that belief based on? Have you considered that your own bias may be keeping you from seeing all sides of the issue fairly, or at all?

CONFIRMATION BIAS is the tendency to favor and seek out information that confirms what we already believe and to reject and ignore information that contradicts those beliefs. Many studies have documented this phenomenon. For example, a Stanford University experiment gathered forty-eight students, half of whom favored capital punishment and thought it was a deterrent to crime and half of whom opposed capital punishment. Researchers then asked students to respond to two studies: one provided data that supported capital punishment as a deterrent to crime; the other provided data that called this conclusion into question. Sure enough, the students who were in favor of capital punishment rated the study that showed evidence that it was a deterrent as "more highly credible," while the students who were against capital punishment rated the study that showed evidence that it did not deter crime as "more highly credible"—in spite of the fact that both studies had been made up by the researchers. Moreover, by the end of the experiment, each side had doubled down on its original beliefs.

That's confirmation bias at work, and it works on all of us. It affects the way we search for information and what we pay attention to, how we interpret it, and even what we remember. So don't assume information is trustworthy just because it confirms what you already think. Ask yourself if you're seeing what you want to see. And look for confirmation bias in your sources; do they acknowledge viewpoints other than their own?

Read Defensively—and Laterally—to Find the Good Stuff

Well over 2,000 years ago, the philosopher Aristotle said that one reason people need rhetoric is self-defense, for making sure that we aren't being deceived, manipulated, or lied to. Today, the need for such caution may be more important than ever when false stories often look authentic and appear right next to accurate, factual information online. These times call, then, for what we think of as defensive reading—the kind of reading that doesn't take things at face value, that questions underlying assumptions, that scrutinizes claims carefully, and that does not rush to judgment. This is the kind of reading that media and technology critic Howard Rheingold calls "crap detection." Crap, he says sardonically, is a "technical term" he uses to describe information "tainted by ignorance or deliberate deception." He warns us not to give in to such misinformation:

> Some critics argue that a tsunami of hogwash has already rendered the web useless. I disagree. We are indeed inundated by online noise pollution, but the problem is soluble. The good stuff is out there if you know how to find and verify it.
>
> —HOWARD RHEINGOLD, "Crap Detection 101"

As Rheingold and many others note, there is no single foolproof way to identify misinformation. But we can offer some advice, along with some specific strategies, all of which can also help you vet the accuracy of AI-generated material.

Triangulate—and use your judgment. Find three different ways to check on whether a story can be trusted. Google the author or the sponsor. Check *FactCheck.org* or *Snopes*. Look for other sources that are reporting the same story, especially if you first saw it on social media. If it's true and important, you should find a number of other reputable sources reporting on it. But however carefully you check, and whatever facts and evidence you uncover, it's up to you to sort the accurate information from the misinformation—and to use your own judgment.

Before reading an unfamiliar source, determine whether it's trustworthy. History professor Sam Wineburg and his research team have found that professional fact-checkers don't even start to read an unfamiliar website until they've determined that it's trustworthy. Instead, they practice LATERAL READING —that is, going outside of the source to open new tabs for finding out what others are saying about the unfamiliar source. Wineburg's team found that those who tried to evaluate a source by focusing only on the source itself were often taken in by false information that looked genuine enough in the context of the source. Here's how lateral reading can work for you:

- Open a new tab and do a search about the author or sponsor. What's the author's expertise? Be wary if there's no author. Does the author belong to any organizations you don't know or trust? Look up any unfamiliar organizations to see what reliable sources have to say. And do a search about the site's sponsor. If the website is run by an organization you've never heard of, find out what it is—and whether it actually exists. What do reliable sources say about it? Read the site's About page, but check up on what it says. As Wineburg says, "If an organization can game what they are, they can certainly game their About page!"

- Check any links to see who sponsors the site and whether they are trustworthy sources. Do the same for works cited in print sources.
- Be careful of over-the-top headlines, which often serve as clickbait to draw you in. Check to see that the story and the headline actually match. Question any exaggerated words like "amazing," "epic," "incredible," or "unbelievable." (In general, don't believe anything that's said to be unbelievable!)
- Pay attention to design. Be wary if it looks amateurish, but don't assume that a professional-looking design means the source is accurate or trustworthy. Those who create fake news sites often design them to look like real news sites.
- Recognize satire! Remember that some authors make a living by writing satirical fake news articles. The *Onion* is one source that pokes fun at gullible readers. Try this: "Genealogists Find 99% of People Not Related to Anyone Cool." This one's silly enough that it can't possibly be true. But if you're not sure, better check.

Ask questions, and check evidence. Double-check things that too neatly support what you yourself think.

- What's the **CLAIM**, and what **EVIDENCE** is provided? What motivates the author to write, and what's their **PURPOSE**—to provide information? make you laugh? convince you of something?
- Check facts and claims using nonpartisan sites that confirm truths and identify lies. *FactCheck.org*, *Snopes*, and *AllSides* are three such sites. Copy and paste the basics of the statement into the search field; if it's information the site has in its database, you'll find out whether it's a confirmed fact or lie. If you use *Google* to check on a fact, you'll need to check on any sources there—and that even if the statement brings up many hits, that doesn't make it accurate. And remember: most social media sites don't fact-check, so beware!
- Don't assume a story or an image must be true—especially if it seems outrageous. Do research on stories; if they're true, they will be widely reported. On the other hand, double-check stories that confirm your own beliefs; assuming they're true might be **CONFIRMATION BIAS** at work.

> Graphic essays don't usually provide sources, but Ally Shwed cites recent studies and historical documents as evidence. Her essay (p. 982) could be a good place to practice your fact-checking.

- Look up any research that's cited. You may find that the research has been taken out of context or misquoted—or that it doesn't actually exist. Is the research itself reliable? Pay close attention to quotations: Who said it, and when? Is it believable? If not, copy and paste the quotation into *Google* or check *FactCheck.org* to verify that it's real.

Fact-Check Photos and Videos

Is a picture really worth a thousand words? In some cases, but only if the picture is an accurate depiction. It's never been easier to falsify photographs. Look at the image below of a pilot leaning from the cockpit of a commercial airliner

Brazilian pilot Daniel Centeno used *Photoshop* to superimpose a selfie over a photo of a plane in flight. See the airport runway reflected in his sunglasses.

to snap a selfie as the plane departs. While his shadow on the plane might seem authentic, look again: airspeed at that altitude would have sucked him out and into the engine. Besides, in his original caption he noted: "Photoshop mode ON!" Be vigilant and examine images (and information) closely!

There are no simple, foolproof ways to identify doctored photos, but experts in digital forensics recommend various steps we can take. Here's advice from Hany Farid, a computer science professor at the University of California at Berkeley:

- Do a reverse image search, using *Google Images* or *Tin Eye*, to see if an image has been recirculated or repurposed from another website. Both sites allow you to drag an image or paste a link to an image into a search bar to learn more about the image's source and see where else the image appears online.
- Check *Snopes*, where altered images are often identified, by typing a brief description of the image into the *Snopes* search box.
- Look carefully at shadows and reflections: an image may have been altered if you find shadows where you don't expect them or don't see them where you do expect them.

With powerful AI tools available to nearly everyone, it's harder than ever to detect fake or manipulated images. So keep an eye on evolving ways to certify the trustworthiness of an image, such as icons or watermarks embedded in images to act like a nutrition label does on food. Camera companies, including Canon, Nikon, and Sony, have announced plans to embed such watermarks in photos, while a free, web-based tool called *Verify*, lets its users see an image's digital signature. If an image has no such signature, *Verify* labels it "no content credentials." However, there are already ways to get around such efforts at verification. Especially when it comes to AI "deepfakes," no verification program available today is foolproof.

As Farid and other experts on the manipulation of images point out, our best defense against false or fabricated photos is to stop and think long and hard about the source, especially before you share it with others. After a shooter killed seventeen people at a Florida school in 2018, an altered photo of X González, one student survivor who advocated for stronger gun laws, went viral, showing them tearing up a page of the US Constitution. In fact, they were actually tearing up a shooting target as part of their advocacy for gun control.

The same advice holds true for researching suspicious videos, which are also easy to falsify. If they flicker constantly or consist of just one short clip, they are questionable, as are videos of famous people doing things that seem highly unlikely. In 2024, a rash of AI-generated deepfakes announced that iconic landmarks like London's Big Ben and the Eiffel Tower in Paris were on fire. Nope—not in real life but only online! In both of these cases, the deepfakes were quickly contradicted by people on the ground who guaranteed that the buildings were standing safe and sound. But other fake videos are harder to disprove and require substantial fact-checking.

Such fabricated videos and deepfakes proliferate, especially on *YouTube* and *TikTok*. The *Guardian* warns that "advances in artificial intelligence and computer graphics . . . allow for the creation of realistic looking footage of public figures appearing to say, well, anything." We hope that using the fact-finding and defensive-reading strategies in this chapter will help you

Big Ben on fire? AI might say so (left) but not in real life (right).

sort out fact from falsehood, figure out who and what you can trust, and have some fun, whether you are keeping up with the news, scrolling social media, conducting research for a school project, or looking for the best deal on a new pair of headphones. Happy reading!

 **REFLECT**

Look back through this chapter, reviewing the advice about how to tell truth from lies and to detect misinformation and deepfakes. What strategies did you learn that were new to you? What ones have you used yourself in checking your sources? Finally, review the discussion of confirmation bias on page 101 and see if you can remember a time when such bias was at work in your own thinking. How might you avoid such bias in the future?

PART III

Writing Processes

Writing is an exploration. You start from nothing and learn as you go.

—E. L. DOCTOROW

HOW WOULD YOU DEFINE your process for writing? You might say it's simple: get words on the screen, complete a draft, and then edit until it's ready to go. But as novelist E. L. Doctorow reminds us, your writing process is a learning process: through writing, you not only learn more about your topic, but you also learn more about *what you think*. As you write, you're discovering what exactly you want to say. The goal of any writing process, then, is not just to complete a draft, but also for you—as a writer, thinker, and contributor—to identify what you have to say and how best to say it.

If that sounds daunting, we hope it's a comfort to remember: writers don't write alone. In studying how writing processes work, researchers recognize that almost all writing is highly social, created by one or more writers in conversation with many others, from those who have influenced us in the past to those who read and respond to our work in the present. That popular image of a writer as a solitary figure (almost always a man) holed up in a tiny room struggling to create an individual work of great genius doesn't really hold true. Instead, a writer is part of an elaborate network, what author Steven Johnson calls "connected minds." The kind of networking available online—especially through social media—surely does involve connected minds. English poet John Donne's insight that no one "is an island, apart from the main" has never been more true than it is today, as evidenced by writers around the globe who collaborate on everything from a *Google Doc* to a protest movement like Black Lives Matter.

 REFLECT

Think of a time you felt really good about something you wrote. What steps did you move through to write it? Did you have a eureka moment when you came up with a new idea? Did you collaborate with others? pause to reflect and change course along the way? Make a list of all you did that led to your writing success.

NINE

Navigating the Writing Process

From Generating Ideas to Drafting and Revising

THINK OF SOMETHING YOU LIKE TO DO: ride a bike, play a certain video game, solve *Wordle*. If you think about it, you'll see that each of these activities involves learning a process that took some effort to get right when you first started doing it. But eventually, the process became familiar, and now you do it almost automatically.

Writing is much the same. It, too, is a process: a series of activities that takes some effort to do well. And as with any process, you can manage the writing process by approaching it in parts. This chapter introduces the various stages of the writing process—from generating ideas and coming up with a topic to drafting and revising—and provides strategies that will help you make the most of the many writing demands you'll encounter at school, at work, and elsewhere.

One important aspect of becoming comfortable with the writing process is figuring out what works best for you. No single process works for every author or every writing task, so try instead to develop a repertoire of strategies that will enable you to become an efficient, productive, and effective writer.

9 Navigating the Writing Process

Writing involves complex processes and often the "work of many hands."

Start with curiosity. You might think the first step in writing is to open a blank document, ask yourself "What do I think?," and then stare at that blinking cursor. If you're like us, drafting from scratch can leave you feeling stalled and a little anxious—with a case of writer's block before you've begun. The good news is there's lots you can do before sitting down to craft a full essay that makes the blinking-cursor moment a whole lot easier.

Setting yourself in a curious frame of mind, asking lots of questions, exploring a multitude of answers, and gathering many ideas will help you learn about a topic before you decide what you want to say. In these

moments you get to identify what you as an author want to say and how you, with your own perspectives and viewpoints, want to enter the conversation. Even if you already know a lot about an issue and have an argument in mind from the start, it's critical to step back and consider what you do and don't know—and what else you could learn before you enter the conversation. Taking time to explore ideas with an open, curious mind is called practicing , and the steps that follow will help you do it yourself.

> ### REFLECT
>
> When was the last time you had writer's block? What were you trying to write, and why did it feel challenging? What did you do to overcome it?

Ask good questions, get the full picture. To gather knowledge and ideas that you can draw from as you think and write, ask questions that will help you see an issue from all sides. Coming up with questions might seem simple, but, in fact, rhetoric scholars have spent a great deal of time studying the art of posing good, specific questions—from ancient Greek philosopher Hermagoras in the third century BCE to contemporary writing scholar/teacher Stacey Waite today. From that study comes a series of questions, called stasis questions, that scholars agree help thinkers wrap their head around an issue.

Use the following questions, based on the stasis model, to get a broad and deep view of the facts, claims, and arguments related to your topic. See one student adapted these questions to explore the debate over cell phone ban policies in high schools:

- *Fact: What has occurred? How does it happen?* Are students using their cell phones during class? To what extent? Have any schools instituted cell phone bans and if so, how and why?

- *Definition: What is the issue? How do we characterize it? What should we call it?* How do we understand students' in-school cell phone use? What does it look like? How can we describe it? What are cell phone bans, and how do they work?

- *Value: How do we evaluate this issue (good, bad, better, worse)?* How do we evaluate students' in-school use of cell phones? Are in-school cell phone bans effective or ineffective?

- *Cause/effect: What caused the issue? What are the effects of it?* What are the effects of students using their phones in school? How does cell phone use affect student learning? What are the effects of these bans for students and teachers? What do the bans do to the learning environment?

- *Procedure: What do we do about the issue?* How do schools institute cell phone bans? What specific steps have schools made/could schools make to institute a policy?

- *Authority: Who oversees this issue? Who should decide what to do? Who has the power to make change?* Who is allowed to institute these policies? How are various parties (students, parents, teachers, administrators) invited into this policymaking process? Who has a voice in the process?

Generating responses to these questions often involves conducting `RESEARCH`. The student working on cell phone bans consulted sources

---

We don't know where Keren Landman was when she noticed that full-body deodorants were everywhere, but her observation led her to follow interesting lines of inquiry and write a thorough report about a curious cultural trend. Read her essay on p. 938.

through a library database search and then interviewed a few teachers, parents, and school officials for firsthand accounts. The goal of asking good questions—and seeking out answers—is to explore your topic deeply and get a sense of the full picture. Posing questions and digging for answers also gives you time and space to think—to reflect on your own developing ideas and arguments and how they relate to those held by others.

Explore your own connection. After you do some research to learn the facts and see what others are saying, you'll also want to ask yourself some questions. Getting clear on your connection to the topic will shape your thinking, research, and drafting process. The following questions can help:

- If you're able to choose the issue you're writing about, why have you chosen to explore this topic? What is your experience with the topic? Why is (or isn't) it meaningful to you?
- What do you already know about this issue?
- How did you gain this knowledge? Whom have you talked with about it? What reading or research have you already done?
- What *don't* you know about this issue? What do you want to learn? How will you learn it?
- How might your knowledge and previous experience shape your thinking and writing? Be careful to check your own CONFIRMATION BIAS.

See how Tarika Sankar, a student at the University of Maryland, used questions and practiced inquiry for a first-year writing assignment. She describes here how she reconsidered her stance on the issue of nonmedicated prescription drug use on college campuses as she conducted her research:

> To my knowledge, all medications have side effects and using them in a manner different from how they are prescribed can pose serious health risks. Consequently, I was surprised to learn that many students treat using medications without a prescription cavalierly and that my campus administration seems to pay no attention to an issue that could endanger their students' well-being. Naturally, this led me to wonder just how prevalent nonmedical use of prescription drugs on college campuses is, and why it seems like such an acceptable and normal behavior to students.

Sankar identified what she knows and doesn't know about students' nonmedical prescription drug use and how her preconceived ideas shaped her early thinking. She gathered facts by researching the prevalence of non-medical prescription drugs on college campuses (what's happening and how it is happening?), and she looked into students' values and perspectives on the topic (is the current situation good or bad?). As Sankar moved through her inquiry, she stayed open to new ideas and information so that her own position, and eventually her thesis and draft essay, was well informed and supported by carefully considered evidence.

Generate Ideas

In addition to asking good questions and researching to find answers, writing (and even drawing) can help us explore a topic and lead to new ideas. Here are some activities that can help you sort out the information you've gathered about your topic—and come up with new ideas:

- BRAINSTORMING is a way to generate ideas without worrying about whether they're useful or not. When writers brainstorm, they list ideas about that topic using words or phrases about anything and everything that occurs to them about the subject. Then they review what they have written, looking for ideas that seem promising and relationships that can be developed. There are no right answers at this point!

- FREEWRITING is a strategy for writing down ideas quickly, without stopping. To freewrite, writers simply write about whatever comes into their head in relation to a particular idea or topic for several minutes. The point is for writers not to censor themselves here but to just let the ideas flow as freely as possible.

- LOOPING is an extended and more focused kind of freewriting. Writers begin by establishing a subject and then freewrite about it for several minutes. Then they look at what they've written and identify the most important or interesting or promising idea and write a sentence summarizing it. Then they use this sentence to start another "loop" of freewriting, and they repeat this process as many times as necessary.

- CLUSTERING is a strategy for generating and processing ideas visually. Here, writers write a word or phrase that best summarizes or evokes their topic. Then, they draw a circle around their word. From there, they fill in the page by adding related words and ideas, circling them and connecting them to the original word, forming clusters. After that, they

See Ch. 15 in the ebook for a video on generating ideas.

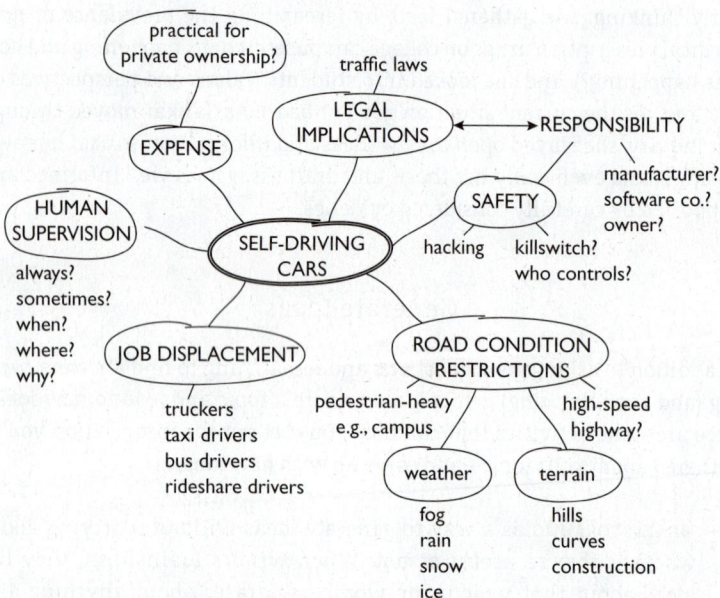

look at all the clusters to see what patterns they can find or where ideas seem to be leading. The image above shows how one writer used clustering to get ideas about self-driving cars.

Once you've asked questions, dug around to find answers, and generated lots of ideas along the way, you'll get to a point when it's time to draft. Even as you begin writing and revising, you can always return to inquiry practices to ask more questions and contemplate new ideas. As author Joan Didion once said, "I don't know what I think until I write it down." For Didion and so many of us, writing is a mode of thinking, and as even as we write, we continue to figure out what we know and exactly what we want to say.

REFLECT

Think of a time when you came up with a new idea while you were writing, experiencing what Joan Didion describes above. What were you working on? When in the process did the new idea strike you? How did you feel when it happened? Summarize the experience.

WRITING PROCESSES / A Roadmap

Everyone's writing process is different, and one writer's process can even change from project to project. As you approach a writing task, think about what often works for you and how you can adjust your process to fit the situation before you. Do you find it helpful to draw up outlines early on? Do you use note cards or sketches to reorganize a draft? Do you write best at a particular time of the day? Do you prefer solitude and quiet, or do you play music? Think about how you'll include those habits that help you produce your best work. Whatever processes you find most productive, following are some tips that provide general guidance. If and when you decide on a particular genre, you'll find genre-specific guidance in the Roadmaps in Chapters 14–19.

Understand your assignment. If you're writing in response to an assignment, make sure you understand what it asks you to do. Does it specify a topic? a theme? a genre? Look for words like "argue," "evaluate," and "analyze"—words that specify a GENRE and thus point you to approach your topic in a certain way. An assignment that asks you to analyze, for example, lets you know that you should break down your topic into parts that can then be examined closely. If your assignment doesn't name a genre, think about which genre will best suit your rhetorical situation.

Come up with a topic. If you get to choose your topic, think of things you are particularly interested in and want to know more about—or something that puzzles you, poses a problem you'd like to solve, or gets you fired up. If your topic is assigned, try to find an aspect or angle that interests you. Looking for a particular angle on a topic can help you narrow your focus, but don't worry if the topic you come up with right now isn't very specific: as you do research, you'll be able to narrow and refine it. The strategies on pages 115–16 can help.

Consider your RHETORICAL SITUATION. Whether you're writing an argument or a narrative, working alone or with a group, you'll have an audience, a purpose, a stance, a genre, a medium and design, and a context. You'll also make choices about language. These are all things you should be considering as you move through your writing process.

- *Audience.* Whom are you addressing? What do they likely know or believe about your topic? What do you want them to think or do in response to your writing?

- *Purpose.* What is your goal in writing? What has motivated you to write, and what do you wish to accomplish?

- *Stance.* What is your attitude toward your topic? What perspective do you offer on it? What's your relationship with your audience, and how do you want to be seen by them?

- *Genre.* Have you been assigned a specific genre? If not, which genre(s) will best suit your purpose and audience?

- *Medium and design.* What medium or media will best suit your audience, purpose, and message? What design elements are possible (or required) in these media?

- *Context.* Consider the conversation surrounding your argument. What has been said about your topic, and how does that affect what you say? What about your immediate context—when is your writing due, and are there any other requirements or constraints?

- *Language.* What are your audience's expectations for language and style? Do you want to meet those expectations? challenge them? What do you want your language to say about you? What risks might you be willing to take with your language?

Schedule your time. Think about how to fit your writing project into your schedule. Taking a series of small steps is easier than doing it all at once. So schedule periodic goals for yourself: meeting them will build your confidence and reinforce good writing habits.

Come up with a tentative THESIS, a statement that identifies your topic and the point you want to make about it. You'll rarely, if ever, have a final thesis when you start writing, but establishing a tentative one will help focus your thinking. Here are some prompts to get you started:

1. *What point do you want to make about your topic?* Try writing it out as a promise to your audience: "In this essay, I will present reasons for people to limit their social media use."

2. ***Try plotting out a tentative thesis in two parts,*** the first stating your topic, the second making some claim about the topic:

   ┌─────── TOPIC ───────┐ ┌─────────── CLAIM ───────────
   Limiting your social media time will improve your self-esteem, provide

   ───┘
   real-life social opportunities, and reduce vulnerability to hacking.

3. ***Ask some questions about what you've written.*** What's your claim? Is it debatable? Will your claim and your supporting ideas engage your audience? There's no point in staking a claim that is a fact, or one that no one would disagree with.

4. ***Do you need to narrow or*** QUALIFY ***your thesis?*** Can you do what you say you will, given the time and resources available? You don't want to overstate your case—or make a claim that you'll have trouble supporting. Adding words such as "could," "might," "likely," or "potentially" can qualify what you say: "Limiting the time you spend on social media might provide more real-life social opportunities, and it could improve self-esteem as well as reduce vulnerability to hacking."

5. ***Is the thesis clear and focused?*** Will it tell readers what's coming? And will it help keep you (and your readers) on track?

At this point in your process, this is a tentative thesis, one that could change. As you move through the writing process you may well find that you want to revise your thesis. This is a good thing! Your position on your topic should change as you learn and think about it more. Once you're satisfied that your thesis makes a clear claim that you can support, and one that will interest your readers, gather together the notes from your research. This is the information you'll draw from as support for your thesis.

ORGANIZE **your ideas.** Outlining can help you see connections between ideas and organize information, especially if you're writing about a complex subject. Begin by listing your main ideas in an order that makes sense. Then add supporting evidence or details under each main idea, indenting these subpoints to mark the different levels, as shown below:

   First main idea
       Supporting evidence or detail
       Supporting evidence or detail
   Second main idea
       Supporting evidence or detail
       Supporting evidence or detail

Whether you like to write out an outline or prefer to do most of your planning on note cards or sticky notes (or in your head!), you'll want to think about how best to organize your text before beginning to write. Writing about events generally works best when told in CHRONOLOGICAL ORDER. And facts, data, and other EVIDENCE are usually most effective when stated in order of importance, starting with the information that's most crucial to your argument before stating the less important information. If you're describing something, you might organize your information SPATIALLY, beginning at one point and moving from left to right, or top to bottom. There's no one way to organize your writing; the order in which you present your points will depend on the topic and what you have to say about it.

Write out a draft. Keep your tentative thesis statement and any other notes and outlines close by as you start writing. A complete draft will include an introduction, a body, and a conclusion, though you may not necessarily draft them in that order.

- *The* INTRODUCTION is often the most difficult part to write, so some authors decide to write it last. But just as a well-crafted opening can help guide your readers, it can also help you get started writing. A good introduction should grab readers' attention, announce your topic and your claim, and indicate how you plan to proceed. A provocative question, an anecdote, a startling claim—these are some of the ways you might open an essay.

- *The body* of an essay is where you will develop your argument, point by point, paragraph by paragraph. Strategies such as COMPARISON, DESCRIPTION, NARRATION, and others can help you develop paragraphs to present EVIDENCE in support of your THESIS.

- *The* CONCLUSION should sum up your argument in a way that readers will remember. You might end by restating your claim, discussing the implications of your argument, calling for some action, or posing further questions—all ways of highlighting the significance of what you've said.

Be flexible, and make changes if you need to. Even the most well-planned writing doesn't show its true shape until you've written a full draft, so don't be surprised if you find that you need to reorganize, do additional research, or otherwise rethink your argument as you go. Be flexible! Rather than sticking stubbornly to a plan that doesn't seem to be working, use each draft and revision as an opportunity to revisit your plan and to think about how you can strengthen your argument or your appeal.

The ancient Greeks had a word for thinking about the opportunities presented by a particular rhetorical situation. They called it "kairos," and it referred to the ability to seize an opportune and timely moment. Kairos was the ancient Greek god of opportunity and perfect timing, qualities every author needs. He was often depicted as a young man running, and it was said that you must seize the forelock of his hair as he passes by; once he's passed, there's nothing to cling to because the back of his head is completely bald—you've missed your opportunity.

Kairos

This is a concept that can be especially helpful when you're drafting—and that can also help you revise. As you work, think of each paragraph and sentence as an opportunity to add (or eliminate) detail, to reorganize, or to improve your point in some other way. Think about how your sentences and paragraphs might be received by your audience—and about how you can get readers to pay attention to and value what you say.

Get responses from others—from your instructor, a classmate, a writing center tutor. Be sure to tell them about any questions or concerns you have about the draft, and ask for their advice. But remember: you don't have to take all the advice you get, just what you consider helpful. You're the author!

Look at your draft with a critical eye and revise. You'll find genre-specific guidelines for reading a draft carefully and revising in the chapters on ARGUMENTS, NARRATIVES, ANALYSES, REPORTS, REVIEWS, and PROPOSALS. For more general advice, following are some prompts to help you read over a draft, either your own or one you're peer-reviewing for a fellow writer.

▶ See the ebook for a video on revision strategies.

- How does the INTRODUCTION capture readers' attention and make them want to read on? Does it indicate that (or why) the topic matters? How else might it begin?

- How do you as the author come across—as well informed? passionate? serious? something else?

- Is it clear what motivated you to write? Consider the larger CONTEXT: what else has been said about the topic, and have you considered perspectives other than your own?

- Is there an explicit THESIS? If not, does there need to be? If so, does it make clear what you are claiming about the topic?

- Is there sufficient support for the thesis? What REASONS and EVIDENCE do you provide? Will they be persuasive for the intended audience?

- Is the draft ORGANIZED in a way that is easy to follow? Check to see how each paragraph supports the thesis, and whether it is developed fully enough to make its point. Are there headings—and if not, should there be? Is there any information that would be easier to follow if set off as a list? Are there explicit TRANSITIONS to help readers follow the text—and if not, are they needed?

- What LANGUAGE and STYLE choices have you made? How are your choices meeting or challenging the expectations of your audience and context? How might your language and style choices do more to enliven your writing, engage your audience, and reflect your persona as an author?

- How does the text CONCLUDE? What does it leave readers thinking? How else might it conclude?

- Is there a title? If so, does it tell readers what your topic is and make them want to read on? If not, think in terms of KAIROS: the title is your first opportunity to indicate that this is a text about something that matters and that readers should care about.

Edit and proofread. Now's the time to pay close attention to the details. Review each sentence and edit so that every word (and punctuation mark!) supports the message you want to convey. Finally, take the time to proofread. Read with an eye for typos and inconsistencies. Make sure all your sentences are complete. Run a spellchecker, but be aware that it is no substitute for careful proofreading.

Reflect. An important part of your writing process is to reflect on it: examining the processes you've used, weighing the success of those processes, and identifying practices you want to keep—and those you want to drop or change. Chapter 12 provides advice on reflecting and the ways it can help you gain more awareness of your writing processes and yourself as a writer.

Approach your writing pragmatically

Even if you have a writing process that works well for you, that doesn't mean you complete all writing tasks the same way—or that you should. It's just common sense that you spend more time and take more care with your writing process for a fifteen-page research paper that counts for 40 percent of your final grade than you do for a much briefer, less formal essay that counts for 10 percent of that grade. Approach your writing pragmatically: consider how important your task is, what time constraints you face, what else you may have to do, what the nature of the task itself requires, and how well prepared you feel to complete it. Then make realistic decisions. What do you *need* to do to complete an assignment effectively—and what *can* you do?

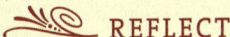 **REFLECT**

Take some time to think about your writing process. What works well? What tends to be a struggle? What do you want to try to do differently? Think about the various ways and places in which you've been able to do good writing. Are you able to make them a regular part of your writing process?

TEN

Collaborating with Others
Peer Review and Group Work

RITERS SELDOM—if ever—write alone. Think about it: some 400 contributors—and counting—have revised the *Wikipedia* page for Caitlin Clark; a journalist on *Instagram* asks students how often they use AI for schoolwork, then uses their responses in an article on the topic; a student talks with a classmate about their essay draft and walks away with a plan to revise. Collaboration has always been inevitable and essential to working out ideas and composing texts.

Think about how collaboration shows up in your writing outside of school. Whether you're creating content for an audience on *TikTok* or leaving comments on *YouTube* videos, these kinds of writing assume a back-and-forth. You might be an author, an audience member, or both. Collaboration is, in fact, today's main tool for social engagement. So collaboration is a necessity. This chapter will help you make the most of opportunities to collaborate in the work you do as an author and a reader, especially in group work and as a peer reader of others' writing.

What Collaboration Means for You as a Student

Academic writing calls on you to engage with the ideas of others—to listen to and think about what they say, to respond, and to weave the ideas of others (those you agree with and those you don't) into your own

10 Collaborating with Others

arguments. Often you'll present your views as a response to what others say—in fact, when you think about it, the main reason we make arguments at all is because someone has said or done something that we want to respond to. And one reason we make academic arguments is to add our voices to conversations about topics that we're studying, things that matter to us.

In your classes you'll collaborate in many forms. Engaging with peers in your writing class is an opportunity to get to know people, learn by exchanging ideas with those from varied backgrounds, and gain multiple perspectives on a range of topics. Think about working with classmates as a chance to practice skills you'll need in your career—listening, engaging productively with others, being open-minded and flexible. Working with team members is foundational in almost every workplace—as the images below demonstrate. Where better to gain experience collaborating with a team than your first-year writing class?

See Ch. 20 in the ebook for a video on understanding academic argument.

Collaboration is everywhere: students at a campus writing center discuss their work (top left); a marketer leads a virtual focus group (top right); a software engineer contributes to a team writing code (bottom left); a nurse gathers patient history notes for the team providing care (bottom right).

 **REFLECT**

Make a list of the kinds of collaboration you've seen happen outside of school. For each, note who was involved and why they were working together—what was their shared purpose? Why do you think they chose to work together instead of alone?

Collaborating in Small Groups

Sometimes your class collaborations will be quick and have low stakes—for example, working with a group to respond to a reading and then sharing that response with the class. Other collaborations are more extended and will have higher stakes, as when you pick lab partners for the whole term or have a major group project that will count toward everyone's final grade.

Extended collaborative assignments can be a challenge. Some people take to group work more than others. An introvert may have much to offer but is hesitant to speak up. An extrovert may be so comfortable that they dominate the meeting. And some members, for a variety of reasons, might not do their part at all. Additionally, the logistics of collaborating can be a challenge. Here are some tips that can help set up efficient, friendly, and

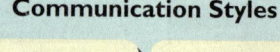
Communication Styles

Analytical Communicators
- take a data-driven approach
- are likely to be comprehensive, examining all angles
- value the practical over the emotional

Intuitive Communicators
- have a direct, concise communication style
- focus on overarching strategy over smaller steps
- trust their instincts, make decisions quickly

Functional Communicators
- are meticulous and thorough
- break issues down into clear, logical pieces
- deliberate over options before making decisions

Personal Communicators
- consider the human element when making decisions
- bring empathy and sensitivity for others to all interactions
- value building relationships

Which of these styles best describes you? Share your style with your collaborators.

productive team relationships when you're working on an extended shared project:

- **Learn something about each other when you first meet.** Find ways to connect. The more common ground you find, the more trust and understanding you'll share. At your first meeting, introduce yourself and one personal detail, like your major or where you're from; share a strength you'll aim to bring to the group's project; and complete the sentence "I do my best writing when . . ."
- **Establish some ground rules.** Whether online or face-to-face, the way your group runs its meetings can make or break your collaborative effort. Spend part of your first meeting discussing how often the group will meet, what method of communication you'll use (email is easier to reference than text messages), and who will make the agenda.
- **Come up with a plan and build a schedule.** Look at the assignment instructions together and create a document listing the tasks that need to be done and who will be responsible. Building a plan helps you share ideas, break the project into parts, and make decisions about how each member will contribute. Specify due dates for each task. Share your plan with your instructor for feedback.
- **Start each meeting with individual reporting.** Ask each group member to report on what they've accomplished and what barriers they're facing, if any. These reports build in accountability and can help keep members on task.
- **Listen carefully**—and respectfully—to every group member. Look for opportunities to invite others into the discussion to be sure everyone's ideas are heard. And speak up yourself, trusting your peers will listen when you have ideas and feedback.
- **Use constructive language to give feedback.** Rather than stating a member's ideas are unclear, you might say, "I'm having trouble making the connection between your suggestion and my understanding of what we're discussing." A simple shift from "your" to "my" can defuse difficult situations. Remember that tact, thoughtfulness, and a sense of humor can go a long way toward resolving issues.
- **Expect the unexpected and be flexible.** Someone's computer may crash, interlibrary loan materials may arrive late, someone may be sick when they're supposed to write a key section. Try to build in extra time for the unexpected and help one another out, working on a solution together when extra teamwork is needed.

> The collaborative projects that Taté Walker describes in her report (p. 1003) deal with agriculture rather than writing. Read her report to see how each project requires good, clear communication.

- ***Know when to ask for your instructor's help.*** Combining different working styles for one shared goal is not always smooth. If you're facing a major conflict, like a group member who isn't contributing or a heated disagreement you can't get past, reach out to your instructor for advice on how to resolve the obstacle together.

Remember that when you engage in group work, you attend to both the task and the group. Completing the assigned project is only one part of successful teamwork. Another part is making sure that group members feel valued as you contribute to a shared goal, a skill you'll need to succeed in virtually any career or field today.

Collaborating through Peer Review

Peer review involves writers sharing their work with others to find out how readers interact with their texts—from academic essays and websites to infographics and podcasts. Writing teachers Charlotte Brammer and Mary Rees point out that "collaboration rather than correction is . . . essential to successful peer review." Why? Because peer review is about exchanging ideas, not simply fixing grammar. Peer review means supporting a writer through honest, respectful discussion of the strengths of their work and the areas that need improvement.

Peer review is as much about being a good reader as it is about being a good writer. When you read with care and with the writer's goals in mind, you can provide useful feedback and model the kind of feedback you hope to receive, too. Participating in this collaborative exchange helps you do the following:

- ***See how others react to your ideas and language.*** Are your words too formal or too casual? Do they get your point across clearly? Do you need more examples? When one of our students, Kienna Whitman, reflected on her undergraduate peer review experience, she stated: "Peer review helped me identify where I needed to expand. My reviewers were quick to point out where background or evidence was lacking, so I could flag those sections and return later."

- ***Gain a different perspective.*** Maybe your peer reviewers point out that your example could be interpreted as offensive, something you did not mean. Maybe they recommend a source to help with an idea you're struggling with. Maybe you get the encouragement you need to move forward with an idea that you're not sure about. As writing researchers Robert Brooke, Ruth Mirtz, and Rich Evans state in their book *Small*

Groups in Writing Workshops, peers' "response to particular drafts can often help writers see new possibilities and problems in their pieces, often leading to revisions that significantly improve the writing."

- **Learn by doing.** Our students tell us that they often benefit more from providing feedback to peers than receiving feedback because they learn about a range of topics. They also practice their rhetorical skills—employing empathy, crafting clear messages, and being supportive while offering concrete advice. Note how Aurora Boothby, a student at Ohio State University, describes how valuable being a peer reviewer is for her own writing: "Being able to analyze the work of students with more writing experience than me, and then having to critique and help them improve that work, came with such a high value. I held on to the [feedback] I gave on their work and then applied that feedback to my own writing; not only did I do this throughout the course of this class but also in my other courses and beyond."

- **Foster relationships.** If you think about writing as a social act, peer review is one vehicle through which social interaction can take place. In their article titled "Student Perceptions of and Attitudes about Peer Review," researchers Dianne Moneypenny, Margaret Evans, and Amanda Kraha reported the majority of students surveyed suggested that "peer review activities increase[d] the interaction between [their] classmates and [them]." So, peer review is an opportunity to do more than improve your writing; it's a chance to get to know classmates and create community.

Give good feedback. When a classmate is depending on you to help improve a draft, you might wonder, "Am I good enough to give advice?" Maybe you're not sure where to begin, worrying, "Will I be too critical or not critical enough?" Being a good peer reviewer takes practice; you'll get more comfortable the more you do it. Our first piece of advice is to relax and trust yourself. Remember, your job is not to take on the role of a writing teacher. If you read closely and with care, you are well on your way to providing helpful observations. The following steps will help:

- First, ask the writer what they think works well in their draft and what areas they want to work on. Are there specific questions they hope you'll answer about their writing? Are there particular issues they want help improving?
- Read the draft once through completely without making any written comments for the writer. On the first read, look to understand the major points and how those claims are supported.

- Read the draft a second time, with an eye toward the areas of concern and areas of strength the writer identified. Make notes about what you find most compelling and what questions you have.
- If you're not sure what to focus on, use the suggested list of review questions for ARGUMENTS on pages 201–2, NARRATIVES on pages 236–37, ANALYSES on pages 284–85, REPORTS on pages 325–26, REVIEWS on pages 368–69, and PROPOSALS on pages 394–95.
- As you make notes for the writer, remember that you're engaging in a conversation and working together to help them achieve their goals. Begin by addressing what you see as the strengths of the draft with notes such as "I like how you . . ." and ". . . really grabbed my attention and made me think."
- Be specific. "This is really good" or "this is boring" aren't as helpful as specifics about which sentences affected you and why. For example, "I got a clear sense of your emotional response when you compared your feelings to a powerful, unexpected storm" points to a specific part and why it stood out. Offer concrete advice when you can. You can try pointing to a specific claim and asking for credible evidence to let the writer know valuable information is missing.
- If you don't understand something, ask the writer to explain it: "Can you explain to me again how this example supports your thesis?" If possible, talk through points of confusion since we tend to explain things more clearly in conversation than in writing. Jot down notes if you hear the writer say something out loud that you think should be added to their text to help clarify.
- After you've discussed your feedback with the writer, ask the writer about their plans for revision. If they're not sure what to focus on, suggest two or three key areas or tasks. Aim to not overwhelm the writer.
- Do not hesitate to suggest the writer ask their instructor about anything they are still confused about in the assignment.

Get good feedback. You won't just participate in peer review as a reader—you'll also benefit from your peers' reactions to your own writing. Because peer review is a collaboration, you're still an active participant as the writer. You won't sit back while your reader does all the work. So what can you do to help your reader generate useful feedback—and how can you make the most of what you learn? The following tips can help:

- If your reader isn't already familiar with the assignment, explain how you understand the writing task and your goals for the next draft.
- Identify one or two strengths in your text and one or two areas that you're unsure about. Be specific. For example, you might identify your transitions from one paragraph to the next as a strength because they indicate a cause-effect relationship—one of your assignment goals. Or you might ask your peer reviewer how persuasive your use of a personal example is to support your thesis.
- During review, if possible, reread your own draft at the same time your reader is working with it. Try to see it objectively, like someone else's work. Read through it completely without stopping to make notes, and then read it again, this time marking areas that are working well and those you're less sure about. Compare your notes with the feedback from your reader and follow up if they don't address the areas that you still have questions about.
- If you get time to talk about your work, take notes on your reader's main suggestions and reactions. Jot down your top two to three revision priorities near the end, and share your plan aloud to see if your reader agrees.
- Remember that as the author, you have agency in a peer review session. That means you can help keep the feedback focused on meeting your goals. Redirect or ask to return to a topic if you want to be sure to address it. At the same time, stay open to the suggestions your peers make; you might be surprised what a fresh set of eyes uncovers.

See Ch. 12 in the ebook for a video on using peer review for revision.

Collaborating at the Writing Center

Most schools have a writing center, and it's often a place you can go (online or in person) to consult with a trained tutor on some aspect of a class assignment. All writers need good readers, and a tutor can work with you at any stage of the process—brainstorming ideas, creating an outline, polishing, clarifying, documenting sources. The good news is that the writing center probably doesn't charge a cent for what it offers. (Or rather, you've already paid for it as part of your tuition and fees, so you might as well take advantage.)

The more prepared you are for your writing center session, the more you'll get out of it. First, figure out what you'd like to accomplish in your session and share that information with your tutor early. Discuss your ideas, goals, doubts, and questions. Your tutor may suggest a different focus for your session; be open and flexible to such suggestions and reasoning. Let the session be a collaboration. A lot of ideas and information will be discussed during your session, so it's important that you take good notes to be able to remember it all. You may want to sit down immediately after your session and add more details to your notes while your memory is still fresh. Finally, write out a plan of action for what you'll do next; this plan will guide you when you get back to your assignment. We also recommend that you schedule your next appointment before leaving the writing center, because having an appointment can be a soft deadline for advancing your project. Finally, think about how the advice in previous sections may help you prepare for and participate in a writing center session.

 **REFLECT**

Go to your school's writing center website. What services and resources do they offer for students? How can you make an appointment? Where is the writing center located?

A SAMPLE PEER-REVIEWED ESSAY

On the following pages, you'll find student Sierra Jaquez's first draft essay for a first-year writing course at San Jose State University, with comments from a classmate. Jaquez and her peer reader first looked over the assignment, which says to:

> Compare two or three case studies in cultural creativity. Your essay should make an overarching argument about creativity by putting your chosen case studies together—comparing and contrasting them—and should end with a call to action for the reader. Your essay should draw on substantial library research, and you should cite at least eight outside sources.

The peer reader offered the comments and suggestions you see in the yellow boxes in margins, keeping in mind Jaquez's goal of working on strong evidence that directly supports the thesis and smooth source integration, two key pieces of the grading rubric.

PEER REVIEW / An Annotated Example

Draft 1:
How Harries and Swifties Changed the Outlook on Modern Concert Fashion

SIERRA JAQUEZ

Two of the world's most popular artists, Harry Styles and Taylor Swift, have dominated the music industry for many years, each with their own unique style. Their recent multimillion-dollar tours, Styles's *Love on Tour* and Swift's *The Eras Tour*, garnered attention not only for their music but also for the outfits they wore to perform—and the outfits their fans wore to attend. By looking at clothing expression through the lens of these tours, we can see that various factors outside of the artists' music, such as personal expression and overall confidence, went into the creation of the outfits fans chose to wear, which shows that these artists' influence on their fans goes beyond just music.

Aside from being ex-lovers, Styles and Swift are connected by a common trend among their fan bases (Harries and Swifties, respectively): at their concerts, fans showed up in unique and creative ensembles, which can be seen as an outpouring of creativity and self-expression. When it comes to Styles's *Love on Tour*, some staple pieces incorporated into many outfits included boas, sparkles, fruits, and fun colors. An article from *The Sydney Morning Herald* includes a quote from a fan who stated, "Harry and his stylist work hard to have an eclectic vibe, he doesn't rock up in jeans and t-shirt. He puts on a show, so as fans we want to bring it back to him" (Economos and Ironmonger). Styles's unique style is something well known by fans and non-fans alike. His bright-colored, sparkly outfits are often accompanied by one-of-a-kind accessories, which reminds me of author Adam Grant's definition of an "original" in his book *Originals: How Non-Conformists Move the World*: "a thing of singular or unique character; a person who is different from other people in an appealing or interesting way; a person of fresh initiative or inventive capacity" (3). Styles's outlook on fashion is definitely "fresh" and different from many of his peers, which causes him to stand out in a confident and poised way.

Similarly, Swifties spend countless hours constructing the perfect concert look, except their common outfit staples are slightly different than those worn to Styles's shows. While sparkles are also very prevalent, the re-creation of past

---

Your intro drew me in. Style choice is a unique way of analyzing pop stars and fans.

Your thesis seems long. Is your main idea that the clothes Styles and Swift wear on their tours influences their fans' outfits?

Are you talking about fan outfits, Styles's outfits, or both?

Nice quote from an expert. Could you say more about Grant's background?

To tie your main point to your thesis, could you say how Styles's fans' POV relates to your bigger ideas of confidence and creativity?

Is being "fresh" the same as being "original"?

Swift concert outfits is not. Instead of copying an outfit worn in the past by her, fans tend to implement certain elements of Swift's style and "vibe" into their outfits, which may include wearing a "Junior Jewels" shirt seen in the *You Belong with Me* music video or wearing a specific color that coincides with a certain era. A pop culture article appearing on the *Today* website explains how one fan went for a *Midnights*-era look and decided to rock a "purple costume, featuring a sequin skirt and heart-shaped sunglasses, inspired by the 'Lavender Haze' music video" (Greene).

> *Details or a photo would help us picture Swift's overall "vibe."*

Popular artists influence their fans in all kinds of ways, and clothing is clearly powerful. Styles stands out because unlike most male artists today, he dresses in ways that defy traditional masculinity. In an article about Styles's fashion choices, student newspaper writer Alayna Yates describes how he conveys the idea that "fashion shouldn't be limited to women's and men's clothing. As far as the former One Direction member is concerned, clothing doesn't have gender." This statement can be supported by Styles's fashion choices: he frequently wears rhinestones and sequins, loves to accessorize, and was even seen wearing a dress in a *Vogue* issue centered on him and his life. In that same *Vogue* interview conducted in 2020, Styles himself stated, "There's so much joy to be had in playing with clothes. I've never thought too much about what it means—it just becomes this extended part of creating something" (Bowles). This statement from him clearly supports the idea that fashion has no barriers; if he wishes to wear a certain piece of clothing, he will, no matter who he angers in the process. His style has changed over the years, though. After emerging in the public eye back in 2010 with the rest of the iconic boy band One Direction his clothing choices were limited. He and his band were constantly seen wearing cohesive colors and patterns, which limited their individuality. Since emerging for the first time in 2017 after One Direction's hiatus, he has shown a new side of himself that allows his personality to shine.

> *I wasn't sure how this par. supports your main argument. What do Swiftie outfits say about creativity and confidence?*

> *These sources add good context for Styles's fashion journey.*

As for Swift's influence on her fans, style evolution has also played an important role. Up until around late 2014, Swift portrayed herself as an innocent rule follower. After releasing her album *1989*, she began to gain the confidence to break out of the "good girl" image and show her edgier side. This side of her was highlighted even more in her 2017 album *Reputation*, and the *Billboard* article titled "Taylor Swift's Style Evolution, from 2006 to Now" displays this development of style—showing how her outfit colors strayed from super bright to more neutral and dark (Longo). A fan even expressed in an article on *TribLive* how Swift's "rep era" was fun and edgy (Daugherty). 5

> *I like how you explain each artists' changing images.*

Her change in self-expression did not go unnoticed, and it even led to fans gaining confidence the way Swift did. One example of Swift breaking out of her shell and expressing her true self was at the 2014 Video Music Awards, where she rocked a short blue bodysuit, messy hair, maroon pumps, and a sparkly blue smoky eye. Instead of continuing to dress in a softer and more modest way, the way the public expected her to, she chose to put on an outfit she felt confident in—one that she felt truly displayed the way she wanted to express herself.

Nice tie back to confidence. How does this relate back to your point about creativity?

After exploring the fun and diverse fashion world of the Harries and Swifties, it is clear that both of these artists attract loyal fan bases by modeling what it means to be a bold, creative, and confident person. They give people permission to boldly express themselves and to play with creative expression. Instead of replicating Styles's and Swift's every move, these fans take inspiration from elements of the artists that resonate most with them. And then they try to do what the artists themselves do: make something their own and have fun doing it. As time goes on, pop music's creativity in the fan fashion department continues to evolve, not only with Harries and Swifties but also with the BeyHive at Beyoncé's *The Renaissance Tour* and the Bunnies at Bad Bunny's *World's Hottest Tour*, to name a couple of examples. As artists and their musical personalities and fashion evolve, so does the imagination of their fans. As a result, these tours and artists will be remembered for their bold creative expressions and how they empowered a generation of fans to express themselves, too, through fashion choices and beyond.

This restatement of your main argument feels clearer than your thesis. Maybe use it earlier on?

The assignment says to end with a call to action. What should readers, like a fashion or artist merch company, do after reading your analysis?

Works Cited

Bowles, Hamish. "Playtime with Harry Styles." *Vogue*, 13 Nov. 2020, www.vogue.com/article/harry-styles-cover-december-2020.

Daugherty, Haley. "Taylor Swift Eras Tour Outfits: Fans Dress to the Nines in Styles with Meaning behind the Music." *TribLive*, 24 Nov. 2024, triblive.com/aande/music/taylor-swift-eras-tour-outfits-fans-dress-to-the-nines-in-styles-with-meaning-behind-the-music.

Economos, Nicole, and Lauren Ironmonger. "Bigger than a Formal: Why Fans Spend Months on DIY Harry Styles Concert Outfits." *The Sydney Morning Herald*, 19 Feb. 2023, www.smh.com.au/lifestyle/fashion/bigger-than-a-formal-why-fans-spend-months-on-diy-harry-styles-concert-outfits-20230202-p5chig.html.

Grant, Adam. *Originals: How Non-Conformists Change the World.* W. H. Allen, 2017.

Greene, Jordan. "Taylor Swift Fans Are Going Viral for the DIY Costumes They're Wearing to Her Tour." *Today*, 27 Mar. 2023, www.today.com/popculture/taylor-swift-eras-tour-fan-concert-outfits-rcna76011.

Longo, Allie. "Taylor Swift's Style Evolution, from 2006 to Now." *Billboard*, 30 Aug. 2023, www.billboard.com/photos/taylor-swift-style-evolution-photos-429884.

Styles, Harry. *Love on Tour.* 4 Sept.–22 July 2023, Europe, South America, North America.

Swift, Taylor. *The Eras Tour.* 17 Mar. 2023–8 Dec. 2024, Asia, Australia, Europe, North America, South America.

Yates, Alayna. "Breaking Down Barriers: Harry Styles Shows Clothes Have No Gender in Recent *Vogue* Issue." *Flyer News* [Dayton], 29 Dec. 2020, flyernews.com/ae/breaking-down-barriers-harry-styles-shows-clothes-have-no-gender-in-recent-vogue-issue/12/29/2020.

> **REFLECT**
>
> What two or three revision priorities do you think Sierra Jaquez settled on after receiving their peer reader's feedback? If you were the peer reader working with Jaquez, how would you go about helping the writer make a revision plan before leaving the session?

ELEVEN

Navigating AI as an Author

"THE COLLEGE ESSAY IS DEAD," declared cultural critic Stephen Marche way back in 2022, pointing to AI as the culprit. Marche claimed generative AI tools like *ChatGPT* had gotten so good at cranking out traditional college essays that teachers needed to find something else for students to write. But you're still here, reading this book for a class requiring you to write essays! So maybe the college essay has some life left after all. And yet AI is still here, too—showing no signs of slowing down, much less going away. So what now? And what, exactly, is generative AI anyway? Should you use it in your own writing? This chapter will help you think through these key questions and explore strategies for evaluating the benefits and drawbacks of using generative AI in your academic writing.

 REFLECT

What's your experience with *ChatGPT* or other tools like it? What do you use it for and why? If you don't use it, why not? What concerns or questions do you have about AI and academic writing?

What Is Generative AI?

"Artificial intelligence" is a misnomer, an inaccurate term—it's not intelligent in the way that we think of the human mind. Instead, *ChatGPT*, *Microsoft Copilot*, *Google Gemini*, and other generative AI tools work sort of like a sophisticated auto-complete. They're called "generative AI" because they predict—and then generate—what a human might say, given all the tool has "read" of human writing. So they are making guesses based on a whole lot of information, but they aren't thinking in the ways that humans do. However, because they're often set up to chat with you and refer to themselves as "I," they may seem like they're "thinking."

AI tools advertised to help you with writing or reading—in word processors, search engines, your phone—are built with something called a large language model (LLM) under the hood. LLMs rely on two main components: large datasets of text and algorithms to process all that data and then reproduce patterns from it. LLMs reflect the data that they're trained on, which is often scraped from the web—everything from *Reddit* forums and news sites to *Wikipedia* entries and pirated books. Some LLMs produce images, graphs, audio, or video, so they've been trained with what is most likely web-based examples of those media as well.

LLMs can produce amazingly complex content, but critics of generative AI point out that they are also prone to producing falsehoods, toxicity, and bias—sometimes obvious and sometimes very subtle. Because most generative AI tools keep the data and algorithms that fuel their product secret, we can't simply take it on faith that the output is accurate, unbiased, or original (that is, not a direct copy of someone else's work); one of the many challenges we face is understanding how, and to what extent, we can verify accuracy and originality for ourselves, using our human intelligence.

You won't be surprised to hear that generative AI is at work all around us, embedded in everything from apps like *Snapchat* and *Google Docs* to programs used for business communication and hiring new employees. In other words, AI is part of our everyday lives, and though we don't always have a choice, when you *do* have a choice whether to use it or not, you'll want to be mindful about how and when you turn to it—making the most of your agency as an author.

Navigating AI as an Author

This illustration appeared on the cover of the *New Yorker* following *ChatGPT*'s release. How would you represent the relationship between humans and robots in this age of AI—using visuals alone, without words?

Authorship, Agency, and AI

If you ever needed more convincing that AI isn't about to take the place of real humans, check out how tech writer Meghan O'Gieblyn responds to a reader who's questioning their own human status. Find it on p. 967.

If everyone is an author, does that include AI? In a word, no. "Author" means someone who invents, creates, or originates—and this act of creation carries *authority*. So writing as an author is more than producing words: authors create new knowledge by **THINKING RHETORICALLY** —listening; considering the perspectives of others; choosing effective genres, media, and modes; and evaluating the context of any situation in which they're called to write.

Marketers might have you think that AI products are all you need to write, and write with authority. Sure, AI chatbots can compose sentences. But what about the rest of what it takes to be an author? The academic journal *Nature* says: "Authorship carries with it *accountability* for the work, which cannot be effectively applied to LLMs." Put another way, AI can string together words—even words that might sound like you!—but it cannot be accountable for those words. And see how the University of Pittsburgh's academic integrity policy puts accountability front and center: "Just as faculty and students must be free to seek truth and to search for knowledge with open minds, they must also accept the responsibility that these activities entail." AI can't think for you, and it certainly won't take responsibility for the consequences of what it writes. As an author, you—and only you—are accountable for work with your name on it.

Authorship also requires agency, taking control and ownership of what you do and how you do it. AI does not have agency, but it does have some power to rob you of yours if you rely on it too much. For example, many of the available generative AI products default to **STANDARDIZED ENGLISH**, a style that works well in some situations and not so well in others, depending on your purpose, audience, and context. You, on the other hand, have your own unique writing voice and only you are able to put that voice to work in achieving your unique goals—with authority, agency, and style. Don't erase that voice with AI! And only you can practice **CRITICAL LANGUAGE AWARENESS**, considering how power and privilege affect the words you use and how your audience receives them. All of this is why one of our students decided to steer clear, saying, "*ChatGPT* has a distinctive style that is different from mine, so to preserve my voice and authenticity, I don't use it."

Questions to Consider before Using Generative AI

In an ad for *Google Gemini* that ran during the 2024 Summer Olympics, a dad asks the chatbot to write his daughter's fan letter to her idol, US Olympic gold medalist hurdler Sydney McLaughlin-Levrone. He says AI will help

Google's ad for when you need "a little help from Gemini."

get her words "just right." In this ad, and many others, AI is presented like a magic wand for making things easier or "unleashing creativity," allowing people to produce polished prose, art, or songs much better and quicker than they could on their own. But the goal for creative work is often the process itself—what you learn and gain along the way—not simply the end product. And for many writing situations, a unique style and voice is more important than "correct" grammar. The *Gemini* ad bombed, and it was quickly pulled from the air. Many viewers pointed out that getting the words "just right" in a girl's fan letter just misses the point.

In other words, be cautious of the promises about AI making your life or work easy. Think carefully about your situation before using generative AI in your academic writing. The following checklist can help:

- **What does your instructor say about AI?** Defer to your instructor's AI policy for class assignments. You'll find it in the syllabus or assignment prompt—or ask them directly. Some instructors specify the tasks AI can be used for and which ones it cannot. Others require certain steps if you rely on AI, like a copy of the transcript or a statement detailing how you used it. Some ban AI outright. If you can't find a policy or you're unsure what's allowed, ask. The penalties for misusing AI can be severe and could include failing an assignment or class.

- **What's your PURPOSE *for writing*?** What do you want to gain from doing this assignment—beyond earning a good grade and getting it done? What's your instructor looking for you to practice? Often the point of writing assignments is more about what you learn along the way than a final product that's "just right." For example, asking AI to write a reading response may get you a list of main points quickly, but it won't help you connect the ideas to discussions from class. If you're looking to

AI for help completing an assignment, why? Which tasks in your process are suited to AI's help and which are not? Consider if and where AI will help you achieve your goals or work against them. You might be surprised how often you decide it's quicker and better to do something yourself.

- **What's the best tool for the job?** You wouldn't use a hammer to paint your room. The same goes with technologies that you use in writing. Different AI tools are suited for different jobs. (And remember sometimes the best tool is the most powerful one of all: your brain!) So, if you're using AI, pay attention to the features of the product you choose. One AI tool might be easy to use but doesn't provide links to real sources—making it not good for research help. Another might be free but offers no privacy protections and uses your data to train itself, so you should avoid it when writing about a sensitive personal topic. To grasp the benefits and drawbacks of a tool, play around with it yourself, read about it, and remember AI products evolve rapidly, so those tradeoffs might shift, too.

- **What's your prompt?** To use any AI chatbot well, you'll need some practice writing prompts to figure out what works well. Sometimes it's helpful to ask a chatbot to walk you through a process step-by-step, like "I need to conduct research interviews; help me break this task down into steps. Where do I begin?" You can assign it a role—a mentor, tutor, or travel guide—in order to get suggestions from a particular perspective. Specify the format you'd like the output in, and the context of the task you're asking it to do. If it's not what you're looking for, then keep the conversation going: ask the AI to do something a little differently to get what you want. And when in doubt, check out the "Help" section.

- **What about ethical issues?** Before you cut-and-paste into an AI product, think about what happens to the text you put in. Many AI tools use what people input to train their models. So consider: What responsibility do you have to the writer of a text? Would the author want to have it shared with an AI company without being asked for their permission? Do you want to share your own work? And don't put your peers writing or essay drafts into an AI tool.

If the questions above lead you to use AI, take a moment to **REFLECT** on how it went near the end of a project. Did it help expand your thinking? improve your writing process? give you more time for the parts of the process you wanted to do yourself? Would it have been easier if you hadn't used AI, or would you have learned more without it?

One of our students, Kermina Abdelsayed at the University of Pittsburgh, wasn't so sure it helped: "Overall, I think the use of AI for this assignment helped the writing process, but I am not sure that it made a better end product. I think if I'd had time to just sit and think about what I had to write, it would have been more authentic and possibly higher quality." As you reflect, consider: what will you do differently—or the same—next time?

>  **REFLECT**
>
> Read your instructor's AI policy carefully and restate it in your own words. Why is your instructor taking this stance? Which parts stand out to you? How will you need to adjust your use of AI?

Some Ways AI Can Help

Both playing and watching soccer can be fun. Watching a soccer game can teach you about plays, how a team works together, or shooting strategies. But it doesn't give you the endurance, ball control skills, and power that you really need to play. To play soccer well, you need to get out and move yourself.

The same is true for writing and reading. You may find AI tools that claim to do the hard work of writing for you: coming up with ideas, organizing arguments, crafting good sentences, revising. But there simply isn't a magic tool that will produce strong essays and help you strengthen your own writing skills at the same time. As one of our students said, "What's the point in taking a writing class if there's a program to do it for you? The purpose of a writing class is to learn how to write well on your own." So, as you write, consider whether offloading a task to AI is worth losing the chance to develop those skills yourself. However, if your instructor's policies allow, below are a few focused ways that AI might help—as well as important limitations to keep in mind.

Managing your time. If you're like many students, you're balancing a lot—classes, a job, a social life, family care, and general maintenance, like cooking and exercise. It can be overwhelming! Personal trainers, dining halls, and therapists might help you manage—but so can AI. Here are some prompts that might help. Note the blue underlined text indicate places where you would supply your own words.

- "I have an essay assignment due in two weeks. I have to turn in an annotated bibliography, two drafts with substantial revision, a 1,000-word essay, and a reflection statement that describes my process. I'm attaching screenshots of my calendar for the next two weeks. Please make a draft schedule for completing the assignment on time."
- "I am trying to procrastinate less on my writing this term. Here's a screenshot of my calendar for a typical week this month. Can you give me some ideas for how I can get my writing process started earlier and work more steadily on it?"
- "I'm a college student at Hampton University struggling to manage all my classes and obligations. What are some campus resources I could use to help me?"

Understanding challenging texts. Like writing, reading can be hard, and we grow as readers when we practice and wrestle with texts ourselves. It might be tempting to turn to AI to "read" for you, especially when you're crunched for time, but remember that we can't trust AI tools to provide accurate information and any brief description of a text is going to cut out details from the original that might be important. AI shortens texts but it doesn't always "get" what's relevant or crucial about them, and it doesn't take into account your context. So, for important texts like your course's assigned reading, stick to doing it yourself, even if you turn to AI for some support. For especially challenging material, AI might be helpful for clarifying key points and simplifying jargon. Here are some other ways that AI might help you understand difficult texts, after you've already read them yourself:

- List a text's main arguments or the main point of a dense paragraph.
- Define unfamiliar terms in simpler words.
- Provide context for a text, like identifying previous research on the topic or any debate surrounding the text.
- Break the reading process into parts, using a prompt such as "Act as a college tutor who is helping me be sure I understand a text I'm reading. Pose a series of questions designed to help me break down the text and grasp what it says and how it works. Pose one question at a time

and wait for my answer. After five questions and answers, offer me an assessment on my understanding of the text. Do not give me hints or answers to your questions."

Refining your own ideas. Before you ask AI for ideas, come up with some yourself. It's one thing to test out your ideas with AI's help, but it's another to let it do your thinking for you. Once you've got a direction in mind, AI can help refine your thinking. We've found it useful for identifying an aspect of a topic that's not yet heavily researched. A lot of times an AI tool's ideas aren't very good, but its suggestions can help you see what you *don't* like, sparking your own new ideas in a different direction. Try the following prompts for AI's help in refining ideas:

> See the ebook for a video on using AI as a resource in your writing process.

- "I'm writing an essay on university support for students, and I've come up with the following list of possible topics. Give me five more ideas related to my original list."
- "I'm figuring out who my audience should be for a proposal essay on installing safety cameras at campus crosswalks. What are five groups of people who have a stake in my topic?"
- "I'm working on a paper about seasonal affective disorder and high school start times, and I feel stuck. Here are the goals for the assignment and my ideas so far. Can you give me a few tips for what my next steps could be?"
- "I'm drafting a proposal for starting a student group focused on fostering animals. What are five potential names for this group that would make the acronym MEOW?"

Navigating early research. When turning to AI for help with research, stick with tools that are connected to databases or linked to real sources. For instance, some available tools (as of this writing, *Elicit* is one) draw on a database of academic papers and generate a list of suggested sources if you provide a question related to your research topic. You can filter results based on journal quality and methodology, and it will describe those papers so that you can select which ones might be most useful to your further research. *SciSpace* currently allows you to upload select materials and have AI draw its responses from those texts only, which can help you explore specific research questions from a body of vetted sources. Yet even AI services that draw from academic databases may have drawbacks: some, for example, reproduce quotations from original sources in their summaries and omit quotation marks, which depending on other factors—may be **PLAGIARISM**. In short, always proceed with caution.

AI tools that don't link to the sources of their information are not good for research because there is no way to know if they are simply making up sources, and you can't review the material they pull information from. In other words, AI can't substitute for your own reading and research, but it may help you to wade through a large volume of sources. The following prompts can be helpful starts for research:

- With a research-focused AI tool, try: "What are the benefits of colleges to their regional economies?" Read through the source descriptions and links AI offers to choose a few sources to explore more deeply yourself. Try filtering results to high-quality journals only or articles published after a certain date.
- In a chatbot, try: "What are the main arguments researchers have made about my research question, In what ways do colleges drive economic growth in a region? Give me the names of real researchers and cite your sources so I can go read the most relevant ones myself."
- "I'm writing a paper on the history of the typewriter. Here are some citations of articles I've found. Please tell me which articles I've provided will be the most useful for my topic, and why."
- "I'm working through ideas on a research paper about seasonal affective disorder and students. I'd like to have a dialogue with you about my ideas and research so far. Please ask me questions that will help me narrow my topic."

Getting additional feedback. AI tools aren't great at coming up with interesting writing, but they can offer one more source of quick feedback for your drafts. Remember, though, that AI is no substitute for human **COLLABORATION**—a peer review session or an appointment at your campus writing center—where people help you hone your writing to the goals of your course and assignment and know the local context of your school. Instead, think of AI as one more sounding board for generating revision ideas for you to consider. The more specific you make your questions, the better the AI's response will be. And the more you specify about your **CONTEXT**, **AUDIENCE**, **PURPOSE**, and **GENRE**, the more you're thinking and learning about your own writing, too. Here are some suggestions for ways you might consider using AI to generate feedback:

- Generate focused feedback, with a prompt like "Please act as a peer reviewer focused on helping with source integration. Review the following draft and analyze how effectively I've used quotes and sources. Provide a list of suggestions for improvement. Do not revise for me. Here's my essay:..."
- Provide suggestions for reaching your audience by prompting "I'm writing an op-ed essay for my local paper where I'm arguing that our town should support community farms. My main audience is local homeowners. List a few ways I might adjust my tone and vocabulary to help me reach that audience. Explain your advice so that I can improve my writing in this genre. Do not revise for me. Here's my essay:..."

Proofreading and formatting. Many students say AI is most helpful during the final steps of their writing process: fixing issues with format, grammar, and spelling. *Grammarly* is a popular platform for suggestions on improving grammar and style. Other AI products, like *ChatGPT*, can format bibliographies and reduce PASSIVE VOICE. However, beware: using AI to rewrite whole sentences can flatten your writing and make it sound a lot less like you—and may even steer you into unwitting PLAGIARISM if you end up quoting without attribution. Your writing voice is like a unique

© marketoonist.com

fingerprint, and your teacher doesn't want to read a stack of essays that all sound the same. Consider AI's suggestions and decide yourself which revisions to make instead of letting it re-write for you. Here are some prompts for getting AI's help on proofreading and formatting:

- "Format a bibliography in APA 7th edition style for the following sources: notes on all sources consulted." It's up to you to double-check against a trusted source that the information is correct, by consulting, for example, Chapter 33 of this book.

- "Please identify in my draft all uses of passive voice and details that seem unnecessary. Mark the areas in bold text, but do not correct them." Then work on revisiting those sections of your paper.

Proceed with Caution

Do you pay attention to where your clothes are manufactured? the materials used? the treatment of the workers involved? Do you ever choose to save gas by carpooling or taking public transit? These are examples of personal habits that can make small impacts on broader social issues. Similarly, researchers such as Emily Bender, Timnit Gebru, Margaret Mitchell, and Angelina McMillan-Major have pointed out there are serious social and environmental costs associated with AI products. From guzzling natural resources, like the millions of gallons of water required to cool off servers, to exploiting workers involved in training chatbots for very low pay, the growth of AI tools has some significant global drawbacks. In fact, some industries have protested AI's use to protect the value of their own work—and of our world! You may be interested in considering these broader issues when you think about using AI yourself.

↪ For more on the global impacts of AI on our world, you can find readings at everyonesanauthor.tumblr.com.

As a writer, if your instructor's policy allows and you choose to enlist AI for help, there are a few common pitfalls to guard against. Use these questions to help reduce the chances of AI's issues showing up in your own writing:

How accurate is the output? Because they predict language by using statistics rather than by relying on verified facts, AI tools sometimes produce wrong information, often called "hallucinations." At the time of this printing, AI tools simply aren't reliable sources of factual information. One attorney, dubbed the "ChatGPT lawyer," found this out the hard way when

11 🖋 Navigating AI as an Author [149]

Nurses raise awareness about the dangers of using AI in health-care settings (left). In Hollywood, writers and actors demonstrate with a message that "AI is not art" (right).

he used *ChatGPT* to find cases for him—and then discovered that the LLM had made them up. Double-check any fact or claim an AI tool provides using the advice for **READING LATERALLY** and checking facts on pages 529–32. A good first step: open a new tab and paste the claim or fact into a search engine to see what other trusted sources say about it.

What cultural and linguistic bias do you see? English is by far the language most represented in the datasets that LLMs draw from, so AI tools tend to have a bias toward English grammar and a narrow Anglophone worldview. Also, many varieties and dialects of English are underrepresented in the data. As a result, certain identities, languages, and viewpoints are poorly represented—or completely missing—in the material AI creates. It's always a good idea to reflect on possible cultural and linguistic bias in your writing, and this goes double for AI-generated content. Use the advice on pages 42–44 to practice **CRITICAL LANGUAGE AWARENESS** when working with AI.

Are you avoiding PLAGIARISM? You already know that when you quote or draw information from outside sources, you need to **CITE** and **DOCUMENT** those sources. What about AI? Tons of research papers, books, and news articles are in the dataset for LLMs. AI sometimes generates text that includes close **PARAPHRASES**, direct **QUOTES**, or information lifted from sources—without indicating where its text came from or that it's copied from elsewhere at all. If you use this uncited AI-generated text, you can be on the hook for **PLAGIARISM**—even if you never saw the source and don't know you're quoting from it! For this reason, we don't recommend pasting AI-generated material into your work. However, if you do use AI-generated material, verify it's not drawn from someone else's work first, and always cite your use of AI according to your instructor's directions or the style you're following, like MLA (p. 578) or APA (p. 635). And include an **AI ACKNOWLEDGMENT STATEMENT** (p. 576).

Are you investing in yourself as a writer? It can be tempting to use AI for many aspects of your writing, but be careful you're not shortchanging your own thinking and learning. Any time you use AI, consider carefully if you are benefiting from the experience.

The Future of AI

Business professor Ethan Mollick reminds us that the AI tools we work with today are the worst models we will ever use because they are still relatively new. Their ability to emulate human writing and work across media such as audio and video will improve—and will do so rapidly. As AI technology evolves, as regulations on AI are established, and as people's attitudes toward AI shift, the role that AI plays in your academic writing and career will likely change, too. Part of learning about writing processes is becoming comfortable with those continual changes in the available tools to support those processes. In fact, it seems likely that you and AI are going to grow and evolve together: this book aims to make sure that you are the one using AI—and not the other way around!

 **REFLECT**

Research how AI is being used in the profession or discipline you hope to work in. Many fields have AI tools targeted for their specific circumstances and needs—does yours? Based on what you find, how do you expect your use of AI in your career to differ from your use in this class or as a college student more generally?

TWELVE

Reflecting on Your Writing

T HIS HIGH SCHOOL GRADUATION, Akash Bobba spoke to his classmates, reflecting on what they had endured: "From unthinkable loss fueled by a pandemic, to civil unrest sparked by the death of George Floyd, . . . this last year has undoubtedly been painful and difficult for us as Pirates. . . ." But Bobba didn't stop there. In light of the strains he and his peers have faced, he went on to consider what's next, offering this advice:

> We live in an age where simplicity reigns supreme, where 30-second TikToks and [social media posts] define our identities. This . . . willingness to simplify even the most complex narratives into sensational tidbits perpetuates misinformation and in the process divides the communities, families, and relationships we cherish. What's the solution, you might ask? Seek discomfort. If there's anything South [High School] has taught us, it's that the answers we deserve demand discomfort. From solving polynomials in Algebra II to breaking down Jacksonian democracy in [AP US History], our quest for understanding was often complex and difficult, challenging us to think past the superficial.

It is through reflecting—taking stock of the circumstances and contemplating what comes next—that Bobba imagines ways forward.

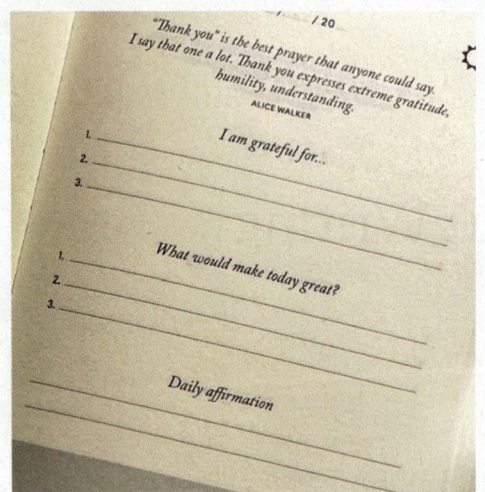 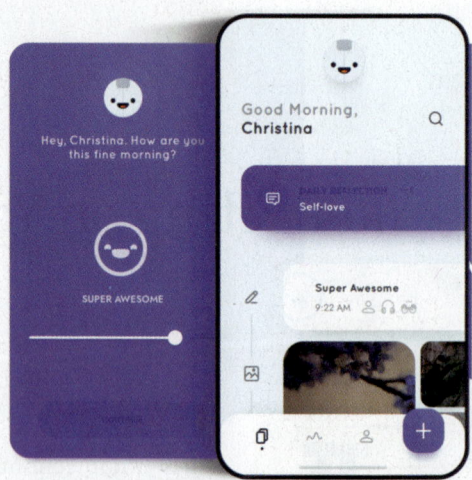

Print journals and apps, like *The Five-Minute Journal* (left) and *Reflectly* (right), help make reflection a daily habit.

Big life moments—graduations, milestone accomplishments, the loss or gain of a loved one, moving to a new place—often prompt us to step back, make sense of what's happened, and plan for what's next. But you likely practice reflection more regularly, too, maybe as you exercise, listen to music, or fall asleep at night. Jotting down what you're thinking can even enable it. You might have seen—or used—a journal with daily prompts to appreciate meaningful moments. Writing helps you pause, consider more deeply, and sometimes come away with new knowledge. So reflecting is powerful: it helps you unpack why things are the way they are, gain a deeper understanding of what you think about them, and even come up with ideas for change.

 **REFLECT**

Think about moments in your life, or even just in the past day, when you've paused to reflect—on how something went, on what you wish you'd done differently, etc. What prompted you to stop and think? How did you go about doing it—were you lost in thought for a few moments? scribbling notes in a journal? talking it out with a friend? What did you realize or learn as a result of reflecting?

Reflecting as a Writer

So writing fosters reflection, but what does reflection do for writing—and for you as a writer? A lot! Reflection can help you better understand the writing strategies and processes you use, why you make certain decisions, and, ultimately, how you might become a more effective author. That's why many writing teachers assign reflection: it prompts writers to study what they've written with the goal of identifying what worked, what didn't, and how to improve. This chapter offers strategies for developing that self-awareness as a writer and guidelines for writing reflections. Here are the main kinds of reflection you can practice.

Reflect to assess your past experiences as a writer. Try this before jumping into a new writing task to help you see how previous experiences affect the way you approach writing now. Consider assignments, courses, and writing done outside of school—the good and the bad—that've shaped the way you think about writing. Reflecting in this way might result in

THINK BEYOND WORDS

➦ WATCH A VIDEO of three high school students *reflecting on writing their award-winning essays for the* New York Times *annual student editorial contest. What do these writers say they've learned about themselves and their writing? How might their reflections be different if written instead of spoken into a camera? What does the format make possible that you'd miss if relying on print or audio alone? Go to* everyonesanauthor.tumblr.com *to watch the video.*

a **LITERACY NARRATIVE**, like Paloma Garcia's on page 249, in which she describes her love of reading and how facing language discrimination detracted from her confidence for a time. Such narratives offer opportunities for you to take stock of your relationship to writing and to see how your practices shift across circumstances.

Reflect to identify your processes and strategies. No two writers use the same process. Like any skill that takes practice, writing requires experimenting to see what works. Through reflection, you can break down the steps you took. For an essay assignment, maybe you brainstormed topics, freewrote to narrow your stance, outlined for organization, talked about your project with a friend, wrote a full draft before visiting the writing center, and revised along the way. Or maybe you sat down and finished a draft in one go. Reflection gives you the space to see all the steps you took and to evaluate them. Start by listing what you did without judging if a step was good or bad. Then assess each strategy. What helped move the project forward and what led to a dead end or took more time than it was worth? You'll see the practices you want to keep as they are, to keep but improve, or to eliminate. Take a look at how Annie Schmittgens, a student at DePaul University, identified peer review as an integral step in her writing process:

> I now understand that peer reviewing is the most important component to my writing process. . . . Peer reviewing has helped me become a more attentive reader, expanded my outlook, and strengthened my writing. It's also made me a better reader because I quickly learned that skimming was not effective. When reviewing a classmate's paper, each word and sentence has to be carefully considered. Becoming a deliberate reader has . . . also helped my reading outside of English class, as well as my writing. When it's time to edit, I look at each word and each sentence and make sure I am expressing my thoughts clearly.

Reflect to understand your decisions. Effective writing is all about smart choices based on your **RHETORICAL SITUATION** —what best suits your audience, purpose, and context. Reflecting offers one way to make sense of those decisions by studying your writing on its own. Once you've got a draft, take stock of the choices you made. What motivated those choices and how did they play out? What **GENRE** did you choose, and why? Did it help achieve your purpose or reach your audience? Why did you choose a particular writing STRATEGY (narrative, description, compare/contrast, etc.)? How did you decide on the STYLE or language variety you used? Aim to identify the important decisions you made and interrogate the reasons behind your choices.

This kind of reflection can also help you TRANSFER effective strategies from one context to another. For example, what you perfected in writing lab reports for general chemistry could be useful when you're assigned to analyze data in microeconomics. When faced with a new writing task, consider how strategies you already know might work in this unfamiliar context. Analyze your rhetorical situation, compare it to those you've been in before, and reflect on how you might draw on your existing skills. You might find that some skills and strategies should *not* carry over. That's good to know, too!

Reflect to plan out what's left to do. Try reading a draft once over with an eye toward what you're liking so far and what you want to work on. Pausing to take stock while you write is the key to REVISING and improving your work. You might use this moment to recall a strategy you've learned about and want to try in this piece of writing. Through reflection, you can identify what you still need to do and make a plan to get it done. Maybe you need to conduct more research, revisit your introduction, replace a weak example, or experiment with language choices. You'll end up with a to-do list and maybe even a revision plan.

Reflect to grow and improve. All these practices create the space for you to see what's working and what's not, which habits are leading to success or holding you back, and how you can improve along the way. Ultimately, reflection offers you the opportunity to deepen your writing knowledge and awareness so that you can make smarter choices in the future. You might even take a moment in your reflection to map a path forward, noting the practices you plan to take along as you move on to new projects.

See the ebook for a video about reflecting on your writing.

Make Reflecting a Habit

You may have noticed that this book includes "reflect" prompts throughout, which invite you to think about how the concepts covered relate to your experiences and your writing. These brief activities can help you make

Journalism student Jenna Bloom wrote about her experience of quitting social media for a year. Her reflections on the experience make up the core of her narrative. Check out what she wrote on p. 870.

connections, to see how the writing practices being discussed are ones you've encountered before and to consider how they relate to your current writing assignments. By making connections, it's more likely information will "stick" because you're taking a moment to apply this new knowledge by building on previous experiences. We also hope these prompts get you in the habit of pausing to assess your reading, writing, and learning experiences— a practice that will surely benefit you as a student and as an author.

 REFLECT

Think about a time when you've taken a writing strategy (addressing counterarguments, citing evidence, defining terms, etc.) you already knew and used it in a different context—from one course to another, or from school to work. Maybe you took what you learned about using stories to hold people's attention in a writing course and applied it in an article for the school newspaper or in a *TikTok* video. Why did you use this strategy? What skills or practices did you transfer? What about the new situation called for it? How did it go?

WRITING A REFLECTION / A Roadmap

While reflecting doesn't always require writing, you may be assigned to document your reflective observations. In many cases, the key to reflective writing is to identify what you've learned about yourself and to explain how it's changed the way you work, using specific examples as evidence. The following guidelines will help you compose a reflection.

Understand your assignment. You'll usually receive a prompt to guide your reflection. For example, your instructor might ask you to compose a LITERACY NARRATIVE about one writing experience or to ANALYZE your revisions for a specific assignment. You might be asked to submit a PORTFOLIO in which you collect and then reflect on pieces of your writing in a letter to your instructor. Or maybe you're prompted to write brief, informal reflections in a journal or on a discussion board. Inspect the prompt carefully and focus your reflection accordingly. What kind of reflection does the prompt ask you to take on? What texts or experiences should you reflect on? How are you expected to deliver your reflection? What details and examples are you asked to include? What writing strategies or processes should take center stage?

Visit the ebook at digital.wwnorton.com/everyone5r for a bonus chapter of advice on assembling a portfolio.

Consider your rhetorical situation

Identify your AUDIENCE. A key audience for your reflection is *you*, since one goal is to discover something about yourself as a writer. Your instructor is also likely part of your audience, and your peers might be, too. Consider these questions about your audience: Who are you trying to reach, and why? What are they expecting to learn from your reflection? What topics are important to them? Revision work? Decision making? Previous writing experience? Processes?

Think about your PURPOSE. Why are you writing this reflection? To explain your revisions? consider your growth as a writer? examine your process? analyze how you transferred writing knowledge from one situation to another? What do you want your audience to know and understand after reading your reflection?

Examine the larger CONTEXT. What background information do you need to provide? How, for instance, does the writing you're reflecting on fit into your larger coursework? You might provide materials for your audience to reference, like an original draft. Offering context could also mean connecting your writing decisions to concepts discussed in class, like argument strategies or source integration. If you're explaining how you've transferred a practice from one context to another, what do you need to say about each situation so readers can follow?

Consider your GENRE, MEDIUM, and DESIGN. Reflective writing can take many forms, from memos and letters to literacy narratives and analyses. Let your prompt and your purpose guide you. You'll also want to consider which STRATEGIES are best suited to your genre and purpose, like DESCRIPTION (what you did in your writing), ANALYSIS (examining your writing), and EVALUATION (assessing your writing). Finally, how can your medium and design convey your points most clearly? If you're submitting a portfolio or you refer to other pieces of writing, think about how best to represent those artifacts. And, if you're providing reference materials, how will you signal what readers should focus on? You might highlight important passages or use the "comment" function to add notes in the margins.

Think about your LANGUAGE. You likely use a number of DIALECTS —and maybe even languages—in your everyday life, which means you have many options for composing a reflection. Which option will be most effective for what you're trying to accomplish? Will your audience expect a certain kind of language or style? Do you want to meet those expectations? challenge them? What do you want your language to say about you? What risks might you be willing to take? See Chapters 4 and 35 for more advice about language choices.

Explore your writing and reflect

Gather the materials you're reflecting on, which can include pieces of your writing (essays, drafts, etc.), artifacts that represent your writing process (notes; outlines; instructor, peer, or tutor feedback), or any related documents (assignment prompts, brainstorming doodles, emails, etc.). Depending on your focus, you might need all your writing for a single course or just the writing and notes from one assignment. Do you have revised versions you can compare to original drafts to see what changed? Grab anything that helps you see evidence of your writing choices and processes.

Think about how to organize what you've gathered. Will you create a folder on your laptop and view everything on-screen? Do you prefer to print files and store them in a physical folder? What storage system will help you to curate (and find!) all the writing artifacts you need?

Reread and take notes. Once you've gathered your materials, review them with the goals of your assignment in mind. Take notes to keep track of what you notice, especially any memories, thoughts, and feelings that aren't visible on the page. Consider the following questions:

- What do you remember about your writing process? What trends do you see in your writing over the course of a project or a semester?
- What do you like most about this piece of writing—a particular section, a sentence, a passage that reflects your personality—and why?
- Where do you see successful writing, and how did you make it happen? Did you have any "aha!" moments when an idea or writing strategy clicked?
- What struggles did you encounter while drafting, and how did you work through them? Which strategies, texts, or ideas gave you trouble, and why?
- What decisions changed the direction of your work? How did peer or instructor feedback shape your writing?
- Did you experiment with language or try different media (text, photos, audio, video)? Why or why not? What were the intended effects?

Generate ideas. FREEWRITING will help jog your memory and pinpoint what stands out to you most and therefore could become the focus of your reflection. The following questions can help get your creative juices flowing:

- What important steps and thinking happened off the page but influenced your project? What circumstances helped or impeded your writing? Did a morning run clear your mind, or did a noisy roommate make composing difficult?

- Consider your emotional responses. What kinds of writing have excited and interested you? When have you felt challenged as a writer? What emotions emerged as you composed, received feedback, and revised? How did these emotional responses shape your work?

Identify significant patterns and major decisions. After you've reviewed your materials, taken notes, and generated ideas, step back and identify the patterns and themes in your writing and writing process. Focus on your most substantive observations—the ones that most significantly impacted you and your writing. What you come up with should help you craft a thesis.

- What common trends do you notice in your writing or process? Maybe anecdotes are your primary form of evidence or peer feedback always prompts your heaviest revisions. Are there issues that pop up frequently?

- What were your greatest successes (and obstacles)? What are you most proud of? What do you want to do differently or better?

- What decisions were most impactful on your writing and process? Maybe it made a big difference when you switched topics or chose to get feedback even when the draft felt final.

- What were the major changes you made as you revised?

Organize and start writing

As you draft, consult your freewriting and your notes. Remember your rhetorical situation, and if you're responding to a specific assignment, return to the prompt to be sure you're addressing it.

Draft a THESIS. Some, though not all, reflective writing includes a central claim or thesis. Your thesis should focus on the key insights you've gained from reflecting on your writing and signal the main points to follow. As you consider your thesis, pinpoint the important takeaways you arrived at as you reflected on your writing. The work you did to identify significant patterns and major decisions will be a big help.

Craft and ORGANIZE supporting paragraphs or sentences. While your thesis statement concisely identifies the focus of your reflection, your paragraphs or sentences should support your main claim by providing evidence. If you're writing a full essay, each paragraph might center on one of those significant patterns or decisions you uncovered. Think about how best to arrange your supporting points: which observations about your writing should come first, last, or somewhere in between?

Include EVIDENCE from your writing to develop each point. If you're highlighting your use of instructor and peer feedback, you might quote directly from a note you received. If you're analyzing your use of language varieties, show a passage from your writing as an example. Consider which examples from your writing offer the clearest insights to the decisions you've made. Think, too, about which revisions show how you've experimented with new ideas or strategies. Such examples help your readers see what your reflective takeaways are based on.

Explain why and how. Strong reflective writing explains *how* your decisions and experiences have affected you as a writer and *why* you've made the choices you have. In other words, you want to make clear the significance of your decisions and experiences so that readers see the meaning these choices hold for you and your writing. These explanations help your readers—and you!—understand the awareness you've gained about your writing. One way to ensure you're including the "how" and "why" is by using "because" statements: "I made this decision because. . ." or "I experimented with this writing strategy because. . . ." Aim to answer the following questions: Why did I make these decisions, take up these practices, or experience writing in this way? What effect have specific decisions, practices, or experiences had on my writing and on me as a writer? How do particular decisions and experiences show my writing awareness or growth?

Identify plans for future writing. You can use reflection not only to look back at what you've done but also to look ahead, mapping out the kind of writer you want to be and the writing processes you want to use in the future. For example, you might realize that draft workshops are central to your writing process, so you plan to visit the writing center more regularly. Consider the practices that have held you back, too, and strategize ways to overcome them. How will you employ strategies that work for you in the future? Looking forward, how will you address areas that give you trouble?

Draft an INTRODUCTION. Your opening should orient your readers to the main ideas and concerns you'll focus on as well as the kind of reflection you're undertaking—a specific assignment, all the assignments for a term or course, your writing process, a significant writing experience, or a combination of these. Provide any background information your audience may need. This is where your thesis will likely go.

Draft a CONCLUSION. Use your conclusion to consider the big picture: What were the major takeaways that your reflection helped you realize? Why do those takeaways matter to you? Your conclusion is a great place to describe your future writing plans given what you've learned through reflection.

Look critically at your draft, get responses—and revise

Read your draft slowly and carefully to see whether your reflection responds to the prompt and that it delivers on the reflective work you set out to do. Make sure you've composed a clear thesis and supporting paragraphs that include examples to help readers see what you've learned. Then ask others to read and respond to your draft. Here are some questions that can help you or others read over a draft of reflective writing:

- *Is your* **THESIS** *clear?* Do you make a specific claim about your writing or writing process? Does the thesis center readers' attention on significant writing strategies and decisions?

- *How does the* **OPENING** *preview the work of your reflection?* Does it focus readers' attention on the aspects of reflection most important to you? Does it provide relevant background information?

- *How do the supporting sentences or paragraphs develop the ideas discussed in your thesis and opening?* Do they center on major writing concerns instead of minor issues? Does each point support your thesis?

- *What details and examples do you provide?* Where might you add details to clarify a point? Do you include examples of your own writing?

- *Where do you explain your plans for future writing tasks,* given the knowledge you've gained through this reflection?

- *How does your reflection* CONCLUDE*?* Does it explain what you've learned and why it matters?

Revise your draft in light of your own observations and any feedback from others—keeping your audience and purpose firmly in mind, as always.

REFLECTION / An Annotated Example

Becoming the Writer I Am: A Reflection on My First-Year Composition Class

ANNAYA BAYNES

BEFORE ATTENDING SPELMAN college, I excelled in my writing classes without being pushed past my intellectual boundaries. In high school, I would often hastily throw together papers without much purpose. My first-year composition course at Spelman, however, prepared me for the rest of my career as a college student. I learned to write papers that were intellectually curious; in the process, my writing became better, and I learned more about myself as a writer. In high school, my teachers taught me the mechanics of writing, but my composition professor taught me how to *write* by pushing me and my peers to ask more complex questions of texts and of ourselves. I learned that revision can include developing ideas rather than focusing on mechanics. By reflecting on the writing and revision process for my first paper in a college writing course, I saw how this course helped improve my writing overall. In this essay, I describe the changes I made to my writing process as a result of one assignment in my first-year writing course.

ANNAYA BAYNES wrote this essay when prompted to reflect on their growth as a writer while attending Spelman College. Baynes reflects on completing a first-year writing assignment, describing a more rigorous process than the one they used in high school.

Opens with important CONTEXT: *a description of the writer in high school so readers can gauge their changes as a first-year writing student.*

Sets out a THESIS *for the reflection.*

As I entered college, I knew that I would have to change my work ethic to be a successful student, but I had no clue what writing at a college level meant. Thus, when my writing instructor assigned our first essay topic—to explore Black love in Tera W. Hunter's text *Bound in Wedlock: Slave and Free Black Marriage in the Nineteenth Century* and to put Hunter's ideas in conversation with Plato's *Phaedrus* and *The Symposium*—I had the sense that I needed to do something different; I just didn't know what. I started by going about my usual process. I gathered salient quotes from the texts assigned and organized them into potential body paragraphs. Then I just sat down to write, starting with the introduction, and I knocked out the paper in one sitting. I read it once to find any errors and then submitted it. When I received my grade for the essay, I was shocked. The lowest grade I'd ever received for a paper was an A-, but my first collegiate essay earned a B. That was the wake-up call that showed me I needed to rethink my writing process to uphold the standard I set for myself. My professor gave the class the opportunity to revise, so I decided to take the time to develop a more intellectually rigorous paper.

In high school, I was too protective of my writing. I never wanted anyone (besides the teacher, but only once submitted) to see my work. I placed a lot of pressure on myself to be a perfect writer, and I saw any constructive criticism as an attack on my intelligence and character. Therefore, I retreated to work alone rather than be vulnerable and allow others into my editing and revision process. With my first college writing assignment, I realized that I did not have all the answers to improve my writing. I needed help. I paid attention to the professor's notes on my paper, and I revised as best I could. Then, I took a big step and showed my friend the revised draft. She pointed out moments where she could not follow my line of thinking and where my argument was not developed fully. I revised the essay again with her notes in mind, and then took an even bigger leap: I met with my instructor.

In talking with my instructor about my essay and revision ideas, I gained clarity not only on this one essay's weaknesses but also on what I needed to work on as a writer. I was anxious before the meeting because I felt like I failed in the original essay. The meeting itself was not as scary as I had feared. We went over my revised paper, and my instructor highlighted areas for improvement. For example, my paragraphs were disjointed with no transition sentences, and my

---

BACKGROUND INFORMATION *about the class and the assignment being discussed.*

A DESCRIPTION *of the author's writing process and how it compares to what they did in high school.*

Pinpoints a significant moment *that prompted a change in the author's writing process.*

Considers the EFFECTS *of not sharing their work with others previously.*

Explains an important realization: sharing work with others can improve one's writing.

Highlights another major change in their writing process: getting feedback from their instructor.

instructor suggested ways that I could more effectively move from idea to idea. I realized that just because my thoughts made perfect sense to me did not mean that the reader would always follow my logic. Working alone, without feedback, had prevented me from considering a reader's experience of my essay.

Further, I realized I also had difficulty making my essay cohesive. I had so many ideas, but I needed to be more economical in choosing what to include. My instructor suggested I assess each argument—and even each sentence—and question how it was supporting my thesis. I applied this approach to the following passage, which appeared in my first draft:

> Whites tried to exert control over black bodies through rape, but enslaved black people rejected this attempt by forming their own consensual relationships. Enslavers had the power to force copulation but not attachment. Black people were the only ones capable of forming those bonds for themselves. Before emancipation, marriages for African Americans combatted white supremacy by illustrating just how powerless enslavers truly were in the face of romantic relationships between enslaved people.

This section took too many words to state my point. In revising, I condensed this point into two sentences: "Whites tried to impose control over black bodies through rape, but enslaved people rejected this attempt by forming their own consensual relationships. Before emancipation, African American marriages helped combat white supremacy by illustrating just how powerless enslavers were in the face of romantic relationships between enslaved people." By focusing my point, I was able to dedicate more space to developing my argument. Previously, I viewed writing as a single action instead of a process; I'd think "just sit down, write the essay, and get it done." Now, I understand that writing is as much about the initial draft as the constant revision that follows.

I also sharpened my language choices while revising. For example, in the original essay, I wrote, "For the reasons listed previously, marriage was not merely the consummation of a romantic relationship for black people." I revised this sentence to read: "The ability to marry was important not only as a consummation of love but also as a tool to combat white supremacy." The initial sentence states that marriage had some importance beyond romance for Black people, but it does not say what that importance is. The latter sentence makes explicit that marriage was also "a tool to combat white supremacy."

I am now a junior, but I haven't forgotten all I learned in freshman composition. On the contrary, I have successfully taken these lessons into all my courses and writing since. In fact, I am also now a writing center tutor, and a lot of the advice I give pushes students to think more deeply about their writing in the same way I learned to in my composition course. Being open and receptive to feedback from peers and my instructor helped develop my writing style and process. I no longer hoard my writing away from critical eyes like a literary dragon. I rely on my community to offer feedback on my work. Also, my writing contains considerably less fluff, as I always evaluate whether what I am writing (at the argument and sentence level) reinforces my thesis. Of course, my writing is not perfect, but it now has the quality that I searched for but could not find at the start of my college career. My strengths and weaknesses are clear to me. Without the work I did in my composition course my first year of college, I would not be the writer I am today.

In CONCLUSION, *the author explains how what they've learned has transferred to other writing situations, like their work as a writing tutor.*

REFLECT

Reflect on a writing project that you especially enjoyed or that you found rewarding. What made the project successful? How did you move through your writing process? What parts of that process could you carry forward to future assignments? Let reflection help you feel good about what you've achieved and take time to appreciate your successes and your strengths!

PART IV

Genres of Writing

"Genres aren't closed boxes. Stuff flows back and forth across the borders all the time."

—MARGARET ATWOOD

COMICS HAVE MANGA, superheroes, and fantasy. Music has hip-hop, country, and folk. Internet aesthetics? Think cottage core, dark academia, and e-girl. How about restaurants? Try Italian, Vietnamese, Tex-Mex, vegan, or Southern soul food. Or movies: sci-fi, thrillers, drama, comedy. These are all genres, and they are one important way we structure our world. You see genres everywhere—in literature (think poetry, fiction, drama), in sports (baseball, basketball, volleyball), or in dance (tap, ballet, jazz). And when we talk about writing, we often talk in terms of genres, too: narratives, lab reports, project proposals, movie reviews, argument essays, and so on. Like all genres, those associated with writing are flexible: they expand and change over time as writers find new ways to communicate and express themselves.

Instructors will often ask you to use particular genres, most likely including the ones taught in this book: arguments, narratives, analyses, reports, reviews, and proposals. You may need to write a rhetorical analysis of a speech, for instance, or to analyze the causes of the increased frequency of wildfires in California. In either case, knowing the characteristic features of an analysis will be helpful. And you may want or need to combine genres—to introduce an analysis with a short narrative or to conclude it with a proposal of some kind.

The chapters that follow introduce most of the genres you'll be assigned in college. Each chapter explains the genre's characteristic features; discusses how, when, where, and why you might use the genre; provides a roadmap to the process of writing in that genre; and includes several example essays. We hope that you'll use these chapters to explore these common academic genres—and to adapt them as needed to your own purposes and goals.

REFLECT

What do you like to do in your spare time? Make a list of three or four favorite activities. Categorize them by genres. How do you know which activity fits in which genre? List the features that help you identify it as belonging to a particular genre. What do you know about that genre? Name a few other examples of that genre, and then think about what features they have in common.

THIRTEEN

Choosing Genres

GENRES ARE CATEGORIZATIONS, ways of classifying things. The genres this book is concerned with are kinds of writing, but you can find genres anywhere you look. In fact, rhetorician and researcher Carolyn Miller has been tracking the use of the word "genre" and has found it everywhere, including on many of the sites you visit every day. *Netflix* lists nineteen film genres, from action and drama to sports and thrillers—and thousands of subgenres within each of these. *YouTube* has twenty-four genres, and one of the most popular, gaming videos, has 40 million overall subscribers and offers a variety of subgenres like reviews, live play, and game hacks. *Spotify*'s algorithm draws from more than 6,000 distinct genres as this book goes to press. Indeed, there is now such a proliferation of genres that they've become the subject of parody, with comedians mixing musical genres to make new ones, like honky tonk and techno to make "honky techno" or folk and dubstep to make "folk step." To get a sense of the result, just take a look at the cartoon on the next page.

What You Need to Know about Genres of Writing

Genres are kinds of writing that you can use to accomplish a certain goal and reach a particular audience. As such, they have well-established

In this cartoon, Roz Chast comes up with her own new movie genres: sci-fi/Western, musical/self-help, sports/horror, and documentary/romance. What new hybrid movie genre can you suggest?

features that help guide you in your writing. However, they're not fill-in-the-blank templates; you will adapt them to address your own rhetorical situations.

Genres have features that can guide you as a writer and a reader. Argument essays, for instance, usually take a position supported by reasons and evidence, consider a range of perspectives, and so on. These features help guide you as an author in what you write—and they also set up expectations for you as a reader, affecting the way you interpret what you read. If something's called a report, for instance, you are likely to assume that it presents information—that it's in some way factual.

This book covers those genres that are most often assigned in school—ARGUMENTS, ANALYSES, REPORTS, NARRATIVES, REVIEWS, PROPOSALS, and ANNOTATED BIBLIOGRAPHIES —and some subgenres: VISUAL ANALYSES, PROFILES, LITERACY NARRATIVES, LITERATURE REVIEWS, and PROJECT PROPOSALS. These are kinds of writing that have evolved over the years as a useful means of creating and sharing knowledge. As you advance in a major, you will become familiar with the most important genres and subgenres in that field. Especially when you are new to a genre, its features can serve as a kind of blueprint, helping you know how to approach an assignment.

Genres are flexible. Keep in mind that genres can be both enabling and constraining. Sometimes you'll have reason to adapt genre features to suit your own goals. One student who was writing an analysis of a sonnet, for example, wanted to bend the analysis genre just a little to include a poem that experimented with the sonnet form. He checked with his teacher, got approval, and it worked. You might not want to stretch a lab report in this way, however. Lab reports follow a fairly set template, covering purpose, methods, results, summary, and conclusions to carry out the goals of the scientific fields that use them; they would not be fitting (or effective) in a creative writing class.

You may also have occasion to combine genres—to tell a story in the course of arguing a position or to conclude a report with a proposal of some kind. If you ever decide to adapt or combine genres, think hard about your rhetorical situation: What genres will help you achieve your purpose? reach the audience you're addressing? work best in the medium you're using?

See how Dana Canedy's narrative about a conversation with her son makes an argument on p. 883.

Genres evolve. While it is relatively easy to identify some characteristic genre features, such features are not universal rules. Genres evolve across time and in response to shifting cultural contexts. Letters, for example, followed certain conventions in medieval Europe (they were handwritten, of course, and they were highly formal); by the twentieth century, letters had developed dozens of subgenres (thank-you notes, letters to the editor, application letters). Then, in the 1990s, letters began to morph into email, adapting in new ways to online situations. Today, text messages and social media posts may be seen as offshoots of the letter genre.

Deciding Which Genres to Use

Sometimes you'll be assigned to write in a particular genre. If that's the case, think about what you know about the genre and about what it expects of you as a writer, then turn to the corresponding chapter in this book for guidance. But other times your assignments won't make the genre clear. The following advice can help determine which genre(s) to use when the choice is yours. Remember to consider your **PURPOSE** for writing and the **AUDIENCE** you want to reach in deciding which genres would be most useful.

Look for clues in the assignment. Even without a clearly assigned genre, your assignment should be your starting point. Are there any keywords that suggest one? "Discuss," for example, could indicate a **REPORT** or an **ANALYSIS**. And you might also need to consider how such a keyword is used in the discipline the assignment comes from—"analyze" in a chemistry assignment doesn't likely mean the same thing as in a literature assignment. In either case, you should ask your instructor for clarification.

Consider this assignment from an introductory communications course: "Look carefully at letters to the editor in one newspaper over a period of two weeks, and write an essay describing what you find. Who are the letter writers? What issues are they writing about? How many different perspectives are represented?" Though this assignment doesn't name a genre, it seems to be asking students for a report: to research a topic and then report on what they find.

But what if this were the assignment: "Look carefully at letters to the editor in one newspaper over a period of two weeks, and write an essay describing what you find. Who are the letter writers? What issues are they writing about? How many different perspectives are represented? What rhetorical strategies do the writers use to get their points across? Draw some conclusions based on what you find." This assignment also asks students to research a topic and report on what they find. But in asking them to identify rhetorical strategies and draw some conclusions based on their findings, it is also prompting them to do some analysis. As you look at your own assignments, look for words or other clues that will help you identify which genres are expected.

If an assignment doesn't give any clues, here are some questions to ask in thinking about which genre may be most effective:

- *What discipline is the assignment for?* Say you're assigned to write about obesity and public health. If you're writing for a journalism course, you might write an op-ed essay ARGUING that high-calorie sodas should not be sold in public schools. If, on the other hand, you're writing for a biology class, you might REPORT on experiments done on eating behaviors and metabolic rates.

- *What is the topic?* Does it call for a specific genre? If you are asked, for example, to write about the campaign speeches of two presidential candidates, that topic suggests that you're being asked to ANALYZE the speeches (and probably COMPARE them). On the other hand, if you're writing about an experiment you conducted, you're probably writing a REPORT and should follow the conventions of that genre.

- *What is your purpose in writing?* If you want to convince your readers that they should "buy local," for example, your purpose will likely call for an ARGUMENT. If, however, you want to explain what buying local means, your purpose will call for a REPORT.

- *Who is the audience?* What interests and expectations might they have? Say you're assigned to write about the growth of competitive video gaming in the United States for a first-year seminar. There, your audience would include other first-year students, and you might choose to write a NARRATIVE about what drew you to esports. Imagine, however, writing on the same topic for a marketing course; most likely, you will REPORT on what strategies companies have used to market esports in the United States and to whom the marketing was targeted, and you will ANALYZE the effectiveness of the strategies.

- *What style and/or language does your assignment call for and how does that affect your choice of genres?* What style (formal or informal, humorous or serious, academic or conversational) will your audience expect you to use in the genre you choose? Do you want to meet those expectations—or perhaps challenge them in some way? What do you want your choice of style and/or language to reflect about you?

- *What medium will you use?* Are there certain genres that work well— or not—in that medium? If you are assigned to give an oral presentation, for example, you might consider writing a NARRATIVE because listeners can remember stories better than they are able to recall other genres. Even if you decide to write an analysis or a report, you might want to include some narrative.

If the assignment is wide open, draw on what you know about genres. Sometimes you may receive an assignment so broad that not only the genre but even the topic and purpose are left up to you. Consider, for example, a prompt one of the authors of this book encountered in college: in an exam for a drama class, the professor came into the room, wrote "Tragedy!" on the blackboard, and said, "You have an hour and a half to respond." We hope you don't run into such a completely open-ended assignment, especially in a timed exam. But if you do, your knowledge of genre can help out. If this assignment came in a Shakespeare course, for example, you might ARGUE that *Hamlet* is Shakespeare's most complex tragedy. Or you could perhaps ANALYZE the role of gender in one of his tragedies.

Luckily, such wide-open assignments are fairly rare. It's more likely that you will encounter an assignment like this one: "Choose a topic related to our course theme and carry out sufficient research on that topic to write an essay of eight to ten pages. Refer to at least six sources and follow MLA citation style." In this instance, you know that the assignment calls for some kind of research-based writing and that you need a topic and thesis that can be dealt with in the length specified. You could write an ARGUMENT, taking a position and supporting it with the research you have done. Or you could write a REPORT that presents findings from your research. But you might also choose to write a NARRATIVE that presents your research in story form. At this point, you would be wise to see your instructor to discuss your choices. Once you have decided on a genre, turn to the corresponding chapter in this book (Chapters 14–19) to guide your research and writing.

When an assignment is wide open, try using what you know about genres as a way to explore your topic:

- What are some of the POSITIONS on your topic? What's been said or might be said? What controversies or disagreements exist? What's your own perspective?

- What stories— NARRATIVES —could you tell about it?

- How might you ANALYZE your topic? What are its parts? What caused it—or what effects might it have? Does it follow a certain process?

- What information might be important or interesting to **REPORT** on?
- How can your topic be evaluated, or **REVIEWED**?
- What problems does your topic present for which you can **PROPOSE** a solution?
- In our current remix culture, you might decide to do some **REMIXING** of your own, taking something written in one genre and transforming it for a different genre altogether. A **REPORT** on internet access across your campus might become a **PROPOSAL**, an **ARGUMENT**, or even a **NARRATIVE** aimed at closing the "access gap" that your report demonstrated. See Chapter 39 for more on remixing your writing.

See the ebook for a video on adapting thesis statements to fit your genre.

REFLECT

Look at three writing assignments you have been given for any of your classes. Did the assignments specify a genre? If so, what was it? If not, what genres would you say you were being asked to use—and how can you tell?

FOURTEEN

"This Is Where I Stand"
Arguing a Position

"**SO WHERE DO YOU STAND ON THIS ISSUE?**" This familiar phrase pops up almost everywhere, from talk radio to social media, from political press conferences to classroom seminars. In fact, much of the work you do as an author responds, in some way, to this question.

After all, taking a position is something you do many times daily: you talk with your academic advisor to explain your reasons for changing your major; you text a friend the reasons she should see a certain film with you; in an economics class discussion, you offer your position on consumer spending patterns in response to someone else's; you survey research on electric vehicle charging stations and then post a message in your neighborhood *Facebook* group advocating (or protesting) the installation of new charging stations. In all these cases, you're doing what philosopher Kenneth Burke calls "putting in your oar," taking and supporting positions of your own in conversation with others around you.

Look around, and you'll see other positions being articulated all over the place. Here's one we saw recently on a T-shirt:

Work to eat.
Eat to live.
Live to bike.
Bike to work.

The central argument here is clear: bike to work. One of the reasons it's so effective is the clever way that the last sentence isn't quite parallel with the others. (In the first three, "to" can be replaced by "in order to"; in the last case, it can't.) Another reason it works well is the form of the argument, which is a series of short commands, each beginning with the same word that the previous sentence ends with.

This chapter offers guidelines for writing an academic essay that takes a position. While taking a position in an academic context often differs in crucial ways from doing so in other contexts, many of the principles discussed will serve you well when stating a position generally.

See Ch. 20 in the ebook for a video on understanding academic argument.

> **REFLECT**
>
> Stop for a moment and jot down every time you remember having to take a position on something—anything at all—in the last day or two. The list might get long if you're like most of us. Then write down the times you noticed someone around you take a position during the same period. This informal research should convince you that the rhetorical genre of taking a position is central to many of your daily activities.

Across Academic Disciplines

Position papers are written in many fields, and a number of disciplines offer specific guidelines for composing them. In philosophy, a position paper is a brief persuasive essay designed to express a precise opinion about some issue or some philosopher's viewpoint. In computer science, a position paper considers a number of perspectives on an issue before finally offering the writer's own position. In political science, a position paper often critiques a major argument or text, first summarizing and analyzing its main points and then interpreting them in the context of other texts. Many college courses ask students to take a position in response to a course reading, specifying that they state their position clearly, support it with evidence and logical reasons, and cite all sources consulted. So one challenge you'll face when you're asked to write a position paper in various disciplines will be to determine exactly what is expected of you.

Across Media

Different media present different resources and challenges when it comes to presenting your position. Setting up a website that encourages people to take action to end animal abuse gives you the ability to link to additional information, whereas writing a traditional essay advocating that position for a print magazine requires that you provide all the relevant evidence and reasons on the page. It is very easy to incorporate color images or video clips in the webpage, but the magazine's budget may not allow for color at all. If you make the same argument against animal abuse in an oral presentation, you'll mostly be talking, though you may use slides to help your listeners follow your comments, to remind them of your main points, and to show graphs or photos that will appeal to their sense of reason or their emotions.

Remember that persuasion is always about connecting with an audience, meeting them where they are, and helping them see why your position is one they should take seriously or even adopt. To achieve that goal, you have to convey your position in a medium your audience will be receptive to—and can access. Different media serve different purposes, and you will want to consider your own goals as well as your audience's expectations.

THINK BEYOND WORDS

➦ *TAKE A LOOK at the website of the animal shelter serving Harrisonburg, Virginia, where you can see photos of available pets, find out about fostering a dog, and more. Click "Engage" to see the organization's appeal for donations, along with photos of your potential "new best friend." How compelling do you find the organization's argument? How does the use of words and images contribute to its appeal—is one more important? How would you revise this site to make it more effective? Add more video? audio? statistics? testimonials? Include more written information (or less)? Go to everyonesanauthor.tumblr.com to access the site.*

Across Cultures and Communities

Taking a position in cultures or communities other than your own poses special challenges. Advertising—a clear case of taking a position—is full of humorous tales of cross-cultural failure. When Pepsi first sought to break into the Chinese market, for example, its slogan, "Pepsi Brings You Back to Life," got mangled in translation, coming out as "Pepsi Brings Your Ancestors Back from the Grave."

Far more problematic than questions of translation are questions of STANCE. When taking a position in American academic contexts, you're almost always expected to state your position explicitly while showing your awareness of other possible positions. In contrast, in some cultures and communities, you would generally avoid stating your opinion directly. In yet others, you would be expected to state your mind forthrightly, paying little attention to what others think about the issue or to how your words might make them feel. So as an author, you always need to understand and respect the cultural context you are writing in.

But cultures and communities are not monolithic. Remember, then, that how people are expected to frame positions they take may well vary within a community, depending on their place in the social hierarchy as supervisor or employee, teacher or student, ruler or governed. To complicate matters, the expectations with respect to outsiders are almost always different from those for the locals. Most people might be quick to criticize their own government among friends, but they don't necessarily grant outsiders the same privilege. A word to the wise: humility is in order, especially when taking a position in communities or cultures of which you're not a member. Don't assume that what works at home will work elsewhere. A safe first step is to listen and observe carefully when in a new context, paying special attention to how people communicate any positions they are taking.

Across Genres

See how video game publisher Activision-Blizzard states its position on mobile gaming and other trends in its 2021 annual report. Go to everyonesanauthor.tumblr.com to see the report.

Arguing a position, as we've pointed out, is something that we do, in small ways or large, almost every day—and even across a range of genres. You might, for instance, write a letter to the editor of your local newspaper lamenting the closure of the local library—and setting forth your POSITION that it must be kept open at all costs. Similarly, a company's annual REPORT would likely set out its position that collective bargaining with suppliers will improve the company's bottom line. After taking in a highly anticipated film, you might post a brief REVIEW, arguing that it wasn't as good as you'd expected. In each case, the text states a position.

> ### REFLECT
> Think about where and how positions are expressed around you, considering posters, editorials, songs, social media posts, commercials, and so on. Then choose one that most interests you—or that most irritates you—and spend some time thinking about how it presents its position. How does it appeal to you—or why does it fail to appeal? What kinds of words, images, or sounds does it offer as support for its position? If you were going to revise it for a different audience, what would you do? If you were going to create it in another medium, how would it be different?

CHARACTERISTIC FEATURES

Given the many different forms of writing that take a position, no one-size-fits-all approach to composing them is possible. We can, however, identify the following characteristic features common to writing in which the author is arguing a position:

- An explicit position (p. 181)
- A response to what others have said or done (p. 183)
- Useful background information (p. 185)
- A clear indication of why the topic matters (p. 188)
- Good reasons and evidence (p. 189)
- Attention to more than one point of view (p. 191)
- An authoritative tone and stance (p. 193)
- An appeal to readers' values (p. 194)

An Explicit Position

Stating a position explicitly is easier said than done, since the complexity of most important issues can make it hard to articulate a position in a crystal-clear way. But it's very important to do so insofar as possible; nothing will lose an audience faster than drowning your position in a sea of qualifications. At the same time, in most contexts, a position stated baldly with no qualifications or nuances may alienate many readers.

In an opinion article published by the *Honolulu Star-Advertiser*, high school student Rihanna Joaquin states her position on banning *TikTok*:

> *TikTok* should be banned because it is infecting the minds of youth, poses a national security concern, and creates the potential for theft of sensitive personal information.
>
> —RIHANNA JOAQUIN, "Column: *TikTok* Affecting Social Development, Mental Health"

Now take a look at another student's response from a different angle in an editorial on the same topic:

> Banning *TikTok* would be blatant censorship and would threaten the democratic fabric of our society. Given the millions of Americans who utilize the platform to communicate and advocate, along with the dangers of censorship that history and literature have warned us about, *TikTok* should not be banned.
>
> —BRAYDEN JADULANG, "Column: Censoring *TikTok* Would Harm Democratic Fabric"

In both cases, readers have a clear sense of not only where the author stands but also their reasons for and against banning *TikTok*. The writers have set up for readers an expectation of how their arguments will proceed. And there's certainly no mistaking either writer's position.

There are times, however, when you will want to **QUALIFY** your position by using words like "many," "some," or "maybe"—or writing "could" rather than "will." Not every position you take can be stated with absolute certainty, and a qualified claim is generally easier to support than an unqualified one. Notice how Sofia Aguilar, a columnist for Syracuse University's student paper, *The Daily Orange*, is careful to qualify the claim that many cities' policies lead to criminalizing homelessness. By using the phrase "it's not technically illegal," Aguilar stops short of an assertion that cannot be supported:

> While it's not technically illegal to sleep in public, there are a myriad of ways the government discourages it, like banning overnight parking or sleeping at rest stops and public parks.
>
> —SOFIA AGUILAR, "Criminalizing Homelessness Is Ushering in a New Form of Capitalism"

In a report on the financial risks and benefits of college, a team of economists from the St. Louis Federal Reserve use the qualifiers "many," "one of the most," and "one of the best" to clarify their position that in spite of the high costs, college degrees are still valuable:

> Students have many options for life after high school. One of the most popular options is college. Even though college enrollment has dropped and people have a more dismal outlook on the returns on investing in a college education, the data suggest it is still one of the best investments a person can make.
> —SCOTT A. WOLLA, GUILLAUME VANDENBROUKE & CAMERON TUCKER, "Is College Still Worth the High Price? Weighing Costs and Benefits of Investing in Human Capital"

Their position is clear, but because their study was limited to financial investment in attending college, they are careful to not overstate their claims. By qualifying, the authors recognize that there may be other types of investment (social or familial, for example) with different benefits and drawbacks.

Keep in mind that while it may be useful, even necessary, to qualify a statement, you should be careful not to overdo it. You don't want to sound unsure of your position. Take a look back at Joaquin's and Jadulang's claims about *TikTok*. What qualifiers might be appropriate to add? How would adding a qualifier affect how you view their position statements? What would an overqualified version of their statements look like?

A Response to What Others Have Said or Done

Crucially, position papers respond to other positions. That is, they are motivated by something that has been said or done by others—and are part of an ongoing conversation. The students writing about *TikTok* in the *Honolulu Star-Advertiser* are responding to arguments for and against enforcing a ban. They are entering an existing debate.

And that was certainly the case with Dove soap's ad campaign encouraging girls to participate in sports. Responding to the fact that criticism of girls' bodies is a major reason they give up on sports, Dove ran an ad titled "These Legs" during the 2025 Superbowl. The brief video features a little girl dashing down a tree-lined sidewalk—sheer exuberance in motion. A caption declares "At 3, these legs are unstoppable." Then, these words appear: "At 14, she'll think they're unbearable," followed by a stark statistic: "1 in 2

See Ch. 21 in the ebook for a video on different ways to respond to the views of others.

THINK BEYOND WORDS

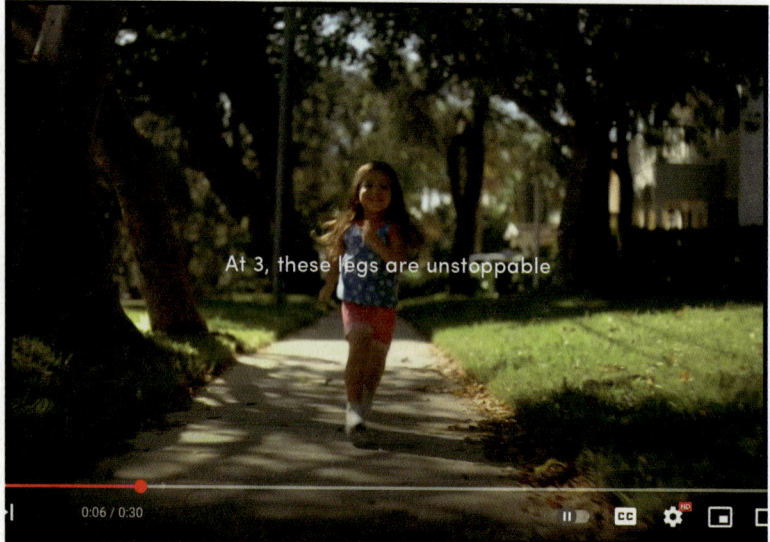

➦ **WATCH THE VIDEO of Dove's "These Legs" ad.** *Consider how the media elements (video, music, and minimal words appearing on screen) contribute to the power of the argument. You can watch the video at* everyonesanauthor.tumblr.com.

girls who quit sports are criticized for their body type." Finally, alongside the Dove logo, they state their position directly: "Let's change the way we talk to our girls #KeepHerConfident." Dove packs a lot into a short ad: early on, girls lose confidence in and appreciation for their bodies' strength, and as a result, often give up on sports. So, Dove responds, we must "change the way we talk to our girls" to increase, rather than diminish, their confidence.

In an essay published on *Medium*, data scientist Sahin Ahmed stakes out a position on the value of a humanities degree. In response to a flood of articles declaring "The End of the English Major" and "The Humanities Are in Crisis," Ahmed argues for its value. See how Ahmed positions his stance in the opening of his essay:

> In today's rapidly advancing society, the value of humanities education is under siege. Subjects like philosophy, literature, and history are increasingly viewed as impractical and outdated compared to the seemingly boundless opportunities in STEM ... fields. This shift in perception has led to a

dramatic decline in the pursuit of humanities degrees, influenced by economic pressures and a market-driven approach to education.

However, it is crucial to revalue humanities education not only to preserve our cultural and intellectual heritage but also to ensure a balanced approach to technological and societal progress. Humanities disciplines foster critical thinking, ethical reasoning, and a deeper understanding of the human condition—all essential for navigating the complexities of modern life.

—SAHIN AHMED, "The Death of Humanities Education: Why We Need to Revalue the Arts and Sciences"

In a short space, Ahmed identifies an argument that others have made and responds to it directly. In academic position papers, authors are expected to acknowledge and address other positions directly in this way. That is often not the case when you take a position in other contexts and in some cultures. In online writing, for instance, it's not unusual for authors to simply provide a brief mention with a link to refer readers to another position within an ongoing conversation.

 REFLECT

Think about your writing as part of a larger, ongoing conversation. Examine something that you have recently written—an email, a social media post, an essay for a class—that expresses a position about an issue that matters to you. Check to see whether it makes clear your motivation for writing and the position(s) to which you were responding. If these aren't clear, try revising your text to make them more explicit.

Useful Background Information

The amount of background information needed—historical background, definitions, contextual information—will vary widely depending on the scope of your topic, your audience, and your medium. If you are preparing a position paper on the effects of global warming for an environmental group, any background information provided will represent extensive, often detailed, and sometimes highly technical knowledge. If, on the other hand, you are preparing a poster to display on campus that summarizes your position on an increase in tuition, you can probably assume your audience will need little background information—for which you will have only limited space anyway.

Dove's "These Legs" ad makes an argument with very little background information. The commercial's creators center the ad on a few major claims like "1 in 2 girls who quit sports are criticized for their body type." This statement serves as background information to support the ad's argument, but unlike what's expected in an academic setting, no source for the statistic is offered. Because it's a brief television ad, the creators depend on viewers noticing that "These Legs" is part of a larger campaign, which they signal by including #KeepHerConfident. The hashtag provides important context as does the music. In a quick visual ad like Dove's, the creators are counting on viewers to connect what they see and hear in the ad to background information they already have about girls' body confidence and sports.

In academic contexts, writers are generally expected to provide a great deal of background information to firmly ground their discussion of a topic. When the former president of Rensselaer Polytechnic Institute, Shirley Ann Jackson, spoke at a symposium celebrating women in science and engineering, she argued that while the number of women graduating with degrees in STEM fields has increased, major obstacles still stand in the way of women academics in the sciences at research universities. To make this argument, she first provided background information about the number of women PhDs leaving the research science track:

> Writing for the *New York Times*, Steven Greenhouse noted that, based on a University of California, Berkeley, study, "Keeping Women in the Science Pipeline," women are far more likely than men to "'leak' out of the research science pipeline before obtaining tenure at a college or university." After receiving a PhD, married women with young children are 35 percent less likely to enter a tenure-track position in science than are married men with young children and PhDs in science. According to the report from the University of California, "women who had children after becoming postdoctoral scholars were twice as likely as their male counterparts to shift their career goals away from being professors with a research emphasis—a 41 percent shift for women versus 20 percent for men." And a 2005 report from Virginia Tech found a disproportionate share of women made up "voluntary departures" from the faculty. Although women represented one-fifth of the faculty, they accounted for two-fifths of departures.

> At every step along the way—from entering college as a science or engineering major to graduating with a technical degree, from entering graduate school to exiting successfully, to getting a postdoc, to succeeding as faculty, to attaining tenure—we need to provide women with bridges to the next level. As is clear from the studies I mentioned, the unequal burden of family life turns the gaps in the road into chasms. Help with childcare, which has been provided at MIT, and the establishment of parental childbirth leave, which has been provided at Rensselaer, can help. But there is more to be done.
>
> —SHIRLEY ANN JACKSON, "Leaders in Science and Engineering: The Women of MIT"

Hearing about specific research studies helps Jackson's audience see that a disproportionately high number of women scientists are "shift[ing] their career goals away from being professors with a research emphasis"—and supports her argument that universities must do more to ease the "unequal burden of family life" that young women scientists bear.

Background information is not always statistical and impersonal. Chanel Smith, a family court attorney, begins her *Teen Vogue* essay on the need to recognize the challenges many public service workers (like teachers, social workers, and family court attorneys) endure with a personal story:

> My heart was beating fast as I listened to the words leave my colleague's mouth: "I hope you are sitting down, Chanel. I have some bad news to tell you about your client's family." After hanging up the phone moments later, I was left stunned. I had just learned that the mother of the eight-year-old I was representing had been murdered the night before. It would take me three days to process the news; every time I thought about my client, I was overcome with sadness.
>
> —CHANEL SMITH, "Secondary Trauma at Work: Why We Experience and How We Cope"

By opening her essay with this shocking story and how she must deal with the devastating news immediately helps readers understand the topic, work trauma, that Smith discusses in the remainder of the essay. It's this dramatic, personal **NARRATIVE** that serves as important background information for Smith's central question: "how do we overcome the emotional challenges of working in public service and continue to show up for the people and communities we serve?"

A Clear Indication of Why the Topic Matters

No matter the topic, one of an author's tasks is to demonstrate that the issue is real and significant—and thus to motivate readers to read on or listeners to keep listening. Rarely can you assume your audience sees why your argument matters.

As a student, you'll sometimes be assigned to write a position paper on a particular topic; in those cases, you may have to find ways to make the topic interesting for you. On other occasions, you may get to choose to write about something you care deeply about, in which case you will need to help your audience understand why they should care as well.

See how Mellody Hobson, CEO of the first Black-owned mutual fund in the United States and chairwoman of Starbucks, tells a personal story in a conversation with journalist Jonathan Capehart that illustrates why being the "first and only [Black person] is not enough." Opening with "it's a true story," she tells Capehart,

> Harold Ford was running for the U.S. Senate, and he called me one day. We were very good friends, and are. And he said, "You know, Mellody, I need some national press. Do you have any ideas?" We're just like pipsqueaks. But I had a friend who was a major, major person, one of the biggest media companies in the world, and so I reached out to her and I told her what we were trying to accomplish. And she said, "Why don't you come and do editorial board lunch? . . ."
>
> [Harold and I] were wearing our best suits. You know, we looked like shiny, new pennies. We were so excited for this opportunity. And we get upstairs, and the receptionist says, "Follow me." . . . And all of a sudden, we enter this room completely stark, empty. And she turns and looks at us and she says, "Where are your uniforms?"
>
> And we were like stunned, I mean, just really stunned. And all of a sudden, my friend runs in, because she knew we were taken to the wrong place, clearly. We were the lunch. And all of the color drained out of her face. And I joked with her. I looked at her and I said, "Now, don't you think this is the reason why we need more than one Black person in the U.S. Senate?" because at that time we only had Barack Obama.
>
> —MELLODY HOBSON, *Washington Post Live* interview

By sharing this story about how she and Ford were assumed to be kitchen workers on the basis of their race, Hobson establishes in a vivid way why

Mellody Hobson, the first Black woman to chair the Economic Club of Chicago.

it matters that business and government entities go well beyond having a "first and only" Black person, so that such inaccurate and injurious assumptions can no longer be so readily made.

In Dove's "These Legs" ad, images, text, and music combine to demonstrate that the creators of the commercial care greatly about advocating for young girls to receive positive messages about their bodies. In all these cases, the writers share the conviction that what they're writing about matters not just to them but to us all, and they work hard to make that conviction evident.

Good Reasons and Evidence

Positions are only as good as the reasons and evidence that support them, so part of every author's task in arguing a position is to provide the strongest possible reasons for the position, and evidence for those reasons. Evidence may take many forms, but among the most often used, especially in academic contexts, are facts; firsthand material gathered from observations, interviews, or surveys; data from experiments; historical data; examples;

expert testimony (often in the form of what scholars have written); precedents; statistics; and personal experience.

EdTech magazine writer Adam Stone argues that colleges are using esports as a tool to attract more students. Note the evidence Stone provides to support this claim, beginning with quantitative data on the number of schools with esports teams, examples from specific schools, and quotes from knowledgeable experts:

> More than 200 colleges and universities are now home to varsity teams in the field of competitive video gaming.... As college enrollments drop, campus leaders are searching for new ways to draw potential students. With new high school esports clubs forming all the time, gamers represent a strong potential demographic in the eyes of recruiters.
>
> ... Schools aren't using esports to recruit only players. A college esports program typically involves media production, graphic design, broadcasting and a host of other skills.... The UMass Dartmouth esports program, for example, has the potential to support the university's College of Engineering and College of Visual and Performing Arts programs. "We hope to get to a point where game design and software design students will be able to test their games with our esports players," [Stacy] Ploskonka [assistant director of student activity] says.
>
> —ADAM STONE, "Collegiate Esports Programs Serve as Recruitment and Retention Tools"

See how a TV reporter uses students' perspectives on esports' growth in covering the topic by visiting everyonesanauthor.tumblr.com.

Stone recognizes that stating the numbers of schools with esports teams, while impressive, may not be enough to persuade readers that having a competitive video gaming team is a powerful recruiting and retention tool. By quoting administrators who connect esports to career opportunities in graphic and game design and by giving the specific example of how esports at UMass Dartmouth support academic programs, Stone provides different types of evidence to support his position.

The scientific community typically takes the long view in terms of gathering evidence in support of the positions it takes. That certainly seems to have been the case with the slow accumulation of evidence to suggest cow's milk may not be as good for us as we once thought. Until recently, US dietary guidelines recommended drinking three glasses of milk a day. But over time, scientists questioned this guideline (heavily promoted by the milk industry), showing in numerous studies that too much milk harms both people and the planet. In a report published by *The New*

England Journal of Medicine, Harvard professor of epidemiology and nutrition Walter Willett and Harvard professor of pediatrics David Ludwig make the following case:

> For adults, the overall evidence does not support high dairy consumption for reduction of fractures, which has been a primary justification for current U.S. recommendations. Moreover, total dairy consumption has not been clearly related to weight control or to risks of diabetes and cardiovascular disease. High consumption of dairy foods is likely to increase the risks of prostate cancer and possibly endometrial cancer but reduce the risk of colorectal cancer.
> —WALTER C. WILLETT & DAVID LUDWIG, "Milk and Health"

In this case, the researchers analyzed evidence gathered over many years before reaching their conclusion.

Attention to More than One Point of View

Considering multiple, often opposing, points of view is a hallmark of any strong position paper, particularly in an academic context. By showing that you understand and have carefully evaluated other viewpoints, you show respect for the issue's complexity and for your audience, while also showing that you have done your homework on your topic.

In a journal article on human-caused climate change, Naomi Oreskes takes a position based on a careful analysis of 928 scientific articles published in well-known and respected journals. Some people, she says, "suggest that there might be substantive disagreement in the scientific community about the reality of anthropogenic climate change. This is not the case." Yet in spite of the very strong consensus on which Oreskes bases her claim, she still acknowledges other possible viewpoints:

> Admittedly, [some] authors evaluating impacts, developing methods, or studying paleoclimatic change might believe that current climate change is natural. . . . The scientific consensus might, of course, be wrong. If the history of science teaches anything, it is humility, and no one can be faulted for failing to act on what is not known.
> —NAOMI ORESKES, "Beyond the Ivory Tower: The Scientific Consensus on Climate Change"

Danielle K. Brown offers statistics in her article criticizing media reports of campus protests. However, she also points out exceptions to the trends—a good move that boosts her credibility. See how she does it on p. 876.

Oreskes acknowledges that the consensus she found in the articles she examined might be challenged by other articles she did not consider and that any consensus, no matter how strong, might ultimately prove to be wrong. The most recent United Nations Intergovernmental Panel on Climate Change offers no such qualifications, however, reporting that "human activities, principally through emissions of greenhouse gases, have unequivocally caused global warming." The conclusion reached by 743 scientists, officials, and contributing authors from 195 member countries are divided into working groups to analyze data and write reports.

Sometimes you'll want to both acknowledge and reply to other viewpoints, especially if you can answer any objections persuasively. Here is college admissions officer Jennifer Delahunty, noting—and ruling out—the possible criticism that college admissions officers do not give careful consideration to all applicants:

> Rest assured that admissions officers are not cavalier in making their decisions. Last week, the 10 officers at my college sat around a table, 12 hours every day, deliberating the applications of hundreds of talented young men and women. While gulping down coffee and poring over statistics, we heard about a young woman from Kentucky we were not yet ready to admit outright. She was the leader/president/editor/captain/lead actress in every activity in her school. She had taken six advanced placement courses and had been selected for a prestigious state leadership program. In her free time, this whirlwind of achievement had accumulated more than 300 hours of community service in four different organizations.
>
> Few of us sitting around the table were as talented and as directed at age 17 as this young woman. Unfortunately, her test scores and grade point average placed her in the middle of our pool. We had to have a debate before we decided to swallow the middling scores and write "admit" next to her name.
>
> —JENNIFER DELAHUNTY, "To All the Girls I've Rejected"

Delahunty provides evidence from a specific case, demonstrating persuasively that the admissions officers at her college take their job seriously.

Take a look at how scholars Varun Pratap Singh, Ashwani Kumar, Chandon Swaroop Meena, and Gaurav Dwividi, who argue for the increased use of electric vehicles (EVs), use a visual diagram to present other points of view—namely, the challenges of EVs:

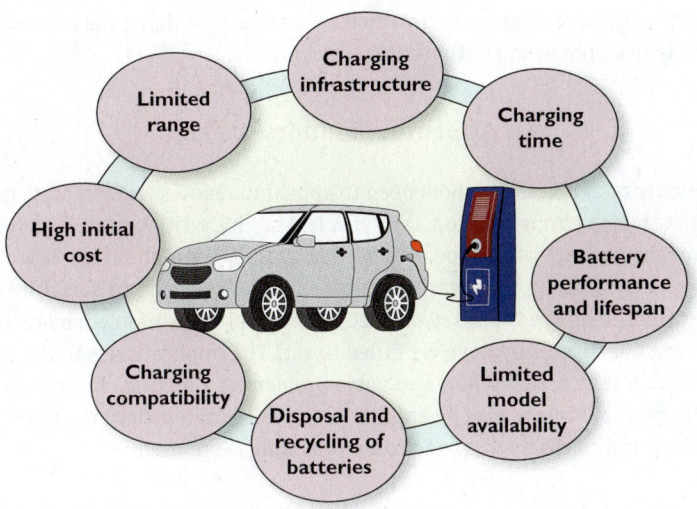

A diagram shows the authors' take on "challenges in making energy-efficient vehicles accessible and affordable."

An Authoritative Tone and Stance

Particularly in academic contexts, authors make a point of taking an authoritative tone. Even if your goal is to encourage readers to examine a number of alternatives without suggesting which one is best, you should try to do so in a way that shows you know which alternatives are worth examining and why. Likewise, even if you are taking a strong position, you should seek to appear reasonable and rational. The 1964 surgeon general's report on the consequences of smoking does not waver: smoking causes cancer. At the same time, in taking this position, it briefly outlines the history of the issue and the evidence on which the claim is logically based, avoiding emotional language and carefully specifying which forms of smoking ("excessive" cigarettes) and cancer (lung) the claim involves.

Jennifer Delahunty establishes her authority in other ways. Her description of ten admissions officers putting in twelve-hour days going through hundreds of applications and "poring over statistics" backs up her forthright assertion, "Rest assured that admissions officers are not cavalier in making their decisions." Delahunty not only demonstrates that she knows what she is writing about but also invites readers to think about the complexity of the situation without offering them any easy answers. In short, she is simultaneously reasonable and authoritative.

An Appeal to Readers' Values

Implicitly or explicitly, authors need to appeal to readers' values, especially when taking a strong position. Dr. Vivek H. Murthy, writing as surgeon general of the United States, appeals to readers' values throughout his *New York Times* essay arguing that warning labels should be added to social media platforms. (Read the full essay on p. 205.) He situates the problem by raising a simple question: why have we failed to act? The implication is that a society should take action when a solvable problem is affecting children. Note in the example below how he appeals to the need for a society to protect its children and connects this need to a moral obligation to act:

> Why is it that we have failed to respond to the harms of social media when they are no less urgent or widespread than those posed by unsafe cars, planes, or food? These harms are not a failure of willpower and parenting; they are the consequence of unleashing powerful technology without adequate safety measures, transparency or accountability. The moral test of any society is how well it protects its children. Students and mothers do not want to be told that change takes time, that the issue is too complicated or that the status quo is too hard to alter. We have the expertise, resources and tools to make social media safe for our kids. Now is the time to summon the will to act. Our children's well-being is at stake.
>
> —DR. VIVEK H. MURTHY, "Surgeon General: Why I'm Calling for a Warning Label on Social Media Platforms"

Murthy puts forward an urgent call to live up to America's values, and he reminds readers that inaction signals a moral failure to use one's resources and expertise on behalf of a vulnerable population.

ARGUING A POSITION / A Roadmap

Choose a topic that matters—to you, and to others

If you get to select your topic, begin by examining your own interests and commitments in light of the context you are writing for. Climate change might be a fitting topic for a course in the life sciences or social sciences, but it's probably not going to serve you well in a course in medieval history unless you can find a direct link between the two topics. You might consider focusing on some issue that's being debated on campus (Are those new rules for dropping classes fair?), a broader political or ethical issue (Is eating meat by definition unethical?), or an issue in which you have a direct stake (Does early admission penalize those who need financial aid?).

If you've been assigned a topic, do your best to find an aspect of it that interests you. (If you're bored with your subject, you can be sure your readers will be.) If, for example, you're assigned to write about globalization in an international studies course, you could tailor that topic to your own interests and write about the influence of American hip-hop on world music.

Be sure that your topic is one that is arguable—and that it matters. Short of astounding new evidence, it's no longer worth arguing that there is no link between smoking and lung cancer. It's a fact. But you can argue about what responsibility tobacco companies now have for tobacco-related deaths, as recent court cases demonstrate.

One sure way to find out whether a topic is arguable is to see if it *is* being debated—and that is a good first step as you explore a topic. You can probably assume that any topic that's being widely discussed matters—and of course you'll want to know what's being said about it in order to write about it. Remember that your essay is part of a larger conversation about your topic: you need to become familiar with that conversation in order to contribute to it.

Keep an open mind. A good, arguable topic will surely trigger at least several different points of view. Keeping an open mind and considering those points of view fairly and carefully at the start is always a good idea. And it will make your argument stronger by showing that you can be trusted to consider all sides of an issue, especially those you may not agree with.

> Do you like watching TV? So does César Albarrán-Torres. He uses his own viewing experiences to make a compelling argument about how streaming services can allow us to enjoy shows in a variety of languages. Check it out on p. 838.

Consider your rhetorical situation

Focus on your AUDIENCE. Who are you trying to reach, and what do you hope to persuade them to think or do?

- What are they likely to know about your topic, and what background information will you need to provide?
- How are they like or unlike you—and one another? Consider such things as age, education, gender, abilities and disabilities, cultural and linguistic heritage, and so on. How will such factors influence the way you make your argument?
- What convictions might they hold about the topic you're addressing— and how sympathetic are they likely to be to your position?

If you're trying to convince your fellow business majors of the virtues of free-market capitalism, your task is quite different than if you're trying to convince members of the campus socialist organization. In the first case, you would almost surely be preaching to the choir, whereas in the second, you would likely face a more skeptical audience.

Keep in mind that there's always danger in speaking only to those who already agree with you; if you keep audiences with differing values and viewpoints in mind, you will be more likely to represent all views fairly and hence encourage others to consider your position seriously.

Think hard about your PURPOSE. Why are you arguing this position? What has motivated you to write on this topic? What do you hope to learn by writing about it? What do you want to convince your audience to think or do? How can you best achieve your purpose or purposes?

Think about your STANCE. Start by asking yourself where you are coming from in regard to this topic. What about the topic captured your interest, and how has that interest led you to the position you're taking on it? Why do you think the topic matters? How would you describe your attitude toward the topic: Are you an advocate, a critic, an observer, or something else? How can you establish your authority in writing on this topic?

Consider the larger CONTEXT. What are the various perspectives on the issue? What have others said about it? If you're writing about the use of ethanol as a fuel source, for instance, you'll need to look at what circumstances led to its use, at who's supported and opposed it (and why), and at the economic ramifications both of producing ethanol for fuel and of not doing so. As you come to understand the larger context, you'll become aware of various positions you'll want to consider and what factors will be important to consider as you develop your position.

Consider your LANGUAGE. Almost any argument can be presented in a number of ways. Regardless of how many languages and dialects you use in your everyday life, you have many options to consider in taking a position. Will your audience expect a certain kind of language or style? Do you want to meet those expectations? challenge them? What do you want your language choices to say about you? What risks might you be willing to take with your language? How will your choice of medium and the larger context limit or expand the language options available to you? (You may want to consult Chapters 4 and 35 for more information about language options.)

Consider your MEDIUM. Will your writing take the form of a print essay? Will it appear as an editorial in a local paper? on a website? as an audio essay for a podcast? as an oral or multimedia presentation for a class you are taking? The medium you choose should be one that suits both your purpose and your audience.

Consider matters of DESIGN. Think about the "look" you want to achieve and how you can format your text to make it easy to follow. Do you need headings? illustrations? any other graphics? color? Does the discipline you're writing in have any conventions you should follow? Does your medium allow for certain elements such as audio or video links that will help you achieve your purpose?

Research your topic

Begin exploring the topic by looking at it from different points of view. Whatever position you take will ultimately be more credible and persuasive if you can show evidence of having considered other positions.

Begin by assessing what you know—and don't know—about the topic. What interests you about the topic, and why? What more do you want or need to find out about it? What questions do you have about it, and where might you go for answers? To answer these questions, you might try BRAINSTORMING or other activities for GENERATING IDEAS.

What have others said? What are some of the issues that are being debated now about your topic, and what are the various positions on these issues? What other POSITIONS might be taken with respect to the topic? Seek out sources that represent a variety of perspectives.

Where should you start your research? Where you start and what sources you consult depend on your topic and what questions you have about it. If you are focusing on a current issue, turn to news media and to websites, listservs, or other online groups devoted to the issue. If you are investigating a topic from the distant past, be sure to look for both older sources and more recent scholarship on the topic. For some issues, you might want to interview everyday folks, local experts, or community-based sources—or conduct other sorts of FIELD RESEARCH. If your instructor's policies allow, generative AI tools might help give background information about a topic, but remember to verify any facts AI provides.

Do you need to cut your topic down to size? Few among us know enough to make strong general claims about climate change. While that fact should not keep us from having opinions about the issue, it suggests that the existence of global warming is much too broad a topic to be well suited to a college essay. Instead, you'll need to focus on some aspect of that topic for your essay. What angle you take will depend on the course you're writing for. For a geology class, you might focus on the effects of rising temperatures on glaciers; for an international relations course, you could look at climate shift and national security debates. Your goal is to take an informed position, one that you can support well.

Formulate an explicit position

Once you have sufficient information about your topic and some understanding of the complexity of the issue, you'll need to formulate a position that you can state explicitly and support fully. Let's say you decide to take a position on a current controversy among scientists about climate change. Here's how one author formulated a position:

> Many scientists have argued that climate change has led to bigger and more destructive hurricanes and typhoons. Other researchers, however, have countered by saying that climate change is not linked causally to an increase in hurricane strength. After reviewing both sides of this debate, I see two strong reasons why changes in our climate have not necessarily led to more severe hurricanes.
> —SOFI MINCEY, "On Climate Change and Hurricanes"

These three sentences articulate a clear position—that climate change is not necessarily to blame for bigger hurricanes—and frame that position as a response to an existing debate. Notice also how the writer qualifies her claim: she does not claim definitively that climate change has not led to bigger hurricanes; rather, she promises to present reasons that argue for this view.

By arguing only that the claims of many scientists *may* be wrong, she greatly increases the likelihood that she can succeed in her argument, setting a reasonable goal for what she must achieve. Note that her position still requires support: she needs to present reasonable evidence to challenge the claim that climate change has "necessarily" led to bigger hurricanes.

State your position as a tentative THESIS. Once you formulate your position, try stating it several different ways and then decide which one is most compelling and clear. Your statement should let your audience know where you stand and be interesting enough to attract their attention.

Then think about whether you should QUALIFY your position. Should you limit what you claim—is it true only sometimes or under certain circumstances? On the other hand, does it seem too weak or timid and need to be stated more forcefully?

Remember that a good thesis for a position paper should identify your specific topic and make a CLAIM about that topic that is debatable. The thesis should also give your audience your reasons for making this claim. Consider the following thesis statement from two scholars at a public policy institute:

> The case against raising the minimum wage is straightforward: A higher wage makes it more expensive for firms to hire workers.
> —KEVIN A. HASSET & MICHAEL R. STRAIN, "Why We Shouldn't Raise the Minimum Wage"

See the ebook for a video on developing an argumentative thesis statement.

Hasset and Strain's claim about raising the minimum wage is explicitly stated (they are "against" it), as is a major reason for that position.

Come up with REASONS and EVIDENCE. List all the reasons supporting your position that you discovered in your research. Which ones will be most persuasive to your audience? Then jot down all the evidence you have to support those reasons—facts, quotations, statistics, examples, testimony, visuals, and so on. Remember that what counts as evidence varies across audiences and disciplines. Some are persuaded by testimonials, while others want statistical data. In some cases, NARRATIVES can underscore or illustrate the importance of your argument. Finally, look for any FALLACIES or weak reasons or evidence, and decide whether you need to do further research.

Identify other positions. Carefully consider COUNTERARGUMENTS and other points of view on the topic and how you will account for them. At the very least, you need to acknowledge other positions that are prominent in the larger conversation about the topic and to treat them fairly. If you disagree with a position, you need to offer reasons why and do so respectfully.

Organize and start writing

Once you have a fair sense of how you will present your position, it's time to write out a draft. If you have trouble getting started, it might help to think about the larger conversation about the topic that's already going on—and to think of your draft as a moment when you get to say what *you* think.

Be guided by your THESIS. As you begin to organize, type it at the top of your page so that you can keep looking back to it to be sure that each part of your text supports the thesis.

Give REASONS for your position, with supporting EVIDENCE. Determine an order for presenting your reasons, perhaps starting with the one you think will speak most directly to your audience.

Don't forget to consider COUNTERARGUMENTS. Acknowledge positions other than your own, and respond to what they say.

Draft an OPENING. Introduce your topic, and provide any background information your audience may need. State your position clearly, perhaps as a response to what others have said about your topic. Say something about why the issue matters, why your audience should care.

Draft a CONCLUSION. You might want to end by summing up your position and by answering the "so what" question: why does your topic matter—and who cares? Make sure you give a strong takeaway message. What are the implications of your argument? What do you want readers to remember or do as a result of reading what you've written?

Look critically at your draft, get responses—and revise

Go through your draft carefully, looking critically at the position you stake out, the reasons and evidence you provide in support of it, and the way you present them to your audience. For this review, play the "doubting game" with yourself by asking "Who says?" and "So what?" and "Can this be done better?" at every point.

Being tough on yourself now will pay off by showing you where you need to shore up your arguments. As you work through your draft, make notes on what you plan to do in your revision.

Next, ask some classmates or friends to read and respond to your draft. Here are some questions that can help you or others read over a draft of writing that takes a position:

- *Is the position stated explicitly?* Is there a clear **THESIS** sentence? Does it need to be qualified, or should it be stated more strongly?

- *What positions are you responding to?* What is the larger conversation?

- *Is it clear why the topic matters?* Why do you care about the topic, and why should your audience care?

- *How effective is the* **OPENING**? How does it capture your audience's interest? How else might you begin?

- *Is there sufficient background information?* What other information might the audience need?

- *How would you describe the* **STANCE** *and* **TONE** —do they reflect your purpose and appeal to your audience?

- *What* **REASONS** *do you give for the position, and what* **EVIDENCE** *do you provide for those reasons?* What are the strongest reasons and evidence given? the weakest? What other evidence or reasons are needed to support this position?

- *How trustworthy are the sources you've cited?* Are **QUOTATIONS**, **SUMMARIES**, and **PARAPHRASES** smoothly integrated into the text—and is it clear where you are speaking and where (and why) you are citing others?

- *What other positions do you consider, and do you treat them fairly?* Are there other **COUNTERARGUMENTS** you should address as well? How well do you answer possible objections to your position?

- *How is the draft organized?* Is it easy to follow, with clear **TRANSITIONS** from one point to the next? Are there headings—and if not, would they help? What about the organization could be improved?

- *Does the* **STYLE** *fit with your purpose and appeal to your audience?* Could the style—choice of words, kinds of sentences—be improved in any way?

- *How effective is your text* **DESIGN** *?* Have you used any visuals to support your position—and if so, have you written captions that explain how they contribute to the argument? If not, what visuals might be helpful? Is there any information that would be easier to follow if it were presented in a chart or table?

- *How does the draft* **CONCLUDE** *?* Is the conclusion forceful and memorable? How else might you conclude?

- *Consider the title.* Does it make clear what the text is about, and does it make a reader want to read on?

- *What is your overall impression of the draft?* Will it persuade your audience to accept the position—and if not, why? Even if they don't accept the position, would they consider it a plausible one?

Revise your draft in light of your own observations and any feedback from others—keeping your audience and purpose firmly in mind, as always.

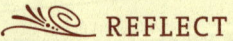# REFLECT

Once you've completed your essay, let it settle for a while and then take time to **REFLECT** . How well did you argue your point? What additional revisions would you make if you could? Research shows that such reflections help "lock in" what you learn for future use.

Work Is a Blessing
RUSSEL HONORÉ

I GREW UP IN Lakeland, Louisiana, one of 12 children. We all lived on my parents' subsistence farm. We grew cotton, sugarcane, corn, hogs, chickens and had a large garden, but it didn't bring in much cash. So when I was 12, I got a part-time job on a dairy farm down the road, helping to milk cows. We milked 65 cows at 5 in the morning and again at 2 in the afternoon, seven days a week.

In the kitchen one Saturday before daylight, I remember complaining to my father and grandfather about having to go milk those cows. My father said, "Ya know, boy, to work is a blessing."

I looked at those two men who'd worked harder than I ever had—my father eking out a living on that farm and my grandfather farming and working as a carpenter during the Depression. I had a feeling I had been told something really important, but it took many years before it sunk in.

Going to college was a rare privilege for a kid from Lakeland, Louisiana. My father told me if I picked something to study that I liked doing, I'd always look forward to my work. But he also added, "Even having a job you hate is better

---

RUSSEL HONORÉ wrote this essay for *This I Believe*, a not-for-profit organization that sponsors "a public dialogue about belief, one essay at a time." The essay was later broadcast on NPR's *Weekend Edition*. Honoré is a retired lieutenant general in the US Army who has contributed to response efforts to Hurricane Katrina in 2005 and other natural disasters. In 2021 he was tasked with investigating security failings at the January 6 attack on the US Capitol.

than not having a job at all." I wanted to be a farmer, but I joined the ROTC program to help pay for college. And what started out as an obligation to the Army became a way of life that I stayed committed to for 37 years, three months and three days.

In the late 1980s, during a visit to Bangladesh, I saw a woman with a baby on her back, breaking bricks with a hammer. I asked a Bangladesh military escort why they weren't using a machine, which would have been a lot easier. He told me a machine would put that lady out of work. Breaking those bricks meant she'd earn enough money to feed herself and her baby that day. And as bad as that woman's job was, it was enough to keep a small family alive. It reminded me of my father's words: To work is a blessing.

Serving in the United States Army overseas, I saw a lot of people like that woman in Bangladesh. And I have come to believe that people without jobs are not free. They are victims of crime, the ideology of terrorism, poor health, depression and social unrest. These victims become the illegal immigrants, the slaves of human trafficking, the drug dealers, the street gang members. I've seen it over and over again on the U.S. border, in Somalia, the Congo, Afghanistan and in New Orleans. People who have jobs can have a home, send their kids to school, develop a sense of pride, contribute to the good of the community, and even help others. When we can work, we're free. We're blessed.

I don't think I'll ever quit working. I'm retired from the Army, but I'm still working to help people be prepared for disaster. And I may get to do a little farming someday, too. I'm not going to stop. I believe in my father's words. I believe in the blessing of work.

Citing his father, Honoré shows his attention to more than one POINT OF VIEW about work.

REASONS and EVIDENCE for how the author came to see work as a blessing.

Specific EXAMPLES indicate why the topic matters and show the author's awareness of his AUDIENCE's values.

The author CONCLUDES by stating his position explicitly.

 REFLECT & WRITE

In this essay, Russel Honoré relies on his personal experience to establish what he sees as distinct differences between people who have jobs and people who don't. He argues that "people without jobs are not free." What kind of evidence does he provide to support this claim? What do you find persuasive about his position? Where do you see gaps in his argument? Write a brief response to Honoré's argument that "work is a blessing" with your own stance, provide evidence for your position, and try using your own personal experience as one element of support.

Social Media Platforms Need Warning Labels

VIVEK H. MURTHY

ONE OF THE MOST IMPORTANT LESSONS I learned in medical school was that in an emergency, you don't have the luxury to wait for perfect information. You assess the available facts, you use your best judgment, and you act quickly.

The mental health crisis among young people is an emergency—and social media has emerged as an important contributor. Adolescents who spend more than three hours a day on social media face double the risk of anxiety and depression symptoms, and the average daily use in this age group, as of the summer of 2023, was 4.8 hours. Additionally, nearly half of adolescents say social media makes them feel worse about their bodies.

It is time to require a surgeon general's warning label on social media platforms, stating that social media is associated with significant mental health harms for adolescents. A surgeon general's warning label, which requires

---

DR. VIVEK H. MURTHY's guest essay was published in the opinion section of the *New York Times* in 2024. He served as the surgeon general of the United States under Presidents Obama and Biden and as the vice admiral of United States Public Health Service Commissioned Corps in charge of more than 6,000 public health officials across the country. Dr. Murthy prioritized fighting against misinformation and providing affordable health care. In the essay, as it appears in the *New York Times*, Dr. Murthy uses hyperlinks, which are underlined in the text presented here.

congressional action, would regularly remind parents and adolescents that social media has not been proved safe. Evidence from <u>tobacco studies show</u> that warning labels can increase awareness and change behavior. When asked if a warning from the surgeon general would prompt them to limit or monitor their children's social media use, 76 percent of people in one <u>recent survey</u> of Latino parents said yes.

To be clear, a warning label would not, on its own, make social media safe for young people. <u>The advisory I issued a year ago about social media and young people's mental health</u> included specific recommendations for policymakers, platforms and the public to make social media safer for kids. Such measures, which already have strong bipartisan support, remain the priority.

Legislation from Congress should shield young people from online harassment, abuse and exploitation and from exposure to extreme violence and sexual content that too often appears in algorithm-driven feeds. The measures should prevent platforms from collecting sensitive data from children and should restrict the use of features like push notifications, autoplay and infinite scroll, which prey on developing brains and contribute to excessive use.

Additionally, companies must be required to share all of their data on health effects with independent scientists and the public—currently they do not—and allow independent safety audits. While the platforms claim they are making their products safer, Americans need more than words. We need proof.

The rest of society can play a role also. Schools should ensure that classroom learning and social time are phone-free experiences. Parents, too, should create phone-free zones around bedtime, meals and social gatherings to safeguard their kids' sleep and real-life connections—both of which have direct effects on mental health. And they should wait until after middle school to allow their kids access to social media. This is much easier said than done, which is why parents should work together with other families to establish shared rules, so no parents have to struggle alone or feel guilty when their teens say they are the only one who has to endure limits. And young people can build on teen-focused efforts like the <u>Log Off movement</u> and <u>Wired Human</u> to support one another in reforming their relationship with social media and navigating online environments safely.

Others must help, too. Public health leaders should demand healthy digital environments for young people. Doctors, nurses and other clinicians should raise the issue of social media with kids and parents and guide them toward safer practices. And the federal Kids Online Health & Safety Task Force must continue its leadership in bringing together the best minds from inside and outside government to recommend changes that will make social media safer for our children.

One of the worst things for a parent is to know your children are in danger yet be unable to do anything about it. That is how parents tell me they feel when it comes to social media—helpless and alone in the face of toxic content and hidden harms. I think about Lori, a woman from Colorado who fought back tears as she told me about her teenage daughter, who took her life after being bullied on social media. Lori had been diligent, monitoring her daughter's accounts and phone daily, but harm still found her child.

There is no seatbelt for parents to click, no helmet to snap in place, no assurance that trusted experts have investigated and ensured that these platforms are safe for our kids. There are just parents and their children, trying to figure it out on their own, pitted against some of the best product engineers and most well-resourced companies in the world.

Parents aren't the only ones yearning for solutions. Last fall, I gathered with students to talk about mental health and loneliness. As often happens in such gatherings, they raised the issue of social media.

After they talked about what they liked about social media—a way to stay in touch with old friends, find communities of shared identity and express themselves creatively—a young woman named Tina raised her hand. "I just don't feel good when I use social media," she said softly, a hint of embarrassment in her voice. Her confession opened the door for her classmates. One by one, they spoke about their experiences with social media: the endless comparison with other people that shredded their self-esteem, the feeling of being addicted and unable to set limits and the difficulty having real conversations on platforms that too often fostered outrage and bullying. There was a sadness in their voices, as if they knew what was happening to them but felt powerless to change it.

As a father of a 6- and a 7-year-old who have already asked about social media, I worry about how my wife and I will know when to let them have accounts. How will we monitor their activity, given the increasingly sophisticated techniques for concealing it? How will we know if our children are being exposed to harmful content or dangerous people? It's no wonder that when it comes to managing social media for their kids, so many parents are feeling stress and anxiety—and even shame.

It doesn't have to be this way. Faced with high levels of car-accident-related deaths in the mid- to late 20th century, lawmakers successfully demanded seatbelts, airbags, crash testing and a host of other measures that ultimately made cars safer. This January the F.A.A. grounded about 170 planes when a door plug came off one Boeing 737 Max 9 while the plane was in the air. And the following month, a massive recall of dairy products was conducted because of a listeria contamination that claimed two lives.

> *Compares actions taken by lawmakers when faced with other serious threats to the safety of citizens as EVIDENCE of what's possible.*

Why is it that we have failed to respond to the harms of social media when they are no less urgent or widespread than those posed by unsafe cars, planes or food? These harms are not a failure of willpower and parenting; they are the consequence of unleashing powerful technology without adequate safety measures, transparency or accountability. 15

> *Points out a gap between his audience's VALUES and action on this topic.*

The moral test of any society is how well it protects its children. Students like Tina and mothers like Lori do not want to be told that change takes time, that the issue is too complicated or that the status quo is too hard to alter. We have the expertise, resources and tools to make social media safe for our kids. Now is the time to summon the will to act. Our children's well-being is at stake.

> *CONCLUDES with a forceful appeal to take action in order to uphold a core value: protecting America's children.*

❧ REFLECT & WRITE

Dr. Vivek H. Murthy takes a position that some may consider controversial, and he uses different strategies for addressing opposing points of view. Identify places where he speaks to counterarguments, both implicitly and explicitly. Do you agree with Murthy's argument or identify with an opposing point of view—or a little of both? Write a brief argument of your own in response to Murthy, explaining what claims you agree with, which you don't, and why. Consider what counterargument you might make to Dr. Murthy's position or any additional support for his position you can add.

Sampling or Stealing?
Copyright Infringement and Hip-Hop

ALEKSANDER LAM

HIP-HOP, a genre of music that combines "chest-thumping beat[s]" with "rapid-fire lyrics rapped into a handheld mic," is known for spilling into other genres, pulling in artists from other traditions, and inventing new sounds (McCollum). Hip-hop's tradition is one that samples other genres such as funk, soul, and R&B to add to the musical conversation. However, US copyright law often mislabels this technique as copyright infringement. The definition of "stealing" in copyright cases against hip-hop artists often punishes those who sample other tracks. This view has created a rift between hip-hop artists who want to keep the tradition alive and American courts looking to label music as either original or stolen material. The US federal district courts ignore hip-hop's roots when they analyze music for copyright infringement. In order to preserve the creative history of the genre, courts must consider the musical conversation hip-hop artists are responding to.

A **POSITION** *in response to a clearly identified problem.*

ALEKSANDER LAM wrote this essay as a student in his first year at Chapman University for an honors class exploring copyright laws. Lam's essay raises questions about the applicability of copyright laws for diverse music genres.

Defines a key term and important BACKGROUND INFORMATION.

Stakes a claim and backs it up with evidence, setting an AUTHORITATIVE TONE.

A brief history gives readers the CONTEXT *they need.*

Quotes an artist as supporting EVIDENCE.

Gives reasons and EXAMPLES *for why sampling is valued.*

Hip-hop artists employ a unique process, called sampling, for making music that builds on the genre's history. According to *Avid*'s "Guide to Using Samples in Music and Digital Audio Production," "sampling is the craft of taking pieces from existing audio tracks or recorded sounds and weaving them into new compositions." A common practice in hip-hop and other genres such as electronic dance music (EDM), producers take samples from other artists, often from the pioneers of a particular genre, to make new music ("Guide"). This process involves "transforming and incorporating these elements in ways that they become something entirely new and different" ("Guide"). Hip-hop artists often sample from tracks of soul, jazz, and R&B. Sampling is integral to hip-hop—the genre wouldn't exist without sampling, and its popularity is *because* of the innovative sampling techniques developed by artists and DJs (Johnson 238). One DJ in particular, DJ Kool Herc, is often credited with starting hip-hop in the early 1970s. He spun twin records on a turntable in the Bronx, New York City, isolating and extending the drum breaks on a song as breakdancers flaunted their skills on the dance floor (McCollum). This technique was an early form of sampling, and it evolved into a way for modern artists to respond to tracks and artists from hip-hop's history.

As hip-hop's popularity grew and artists picked up recording deals, sampling allowed artists to add to the musical conversation of the genre. Hip-hop artists rely on sampling to pay homage to older artists, introduce music to their audience, and comment on culture and society. "Listening for songs within songs" became a key part of the creative process as artists searched for music to sample from (McCollum). By rapping over older beats, hip-hop artists lament, celebrate, and criticize their current world in tandem with the music of artists that came before. Grammy Award–winning rapper and producer, Tyler, the Creator, commented on his affinity for an older song that inspired and contributed to his 2018 track "Potato Salad" via a post on *X*. He wrote, "knock knock by monica i was tryna rap on that for 10 years ha" (@tylerthecreator). "Knock Knock," a track by the artist Monica that was released in 2003, was the backing track that Tyler, the Creator rapped over in "Potato Salad." Tyler used sampling to pay homage to Monica, and by doing so, he was able to bring her work to modern-day listeners.

Although hip-hop artists see sampling as transformative, federal district courts disagree and often analyze music in a way that does not consider the artistic and creative value of this technique. According to Cornell Law School, federal courts define copyright infringement as "the act of unlawful copying of material under intellectual property law" (United States Code). For something to be considered "an infringement, the derivative work must be based upon the copyrighted work" (United States Code). Artists creating music in other genres may benefit from this definition, especially if they want to protect their original ideas from being replicated by other artists who may profit from them without seeking permission first. For example, Marvin Gaye's estate felt cheated when they alleged Robin Thicke and Pharrell Williams's 2013 pop song, "Blurred Lines," stole material from Gaye's hit "Got to Give It Up" released decades earlier; the courts agreed and awarded millions in damages to be paid to the Gaye estate (Gibbs). In the context of sampling, however, this definition concludes that hip-hop songs that sample other tracks are based on previously copyrighted work, so any artist engaging in sampling is potentially guilty of copyright infringement. Rather than analyzing music and resulting samples in a way that considers artistry and cultural context, courts instead only seem to understand music as a "tangible medium of expression" that "can be perceived, reproduced, or otherwise communicated, either directly or with the aid of a machine or device" (United States Code). This line of thinking reduces the creative technique of sampling to an illegal practice and, as a result, threatens the tradition at the heart of hip-hop (Johnson).

Cites an authoritative source to include an opposing POINT OF VIEW.

A clear indication of why this issue matters.

The legal definition of "stealing" in copyright cases has, indeed, resulted in punishing hip-hop artists who sample other tracks. In the 1991 case *Grand Upright v. Warner*, rapper Biz Markie faced legal trouble after sampling Gilbert O'Sullivan's song, "Alone Again (Naturally)" in a song titled "Alone Again," a clear reference to the original song sampled (*Grand Upright v. Warner*). Because Biz Markie did not receive permission to sample from the original track, Gilbert O'Sullivan saw this as copyright infringement. A blog post from the George Washington University Law School points out that Markie only included "unauthorized use of three words, and the accompaniment ostinato" from the original song (*Grand Upright v. Warner*). Notably, Markie's defense team urged the court to consider how unapproved sampling was common in the hip-hop industry. Judge Kevin Thomas Duffy disputed the defense team's argument in his ruling, mentioning that "the defendants in this action for copyright infringement would have this court believe that stealing is rampant in the music business and, for that reason, their conduct here should be excused" (*Grand Upright v. Warner*). In the end, Duffy concluded that "the conduct of the defendants . . . violates not only the Seventh Commandment, but also the copyright laws of this country." Biz Markie was found guilty of copyright infringement, and the

Citing examples from specific legal cases along with expert analysis adds CREDIBILITY.

ruling set a precedent that any sample had to be cleared by the respective copyright owners (*Grand Upright v. Warner*). In this case, Duffy incorrectly concluded that sampling, in any form, is stealing. Furthermore, this definition of stealing fails to acknowledge or consider that sampling is extremely common in the hip-hop industry. Because federal courts and hip-hop artists have different understandings of sampling, many artists like Biz Markie are found guilty of copyright infringement when they are simply upholding the tradition of hip-hop by honoring other artists in their work.

> *Addresses another* POINT OF VIEW *from a different genre.*

Federal courts have identified one "permissible" form of sampling, which tends to protect artists in other genres, but not hip-hop (Johnson). Artists in other genres engage in sampling as well, often using a much smaller part of another track compared to hip-hop's style. In a 2013 court case, record label Salsoul sued pop artist Madonna, arguing her 1990 song "Vogue" broke copyright law by stealing from a Salsoul song. Madonna sampled a 0.23-second horn hit from the 1976 song "Love Break." In a 2016 appeal, the court ruled that the sample was too inconsequential to be violating copyright laws—a concept known as *de minimis* (Gardner). California 9th Circuit Judge Susan Graber expanded on her decision, explaining that "even if a listener recognized some similarities between the horn hits in the two songs, it is hard to imagine that he or she would conclude that sampling had occurred" (qtd. in Gardner). The lawsuit set a precedent: if a sample was deemed brief enough, then it was legally permissible. Sampling in this way might happen in other genres, but is not common in hip-hop, where the point is to create a conversation between musicians, weaving in the work of others so others recognize it. In Madonna's track, the original artist sampled is barely recognizable—as the judge noted: "Without careful attention, the horn hits are easy to miss" (qtd. in Gardner). As a result, the only legally acceptable form of sampling without prior permission is not sampling at all—it is the act of dropping a sound into a track and hoping no one

> *Uses* COMPARISON *and definition to develop the main argument.*

will notice. Courts are focused on whether a sample is recognizable enough to be deemed "stolen" instead of considering an artist's context and creative process (Johnson). This disagreement about if and when sampling is a criminal act could be attributed to cultural differences between the legal community and hip-hop artists. Is there a solution that does not criminalize the actions of this one group, hip-hop artists, more so than others?

> PROPOSES *a solution to the problem.*

When sampling copyright cases arise involving hip-hop tracks, federal courts should consider the genre context, tradition, and creative process behind a sample's use. In his 2019 track "A BOY IS A GUN*," Tyler, the Creator samples vocals and instrumentals from "Bound," a song released in 1971 by the R&B group Ponderosa Twins Plus One. Tyler, the Creator sampled eleven seconds of "Bound," and those eleven seconds repeat throughout his track. If the Ponderosa Twins Plus One were to sue Tyler, the Creator for copyright infringement, federal courts could take a new approach. First, they might still determine if the sample is easily recognizable. And in this case it is, so it is not privy to the *de minimis* exception. However, instead of stopping here, the court could take into account the creative purpose and context behind the sample, leading to an analysis of the musical conversation the artists are having. While the Ponderosa Twins Plus One—an all-male group—sang about being "bound" to fall in love with a woman, Tyler raps about a man's unrequited feelings for another man, and he does so directly over the original track. In doing so, he expands the traditional heteronormative love story of "Bound" by connecting it to unreciprocated homosexual love. Tyler is using the art of sampling both to pay homage to artists from the past and to continue to add to the musical conversation. By taking the step to consider the creative merits of the track in the context of a genre's tradition, federal courts would be able to acknowledge and judge the value of sampling more fairly and appropriately across genres, including hip-hop.

Hip-hop is a distinct genre of American music, and yet the US federal court system fails to take into account hip-hop's roots of creative expression when dealing with copyright cases. This reality deters hip-hop artists from experimenting with sampling in fear of being accused of copyright infringement. Instead, by making a change to consider the history of hip-hop and its tradition of artists adding to an ongoing musical conversation, courts can better promote creative freedom for musicians across all genres of American music today.

CONCLUDES by restating the main argument and reminding readers what's at stake.

Works Cited

Gardner, Eriq. "Madonna Gets Victory over 'Vogue' Sample at Appeals Court." *The Hollywood Reporter*, 2 June 2016, www.hollywoodreporter.com/business/business-news/madonna-gets-victory-vogue-sample-898944.

Gibbs, Adrienne. "Marvin Gaye's Family Wins 'Blurred Lines' Appeal; Pharrell, Robin Thicke Must Pay." *Forbes*, 21 Mar. 2018, https://www.forbes.com/sites/adriennegibbs/2018/03/21/marvin-gaye-wins-blurred-lines-lawsuit-pharrell-robin-thicke-t-i-off-hook. Accessed 25 Apr. 2024.

Grand Upright v. Warner. Music Copyright Infringement Resource, Jacob Burns Law Library, blogs.law.gwu.edu/mcir/case/grand-upright-v-warner. Accessed 22 Apr. 2024.

"Guide to Using Samples in Music & Digital Audio Production." *Avid*, 19 Oct. 2023, www.avid.com/resource-center/music-sampling-guide.

Johnson, Vincent R., II. "Sampling as Transformation: Re-evaluating Copyright's Treatment of Sampling to End Its Disproportionate Harm on Black Artists." *American University Law Review*, vol. 70, 2021, 227–79, aulawreview.org/blog/sampling-as-transformation-re-evaluating-copyrights-treatment-of-sampling-to-end-its-disproportionate-harm-on-black-artists.

McCollum, Sean. "Hip-Hop: A Culture of Vision and Voice." Edited by Lisa Resnick, *The Kennedy Center*, John F. Kennedy Center for the Performing Arts, www.kennedy-center.org/education/resources-for-educators/classroom-resources/media-and-interactives/media/hip-hop/hip-hop-a-culture-of-vision-and-voice. Accessed 22 Apr. 2024.

@tylerthecreator. "knock knock by monica i was tryna rap on that for 10 years ha." *X*, 23 July 2018, 11:25 p.m., x.com/tylerthecreator/status/1021597099844988928.

United States Code. 17 U.S. Code §102—Subject Matter of Copyright: In General, *Legal Information Institute*, Cornell Law School, www.law.cornell.edu/uscode/text/17/102.

REFLECT & WRITE

Aleksander Lam argues that federal copyright laws disadvantage hip-hop artists because their sampling practices, which are foundational to that genre, are considered stealing under the law. He defines a few ways of thinking about sampling and several examples from cases and artists themselves. Are there other points of view or examples you think Lam should have included? Are you convinced by Lam's argument? Why or why not? Write a brief response stating your position and include at least one example from Lam's argument and one example you find yourself.

FIFTEEN

"Here's What Happened"
Writing a Narrative

"**So, tell me what happened.**" Anytime we ask someone about an incident at work or an event at school, we are asking for a narrative. Narratives are stories, and they are fundamental parts of our everyday lives. When we tell someone about a movie we've seen or a basketball game we played in, we often use narrative. When we want someone to understand something that we did, we might tell a story that explains our actions. When we post to *Instagram*, we often use photos and text to share something we've just done or seen.

If you wrote an essay as part of your college applications, chances are that you were required to write a narrative. Here, for instance, are instructions from two colleges' applications:

> The lessons we take from obstacles we encounter can be fundamental to later success. Recount a time when you faced a challenge, setback, or failure. How did it affect you, and what did you learn from the experience?
>
> —SPELMAN COLLEGE

> Describe an example of your leadership experience in which you have positively influenced others, helped resolve disputes or contributed to group efforts over time.
>
> —UNIVERSITY OF CALIFORNIA SYSTEM

Each of these prompts asks applicants to write a narrative about some aspect of their lives. In each case they need to do more than just tell a good story; they need to make a clear point about why it matters.

Narrative is a powerful way to get an audience's attention. Telling a good story can even help establish your authority as a writer. Take a look, for example, at the opening to Lynda Barry's narrative of a childhood experience in her essay "The Sanctuary of School":

> I was 7 years old the first time I snuck out of the house in the dark. It was winter and my parents had been fighting all night. They were short on money and long on relatives who kept "temporarily" moving into our house because they had nowhere else to go.

You can read Linda Barry's full essay on p. 849.

That grabbed your attention, didn't it? You want to keep reading, to know what happened to that child, where she went, what she did outside in the winter dark. (Spoiler alert: she went to her school, where she always felt safe. And she grew up to become an award-winning author and cartoonist.)

Images, too, can tell stories. What are the kids in the picture on the next page doing? Might they be trick or treating at the doorstep of a very tall neighbor? That's *almost* believable, but we know better. They're watching a solar eclipse, as did millions of others across parts of Canada, the United States, and Mexico in the spring of 2024. Paper plates have been affixed to their protective glasses to help hold them in place and ensure that no damaging rays reach their eyes (pretty good idea, right?). We can see the kids' expressions of rapt wonder even though most of their faces are hidden from view. Their mouths, their hands, their postures—all those details communicate the awe and joy of the moment.

Think about some of the powerful personal narratives you've read, perhaps the *Narrative of the Life of Frederick Douglass* or Anne Frank's *Diary of a Young Girl*. We could, of course, read about their lives on *Wikipedia*, but a good narrative provides more than just the facts; it gives us a well-told story that captures not only our attention but also our imagination.

15 　 Writing a Narrative

Pictures can tell stories. Here, kids watch a solar eclipse.

So what exactly is a narrative? For our purposes, narrative is a kind of writing that presents events in some kind of time sequence with a distinct beginning, middle, and ending (but not necessarily in strict chronological order) and that is written for the purpose of making a point. That is, to write a narrative it is not enough to simply report a sequence of events ("this happened, then that happened"), which is often what children do when they tell stories. Narrative essays, especially in college, are meaningful ways of making sense of our experiences, of what goes on around us—and of illustrating a point, making an argument, or writing about the lives of others.

REFLECT

Think about some stories that are told in your favorite songs or music videos, that you hear in sermons, or that your older relative tells. Make a list of the stories that you hear, read, see, or tell in one day and the subjects of those stories. You'll begin to see how narratives are an important way that we communicate with each other.

Across Academic Disciplines

The narrative essay is a common assignment in the humanities and increasingly in other academic fields as well. In a composition class, you may be asked to write a literacy narrative about early memories of reading or writing, or a personal narrative about an important person or experience in your life. In a history class, you may be asked to take data from archives and construct a narrative about a particular historical event. (Some think that historians focus on dates and facts about incidents from the past, but actually they are generally piecing together narratives that provide a context for interpreting what those dates and facts mean.) In medicine, patient accounts and medical histories play a key role in diagnosis and treatment. In the sciences, lab reports tell the story of how researchers conducted an experiment and interpreted the data they collected. Since narratives take different forms across disciplines, one challenge you'll face will be to determine which narrative elements are valued or even required in a particular situation.

↪ Visit the Digital Archive of Literacy Narratives (thedaln.org), a site sponsored by Ohio State and Georgia State where you can read literacy narratives as well as post your own.

Across Media

The medium you use makes a big difference in the way you tell a story. Video, for example, presents a wide range of possibilities. *TikTok* is full of mini-stories told through video in a variety of ways, and anyone can participate. In TV broadcasts of football games, for example, commentators review plays in slow motion or diagram them on the screen to give viewers a more complete picture of what's happening on the field. The fast pace of basketball games presents a challenge for play-by-play announcers, whose descriptions must race along to keep up with the ball. Even a still photo, however, can catch a split-second narrative, like the one on the next page: two Spartans, two Badgers, four faces intent and focused, five hands stretched and tangled reaching for one ball, all in a tiny but packed moment of drama. The same story would be told differently in print, through video, or using a combination of media to describe the game play.

So when you're writing a narrative, you'll want to think about what media will best suit your audience and purpose. But you won't always have a choice. If you're assigned to work in a specific medium, think about whether a narrative would help get your message across. Well-told stories are a good way to engage your audience's attention in an oral presentation, for instance, and to help them remember what you say.

Several players compete for a rebound during a Wisconsin vs. Michigan State game.

REFLECT

Compare narratives in different media. From the many kinds of narratives you encounter in one day—in books or magazines, on *YouTube* and *TikTok* or in video games, in textbooks or conversations with friends—choose two narratives on the same topic from different media that you find most interesting. Think about the similarities and differences between the ways the two stories are told. What would change about each narrative if it were presented in a different medium?

Across Cultures and Communities

What makes a good story often depends on who's telling the story and who's listening. Not only is that the case for individuals, but different communities and cultures also tell stories in unique ways and value particular things in them.

Many Native American tribes consider narrative an important tradition and art form, so much so that storytellers hold a place of honor. In much of West Africa, the griots are the official storytellers, entrusted with telling the history of a village or town through recitation and song. And in many Appalachian communities, storytelling functions as a way to pass down family and community history. As in West Africa, good storytellers enjoy high status in Appalachia.

In many cultures and communities, stories are the way that history is passed down from generation to generation. Think about the ways that family histories are passed down in your family or community—through oral stories? photo albums? home videos?

Precisely because stories provide a strong foundation for history and for belief systems, it's worth adding a caution here about what author Chimamanda Ngozi Adichie calls "the danger of a single story." When one story is told about a people or a place, it tends to become *the* story. As Adichie points out, "The single story creates stereotypes. And the problem with stereotypes is not that they are untrue, but that they are incomplete. They make one story become the only story." As a writer, you'll want to make sure that the story you tell isn't simply a variation of "the single story."

Watch Adichie's TED talk in which she warns against the danger of a single story by visiting everyonesanauthor.tumblr.com.

THINK BEYOND WORDS

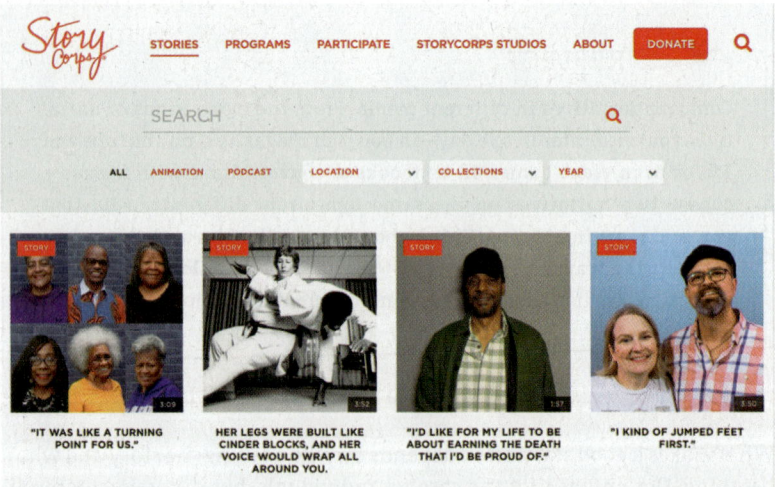

GO TO storycorps.org, the online home of StoryCorps, an archive containing hundreds of short narratives told by ordinary people about memorable events or people in their lives. Listen to a few of the narratives that draw your attention. Which one do you find most powerful, and why? How much of the narrative's effectiveness is due to its content and how much to how it's told?

Across Genres

Narrative is often a useful strategy for writers working in other genres. For example, in an essay **ARGUING A POSITION**, you may use a narrative example to prove a point. In a **REVIEW** of a film, in which evaluation is the main purpose, you may need to tell a brief story from the plot to demonstrate how the film meets (or does not meet) a specific evaluative criterion. These are only two of the many ways in which narrative can be used as part of a text.

CHARACTERISTIC FEATURES

There is no one way to tell a story. Most written narratives, however, have a number of common features, revolving around the following characteristics and questions:

- A clearly identified event: What happened? Who was involved? (p. 221)
- A clearly described setting: When and where did it happen? (p. 222)
- Vivid, descriptive details: What makes the story come alive? (p. 223)
- A consistent point of view: Who's telling the story? (p. 225)
- A clear point: Why does the story matter? (p. 227)

A Clearly Identified Event: What Happened? Who Was Involved?

Narratives are based on an event or series of events, presented in a way that makes audiences want to know how the story will turn out. Consider this paragraph by Mike Rose, in which he narrates how he, as a marginal high school student with potential, got into college with the help of his senior-year English teacher, Jack MacFarland:

> My grades stank. I had A's in biology and a handful of B's in a few English and social science classes. All the rest were C's—or worse. MacFarland said I would do well in his class and laid down the law about doing well in others. Still the record for my first three years wouldn't have been

acceptable to any four-year school. To nobody's surprise, I was turned down flat by USC and UCLA. But Jack MacFarland was on the case. He had received his bachelor's degree from Loyola, so he made calls to old professors and talked to somebody in admissions and wrote me a strong letter. Loyola finally accepted me as a probationary student. I would be on trial for the first year, and if I did okay, I would be granted regular status. MacFarland also intervened to get me a loan, for I could never have afforded a private college without it. Four more years of religion classes and four more years of boys at one school, girls at another. But at least I was going to college. Amazing.

—MIKE ROSE, *Lives on the Boundary*

It's not the actual facts that make this narrative worth reading; rather, it's the way the facts are presented—in other words, the way the story is told.

The narrator grabs our attention with his first sentence ("My grades stank"), then lays out the challenges he faced ("turned down flat by USC and UCLA"), and ends with a flourish ("Amazing"). He could have told us what happened much more briefly—but then it would have been just a sequence of facts; instead, he told us a story. As the author of a narrative, you'll want to be sure to get the facts down, but that won't be enough. Your challenge will be to tell about "what happens" in a way that gets your audience's attention and makes them care enough to keep on reading.

A Clearly Described Setting: When and Where Did It Happen?

Narratives need to be situated clearly within time and space in order for readers to understand what's going on. For that reason, you will generally arrange your story in **CHRONOLOGICAL ORDER** starting at the beginning and moving straight ahead to the end. There are times, though, when you may choose to present a narrative in reverse chronological order, starting at the end and looking back at the events that led up to it—or with a flashback or flash-forward that jumps back to the past or ahead to the future. Whether you tell your story in chronological order or not, the sequence of events needs to be clear to your audience.

Also important is that your audience get a clear idea of the place(s) where the events occur. Time and space work together to create a scene that your audience can visualize and follow, as they do in the following example

15 ✏️ Writing a Narrative

from student Minh Vu's essay "Dirty Nails," which documents growing up in his family's nail salon.

> I was born in my family's nail salon. It was in the waxing room, and my first swaddle was made up of giant waxing strips. Normally, they're used to tear the hair off people. For me, they were warmth and protection.
>
> I was raised within glass doors kept shiny with diluted Windex, among towering boxes of acetone, and atop giant pedicure thrones. Such was my childhood kingdom. Alphabet blocks were replaced by white Arial stickers I used to spell out "JEL MANICURE" and "BIKIKNEE WAX" on the price board. Instead of bicycles I rode bumper cars with the pedicure stools. And the rest of my time I spent trying to fit my toddler toes into the pastel foot separators that looked like mini combs. . . . The pallor of peeling plaster was rolled over with a deep textured azure, like the ocean [my grandma] immigrated across in the 1970s. Dim overhead lights were torn down and replaced with a crystal chandelier that, albeit fake, brought illumination in a time of immigrant loneliness. And red leather diner stools from the space's past life were refurbished into sleek manicure chairs.
>
> The nail salon was my world. It was where all of life existed.
>
> —MINH VU, "Dirty Nails"

Minh Vu establishes the setting by providing vivid, descriptive language of the nail salon that makes up the center of his story. His first statement—"I was born in my family's nail salon"—establishes the setting of the story, but it's the details that come after that that paint a picture for readers: "giant pedicure thrones" and "pastel foot separators." These details help readers, especially those who have been to nail salons, visualize where and how the writer grew up.

Vivid, Descriptive Details: What Makes the Story Come Alive?

You may remember English teachers telling you that good writers "show rather than tell." It's an old adage that applies to narratives in particular. Vivid, descriptive detail makes the people, places, and events in a narrative come alive for an audience, helping them see, hear, smell, taste, and feel "what happened." In the following example from a 2024 essay published on the *Bitter Southerner* website, author Kiese Laymon evokes the sights, sounds, smells, and sense of well-being of a summer evening in childhood spent with his grandmama and her boyfriend.

> They'd sit in the front cab of a raggedy Ford listening to a Tina Turner tape. I'd sit in the back, next to burnt orange pine needles, a few broken lawnmowers, and all forms of rust. Friday nights smelled like dead chickens, piney woods, browning water, burning yard, and the insecticide that the mosquito man sprayed over every mile of Forest. . . . I have no idea what I wore any of those Friday nights. I just knew that there was no more regal way to move through space in Forest, Mississippi, at 8 years old, no matter how you were dressed, than the back of a pickup truck near dusk.
> —KIESE LAYMON, "My Favorite Restaurant Served Gas"

Read Kiese Laymon's full essay on p. 946.

The narrative offers a sensory-rich serving of vivid details—the colors of the pine needles, the ambient aromas, the music of Tina Turner, the fading light of dusk. "A few broken lawnmowers" is specific, and yet the image leaves plenty of room for readers' own imaginations. Are they push mowers? Gas powered? Are they intact or dismantled? We don't really need to know; just that short phrase is enough. Laymon's mention of his age offers a wealth

A pickup truck parked on a sleepy small town Main Street.

of information in few words, and it invites readers to remember their own childhood summers.

Think about how much detail and what kind of detail your narrative needs to "come to life" for your audience. Remember that you are likely writing for readers (or listeners) unfamiliar with the story you are telling. That means that you need to choose details that help them get a vivid picture of the setting, people, and events in the narrative. When deciding whether to include direct quotations or dialogue, ask yourself if doing so would paint a scene or create a mood more effectively than a summary would.

A Consistent Point of View: Who's Telling the Story?

A good narrative is generally told from one consistent point of view. If you are writing about something that happened to you, then your narrative should be written from the first-person point of view (I, we). First person puts the focus on the narrator, as Georgina Kleege does in the following example, which recounts the opening moments of one of her classes:

> I tell the class, "I am legally blind." There is a pause, a collective intake of breath. I feel them look away uncertainly and then look back. After all, I just said I couldn't see. Or did I? I had managed to get there on my own—no cane, no dog, none of the usual trappings of blindness. Eyeing me askance now, they might detect that my gaze is not quite focused. My eyes are aimed in the right direction but the gaze seems to stop short of touching anything. But other people do this, sighted people, normal people, especially in an awkward situation like this one, the first day of class. An actress who delivers an aside to the audience, breaking the "fourth wall" of the proscenium, will aim her gaze somewhere above any particular pair of eyes. If I hadn't said anything, my audience might understand my gaze to be like that, a part of the performance. In these few seconds between sentences, their gaze becomes intent. They watch me glance down, or toward the door where someone's coming in late. I'm just like anyone else. Then what did I actually mean by "legally blind"? They wait. I go on, "Some people would call me 'visually challenged.'" There is a ripple of laughter, an exhalation of relief. I'm making a joke about it. I'm poking fun at something they too find aggravating, the current mania to stick a verbal smiley-face on any human condition which deviates from the status quo. Differently abled. Handicapable. If I ask, I'm sure

> some of them can tell jokes about it: "Don't say 'bald,' say 'follicularly challenged.'" "He's not dead, he's metabolically stable." Knowing they are at least thinking these things, I conclude, "These are just silly ways of saying I don't see very well."
>
> —GEORGINA KLEEGE, "Call It Blindness"

Notice how the first-person point of view—and the repetition of "I"—keeps our attention focused on Kleege. Like the students in her class, we are looking right at her.

If your narrative is about someone else's experience or about events that you have researched but did not witness, then the narrative should probably be written in third person (he, she, they, it). Unlike a first-person narrative, a third-person narrative emphasizes someone or something other than the narrator. Historical and medical narratives are usually written in third person, as are newswriting and sportswriting. Look at the following description of a play by tennis star Roger Federer:

> The ball comes toward Federer and, as he sees it, his body is suddenly in the air, turning effortlessly, his arms unfurling like two waves moving in opposite directions, and he hits his one-handed backhand. As he extends through the shot, his chest opens wide and his arms keep reaching, away, and the movement ripples down through his fingers, which are so relaxed that they look weightless, fluttering briefly in the breeze, and it is beautiful so beautiful.
>
> —CHLOÉ COOPER JONES, "Champion Moves"

Notice how Jones's narration puts the action in slow motion, allowing readers to notice every detail of the motion of Federer's body—arms, chest, fingers.

Compare the points of view of Georgina Kleege's first-person narrative and Chloé Cooper Jones's third-person one. Notice that there is one consistent point of view in each example. As an author, you will have to determine whether your narrative is most effective told from the first-person or third-person point of view. No matter what you may have been taught in high school, the first person is acceptable in many (though not all) academic contexts. Whatever point of view you use, however, do so consistently. That is, if you refer to yourself in the narrative, do not switch between first (I, we) and third (he, she, they) person. (Rarely is a narrative told from a second-person—"you"—point of view.)

Roger Federer stretches to make a one-handed backhand at the Australian Open.

Part of maintaining a consistent point of view is establishing a clear time frame. Notice Chloé Cooper Jones's use of present-tense verbs in the example about Federer. By consistently narrating the actions in the present tense, Jones places the reader in the moment of the story being told. Using a consistent verb tense situates the actions of the event within a clear time frame.

A clear time frame does not mean that every verb in the narrative has to be in the same tense, only that the writer establishes one primary tense—usually present or past—for the main action of the story. In the example by Mike Rose on page 972, most of the verbs are in the past tense: "said," "made," "talked." But other tenses are used to indicate events that, in relation to the main action of the narrative, occurred earlier ("He had received his bachelor's degree from Loyola") or might occur later ("I would be granted regular status").

A Clear Point: Why Does the Story Matter?

Good narratives tell stories that matter. In academic writing in particular, narratives are told to make a point. Whether they begin by stating the point explicitly in a thesis or build toward a point that is expressed at the end, the

> See how Zeynep Tufekci's personal narrative gives an ordinary trip to the post office a whole new perspective on p. 989.

purpose of the narrative needs to be clear to the audience. Nothing irritates an audience more than reading or listening to a story that has no point. Even if a story is interesting or entertaining, it will most likely be deemed a failure in an academic context if it does not make clear why the events matter. Consider how the late author and English professor bell hooks makes a point about learning to value work:

> "Work makes life sweet!" I often heard this phrase growing up, mainly from old black folks who did not have jobs in the traditional sense of the word. They were usually self-employed, living off the land, selling fishing worms, picking up an odd job here and there. They were people who had a passion for work. They took pride in a job done well. My Aunt Margaret took in ironing. Folks brought her clothes from miles around because she was such an expert. That was in the days when using starch was common and she knew how to do an excellent job. Watching her iron with skill and grace was like watching a ballerina dance. Like all the other black girls raised in the fifties that I knew, it was clear to me that I would be a working woman. Even though our mother stayed home, raising her seven children, we saw her constantly at work, washing, ironing, cleaning, and cooking (she was an incredible cook). And she never allowed her six girls to imagine we would not be working women. No, she let us know that we would work and be proud to work.
>
> —BELL HOOKS, "Work Makes Life Sweet"

Professor hooks opens with her main point, that "work makes life sweet!" In the sentences that follow, she explains how she learned this lesson from "old black folks who did not have jobs in the traditional sense." Through specific examples, she illustrates how they "took pride in a job done well" and passed on this pride in their work to hooks and her sisters. The explicit restatement of the point in the final sentence—that hooks and her six sisters learned from their mother that they would "work and be proud to work"—recasts the notion of "working woman" in a unique and engaging way.

In contrast to bell hooks, author and activist Roxane Gay, in a speech to publishers, withholds her main point even after announcing to the audience that she had anticipated what topic she would be asked to address:

> When I received the invitation to speak at Winter Institute, I knew, even before I got the details, that I would be asked to talk about diversity in some form or fashion. This is the state of most industries,

and particularly contemporary publishing. People of color are not asked about our areas of expertise as if the only thing we are allowed to be experts on is our marginalization. We are asked about how white people can do better and feel better about diversity or the lack thereof. We are asked to offer "good" white people who "mean well" absolution from the ills of racism.

—ROXANE GAY, speech to *Publishers Weekly*'s Winter Institute, 2017

Rather than announcing her main point right away, Gay provides a bit of context on the word "diversity," including the current state of discussions about diversity. After giving this background and making a bold admission, she *then* states her main point:

> The word diversity has of late become so overused as to be meaningless. In a 2015 article for *The New York Times Magazine*, Anna Holmes wrote about the dilution of the word diversity, attributing its loss of meaning to "a combination of overuse, imprecision, inertia, and self-serving intentions."
>
> The word diversity is, in its most imprecise uses, a placeholder for issues of inclusion, recruitment, retention and representation. Diversity is a problem, seemingly without solutions. We talk about it and talk about it and talk about it and nothing much ever seems to change. And here we are today, talking about diversity yet again.
>
> I am so very tired of talking about diversity.
>
> Publishing has a diversity problem. This problem extends to absolutely every area of the industry. I mean, look at this room, where I can literally count the number of people of color among some 700 booksellers. There are not enough writers of color being published. When our books are published, we fight, even more than white writers, for publicity and reviews. People of color are underrepresented editorially, in book marketing, publicity, and as literary agents. People of color are underrepresented in bookselling. On and on it goes.

Gay states her main point—"Publishing has a diversity problem"—and provides further clarification and evidence of the problem. She makes the main point even more visible by focusing on the lack of diversity in the audience. In contrast to hooks, Gay moves more slowly toward her main point, describing her reaction to both the speaking invitation and the topic she was asked to cover before offering her main message outright: "People of color are underrepresented in bookselling."

As an author, don't assume that your readers will recognize the point you're trying to make. No matter how interesting you think your story is, they need to know why they should care. Why is the story important? State your main point as bell hooks and Roxane Gay do.

 **REFLECT**

Look at a narrative in a newspaper or magazine article or on a blog or other website to see what main point it makes and how it does so. Is the main point explicitly stated in a thesis, or is it only implied? Does the narrative make clear to readers why the story is important or why they should care about it?

LITERACY NARRATIVES

Literacy narratives focus on meaningful experiences involving some kind of reading or writing: stories, music, computer code, learning a foreign language, and so on. The focus on learning and literacy makes this sort of narrative a common assignment in first-year writing classes. Professional writers also use the genre to reflect on their craft. Literacy narratives can serve various purposes, but they generally have the following characteristic features.

A Well-Told Story

Whether you're writing about the joys or struggles (or both) of learning to do something or why you've always loved a certain book or song, there are some tried-and-true storytelling techniques that can help your literacy narrative interest readers. If you write about something you struggled to learn, for instance, readers will want to know how your struggle turned out, how the story ends. And whatever your topic, make sure your narrative has a clear arc, from a beginning that engages your audience to a conclusion that leaves them understanding why the experience you wrote about matters to you.

A Firsthand Account, Often (but Not Always) about Yourself

You'll want to write about an experience that you know firsthand, not one that you've only read about. Writing about your own experience is the most common way of achieving this close perspective, but you may also reflect on the experiences of others. Perhaps you've observed or had a hand in helping someone else learn to read or write and are able to speak about it firsthand. This, too, could be a productive topic for a literacy narrative.

An Indication of the Narrative's Significance

Readers quickly lose patience with stories that seem to have no point, so you need to make clear what significance your narrative has for those involved. Sometimes you may have an explicit THESIS that makes the point clear from the start; other times, you may prefer to let the narrative play out before explaining its significance.

See an annotated model literacy narrative on page 249.

WRITING A NARRATIVE / A Roadmap

Choose a topic that matters—to you, and to others

Whether you write a narrative for personal reasons or in response to an assignment, choose your own topic or work with an assigned topic, try to write about something that matters to you—and try to make sure that it will matter to your audience as well.

See the ebook for a video on generating ideas for a literacy narrative.

If you are writing a personal narrative, choosing a topic can be difficult. You will need to choose an experience or event that you feel comfortable sharing, in some detail, with an audience. Be sure that the experience is not only important to you but also of enough general interest to engage your audience.

If your narrative is not a personal one, you still want it to be compelling. Narratives that aren't personal are often part of a larger conversation about an event, or some topic that the event represents, which gives the story significance. For example, if you are writing a narrative about how specific students' academic performances changed when their school began participating in a school lunch program, you need to recognize that such stories are part of an ongoing educational and political debate about the effectiveness and public benefit of such programs. You may need to do some research to understand this debate and how your narrative fits into it.

Consider your rhetorical situation

Whenever you write a narrative (or anything, for that matter), you need to consider the following elements of your rhetorical situation:

Think about your AUDIENCE. Who will be reading what you write, and what's your relationship with them?

- Will your audience have any knowledge about your topic? Will you need to explain anything or provide any background information?

- How are they like or unlike you? Consider age, gender, income, cultural heritage, political beliefs, and so on. How will such factors affect how you tell the story?

- Can you assume they'll be interested in what you write? How can you get them interested?

- How are they likely to react to your narrative? What do you want them to think or do as a result of reading what you say?

Think about your PURPOSE. Why are you writing this narrative? What is the significance of this story, and what do you hope it will demonstrate to your readers? Remember that your narrative needs to do more than just tell an engaging story; it needs to make a point of some kind.

Think about your STANCE. Are you telling a story that is very personal to you, or is it one you have some distance from? How do you want to present yourself as the narrator? Do you want to come across as witty and amusing, if you're telling a humorous family story? as knowledgeable but impersonal, if you're recounting historical events for a political science essay? Whatever your stance, how can you make your writing reflect that stance?

Consider your LANGUAGE. Almost everything can be said in a variety of ways. Regardless of how many dialects or languages you use in your everyday life, you have many options for your narrative. Will your audience expect a certain kind of language or style? Do you want to meet those expectations? challenge them? What do you want your language to say about you? What risks might you be willing to take with your language? How will the medium and larger context limit or expand the language options that are available to you? (You may want to consult Chapters 4 and 35 for more advice about language options.)

Consider the larger CONTEXT. What broader issues are involved in your narrative? What else has been said and written about this topic? Even if your narrative is personal, how might it speak to some larger topic—perhaps a social or political one? Considering the larger context for your narrative can help you see it from perspectives different from your own and present it in a way that will interest others.

Consider your MEDIUM. If you have a choice, think about which medium best suits your goals and audience. The kinds of details you include, the language you use, the way you present materials from sources, and many other things depend on the medium. The conventions of a print essay, for instance, in which you can use written words and images, differ markedly from those of an audio essay (in which you can use sounds but no written words or images).

Consider matters of DESIGN. Does your narrative need headings? Is there anything in the story that could be conveyed better with a photograph than with words alone? Will embedded audio or video clips help you engage your audience? Often in academic writing, you may have to conform to a specific design format. If you can determine the look of your text, though, remember that design has a powerful impact on the impression your narrative makes.

Explore your topic and do any necessary research

If you are writing a personal narrative, write down all that you remember about your topic. Using FREEWRITING or other activities for GENERATING IDEAS, write down as many specific details as you can: sounds, smells, textures, colors, and so on. What details will engage your audience? Not all the details that you jot down in this exploratory stage will make it into your essay. You'll need to choose the ones that will engage your audience and support your main point. In addition to sensory details, try to write down direct quotations or dialogue you can remember that will help bring your story to life.

If your narrative is not a personal one, you'll likely need to conduct RESEARCH so that you can provide accurate and sufficient details about the topic. Whether your research takes you to sources in the library or online, or into the community to conduct interviews, it's important to get the what, when, and where of the narrative right, and consulting sources will help you do that.

Decide on a point of view

The subject that you choose to write about will usually determine the point of view from which you write. If you're telling a story in which you are a central participant, you will usually use the first person (I, we). In some academic disciplines, however, or if you're narrating a story that is not personal, the third person (he, she, they) may work better.

Also think about what verb tense would be most effective for establishing the point of view in your narrative. Most personal narratives that are arranged in chronological order are written in the past tense ("When I was twelve, I discovered what I wanted to do for the rest of my life"). However, if you want readers to feel like they are actually experiencing an event, you may choose to use the present tense, as Georgina Kleege and Chloé Cooper Jones do in examples earlier in this chapter.

Organize and start writing

Once you've chosen a subject and identified your main point, considered your rhetorical situation, come up with enough details, and decided on a point of view (not necessarily in this order), it's time to think about how to organize your narrative.

Keep your main point in mind. As you begin to draft, type out that point as a tentative THESIS and keep your eye on it as you write; you can decide later whether you want to include it in your text.

Organize your information. What happened? Where? When? Who was there? What details can you describe to make the story come alive? Decide whether to present the narrative in CHRONOLOGICAL ORDER, in reverse chronological order, or in some other order.

Draft an OPENING. A good introduction draws your audience into the story and makes them want to know more. Sometimes you'll need to provide a context for your narrative—to describe the setting and introduce some of the people before getting on with what happened. Other times you might start in the middle of your story, or at the end—and then circle back to tell what happened.

Draft a CONCLUSION. However you organize your narrative, make sure your readers see the point of your story; if you haven't made that clear, you might end by saying something about the story's significance. Why does it matter to you? What do you want readers to take away—and remember?

Look critically at your draft, get responses—and revise

Read your draft slowly and carefully. Try to see it as if for the first time: Does the story grab your attention, and can you follow it? Can you tell what the point is, and will your audience care? If possible, get feedback from others. Following are some questions that can help you or others examine a narrative with a critical eye:

- *How does the* OPENING *capture the audience's interest?* Is it clear why you're telling the story, and have you given readers reason to want to find out what happened? How else might the narrative begin?

- *Who's telling the story?* Have you maintained a consistent POINT OF VIEW?

- *Is the setting of your story clear?* Have you situated the events in a well-described time and place?

- *Is the story easy to follow?* If it's at all confusing, would TRANSITIONS help your audience follow the sequence of events? If it's a lengthy or complex narrative, would headings help?

- *Are there enough vivid, concrete details?* Is there a good balance of showing and telling? Have you included any dialogue or direct quotations—and if not, would adding some help the story come alive?

- *Are there any visuals?* If not, would adding some help bring the narrative to life?

- *How do you establish* AUTHORITY *and credibility?* How would you describe the STANCE and TONE? Do they reflect your purpose and appeal to your audience?

- *Does the story have a clear point?* Is the point stated explicitly—and if not, should it be? If the main point is implied rather than stated, is the significance of the narrative still clear?

- *How satisfying is the* CONCLUSION*?* What does it leave the audience thinking? How else might the narrative end?

- *Does the title suggest what the narrative is about,* and will it make an audience want to read on?

Revise your draft in light of any feedback you receive and your own critique, keeping your purpose and especially your audience firmly in mind.

> 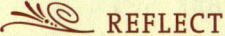 **REFLECT**
>
> Once you've completed your narrative, let it settle for a while and then take time to **REFLECT**. How well did you tell the story? What additional revisions would you make if you could? Research shows that such reflections help "lock in" what you learn for future use.

READINGS / Annotated Model Narratives

At the VA, Healing the Doctor-Patient Relationship

RAYA ELFADEL KHEIRBEK

THE MAN'S VOICE over the phone was angry: "The VA provides terrible care!" I had promised the Veterans Affairs (VA) Medical Center's Patient Advocate office that I would connect with the man, Mr. Davis, who had called three times before to complain about his care. I was warned beforehand that he was displeased, to say the least.

With him on the line, I took a deep breath and began to look up his records. "I am sorry to hear this, Mr. Davis," I said. "Would you please tell me specifically what is bothering you? I am covering for your doctor and will do my best to help."

Mr. Davis needed to have an MRI for his right shoulder, as was recommended by his military doctor before he separated from the service. He also was having back pain and wasn't exercising enough. He had gained twenty pounds in six months and asked if we offered liposuction.

RAYA ELFADEL KHEIRBEK is a professor at the University of Maryland School of Medicine in Baltimore, Maryland. She has served in several roles within the Department of Veterans Affairs. This 2017 essay was originally published in *Health Affairs*, an American journal about national and global health policy and research issues.

He had met his primary care clinician, Dr. Kumar, for the first time a couple of weeks earlier and was very uncomfortable when he saw her. To him, there was great insensitivity in the VA's decision to assign him a doctor who he believed was originally from the Middle East.

"Those people wanted to kill me," he remarked to me on the phone, "and I do not appreciate having a doctor who is one of them."

"If you had a woman who was subjected to repeated rape, would you let her be examined by a male doctor?" he continued.

I knew that our policy would allow him to switch doctors, but I had no idea what to say. I had been practicing medicine for a couple of decades and naturally had encountered many types of unusual behavior. Yet I had never heard this type of comment from a patient. I composed myself and quietly explained to Mr. Davis that Dr. Kumar's family came from India. Dr. Kumar herself was born and raised in Pennsylvania and had no connection to the Middle East whatsoever.

But Mr. Davis was insistent on having a doctor who looked like him.

And he was angry.

"I am not your typical patient," he fired back. "I am smart, educated, and highly trained. I do not need your opinion. I have lived in my body for three decades. I know what I want, and your job is to deliver."

I told him that I wanted to meet with him to help resolve these issues and blocked off an hour the following week to meet during my administrative time. He was excited that I would be able to see him quickly, given what he referred to as the long wait time to get an appointment in the VA. He added that, based on our conversation, I seemed to be a good doctor.

While I was determined to meet and help Mr. Davis, a potential challenge loomed. I am of Middle Eastern origin. I wondered if I should reveal this information after coordinating his care and give him another opportunity to seek a different clinician. My colleagues advised me to stand tall and not give him that choice. To them, his views represented bigotry.

Yet Mr. Davis was not the only one struggling with the past. For me, encountering Mr. Davis brought back painful memories and forced me to stop and reflect on my years of service in the VA, my belief system, and my biases. I wondered if his "bigotry" was really so alien to the human nature in us all.

A Veterans Affairs health-care center in Phoenix, Arizona—similar to the one where Mr. Davis and Dr. Kheirbek met.

An Occupational Hazard

As a primary care physician working in the VA, I have heard countless stories from soldiers reliving their experiences in war zones. As an Arab American immigrant, I had followed the Iraqi war and—later—the promising start of the Arab Spring and then watched them both spiral into the chaos of death and destruction, including a civil war in my native country, Syria. I felt privileged to be a physician and an American, especially as violence took hold overseas. I could have been back home, along with everyone I worried about. I could be dead. Feeling powerless, I forced myself to watch and listen to the news. The least I could do was to be aware.

Details about the author's experience move the story along.

Meeting Mr. Davis

I introduced myself to Mr. Davis on a Tuesday in March 2017, less than a week after our initial phone conversation. A white man in his early thirties, he was tall and well-built, with a rectangular face; a defined, slightly pointed

Reestablishing the timeline makes the progression of events clear.

chin; and a sturdy jaw line. He had light brown hair, small blue eyes, and a straight nose. The jacket he wore over his broad shoulders had neatly polished buttons and was slightly frayed in places. Part of his right hand was missing. He glanced at me with a smile. I am a white woman with green eyes and brown hair.

"I am very happy you were able to make it to this meeting," I said with a big smile.

He nodded in silence and avoided making eye contact.

"I had a chance to review your chart. I think I can help with your physical needs," I added. "But I am also suspecting there are mental health issues that might need to be addressed."

Given his sentiments about Middle Eastern doctors, I thought he had a plausible PTSD diagnosis. When I began to suggest as much, he cut me off.

"This is all stereotyping," he asserted. "I did what I was supposed to do. I will heal through going back to work and being productive."

I caught him looking at my name badge.

"I understand," I said. "Thank you for clarifying."

I asked how he had ended up in the military. He said he'd signed up simply because college was "so damn expensive." He was not a "military brat" and didn't enlist out of a sense of obligation. He was not angry or in need of some form of revenge. It's not that he felt enlisting was brave or important.

Mr. Davis had been in three combat deployments—Iraq in 2010 and Afghanistan in 2011 and 2013—as a member of the US Army Special Forces. He'd been involved in multiple close-range blasts, traumatic jumps, and firefights. Many of the people he had served with had been killed. Since his return to the United States, he had been having constant pain in his right shoulder. He had nightmares one or two times a week, and recently they'd become more frequent.

"What kept you going during all the deployments?" I asked.

"I closed my eyes while hiding from fire and remembered family trips skiing with my little sister and laughing on the slopes of Jackson Hole." He looked up and smiled. I saw a glimpse of the little boy in his face and knew he was in pain. I wanted to reach out and touch his hand, but I was afraid he would not welcome my gesture.

VIVID DETAILS paint a picture of Mr. Davis's physical appearance.

DIALOGUE makes us feel as if we're witnessing the conversation.

Details establish the intensity of Mr. Davis's combat experiences.

A TURNING POINT signals the growing bond between doctor and patient.

I asked if he'd had any good experiences in Iraq. Yes, he said. It touched him to see families with young children walking for many miles to collect American parachutes to help build houses. The local people found something useful to do with even the trash that Americans had left. All his memories, however, were haunted by the killings he had witnessed and the poverty of the places he had been.

I felt it was then time to address his comments about Dr. Kumar. I said: "You know, Mr. Davis, you are a man of tremendous courage. It is not easy to share your experiences with someone else, especially experiences of this nature."

He looked out the window.

"You mentioned to me in our phone conversation last week that you were uncomfortable with a doctor from the Middle East."

I paused, then continued. "I want you to be comfortable, and I am very happy we met today. I want to thank you for allowing me into your life and for the opportunity to help. I owe to you the knowledge that I was born and raised in Syria."

The few seconds of silence that ensued felt like an eternity.

Then Mr. Davis abruptly got to his feet and raised his severed hand. "I am so sorry I was being a jerk. I would really like you to be my physician—unless you do not feel comfortable caring for me, based on my earlier comments."

I stood up and extended my hand to him. "It was important for us to talk. Please keep doing so, as it's the only way for us to deal with such emotions."

His face broke out into a wide smile. He was absolutely thrilled at the prospect of us working together. I was, too.

Healing Takes Time

Though I have served in the VA for many years and in different roles, my focus has always been on patients. The sacred time spent with patients in an exam room is the only lasting truth in medicine. In this large bureaucratic system, all else can wait. Yet many priorities compete for our attention during a single visit. It might not be possible to spend the needed time on each important issue. While a slew of mandatory screenings for diseases has improved our medical care, it is equally crucial to take the time to develop a relationship with the patient, exploring his or her service history and the lived experiences that may come with that. It is not always easy. In my work, I know what it is like to be discriminated against, and what it is like to have stereotypes of my own. Yet an admission of our own vulnerability and opening the door to a conversation about self-care, compassion, understanding, and human connection is how we attend to all aspects of our patients' suffering—and perhaps some of our own.

 REFLECT & WRITE

Analyze a short nonfiction narrative that you find in a magazine or on a website. Look at the list of five characteristic features of narratives on page 221 and annotate the essay to point out these features, using Kheirbek's essay as a model. Then look at your annotations and the parts of the text they refer to and evaluate how well your chosen narrative illustrates the characteristic features. For example, is the setting clearly described? How vivid are the details?

It'll Grow Back. It Always Does.

ANGELINA X. NG

> *A dramatic opening gives important* CONTEXT *information—when, where, who, what, how—and leaves us wanting to know the why.*

O NE SATURDAY IN NINTH GRADE, I sat on the stage of a shopping mall in Singapore as a man I didn't know stood behind me—electric razor buzzing—ready to shave all my hair off. In front of me, a motley assortment of friends, family, and strangers cheered, their phones clicking away. I kept a smile plastered on my face, even though I was quickly realizing what a colossal mistake I had made.

> *Signals a shift in time to an earlier conversation.*

One month before, a friend said, "Wouldn't it be great if we all did Hair for Hope?" She was referring to the annual fundraiser hosted by the Children's Cancer Foundation, which involved participants shaving their heads to raise awareness for childhood cancer. Laughing, I'd agreed. Wouldn't it be meaningful, raising money for a good cause? And wouldn't it be a laugh, doing something memorable with all my best friends?

No, it really wasn't a laugh, I realized as the razor sounded dangerously close to my head. I would soon be painfully familiar with the fact that human

---

ANGELINA X. NG *studies social policy and economics at Harvard University and is a staff writer for the* Harvard Crimson, *where this essay was published in April 2024.*

hair grows just half an inch every month, no matter how much tugging or rosemary oil one massages into their head; the fact that I relied heavily on my hair to conceal the pimples on my forehead; and the fact that some people could pull off a bald head, but I, alas, could not count myself among the blessed few.

As I felt pounds of my hair slide off my head, I cast my mind wildly for a positive spin on my new reality (Wigs? Homeschool? House arrest?). But I could latch on to only one thing: At least this would be the beginning of something new.

Reinvention's becoming a corporate term now—a quick *Google* search brings up buzzwords like "growth model," "technological disruption," and "business trends." Like most business buzzwords, they're devoid of any actual technical meaning, but that desire to change it up feels indicative of a larger societal impulse for a clean slate.

I'm skeptical of how useful these reinventions actually are. They feel like PR gimmicks, creating nothing more than a more marketable, more appealing facade. Yet I wasn't immune to the allure of it either. "This is the week," I swore to friends on weekends, "that I'm getting my shit together and cleaning my room." Then I would go home, do my laundry, make a *Spotify* playlist, and then lie on my newly made bed for three hours to read a book, foolishly proud of the new me that I had just invented.

Most of my frantic reinventions stemmed from a desire to fix some issue I'd identified in myself. The inability to care for myself, for instance, or feeling shitty about my exercising habits, or my general disorganization. But the consequent changes I made—a new running routine, or new skincare products, or increasingly complicated ways of arranging the various knickknacks on my desk—didn't manifest in a brand-new identity any more than they manifested in new ways of hiding what I didn't like about myself.

I treated myself as a palimpsest, plastering over the things that I didn't like with a shiny new bumper sticker. Meanwhile, all my existing tendencies accumulated below the surface, hidden under layers and layers of superficially built habits and artificial declarations of becoming a new person.

A friend recently taught me about the Big Bang Theory's counterpart, the Big Crunch, which is the idea that the Universe could eventually collapse just as quickly as it was formed. I'm not a science person, but the notion

In these four introductory paragraphs, the author VIVIDLY DESCRIBES a significant event and suggests that we will read about its consequences and its importance in her life.

Pivots to a more general discussion of "reinvention," beginning with the use of the word in public discourse to a more personal application.

Specific EXAMPLES with a humorous TONE demonstrates that the author doesn't take herself too seriously.

that everything that we create can be destroyed in less than a second made sense. All my reinventions tended to collapse within days of being instituted, because—as I was well aware—I was very much the same person, but with slightly cuter shelves.

Maybe that was why shaving my head was so crazy, because it meant, literally and figuratively, that I had nothing to hide behind. You can't cut bangs when your hair is gone. There was nothing I could change about my appearance to rectify the situation. For the first time, I had to face the world un-reinvented, bumper stickers peeling slightly for everyone to see.

Two days after The Event, I had an ultimate Frisbee tournament. On the train I found myself tucking phantom strands behind my ear, grasping at nothing. A woman offered her seat up to me, and I felt too embarrassed to decline.

I loved my teammates, who were friends that I'd known since elementary school, but we shared a brutal honesty born from years of insulting each other. As I walked across the field, my flip-flops crunching the wet grass, I doubted whether I could trust them with this—if these people whom I'd known longer than I didn't would understand how vulnerable I felt. Goose bumps pricked my skin as I approached.

"Nice head shape," someone said. Everyone laughed, and then we moved on, as if nothing happened, as if I was the same person I always had been. And I guess I was, but it felt like a miracle that that was true.

When it came down to it, what I really loved about the idea of a reinvention was the notion that I could turn my whole life around. Don't we all think that? That there is just one thing that's been holding us back, and that making this tiny change will fix everything else that's going wrong in our lives?

Shaving my head was the first time I realized that the reverse was true. For once, I had nothing that I could hide behind—and nothing, fundamentally, had changed. The bumper stickers—those tiny attempts at reinvention—weren't actually what was holding me together. The very thing I was trying to reinvent, after all, was my self.

In the coming months, my hair began to grow out. First, a soft fuzz covering my head, the length where I would debate whether to use shampoo or soap. The worst period, I came to realize, wasn't being bald, but rather the months following it: too short to properly style, but long enough to unattractively stick out in multiple directions.

Others agreed. "I'll never shave my head," a friend said to me. "It's not even about being bald, but how bad it looks when it's growing out." As she talked, I stared at her, my hair standing up on end.

But I let it slide, like how I learned to let so many comments slide. I had to, for the sake of self-preservation, because not every encounter was as happy as the one with my Frisbee team. On vacation with my parents and sister, we were seated for dinner with an older couple we had never met. "What a beautiful family," the woman cooed. "So perfect, having a girl and a boy!" I laughed, because the alternative was to get upset and scream.

Sometimes, though, I loved being bald. I had made my peace with being imperfect, rather than burying myself in an avalanche of reinventions. Each little lifestyle switch I made, I began to understand, didn't have to signify some bigger cosmic change. And in a way, that realization was freeing.

My hair took two years to hit my shoulders, and when it finally did, I took 20 to cutting my own bangs, whenever I felt like it. I would try to emulate whatever hairdressers do, angling the scissors vertically to layer, or pinching my hair between two fingers like chopsticks, but I suspect that the method had little bearing on the result.

Either way, it doesn't matter. My hair is no longer a symbol of some seismic shift in my character or personality—it's just something that I alter out of curiosity, or even boredom. Because I am not the Universe, and this isn't the Big Bang Theory. I wouldn't become a new person, for better or for worse, the instant I cut curtain bangs.

Recently, I've made another bad hair decision. Emerging from a shower, I stared in the mirror, took a pair of Fiskars scissors, and cut my bangs again. I didn't realize my error until I woke up the next morning, hair dry, and stared into the mirror again. My new bangs covered only half my forehead. I looked like Daphne in *Bridgerton*, except without the fancy gowns and demeanor to pull it off.

But it was all right. I was calm, even as I texted a friend a picture accompanied by a text in all caps: "SEND HELP I MADE A MISTAKE." Because, as she replied: "It'll grow back." And she's right. It always does.

Explains the evolution of an attitude shift.

With this dramatic claim, the author signals the final attitude shift that leads to the lesson learned.

What this story means—and why it matters.

The author takes a chance that her AUDIENCE of college student peers will be familiar with this specific cultural reference.

CONCLUDES with one final example that illustrates the lesson learned and her new attitude.

REFLECT & WRITE

At some moment in your life, you've likely had a memorable haircut. Reflect on your experience of it—during, immediately afterward, and possibly today, looking back. Why was it memorable? How did you feel about it? Did the experience prompt you to make any changes in your life or, in contrast, reinforce your commitment to not change? How would you tell the story? Write a paragraph summarizing how you'd structure the narrative of that event. If you have ever refused to get a haircut despite expectations to get one, or if you've never had a haircut, you might reflect on that experience and the reasons for your stance.

An Annotated Literacy Narrative

First Day of School
PALOMA GARCIA

It was a warm morning at *el ranchito*, and a special one, too—it was the opening of my day-school, and my first day as a teacher, or so I liked to think. Although at the time I was only seven years old, I knew I wanted to be a teacher and help others learn. Ironically, even though I was never read to at home, I loved reading, and I especially loved (and still do) going to school and learning as much as I could from my teachers. I would go home from school and tell my mom what I had learned in class, an everyday ritual she and I shared. This daily report of what I learned helped me see that I wanted to share knowledge and teach others. This is how I got the idea to become a teacher, and before my mother knew my brilliant plan, half the kids in our neighborhood were knocking on our door, anxiously waiting for me to come outside and begin class.

I began class by reading my first and favorite book: *Pulgarcito*, or *Tom Thumb* in English. I can still see the look in my friends' faces; they seemed to be so

The compelling OPENING draws readers in by setting up a surprise: the "teacher" is only seven years old.

Here the author moves from general description to a specific moment, which she signals clearly with "I began class..."

PALOMA GARCIA was a student at Santa Clara University when she wrote this literacy narrative for her Literacy and Social Justice class, which was then published by the Digital Archive of Literacy Narratives (thedaln.org). Today she is chief of staff at New York University's Metropolitan Center for Research on Equity and the Transformation of Schools.

engaged in the story, very attentive, and extremely quiet. I could hear my own breathing and feel my heart beat at times. After I finished reading, I would ask what my "students" had learned, what they had most liked, and what did not interest them much. Then came "*las clases de escritura*," or the writing classes, as I would call them. I would go over vowels and the whole alphabet, giving a brief explanation and an example word for each letter. Despite my young age, I felt I was truly helping my students, and I loved how they sometimes called me "*maestra*," or teacher, even if they only did so playfully or to tease me. To me, it was real. I knew I was their teacher.

Soon enough, I wanted to teach something to everyone that I encountered, especially family and friends who visited our home. I grew confident and proud of my improved reading and writing skills, my ability to address large groups without overwhelming fear, and my knack for talking and connecting with others no matter their age or gender. Unfortunately, this was all soon to change, and it happened when I least expected it.

One day when I arrived home from school, my mother didn't welcome me with a hug and kiss like she usually did, and I knew something was wrong. I was told we were immigrating to *El Norte*, or the North. I knew my life was never going to be the same. We made the move, and on my first day at my new school, Los Padres Elementary, I cried and begged my mom to take me back to our old home. I knew I was going to be at a disadvantage for not knowing a single word in English.

Only because of my mom's assurances and blessings, I gathered my strength and walked into Ms. Camaney's third-grade classroom. About a month or so into class, Ms. Camaney asked several students to read aloud, and my worst fear was realized: she asked if I could continue reading the story—in English, of course. I felt my face turn red hot with embarrassment, and I asked to be excused from reading, since I still wasn't comfortable with English, especially reading it out loud to the rest of the class. But Ms. Camaney insisted. I began reading with my heavy accent, mispronouncing almost every word, while my classmates laughed.

It was an enormous challenge to be so young in a foreign place with no knowledge of the language, and incidents like the read-aloud debacle at school made me feel like I was living through a war where I was wounded and defeated constantly as everything and everyone plotted against me. Although I tried to continue to read—something that gave me comfort before—no words came out. Instead, tears would stream down my cheeks. Here I was, scared but hopeful for a helping hand and an opportunity to try my best, but instead I was laughed at and ridiculed for trying.

This incident in Ms. Camaney's class marked a turning point in my life; I began to lose my interest in and passion for reading, and I wasn't interested in learning English. Now I was afraid of being laughed at and humiliated for mispronouncing a word or stumbling through a sentence. My fear overwhelmed my love of learning and killed my interest in practicing a new language. I began to isolate myself from others, avoiding any social interactions that required English, since I felt inferior to my fluent classmates.

As I reflect on these years of my childhood, I know that this experience with language, reading, and education affected both my self-esteem and my academic performance and ambition. I went from a kid who loved reading and writing and dreamed of becoming a teacher to a student who lacked confidence and dreaded school. Humiliation and discrimination turned into fear, and fear kept me from participating in class, from asking questions, and ultimately, from believing in my own abilities and strengths to excel as a student. As time passed in my new life in the US, however, I learned to believe in my own will power and to reconnect with my passion for language, learning, and teaching. Incidents of language discrimination were painful; they have also shaped me, in part, into the person I'm proud to be today: bold, determined, and not afraid to speak up for my beliefs and ideals. My passion for reading and teaching others slowly returned and is stronger than ever because I learned how precious and fragile our relationships to language and education can be.

> *The author shifts from recounting a specific event to* REFLECTING *on its impact.*

> *A clear contrast between "before" and "after" points to the story's* LARGER SIGNIFICANCE.

> *The* CONCLUSION *indicates why this story is so meaningful—and why it matters to the author.*

REFLECT & WRITE

Reflect on your own experiences as a reader, writer, or language learner, and identify one experience that played a key role in your developing literacy. What did you learn, and how? What impact has it had on your life?

SIXTEEN

"Let's Take a Closer Look"
Writing Analytically

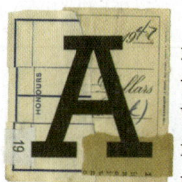

NALYSIS IS A NECESSARY STEP in much of the thinking that we do, and something that we do every day. When you analyze something, you break it down into its component parts and think about those parts methodically in order to understand it. Since our world is awash in information, the ability to read it closely, examine it critically, and decide how—or whether—to accept or act on it is essential. To navigate this sea of information, we rely on our ability to analyze.

Case in point: you want a new tablet, both for school and at home, but how do you choose which is best for you? The latest iPad? A hand-me-down Microsoft Surface? Or maybe the cheapest thing available? As you consider your needs and your options, focus your analysis with questions: What's most important to you—screen size? price? portability? battery life? compatibility with your other devices? When and where will you most often be using it? How much storage will you need? You could ask friends for their opinions, and you might check websites, like *Wirecutter*, *CNET*, or even *YouTube*, that provide analysis as well as price comparisons. Analyzing your options will enable you to understand what each offers and decide based on your goals.

While you've analyzed literary texts in English classes, in many college classes you'll be expected to conduct different kinds of analyses—of texts, but also of events, issues, arguments, and more. Analysis is critical to every academic discipline and useful in every professional field. This chapter provides guidelines for conducting an analysis and writing analytically, with specific advice for rhetorical, causal, discourse, process, data, and visual analysis.

>  **REFLECT**
>
> How many decisions—large and small—have you made in the last week? From small (what to have for breakfast) to major (which classes to take), make a chart listing a sample of these decisions and what areas of your life they affected. Then note the information you gathered in each case before you came to a final decision. What does this chart tell you about your interests, activities, and priorities? You've just completed an analysis.

Across Academic Disciplines

Some form of analysis can be found in every academic discipline. In a history class, you may be asked to analyze the causes of the US Civil War. In biology, you might analyze how the body responds to exercise. In economics, you might analyze the trade-off between unemployment and inflation rates. In a technical communication course, you might analyze a corporate website. In your composition course, you'll analyze your own writing for many purposes, from thinking about how you've appealed to your audience to deciding how you need to revise a draft. So many courses require analysis because looking closely and methodically at something—a text, a process, a philosophy—helps you discover connections between ideas and think about how things work, what they mean, and why.

Across Media

Your medium affects the way you present your analysis. In print, you'll be writing mostly in paragraphs, and you might include photos, tables, graphs, diagrams, or other images to make your analysis clear. If you're making an oral presentation, you might share information on handouts or presentation slides. A digital text allows you to blend words, images, and audio—and you can link to more information elsewhere. In an analysis of Caitlin Clark's signature basketball moves published on the website *HoopsKing*, author Chris Hungerford includes images and video to accompany the following description so that readers can see the specific moves in action:

> Under intense pressure, Caitlin Clark excels at racking up points using her repertoire of unique moves. One such move is the one-dribble step back. Her go-to maneuver, the one-dribble step back, effortlessly puts distance between her and any defender. . . .
>
> In the half-court, Clark often resorts to this go-to technique. It starts with a quick dribble to her left followed by a swift step back, creating enough distance from her defender to get off a clean shot. Its charm springs from the straightforward yet potent manner it achieves the perfect gap. . . .
>
> . . . Amidst the relentless defense, her display of both physical prowess and mental resilience in executing these plays truly stands out as remarkable.
>
> —CHRIS HUNGERFORD, "Breakdown of Caitlin Clark's Game: Skills, Stats & Impact"

WNBA Indiana Fever phenom Caitlin Clark dribbling.

THINK BEYOND WORDS

➦ *WATCH THE VIDEO of the first-ever female beatbox battle world champion, Antoinette Clinton*, who goes by the stage name Butterscotch, defining and explaining beatboxing in thirteen levels of complexity. Her video pairs verbal explanation with visual and auditory demonstrations for the moves of each "instrument" she's mimicking. How do the visuals and sounds contribute to this analysis? Go to *everyonesanauthor.tumblr.com* to watch the video.

Across Cultures and Communities

Communicating with people from other communities or cultures challenges us to examine our assumptions and think about our usual ways of operating. Analyzing and understanding beliefs, assumptions, and practices that we are not familiar with may take extra effort. We need to be careful not to look at things only through our own frames of reference.

Pastor Don Mackenzie, Rabbi Ted Falcon, and Imam Jamal Rahman put in this extra effort in writing their book, *Getting to the Heart of Interfaith: The Eye-Opening, Hope-Filled Friendship of a Pastor, a Rabbi & an Imam*. In this book, they take on the challenge of working toward interfaith understanding, saying that religion today "seems to be fueling hatred rather than expanding love" and that in order to heal the divisions, we must "find ways of entering into conversation with those different from us." And they say that analysis—what they call "inquiring more deeply"—is essential to their ongoing journey toward understanding issues central to each faith.

All three agree that it is critical to discuss the difficult and contentious ideas in faith. For the minister, one "untruth" is that "Christianity is the only way to God." For the rabbi, it is the notion of Jews as "the chosen people." And for the imam, it is the "sword verses" in the Koran, like "kill the unbeliever," which when taken out of context cause misunderstanding.

Their book embodies cultural sensitivity and describes the process of practicing analysis that's respectful of difference. Reading a sentence that the imam had written about the security wall in Israel, the rabbi responded, "If that line is in the book, I'm not in the book." Then they analyzed and discussed the sentence, and Imam Rahman revised the wording to be "respectful of [both] their principles."

Having respect for the principles, values, and beliefs of others means recognizing and being sensitive to differences among cultures. The best way to demonstrate cultural sensitivity is to use precise language that avoids negative words or stereotypes about gender, religion, race, ethnicity, and such—in short, by carefully selecting the words you use.

Across Genres

Seldom does any piece of writing consist solely of one genre; in many cases, writers draw on multiple genres as the situation demands. Analysis is a crucial step in writing for many purposes. To **ARGUE A POSITION** on an issue, you'll need to analyze that issue before you can take a stand on it. To compose a **REPORT**, you sometimes have to first analyze the data or the information that the report will be based on. And a **REVIEW** —whether it's of a film, a website, a book, or something else—depends on your analyzing the material before you evaluate it. Likewise, you might use a short **NARRATIVE** as an introductory element in a process or causal analysis.

 **REFLECT**

Look for analysis in everyday use. Find two websites that analyze something you're interested in—tablets, cell phones, sneakers, places you want to go, things you want to do. Study the analyses and decide which one is more useful. What makes it better? Is it the language? the images? the amount of detail? the format? Keep these observations in mind as you write and design your own analyses.

16 ~ Writing Analytically

CHARACTERISTIC FEATURES

While there are nearly as many different kinds of analysis as there are things to be analyzed, we can identify five common elements that analyses share across disciplines, media, cultures, and communities:

- A question that prompts you to take a closer look (p. 257)
- Some description of the subject you are analyzing (p. 258)
- Evidence drawn from close examination of the subject (p. 260)
- Insight gained from your analysis (p. 270)
- Clear, precise language (p. 272)

A Question That Prompts You to Take a Closer Look

Look at the examples cited earlier in this chapter, and note that each is driven by a question that doesn't have a single "right" answer. Which tablet best meets your needs? How can we begin to achieve interfaith understanding? Each question requires some analysis. While an author may not explicitly articulate such a question, it will drive the analysis—and their writing. In the example below, note how the author provides a prompt that requires taking a closer look:

> Multiple well-respected journalistic outlets have announced to much fanfare that, having reflected on the rapidly shifting American racial landscape, they will be capitalizing "Black" as designations for people and cultures. Some have also clarified why they're not capitalizing "white." . . . I haven't always capitalized "White" in my own writing, but I do now. Here's why.
>
> Whiteness is not only an absence. It's not a hole in the map of America's racial landscape. Rather, it is a specific social category that confers identifiable and measurable social benefits. . . . As long as White people do not ever have to interrogate what Whiteness is, where it comes from, how it operates, or what it does, they can maintain the fiction that race is other people's problem, that they are mere observers in a centuries-long stage play in which they have, in fact, been the producers, directors, and central actors.
>
> Other than the demonstrably untrue idea that White "merely" describes skin color, there are other interesting arguments to consider

for keeping it lowercase. For instance, many Black people I know say that they capitalize Black as a show of respect, pride, and celebration, and they don't want to afford the same courtesy to Whiteness. But we frequently capitalize words for reasons other than respect—words like Holocaust, or Hell, which can be capitalized to indicate specificity or significance. When we ignore the specificity and significance of Whiteness—the things that it is, the things that it does—we contribute to its seeming neutrality and thereby grant it power to maintain its invisibility.

Some outlets have also noted that White supremacist hate groups capitalize White, so we shouldn't. To that, I respond with an ancient African American proverb: *I ain't studdin' them.*

—EVE L. EWING, "I'm a Black Scholar Who Studies Race. Here's Why I Capitalize 'White.'"

Even though Ewing doesn't pose an explicit question, her early statement—"I haven't always capitalized 'White' in my own writing, but I do now"—invites readers to consider why she's changed her mind. Then she takes a closer look, providing an analysis of the social conditions that support her stance, as well as an analysis of counterarguments. You might not always start an analytical essay by asking an explicit question, but your analysis will always be prompted by a question of some kind.

Some Description of the Subject You Are Analyzing

To help your audience fully understand your analysis, you need to first describe what you are analyzing, focusing on the elements that support your claims. How much description you need depends on your subject, your audience, and your medium. For example, in analyzing the reasons for the success of the movie *Barbie* published on *ScreenRant*, writer Adrienne Tyler provides a summary of the film's plot and a description of its phenomenal financial success at the box office:

> Among the most anticipated movie releases of 2023 was Greta Gerwig's *Barbie*, which took the famous Mattel doll and brought it to life in a story that explored both Barbieland and how a Barbie-led society works and the inequality and struggles women go through in the real, human world.

Barbie (played by Margot Robbie) in her classic pink convertible.

Barbie follows Stereotypical Barbie (Margot Robbie), who after going through sudden changes like flat feet and questioning her mortality, goes on a journey to the real world accompanied by Stereotypical Ken (Ryan Gosling) to find the girl who plays with her and fix the portal between Barbieland and the real world. *Barbie* has been praised by critics and it has become a massive box office success, breaking records and earning a place on the list of highest-grossing films of 2023. At the time of writing, *Barbie* has grossed over $1 billion worldwide.

—ADRIENNE TYLER, "10 Reasons *Barbie* Made $1 Billion in Just 3 Weekends (& How Much Will It Make?)"

After providing this important background information, the author goes on to state ten reasons *Barbie* was such a smash hit. Tyler supports each reason with specific examples of how the marketing campaign succeeded in selling "the movie to its target audience and to viewers outside of it, who were drawn to it because of its humor, design, and its then-intriguing premise." She uses her medium effectively by preceding each reason with a still from the film, followed by an explanation of her claim in more detail.

Just as Tyler does, when composing a text that will be read by an audience that may not know your topic well, provide any necessary description and details. You might also include an image, embed a video, or include a link to a site offering more information if the medium you're writing in allows it.

Evidence Drawn from Close Examination of the Subject

Examining the subject of your analysis carefully and in detail and then thinking critically about what you find will help you discover key elements, patterns, and relationships—all of which provide you with the evidence on which to build your analysis. For example, if you are analyzing a poem, you might examine word choice, rhyme scheme, figurative language, repetition, and imagery. If you are analyzing an ad in a magazine, you might look at the use of color, the choice of typefaces, and the placement of figures or logos. Each element contributes some part of the message being conveyed. The kinds of elements you examine and the evidence you draw from them will depend on the nature of your subject as well as the kind of analysis you are conducting. Following are discussions and examples of five common kinds of analysis: rhetorical analysis, discourse analysis, process analysis, causal analysis, and data analysis.

Rhetorical analysis. This kind of analysis can focus on a written text, a visual text, an audio text, or one that combines words, images, and sound. All these are rhetorical analyses; that is, they all take a close look at how authors, designers, or artists communicate a message to an audience. Whether they are using words or images, adjusting typeface sizes or colors, they all are trying to persuade a particular audience to have a particular reaction to a particular message—theirs.

See how the following example from an article published on *Branding Strategy Insider*, a blog about brand strategy, analyzes Nike's thirtieth anniversary Just Do It campaign and the company's choice to feature Colin Kaepernick, a former NFL quarterback who sat and knelt during the national anthem at 49ers games in the 2016 season as a protest against the oppression of Black people and people of color:

> Is the new Kaepernick 30th Anniversary Just Do It Campaign a smart move for the Nike brand? ... Perhaps the first question to ask about this campaign from a brand planner's perspective is: *What is it about Colin Kaepernick's character that Nike finds so important to attach it to the Nike brand?*
>
> Developing brand character has many things in common with screenwriting and the attempt to develop relatable characters for film

and TV. Relatable characters are . . . sympathetic heroes on a mission to achieve worthy goals. They're often created as original, attractive, intelligent and provocative, and definitely not cliché, predictable or superficial. They have a definite point of view and a convincing way of getting it across. . . . Above all, relatable characters get people talking about them.

In Nike's current campaign, Kaepernick has certainly demonstrated that he has character, conviction about his beliefs, concern for social justice and he certainly has people talking about him. But, is he really a sympathetic hero? To segments of society struggling with [or sympathetic to] experiences of social injustice he definitely is. . . . To [others] . . . he carries strong and negative emotional associations.

Risk or Reward? In launching this new campaign Nike is risking alienating a huge segment of its U.S. consumer base, perhaps as much as half. Why would they do that? Perhaps they are thinking that it will tighten the tribe with millennials, who tend to be involved in protest movements, particularly when political leaders and other authority figures are not aligned with their feelings and values. They see Kaepernick as a champion of individual rights, fighting for a sense of social justice. . . .

This campaign will [also] scatter parts of the Nike tribe. . . . These people see not standing for the national anthem at a sporting event as an outward sign of disrespect for the idea of America and all the sacrifices made in the name of the nation. They see the gestures taken by Colin Kaepernick as a sign of questionable character. They see his public gestures as inappropriate and out of place.

—JEROME CONLON, "Analyzing Nike's Controversial Just Do It Campaign"

In the rest of the article, Conlon goes on to analyze how two different and opposing audiences are likely to react to the ad: those who will "like that Nike is supporting individual athlete rights, acts of moral conscience, conviction and protest," and those who will see the choice as disrespectful to the American values they embrace. As a former director of marketing for Nike, Conlon also analyzes the advertisement—and its likely impact—by looking at the history of the Just Do It campaign, which was designed to celebrate "the joy of all kinds of sports and fitness activities . . . for everyone, pro sports athletes to fitness amateurs, young and old, men and women, people in America, people around the world. No one was excluded."

To see Nike's Just Do It campaign videos and posters, go to everyonesanauthor.tumblr.com.

Nike's Just Do It ad campaign featuring former football quarterback Colin Kaepernick.

Conlon concludes with a prediction and wider implications of the ad: "Short-term pain for Nike's brand, but long-term gain. The social discussion around the campaign will elevate public understanding of the greatness of America and the need for more respect and regard for all people, of all colors and classes." Note how the author begins with a question and then presents evidence by analyzing the ad's tone, stance, context, and how all these elements will play with specific audiences.

In the following example from her study of a literacy tradition in African American churches, rhetorician Beverly Moss uses direct quotations from her field notes to illustrate a key rhetorical pattern she noticed in one preacher's sermons.

> One of the patterns that leapt out at me as I sat in the pew during all the sermons and as I listened to tapes and reviewed fieldnotes was the high level of participation in the sermons by the congregation.... It is a pattern that almost any discussion of African American preaching addresses.

Just as in the three churches highlighted [earlier], in this church, the congregation and Reverend M. engaged in a call-and-response dialogue. At times during the revival sermons, the feedback from the congregation was so intense that it was impossible to separate speaker from audience. Consider the following exchange. . . .

> When you shout before the battle is over (Preach!)
> It puts things in a proper perspective (Yeah!)
> It puts you in a posture of obedience (Yeah!)
> And it puts things in a proper perspective
> But finally
> When you shout before the battle is fought
> It puts the enemy in confusion (Yeah! That's right!)

The parenthetical expressions, responses from the congregation, do not appear on separate lines because there was little or no pause between the minister's statement and the congregation's response. Often, the congregation's response overlapped with the minister's statement. This type of feedback was typical in the sermons Reverend M. preached to this congregation, as was applause, people standing, cheering, and so on. Practically every sermon Reverend M. preached ended with the majority of the congregation on their feet clapping and talking back to Reverend M.

—BEVERLY MOSS, *A Community Text Arises*

Members of a congregation move and shout in response to the preacher's words.

Moss analyzes and presents evidence from a spoken text. Because she was writing a print book, she could not include the actual audio of the sermon, but still she presents evidence in a way that demonstrates a key point of her analysis: that the closeness of the preacher's "call" and the congregation's "response" made it almost "impossible to separate speaker from audience." This quoted evidence shows a specific example of how the congregation's response becomes a part of the sermon, filling the church with "applause, people standing, cheering."

Discourse analysis. This kind of analysis can focus on any spoken or written language used in a particular social context. Discourse analysis often entails analyzing the communication practices of a specific community—people who share basic values, practices, and goals. For example, a community of scholars such as the teachers at your school all likely value education, believe in helping students grow intellectually, and practice their profession by providing instruction to enable students to achieve their goals. You've probably noticed that most of your teachers—especially those in a particular discipline or department—share a specific vocabulary. This holds true for any field, any profession, any group of people with shared interests; they develop ways of interacting and communicating most effectively with each other. In order to analyze how a specific group communicates, you'll examine that community's practices, an effort that requires careful observation and even immersion when possible.

Look at the following example by Alberta Negri, a student at the University of Cincinnati, that analyzes the communication practices of a local group of bikers. Note how the introduction draws you in with a brief narrative and specific sensory details before offering background information. The author moves from common misperceptions of bikers to her specific subject, a group she refers to as the "Shell Station Squad." Note that Negri gives a rationale for focusing on this group; she tells readers why it matters.

> It's 8:56 p.m. on a Tuesday evening, and from my third-floor dorm room, I can once again hear the aggressive growls of 600-pound motorcycles as they roll into the parking lot of the Shell station across the street. The riders meet every night around 9:00 and face the usual apprehensive looks from bystanders.... Few investigations have been done from within the biking community; even fewer have examined the inner workings of the communication among members.... The following research makes the effort to peek into this unexplored group and discuss the less

action-packed qualities, including its status as a discourse community, the process of club enculturation, and how a member's new identity can complicate their previous social roles.

—ALBERTA NEGRI, "Underneath the Leather Jackets and Chrome Pipes: Research into a Community of Local Bikers"

Negri goes on to explain the methods used to conduct her research—including firsthand observation—and then she begins her analysis:

> What do these men have in common? The riders of the Shell Station Squad have separate personal lives: full-time gunsmith, engineering firm representative, college student and *Call of Duty* gamer among them, but they all plan to meet every night and anticipate their 9 p.m. ride all day. Their passion to ride is often their only unifying characteristic. There is no need for them to begin each ride with a preface, stating the goals for the ride for the night, or what they hope to accomplish as a team. There is a simple, unspoken understanding that if you pull into that gas station parking lot, you're there for the chance to revel in the thrill of weaving through streets on a motorcycle, while flocking as a group to make the experience a little safer for all involved. . . .
>
> Their primary mode of correspondence is *Facebook*; they use social media to create a private group for discussing matters such as driving routes and safety updates. . . . There is no clear pecking order. The peer-appointed leader never dominated the discourse. More often, he would push for more interaction from those who were recently recruited: addressing questions to them to get individual opinions and inviting them to special weekend rides. [This leader] went as far as directly introducing new riders, saying, "Guys: new kid with us tonight. Thomas is a student at [the university], new rider, let's make sure to make him feel welcome tonight, alrite? Good kid, i think" [sic] (Lucius). His digital diction was a tad gentler in these interactions compared to his brash joking with the more experienced riders.

Negri analyzes the shared motivations and passions that build kinship among the group members—"the thrill of weaving through streets on a motorcycle"—and acknowledges what sets them apart from one another, too: their personal lives outside of biking. She goes on to examine the group's way of communicating and building community, in person and online, in order to understand how the community operates. To conduct her analysis,

Visit **everyones anauthor.tumblr .com** for a link to Negri's complete analysis.

Negri relies on interviews with group members as well as primary texts: text messages, *Facebook* posts, and hand signals.

Process analysis. Analyzing a process requires you to break down a task into individual steps and examine each one to understand how something works or how something is done. Thus there are two kinds of process analyses: **INFORMATIONAL**, showing how something works, and **INSTRUCTIONAL**, telling how something is done. An analysis of the chemistry that makes a cake rise would be informational, whereas an analysis of how to make a cake would be instructional.

The following example analyzes the process of how skaters make high-speed turns. This is the most critical element in speed skating, for being able to consistently make fast turns without slipping can be the difference between winning and losing. This analysis from *Science Buddies*, a website for students and parents, closely examines the key steps of the process. Note how the author provides some information about the basic physics of speed and turns and then systematically explains how each element of the action—speed, angle, push-back force from the surface—contributes to the total turn.

> Whether it's ice, wood, or a paved surface, the science that governs a skater's ability to turn is essentially the same. It's based on a couple of basic laws of physics that describe speed and the circular motion of turns. The first is Newton's *law of inertia* that says a body in motion will stay in motion unless there is some outside force that changes it. To skaters hoping to make a turn after they speed down the straightaway, that means the force of inertia would tend to keep them going straight ahead if there wasn't a greater force to make them change direction and begin turning.
>
> The force that causes the change in direction comes from the skater's blades or wheels as they cross over at an angle in front of the skater leaning to make a turn. Newton's *law of reaction* explains that the push from the skater's skates generates an equal but opposite push back from the ice or floor. This push back force draws the skater in towards the track and is described as a "center seeking" or *centripetal* type of force. It's the reason why turns are possible in any sport. The wheels of a bicycle, for example, also angle into the road surface when the cyclist leans to begin a turn. As the road pushes back on both bike and rider, it supplies the inward centripetal force to generate the turning motion.
>
> The more a skater leans into a turn, the more powerful the push from the skate, and the greater centripetal force produced to carry the skater through the turn. Leaning in also creates a smaller arc, or tighter

Skaters from around the world compete in the Short Track Speed Skating World Cup.

turn, making for a shorter distance and a faster path around the turn. However, there's a catch. As the skater leans more and more into the track, the balancing point of the body, or the skater's *center of gravity*, also shifts more and more to the side. If it shifts too far, the skater no longer can maintain balance and ends up splayed out onto the rink rather than happily heading round the turn to the finishing line.

So success in turns, especially fast ones, means skaters must constantly find their center of gravity while teetering on the edge of their skates. To make the turn at all requires that the skater push the skates against the ice with sufficient power to generate enough inward centripetal force to counter the inertia of skating straight ahead. And to keep up speed in a race, a skater must calculate and execute the shortest, or tightest, turns possible around the track.

—DARLENE JENKINS, "Tightening the Turns in Speed Skating: Lessons in Centripetal Force and Balance"

To read the full analysis and see a video analysis, go to everyonesanauthor.tumblr.com.

This kind of close examination of the subject is the heart of analysis. Darlene Jenkins explains the key elements in the process of making a high-speed turn—speed, angle, push-back force—and also examines the relationships among these elements as she describes what happens in minute detail, revealing how they all combine to create the pattern of movement that leads to a successful high-speed turn. By including a photograph that shows skaters leaning into a turn, blades and bodies angled precariously, Jenkins shows what the process entails, and readers can actually see what's being described.

Causal analysis. Why is the Arctic ice pack decreasing in volume? What causes extreme droughts in California? These and other questions about why something occurs or once occurred call on you to analyze what caused a certain event, the possible effects of an event, or the links in a chain of connected events. Put most simply, causal analyses look at why something happened or will happen as a result of something else.

Go to everyonesanauthor.tumblr.com to link to the full article, "The Cry Embedded within the Purr."

Behavioral ecologist Karen McComb, who studies communication between animals and humans, wanted to understand why cat owners so often respond to purring cats by feeding them. To answer this question, McComb and a team recorded a number of domestic cats in their homes and discovered what the team termed "solicitation purring"—an urgent high-frequency sound, similar to an infant's cry, that is embedded within the cats' more pleasing and low-pitched purring and that apparently triggered an innate nurturing response in their owners. In an article presenting their findings, the team provided quantitative data about the pitch and frequency of different kinds of purring to support their conclusion about what the data showed: that the similarities in pitch and frequency to the cries of human infants "make them very difficult to ignore."

Using data like these to support an analysis is common in science classes, while in the humanities and social sciences, you're more likely to write about causes that are plausible or probable than ones that can be measured. In a literature class, for example, you might be asked to analyze the influences that shaped F. Scott Fitzgerald's creation of Jay Gatsby in *The Great Gatsby*—that is, to try to explain what caused Fitzgerald to develop Gatsby the way he did. In a sociology class, you might be asked to analyze what factors contributed to a population decline in a certain neighborhood. In both cases, these causes are probabilities—plausible but not provable.

Data analysis. Some subjects will require you to examine data. **QUANTITATIVE** analysis looks at numerical data; **QUALITATIVE** analysis looks at data that's not numerical.

16   Writing Analytically

When Beverly Moss analyzed the rhetoric of three ministers, she worked with qualitative data: transcripts of sermons, personal testimonies, her own observations from the church pews. Her data came mostly in the forms of words and text, not statistics.

Now see how blogger Will Moller analyzes the performances of ten major-league baseball pitchers using quantitative data—baseball statistics, in this case—to answer the question of whether New York Yankees pitcher Andy Pettitte is likely to get into baseball's Hall of Fame.

> I prefer to look at Andy versus his peers, because simply put, it would be very odd for 10 pitchers from the same decade to get in (though this number is rather arbitrary). Along that line, who are the best pitchers of Andy's generation, so we can compare them?

	Wins	Win%	WAR	ERA+	IP	K	K/BB	WAR/9IP
Martinez	219	**68.7%**	89.4	**154**	2827	3154	**4.15**	0.28
Clemens	354	65.8%	**145.5**	143	4917	**4672**	2.96	0.27
Johnson	303	64.6%	114.8	136	4135	4875	3.26	0.25
Schilling	216	59.7%	86.1	128	3261	3116	**4.38**	0.24
Maddux	**355**	61.0%	120.6	132	5008	3371	3.37	0.22
Mussina	270	63.8%	85.6	123	3563	2813	3.58	0.22
Smoltz	213	57.9%	82.5	125	3473	3084	3.05	0.21
Brown	211	59.4%	77.2	127	3256	2397	2.66	0.21
Pettitte	240	63.5%	66.9	117	3055	2251	2.34	0.20
Glavine	305	60.0%	67.1	118	4413	2607	1.74	*0.14*

> The above table tells the story pretty well. I've bolded the numbers that are particularly absurd, and italicized one in particular which should act as a veto. Though I imagine most of the readers of this blog know full well what these statistics mean at this point, for those of you who don't, a primer:
>
> WAR stands for Wins Above Replacement, and is a somewhat complicated equation which estimates the true value of a pitcher, taking into account league, ERA, park effects, etc. For instance, a pitcher that wins a game but gives up 15 earned runs has probably lost value in their career WAR, even though they get the shiny addition to their win-loss record. We like WAR around these parts.

ERA+ is a normalized version of ERA centered on 100, basically showing how much better or worse a pitcher was compared to their league average (by ERA). 110, for example, would indicate that the pitcher's ERA was 10% better than average. 95, on the other hand, would be roughly 5% worse than average. This is a good statistic for comparing pitchers between different time periods—a 4.00 ERA in 2000 doesn't mean the same thing as a 4.00 ERA in 1920, for example.

K/BB is how many strikeouts a pitcher had per walk. More is better, less is worse.

As you can see, the above table doesn't do Andy any favors. He's 6th in wins and 5th in winning percentage, but he's 9th in ERA+ and dead last in WAR. His K/BB beats only Tom Glavine, who comes off looking pretty bad on this list. The only thing he has going for him is his playoff record—and frankly, the team he was on won a whole bunch of playoff games while he was on the team, even when he wasn't pitching. Besides, we're pretty much past the point of taking W/L record as a good indication of pitcher skill—why is it that when we slap the word "postseason" onto the statistic, we suddenly devolve 10 years to when such things seemed to matter?

—WILL MOLLER, "A Painful Posting"

Moller's guiding question, "Should Andy Pettitte be in the Hall of Fame?," is unstated in this excerpt, but it is made clear earlier in the piece. He presents the data in a table for readers to see—and then walks us through his analysis of that data. It's critical when using numerical data like these not only to present the information but also to say what it means. That's a key part of your analysis. Using a table to present data is a good way to include numerical evidence, but be careful that you don't just drop the table in; you need to explain to readers what the data mean and to explain any abbreviations that readers may not know, as Moller does. Though he does not state his conclusions explicitly here, his analysis makes clear what he thinks.

Insight Gained from Your Analysis

One key purpose of an analysis is to offer your audience some insight on the subject you are analyzing. As you examine your subject, you discover patterns, data, specific details, and key information drawn from the subject—which will lead you to some insight, a deeper understanding of the subject you're analyzing. The insight that you gain will lead you to your thesis. When the imam, pastor, and rabbi mentioned earlier in this chapter analyzed a sentence in their book that offended the rabbi, each gained insight into the others' principles, which led them to further understanding. In "I'm a Black Scholar Who Studies Race. Here's Why I Capitalize 'White,'" Eve L. Ewing makes clear the insights she derived from analyzing the reasons for and against capitalizing "White" and especially why she believes it's an important topic:

> Ultimately, it's good that we're having this public conversation. Plenty of other scholars who study race and racism will disagree with me on this, and that's fine. In fact, I disagree with myself from two years ago. . . . I might change my mind again. Language and racial categories have some important things in common: They are fluid, they are inherently political, and they are a socially constructed set of shared norms that are constantly in flux as our beliefs and circumstances change.
>
> The terms we use, and the ways we write them, are less about saying or doing the "correct" thing, the thing that will prevent you from getting flamed on Twitter or earning an eye roll in a staff meeting. Rather, it's about what we want words to do for us and the arguments we're trying to make about ourselves and the world through the words we choose.
>
> —EVE L. EWING, "I'm a Black Scholar Who Studies Race. Here's Why I Capitalize 'White.'"

Ewing makes clear that the words we use—and how we style them—are powerful tools for reflecting and engaging with the world around us.

Summarizing the study of the way humans react to a cat's purr, Karen McComb and her team note parallels between the isolation cry of domestic cats and the distress cry of human infants as a way of understanding why the "cry embedded within the purr" is so successful in motivating owners to feed their cats. They conclude that the cats have learned to communicate their need for attention in ways that are impossible to ignore, ways that prompt caring responses from people. Thus, their work suggests that much can be learned by studying animal-human communication from both directions, from animals to humans as well as the reverse.

Remember that any analysis you do needs to have a purpose—to discover how cats motivate their owners to provide food on demand, to understand the power behind word and style choices, to explain why a favorite baseball player's statistics probably won't get him into the Hall of Fame. In writing up your analysis, your point will be to communicate the insight you gain from the analysis.

Clear, Precise Language

Since the point of an analysis is to help an audience understand something, you need to pay extra attention to the words you use and the way you explain your findings. You want your audience to follow your analysis easily and not get sidetracked. You need to demonstrate that you know what you are talking about. You've studied your subject, looked at it closely, thought about it—*analyzed* it; you know what to say about it and why. Now you have to craft your analysis in such a way that your readers will follow that analysis and understand what it shows. Andy Pettitte doesn't just rank low by his statistics; "he's 9th in ERA+ and dead last in WAR." It's not just that White people don't have to think about their race while others do: "White people get to be only normal, neutral, or without any race at all, while the rest of us are saddled with this unpleasant business of being racialized." Like Moller and Ewing, you should be precise in your explanations and in your choice of words.

Analyzing an intricate process or a complicated text requires you to use language that your audience will understand. The analysis of speed skating turns earlier in this chapter was written for an audience of young people and their parents. The language used to describe the physics that govern the process of turning works well for such an audience—precise but not technical. When the author refers to Newton's law of inertia, she defines "inertia" and then explains what it means for skaters. The role of centripetal force is explained as "the more a skater leans into a turn, the more powerful the push from the skate." Everything is clear because the writer uses simple, everyday words—"tighter turn," "teetering on the edge of their skates"—to convey complex science.

You need to consider what your audience knows about your topic and what information you'll need to include to make sure they'll understand what you write. You'll also want to be careful to state your conclusions explicitly—in clear, specific language.

VISUAL ANALYSIS

Photos, cartoons, ads, movies, *YouTube* videos, *TikTok*s—all are visual texts, ones that say something and, just like words alone, make some kind of claim that they hope we will accept. When you analyze a visual, you ask the same questions you would of any text: How does it convey its message?

How does it appeal to audiences? To answer such questions for a visual text, you'd begin by considering each of its elements—its use of color, light, and shadow; its perspective; any words or symbols; and its overall composition. Visual analysis takes various forms, but it generally includes the following features.

A Description of the Visual

Include an image of the visual in your analysis, but if that's not possible—in a print essay analyzing a video, for instance—you'll need to describe it. Your description should focus on the most important elements and those you'll point to in your analysis. What draws your eye first, and why? What's most interesting or seems most important? Does any use of contrast affect what you see? Consider the cartoon below. Your eyes were probably first drawn to the road signs because they come at the top and use capital letters. Then you may have noticed Uncle Sam next, the only human figure included, wearing red, white, and blue clothing that stands out against the white road.

Some Contextual Information

You'll need to provide contextual information about your subject. What's its purpose, and who's the target audience? Is there any historical, political, or cultural context that's important to describe? Such factors are important to think about—and to describe in your analysis. The Uncle Sam at a crossroads cartoon by John Darkow appeared in the *Columbia Missourian*, a local newspaper in Columbia, Missouri, in 2021 and reflects the concern many had at the time about political divisions and extremism in the United States.

Attention to Any Words

If the visual includes any words, what do they add to its message? Whatever the words—the name of a sculpture, a caption beneath a photo, a slogan in an ad, the words in a speech balloon—you'll want to discuss how they affect the way we understand the visual. The same is true of the typography: words in boldface are likely ones the author wants to emphasize; the typefaces affect the tone. If you were analyzing the Uncle Sam cartoon, for instance, you might point out that the road signs suggest that both fascism and authoritarianism oppose the traditional path of the United States since those two signs point one way while the "democracy" sign points in the opposite direction.

Close Analysis of the Message

What elements are most important in conveying the message? Probably the most compelling in the Uncle Sam cartoon is the placement of Uncle Sam himself, a figure often used as a traditional symbol of the United States. What does his posture suggest? He's still, hands at his sides, baggage in tow, looking in democracy's direction and not at the signs above. The fact that he's showing little emotion, other than his stillness, might be read as his own concern and deliberation—worry that the direction he chooses could be terribly important and thus worthy of serious consideration. You might also note that the sun seems to be setting—or is it rising?—on the land labeled as "democracy."

Insight into What the Visual "Says"

Your analysis of the visual will lead you to an understanding of what it's saying. In the Uncle Sam cartoon, the character's position and posture at a literal crossroads suggests the country is at a pivotal moment when a path other than democracy might take us into the future. Whenever you analyze a visual—a cartoon, an advertisement, a slogan on a sign or T-shirt—you know it's trying to persuade you to take an action, to have an emotional response, to desire—and perhaps purchase—something. When you analyze visuals, you need to think about how the image makes you feel. What is it suggesting you think or do? And what techniques does it use to draw that reaction from you?

Precise Language

It's especially important to use precise words in writing about a visual. Saying that the Uncle Sam cartoonist "places a symbol of the United States at a crossroads" doesn't say much. This is better: "the vivid red, white, and blue of Uncle Sam's clothes are in contrast to the stark crossroads he stands on—all while he looks ahead and into the sun, which might be rising or setting on democracy." When you write about a visual, you need to use language that will help readers see the things that matter.

You'll find an annotated model of a visual analysis, "What Is the Invisible Problem with *TikTok*" by Sydney Sallman, on page 286.

THINK BEYOND WORDS

➦ *TAKE A LOOK at "Paradise, Paved,"* a photo essay about travelers spending the night in Walmart parking lots. Click through the images and read the surrounding text. Then pick one image to analyze. How are the people in the image portrayed? How is the image itself composed? If this photo essay had a thesis, what would it be? Go to everyonesanauthor.tumblr.com *to access the entire piece.*

WRITING ANALYTICALLY / A Roadmap

Find a topic that matters to you—and to others

Whether you can choose your topic or have to respond to a specific assignment, find an angle that appeals to you—and to your audience. Write about something that you care about, that engages you. No audience will want to hear about something that you are not interested in writing about.

If you can choose your topic, begin by considering your interests. What do you like to do? What issues do you care about? If you are a dedicated fan of Billie Eilish, you might analyze her musical influences or how her approach has changed over her career. If you are interested in sports, you might examine statistical data on a favorite athlete or analyze the process of doing something in a particular sport.

If you've been assigned a topic, say, to conduct a rhetorical analysis of the Gettysburg Address, find an angle that interests you. If you're a history buff, you might research the particular occasion on which Lincoln spoke and look at how his words were especially fitting for that audience and event. Or perhaps your interests lie more in current politics, in which case you might compare Lincoln's address to the speeches politicians make today.

Make your topic matter to your audience. Some topics matter to everyone, or nearly everyone; you might be able to identify such topics by checking the media for what's being debated and discussed. But when you're writing about something that may not automatically appeal to a wide audience, it's your responsibility as the writer to tell them why they should care about it.

Consider your rhetorical situation

Keep in mind the elements of your particular situation—your audience, your specific purpose, your stance, and so on—and how they will or should influence the choices you make in your writing.

Identify your AUDIENCE. Whom do you want to reach, and how can you shape your analysis so that you get through to them? Karen McComb and colleagues' analysis of cat purring was for an audience of scientific peers, whereas Sydney Sallman's analysis of comedian Ro Ramdin's discussion of *TikTok* on page 286 is written for a general audience of her peers. Very different audiences, very different purposes—very different analyses. You, too, should think carefully about whom you are trying to reach.

- What do you know about them—their age, gender, cultural and linguistic background?
- What are they likely to know about your subject, and what background information will you need to provide?
- How might they benefit from the analysis and insight you offer?
- Will your subject matter to them—and if not, how can you make them care about it?

If you are writing for the internet, you will likely reach a broad audience whose characteristics you can't predict, so you need to assume a range of readers—just as Will Moller does in his blog post about Andy Pettitte. Even though his primary audience comprises Yankees fans, he knows that some readers won't know much about statistics, so he provides the definitions they need to understand his analysis.

Articulate your PURPOSE. Even if you're writing in response to an assignment, here are some questions that can help you narrow your focus and articulate some more specific purposes:

- What are you analyzing? A text? A community? A process? Causes? Data? A visual?
- What's motivated you to write? Are you responding to some other text or author?
- What do you want to accomplish by analyzing this subject? How can you best achieve your goals?
- What do you want your audience to take away from your analysis?

Think about your STANCE. How do you want to come across as an author? How can your writing reflect that stance? If your subject is surfing and you're writing on a surfers' blog about how to catch a wave for an audience of beginners, your stance might be that of an experienced surfer or a former beginner. Your language would probably be informal, with little or no surfing jargon. If, on the other hand, you're writing an article for *Surfing Magazine* analyzing the process Laird Hamilton developed to ride fifty-foot waves, your stance might be that of an objective reporter, and your language would need to be more technical for that well-informed audience. No matter what your stance or target audience, you need to consider what kind of language will work best, what terms need to be defined, and how you can establish your authority as an author.

Consider the larger CONTEXT. If you are analyzing an ad in a composition class, you will want to look at relevant information about its original context. When was the ad created, and who was the target audience? What were the social, economic, and political conditions at the time? All that is contextual information. If you are preparing a load analysis for an engineering class, you'll need to consider factors such as how, when, and where the structure will be used. Other contextual information comes from what others have said about your subject, and your analysis adds to the conversation.

Consider your LANGUAGE. Almost any analysis can be presented in a number of ways. Regardless of how many languages and dialects you use in your everyday life, you have many options to consider in crafting an analysis. Will your audience expect a certain kind of language or style? Do you want to meet those expectations? challenge them? What do you want your language choices to say about you? What risks might you be willing to take with your language? How will your choice of medium and the larger context limit or expand the language options available to you? (You may want to consult Chapters 4 and 35 for more information about language options.)

Consider MEDIA. Will your analysis be delivered in print? on a website? in an oral presentation? Are you writing for an online class? a blog? your campus newspaper? If you get to choose your medium, the choice should depend on how you can best present your subject and reach your intended audience. Do you need to incorporate visuals, audio, and/or video? Or, do you need to speak directly to your audience in person? Whether you have a choice or not, the media you use will affect how you design and deliver your analysis.

Consider matters of DESIGN. Think about how to best present your information and whether you need to follow any disciplinary conventions. Does your analysis include data that is easiest to understand in a chart or graph? Would headings help readers follow your analysis? Would illustrations make your point clearer?

Analyze your subject

What kind of analysis is needed for your subject and purpose? You may be assigned to conduct a certain kind of analysis, or you may be inspired by a question, as Shaan Sachdev is in analyzing the reasons for Beyoncé's enduring popularity (see p. 292). But sometimes you may be asked simply to "analyze *x*"—an ad, a game, a historical event, profiles of several companies—in which case you'll need to determine what kind of analysis will work best. The kind of analysis you need to do—rhetorical analysis, discourse analysis, process analysis, causal analysis, data analysis, visual analysis—will determine the way you study your subject.

If you're analyzing rhetoric, you need to look at what the text you're examining says and how it supports its claims.

- What question are you asking about this text? What specifically are you looking for?
- What CLAIM is the text making—and what REASONS and EVIDENCE does the author provide for the claim? Do they convince you?
- Does the writer acknowledge or respond to COUNTERARGUMENTS or other opinions? If so, are they presented fairly?
- Are there any words that indicate what the author thinks—or wants you to think?
- How does the author establish AUTHORITY to address the topic?
- Does the text use any EMOTIONAL APPEALS ? If so, how?

If you're analyzing a discourse community, you're trying to understand the community whose language practices you are focusing on. And you'll want to be clear about both your reasons for choosing a particular community and the questions you're striving to answer about your subject.

Are you primarily concerned with how a given community creates cohesion through its discourse practices? Or are you interested in narrowing your focus to a particular type of exchange, focusing on vocabulary choices, figurative language, rhetorical elements, or preferred types of argument? Are you interested in understanding how the community establishes its social relationships through language? Or do you want to chart this particular community's similarities to and differences from other groups? Or perhaps you want to focus on how a given individual manages the discourses

> Would you say that *Yelp* reviews are a form of discourse that can be analyzed? We would. Kevin M. Kearney examines one-star *Yelp* reviews and comes to some surprising conclusions. Read his analysis on p. 927.

of multiple communities: an engineering student who is also a birder and a church choir member. Enacting one's identity in multiple communities requires using language at least somewhat differently in each. The following questions can guide your research and analysis:

- Why have you chosen this particular community? Or this specific discourse?
- What questions are you trying to answer about your subject?
- What existing texts—written, visual, recorded—can you draw on for background information?
- What kinds of research will you need to do to observe your subject's communication practices? Textual analysis? Data collection? Interviews?
- Do you observe any patterns or habits? Does what you observe match your expectations or surprise you?
- Can you observe your subject firsthand? Who might help you access the community you're interested in? Will you need permissions from your subjects or your university?

If you're analyzing a process, you'll need to decide whether your analysis will be INFORMATIONAL (how something works) or INSTRUCTIONAL (how to do something). Writing about how solar panels convert sunshine to energy would be informational, whereas writing about how to install solar panels would be instructional—and would need to explicitly identify all materials needed and then tell readers step-by-step exactly how to carry out the process. Once you've determined the kind of analysis, you might then consider questions like these:

- What question is prompting your analysis?
- If the process is instructional, what materials are needed?
- What are the steps in the process? What does each step accomplish?
- What order do the steps follow? Whether a process follows a set order (throwing a curveball, parallel parking a car) or not (playing sudoku), you'll need to present the steps in some order that makes sense.

If you're analyzing causes, you're looking for answers to why something happened. Why, for instance, are Americans waiting longer to get married? Is it because more people—especially young women—are putting their educations and careers first? Or because more young people have seen their parents divorce? Or because they are less financially able to spend on a large event than previous generations?

16 ⁂ Writing Analytically

Questions about causes can rarely be answered definitively, so you'll usually be ARGUING that certain causes are the most plausible or the primary ones, and that others are less likely or secondary. In addition, although an immediate cause may be obvious, less obvious long-term causes may also have contributed. You'll need to consider all possible causes and provide evidence to support the ones you identify as most plausible.

As you determine which causes are more or less likely, be careful not to confuse coincidence with causation. That two events—such as higher divorce rates in older people and later marriages in younger people—occurred more or less simultaneously, or even that one event preceded the other, does not prove that one *caused* the other.

You'll often need to do some RESEARCH to understand all the possible causes and whether they are primary or contributing, immediate or long-term causes. The following questions can guide your research and analysis:

- What question is prompting your analysis?
- List all the causes you can think of. Which seem to be the primary causes and which are contributing or secondary causes? Which are immediate causes and which are long-term causes?
- Might any of the causes on your list be merely coincidences?
- Which causes seem most plausible—and why?
- What research do you need to do to answer these questions?

If you're analyzing data, you're trying to identify patterns in information that you or someone else has gathered in order to answer a question or make an argument. The information collected by the US Census is quantitative data. Social scientists looking for patterns to help them make arguments or predictions about population trends might analyze the data on numbers of families with children in urban areas.

Although the mathematical nature of analyzing QUANTITATIVE DATA can often make it more straightforward than other kinds of analysis, identifying statistical patterns and figuring out their significance can be challenging. Finding and interpreting patterns in QUALITATIVE data can also be tricky, especially as the data is more free-form: words, stories, photographs, and so on. Here are some questions to consider when analyzing data:

- What question are you trying to answer?
- Are there any existing data that can help answer your question? If so, will they provide sufficient information, or do you need to conduct any RESEARCH of your own to generate the data you need?

- If you're working with existing data, who collected the data, using what methods, and why? How do the data relate to the analysis you're conducting?
- Do the data show the full picture? Are there other data that tell a different story?
- Can you identify patterns in the data? If so, are they patterns you expected, or are any of them surprising?

If you're analyzing a visual, how do specific visual elements convey a message or create an effect?

See the ebook for a video on examining a visual text closely.

- What draws your eye first, and why? What seems most interesting or important?
- What's the PURPOSE of this visual, and who's its target AUDIENCE?
- Is there any larger historical, cultural, or political CONTEXT to consider? Could AI help you research the context? (Check your instructor's policy before using AI.)
- Are there any words, and what do they tell you about the message?
- What's the overall ARGUMENT or effect? How do you know?

Determine what your analysis shows

Once you've analyzed your subject, you need to figure out what your analysis shows. What was the question that first prompted your analysis, and how can you now answer that question? What have you discovered about your subject? What have you found that interests you—and how can you make it matter to your audience?

State your insight as a tentative THESIS. Once you've determined what insight your analysis has led to, write it out as a tentative thesis, noting what you've analyzed and why and what conclusions or insights you want to share. Your thesis introduces your point, what you want to say about your subject. Let's say you're writing a rhetorical analysis of the Gettysburg Address. Here's how you might introduce an analysis of that speech:

> Following Edward Everett's two-hour oration, President Lincoln spoke eloquently for a mere two minutes, deploying rhetorical devices like repetition, contrast, and rhythm in a way that connected emotionally with his audience.

This sentence tells us that the writer will describe the event, say something about the length of the speech, and explain how specific words and structures resulted in an eloquently simple but profoundly moving speech.

As you formulate your thesis, begin by thinking about your **AUDIENCE** and how you can make your analysis most compelling to them. What aspects of your analysis will they care most about? How might it apply to them? Does your analysis have important implications beyond the immediate subject, as Eve L. Ewing's analysis of a single word does?

Then list the evidence you found that supports your analysis—examples, quotations, significant data points, and so forth. What of all your evidence will best support your point, and what will your audience find most persuasive?

Organize and start writing

Start with your tentative thesis, being sure that it identifies what you're analyzing, what insights you have to offer, and why your ideas are significant. As you write, be sure you're supporting your thesis—and that it's working. That said, don't hesitate to revise it if you have difficulty supporting it.

Give EVIDENCE that supports your thesis. Depending on the kind of analysis, evidence could include examples, statistics, quotations, definitions, and so on.

Cite other sources, but remember that this is *your* analysis. Your audience wants to hear your voice and learn from your insights. At the same time, don't forget to acknowledge other perspectives.

Draft an OPENING. You might begin by describing what you're analyzing and why, explaining what question prompted you to take a closer look at your topic. Provide any background information your audience might need. State your thesis: what are you claiming about your subject?

Draft a CONCLUSION. You might reiterate what you've learned from your analysis and what you want your audience to understand about your subject. Make sure they know why your analysis matters, to them and to you.

Look critically at your draft, get responses—and revise

Read your draft slowly and carefully to see whether you've made your guiding question clear, described your subject sufficiently, offered enough evidence to support your analysis, and provided your audience with some insight about your subject.

Then ask others to read and respond to your draft. If your school has a writing center, try to meet with a tutor, bringing along any questions you have. Here are some questions that can help you or others read over a draft of analytical writing:

- *Is the question that prompted your analysis clear?* Is it a question worth considering?
- *How does the* OPENING *capture the audience's interest?* Does it indicate why this analysis matters? How else might you begin?
- *Is the point of your analysis clear?* Have you stated the point explicitly in a THESIS —and if not, do you need to?
- *Is the subject described in enough detail for your audience?* Is there any other information they might need in order to follow your analysis?
- *What* EVIDENCE *do you provide to support your point?* Is it sufficient?
- *What insights have you gained from the analysis?* Have you stated them explicitly? How likely is it that readers will accept your conclusions?
- *If you've cited any sources, are they credible and convincing?* Have you integrated them smoothly into your text—is it clear what you are saying yourself and where (and why) you are citing others? And have you DOCUMENTED any sources you've cited?
- *Have you addressed other perspectives?* Do you need to acknowledge possible COUNTERARGUMENTS ?
- *How would you describe the* TONE *, and does it accurately convey your* STANCE *?* Is the tone well suited to your audience and purpose?
- *How is the analysis organized?* Is it easy to follow, with clear TRANSITIONS from one point to the next? Are there headings—and if not, would adding them help? If you're analyzing a process, are the steps in an order that your audience will be able to follow easily?
- *Consider* STYLE . Look at the choice of words and kinds of sentences—are they fitting for the audience and purpose? Could the style be improved in any way?

- *How effective is the* DESIGN*?* Have you included any images or other visual elements—and if so, how do they contribute to the analysis? If not, is there any information that might be easier to understand if presented in a table or chart or accompanied by an image?
- *How does the draft* CONCLUDE*?* Is the CONCLUSION forceful and memorable? How else might the analysis conclude?
- *Consider the title.* Does it make clear what the analysis is about, and will it make your audience interested in reading on?

Revise your draft in light of your own observations and any feedback you get from others, keeping your audience and purpose firmly in mind. But remember: *you* are the analyst here, so you need to make the decisions.

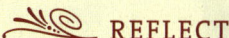 REFLECT

Once you've completed your analysis, let it settle for a while and then take time to REFLECT. How well did you analyze your subject? What insights did your analysis lead to? What additional revisions would you make if you could? Research shows that such reflections help "lock in" what you learn for future use.

READINGS / An Annotated Visual Analysis

What Is the Invisible Problem with *TikTok*?

SYDNEY SALLMAN

An engaging OPENING *draws readers in and introduces the topic.*

A GUIDING QUESTION *that prompts a closer look.*

A THESIS *states the main insights from conducting this analysis.*

"OH! I'M GETTING a prophetic message from God that I need to get back to the topic," Ro Ramdin jokes as she transitions from a sponsorship ad to the central topic of her *YouTube* video: *TikTok*. In "The Invisible Problem with *TikTok*," Ramdin, a *YouTube* comedian and commentator, explores the history of the social media app and its problems, ultimately crafting an argument against using the app. In doing so, Ramdin identifies the central demographic she is hoping to reason with as *TikTok* users. However, using *YouTube* as a medium creates a challenge as *TikTok* users are conditioned toward short-form content and constant dopamine hits. So how does Ramdin engage and reason with an audience addicted to a style of content designed to hold their attention elsewhere? Ultimately, it is through her skillful weaving of logical, emotional, and ethical rhetorical appeals as well as through uses of humor, sarcasm, and a fast pace that Ramdin effectively informs her audience while simultaneously entertaining them.

↗ Visit everyonesanauthor.tumblr.com to watch Ramdin's *YouTube* video.

SYDNEY SALLMAN wrote this essay for her first-year composition and rhetoric class at DePaul University. At the time of this book's printing, she's a third-year film and television major with a concentration in creative producing, aiming to pursue "a career devoted to storytelling in any form."

From the very beginning of the video, Ramdin relies on humor and speed to draw viewers in. As she walks viewers through the origins of social media, Ramdin speaks at an incredibly fast pace with steady jokes between every piece of information. Rapid cuts come after almost every line delivered; her next sentence always seems to nip at the heels of the previous one. This technique not only keeps the audience engaged with constant humor but also almost forces the audience to be closely attentive as every line quickly blends into the next. This is particularly important in engaging people who are used to short-form content. The fast pace and steady humor don't leave space for a viewer to become disengaged and turn to another source of entertainment. For example, Ramdin introduces the main topic of her video by stating "I don't think in my life I've seen something half as scary as *TikTok*. Unless you count the time I went to the premiere of Pixels. Huh, timely and funny. That's what you get when you click on a Ro Ramdin video—it's timely and funny" (7:01). With quick jokes like this, particularly self-deprecating jokes that indicate an awareness of the need to be entertaining, there is an unspoken promise to the audience that the remainder of the video will be just that: entertaining.

Ramdin makes her first nod toward establishing her credibility and making an ethical appeal by directly acknowledging the question of her credentials, stating: "I can hear you now: 'Oh, but Rose [Ro], what gives you the right to lecture me on this social media application?' Well, I'll have you know that I have a master's in media studies from your mother's bedroom" (8:39). Though Ramdin initially blows off potential naysayers with a joke, she goes on to clarify that she has been a *TikTok* user for years and even amassed a follower base of over three hundred thousand people. Having reeled in the audience with her fast-paced humor and her credibility to speak on the subject at the start, Ramdin moves into examining *TikTok*'s early days.

In an early segment of her video, Ramdin provides context by reporting on *TikTok*'s original user base, an effective logical appeal to viewers. She informs viewers that *TikTok* originally operated under the name *Musical.ly*, promoting itself as a lip-syncing app where users could record videos of themselves lip-syncing to a plethora of songs, audio recordings, or sound bytes. However, Ramdin explains that "cringe" content quickly took over when the platform was sold and rebranded as *TikTok*. As Ramdin explains, *TikTok*'s start was "based in reactionary bullying of subcultures . . . especially subcultures that had a hard time standing up for themselves, so what kind of app results from this sort

---

A DESCRIPTION *of a key element of the video.*

The author cites specific EXAMPLES *as evidence of humor.*

Provides supporting evidence from the video for how Ramdin establishes CREDIBILITY.

Points out how Ramdin makes a LOGICAL APPEAL, *and offers evidence.*

of thing? . . . An app full of young very volatile users who are looking for constant entertainment" (13:50). With this statement, Ramdin makes an emotional appeal to the audience's morality. Particularly with the distinction that those being bullied "had a hard time standing up for themselves," the audience feels a sense of moral obligation to stand against this behavior. While Ramdin notes that neither the bullies nor the bullied would become the central idea people associated with the app, the reactionary atmosphere *TikTok* was built on still stands.

Ramdin also provides statistics, appealing to the viewers' logic. She notes that at the time of creating her video, forty-seven percent of *TikTok* users were under the age of twenty-nine and twenty-five percent of users were under the age of nineteen. Even though Ramdin doesn't disclose her exact source, the use of outside sources continues to promote Ramdin's credibility while strengthening her appeal to the audience's logic. A substantial portion of *TikTok*'s users are younger, impressionable people exposed to this reactionary setting. By presenting these data, Ramdin forces her audience to reckon with the fact that *TikTok* is not the harmless environment they might have convinced themselves it is.

Expanding on the impact on impressionable minds, in her following segment, Ramdin calls back to her personal experience with growing up with social media. Ramdin notes that she used *YouTube*, which at the time was also boosting short-form, attention-grabbing, and often age-inappropriate content. Regarding personal impacts, Ramdin notes that *YouTube* had her "attention span soaked in vinegar and pickled," adding that she still struggles to devote full attention to television shows and movies (15:54). Additionally, Ramdin describes the role *YouTube* had in establishing many of her insecurities. She then applies these impacts to *TikTok*, illustrating how the platform has even shorter content, contains a more addictive and targeting algorithm, and promotes stereotypes and insecurities. Citing a specific example, Ramdin details how when a user goes live on *TikTok*, a face filter is automatically applied to their video that makes their eyes larger, skin smoother, and face slimmer. In doing so, the app perpetuates Eurocentric beauty standards and implies an imperfection with the way people look naturally.

By recounting the personal impacts social media has had on her and applying them to *TikTok*, Ramdin further solidifies her credentials and appeals to the audience's emotions. She is established as a person with credibility to speak on the impacts of social media and, in describing the negative effects, appeals to the audience's desire to protect themselves and others. Furthermore, there is an appeal to morality in revealing evidence of *TikTok*'s unethical practices, which is compounded by the previous statistics showcasing the young age of users. Ramdin explores this further as she approaches the conclusion of the video.

In the final section of the video, the style shifts from Ramdin talking directly to the camera to a voiceover playing over cinematic shots of a dark room, and the aspect ratio shifts from that of a classic *YouTube* video to one more commonly used in film. This deliberate editing choice signals a shift, which helps keep the audience's attention near the end of this forty-two-minute video. We hear Ramdin explain that she still uses *TikTok* despite recognizing all of its issues. She describes how she feels known and seen by the algorithm. In doing so, she relates to her audience; she doesn't demonize or talk down to them for their use of *TikTok*. As the voiceover plays, Ramdin discusses how *TikTok* is "an all-encompassing pathological people pleaser that has burrowed its way into [her] conscious and [her] subconscious, emboldening [her] most self-righteous pursuits and [her] most shameful innate biases, all the while distracting [her] from

CITES *Ramdin's own words in analyzing her use of emotional appeals.*

The style shifts from Ramdin talking directly to the camera to cinematic shots like this one, with voiceover narration.

VISUALS *illustrate a meaningful shift in style.*

those very processes that it exploits" (35:49). Ramdin is incredibly open about *TikTok*'s personal impact, drawing attention to a user experience that many have likely had, but perhaps not given much thought to. Yet she still brings up the harmful things *TikTok* emphasizes, such as her "most shameful innate biases." She reveals a viewpoint and experience many wouldn't want to admit to. This further builds her credibility as she is willing to share not only her personal experience with the platform but also experiences that often go unspoken. Her vulnerability about her interactions with the app is emphasized again when she states that "*TikTok* knew [she] was transgender before [she] did" (35:50). By stating this, Ramdin reveals a very personal and extreme example of the impact of the *TikTok* algorithm and its design to cater individualized content to each user.

> *Provides more EVIDENCE of how the video's creator builds credibility.*

In her conclusion, Ramdin makes a powerful emotional appeal through her use of visuals and closing statements. She discusses her attempt to report a user for hate speech and the response she received from *TikTok*, telling her that the user's content would be looked into. Following this, the screen cuts to black, forcing the viewer to pay close attention to the words she speaks. The section ends with the statement "the video is still up, nothing . . . really changed" (39:21). The bleakness of this statement in conjunction with a lack of visuals leaves the viewer feeling empty and hollow. By describing and depicting her inability to escape *TikTok*, as well as the failure to bring change to the platform, Ramdin leaves the audience feeling an overwhelming absence of hope for the future of *TikTok*.

> *Offers insight on the impact of Ramdin's language and message.*

By rapidly moving between the ethical, logical, and emotional rhetorical appeals combined with moments of levity, Ro Ramdin is able to effectively engage and educate her audience on the myriad of problems with *TikTok*. However, as she ends the video, we are not left with a clear-cut answer on where to go next. Ramdin passionately argues that we should do what we can to separate ourselves from the platform while also acknowledging the difficulty of doing so. However, Ramdin reminds the audience that *TikTok* "is constantly indebted to the users for existing on its platform, regardless of how it treats them. . . . It will show us whatever we need to see so that we will stay" (36:51). Perhaps it is that very sentiment that will allow us to leave.

> *CONCLUDES by summarizing what the video "says" and why it matters.*

10

Work Cited

"The Invisible Problem with *TikTok*." *YouTube*, uploaded by Ro Ramdin, 31 May 2022, www.youtube.com/watch?v=o9EIR7F2liU.

REFLECT & WRITE

Sydney Sallman focuses on four of the six parts of Ro Ramdin's *YouTube* video (Parts 1, 2, 4, and 6). Take a look at Ramdin's video for yourself, especially noting the two parts (Part 3 at 14:34 and Part 5 at 28:32) Sallman does not comment on. Why do you think Sallman chose to analyze the four parts and omit the other two? What in those omitted parts seems most pertinent to Sallman's thesis (or not)? Write a message to Sallman explaining why you would or would not recommend including one or both of the omitted parts in her analysis—and also letting her know if and how this analysis essay in any way changed your thinking about *TikTok*.

The Key to Beyoncé's Lasting Success
SHAAN SACHDEV

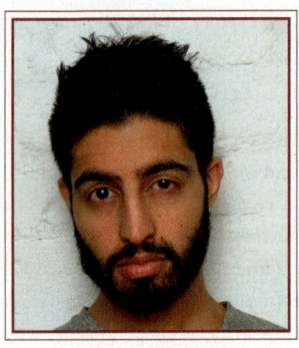

FIFTY THOUSAND PEOPLE—more Black and brown than white, more gay than straight—comprise a studious frenzy. Sure, there are some in the crowd who chatter amongst themselves as Beyoncé successively runs through "Mine," "Baby Boy," "Hold Up," and "Countdown," in one of the more exhilarating mid-concert medleys in modern pop history, but this show is neither for casual spectators nor about casual spectatorship. It's about memorizing and mirroring her choreography in the stadium's narrow aisles. It's about obeying her commands, six times per song, that everyone "sing!", these interruptions the only sign her pristine vocals are live and not lip-synched. It's about ecstasy, tears, and breathlessness. The least breathless person in the stadium, it seems, is Beyoncé. . . .

As Beyoncé turns 40, her legacy might already be cemented even as it is evolving. So perhaps it is opportune to point to precisely what distinguishes her from the glittery cadre of millennial pop princesses (Rihanna, Lady Gaga, Britney Spears, Ariana Grande, Katy Perry, Pink, and yes, Mariah Carey, Jennifer Lopez, and Madonna too)—making her "the result, the logical end point, of a century-plus of pop," as Jody Rosen wrote in 2013.

SHAAN SACHDEV wrote this article in 2021 analyzing why Beyoncé enjoys such enduring success. It was published by *Slate*, an online magazine and podcast network that offers "analysis and commentary about politics, news, business, technology, and culture."

Beyoncé performing at New Jersey's MetLife Stadium.

The answer lies in her live performances.

Stadium-sized live concerts are the closest things we have to the artistic mass ritual. But the burden of a hundred thousand eyes and ears is so taxing that the superstars who bear them often crack, fizzle, or are simply conceded lowered expectations. Because Beyoncé approaches her performances with the sort of ferocious discipline more commonly associated with professional athletes than with pop stars—she practices until her feet bleed—she is our most physically capable living superstar.

Here's the INSIGHT *that the analysis will develop.*

She brings her music and visions to life with the force and glitz of a cultural deity. None of the aforementioned pop princesses—and no one else in our constellation of arena-filling performers—can sing and dance in six-inch heels for two and a half hours with the same unremitting vocal wattage and choreographic mastery. Her musical athleticism is unrivaled. And for atheists, agnostics, queers, and aesthetes, what is a deity, a goddess, if not a buxom diva striking a silhouetted posture of superlative womanhood—and then *embodying* it—before millions of congregants around the world?

5

Critics, scholars, and professors of voice performance tend to name just five virtuosos in the history of pop music who rival Beyoncé's strenuous showmanship. Or rather, whom *she* rivals, since four of the five are dead, and the only one still alive, the fabulous Tina Turner, is now over 80. After Tina and Sammy Davis Jr. and James Brown and Prince, the experts usually settle upon one name.

"I think she is, in some ways, the inheritor of Michael Jackson's legacy—the truest inheritor that we have today," says Jason King, Chair of NYU's Clive Davis Institute of Recorded Music. Jackson was crowned "King of Pop" precisely because of his supernatural aura on stage, a dazzling amalgam of dance, vocals, and visual effects. But the resemblance between the two stars has its limits—Jackson's legacy has since been clouded by abuse allegations in ways Beyoncé's has not. . . .

[Quoting an expert provides EVIDENCE for the author's analysis.]

Perhaps it isn't altogether surprising that Beyoncé's father, Matthew Knowles, is sometimes compared to Michael Jackson's father, Joe Jackson. But where Joe Jackson was a violent martinet, tales of Knowles portray more of a drill sergeant who'd wake a young Beyoncé early in the morning, along with the other founding members of Destiny's Child, and make them jog for miles around Houston's Hermann Park *while singing*.

[Background information provides CONTEXT and supports the author's claim of Beyoncé's athleticism.]

Beyoncé eventually confirmed the stories to the *Times of India*, and years later, celebrity trainer Mark Jenkins told Insider Magazine that he'd similarly have Beyoncé sing an entire album while running in the Georgia heat—and "make it sound good." The result? Some of the best breath control on the Billboard Hot 100—and "bionic" onstage execution.

When Beyoncé says, "I've worked harder than probably anyone I know, at least in the music industry," she sounds more matter-of-fact than arrogant. While Michael Jackson was scarred by his father's tyrannical exploitations, Beyoncé fired her father, took possession of the torch, and kept on perfecting.

"One of the reasons I connect to the Super Bowl is that I approach my shows like an athlete," she told *GQ* in 2013, finally using the A-word. "You know how they sit down and watch whoever they're going to play and study themselves? That's how I treat this."

[Beyoncé's own words are included to illustrate the main point.]

She wasn't overstating. When she's on tour, Beyoncé said she watches a recording of the show she's just performed every night before bedtime, handing her dancers, bandmates, and crew pages of notes the next day. Her 2016 VMA and 2016 BET Awards performances, both amid her Formation World Tour, supplied the national airwaves with outrageously incontrovertible evidence that her method was working.

10

"I promise I will always give you a hundred percent of myself," she said to 185,000 fans at the end of her 2011 Glastonbury set (to their—and George Michael's—roaring approval). It was less a "thank you for coming" and more a declaration of her creed. . . .

"A Broadway show is about the show. Even if there's a celebrity in it, it's still about the context of the show itself," says King. "With Beyoncé, it's really about the cult of her celebrity and the kind of deification of her on stage working very hard on *our* behalf, not even just her behalf. There's an element of this power and ferocity that is a kind of martyrdom. You have to leave it all on stage. You have to give it all up." . . .

If her songs sounded like those of Lady Gaga or Katy Perry, her performances would be campy and fun, but she'd qualify neither as a queen nor a genius. Her musical athleticism, in other words, would be moot if her songs didn't merit this divine breath of life.

Thankfully, Beyoncé's music is pretty damn good. Lyrical simplicities aside, her songs are weird, distinctive, beautiful, ranging, and complicated. She can do maternal power pop and outlandish anthems, rap and eerie ballads. No superstar pays more attention to production. "Countdown" might be the strangest R&B song of the new millennium, while "Love on Top" might number among the most difficult to sing live. (Linda Balliro even shows Beyoncé's performance of "Love on Top" at the 2011 MTV Music Awards to her students at Berklee as an exemplar of stamina and energy, likening the four key changes to running a marathon.)

Prince may have lost the "black-queen vote"—or at least Hilton Als's faith—in the 80s, but Beyoncé continues to win the pop-queen vote because she inspirits an identification that is much more viscerally thrilling than genuine political subversiveness. She also wins the critical and celebrity vote. As a matter of fact, she is the celebrity of celebrities—the rare untouchable who makes Oscar winners nervous and giddy, talk show hosts grill guests about their interactions with her, comedians speechless, rappers gush, musicians gush, other singers gush, the old guard applaud, and First Ladies want to trade places.

Perhaps it's not only queens, misfits, and artistes who identify with Beyoncé as she transforms from woman to goddess—a singular amplified voice and spectacle, serenading the masses' desire for straightforward rhapsodic pleasure. Goddesses, after all, give us energy, glory, beauty, and joy. Most of us wouldn't mind *being* divine, if it didn't take so much damn practice, stamina, and lung power. Instead we exalt, and we are deified vicariously.

❦ REFLECT & WRITE

Clearly captivated himself, Shaan Sachdev provides numerous examples of how Beyoncé draws in her audiences, focusing on specific details of her performances to identify "precisely what distinguishes her from the glittery cadre of millennial pop princesses." Which of his key points do you find most compelling? Her "ferocious discipline?" "unremitting vocal wattage"? "choreographic mastery"? "musical athleticism"? Is there anything in his argument you find unconvincing or overdone? If so, why? Compose a brief response summarizing your position on his argument and citing specific evidence from Sachdev's argument to support your stance.

Advertisements R Us
MELISSA RUBIN

A DVERTISEMENTS ARE WRITTEN to persuade us—to make us want to support a certain cause, buy a particular car, drink a specific kind of s o d a . But *how* do they do it? How do they persuade us? Since the beginning of modern consumer culture, companies have cleverly tailored advertisements to target specific groups. To do so, they include text and images that reflect and appeal to the ideals, values, and stereotypes held by the consumers they wish to attract. As a result, advertisements reveal a lot about society. We can learn a great deal about the prevailing culture by looking closely at the deliberate ways a company crafts an ad to appeal to particular audiences.

This ad that appeared in the August 1950 *Coca-Cola Bottler* magazine, a trade magazine for Coca-Cola bottlers (fig. 1), features a larger-than-life red Coca-Cola vending machine with the slogan "Drink Coca-Cola—Work *Refreshed*" (Advertisement for Coca-Cola). Set against a bright blue sky with puffy white clouds, an overlarge open bottle of Coke hovers just to the right and slightly above the vending machine, next to the head of "Sprite Boy," a pixie-ish character and onetime Coke symbol, who sports a bottle cap for a hat. Sprite

The author begins with CONTEXTUAL *information: the purpose behind ads.*

States the QUESTION *that prompts the author to take a closer look.*

A THESIS *statement sums up the author's main insight.*

BACKGROUND *information, this time for a specific example.*

A DESCRIPTION *of the visual, using clear, precise language.*

MELISSA RUBIN wrote this analysis when she was a student at Hofstra University using an early draft of this chapter. She has taught creative writing and composition at Hofstra University and Touro College.

Fig. 1. 1950 ad from *Coca-Cola Bottler* magazine. Advertisement for Coca-Cola.

Includes the ad being analyzed so readers can see for themselves.

Boy's left hand gestures past the floating Coke bottle and toward a crowd congregating before the vending machine. The group, overwhelmingly male and apparently all white, includes blue-collar workers in casual clothing, servicemen in uniform, and businessmen in suits in the foreground; the few women displayed are in the background, wearing dresses. The setting is industrialized and urban, as indicated by the factory and smokestacks on the far left side of the scene and by the skyscrapers and apartment building on the right.

Practically since its invention, Coca-Cola has been identified with mainstream America. Born from curiosity and experimentation in an Atlanta pharmacy in 1886, Coke's phenomenal growth paralleled America's in the industrial age. Benefiting from developments in technology and transportation, by 1895 it was "sold and consumed in every state and territory in the United States" ("Coca-Cola Company"). In 2010, Diet Coke became the second-most-popular carbonated drink in the world . . . behind Coca-Cola (Esterl). In the immediate postwar world, Coke became identified with American optimism and energy, thanks in part to the company's wartime declaration that "every man in uniform gets a bottle of Coca-Cola for 5 cents, wherever he is, and whatever it costs the Company" ("Coca-Cola Company"). To meet this dictate, bottling plants were built overseas with the result that many people other than Americans first tasted Coke during this war that America won so decisively, and when peace finally came, "the foundations were laid for Coca-Cola to do business overseas" ("Coca-Cola Company").

Given the context, just a few years after World War II and at the beginning of the Korean War, the setting clearly reflects the idea that Americans experienced increased industrialization and urbanization as a result of World War II. Factories had sprung up across the country to aid in the war effort, and many rural and small-town Americans had moved to industrial areas and large cities in search of work. In this advertisement, the buildings surround the people, symbolizing a sense of community and the way Americans had come together in a successful effort to win the war.

The author's insight into what the visual "says."

The ad suggests that Coca-Cola recognized the patriotism inspired by the war and wanted to inspire similar positive feelings about their product. In the center of the ad, the huge red vending machine looks like the biggest skyscraper of all—the dominant feature of the urban industrial landscape. On the upper right, the floating face of Coca-Cola's Sprite Boy towers above the scene. A pale character with wild white hair, hypnotic eyes, and a mysterious smile, Sprite

5

DESCRIBES *specific elements of the visual as* EVIDENCE *of her analysis.*

Boy stares straight at readers, his left hand gesturing toward the red machine. Sprite Boy's size and placement in the ad makes him appear godlike, as if he, the embodiment of Coca-Cola, is a powerful force uniting—and refreshing—hardworking Americans. The placement of the vending machine in the center of the ad and the wording on it evoke the idea that drinking Coca-Cola will make a hardworking American feel refreshed while he (and apparently it was rarely she) works and becomes part of a larger community. The text at the bottom of the ad, "A welcome host to workers—*Inviting you to the pause that refreshes with ice-cold Coca-Cola*"—sends the same message to consumers: Coke will refresh and unite working America.

> *A close analysis of the vending machine—the words on it and how it's placed.*

The way that Coca-Cola chooses to place the objects and depict men and women in this ad speaks volumes about American society in the middle of the twentieth century: a white, male-dominated society in which servicemen and veterans were a numerous and prominent presence. The clothing that the men in the foreground wear reflects the assumption that the target demographic for the ad—people who worked in Coca-Cola bottling plants—valued hard workers and servicemen during a time of war. White, uniformed men are placed front and center. One man wears an Army uniform, the one next to him wears a Navy uniform, and the next an Air Force uniform. By placing the servicemen so prominently, Coca-Cola emphasizes their important role in society and underscores the value Americans placed on their veterans at a time when almost all male Americans were subject to the draft and most of them could expect to serve in the military or had already done so. The other men in the foreground—one wearing a blue-collar work uniform and the other formal business attire—are placed on either side of and slightly apart from the soldiers, suggesting that civilian workers played a valuable role in society, but one secondary to that of the military. Placing only a few women dressed in casual day wear in the far background of the image represents the assumption that women played a less important role in society—or at least in the war effort and the workforce, including Coke's.

> *A close reading of another element of the ad: how gender roles are depicted.*

The conspicuous mixture of stereotypical middle-class and working-class attire is noteworthy because in 1950, the US economy had been marked by years of conflict over labor's unionization efforts and management's opposition to them—often culminating in accommodation between the two sides. The ad seems to suggest that such conflict should be seen as a thing of the past, that men with blue-collar jobs and their bosses are all "workers" whom Coca-Cola, a generous "host," is inviting to share in a break for refreshments. Thus all economic classes, together with a strong military, can unite to build a productive industrial future and a pleasant lifestyle for themselves.

From the perspective of the twenty-first century, this ad is especially interesting because it seems to be looking backward instead of forward in significant ways. By 1950, the highly urban view of American society it presents was starting to be challenged by widespread movement out of central cities to the suburbs, but nothing in the ad hints at this profound change. At the time, offices and factories were still located mostly in urban areas and associated in Americans' minds with cities, and the ad clearly reflects this perspective. In addition, it presents smoke pouring from factory smokestacks in a positive light, with no sign of the environmental damage that such emissions cause, and that would become increasingly clear over the next few decades.

Another important factor to consider: everyone in the ad is white. During the 1950s, there was still a great deal of racial prejudice and segregation in the United States. Coca-Cola was attuned to white society's racial intolerance and chose in this ad to depict what they undoubtedly saw as average Americans, the primary demographic of the audience for this publication: Coca-Cola employees. While Coke did feature African Americans in some ads during the late 1940s and early 1950s, they were celebrity musicians like Louis Armstrong, Duke Ellington, Count Basie, or Graham Jackson (the accordion player who was a huge favorite of Franklin Delano Roosevelt) or star athletes like Marion Motley and Bill Willis, the first men to break the color barrier in NFL football ("World"). The contrast between these extremes underscores the prejudice: "ordinary" people are represented by whites, while only exceptional African Americans appear in the company's ads.

Offers a **COUNTERARGUMENT** *to the ad's message, with contextual information as evidence.*

In 1950, then, the kind of diversity that Coke wanted to highlight and appeal to was economic (middle-class and working-class) and war-related (civilian and military). Today, such an ad would probably represent the ethnic diversity missing from the 1950 version, with smiling young people of diverse skin colors and facial features relaxing with Cokes, probably now in cans rather than bottles. But the differences in economic, employment, or military status or in clothing styles that the 1950 ad highlighted would be unlikely to appear, not because they no longer exist, but because advertisers for products popular with a broad spectrum of society no longer consider them a useful way to appeal to consumers.

> **CONCLUDES** by summarizing the author's analysis of what the ad "says" and its impact on American identity.

While initially the ads for Coca-Cola reflected the values of the time, their enormous success eventually meant that Coke ads helped shape the American identity. In them, Americans always appear smiling, relaxed, carefree, united in their quest for well-deserved relaxation and refreshment. They drive convertibles, play sports, dance, and obviously enjoy life. The message: theirs is a life to be envied and emulated, so drink Coca-Cola and live that life yourself.

Works Cited

> The author cites sources, using **MLA STYLE**, which lends to her authoritative tone and **CREDIBILITY** on the topic.

Advertisement for Coca-Cola. *Vintage Ad Browser*, 1950, www.vintageadbrowser.com/coke-ads-1950s/6#adjjm2v0hc7efog6. Accessed 5 May 2011.

"The Coca-Cola Company Heritage Timeline." *Coca-Cola History*, Coca-Cola Company, www.coca-colacompany.com/history/. Accessed 26 June 2011.

Esterl, Mike. "Diet Coke Wins Battle in Cola Wars." *The Wall Street Journal*, 17 Mar. 2011, p. B1.

"The World of Coca-Cola Self-Guided Tour for Teachers. Highlights: African American History Month." *World of Coca-Cola*, www.worldofcoca-cola.com/wp-content/uploads/sites/3/2013/10/aahhighschool.pdf. Accessed 26 June 2011.

 **REFLECT & WRITE**

To support her position that "we can learn a great deal about the prevailing culture by looking closely at the deliberate ways a company crafts an ad to appeal to particular audiences," Melissa Rubin analyzes one specific advertisement by looking at its details and describing how and why it appealed to particular audiences. What do you find most persuasive in her analysis? Do any of her claims fail to convince you? What, and why? Compose a brief response to Rubin's take on this ad and be sure to support your own stance with concrete evidence from both the ad and her analysis.

SEVENTEEN

"Just the Facts"
Reporting Information

REPORTS HAVE PROBABLY played an important role in your life for a long time: Of course, all those report cards from school summed up how you were doing; and they could have been encouraging—or just the opposite. Or think of the reports you received after taking the SAT or ACT or any other tests, including your driver's license exam, if you drive. If you've had medical checkups, you've likely received reports on the state of your health. And you've no doubt written your share of reports, beginning in elementary school with reports on what you read over summer break or on a book your class was reading, and moving to lab reports in middle school science classes—and on and on.

Reports contain information that is factual in some way. As you no doubt realize, separating what is factual from what is opinion can be a challenge, especially when the topic is controversial.

The primary goal of a report is to present factual information to educate an audience in some way. The stance of those who write reports is generally objective rather than argumentative. Thus, newspaper and television reporters—note the word—in the United States have traditionally tried to present news in a neutral way. Writers of lab reports describe as carefully and objectively as they can how they conducted their experiments and what they found. And institutions like the Pew Research Center produce reports on a wide range of topics that state the facts on trends

This cartoon shows a familiar moment for many students who may wish to redact, or edit out, portions of their report cards.

in our everyday world. For example, a recent Pew report titled *Teens and Video Games Today* opens by stating the objective findings of their research: "85% of U.S. teens say they play video games . . . [and] teens see both positive and negative sides of video games—from problem-solving and making friends to harassment and sleep loss." Perhaps even more than authors in other genres, therefore, writers of reports aim to create an **ETHOS** of trustworthiness and reliability.

This chapter offers guidelines for composing reports, including profiles, a kind of report often assigned in college. As you'll see, writing effective reports requires you to pay careful attention to your purpose, audience, and stance as well as to whatever facts you're reporting.

 REFLECT

Think about reports you've read, heard, seen, or written recently, and make a list of them. Your list may include everything from a lab report for a biology class, to a documentary film, to a *PowerPoint* presentation that you and several classmates created for a course. What features do these reports share—and how do they differ?

Across Academic Disciplines

Reports are found everywhere in academic life. You're certainly familiar with book reports, and you're probably familiar with lab reports from science courses. Students and practitioners in most fields in the physical sciences, social sciences, and applied sciences regularly write reports, generally based on experiments or other kinds of systematic investigation.

Many scientific reports share a common format—often labeled IMRAD (introduction, methods, results, and discussion)—and a common purpose: to convey information. The format mirrors the stages of inquiry: you ask a question, describe the materials and methods you used to try to answer it, report the results you found, and discuss what your results mean in light of what you and others already know.

Another kind of report students often write, especially in courses that focus on contemporary society in some way, is the profile, a firsthand report on an individual, a group, an event, or an institution. A profile of a person might be based on an interview, perhaps with an American soldier who served in Afghanistan, for example, or the first woman professor to receive tenure in your college's economics department. Similarly, a profile of an institution might report on the congregation of a specific house of worship, an organization, or a company; such reports often have a specific audience in mind, whether it is donors, investors, members, or clients.

Across Media

As you might expect, reports and the research they convey are presented through all different forms of media. Throughout this chapter, we'll refer to the 2024 *World Happiness Report*, the result of a massive survey distributed to 100,000 people in 130 countries that posed questions about happiness at different stages of life from childhood to old age. The report—a 154-page document filled with discussion, images, tables, and figures—was collaboratively produced by the US-based analytics firm Gallup, Great Britain's Oxford Wellbeing Research Centre, and the United Nations' Sustainable Development Solutions Network.

You might be thinking, "What's so scientific about happiness?" The report's authors say their research "reflects a worldwide demand for more attention to happiness and wellbeing as criteria for government policy." And who wouldn't want to know the key to happiness? The 2024 *World Happiness Report* was covered in news outlets from *Vox* and the *New York Times* to NBC News and National Public Radio. A flood of *TikTok* and *Instagram* posts commented on the subject, and a *YouTube* explainer video appeared from

Find the full report by visiting everyonesanauthor.tumblr.com.

one of the report's funding organizations. Many outlets focused on the big questions: which country is happiest (Finland), and what makes people who live there so happy (social support, healthy life expectancy, and freedom)? As you consider these reports throughout this chapter, you'll get a clear idea of the ways media influence not only how information is reported but also what kinds of information can be covered.

Across Cultures and Communities

Wherever you find formal organizations, companies, and other institutions, you'll find reports of various kinds. For example, a school board exploring new models for bilingual education will surely rely on information in reports written by education researchers, parents' organizations, community groups, teachers' unions, or outside consultants. Odds are that the reports from each of these groups would differ in focus, tone, and even language. Some of these reports might be based primarily on research and

THINK BEYOND WORDS

↪ *WATCH THE VIDEO by the United Nations' Sustainable Development Solutions Network that summarizes the 2024* World Happiness Report. *Pay attention to how the video explains the study and its discussion of the six explanatory factors. Focus on how the visuals aid in the video's explanations. Imagine other possibilities: how else might the video have used visuals, audio, or text to convey the study's findings? Go to* everyonesanauthor.tumblr.com *to access the video.*

statistical data while others might feature personal testimonies. Those created by outside consultants would likely be very formal and data-driven and might include a presentation to the school board followed by a question-and-answer period. In contrast, a report from a parents' group could include a homemade video consisting primarily of conversations with students.

And, of course, the language you choose is an important consideration for report writing. For example, the report below about San Antonio's Independent School District's revised bilingual immersion program is

En una ciudad bilingüe como San Antonio, la educación de lenguaje dual es clave

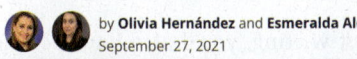

by **Olivia Hernández** and **Esmeralda Alday**
September 27, 2021

This *San Antonio Report* article, "In a Bilingual City Like San Antonio, Dual Language Education Is Key," is available in Spanish and English to reach those most interested in the city's dual language programs.

available in both English and Spanish, so that community members who read in either (or both!) of these languages can learn more. Even the English-language version demonstrates the value of a bilingual community by weaving in some Spanish. The report concludes this way: "For a long time now, the societal marketplace of this city has been calling for a bilingual education program that produces bilingual and multicultural individuals who can run our social systems and take them boldly into the future. . . . Today, that call is stronger than ever, and San Antonio [Independent School District] has taken a wonderful opportunity to respond to it loudly, decisively *y con mucho orgullo* [and with much pride]."

As a student, you'll be working in various academic communities, and you will need to pay attention to the way information is reported across disciplines and communities—and to what is expected of you in any reports that you write.

Across Genres

While reports are a common genre of writing, you'll also have occasion to report information in other genres. NARRATIVES, ANALYSES, REVIEWS, ARGUMENTS, and many other kinds of writing contain factual information often presented as neutrally as possible—and you will often report factual evidence to support your claims.

On the other hand, some documents that are called reports present more than facts alone and cross the line to ANALYZE and interpret the information presented or go on to make a PROPOSAL that offers recommendations for the future. These recommendations, though, should follow carefully reported information (as well as considerable analysis of that information).

For example, travel writer Mikeala Ruland mixes reporting with NARRATION in an article for *Outside* magazine. Inspired by the *World Happiness Report*, she reports on Finland's status as "the happiest place on earth" and narrates her experience visiting the country:

> On my first inhale after leaving the puddle jumper that had brought us to the Kittila Airport, my nose hairs froze. Despite it being 9 a.m., the stars still winked overhead, here at the top of the world. It was minus 4 degrees outside. . . . I'd gotten incredulous questions from more than a few people before coming here. Northern Finland? In January? Really? I, myself, had dubiously seen Finland atop the World Happiness Report since 2018—it was once again named #1 in 2024—and wondered how a country known

Ruland's report in *Outside* magazine includes an image to show some of what she describes, the awe-inspiring northern lights and cozy homes.

> for pickled herring and the wild vacillations between light and darkness could really be the happiest on earth.
>
> —MIKEALA RULAND, "What I Discovered about Happiness in Finland"

Ruland goes on to explain the *World Happiness Report*'s findings, weaving in her firsthand experience with Finnish Indigenous culture, cross-country skiing, saunas, freezing temperatures, and more. Even her concluding sentence draws on a bit of narration and a bit of reporting: "I do know how Finland made me feel. Happy."

 REFLECT

For Ruland, the *World Happiness Report* inspired a trip to Finland and a piece of writing that reported on that country, happiness, and her personal adventure. What other kinds of writing might you imagine this report could inspire people to compose? An argument on some aspect of its findings? A proposal for some kind of change? What else?

CHARACTERISTIC FEATURES

While you can expect differences across media and disciplines, most of the reports you will write share the following characteristics:

- A topic carefully focused for a specific audience (p. 310)
- Definitions of key terms (p. 311)
- Trustworthy information (p. 313)
- Effective organization and design (p. 314)
- A confident, informative tone (p. 315)

A Topic Carefully Focused for a Specific Audience

The most effective reports have a focus, a single topic that is limited in scope by what the audience already knows and what the author's purpose is. For example, every year the *U.S. News & World Report* ranks colleges and universities in terms of various criteria—top historically Black colleges and universities, best engineering programs, and schools with the highest value. The authors have in mind their main audience: high school students (and their parents or guardians) who are deciding where to apply. The 2024 report highlighted "14 environmentally friendly college campuses" that "demonstrate a strong interest in environmental protection." The opening of the report speaks right to its audience:

> For college hopefuls who are passionate about the environment, an institution's policies on sustainability may be a major factor they consider in their school search. While some colleges take small steps toward creating a greener campus, others put it at the core of their mission. The following 14 colleges and universities have focused on reducing their negative environmental impact through different initiatives, such as pledging to reduce carbon emissions, limiting food waste or mandating environmental literacy courses.
>
> —ILANA KOWARSKI & SARAH WOOD, "14 Environmentally Friendly College Campuses"

The report goes on to name the schools, elaborating on the environmental programming and opportunities at each campus. Visuals add depth and photographic evidence—like the snapshot of University of Dayton's

University of Dayton (OH)

The University of Dayton offers Bachelor of Arts and Bachelor of Science degrees in sustainability, both designed for undergraduates pursuing double majors such as environmental biology and sustainability. The campus also has a "solar prairie," an eight-acre lawn filled with solar panels and prairie plants that provides opportunities for research and internships.

One entry in a report of top environmentally friendly campuses.

"solar prairie," an eight-acre lawn filled with solar panels and prairie plants that provides opportunities for student research.

While high school students aspiring to careers in environmental studies might use the report to help them decide where to apply, there could be other possible audiences: for example, a current university student or administrator might consult it to find ways their institution could do more. Just as the authors of this report have done, keep your topic carefully focused and keep in mind the main audience you're addressing and their reasons for reading, as well as what they know about your topic and what new information they expect to find.

Definitions of Key Terms

Effective reports always define key terms explicitly. These definitions serve several functions. Some audience members may not understand some of the technical terms. And even those familiar with the terms pay attention to the definitions for clues about the writer's stance or assumptions.

The authors of the *World Happiness Report* (and the creators of the related *YouTube* video) do a lot of defining. One of the first and most important terms defined is "the Cantril ladder," a method researchers use to assess participants' happiness by asking them to first "think of a ladder, with the best possible life for them being a 10 and the worst possible life being a 0" and second to specify "on which step" they stand right now. This definition is necessary for readers to understand how the researchers gather and analyze information from respondents. Both words and visuals help explain it, as the image on page 312 shows. And in the *YouTube* video summarizing the report, an animation helps explain what the Cantril ladder is and how it's used to measure happiness.

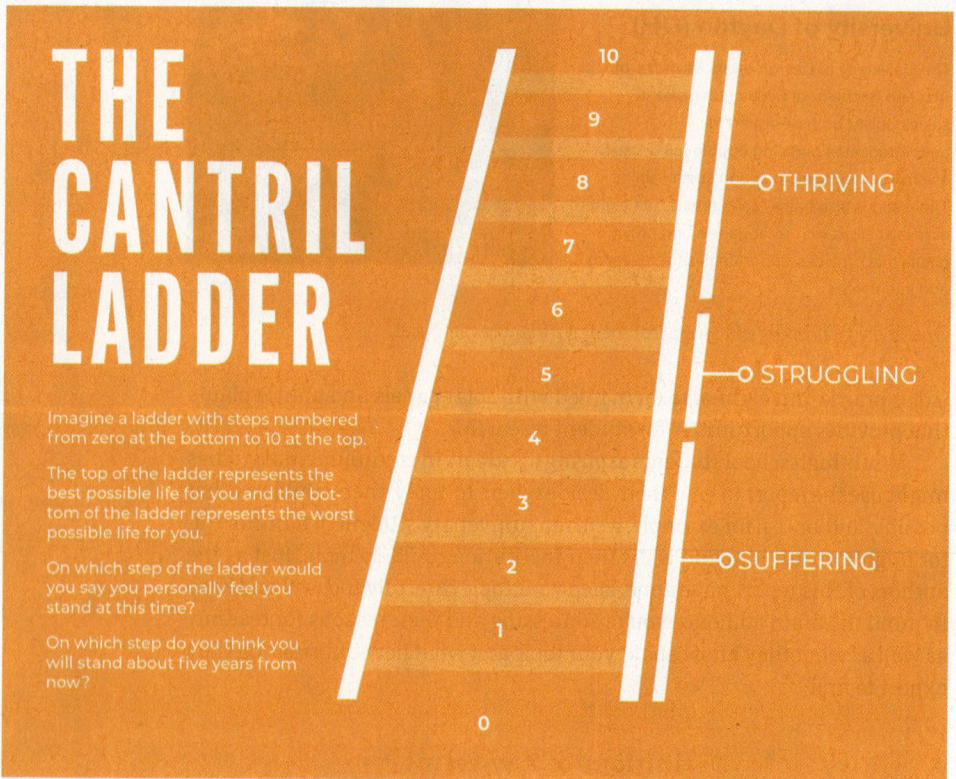

This image defines the key tool researchers use to learn about people's happiness levels.

 The authors go on to offer more definitions, including ones for each of the six "explanatory factors" that break down the "different levels of happiness" that participants experience: social support, healthy life expectancy, freedom to make life choices, generosity, corruption, and GDP per capita. In the report's *YouTube* video, social support is defined as the confidence someone has that "at least one person would care for them when in need," and generosity is defined as "how charitable people are." The video's text on the screen, simple animations, and a voiceover track work together to make these key concepts easy to understand. Finally, in the report's section of frequently asked questions, the authors anticipate questions about specific research terms and provide brief, clear definitions for terms like "data wave," "confidence interval," and "residuals." Clearly defined terms throughout this report help readers get a good sense of how the research was conducted and why it all matters.

Trustworthy Information

Effective reports present information that readers can trust to be accurate. In some cases, writers provide documentation to demonstrate the veracity of their information, including citations of published research, the dates of interviews they have conducted, or other details about their sources.

In a report for a writing class at Chapman University, Kelley Fox presents information in ways that lead readers to trust the details she offers and, ultimately, the author herself. The report describes how Griffin, Simon, and Andy, three roommates in Room 115 of Fox's dorm, create their identities. Beginning with Muhammad Ali's line "Float like a butterfly, sting like a bee," which is the caption on a large poster of Ali on Griffin's wall, Fox seeks to characterize Griffin as someone who floats at "the top of the pecking order" and who seems "invincible":

> In a sense, Griffin is just that: socially invincible. A varsity basketball athlete, Griffin has no shortage of friends, or of female followers. People seem to simply gravitate toward him, as if being around him makes all their problems trivial. Teammates can often be found in his room, hanging out on his bed, watching ESPN. Girls are certainly not a rarity, and they usually come bearing gifts. It happens often, and I have a feeling this "social worship" has been going on for a while, although in myriad other forms. Regardless, the constant and excessive positive attention allows Griffin to never have to think about his own happiness; Griffin always seems happy. And it is because of this that, out of the three roommates, it is easiest to be Griffin.
>
> —KELLEY FOX, "Establishing Identities"

Fox's description demonstrates to readers that she has spent considerable time in or around Room 115 and that she knows what she is writing about. Her use of specific details convinces us that Griffin is real and that the things she describes in fact occur—and on a regular basis.

In a report on early language development in children written for a linguistics class at Portland State University, Katryn Sheppard demonstrates the trustworthiness of her information differently, citing both published

In crafting his report on country music's response to the opioid crisis, Jeff Gage cited artists and songs that would be well-known to his audience, reinforcing the trustworthiness of the information. Read his report on p. 899.

research and her own primary research on a speech transcript of one-year-old Allison:

> One feature of Allison's utterances that did adhere to what is expected for a typical child at this age was related to her use of negatives. Although she used only one negative word—"no"—the word was repeated frequently enough to be the fourth most common category in the transcript. Her use of "no" rather than any other negative conformed to Brown's (1973) finding that other forms of negation like "not" and "don't" appear only in later stages (Santelmann, 2014). In Allison's very early stage of linguistic development, the reliance on "no" alone seems typical.
>
> —KATRYN SHEPPARD, "Early Word Production"

By citing both published research and examples from her own primary research, Sheppard demonstrates that she has spent considerable time researching her topic and can thus make informed observations about Allison's speech. These citations not only let readers know that Sheppard can support her claims, but they also indicate where readers can go to verify the information if they so choose; both strategies demonstrate trustworthiness.

Although Fox and Sheppard use different techniques, both of them convince readers that the information being presented and the writers themselves can be trusted.

Effective Organization and Design

There is no single best strategy for organizing the information you are reporting. In addition to **DEFINING** (as the *World Happiness Report* does), you'll find yourself **DESCRIBING** (as Kelley Fox does), offering specific **EXAMPLES** and data (as the *U.S. News & World Report* does), and **ANALYZING** causes and effects (as Mikeala Ruland does). The specific organizational strategies you'll use will depend on the information you want to report.

In many cases, you'll want to include visuals of some sort, such as photographs, charts, figures, or tables. See, for example, the diagram explaining the Cantril Ladder. Displaying information visually helps deepen the impact of the sentence-level descriptions and definitions in the report. And as noted on page 310, *U.S. News & World Report* also uses photos to make the report more interesting and appealing.

Graphic essays need to present information concisely, so their organization and design are key. See how Dan Nott and Scott Cambo's report on humans and AI weaves explanation and illustration together to make each panel effective. Check it out on p. 960.

Sometimes the way you organize and present your information will be prescribed. If you're writing a report following the **IMRAD** format, you will have little choice in how you organize and present information. Everything from the use of headings to the layout of tables to the size of typefaces may be dictated.

Some disciplines specify certain format details. Students of psychology, for example, are expected to follow **APA STYLE**. On the other hand, a report for a composition class may have fewer constraints. For example, you may get to decide whether you will need headings and whether to use personal examples. Ask your instructor about the format they'd like you to use.

A Confident, Informative Tone

Effective reports have a confident tone that assumes the writer is presenting reliable information rather than arguing or preaching. The authors of the *World Happiness Report* and the *U.S. News & World Report* both sound like they know what they're writing about. In both cases, we as readers are getting the facts about the subject, though it is apparent that the authors have clear convictions about people's happiness and environmentally invested colleges.

The line between informing and arguing can become fuzzy, however. If you read reports on any number of hot-button issues—voting rights, the economy, transgender rights, abortion—you'll find that they often reflect some kind of position or make recommendations that convey a stance. But the authors of such reports usually try to create an informative tone that avoids indicating their own opinions.

You may sometimes find yourself struggling with this line, working to present information while stopping short of telling readers what to think about or how to feel about a topic. Here, we can offer two pieces of advice. First, keep in mind that you're aiming to explain something to your audience clearly and objectively rather than to persuade them to think about it a certain way. You'll know you've succeeded if someone reading a draft of your report can't tell exactly what your own position on the topic is. Second, pay special attention to word choice because the words you use give subtle and not-so-subtle clues about your stance. Referring to "someone who eats meat" is taking an objective tone; calling that person a "carnivore" is not.

PROFILES

Profiles provide firsthand accounts of people, places, events, institutions, or other things. Newspapers and magazines publish profiles of interesting subjects; college websites often include profiles of the student body; investors may study profiles of companies before deciding whether or not to buy stock. Profiles take many different forms, but they generally have the following features.

A Firsthand Account

In creating a profile, you're always writing about something you know firsthand, not merely something you've read about. You may do some reading for background, but reading alone won't suffice. You'll also need to talk with people or visit a place or observe an event in some way. Lucy Diavolo opens her *Teen Vogue* profile on climate activist Greta Thunberg by narrating the moments leading up to their first meeting (including her regret for not being better environmentally prepared):

> I'm on the subway headed to Manhattan to meet Greta Thunberg, the 16-year-old Swedish climate activist who pioneered the climate strike movement, and I'm absolutely kicking myself for forgetting my travel mug. The iced coffee I'm sipping is in a single-use plastic cup—straw and all—and here I am on my way to meet arguably the most visible climate activist in the world.
>
> —LUCY DIAVOLO, "Greta Thunberg Wants You—Yes, You—to Join the Climate Strike"

Once she gets over her embarrassment, Diavolo settles in to her meeting with Thunberg, and the profile proceeds with Diavolo considering how Thunberg is both disrupting and confirming the expectations Diavolo had of the activist.

> Having completed a transatlantic journey by sailboat, Greta is scheduled to speak at the United Nations General Assembly's Climate Action Summit, another chance she'll have to make her no-nonsense appeal to world leaders about the urgent necessity of international action on the climate crisis. She's famous for being ruthlessly frank with the global elite,

so when I meet her in a midtown conference room on a recent Friday morning, I'm surprised to find a reserved young woman who speaks softly after carefully considering each question I ask.

What's less surprising is the steadfast confidence and grave seriousness that emanates from this teenager who has given voice to an entire generation's existential fear and energized a worldwide movement demanding everything necessary and possible to save our planet.

Diavolo's in-person meeting and interview enables her to gain insight on Thunberg and share that insight with readers. That we're reading a profile through Diavolo's eyes is clear: Diavolo notes her embarrassment for forgetting her travel mug, and she marks her "surprise" at Thunberg's soft-spokenness, when her previous knowledge of Thunberg was that the young woman was "urgent," "frank," and "no-nonsense." Though the profile offers factual information, it is enriched by Diavolo's firsthand account of her interactions with Thunberg.

Detailed Information about the Subject

Profiles are always full of details—background information, descriptive details (sights, sounds, smells), anecdotes, and dialogue. Ideally, these details help bring the subject to life—and persuade your audience that whatever you're writing about is interesting, and worth reading about. What makes the *Teen Vogue* profile so successful is the kind of details about Thunberg the author provides. Diavolo zeroes in on Thunberg's experiences with both Asperger's syndrome and depression and includes quotations from Thunberg to help readers gain a keen sense of Thunberg's ideas on these topics. For instance, Thunberg explains to Diavolo the importance of listening to people who "think a bit outside the box and who can see things from a different, new perspective." Diavolo then includes a longer quotation so readers can learn more directly from Thunberg:

> We need these people, especially now, when we need to change things and we can't see it just from where we are. We need to see it from a bigger perspective and from outside our current systems. . . . That's why people who are different are so necessary: because they contribute so much. Therefore we need to really look after the people who may not be heard. We need to listen to those and to look after each other.

These inspirational words enable readers to grasp Thunberg's understanding of difference and the role of difference in activism. The author also includes more mundane yet still compelling details that help readers come to know Thunberg. Diavolo reports that when she asked how Thunberg has liked her visit to the States and especially New York City, Thunberg replies that she

Greta Thunberg holds a protest sign that says *Skolstrejk för klimatet*, Swedish for "School strike for climate." School strikes were Thunberg's early form of activism.

has been "keeping up her routine of unwinding with long walks by strolling through Central Park and visiting New York's museums." Diavolo notes that it's especially "fitting" that Thunberg's favorite museum is the American Museum of Natural History—a specific detail that adds even more nuance to the picture Diavolo draws for readers.

Another way that writers of profiles bring their subjects "to life" is by including photos, letting readers see their subjects in action. In the photo on the previous page (which was featured in the *Teen Vogue* profile), Thunberg is in her element, holding a protest sign with a solemn expression on her face, letting us see some of what Diavolo describes.

An Interesting Angle

The best profiles present a new or surprising perspective on whatever is being profiled. In other words, a good profile isn't merely a description; rather, it captures something essential about its subject from an interesting angle, much like a memorable photo does. When you plan a profile, try to come up with an angle that will engage readers. This angle will dictate what information you include. In addition to the smaller details that bring to life Thunberg's personality throughout Diavolo's profile, the author takes an interesting angle in the concluding paragraphs when she reflects on the importance of "perspective," which came up several times in conversation with Thunberg. Diavolo considers how this term resonates for herself and for people interested in supporting Thunberg's activism:

> The fact that "perspective" came up twice during our interview doesn't surprise me, nor does it surprise me that Greta talks about the view of the stars from her sailboat or the way she views Asperger's as her superpower. Youth climate activists have a way of giving those of us who might be older and more jaded the perspective to see the potential for a future without crisis, but meeting Greta affirms that this is more than just hijacking youthful activism. It is about welcoming the perspective of a generation that is fighting for its own future—for the right to live.

You'll find an annotated model of a profile, "Heart and Sole: Detroiter Walks 21 Miles in Work Commute" by Bill Laitner on page 341.

REPORTING INFORMATION / A Roadmap

Choose a topic that matters—to you, and to others

If you get to select your topic, begin by considering topics that you know something about or are interested in learning more about. Whatever your topic, be sure it's one you find intriguing and can be objective about. If you're a devout Catholic and believe that the church is wrong—or right—in its stance on birth control, you're likely to have trouble objectively sticking to the facts, which is necessary for writing a good report.

The more controversial the topic, the more challenging it may be to report fairly and accurately on it because the facts themselves likely will be the subject of controversy. So if you're going to write about a controversial topic, you might consider reporting on the controversy itself: the major perspectives on the issue, the kinds of evidence cited, and so on.

If you've been assigned a topic, find an aspect of it that is both interesting and focused. Unless you've been specifically instructed to address a broad topic (for example, the consequences of World Bank policies for developing economies), focus on a narrower aspect of the topic (take a single country that interests you and report on the consequences of World Bank policies for that economy). Even when you are asked to report on a broad topic, see if it is possible to start out with a specific case and then move to the broader issue.

Consider your rhetorical situation

Analyzing your audience, purpose, and other elements of your rhetorical situation will help you make the decisions you'll face as you write.

Think about the best way to address your AUDIENCE. If you're writing a report for an audience you know—your classmates, your instructor—you can sometimes assume what they will and won't know about your topic. But if you're writing for a broader audience—all students on campus, readers of a blog—you'll probably be addressing people with different levels of knowledge. Your challenge will be to provide enough information without including irrelevant details. Here are some questions that might guide you in considering your audience:

- What do you know about your audience? To what extent are they like or unlike you—or one another?
- What background information will your audience need on your topic? Will their knowledge of it vary?
- What terms need to be defined or illustrated with examples? What sorts of examples will be most effective for your audience?
- What interest does your audience have in your topic? If they're not already interested in it, how can you get them interested—or at least to see that it matters?

Be clear about your PURPOSE. Consider why you are writing a report on this topic for this particular audience. Odds are that you want your report to do more than merely convey information. If you're writing it for a course, you want to learn something and to get a good grade. If the report is part of a large project—a campaign to encourage composting on campus, for example—a lot may be riding on the quality of your work. What short-term goals do you have in writing, and do they relate to any longer-term goals?

Consider your STANCE. Think about your own attitudes toward your topic and your audience: What about this topic captured your interest? Why do you think it matters—or should matter—both in general and to your audience? How can you establish your authority on the topic and get your audience to trust you and the information you provide? How do you want them to see you? As a fair, objective reporter? As thoughtful? serious? curious? something else?

Consider your LANGUAGE. Almost everything can be said in a variety of ways. Regardless of how many dialects or languages you use in your everyday life, you have many options for your report including, for example, your level of formality. Which option will be most suitable and effective for what you are trying to accomplish? Will your audience expect a certain kind of language or style? Do you want to meet those expectations? challenge them? What do you want your language to say about you? What risks might you be willing to take with your language? How will the medium and larger context limit or expand the language options that are available to you? You may want to consult Chapters 4 and 35 for more advice about language options.

Consider the larger CONTEXT. What are the various perspectives on the topic, and what else has been said about it? What larger conversations, if any, is this topic a part of? For a report that's part of a campaign to encourage composting on campus, for example, you'd need to become familiar with how such programs have been conducted at other schools, and what the main challenges and arguments have been.

Think about MEDIA. As the *World Happiness Report* makes clear, the medium you use plays a big role in determining the message you convey. If you have a choice, will your text be presented in print? online? as an oral report? via a podcast? Which will be most effective for your subject and audience? If you've got audio of an interview, can you embed it in an online report or incorporate it into an oral report? If your report will be in print, can you summarize or quote from the interview? If your report will be oral, should you prepare slides to help your audience follow your main points?

Think about DESIGN. Consider what design elements are available to you and will help you convey your information in the clearest, most memorable way. For example, much of the effectiveness of the United Nations' *World Happiness Report* video comes from the animation and voiceover explanation of the report's findings. Think about whether your report will include any elements that should be highlighted. Do you need headings? Would photos, charts, tables, or other visuals help you convey information more effectively than words alone? Do you have the option of using color in your text—and if so, what colors will set the right tone?

Research your topic

Your goal in researching your topic is first to get a broad overview of what is known about it and second to develop a deeper understanding of the topic. While most high school reports discuss the research of others, those you write in college may call on you to gather data yourself and then write about the data in light of existing research.

LAB REPORTS, for example, describe the results of experiments in engineering and the natural sciences, and reports based on ethnographic observation are common in the social sciences. And whatever your topic or field, reading SECONDARY SOURCES will help you see how your findings relate to what people already know.

Thus, your first task is to read broadly enough to get a feel for the various issues and perspectives on your topic so that you know what you're talking about and can write about it authoritatively. If your instructor's policies allow, generative AI tools might help you find background information about a topic, but remember to verify any facts AI provides.

Begin by assessing what you know—and don't know—about the topic. What aspects of your topic do you need to learn more about? What questions do you have about it? What questions will your audience have? To answer these questions, you might try BRAINSTORMING or other activities for GENERATING IDEAS. Such activities may help you focus your topic and also discover areas you need to research further.

Find out what others say. You can research others' POSITIONS and perspectives in many different ways. If your topic is a local one, such as alcohol use at your college, you may want to conduct a student survey, interview administrators or counselors who deal with campus drinking problems, or do a search of local newspapers for articles about alcohol-related incidents. But it would also be a good idea to look beyond your own community, in order to gain perspective on how the situation at your school fits into national patterns. You could consult books and periodicals, databases, websites, or online forums devoted to your topic. If your topic doesn't have a local focus, you will likely start out by consulting sources like these. You may also interview people at your school or in the community who are experts on your topic.

Decide whether you need to narrow your topic. What aspect of your topic most interests you, and how much can you cover given the constraints of your assignment? If your political science professor has assigned a five-minute oral report on climate-change legislation, for example, you will need to find a more specific focus than you would for a twenty-page written report on the same general topic.

See Ch. 23 in the ebook for a video on narrowing your topic.

Organize and start writing

Once you've narrowed your topic and have some sense of what you want to say about it, you need to think about how you can frame your topic to appeal to your audience and how you can best organize the information you have collected. As you draft, you may discover that you need to do some additional research as new questions and ideas arise. But for now, just get started.

Come up with a tentative thesis. State your topic and the gist of what you have to say about it in a tentative **THESIS** statement, trying to make it broad enough to cover the range of information you want to share with your audience but limited enough to be manageable—and keeping in mind that your goal is to report information, not to argue a position.

Organize your information. Make a list of the information you want to convey, and think about what details you want to include. You'll find that you need various strategies for presenting information— **DESCRIPTION**, **DEFINITION**, **ANALYSIS**, **EXAMPLES**, and so on.

Then consider how to arrange your material. Some topics call for a **CHRONOLOGICAL** structure, moving from past to present, maybe even projecting into the future. Or you may find that a **SPATIAL ORGANIZATION** works well—if you're reporting on the design of a new building, for instance—moving from exterior to interior or from top to bottom. There are any number of ways to organize a report in addition to these; you'll just need to work out a structure that will help your audience understand your topic in a systematic way.

Don't be surprised if you find that you do not need to use all the information that you have collected. Authors often gather far more information than they finally use; your task is to choose the information that is most relevant to your thesis and present it as effectively as possible.

Draft an OPENING. Why do you care about your topic, and how can you get your audience interested in it? You will want to open by announcing your subject in a way that makes your audience want to know more about it. Consider opening with an intriguing example or a provocative question. Perhaps you have a memorable anecdote. It's usually a good idea also to include the thesis somewhere in the introduction so that your audience can follow from the outset where your report is heading and don't have to figure this out for themselves.

Draft a CONCLUSION. What do you want your audience to take away from your report? What do you want them to remember? You could end by noting the implications of your report, reminding them why your topic matters.

You could summarize your main points. You could even end with a question, leaving them with something to think about.

Look critically at your draft, get responses—and revise

Try rereading your draft several times from different perspectives and imagining how different readers will experience your text. Will readers new to the topic follow what you are saying? Will those who know about the topic think that you have represented it accurately and fairly? If possible, get feedback from a classmate or a tutor at your school's writing center. Following are some questions that can help you and others examine a report with a critical eye:

- *How does the report* OPEN *?* Will it capture your audience's interest? How else might it begin?

- *Is the topic clear and well focused?* Are the scope and structure of the report set out in its opening paragraphs? Is there a THESIS statement—and if not, would it help to add one?

- *Is it clear why the topic matters*—why you care about it and why others should?

- *How does the draft appeal to your* AUDIENCE *?* Will they be able to understand what you say, or do you need to provide more background information or define any terms?

- *How do you establish your* AUTHORITY *on the topic?* Does the information presented seem trustworthy? Are the sources for your information credible, and have you provided any necessary DOCUMENTATION ?

- *Is the* TONE *suited to your audience and purpose?* If it seems tentative or timid, how could you make it more confident? If it comes across as argumentative, how could you make it focus on the facts alone?

- *How is the information organized?* Past to present? Simple to complex? Some other way? Does the structure suit your topic and MEDIUM ? What strategies have you used to present information— COMPARISON , DESCRIPTION , NARRATION ?

- *What* MEDIA *will the report be presented in,* and how does that affect the way it's written? You might consider, for example, including photos in a print report, videos and links in an online report, or slides to go along with an oral presentation.

- *Is the report easy to follow?* If not, try adding TRANSITIONS or headings. If it's an oral report, you might put your main points on slides.

- *If you've included illustrations,* are there captions that explain how they relate to the written text? Have you referred to the illustration in your text? Is there information in your text that would be easier to follow in a chart or table?

- *Is the* STYLE *effectively engaging your audience?* How are you speaking to their language backgrounds and expectations? How might you challenge those expectations and for what purpose? Consider choice of words, level of formality, and so on.

- *How effective is your* CONCLUSION *?* How else might you end?

- *Does the title tell readers what the report is about,* and will it make them want to know more?

Revise your draft in response to any feedback you receive and your own analysis, keeping in mind that your goal is to stick to the facts.

# REFLECT

Once you've completed your report, let it settle for a while and then take time to REFLECT . How well did you report on your topic? How successful do you think you were in making the topic interesting to your audience? What additional revisions would you make if you could? Research shows that such reflections help "lock in" what you learn for future use.

READINGS / Annotated Model Reports

How Digital Beauty Filters Perpetuate Colorism
TATE RYAN-MOSLEY

WHEN LISE WAS A YOUNG TEENAGER in Georgia, her classmates bullied her relentlessly. She had moved with her family from Haiti a few years earlier, and she didn't fit in with the other students. They teased her about her accent, claimed she "smelled weird," and criticized the food she ate. But most often they would attack her with remarks about her dark complexion. Sometimes teachers would send her home from school because she couldn't stop crying. "I remember going home and I would take those copper wire things that you scrub dishes with," she says. "I would go to the bathroom and I would take my mom's bleach cream and scrub my skin with it."

And it wasn't just white classmates. Black students harassed her too—for being an outsider, for being too different. She remembers them asking, "Why is she so dark?"

Just when she thought it couldn't get worse, the phone in her palm became an endless stream of pictures of beautiful, lighter-skinned women getting dozens, hundreds, or even thousands of likes and affirming comments. She slowly began to notice that the world wanted parts of her—like her curves and her lips—but not things like her dark skin or her hair. Not her whole self, all together.

The **INTRODUCTION** *sets up the issue that the report will cover by offering a teenager's real-life experience with colorism.*

TATE RYAN-MOSLEY is a reporter for *MIT Technology Review*, where she writes about the social impact of new technologies. Ryan-Mosley's articles for *MIT Technology Review* have focused on police use of facial recognition, internet shutdowns, artificial intelligence, and disinformation. This report was published in August 2021.

As she struggled to cope with the abuse, Lise convinced herself that the darkness of her skin was to blame. And social media platforms and the visual culture of the internet suggested the same thing.

Even among those closest to her, the undesirability of her darkness was reinforced. She grew to realize that her mom, aunts, and friends all used the skin-lightening creams she'd borrowed after school, many of which contain toxins and even carcinogens. It was confusing: her community fought hard against racism, but some of the prejudice she experienced came from Black people themselves.

And social media was just making it worse.

The prejudice Lise experienced—colorism—has a long history, driven by European ideals of beauty that associate lighter skin with purity and wealth, darker tones with sin and poverty. Though related to racism, it's distinct in that it can affect people regardless of their race, and can have different effects on people of the same background. . . .

These prejudices have been part of the social and media landscape for a long time, but the advent of digital images and *Photoshop* created new ways for colorism to manifest. In June 1994, notoriously, *Newsweek* and *Time* both ran cover images of O.J. Simpson's mug shot during his murder trial—but on *Time*'s cover, his skin was markedly darker. The difference sparked outrage: *Time* had darkened the image in what the magazine's photo illustrator claimed was an attempt to evoke a more "dramatic tone". But the editing reflected that the darker the man, the more criminal the American public assumes him to be.

This association has very real consequences. A 2011 study from Villanova University found a direct link between the severity of sentences for 12,000 incarcerated women and the darkness of their complexion.

And today, thanks to the prevalence of selfies and face filters, digital colorism has spread. With *Snapchat*, *Instagram*, *TikTok*, and *Facebook* a part of billions of people's everyday lives, many of us find that people see far more pictures of us than ever before. But there are biases built into these systems. At a basic level, the imaging chips found in most personal cameras have pre-set ranges for skin tones, making it technically impossible to accurately capture the real variety of complexions.

And the images that do get taken are often subject to alteration. *Snapchat* reports that over 200 million people use its filter product, Lenses, every day. Some of them use it to lighten their skin tone; other filters and automatic enhancing features can do the same on *Instagram* and *TikTok*. Photo technologies and

---

Tate-Mosley DEFINES *the experience she described in the opening paragraphs as colorism.*

The report pinpoints more EXAMPLES *of colorism at work and research that identifies its negative effects.*

Consider the ORGANIZATION: *the author opened by establishing colorism before moving into how colorism operates through social media filters.*

Examples and research add to the author's informative and TRUSTWORTHY TONE.

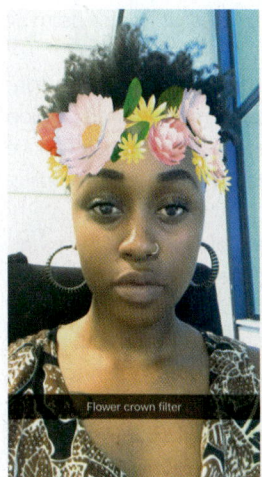  

Snapchat filters alter a user's skin tone.

image filters can do this in ways that are almost imperceptible. Meanwhile, social media algorithms reinforce the popularity of people with lighter skin to the detriment of those with darker skin. Just this week, *Twitter*'s image-cropping algorithm was found to prefer faces that are lighter, thinner, and younger.

Selfie-Esteem

... The [filter] phenomenon has led to the concept of the "Instagram face," a particular look that's easily accessible through the proliferation of editing tools. Photos reflecting this look, with a small nose, big eyes, and fuller lips, attract more comments and likes, leading recommendation algorithms to prioritize them. We also interviewed researchers who say beauty ideals are narrowing even more dramatically and quickly than they expected—with especially profound effects on the way young girls, in particular, see themselves and shape their identity.

But it could be particularly catastrophic for women with darker complexions, says Ronald Hall, a professor at Michigan State University and an expert on colorism. As more European looks are increasingly held up as an ideal, "these young girls imitate these behaviors, and those who are super dark-complected

> *The author* **DEFINES** *a key term, "Instagram face."*

see no way out," he says. "Those are the ones who are most at risk for harming themselves."

That harm can involve bleaching or other risky body treatments: the skin-lightening industry has grown rapidly and is now worth more than $8 billion worldwide each year. But beyond physical risks, researchers and activists have also begun documenting troubling emotional and psychological effects of online colorism.

Amy Niu researches selfie-editing behavior as part of her PhD in psychology at the University of Wisconsin, Madison. In 2019, she conducted a study to determine the effect of beauty filters on self-image for American and Chinese women. She took pictures of 325 college-aged women and, without telling them, applied a filter to some photos. She then surveyed the women to measure their emotions and self-esteem when they saw edited or unedited photos. Her results, which have not yet been published, found that Chinese women viewing edited photos felt better about themselves, while American women (87% of whom were white) felt about the same whether their photos were edited or not.

Niu believes that the results show there are huge differences between cultures when it comes to "beauty standards and how susceptible people are to those beauty filters." She adds, "Technology companies are realizing it, and they are making different versions [of their filters] to tailor to the needs of different groups of people."

This has some very obvious manifestations. Niu, a Chinese woman living in America, uses both *TikTok* and *Douyin*, the Chinese version (both are made by the same company, and share many of the same features, although not the same content). The two apps both have "beautify" modes, but they are different: Chinese users are given more extreme smoothing and complexion lightening effects.

She says the differences don't just reflect cultural beauty standards—they perpetuate them. White Americans tend to prefer filters that make their skin tanner, teeth whiter, and eyelashes longer, while Chinese women prefer filters that make their skin lighter.

Niu worries that the vast proliferation of filtered images is making beauty standards more uniform over time, especially for Chinese women. "In China, the beauty standard is more homogeneous," she says, adding that the filters "erase lots of differences to our faces" and reinforce one particular look.

"It's Really Bad"

Amira Adawe has observed the same dynamic in the way young girls of color use filters on social media. Adawe is the founder and executive director of Beautywell, a Minnesota-based nonprofit aimed at combating colorism and skin-lightening practices. The organization runs programs to educate young girls of color about online safety, healthy digital behaviors, and the dangers of physical skin lightening.

Adawe says she often has to inform the girls in her workshops that their skin is being lightened by social media filters. "They think it's normal. They're like, 'Oh, this is not skin lightening, Amira. This is just a filter,'" she says. "A lot of these young girls use these filters and think, 'Oh my God, I look beautiful.'"

Another INTERVIEW with an expert on this issue offers a different perspective.

It's so easy to do—with a few clicks, users can make their appearance more similar to everyone else's ideal—that many young women end up assuming a lighter-skinned identity online. This makes it easier to find acceptance in the digital world, but it can also make it harder for them to identify with their real complexion.

When Adawe explains how using a face filter can be part of a cycle of colorism, she is often met with resistance. The filters have become essential to the way some girls see themselves.

"It's really bad," she says. "And it's contributing to this notion that you're not beautiful enough."

And it's complicated regardless of your skin tone.

Halle, a single biracial woman in her mid-20s, thinks a lot about her own racial identity. She says most people would use the term "ambiguous" to describe her appearance. "I have whiter features," she says. "My skin complexion is lighter than some other mixed-race girls', and my hair is less curly." She also used to be a regular user of dating apps. And from conversations with her friends who have darker complexions, she realized that her experience on dating apps was very different from theirs.

"Quite candidly, we compare matches and number of matches," she says. "That is where I started to realize: wait a minute, there's something going on here. My friends who identify as Black or Afro-Latina don't get as many matches."...

Halle says her experience on these apps reflects the wider world, too. "This is deeply rooted in racism, colorism, and everything that's happening in our society," she says. The experience became so frustrating for her that she deleted all her dating apps. *MIT Technology Review* has reached out to many dating sites to ask whether they use beauty-scoring algorithms for matches, but none will confirm or deny. . . .

Meanwhile, platforms including *TikTok* have been accused of intentionally "shadow-banning" content from some Black creators, especially those discussing the Black Lives Matter movement or racism in general. That diminishes their reach, and the cycle reinforces itself further. (In a statement, a *TikTok* spokesperson said "We unequivocally do not moderate content or accounts on the basis of race.")

Michigan State's Ronald Hall says he's "extremely worried" about the impact on women of color in particular: "Women of color are constantly bombarded with these messages that you gotta be light in order to be attractive."

Adawe, meanwhile, thinks the only solution is an all-out ban on filters that lighten faces. She says she has emailed *Snapchat* asking for just that. "Social media companies keep [creating] filters because the demand is so high," she says. "But to me, I think they're promoting colorism, whether they realize it and whether it's intentional or not."

A spokesperson for Snap told *MIT Technology Review*, "Our goal is to build products that are fully inclusive of all Snapchatters, and we've put in place a number of processes and initiatives to help us do that. Our guidelines for all Snapchatters—which also apply to Lens submissions—prohibit discrimination and the promotion of stereotypes, and we have an extensive review process in place for Lenses, which includes testing them on a wide range of skin tones."

The company says it is partnering with experts for advice, and earlier this year it launched an initiative to build an "inclusive camera," which is meant to be better at capturing a broader range of skin tones.

A Completely Different Lens

Lise, who now lives in Minnesota, struggled with the effects of colorism for a long time. She went to therapy, watched endless *YouTube* tutorials on photo editing, and even bought a $600 camera that she hoped would make her look less dark in photos. Eventually she came to realize how harmful it had been.

"Now I just view everyone's social media page with a completely different lens," she says. . . .

The reporter makes clear she contacted dating sites to learn their PERSPECTIVE on this issue.

Moves into how experts question social media's responsibility in perpetuating colorism.

She says she wants to see more raw photos online that show beautiful women who look like her. She no longer edits her skin color in photos, and she tries hard to stop the negative thoughts in her head, though it can be hard. "Oh, I'll be darned if I see someone saying anything to a beautiful dark-skinned woman," she says. "I don't care if it's online, I don't care if it's in person—I'm going to call you out. I just can't be quiet about it anymore. . . ."

The report begins and ends with Lise NARRATING her experience with colorism.

 REFLECT & WRITE

Tate Ryan-Mosley's report describes the harmful, and unequal, effects that digital technologies like photo-editing tools have on users and how some technology companies are responding. She quotes a *Snapchat* representative who says, "Our goal is to build products that are fully inclusive of all Snapchatters, and we've put in place a number of processes and initiatives to help us do that. Our guidelines for all Snapchatters . . . prohibit discrimination and the promotion of stereotypes, and we have an extensive review process in place for Lenses, which includes testing them on a wide range of skin tones." Do your own research into what companies with beauty filter features are doing in response to the information Ryan-Mosley reports. Do these companies have a responsibility to ensure their products don't promote discrimination? If so, are these companies doing enough? Write an essay that takes a POSITION on these questions.

This article has been edited specifically for this textbook. The original article can be found online at https://www.technologyreview.com/.

The Future of the American City: Omaha's Hope
MCCADE GOWDY

Opens with a brief narrative to set up the report's TOPIC.

WHEN BENNY FOLTZ COMMUTES to his office, he often relies on his bike. His 13-mile route consists of trails, bike lanes and dodging cars on his way to his office in downtown Omaha. Sure, he could hop in a car and make the drive in a few minutes. It would be convenient. But that convenience is what got him to start riding to work in the first place.

"When I was at a tech company, we had this huge parking lot. And fast-food restaurants were on the other side of the parking lot," he said. "People would walk out of the office building to their car, drive to the fast-food restaurant, go through the drive-through and bring it back. It just blew my mind."

He thought more people should bike to work. At the time, Omaha was in the infancy of a bikeshare program. Foltz was inspired, so much so he started a similar bike-share at his work. It was "wildly unsuccessful." Everyone just kept using cars.

One main EXAMPLE, *returned to throughout, helps organize the report.*

That didn't deter Foltz, though. Fast forward to today and Foltz is now the executive director of ROAM bike share, the organization that originally inspired him. And the timing couldn't be better.

MCCADE GOWDY wrote this report, which won a Mark of Excellence Award from the Society for Professional Journalists, as a student at Drake University. It was published on the *Urban Plains* website by the organization of the same name that aims to "provide eye-opening profiles, engaging visuals, and first-hand accounts from the people who call [the Midwest] home." In this essay, underlined text indicates hyperlinks in the original.

Change on the Horizon

Like many American cities, Omaha is at an inflection point. The city has undergone decades of suburban development, creating a complex web of strip malls and cul-de-sacs that stretch for miles. And for decades, that expansion outward was viewed as progress. After all, the more land you have, the better off you are. Right?

Maybe not. Omaha has hit an invisible wall. Once a <u>powerful annexation force</u>, swallowing communities of less than 10,000 whole without so much as a vote from that town, Omaha is now running out of space to grow.

To the south, there are already multiple cities with populations too big to gobble up, making growth in this direction impossible. They also can't expand to the east over the Missouri River—that's Iowa and already claimed by Omaha's sister city, Council Bluffs. And the hilly north is too difficult to develop.

A new bus on the ORBT system sits at a station with several bikes nearby. Part of ROAM's Heartland Bike Share includes the "first/last" mile, which ensures people have a way to get to and from these stops.

Questions and answers establish an engaging TONE, *inviting readers in.*

Uses an OBJECTIVE TONE *to relay the facts of Omaha's situation.*

That just leaves west of the city. Yet a single ridge challenges the whole plan. Over that ridgeline lies a separate watershed, which requires its own sewage system. There would also be new roads, new electrical lines—all of it more costly when they must travel farther and serve fewer people.

So Omaha, like other hemmed-in Midwest cities like Des Moines and Kansas City, is looking to change the land it's already using. Its future is tied up in making the city denser. That means adjusting the space the city already occupies. It means rethinking its transit system. And it means making the city more walkable—or in Foltz's case, more rideable—as well. Omaha is about to get a makeover—and it could have massive implications for its citizens, the climate and more. If they can get people to buy into it.

The Car Revolution

To understand how we got to a car-centered suburbia today (and why we're trying to get out of it), we have to look at how American cities developed. In the early 1900s, many cities were walkable and had public transportation.

"At the turn of the 20th century, American cities were at their most accessible," said Bradley Lane, an associate professor of urban planning at the University of Kansas. "Everything remotely resembling a village in the United States had a trolley system. And going into the 1920s and '30s and '40s, we had the largest urban rail network in the world."

Omaha was no different. The original downtown was small, and the city had an extensive streetcar network.

But then came Henry Ford and his mass-production of shiny new automobiles. The accessibility of the modern car changed the landscape of city planning.

"Around the country in the latter half of the 20th century, there's basically a complete focus on automobile-oriented suburban sprawl," said Kevin Carder, an Omaha city planner.

From then on, Omaha—and every other city in America—focused on constructing large roadways and interstates. The cost of living was cheaper in the suburbs. Residents could commute downtown to work. Walkability didn't just suffer; it was ignored.

Steve Jensen, former planning director for the City of Omaha, saw this when he began work in the 1970s. In his early days, he was tasked with planning roadways. His bosses told him to make six-lane roads everywhere. Jensen questioned this.

"I asked 'Why would we do that?'" Jensen said. "'Why would we need that many lanes to handle the traffic?' And the reaction from Public Works was,

'Well, because we have no idea how much development is going to occur . . . just to be safe, let's make everything six lanes.'"

And that just made room for more cars. In fact, research has shown that <u>building more lanes does not equal less traffic</u>.

"If we are solving problems from today's car-centric perspective, and add another lane, we are going to just see more cars," said Alenka Poplin, associate professor of community and regional planning at Iowa State University. "We will not be able to reduce the number of cars because we didn't offer an alternative."

Get Out of the Car

Across the country, cities are trying to come up with those alternatives, but it's not easy. It's a geography problem. Cities are spread out labyrinths of strip malls, fast food restaurants and supermarkets. And they all have massive parking lots, vast asphalt lakes connected via multilane road tributaries. Even when something is close—say, going across one of those parking lots for a coffee—people still drive.

Poplin believes you can begin to change this if you give attention to people, not cars.

"What would be a city that would make citizens happy?" she asked. "A happy city would be able to adapt quickly to new situations."

Poplin's research focuses largely on what she calls "smart cities." Sure, that can mean the cities are technologically advanced, but that's not all. It can also mean intentional. She asks folks what they want to see in urban settings. They want cities that are walkable. With parks and shopping centers. That are easy to navigate. Then she gives it to them.

Sort of.

Using a melding of video games, social media and surveys, Poplin creates virtual environments where users can create their own ideal public space. Cities that meet residents' real needs, not whatever the government imagines the common person must want.

"There's a lot of pent-up consumer demand for more and more options," Lane said. "More walkability. Easier, closer access to things."

That, of course, means creating more mixed-use areas, where housing and shopping are intertwined. Where there's more multifamily housing. Where there's less need for cars. But that's easier said than done. . . .

> DEFINITION *of a key term.*

A Changing City for a Changing Climate

Cars don't just impact citizens—they impact the planet. In 2020, transportation accounted for 27% of total emissions in the U.S. Within that, cars are a major contributor, comprising 57% of this category. And this means something needs to change.

In many ways, the solution has been to shift to electric vehicles. But this comes with its own problems, namely that our electric grids aren't adapted to charging all these cars.

"We do not currently have the capacity to deliver the amperage to charge those vehicles all at once. And there isn't a solution for that," Lane said.

While Lane sees potential for innovation in electric vehicle charging, it's still a massive challenge. So he has another idea, one that's easier: a focus on shared vehicles. Right now, the average vehicle occupancy is "generously 1.2," according to Lane.

If you can increase occupancy to an average of two people, a lot changes. Miles traveled per person drops dramatically since you have one car commuting instead of two. Lane estimates that alone could "presumably cut travel by 80%." Even if that's an overestimate, it still significantly cuts down on emissions. It cuts down on gas. It cuts down on the number of cars that need charging. It's a different approach to climate change. It looks at changing our behavior instead of our energy source.

Biking to Work

Back to Foltz. He doggedly bikes those 13 miles to work every day, dodging traffic and pedestrians alike. For him, biking is transit, and bike-share is more than getting exercise or having fun. ROAM's investment and implementation of e-bikes has shown that.

"Imagine if you didn't have a car, or you didn't have a bus stop and you had access to an e-bike like this," he said. "You don't have to maintain it and it's available year-round. It's a great thing happening in the bike-share world."

In fact, ROAM just announced their move to a 100% electric fleet. It positions the organization to function more like a transportation provider. Which is what Foltz has been building toward. ROAM has more than doubled the number of stations and staff in Omaha since Foltz took over in 2017. They even played a part in the protected bike lane in the new development of the downtown region. Along that route alone they installed five stations.

"The No. 1 reason people aren't riding is because of safety," Foltz said. "To overcome that, we need more infrastructure."

ROAM goes beyond providing bikes for people. They also research how people use bikes within the region.

"We've provided enough data that this type of infrastructure is allowing more folks to ride their bikes safely and that's where they want to ride, as opposed to on the street," Foltz said.

For Foltz, growing the e-bike system is all about educating the public. He said people don't realize how useful these bikes can be, and he thinks it could change transit.

Equitability

Retrofitting cities does more than help middle-class citizens. It helps everyone. There are plenty of people that can't afford cars. Lessening the need for a car, or even removing that need altogether, impacts everyone up and down the socioeconomic ladder.

> *Describes another key effect of relying less on cars, and provides more research.*

It's one of the things the Metropolitan Area Planning Agency (MAPA) is considering. MAPA is focused on the Omaha–Council Bluffs region, spanning across six counties and two states. They assist local governments with creating sustainable growth, and their long-term goal looks toward the year 2050. They envision the region hosting an additional 500,000 residents.

Mike Helgerson, MAPA's executive director, said their planning doesn't focus on traditional transportation planning like efficiency of traffic or freight movement. Similarly to Poplin's research, it's concentrated on people.

"Our first goal is access to opportunity," Helgerson said. "What role does transportation have in connecting people to educational opportunities, employment opportunities and daily needs like health care?"

MAPA works closely with Omaha Metro Transit. They assisted with ORBT, a new rapid bus transit line in the city. This resulted in $35 million of new investment in an area with some of the largest employers in the region.

"That's kind of our forte, helping community leaders think long-term about some of these issues," Helgerson said. "And then on the back end, trying to connect them with the resources to implement the plans."

The next targeted area will be along 24th Street, a corridor that connects north and south Omaha—areas that have large Black and Latino populations. They are also areas of poverty and have been victims of redlining.

To work toward equitable transportation, ROAM also has focused on making bikes accessible. They partner with food shelters, nonprofits working to help people find employment and nonprofits that help incarcerated people with transition.

"If someone can't afford a membership, we pretty much will give you one," Foltz said. "We firmly believe in this."

They were one of the first to implement this type of program in the nation, making access to transit more viable.

Automating the Future

City plans are long term. They can't be changed from year to year and can be slow to adapt. Intentional planning is patient. Technology is not. How people navigate cities could change drastically in the future. From <u>flying taxis</u> to <u>convertible bus-trains</u>, there are countless new ideas and innovations in the pipeline.

Autonomous cars alone might force cities to adjust in massive ways. They could change how we view ownership. People may simply call a car from a ride-share app. Or send their car home after it drives them to work.

These changes in technology could threaten new plans for transit and walkability. But they're not here yet.

"It's a really interesting juncture right now for the future of the American city," Lane said. Omaha's hope: That its citywide makeover helps define that future for everyone.

Ends with why the topic matters to a broad AUDIENCE.

REFLECT & WRITE

McCade Gowdy's report focuses on accessibility in Omaha, Nebraska, and more broadly on the topic of city planning. What kind of research does Gowdy conduct to compose this report? Whom does he talk to and what does he observe? What strategies does he use to weave this research into the report? Consider composing this kind of report about your own town or city. What do you already know or think about accessibility where you live? What kind of research would you aim to do in order to learn more? Write some brainstorming notes for how you'd approach conducting research and composing a report of your own inspired by Gowdy's work.

An Annotated Model Profile

Heart and Sole:
Detroiter Walks 21 Miles in Work Commute

BILL LAITNER

LEAVING HOME IN DETROIT at 8 a.m., James Robertson doesn't look like an endurance athlete.

Pudgy of form, shod in heavy work boots, Robertson trudges almost haltingly as he starts another workday.

But as he steps out into the cold, Robertson, 56, is steeled for an Olympic-sized commute. Getting to and from his factory job 23 miles away in Rochester Hills, he'll take a bus partway there and partway home. And he'll also walk an astounding 21 miles.

Five days a week. Monday through Friday.

It's the life Robertson has led for the last decade, ever since his 1988 Honda Accord quit on him.

Every trip is an ordeal of mental and physical toughness for this soft-spoken man with a perfect attendance record at work. And every day is a tribute to how much he cares about his job, his boss and his coworkers. Robertson's

The profile opens with DESCRIPTIVE DETAILS *that introduce readers to the subject—and make us want to read on.*

BILL LAITNER covers local news for the *Detroit Free Press*, specializing in social and political issues and human interest stories like this one. The following profile, published in the *Free Press* in January 2015, inspired a nationwide response.

James Robertson commutes twenty-three miles to and from his job every day—most of it on foot.

Placing Robertson's challenging commute in the context of the struggles faced by other Detroiters gives it an interesting and MEANINGFUL ANGLE.

daunting walks and bus rides, in all kinds of weather, also reflect the challenges some metro Detroiters face in getting to work in a region of limited bus service, and where car ownership is priced beyond the reach of many.

But you won't hear Robertson complain—nor his boss.

"I set our attendance standard by this man," says Todd Wilson, plant manager at Schain Mold & Engineering. "I say, if this man can get here, walking all those miles through snow and rain, well I'll tell you, I have people in Pontiac 10 minutes away and they say they can't get here—bull!"

Another INTERESTING ANGLE: *Robertson's extraordinary work ethic in spite of the challenging circumstances.*

As he speaks of his loyal employee, Wilson leans over his desk for emphasis, in a sparse office with a view of the factory floor. Before starting his shift, Robertson stops by the office every day to talk sports, usually baseball. And during dinnertime each day, Wilson treats him to fine Southern cooking, compliments of the plant manager's wife.

Interviews with Robertson and his coworkers provide detailed FIRSTHAND INFORMATION.

"Oh, yes, she takes care of James. And he's a personal favorite of the owners because of his attendance record. He's never missed a day. I've seen him come in here wringing wet," says Wilson, 53, of Metamora Township.

With a full-time job and marathon commutes, Robertson is clearly sleep deprived, but powers himself by downing 2-liter bottles of Mountain Dew and cans of Coke.

"I sleep a lot on the weekend, yes I do," he says, sounding a little amazed at his schedule. He also catches zzz's on his bus rides. Whatever it takes to get to his job, Robertson does it.

"I can't imagine not working," he says.

"Lord, Keep Me Safe"

The sheer time and effort of getting to work has ruled Robertson's life for more than a decade, ever since his car broke down. He didn't replace it because, he says, "I haven't had a chance to save for it." His job pays $10.55 an hour, well above Michigan's minimum wage of $8.15 an hour but not enough for him to buy, maintain and insure a car in Detroit.

As hard as Robertson's morning commute is, the trip home is even harder.

At the end of his 2–10 p.m. shift as an injection molder at Schain Mold's squeaky-clean factory just south of M-59, and when his coworkers are climbing into their cars, Robertson sets off, on foot—in the dark—for the 23-mile trip to his home off Woodward near Holbrook. None of his coworkers lives anywhere near him, so catching a ride almost never happens.

Instead, he reverses the 7-mile walk he took earlier that day, a stretch between the factory and a bus stop behind Troy's Somerset Collection shopping mall.

"I keep a rhythm in my head," he says of his seemingly mechanical-like pace to the mall.

At Somerset, he catches the last SMART bus of the day, just before 1 a.m. He rides it into Detroit as far it goes, getting off at the State Fairgrounds on Woodward, just south of 8 Mile. By that time, the last inbound Woodward bus has left. So Robertson foots it the rest of the way—about 5 miles—in the cold or rain or the mild summer nights, to the home he shares with his girlfriend.

"I have to go through Highland Park, and you never know what you're going to run into," Robertson says. "It's pretty dangerous. Really, it is dangerous from 8 Mile on down. They're not the type of people you want to run into.

"But I've never had any trouble," he says. Actually, he did get mugged several years ago—"some punks tuned him up pretty good," says Wilson, the plant manager. Robertson chooses not to talk about that.

So, what gets him past dangerous streets, and through the cold and gloom of night and winter winds?

"One word—faith," Robertson says. "I'm not saying I'm a member of some church. But just before I get home, every night, I say, 'Lord, keep me safe.'"

The next day, Robertson adds, "I should've told you there's another thing: determination."

A Land of No Buses

Robertson's 23-mile commute from home takes four hours. It's so time-consuming because he must traverse the no-bus land of rolling Rochester Hills. It's one of scores of tri-county communities (nearly 40 in Oakland County alone) where voters opted not to pay the SMART transit millage. So it has no fixed-route bus service.

Once he gets to Troy and Detroit, Robertson is back in bus country. But even there, the bus schedules are thin in a region that is relentlessly auto-centric.

"The last five years been really tough because the buses cut back," Robertson says. Both SMART and DDOT have curtailed service over the last half decade, "and with SMART, it really affected service into Detroit," said Megan Owens, executive director of Transportation Riders United.

> DETAILED INFORMATION about Robertson's commute, including a graphic with time stamps, helps readers understand it more clearly—and why it's so incredible.

> The local angle on this story as an EXAMPLE of the struggles many face in Detroit leads Laitner to include information about the city's transportation services.

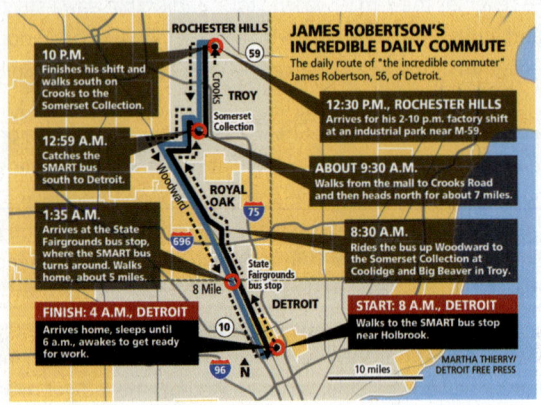

Buses provide sparse service on Robertson's long work commute, leaving him to walk most of the way on foot.

Detroit's director of transportation said there is a service Robertson may be able to use that's designed to help low-income workers. Job Access and Reverse Commute, paid for in part with federal dollars, provides door-to-door transportation to low-income workers, but at a cost. Robertson said he was not aware of the program.

Still, metro Detroit's lack of accessible mass transit hasn't stopped Robertson from hoofing it along sidewalks—often snow-covered—to get to a job.

At Home at Work

Robertson is proud of all the miles he covers each day. But it's taking a toll, and he's not getting any younger.

"He comes in here looking real tired—his legs, his knees," says coworker Janet Vallardo, 59, of Auburn Hills.

But there's a lot more than a paycheck luring him to make his weekday treks. Robertson looks forward to being around his coworkers, saying, "We're like a family." He also looks forward to the homemade dinners the plant manager's wife whips up for him each day.

"I look at her food, I always say, 'Excellent. No, not excellent. Phenomenal,'" he says, with Wilson sitting across from him, nodding and smiling with affirmation.

Although Robertson eats in a factory lunchroom, his menus sound like something from a Southern café: Turnip greens with smoked pork neck bones, black-eyed peas and carrots in a brown sugar glaze, baby-back ribs, cornbread made from scratch, pinto beans, fried taters, cheesy biscuits. They're the kind of meal that can fuel his daunting commutes back home.

Though his job is clearly part of his social life, when it's time to work this graduate of Northern High School is methodical. He runs an injection-molding machine the size of a small garage, carefully slicing and drilling away waste after removing each finished part, and noting his production in detail on a clipboard.

Strangers Crossing Paths

Robertson has walked the walk so often that drivers wonder: Who is that guy? UBS banker Blake Pollock, 47, of Rochester, wondered. About a year ago, he found out.

Pollock tools up and down Crooks each day in his shiny black 2014 Chrysler 300.

"I saw him so many times, climbing through snow banks. I saw him at all different places on Crooks," Pollock recalls.

Last year, Pollock had just parked at his office space in Troy as Robertson passed. The banker in a suit couldn't keep from asking the factory guy in sweats, what the heck are you doing, walking out here every day? They talked a bit. Robertson walked off and Pollock ruminated.

From then on, Pollock began watching for the factory guy. At first, he'd pick him up occasionally, when he could swing the time. But the generosity became more frequent as winter swept in. Lately, it's several times a week, especially when metro Detroit sees single-digit temperatures and windchills.

"Knowing what I know, I can't drive past him now. I'm in my car with the heat blasting and even then my feet are cold," Pollock says.

Other times, it's 10:30 or 11 p.m., even after midnight, when Pollock, who is divorced, is sitting at home alone or rolling home from a night out, and wondering how the man he knows only as "James" is doing in the frigid darkness.

On those nights, Pollock runs Robertson all the way to his house in Detroit.

"I asked him, why don't you move closer" to work. "He said his girlfriend inherited their house so it's easy to stay there," Pollock said.

On a recent night run, Pollock got his passenger home at 11 p.m. They sat together in the car for a minute, outside Robertson's house.

"So, normally you'd be getting here at 4 o'clock (in the morning), right?" the banker asks. "Yeah," Robertson replies. Pollock flashes a wry smile. "So, you're pretty early, aren't you?" he says. Robertson catches the drift.

"Oh, I'm grateful for the time, believe me," Robertson says, then adds in a voice rising with anticipation: "I'm going to take me a bath!"

After the door shuts and Pollock pulls away, he admits that Robertson mystifies him, yet leaves him stunned with admiration for the man's uncanny work ethic and determination.

"I always say to my friends, I'm not a nice guy. But I find myself helping James," Pollock says with a sheepish laugh. He said he's picked up Robertson several dozen times this winter alone.

Laitner notes details such as Pollock's "wry smile" and "sheepish laugh" that signal that he is providing details from conversations he heard, adding CREDIBILITY *to his writing.*

Has a Routine

At the plant, coworkers feel odd seeing one of their team numbers always walking, says Charlie Hollis, 63, of Pontiac. "I keep telling him to get him a nice little car," says Hollis, also a machine operator.

Echoes the plant manager Wilson, "We are very much trying to get James a vehicle." But Robertson has a routine now, and he seems to like it, his coworkers say.

"If I can get away, I'll pick him up. But James won't get in just anybody's car. He likes his independence," Wilson says.

Robertson has simple words for why he is what he is, and does what he does. He speaks with pride of his parents, including his father's military service.

"I just get it from my family. It's a lot of walking, I know."

The CONCLUSION *brings up another interesting angle to Robertson's story: how he connects his walking to a strong work ethic he inherited from his parents.*

 REFLECT & WRITE

Bill Laitner profiles an ordinary person whose extraordinary commute brought nationwide attention to the challenges of getting to work without a car or public transportation. Think about someone you know whose story might prove significant in this way. Write a paragraph about this person, briefly describing what details would bring them to life and what angle you would take in a full profile essay to make their story matter to others.

EIGHTEEN

"Two Thumbs Up"
Writing a Review

RESTAURANTS, CELL PHONES, BOOKS, movies, TV shows, cars, toaster ovens, employees—just about anything can be reviewed. Many people don't buy a new product or try a new restaurant without first checking to see what others have said about it online—and even posting their own thoughts on it afterward.

You've probably given casual reviews of this sort yourself. If a friend asks what you think of the TV series *The Handmaid's Tale* (based on Margaret Atwood's dystopian novel), your response would probably constitute a brief review: "This last season was probably the most exciting. The acting was terrific throughout, but sometimes the plot kind of got lost. I'll probably keep watching through the final season, though, to see how it ends." Even this offhand opinion includes two basic elements of all reviews: a judgment ("terrific," "got lost") and the criteria used to arrive at that judgment, in this case the quality of the acting and the plot, and the season's overall excitement.

Reviews can vary a good deal, however, as you can see in these examples from other reviews of *The Handmaid's Tale*.

> I say it almost every year, and I'm not afraid to write it: you're not prepared for what's coming. Season 5 exemplifies masterful character development, with eye-catching direction and evenly paced, riveting

18 Writing a Review

A still from *The Handmaid's Tale*.

> writing. The new chapter includes scenes that will undoubtedly come back to haunt you as you contemplate the fate of *The Handmaid's Tale* characters, cheering for them, crying with them, and waiting impatiently for the Gilead to turn to dust.
>
> —ZOFIA WIJASZKA, "'The Handmaid's Tale' Review: Season Five Delivers Another Shocking Entry about Grief, Retaliation and Bodily Autonomy"

This brief excerpt from Wijaszka's review, published on the *AwardsWatch* website, makes clear her criteria: the show's character development, outstanding direction and writing, and haunting cinematography. The rest of the review elaborates on and gives examples of these qualities.

On the other hand, the *Metacritic* website gives ratings by gathering numerical scores from multiple sources and calculating an average—63 out of 100 in the case of this series, on the high end of "Generally Favorable." The site also provides excerpts and links to full reviews, and lets visitors add their own reviews. On *Metacritic*, everyone can be a reviewer.

This chapter provides guidelines for writing reviews—whether an academic book review for a political science class, a product review on *Amazon*, or a movie review in your campus newspaper.

 REFLECT

Think about reviews you've read. All reviews evaluate something, and they do so using relevant criteria. Someone reviewing a movie, for instance, would generally consider such factors as the quality of the script, acting, directing, and cinematography. Think about a product you are familiar with or a performance you have recently seen. Develop a list of criteria for evaluating it, and then write an explanation of why these criteria are well suited to your subject. What does this exercise help you understand about the process of reviewing?

Across Academic Disciplines

Reviews are a common genre in all academic disciplines. As a student, you will often be assigned to write a review of something—a book, a work of art, an engineering design, a musical performance—as a way of engaging critically with the work. While students in the humanities and social sciences are often asked to write book reviews, students in the performing arts may review a performance. In a business course, you may be asked to review products or business plans.

In each of these cases, you'll need to develop criteria for your evaluation and to support that evaluation with substantial evidence. The kind of evidence you show will vary across disciplines. If you're evaluating a literary work, you'll need to show evidence from the text (quotations, for example), whereas if you are evaluating a proposed tax policy for an economics class, you're probably going to be required to show numerical data demonstrating projected outcomes.

Across Media

Reviews can appear in many media—from print and online to television and radio. Each medium offers different resources and challenges. A television film critic reviewing a new movie can intersperse clips from the film to back up their points, but their own comments will likely be brief. A different critic, writing about the same film for a print magazine, can develop a fuller, more carefully reasoned review but will be limited to still images rather than video clips.

The same choices may be available to you when you are assigned to review something. For instance, if you give an oral presentation reviewing

↪ *LOOK AT this photo of Immersive Van Gogh, a traveling art exhibit that immerses visitors in the Impressionist artist's famous works. A similar photo was included in Keisha Raines's review of the exhibition in Los Angeles, published on* Thrillist. *According to Raines, "The artist's works are brought to life in a production that includes 60,600 frames of captivating video totaling 90 million pixels and 500,000+ cubic feet of projections set to original song compositions." The brief review, which you can see at* everyonesanauthor.tumblr.com, *includes several photos. How else could a review published online take advantage of the medium—with music? video? What else?*

an art show, you might create slides that show some of the art you discuss. Perhaps your review could take the form of a video that includes not only images of the art but also footage of viewers interacting with it. If you get to choose media, you'll need to think about which ones will allow you to best cover your subject and reach your audience.

Across Cultures and Communities

Conventions for reviewing vary across communities and cultures. In most US academic contexts, reviews are quite direct, explicitly stating whether something is successful or unsuccessful, and why. Especially online, reviews are often very honest, sometimes even brutal, calling attention to the ethics of reviewing. In other contexts, reviewers have reason to remember that there are almost always real people—with feelings—on the other end of reviews. When the *Detroit News* reviews a new car, for instance, its writers have to keep in mind the sensitivities of the community, many of whom work, and work very hard, in the auto industry, and of the company that produces that car, which may be a major advertiser in the newspaper. *Consumer Reports* might review the same car very differently, since it is supported not by advertisers but by subscribers who want impartial data and information that will help them decide whether or not to purchase that car.

Across Genres

Evaluation is often used as a strategy in other genres. **PROPOSALS** offer solutions to problems, for example, and in that process they must consider—and review and evaluate—various other solutions. Evaluation and **ANALYSIS** often go hand in hand as well, as when *Consumer Reports* analyzes a series of smartphones in order to evaluate and rank them for its readers. Even **ARGUMENTS** sometimes call for some type of review.

REFLECT

Look for several reviews of a favorite movie. You're likely to find many reviews online, but try also to find reviews in print sources or online versions of print publications. How do the reviews differ from one medium to the next? What, if anything, do the online reviews have that the print versions do not? Then check out some fan sites or social media posts about the same movie. How does the medium affect the decisions that a reviewer makes about content, length, style, and design?

CHARACTERISTIC FEATURES

Kate Aronoff's essay about Taylor Swift and carbon offsets incorporates many elements of a review. Read the essay on p. 843, and notice how she pays attention to her audience's needs.

Whatever the audience and medium, the most successful reviews share most of the following features:

- Relevant background information about the subject (p. 353)
- Criteria for the evaluation (p. 354)
- A well-supported evaluation (p. 357)
- Attention to the audience's needs and expectations (p. 359)

- An authoritative tone (p. 360)
- Awareness of the ethics of reviewing (p. 362)

Relevant Background Information about the Subject

The background information needed in a review may entail anything from items on a restaurant menu to a description of the graphics of a video game to the plot summary of a novel or movie. What information to include—and how much—depends on your rhetorical situation. In the case of an academic review, your instructor may specify a length, which will affect how much information you can provide. What's needed in nonacademic reviews varies depending on the audience and publication. Someone reviewing a new album by an indie group for *Rolling Stone* may not need to provide much background information since readers are already likely to be familiar with the group. This would not be the case, however, if the same author were writing a review for a more general-interest magazine, such as *Time*.

Reviews of films, books, and music albums often provide background information about the subject matter, the research process, or the story (depending on the genre of the work being reviewed). See how Julianne Escobedo Shepherd provides background information that will help readers put her review of Beyoncé's *Country Carter* album in context. Shepherd begins with a flashback to an album that preceded it, *Lemonade*:

> *Lemonade*, as it happened, may have helped plant the seed for *Cowboy Carter*, which was "born out of an experience that I [Beyoncé] had years ago where I did not feel welcomed . . . and it was very clear that I wasn't." It seems she is referring to her 2016 appearance at the Country Music Association Awards, in which she performed *Lemonade*'s Texas country triumph "Daddy Lessons" with the Chicks, who were also once exiled by the entire country music apparatus. As they played the song and after it ended, Beyoncé was met with reactions that ranged from cool sneers to racist vitriol, both in the crowd and online.
>
> At that moment, it was clear that even Beyoncé's Texas bona fides wouldn't protect her from the longstanding racism and sexism that still existed in the country mainstream, despite Black musicians creating the spark of country music and Black Americans creating the foundations of the country itself. "Because of that experience," she wrote, "I did a deeper dive into the history of country music and studied our rich musical archive . . . the criticisms I faced when I first entered this genre forced me

Beyonce's *Cowboy Carter* album, advertised on a billboard.

> to propel past the limitations that were put on me." The country music establishment got Beyoncé doing homework. The guns they are a-blazin'.
> —Julianne Escabedo Shepherd, "*Cowboy Carter*: Beyoncé"

In the opening of this review of *Cowboy Carter*, Shepherd backs up to give readers information about how Beyoncé got inspired (or incensed enough) to do research on Black country music and then to stake her claim to being part of that tradition, with her musical guns "a-blazin'."

Criteria for the Evaluation

Underlying all good reviews are clear criteria. As an author, then, you'll need to establish the criteria for any review you write. Sometimes the criteria are obvious or can be assumed: criteria for reviewing cars, for example, would almost assuredly include price, style, comfort, performance, safety, gas mileage, and so on. Often, however, you may want to shape the criteria for specific purposes and audiences. Now see how *Consumer Reports*, a nonprofit publication dedicated to product reviews, provides specific criteria for evaluating bicycle helmets. First, they specify that "fit, comfort, and durability are

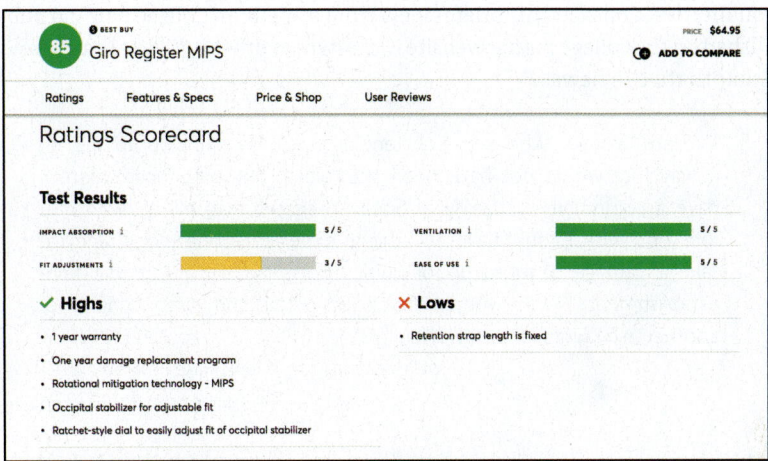

Consumer Reports rating scorecard for the Giro Register MIPS bike helmet.

important factors when you choose a helmet." Then they use those criteria to review, rate, and recommend their top pick, the Giro Register MIPS:

> This adult bike helmet is one of the best CR has tested. It rates Excellent for absorbing impact forces in a crash. And it includes a multidirectional impact protection system (MIPS), a promising technology designed to reduce the risk of concussion. This relatively lightweight, easy-to-use helmet also provides excellent ventilation. Its one less-than-stellar quality concerns fit adjustability: It comes in a universal size and not all the straps are adjustable.
> —CONSUMER REPORTS, "Giro Register MIPS Bike Helmet"

Consumer Reports presents its review in multiple formats. For readers who are very familiar with helmets already or want just the highlights, it offers a "ratings scorecard" and a list of "highs" and "lows." For readers who may want a bit more detail or need background information, *Consumer Reports* provides a narrative explanation as well as verified users' reviews. In this case, the criteria are flexible enough that they work for these different audiences and formats.

However, **QUALITATIVE** criteria can be as persuasive as **QUANTITATIVE** criteria, and many reviews combine both. For example, that's often what you'll find when examining reviews of colleges and universities. Student-written and alumni evaluations of colleges and universities tend to be qualitative. Consider this brief review from a Spelman College alumna published on the college profile website *Niche* (which offers both qualitative and quantitative reviews):

> We are women who serve. Attending Spelman empowered me in a way that would not have been possible at any other institution. I have a community or family of Spelman sisters that will be with me forever. I wish I could have my college experience one more time to take advantage of more opportunities presented to me at that fine establishment. Black women being educated and supporting one another is beautiful and powerful.
>
> —SPELMAN COLLEGE ALUMNA, Review on *Niche*
> (© Niche.com, Inc. 2022)

This reviewer uses qualitative criteria such as personal feelings and values ("Spelman empowered me" and "I have a community or family") to signal the strengths of this college. This qualitative review complements the following quantitative assessment of Spelman that appeared in *U.S. News & World Report*. Note the rankings process that this publication uses, relying on numerical ranking rather than qualitative experience:

> Spelman College Rankings: See where this school lands in our other rankings to get a bigger picture of the institution's offerings:
>
> #54 in National Liberal Arts Colleges (tie)
> #24 in Best Undergraduate Teaching (tie)
> #90 in Best Value Schools
> #7 in Most Innovative Schools (tie)
> #4 in Top Performers on Social Mobility (tie)
> #1 in Historically Black Colleges and Universities
> #33 in Study Abroad (tie)
> #9 in Learning Communities (tie)
> #21 in Service Learning (tie)
>
> —U.S. NEWS & WORLD REPORT, "Spelman College Rankings"

As you consider writing reviews, keep in mind how the criteria you use presents a particular story about what you are reviewing. Think about both your subject and the discipline you're writing within to help determine how you'll use qualitative and quantitative criteria.

A Well-Supported Evaluation

The foundation of every review is a clear evaluation, a claim that something is good or bad, right or wrong, useful or not. Whatever you're reviewing, you need to give reasons for what you claim and sufficient evidence to support those reasons. And because rarely is anything all good or all bad, you also need to acknowledge any weaknesses in things you praise and any positives in things you criticize. Also, remember to anticipate and acknowledge reasons that others might evaluate your subject differently than you do. In other words, you need to consider other possible perspectives on whatever you're reviewing.

Journalist Amy Goldwasser approached a number of passengers on a New York subway and asked them for impromptu reviews of what they were reading. She then collaborated with the illustrator Peter Arkle to compose graphic reviews for the *New York Times Book Review*. Here's what two readers had to say:

MARIAH ANTHONY, 18, high school senior, on p.133 of THE KITE RUNNER, by Khaled Hosseini (paperback)

I read every day. Every. Day. I'm not a novel-reader. I'm more self-help and psychology. But this is an *amazing* book. You should read it. The author went way into depth. Where I'm at, the main character's 18. He and his father moved to San Francisco from Kabul... they were refugees who had to be smuggled into the States. He had to travel *inside an oil tank* to be here. I don't think I can exactly relate, but it's about how people go through things. It's beautiful.

DON SHEA, 70, fiction writer, on p.214 of LIT, by Mary Karr (paperback)

This is her third book. I've read the first two. She's a poet.... I've been struck by the **wonderful** metaphors. I'm always surprised when poets really write superb prose. It gets a little draggy in the rehab part. She just keeps **slipping and slipping**. But it's good—all her stuff is good.

Both readers clearly stated what they thought of the books they were reading ("an amazing book," "it's good"). And then they gave reasons ("the author went way into depth," "all her stuff is good") and evidence to support those reasons ("he had to travel *inside an oil tank* to be here," "wonderful metaphors"). Note as well that one of the readers, Don Shea, acknowledges one weakness in Mary Karr's book ("It gets a little draggy in the rehab part").

When you're writing a review for a college class, you'll need to be more systematic and organized than these off-the-cuff reviews—with an

A still from *Dune: Part Two* (2024).

explicitly stated evaluation, for one thing. See how Dana Stevens recalls her review of the 2021 *Dune* film as a way of setting up the claim that *Dune: Part Two* exceeds expectations:

> With the release of *Dune: Part Two*, all the meticulous (some might say exhausting) attention Villeneuve paid to building out the first movie's vast and complex world . . . pays off. More than any science-fiction epic I can think of in recent years, the *Dune* movies…belong to the tradition of speculative science fiction that Frank Herbert's original 1965 novel partook of and helped to establish: They are movies as much about mass belief systems and political power struggles as they are about characters and relationships . . . . I was not even a huge fan of *Dune: Part One*, which struck me as more visually and sonically hypnotic than it was narratively coherent. I was also among the critics who found its truncated ending almost comically abrupt. But to his great credit, Villeneuve has followed through on the task he set for himself in *Dune*'s moody, enigmatic, and expansive first chapter: He now returns to the world he so painstakingly established, ready to orchestrate the grand-scale conflicts that are about to tear it apart.
>
> —DANA STEVENS, "The Spectacular New *Dune* Will Turn Even Skeptics into Believers"

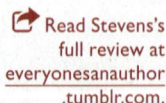

Read Stevens's full review at everyonesanauthor.tumblr.com.

Stevens's full review includes the characteristic features introduced earlier in this chapter on pages 352–53. It offers necessary background information about the complex plot and the challenges of making a sequel that would overcome the previous film's shortfalls. Criteria for evaluation and vivid evidence from the film work to support the evaluation. Equally important is Stevens's credibility as a well-known and experienced film critic, who is also the host of a popular culture podcast and author of a book on Hollywood films.

Attention to the Audience's Needs and Expectations

All authors need to consider what their audience expects from them. But this consideration plays a particularly important role in the case of reviews. In many situations, some audience members will be familiar with what you're reviewing, whereas others will need a detailed summary or description; some will need an explicit statement of the criteria for the evaluation, while others will know what the criteria are without being told. When in doubt about audience knowledge, provide criteria and more details.

Audience considerations can also influence the criteria that reviewers identify as most crucial for their evaluation. Consider, for example, reviews of self-driving cars. Potential customers might expect one set of criteria, perhaps focusing on comfort, cost, and availability. Government regulators might look for entirely different criteria, ones that focus on safety first of all. Take a look at how *Business Insider* chief correspondent Peter Kafka keeps needs and expectations of readers in mind in a review of self-driving Waymo taxis:

> While Waymo says it drives tens of thousands of trips a week, even the most tech-savvy people I talk to have yet to ride in one. And it's reasonable to have concerns about this tech as it rolls out. Waymo's rival Cruise halted its service last fall after a slew of incidents, including a grisly one where a self-driving Cruise dragged a pedestrian who had been hit by a human-driven car.

Kafka recognizes that for all the hype around self-driving vehicles, they are still not readily available—or always safe for potential customers reading this review. With these cautions in mind, Kafka recommends trying out a Waymo:

> Right now, beyond the novelty, the big upside for me is that the fleet's cars—electric Jaguars—are comfortable and clean. And that the pre-trip cost is about the same as an Uber Comfort (one level up from the base Uber X fare)—but really a bit cheaper, since you're not tipping your robot driver.
> —PETER KAFKA, "It's Easy to Bash Tech, but I've Started Taking Robotaxis—and They're Awesome"

Writing for a general audience, Kafka focuses on the novelty of this intriguing invention instead of describing how the technology works in detail. However, like all good reviews, this one provides a clear evaluation using explicit criteria and demonstrating knowledge of the self-driving car industry in general.

 **REFLECT**

Find two reviews of the same subject (a movie, a band, whatever) from two different sources: *Yelp* and *Travel + Leisure*, perhaps, or *Salon* and *Time*. Look over each source and decide what kind of audience each one addresses. Young? Affluent? Intellectual? A general audience? Then study each review. How much prior knowledge does each one expect of its readers? Do the two reviews use the same criteria—and if not, what might account for the difference? What does this analysis suggest about the role that audience plays in the way reviews are written?

An Authoritative Tone

As important as the reviews themselves is the credibility of the reviewers. Authors of reviews establish their authority and credibility in a variety of ways, including demonstrating their knowledge of the subject, balancing praise and critique, and establishing a relationship with the audience early on. Note how *Washington Post* TV critic Inkoo Kang connects the HBO docuseries *Black and Missing* to another widely known story in the news at the time.

> In March 2014, 8-year-old Relisha Rudd, who had been living with her family at a homeless shelter in Washington, D.C., went missing. The second-grader was last seen alive on the day of her disappearance: Cameras caught her entering a motel room with 51-year-old Kahlil Tatum, a janitor at the shelter who had served long stints in prison. . . .
>
> Her case . . . was assiduously covered by the local media but hardly registered on the national consciousness. Gabby Petito-style news coverage has traditionally been reserved for girls and women who look like Gabby Petito, and Rudd did not.
>
> Rudd's disappearance is one of several explored in the HBO docuseries "Black and Missing." Part of a steady drip of programming attempting to reform the fire hose of true-crime entertainment, the two-night,

four-part series profiles the sisters-in-law founders of the Maryland-based Black and Missing organization—and attests to why their work of circulating the names, photos and identifying details of Black missing people is regrettably necessary.

True crime, as we know it today, is a White genre, focusing overwhelmingly on White victims and White perpetrators, with a tendency to ally with law enforcement and uphold the prison-industrial complex. That gives its consumers a distorted sense of the world, as the factors that lead to missing girls and women—poverty, mental illness, domestic violence and police indifference—disproportionately impact Black (and Native) Americans. One of the primary aims of the docuseries is to redirect the media spotlight on the groups most likely to suffer victimization.

—INKOO KANG, "'Black and Missing' Attempts a Much-Needed Reform of True-Crime Storytelling. It Mostly Succeeds."

The dramatic, horrifying opening example and comparison to a well-known news story captures readers' attention while demonstrating Kang's deep knowledge of the subject. In addition, the review's title, "'Black and Missing' Attempts a Much-Needed Reform of True-Crime Storytelling. It Mostly Succeeds"—particularly the final statement—previews Kang's critical stance. Readers can trust Kang is a credible reviewer.

Finally, here is the introduction to a review of Steven Spielberg's 2021 adaptation of *West Side Story* written by University of California, Berkeley,

Scenes from *West Side Story*, the 1961 film (left) and the 2021 adaptation (right).

student Joy Diamond and published in the *Daily Californian*, the independent student-run newspaper at her university:

> "West Side Story" has an outstanding legacy. The original musical, with lyrics by Stephen Sondheim, won two Tony Awards and marked a turning point in musical theater with its dark themes and emphasis on social problems. The 1961 film adaptation was nominated for 11 Oscars and won 10, including the Academy Award for Best Picture, and the film has been deemed "culturally, historically or aesthetically significant" by the Library of Congress. Needless to say, the 2021 film adaptation of "West Side Story" has some large dancing shoes to fill—but equally obvious is its inability to do so.
>
> —JOY DIAMOND, "Devoid of Spark, 'West Side Story' Is Rough, Unfortunate Film Adaptation"

This introduction shows that the reviewer is knowledgeable about *West Wide Story*'s history and accolades.

If you get to choose your subject, select a topic that you know (and care) about, and share some of what you know in your introduction. Telling your audience something interesting about your subject and giving some sense that it matters will help establish your credibility and make them want to know more.

Awareness of the Ethics of Reviewing

Depending on the context and purpose, a review can have substantial—or minimal—consequences. When the late, widely syndicated film reviewer Roger Ebert gave a Hollywood movie a thumbs-up or thumbs-down, his judgment influenced whether the movie was shown in theaters across America or went immediately to DVD. Those reviewing Broadway plays for publications like the *New York Times* hold similar powers. And reviews in *Consumer Reports* influence the sale of the products they evaluate.

By comparison, a review of a local high school musical will not determine how long the musical will run or how much money it will make, but an especially negative review, particularly if it is unjustified, will certainly wound the feelings of those involved in the production. And a movie review on the *Internet Movie Database* (*IMDb*) that gives away key elements of a plot without including a "spoiler alert" will ruin the film for some of the audience. So an ethical reviewer will always keep in mind that a review has power—whether economic, emotional, or some other kind—and take care to exercise that power responsibly.

An ethical reviewer also considers how their background influences their evaluation. How might your previous experiences factor into your review? For example, your background as a veteran will likely be a filter through which you review a military-oriented video game or film. That background may help you identify inaccuracies, but it may also make you less open to experiences different from your own. Think about how best to be fair-minded.

Considering the likely effect of your review on those who created whatever you're reviewing is part of the ethics of reviewing as well. It's one thing to criticize the latest episode of *The Handmaid's Tale* (the creators of that series can likely afford to laugh all the way to the bank) but quite another when you're reviewing a new restaurant in town. It's not that you should hold back criticism (or praise) that you think the subject deserves, but you do need to think about the effect of your judgments before you express them.

WRITING A REVIEW / A Roadmap

Choose something to review and find an interesting angle

If you get to choose your topic, pick a subject you're interested in and know something about. Perhaps you're an artist or art lover who is interested in the works of Van Gogh and therefore choose to review the *Immersive Van Gogh* exhibit. Or maybe you love mountain biking: you could review three best-selling bikes. Remember that many things can be reviewed—shoes, appliances, restaurants, books, music.

If your topic is assigned, try to tailor it to your interests and to find an angle that will engage your audience. For instance, if your assignment is to review a specific art exhibit, see if you can focus on some aspect of the work that intrigues you, such as the use of color or the way the artist represents nature. If you are assigned to review a particular book, try to center your review on themes that you find compelling and that might interest your audience.

Consider your rhetorical situation

Think about what your AUDIENCE knows and expects. If your review is for an assignment, consider your instructor to be your primary audience (unless they specify otherwise) and know what's expected of a review in your discipline. If, however, you're writing for a specific publication or another audience, you'll have to think about what's expected in that situation. Here are some things to consider:

- Who are you trying to reach, and why?
- In what ways are they like or unlike you? Are they likely to agree with you?
- What do they probably know about your subject? What background information will you need to provide?
- Will the subject matter to your audience? If not, how can you persuade them that it matters?
- What will they be expecting to learn from your review? What criteria will they value?

Think about your PURPOSE. Why are you writing this review? If it's for a class, what motivations do you have beyond getting a good grade? To recommend a book or film? evaluate the latest smart device? introduce your classmates to a new musical group? What do you expect your audience to do with the information in your review? How can you best achieve your purpose?

Consider your STANCE. Think about your overall attitude about the subject and how you want to come across as an author. Are you extremely enthusiastic about your subject? firmly opposed to it? skeptical? lukewarm? How can you communicate your feelings? Think also about how you want your audience to see you as author. As well informed? thoughtful? witty? How can your review reflect that stance?

Think about the larger CONTEXT. What, if any, background information about your subject should you consider—other books on the same subject or by the same author? movies in the same genre? similar products made by different companies? What else has been said about your subject, and how will you respond to it in your review?

Consider your LANGUAGE. Almost any review can be presented in a number of ways. Regardless of how many languages and dialects you use in your everyday life, you have many options to consider in crafting a review. What variety of language or dialect will best suit your audience and help you achieve your goals as a writer? Will your audience expect a certain kind of language or style? Do you want to meet those expectations? challenge them? What risks might you be willing to take with your language? How will your choice of medium and the larger context limit or expand the language options available to you? See Chapters 4 and 35 for more information about language options.

Consider MEDIA. Whether or not you have a choice of medium—print, spoken, or electronic—you need to think about how your medium will affect what you can do in your review. If you're presenting it online or to a live audience, you may be able to incorporate video and audio clips of a film or a concert. If your review will appear in print, can you include still photos? And most important of all: if you get to choose your medium, which one will best reach your audience?

Consider matters of DESIGN. If you are writing for an academic assignment, be sure to follow the format requirements of the discipline you're writing in. If you're writing for a particular publication, you'll need to find out what design options you have. But if you have the option of designing your text yourself, think about what will help readers understand your message. Should you include illustrations? Are you including any information that would be best presented in a list or a graph? Product reviews, for example, often display data in a table so that readers can compare several products.

Consider GENERATIVE AI. If your instructor's course policies allow you to use generative AI tools, consider whether you'd find it helpful to run ideas by a chatbot or get feedback on your review. If you are having a hard time deciding on a subject for your review, you might share some interests with a chatbot and have it suggest related products, books, films, or music to explore. Or if you have decided to review a product—perhaps the latest smartphone camera—you might prompt a bot to help identify the most important characteristics of such a product to focus on. Or if you have completed a draft of a review, you might ask a bot to respond to the draft, suggesting two or three ways you could make it more convincing or interesting. Remember that while AI can be helpful to your writing process, the information it provides isn't always right!

Evaluate your subject

Think about your own first impressions. What about the subject got your interest? What was your first reaction, and why? What is the first thing you would tell someone who asked your opinion on this subject?

Examine your subject closely. If you're reviewing a performance, take notes as you're watching it; if you're reviewing a book, read it more than once. Look for parts of your subject that are especially powerful, or weak, or unexpected to mention in your review.

Do any necessary RESEARCH. Your subject will be your primary source of information, though you may need to consult other sources to find background information or to become aware of what else has been written about your subject. Would learning more about a book's author or a film's director help you evaluate your subject? If you're writing an academic review, do you need to find out what else has been said about your subject?

Determine the CRITERIA for your evaluation. Sometimes these are obvious: film reviews, for instance, tend to focus on criteria like acting, directing, script, and so forth. At other times, you'll need to establish the criteria that will guide your review. If you're unsure what criteria are most well suited to your subject, look up reviews others have written on a similar topic. What criteria do those models use effectively?

Make a judgment about your subject. Based on the criteria you've established, evaluate your subject. Remember that few things are all good or all bad; you will likely find some things to praise, and others to criticize. Whatever you decide, use your criteria to examine your subject carefully, and look for specific EVIDENCE you can cite—lines or scenes from a movie, particular features of a product, and so on.

Anticipate other points of view. Not everyone is going to agree with your evaluation, and you need to acknowledge COUNTERARGUMENTS to what you think. Even if you don't persuade everyone in your audience to accept your judgment, you can demonstrate that your opinion is worth taking seriously by acknowledging and responding respectfully to those other perspectives.

Think about your mix of DESCRIPTION or SUMMARY and EVALUATION. You need to describe or summarize your subject enough so that readers will understand it, but remember that your primary goal is to evaluate it. The balance will depend on your purpose. Some reviews are expected to give a simple star rating, or a thumbs-up (or thumbs-down). Others require more complex judgments.

Organize and start writing

Once you've determined your overall evaluation of your subject, compiled a list of its strengths and weaknesses, and assembled EVIDENCE you can draw on to support that evaluation, it's time to organize your materials and start writing. To organize your review, think about what you want to tell readers about your subject, what your evaluation of it is, and why.

Come up with a tentative THESIS. What major point do you want to make about your subject? Try writing this point out as a tentative thesis. Then think about whether the thesis should be stated explicitly or not. Also consider whether to put the thesis toward the end of your introduction or save it for the conclusion.

DESCRIBE or **SUMMARIZE** the subject you're reviewing, and provide any background information your audience may need.

Evaluate your subject. Using the **CRITERIA** you identified for your review, present your subject's strengths and weaknesses, generally in order of importance. Provide **REASONS** and specific **EVIDENCE** to back them up. Don't forget to acknowledge other points of view.

Draft an **OPENING**. Introduce your subject in a way that makes clear what you're reviewing and why your audience should care about it—and shows that you know what you're talking about!

Draft a **CONCLUSION**. Wrap up your review by summarizing your evaluation. If you have any recommendations, here's where to make them.

Look critically at your draft, get responses—and revise

Once you have a complete draft, read it over carefully, focusing on your evaluation, the reasons and evidence you provide as support, and the way you appeal to your audience. If possible, ask others—a writing center tutor, classmate, or friend—for feedback. Be sure to give your readers a clear sense of your assignment or purpose and your intended audience. Here are some questions that can help you or others respond:

- *Is the evaluation stated explicitly?* Is there a clear **THESIS**—and if not, is one needed?

- *How well does the introduction capture the audience's interest?* How well does it establish your **AUTHORITY** as a reviewer? Does it make clear what the review is about? How will it engage your audience's interest? How else might it begin?

- *Is the subject* **DESCRIBED** *or* **SUMMARIZED** *sufficiently for your audience?* Is any additional description or background information needed?

- *How much of the review is* DESCRIPTION *and how much is* EVALUATION — and does the balance seem right for the subject and purpose?
- *What are the* CRITERIA *for the evaluation?* Are they stated explicitly—and if not, should they be? Do the criteria seem suitable for the subject and audience? Are there other criteria that should be considered?
- *What good* REASONS *and* EVIDENCE *support the evaluation?* Will your audience be persuaded?
- *What other viewpoints do you consider,* and how well do you respond to these views? Are there other views you should consider?
- *How would you describe the* STANCE *and* TONE *?* Are they authoritative? What words or details create that impression?
- *How is the draft organized?* Is it easy to follow, with clear TRANSITIONS from one point to the next?
- *What about* DESIGN *?* Should any material be set off as a list or chart or table? Are there any illustrations—and if not, should there be?
- *Is the* STYLE —choice of words, kinds of sentences, level of formality—well suited for the intended audience?
- *How does the draft* CONCLUDE *?* Is the conclusion decisive and satisfying? How else might it conclude?
- *Is this a fair review?* Even if readers do not agree with the evaluation, will they consider it fair?

REFLECT

Once you've completed your review, let it settle for a while and then take time to REFLECT . How well did you argue for your evaluation? How persuasive do you think your readers will find your review? Will those who do not agree with your evaluation consider it fair? What additional revisions would you make if you could? Research shows that such reflections help "lock in" what you learn for future use.

READINGS / Annotated Model Reviews

Thirsty Suitors: I Feel Seen by This Game

SWAPNA KRISHNA

The "Wired and Tired" feature of all reviews on this website provides a preview of positive and negative points.

WIRED: If you're South Asian, this game will speak directly to you. If not, it's a hilarious romance action game. The gameplay is simple and fun, and the characters are endearing. TIRED: A little short at around 10 hours, but it's only bad because I wish it were longer.

Growing up as the child of Indian immigrants to the United States, I'm very used to feeling like I'm on the outside looking in. As a kid, I felt like I didn't belong anywhere; my skin color set me apart from my mostly white peers growing up in Oklahoma, and I didn't quite fit in at the temple either. My Indian friends and I felt like in-betweens, not quite belonging anywhere, and it's something I've gotten used to as an adult.

Use of personal experience appeals to AUDIENCE members, many of whom can probably relate.

That's why it came as such a shock to feel like I belonged, to feel seen, among the misfit characters in the video game *Thirsty Suitors*.

SWAPNA KRISHNA is a journalist specializing in space, science, technology, and sci-fi who has written for *Wired* (where this review appeared in 2023) as well as for *Gizmodo, Newsweek, New Scientist,* and the *Verge*.

Thirsty Suitors Is Wildly Creative

The premise of *Thirsty Suitors*, from Outerloop Games, is that you play as Jala Jayaratne, a South Asian (by way of Sri Lanka and Bangalore, India) American woman returning to her small hometown for the first time in three years. Jala left Timber Hills without so much as a word, leaving brokenhearted exes in her wake, along with a loving family. She has some apologies to make, starting with her older sister Aruni, who's getting married—but Jala doesn't even know her soon-to-be brother-in-law's name.

    The story seems simple, and it could be a little boring in someone else's hands—but thanks to the unique gameplay, excellent art style, and wonderful scripting, it's anything but. Jala must confront each person in her life, everyone she's wronged in the past, and fight them in order to forge ahead with a new friendship.

    The battle mechanics are a lot of fun: Jala can attack normally, or she can taunt her suitors, making them thirsty, angry, or even impressed, and then take advantage of their status effects to inflict extra damage with special attacks. These rely on specific button presses and timing, but if you struggle with that, accessibility tweaks can help. The battles with suitors are long, but they reveal a lot about both Jala and her opponent.

    It's not just the people from your past that you can fight. There are other random encounters along the way. Jala's grandmother, Paati, tries to play matchmaker and sends along suitors from matrimonial ads, while the local skate park is being taken over by a creepy guy wearing a brown bear suit (seriously). The skate park is an interesting mystery with an ambiguous ending, but the Shaadi.com-style suitors had me laughing out loud every time I ran into them. It was genuinely a delight to fight these guys off.

    Besides her personal journey and the skate park, Jala chats with her parents, tries to make amends with her sister Aruni, and skates around town visiting her aunt, shops, the diner, and the bar. She even cooks with her parents, making traditional Indian and Sri Lankan recipes, a personal highlight for me.

    My only complaint with *Thirsty Suitors* is the game's length—at around 10 hours to complete the main story along with suitor side quests, it feels short. However, the narrative is tight and well plotted, and if it had been any longer, that might not have been the case. Compared to the epic, exhausting, never-ending games that are increasingly popular, though, the length of *Thirsty Suitors* feels like a breath of fresh air.

This Game Is for *Me*, and That's Revolutionary

The gameplay of *Thirsty Suitors* is great, but it's the story and characters that really stuck with me. It's easy to get dazzled by the flash of the game—the bright colors and art style are fantastic, and they really draw you in and make you want to keep playing. But it's the characters that have stuck with me.

Jala is not a great person at first glance; she's made a lot of mistakes. She's not really home by choice, but because her latest mistake has caught up with her. The player has discretion over how she acts toward others—is she a heart-breaker? Is she a people pleaser?—but the result is the same: making amends for the hurt she's caused, accepting responsibility, and forging a new path forward.

There's also a lot of substance here. This is a game made for the South Asian American community—those who immigrated as kids or, like myself, were born in the United States to immigrant parents and found themselves caught between two worlds. The main purpose of this game is to make us, who are often so forgotten in modern media and pop culture, feel seen. We're so used to seeing ourselves in people who don't look like us, don't act like us, and don't have our mixed backgrounds and cultures because it's all we've had.

And often, the representation we have now in pop culture isn't actually about us. Instead, it's about educating other communities about us. Sure, I can relate to those characters, but it's not really feeling *seen*. That's why it's so revolutionary to experience something that feels like it was made *for* me and for people like me, which clearly *Thirsty Suitors* was.

The game is brimming with its cultural heritage. It features the good—food, loving families—but doesn't paper over the bad: Jala's loving parents accept her queer identity, but she has other LGBTQ+ South Asian friends whose families have cut off contact. At home, Jala chats with her parents and raids the fridge at night for her favorite childhood dishes: parathas, jalebi, and dal. Certainly anyone without a South Asian background can enjoy playing the game and making these dishes, but to me it's comforting and familiar because it's what I know. Jala also confronts her parents about cultural trauma and expectations, something that our communities often don't talk about enough.

And that's what's amazing about this game. Many of these characters are purposefully exaggerated caricatures, but they feel familiar and the conversations (and the pain behind them) are real.

In the end, *Thirsty Suitors* is a game about a group of misfits who try to find peace. And it was nice, for just a little while, to feel like I belonged among them.

> *More reasons to value this game: the characters feel familiar and real.*
>
> *Concludes with a statement about why the game matters, ending on a positive note of what it feels like to belong.*

REFLECT & WRITE

Swapna Krishna claims in her review of *Thirsty Suitors* **that the game succeeds in its aim "to make us, who are often so forgotten in modern media and pop culture, feel seen." What evidence and good reasons does she offer in support of this claim, and how convincing do you find her argument? Note that she draws on her own personal experience a great deal in this review. What other kinds of evidence might she have called on? Write a response back to Krishna, telling her what seemed most effective and memorable about her review and explaining why you found her overall argument persuasive (or not).**

Guts (spilled) by Olivia Rodrigo: An Album for the Ages
KENNEDI L. GOODE-BEY

Opens with a personal experience to draw readers in.

Friendly TONE *and everyday language engage readers' attention.*

First criterion for evaluation: a trans-generational appeal.

I STARTED LISTENING to Olivia Rodrigo in 2021, with the release of her song "Drivers License"—the song that hooked my mom, my friends, and me from the moment we heard it. At the time, we were all recovering from the hysteria of the COVID-19 pandemic and trying to figure out how to adapt to the new normal in our lives. I was surprised when my mom said she enjoyed Rodrigo's songs, because my parents often tell me they aren't fond of the music most singers are creating today—since the 1990s, they feel, the music industry hasn't really produced "real music." I disagree (of course!), but at times I can see their perspective. After all, as my mom points out, today's songs use a lot more curse words, even songs that are played on the radio. But I think the main reason my parents don't think singers today make "real" music anymore is that the subject matter seems trivial or unimportant to them. So although it surprised me at first that my mother enjoyed the pop music made by this Gen Z teen, I soon realized it's because Rodrigo is truly a trans-generational artist who speaks to the teenager buried in all of us.

KENNEDI L. GOODE-BEY, who wrote this review especially for our book, is a second-year student at North Carolina A&T University, where she is majoring in journalism and mass communication. A reporter and frequent reviewer for the *A&T Register*, she aims to become a journalist writing for publications like the *New York Times*.

Goode-Bey / Guts (spilled) by Olivia Rodrigo: An Album for the Ages

Olivia Rodrigo performing on tour and holding her Grammy awards.

This trans-generational aspect is a hallmark of Rodrigo's most recent album, the 2023 *Guts,* whose songs grabbed the attention of parents, millennials, and teenagers alike. In "Bad Idea Right?" Rodrigo sings, "Yes, I know that he's my ex, but can't two people reconnect? / . . . I only see him as a friend, I just tripped and fell into his bed." Her song about a former relationship is one that all generations of listeners can relate to.

Guts has been a roaring success, offering twelve songs, not counting the additional five that were released a few months later by the singer. The album with all seventeen songs is titled *Guts (spilled)*, so titled because Rodrigo spilled her entire heart, guts, and collection of big feelings in the music and spirited lyrics. In "Pretty Isn't Pretty," Rodrigo sings, "When pretty isn't pretty enough, what do you do? / And everybody's keeping it up, so you think it's you." Tapping into the angst that young women feel as society pulls them in conflicting directions, she reveals in this song how her efforts to conform to society's expectations of how she should act, dress, and look were never enough. This pressure took such a toll on her self-confidence that she "bought a new prescription to try and stay calm / 'Cause there's always somethin' missin'." The personal experiences Rodrigo shares in her songs are relatable to a whole range of audiences who have all felt overwhelmed by the impending pressures of young adulthood. But even aside from the fact that her music can be clearly understood, the artist is up-front about the fact that she has imperfections just like the rest of us. Life as a teen can be messy, stressful, and confusing, a message her album encapsulates and one that young people everywhere relate to.

Rodrigo first came into the spotlight when she was on the Disney show *Bizaardvark*, but the pop sensation had long had a passion for singing and making music.

BACKGROUND information provides context and helps establish the author's CREDIBILITY: she knows Rodrigo's work well.	When she played the role of Nini in *High School Musical: The Musical: The Series*, viewers fell in love with Rodrigo's character and the songs she sang. From the time that Rodrigo began performing, she has made it clear that songwriting was a serious passion of hers, which is why she ultimately left the Disney show in season 3.
More criteria for evaluation introduced and supported with examples of Rodrigo's awards and accolades as well as her artistry.	That passion is evident in the quality of her solo-delivered lyrics and musical composition, as well as her sheer storytelling power, which has been recognized with three Grammy awards and several Billboard Hot 100 number one singles. In *Guts*, the song "Lacy" exemplifies her artistry in a story that grips the audience and transports them into a tumultuous platonic relationship of Rodrigo's. "Lacy" is about someone Rodrigo loves and admires, but is also wary of—because Rodrigo might have ulterior motives for their friendship: "And I despise my jealous eyes and how hard they fell for you / Yeah, I despise my rotten mind and how much it worships you." The imagery and dialogue in these powerful lyrics hold listeners at rapt attention; the musical score starts off gentle but builds into a melody with a striking intensity.
Title of album analyzed for its appropriateness and power.	Rodrigo's provocative titles also reflect her artistic intent: the names of her songs and albums are intentional and bold. Fans who at first found the *Guts* title jarring later decided it was fitting for a song collection about the aching growing pains young people experience as they reach their twenties. This album focuses on Rodrigo's feelings and reactions—her guts—as she processes and internalizes events happening to her. The title is original and abrupt, easily resonating with the teenager within all of us.
The echo of the title helps draw the review to a conclusion along with a summary of the criteria of evaluation.	When I take the time to reflect, I realize that the younger version of myself needed Olivia Rodrigo's music to help me voice complicated thoughts and feelings I have as I grow into a young adult in this ever-changing country and world. When I listen to her songs now, I feel confident and excited for the life ahead of me. Overall, *Guts* is an album for the ages, one rich with replay value and timeless storytelling. Rodrigo's easily relatable music transcends generations, and the lyricism partnered with artistic talent that shines through her visuals signifies that she is truly the voice of today—and tomorrow.

Works Cited

Bizaardvark. Created by Kyle Stegina and Josh Lehrman, Disney Channel, 2016–19.

High School Musical: The Musical: The Series. Created by Tim Federle, Disney+, 2019–23.

Rodrigo, Olivia. "Bad Idea Right?" *Guts*, Geffen Records, 2023.

———. "Lacy." *Guts*, Geffen Records, 2023.

———. "Pretty Isn't Pretty." *Guts*, Geffen Records, 2023.

REFLECT & WRITE

Kennedi L. Goode-Bey realizes that her younger self "needed Olivia Rodrigo's music to help [her] voice complicated thoughts and feelings," and she points to Rodrigo's provocative titles and original lyrics as two aspects of the music that were particularly helpful. What other criteria does Goode-Bey offer in her assessment of Rodrigo's success—and what evidence/examples does she present to support the criteria? Can you identify a singer or singer/songwriter (or another kind of artist altogether) who has played a similar role in helping you articulate your thoughts and feelings? Write two or three paragraphs introducing that artist and explaining, in detail and with examples, what aspects of their music was particularly helpful to you.

NINETEEN

"Here's What I Recommend"
Making a Proposal

WILL YOU MARRY ME? There is no clearer proposal than the one this question represents. It proposes something that at least one person thinks ought to occur. Proposals are just that: recommendations that something be done, often to bring about some kind of change or to solve a problem. You'll likely have occasion to write proposals for various purposes; and if you're reading this chapter now, you've probably been assigned to write one for a composition class.

You might propose more transparent financial aid options, a more efficient way of recycling, a possible solution to housing insecurity among students. Like a marriage proposal, each suggests change; unlike a marriage proposal, however, each of these cases addresses a problem and calls for careful analysis of several possible courses of action. While it may be obvious to your beloved that you are the one, it's less obvious how a more transparent financial aid system can actually ease the burden of student debt, how to motivate people to recycle, or how to respond to a problem as complex as housing insecurity. Proposals of this kind argue for clear solutions to specific problems; and as with any argument, they build a convincing case that what they recommend should be considered—and even acted on.

19 ✤ Making a Proposal

This chapter provides guidelines for writing proposals that will be taken seriously, ones that say, "Here's what I recommend—and why you should take my advice."

> ## REFLECT
>
> Proposals are part of daily life, but some are more compelling than others. Find a proposal that interests you, perhaps an op-ed on a social issue such as gun rights or free speech or a Get Out the Vote campaign. How does the proposal convince—or fail to convince—you that it's important and that the recommended solution is worth your support?

Across Academic Disciplines

When you're assigned to write a research-based essay, chances are your instructor will ask you to present a proposal before you begin researching and drafting. Such proposals give you a chance, early on, to show that your topic is viable and your plan for completing the proposal is doable—and that you are addressing the assignment. You'll likely have occasion to write such proposals in many courses. For an engineering course, an assignment may call for you to propose the creation of a new product, explaining the need it fills and how it'll work. In a public policy course, you might work with a group to analyze a specific policy—perhaps your city's plan to go electric for all city transportation vehicles—and to propose changes. In each case, you'll need to think about what's expected, given the topic and the discipline.

Across Media

Today, authors of proposals most often use multiple media to present their recommendations. Crowdfunding sites like *Kickstarter* may use video to show their projects in action or bring audiences face-to-face with their cause. Op-ed columnists writing for newspapers rely on carefully crafted words to make their points, but online versions of the papers include links to supporting materials. If you're presenting a proposal as a part of an oral presentation, slides will help illustrate what you're recommending—and you may be asked to provide a print document to elaborate on what you propose.

**THINK
BEYOND
WORDS**

 CROWDFUNDING SITES *are filled with proposals.* Take a look at the proposal that former flight attendant Robin Wearly created on Kickstarter *for a disabled passenger transfer sling (ADAPTS) that permits air travelers who use wheelchairs to get off the plane quickly and safely in case of evacuation. It states a problem and proposes a solution. Go to* everyonesanauthor.tumblr.com *to see the full proposal. Note how the campaign page uses written text, images, and videos. Imagine how Wearly might present this proposal in a meeting with potential investors. What information would be best presented as speech, on slides, as an embedded video, or in a handout? What additional information might investors want that the website does not contain?*

Across Cultures and Communities

Proposals of various sorts are common in the United States. At your school, for example, students might propose a new policy for dealing with matters of sexual assault or propose the creation of a free food pantry on campus. In business, many companies encourage employees at all levels to share ideas for improving the company's products or services. And in many states, voters can propose ballot initiatives to change existing laws.

Proposals are common in cultures and industries that thrive on open discussion and innovation, but not every community is receptive to input from just anyone. Many governments, organizations, and households around the world value the judgment of authorities and community leaders, and proposals from others may be seen as disrespectful. So be aware of the context you're writing in and the audience you are speaking to, not just to avoid offending someone but also to determine how to present your ideas so they'll have the greatest chance of succeeding.

Across Genres

Proposals occur in many kinds of writing. REVIEWS may sometimes end with proposals for how a product under review could be improved, and many REPORTS, especially those on pressing social issues, conclude by proposing a course of action to address the issue.

A fully developed proposal is based on a detailed ANALYSIS of a problem or situation. It requires REPORTING trustworthy information, and often involves NARRATING one or more past events as part of that reporting.

> **REFLECT**
>
> Find two proposals that address the same issue, perhaps one students are currently debating on your campus. How does each proposal define the issue, what solutions does each of them offer, and what evidence does each provide to show that its solutions will work? Which of the two proposals do you find more persuasive, and why?

CHARACTERISTIC FEATURES

Although there will be variation depending on the topic, you'll find that nearly all strong proposals share the following characteristics:

- A precise description of the problem (p. 381)
- A clear and compelling solution to the problem (p. 384)
- Evidence that your solution will address the problem (p. 384)
- Acknowledgment of other possible solutions (p. 385)
- A statement of what your proposal will accomplish (p. 386)

A Precise Description of the Problem

The goal of all proposals is to offer a solution for some problem, so most of them begin by explicitly stating the problem and showing that it is serious enough to call for a solution. Some problems are obvious—that there's a severe water shortage in the Southwest, for instance, or your campus needs more resources to support mental health—so you won't have to say very much to convince your audience that they matter. In other cases, though, you'll need to describe the problem in detail and provide data, examples, and other evidence to convince readers that it's serious enough to require a solution.

For example, see how the Editorial Board of the University of Pittsburgh's daily student newspaper, the *Pitt News*, begins a proposal by describing a problem faced by many of the paper's readers:

> Walking back home after you pick up your takeout from Shah's on Semple Street should be a harmless affair, but tragically, many people must take their dinner home across the death trap that is the intersection of Semple and Bates Street.
>
> With its southern curb perpetually lined with parked cars, pedestrians crossing in the direction of campus cannot see oncoming traffic through this thick metal facade. They must either walk into the road with the blind faith that a car isn't approaching quicker than 20 miles per hour or carefully inch into the intersection, straining their neck to see, like a wounded giraffe. . . .
>
> Semple and Bates is only one of many spots around Oakland where the grim reaper hangs out, dancing where a stop sign should be. The intersection of North Dithridge and Bayard Street has the same heavy foot traffic with no real signage to protect pedestrians. As unfortunate as it is, a yellow yield sign has the same authority for cars as the No Jaywalking signs have for students crossing Forbes Avenue outside Hillman Library.
>
> Oakland needs stop signs and stoplights consistently throughout its intersections for the safety of pedestrians. One block over from Semple's death trap, the intersection of Bates and Atwood Street has traffic lights, so students don't need to worry about being struck by two tons of steel on their daily walk to class. The stoplight rarely backs up traffic, and people can save their gambling luck for a scratch-off rather than wasting it blindly walking across the street.
>
> Traffic lights are generally a better solution than stop signs because just as cars ignore yield signs, students often ignore the crossing order at stop signs. . . . While stop signs can work just fine on the outskirts of Oakland's residential areas, the high-traffic areas of the neighborhood would benefit most from a simple stoplight.
>
> We must prioritize the safety of pedestrians, especially in a neighborhood with students wandering the streets at all hours of the day and night. A high-speed block of metal has the potential to ruin somebody's life at every intersection it cruises through—we shouldn't

19 Making a Proposal

jeopardize the safety of Oakland's residents just so a car doesn't have to wait for a few seconds at a red light.

—PITT NEWS EDITORIAL BOARD, "Oakland Desperately Needs to Improve Its Traffic Signage."

In the opening paragraph of its proposal, the Editorial Board sets a scene that captures the significance of the problem: lives are at stake. The following paragraphs provide specific examples of intersections that pose dangers for pedestrians, describing in detail the choices they face in getting across safely and then going on to recommend a solution: "stop signs and stoplights consistently throughout" the area of Pittsburgh that surrounds the university.

Robin Wearly, author of the *Kickstarter* proposal illustrated on page 380, begins her proposal by stating the problem in terms that appeal to readers' emotions and logic in a culture that values individual responsibility and thinking ahead: "Emergencies happen. What if you or a loved one rely on a wheelchair? What's the plan?" She then provides a series of brief but vivid scenarios that confront readers with the reality of the problem:

> Wheelchairs are checked in cargo on airplanes. Elevators are shut down in hotel emergencies. So did you ever wonder how wheelchair travelers escape a burning airplane, a derailed train, a bus accident, a cruise ship disaster, or hotel room when told to evacuate? What if they can't wait for rescue personnel and their only hope is the crew or kindness of strangers? What if you have less than 90 seconds to make it to an emergency exit? Will a trapped person leave both your lives in peril? Here's how ADAPTS comes to the rescue!
>
> —ROBIN WEARLY, "ADAPTS, the First Evacuation Sling for Wheelchair Users"

These descriptions remind readers, especially able-bodied ones, of things that can go wrong and the consequences of such situations for wheelchair users. These high-stakes scenarios define the problem that the proposal will then address.

As in these examples, proposals you write should identify and define the problem clearly and foreshadow the clear and realistic recommendations you will be making. In the case of Wearly's proposal, preventing emergencies that endanger individuals with various mobility issues is a tall order, but the solution proposed seems entirely doable.

A Clear and Compelling Solution to the Problem

> Missy Watson wants writing instructors (and you) to examine and challenge some of their own beliefs about language. How well does she make her case? Check it out on p. 1010.

Successful proposals offer a compelling solution to the problem at hand. That is, it's not enough just to have a good idea; in a proposal, you'll have to convince readers that your idea squarely addresses the problem as you've defined it. You'll want to explain the solution succinctly but in enough detail to make a clear and confident case for it.

Consider a proposal for a policy that would provide more affordable housing in Portland, Oregon, from an article by a member of Portland's city council. This article was published in *Street Roots*, a weekly newspaper often sold by people who are experiencing homelessness:

> We can't require developers to build affordable housing; state law prevents it. But we can encourage those who want to build here to be part of the solution. . . . The city currently provides "density bonuses" to developers for including certain public benefits in their projects—meaning they can build taller buildings or get more floor space than would normally be allowed in exchange for including features like eco-roofs or bicycle parking.
>
> Now is the time to restructure our density bonus regulations to prioritize affordable housing development. . . .
>
> Under a proposal that will go before the council on July 9, developers seeking a density bonus must either provide affordable housing within their development or pay a fee into a fund for the creation and preservation of affordable housing. This proposal . . . would require them to contribute to the creation of affordable housing in order to receive the maximum density that our zoning currently allows.
>
> —DAN SALTZMAN, "Incentive for Developers Would Spur Affordable Housing"

Saltzman's proposal addresses the problem clearly: to build the largest permissible buildings (and hence make more money), developers must include affordable units in the development *or* contribute to a fund for creating affordable housing. In return for something a developer wants, the city gets something it wants: more affordable housing.

Evidence That Your Solution Will Address the Problem

A proposal is convincing when the evidence it provides shows that the solution being proposed will, in fact, address the problem. What counts as convincing evidence will vary depending on what it is you're proposing and to whom.

If you're pitching a new business venture to potential investors, your evidence would include numbers showing the projected returns on investment. If you're proposing a new honor code at your school, your evidence would likely include testimonies and examples of how it would improve the learning environment. In his article on the Portland affordable housing proposal, Dan Saltzman provides data projecting what the proposal could accomplish:

> This "affordable housing incentive zoning proposal" could result in as many as 60 additional units of affordable housing a year on top of those already being developed by the city, or it could mean an additional $120 million to $200 million in funds for affordable housing over the next 20 years.
>
> This proposal alone will not solve our affordable-housing crisis but is a critical step to ensuring more affordable housing in our city.

By acknowledging that this proposal will not totally solve the problem of affordable housing but demonstrating its potential benefits, Saltzman limits his solution to one that Portland will be able to address at the time, thus making a persuasive case that what he is suggesting is realistic and feasible.

Another example comes from Appleton, Wisconsin, a city facing the challenge of redesigning its streets and transit systems to accommodate pedestrians and bicyclists. In an eighty-page proposal laying out a twenty-year plan to improve such access, the city's designers offer plenty of evidence to support their ideas: diagrams showing how specific roads will be reconfigured to include bike lanes, charts of costs and funding sources, and a timetable for completing the project over the twenty-year construction period. Some of this evidence illustrates that the proposed changes will achieve the city's goal; other evidence shows that they will do so in a feasible manner.

Acknowledgment of Other Possible Solutions

Part of crafting a persuasive proposal is making it clear that your solution is the best course of action—and hence better than other options. To do so, you need to account for other possible solutions and demonstrate the comparative advantages of the solution you're suggesting.

In an article for the *Stanford Daily*, Mark Allen Cu argues that the residence hall he lives in at Stanford University should get a new name. Why? Because Wilbur Hall honors Ray Lyman Wilbur, "a eugenicist who feared the expansion of various ethnic groups in the United States, including Asian immigrants." In the article, Cu recognizes reasons for remembering Wilbur, saying that he was:

> a lifelong friend of Herbert Hoover, a politician in his own right and the University's longest serving president, [whom] Stanford Magazine referred to as "the doctor-president who made Stanford better." . . . The Iowa-native also served as the U.S. secretary of the interior and [was noted for] public health advocacy. . . . It is undeniable that Wilbur's life accomplishments are far-reaching; however, Stanford's idolization of him does not discount his involvement with one of the most harmful scientific movements in American history.
>
> —MARK ALLEN CU, "Stanford Should Rename Wilbur Hall"

And it is for this compelling reason that Cu calls for renaming his residence hall. The problem Cu addresses is one that can be remedied with one solution: replacing a name.

Other situations call for proposals that consider several possible solutions at the same time, as in the case of the one for creating bicycle and pedestrian access in Appleton, Wisconsin. Because there's no one-size-fits-all solution that will work for every street in the city, the authors of this proposal suggest several possible configurations, including those shown in Figures 19.a and 19.b.

Bike lanes (only for cyclists) and shared lanes (for bicycles and cars) are two of the possible configurations the authors explore. They provide detailed information about each option, describing its purpose, listing its advantages and disadvantages, and including visuals that provide information words alone could not. In situations that call for multiple solutions, weighing all possibilities shows that you have fully considered the problems' complexity.

A Statement of What Your Proposal Will Accomplish

So what if readers decide to follow your proposal? What can they expect it to accomplish? The strongest proposals answer that question explicitly. Given that your goal is to persuade readers to agree with your recommendation and perhaps to take some action, you need to help them understand the likely outcomes. Many proposals end by making clear what's to be gained, what outcomes, large and small, they might bring about.

After calling the University of Texas at Austin's Counseling and Mental Health Center (CMHC) and being told to call back two hours later in order to speak with someone, Michael Lazenby, a columnist for the university's student newspaper, the *Daily Texan*, wrote that it seemed like his problems

19 Making a Proposal

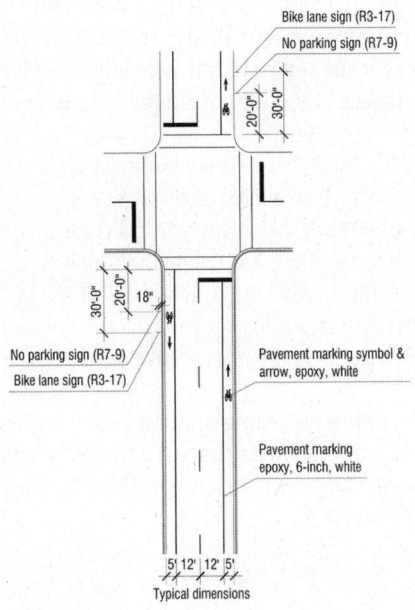

Fig. 19.a BIKE LANE

Description/Purpose: Marked space along length of roadway for exclusive use of cyclists. Bike lanes create separation between cyclists and automobiles.

Advantages
- Provides bicycle access on major through streets
- Clarifies lane use for motorists and cyclists
- Increases cyclists' comfort through visual separation

Disadvantages
- Space requirements may preclude other possible uses like parking or excess travel lane width

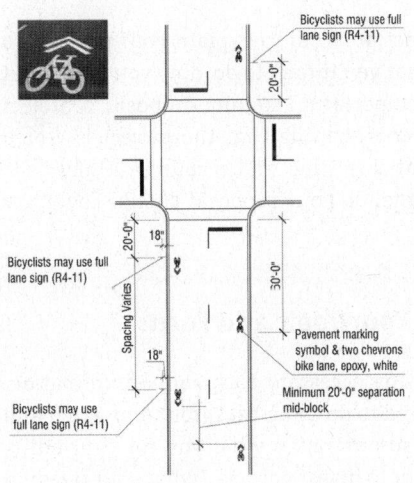

Fig. 19.b SHARED LANE

Description/Purpose: Shared roadway pavement markings, or "sharrows," are markings used to indicate a shared lane environment for bicycles and automobiles. Sharrows identify to all road users where bicycles should operate on a street where a separated facility is not feasible.

Advantages
- Helps cyclists position themselves in lanes too narrow for a motor vehicle and a bicycle to travel side by side
- Provides pavement markings where bike lanes are not possible

Disadvantages
- Maintenance requirements
- Not as effective as a separated bicycle facility

—WISCONSIN DEPARTMENT OF TRANSPORTATION, *City of Appleton On-Street Bike Plan*

"didn't matter." After speaking with other students, he proposed that UT create an app where students sign up for appointments, an idea that the associate director of clinical services at the center found to be a "beneficial" and "feasible" way to "reduce . . . barriers." Lazenby concludes his proposal:

> Students have access to grades, emails, and other miscellaneous announcements from UT in their back pocket. While these are important for students to keep track of, they don't hold a candle to student mental health. Being able to schedule a session with one of the CMHC's counselors in a matter of seconds rather than hours can make all the difference for a student seeking help.
>
> —MICHAEL LAZENBY, "Make Mental Health Accessible"

By comparing the usefulness of an app to schedule appointments with a counselor to other online campus communications that, in a time of crisis, are far less important, Lazenby makes clear what his proposal will accomplish in a compelling and persuasive way.

PROJECT PROPOSALS

You may be asked to write a project proposal to explain your plans for a large or long-term assignment: what you intend to do, how you'll go about doing it, and why the project is important. Like any proposal, a project proposal makes an argument, demonstrating that the project is worth doing and feasible given the available time and resources. Unless the assignment names other requirements, your proposal should cover the following ground.

An Indication of Your Topic and Focus

Explain what your topic is, giving any necessary background information. In some cases, you might be required to do some background research and to include a LITERATURE REVIEW summarizing what you find, including any issues or controversies you want to investigate. Say what your research focus will be, with the RESEARCH QUESTION you plan to pursue and a tentative THESIS. Finally, say why the topic matters—so what, and who cares?

An Explanation of Why You're Interested in the Topic

Briefly explain what you already know about your topic and why you've chosen to pursue this line of inquiry. You might describe any coursework, reading, or experience that contributes to your knowledge and interest. Also note what you don't yet know but intend to find out.

A Plan

Explain how you will investigate your research question. What types of sources will you need, and what will your research methods be? If you plan to do FIELD RESEARCH, how will you conduct your study? And what GENRE and MEDIUM will you use to present your findings? What steps will be required to bring it all together into the final document?

A Schedule

Break your project into tasks and make a schedule, taking into account all the research, reading, and writing you'll need to do. Include any specific tasks your instructor requires, such as handing in a draft or an ANNOTATED BIBLIOGRAPHY. Be sure also to leave yourself time to get feedback and revise.

See page 407 for a model annotated project proposal.

WRITING A PROPOSAL / A Roadmap

Think of a problem you can help solve

If you get to select the topic, identify an issue you know something about. You'll find it easiest—and most rewarding—to tackle an issue on which you can have some real impact. Try choosing a topic you have authority to speak on and one that is narrowly focused or local enough that your suggestions may be heard.

If you've been assigned a topic, consider ways that you can make it interesting to you and your readers. This may mean finding a particular angle on the topic that appeals to you, or, if the assignment is framed in general terms, finding a specific aspect that you can address with a specific solution.

Consider your rhetorical situation

Once you have a topic, thinking about your rhetorical situation will help you focus on how to proceed.

Think about your AUDIENCE. Who do you want your proposal to reach, and why? If you're proposing changes to a campus policy, you would do so differently if you're writing to school administrators in charge of that policy than if you're writing a piece for the newspaper. Here are some things to consider:

- What do you know about your audience? In what ways are they like or unlike you—and one another?

- What will they likely know about your topic? What background information will you have to provide?

- What interest or stake are they likely to have in the situation you're addressing? Will you need to convince them that the problem matters—and if you do, how can you do so?

- What sorts of evidence will they find most convincing?

- How likely are they to agree with what you propose?

Be clear about your PURPOSE. Odds are that you'll have multiple purposes—everything from getting a good grade, to demonstrating your understanding of a situation, to making your community a better place for everyone. The more you understand your own motivations, the clearer you can be with your audience about what is at stake.

Be aware of your STANCE. What is your attitude about your topic, and how do you want to come across to your audience? How can your choice of words help convey that stance?

Examine the larger CONTEXT. What do you know about the problem you're tackling? What might you need to learn? How have others addressed it? What solutions have they proposed and how well have they worked?

Consider your LANGUAGE. Almost any proposal can be presented in a number of ways. Regardless of how many languages and dialects you use in your everyday life, you have many options to consider in crafting a proposal. What variety of language or dialect will best suit your audience and help you achieve your goals as a writer? Will your audience expect a certain kind of language or style? Do you want to meet those expectations? challenge them? What do you want your language choices to say about you? What risks might you be willing to take with your language? How will your choice of medium and the larger context limit or expand the language options available to you? See Chapters 4 and 35 for more information about language options.

Think about MEDIA. If the choice is yours, what medium will best reach your audience and suit your purpose? If you're assigned to use a particular medium, how can you use it best? If, for example, you're giving an oral presentation, slides can help your audience follow the main points of your proposal, especially if you're presenting quantitative data.

Think about DESIGN. If you have the option of designing your proposal, think about what it needs. If it's lengthy or complex, should you use headings? Is there anything in your proposal that would be hard to follow in a paragraph—and easier to read in a chart or a graph?

Consider GENERATIVE AI. If your instructor's course policies allow you to use generative AI tools, consider whether you'd find it helpful to run ideas by a chatbot, generate images, or get feedback on your proposal. If you are having a hard time thinking of and considering alternatives to your proposal, you might ask a chatbot to suggest some alternatives—and then do some research on any suggestions you want to address so that you can study them yourself. Or once you have completed a draft of your proposal, you might ask a bot to respond to the draft, suggesting two or three ways you could make it livelier and more engaging to your target audience. And remember that while AI can be helpful to your writing process, the information it provides isn't always right!

Study the situation

Whatever the problem, you have to understand it in all its complexity and think about the many ways in which different parties will likely understand it.

Begin by thinking about what you know about the situation. What interests you about the issue, and why do you care? What more do you need to find out about it? To answer these questions, try BRAINSTORMING or other activities for GENERATING IDEAS.

Be sure you understand the problem. To do so, you'll surely need to do some RESEARCH. What CAUSED this problem, and what are its EFFECTS? How serious is it? Who cares about it? What's been said about it? What efforts have already been made to address the problem, and how have they succeeded? How have similar problems been handled, and what insights can you gain from studying them?

Consider how you can best present the problem for your AUDIENCE. If they're aware of the problem, how much do they care about it? Does it affect them? If they're not aware of it, how can you make them aware? What kind of evidence can you provide to make them recognize the potential consequences? Why do you think the issue matters, and how can you persuade others to take it seriously?

For example, if you were writing about the need for a program to raise awareness of the effects of hate speech on campus, you might open with an anecdote about hateful things that have been said about others to make those not otherwise concerned with the topic aware of the issue. And you could then appeal to their goodwill and concern for fellow students to understand why it's a problem that needs to be tackled.

> What Missy Watson is proposing is no small ask—that thousands of individuals make a huge and sustained effort. Does she succeed in getting her audience to care about the problem and take it seriously? Check out her proposal on p. 1010.

Determine a course of action

Once you've got a thorough understanding of the problem and what others think about it, you can start thinking about possible solutions.

Come up with some possible solutions. Start by making a list of options. Which ones seem most feasible and most likely to solve the problem? Is there one that seems like the best approach? Why? Will it solve the problem entirely, or just part of it?

If, for example, you're proposing a program to raise awareness about hate speech on campus, what are the options? You could suggest an open forum, or a teach-in. Maybe you could get an outside speaker to visit campus.

Decide on the best solution. Determine which of the options would be feasible and would work the best. Then think about how far it would go toward actually solving the problem. Hate speech is not easily solved, so this might well be a case where you can realistically only raise awareness of the problem.

Organize and start writing

Once you've clearly defined the problem, figured out a viable solution, and identified evidence to support your proposal, it's time to organize your materials and start drafting.

Come up with a tentative THESIS that identifies the problem it proposes to solve. Use this statement to guide you as you write.

Provide EVIDENCE showing that the problem in fact exists, that it is serious enough to demand a solution, and that your proposed solution is feasible and the best among various options.

Acknowledge other possible solutions. Decide how and at what point in your proposal you will address other options. You might start with them and explain their shortcomings, or you could raise them after presenting your own solution, comparing your solution with the others as a way of showing that yours is the most feasible or the most likely to solve the problem.

Draft an **OPENING**. Identify and describe the problem, making clear why the issue matters—and why the problem needs a solution.

Draft a **CONCLUSION**. Reiterate the nature of the problem and the solution you're proposing. Summarize the benefits your proposal offers. Most of all, remind readers why the issue matters, why they should care, and why they should take your proposal seriously (and perhaps take action).

Look critically at your draft, get responses—and revise

Once you have a complete draft, read it over carefully, focusing on how you define the problem and support the solution you propose—and the way you appeal to your audience. If possible, ask others to read it over as well. Here are some questions to help you or others read over the draft with a critical eye:

- *How does the proposal* **OPEN***?* Will it capture readers' interest? Does it make clear what problem will be addressed and give some sense of why it matters? How else might it begin? Does the title tell readers what the proposal is about, and will it make them want to know more?

- *Is the problem* **DESCRIBED** *in enough detail?* Will any readers need more information to understand that it's a problem that matters? Have you said anything about its **CAUSES** and consequences—and if not, do you need to?

- *Is the proposed solution explicit and compelling?* Have you provided enough **EVIDENCE** to show that it's feasible and will address the problem—and that it's better than other possible solutions? Is there an explicit statement of what it will accomplish?

- *Have other possible solutions been acknowledged fairly?* How well have you responded to them? Are there any other solutions to be considered?

- *Is the proposal easy to follow?* If not, try adding **TRANSITIONS** or headings.

- *How have you established your* **AUTHORITY** *to write on this topic?* Does the information seem trustworthy? How do you come across as an author—passionate? serious? sarcastic?—and how does this tone affect the way the proposal comes across to readers?

- *How would you characterize the* STYLE *?* Is it fitting for your intended audience? Consider the choice of words, the level of formality, and so on.
- *How about* DESIGN *?* Are there any illustrations—and if so, how do they contribute to the proposal? If not, is there any information that would be easier to show with a photo or in a chart? What about the typeface: is it right for a proposal of this kind? Is the design well suited to the MEDIUM ?
- *How does the proposal* CONCLUDE *?* Will it inspire the change or action you're calling for? How else might it conclude?

Revise your draft in response to any feedback you receive and your own analysis.

REFLECT

Once you've completed your proposal, let it settle for a while and take time to REFLECT . How well did you define the problem? How thoroughly did you support your proposed solution? How persuasively have you demonstrated the feasibility of your solution? How fairly did you acknowledge and respond to other possible solutions? Research shows that such reflections help "lock in" what you learn for future use.

READINGS / Annotated Model Proposals

Uses for AI in the Criminal Justice System
EMI VAUGHAN

Opening establishes her CREDIBILITY as a resident of Vermont and a student of the justice system—and points to the problem to address: AI.

Demonstrates knowledge of the state's positive actions to date, further establishing her credibility.

Dear Patricia Gabel, Vermont's State Court Administrator,

As a criminal justice major at Endicott College and a resident of Vermont, I am strongly invested in the future of my home state's legal system. Something that will undoubtedly shape this future, not only in Vermont but also across the nation, is artificial intelligence (AI).

It is exciting to see that our state government has already begun to embrace AI technology, even establishing the Vermont Artificial Intelligence Task Force to oversee its adoption and ensure its ethical use. It is no wonder that Vermont would take steps in this direction, with AI promising to make justice systems across the country more manageable, efficient, and equitable. However, this evolving technology also presents serious concerns that merit careful consideration (*Artificial Intelligence Task Force*). Perhaps the most widely researched concern among these is that of bias, particularly in risk assessment tools that help predict offenders' likelihood of recidivism, violence, and returning to court. Although these tools—which have already been widely adopted across the

---

EMI VAUGHAN wrote this proposal for a Writing with AI course at Endicott College—though she decided not to use AI in the process! Assigned to "write a letter to a leader" in her future professional field on how the field may adapt to the rise of generative AI, Vaughan, who plans to pursue a career in criminal justice, focused on her home state's court system and the dangers AI can pose if used indiscriminately.

United States—are meant to serve as objective, data-driven decision makers, numerous studies have found that they can reinforce existing racial prejudices rather than reduce them. This is especially concerning in Vermont, the state with the second-Whitest population and highly disproportionate arrest and incarceration rates of its Black citizens.

In your role as the Vermont State Court administrator overseeing court staff procedures and the procurement or modification of technology, it is imperative that your decisions regarding the implementation of AI technology in our state's justice system be both deeply informed and in the best interest of our residents ("Standard Practices Committee"). As such, I would like to elaborate on concerns surrounding the use of these tools, drawing on in-depth research and insights from an honors-level college course on AI technology. In particular, I propose that Vermont not make use of risk assessment tools that will amplify our legal system's racial biases but instead use AI as an organizational tool during other pretrial processes to achieve greater efficiency.

Risk assessment tools sit at the forefront of discussions regarding AI and criminal justice, garnering mostly positive responses from judges across the nation. In a process of statistical analysis using previous arrest and court appearance data, risk assessment tools score defendants on a scale of low to high risk of recidivism, violence, and failing to show at court during the pretrial phase. These scores can then help judges decide whether to release or detain defendants until their trial and determine sentences for convicted offenders (Buskey and Woods).

The benefits of this may seem remarkable: risk assessment tools can help judges make decisions more efficiently and more impartially. However, the development of these tools relies on historical data—and historically, decisions made by law enforcement, corrections, and judicial officers have not always been fair. People of color have long been systematically disadvantaged by the U.S. justice system, often being subjected to harsher judgments and legal practices than White citizens. Consequently, any risk assessment tool that is trained using records of these racist practices may reflect those same patterns in their assessments (Freeman and McGilton).

This has been the case for one prominent risk assessment tool, the Correctional Offender Management Profiling for Alternative Sanctions (COMPAS). In 2016 ProPublica conducted a study utilizing COMPAS to evaluate ten thousand defendants in a county in Florida and found racial disparities in the system's results (Larson et al.). The researchers discovered that Black defendants were

States one problem AI presents to the state's legal system: bias.

Appeals directly to the administrator's role in serving the people of Vermont.

Further establishes her authority to speak on this issue.

States the proposed solution clearly and concisely.

Presents EVIDENCE in favor of the use of AI in risk assessment.

BACKGROUND information ensures readers understand the basics.

Presents COUNTERARGUMENTS drawing on credible sources to question the use of AI for assessing risk.

A specific example supports the author's claim.

"45 percent more likely to be assigned higher risk scores than white defendants" and almost twice as likely to be misclassified as being high risk for both standard recidivism and violent recidivism compared to White defendants (Larson et al.). These revelations clearly suggest that tools like COMPAS operate based on preexisting racial prejudices in our justice system.

Concerns like these extend beyond COMPAS, though: numerous groups have called for the cessation of all risk assessment tool use due to issues of bias. The Pretrial Justice Institute, once a staunch advocate for risk assessment technology, reversed its stance in 2020 when it stated that "these tools [were] derived from data reflecting structural racism and institutional inequity" and warned that using these data would only reinforce that inequity (Wolfe). The Science, Technology, and Public Policy program at the University of Michigan came to similar conclusions (McCoy), which were echoed by the American Civil Liberties Union (Woods and Allen-Kyle). Considering these words of caution from so many researchers, it is not advisable that Vermont's justice system adopt any current risk assessment tools if we truly seek to achieve racial equality.

Proponents of risk assessment tools may argue that despite these concerns, this technology provides too many benefits to be thrown out entirely. After all, there are various factors that can unduly influence a judge (or other judicial member's) decision making, including how recently they ate or how their favorite football team is performing (Chohlas-Wood). As such, it could be argued that judges should still use risk assessment tools as a guide but not rely on them as an end-all determinant if they believe racial bias has tainted the evaluation.

However, whether judges believe they are neglecting a defendant's risk assessment score or not, research has shown that their pretrial decision making can be subconsciously altered by these evaluations. Professors from Harvard University and the University of Michigan conducted a study revealing that "risk assessments can systematically alter how people balance risk with other factors when making policy-relevant decisions" (Green and Chen). For example, participants of the study were presented with information about hypothetical defendants and asked to either detain or release them before trial. When presented with the defendant's risk assessment score alongside their background information, participants became more sensitive to the factor of risk. More alarmingly, when asked to reflect on their decision-making process, "participants did not seem to recognize that the risk assessment had altered how they consider risk" (Green and Chen).

To back up her STANCE, *draws on statements by three respected organizations that argue against the use of risk assessment tools because of their inherent bias.*

Acknowledges the reasonable arguments of those who support the use of risk assessment tools.

Introduces a research study from respected institutions as EVIDENCE *countering those who argue in favor of these tools.*

This evidence suggests that even if a judge suspects a risk assessment score is racially biased and chooses not to consider it as a factor, they may still be unknowingly influenced by the AI evaluation. As such, it is safer to withhold risk assessment scores from Vermont's judicial decision makers altogether. Otherwise, the scores will likely only exacerbate issues of racial bias facing our state's courts and correctional facilities. As the ACLU of Vermont wrote in their 2021 Statement on Racial Disparities in Vermont Prosecutions, our state prisons "have some of the worst racial disparities in the country," with Black residents being six times more likely to face incarceration than their White counterparts ("ACLU of Vermont"). Risk assessment tools will likely not stop these trends, but reflect and uphold them. Until Vermont's justice system can achieve racial equality, I strongly recommend that we abstain from adopting AI-powered risk assessment tools.

And yet, Vermont's criminal justice system does not need to reject AI technology entirely. There are other ways AI tools can help our judicial employees achieve greater efficiency without putting certain communities at risk. In particular, one major task of the judicial process that could benefit from AI technology is the reviewing and organizing of legal documents. Judges are responsible for reading and analyzing documents relevant to their cases, including motions, claim applications, and legal briefs. Prosecutors and defense lawyers have similar responsibilities. In a recent lecture, American court system professor Dr. Ethan Boldt pointed out that most of an attorney's time is dedicated to reading documents relevant to their cases. Because legal writing is often dense, judicial employees may struggle to retain important details without rereading the documents several times or taking notes—both of which are tedious and time-consuming. Platforms like *ChatGPT* and other customized tools that are likely to be developed in the years ahead can be used to alleviate these challenges by summarizing and organizing the readings.

To demonstrate how *ChatGPT* can be used to organize legal documents, consider a sample brief provided by the US Court of Appeals Fifth Circuit, for a random case, No. 13-30972. Included in this sample brief is a thirteen-page "Statement of the Case," which chronicles various interactions between the plaintiff and defendants (United States, Court of Appeals). The involved judge and attorneys are responsible for understanding this series of events and may want to refer to specific details during trial. Given the document's length, neither of these is an easy task. The writing can be copied and pasted into

Sums up the danger of relying on AI-generated risk assessment scores.

Offers a solution to the problem: don't use the risk assessment scores!

Brings the argument back close to home, stating why the topic matters.

Proposes other ways that AI could be used ethically and effectively in the Vermont legal system.

Provides specific **EXAMPLES** *of how AI could be helpful.*

ChatGPT following the prompt, "Organize the main points of this passage into a cohesive timeline." Within seconds, ChatGPT provides what may have taken significant time and energy for a human to complete: a numbered list of the events featured in the sample case statement, organized by date. Attorneys and judges can use this timeline to review important case details and quickly reference them while making their case in court. If they feel specific points are missing, they can manually add them or ask ChatGPT to redo its process, including more information for each timeline point.

When considering this method of using AI, criminal justice professionals like yourself may have doubts about ChatGPT's capabilities. Tech experts like Doug Aamoth have raised concerns about this, noting how inaccuracies and the exclusion of important details in the AI platform's summaries could weaken a judge or attorney's case knowledge and court argument. These concerns are legitimate; I certainly do not suggest ChatGPT as a replacement for legal reading altogether. Judges and attorneys should still be expected to review legal documents in order to understand the full scope of the case they are working on. They also may need to fact-check ChatGPT's work and manually add neglected details. The process of using ChatGPT to summarize writing simply allows court participants to organize their thoughts, highlight main points, and quickly identify important case details without having to reread the same document several times or rifle through endless pages of legal documentation while on the stand.

By using AI tools in this way—for organizing and summarizing legal writing rather than predicting defendants' risk of criminality—Vermont's justice system can embrace the rise of generative AI technology without worsening racial disparities. Avoiding practices that perpetuate racial injustice is crucial toward fostering a community that is safe for all in Vermont, including the state's underrepresented Black citizens. Current risk assessment tools enable the oppression of this population, but our justice system has the opportunity to reconsider how they use this AI technology. Text generation tools such as ChatGPT can reduce the time judicial employees spend on tedious tasks and allow them to focus on more important responsibilities. This, in turn, can accelerate legal processes and improve our state's justice system as a whole.

As previously stated, it is wonderful to see Vermont embracing AI technology within the justice system that I one day hope to work for myself. There is no doubt that our state can implement AI tools in powerful ways,

---

Provides an extended example of how ChatGPT could organize events in a lengthy document, saving human time and effort.

Addresses the administrator directly, acknowledging concerns and citing tech experts who also raise concerns about ChatGPT's abilities.

Acknowledges the legitimacy of these concerns but offers ways to fact-check and question ChatGPT.

Sums up how Vermont can use AI to improve its legal system without worsening racial disparities that the use of risk assessment tools entails.

Reiterates the problem.

Reiterates the appropriate ways AI can be used to improve the Vermont legal system.

15

and I hope you will take my proposals here into consideration as you explore these possibilities in order to ensure the safety of some of our most vulnerable citizens.

Ends on a personal note, showing a personal investment in the future of Vermont's legal system and the role AI can play in it.

Works Cited

Aamoth, Doug. "This ChatGPT Feature Has Huge Potential—but Really Needs Work." *Fast Company*, 22 Feb. 2023, www.fastcompany.com/90851964/chatgpt-summarization.

"ACLU of Vermont Statement on Racial Disparities in Vermont Prosecutions." *ACLU of Vermont*, 18 Nov. 2021, www.acluvt.org/en/press-releases/aclu-vermont-statement-racial-disparities-vermont-prosecutions.

Artificial Intelligence Task Force: Final Report. State of Vermont, Agency of Commerce and Community Development, 15 Jan. 2020, accd.vermont.gov/economic-development/artificial-intelligence-task-force.

Boldt, Ethan. "Attorney Responsibilities." Lecture. Criminology, 11 Dec. 2023, Endicott College.

Buskey, Brandon, and Andrea Woods. "Making Sense of Pretrial Risk Assessments." *National Association of Criminal Defense Lawyers*, www.nacdl.org/Article/June2018-MakingSenseofPretrialRiskAsses. Accessed 4 Dec. 2023.

Chohlas-Wood, Alex. "Understanding Risk Assessment Instruments in Criminal Justice." *Brookings*, 19 June 2020, www.brookings.edu/articles/understanding-risk-assessment-instruments-in-criminal-justice.

Freeman, Kelly Roberts, and Mari McGilton. "The Problem Is Not the Criminal Justice Risk Assessment Tool: It's Systemic Racism." *Urban Institute*, 3 Aug. 2020, www.urban.org/urban-wire/problem-not-criminal-justice-risk-assessment-tool-its-systemic-racism.

Green, Ben, and Yiling Chen. "Algorithmic Risk Assessments Can Alter Human Decision-Making Processes in High-Stakes Government Contexts." *Proceedings of the ACM on Human-Computer Interaction*, vol. 5, no. CSCW2, 18 Oct. 2021, https://doi.org/10.1145/3479562.

Larson, Jeff, et al. "How We Analyzed the COMPAS Recidivism Algorithm." *ProPublica*, 23 May 2016, www.propublica.org/article/how-we-analyzed-the-compas-recidivism-algorithm.

McCoy, Ember. "The Risks of Pretrial Risk Assessment Tools: Policy Considerations for Michigan." *Gerald R. Ford School of Public Policy*, University of Michigan, May 2023, stpp.fordschool.umich.edu/research-projects/risks-pretrial-risk-assessment-tools-policy-considerations-michigan.

"Standard Practices Committee." *Vermont Judiciary*, 2021, www.vermontjudiciary.org/about-vermont-judiciary/boards-and-committees/standard-practices.

United States, Court of Appeals for the Fifth Circuit. *Resa Latiolais v. Donald Cravins, Sr.* Docket no. 13-30972, 6 Sept. 2013. *United States Court of Appeals for the Fifth Circuit*, www.ca5.uscourts.gov/documents/SampleBriefs.pdf.

Wolfe, Dawn R. "Criminal Justice Group Drops Support for Pretrial Risk Assessment Tools as Ohio Justices Seek to Blo." *Pretrial Justice Institute*, 12 Feb. 2020, www.pretrial.org/about/newsroom/2020/02/12/criminal-justice-group-drops-support-for-pretrial-risk-assessment-tools-as-ohio-justices-seek-to-blo.

Woods, Andrea, and Portia Allen-Kyle. "A New Vision for Pretrial Justice in the United States." *ACLU Smart Justice*, American Civil Liberties Union, Mar. 2019, www.aclu.org/wp-content/uploads/publications/aclu_pretrial_reform_toplines_positions_report.pdf.

REFLECT & WRITE

Emi Vaughan is careful throughout the letter to acknowledge and address alternative perspectives on AI in general and risk assessment tools in particular. Read back through the letter, marking each acknowledgment and consideration of counterarguments. How would you describe Vaughan's **STANCE** in this letter, and how is that stance related to consideration of alternative perspectives? How effective do you find it? Do you think this letter will be convincing to the administrator it addresses? Why or why not? Do you agree with Vaughan's stance or find one of the noted counterarguments more persuasive? Write a brief response weighing in on the topic and be sure to address counterarguments to clarify your own stance.

To Unite a Divided America, Make People Work for It
JONATHAN HOLLOWAY

I F WE AMERICANS listened to one another, perhaps we would recognize how absurd our discourse has become. It is our own fault that political discussions today are hotheaded arguments over whether the hooligans storming the halls of the Capitol were taking a tour or fomenting an insurrection; if we broadened our audiences, perhaps we would see the fallacy of claims that all Republicans are committed to voter suppression and that all Democrats are committed to voter fraud.

It seems like an easy challenge to address, but we lack the incentives to change our behavior. We are all, regardless of where we sit on the political spectrum, caught in a vortex of intoxication. We have fooled ourselves into thinking that our followers on social media are our friends. They aren't. They are our mirrors, recordings of our own thoughts and images played back to us, by us and for us. We feel good about ourselves, sure, but do we feel good as citizens? Do we feel good as Americans? Are we better off? Is America?

There are many problems in America, but fundamental to so many of them is our unwillingness to learn from one another, to see and respect one another,

Use of first person plural ("we," "our") attempts to connect with readers, suggesting that we are all in this together.

Concise statement of the problem.

Second and third paragraphs elaborate on the problem: Americans won't listen to or learn from one another.

JONATHAN HOLLOWAY is an American historian, former president of Rutgers University, and the author of several books on race in America—most recently *The Cause of Freedom: A Concise History of African Americans* (2021). This essay was published in the *New York Times* in 2021 as part of a series dedicated to "exploring bold ideas to revitalize and renew the American experiment."

to become familiar with people from different racial and ethnic backgrounds and who hold different political views. It will take work to repair this problem, but building blocks exist. A good foundation would be a one-year mandatory national service program.

> *Proposed solution introduced: a new national service program.*

Nearly 90 years ago, in response to the Great Depression, President Franklin Roosevelt created the Civilian Conservation Corps, what was then America's largest organized nationwide civilian service program. About 30 years later, President Lyndon Johnson brought to fruition President John Kennedy's "domestic Peace Corps" initiative, the Volunteers in Service to America program, known as VISTA. Today, domestic civilian service is dominated by AmeriCorps and nongovernmental programs like Teach for America.

> *EXAMPLES of previously effective service programs are offered in support of the solution.*

Taken together, these programs have been enormously successful at putting people to work, broadening the reach of basic social services related to education, health and welfare. Most important, they have helped citizens see the crucial role that they can play in strengthening our democracy. Given that we know service programs can be so effective in shoring up the nation in moments of crisis, the time has come for a broader initiative, with higher aspirations and goals. The time has come for compulsory national service for all young people—with no exceptions.

> *EVIDENCE that prior programs have put people to work for the good of the country.*

Universal national service would include one year of civilian service or military service for all adults to be completed before they reach the age of 25, with responsibilities met domestically or around the world. It would channel the conscience of the Civilian Conservation Corps and put young people in the wilderness repairing the ravages of environmental destruction. It would draw on the lessons of the Peace Corps and dispatch young Americans to distant lands where they would understand the challenges of poor countries and of people for whom basic health and nutrition are aspirational goals. It would draw on the success of our military programs that in the past created pathways toward financial stability and educational progress for those with limited resources while serving as great unifiers among America's races, religions and social classes.

> *Details of how the solution could work deepen the author's CREDIBILITY.*

These are but three examples. A one-year universal national service program could take many other forms, but it is easy to imagine that it could be a vehicle to provide necessary support to underserved urban and rural communities, help eliminate food deserts, contribute to rebuilding the nation's

> *States the positive outcomes that the proposed service program would lead to.*

infrastructure, enrich our arts and culture, and bolster our community health clinics, classrooms and preschools.

Furthermore, because service would be mandatory, it would force all of our young people to better know one another, creating the opportunities to learn about and appreciate our differences. Speaking as an educator, I know that we get better answers to complex problems when we assemble teams from a wide range of backgrounds. Once these teams realize that they have a common purpose, their collective differences and diversity in race, gender, expertise, faith, sexual orientation and political orientation start to emerge as a strength. If you look at the state of our civic culture, it is clear that we have a long way to go before we can claim that we are doing the best that we can. The kind of experiential education I am advocating could change a life, could open a mind and could save a democracy.

> *Additional positive outcomes presented in support of the proposal.*

A sensible system of compulsory national service would build bridges between people and turn them into citizens. It would shore up our fragile communities and strengthen us as individuals and as a nation. Compulsory national service would make us more self-reliant and at the same time more interdependent. It would help us to realize our remarkable individual strengths and would reveal the enormous collective possibilities when we pull together instead of rip apart.

> *Notes ways in which the proposal would benefit individual citizens.*

At its core, we need to heed the call for citizenship. We need to take the natural inclination to help out our friends and families and turn it into a willingness to support strangers. We need to inspire people to answer the call to serve because in so doing, they will discover ways to have their voices heard and their communities seen and respected.

> *Connects the proposal to building a sense of committed citizenship among the populace.*

This is neither a new nor a partisan idea. This call to serve and inspire is written into the preamble of the United States Constitution. When the founders sought to "form a more perfect union, establish justice, ensure domestic tranquility, provide for the common defense, promote the general welfare, and secure the blessings of liberty," they were talking about establishing an ethos of citizenship and participation.

Compulsory national service is not a panacea, but neither is it a mere placebo. It could be a very real solution to a very real problem that already has wrought havoc on our democracy and that threatens our future as a nation, our viability as a culture and our very worth as human beings. This nation and its democratic principles need our help. We can and must do better.

> *Acknowledges that the proposal is not a cure-all but sums up why it should be adopted as the best option for success.*

REFLECT & WRITE

Jonathan Holloway's proposal is based on a cause-effect argument: establish a one-year mandatory national service program (cause) and get ... what results? Make a list of all the positive effects Holloway argues will come from adopting this proposal. What evidence does he provide to suggest that the cause would indeed lead to those effects? Are you persuaded by Holloway's argument and evidence? Write a brief argument of your own in response to Holloway and point to specific effects he cites that you agree or disagree will occur—and why you think so.

An Annotated Project Proposal

The Economic Impact of Investing Public Funds in Sports Franchises

DAVID PASINI

Since the 1960s, local governments have provided increased funding and subsidies for professional sports franchises. Taxpayer money has gone toward facilities like stadiums and arenas, and many cities have offered tax exemptions and other financial incentives to keep a team in town that has threatened to relocate. Proponents of public funding for privately owned sports franchises argue that cities gain more from the arrangement—namely, jobs, status, and tourist dollars—than they lose. Opponents argue that using public funds for these purposes results in long-term financial drains on local governments and point out that many communities have been abandoned by teams even after providing substantial benefits.

Writing in *The New York Times*, Ken Belson gives an example of one such government-funded project: "The old Giants Stadium, demolished to make way for New Meadowlands Stadium, still carries about $110 million in debt, or nearly $13 for every New Jersey resident, even though it is now a parking lot." The image included here shows the governor of New Jersey looking over a drawing of the Giants Stadium, which was completed in 1976 and destroyed in 2010 (fig. 1).

The introduction announces the TOPIC and summarizes a controversy the project will focus on.

DAVID PASINI wrote this project proposal for a first-year writing course at The Ohio State University on the theme of sports in American society.

Fig. 1. Left to right: The governor of New Jersey, William T. Cahill; the owner of the Giants, Wellington Mara; and chairman of the New Jersey sports authority, Sonny Werblin, admire a drawing of Giants Stadium. Neal Boenzi, 1971. "As Stadiums Vanish, Their Debt Lives On," by Ken Belson. *The New York Times*, 8 Sept. 2010, p. A1.

Given the high stakes involved—and particularly the use of taxpayer dollars—it seems important, then, to ask what these sports franchises contribute (or do not contribute) to their cities and wider metropolitan areas. Do these teams "generate positive net economic benefits for their cities," or do they "absorb scarce government funds" that would be better spent on programs that have "higher social or economic payoff" (Noll and Zimbalist 55)? My research project will investigate these questions.

The question of public funding for sports is important to any resident of a community that has a professional sports franchise or is trying to lure one, as well as to any citizen who is interested in local economic and political issues. I am in the latter group, a nonfan who is simply interested in how public monies are being used to support sports, and whose knowledge about the issues is primarily in the economic domain. At this point, I am neither a proponent nor an opponent of investing in sports, but I think that it's important to consider how much professional sports contribute to the economic well-being of the government that funds them.

How much of the money that teams generate supports local businesses, school districts, or other entities that benefit all citizens? How much of it stays in the owners' pockets? Do the franchises "give back" to their communities in tangible or intangible ways? The franchises themselves should consider these questions, since the communities that invest in their success have a right to expect something in return.

An explicit statement of his RESEARCH QUESTIONS.

A statement of why this topic matters, and to whom.

Pasini explains his interest in the topic and his current knowledge of it.

More focused research questions, leading to a tentative THESIS *statement.*

To learn more about investment in sports teams and the teams' economic impact, I will consult business and sports management journals and appropriate news sources, both print and digital. I will also interview stakeholders on both sides of the debate as well as experts on this topic. I will consider the many factors that must be taken into account, such as the benefits of tourism and the costs of "creating extra demand on local services" (Crompton 33). As a result of my research, I hope to offer insight on whether public funds are in fact put to good use when they are invested in major sports franchises.

A research plan, including kinds of sources he'll consult and field research he plans to conduct.

The CONCLUSION *restates why this research matters.*

Proposed Schedule

Do library and internet research	April 6–20
Submit annotated bibliography	April 20
Schedule and conduct interviews	April 21–25
Turn in first draft	May 10
Turn in second draft	May 18
Turn in final draft	May 25

A schedule that allows time for research, writing, and revising—and lists assignment deadlines.

Preliminary Works Consulted

Belson, Ken. "As Stadiums Vanish, Their Debt Lives On." *The New York Times*, 8 Sept. 2010, p. A1.

Crompton, John L. "Economic Impact Analysis of Sports Facilities and Events: Eleven Sources of Misapplication." *Journal of Sport Management*, vol. 9, no. 1, 1995, pp. 14–35.

Noll, Roger G., and Andrew Zimbalist, editors. *Sports, Jobs, and Taxes: The Economic Impact of Sports Teams and Stadiums*. Brookings Institution Press, 1997.

Robertson, Robby. "The Economic Impact of Sports Facilities." *The Sport Digest*, vol. 16, no. 1, 2008, www.thesportdigest.com/archive/article/economic-impact-sports-facilities.

Pasini uses MLA STYLE *for a preliminary list of works consulted.*

REFLECT & WRITE

If you're reading about project proposals, you've probably been assigned to write one. Analyze what your assignment is asking for, comparing it with the features listed on page 381. What does this exercise help you appreciate about how such a proposal works? What you can learn from doing one?

PART V

The Centrality of Argument

A huge amount of our everyday thinking—powerful, creative, and resonant stuff—is done socially, talking to other people [and] arguing with them.

—CLIVE THOMPSON

I like arguments.

—PRINCE

HANCES ARE, your early attempts to communicate were arguments: "More!" "No!" "Cookie!" All arguments. So if you think that argument is just about disputes or disagreements, think again. In rhetorical terms, argument refers to any way that human beings express themselves to try to achieve a particular purpose—in other words: everything is an argument. That's no doubt why Prince said he liked arguments. And so do we: understanding and analyzing them is one way we protect

ourselves from misinformation and outright lies, and writing them for ourselves is a major way we think and share our ideas.

You'll find plenty of arguments in this book: an opinion article offers a position on a social issue; a media critic writes a rave review of a video game; an infographic makes a case for action—as do many other speeches and essays included here, too. And beyond this book, you encounter arguments in all your classes, in groups you belong to, and in the media surrounding you 24/7. In addition, you make arguments of your own. When you post on *TikTok*, you're arguing that your topic will be important or perhaps amusing to your followers. When you recommend a new TV show to a friend, you're arguing that it's good and worth their time. Even when you write a lab report, you describe and interpret the results of an experiment, thus arguing that your findings have important implications.

We want to get you thinking hard about the arguments surrounding you and about how you can understand and control them—rather than letting them control you—and how you can create arguments that are persuasive, powerful, and ethical.

> **REFLECT**
>
> Jot down the arguments you encountered so far today—on T-shirts and bumper stickers and ads; on podcasts, social media posts, and TV; in textbooks and class meetings; in talking with friends. Then take a look at your list: where and when did you encounter most of the arguments? How can you categorize them? Does anything surprise you about them? How did you respond to some of them—mostly positively? negatively? Why?

TWENTY

Recognizing Arguments

IT WILL COME AS NO SURPRISE to you to hear that you are immersed in argument. You might have had an argument with yourself over what to wear this morning. You might have passed a barrage of posters asking you to support certain causes on your way to class. In your biology lecture, you might have heard the professor explain the conflicting arguments about global warming's causes. If you've scrolled your social media feed, you certainly faced a flood of claims and arguments there. Maybe you ended the day agreeing to disagree with a friend about who is the GOAT—Michael Jordan or LeBron James—or Simone Biles! The point we want to make is simple: you are the author of many arguments and the target of many more—and you'll be a better reader and writer of your own arguments if you recognize them and understand how they work.

Arguments Are Multimodal

Arguments today most often consist of more than just words, from a park sign signaling people to "make way for ducklings," to a big "thumbs up," to an ad for McDonald's. These familiar images demonstrate how images, often along with words, make strong visual arguments. As a reader and analyzer of arguments, this means that you will need to pay very careful

Words, graphics, and images can be combined to make strong visual arguments.

attention not only to the words of a message but also to its layout—the way it is visually presented—as well as to any images it contains.

If you saw the early trailer for Francis Ford Coppola's 2024 movie *Megalopolis* before it was pulled, for example, you could have studied how the trailer's elements made a strong argument that the film is worth the price of admission, even if it faced harsh critics at the start. Those elements included movie scenes, text quoting negative reviews of Coppola's earlier masterpieces like *The Godfather*, and a voiceover soundtrack. However, observant viewers immediately spotted something wrong with a lot of those quotes; they were completely fake or patched together from a medley of negative reviews. And, as it turned out, they were crafted using AI. Lionsgate quickly pulled the trailer and apologized, saying, "We screwed up," but this episode is one more clear warning to all of us: compelling multimodal arguments like this trailer (aiming to convince us that *Megalopolis* is worth seeing no matter the reviews because the masterpieces Coppola is known for were all once dismissed by critics) must be read and viewed with a careful and critical eye.

▶ See the ebook for a video on understanding academic argument.

Arguments Have a Purpose

Multimodality—drawing us in with engaging images, sounds, and experiences—is just one reason that arguments today are more seductive than ever. A single social media post can sway thousands of voters (as Taylor Swift's *Instagram* post did in 2024 when she shared a link that resulted in 405,999 new voter registrations within twenty-four hours). A song you

A still from the trailer for *Megalopolis*, which made a strong argument—with flaws.

loved as a twelve-year-old now boosts sales of soft drinks. Celebrities write op-ed essays on issues they care about. Even your school mounts arguments to attract prospective students—and, later, to motivate alumni to give generously. Check out your school's website, and you'll find appeals intended to attract both applications and contributions.

Perhaps you think that such arguments are somewhat manipulative, intended to trick you into buying a product or contributing to a cause (or paying good money to see a movie). You would be right! But remember that all arguments are trying to achieve some specific PURPOSE, so it is up to you both as a reader and as a writer to distinguish the good from the bad. And arguments can, of course, be used for good (think of Martin Luther King Jr.'s powerful arguments for human rights) or ill (think of Hitler's diabolical but hypnotic speeches). Thus they can also be dangerous. Research shows that arguments based on misinformation tend to attract more "clicks" online than truthful ones do, reminding us of poet Jonathan Swift's warning more than 300 years ago: "falsehood flies, and truth comes limping after it." All the more reason to be aware of the arguments around you—and to be a careful analyst of them all.

But mixed in with misleading arguments are many that are research- and fact-based, and thus deserve your attention. If all of the arguments that swirl around us aim to achieve some purpose, trying to grasp that purpose

> Charlotte Clymer's purpose in her argument about gender may not be stated explicitly, but it would be hard to miss. Check out her essay on p. 888.

can help guide you. Of the many purposes we might name, here are some of the most important that you're likely to encounter or pursue in your own arguments:

- *to convince or persuade*—to bring others around to your way of thinking through the use of ethical, emotional, and logical appeals
- *to explore*—to seek information, experiment with it, see where it may lead
- *to understand*—to fully "hear" what an argument is saying openly, respectfully, and fairly before coming to judgment on it
- *to seek consensus*—to look for common ground, for ways to bring people together
- *to make decisions*—to carefully weigh options and look at different perspectives, to come to the best solution or decision

As you begin developing any argument, it makes good sense to look very closely at your purpose or purposes for making that argument: whose interests does your purpose serve?

>  REFLECT
>
> Visit a social media feed that's familiar to you and look for all the posts that make arguments. Which one impacts you the most, either positively or negatively, and why? Is that post based on research? on opinion? on shaky facts (or even misinformation)? What is its purpose—and how did the creator achieve that purpose, if at all? Do you still have the same reaction to the post after considering these questions? Why or why not?

Arguments Are Contextual

Keep in mind that arguments are always embedded in particular CONTEXTS — and that what is persuasive will vary from one context to another, from one culture to another. The most persuasive evidence in one community might come from religious texts; in another, from the knowledge of revered elders; in still another, from facts or statistics. Especially when arguments often take place online and reach people all around the world, it's important to be aware of and to respect such differences.

During the 2020 Tokyo Olympics, gymnast Simone Biles withdrew from multiple events, citing mental health and safety issues, which included dealing with the "twisties," a disconnect that can occur between a gymnast's body and mind while performing, resulting in loss of sense of space. While many rallied around Biles, others were quick to criticize her, labeling her a "quitter." But those critics had failed to contextualize their arguments. Had they done so, they would have learned that the "twisties" are no joke. Craig Meyer, writing for *USA Today*, explained that "dealing with the twisties can prevent a gymnast from landing safely on the mat, which could result in serious injury." Biles herself tried to educate others in a series of *Instagram* posts, where she said that her "mind and body [were] simply not in sync" and that she didn't think people "realize[d] how dangerous this [was] on hard/competitive surfaces." Putting Biles's withdrawal in full context allows us to better evaluate arguments for and against her actions. That context is also important in understanding the full significance of her triumphant return to the 2024 Paris Olympics.

To take another brief example of the role context plays in arguments, consider a 2024 ad for the Apple iPad Pro. Apple's "Crush" commercial featured a huge hydraulic press literally crushing all kinds of creative tools, from pianos and other musical instruments to record players, books, and cameras—flattening them all to reveal "the most powerful iPad ever." The creators of the ad may have intended to send a positive message about all the wonderful and creative things the latest iPad can do. They apparently

Apple's "Crush" ad, selling "the most powerful iPad ever."

failed, however, to consider the context surrounding the ad, which evoked a huge backlash. As one professor of marketing put it, "I think the way it came across is, here is technology crushing the [creative] life." Others noted that the ad was particularly tone-deaf in a time when many people fear that big tech and artificial intelligence tools may take their jobs away—along with their creativity. Realizing their misreading of the context, Apple quickly pulled the ad and apologized. But the damage was done.

During his lifetime, Martin Luther King Jr. did not have the benefit of the internet, but the arguments he made eventually reverberated around the world. In his "Letter from Birmingham Jail," King was responding to a statement written in 1963 by eight White Alabama clergymen who had urged him to stop his campaign of civil disobedience to protest racial discrimination. This particular context—the US South at the height of the civil rights struggle—informs his argument throughout. And while King's argument remains the same, having been republished countless times, its interpretation varies across time and cultures. When the letter first appeared, it responded point by point to the statement by the eight clergymen, and it was read as an answer to their particular charges. Today, however, it is read as a much more general statement about the importance of civil rights for all people. King's famous conclusion to this letter sums up his argument and consciously addresses an audience that extends far beyond the eight clergymen:

> Let us all hope that the dark clouds of racial prejudice will soon pass away and the deep fog of misunderstanding will be lifted from our fear-drenched communities, and in some not too distant tomorrow the radiant stars of love and brotherhood will shine over our great nation with all their scintillating beauty.
> —MARTIN LUTHER KING JR., "Letter from Birmingham Jail"

As with all arguments, the effectiveness of King's letter has always varied according to the context in which it is read and, especially, the audience that is reading it. In most of his letter, King addresses eight specific people, and they are clearly part of his primary audience. But his use of "us" and "our" in the passage above works to broaden that audience and reaches beyond that time and place to many other readers and listeners.

King's letter was a written text and meant to be read. But like his spoken texts, it can also be heard—what Nicole Furlonge, author of *Race Sounds: The Art of Listening in African American Literature,* calls "listening

Martin Luther King Jr. in a jail cell in Birmingham, Alabama.

in print." This kind of listening calls on us to concentrate on the soundscape of a text, what we can hear in our aural imagination that can add a great deal of richness to what we are seeing with our eyes. Imagine King speaking this text and listen for his pacing, his cadences, and his strong baritone voice.

Because arguments are so central to our lives, it's important to recognize them around us and to understand how they work. To make effective arguments of your own, you'll practice paying very careful attention to your purpose, your context, and the rest of your rhetorical situation—as well as to the media tools available to you. The next two chapters focus on how good arguments work and some strategies you can use to support the arguments that you make.

TWENTY-ONE

Analyzing and Constructing Arguments
Those You Read, Those You Write

THE CLOTHES YOU CHOOSE TO WEAR argue for your sense of style; the courses your college requires argue for what educators consider important; the kind of transportation you take, the food you eat (or don't eat)— almost everything represents some kind of argument. So it is important to understand all these arguments, those you encounter and those you create. Consider a couple of everyday examples.

What's in a social media handle? What about an email address? You may not have thought much about the argument that these chosen titles make, but they certainly do make a statement about you. One student we know chose @2hot2handl as an *Instagram* handle. But when it came time to look for meaningful employment, he began to think about what that username might suggest about him. As a result, he chose something more fitting for the image he wanted to convey: @jabariblake22.

It's also important to understand the arguments that come from others. Take a look, for example, at the two visuals on the next page. The first is a poster featuring a raised fist, calling on people to attend a National Women's Strike in Portland to protest for "equal rights, reproductive freedom & to end gender-based violence." The poster's argument

Activists' signs make decidedly different arguments about women's rights in America.

is aimed directly at protecting women's rights. The second image shows anti-abortion protesters rallying on the same day, June 24, 2024. Like all arguments, these images exist in a larger **CONTEXT** : the date is significant to both visuals, since it marks the second anniversary of the US Supreme Court decision to overturn *Roe v. Wade*, which ended federal protections for the right to have an abortion. The first image may call to mind the famous image of Tommy Smith and John Carlos raising their fists during their 1968 Olympics medal ceremony as a silent protest of violence against Black people. The second image also shows raised hands, holding signs—written in Spanish and English—in Washington, DC, at the site of the Supreme Court ruling. The images make very different arguments about women's rights and responsibilities, arguments that continue today.

Arguments, in short, don't appear out of thin air: every argument begins as a response to some other argument—a statement, an event, an image, or something else. From these images we see how important it is to analyze any argument you encounter—and consider the other side—before deciding where you yourself stand. That goes for arguments you read and for ones you write. Either way, all arguments are part of a larger conversation. Whether you're responding to something you've read, discussing a film you've seen, or writing an essay that argues a position, you enter into a dialogue with the arguments of others.

This chapter will help you analyze the arguments you encounter and compose arguments of your own.

WHERE'S THE ARGUMENT COMING FROM?

As a reader, you need to pay special attention to the source of an argument—literally to where it is coming from. It makes a difference whether an argument appears in the *New Pittsburgh Courier* or a school newspaper, in *Physics Review* or on the social media feed of someone you know nothing about, in an impromptu speech by a candidate seeking your vote or in an analysis of that speech done by the nonpartisan website *FactCheck.org*. And even when you know who's putting forward the argument, you need to dig deeper to find out where—what view of the world—that source itself is "coming from."

For example, see the homepage of the website of Public Citizen, a nonprofit organization founded in 1971 by consumer advocate and social critic Ralph Nader. So what can we tell about where this argument is coming from? We might start with the image in the upper-left corner of Lady Liberty holding up her torch right next to the headline "PUBLIC CITIZEN." Below that is the menu bar and a statement of the organization's goal:

> We fight for you and take on corporate power. Corporations have their lobbyists. The People need advocates too.

Based on its website and its stated goal, we can surmise, then, that Public Citizen supports the rights of ordinary citizens and liberal democratic values and opposes the influence of corporations on government. Indeed, if we look a bit further, to the About page, we will find the following statement:

> Public Citizen is a nonprofit consumer advocacy organization that champions the public interest in the halls of power. We defend democracy, resist corporate power, and fight to ensure that government works for the people—not for big corporations. Founded in 1971, we now have 500,000 members and supporters throughout the country.
>
> ... [W]e don't participate in partisan political activities or endorse any candidates for elected office. We take no government or corporate money, which allows us to remain fiercely independent and call out bad actors—no matter who they are or how much power and money they have.

Together, these images and statements tell us a lot about Public Citizen's stance, where the organization is coming from. Checking a few other trustworthy sources confirms this stance, since they call Public Citizen a

The homepage of Public Citizen's website: https://www.citizen.org.

"progressive" and "liberal" organization that practices "lobbying and advocacy." As savvy readers, we then have to assess the claims Public Citizen makes on its website and elsewhere in light of this knowledge: knowing where an organization is coming from and how it is seen by others affects how willing or skeptical we are to accept what it says.

Or consider a more lighthearted example, this time from political pundit David Brooks:

> We now have to work under the assumption that every American has a tattoo. Whether we are at a formal dinner, at a professional luncheon, at a sales conference or arguing before the Supreme Court, we have to assume that everyone in the room is fully tatted up—that under each suit, dress or blouse, there is at least a set of angel wings, a barbed wire armband, a Chinese character or maybe even a fully inked body suit. We have to assume that any casual anti-tattoo remark will cause offense, even to those we least suspect of self-marking.
>
> —DAVID BROOKS, "Nonconformity Is Skin Deep"

What can we know about where Brooks is coming from? For starters, a quick *Google* search will bring up photos showing a middle-aged White man, and other sources describing Brooks as a conservative journalist whose work appears in many publications across the political spectrum and who often appears as a television commentator on the *PBS NewsHour*. We also know that this passage comes from one of his opinion columns for the *New York Times*. His professional photo on the *Times* website presents him in jacket and tie.

What more can we tell about where he's coming from in the passage itself? Probably first is that Brooks is representing himself here as somewhat old-fashioned, as someone who's clearly an adult and a member of what might be called "the establishment" in the United States (note his off-handed assumption that "we" might be "at a formal dinner" or "arguing before the Supreme Court"). And he's someone who almost certainly does not have a tattoo! He's also comfortable using a little sarcasm ("everyone in the room is fully tatted up") and exaggeration ("every American has a tattoo") to make a humorous point. Finally, we can tell that he is a self-confident—and persuasive—author and that we'll need to be on our toes to understand the argument that he's actually making.

David Brooks

As an author, you should always think hard about where *you* are coming from in the arguments you make. What's your STANCE , and why? How do you want your audience to perceive you? As reasonable? knowledgeable? opinionated? curious? something else?

How can you convey your stance? Through your choice of words, of course—both *what* you say and *how* you say it—but also through any images you include and the way you design your text. The words you choose not only convey your meaning, but they also reveal a lot about your attitude—toward your subject and your audience. Introducing a quotation with the words "she insists" indicates a different attitude than the more neutral "she says."

WHAT'S THE CLAIM?

You run into dozens of claims every day. Your brother says that Shang-Chi is the best Marvel superhero ever; your news feed predicts that the Boston Celtics will win the next NBA championship; a friend texts to say it's a waste of time and money to eat at Subway. Each of these statements makes a claim and argues implicitly for you to agree. The arguments you read and write in college often begin with a claim, an arguable statement that must then be supported with good reasons and evidence.

Billy Porter as Cinderella's fairy godperson.

In 2021, famed Broadway singer and actor Billy Porter, shown below in a luscious gold and orange sequined gown, played Cinderella's fairy godmother in a remake of the classic story. Porter is well known for pushing boundaries of all kinds in his work. For example, in 2019 he won an Emmy for his role in the series *Pose*, making him the first openly gay Black man to win that prize for lead actor in a drama series. And in 2024, he was awarded the Isabelle Stevenson Tony Award for his activist LGBTQ+ humanitarian work, specifically for the Elizabeth Taylor AIDS Foundation and the Entertainment Community Fund. About his decision to play a genderless fairy godperson, Porter took the director's challenge that "it's time to shake it up" seriously. Noting that "magic has no gender," Porter says he was happy playing this powerful genderless role, making a "classic fairytale for a new generation"; he believes "the new generation is really ready. The kids are ready. It's the grownups that are slowing stuff down." So what's the claim? Porter's role as a fairy godperson whose gender is indeterminate—depicted below in the character's signature outfit—suggests that gender doesn't have a role to play in helping make dreams true.

The easiest claims to identify are those that are stated directly as an explicit THESIS. Look, for instance, at the following paragraph from a journal article by civil rights activist W. E. B. Du Bois in 1922. As you read each sentence, ask yourself what Du Bois's claim is.

> Abraham Lincoln was a Southern poor white, . . . poorly educated and unusually ugly, awkward, ill-dressed. He liked smutty stories and was a politician down to his toes. Aristocrats—Jeff Davis, Seward and their ilk—despised him, and indeed he had little outwardly that compelled respect. But in that curious human way he was big inside. He had reserves and depths and when habit and convention were torn away there was something left to Lincoln—nothing to most of his contemners. There was something left, so that at the crisis he was big enough to be inconsistent—cruel, merciful; peace-loving, a fighter; despising Negroes and letting them fight and vote; protecting slavery and freeing slaves. He was a man—a big, inconsistent, brave man.
>
> —W. E. B. DU BOIS, "Abraham Lincoln"

We think you'll find that the claim is difficult to make out until the last sentence, which lets us know in an explicit thesis that the contradictions Du Bois has been detailing are part of Lincoln's greatness, part of what made him "big" and "brave." Take note as well of where the thesis appears in the text. Du Bois holds his claim for the very end.

Here is a very different example, from a newspaper column about legendary dancer Judith Jamison. Note that it begins with an explicit thesis stating a claim that the rest of the passage expands on—and supports:

> Judith Jamison is my kind of American cultural icon. . . . She has many accolades and awards—among them the National Medal of Arts, the Kennedy Center Honors and an Emmy. . . .
>
> But when I met her . . . she said with a huge smile, "Yes, honey, but you know I still have to do the laundry myself, and no one in New York parts the sidewalk 'cause I am comin' through!"
>
> I like icons who are authentic and accessible. I think our country benefits from that. It can only serve to inspire others to believe that they can try to do the same thing.
>
> —MARIA HINOJOSA, "Dancing Past the Boundaries"

Notice that although Hinojosa's claim is related to her own personal taste in American cultural icons, it is not actually about her taste itself. Her argument is not about her preference for cultural icons to be "authentic and

Robin Wall Kimmerer's claim also challenges her audience, so she states it after providing a delicious narrative about wild strawberries. Read her essay on p. 932.

Judith Jamison dancing with the Alvin Ailey American Dance Theater.

accessible." Instead, she's arguing that given this criterion, Judith Jamison is a perfect example.

As an author making an argument of your own, remember that a claim shouldn't simply express a personal taste: if you say that you feel lousy or that you hate the New York Yankees, no one could reasonably argue that you don't feel that way. For a claim to be *arguable*—worth arguing—it has to take a POSITION that others can logically have different perspectives on. Likewise, an arguable claim can't simply be a statement of fact that no one would disagree with ("Violent video games earn millions of dollars every year"). And remember that in most academic contexts, claims based on religious faith alone often cannot be argued since there are no agreed-upon standards of proof or evidence.

In most academic writing, you'll be expected to state your **CLAIM** explicitly as a **THESIS**, announcing your topic and the main point(s) you are going to make about that topic. Your thesis should help readers follow your train of thought, so it's important that it state your point clearly. A good thesis will also engage your audience's interest—and make them want to read on.

Be careful, however, not to overstate your thesis: you may need to **QUALIFY** it with words like "some," "might," or "possible"—for example, that "Recent studies have shown that exercise has a limited effect on a person's weight, so eating less may be a better strategy for losing weight than exercising more." By saying that dieting "may be" more effective than exercise, the author of this thesis has limited her claim to one she will be able to support.

See Ch. 14 in the ebook for a video on developing an argumentative thesis statement.

In most US academic contexts, authors are expected to make claims directly and get to the point fairly quickly, so you may want to position the thesis near the beginning of your text, often at the end of the introduction or the first paragraph. When your claim is likely to challenge or surprise your audience, though, you may want to build support for it more gradually and hold off stating it explicitly until later in your argument, as Du Bois does. In other situations, you may not need to make a direct statement of your claim at all. But always make sure in such cases that your audience has a clear understanding of what the claim is.

WHAT'S AT STAKE?

Figuring out the answer to this question takes you to the heart of the argument. Rhetoricians in ancient Rome developed what they called stasis theory, a simple system for identifying the crux of an argument—what's at stake in it—by asking four questions in sequence:

1. What are the facts? What happened?
2. How can the issue be defined?
3. How much does the issue matter, and why?
4. What actions should be taken as a result?

Together these questions help determine the basic issues at stake in an argument. A look at the arguments that swirled around the devastating

2023 wildfires in Maui, Hawaii, and their effects can illustrate how these questions work.

What are the facts? What happened? High winds on the island on August 8, 2023, fueled multiple fires exacerbated by a long, dry summer and low humidity. The blaze destroyed thousands of structures in Lahaina, Kihei, and the upcountry area; took the lives of at least 115 people; and caused an estimated $5.5 billion in damage. Many arguments about the disaster had their crux (or stasis) in claims that "what happened" had as much or more to do with a lack of planning and preparing for the risk of such fires in Hawaii.

How can the issue be defined? In the case of these wildfires, it was easy to define the event as "the deadliest natural disaster in Hawaii's history" but much more difficult to classify the disaster beyond that label. To what extent was it a local disaster only? Was it primarily a natural disaster, or were there human causes (such as changes to land use and the climate)? Was it proof of incompetence on the part of local and state officials? A slow FEMA response? What else?

How much does the issue matter, and why? For an island whose economy runs on tourism, the effects of the wildfires left a huge hole in revenue along with the loss of thousands of jobs and skyrocketing unemployment. Estimates were that Maui was losing at least $11 million a day during and after the fires. In addition, the fires dramatically affected the mental and physical health of residents: rates of depression and anxiety rose significantly, along with smoke-related illnesses. In short, the fires had a negative effect on everyone on Maui, presenting huge challenges for those trying to overcome their losses and rebuild homes, towns, and cities.

What actions should be taken as a result? Of all the stasis questions, this one was the basis for the greatest number of arguments, from those arguing that the federal government should be responsible for funding reconstruction, to those arguing that the government should work with insurance agencies and local and state officials, to those arguing that profit-seeking developers buying up land and property would inevitably force homeowners out and destroy the culture of the island, to those arguing that the hardest-hit areas should never be rebuilt. Thousands of proposals were offered and debated.

Such questions can help you understand what's at stake in an argument—to help you figure out and assess the arguments put forth by others, to identify which stasis question lies at the heart of an argument—and then to decide whether or not the argument answers the question satisfactorily.

As an author, you can use these questions to identify the main point you want to make in an argument of your own. In the Maui wildfire example, for instance, working through the four stasis questions would help you see the disaster from a number of different perspectives and then develop a cogent argument related to them. In addition, these questions may help you decide what GENRE of argument you want to make: a question of fact might lead you to write a NARRATIVE , explaining what happened, while the question of what action(s) should be taken might lead you to compose a PROPOSAL .

▶️ See the ebook for a video on making the stakes clear to your readers.

MEANS OF PERSUASION: EMOTIONAL, ETHICAL, AND LOGICAL APPEALS

Aristotle wrote that good arguments should make use of "all the available means" of persuading an audience and named three in particular, which he labeled emotional appeals (to the heart), ethical appeals (about credibility or character), and logical appeals (to the mind). These universal appeals must always, however, be looked at—and used—in context: what is effective as an emotional appeal in one time and place may be quite different in another. In other words, all appeals exist in specific cultural contexts.

Emotional Appeals

Emotional appeals (also referred to as "pathos") stir feelings and often invoke values that the audience is assumed to hold. The paragraph on Lincoln on page 425, for example, offers a strong appeal to readers' emotions when it represents Lincoln as "big" and "brave," invoking two qualities Americans traditionally value. Images can make especially powerful appeals to our emotions, such as the one on the following page showing Ukrainians leaving teddy bears and other children's toys beneath a sign demanding that Russia return the more than 19,000 children who have been deported to Russia since that country invaded Ukraine in 2022, actions that led the International Criminal Court to issue an arrest warrant for Vladimir Putin.

A public display of toys draws attention to missing children.

The toys are a wrenching reminder of the lost children, as are the images of adults kneeling—almost as if in prayer—to add their own contributions to the resistance. Such images speak volumes to those who see them, encouraging empathy as well as support. As a reader, you'll want to consider how such emotional appeals support an author's claim.

As an author, you should consider how you can appeal to your audience's emotions and how such appeals may work to support your claim and your purpose for your audience. But whatever you decide, remember that the line between persuasion and coercion is easily crossed, so work hard to avoid using images that are manipulative.

Ethical Appeals

Ethical appeals (also referred to as "ethos") invoke the credibility and good character of whoever is making the argument. See how the website for the Interfaith Youth Core, a nonprofit organization building common ground between people with different beliefs, includes information intended to establish founder Eboo Patel's credibility and integrity. Here is part of Patel's "bio" page from the site:

[Eboo] is inspired to build this bridge by his identity as an American Muslim navigating a religiously diverse social landscape.

For over 15 years he has worked with governments, social sector organizations, and college and university campuses to help make interfaith cooperation a social norm. Named by *U.S. News & World Report* as one of America's Best Leaders of 2009, Eboo served on President Obama's Inaugural Faith Council and is the author of *Acts of Faith*, *Sacred Ground*, *Interfaith Leadership: A Primer*, and *Out of Many Faiths: Religious Diversity and the American Promise*. He holds a doctorate in the sociology of religion from Oxford University, where he studied on a Rhodes scholarship.

These days, Eboo spends most of his time on the road, doing what he loves: meeting students, educators, and community leaders to talk about the complex landscape of religious diversity and the power of interfaith cooperation in the 21st century.

—INTERFAITH YOUTH CORE, "Eboo Patel"

All this information, including Patel's numerous degrees and publications and his position advising the US president helps establish his credibility and helps readers decide how much stock they can put in his words and the work of the organization he founded.

Citing scholarly achievements and national positions of influence is only one way of establishing credibility. Here Patel uses another approach during a *PBS NewsHour* interview when he responds to a question about "hostile racial divisions" on campus:

> I'm on 25 college campuses a year. I have probably visited something like 130 in the past eight or 10 years. It's not like things don't ever get tense, but what I read about in the news on college campuses is foreign to me, right, which is to say it is by definition sensational.
>
> How am I not going to be optimistic, really? . . . The beautiful thing is, there's lots of us that feel this way. There's this whole growing network of college student interfaith leaders on American campuses basically saying, where's the divide? Let me bridge it. That's the future of America, or we have no future at all.
>
> —EBOO PATEL, *PBS NewsHour* Interview, "To Narrow Toxic Divides, Students Build Bridges between Faiths"

Charlotte Clymer's essay is based entirely on the personal qualities of decency and respect. Take a look at how she develops her argument on p. 888.

In his comments, Patel lets listeners know that he is basing his claim on a lot of personal experience. And his informal tone suggests that he has a simple,

Eboo Patel speaking on campus.

direct message to give to his audience. His extensive experience gives him confidence to talk with conviction about why he's optimistic in the face of deep differences.

Visit everyonesanauthor.tumblr.com to find Patel's full interview.

Building common ground. Patel's use of simple, everyday language helps establish credibility in another way: by building common ground with his audience. He is not "putting on airs" but speaking directly to them; the concerns so many feel, he seems to say, are his concerns. He also uses **ANALOGIES**, especially those associated with bridges, which can bring people of different views together. Given Patel's goals and the aims of the organization he founded, it's no surprise that he seeks to build common ground with his audience.

While building common ground cannot ensure that your audience is "on your side," it does show that you respect your audience and their views and that you've established, with them, a mutual interest in the topic. Both parties care about the issues that you are addressing. Thus, building common ground is a particularly important part of creating an effective argument. Especially if you are addressing an audience unlikely to agree with your position, finding some area of agreement with them, some common ground you can all stand on, can help give the argument a chance of being heard.

21 ✵ Analyzing and Constructing Arguments

Few if any global leaders have been more successful in building common ground than Nelson Mandela, who became the first Black president of South Africa in 1994 after the country's harsh apartheid system of racial segregation ended. In *Playing the Enemy: Nelson Mandela and the Game That Made a Nation*, the basis for the 2009 film *Invictus*, author John Carlin recounts hearing Mandela say that "sport has the power to change the world . . . the power to unite people in a way that little else does" and that "it is more powerful than governments in breaking down racial barriers." Carlin uses this quotation as an example of Mandela's singular ability to "walk in another person's shoes" and to build common ground even where none seems possible. He goes on to detail the ways in which Mandela used White South Africans' love of rugby to build common ground between them and the country's Black majority, which had long seen the almost all-White national rugby team, the Springboks, as a symbol of White supremacy:

> He explained how he had . . . used the 1995 Rugby World Cup as an instrument in the grand strategic purpose he set for himself during his five years as South Africa's first democratically elected president: to reconcile blacks and whites and create the conditions for a lasting peace. . . . He told me, with a chuckle or two, about the trouble he had persuading his own people to back the rugby team. . . . Having won over his own people, he went out and won over the enemy.
>
> —JOHN CARLIN, *Playing the Enemy*

Mandela understood, in short, that when people were as far apart in their thinking as Black and White South Africans were when apartheid ended, the only way to move forward, to make arguments for the country's future that both groups would listen to, was to discover something that could bring them together. For Mandela—and for South Africa—rugby provided the common ground. His personal meetings with the Springboks players and his support for the team paid off to such an extent that when they won a stunning upset victory in the 1995 World Cup final in Johannesburg, the multiracial crowd chanted his name and the country united in celebration. And establishing that common ground contributed to Mandela's extraordinary ethical appeal—which he put to good use in the difficult arguments he had to make in the transition to a post-apartheid South Africa.

In all the arguments you encounter, you'll want to consider how much you can trust the author. Do they seem knowledgeable? represent opposing positions fairly (or at all)? do anything to build common ground?

President Nelson Mandela, wearing a Springboks cap and shirt, presents the Rugby World Cup to South African captain Francois Pienaar in June 1995.

As an author, you need to establish your own **AUTHORITY** : to show that you know what you're talking about by citing trustworthy sources; to demonstrate that you're fair by representing other positions even-handedly and accurately; and to work toward establishing some common ground with your audience. Remember, though, that on some occasions finding common ground may not be possible. In these cases, it's most important that you remain true to your values, representing them as clearly and as fairly as possible.

Logical Appeals

Appeals to logic (also referred to as "logos") were long regarded in the Western world as the most important of all the appeals, following Aristotle's definition of humans as rational animals. Recent research has made it increasingly clear, however, that people seldom make decisions based on logic alone and that emotion often plays a larger role in our decision making than does logic. Nevertheless, in US academic contexts, logical appeals still count for a lot. When we make an argument, we need to provide **REASONS** and **EVIDENCE** to support our claims. Such evidence may include facts and statistics, data from surveys and questionnaires, direct observations, interviews, testimony, experiments, personal experience, visuals, and more.

Facts and statistics. Facts and statistics are two of the most commonly used kinds of evidence. Facts are claims that have been proven to be true—and that an audience is likely to accept without further proof. Statistics are research-based numerical data. Here *Men's Health* editor David Zinczenko offers facts and statistics as support for an argument in the *New York Times* about the effects of fast foods on Americans:

> Before 1994, diabetes in children was generally caused by a genetic disorder—only about 5 percent of childhood cases were obesity-related, or Type 2 diabetes. Today, according to the National Institutes of Health, Type 2 diabetes accounts for at least 30 percent of all new childhood cases of diabetes in this country.
>
> Not surprisingly, money spent to treat diabetes has skyrocketed, too. The Centers for Disease Control and Prevention estimate that diabetes accounted for $2.6 billion in health care costs in 1969. Today's number is an unbelievable $100 billion a year.

> Shouldn't we know better than to eat two meals a day in fast-food restaurants? That's one argument. But where, exactly, are consumers—particularly teenagers—supposed to find alternatives? Drive down any thoroughfare in America, and I guarantee you'll see one of our country's more than 13,000 McDonald's restaurants. Now, drive back up the block and try to find someplace to buy a grapefruit.
>
> —DAVID ZINCZENKO, "Don't Blame the Eater"

The facts about the proliferation of fast-food chains compared to the relative lack of healthier options will be obvious to Zinczenko's readers, and most of his statistics come from respected health organizations whose authority adds to the credibility of his argument. Statistics can provide powerful support for an argument, but be sure they're accurate, current, from reliable sources, and relevant. And if you base an argument on facts, be sure to take into account all the relevant information. Realistically, that's hard to do—but be careful not to ignore any important available facts. Also, remember that "facts" can be manufactured online and then spread like a virus, and that generative AI tools are limited to the data they are trained on, making them prone to mistaken, false, or even made up information presented as facts. The bottom line: you need to verify your facts. The advice in Chapter 8 will further help you distinguish facts from dis- or misinformation.

Surveys and questionnaires. You have probably responded to a number of surveys or questionnaires, and you will often find them used as evidence in support of arguments. When a college student wondered about the kinds of reading for pleasure her dormmates were doing, she decided to gather information through a survey and to present it in a pie chart.

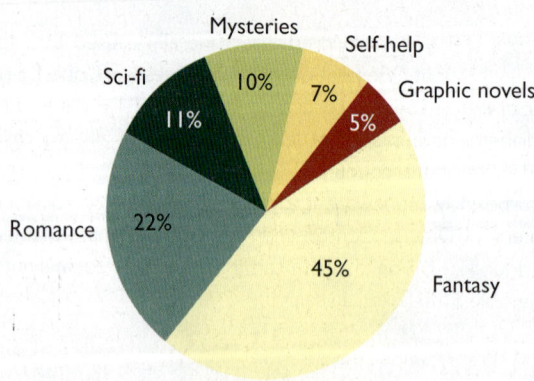

What Genres Students Are Reading

The information displayed in the chart offers evidence that fantasy is the most-read genre, followed by romance, sci-fi, mysteries, self-help, and graphic novels. Before accepting such evidence, however, readers might want to ask some key questions: How many people were surveyed? What methods of analysis did the student use? How were particular works classified? (For example, how did she decide whether a particular book was a "romance" or a "mystery"?) Whether you're reacting to survey data in an essay or a lecture, or conducting a survey of your own, you need to scrutinize the methods used and findings. Who conducted the survey, and why? (And yes, you need to think about that even if you conducted it.) Who are the respondents, how were they chosen, and are they representative? What do the results show?

Observations. A 2024 study reported in *Salon*'s Science section demonstrates how direct observations can form the basis for an argument. In this study, researchers in Zimbabwe observed the way African Savannah elephants communicate, and their findings support arguments about the complexity and multimodality of elephants' communicative practices. What some scientists had previously argued were "nonsense" behaviors—rumbling, flapping ears, rubbing their trunks, and so on—turned out after extensive observation to be purposeful multimodal expressions. As researcher Vesta Eleuteri puts it, their team found that

> Elephants greet by appropriately targeting visual, acoustic, and tactile gestures at their audience depending on the audience's state of visual attention. For example, if we're in a noisy bar and I want to tell you "let's leave" and you are looking at me, I might use a visual gesture, but if you are not, I might touch you. . . . [F]inding this capacity between elephants, although quite expected for people who know elephants, was also novel.
> —MATTHEW ROZSA, "Researchers Decode How Elephants Form 'Sentences,' Lending Insight to Their Complex Communication"

Observations that are carried out over time, like those reported here, are particularly useful as evidence. They show that something is not just a onetime event—it might be a persistent pattern. As a college student, you probably won't spend years observing something, but in most cases you'll need to observe your subject more than once.

Interviews and informal conversations. Reporters often use information drawn from interviews to add authenticity and credibility to their articles.

African Savannah elephants in Cape Town, South Africa.

For an article on the danger concussions cause to athletes and the number of such unreported injuries, Kristin Sainani, a professor of health policy, interviewed Stanford neuroscientists conducting research on concussions as well as one athlete who had suffered several. Here is basketball star Toni Kokenis describing the effects her concussions had on her:

> "I felt withdrawn from everything. It was like I was there, but in slow motion," she says. "I didn't feel comfortable shooting three-pointers because I couldn't focus on the basket long enough to know that the ball was actually going to go near the hoop."
> —KRISTIN SAINANI, "Damage Control"

Sainani also cites information she learned from researcher David Camarillo, whose lab is at work on understanding concussions—a science, he says, that is still in its infancy. Preventing concussions won't be possible, he tells us, until we understand them. Camarillo then goes on to describe, in everyday language, what happens during a concussion: "You've got this kind of gelatinous blob in a fluid floating in a sealed pressure vessel. A concussion occurs when the brain is sloshed and bounced around in this fluid."

Unfortunately, he tells Sainani, wearing a helmet does little to prevent concussions, and so his lab is conducting research to "change the industry standards" for protective equipment.

Throughout this article, Sainani uses evidence drawn from interviews to engage readers and convince them that equipment to protect against concussions "needs to be better." As an author, be sure that anyone you interview is an authority on your subject whom your audience will consider trustworthy.

You may also gather important and useful information through informal conversations. Especially in cultures or communities where formal, scripted interviews might not be accepted—or could even be offensive—consider alternative possibilities. Two Navajo students, for example, wanted to gather information about how elders in their home community had managed to cope during the COVID-19 pandemic. They did so by asking to visit each elder in their home. Rather than arriving with a list of set questions, they arrived with a gift for the elder and expressed a desire to join the elder in some activity (sometimes cooking, sometimes gardening, sometimes walking), during which time they shared information about their lives during the pandemic and listened actively and respectfully to what the elder said in response. Whether your research involves formal interviews, informal conversations, or something in between, make sure you understand and respect the expectations of those you are speaking with, as well as their cultural values.

Testimony. Most of us depend on reliable testimony to help us accept or reject arguments: a friend tells us that *Will & Harper* is the best documentary, and likely as not we'll try to catch it, if only to agree or disagree with the friend's argument. Testimony is especially persuasive evidence when it comes from experts and authorities on a topic. When you cite authorities to support an argument, you build your own credibility as an author; readers know that you've done your homework and are aware of the different perspectives on your topic. In the example on page 437 about the communication strategies of elephants, for example, the *Salon* report notes testimony from one of the scientists who conducted the research.

Experiments. Evidence based on experiments is especially important in the sciences and social sciences, where data are often the basis for supporting a claim. In arguing that multitaskers pay a high mental price, Clifford Nass, a professor of communications, based his claims on a series of empirical

> In her article about body deodorants, Keren Landman cites medical research as well as investigations by sociologists and marketers. Read how she does it on p. 938.

studies of college students who were divided into two groups, those identified as "high multitaskers" and those identified as "low multitaskers." In the first studies, which measured attention and memory, Nass and his fellow researchers were surprised to find that the low multitaskers outperformed high multitaskers in statistically significant ways. Still not satisfied that low multitaskers were more productive learners, the researchers designed another test, hypothesizing that if high multitaskers couldn't do well in the earlier studies on attention and memory, maybe they would be better at shifting between tasks more quickly and effectively than low multitaskers.

> Wrong again, the study found.
> The subjects were shown images of letters and numbers at the same time and instructed what to focus on. When they were told to pay attention to numbers, they had to determine if the digits were even or odd. When told to concentrate on letters, they had to say whether they were vowels or consonants.
> Again, the heavy multitaskers underperformed the light multitaskers.
> "They couldn't help thinking about the task they weren't doing," the researchers reported. "The high multitaskers are always drawing from all the information in front of them. They can't keep things separate in their minds."
> —ADAM GORLICK, "Media Multitaskers Pay Mental Price"

As Gorlick notes, these researchers had evidence to support their hypothesis. Nevertheless, they realized the dangers of generalizing from one set of students to all students. Whenever you use data drawn from experiments, you need to be similarly cautious not to overgeneralize.

> See Ch. 22 in the ebook for a video on using personal stories in academic writing.

Personal experience can provide powerful support for an argument since it brings "eyewitness" evidence, which can establish a connection between author and audience. In an interview published in British fashion and culture magazine *The Face*, Raquel Willis, director of communications for the Ms. Foundation for Women, talks about the role personal stories play in her memoir, where she argues for the importance of Black trans lives.

> I'm excited to be working on this book and releasing it because I feel like we don't tell our stories enough. We can never share our insights enough, and for me as a Black trans woman from Augusta, Georgia, it is important for me to elevate the ways that my life has been impacted by systems of oppression, but also the ways that I have figured out how to come up from under the thumb of oppression. And then also the way

that the stories of the spaces and the movements I've been in and the relationships that I've had are complicated. I'm talking about the way that gender and identity is messy. The ways that our movements are messy, the ways that being empowered and successful is messy. I'm excited to put all that out there.

—RAQUEL WILLIS, "Why Activist Raquel Willis Believes in Black Trans Power"

In your own writing, your personal experience can often provide important and relevant support for your argument, so make use of it when you can, remembering that personal stories can make a strong impact on your audience.

Charts, images, and other visuals. Visuals of various kinds often provide valuable evidence to support an argument. Pie charts like the one showing the literary genres favored in a college dorm, photos depicting African elephants in the wild, and many other kinds of visuals—including drawings, bar and line graphs, cartoons, screenshots, videos, and advertisements—can make it easier for an audience to see certain kinds of evidence. Imagine how much more difficult it would be to take in the information shown in the pie chart about the genres read by students in the dorm had the data been presented in a paragraph. Remember, though, that visual evidence usually needs to be explained—photos need captions, and any visuals need to be referenced in the accompanying text.

As an author, keep in mind that the MEDIUM you're using affects the kind of EVIDENCE you choose and how you present it. In a print text, evidence has to be in the text itself; in a digital medium, you might link directly to statistics, images, and other information. In a spoken text, any evidence needs to be said or shown on a slide or a handout—and anything you say should be simple, direct, and memorable. In every case, any evidence drawn from sources needs to be fully DOCUMENTED.

Are There Any Problems with the Reasoning?

Some kinds of appeals use reasoning that some may consider to be unfair, unsound, or an example of lazy or simpleminded thinking. Such appeals are called fallacies, and because they can often be very powerful and persuasive, it's important to be alert for them in arguments you encounter—and in your own writing. Here are some of the most common fallacies.

Ad hominem (Latin for "to the man") arguments make personal attacks on those who support an opposing position rather than addressing the position itself: "Of course council member Acevedo doesn't want to build a new high school; she doesn't have any children herself." The council member's childlessness may not be the reason for her opposition to a new high school, and even if it is, such an attack doesn't provide any argument for building the school.

Bandwagon appeals simply urge the audience to go along with the crowd: "Join the millions who've found pain relief through Weleda Migraine Remedy." "Everybody knows you shouldn't major in a subject that doesn't lead to a job." Such appeals often flatter the audience by implying that making the popular choice means they are smart, attractive, sophisticated, and so on.

Begging the question tries to support an argument by simply restating it in other language, so that the reasoning goes around in circles. For example, the statement "We need to reduce the national debt because the government owes too much money" begs the question of whether the debt is actually too large, because what comes before and after "because" say essentially the same thing.

Either-or arguments, also called false dilemmas, argue that only two alternatives are possible in a situation that actually is more complex. A candidate who declares, "I will not allow the United States to become a defenseless, bankrupt nation—it must remain the military and economic superpower of the world," ignores the possibilities in between.

Faulty analogies are comparisons that do not hold up in some way crucial to the argument at hand. Accusing parents who homeschool their children of "educational malpractice" by saying that parents who aren't doctors wouldn't be allowed to perform surgery on their children, so parents who aren't trained to teach shouldn't be allowed to teach their children makes a false analogy. Teaching and surgery aren't alike enough to support an argument that what's required for one is needed for the other.

Faulty causality, the mistaken assumption that because one event followed another, the first event caused the second, is also called post hoc, ergo propter hoc (Latin for "after this, therefore because of this"). For example, a mayor running for reelection may boast that a year after their administration began having the police patrol neighborhoods less frequently, the city's crime rate has dropped significantly. But there might be many other possible causes for the drop, so considerable evidence would be needed to establish such a causal connection.

Hasty generalizations draw sweeping conclusions on the basis of too little evidence: "Both of the political science classes I took were deadly dull, so it must be a completely boring subject." "You shouldn't drink so much coffee—that study that NPR reported on today said it causes cancer." Many hasty generalizations take the form of stereotypes about groups of people, such as men and women, young and elderly, and ethnic or religious groups. It's difficult to make arguments without generalizing, but they always need to be based on sufficient evidence and qualified with words like "most," "in many cases," "usually," "in this state," "in recent years," and so on.

Paralipsis (from the Greek for "omission") statements provide information after claiming such information won't be included. For example, during Socrates's trial for supposedly corrupting the youth of Athens (by inviting them to think!), the philosopher is believed to have said, "I will not mention here my grieving wife and children," and thereby of course, mentions them. That is an example of paralipsis, saying what you supposedly will not say. Robert Downey Jr.'s character in *Iron Man* uses paralipsis when he says: "I'm not saying I'm responsible for this country's longest run of uninterrupted peace in thirty-five years!"

Setting up a straw man misrepresents an opposing argument, characterizing it as more extreme or otherwise different than it actually is, in order to attack it more easily. The misrepresentation is like an artificial figure made of straw that's easier to knock down than a real person would be. For example, in disagreements about online content moderation, critics sometimes claim that advocates for moderation want to censor all opinions they disagree with or eliminate free speech. In reality, most content moderation strategies focus on limiting hate speech, misinformation, and harmful content while still allowing a wide range of viewpoints to be shared.

Red herring arguments are ones that distract attention from the real issue (as smelly red herring fish were once put on a trail to distract dogs from the hunters' kills). In a 2024 presidential debate, a moderator asked Vice President Harris why the current administration held off imposing border asylum restrictions until an election year. In response, Harris talked about the fact that Republicans had failed to pass a border reform bill and then turned to talking about her opponent's political rallies, saying, "[W]hat you will also notice is, that people will start leaving [Trump] rallies early out of exhaustion and boredom." That response represented a red herring aimed at distracting Trump and shifting attention away from the question asked.

Slippery slope arguments contend that if a certain event occurs, it will (or at least might) set in motion a chain of events that will end in disaster, like a minor misstep at the top of a slick incline that causes you to slip and then slide all the way to the bottom. For example, opponents of physician-assisted suicide often warn that making it legal for doctors to help people end their lives would eventually lead to an increase in the suicide rate, as people who would not otherwise kill themselves find it easier to do so, and even to an increase in murders disguised as suicide. Slippery slope arguments are not always wrong—an increasingly catastrophic chain reaction does sometimes grow out of a seemingly small beginning. But the greater the difference is between the initial event and the predicted final outcome, the more evidence is needed that the situation will actually play out in this way.

WHAT ABOUT OTHER PERSPECTIVES?

In any argument, it's important to consider perspectives other than those of the author, especially those that would not support the claim or would argue it very differently. As a reader, you should question any arguments that don't acknowledge other positions, and as a writer, you'll want to be sure that you represent—and respond to—perspectives other than your own. Acknowledging other arguments, in fact, is another way of demonstrating that you're fair and of establishing your credibility—whereas failing to consider other views can make you seem closed-minded or lazy, unfair or manipulative. Think of any advertisements you've seen that claim, "Doctors recommend drug X."

The famous Got Milk? ads, run for decades by the milk industry, often suggested that milk was the secret ingredient of good health, strength, and athletic achievements. These ads, funded and produced by the US milk industry, routinely omitted any mention of alternative points of view—for example, that milk is a major source of saturated fats in American diets or that many people, including athletes, are lactose intolerant. That might be one reason sales of milk had been falling quickly for the past few decades,

Got Milk? ad, 2021. Visit everyonesanauthor.tumblr.com to watch the video.

though the increasing popularity of nondairy beverages, including soft drinks and sports drinks, were surely at play as well. This situation led the milk industry to launch new campaigns, including Milk Life and Gonna Need Milk ads that go directly after the competition. The new ads compare milk (very favorably) with its competitors, focusing on milk's nutritional benefits. But does it address alternative views enough to boost milk sales? It's still too early to say.

Compare such partial or one-sided arguments with the following detailed discussion of contemporary seismology:

> Jian Lin was 14 years old in 1973, when the Chinese government under Mao Zedong recruited him for a student science team called "the earthquake watchers." After a series of earthquakes that had killed thousands in northern China, the country's seismologists thought that if they augmented their own research by having observers keep an eye out for anomalies like snakes bolting early from their winter dens and erratic well-water levels, they might be able to do what no scientific body had managed before: issue an earthquake warning that would save thousands of lives.
>
> In the winter of 1974, the earthquake watchers were picking up some suspicious signals near the city of Haicheng. Panicked chickens were

squalling and trying to escape their pens; water levels were falling in wells. Seismologists had also begun noticing a telltale pattern of small quakes. "They were like popcorn kernels," Lin tells me, "popping up all over the general area." Then, suddenly, the popping stopped, just as it had before a catastrophic earthquake some years earlier that killed more than 8,000. "Like 'the calm before the storm,'" Lin says. "We have the exact same phrase in Chinese." On the morning of February 4, 1975, the seismology bureau issued a warning: Haicheng should expect a big earthquake, and people should move outdoors.

At 7:36 p.m., a magnitude 7.0 quake struck. The city was nearly leveled, but only about 2,000 people were killed. Without the warning, easily 150,000 would have died. "And so you finally had an earthquake forecast that did indeed save lives," Lin recalls. . . .

Lin is now a senior scientist of geophysics at Woods Hole Oceanographic Institution, in Massachusetts, where he spends his time studying not the scurrying of small animals and fluctuating electrical current between trees (another fabled warning sign), but seismometer readings, GPS coordinates, and global earthquake-notification reports. He and his longtime collaborator, Ross Stein of the U.S. Geological Survey, are champions of a theory that could enable scientists to forecast earthquakes with more precision and speed.

Some established geophysicists insist that all earthquakes are random, yet everyone agrees that aftershocks are not. Instead, they follow certain empirical laws. Stein, Lin, and their collaborators hypothesized that many earthquakes classified as main shocks are actually aftershocks, and they went looking for the forces that cause faults to fail.

Their work was in some ways heretical: For a long time, earthquakes were thought to release only the stress immediately around them; an earthquake that happened in one place would decrease the possibility of another happening nearby. But that didn't explain earthquake sequences like the one that rumbled through the desert and mountains east of Los Angeles in 1992. . . .

Lin and Stein both admit that [their theory] doesn't explain all earthquakes. Indeed, some geophysicists, like Karen Felzer, of the U.S. Geological Survey, think their hypothesis gives short shrift to the impact that dynamic stress—the actual rattling of a quake in motion—has on neighboring faults.

—JUDITH LEWIS MERNIT, "Seismology: Is San Francisco Next?"

As this example shows, Lin and Stein's research supports the claim that earthquakes can be predicted some of the time, but they—and the author of the article about them—are careful not to overstate their argument or to ignore those who disagree. The author responds to other perspectives in three ways. She acknowledges the "all random" theory held by "some established geophysicists"; she provides evidence (not shown here) to refute the idea that "earthquakes release only the stress immediately around them." And in the last paragraph she accommodates other perspectives by qualifying Lin and Stein's claim and mentioning what some critics see as a weakness in it.

As an author, remember to consider what other perspectives exist on your topic—and what **COUNTERARGUMENTS** someone might have to your position. You may not agree with them, but they might lead you to **QUALIFY** your thesis—or even change your position. Whatever you think about other viewpoints, be sure to acknowledge them fairly and respectfully—and to accommodate or refute them as possible. And carefully investigate your reactions to opposing positions to be sure you aren't falling prey to **CONFIRMATION BIAS** or **ATTRIBUTION BIAS**. They will help you to sharpen your own thinking, and your writing can only improve as a result.

See the ebook for a video on anticipating counterarguments.

WAYS OF STRUCTURING ARGUMENTS

You can organize arguments in several ways. You may decide to approach a controversial or surprising argument slowly, building up to the claim but withholding it until you have established plenty of evidence to support it, as in this introductory paragraph from an essay about sports injuries:

> The flood of media attention highlighting damaged brains, dementia, and suicides in retired NFL players has made concussions synonymous with football. That attention was greatly needed: the debilitating consequences of brain injuries in football players of all ages has been severely overlooked. But the focus of this controversy has been far too narrow. It's true that young players need better equipment and stricter safety standards on the gridiron. But in many of the most popular sports, boys aren't the ones most likely to be afflicted by concussions. Girls are.
> —MARJORIE A. SNYDER, "Girls Suffer Sports Concussions at a Higher Rate than Boys. Why Is That Overlooked?"

On the other hand, you may choose to start right off with the claim and then build support for it piece by piece by piece, as in this opening from an essay in the *Atlantic* about François Poulain de la Barre, a very early advocate of women's rights who argued that the labor of motherhood should be fairly compensated and other way-ahead-of-his-time ideas:

> What if I told you that the first modern feminist was a man, lived in the 17th century, and was a priest? I'm guessing you'd be especially skeptical about the priest part, so I'll add that when this father of feminism wrote his vindications of women's rights, he wasn't a priest yet. He became one later, probably because he was broke.
> —JUDITH SHULEVITZ, "I Found the Feminism I Was Looking for in the Lost Writings of a 17th-Century Priest"

See the ebook for a video on different ways to respond to the views of others.

Another common way to begin is to note what others have said about your topic and then to present your own ideas—your claim—as a response. See how the secretary of the Smithsonian Institution, Lonnie G. Bunch, uses this strategy in describing how he created *The Smithsonian's America: An Exhibition on American History and Culture* for a festival in Japan:

The Smithsonian's America exhibit in Chiba, Japan, in 1994.

21 ~ Analyzing and Constructing Arguments

The Japanese team wanted the exhibition to reintroduce the ideals of the United States to a new generation of Japanese citizens.... They urged us to focus on technological advancement, the presidents, and the wild west. We insisted on telling a more comprehensive and complicated story ... unified by the throughline of the contested promise of American life. For instance, the exhibition included the original model for the Statue of Liberty, with broken chains at Lady Liberty's feet to symbolize the end of slavery; it discussed the incremental expansion of civil liberties to women and African Americans; and it told the story of how migration diversified the American West far beyond the "cowboys and Indians" stereotype.
— LONNIE G. BUNCH, "Whole of Our History"

Whatever the approach, arguments are inherently social, involving an author and an audience. They always have certain purpose(s) and make debatable claims that the author presents as true or beneficial. In addition, they all provide reasons and evidence as support for their claims, though what counts as good evidence varies across fields and communities. And finally, arguments almost always rely on assumptions that may not be explicitly stated but that the audience must agree with in order to accept the argument. For example:

Claim: Colleges should not return to a reliance on standardized tests for admission.

Reason: Such tests are socioeconomically biased.

Evidence: The disparity in test scores among various groups has been linked to cultural biases in the types of questions posed on such tests.

Assumption: Questions that favor any group are inherently unfair.

Now let's consider four ways of approaching and structuring an argument: CLASSICAL, TOULMIN, ROGERIAN, and INVITATIONAL.

Classical Arguments

Originating in the ancient Greek law courts and later refined by Roman rhetoricians, the system of argumentation often referred to as "classical" is still favored by writers in many different fields. Throughout a classically structured argument, you'll rely on ETHICAL, EMOTIONAL, and LOGICAL appeals to your audience. Ethical appeals (those that build your credibility) are especially effective in the introduction, while logical and emotional appeals are useful anywhere.

The introduction engages the interest and attention of its audience by establishing the importance of the issue, establishing COMMON GROUND with the audience and showing how they are affected by the argument, and establishing the author's CREDIBILITY. To engage the audience, you might begin with an anecdote, ask a provocative question, or state the issue explicitly. Most writers taking a classical approach state the CLAIM in the introduction; students making an academic argument usually do so in an explicit THESIS statement.

The body of the argument provides any necessary background information, followed by REASONS and EVIDENCE in support of the claim. In addition, this section should make clear how the argument you're making is in the best interests of the audience. Finally, it should acknowledge possible COUNTER-ARGUMENTS and alternative points of view, presenting them fairly and respectfully and showing how your own argument is preferable.

The conclusion may summarize your argument, elaborate on its implications, and make clear what you want those in your audience to do in response. Just as it's important to open in a way that will engage their attention, you'll want to close with something that will make them remember your argument—and act on it in some way.

Let's suppose you've been assigned the topic of free speech on campus, and you believe that free speech must always be protected. That's a fairly broad topic, so eventually you decide to focus on a tendency at some colleges to withdraw invitations to speakers holding controversial viewpoints. You might begin your introduction with a provocative statement, followed by some facts that will get your readers' attention (both ways of appealing to emotions) and culminating in a statement of your claim:

> One of our most cherished American freedoms is under attack—and not from abroad. On numerous campuses in recent years, an increasing number of invited speakers have been disinvited or canceled or driven to decline because various members of the campus community find it offensive to hear from people who hold beliefs or positions that they or

others disagree with. However, true freedom of speech requires us to encounter ideas and even language we don't like, don't agree with, or find offensive. As students, we need to wrestle with ideas that challenge us, that make us think beyond our personal beliefs and experiences, and that educate us in and out of the classroom.

You might then introduce some background information about this issue, identifying points you'll develop later as support for your claim. Here you might note examples of disinvitation or "deplatforming" campaigns. Using specific examples will make your argument more credible:

> The Foundation for Individual Rights in Education (FIRE) documented 626 successful disinvitation or deplatforming events as of April 2024, 110 of which occurred in the first four months of that year.

And you might well include a visual to help underscore and support your argument like the one below.

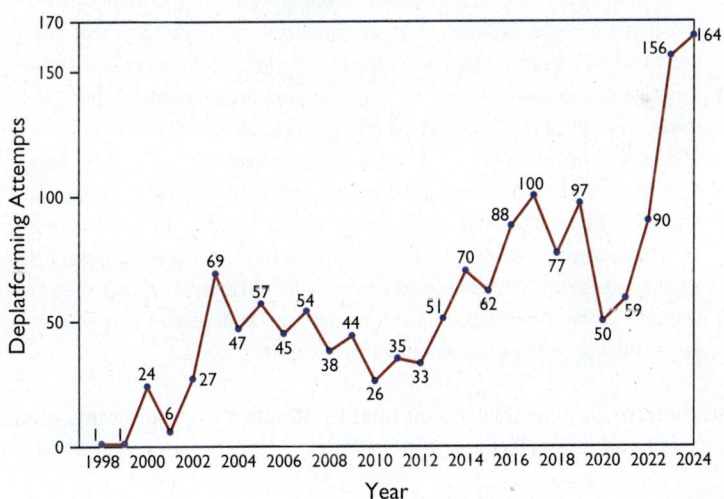

This database includes attempts to cancel performances, remove art exhibits, prevent the showing of a film, and disinvite speakers. It includes attempts that occurred before or during an event, not after.

Then you might provide support for your claim by noting specific instances where invitations to speak have been withdrawn or speeches have been derailed and giving reasons that free speech applies to everyone:

> Conservative media pundit Ann Coulter, former secretary of state Hillary Clinton, author and political commentator Michael Eric Dyson, US ambassador to the United Nations Linda Thomas Greenfield, sports activist Paula Scanlan, and Judge Kyle Duncan have been uninvited and/or silenced by hecklers as they attempted to speak or even before they had the opportunity to speak on campus. When we accept only speakers whose political philosophies are ones no one would disagree with, free speech becomes "free only if you agree with me" speech. And then we may as well give up the notion of independent thought.

Acknowledging and responding to counterarguments strengthens your argument by showing you to be well informed, fair, and open-minded:

> Of course, some resistance may well be justified, as when many attendees of CPAC, the Conservative Political Action Conference, protested the 2020 appearance of musician Young Pharaoh, who had posted anti-Semitic remarks and conspiracy theories (for example, that the pandemic had been "staged"). Moreover, the focus on disinvitations and cancellations ignores the fact that many controversial figures continue to speak without protest: economist Jeffrey Sachs compiled a long list on *X* of schools where controversial speeches took place without incident. And in an essay for *Deseret News*, Jacob Hess offers other examples of schools that do not give in to protests for cancellations, including this one about a commencement speaker at Utah Valley University: "After getting pressure by activists on and off campus to cancel Sister [Wendy] Nelson's speech because of her traditional views on marriage and sexuality, university leaders did something brave. They stuck with their plans."

And then in your conclusion you might reiterate the major points of your argument and rephrase your claim:

> We should strive to accept diverse voices and viewpoints on campus. Our conversations should challenge us to question our own long-held beliefs and closely examine those of others. We can do so only if we protect and truly embrace the right to freedom of speech—for one and all.

Toulmin Arguments

British philosopher Stephen Toulmin developed a detailed model for analyzing arguments, one that has been widely used for writing arguments as well.

The introduction presents a `CLAIM`, one that others will find debatable. If need be, you'll want to carefully `QUALIFY` this claim using words like "often" or "it may be" that limit your argument to one you'll be able to support.

The body of the argument presents good `REASONS` and `EVIDENCE` (which Toulmin calls "grounds") in support of the claim and explains any underlying assumptions (Toulmin calls these "warrants") that your audience needs to agree with in order to accept your argument. You may need to provide further evidence (which Toulmin calls "backing") to illustrate the assumptions. Finally, you'd acknowledge and respond to any `COUNTERARGUMENTS`.

The conclusion restates the argument as strongly and memorably as possible. You might conclude by discussing the implications of your argument, saying why it matters. And you'll want to be clear about what you want readers to think (or do).

For example:

> *Claim:* Our college should ban vape pens.
>
> *Qualification:* The ban should be limited to public places on campus.
>
> *Good reasons and evidence:* Vape pens contain some of the same toxins as cigarettes; research shows that they are a hazard to health.
>
> *Underlying assumptions:* Those who work and study here are entitled to protection from the harmful acts of others; the US Constitution calls for promoting "the general welfare" of all citizens.
>
> *Backing for the assumptions:* Other colleges and even some cities have banned vape pens; highly respected public health advocates have testified about their ill effects.
>
> *Counterarguments:* Vape pens are less harmful than traditional cigarettes; smokers have rights too. However, this argument limits the ban to public spaces, which means smokers can still use vape pens in their homes and other private places.
>
> *Conclusion:* Our school should ban the use of vape pens in public places to protect the health of all who work and study here.

Now let's see how an argument about free speech on campus would work using Toulmin's model. You'd begin with your claim, carefully qualified if need be. The underlined words in the following example are qualifiers:

> To be successful as college students, to truly develop into independent thinkers, we need to wrestle with ideas that challenge us and that make us think beyond our personal beliefs and experiences, both in and out of the classroom. Such intellectual challenges are being diminished at <u>many</u> colleges as <u>some</u> on campus decide that ideas they or others disagree with are more threatening than educational. On numerous campuses in recent years, a number of invited speakers have been disinvited or driven to decline because some on campus find it offensive to hear from those who hold beliefs different from theirs.

You would then follow that claim with the reasons and evidence that support your claim:

> Education requires exposure to multiple points of view, at least according to Aristotle and Martin Luther King Jr. Aristotle notes in his *Metaphysics* that "it is the mark of an educated mind to be able to entertain a thought without accepting it." More than 2,000 years later, King defined the purpose of education as enabling a person to "think incisively and to think for one's self . . . [and not to] let our mental life become invaded by legions of half truths, prejudices, and propaganda."

Then you would make clear the assumptions on which you base your claim:

> Considering a variety of viewpoints is a hallmark of intelligent thinking. Freedom of speech is the right of every American.

And you'd add backing to support your assumptions:

> Freedom of speech requires us to encounter ideas, language, or words we don't like, don't agree with, or find offensive. To truly protect our own right to free speech, we need to protect those rights for everyone.

Next you'd acknowledge and respond to counterarguments and other views, showing yourself to be well informed, fair, and open-minded:

Sometimes, supporting free speech calls for just the kind of protests that have led to disinviting speakers. For example, students and faculty at Brown University protested a speech by New York police commissioner Ray Kelly, arguing that it took a disruption to have their voices heard.

Finally, in your conclusion you'd remind your readers of your claim, reiterate why it matters, and let them know what you want them to think or do.

Free speech is a bedrock value of American life. It's up to all of us to protect it—for ourselves as well as for others.

Rogerian Arguments

Noting that people are more likely to listen to you if you show that you are really listening to them, psychologist Carl Rogers developed a series of nonconfrontational strategies to help people involved in a dispute listen carefully and respectfully to one another. Rhetoricians Richard Young, Alton Becker, and Kenneth Pike developed an approach to argument based on Rogers's work as a way to resolve conflict by coming to understand alternative points of view. Rogerian argument aims to persuade by respectfully considering other positions, establishing `COMMON GROUND`, encouraging discussion and an open exchange of ideas, and seeking mutually beneficial compromise. Success depends on a willingness to listen and to try to understand where others are coming from.

The introduction identifies the issue and `DESCRIBES` it as fully and fairly as possible. It then acknowledges the various viewpoints on the issue, using nonjudgmental language to show that you respect the views of others.

The body of the argument discusses the various `POSITIONS` respectfully and in neutral language, presenting `REASONS` and `EVIDENCE` that show how each position might be acceptable in certain circumstances. Then state your own position, also using neutral language. You'll want to focus on the commonalities among the various positions—and if at all possible, show how those who hold other positions might benefit from the one you propose.

The conclusion proposes some kind of resolution, including a compromise if possible and demonstrating how it would benefit all parties.

Now let's take a look at how you'd approach the topic of free speech on campus using Rogerian methods. You could begin by identifying the issue, noting that there are a number of different viewpoints, and describing them respectfully:

> On many campuses today, reasonable people are becoming increasingly concerned about the unwillingness of some students and others to listen to people with viewpoints they disagree with—or even to let them speak. As Americans, we can all agree that our right to speak freely is guaranteed by the US Constitution. Yet this principle is being tested at many colleges. Some say that controversial figures should not be invited to speak on campus; others have even argued that certain people who've been invited to speak should be disinvited.

Next you'd discuss each position, showing how it might be reasonable. Then explain your position, being careful to use neutral language and to avoid seeming to claim the moral high ground:

> It's true that some speakers may bring messages based on untruths, lies, violence, or hate. If such speakers represent a credible threat to campus life and safety, it seems reasonable that they be disinvited or simply not invited in the first place. Others feel that speakers who hold extreme or radical positions—on either the right or the left—should not be invited to speak on our campuses. In some cases, this position might be justified, especially if the speaker's position is irrelevant to higher education. Except in such extreme circumstances, however, a very important part of a college education involves exposure to multiple points of view. Such great thinkers as Aristotle and Martin Luther King Jr. have expressed this better than I can: in the *Metaphysics*, Aristotle notes that "it is the mark of an educated mind to be able to entertain a thought without accepting it," and more than 2,000 years later, King defined the purpose of education as enabling a person to "think incisively and to think for one's self."

Try to conclude by suggesting a compromise:

> Speakers who threaten campus life or safety may be best left uninvited. But while controversial figures may sometimes cause disruption, our community can learn from them even if we disagree with them. Rather than disinviting such speakers, let's invite discussion after they speak—and make it open to all of the interested parties.

Invitational Arguments

Feminist scholars Sonja Foss and Cindy Griffin have developed what they call "invitational" arguments, using an approach that aims to foster conversation and understanding instead of confrontation. Rather than trying to convince an audience to accept a position, invitational argument aims to get people to work together toward understanding. This approach begins with demonstrating to your audience that you understand and respect their position, setting the stage for discussion and collaboration in which all parties can benefit.

As you can see, invitational arguments have much in common with the Rogerian approach. One important difference, however, lies in the emphasis on openness and the focus on a shared goal. Rather than presenting the audience with a predetermined position that you then attempt to convince them to accept, an invitational argument starts out by assuming that both author and audience are open to changing their minds.

The introduction presents the topic, acknowledges that there are various POSITIONS and perspectives on it, and makes clear that the goal is to understand each viewpoint so that readers can decide what they think.

In the body of the argument, you'd DESCRIBE each perspective fairly and respectfully. If you can, QUOTE those who favor each viewpoint—a way of letting them speak for themselves.

The conclusion looks for COMMON GROUND among the various perspectives, calling on readers to consider each carefully before making up their minds.

Using an invitational approach to the subject of disinvitations and free speech on campus, you could begin by focusing on the complexity of the issue, noting the ways that well-meaning people can have strong differences of opinion but still aim for a common goal:

> On many campuses today, well-meaning people are increasingly concerned about a tendency to reject others' viewpoints out of hand, without even listening to them. This trend has led to such acts as disinviting speakers to campus or preventing them from speaking, once there. This issue might seem to pit freedom of speech against the right to resist speakers whose views may be harmful in certain ways. Yet looking only at this dichotomy ignores the many other possible perspectives people hold on this issue.

> The goal of this essay is to bring the major perspectives on free speech on campus together in order to understand each one thoroughly, to identify any common ground that exists among the perspectives, and to provide readers with the information they need to make informed decisions of their own.

Next, you would discuss each perspective fairly and openly, showing its strengths and weaknesses.

> There seem to be at least four perspectives on the issue of free speech on our campus. First, there are those who believe that the principle of free speech is absolute and that anyone should be able to speak on any issue—period. A second perspective holds that free speech is "free" in context; that is, the right to free speech goes only so far and when it verges on harming others, it is "free" no more. Still a third perspective argues that universities must accept the role of "in loco parentis" and protect students from speech that is offensive, even if it potentially offends only a small group of students. Finally, some hold that universities are indeed responsible for maintaining a safe environment—physically, mentally, and emotionally—and that they can do so while still honoring free speech in most circumstances.

You could then look in detail at the four perspectives, allowing proponents of each to speak for themselves when possible (through quoted and cited passages) and exploring each respectfully and fairly. Following this discussion, you could identify any commonalities among the perspectives:

> Each perspective on this issue has good intentions. Let us use that common ground as the starting point for further exploration, seeing if we can develop guidelines for protecting free speech on campus while also keeping our campus safe. It may well be that considering these perspectives carefully, honestly, and fairly will lead some to change their minds or to come together in certain areas of agreement. I hope that readers of this essay will do just that before taking a position on this issue.

These four methods of organizing arguments are certainly not the only ones available to you. African American methods, for example, might employ a "call and response" organization, in which the writer or speaker issues a call or series of calls and then provides a compelling response to the call. Indigenous methods might use storytelling as the basis for organizing an argument. As you begin to build an argument, we encourage you to think about your own culture's ways of organizing arguments and to draw on this knowledge in creating arguments that reflect your own values and ways of knowing.

 **REFLECT**

Look for an argument you've read or heard recently that caught your attention and revisit it with an eye for the argumentative strategies it uses. Does it use one particular approach—classical? Toulmin? Rogerian? invitational?—or does it mix strategies from more than one approach? Is the argument persuasive? If not, try revising it using strategies from one of these approaches.

MATTERS OF STYLE

An argument's style usually reinforces its message in as many ways as possible. The ancient Roman orator Cicero identified three basic speaking styles: "high," "middle," and "low." After surveying a wide range of prose from the mid-twentieth century, professor of English Walker Gibson identified three prominent written styles: "tough," "sweet," and "stuffy." Today, Hip Hop International hosts competitions for a number of distinct hip-hop dance styles, from "popping and locking" to "krumping" and "breakdancing." Whether you are speaking, writing, or dancing, you will have a style, one that can help to get your message across powerfully. Authors today have at their disposal a wide range of styles, from the highly formal language of US Supreme Court opinions, to the semiformal style of much business and professional writing, to the informal style of everyday written communication such as texts and emails, to the colloquial or vernacular styles of much spoken language.

You can learn a lot by looking closely at the stylistic choices in an argument—the use of individual words and phrases of figurative language, of particular dialects and varieties of language, of personal pronouns (or not), of vivid images (verbal and visual), of design and format. Savvy readers will be alert to the power of stylistic choices in these messages.

See how NBA player Reggie Bullock uses language in an essay about his sisters' murders:

> That's why I wanted to write something about my sisters for National Gun Violence Awareness Day. I don't want to preach or nothing. I don't have some big public service announcement about gun violence. And I don't have all the answers about how to make communities safer. I just wanna try and treat this as a day of remembrance, if that's alright with y'all. I just want to say my sisters' names. That way they live on through their memory.
>
> —REGGIE BULLOCK, "I Just Wanna Say My Sisters' Names"

Here, Bullock is speaking from the heart, addressing his many fans and friends, and he chooses everyday colloquial language to do so. His use of multiple negation in the second sentence ("I don't want to preach or nothing") is a hallmark of Black language, made more powerful by the repetition. Using "wanna" instead of "want to" and "if that's alright with y'all" creates the overall impression of speaking directly, and personally, to his audience.

As an author, you will need to make such important stylistic choices, beginning—as is almost always the case—with the overall effect you want to create. Try to identify that overall effect in a word or phrase (for instance, concern, outrage, sympathy, or direct action), and then use it to help you choose specific words, images, and design elements that will create that effect and convey it most powerfully to your audience.

TWENTY-TWO

Strategies for Supporting an Argument

ARGUMENTS ARE ONLY AS STRONG as the good reasons and evidence that support them. Just as a house built on weak foundations is likely to crumble, so it is with arguments. As an author arguing a point, then, you will need to provide good, strong, reliable evidence to support your position. Rhetoricians throughout the ages have developed strategies for finding such support, strategies that continue to serve us well today. This chapter introduces you to some of those strategies, arranged alphabetically from analogy to signifying.

Analogy

Analogies are comparisons that point out similarities between things that are otherwise very different. Authors often use them to create vivid pictures in a reader's mind and make abstract ideas more concrete. Analogies can be especially powerful in an ARGUMENT, demonstrating that what is true in one case is true in another, usually more complicated, case. Here, Annie Dillard draws an analogy between a writer's words and various tools:

> When you write, you lay out a line of words. The line of words is a miner's pick, a wood-carver's gouge, a surgeon's probe. You wield it, and it digs a path you follow. Soon you find yourself deep in new territory. Is it a dead end, or have you located the real subject? You will know tomorrow, or this time next year.
>
> —ANNIE DILLARD, *The Writing Life*

See the ebook for a video about using different strategies for supporting sentences in a paragraph.

Dillard uses this analogy to suggest that writers can use words as tools for exploring a topic—to "probe" or "dig a path" into their subject.

Now see how Malala Yousafzai uses an analogy in a speech to the United Nations to support her argument that education is the best means of overcoming poverty and injustice:

> We will continue our journey to our destination of peace and education for everyone. No one can stop us. We will speak for our rights and we will bring change through our voice. We must believe in the power and the strength of our words. Our words can change the world because we are all together, united for the cause of education. And if we want to achieve our goal, then let us empower ourselves with the weapon of knowledge and let us shield ourselves with unity and togetherness.

Malala Yousafzai addressing the United Nations.

> Dear brothers and sisters, we must not forget that millions of people are suffering from poverty, injustice, and ignorance. We must not forget that millions of children are out of schools. We must not forget that our sisters and brothers are waiting for a bright, peaceful future.
>
> So let us wage a global struggle against illiteracy, poverty, and terrorism and let us pick up our books and pens. They are our most powerful weapons.
>
> —MALALA YOUSAFZAI, Speech at the United Nations

Yousafzai, a Pakistani activist for girls' education and Nobel Prize winner, builds her argument on an analogy that compares "the power and strength of our words" to the power of weapons used by the Taliban and others who would deny women education. She draws this analogy throughout her speech, calling upon us to use knowledge to "empower," unity to "shield," and books and pens to "wage a global struggle" against illiteracy, poverty, and terrorism. If these are our weapons, she says, then "no one can stop us." As an author, when you use an analogy, check to be sure it isn't a faulty analogy. In other words, compare things that are alike enough to support your claim; compare apples to apples, not apples to oranges.

Cause / Effect

When we analyze causes, we're trying to understand and explain why something happened. Why has there been so much extreme weather in recent years? Why did your chocolate chip cookies all run together on the cookie sheet? And when we think about effects, we speculate about what might happen. How will recent weather patterns affect crop yields? Will the cookies still run if you let the cookie sheet cool between batches?

Authors of **REPORTS** might focus on multiple causes for the last economic downturn, whereas someone writing a **PROPOSAL** may argue that a specific, avoidable cause had a particular effect. And in a **NARRATIVE**, you might use cause-and-effect reasoning to describe and explain an event.

Arguing about causes and effects can be tricky, because often it's almost impossible to link a specific cause to one specific effect. That's why it took decades of research to establish a strong enough link between cigarette smoking and cancer to label tobacco products with a warning: researchers had to be able to discount many other possible causes. For decades, physicists have looked for cause-effect patterns in the behavior of black holes,

A memory of having tea with her beloved great-uncle caused a life-changing realization for Ling Ling Huang. Read how she describes it on p. 923.

particularly since Stephen Hawking's discovery that black holes emit thermal radiation. Almost fifty years later, in 2021, scientists at the University of Sussex were able to confirm that black holes exert some very small but measurable pressure on their environment, a discovery they hope will lead to better descriptions of black holes.

As this example suggests, exact cause-effect relationships are difficult to determine. In 2014, the United Nations released a report on climate change, stating the possible environmental effects if we continue to burn fossil fuels. Notice how the report's authors **QUALIFY** their statements by noting what effects greenhouse emissions "could" cause to happen:

- The emission of greenhouse gases could cause dangerous warming and long-lasting changes in the climate system, severely impacting people and ecosystems.
- Failure to reduce emissions . . . could cause food shortages, flooding of cities and even nations and a dangerous climate during the hottest times of the year.

—*Climate Change 2014: Synthesis Report*

In 2024, however, the United Nations reports an unequivocal connection between human activity and climate change:

> Natural changes in the sun's activity or large volcanic eruptions have caused ancient shifts in the Earth's temperatures and weather patterns, but over the last 200 years, these natural causes have not significantly affected global temperatures. Today, it's human activities that are causing climate change, primarily due to the burning of fossil fuels like coal, oil, and gas.
>
> —UNITED NATIONS, "FACT: Climate Change Is Caused by Human Activity"

Causal analysis can sometimes be easier to understand in a chart or graph than in words alone. See an especially famous example in the history of information graphics on the following page, a map created in 1869. It depicts the horrific loss of life resulting from Napoleon's decision to march on Moscow in 1812. Its creator, Charles Joseph Minard, plotted information about troop numbers and locations, dates, direction and distances traveled, longitude and latitude, and the temperatures as soldiers retreated from Moscow. He used the width of the tan line to show the troops going into Russia (initially 680,000) and the much narrower black line to show those retreating (27,000). His causal argument was clear as he linked the dropping

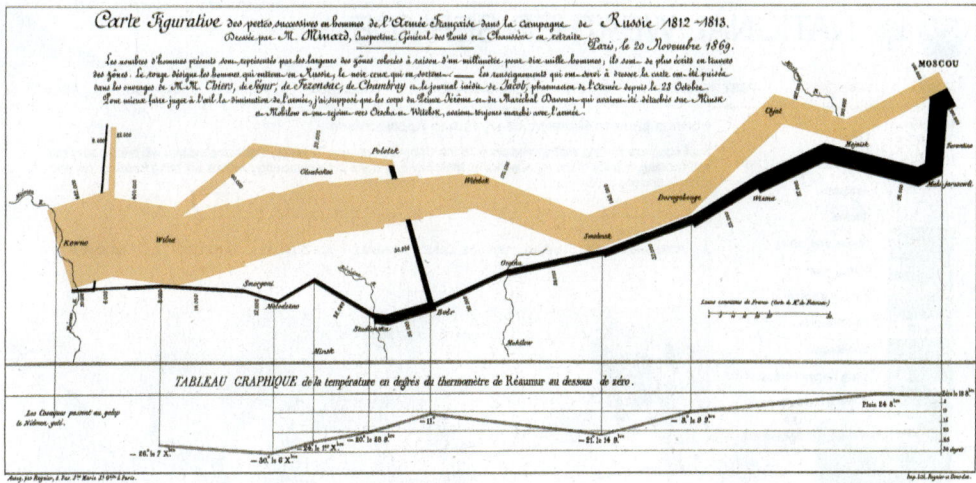

A map showing Minard's analysis of Napoleon's failed invasion of Russia in 1812.

temperatures to the retreat: the colder the temperature, the fewer soldiers who survived.

Classification

When you classify, you group items into categories according to similarities. Tomatoes, for example, can be classified according to their varieties: cherry, plum, grape, heirloom, and so on. Authors frequently turn to classification in order to organize and elaborate on a topic. Here George Packer, a staff writer at the *Atlantic*, argues that there are four versions of America: free America, smart America, real America, and just America:

> Free America celebrates the energy of the unencumbered individual. Smart America respects intelligence and welcomes change. Real America commits itself to a place and has a sense of limits. Just America demands a confrontation with what the others want to avoid. They rise from a single society. . . . But their tendency is also to divide us, pitting tribe against tribe.
> —GEORGE PACKER, "How America Fractured into Four Parts"

Classification is an essential feature of all websites, one that makes accessible the enormous amount of information available on a site. Take a look at the homepage on the National Weather Service's website at weather.gov and

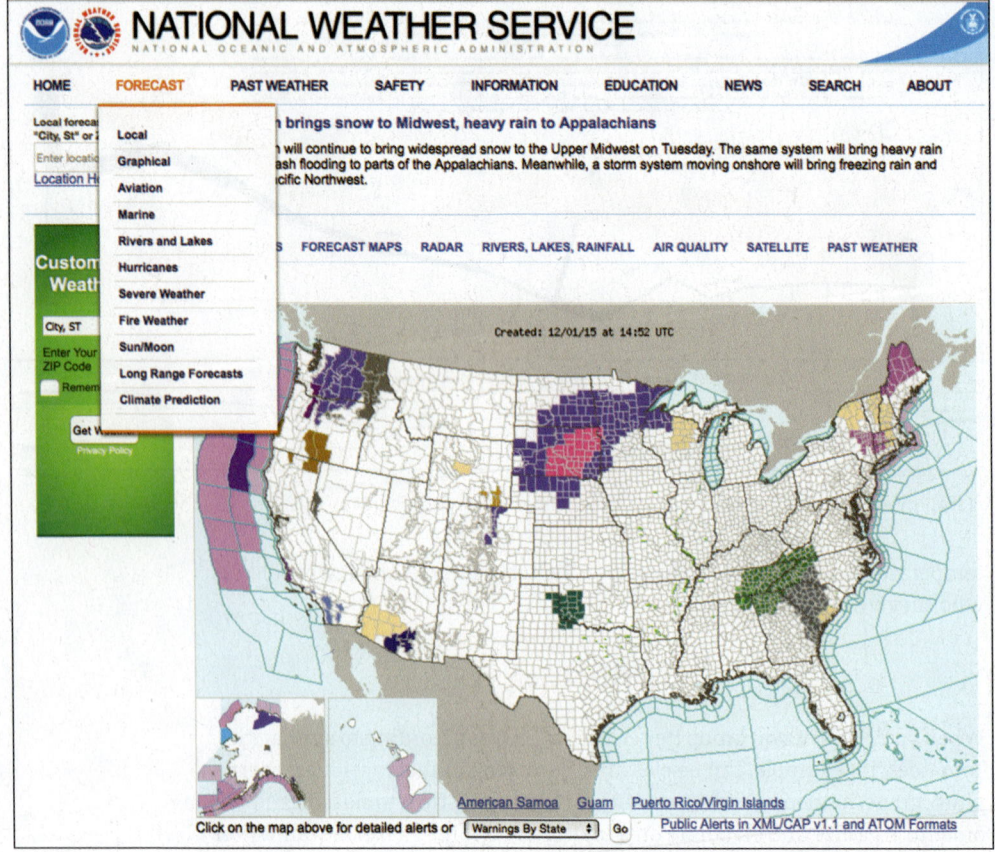

you'll find various kinds of classification, starting with the horizontal menu bar at the top that categorizes the information on the site into commonly consulted topics: Forecast, Safety, News, and so on. Hovering your mouse over "Forecast" opens a drop-down menu that classifies forecasts into various categories: Aviation, Marine, Hurricanes, Fire Weather, and so on.

Comparison / Contrast

When you compare things, you focus on their similarities, and when you contrast them, you look at their differences. Both strategies can be very useful in developing an argument, helping explain something that is unfamiliar by comparing (or contrasting) it with something more familiar. In a **REVIEW**, for example, you might compare *Netflix's Baby Reindeer* with HBO's *I May Destroy You*, or in a **REPORT** on the crisis of homelessness in your state, you might compare the results of approaches two different cities have taken to address the problem.

You might consider two ways that comparisons can be organized: block method and point by point. Using the block method, you present the subjects you're comparing one at a time, as in the following paragraphs by award-winning humorist Dave Barry:

> Most men, I believe, think of themselves as average-looking. Men will think this even if their faces cause heart failure in cattle at a range of 300 yards. Being average does not bother them; average is fine, for men. This is why men never ask anybody how they look. Their primary form of beauty care is to shave themselves, which is essentially the same form of beauty care that they give to their lawns. . . .
>
> Women do not look at themselves this way. If I had to express, in three words, what I believe most women think about their appearance, those words would be: "not good enough." No matter how attractive a woman may appear to be to others, when she looks at herself in the mirror, she thinks: woof. —DAVE BARRY, "Beauty and the Beast"

Barry clearly exaggerates and overgeneralizes for laughs, but note that he engages in some pretty strong stereotyping as well, comparing "men" and "women" as if they were the only two categories available.

Or you can organize your comparison point by point, discussing your subjects together, one point at a time, as Pamela Paul does in a tongue-in-cheek comparison of dog and cat owners:

> The swinging dog owner is out and about at the dog run, but the single cat owner? Happy to stay at home. Give a guy a cat in the movies and that tells you he's a real schlub. Take the film "Hit Man": Glen Powell's lonely and sad loser Gary has two cats. Sexy, married Gary? He's got dogs.
> —PAMELA PAUL, "The Saying Goes: Dogs Are Man's Best Friend. but Cats Are Better"

Comparisons of data can often be easier to understand in a chart or graph than in paragraphs. Take a look at Visual Capitalist's chart showing the world's population, which reached 8 billion in 2022:

THE CENTRALITY OF ARGUMENT

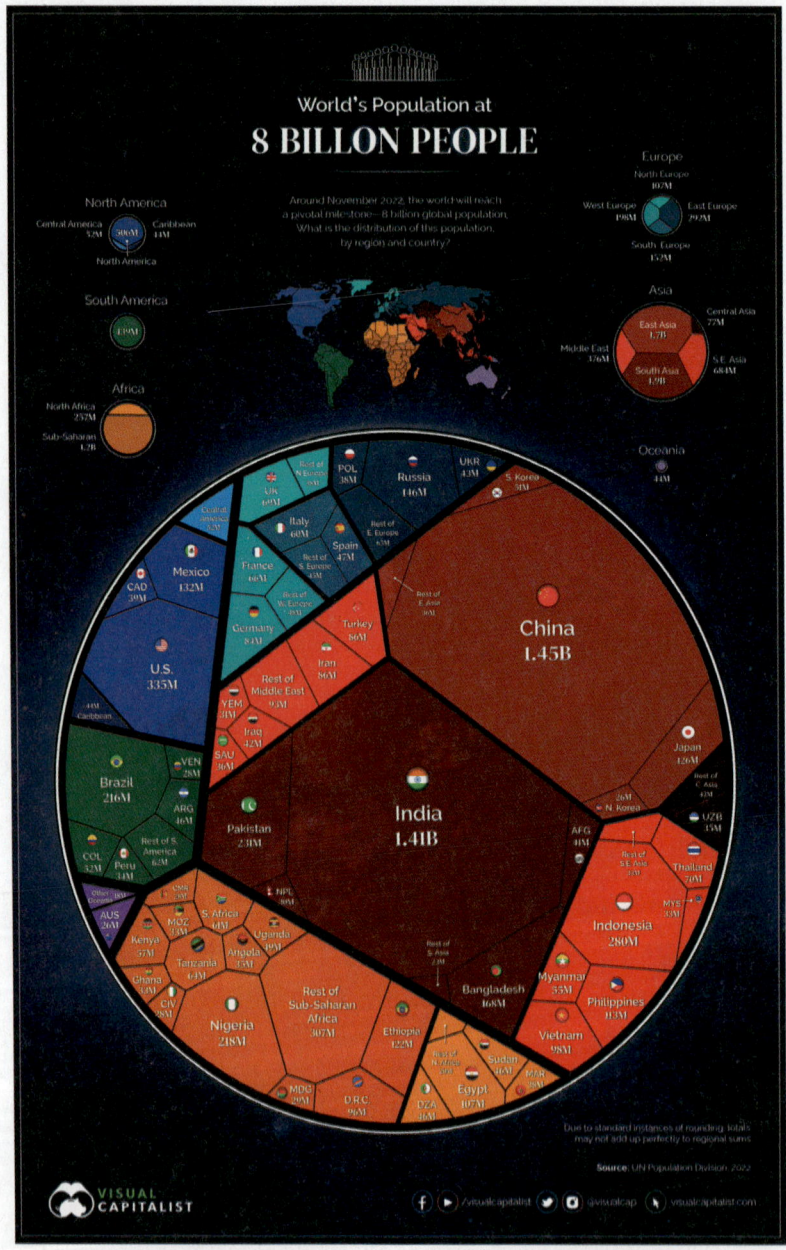

Visuals help to compare and contrast the population of different countries.

The use of a simple circle to represent the earth, along with colors to represent continents and lines to separate countries makes comparisons related to the vast complexity of our world's population more straightforward and easier to grasp than words alone could capture.

Definition

Definitions often lie at the heart of an argument: if readers don't agree with your definition of "the good life," for example, they aren't likely to take your advice on how to achieve one. As such, definitions themselves are rhetorical choices, especially in the case of controversial topics. Whether you're writing an ANALYSIS, a REPORT, or using some other genre, you'll often have reason to include definitions. Good definitions provide clear explanations of a word, concept, or idea, often by listing its characteristic features, noting distinguishing details, and perhaps providing an illustration as well. A good definition tells readers what something is.

> Mike Rose takes on the way intelligence is defined and demonstrated in our culture. Check out what he says on p. 972.

In 2020, Kennedy Mitchum—a recent college grad—noticed that in online debates about racism, some people were relying on a definition of the term from Merriam-Webster's dictionary to argue that they were not racist because, as individuals, they did not think themselves superior to people of other races. These arguments depended on Merriam-Webster's website's definitions of "racism" at the time: "1. a belief that race is the primary determinant of human traits and capacities and that racial differences produce an inherent superiority of a particular race. 2. a doctrine or political program based on the assumption of racism and designed to execute its principles." "Racial prejudice" was not mentioned until the third and final definition provided.

Mitchum wrote to the Merriam Webster, pointing out that people she knew never looked beyond the first definition and arguing that "racism is not only prejudice against a certain race due to the color of a person's skin, as it states in your dictionary. . . . It is prejudice combined with social and institutional power. It is a system of advantage based on skin color." To Mitchum's surprise, she got an almost immediate reply from a Merriam-Webster editor saying that the definition of racism had not been revised in decades and agreeing that it needed updating. The revised definitions recognize the systemic nature of racism today:

1. a belief that race is a fundamental determinant of human traits and capacities and that racial differences produce an inherent superiority of a particular race

2. a. the systemic oppression of a racial group to the social, economic, and political advantage of another
   b. a political or social system founded on racism and designed to execute its principles

   —MERRIAM-WEBSTER.COM, "racism"

One term that is the focus of many arguments is "capitalism," and such arguments often begin with or include a definition of the word. Here is anarchist Emma Goldman, who argued that capitalism was simply not compatible with liberty:

> The only demand that property recognizes is its own gluttonous appetite for greater wealth, because wealth means power; the power to subdue, to crush, to exploit, the power to enslave, to outrage, to degrade . . . [leading to] the crime of turning the producer into a mere particle of a machine, with less will and decision than his master of steel and iron.
>
> —EMMA GOLDMAN, *Anarchism and Other Essays*

In a keynote address to an international conference on economies and nation-states, theologian Michael Novak takes a very different view of capitalism, which he defines in glowing terms at much greater length by focusing on what capitalism *does*:

> Finally, capitalism instills in tradition-bound populations a new and in some respects a higher personal morality. It demands transparency and honest accounts. It insists upon the rule of law and strict observance of contracts. It teaches hard work, inventiveness, initiative, and a spirit of responsibility. It teaches patience with small gains, incremental but steady and insistent progress. During the 19th century, Great Britain achieved an average of one-and-a-half percent of GDP growth every year, with the happy result that the average income of the ordinary laborer in Britain quadrupled in a single century. . . .
>
> Capitalism brings in its train immense transformation, and the root of this transformation is moral. Those peoples and nations that neglect the moral ecology of their own cultures will not enjoy the fruits of such a transformation—or, having tasted them, will fall into rapid decline.
>
> —MICHAEL NOVAK, "The Spirit of Capitalism"

Visuals can help in making arguments that hinge on definition. On the facing page is a case in which the way the word "capitalism" is designed

Image from *Daily Wallpapers* blog.

argues for yet another definition of that word. What argument(s) do you find in this illustration?

Description

When you describe something, you explain how it looks (or sounds, smells, tastes, or feels). Good descriptions focus on distinctive features and concrete details that add up to some **DOMINANT IMPRESSION** and help readers or listeners imagine what you are describing. In arguing that we have become separated from the food we eat in ways that are destructive of both us and our environment, Potawatomi botanist Robin Kimmerer describes what she sees as our current situation:

> Something is broken when the food comes on a Styrofoam tray wrapped in slippery plastic, a carcass of a being whose only chance at life was a cramped cage. That is not a gift of life; it is a theft.
> —ROBIN WALL KIMMERER, *Braiding Sweetgrass: Indigenous Wisdom, Scientific Knowledge and the Teachings of Plants*

In two sentences, Kimmerer's description captures a sense of alienation: we see that "Styrofoam tray"; we feel that "slippery plastic"; we back off from the "carcass" it holds.

You'll have occasion to use description in most of the writing you do—in a PROFILE of a neighborhood, you might describe the buildings and people; in a NARRATIVE, you'll likely describe people, places, and events. In a REPORT, you'll describe the event or situation or even the data set you are reporting on. In writing about atomic testing in Utah in her 1991 memoir *Refuge: An Unnatural History of Family and Place*, writer and activist Terry Tempest Williams uses description to set the scene for the facts she then presents about the high incidence of breast cancer there. She tells her father of a recurring dream she has, of a flash of light in the desert. Hearing this story, he has a sudden realization:

"You did see it," he said.
"Saw what?"
"The bomb. The cloud. We were driving home from Riverside, California. You were sitting on [your mother's] lap. . . . In fact, I remember the day, September 7, 1957. We had just gotten out of the Service. We were driving north, past Las Vegas. It was an hour or so before dawn, when this explosion went off. We not only heard it, but felt it. I thought the oil tanker in front of us had blown up. We pulled over and suddenly, rising from the desert floor, we saw it, clearly, this golden-stemmed cloud, the mushroom. The sky seemed to vibrate

Fiery mushroom cloud rising above Nevada atomic bomb test site, 1957.

22 · Strategies for Supporting an Argument

with an eerie pink glow. Within a few minutes, a light ash was raining on the car."

—TERRY TEMPEST WILLIAMS, "The Clan of One-Breasted Women"

Williams's description lets readers see the "golden-stemmed cloud" and feel the sky "vibrate"—and understand what it must have been like when the bomb exploded. Compare her description with a photograph of the atomic bomb test. Which do you find more powerful—the description of what it was like to be there when the bomb exploded or the photograph of the actual explosion? Would adding the photo have made Williams's description—and her argument—even more forceful?

Examples

If a picture is sometimes worth a thousand words, then a good example runs a close second: examples can make abstract ideas concrete and provide specific instances to back up a claim. See how novelist Gretel Ehrlich uses two examples to support her ANALYSIS of courage in a cowboy context:

> In a rancher's world, courage has less to do with facing danger than with acting spontaneously—usually on behalf of an animal or another rider. If a cow is stuck in a boghole, he throws a loop around her neck, takes his dally (a half hitch around the saddle horn), and pulls her out with horsepower. If a calf is born sick, he may take her home, warm her in front of the kitchen fire, and massage her legs until dawn.
>
> —GRETEL EHRLICH, "About Men"

You can sometimes draw on personal experience for powerful examples, provided that the experience you cite is pertinent to your point. In a letter to the editors of the *Atlantic*, reader James A. Gibson uses an example to explain an important change in his way of seeing the world during a tour of the gardens at Middleton Place in South Carolina, a former plantation that is now a historical landmark and museum:

> The grounds were immaculate and the guides enthusiastic, [and] I looked to our guide for more information. "It took 100 slaves 10 years to do this work!" I will never look at a plantation again without wondering in anger and sadness who built the home, who planted and tended the garden, who wept at night over the forced labor, and who made southern life possible by being brutalized daily.
>
> —JAMES A. GIBSON, letter to the *Atlantic*

Humor, Sarcasm, and Exaggeration

> Comedian John Oliver uses humor to stake his claims. See an example by visiting everyones anauthor.tumblr.com.

Humor can often be used to good effect to support an argument—as long as the humor fits the context and audience. Of course, humor comes in many forms, from a self-deprecating story to a gentle parody or satire, from biting ridicule to a tired joke. While few of us are talented enough to write an argument based entirely on humor, it's possible to learn to use it judiciously. Doing so can help you to connect with your audience, provide some relief from a serious topic, or just vary the tone of your argument.

You'll want to make sure that most members of your audience will understand the humor. Jokes are notoriously difficult to translate, and what's funny in one language rarely comes through the same way in another. Sometimes attempts to translate advertisements into various languages are a source of humor themselves, as when KFC's "finger lickin' good" came out in Chinese as "eat your fingers off"! And cultural context can also determine if something will be funny at all—if it will fall flat, or worse, offend. For example, a story beginning "two cows walked into a bar" might seem like a humorous way to introduce an argument about overproduction of beef in the United States, but it probably wouldn't sit too well in India, where cows are sacred.

The late journalist Molly Ivins was famous for using humor and exaggeration in arguing serious positions. In the following interview on *Nightline*, Ivins is arguing in favor of gun regulation, but she uses humorous exaggeration—and a bit of real silliness—to help make her point:

> I think that's what we need: more people carrying weapons. I support the [concealed gun] legislation but I'd like to propose one small amendment. Everyone should be able to carry a concealed weapon. But everyone who carries a weapon should be required to wear one of those little beanies on their heads with a little propeller on it so the rest of us can see them coming.
> —MOLLY IVINS

Humor and exaggeration are key tactics used by Pepper Dem Ministries (PDM), a group of Ghanaian feminists who have worked to disrupt the tradition of all-male panels in political, civic, and social discussions. Referring to such panels as "manels"—like one featuring five men talking about women's issues in order to "break myths about periods"

The strategic humor (and sarcasm) in this image intends to make us laugh—but also to make us think hard about its serious, if implicit, message.

during World Menstrual Hygiene Day—a group of Ghanaian feminists employed PDM's tactic of humor and sarcasm and responded with a counter flyer of their own.

Narration and Narrative Sequencing

A good story well told can engage your audience and help support an argument. Both writers and speakers use narratives often—in REPORTS, MEMOIRS, and many other genres. Be sure, however, that any story you tell supports your point and that it is not the only evidence you offer. In most academic contexts, you shouldn't rely only on stories to support an argument, especially personal stories.

In the following example, author Bich Minh Nguyen writes about her experiences becoming "the good immigrant student." In this essay, she uses narration to capture the tension she felt between wishing to fit in and wanting to rebel as well as to document the racist behavior she endured.

See the ebook for a video on using personal stories in academic writing.

More than once, I was given the assignment of writing a report about my family history. I loathed this task, for I was dreadfully aware that my history could not be faked: it already showed on my face. When my turn came to read out loud the teacher had to ask me several times to speak louder. Some kids, a few of them older, in different classes, took to pressing back the corners of their eyes with the heels of their palms while they chanted, "Ching-chong, ching-chong!" during recess. This continued until Anh [Nguyen's sister], who was far tougher than me, threatened to beat them up.

    I have no way of telling what tortured me more: the actual snickers and remarks and watchfulness of my classmates, or my own imagination, conjuring disdain. My own sense of shame. At times I felt sickened by my obedience, my accumulation of gold stickers, my every effort to be invisible.   —BICH MINH NGUYEN, "The Good Immigrant Student"

Advertisements use narrative to appeal to viewers, as in this ad campaign for animal adoption. With three frames and eight words, the cartoon below tells a story to make an argument.

NARRATIVE SEQUENCING, a feature of much Black discourse, links stories or parts of stories to make what might be abstract points in an argument into memorable and concrete narratives. Professor Geneva Smitherman elaborates on the use of narrative sequencing when she explains:

> Black English speakers will render their general, abstract observations about life, love, people in the form of a concrete narrative. . . . The

relating of events (real or hypothetical) becomes a black rhetorical strategy to explain a point, to persuade holders of opposing views to one's own point of view. . . . This meandering away from the "point" takes the listener on episodic journeys and over tributary rhetorical routes, but like the flow of nature's rivers and streams, it all eventually leads back to the source.

—GENEVA SMITHERMAN, *Talkin and Testifyin: The Language of Black America*

In her address to the 2016 Democratic National Convention, former First Lady Michelle Obama used this strategy, speaking personally and drawing on her own unique life experiences in the opening of her talk by flashing back to comments she had made four years earlier in arguing that her husband would make a good president:

Remember how I told you about his character and convictions, his decency and his grace, the traits that we've seen every day that he's served our country . . . ? I also told you about our daughters, how they are the heart of our hearts, the center of our world. . . . When they set off for their first day at their new school, I will never forget that winter morning as I watched our girls, just 7 and 10 years old, pile into those black SUVs with all those big men with guns. And I saw their little faces pressed up against the window, and the only thing I could think was, what have we done?

—MICHELLE OBAMA, "Remarks by the First Lady at the DNC, 2016"

Obama uses this moving story to launch her discussion of what her husband had done to protect his own (and all) children, focusing on how all parents can be role models who practice her mantra: "When they go low, go high." Later in the speech, she returns to the narrative strategy, linking her family and daughters' story to those of her ancestors:

The story of generations of people who felt the lash of bondage, the shame of servitude, the sting of segregation, but who kept on striving and hoping and doing what needed to be done so that today I wake up every morning in a house that was built by slaves. And I watch my daughters, two beautiful, intelligent, black young women playing with their dogs on the White House lawn.

In this speech, Obama uses indirection and interwoven narrative (rather than a direct, linear argument) to argue for a particular vision of America. Obama's narrative sequencing brings the argument up close and personal, appealing to everyone who has hopes and dreams for their children.

Problem / Solution

Most **PROPOSALS** articulate a problem and then offer a solution that addresses that problem. The following passage from an article in the *Community College Daily* sets out a problem (food insecurity on college campuses) and offers possible solutions:

> Too many California college students spend too much time figuring out where their next meal may come from, or how to pay for it. When students have proper access to food, they stay enrolled and do better in school—and California policymakers can make that happen. The Hope Center found that three out of five students nationally struggle with food insecurity and the California Student Aid Commission found that 56% of California Community College students reported rising weekly food costs. Black, Latinx, American Indian and Alaska Native students experience food insecurity at consistently higher rates. . . . AB 1746, legislation sponsored by Assembly member Jose Medina (D-Riverside), would help to address this crisis by streamlining the existing Cal Grant entitlement programs and allow more than 120,000 additional community college students to qualify. More broadly, programs need to be reworked or created to be fast-acting for students who need cash quickly. Hunger, medical emergencies, and sick kids don't wait for paperwork to be filed and approved.
> —ELOU ORTIZ OAKLEY & ANGELICA CAMPOS, "California Can Solve Community College Students' Food Insecurity Crisis. Here's How"

Often writers open with a statement of the problem, as Rhoi Wangila and Chinua Akukwe do in their article on HIV and AIDS in sub-Saharan Africa:

> Simply stated, Africans living with H.I.V./AIDS and the millions of others at high risk of contracting H.I.V. are not benefiting significantly from current domestic, regional, and international high profile remedial efforts.
> —RHOI WANGILA & CHINUA AKUKWE, "H.I.V. and AIDS in Africa: Ten Lessons from the Field"

22 ⌘ Strategies for Supporting an Argument [479]

Children in sub-Saharan Africa who have lost parents to AIDS.

Wangila and Akukwe's article includes a photograph of African children affected by AIDS, which enhances their statement of the problem. The remainder of their essay then tackles the staggering complexities involved in responding to this problem.

Infographics are often used to present problems and solutions. On the following page, you'll find the final panel of an infographic that Chloe Colberg created about saving rhinos from illegal poaching. It identifies three ways of helping solve the problem: "get informed," "spread the word," and "support a campaign." The same information could be communicated in a paragraph or a bulleted list, but the large bold type makes the message much more visible.

Repetition, Reiteration, and Call and Response

A form of repetition, reiteration helps support an argument through emphasis: like a drumbeat, the repetition of a keyword, phrase, image, or theme can help drive home a point, often in very memorable ways. Reiterating is especially powerful in presentations and other spoken texts—think "Yes, we can!" and Sojourner Truth's "Ain't I a Woman?" Martin Luther King Jr. was a

What can you do to make a difference?
There are a number of different ways to get involved.

GET INFORMED

Continue to educate yourself on this issue. Visit the WWF website to learn more specifics and details about the rhino crisis.

SPREAD THE WORD

The more people that know about this issue, the better! Let your colleagues, friends and families know about this serious problem.

SUPPORT A CAMPAIGN

Support the WWF and other organizations' campaigns by learning about their efforts and considering a financial contribution.

SOURCES:
http://www.bbc.co.uk/news/uk-england-11477508
http://www.cites.org/eng/news/pr/2013/20131106_forensics.php
http://www.savetherhino.org/rhino_info/poaching_statistics
http://www.savetherhino.org/rhino_info/thorny_issues/
http://www.worldwildlife.org/species/rhino

DESIGNED FOR:
World Wildlife Fund
Chloe Colberg
December 2013

master of effective repetition, as is evident in the famous speech he delivered on the steps of the Lincoln Memorial in 1963. Just think for a moment what would be lost in this speech without the power of that repeated phrase, "I have a dream."

> *I have a dream* that one day this nation will rise up and live out the true meaning of its creed: "We hold these truths to be self-evident, that all men are created equal." *I have a dream* that one day on the red hills of Georgia, the sons of former slaves and the sons of former slave owners will be able to sit down together at the table of brotherhood. *I have a dream* that one day even the state of Mississippi, a state sweltering with the heat of injustice, sweltering with the heat of oppression, will be transformed into an oasis of freedom and justice. *I have a dream* that my four little children will one day live in a nation where they will not be judged by the color of their skin but by the content of their character.
> *I have a dream today!*
>
> —Martin Luther King Jr., "I Have a Dream"

Here's part of a frame from *Persepolis*.

Reiteration also works in visual texts and is a hallmark of graphic novelist Marjane Satrapi's work. Born and raised in Iran before being sent abroad in 1984 to escape what became the country's Islamic revolution, Satrapi recounts her childhood in *Persepolis I*, arguing implicitly that repressive regimes squelch individuality. In the detail of a frame shown here, Satrapi depicts a class of female students, using reiteration to make her point: all these girls are dressed exactly the same.

A little reiteration can go a long way. In an article published in *Ebony* magazine about the future of Chicago, see how it drives an argument that Chicago is still a home of Black innovation and creativity:

> [Chicago]'s the place where organized Black history was born, where gospel music was born, where jazz and the blues were reborn, where the Beatles and the Rolling Stones went up to the mountaintop to get the new musical commandments from Chuck Berry and the rock 'n' roll apostles.
> —LERONE BENNETT JR., "Blacks in Chicago"

Here the reiteration of "where" and the parallel clauses help establish a rhythm of forward movement that drives the argument.

CALL AND RESPONSE, a familiar form of reiteration, grows out of African traditions of participation in such things as public gatherings, religious ceremonies, and musical performances. During the 2020 March on Washington, the civil rights activist, TV host, and Baptist minister Al Sharpton repeatedly asked the crowd, "What do we want?" to which they replied, "Justice," creating a drumbeat demand at the heart of the argument for true equity.

In a religious context, professor of English Beverly Moss studied the sermon styles of several Black ministers, noting the use of call and response as the congregation responds to the preacher throughout the sermon, punctuating the minister's argument with their affirmation:

> Minister: "When you shout before the battle is over"
> Congregation: **"Preach!!"**
> Minister: "It puts things in a proper perspective"
> Congregation: **"Yeah!"**
> Minister: "It puts you in a posture of obedience"
> Congregation: **"Yeah!"**

Call and response may be most familiar, however, from its widespread use in music, where one instrument answers another, part of a musical composition responds to another, or a performer offers a call and others provide a response.

Signifying

SIGNIFYING is a strategy for underscoring something true or important through humor, irony, and indirection. Scholar of African American literature Henry Louis Gates Jr. traces this practice to the trickster figure found in African folklore and mythology, and particularly in stories in which the "signifying monkey" gets the best of the all-powerful lion through the use of puns and other forms of humorous linguistic substitution.

Sometimes gentle, sometimes sharp, you will see signifying putdowns at work in American films, TV shows, and books. Take, for example, the plot of *American Fiction*, a film based on Percival Everett's novel *Erasure*. The main character, Monk, is a frustrated Black academic whose books on Greek mythology have not sold well and are miscategorized as "African American Studies," even though, as Monk points out, the only African American thing about his books is the "jacket photograph." Irritated by another Black author who is being celebrated for writing the latest "so Black" hot ticket, *We's Lives in da Ghetto*, Monk dashes off a patronizing fake autobiography he calls *My Pafology*, using a pseudonym of a supposed fugitive felon he calls Stagg R. Lee.

This move is a monumental act of signifying—his fake book is a putdown of other authors pandering to White readers' appetite for crass caricatures of Black life presented as "authentic." And the move backfires (or perhaps doubly succeeds?) when Monk finds himself caught up in a rush of rave reviews for the new work. Irony piles upon irony, culminating in Monk's fake book being nominated for a prestigious literary award. The award committee has five members: two Black authors (one of whom is Monk) and three White authors. The three White authors vote for Stagg R. Lee's book to win; the two Black authors argue against it. One of the White authors sums up: "Well, it's two versus three so [our choice] is the winner." Another White author comments, "You know it's not just that it's so affecting. I just think it's essential to listen to black voices right now." The movie script direction adds: "In a wide shot, we see the division of the room: the three white judges on one side, the overruled black judges on the other." And in the film, the look on Monk's face—frozen in contempt, with a slight eyebrow twitch—is a visual piece of signifying that has the last, silent, word: look whose voices *are still* not being listened to.

Signifying, along with irony and exaggeration, can provide strong support for an argument, in this case through the irony that actual Black voices are ignored. You can also see signifying at work in much of today's popular music, especially hip-hop, which Gates describes as "signifying on steroids."

REFLECT

Choose an example in this chapter that's all words. Think about whether the same argument could be made visually—in a chart, with a photo and caption, and so on. If that doesn't seem possible, how might you illustrate the example, and which of the rhetorical strategies described in this chapter could you employ to further strengthen the example?

PART VI

Research

Research is formalized curiosity. It is poking and prying with a purpose.

—ZORA NEAL HURSTON

RESEARCH, LIKE WRITING, is a process fueled by curiosity. And it's a process of inquiry. When you research, you begin with questions that you're curious to answer. To find those answers, you might use a variety of methods—fieldwork, lab experiments, internet searches—and you'll find information in a variety of sources—books, articles, news reports, databases, websites, letters, photographs, historical records, social media, community knowledge. Research will help you to find some answers, but it's also more than that. Your exploration and inquiry through research will take you on a journey of discovery and learning.

As a student, you'll engage in research in many of the courses you take and in a variety of disciplines. Research is likely to be part of your work life as well. People working in business, government, and industry all need to follow research in order to make important decisions and keep up with new developments in their fields. Restaurant owners need to do research, for instance, to discover how to maximize profits from menu options and delivery methods. Engineers constantly do research to find the best equipment and supplies. And we know social media giants like *Facebook* certainly do research to learn more—and more—about user behaviors.

When you take on academic inquiry and research, you'll often be studying a topic that scholars before you have examined. You'll want to start by learning what has been written about your topic and then thinking carefully about questions you want to pursue. In this way, you'll be engaging with the ideas of others and participating in discussions about topics that matter—and joining the larger academic conversation along the way. The following chapters can help you do so.

REFLECT

Think about a time when your research was inspired by your curiosity. It could be a time inside or outside of school. What did you research and what did you learn? What was the end result of this experience? Did you do anything different based on what you learned?

TWENTY-THREE

Starting Your Research
Joining the Conversation

WHAT DO YOU FIND MOST DIFFICULT about doing research? Gathering data? Writing it up? Documenting sources? For many of us, the hardest part is just getting started. Researchers from Project Information Literacy, a nonprofit research institute conducting ongoing national studies of college learning practices, report that US students doing course-related research have the most difficulty with three things: getting started, defining a topic, and narrowing a topic. This chapter will help you tackle these tricky first steps, identify specific questions that will drive your research, and make a schedule to manage the many tasks involved in a research project.

At the same time, we aim to show you that doing research means more than just finding sources. College-level research is a discovery process: it's as much about the search for knowledge and answers as it is about managing sources. When we search, we go down expected and unexpected paths to answer important questions, discover solutions to problems, and come to new perspectives on old issues. While this chapter suggests a sequence of activities for doing research, keep in mind that you probably won't move through these stages in a fixed order. The research process is messy, and you may find yourself circling back to a question or stumbling on something that sends you in a new direction. That's all part of the fun.

Find a Topic That Fascinates You

At its best, research begins as a kind of treasure hunt, an opportunity for you to investigate a subject that you care or wonder about. So finding that topic might be the single most important part of the process.

If you've been assigned a topic, study the instructions carefully so that you understand exactly what you are required to do. Does the assignment give you a list of specific topics to choose from or a general topic or theme to address? Does it specify the research methods? number and kinds of sources? a GENRE in which to write up your findings? Even if you've been assigned a particular topic and told how to go about researching it, you'll still need to decide what aspect of the topic you'll focus on. Consider the following assignment:

> Identify a current language issue that's being discussed and debated nationally or in your local community. Learn as much as you can about this issue by consulting reliable print and online sources. You may also want to interview experts on the issue or take a poll of everyday people's thinking on the issue. Then write a 5-to-7-page informative essay following MLA documentation style. And remember, your task is to report on the issue, not to pick one side over others.

This assignment identifies a genre (a report), research methods (interviews, a survey, and published sources), a documentation style (MLA), and a general topic (a current language issue), but it leaves the specific issue up to the author. You might investigate how your local school district handles bilingual education, for example, or you could research the debate about standardized English in US classrooms.

While this particular assignment is broad enough to allow you to choose a particular issue that interests you, even assignments that are more specific can be approached in a way that will make them interesting to you. Is there some aspect of the topic related to your major that you'd like to look into? For example, a political science major might research court cases about dealing with language biases.

If you get to choose your topic, think of it as an opportunity to learn about something that intrigues you. Consider topics related to your major, or to personal or professional interests. Are you a hunter who is concerned about

If the debate about standardized English catches your attention, read Missy Watson's argument on p. 1010.

> For ideas and inspiration, visit TED.com, a site devoted to "ideas worth spreading." While there, check out Steven Johnson's talk, "Where Good Ideas Come From."

legislation that impacts gun rights in your hometown? Do you spend time watching *TikTok* videos and want to learn more about how the algorithm operates? Maybe you're an environmentalist interested in your state's policies on fracking.

In addition to finding a topic that interests you, try to pick one that has not been overdone. Chances are, if you're tired of hearing about an issue—and if you've heard the same things said repeatedly—it's not going to be a good topic to research. Instead, pick a topic that is still being debated: the fact that people are talking about it will ensure that it's something others care about as well.

If you're having trouble deciding on a topic, and if your instructor allows it, it could be helpful to enlist GENERATIVE AI to interview you about your interests and then offer some tips for what to do next. Whenever you use AI for brainstorming, we suggest using it as a guide to get your own ideas out of *you*, not to spit out ideas for you to adopt. Telling it to ask you questions is one strategy; another is to be direct and tell it what *not* to do, like "ask me questions; don't give me ideas." Here's a prompt one of our students used early in their research: "I'm in a first-year writing class and I'm supposed to find an issue about language that I can research and write a 5-to-7-page paper on. I would like your help choosing a topic. Please ask me some questions about my interests and local context; don't give me ideas. Ask me questions one at a time and adjust your next question based on my answers. Ask me a few questions and then offer suggestions for next steps I can take to decide on a topic that I'm interested in that meets my assignment goals."

Think about doing research as an invitation to explore a topic that really matters to you. If you're excited about your topic, that excitement will take you somewhere interesting and lead you to ideas that will in turn inform what you know and think.

Consider Your Rhetorical Situation

As you get started, think about your rhetorical situation, starting with the requirements of the assignment. You may not yet know your genre, and you surely won't know your stance, but thinking about those things now will help you when you're narrowing your topic and figuring out a research question.

- AUDIENCE. Who will be reading what you write? What expectations might they have, and what are they likely to know about your topic? What kinds of sources will they consider credible? What is your relationship to your audience?

- **PURPOSE**. What do you hope to accomplish by doing this research? Are you trying to report on the topic? argue a position? analyze the causes of something? something else?
- **GENRE**. Have you been assigned to write in a particular genre? Will you **ARGUE A POSITION**? **NARRATE** a historical event? **ANALYZE** some kind of data? **REPORT** information? something else?
- **STANCE**. What is your attitude toward the topic—and toward your audience? How can you establish your authority with them, and how do you want them to see you? As a neutral researcher? an advocate for a cause? something else? Check your biases—is **CONFIRMATION** or **ATTRIBUTION BIAS** keeping you from considering all sides fairly?
- **LANGUAGE**. Will you use more than one language or variety of language, and why? Will your audience expect you to use certain kinds of language or levels of formality, and will you meet—or perhaps challenge—those expectations?
- **CONTEXT**. Does the assignment have any length requirements? When is the due date? What other research has been done on your topic, and how does that affect the direction your research takes?
- **MEDIA**. Are you required to use a certain medium? If not, what media will be most effective for your audience, topic, and main point? Will you want or need to include links to other information? audio? video?
- **DESIGN**. Will you include photographs or other illustrations? present any data in charts or graphs? highlight any parts of the text? use headings or lists? Are you working in a discipline with specific format requirements?

Don't worry if you can't answer all of these questions at this point or if some elements change along the way. Just remember to keep these questions in mind as you work.

Narrow Your Topic

A good academic research topic needs to be substantive enough that you can gather adequate information but not so broad that you become overwhelmed by a flood of sources on it. The topic "women in sports," for example, is too general; a quick search on *Google* will display hundreds of subtopics, from "Title IX" to "women's sports injuries." One way to find an aspect of a topic that interests you is to scan the subtopics listed in online search results. Additionally, online news sites like *Google News* and *NPR Research News* can give you a sense of current conversations related to your topic. Your goal is to move from a too-general topic to a manageable one, as shown here:

General topic: women in sports

Narrower topic: injuries among women athletes

Still narrower: injuries among women basketball players

Even narrower: patterns of injuries among collegiate women basketball players compared with their male counterparts

Notice how the movement from a broad topic to one with a much narrower focus makes the number of sources you will consult more manageable. But just as a topic that is too broad will yield an overwhelming number of sources, one that is too narrow will yield too little information. The topic "shin splints among women basketball players at Florida International University," for example, is so narrow that there is probably not enough information available.

See the ebook for a video on narrowing your topic.

Practice INQUIRY to help narrow your topic further by asking good questions and exploring your own connection to the subject. Your research process and your writing process are closely linked. In both, you're generating ideas, learning more about what others (and you!) think about a topic, and figuring out the angle you want to take. The questions on page 113 will help you focus in on the specific debates related to your topic. How, for instance, do people understand the causes and effects of the issue you're studying? What are the specific claims people make about what should be done about the issue? As you move through these questions, you'll uncover aspects of your topic that draw you in the most—the ones you want to focus on through your research and writing.

Another mode of inquiry for narrowing your topic is to explore your connection to the issue by identifying what you already know (and don't know) about the topic and reflecting on the experiences you've had with it. The questions on page 114 can help you map out your connection and lead you to see where you might conduct more research by identifying what else there is to learn.

Finally, you can narrow your topic by making use of the inquiry activities on page 115, which include BRAINSTORMING, CLUSTERING, and LOOPING. These activities should help you to get your thoughts on the page and make connections among different ideas.

> **REFLECT**
>
> Review your research assignment. Make a list of three topics that you're considering and jot down what you already know about each. Review those notes. What do they suggest to you about your interest in these topics? Finally, narrow each one to a specific, manageable research topic. Which of the three now seems most promising?

Do Some Background Research

Existing research on your topic can provide valuable background information and give you an overview of the topic before you dive into more specialized sources. It can also help you discover issues that have not been researched—or perhaps even identified. At this point, your goal should be to see your topic in a larger context and to begin formulating questions to guide the rest of your research.

You may want to take a look at some online encyclopedias like *Wikipedia*, explanatory resources like the *World Almanac* or *World Factbook*, and other REFERENCE WORKS, which can provide an overview of your topic and point you toward specific areas where you might want to follow up. Subject-specific encyclopedias provide more detail, including information about scholarly books to check out.

Finally, you might begin your background research by reading articles on popular news magazines' or newspapers' websites to get a sense of who's talking about the topic and what they're saying.

Articulate a Question Your Research Will Answer

Once you have sufficiently narrowed your topic, you will need to turn it into a question that will guide your research. Start by asking yourself what you'd like to know about your topic. A good research question should require more than a "yes" or "no" answer. Instead, ask an open-ended question that will lead you to gather more information and explore multiple perspectives on your topic. For example:

> *Topic*: injuries among WNBA players
>
> *What you'd like to know:* What are the current trends in injuries among WNBA players, and how are athletic trainers responding?

An athletic trainer for the Los Angeles Sparks checks on Riquna Williams midgame.

This is a question that's focused, complex, and meaningful. Before settling on a research question, you should consider why the answer to that question matters. Why is it worth looking into and writing about? And why will others want to read about it? Answering the above question, for instance, can help athletic trainers see if their approach can be improved.

Keep your rhetorical CONTEXT in mind as you work to be sure your research question is manageable in the time you have and narrow or open enough to address in the number of pages you plan to write. Consider also any GENRE requirements. If you're assigned to argue a position, for example, be sure your research question is one that will lead to an argument. Notice how each question below suggests a different genre:

A question that would lead to a REPORT : What are the current trends in injuries among WNBA players?

A question that would lead to an ANALYSIS : Why do women basketball players suffer specific types of injuries during training?

A question that would lead to an ARGUMENT : At what age should young girls interested in basketball begin serious athletic training to minimize the chance of injury?

Once you've settled on a research question, your next step is to do some more research. Keeping your question in mind will help you stay focused. Your goal at this point is to look for possible answers to your question—to get a sense of the various perspectives on the issue and to start thinking about where you yourself stand.

>  **REFLECT**
>
> Write a research question for your narrowed topic that would lead to a report, one that would lead to an analysis, and one that would lead to an argument. Remember, try to avoid "yes" or "no" questions.

Plot Out a Working Thesis

Now it's time to think about what answers to your research question are emerging—in sources you consult and in your own mind. When you think you've found the best possible answer, the next step is to turn it into a working thesis. Basically, a working thesis is your hypothesis, your best guess about the claim you will make based on your research thus far.

But your working thesis may not be your final thesis. As you conduct more research, you may find more support for it or new information that prompts you to rethink your position. Consider one working thesis on the question about why WNBA players experience so many injuries during training:

> WNBA players suffer 60 percent more injuries than their NBA counterparts because of a very short pre-draft period and little to no off-season.

This working thesis makes a clear, arguable claim and provides reasons for that position.

Keep in mind that your working thesis may well change as you learn more about your topic; stay flexible—and expect to revise it as your ideas develop. The more open your mind, the more you'll learn.

See Ch. 14 in the ebook for a video on developing an argumentative thesis statement.

Establish a Schedule

A research project can seem daunting if you think of it as one big undertaking, rather than as a series of smaller tasks. Establishing a schedule will help you break your research into manageable steps, stay organized, and focus on the task at hand. The following template can help you make a plan:

Working title:

Working thesis:

	Due date
Choose a topic	_____
Analyze your rhetorical situation	_____
Do some preliminary research	_____
Narrow your topic and decide on a research question	_____
Plot out a working thesis	_____
Do library and web research	_____
Start a working bibliography	_____
Turn in your research proposal and annotated bibliography	_____
Plan and schedule any community-based or other field research	_____
Conduct community-based or other field research	_____
Draft a thesis statement	_____
Write out a draft	_____
Get response	_____
Do additional research, if needed	_____
Revise	_____
Prepare your list of references or works cited	_____
Edit	_____
Write your final draft	_____
Proofread	_____
Turn in the final draft	_____

TWENTY-FOUR

Finding Sources
Online and at the Library

**F YOU'VE SEEN** *The Amazing Race*, a reality show that sends teams of contestants to overcome challenges as they race around the world, then you know what has kept it winning Emmys for over three decades. Each season, we see the teams learning about cultural traditions in small Greek villages, famous art in German museums, and social practices in little-known regions of the world—all during their wild race to the finish line.

What we don't see is the research on those locations and cultures conducted by more than 2,000 crew members who explore potential sites, interview residents and town officials, read histories, pore over maps, and seek information from as many sources as they can before sending the contestants out on their quests.

Like the *Amazing Race* crew, student researchers today have access to a vast number of resources. And with so much information out there—held by knowledgeable people from grandparents to government experts and housed in libraries, archives, museums, and online—you, too, face the challenge of sifting through a lot of information to find the most helpful sources. Much like finding your way to an unfamiliar location, finding sources is a process of exploration that will lead to new discoveries.

This chapter will help teach you how to use resources ranging from library catalogs, reference works, online search engines, and social media, to those gathered from community-based and other firsthand field research. The following sections introduce you to different types of sources by explaining what's out there, where to find it, how to access it, and how to use it.

Starting with *Wikipedia* or Social Media

Casual or informal sources like *Wikipedia, YouTube*, and other social media can offer excellent starting points for your research. Of course, whenever you use online sources like these, it's crucial to read defensively—checking out the information you find to be sure it's trustworthy.

One student we know saw a *YouTube* review of a video game developed by Native Alaskans. Curious, she googled the game and found links to information about its origins and artwork, along with a statement about the purpose of the project: "We want to take back our culture out of the museum . . . to share who we are with the world." This statement got our student thinking about how Native Alaskans were representing their own culture in this game compared to how museums were representing it in exhibitions. So she searched the internet for more information about the game, visited the Native American Cultural Center on campus as well as her campus library for books and articles on Native Alaskan culture, and perused museum websites to investigate their presentation of it. She fact-checked her sources along the way, especially those turned up by *Google* searches. A *YouTube* video led this student all the way to the Smithsonian!

That's how research often develops: curiosity, and the questions that grow from it, leads to valuable and relevant sources. Today, those sources are more wide ranging than ever. As professor of education Adam Banks points out, you can often learn as much about visual rhetoric, for instance, from *TikTok* and *Instagram*, as you can from professional designers.

As the student example above also demonstrates, the questions that emerge as you examine sources will determine the kinds of information you will seek out. Do you need to learn the history of a group of people or an event? Do you need to research different perspectives on an issue? Do you need statistical data? personal narratives? Once you've determined the types of information that will best address your questions, you will need to figure out where to find this information—what sources you will need to locate or what studies you will need to conduct.

WHAT KINDS OF SOURCES DO YOU NEED?

The decisions you make about what types of sources you seek, where you look for them, and how authoritative you need them to be will be guided not only by the requirements of your assignment but also by your PURPOSE, AUDIENCE, and other elements of the RHETORICAL SITUATION. For the research you do in college, an important part of that rhetorical situation may be the discipline you are working in; for example, scientists tend to value research done through observation and experimentation whereas historians tend to value research done in libraries and archives or with living subjects, as in oral history projects.

You may not always be able to anticipate who will read your writing, especially if you're posting online, but you can analyze other aspects of your rhetorical situation to determine what types of sources you'll need. For instance, if your purpose is to convince voters of a political candidate's honesty, what information will be most persuasive and where will you find it? If you're writing about this candidate for a website, what kinds of sources do other writers cite on that site? Who's the site's primary audience? Will you find what you need in the library or online, or will you need to go out and talk to voters? Or will you need to use a variety of sources?

For academic research, you'll also want to keep several other distinctions in mind: the differences between primary and secondary sources, scholarly and popular sources, and older and more current sources.

Primary and secondary sources. Primary sources are original documents or materials, firsthand accounts, or field research, like interviews or observations. Secondary sources are texts that analyze and interpret primary sources; they offer background and context that can help you gain perspective on your topic. Secondary sources on a subject might include scholarly books and journal articles about the topic, magazine and newspaper reviews, government research reports, or annotated bibliographies. The student who researched the video game that drew on Native Alaskan culture conducted primary research when she analyzed the game itself and secondary research when she turned to articles about the game's development and books about the politics surrounding the representation of Native Alaskans.

Whether a particular source is considered primary or secondary often depends on what the topic is. If you are analyzing an artistic work, say a film, then the film itself is a primary source, while A. O. Scott's review of the

---

César Albarrán-Torres did the bulk of his research by watching TV. You may not be that lucky but be alert for possible sources in your everyday life. Check out Albarrán-Torres's article on p. 838.

film is a secondary source. But if you are researching Scott's work as a critic, then his review would be a primary source.

Scholarly and popular sources. For most academic assignments, you'll want to consult scholarly sources: articles, books, conference papers, and websites written by authorities in a given field. Such sources have usually been peer-reviewed, evaluated by experts in the field before publication. Because they are written for a knowledgeable audience, scholarly texts go into more depth than popular sources do, citing research and including detailed documentation.

Popular sources, by contrast, are written by journalists and writers for a general audience. They are often fact-checked, but they are not likely to be evaluated by experts before publication. Popular magazines can be a good source of information on current issues since they're published so frequently. Like scholarly sources, they often cite research, but rarely do they document those citations. Make sure that any such sources you use serve your subject and purpose. If, for instance, you're writing about fashion, *Vogue* might be a useful source—but its brief reviews of new books would not be the best sources in a literary analysis. Social media posts and conversations can often serve as popular sources, too, especially when a topic has not yet been studied very much, or not much has been published on it.

DETERMINING IF A SOURCE IS SCHOLARLY

- *What are the author's credentials* to write on the topic? Look authors up to confirm they are who they say they are.

- *Who's the publisher or sponsor?* Look for academic presses, professional organizations, or academic institutions. And see what others say about the source to ensure it's legitimate.

- *Does the source include original research* or interpret research by others that it cites?

- *Does it provide documentation?* Look for a list of works cited or references at the end and parenthetical documentation within the text. Check out a few cited sources to see that they're reputable.

- *Does the text seem authoritative?* Most scholarly texts use FORMAL language and provide evidence that shows the author can be trusted.

- **Does the text look academic?** Scholarly texts tend to use conservative typefaces and often include tables and charts. Popular texts are more likely to include color photos and to highlight certain things in sidebars.

- **Are there ads?** Scholarly texts have few, if any, ads; popular articles and sites often have ads.

Considering these questions can help you distinguish between sources such as the two on the following page, one from the popular magazine *Wired*, the other from the scholarly journal *Sustainability*. While both sources address gene editing of livestock, note their differences in focus and design. *Wired* displays on its cover and in the article's first pages striking, high-contrast images of cows and very little text; the magazine's typography and layout emphasize decorative elements. These visuals attract readers' attention. By contrast, the journal's cover includes its name, technical diagrams and images from a featured article, and publication information. The article certainly looks scholarly; the first page includes its genre (review), its title ("Sustainable Food Production: The Contribution of Genome Editing in Livestock"), the author's name, keywords, citation information, and an abstract.

While the questions above can help you judge whether a source is scholarly or popular, keep in mind that some sources are designed to look, act, and feel scholarly, but aren't. You'll need to be vigilant about checking out all the sources you consult—even those that seem scholarly—to ensure you aren't relying on **MISINFORMATION**. For example, some predatory publishers pose as legitimate even while they publish anything someone pays to have published—without conducting any peer review or fact-checking. These predatory journals have names, websites, and published works that look and seem scholarly. **READING DEFENSIVELY** by checking out what others say about the source will help you steer clear of these unreliable sources.

Older and more current sources. You will need to determine whether older or more current sources are best suited for your topic, purpose, and audience. Although you will always want to investigate the latest news and research about your topic, sometimes older works will serve as better sources of essential information. Your research question and your discipline may dictate the balance between using older or more current sources. In scientific and technological fields, the most current scholarly sources are usually favored, since change is occurring so rapidly, while in history or literature, older sources that have stood the test of time may offer the best and most fitting information.

Popular source

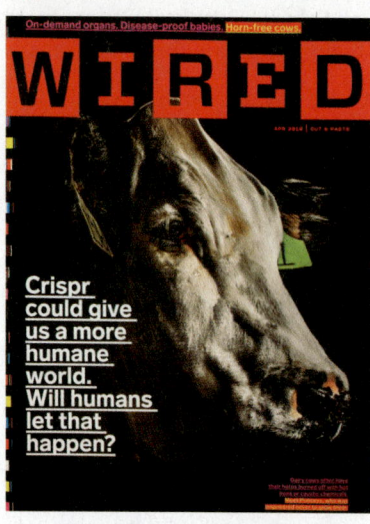
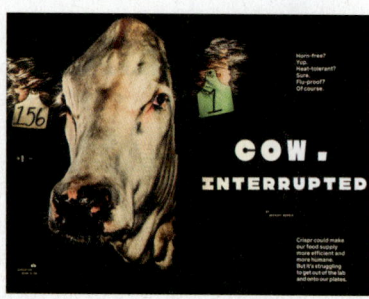

Scholarly source

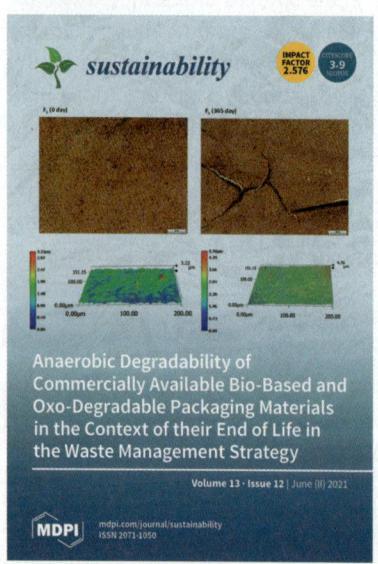
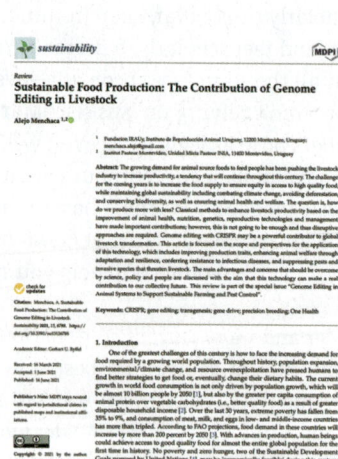

Remember that your professors may expect—or require—certain kinds of sources. They may, for instance, want you to use only scholarly books and articles. Most projects, however, call for information drawn from many types of sources. For a report on the impact of recent floods on small local farms, for example, you may want to conduct primary research by interviewing local farmers to gather personal narratives about how they have been affected; carry out secondary research online for news reports, photographs, and videos that document the floods; and use library sources to document flood conditions in the past.

TYPES OF SOURCES—AND WHERE TO FIND THEM

Reference Works

General reference sources include general encyclopedias (*Encyclopaedia Britannica, Columbia Encyclopedia*), dictionaries (*Merriam-Webster's, Oxford English Dictionary*), almanacs (*The World Almanac and Book of Facts*), and atlases (*The National Atlas of Canada*), among others. Besides brief overviews of your topic, such sources can be helpful for gathering background information, defining core concepts and terms, and understanding the larger context of your topic—or narrowing it if need be—as well as for getting leads to more specific sources. Your library may have print versions of some of these resources and online subscriptions to others. Still other dictionaries and encyclopedias, such as *Wikipedia*, are online only, free to access, and good places to start research.

Specialized encyclopedias and wikis can give information that is more specifically related to your topic or discipline than general reference works. Through your library or the library website you'll find subject-specific resources ranging from the *Encyclopedia of Ethics* to the *Encyclopedia Latina* and many more. Specialized wikis put similar information online in groups of pages about everything from health and medicine to comic book superheroes of the Marvel universe. Wikis can connect you to information and communities online, but keep in mind that their open, collaborative authoring policy means that anyone can edit the information on a page. So be sure to evaluate the source carefully.

Bibliographies, also called references or works cited, are lists of publications that appear at the end of books or articles. If you've located a useful source, check its bibliography to find additional sources related to your topic. You may find longer, standalone bibliographies for popular or widely researched subjects; ask your librarian about availability. Many bibliographies include descriptive annotations for sources, and *Wikipedia*'s bibliographies often contain links that will take you right to the cited source.

Books

In addition to the thousands of print books available through your campus library, which you can search through the library website, you can also access many books online. *Project Gutenberg* makes freely available over 57,000 ebooks and digitized texts that are in the public domain. *Google Books* also provides free digital access to books in the public domain, and it makes these texts searchable.

Rarely will an entire book be relevant to your specific topic, so you'll need to be selective. Reading the table of contents, skimming chapter headings and sections, and examining the list of keywords and topics in the book's catalog or database entry can tell you whether all or part of a book is relevant to your research.

Periodicals

Articles from newspapers, magazines, and scholarly journals are available online through news sites, academic search engines, journal websites, and open-access databases. In addition to these, many more articles may be available to you in your library in print or online or both, depending on the library and the periodical; you can locate such articles through indexes and databases to which the library subscribes. If you can't access an index electronically through your library, ask a reference librarian to help you locate the print version on the library shelves.

Journal articles can be found online through academic search engines such as *Google Scholar* and *JURN*, which yield results from electronic journals and works from academic publishers. *Google Scholar* tends to produce more results in the sciences than in the humanities, while *JURN* focuses on humanities and the arts. You may come across a site that offers an abstract but charges to unlock the full text. In such cases, see whether your library gives you access to the journal. Your campus library may also give you access to subscription-only articles that simply don't turn up on *Google Scholar* and *JURN*, which find a portion of the scholarly texts available online but can miss content held behind paywalls. For this reason, library databases are a good place to go when searching for articles from scholarly journals.

Magazine and news articles are available online through news organizations' websites that provide searchable access to current and archived articles, photos, podcasts, videos, and streaming broadcasts. Many sites, like that of the *New York Times*, provide only limited access or require subscriptions, but some are available for free online. News aggregators like *Google News* are also useful for searching news on specific subjects, turning up articles from a range of international or local news sources; often you can personalize such aggregators to track news on specific subjects.

For newspapers that do not archive their articles online, and for older or historical articles that have not been digitized, you can turn to your library's indexes and databases. To find articles published before 1980, you'll most likely need to search indexes such as *The Readers' Guide to Periodical Literature* and *National Newspaper Index*. Many databases also include newspaper as well as journal articles and might give you access to articles not openly available online. Remember to carefully scrutinize and evaluate news sources you encounter so that you aren't duped by FAKE NEWS or material that seems trustworthy but isn't based on facts.

Government and Legal Documents

Official reports, legislative records, laws, maps and photos, census data, and other information from federal, state, and local governments are available for free online. Check the websites of government departments and agencies for these resources; you can access such resources for the US government through *USA.gov*. The Library of Congress website provides a large archive of photographs, maps, and other US historical and cultural materials.

Primary and Historical Documents and Oral Forms of Knowledge

Most university libraries include among their holdings rare and unique materials—books, photographs, fine art, cultural artifacts, maps, oral histories, and other material—held in the library's archives or special collections. These materials are usually searchable through the library's online catalog, but because the items are often rare and hard, if not impossible, to replace, you'll probably need to contact your library for access.

Some libraries also house digital images of rare documents in online archives; this is one way of viewing documents held by another institution that you cannot access in person. Many museums, cultural institutions, and historical societies also make their holdings available for viewing through their own online archives—you can explore many rooms of the Smithsonian this way—or through open-access archives like *Google Arts and Culture*. Remember too that, if you have access to them, oral forms of knowledge—songs, chants, riddles, folktales, parables, and other story forms—can be sources of profound cultural knowledge passed on from one generation to another.

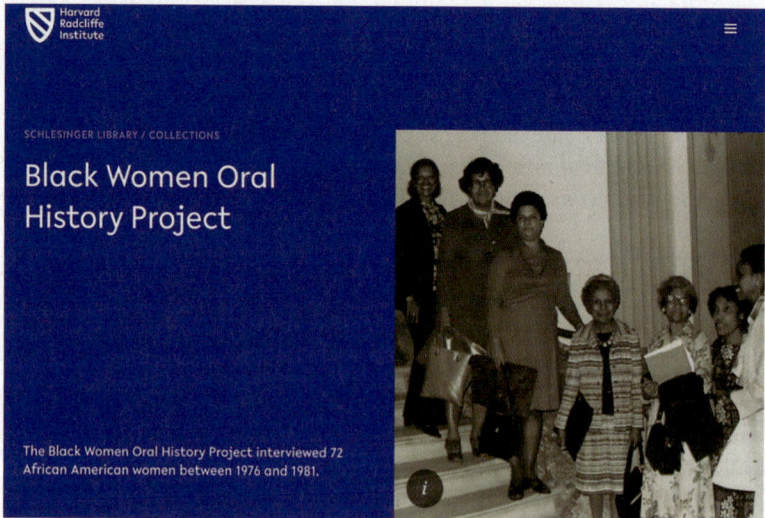

This website provides digital access to the Harvard Radcliffe Institute's Black Women Oral History Project and hosts audiovisual materials of Black women who "made significant contributions to American society during the first half of the 20th century."

RESEARCH SITES: ON THE INTERNET, IN THE LIBRARY

Researchers often turn to the internet first for answers to all sorts of questions. Convenient and powerful the internet may be, but given the prevalence of false and misleading information, using this vast resource requires caution in order to verify the accuracy of what you uncover.

Some people turn to **GENERATIVE AI** for help finding sources. If your instructor allows it and you choose to use AI to conduct research, you will want to exercise similar caution as you do when using the internet for research by **READING DEFENSIVELY** and double-checking facts. AI can make up or "hallucinate" entire sources, though some platforms connected to scholarly databases are less likely to do so. The advice on page 507 will help you weigh the benefits and drawbacks of using AI platforms for early research.

Remember, academic libraries still provide access to a wealth of reliable resources, from reference works to bibliographies to **PRIMARY SOURCES** and **SECONDARY SOURCES**. Most college libraries provide free online access to electronic resources such as indexes, databases, and the library catalog remotely. The following sections introduce you to some tools for finding sources online and in the library; knowing how to use these tools effectively will help you take advantage of all that these sites have to offer.

Search sites. Search engines like *Google* help you locate information on general sites like *Wikipedia*, government information sites like the Library of Congress, and social media sites like *Instagram* or *TikTok*, as well as public sites for colleges and professional organizations. Through them, you can also access local, national, and international news sites, though some will require you to subscribe in order to access their materials.

General search sites like these are a good starting point, but you can find more specialized sources on your topic by identifying which sites will be most relevant to your search. For academic searches, try *Google Scholar* or *JURN*. *Google Scholar* locates peer-reviewed articles, books, abstracts, and technical reports by searching the websites of academic publishers, professional societies, and universities. A variety of search sites are useful for specific types of searches, including those devoted to maps or image searches (*Google Maps*, *Flickr*), news aggregators (*Google News*, *NewsNow*), and so on.

As you use search terms to further your research, move from general concepts to more specific ones by configuring short, increasingly narrowed combinations of **KEYWORDS**. Most search sites also allow advanced searches that help you limit results by date, type of source, or other criteria; check the site's search tips for guidelines that are specific to the search engine you're using.

Keep in mind that some search sites allow websites to pay for higher placement or ranking in search results, which means that what comes up first in a search may not be the most useful or relevant to your topic. And we know that many search engines collect information on us each time we search, which impacts what we see in future searches. So don't take search results at face value—scroll beyond the initial AI-generated summary and the first few results and see what multiple search engines produce, not just one. You can also seek out search engines that don't track users, like *DuckDuckGo*.

Social media may be something you search unconsciously as you scroll through your personal feeds. Sites and apps like *TikTok*, *Instagram*, *YouTube*, and *Facebook* are useful as "sources of sources," where you can connect with people who share your interests to find and share information and sources about those interests. With so many prominent people posting on social media, these sites can also provide you with primary source material. By following experts in the field you're researching, you can find relevant quotes or introductions to a larger discussion.

Online forums, groups, and discussion lists can also connect you with people who share an interest or expertise in specific topics. Many forums and discussion lists archive past posts and threads that you can search to see if your topic has come up in the discussion before; you can also join current discussions and post questions or requests for information.

While social media lets you see what others are reading and allows them to recommend sources you might otherwise miss, recent research tells us that people tend to follow like-minded individuals from similar social circles; that is, the view from your feed may be more like an echo chamber of similar views rather than truly representative of a larger reality. And we know that social media sites are where **FAKE NEWS** and **MISINFORMATION** spread most quickly. So be sure to evaluate every source: Is the person you are quoting actually an expert? Can you confirm the information in the post and follow it to a larger discussion? Have you checked sites like *Snopes* and *FactCheck.org* to be sure you aren't relying on something phony? See Chapters 27 and 8 for more on how to evaluate sources and avoid misinformation.

Generative AI platforms are not search engines, authors, databases, or sources themselves. But they will generate lists of potential sources if you ask them. Because of the way generative AI tools work, however, you should be careful about trusting their suggestions. They may suggest a source that doesn't exist or get some part of a source wrong. For instance, an AI chatbot may get the title of a source wrong even when the author and date are accurate. If your instructor allows you to use AI for finding sources, we suggest trying an AI platform that draws from scholarly databases of real sources. For instance, at the time of this writing, *Elicit* and *SciSpace* are AI-powered research tools that claim to draw results from a massive collection of scientific research papers and provide links to the real papers for you to review. AI research platforms have different features, and they change rapidly, so play around with them to evaluate which one works best for your purpose. While AI can be one way to locate sources, it is not a good source itself. If you use AI to find a source, visit that source and cite the source directly, not the AI platform.

Libraries. College libraries, and their librarians, are especially valuable resources. All college libraries are staffed with reference librarians whose major responsibility is to help faculty and students with their research inquiries. While they will not do the research for you, reference librarians can be enormously helpful in showing you where you can find materials specific to your research question or topic and how you can search for them most efficiently. Their advice can save you considerable time and frustration.

In addition to reference librarians, many libraries have specialists in specific academic disciplines. Discipline (or subject) librarians work closely with academic departments to make sure that the relevant journals, databases, and books for that discipline are available to students and faculty.

Schedule a meeting with a reference or discipline librarian, and come to the meeting prepared to discuss your research question or topic. This is also your chance to ask about library resources available on your topic or any specific kinds of sources you're looking for.

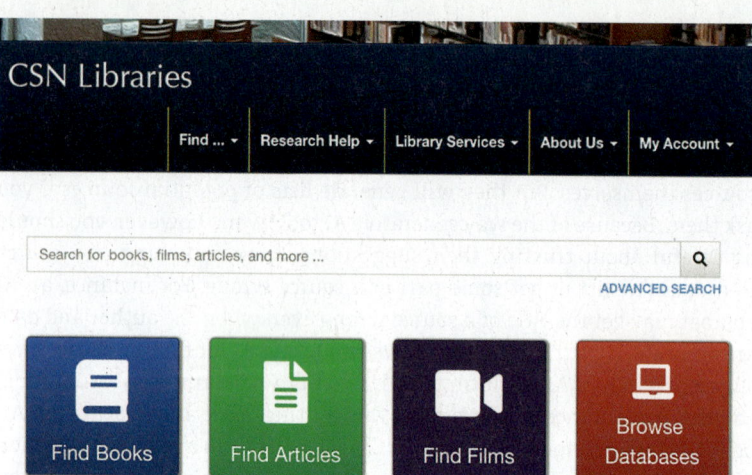

The library homepage for the College of Southern Nevada.

Library websites. In addition to information about hours, location, and holdings, library websites often provide useful guides or tutorials to using the library. College libraries often provide online research guides that list databases, references, websites, organizations, and other discipline- or subject-specific resources. The image above shows the homepage of the College of Southern Nevada library. Note the links that allow you to search in various ways and access specific services, including getting help from research librarians. In addition to multiple libraries on campus and special collections, many universities offer research guides by discipline. If you're conducting research in a particular discipline, these guides can help you understand conventions and search for books, journals, and articles in that field.

Library catalogs. Most libraries have electronic catalogs that account for all their holdings. Searching the catalog is the best method for locating books and other materials, such as audio and video recordings, that you can access through the library. The record for each item includes the author, title, and publication information; a physical description of the item; and sometimes a summary or overview of the contents. The electronic catalog also provides a call number that tells you where the item is physically located in the library stacks (or a networked library), and whether or not it is currently available.

You can search a library catalog by author, title, series, subject, or keyword—or some combination of those in an advanced search. The

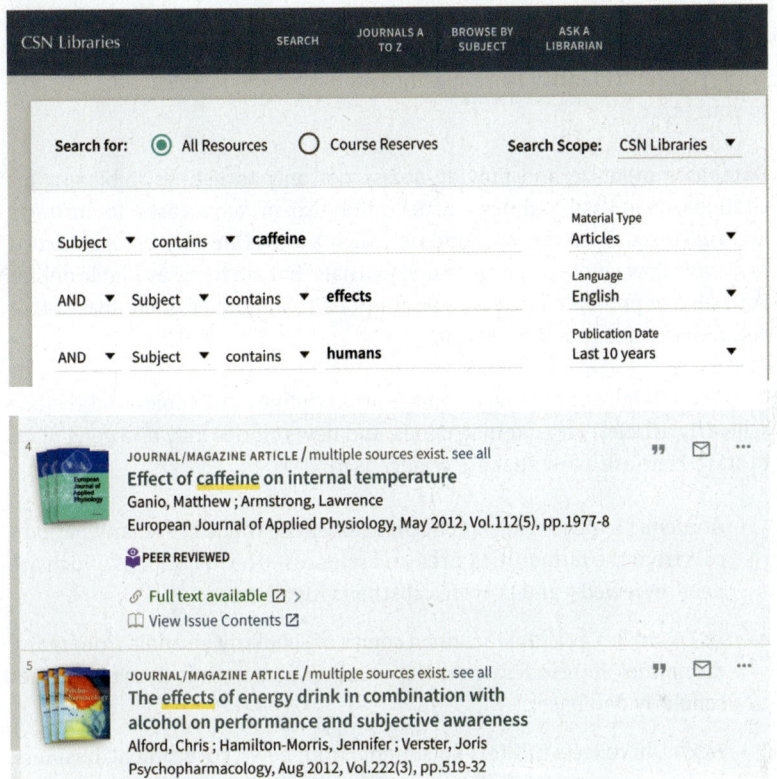

image above shows the initial search terms for a paper in an introduction to biology course. The student researcher, intrigued by the conflicting stories they had heard about the impact of caffeine on the human body, searched by selecting filters (subject terms include "caffeine," "effects," and "humans"), limited the type of source (articles only), selected a specific language (English), and specified a date range (the last ten years).

These search criteria turned up 184 results in the College of Southern Nevada library catalog. All the results yielded peer-reviewed articles, so the student knows they can trust them. Analyzing the results reveals a variety of ways the researcher could narrow their focus. For example, several of the articles examine the effects of combining caffeine with energy drinks or alcohol or high-calorie foods; others look at behavioral effects at a variety of consumption levels. The point is that doing the initial search of a library's full catalog, depending on your findings, can help you focus—or broaden—your scope and identify more specific databases that include works relevant to your topic.

Databases organize and provide access not only to listings (bibliographic citations) of journal and news articles but also, in many cases, to abstracts and full texts. Open-access databases, such as the *Directory of Open Access Journals*, allow you to search research journals that are freely available online. Your library probably also has subscriptions to a number of databases that you can access through its website.

General databases that cover a range of disciplines and topics and include scholarly articles, popular magazines, and news stories may be a good place to start. Here are a few that are widely used:

- *Academic Search Premier* (EBSCO) includes the full text of many periodicals from the humanities, arts, and sciences—the majority of which are peer-reviewed—and provides abstracts for others.
- *JSTOR* makes available scanned copies of scholarly journals from many disciplines. It includes issues from further back in time than most other scholarly databases.
- *Nexis Uni* collects full-text documents from news, government, business, and legal sources. This database includes transcripts of broadcast news sources.
- *ProQuest One* provides full-text articles from journals, periodicals, dissertations, newspapers, and video broadcasts.

Subject-specific databases are useful when you have a focused topic and research question. For example, if you are conducting research on sustainable farming efforts in urban areas, you might begin by searching databases that focus on food and nutrition, such as *Food Science and Technology Abstracts*. If you are searching for information on trends in sports injuries among basketball players, you might search a sports research database like *SPORTDiscus*. Ask a subject or reference librarian to direct you to the most relevant databases to your topic.

RUNNING SEARCHES, NARROWING RESULTS

Whether you're looking for sources online or in the library, the search typically starts with a website and an open search bar. The following tips will help you conduct searches and narrow your results, whether you're using search sites, library catalogs, or electronic databases.

Keyword searches allow you to use words and phrases, including author names, titles, and descriptions, to locate sources—but keep in mind that you may need to adjust your **KEYWORDS** or use synonyms if your initial searches don't yield useful results. If searching for "women's sports injuries" doesn't yield much, try "female athlete injuries." You may also need to try broader keywords ("women sports medicine"). If your search returns too many results, try narrowing your term ("women's sports injuries basketball"). Here's another strategy: once you've found a relevant article on your topic, look at the subject terms listed for that article in the library catalog or note jargon you find in the article. These subject terms might give you ideas for keywords that you can use for additional searching.

Following are some advanced search techniques that can help you focus your search.

Quotation marks can be used around terms to search for an exact phrase, such as "International Monetary Fund" or "obesity in American high schools." Using quotation marks may exclude useful results, however—for example, searching for "factory farms" may omit results with "factory farming" in a library search.

Boolean operators (AND, OR, and NOT) let you refine your search by combining keywords in different ways to include or exclude certain terms. Using AND narrows a search to include all terms joined by AND; using OR broadens a search to include items with any of the terms joined by OR; and using NOT limits a search to exclude items with any term preceded by NOT. For example, if you're researching solar energy, typing in "alternative energy" will bring up many more options than "alternative energy AND solar," which reduces the number to only those that include the term "solar." Typing in "alternative energy NOT wind" narrows the search to results that exclude the term "wind."

Parentheses allow you to combine Boolean searches in a more complex way. For example, a search for "alternative energy AND (solar OR wind)" yields only those items that contain both "alternative energy" and "solar" or both "alternative energy" and "wind." Searching "alternative energy NOT (solar OR wind)" yields only items that contain "alternative energy" but do not contain either "solar" or "wind"; this kind of search might be useful, for example, if you are specifically researching forms of alternative energy other than solar or wind energy.

 REFLECT

Consider the sources you have gathered so far in your research. Which ones are primary, which ones secondary—and why did you choose them? How many of them come from popular sources or from social media? What use have you made of *Wikipedia*, and how has it helped you (or not)? At this point, do you need to identify additional sources? If so, what kind?

TWENTY-FIVE

Conducting Research in the Field

OURNALISTS WHO INTERVIEW eyewitnesses, researchers who spend months observing the behavior of a particular population, historians who study archival records, pollsters who conduct surveys on the general public's attitudes about current government policies, and students who gather oral histories from local heroes or beloved grandparents—all are engaging in field research. Depending on your research question, you, too, may need to go "into the field" to conduct research, using data-gathering methods that rely on firsthand accounts. This chapter offers advice on doing field research using the three most common discovery methods: observation, interviews, and surveys or questionnaires.

Keep in mind that conducting field research on human subjects may require prior approval from your college's Institutional Review Board (IRB), a group responsible for making sure that a study will not harm research participants. Observing what kinds of clothing people wear to the mall may not need permission, but observing interactions in a private space like a doctor's office or doing any kind of field research with children probably will. Check with your instructor to find out if your project requires approval. If it does, be sure you understand the approval process and the time required to complete it.

Observations

Observation as a field research method calls for a lot more than casual "people watching." It involves taking careful notice of environments and behaviors, with a clear sense of your purpose and of how your observations will help you answer your research question. Many disciplines use observation to collect data about individuals and communities in order to answer questions about how and why they organize, relate to, or interact with one another and the world around them. In many cases, observation is the best and often the only means of gathering field data.

When reference librarian Linda Bedwell and graduate student Caitlin Banks wanted to find out how the study areas in Canada's Dalhousie University Library were being used, they observed students there, noting behaviors and paying attention to how they themselves used the spaces. Bedwell and Banks were conducting **PARTICIPANT OBSERVATION**, which operates on the principle that researchers can learn by doing as well as by watching. In non-participant observation, on the other hand, researchers focus on the actions of others but do not participate in the situations they're observing.

The process (and resulting information) will differ significantly depending on the type of observation, and you should choose the type most suitable to the situation and for addressing your research topic and question. If you're studying the winning strategies of video gamers, you might choose to do participant observation if you're an expert gamer yourself and if playing the games would result in more insightful data. If you are researching careers in medicine and want to learn about the typical day of a nurse, participant observation would not be an option—unless you have the credentials, training, and legal standing to provide patient care.

Keep your research question clearly in mind when conducting observations and carefully record what you see. Following are some additional tips for conducting effective observations:

- *Determine your purpose and method for observing.* Is participant observation the most suitable method to pursue your research question? Or do you need to focus only on the actions of others—and not to participate yourself? How do you expect to use the data?

- *Plan ahead.* Decide where you will observe and what materials you'll need—and make sure your equipment is ready and working. Determine whether you'll need permission to observe, photograph, and/or record;

Judith Newman writes about conversations with her son. Does it still count as participant observation? We think it does. Read her essay on p. 952, and notice whether she follows the advice here.

if so, secure necessary permissions ahead of time. Keep in mind that it may not be permissible to take photographs or record video in some sites—at a church service, for instance.

- *Record your observations.* Take detailed descriptive notes, even if you are also recording audio or video; your notes will add necessary texture. Note who is present, the activities they engage in, where they're situated, and pertinent details about the setting such as the physical design of the space. Be sure to record the date, time, and location. As you observe, focus on recording and describing; save the interpretation and analysis for later, when you review your notes and recordings.

- *Be guided by your purpose for observing,* but don't let that purpose restrain you. Be open to whatever you encounter. Sometimes in the process of looking for one thing, you may find something else that is equally interesting or important. And don't look only for extraordinary behavior. The goal of observation is generally to look for the routine and for patterns, things that are important because they happen regularly.

- *After your observation,* take a moment to flesh out what you've recorded with notes about any additional thoughts or reflections you have.

- *Review your observation notes* and any audio or video recordings, looking for patterns that emerge. Look for actions that recur, for topics that are repeatedly addressed, for individual participants who seem to play important roles. Also note when deviations from patterns occur and what seems to prompt the deviation. You should also consider whether those you observe have changed their behavior because they are being observed and, if so, how these changes may affect your data. You won't be able to correct for these effects, but you can consider and acknowledge them in your analysis. Your goal at this point is to start to analyze and look for an answer to your research question.

Interviews

You may find that the best way to answer your research question is to interview people who have a valuable perspective on your topic, such as experts, witnesses, or key participants in an event. Interviews can provide information that may not be available elsewhere; they can also complement other research and data-gathering methods, such as observations and library research. Just as with observations, you'll need to consider your purpose for conducting an interview and how the information you gain from it will speak to your research question.

You'll also need to decide whom to interview. Will one interview provide the needed information, or will you need several? And how qualified are those you're considering to address your research question? As a veteran of the war in Afghanistan, an uncle may not be the most neutral source for a detailed analysis of the history of US involvement in the region; print sources may be a better starting place for that type of background information. But your uncle probably *would* be a valuable, reliable source for a first-hand account of the combat experience and could probably provide details that you would never get from a book.

In any case, remember to ask your interviewees for their written consent to the interview, especially if your work will be published online or elsewhere. Following are additional tips for conducting successful interviews:

- *Plan to conduct your interviews early in your research* in case you have to do follow-up interviews. Contact interviewees well before your research project is due to set up appointments.

- *Do some background research* on your topic before the interview so that you can ask informed questions.

- *Write out a list of questions* that you will ask in the interview. These questions should be directly related to your research. Avoid questions that are too general that lead to one-word answers like "yes" or "no." Also avoid leading questions, ones that prompt answers that you want. The question "Don't you think his campaign tactics were dishonest?" allows the interviewee to disagree, but it still suggests a particular response. A better question would be "What is your opinion on the candidate's campaigning methods?"

- *Practice your interview skills.* Writing teacher Katherine Welsh points out that you can use an AI platform to rehearse your interview. If your instructor allows AI use, prompt it to play the role of the person you plan to interview in response to the questions you pose. Interviewing AI is not a substitute for talking to a real person, but it can help you prepare and alleviate some nerves before the real meeting. Here's a prompt one of our students used with *ChatGPT*: "I'm planning to interview a local librarian about the public library's strategies and programming to attract teens. Please play the role of this librarian to help me prepare. I will ask you 10 questions and you should answer them from the perspective of a librarian in charge of Teen Services at a public library in Rockford, IL. This librarian has 20 years of library experience and was a former high school history teacher. Once I'm done, please offer some suggestions for additional questions and how I might improve my existing questions."

- *Decide how you'll record the interview.* Will you rely solely on note-taking, or will you combine it with audio or video recording? Remember to ask permission before you tape any part of an interview.

- *If your interview requires any electronic equipment,* test it before the interview. And have a backup plan; there's nothing more frustrating than finding out that you've lost the data from a wonderful interview because your batteries died.

- *Be polite.* Remember that the person you're interviewing is doing you a favor by agreeing to speak with you. Send a thank-you note to anyone you interview.

- *Record the date, time, and location* of every interview that you conduct, and write down contact information for the interviewee.

- *Check facts, dates, and other information* the interviewee provides, especially about anything controversial. If any of the information seems questionable, try to interview others who can corroborate it or provide another perspective.

Remember that such highly structured interviews, a hallmark of Western research methods, may not be best suited for all cases. Interviewing children, for example, may call for more informal methods. Or members of some cultural communities may not wish to participate in structured events or may view such events as suspect (at best). In such cases, think about using a semistructured interview, or an informal conversation, which will leave more room for open responses. In such an interview or conversation, using open-ended questions will let those you are talking with tell you about their own experiences in their own way—so leave time for silence and for thinking.

You may not want to ask questions at all, but just listen intently as the conversation develops in its own way. The goal of such semistructured interviews is to share and gather stories, not answer a list of set questions. Such stories can be especially important in helping preserve the experiences of those whose voices have been ignored or unheard, and in letting people speak for themselves in their own times and places.

Surveys and Questionnaires

You've probably been asked to participate in marketing surveys that review products or services, or maybe you've completed questionnaires for course evaluations. Such surveys and questionnaires can be useful in soliciting information from a large number of people. Most often they aren't meant to poll an entire population; rather, they usually target a representative sample, a selected subset of a group that accurately reflects the characteristics of the whole group. The most reliable way to select such a group is by random sampling. A true random sample is one in which every member of the target population has the same chance of being selected to participate. Say you want to survey the first-year students in your school. You could try to track down each one—not a problem in a tiny school, but how about a school with 5,000 students? Not feasible. Or you could acquire a list of names from the registrar, assign each name a number (you can use *Excel* to assign random numbers), and then select a certain percentage of these people.

Unlike interviews, most surveys or questionnaires do not solicit detailed information; generally, researchers use them to gauge trends and opinions on a rather narrow topic. Following are some tips for deciding when to use surveys and how to design and administer them.

Consider your PURPOSE. If you are trying to find out how first-year medical residents negotiate the challenges of their demanding schedule, a survey is not likely to provide you with the level of detail you will need; interviews might be effective. However, if you are researching how the residents account for their time in a typical day, a survey would likely be your best method.

Once you've decided that a survey is the practical way to proceed, think about how you will use the results. Will the results provide essential support for your argument or anecdotal details to make your discussion more interesting and concrete? These considerations will determine the number of people you survey and what sorts of questions you ask them.

Determine your sample. Unless you are only after anecdotal information, you should aim to survey a representative sample, a randomly selected subset of a group that reflects the characteristics of the whole group. If you want to discover your college community's level of satisfaction with campus dining services, for example, you'll need to solicit a sample that represents all those who use the services—students, faculty, administrative staff, and visitors—while also reflecting the range of ages, genders, ethnicities, and so on. Including only students who eat breakfast in the dining halls on weekends is not likely to give you a viable sample. Most importantly, decide how many people you will contact; generally, the more of the target population you sample, the more reliably you will be able to claim that your results represent trends in that population.

Choose your distribution method. Will you administer the survey over the phone or face-to-face? send a written survey through text message? Or will you use an online service like *Qualtrics*, *SurveyMonkey*, or *Google Forms*? Most universities provide access to one of these tools; check with the Office of Research on campus. And don't expect a 100 percent response rate. Researchers often distribute surveys multiple times to get as many people in their targeted population to respond as they can.

Surveys must be carefully designed—or respondents may revolt!

Write the questions and an introduction, and test the survey. Respondents tend not to complete long or complicated surveys, so the best surveys include only a few questions and are easy to understand. Sequence questions from simple to complex unless there is a good reason not to do so. Also decide what kinds of questions are most likely to yield the information you're after. Here are examples of four common kinds of survey questions: open-ended, multiple-choice, agreement scale, and rating scale.

Open-ended

What genre of books do you like to read?

Multiple-choice

Please select your favorite genre of book (check all that apply):
__ nonfiction __ autobiography __ self-help __ histories __ sci-fi / fantasy

Agreement scale

Indicate your level of agreement with the following statements:

	Strongly Agree	Agree	Disagree	Strongly Disagree
The library should provide both ebooks and print books.	☐	☐	☐	☐

Rating scale

How would you rate your campus library?
__ Excellent __ Good __ Fair __ Poor

Your questions should focus on specific topics related to your research question. For example, undergraduate researcher Steven Leone believed that solar energy provided by thin-film solar cells could be an alternative to fossil fuels as an energy source, but he knew many homeowners resist expensive solar installations. His project, "The Likelihood of Homeowners to Implement Thin-Film Solar Cells," was designed to discover the relationship between homeowners' socioeconomic status and their attitudes about alternative energy sources in order to gauge how likely they are to adopt this new technology. These are the questions he asked in a survey of homeowners. Notice that some call for short answers while others ask for detailed responses.

1. What is your combined annual household income?
2. What is the highest level of education you have completed?
   __ high school __ some college __ college __ graduate school
3. How is your home currently heated?
4. How much are you currently spending each year on home energy costs?
5. Which is more important to you—saving money or going green? Why?
6. Have you considered using solar energy as your home energy source? Why or why not?
7. Thin-film solar cells cost significantly less than conventional solar installations and offer an energy-cost payback that is twice as fast. How much more likely does this information make it that you will implement this technology?
   __ very likely   __ somewhat likely
   __ somewhat unlikely   __ very unlikely
8. Thin-film solar cells will increase the resale value of your home. How much more likely does this information make it that you will implement the technology?
   __ very likely   __ somewhat likely
   __ somewhat unlikely   __ very unlikely

Leone's questions provided him with data that he then analyzed to determine patterns (education, income, lifestyle) of attitudes on his topic.

Once you're satisfied with your questions, write a brief introductory statement that will let participants know the purpose of the survey and what they can expect, including an estimate of how long it will take to complete.

Manage your results. When you are done collecting data, be sure to carefully record and store your responses. If you are using a print survey, one simple method is to use a blank survey and tally responses next to each question. You can also use a spreadsheet to track your findings. If your survey includes open-ended questions, you may want to choose some responses to quote from when you present your results.

ANALYZE your results. After you have tallied up the results, you need to analyze them, looking for patterns that reveal trends and explaining what those trends may mean. Data from survey results do not speak for themselves. You need to analyze the data by looking for similar responses to questions you've asked. Group those that are similar, and label them accordingly. What does that pattern or trend in responses indicate about your research question? When you move from describing the patterns and trends to discussing what they mean, you are interpreting your results. For example, suppose you survey 200 classmates about a recent increase in student fees for using the on-campus fitness center and find that the students, by a significant majority, think the fees are cost-prohibitive. Based on your survey results, your interpretation is that the fee increase is likely to lead to decreased use of the fitness center. You didn't just report the results; you interpreted them as well.

REFLECT on how well the survey worked. When you present your results, be sure to acknowledge any limitations of your survey. What topics were not covered? What populations were not surveyed? Was your sample truly representative?

Information today lives everywhere: in traditional libraries, on the internet, and out "in the field." Your research question and your rhetorical situation—including who will read your research—dictate what kinds of sources you consult and cite. But ultimately, research should be a voyage of discovery, driven by *your* questions based on *your* desire to find out something you didn't know before.

 **REFLECT**

Now that you have thought more about your topic and questions, done some preliminary research, decided on methods, and located some sources, review the types of sources that you've consulted. How did each of those sources help you answer your research question? What other sources do you still need to consult?

TWENTY-SIX

Keeping Track
Managing Information Overload

RESEARCH HAS ALWAYS been a complex, often messy process, but in an age of information overload, it can spiral out of control. Where did you save those notes you took? Did that piece of information come from the book you read or somewhere online? Researchers today have so much information at their fingertips that just managing it has become tough. This chapter aims to help you organize potential chaos by offering tips for keeping track of your sources, taking notes, and maintaining a working bibliography.

Keep Track of Your Sources

The easiest way to keep track of your sources is to save a copy of each one. Especially when your research is spread out over several days or weeks, and when it turns up dozens of potential sources, don't rely on your memory.

Electronic sources. Download and save files, or print them out. Make copies of materials found online, which can change or even disappear: print out what you might use, or take a screenshot and save the image. Some subscription database services let you save, email, or print citations and articles. You might also want to use one of the free online tools, like *Zotero*, *Mendeley*, or *EndNote*, that allow you to organize, store, analyze, and share articles, images, and even audio/video files.

Once you've got copies of your sources, the challenge is to keep them all organized and easy to find. Store all the files for a single project together in one folder, and use a consistent file-naming system so each item is easy to identify. The following example uses the author's last name and keywords from the source's title. All of the sources are saved in a folder under the course title and assignment.

> ENG1102_ResearchProject
> > Ehrenreich_ServingFL
> > Farid_PeriodEquity
> > Kohls_CleanSweep
> > McMillanCottom_NewMoney

You should note the author(s), title, URL, and date of access on each item—and record all the other information needed in a `WORKING BIBLIOGRAPHY`. And be sure to back up your files regularly.

Print sources. Make photocopies, printouts, or scans of everything you think will be useful to your research. Keep a copy of the title and copyright pages of books and of the table of contents or front page of periodicals. Label everything with the author(s), title, and page numbers, and file related materials together in a clearly marked folder.

Take Notes

Experienced researchers have a tip for you: take notes systematically *as you go*. But this doesn't mean you should write down everything; carefully select what details you note to be sure they are pertinent to your project. `ANNOTATING` as you read sources will help you understand and synthesize important information.

Take notes in your own words, and be sure to enclose any words taken directly from a source in quotes. Label anything you `QUOTE`, `PARAPHRASE`, or `SUMMARIZE` as such so that you'll remember to acknowledge and document the original source if you use it—and so that you don't accidentally `PLAGIARIZE`. Consider this example:

> Lyon, G. Reid. "Learning Disabilities." *The Future of Children: Special Education for Children with Disabilities*, vol. 6, no. 1, spring 1996, pp. 54–76. JSTOR, https://doi.org/10.2307/1602494.

Summary: Focuses on problems with reading skills but cautions that early intervention with reading won't address all manifestations of LD.
- Lyon is chief of Child Development and Behavior in the National Institute of Child Health and Human Development at the NIH.
- LD is several overlapping disorders related to reading, language, and math (paraphrase, p. 54).
- Lyon: "[L]earning disability is not a single disorder, but is a general category of special education composed of disabilities in any of seven specific areas: (1) receptive language (listening), (2) expressive language (speaking), (3) basic reading skills, (4) reading comprehension, (5) written expression, (6) mathematics calculation, and (7) mathematical reasoning" (direct quotation, p. 55).

Comment: Lyon breaks down LD into more precise categories. Defines each category. Will help me define LD.

Notice the specific information included in these notes—all details that will help if the researcher decides to reference this article: a full MLA-style citation, a brief summary of the article, and notes about how the source might relate to the research question. And notice, too, that the researcher indicated what's paraphrased and what's quoted from the text, with page numbers in each case. If the researcher does end up citing this source, they'll already have all the necessary documentation information.

Label notes with full citation information—the author(s) and title, publication information, page numbers, and DOI or URL.

SUMMARIZE the main point and any other important points you want to remember in a sentence or two. Be very careful to write your summary using your own words and sentence patterns.

If you copy any passages by hand, take care to do so accurately, paying attention to both words and punctuation and enclosing the entire passage in quotation marks. If you cut and paste any text from electronic sources, put quotation marks around it.

Record your own questions or reactions as you go. Do you see anything that addresses your research question? anything you want to know more about? Consider what role this source might play in your own writing. Does it provide evidence? represent perspectives? show why the topic matters?

Maintain a Working Bibliography

Danielle K. Brown's report includes a works-cited list with twelve sources of various kinds. She might have used the strategies in this chapter to keep it organized. Check out her article on p. 876

It might seem easiest to keep track of only the sources that you know you will cite. But what if your research takes an interesting twist and you need to include some of the sources that you discarded earlier? Rather than having to stop and search for those earlier sources, you could access the source information right away if you keep a working bibliography—a list of all the sources that you consult.

Unlike a final works-cited or reference page, a working bibliography constantly changes as you find more sources to add to it. Keep it on a computer or individual note cards for easy updating. As you update, note for each source whether you have already used it, rejected it, or are still thinking about it. You may even want to annotate your working bibliography with a summary of each source you know you will use. Eventually this information will become your list of works cited or references, so follow whatever DOCUMENTATION style you plan to use. See Chapters 32 and 33 for information on MLA and APA styles.

Consider the working bibliography entries below:

Brueggemann, Brenda. Email interview with the author. 10 July 2025.
> Professor Brueggemann is one of the world's leading scholars in the field of disability studies. This interview focused on the growth of that field.

Ellcessor, Elizabeth. *Restricted Access: Media, Disability, and the Politics of Participation.* New York UP, 2016.
> Drawing on multiple examples from participant observation in blogs and websites, Ellcessor exposes the myth of digital media accessibility to the disabled. Support for my central claim re: "participatory culture"?

WHAT TO PUT IN YOUR WORKING BIBLIOGRAPHY

For books

- Author(s), editors, or translators
- Title
- Edition or volume number
- Publisher, year published

For periodicals

- Author(s)
- Title and subtitle of article
- Name of periodical
- Volume and issue numbers, date
- Page numbers
- URL and date accessed (for online sources)

Additional items for articles accessed via database

- Name of database
- DOI, if there is one, or URL if not

For web sources

- Author(s) and any editors
- Title and subtitle of source
- Name of site
- Date published, posted, or last updated
- Publisher or sponsor of site (if different from name or site)
- Page or paragraph numbers, if any
- URL
- Date accessed

>  **REFLECT**
>
> Review your system for organizing and tracking your sources. Are your sources organized in a way that lets you go back to them easily? Have you recorded the necessary bibliographic information? If you answered "no," take the time now to set up a system that helps you keep track of your sources.

TWENTY-SEVEN

Evaluating Sources

OUR RESEARCH QUESTION: Is it important to address the loss of sea ice in the Arctic? If so, what actions should be taken? To research this topic, rather than merely giving your opinion, you would need to consult reliable sources—that is, sources that can be verified. Which do you trust more: official reports from the National Aeronautics and Space Administration (NASA), the *Wikipedia* page on the issue, or a post on the website *JunkScience.com*? Is it possible that they could all be useful? How will you know?

Your integrity as an author rests to some degree on the quality of the sources you cite. You can probably trust that an article or website recommended by a known expert on your topic is a credible source of information. And sources you find in library catalogs or databases are often vetted for credibility by professionals.

Even so, given the overwhelming amount of information available—not to mention *mis*information—it can be difficult to know which sources will be useful and relevant. Or, as media expert Howard Rheingold puts it, the unending stream of information on the internet calls for some serious "crap detection": we have to know how to separate the credible sources from the questionable ones. This chapter provides advice for determining which sources are well suited to your purposes and for evaluating those sources with a critical eye.

See the ebook for a video example of how we evaluate sources in our everyday lives.

Is the Source Credible and Useful?

A database search turns up fifty articles on your topic. The library catalog shows hundreds. *Google*? Thousands. So how do you decide which sources are reliable and worth your time and careful attention?

To get started, conduct a quick overview; answering a few preliminary questions will help you begin to evaluate the usefulness and reliability of any source:

- *What's the title?* Is it relevant to your topic? Is it serious? ironic or humorous? too good to be true or too extreme? Does the title match the content?
- *Who are the authors?* Are their credentials listed? What institutions are they affiliated with, and how might that affect their viewpoints? What does a quick search of their names reveal about them?
- *Who's the publisher or sponsor?* An academic press? A news organization? A government agency or nonprofit group? If there is an About page, what does it tell you about the publisher? Consider whether the publication or sponsor has a particular agenda or bias.
- *What's the URL?* For online sources, the URL can tell you what kind of organization sponsors the site: ".com" signals commercial organizations; ".edu," colleges and universities; ".org," nonprofits; and ".gov," government agencies.
- *When was it published or updated?* Think about whether your topic calls for current sources or for older historical ones. You may want to consult both, but if your source is on a website, check to see that both the site and its links are still active.
- *What's the genre?* Note especially whether the source is REPORTING information or ARGUING a claim. You'll probably want to look for both, but for those that make an argument, you'll need to identify sources that corroborate your source and/or provide different viewpoints on it.

Practice Lateral Reading

Take a tip from education researcher Sam Wineburg, and don't waste time reading a source online, even after you've conducted a quick overview, until you're sure it's worth your while. Practicing what Wineburg calls

LATERAL READING can help you make this determination. Wineburg and his colleagues have written widely about several studies conducted with undergraduate students, historians, and professional fact-checkers. Asked to determine which of two websites was most credible, among those study participants only the fact-checkers were able to make that determination correctly with any consistency. Why weren't the others? Because the students and historians stayed stuck on the website, looking closely at it and at what it said about itself and assessing its professional "look." But as you know, looks can be deceiving, as can information provided online.

Wineburg says the students and historians were reading "vertically," that is, attending to what was on the website and dutifully scrolling through it—in other words, taking it at its own word(s). The fact-checkers, on the other hand, left the websites in question immediately, opened new tabs, and searched for the title or author or sponsor, and then followed the trail to see what they could find out, based on what others said, about the two sites they were given to compare. They also looked for links leading *to* the sites, not just from them. And—voilà!—they quickly found that one site was legitimate and well respected; the other—not so much.

That's **READING LATERALLY** —moving across the tabs you've opened about a source to investigate it instead of diving into the source itself first. Doing so will help ensure that you spend time digging only into sources that are reputable and thus worth your attention.

Let's say you are conducting preliminary research on climate change and a *Google* search turns up an article titled "On the Linearity of Local and Regional Temperature Changes from 1.5°C to 2°C of Global Warming." You've heard that small temperature increases are significant and the title uses academic language, so this article sounds promising.

Before you read the article itself, however, you open a few new tabs and check out the author and source to make sure they're reliable. Written by seven international scholars, this report is hosted on the American Meteorological Society's page and was published in the *Journal of Climate*. Checking out each author uncovers their individual publishing history and helps verify their expertise. Googling each of the authors' names plus "climate science" further confirms their identities and expertise by uncovering university faculty bios and *Google Scholar* pages listing when their works have been cited by others. You note that the American Meteorological Society's About page says it was established in 1919, has more than 13,000 members, and "is the nation's premier scientific and professional organization

"On the Internet, nobody knows you're a dog."

promoting and disseminating information about the atmospheric, oceanic, and hydrologic sciences." This information paints a picture of a trustworthy source, but don't stop there. Read laterally by opening a new tab to search the society's name and you'll find other trustworthy sources (such as *Forbes* and *JSTOR*) that confirm its mission and stature.

Fact-Check and Triangulate

Those professional fact-checkers who were able to discern reliable from unreliable sources may have worked for one of the fact-checking sites that are available to all writers today: services such as *FactCheck.org*, *PolitiFact*, or *Full Fact*. These sites are easily accessible and easy to use, and while they can, of course, make mistakes, each of them strives for as much objectivity and accuracy as possible. Let them give you a hand in your evaluations.

Checking facts can help you do what social scientists refer to as "triangulation," that is, making sure that you can find sources that corroborate claims

Dan Nott and Scott Cambo write with authority, but graphic essays don't usually document their sources. Read their essay on p. 960, and try verifying some of the facts they present.

made in a source. If a claim or argument is acceptable, then you are sure to find two or three (or more) credible, reputable sources agreeing with it.

Check for Your Own Biases

Remember that you have your own point of view and your own biases (we all do!), and these biases can be silently at work when you are searching for and evaluating sources. Be especially careful, then, to avoid two of the most common of these biases. **CONFIRMATION BIAS** is the tendency to look for and accept information you already agree with—that confirms what you already think—and to reject information that contradicts your beliefs. As mystery writer Louise Penny's Chief Inspector Gamache tells his younger colleagues, "Never believe everything you think." In your search for sources that address climate change in the Arctic, then, make sure that you don't simply gather up the first sources you find that agree with your stance on this issue.

ATTRIBUTION BIAS is another bias common to most of us—the tendency to think that our motivations for believing what we believe are objectively good while thinking that those who we disagree with have objectively wrong motivations. Let's say you find an author writing about loss of sea ice in the Arctic who argues this loss is simply due to "natural variation," and your immediate response is to think "that writer just has his head in the sand and is driven by the need not to know!" That's attribution bias at work. Now, it may well be that the author is indeed ignoring facts, and if so then it's your job to show that's the case, not to dismiss the author for a perceived personality trait ("the need not to know").

Consider Alternative Perspectives

One way to guard against biases—your own as well as those of others—is to consider different perspectives on the topic you are researching, especially those that don't simply confirm what you already think. Looking through bibliographies, footnotes, or abstracts of sources you have already vetted can help you identify alternative viewpoints. The article "On the Linearity of Local and Regional Temperature Changes from 1.5°C to 2.0°C of Global Warming," for example, opens with an abstract containing the keyword "climate change," which links to a list of additional articles on the subject, including one offering a different point of view. And when you check that article, you find that it leads you to yet another take on the subject. Such discoveries are at the heart of the research process—all part of the adventure.

>  **REFLECT**
>
> Read the article titled "The IPCC Report on the Impacts of Climate Change Is Depressing: But Not for the Reasons You Think" on everyonesanauthor.tumblr.com. Underlined words are linked to sources—open a few of these sources and evaluate them, using the questions earlier in this chapter, to determine if they would be credible sources for research on this topic. What are the sources' strengths and weaknesses?

Read Your Sources with a Critical Eye

Once you've determined that a source is credible and useful, you'll need to read it closely, thinking carefully about the author's position, how (and how well) it's supported, and how it affects your understanding of the topic as a whole. As you read your sources, approach each one with a critical eye and practice READING DEFENSIVELY. The following questions can help you do so.

Consider your own RHETORICAL SITUATION. Will the source help you achieve your PURPOSE? Look at the preface, abstract, or table of contents to determine how extensively and directly it addresses your topic. Will your AUDIENCE consider the source reliable and credible? Are they expecting you to cite certain kinds of materials, such as historical documents or academic journals? Does the source confirm what you already believe or expose you to new considerations?

What is the author's STANCE? Does the title indicate a certain attitude or perspective? How would you characterize the TONE? Is it objective? argumentative? sarcastic? How does the author's stance affect its usefulness for your project?

What do you notice about the author's LANGUAGE? What is the level of formality? Does the author favor passive voice? use—or avoid using—first person? What jargon or disciplinary vocabulary does the author use, and why? What languages and/or dialects does the author use, and why?

Who is the AUDIENCE for this work? Is it aimed at the general public? members of a field? policy makers? Sources written for a general audience may provide useful overviews or explanations. Sources aimed at experts may be more authoritative and provide more detail—but they can be challenging to understand.

What is the main point, and what has motivated the author to write? Is the author responding to some other argument? What's the larger conversation on this issue? Is it clear why the topic matters?

What REASONS and EVIDENCE does the author provide as support? Are the reasons fair, relevant, and sound? Is the evidence drawn from credible sources? Is the kind of evidence (statistics, facts, examples, expert testimony, and so on) well matched to the point it's supporting? How persuasive do you find the argument? Check facts and claims you're skeptical of by using nonpartisan sites (*Snopes* and *FactCheck.org*) that confirm truths and identify lies or misinformation.

Does the author acknowledge and respond to other viewpoints? Look for mention of multiple perspectives, not just the author's own view. And be sure to consider how fairly any COUNTERARGUMENTS are represented. The most trustworthy sources represent other views and information fairly and accurately, even (especially) those that challenge their own. Check out the people and ideas cited to be sure they are reliable themselves. The sources and ideas an author is in conversation with can help you uncover more information about the author's own purpose, stance, and bias.

Have you seen ideas given in this source in any other sources? Information found in multiple sources is more reliable than information you can find in only one place. Do other credible sources challenge this information? If so, is what's said in this source controversial, or is it flat-out false? Copy and paste the basics of the questionable statement into a search engine and see what reliable sources say. Even if a search brings up many hits, that doesn't make the information accurate—look for sources you trust to weigh in.

How might you use this source? Source materials can serve a variety of purposes in both your research and your writing. You might consult some sources for background information or to get a sense of the larger context for your topic. Other sources may provide support for your claims—or for

THINK BEYOND WORDS

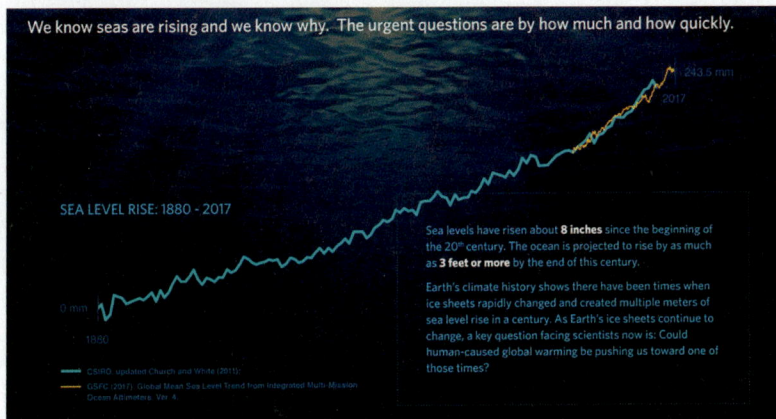

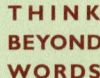 **SUPPOSE YOU'RE RESEARCHING** climate change and come across NASA's site sealevel.nasa.gov. Checking out what others say about the source tells you that NASA stands for "National Aeronautics and Space Administration," and it is an agency of the US government that employs thousands of scientists and publishes information on natural-science topics. If you were writing an essay about how climate change impacts coastal communities, what kinds of information from this site would you consider citing? How does the way information is presented make it seem more or less credible? For instance, compare the site's report "Melting Ice, Warming Ocean" with the infographic shown above. Is one source easier to vet than the other? Does one seem more fitting to cite than the other—and if so, why?

your credibility as an author. Still others will provide other viewpoints, ones that challenge yours or that provoke you to respond. Most of all, they'll give you some sense of what's been said about your topic. Then, in writing up your research, you'll get your chance to say what *you* think—and to add your voice to the conversation.

REFLECT

Choose three or four different sources on your chosen topic—possibly one from a government source, one from an academic journal, one from a popular source, and one from a website. Evaluate each of the sources according to the guidelines laid out in this chapter. Explain what makes each source credible (or not).

TWENTY-EIGHT

Annotating a Bibliography

**NSTRUCTORS ASSIGN ANNOTATED** bibliographies for a variety of reasons: to encourage you to read sources carefully and critically, summarize useful information about them, and think about how and why you expect to use particular ones. The rhetorical purpose of the annotated bibliography is to inform—yourself as well as others. Conscientiously done, annotating a bibliography will help you gain a sense of the larger conversation about your topic and think about how your work fits into that conversation.

In a formal annotated bibliography, you **DESCRIBE** each of the sources you expect to consult and state what role each will play in your research. Sometimes you will be asked to **EVALUATE** sources as well—to assess their strengths and weaknesses in one or two sentences.

Characteristic Features

Annotations should be brief, but they can vary in length from a sentence or two to a few paragraphs. They also vary in terms of style: some are written in complete sentences; others consist of short phrases. And like a works-cited or reference list, an annotated bibliography is arranged in alphabetical order. You'll want to find out exactly what your instructor expects, but most annotated bibliographies include the following features.

Complete bibliographic information, following whatever documentation style you'll use in your essay— MLA , APA , or another style. This information will enable readers to locate your sources—and can also form the basis for your final list of works cited or references.

A brief SUMMARY or DESCRIPTION of each work, noting its topic, scope, and STANCE . If a source reports on research, the research methods may also be important to summarize. Other details you include will depend on your own goals for your project. Whatever you choose to describe, however, be sure that it represents the source accurately and objectively.

Evaluative comments. If you're required to write evaluative annotations, you might consider how AUTHORITATIVE the source is, how up-to-date, whether it addresses multiple perspectives, and so on. Consider both its strengths and its limitations.

Some indication of how each source will inform your research. Explain how you expect to use each source. Does it present a certain perspective you need to consider? report on important new research? include a thorough bibliography that might alert you to other sources? How does each source relate to the others? How does each source contribute to your understanding of the topic and to your research goals? Or if you find that it isn't helpful to your project, explain why you won't use it.

A consistent and concise presentation. Annotations should be consistent: if one is written in complete sentences, they all should be. The amount of information and the way you structure it should also be the same throughout. And that information should be written concisely, summarizing just the main points and key details relevant to your purpose.

Following is a model annotated bibliography with marginal comments that highlight the key features.

An Annotated Bibliography

Nonresistance in the Battle for Freedom
MAGGIE CARSON

Copeman, Jacob. "Violence, Non-violence, and Blood Donation in India." *Journal of the Royal Anthropological Institute*, vol. 14, no. 2, June 2008, pp. 278–96. *RAI*, https://doi.org/10.1111/j.1467-9655.2008.00501.x.

Copeman explores how blood donation in India intersects with ideas of violence and nonviolence, particularly within devotional orders from the *sant* tradition. These groups, committed to the principle of ahimsa (nonviolence), still find themselves indirectly involved in violence by donating blood to soldiers. Copeman shows this tension, explaining how blood donation can be seen as both a form of nonviolent sacrifice and a subtle contribution to military efforts. He also explores the symbolic nature of blood donation, framing it as a modern form of sacrifice in the context of religious and national duty.

One drawback with this source is that it spends more time discussing the blood donors than it does exploring the broader concepts of violence versus nonviolence, which I need to focus on for my project. While the source provides valuable insight into nonviolence from a different cultural perspective, I may not rely on it for citations. Instead, I can use it to broaden my understanding of nonviolence outside the usual framework of revolutionary movements.

MAGGIE CARSON, an international studies major at Dickinson College, wrote this descriptive annotated bibliography for her first-year seminar.

Sidenotes:
- Complete bibliographic information for this source following MLA style.
- Summarizes and describes the source.
- Evaluates the source and explains how this source will inform the project.

Habib, Irfan. "Jallianwala Bagh Massacre: The First Wave of Mass Struggle and Its Aftermath, 1919–26." *Social Scientist*, vol. 47, nos. 5–6, 2019, pp. 3–8. *JSTOR*, https://www.jstor.org/stable/26786184.

> Habib looks into the events leading up to the Jallianwala Bagh Massacre and highlights the impact of World War I on India's revolutionary movements. He points out that India sent over a million soldiers to fight in a war that had little to do with its own interests, leading to about 74,000 deaths. Despite these sacrifices, the country gained very little from Britain's victory, which left many Indians disappointed.
>
> The article also examines the economic hardships of the time, including skyrocketing prices and the devastating influenza outbreak that took millions of lives. Habib critiques the British government's broken promises of political reform, focusing on the oppressive Rowlatt Act, which further fueled public anger. By tracing these tensions, Habib helps us understand why the massacre happened and the mass protests that followed. This article will be a valuable resource for my final project, as it provides important context for the Jallianwala Bagh Massacre and its significance in India's fight for independence.

Komarov, E. N. "Mahatma Gandhi & the Revolution." *India Quarterly*, vol. 26, no. 4, 1970, pp. 368–89. *Sage Journals,* https://doi.org/10.1177/097492847002600404.

> This article covers Mahatma Gandhi's key role in India's fight for independence, focusing on his ability to unite various social classes against British rule. Komarov emphasizes Gandhi's evolving political views, initially rooted in bourgeois nationalism but later influenced by global movements like the Russian revolutions, which inspired his mass mobilization efforts. The article also contrasts two trends in India: the liberal push for reform within British rule and the radical-nationalist demand for complete independence. Gandhi's leadership blended nonviolence with radical nationalism, making his approach unique.
>
> I find this article interesting because it offers a different view of Gandhi, including criticisms and global comparisons that deepen the understanding of his strategies. Komarov's use of historical context makes Gandhi's role clearer, not just within India but in connection with global movements. This perspective will help me add depth to my project, especially when discussing nonviolence and its broader influences.

Includes sources from a range of years, from 1970 to 2019.

Highlights aspects of the source that make it distinctive from the others.

Kuortti, Joel. "'One Thousand Six Hundred and Fifty Rounds': Colonial Violence in the Representations of the Jallianwala Bagh Massacre." *Indialogs*, vol. 1, no. 38, April 2014, pp. 38–50. https://doi.org/10.5565/rev/indialogs.3.

- The article offers a multifaceted analysis of the Amritsar Massacre, emphasizing various perspectives that challenge the often-simplified narratives surrounding this pivotal event in Indian history. By delving into criticisms of Mahatma Gandhi, the authors provide a nuanced examination of his role and the broader sociopolitical landscape of the time. This critical approach distinguishes the article from other literature, as it does not shy away from exploring contentious viewpoints, which contributes to a more comprehensive understanding of the massacre's implications.

  The authors employ a comparative strategy between different historians and scholars. This method allows for a strong analysis of the causes and consequences of the Amritsar Massacre, showing the complexity of historical narratives. This article is interesting because the authors go down many different routes, including criticisms of Gandhi, which is something none of the other articles have. I like their
- strategy of comparing different authors' views to explain the massacre in a more complex way, and I will probably use evidence from this source in my final project.

Nakhre, Amrut. "Meanings of Nonviolence: A Study of Satyagrahi Attitudes." *Journal of Peace Research*, vol. 13, no. 3, 1976, pp. 185–96. *JSTOR*, http://www.jstor.org/stable/423326.

- Amrut Nakhre's article explores the social and psychological aspects of satyagraha, focusing on the experiences of ordinary participants, rather than on Gandhi or its philosophical roots. Through interviews from the Bardoli, Rajkot, and Pardi movements, the study reveals that less-educated satyagrahis viewed nonviolence as a way of life ("creed"), while more educated ones saw it as a tactic. The article shows how true commitment to nonviolence went beyond strategy, influencing practitioners' entire lives. The evidence makes a strong argument for satyagraha, and I plan to use it in my final project on nonviolence.

Each annotation follows the same pattern: summary, evaluation, connection to the larger project.

Explains how the source will be useful in the project.

Evaluates the source, noting its strengths as well as its distinct and helpful perspective.

TWENTY-NINE

Synthesizing Ideas
Moving from What Your Sources Say to What You Say

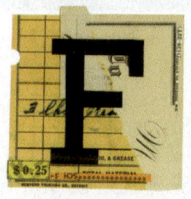"**FRISBEE GOLF, DISC GOLF, FROLF**—whatever you call it, it's a fun and pretty accessible sport that doesn't even require an official course. Grab a frisbee and go to an area that has objects you can use as targets, and you're on your way." This is the opening writer Haines Eason uses to introduce Kansas City's National Public Radio listeners to the "hybrid" sport growing in popularity for locals. Disc golf is a mash-up sport, combining elements of Frisbee and golf, with the objective, as Haines explains it, of "complet[ing] a course, typically consisting of nine or 18 holes, in the fewest number of throws. Each hole has a starting point (tee) and a target (basket or pole hole)." In other words, disc golf and other mash-up sports (think pickle ball) integrate features of different sports into one seamless new experience. In academic terms, the creators of these mashups are engaging in **SYNTHESIS**, bringing together materials from various sources to create something new.

Like any good mash-up artist, you don't just patch together ideas from various sources when you do research. Instead, you synthesize what they say to help you think about and understand the topic you're researching—to identify connections among them and blend them into a coherent whole that at the same time articulates *ideas of your own*. This chapter will help you blend ideas from sources with your own ideas smoothly and effectively—just like a really great mash-up.

Frisbee golf, a new sport created by synthesizing elements of others.

Synthesizing the Ideas in Your Sources

Here are some questions to help you synthesize information as you work with your sources. Try **ANNOTATING** sources with these questions in mind:

- What issues, problems, or controversies do your sources address?
- What else do your sources have in common? Any ideas? facts? examples? statistics? Are any people or works cited in more than one source?
- What significant differences do you find among sources? Different stances? positions? purposes? kinds of evidence? conclusions?
- Do any of your sources cite or refer to one another? Does one source provide details, examples, or explanations that build on something said in another? Does any source respond specifically to something said in another?

Your goal is to get a sense of how the information from your various sources fits together—how the sources speak to one another and what's being said about your topic.

See the ebook for a video on organizing and synthesizing ideas.

One function of a synthesis is to establish **CONTEXT** and set the scene for what *you* have to say. See how the following example, from a scientific article on the effects of extreme weather and climate change, brings together information from four different sources (linked to via superscript numbers) to substantiate the article's claim (and title) that "extreme heat is more dangerous for workers every year."

> Heat-related illness has been recognized as an occupational hazard for decades.[1] Extreme heat conditions are increasing in frequency across the United States, exposing a rising number of workers to conditions that cause injury, illness, and death. For example, during extreme heat events, workers suffer from heat-related illness including heat exhaustion and heat stroke; occupational injuries from high heat exposure such as burns or falls from dizziness; and exacerbation of preexisting conditions such as asthma, kidney disease, or heart disease.[2] These health consequences also have economic impacts, including lost worker productivity, increased health care costs and worker compensation claims, and threats to workers' financial stability from missing work.[3] These risks grow as heat waves spurred by climate change become more frequent, longer lasting, and more intense.[4]
>
> —Jill Rosenthal, Rosa Barrientos-Ferrer & Kate Petosa, "Extreme Heat Is More Dangerous for Workers Every Year"

This article synthesizes critical information to give readers context for what the authors go on to say. For all writers, including you, that's the next step.

> ### REFLECT
>
> Try your hand at synthesizing the sources you've consulted so far for something you're writing. What's being said about your topic? What patterns do you see?

Moving from What Your Sources Say to What You Say

As a researcher, you'll always be working to synthesize the ideas and information you find in your research, to see the big picture and make sense of it all. At the same time, you'll be striving to connect the data you gather to your own ideas and to your research goals. You'll be learning a lot about what many others have discovered or said about your topic, and that will surely affect what you think—and write—about it. Here are some questions that can help you move from the ideas you find in your sources to the ideas that you'll then write about:

- How do the ideas and information in your sources address your RESEARCH QUESTION ? What answers do they give? What information do you find the most relevant, useful, and persuasive?
- How do they support your tentative THESIS ? Do they suggest reasons or ways that you should expand, qualify, or otherwise revise it?
- What viewpoints in your sources do you most agree with? disagree with? Why?
- What conclusions can you draw from the ideas and information you've learned from your sources? What discoveries have you made in studying these sources, and what new ideas have they led you to?

THINK BEYOND WORDS

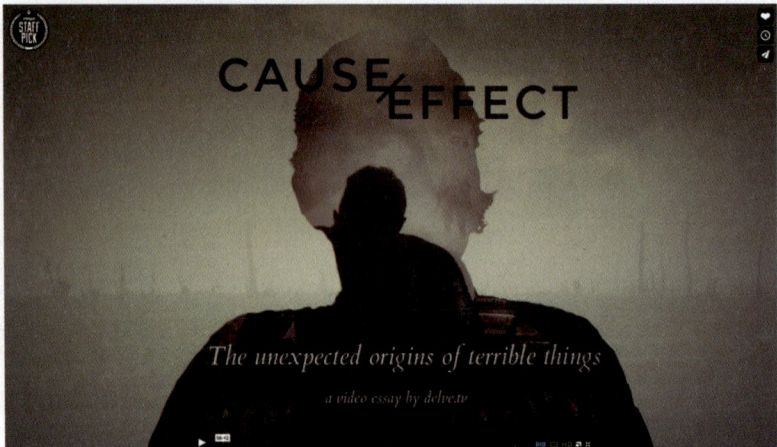

⤴ WATCH Cause / Effect: The Unexpected Origins of Terrible Things, *a video essay by Adam Westbrook that makes a fascinating argument about what caused World War I. (You'll find it at* everyonesanauthor.tumblr.com.) As you'll see, Westbrook synthesizes many kinds of sources and information—history books, maps, cartoons, newspapers, archival photographs and video, data from public records, and more—to build a case for his argument. How does he synthesize all these sources in a video? How does he go about introducing each one and weaving them together with his own ideas?

- Has your research changed your own views on your topic? Do any of your sources raise questions that you can pursue further?
- Have you encountered any ideas that you would like to build on—or challenge?
- From everything you've read, what is the significance of the topic you're researching? Who cares, and why does it matter?

When you work with your sources in this way, you can count on your ideas to grow and change. As we've been saying, research is an act of learning and inquiry, and you never know where it will lead. But as soon as you sit down and write, no matter what you say or how you say it, you will be, as philosopher Kenneth Burke says, "putting in your oar," adding your voice *and your ideas* to the very conversation you've been researching.

Entering the Conversation You've Been Researching

Once you've thought carefully about what others have said about your topic, you can add your own voice to the conversation. Look at the following example from the introduction to an essay tracing the changes in political cartoons in the United States between World War II and the Iraq War. See how the writer synthesized ideas from her research into her writing in a way that set up her own questions and thoughts.

> A cartoon shows carolers at the White House door making a choral argument to then president George W. Bush that "we gotta get out of this place," referring to America's involvement in the war in Iraq (fig. 1). Bush appears completely oblivious to their message.
>
> First published in 2006, this cartoon offered a critique of America's continued presence in Iraq by criticizing the president's actions and attitudes towards the war, exemplifying how political cartoons have long been, and continue to be, a prominent part of wartime propaganda.
>
> Combining eye-catching illustrations with textual critique, such cartoons do more than merely convey messages about current events. Rather, political cartoons serve as a tool for shaping public opinion. In fact, since the 1500s, political cartoons have used satirical critiques to persuade the general public about matters large and small (McCloud 16–17).
>
> In the United States, the political (or editorial) cartoon is a form of editorializing that began as "scurrilous caricatures," according to Stephen Becker, author of *Comic Art in America*. Becker's book looks, in part, at the

Fig. 1. Gary Markstein. Cartoon. *Copley News Service*, 9 Dec. 2006.

See how Judith Newman pairs two seemingly unconnected topics—autism and Apple's personal assistant—when she writes about her autistic son's relationship with Siri on p. 952.

social history of political cartoons and states that it was only after "newspapers and magazines came to be published regularly . . . that caricatures, visual allegories, and the art of design were combined to form . . . modern editorial art" (15). As all-encompassing as that description of "modern editorial art" seems to be, it suggests several questions that remain unanswered: Do cartoonists use common themes to send their critical messages? As society and regulations change from generation to generation, do the style and content of political cartoons change as well? Have political cartoons become "modernized" since World War II? The essay that follows aims to answer as well as draw out the implications of these questions.

—JULIA LANDAUER, "War, Cartoons, and Society: Changes in Political Cartoons between World War II and the Iraq War"

Landauer begins with a cartoon (a primary source) that illustrates a point she is making—that editorial cartoons are known for stinging political critiques. She then refers to a source (McCloud) to provide some background information and then another (Becker) to provide additional commentary on the "modern editorial art" she intends to examine in her essay. At that point, she raises questions "that remain unaddressed"—and says that answering them will be the work of her essay. Thus she uses ideas drawn from her sources to introduce her own ideas—and to weave them all together into a strong introduction for her essay.

In your college writing, you will have the opportunity to come up with a research question, and you will have to dig in and do some research in order to answer it. That digging in will lead you to identify key sources already in conversation about your topic, to read and analyze those sources, and to begin synthesizing them with your own ideas. Before you know it, you won't be just listening in on the conversation: you'll be an active participant in it.

LITERATURE REVIEWS

When instructors refer to "the literature" on a topic, chances are they are not talking about poetry or other literary texts, but they are using an earlier meaning of the term. As early as 1450, "literature" referred to knowledge contained in books or to a body of printed material on any subject. And this meaning of the term continues today, referring to published research on a given topic. In a "literature review," you survey, synthesize, and evaluate that research. You may be assigned to write a full essay reviewing a body of research, or to write a literature review as part of a report on research you've conducted.

Characteristic Features

Survey of relevant research on a focused topic. The "literature" you review should be credible, relevant sources related to your topic. When the choice is yours, a narrow, focused topic is best: a review of literature about colonies and postcolonialism could easily run to dozens of pages or more, whereas a review of what's been said about one particular aspect of those topics would be far easier to manage. For a review that is part of a report, the choice of what literature you review will be guided by your RESEARCH QUESTION and should include all the sources your study is based on. Keep your assignment and particular discipline in mind to determine what kinds and number of sources should be included in your review.

Fair-minded synthesis / summary of the literature. Once you've collected the sources for review, you'll need to `SYNTHESIZE` them, looking for significant connections, trends, and themes, as well as for how the sources agree and disagree with each other. A synthesis of important trends might begin something like this: "Researchers writing about *[topic]* have generally taken one of three perspectives on it," followed by a section discussing each perspective and what it has contributed to understanding of the topic. `SUMMARIZING` the themes and trends shows that you understand how the pieces in your review relate to one another and provides readers with an overview of their significance.

An evaluation of the literature. Your evaluation might point out strengths and weaknesses, as well as any limitations in what the research covers. Are there any important questions that are ignored? claims for which little evidence exists? gaps that future research might address?

Clear organization. To organize your review, think about how the sources relate to one another. Do they follow a clear progression that makes chronological organization most helpful? Do they group by theme? by the authors' perspectives? by research methods? by trends in results? Looking for ways your sources connect with one another will help you not only to synthesize the information but also to organize it in a way that helps readers see significant patterns and trends.

Complete, accurate documentation. Be sure to follow carefully any disciplinary conventions for `CITING` and `DOCUMENTING` sources. For guidelines on following `MLA` or `APA` style, see Chapters 32 and 33.

LITERATURE REVIEW / An Annotated Example

Exploring the Hardships and Stigma Students With Invisible Disabilities Face

KRISTIN PERRY

MORE THAN 42 MILLION Americans are considered to have a severe disability, and 96% of these are hidden (Morgan, 2020). Invisible disabilities are impairments that come with few visual identifiers and are unapparent to an outside observer (Boskovich, 2018). When individuals with invisible disabilities are students, they struggle because they do not receive the help they need to succeed. Many students with invisible disabilities either are not identified as having them or choose not to disclose them because of stigma. This can cause students to be underrepresented in the student body, and it can affect the number of accommodations they receive.

The opening paragraph establishes the research topic and gives background information.

Identifying Students With Invisible Disabilities Is Difficult

Before teachers and schools can do anything to help students with invisible disabilities, they first need to identify these students. This is difficult to do if

Organizes the literature review by topic, with descriptive headings.

KRISTIN PERRY is a student at the University of Maryland, College Park. Perry composed this literature review for her first-year writing course. This review was part of a sequence of assignments that eventually led to a final project: a position paper in which Perry asserted her own arguments about how schools could better support students with invisible disabilities. This literature review helped her develop the knowledge and expertise she relied on to make effective claims in her final paper.

a student is masking, or disguising, their disabilities (Boskovich, 2018). Learning disabilities are the most common hidden disability in education, affecting one out five students, but only a third of those students have been identified (Barto, n.d.). In fact, younger students themselves may not be aware that they have disabilities until they are older, further complicating the task of identifying invisible disabilities (Johnson, 2020). Race and ethnicity tend to complicate the ability of others to identify students possessing disabilities, invisible or not. Asian and Pacific Islander, compared to White, students are underidentified as having an invisible disability and do not receive the proper accommodations (Sullivan et al., 2020). This is because "teachers are less likely to perceive Asian students as having disabilities than they are of students from other racial and ethnic groups" (Sullivan et al., 2020, pp. 451–452). It then puts these students at a disadvantage as teacher referrals are usually the primary way students access special education services.

Stigma Associated With Having an Invisible Disability

Brings together and synthesizes a number of sources.

Throughout history some people have judged or bullied those who are different, and this fact is no different among students with invisible disabilities. One study showed that children with invisible disabilities were two to three times more likely to be bullied than other kids (Adams, 2016). Some people will say "But you don't look disabled" to those with hidden disabilities (United Nations Academic Impact, 2020). Statements like this undermine the struggles people with invisible disabilities face. In higher education, another study found that students who received academic support were stigmatized when they disclosed their invisible disability to faculty and students (Mamboleo et al., 2020). Mamboleo et al. (2020) reported that not only did students with invisible disabilities receive judgment from other students, but the teachers also contributed just as much or even more to these students' stigma. In fact, faculty were found to have exhibited a negative attitude toward students with invisible disabilities. On top of this, in South Korea, for example, 60% of respondents said that there is still discrimination toward students with invisible disabilities (Shin & Choi, 2022). These various forms of stigma cause students to not disclose their invisible disabilities, leaving them at a disadvantage in education.

Students With Invisible Disabilities Are Underrepresented

As I have mentioned before, students who have invisible disabilities are underrepresented in the school and/or disability populations. Shin and Choi (2022) found that the number of students who were identified as having an invisible disability made up only 0.02% of the school population. They further reported that "in 2019, only 1.5% of students receiving special education support were identified as having learning disabilities," which are the most common invisible disability (p. 194). In an article subtitled "But You Don't Look Disabled: Legitimizing Invisible Disabilities," the authors found that even at the college and university levels, students with invisible disabilities were the most marginalized, vulnerable, and excluded groups on campus (United Nations Academic Impact, 2020).

Why Students With Invisible Disabilities Face a Lack of Accommodations

Studies have also shown that students with mild disabilities receive less attention than those with more severe disabilities (Shin & Choi, 2022). Teachers and schools see those with severe disabilities and thus accommodate them more. Many students with invisible disabilities do not receive the accommodations they need and are entitled to. Part of the problem is that even though these disabilities "are legally documented, their invisible nature, along with the stigma sometimes associated with having any disability, keeps many students from requesting the accommodations they need" (Bohanon, 2017). Another problem is that parents of students with invisible disabilities do not know about the accommodations available to their children. Venville et al. (2016) found that many students did not receive accommodations because they did not know how or where to access them, whereas Mamboleo et al. (2020) reported that the main challenges students faced when requesting and utilizing accommodations were a lack of instructor understanding, judgment from other students, and improper facilitation by instructors. These studies point to different reasons for a lack of accommodations but agree that this lack is a problem that needs to be corrected. When students with invisible disabilities are not being identified, are not disclosing their conditions, and are not finding resources, their academic performances and their ability to be accepted socially will continue to be jeopardized.

Topic sentences signal the discussion of research to come.

Conclusion

Experts offer different reasons for the underrepresentation of students with invisible disabilities and different explanations for why these students don't receive proper accommodations. But because students with invisible disabilities are not reaching a level playing field socially or academically, experts agree the problem needs to be fixed. Solutions include creating a more inclusive school environment so students feel safer disclosing their invisible disabilities and providing teachers with greater resources and support to foster these students' continued education and growth.

The conclusion demonstrates Perry's assessment of the literature and the conclusions she's drawing from her sources.

References

Adams, C. (2016, October 19). *10 tips for teaching about invisible disabilities and bullying*. We Are Teachers. https://www.weareteachers.com/10-tips-teaching-invisible-disabilities-bullying/

Barto, A. (n.d.). *The state of learning disabilities: Understanding the 1 in 5*. Learning Disabilities Association of America. Retrieved May 26, 2022, from https://ldaamerica.org/lda_today/the-state-of-learning-disabilities-today/

Bohanon, M. (2017, June 26). Moving beyond stigma to support students with invisible disabilities. *INSIGHT Into Diversity*. https://www.insightintodiversity.com/moving-beyond-stigma-to-support-students-with-invisible-disabilities/

Boskovich, L. (2018, December 18). Invisible disability: Students with invisible disabilities in higher education. *Thompson Policy Institute*. https://blogs.chapman.edu/tpi/2018/12/18/invisible-disability-students-with-invisible-disabilities-in-higher-education/

Johnson, H. M. (2020, March 24). Students with invisible disabilities in higher education. Welcome to the Scholarly Open Access Repository at the University of Southern Indiana, 24 Mar. 2020, https://soar.usi.edu/handle/20.500.12419/576

Mamboleo, G., Dong, S., Anderson, S., & Molder, A. (2020). Accommodation experience: Challenges and facilitators of requesting and implementing accommodations among college students with disabilities. *Journal of Vocational Rehabilitation, 53*(1), 43–54. https://doi.org/10.3233/JVR-201084

Morgan, P. (2020, March 20). Invisible disabilities: Break down the barriers. *Forbes.* https://www.forbes.com/sites/paulamorgan/2020/03/20/invisible-disabilities-break-down-the-barriers/?sh=556ce4affa50

Shin, M., & Choi, N. (2022). The invisible population of students with learning disabilities in South Korea. *Intervention in School and Clinic, 57*(3), 194–197. https://doi.org/10.1177/10534512211014883

Sullivan, A. L., Kulkarni, T., & Chhuon, V. (2020). Making visible the invisible: Multistudy investigation of disproportionate special education identification of U.S. Asian American and Pacific Islander Students. *Exceptional Children, 86*(4), 449–467. https://doi.org/10.1177/0014402920905548

United Nations Academic Impact. (2020, December 14). *Disability and higher education: "But you don't look disabled": Legitimizing invisible disabilities.* https://www.un.org/en/academic-impact/%E2%80%9Cyou-don%E2%80%99took-disabled-legitimizing-invisible-disabilities

Venville, A., Mealings, M., Ennals, P., Oates, J., Fossey, E., Douglas, J., & Bigby, C. (2016). Supporting students with invisible disabilities: Scoping review of postsecondary education for students with mental illness or an acquired brain injury. *International Journal of Disability, Development and Education, 63*(6), 571–592. https://doi.org/10.1080/1034912X.2016.1153050

THIRTY

Quoting, Paraphrasing, Summarizing

WHEN YOU'RE TEXTING or talking with friends, you don't usually need to be explicit about where you got your information; your friends trust what you say because they know you. In academic writing, however, it's important to establish your credibility, and one way to do so is by consulting authoritative sources. Doing so shows that you've done your homework on your topic, gives credit to those whose ideas you've relied on, and helps demonstrate your own authority as an author.

Your challenge in much academic writing is to integrate other voices with your own. How do you let your audience hear from expert sources while ensuring that their words don't eclipse yours? How do you pick and choose brief segments from long passages of text—or condense those passages into much briefer statements—without misrepresenting someone's ideas? How do you then introduce these segments and integrate them with your own words and ideas? This chapter provides guidelines on three ways you can incorporate sources into your writing: quoting, paraphrasing, and summarizing.

A **QUOTATION** consists of someone's exact words, enclosed in quotation marks or set off as a block from the rest of your text. A **PARAPHRASE** includes the details of a passage in your own words and syntax. A **SUMMARY** briefly captures the points of a passage that are important to your purpose, leaving out the other details.

Deciding Whether to Quote, Paraphrase, or Summarize

QUOTE

- Something that is said so well that it's worth repeating word for word
- Complex ideas that are expressed so clearly that paraphrasing or summarizing could distort or oversimplify them
- Experts whose opinions and exact words help to establish your own **CREDIBILITY** and **AUTHORITY** to write on the topic
- Passages that you yourself are analyzing
- Those who disagree or offer **COUNTERARGUMENTS** —quoting their exact words is a way to be sure you represent their opinions fairly

PARAPHRASE

- Passages where the details matter, but not the exact words
- Passages that are either too technical or too complicated for your readers to understand

SUMMARIZE

- Lengthy passages when the main point is important to your argument but the details are not

Whatever method you use for incorporating the words and ideas of others into your own writing, be sure that they support what *you* want to say. You're the author—and whatever your sources say needs to connect to what you say—so be sure to make that connection clear. Don't assume that sources speak for themselves. Introduce any source that you cite, naming the authors and identifying them in some way if your audience won't know who they are. In addition, be sure to follow quotations with a comment that explains how they relate to your point.

And regardless of whether you decide to quote, paraphrase, or summarize, you'll need to credit each source. Even if what you include is not a direct quotation, the ideas are still someone else's, and failing to credit your source can result in PLAGIARISM. Indicate the source in a SIGNAL PHRASE and include in-text documentation.

Quoting

When you include a direct quotation, use the exact words of the original source. And while you don't want to include too many quotations—you are the author, after all—using the exact words from a source is sometimes the best way to ensure that you accurately represent what was said. Original quotations can also be an effective way of presenting a point, by letting other people speak in their own words. But be sure to frame any quotation you include, introducing it and then explaining why it's important to the point that you are making.

Enclose short quotations in quotation marks within your main text. Such quotations should be no longer than four typed lines (in MLA style) or forty words (in APA style).

> Programmer and digital media pioneer Jaron Lanier describes the problems resulting from "lock-in" (in which software becomes difficult to change because it has been engineered to work with existing programs), arguing that lock-in "is an absolute tyrant in the digital world" (8). He means that "lock-in" inhibits creativity as new development is constrained by old software.

30 ⁂ Quoting, Paraphrasing, Summarizing

In MLA style, short quotations of poetry—no more than three lines—should also be enclosed in quotation marks within the main text. Include slashes (with a space on either side) between each line of verse.

> In "When You Are Old," poet William Butler Yeats advises Maud Gonne, the radical Irish nationalist, that when she looks back on her youth from old age, she should consider "How many loved your moments of glad grace, / And loved your beauty with love false or true, / But one man loved the pilgrim soul in you" (lines 5-7). Yeats thus suggests that he is the "one man" who truly loved her so sincerely all these years.

Set off long quotations as a block by indenting them from the left margin. No need to enclose them in quotation marks, but do indent five spaces (or one-half inch) if you are using either MLA or APA style. Use this method for quotations that are more than four lines of prose or three lines of poetry (in MLA) or longer than forty words (in APA).

> In her often-quoted 1976 keynote address to the Democratic National Convention, Texas congresswoman Barbara Jordan reflects on the occasion:
>
>> Now that I have this grand distinction, what in the world am I supposed to say? . . . I could list the problems which cause people to feel cynical, angry, frustrated: problems which include lack of integrity in government; the feeling that the individual no longer counts; the reality of material and spiritual poverty; the feeling that the grand American experiment is failing or has failed. I could recite these problems, and then I could sit down and offer no solutions. But I don't choose to do that either. The citizens of America expect more. (189)
>
> In this passage, Jordan resists the opportunity to attack the opposing party, preferring instead to offer positive solutions rather than simply a list of criticisms and problems.

Go to <u>every onesanauthor .tumblr.com</u> to listen to the full text of Barbara Jordan's speech.

Notice that with block quotations, the parenthetical citation falls *after* the period at the end of the quotation.

Indicate changes to the text within a quotation by using brackets to enclose text that you add or change and ellipses to indicate text that you omit.

Use brackets to indicate that you have altered the original wording to fit grammatically within your text or have added or changed wording to clarify something that might otherwise be unclear. In this example, the author inserted the topic being discussed for clarification:

> Syracuse professor and literacy scholar Marcelle Haddix makes the point that in the field of teacher education, the idea of "social justice" is now being used as a buzzword instead of engaged with as a serious concept. And many agree with Haddix. For example, education professor April Baker-Bell responds: "No doubt! I think this is an important critique [of teacher education]" (*Linguistic Justice* 7).

Use ellipsis marks in place of words, phrases, or sentences that you leave out because they aren't crucial or relevant for your purpose. Use three dots, with a space before each one and after the last, when you omit only words and phrases within a sentence. If you leave out the end of a sentence or a whole sentence or more, put a period after the last word before the ellipsis mark. Note how a writer does both in the example below.

> Warning of the effects of GPS on our relationship to the world around us, Nicholas Carr concludes that "the automation of wayfinding . . . encourages us to observe and manipulate symbols on screens rather than attend to real things in real places. . . . What we should be asking ourselves is, *How far from the world do we want to retreat?*" (137).

When you use brackets or ellipses, make sure your changes don't end up misrepresenting the author's original point, which would damage your own credibility. Mark Twain once joked that "nearly any invented quotation, played with confidence, stands a good chance to deceive." Twain was probably right—it's quite easy to "invent" quotations or twist their meaning by taking them out of context or changing some keyword. You don't want to be guilty of this!

Set off a quotation within a quotation with single quotation marks. In the following passage, the author quotes Nicholas Carr, who himself quotes the writing of anthropologist Tim Ingold:

Nicholas Carr sums up the difference between navigating with and without a GPS device using two terms borrowed from Scottish anthropologist Tim Ingold. As Carr explains, Ingold "draws a distinction between two very different modes of travel: wayfaring and transport. Wayfaring, [Ingold] explains, is 'our most fundamental way of being in the world'" (132). Wayfaring means navigating by our observations and mental maps of the world around us, as opposed to blindly following GPS-generated directions from point A to point B—the mode Ingold and Carr call "transport."

Punctuate quotations carefully. Parenthetical documentation comes after the closing quotation mark, and any punctuation that is part of your sentence comes after the parentheses (except in the case of a block quote, where the parenthetical documentation goes at the very end).

- *Commas and periods* always go inside the closing quotation marks. If there's parenthetical documentation, however, the period goes after the parentheses.

    "Watch your mind," said Joy Harjo, the first Native American US poet laureate, in a 2021 commencement address. "Without training it might run away and leave your heart for the immense human feast set by the thieves of time" (3).

- *Colons and semicolons* always go outside closing quotation marks.

    David Foster Wallace warned as well that there are "whole, large parts of adult American life that nobody talks about in commencement speeches": sometimes, he says, we'll be bored (4).

    He also once noted that when a lobster is put in a kettle of boiling water, it "behaves very much as you or I would behave if we were plunged into boiling water"; in other words, it acts as if it's in terrible pain (10).

- *Question marks and exclamation points* go inside closing quotation marks if they are part of the original quotation, but outside the quotation marks if they are part of your sentence.

> When you include dialogue, the same conventions of quoting apply. Dana Canedy, recounting a difficult conversation with her 8-year-old son, uses quotes. See how she did it on p. 883.

Wallace opened his speech with a now famous joke about how natural it is to be unaware of the world: an old fish swims by two young fish and says, "Morning, boys. How's the water?" They swim on, and after a while one young fish turns to the other and asks, "What the hell is water?" (1).

So what, according to David Foster Wallace, is the "capital-T Truth . . . about life" (9)?

Paraphrasing

When you paraphrase, you restate information or ideas from a source using your words, your sentence structure, your style. A paraphrase should cover the same points that the original source does, so it's usually about the same length—but sticking too closely to the sentence structures in your source could be plagiarizing. And even though you're using your own words, don't forget where the ideas came from: you should always name the author and include parenthetical documentation.

Here is a paragraph about the search for other life-forms similar to our own in the universe, followed by three paraphrases.

Original source

As the romance of manned space exploration has waned, the drive today is to find our living, thinking counterparts in the universe. For all the excitement, however, the search betrays a profound melancholy—a lonely species in a merciless universe anxiously awaits an answering voice amid utter silence. That silence is maddening. Not just because it compounds our feeling of cosmic isolation, but because it makes no sense. As we inevitably find more and more exo-planets where intelligent life *can* exist, why have we found no evidence—no signals, no radio waves—that intelligent life *does* exist?

—CHARLES KRAUTHAMMER, "Are We Alone in the Universe?"

As the underlined words show, the following paraphrase uses too many words from the original.

Unacceptable paraphrase: wording too close to the original

Charles Krauthammer argues that finding our intelligent counterparts in the universe has become more important as the romance of manned space exploration has declined. Even so, the hunt for similar beings also suggests our sadness as a species waiting in vain for an acknowledgment that we aren't alone in <u>a merciless universe</u>. The lack of response, he says, just doesn't make sense because if we keep finding planets that *could* support life, then we should find evidence—like <u>radio waves or signals</u>—of intelligent life out there (A19).

While the next version uses original language, the sentence structures are much too similar to the original.

Unacceptable paraphrase: sentence structures too close to original

As the allure of adventuring into the unknown cosmos has diminished, the desire to discover beings like us out there has grown. There is a sadness to the search though—the calling out into empty space that brings no response. Nothing. Only a vast silence that not only emphasizes our solitary existence but increases our frustration. How can we continue to discover potentially hospitable planets that could sustain life like ours, yet find no evidence—no signs, no data—that such life exists (Krauthammer A19)?

When you paraphrase, be careful not to simply substitute words and phrases while replicating the same sentence structure. And while it may be necessary to use some of the key terms from the original in order to convey the same concepts, be sure to put them in quotation marks—and not to use too many (which would result in plagiarism).

Acceptable paraphrase

Syndicated columnist Charles Krauthammer observes that our current quest to discover other "intelligent life" in the universe comes just as the allure of exploring outer space is dimming. It's a search, he says, that reveals a deep sadness (that we may in fact be living in "cosmic isolation") and a growing frustration: if scientists continue to discover more planets where life like ours can be sustainable, why do we find no actual signs of life (A19)?

Summarizing

Like a paraphrase, a summary presents the source information in your words. However, a summary dramatically condenses the information, covering only the most important points and leaving out the details.

Summaries are therefore much briefer than the original texts, though they vary in length depending on the size of the original and your purpose for summarizing; you may need only a sentence or two to summarize an essay, or you may need several paragraphs. In any case, you should always name the author and document the source. The following example appropriately summarizes Krauthammer's passage in one sentence:

> Charles Krauthammer questions whether we will ever find other "intelligent life" in the universe—or whether we'll instead discover that we do in fact live in "cosmic isolation" (A19).

This summary tells readers Krauthammer's main point and includes in quotation marks two key phrases borrowed from the original source. If we were to work the summary into an essay, it might look like this:

> Many scientists believe that there is a strong probability—given the vastness of the universe and how much of it we have yet to explore, even with advances like the Hubble telescope—that there is life like ours somewhere out there. In a 2011 opinion piece, however, syndicated columnist Charles Krauthammer questions whether we will ever find other "intelligent life" in the universe—or whether we'll instead discover that we do in fact live in "cosmic isolation" (A19).

Three ways a summary can go wrong are if it inaccurately represents the point of the original source, provides so many details that the summary is too long, or is so general that readers are left wondering what the source is about. Consider the following unsuccessful summaries of Krauthammer's passage:

Unacceptable summary: misrepresents the source

> Pulitzer Prize–winning columnist Charles Krauthammer extols the virtues of space exploration.

This summary both misses the point of Krauthammer's questioning our troubled search for "intelligent life" beyond Earth and claims that the author praises space exploration when at no point in the passage does he do so.

Unacceptable summary: provides too many details

Award-winning columnist Charles Krauthammer suggests that while sending people into space is no longer as exciting to us as it once was, we are interested in finding out if there is life in the universe beyond Earth. He laments the feeling of being alone in the universe given that all signs point to the very real possibility that intelligent life exists elsewhere. Krauthammer wonders "why we have no evidence . . . of intelligent life" on other habitable planets. He finds this lack of proof confounding.

This summary is almost a long as the original passage and includes as many details. As a summary, it doesn't let readers know what points are most important.

Unacceptable summary: too general

Charles Krauthammer is concerned about the search for life on other planets.

While the statement above is not false, it does not adequately reflect Krauthammer's main point in a way that will help the reader get the gist of the original passage. A better summary would tell readers what precisely about the search for life concerns Krauthammer.

 **REFLECT**

Return to the quotation from Barbara Jordan on page 557. First, write an appropriate paraphrase of the quotation; then write an appropriate summary.

Incorporating Source Material

Whether you quote, paraphrase, or summarize source material, you need to be careful to distinguish what you say from what your sources say, while at the same time weaving the two together smoothly in your writing. That is, you must make clear how the ideas you're quoting, paraphrasing, or summarizing relate to your own—why you're bringing them into your text.

See the ebook for a video on introducing and explaining quotations.

> Jeff Gage includes direct quotes from country music artists, and he varies the signal verbs and their placement. Take a look at how he does it on p. 899.

Use signal phrases to introduce source materials, telling readers who said what and providing some context if need be. Don't just drop in a quotation or paraphrase or summary; you need to introduce it. And while you can always use a neutral signal phrase such as "the author says" or "the author claims," try to choose verbs that reflect the **STANCE** of those you're citing. In some cases, a simple "says" does reflect that stance, but usually you can make your writing livelier and more accurate with a more specific signal verb.

Use a **SIGNAL PHRASE** and parenthetical documentation to clearly distinguish your own words and ideas from those of others. The following paraphrase introduces source material with a signal phrase that includes the author's name and closes with documentation giving the page number from which the information is taken.

> As Ernst Mayr explains, Darwin's theory of evolution presented a significant challenge to then prevalent beliefs about humanity's centrality in the world (9).

If you do not give the author's name in a signal phrase, include it in the parenthetical documentation.

> Darwin's theory of evolution presented a significant challenge to then prevalent beliefs about humanity's centrality in the world (Mayr 9).

Sometimes you'll want or need to state the author's authority or credentials in the signal phrase, lending credibility to your own use of that source.

> According to music historian Ted Gioia, record sales declined sharply during the Great Depression, dropping by almost 90 percent between 1927 and 1932 (127).

Choose verbs that reflect the author's stance toward the material—or your own stance in including it. Saying "she notes" means something different than saying "she insists" or "she implies."

> Because almost anyone can create a blog, most people assume that blogs give average citizens a greater voice in public dialogue. Political scientist Matthew Hindman questions this assumption: "Though millions of Americans now maintain a blog, only a few dozen political bloggers get as many readers as a typical college newspaper" (103).

Signal phrases do not have to come first. To add variety to your writing, try positioning them in the middle or at the end of a sentence.

"Attracting attention," observes Richard Lanham, "is what style is all about" (xi).

"Hard work beats talent," warns Kevin Durant, "when talent fails to work hard."

SOME USEFUL SIGNAL VERBS

acknowledges	concludes	observes
adds	declares	reports
asserts	implies	responds
claims	objects	suggests

See the ebook for a video on understanding signal phrases.

Verb tenses. The verb tense you use when referring to a text or researcher in a signal phrase will depend on your documentation style. MLA style requires the present tense ("argues") or the present perfect ("has argued"). Using MLA style, you might write, "In *Rhetoric*, Aristotle argues" or "In commenting on Aristotle's *Rhetoric*, scholars have argued." An exception involves sentences that include specific dates in the past. In this case, use the past tense: "In his introduction to the 1960 edition of Aristotle's *Rhetoric*, Lane Cooper argued."

The past tense is conventional in APA style. The present perfect is conventional when referring to an ongoing action that started in the past or to something that didn't occur at a specific time. You might write, "Anderson (1988) argued" or "In commenting on Aristotle's *Rhetoric*, scholars have argued." However, use the present tense when you refer to the results of a study ("the results of Conrad (2012) demonstrate") or when you make a generalization ("writing researchers agree").

Parenthetical documentation. If you're following MLA, you'll need to include page numbers for all quotations, paraphrases, and summaries from print sources in your parenthetical documentation. If you're using APA, page numbers are required for quotations; for paraphrases and summaries, they're optional—but it's always a good idea to include them whenever you can do so.

Incorporating Visual and Audio Sources

Sometimes you will want to incorporate visual or audio elements from sources that you cannot write into a paragraph. For example, you may include charts, photographs, or audio/video clips. Remember that any such materials that come from sources need to be introduced, explained, and documented just as you would a quotation. If you're following MLA or APA style, refer to Chapters 32 and 33 for specific requirements.

Tables. Label anything that contains facts or figures displayed in columns as a table. Number all tables in sequence, and provide a descriptive title for each one. Supply source information immediately below the table; credit your data source even if you've created the table yourself. If any information within the table requires further explanation (abbreviations, for example), include a note below the source citation.

Figures. Number and label everything that is not a table (photos, graphs, drawings, maps, and so on) as a figure and include a caption letting readers know what the image illustrates. Unless the visual is a photograph or drawing you created yourself, provide appropriate source information after the caption; graphs, maps, and other figures you produce based on information from other sources should still include a full credit. If the visual is referenced within your text, you can use an abbreviated citation and include full documentation in your list of WORKS CITED or REFERENCES.

Audio and video recordings. If your medium allows it, provide a link to any recorded element or embed a media player into the text. If you're working in a medium that won't allow linking or embedding, discuss the recording in your text and provide a full citation in your list of WORKS CITED or REFERENCES so your readers can track down the recording themselves.

Captions. Create a clear, succinct caption for each visual or recording: "Fig. 1. The Guggenheim Museum, Spain." The caption should identify and explain the visual—and should reflect your purpose. In an essay about contemporary architecture in Spain, your caption might say "Fig. 1. The Guggenheim Museum, Bilbao. Designed by Frank Gehry."

Sizing and positioning visuals and recordings. Refer to every visual or embedded recording in your text: "(see fig. 1)," "as shown in Table 3," "in the *YouTube* video below." The element may be on the page where it's discussed, but it should not come before you introduce it to your readers. Think carefully about how you will size and position each visual to be most effective: you want to make sure that your visuals are legible and that they support rather than disrupt the text.

Fig. 1. The Guggenheim Museum, Spain.

THIRTY-ONE

Giving Credit, Avoiding Plagiarism

WHO OWNS WORDS AND IDEAS? Answers to this question differ from culture to culture. In some societies, they are shared resources, not the property of individuals. In others, using another person's words or ideas may be seen as a tribute or compliment that doesn't require specific acknowledgment. In the United States, however (as in much of the Western world), elaborate systems of copyright and patent law have grown to protect the intellectual property (including words, images, voices, and ideas) of individuals and corporations. This system forms the foundation of the documentation conventions currently followed in US schools. And while these conventions are being challenged today by the open-source movement and others who argue that "information wants to be free," the conventions still hold sway in the academy and in the law. As a researcher, you will need to understand these conventions and to practice them in your own writing. Put simply, these conventions allow you to give credit where credit is due and thereby avoid **PLAGIARISM** (the use of the words and ideas of others as if they were your own work).

But acknowledging your sources is not simply about avoiding charges of plagiarism (although you would be doing that too). It also helps establish your own **CREDIBILITY** as a researcher and an author. It shows that you have consulted other sources of information about your topic and can engage with them in your own work. In addition, citing your sources acknowledges and honors the hard work of the person(s) who created the source. Finally, citing and documenting your sources allows readers to locate them for their own purposes if they wish; in effect, it anticipates the needs of your audience.

There are some cases, however, in which you do not need to provide citations for information that you incorporate—for example, if the information is common knowledge. This chapter will help you identify which sources you must acknowledge, explain the basics of documenting your sources, and provide strategies for avoiding plagiarism.

Knowing What You Must Acknowledge

As a general rule, material taken from specific outside sources—whether ideas, texts, images, or sounds—should be CITED and DOCUMENTED.

INFORMATION THAT MUST BE ACKNOWLEDGED

- *Direct quotations, paraphrases, and summaries.* Exact wording should always be enclosed in quotation marks and cited. And always cite specific ideas taken from another source, even when you present them using your own words.

- *Controversial information.* If there is some debate over the information you're including, cite the source so readers know whose version or interpretation of the facts you're using. You may not always know whether information in a source is controversial, which is another reason to READ LATERALLY and check out what others have to say about the information.

- *Information given in only a few sources.* If only one or two sources make this information available (that is, it isn't common knowledge widely accessible in general sources), include a citation.

- *Any materials that you did not create yourself—including tables, charts, images, and audio or video segments.* Even if you create a table or chart yourself, if it presents information from an outside source, that's someone else's work that needs to be acknowledged.

- *Material generated by AI tools.* While AI products are not "sources," if you use information from an AI platform, you should indicate that you did so by stating which AI platform or model you used (e.g.,

ChatGPT or *Gemini*) and providing a footnote or a link to the conversation. See models for how to cite AI-generated material in MLA (p. 587) and APA style (p. 642).

A word to the wise: it's always better to cite any information that you've taken from another source than to guess wrong and unintentionally plagiarize. And a second word to the wise: it's an ethical practice to contact social media users and ask permission to use and cite their work. Remember, though, that there are exceptions to all rules, and so there are some times when acknowledging a source is not necessary.

INFORMATION THAT DOES NOT NEED TO BE ACKNOWLEDGED

- *Information that is "common knowledge."* Uncontroversial information ("People today get most of their news and information from the internet"), well-known historical events ("Neil Armstrong was the first person to walk on the moon"), facts ("All mammals are warm-blooded"), and quotations (Armstrong's "That's one small step for man, one giant leap for mankind") that are widely available in general reference sources do not need to be cited.

- *Information well known to your audience.* Keep in mind that what is common knowledge varies depending on your audience. While an audience of pulmonary oncologists would be familiar with the names of researchers who established that smoking is linked to lung cancer, for a general audience you might need to cite a source if you give the names.

- *Information from well-known, easily accessible documents.* You do not need to include the specific location where you accessed texts that are available from a variety of public sources and are widely familiar, such as the United States Constitution.

- *Your own work.* If you've gathered data, come up with an idea, or generated a text (including images, multimedia texts, and so on) entirely on your own, you should indicate that to your readers in some way—but it's not necessary to include a formal citation, unless the material has been previously published elsewhere.

Just remember: when in doubt, err on the safe side and include a citation.

In discussing language and popular media, César Albarrán-Torres mentions many movies and TV shows, as well as articles discussing them. What information does he include in his works-cited list? What's not cited? Take a look at his essay on p. 838.

Fair Use and the Internet

In general, principles of fair use apply to the writing you do for your college classes. These principles allow you to use passages and images from the copyrighted work of others without their explicit permission as long as you do so for educational purposes and you fully cite what you use. When you publish your writing online, however, where that material can be seen by all, then you must have permission from the copyright owner in order to post it.

Students across the country have learned about this limitation on fair use the hard way. One student we know won a prize for an essay she wrote, which was then posted on the writing prize website. In the essay, she included a cartoon that was copyrighted by the cartoonist. Soon after the essay was posted, she received a letter from the copyright holder, demanding that she remove the image and threatening her with a lawsuit. Another student, whose essay was published on a class website, was stunned when his instructor got an angry email from a professor at another university, saying that the student writer had used too much of her work in the essay and that, furthermore, it had not been fully and properly cited. The student, who had intended no dishonesty at all, was embarrassed, to say the least.

Many legal scholars and activists believe that fair-use policies and laws should be relaxed and that making these laws more restrictive undermines creativity. While these issues get debated in public forums and legal courts, however, you are well advised to be careful not only in citing and documenting all your sources thoroughly but in getting permission in writing to use any copyrighted text or image in anything you plan to post or publish online.

Avoiding Plagiarism

In US academic culture, incorporating the words, ideas, or materials of others into your own work without giving credit through appropriate citations and documentation is viewed as unethical and is considered plagiarism. The consequences of such unacknowledged borrowing are serious: students who plagiarize may receive failing grades for assignments or courses, be subjected to an administrative review for academic misconduct, or even be dismissed from school.

See the ebook for a video on understanding plagiarism.

Certainly, the deliberate and obvious effort to pass off someone else's work as your own, such as by handing in a paper purchased online or written by someone else, is plagiarism and can easily be spotted and punished. More troublesome and problematic, however, is the difficulty some students have using the words and ideas of others fairly and acknowledging them fully. Especially when you're new to a field or writing about unfamiliar ideas, incorporating sources without plagiarizing can be challenging.

In fact, researcher Rebecca Moore Howard has found that even expert writers have difficulty incorporating the words and ideas of others acceptably when they are working with material outside their comfort zone or field of expertise. Such difficulty can often lead to what Howard calls **PATCHWRITING**: restating material from sources in ways that stick too closely to the original language or syntax.

But patchwriting can help you work with sources. Some call patchwriting plagiarism, even when it's documented, but we believe that it can be a step in the process of learning how to weave the words and thoughts of others into your own work. Assume, for example, that you want to summarize ideas from the following passage:

> Over the past few decades, scholars from a variety of disciplines have devoted considerable attention toward studying evolving public attitudes toward a whole range of LGBT civil rights issues including support for open service in the military, same-sex parent adoption, employment non-discrimination, civil unions, and marriage equality. In the last 10 years in particular, the emphasis has shifted toward studying the various factors that best explain variation in support for same-sex marriage including demographic considerations, religious and ideological predispositions, attitudes toward marriage and family, and social contact (Baunach, 2011, 2012; Becker, 2012a, 2012b; Becker & Scheufele, 2009, 2011; Becker & Todd, 2013; Brewer, 2008; Brewer & Wilcox, 2005; Lewis, 2005, 2011; Lewis & Gossett, 2008; Lewis & Oh, 2008).
> —AMY BECKER, "Employment Discrimination, Local School Boards, and LGBT Civil Rights: Reviewing 25 Years of Public Opinion Data"

This passage includes a lot of detailed information in complex sentences that can be hard to process. See how one student first summarized it, and why this summary would be unacceptable in an essay of his own:

A patchwritten summary

For more than 20 years, scholars from many disciplines have committed their energies to examining changing public attitudes toward a variety of LGBT civil rights issues. These encompass things like open military service, same-sex parent adoption, equal employment opportunities, civil unions, and marriage equality. Since 2004, focus has moved toward examining those elements that best account for differences in public support for same-sex marriage like demographic considerations, religious and ideological predispositions, attitudes toward marriage and family, and social contact (Baunach, 2011, 2012; Becker, 2012a, 2012b; Becker & Scheufele, 2009, 2011; Becker & Todd, 2013; Brewer, 2008; Brewer & Wilcox, 2005; Lewis, 2005, 2011; Lewis & Gossett, 2008; Lewis & Oh, 2008).

This is a classic case of patchwriting that would be considered plagiarism. The sentence structure looks very much like Becker's, and even some of the language is taken straight from the original article. While such a summary would not be acceptable in any writing you turn in, this sort of patchwriting can help you understand what a difficult source is saying.

And once you understand the source, writing an acceptable summary gets a lot easier. In the acceptable summary below, the writer focuses on the ideas in the long second sentence of the original passage, turning those ideas into two simpler sentences and using a direct quotation from the original.

See Ch. 7 in the ebook for a video on summarizing for reading comprehension.

Acceptable summary

Scholars studying changes in public opinion on LGBT issues have increasingly focused on the growing support for same-sex marriage. In looking at the question of why opinions on this issue differ, these scholars have considered factors such as "demographic considerations, religious and ideological predispositions, attitudes toward marriage and family, and social contact" (Becker 342).

An acceptable summary uses the writer's own language and sentence structures, and quotation marks to indicate any borrowed language. To write a summary like this one, you would need to be able to restate the source's main point (that same-sex marriage has gotten greater scholarly attention lately than other LGBTQ issues) and decide what information is most important for your purposes—what details are worth emphasizing with a quotation or a longer summary. Finally, notice that the citation credits Becker's article, because that is the source this writer consulted, not the research Becker cites. Chapter 30 offers you more guidelines on QUOTING, PARAPHRASING, and SUMMARIZING appropriately.

STEPS YOU CAN TAKE TO AVOID PLAGIARISM

Understand what constitutes plagiarism. Plagiarism includes any unacknowledged use of material from another source that isn't considered common knowledge; this includes phrases, ideas, and materials such as graphs, charts, images, videos, and so on. In a written text, it includes neglecting to put someone else's exact wording in quotation marks; leaving out in-text documentation for sources that you QUOTE, PARAPHRASE, or SUMMARIZE; and borrowing too many of the original sources' words or sentence structures in paraphrases or summaries. Check to see if your school has any explicit guidelines for what constitutes plagiarism. Plagiarism also includes using material generated by AI tools without acknowledgment.

Take notes carefully and conscientiously. If you can't locate the source of words or ideas that you've copied down, you may neglect to cite them properly. Technology makes it easy to copy and paste text and materials from electronic sources directly into your own work—and then to move on and forget to put such material in quotation marks or record the source. So keep copies of sources, note documentation information, and be sure to put any borrowed language in quotation marks and to clearly distinguish your own ideas from those of others.

Know where your information comes from. Because information passes quickly and often anonymously through the internet grapevine, you may not always be able to determine the origin of a text or image you find online. If you don't know where something came from, don't include it. Not only would you be unable to write a proper citation—chances are you haven't been able to verify the information either!

DOCUMENT **sources carefully.** Below you'll find an overview of the basics of documenting sources. More detail on using MLA and APA documentation is given in the next two chapters.

Plan ahead. Work can pile up in a high-pressure academic environment. Stay on top of your projects by scheduling your work and sticking to the deadlines you set. This way, you'll avoid taking shortcuts that could lead to inadvertent plagiarism.

Consult your instructor if necessary. If you're uncertain about how to acknowledge sources properly or are struggling with a project, talk with your instructor about finding a solution. Even taking a penalty for submitting an assignment late is better than being accused of plagiarism that you didn't intend to commit.

Documenting Sources

When you document sources, you identify the ones you've used and give information about their authors, titles, and publication. Documenting your sources allows you to show evidence of the research you've done and enables your readers to find those sources if they wish to. Most academic documentation systems include two parts: `IN-TEXT DOCUMENTATION`, which you insert in your text after the specific information you have borrowed, and an end-of-text list of `WORKS CITED` or `REFERENCES`, which provides complete bibliographic information for every work you've cited. It's also worth noting that hyperlinks are often used to document sources in popular writing—you might have seen linked documentation in news sites and online magazines.

See Ch. 32 in the ebook for a video on understanding in-text citations.

This book covers two documentation systems—those of the Modern Language Association (`MLA`) and the American Psychological Association (`APA`). MLA style is used primarily in English and other humanities subjects, and APA is used mostly in psychology and other social sciences. Chances are that you will be required to use either MLA or APA style or both in your college courses. Note that some disciplines may require other documentation systems, such as CSE (Council of Science Editors) or *Chicago Manual of Style*.

MLA and APA both call for the same basic information; you'll need to give the author's name (or sometimes the editor's name or the title) in the in-text citation, and your end-of-text list should provide the author, title, and publication information for each source that you cite. But the two systems differ in some ways. In APA, for example, your in-text documentation always includes the date of publication, but that is not generally done in MLA. You'll find detailed guidance on the specifics of MLA in Chapter 32 and of APA in Chapter 33, with color-coded examples to help you easily distinguish where the author and editor, title, and publication information appear for each type of work you document. Each of these chapters also includes a student paper that uses that style of documentation.

What about Generative AI?

If you're considering using generative AI for an assignment, your first step is to consult with your instructor and their course policy on AI use. Different instructors will have different perspectives on the role generative AI might play in coursework and whether you can use it in your inquiry, research, invention, drafting, and revision process for specific assignments. If your instructor's policy allows and you do incorporate AI-generated material, be sure to CITE it. Presenting any material you did not create as your own—including material you prompted an AI tool to produce—could be considered plagiarism.

If generative AI use is allowed, many instructors will ask you to provide an AI ACKNOWLEDGMENT STATEMENT, with citations, to help clarify exactly how you used AI. Follow your instructor's specific guidelines for writing an AI acknowledgment statement, since what's expected will vary. However, in most statements, you'll be expected to:

- identify the AI tool you used (ChatGPT, Grammarly, NotebookLM, etc.)
- state the tasks you used the AI tool for
- provide the prompt that generated the material you incorporated
- describe how the tool contributed to your assignment

In considering whether you need to include such a statement, think broadly about what AI "use" includes: it doesn't just mean using text from a tool like *ChatGPT*. If you relied on AI at any stage of the writing process—to brainstorm ideas, create images, explain difficult concepts, consider counterarguments, conduct research, summarize readings, edit drafts, or something else—explain that use in an acknowledgment statement. These statements don't need to be long, but they should include *all* the ways you engaged generative AI tools. Here are a few model AI acknowledgment statements.

For generating images, graphs, or other media

I used *Perplexity* to help add an image into my final research presentation. My prompt was "create an image of a field hockey player," and because the image provided was of a male player, I had to re-prompt it to "make the player female and college aged." I used the image to make the slide about field hockey more visually appealing in my *PowerPoint* presentation reporting on Title IX disputes in college sports.

For generating text and helping with other writing tasks

I used *ChatGPT* for my creative nonfiction narrative essay assignment in which I wrote about my experience having an emergency appendectomy. My prompt was "explain an appendectomy procedure." I used the information generated to compare it to how I remembered my appendectomy experience and to clarify my explanation of the procedure to my readers. I also used *Grammarly* on my rough draft of this essay. I pasted my draft into *Grammarly*, and I looked at each suggestion. I made some of the changes exactly, especially to fix misspelled words. For some suggestions, I revised the sentence on my own to make it shorter, but I didn't make the exact change proposed.

And here's a basic template to help you compose your own:

I used name of AI tool to task AI helped with. My prompt was: list initial prompts and any redirecting prompts. I used the information generated to explain how it fit into your project.

Remember that AI acknowledgment statements are a way to help you and your instructor reflect on how these tools are impacting your thinking and writing. They aren't designed to get you in trouble, so be honest about what you used and why.

 **REFLECT**

Think about the kinds of information you'll need to give when writing about your research. For your topic and your intended audience, what would be considered common knowledge? What might not be common knowledge for a different audience? What do you know about your audience that can help you make that decision?

THIRTY-TWO

MLA Style

LA STYLE CALLS for (1) brief in-text documentation and (2) complete bibliographic information in a list of works cited at the end of your text. The models and examples in this chapter draw on the ninth edition of the *MLA Handbook*, published by the Modern Language Association of America in 2021. For additional information, or if you're citing a source that isn't covered, visit style.mla.org.

A DIRECTORY TO MLA STYLE

In-Text Documentation 581

1. Author named in a signal phrase 581
2. Author named in parentheses 581
3. Two or more works by the same author 582
4. Authors with the same last name 582
5. Two or more authors 582
6. Organization or government as author 583
7. Author unknown 583
8. Literary works 583
9. Work in an anthology 584
10. Encyclopedia or dictionary 584
11. Legal documents 585
12. Sacred text 585
13. Multivolume work 585
14. Two or more works cited together 585
15. Source quoted in another source 586
16. Work without page numbers 586
17. An entire work or a one-page article 587
18. Generative AI 587

32 MLA Style

Notes 587

List of Works Cited 588

Core Elements 588

Authors and Other Contributors 588
Titles 589
Versions and Numbers 589
Publishers 590
Dates 590
Location 591
Punctuation 591
Sources Not Covered 592

Authors and Other Contributors 592

1. One author 592
2. Two authors 592
3. Three or more authors 593
4. Two or more works by the same author 593
5. Author and editor or translator 593
6. No author or editor 594
7. Organization or government as author 594

Articles and Other Short Works 594

Documentation Map: Article in a Print Journal 596
Documentation Map: Article in an Online Magazine 597
Documentation Map: Journal Article Accessed through a Database 599

8. Article in a journal 595
9. Article in a magazine 595
10. Article in a news publication 598
11. Article accessed through a database 598
12. Entry in a reference work 600
13. Editorial or op-ed 600
14. Letter to the editor 601
15. Review 601
16. Comment on an online article 602

Books and Parts of Books 602

Documentation Map: Print Book 603

17. Basic entries for a book 602
18. Anthology or edited collection 604
19. Work in an anthology 604
20. Multivolume work 604
21. Book in a series 605
22. Graphic narrative or comic book 605
23. Sacred text 606
24. Edition other than the first 606
25. Republished work 606
26. Foreword, introduction, preface, or afterword 606
27. Published letter 606
28. Paper heard at a conference 607
29. Dissertation 607

Websites 607

Documentation Map: Work on a Website   609

30. Entire website 608
31. Work on a website 608
32. Blog entry 608
33. Wiki 608

Personal Communication and Social Media 610

34. Personal letter 610
35. Email or text message 610
36. Post to *Instagram* or other social media 610

Audio, Visual, and Other Sources 611

37. Advertisement 611
38. Art 611
39. Cartoon 612
40. Supreme Court case 612
41. Film 612
42. TV show episode 613
43. Online video 614
44. Interview 614
45. Map 615
46. Musical score 615
47. Oral presentation 615
48. Virtual presentation 615
49. Podcast 615
50. Radio program 616
51. Sound recording 616
52. Video game 616
53. Generative AI 617

Formatting a Research Essay 617

Sample Research Essay 619

Glavee Glavee's essay is another that employs MLA style. Check it out on p. 905.

Throughout this chapter, you'll find color-coded models and examples to help you see how writers include source information in their texts and in their lists of works cited: tan for author, editor, translator, and other contributors; yellow for titles; gray for publication information—publisher, date of publication, page number(s), DOIs, and other location information.

author   title   publication

IN-TEXT DOCUMENTATION

Whenever you QUOTE, PARAPHRASE, or SUMMARIZE a source in your writing, you need to provide brief documentation that tells readers what you took from the source and where in the source you found that information. This brief documentation also refers readers to the full entry in your works-cited list, so begin with whatever comes first there: the author, the title, or a description of the source.

You'll need to mention the author, title, or description, either in a signal phrase—"as Toni Morrison writes"—or in parentheses—(Morrison). Name the author, title, or description in either place but not in both places.

Shorten any lengthy titles or descriptions in parentheses by including the first noun with any preceding adjectives but without any initial articles (*Norton Field Guide* rather than *The Norton Field Guide to Writing*). Use the full title if it's short (*What's Your Pronoun?*).

The first examples below show basic in-text documentation of a work by one author. Variations on those examples follow. The examples illustrate the MLA style of using quotation marks around titles of short works and italicizing titles of long works.

See the ebook for a video on understanding in-text citations.

1. Author named in a signal phrase

If you mention the author in a SIGNAL PHRASE, put only the page number(s) in parentheses. Do not write "page" or "p." The first time you mention the author, use their first and last names. Omit any middle initials.

> David McCullough describes John Adams's hands as those of someone used to manual labor (18).

In subsequent references to the author, use their last name only. You can also use a pronoun (use singular "they" if you don't know the author's pronouns) or another term, like "the author."

2. Author named in parentheses

If you do not mention the author in a signal phrase, put the last name in parentheses along with any page number(s). Do not use punctuation between the name and the page number(s).

> Adams is said to have had "the hands of a man accustomed to pruning his own trees, cutting his own hay, and splitting his own firewood" (McCullough 18).

Whether you use a signal phrase and parentheses or parentheses only, try to put the parenthetical documentation at the end of the sentence or as close as possible to the material you've cited—without awkwardly interrupting the sentence. Notice that in the example above, the parenthetical reference comes after the closing quotation marks but before the period at the end of the sentence.

3. Two or more works by the same author

If you cite multiple works by one author, include the title of the work you are citing either in the signal phrase or in parentheses.

> Robert Kaplan insists that understanding power in the Near East requires "Western leaders who know when to intervene, and do so without illusions" (*Eastward to Tartary* 330).

Put a comma between author and title if both are in the parentheses.

> Understanding power in the Near East requires "Western leaders who know when to intervene, and do so without illusions" (Kaplan, *Eastward to Tartary* 330).

4. Authors with the same last name

Give the author's first and last names in any signal phrase, or add the author's first initial in the parenthetical reference.

> *Imaginative* applies not only to modern literature but also to writing of all periods, whereas *magical* is often used in writing about Arthurian romances (A. Wilson 25).

5. Two or more authors

For a work with two authors, name both. If you first mention them in a signal phrase, give their first and last names.

> Lori Carlson and Cynthia Ventura's stated goal is to introduce Julio Cortázar, Marjorie Agosín, and other Latin American writers to an audience of English-speaking adolescents (v).

For a work by three or more authors that you mention in a signal phrase, you can either name them all or name the first author followed by "and others" or "and colleagues." If you mention them in a parenthetical reference, name the first author followed by "et al.," Latin for "and others."

> Phyllis Anderson and colleagues describe British literature thematically (A54–A67).

> One survey of British literature breaks the contents into thematic groupings (Anderson et al. A54–A67).

6. Organization or government as author

In a signal phrase, use the full name of the organization: American Academy of Arts and Sciences. In parentheses, use the shortest noun phrase: American Academy. Omit any initial articles.

> The US government can be direct when it wants to be. For example, it sternly warns, "If you are overpaid, we will recover any payments not due you" (Social Security Administration 12).

7. Author unknown

If you don't know the author, use the work's title in a signal phrase and a shortened version of the title in the parenthetical reference.

> A powerful article in last week's paper asserts that healthy liver donor Mike Hurewitz died because of "frightening" faulty postoperative care ("Every Patient's Nightmare").

8. Literary works

When referring to common literary works that are available in many different editions, give the page numbers from the edition you are using, followed by information that will let readers of any edition locate the text you are citing.

Novels and prose plays. Give the page number followed by a semicolon and any chapter, section, or act numbers, separated by commas.

> In *Pride and Prejudice*, Mrs. Bennet shows no warmth toward Jane and Elizabeth when they return from Netherfield (Austen 105; ch. 12).

Verse plays. Give act, scene, and line numbers, separated by periods.

> Shakespeare continues the vision theme when Macbeth says, "Thou hast no speculation in those eyes / Which thou dost glare with" (*Macbeth* 3.3.96–97).

Poems. Give the part and the line numbers (separated by periods). If a poem has only line numbers, use the word "line" or "lines" only in the first reference.

> Walt Whitman sets up not only opposing adjectives but also opposing nouns in "Song of Myself" when he says, "I am of old and young, of the foolish as much as the wise, / . . . a child as well as a man" (16.330–32).

> One description of the mere in *Beowulf* is "not a pleasant place" (line 1372). Later, it is labeled "the awful place" (1378).

9. Work in an anthology

Name the author(s) of the work, not the editor of the anthology.

> "It is the teapots that truly shock," according to Cynthia Ozick in her essay on teapots as metaphor (70).

> In *In Short: A Collection of Creative Nonfiction*, readers will find both an essay on Scottish tea (Hiestand) and a piece on teapots as metaphors (Ozick).

10. Encyclopedia or dictionary

For an entry in an encyclopedia or dictionary, give the author's name, if available. For an entry without an author, give the entry's title.

> According to *Funk and Wagnall's New World Encyclopedia*, early in his career Kubrick's main source of income came from "hustling chess games in Washington Square Park" ("Kubrick, Stanley").

11. Legal documents

For legal cases, give whatever comes first in the works-cited entry. If multiple entries in your works-cited list start with the same government author, give as much of the name as you need to differentiate the sources.

> In 2015, for the first time, all states were required to license and recognize the marriages of same-sex couples (United States, Supreme Court).

12. Sacred text

When citing a sacred text such as the Bible or the Qur'an for the first time, give the title of the edition as well as the book, chapter, and verse (or their equivalent), separated by periods. MLA recommends abbreviating the names of the books of the Bible in parenthetical references. Later citations from the same edition do not have to repeat its title.

> The wording from *The New English Bible* follows: "In the beginning of creation, when God made heaven and earth, the earth was without form and void . . ." (Gen. 1.1–2).

13. Multivolume work

If you cite more than one volume of a multivolume work, each time you cite one of the volumes, give the volume *and* the page number(s) in parentheses, separated by a colon and a space.

> Carl Sandburg concludes with the following sentence about those paying last respects to Lincoln: "All day long and through the night the unbroken line moved, the home town having its farewell" (4: 413).

If you cite an entire volume of a multivolume work in parentheses, give the author's last name followed by a comma and "vol." before the volume number: (Sandburg, vol. 2). If your works-cited list includes only a single volume of a multivolume work, give just the page number in parentheses: (230).

14. Two or more works cited together

If you're citing two or more works closely together, you will sometimes need to provide a parenthetical reference for each one.

> Dennis Baron describes singular "they" as "the missing word that's been hiding in plain sight" (182), while Benjamin Dreyer believes that "singular 'they' is not the wave of the future; it's the wave of the present" (93).

If you are citing multiple sources for the same idea in parentheses, separate the references with a semicolon.

> Many critics have examined great works of literature from a cultural perspective (Tanner 7; Smith viii).

15. Source quoted in another source

When you are quoting text that you found quoted in another source, use the abbreviation "qtd. in" in the parenthetical reference.

> Charlotte Brontë wrote to G. H. Lewes, "Why do you like Miss Austen so very much? I am puzzled on that point" (qtd. in Tanner 7).

16. Work without page numbers

For works without page or part numbers, including many online sources, identify the source using the author or other information.

> Studies show that music training helps children to be better at multitasking later in life ("Hearing the Music").

If you mention the author in a signal phrase, or if you mention the title of a work with no author, no parenthetical reference is needed.

> Arthur Brooks argues that a switch to fully remote work would have a negative effect on mental and physical health.

If the source has chapter, paragraph, or section numbers, use them with the abbreviations "ch.," "par.," or "sec." ("Graduate Student Unions," par. 2). Don't count sections or paragraphs on your own if they aren't numbered in the source. For an ebook, use chapter numbers. For an audio or video recording, give the hours, minutes, and seconds (separated by colons) as shown on the player: (00:05:21–31).

17. An entire work or a one-page article

If you cite an entire work rather than a part of it, or if you cite a single-page article, there's no need to include page numbers.

> Throughout life, John Adams strove to succeed (McCullough).

18. Generative AI

The results of generative AI are not considered to have an author and don't have titles; instead, identify the source by using the first phrase or clause of your prompt. Use the whole prompt if it's short.

> A light bulb, also known as an incandescent bulb, works "on the principle of incandescence" ("Explain how a light bulb works").

NOTES

Sometimes you may need to give information that doesn't fit into the text itself—to thank people who helped you, to acknowledge the use of AI in your writing process, to provide additional details, to refer readers to other sources, or to add comments about sources. Such information can be given in a footnote (at the bottom of the page) or an endnote (on a separate page with the heading "Notes" or "Endnotes" just before your works-cited list). Put a superscript number at the appropriate point in your text, signaling to readers to look for the note with the corresponding number. If you have multiple notes, number them consecutively throughout your paper.

Text

World (and Word) Building: A Gamer's Literacy[1]

Note

[1] I want to thank those who gave me feedback on a draft of this literacy narrative, including my teacher Vincent Yu and my classmates Karima and Luke. I also want to acknowledge the use of *ChatGPT* to brainstorm ideas early in my writing process. *ChatGPT* helped me

develop the idea of sharing an anecdote about the storytelling skills I learned from playing *Dungeons & Dragons*. I've included my initial prompt and full *ChatGPT* conversation history in an appendix.

LIST OF WORKS CITED

A works-cited list provides full bibliographic information for every source cited in your text. See page 619 for guidelines on formatting this list and page 634 for a sample works-cited list.

Core Elements

MLA style provides a list of core elements for documenting sources, advising writers to list as many of them as possible in the order that MLA specifies. We've used these general principles to provide templates and examples for documenting fifty-three kinds of sources college writers most often need to cite. The following general guidelines explain how to treat each of the core elements.

Authors and Other Contributors

- An author can be any kind of creator—a writer, a musician, a visual artist, and so on.
- If there is one author, list the last name first: Morrison, Toni.
- If there are two authors, list the first author last name first and the second one first name first: Lunsford, Andrea A., and Lisa Ede. Put their names in the order given in the work. For three or more authors, give the first author's name followed by "et al.": Gonzalez, Laura, et al.
- Include any middle names or initials: Heath, Shirley Brice; Toklas, Alice B.
- If the author is a group or organization, use the full name, omitting any initial article: American Psychological Association, United Nations.
- If an author uses a handle that is significantly different from their name, include the handle in square brackets after the name: Ocasio-Cortez, Alexandria [@AOC].

author   title   publication

- If there's no known author, start the entry with the title.
- If there's an editor but no author, put the editor's name in the author position and specify their role: Coates, Ta-Nehisi, editor.
- If you're citing an editor, translator, director, or other contributors, specify their role. For works with multiple contributors, put the one whose work you wish to highlight before the title, and list any others you want to mention after the title. If you don't want to highlight one particular contributor, start with the title and include any contributors after the title. For contributors named before the title, put the label after the name: Fincher, David, director. For those named after the title, specify their role first: Directed by David Fincher.

Titles

- Include any subtitles and capitalize all the words in titles and subtitles except for articles (a, an, the), prepositions (to, at, from, and so on), and coordinating conjunctions (and, but, for, or, nor, yet, so)—unless they are the first or last word of a title or subtitle.
- Italicize the titles of books, periodicals, websites, and other long works (*Pride and Prejudice*, *Wired*).
- Enclose in quotation marks the titles of articles and other short works: "Letter from Birmingham Jail."
- To document a source that has no title, describe it without italics or quotation marks: Letter to the author, Photograph of a tree. For a short, untitled email, text message, social media post, or poem, you may want to include the first few words of the text itself instead: Dickinson, Emily. "Immortal is an ample word." *American Poems*, www.americanpoems.com/poets/emilydickinson/immortal-is-an-ample-word.

Versions and Numbers

- If you cite a source that's available in more than one version, specify the one you consulted in your works-cited entry. Write ordinal numbers with numerals, and abbreviate "edition": 2nd ed. Write out names

of specific versions, and capitalize following a period or if the name is a proper noun: King James Version, unabridged version, director's cut.
- If you cite a book that's published in multiple volumes, indicate the volume number. Abbreviate "volume," and write the number as a numeral: vol. 2.
- Indicate any volume and issue numbers of journals, abbreviating both "volume" and "number": vol. 123, no. 4.
- If you cite a TV show or podcast episode, indicate the season and episode numbers: season 1, episode 4.

Publishers

- Write publishers', studios', and networks' names in full, but omit initial articles and business words like "Company" or "Inc."
- For academic presses, use "U" for "University" and "P" for "Press": Princeton UP, U of California P. Spell out "Press" if the name doesn't include "University": Running Press, MIT Press.
- If the publisher is a division of an organization, list the organization and any divisions from largest to smallest: Stanford U, Center for the Study of Language and Information, Metaphysics Research Lab.

Dates

- Whether to give just the year or to include the month and day depends on the source. In general, give the full date that you find there.
- For books, give the publication date on the copyright page: 1948. If a book lists more than one date, use the most recent one.
- Periodicals may be published annually, monthly, seasonally, weekly, or daily. Give the full date that you find there: 2019, Apr. 2019, spring 2019, 16 Apr. 2019.
- Abbreviate the months except for May, June, and July: Jan., Feb., Mar., Apr., Aug., Sept., Oct., Nov., Dec.
- For online sources, use the copyright date or the full date that you find in the source. If the source does not give a date, use the date of access: Accessed 6 June 2020. Give a date of access as well for online sources you think are likely to change or for websites that have disappeared.

Location

- For most print articles and other short works, give a page number or range of pages: p. 24, pp. 24–35. For those that are not on consecutive pages, give the first page number with a plus sign: pp. 24+.
- If it's necessary to specify a particular section of a source, give the section name before the page numbers: Sunday Review sec., p. 3.
- Indicate the location of an online source by giving a DOI if one is available; if not, give a URL—and use a permalink if one is available. URLs are not always reliable, so ask your instructor if you should include them. DOIs should start with "https://doi.org/" but no need to include "https://" for a URL, unless you want the URL to be a hyperlink.
- For a location, give enough information to identify it: a city (Houston), a city and state (Provo, Utah), or a city and country (Itu, Brazil). For something seen in a museum or elsewhere, name the institution and its location: Maine Jewish Museum, Portland; Portland Museum of Art, Portland, Maine.
- For performances or other live presentations, name the venue and its location: Mark Taper Forum, Los Angeles.

Punctuation

- Use a period after the author name(s) that start an entry (Morrison, Toni.) and the title of the source you're documenting (*Beloved*.).
- Use a comma between the author's last and first names: Morrison, Toni.
- Some URLs won't fit on one line. When necessary, we recommend breaking a URL before a punctuation mark. Do not add a hyphen or a space.
- Sometimes you'll need to provide information about more than one work for a single source—for instance, when you cite an article from a periodical that you access through a database. MLA refers to the periodical and database (or any other entity that holds a source) as "containers." Use commas between elements within each container and put a period at the end of each container. For example:

    Semuels, Alana. "The Future Will Be Quiet." *The Atlantic*, Apr. 2016,
      pp. 19–20. *ProQuest*, search.proquest.com/docview
      /1777443553?accountid+42654.

The guidelines below should help you document kinds of sources you're likely to use. The first section shows how to acknowledge authors and other contributors and applies to all kinds of sources—print, online, or others. Later sections show how to treat titles, publication information, location, and access information for many specific kinds of sources. In general, provide as much information as possible for each source—enough to tell readers how to find a source if they wish to access it themselves.

Sources Not Covered

These guidelines will help you cite a variety of sources, but there may be sources you want to use that aren't mentioned here. If you're citing a source that isn't covered, consult the MLA style blog at style.mla.org, or ask them a question at style.mla.org/ask-a-question.

Authors and Other Contributors

When you name authors and other contributors in your citations, you are crediting them for their work and letting readers know who's in on the conversation. The following guidelines for citing authors and contributors apply to all sources you cite: in print, online, or in some other medium.

1. One author

Author's Last Name, First Name. *Title*. Publisher, Date.

Anderson, Chris. *The Long Tail: Why the Future of Business Is Selling Less of More*. Hyperion, 2006.

2. Two authors

1st Author's Last Name, First Name, and 2nd Author's First and Last Names. *Title*. Publisher, Date.

Lunsford, Andrea A., and Lisa Ede. *Singular Texts/Plural Authors: Perspectives on Collaborative Writing*. Southern Illinois UP, 1990.

3. Three or more authors

1st Author's Last Name, First Name, et al. *Title.* Publisher, Date.

Sebranek, Patrick, et al. *Writers INC: A Guide to Writing, Thinking, and Learning.* Write Source, 1990.

4. Two or more works by the same author

Give the author's name in the first entry, and then use a three-em dash (or three hyphens) in the author slot for each of the subsequent works, listing them alphabetically by the first word of each title and ignoring any articles.

Author's Last Name, First Name. *Title That Comes First Alphabetically.* Publisher, Date.

———. *Title That Comes Next Alphabetically.* Publisher, Date.

Kaplan, Robert D. *The Coming Anarchy: Shattering the Dreams of the Post Cold War.* Random House, 2000.

———. *Eastward to Tartary: Travels in the Balkans, the Middle East, and the Caucasus.* Random House, 2000.

5. Author and editor or translator

Author's Last Name, First Name. *Title.* Role by First and Last Names, Publisher, Date.

Austen, Jane. *Emma.* Edited by Stephen M. Parrish, W. W. Norton, 2000.

Dostoevsky, Fyodor. *Crime and Punishment.* Translated by Richard Pevear and Larissa Volokhonsky, Vintage Books, 1993.

Start with the editor or translator if you are focusing on their contribution rather than the author's. If there is a translator but no author, start with the title.

Pevear, Richard, and Larissa Volokhonsky, translators. *Crime and Punishment.* By Fyodor Dostoevsky, Vintage Books, 1993.

Beowulf. Translated by Stephen Mitchell, Yale UP, 2017.

6. No author or editor

When there's no known author or editor, start with the title.

> *The Turner Collection in the Clore Gallery.* Tate Publications, 1987.

> "Being Invisible Closer to Reality." *The Atlanta Journal-Constitution,* 11 Aug. 2008, p. A3.

7. Organization or government as author

> Organization Name. *Title.* Publisher, Date.

Diagram Group. *The Macmillan Visual Desk Reference.* Macmillan, 1993.

For a government publication, give the name that is shown in the source.

> United States, Department of Health and Human Services, National Institute of Mental Health. *Autism Spectrum Disorders.* Government Printing Office, 2004.

When a nongovernment organization is both author and publisher, start with the title and list the organization only as the publisher.

> *Stylebook on Religion 2000: A Reference Guide and Usage Manual.* Catholic News Service, 2002.

If a division of an organization is listed as the author, give the division as the author and the organization as the publisher.

> Center for Workforce Studies. *2005–13: Demographics of the U.S. Psychology Workforce.* American Psychological Association, July 2015.

Articles and Other Short Works

Articles, essays, reviews, and other short works are found in journals, magazines, newspapers, other periodicals, and books—all of which you may find in print, online, or in a database. For most short works, you'll need to provide information about the author, the titles of both the short work and the longer work, any page numbers, and various kinds of publication information, all explained on the following pages.

8. Article in a journal

Print

Author's Last Name, First Name. "Title of Article." *Name of Journal*, Volume, Issue, Date, Pages.

Cooney, Brian C. "Considering *Robinson Crusoe*'s 'Liberty of Conscience' in an Age of Terror." *College English*, vol. 69, no. 3, Jan. 2007, pp. 197–215.

Online

Author's Last Name, First Name. "Title of Article." *Name of Journal*, Volume, Issue, Date, DOI *or* URL.

Schmidt, Desmond. "A Model of Versions and Layers." *Digital Humanities Quarterly*, vol. 13, no. 3, 2019, www.digitalhumanities.org/dhq/vol/13/3/000430/000430.html.

9. Article in a magazine

Print

Author's Last Name, First Name. "Title of Article." *Name of Magazine*, Volume (if any), Issue (if any), Date, Pages.

Burt, Tequia. "Legacy of Activism: Concerned Black Students' 50-Year History at Grinnell College." *Grinnell Magazine*, vol. 48, no. 4, summer 2016, pp. 32–38.

Online

Author's Last Name, First Name. "Title of Article." *Name of Magazine,* Volume (if any), Issue (if any), Date, DOI *or* URL.

Brooks, Arthur C. "The Hidden Toll of Remote Work." *The Atlantic*, 1 Apr. 2021, www.theatlantic.com/family/archive/2021/04/zoom-remote-work-loneliness-happiness/618473.

Documentation Map (MLA) / Article in a Print Journal

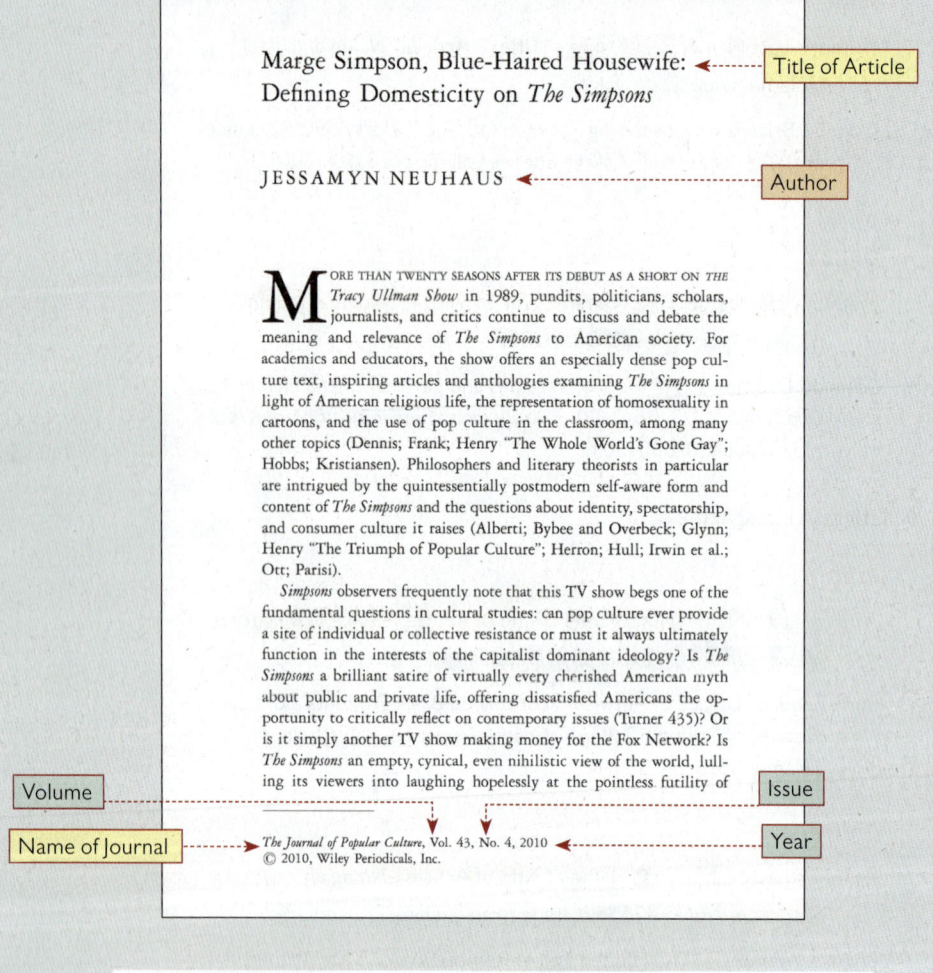

Neuhaus, Jessamyn. "Marge Simpson, Blue-Haired Housewife: Defining Domesticity on *The Simpsons*." *The Journal of Popular Culture*, vol. 43, no. 4, 2010, pp. 761–81.

Documentation Map (MLA) / Article in an Online Magazine

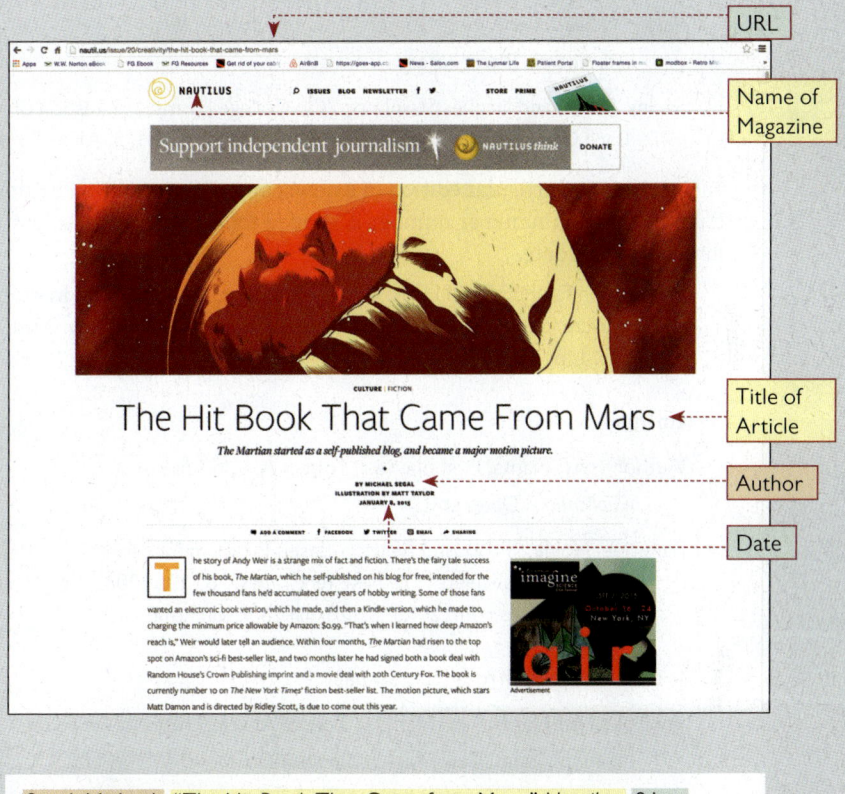

Segal, Michael. "The Hit Book That Came from Mars." *Nautilus*, 8 Jan. 2015, nautil.us/issue/20/creativity/the-hit-book-that-came-from-mars.

10. Article in a news publication

Print

Author's Last Name, First Name. "Title of Article." *Name of Publication*, Date, Pages.

Saulny, Susan, and Jacques Steinberg. "On College Forms, a Question of Race Can Perplex." *The New York Times*, 14 June 2011, p. A1.

To document a particular edition of a newspaper, list the edition before the date. If a section name or number is needed to locate the article, put that detail after the date.

Burns, John F., and Miguel Helft. "Under Pressure, YouTube Withdraws Muslim Cleric's Videos." *The New York Times*, late ed., 4 Nov. 2010, sec. 1, p. 13.

Online

Author's Last Name, First Name. "Title of Article." *Name of Publication,* Date, URL.

Banerjee, Neela. "Proposed Religion-Based Program for Federal Inmates Is Canceled." *The New York Times*, 28 Oct. 2006, www.nytimes.com/2006/10/28/us/28prison.html.

11. Article accessed through a database

Author's Last Name, First Name. "Title of Article." *Name of Periodical*, Volume, Issue, Date, Pages. *Name of Database,* DOI or URL.

Stalter, Sunny. "Subway Ride and Subway System in Hart Crane's 'The Tunnel.'" *Journal of Modern Literature*, vol. 33, no. 2, Jan. 2010, pp. 70–91. *JSTOR*, https://doi.org/10.2979/jml.2010.33.2.70.

Documentation Map (MLA) / Journal Article Accessed through a Database

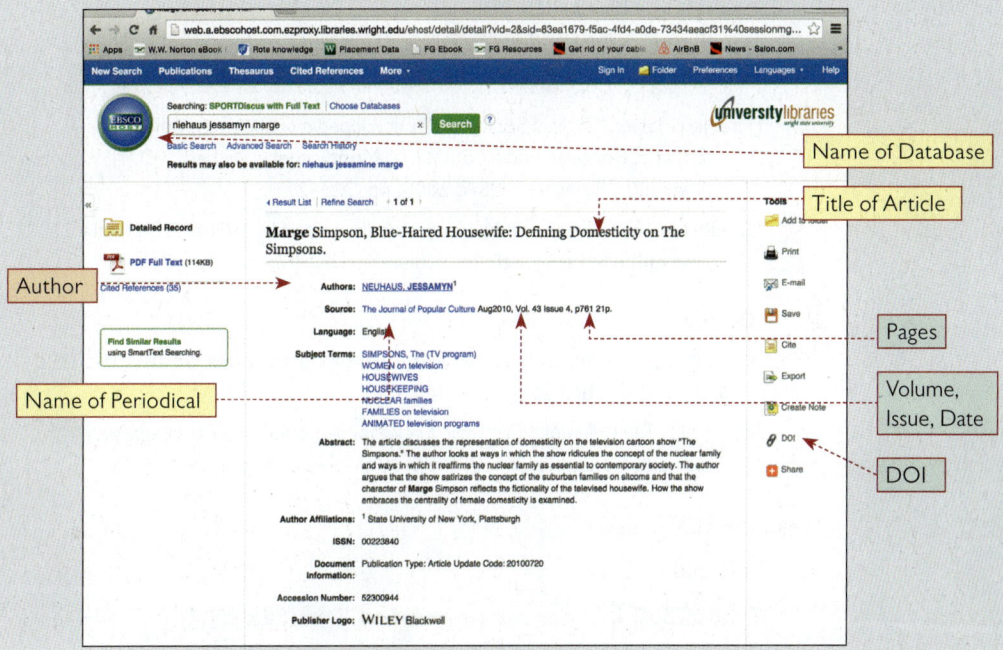

Neuhaus, Jessamyn. "Marge Simpson, Blue-Haired Housewife: Defining Domesticity on *The Simpsons*." *The Journal of Popular Culture*, vol. 43, no. 4, Aug. 2010, pp. 761–81. *EBSCOhost*, https://doi.org/10.1111/j.1540-5931.2010.00769.x.

12. Entry in a reference work

Print

Author's Last Name, First Name (if any). "Title of Entry." *Title of Reference Book*, edited by Editor's First and Last Names (if any), Edition number (if any), Volume (if any), Publisher, Date, Pages.

Fritz, Jan Marie. "Clinical Sociology." *Encyclopedia of Sociology*, edited by Edgar F. Borgatta and Rhonda J. V. Montgomery, 2nd ed., vol. 1, Macmillan Reference USA, 2000, pp. 323–29.

"California." *The New Columbia Encyclopedia*, edited by William H. Harris and Judith S. Levey, 4th ed., Columbia UP, 1975, pp. 423–24.

Online

Document online reference works the same as print ones, adding the URL after the date of publication.

"Baseball." *The Columbia Electronic Encyclopedia,* edited by Paul Lagasse, 6th ed., Columbia UP, 2012, www.infoplease.com/encyclopedia.

13. Editorial or op-ed

Editorial

Editorial Board. "Title." *Name of Periodical*, Date, Page or URL.

Editorial Board. "A New Look for Local News Coverage." *The Lakeville Journal*, 13 Feb. 2020, p. A8.

Editorial Board. "Editorial: Protect Reporters at Protest Scenes." *Los Angeles Times*, 11 Mar. 2021, www.latimes.com/opinion/story/2021-03-11/reporters-protest-scenes.

Op-ed

Author's Last Name, First Name. "Title." *Name of Periodical*, Date, Page or URL.

Okafor, Kingsley. "Opinion: The First Step to COVID Vaccine Equity Is Overall Health Equity." *The Denver Post*, 15 Apr. 2021, www.denverpost.com/2021/04/15/covid-vaccine-equity-kaiser.

If it's not clear that it's an op-ed, add a label at the end.

> Balf, Todd. "Falling in Love with Swimming." *The New York Times*, 17 Apr. 2021, p. A21. Op-ed.

14. Letter to the editor

> Author's Last Name, First Name. "Title of Letter (if any)." *Name of Periodical*, Date, Page *or* URL.

> Pinker, Steven. "Language Arts." *The New Yorker*, 4 June 2012, p. 10.

If the letter has no title, include "Letter" after the author's name.

> Fleischmann, W. B. Letter. *The New York Review of Books*, 1 June 1963, www.nybooks.com/articles/1963/06/01/letter-21.

15. Review

Print

> Reviewer's Last Name, First Name. "Title of Review." *Name of Periodical*, Date, Pages.

> Frank, Jeffrey. "Body Count." *The New Yorker*, 30 July 2007, pp. 86–87.

Online

> Reviewer's Last Name, First Name. "Title of Review." *Name of Periodical*, Date, URL.

> Donadio, Rachel. "Italy's Great, Mysterious Storyteller." *The New York Review of Books*, 18 Dec. 2014, www.nybooks.com/articles/2014/12/18/italys-great-mysterious-storyteller.

If a review has no title, include the title and author of the work being reviewed after the reviewer's name.

> Lohier, Patrick. Review of *Exhalation*, by Ted Chiang. *Harvard Review Online*, 4 Oct. 2019, www.harvardreview.org/book-review/exhalation.

16. Comment on an online article

Commenter's Last Name, First Name *or* Username. Comment on "Title of Article." *Name of Periodical*, Date posted, Time posted, URL.

ZeikJT. Comment on "The Post-Disaster Artist." *Polygon*, 6 May 2020, 4:33 a.m., www.polygon.com/2020/5/5/21246679/josh-trank-capone-interview-fantastic-four-chronicle#comments.

Books and Parts of Books

For most books, you'll need to provide information about the author, the title, the publisher, and the year of publication. If you found the book inside a larger volume, a database, or some other work, be sure to specify that as well.

17. Basic entries for a book

Print

Author's Last Name, First Name. *Title.* Publisher, Year of publication.

Watson, Brad. *Miss Jane.* W. W. Norton, 2016.

Ebook

Author's Last Name, First Name. *Title.* E-book ed., Publisher, Year of publication.

Watson, Brad. *Miss Jane.* E-book ed., W. W. Norton, 2016.

Concise Guide to APA Style. 7th ed., e-book ed., American Psychological Association, 2020.

On a website

Author's Last Name, First Name. *Title.* Publisher, Year of publication, DOI *or* URL.

Ball, Cheryl E., and Drew M. Loewe, editors. *Bad Ideas about Writing.* West Virginia U Libraries, 2017, textbooks.lib.wvu.edu/badideas/badideasaboutwriting-book.pdf.

Documentation Map (MLA) / Print Book

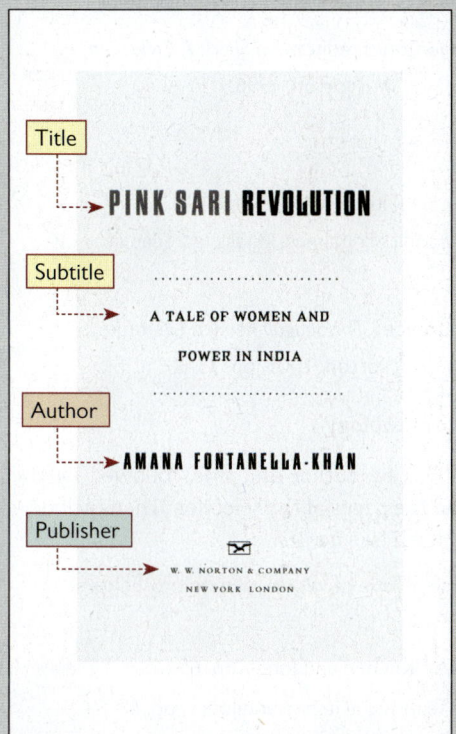
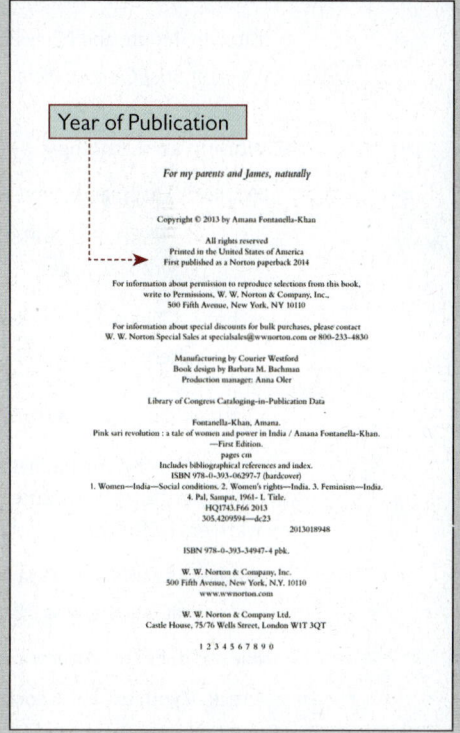

Fontanella-Khan, Amana. *Pink Sari Revolution: A Tale of Women and Power in India.* W. W. Norton, 2014.

18. Anthology or edited collection

Last Name, First Name, editor. *Title.* Publisher, Year of publication.

Kitchen, Judith, and Mary Paumier Jones, editors. *In Short: A Collection of Brief Creative Nonfiction.* W. W. Norton, 1996.

19. Work in an anthology

Author's Last Name, First Name. "Title of Work." *Title of Anthology*, edited by First and Last Names, Publisher, Year of publication, Pages.

Achebe, Chinua. "Uncle Ben's Choice." *The Seagull Reader: Literature*, edited by Joseph Kelly, W. W. Norton, 2005, pp. 23–27.

Two or more works from one anthology

Prepare an entry for each selection by author and title, followed by the anthology editors' last names and the pages of the selection. Then include a separate entry for the anthology itself (see no. 18).

Author's Last Name, First Name. "Title of Work." Anthology Editors' Last Names, Pages.

Hiestand, Emily. "Afternoon Tea." Kitchen and Jones, pp. 65–67.
Ozick, Cynthia. "The Shock of Teapots." Kitchen and Jones, pp. 68–71.

20. Multivolume work

All volumes

Author's Last Name, First Name. *Title of Work.* Publisher, Year(s) of publication. Number of vols.

Churchill, Winston. *The Second World War.* Houghton Mifflin, 1948–53. 6 vols.

Single volume

Author's Last Name, First Name. *Title of Work*. Vol. number, Publisher, Year of publication.

Sandburg, Carl. *Abraham Lincoln: The War Years*. Vol. 2, Harcourt, Brace and World, 1939.

If the volume has its own title, include it after the author's name, and indicate the volume number and series title after the year.

Caro, Robert A. *Means of Ascent*. Vintage Books, 1990. Vol. 2 of *The Years of Lyndon Johnson*.

21. Book in a series

Author's Last Name, First Name. *Title of Book*. Edited by First and Last Names, Publisher, Year of publication. Series Title.

Walker, Alice. *Everyday Use*. Edited by Barbara T. Christian, Rutgers UP, 1994. Women Writers: Texts and Contexts.

22. Graphic narrative or comic book

Author's Last Name, First Name. *Title*. Publisher, Year of publication.

Barry, Lynda. *One! Hundred! Demons!* Drawn and Quarterly, 2005.

If the work has more than one contributor you want to include, start with the one you want to highlight, and label the role of anyone who's not an author.

Pekar, Harvey. *Bob and Harv's Comics*. Illustrated by R. Crumb, Running Press, 1996.

Crumb, R., Illustrator. *Bob and Harv's Comics*. By Harvey Pekar, Running Press, 1996.

To cite several contributors, you can also start with the title.

Secret Invasion. By Brian Michael Bendis, illustrated by Leinil Yu, inked by Mark Morales, Marvel, 2009.

23. Sacred text

If you cite a specific edition of a religious text, you need to include it in your works-cited list.

The New English Bible with the Apocrypha. Oxford UP, 1971.

The Torah: A Modern Commentary. W. Gunther Plaut, general editor, Union of American Hebrew Congregations, 1981.

24. Edition other than the first

Author's Last Name, First Name. Title. Name or number of edition, Publisher, Year of publication.

Smart, Ninian. *The World's Religions*. 2nd ed., Cambridge UP, 1998.

25. Republished work

Author's Last Name, First Name. Title. Year of original publication. Current publisher, Year of republication.

Bierce, Ambrose. *Civil War Stories*. 1909. Dover, 1994.

26. Foreword, introduction, preface, or afterword

Part Author's Last Name, First Name. Name of Part. Title of Book, by Author's First and Last Names, Publisher, Year of publication, Pages.

Tanner, Tony. Introduction. *Pride and Prejudice*, by Jane Austen, Penguin, 1972, pp. 7–46.

27. Published letter

Letter Writer's Last Name, First Name. "Title of letter." Day Month Year. Title of Book, edited by First and Last Names, Publisher, Year of publication, Pages.

White, E. B. "To Carol Angell." 28 May 1970. *Letters of E. B. White*, edited by Dorothy Lobrano Guth, Harper and Row, 1976, p. 600.

28. Paper heard at a conference

Author's Last Name, First Name. "Title of Paper." Conference, Day Month Year, Location.

Hern, Katie. "Inside an Accelerated Reading and Writing Classroom." Conference on Acceleration in Developmental Education, 15 June 2016, Sheraton Inner Harbor Hotel, Baltimore.

29. Dissertation

Author's Last Name, First Name. *Title*. Year. Institution, PhD dissertation. *Name of Database*, URL.

Simington, Maire Orav. *Chasing the American Dream Post World War II: Perspectives from Literature and Advertising*. 2003. Arizona State U, PhD dissertation. *ProQuest*, search.proquest.com/docview/305340098.

For an unpublished dissertation, end with the institution and a description of the work.

Kim, Loel. *Students Respond to Teacher Comments: A Comparison of Online Written and Voice Modalities*. 1998. Carnegie Mellon U, PhD dissertation.

Websites

Many sources are available in multiple media—for example, a print periodical that is also on the web and contained in digital databases—but some are published only on websites. A website can have an author, an editor, or neither. Some sites have a publisher, and some do not. Include whatever information is available. If the publisher and title are essentially the same, omit the name of the publisher. If the site is likely to change, if it has no date, or if it no longer exists, include a date of access.

30. Entire website

Author's Last Name, First Name. *Title of Site.* Date (if any), URL.

Park, Linda Sue. *Linda Sue Park: Author and Educator.* 2021, lindasuepark.com.

Editor's Last Name, First Name, role. *Title of Site.* Publisher (if any), Date (if any), URL.

Proffitt, Michael, chief editor. *The Oxford English Dictionary.* Oxford UP, 2021, www.oed.com.

If a site is likely to change or has no date, include a date of access.

Archive of Our Own. Organization for Transformative Works, archiveofourown.org. Accessed 23 Apr. 2021.

31. Work on a website

Author's Last Name, First Name (if any). "Title of Work." *Title of Site,* Publisher (if any), Date, URL.

Cesareo, Kerry. "Moving Closer to Tackling Deforestation at Scale." *World Wildlife Fund,* 20 Oct. 2020, www.worldwildlife.org /blogs/sustainability-works/posts/moving-closer-to-tackling -deforestation-at-scale.

32. Blog entry

Author's Last Name, First Name. "Title of Blog Entry." *Title of Blog,* Date, URL.

Hollmichel, Stefanie. "Winter Solstice." *A Stone in the River,* 22 Dec. 2021, www.astoneintheriver.net/2021/12/22/winter-solstice.

Document a whole blog as you would an entire website (no. 30) and a comment on a blog as you would a comment on an online article (no. 16).

33. Wiki

"Title of Entry." *Title of Wiki,* Publisher, Date, URL.

"Pi." *Wikipedia,* Wikimedia Foundation, 28 Aug. 2013, en.wikipedia.org /wiki/Pi.

Documentation Map (MLA) / Work on a Website

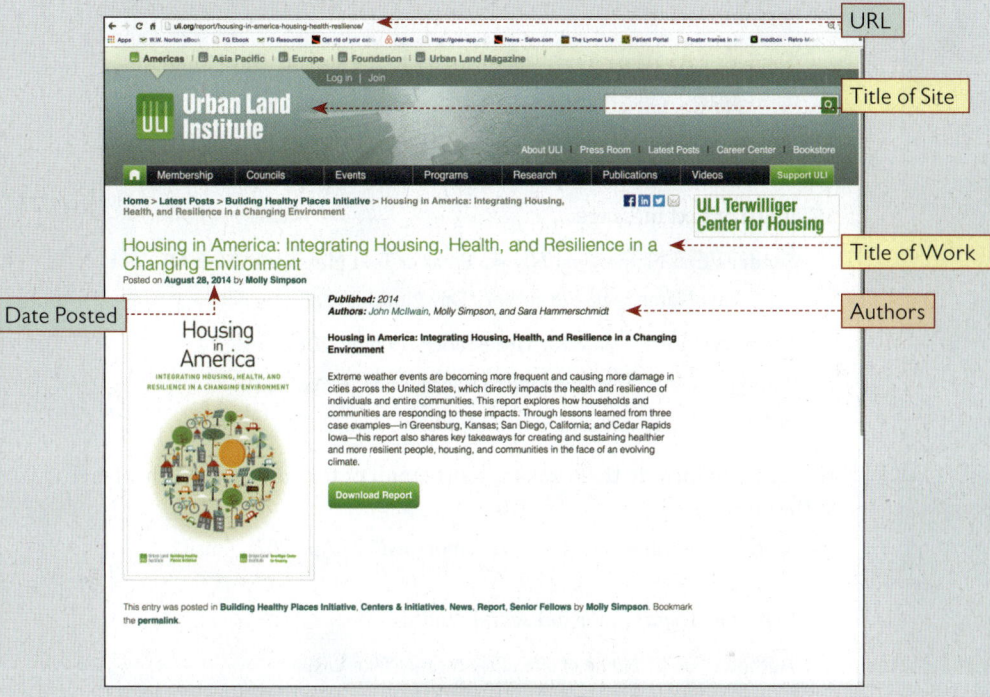

McIlwain, John, et al. "Housing in America: Integrating Housing, Health, and Resilience in a Changing Environment." *Urban Land Institute*, 28 Aug. 2014, uli.org/report/housing-in-america-housing-health-resilience.

Personal Communication and Social Media

34. Personal letter

> Sender's Last Name, First Name. Letter to the author. Day Month Year.

Quindlen, Anna. Letter to the author. 11 Apr. 2013.

35. Email or text message

> Sender's Last Name, First Name. Email *or* Text Message to First Name Last Name *or* to the author. Day Month Year.

Smith, William. Email to Richard Bullock. 19 Nov. 2013.

Rombes, Maddy. Text message to Isaac Cohen. 4 May 2021.

O'Malley, Kit. Text message to the author. 2 June 2020.

You can also include the text of a short email or text message, with a label at the end.

Rust, Max. "Trip to see the cows tomorrow?" 27 Apr. 2021. Email.

36. Post to *Instagram* or other social media

> Author. "Title." *Name of Site*, Day Month Year, URL.

Oregon Zoo. "Winter Wildlife Wonderland." *Facebook*, 8 Feb. 2019, www.facebook.com/80229441108/videos/2399570506799549.

If there's no title, you can use a concise description or the text of a short post.

Millman, Debbie. Photos of Roxane Gay. *Instagram*, 18 Feb. 2021, www.instagram.com/p/CLcT_EnhnWT.

President Obama [@POTUS44]. "It's been the honor of my life to serve you. You made me a better leader and a better man." *X*, 20 Jan. 2017, x.com/POTUS44/status/822445882247413761.

Audio, Visual, and Other Sources

37. Advertisement

Print

Description of ad. *Title of Periodical*, Date, Page.

Advertisement for Grey Goose. *Wine Spectator*, 18 Dec. 2020, p. 22.

Video

"Title." *Name of Site*, uploaded by Company, Date, URL.

"First Visitors." *YouTube*, uploaded by Snickers, 20 Aug. 2020, www.youtube.com/watch?v=negeco0b1L0.

38. Art

Original

Artist's Last Name, First Name. *Title of Art*. Year created, Location.

Van Gogh, Vincent. *The Potato Eaters*. 1885, Van Gogh Museum, Amsterdam.

In a book

Artist's Last Name, First Name. *Title of Art*. Year created, Location. *Title of Book*, by First and Last Names, Publisher, Year of publication, Page.

Van Gogh, Vincent. *The Potato Eaters*. 1885, Van Gogh Museum, Amsterdam. *History of Art: A Survey of the Major Visual Arts from the Dawn of History to the Present Day*, by H. W. Janson, Prentice Hall / Harry N. Abrams, 1969, p. 508.

Online

Artist's Last Name, First Name. *Title of Art*. Year created. *Name of Site*, URL.

Warhol, Andy. *Self-portrait*. 1979. *J. Paul Getty Museum*, www.getty.edu/art/collection/objects/106971/andy-warhol-self-portrait-american-1979.

39. Cartoon

Print

Author's Last Name, First Name. Cartoon *or* "Title of Cartoon." *Name of Periodical*, Date, Page.

Mankoff, Robert. Cartoon. *The New Yorker*, 3 May 1993, p. 50.

Online

Author's Last Name, First Name. Cartoon *or* "Title of Cartoon." *Title of Site*, Date, URL.

Munroe, Randall. "Up Goer Five." *xkcd*, 12 Nov. 2012, xkcd.com/1133.

40. Supreme Court case

United States, Supreme Court. *Name of Case*. Date of decision. *Name of Source Site*, Publisher, URL.

United States, Supreme Court. *District of Columbia v. Heller*. 26 June 2008. *Legal Information Institute*, Cornell Law School, www.law.cornell.edu/supremecourt/text/07-290.

41. Film

Name individuals based on the focus of your project—the director, the screenwriter, or someone else.

Title of Film. Role by First and Last Names, Production Company, Date.

Breakfast at Tiffany's. Directed by Blake Edwards, Paramount, 1961.

Online

Title of Film. Role by First and Last Names, Production Company, Date. Name of Site, URL.

Interstellar. Directed by Christopher Nolan, Paramount, 2014. *Amazon Prime Video*, www.amazon.com/Interstellar-Matthew-McConaughey/dp/B00TU9UFTS.

42. TV show episode

Name contributors based on the focus of your project—director, writers, actors, or others. If you don't want to highlight anyone in particular, don't include any contributors.

Broadcast

"Title of Episode." Title of Program, role by First and Last Names (if any), season, episode, Production Company, Broadcast date.

"The Storm." *Avatar: The Last Airbender*, created by Michael Dante DiMartino and Bryan Konietzko, season 1, episode 12, Nickelodeon Animation Studio, 3 June 2005.

DVD

"Title of Episode." Broadcast Date. Title of DVD, role by First and Last Names (if any), season, episode, Production Company, Release Date, disc number. DVD.

"The Storm." 2005. *Avatar: The Last Airbender: The Complete Book 1 Collection*, created by Michael Dante DiMartino and Bryan Konietzko, episode 12, Nickelodeon Animation Studio, 2006, disc 3. DVD.

Streaming online

"Title of Episode." Title of Program, role by First and Last Names (if any), season, episode, Production Company, Date. Title of Site, URL.

"The Storm." *Avatar: The Last Airbender*, season 1, episode 12, Nickelodeon Animation Studio, 2005. *Netflix*, www.netflix.com.

Streaming on an app

"Title of Episode." *Title of Program*, role by First and Last Names (if any), season, episode, Production Company, Date. *Name of* app.

"The Storm." *Avatar: The Last Airbender*, season 1, episode 12, Nickelodeon Animation Studio, 3 June 2005. *Netflix* app.

43. Online video

"Title of Video." *Title of Site*, uploaded by Uploader's Name, Day Month Year, URL.

"Everything Wrong with *National Treasure* in 13 Minutes or Less." *YouTube*, uploaded by CinemaSins, 21 Aug. 2014, www.youtube.com/watch?v=1ul-_ZWvXTs.

44. Interview

If it's not clear that it's an interview, add a label at the end. If you are citing a transcript of an interview, indicate that at the end as well.

Published

Subject's Last Name, First Name. "Title of Interview (if any)." Interview by First Name Last Name (if given). *Name of Publication*, Date, Pages *or* URL.

Whitehead, Colson. "Colson Whitehead: By the Book." *The New York Times*, 15 May 2014, www.nytimes.com/2014/05/18/books/review/colson-whitehead-by-the-book.html. Interview.

Personal

Subject's Last Name, First Name. Concise description. Day Month Year.

Bazelon, L. S. Telephone interview with the author. 4 Oct. 2020.

45. Map

If the title doesn't make clear it's a map, add a label at the end.

Title of Map. Publisher, Date.

Brooklyn. J. B. Beers, 1874. Map.

46. Musical score

Composer's Last Name, First Name. *Title of Composition*. Publisher, Year of publication.

Frank, Gabriela Lena. *Compadrazgo*. G. Schirmer, 2007.

47. Oral presentation

Presenter's Last Name, First Name. "Title of Presentation." Sponsoring Institution, Date, Location.

Cassin, Michael. "Nature in the Raw—The Art of Landscape Painting." Berkshire Institute for Lifelong Learning, 24 Mar. 2005, Clark Art Institute, Williamstown, Massachusetts.

48. Virtual presentation on *Zoom* or other platform

Author's Last Name, First Name. "Title." Sponsoring Institution, Day Month Year, online.

Budhathoki, Thir. "Cross-Cultural Perceptions of Literacies in Student Writing." Conference on College Composition and Communication, 9 Apr. 2021, online.

49. Podcast

If you accessed a podcast online, give the URL; if you accessed it through an app, indicate that instead.

"Title of Episode." *Title of Podcast*, hosted by First Name Last Name, season, episode, Production Company, Date, URL.

"DUSTWUN." *Serial*, hosted by Sarah Koenig, season 2, episode 1, WBEZ / Serial Productions, 10 Dec. 2015, serialpodcast.org/season-two/1/dustwun.

"DUSTWUN." *Serial*, hosted by Sarah Koenig, season 2, episode 1, WBEZ / Serial Productions, 10 Dec. 2015. *Spotify* app.

50. Radio program

"Title of Episode." *Title of Program*, hosted by First Name Last Name, Station, Day Month Year.

"In Defense of Ignorance." *This American Life*, hosted by Ira Glass, WBEZ, 22 Apr. 2016.

51. Sound recording

If you accessed a recording online, give the URL; if you accessed it through an app, indicate that instead.

Artist's Last Name, First Name. "Title of Work." *Title of Album*, Label, Release Date, URL.

Beyoncé. "Pray You Catch Me." *Lemonade*, Parkwood Entertainment / Columbia Records, 2016, www.beyonce.com/album/lemonade-visual-album/songs.

Simone, Nina. "To Be Young, Gifted and Black." *Black Gold*, RCA Records, 1970. *Spotify* app.

On a CD or Vinyl

Artist's Last Name, First Name. "Title of Work." *Title of Album*, Label, Date. CD *or* Vinyl LP.

Brown, Greg. "Canned Goods." *The Live One*, Red House, 1995. CD.

52. Video game

Title of Game. Version, Distributor, Date of release.

Animal Crossing: New Horizons. Version 1.1.4, Nintendo, 6 Apr. 2020.

53. Generative AI

At the time of this printing, the *MLA Style Center* website gives advice on how to cite content generated by AI tools such as *ChatGPT*. See style.mla.org for more information.

"Prompt fed into AI tool" prompt. *AI Tool*, version, Company, Date, URL.

"Explain how a light bulb works" prompt. *ChatGPT*, 23 Mar. version, OpenAI, 14 Apr. 2023, chat.openai.com.

If you're citing a creative work, you can use the title and a concise description instead of including the prompt. If there's no title, you can use the first few words of the text.

"New sneakers, so fresh . . ." haiku about sneakers. *ChatGPT*, 23 Mar. version, OpenAI, 24 Apr. 2023, chat.openai.com.

FORMATTING A RESEARCH ESSAY

Name, course, title. MLA does not require a separate title page, unless your paper is a group project. In the upper left-hand corner of your first page, include your name, your instructor's name, the course name and number, and the date. Center the title of your paper on the line after the date; capitalize it as you would a book title. If your paper is a group project, include all of that information on a title page instead, listing all the authors.

Page numbers. In the upper right-hand corner of each page, one-half inch below the top of the page, include your last name and the page number. If it's a group project and all the names don't fit, include only the page number. Number pages consecutively throughout your paper.

Typeface, spacing, margins, and indents. Choose a typeface that is easy to read (such as Times New Roman) and that provides a clear contrast between regular text and italic text. Set the font size between 11 and 13 points. Double-space the entire paper, including your works-cited list and any notes. Set one-inch margins at the top, bottom, and sides of your text; do not justify your text. The first line of each paragraph should be indented one-half inch from the left margin. End punctuation should be followed by one space.

Headings. Short essays do not generally need headings, but they can be useful in longer works. Use a large, bold font for the first level of heading, and smaller fonts and italics to signal lower-level headings. MLA requires that headings all be flush with the left margin.

First-Level Heading
Second-Level Heading
Third-Level Heading

Long quotations. When quoting more than three lines of poetry, more than four lines of prose, or dialogue between characters in a drama, set off the quotation from the rest of your text, indenting it one-half inch (or five spaces) from the left margin. Do not use quotation marks, and put any parenthetical documentation *after* the final punctuation.

> In *Eastward to Tartary*, Robert Kaplan captures ancient and contemporary Antioch for us:
>
>> At the height of its glory in the Roman-Byzantine age, when it had an amphitheater, public baths, aqueducts, and sewage pipes, half a million people lived in Antioch. Today the population is only 125,000. With sour relations between Turkey and Syria, and unstable politics throughout the Middle East, Antioch is now a backwater—seedy and tumbledown, with relatively few tourists. I found it altogether charming. (123)
>
> In the first stanza of Matthew Arnold's "Dover Beach," exclamations make clear the speaker is addressing someone who is also present in the scene:
>
>> Come to the window, sweet is the night air!
>> Only, from the long line of spray
>> Where the sea meets the moon-blanched land,
>> Listen! You hear the grating roar
>> Of pebbles which the waves draw back, and fling . . . (lines 6–10)

Be careful to maintain the poet's line breaks. If a line does not fit on one line of your paper, put the extra words on the next line. Indent that line an additional quarter inch (or two spaces). If a citation doesn't fit, put it on the next line, flush with the right margin.

Tables and illustrations. Insert illustrations and tables close to the text that discusses them, and be sure to make clear how they relate to your point. For tables, provide a number (Table 1) and a title on separate lines above the table. Below the table, provide a caption with source information and any notes. Notes should be indicated with lowercase letters. For graphs, photos, and other figures, provide a figure number (Fig. 1) and caption with source information below the figure. If you give only brief source information, use commas between elements—Zhu Wei, *New Pictures of the Strikingly Bizarre #9*, print, 2004—and include full source information in your list of works cited. If you give full source information in the caption, don't include the source in your list of works cited. Punctuate as you would in the works-cited list, but don't invert the author's name: Berenice Sydney. *Fast Rhythm*. 1972, Tate Britain, London.

List of works cited. Start your list on a new page, following any notes. Center the title, "Works Cited," and double-space the entire list. Begin each entry at the left margin, and indent subsequent lines one-half inch (or five spaces). Alphabetize the list by authors' last names (or by editors' or translators' names, if appropriate). Alphabetize works with no author or editor by title, disregarding "A," "An," and "The." To cite more than one work by a single author, list them as in number 4 on page 593.

SAMPLE RESEARCH ESSAY

Walter Przybylowski wrote the following analysis for a first-year writing course. It is formatted according to the guidelines of the MLA (style.mla.org).

Walter Przybylowski

Professor Matin

English 102, Section 3

4 May 2019w

Holding Up the Hollywood Stagecoach:

The European Take on the Western

  The Western film has long been considered by film scholars and enthusiasts to be a distinctly American genre. Not only its subject matter but its characteristic themes originate in America's own violent and exciting past. For many years, Hollywood sold images of hard men fighting savages on the plains to the worldwide public; by ignoring the more complicated aspects of "how the West was won" and the true nature of relations between Native Americans and whites, filmmakers were able to reap great financial and professional rewards. In particular, the huge success of John Ford's 1939 film *Stagecoach* brought about countless imitations that led over the next few decades to American Westerns playing in a sort of loop, which reinforced the same ideas and myths in film after film.

  After the success of German-made Westerns in the 1950s, though, a new take on Westerns was ushered in by other European countries. Leading the Euro-Western charge, so to speak, were the Italians, whose cynical, often politically pointed Westerns left a permanent impact on an American-based genre. Europeans, particularly the Italians, challenged the dominant conventions of the American Western by complicating the morality of the characters, blurring the lines between good and evil, and also by complicating the traditional narrative, visual, and aural structures of Westerns. In this way, the genre motifs that *Stagecoach* initiated are explored in the European Westerns of the 1950s, 1960s, and early 1970s, yet with a striking difference in style. Specifically, Sergio Leone's 1968 film *Once upon a Time in the West* broke many of the rules set by the Hollywood Western and in the process created a new visual language for the Western. Deconstructing key scenes from this film reveals the demythologization at work in many of the Euro-Westerns, which led to a genre enriched by its presentation of a more complicated American West.

Stagecoach is a perfect example of almost all the visual, sound, and plot motifs that would populate "classic" Hollywood Westerns for the next few decades. The story concerns a group of people, confined for most of the movie inside a stagecoach, who are attempting to cross a stretch of land made dangerous by Apache Indians on the warpath. Little effort is made to develop the characters of the Indians, who appear mainly as a narrative device, adversaries that the heroes must overcome in order to maintain their peaceful existence. This plot, with minor changes, could be used as a general description for countless Westerns. In his book *The Crowded Prairie: American National Identity in the Hollywood Western*, Michael Coyne explains the significance of *Stagecoach* to the Western genre and its influence in solidifying the genre's archetypes:

> [I]t was *Stagecoach* which . . . redefined the contours of the myth. The good outlaw, the whore with a heart of gold, the Madonna/Magdalene dichotomy between opposing female

Quotations of more than 4 lines are indented ½" (5 spaces) and double-spaced.

leads, the drunken philosopher, the last-minute cavalry rescue, the lonely walk down Main Street—all became stereotypes from *Stagecoach*'s archetypes. *Stagecoach* quickly became the model against which other "A" Westerns would be measured. (18–19)

Coyne is not exaggerating when he calls it "the model": in fact, all of these stereotypes became a sort of checklist of things that audiences expected to see. The reliance on a preconceived way to sell Western films to the public—where you could always tell the good characters from the bad and knew before the film ended how each character would end up—led to certain genre expectations that the directors of the Euro-Westerns would later knowingly reconfigure. As the influential critic Pauline Kael wrote in her 1965 book *Kiss Kiss Bang Bang*, "The original *Stagecoach* had a mixture of reverie and reverence about the American past that made the picture seem almost folk art; we wanted to believe in it even if we didn't" (52).

There seemed to be a need not just in Americans but in moviegoers around the world to believe that there was (or had been) a great untamed land out there just waiting to be cultivated. More important, as Kael pointed out, Americans wanted to believe that the building of America was a wholly righteous endeavor wherein the land was free for the taking—the very myth that Europeans later debunked through parody and subversive filmmaking techniques. According to Theresa Harlan, author of works on Native American art, the myth was based on the need of early white settlers to make their elimination of American

Indians more palatable in light of the settlers' professed Christian beliefs. In her article "Adjusting the Focus for an Indigenous Presence," Harlan writes that

> Eurocentric frontier ideology and the representations of indigenous people it produced were used to convince many American settlers that indigenous people were incapable of discerning the difference between a presumed civilized existence and their own "primitive" state. (136)

Although this myth had its genesis long before the advent of motion pictures, the Hollywood Western drew inspiration from it and continued to legitimize and reinforce its message. *Stagecoach*, with its high level of technical skill and artistry, redefined the contours of the myth, and a close look at the elements that made the film the "classic" model of the Western is imperative in order to truly understand its influence.

The musical themes that underscore the actions of the characters are especially powerful in this regard and can be as powerful as the characters' visual representation on screen. In *Stagecoach*, an Apache does not appear until more than halfway through the movie, but whenever one is mentioned, the soundtrack fills with sinister and foreboding drumbeats. The first appearance of Indians is a scene without dialogue, in which the camera pans between the stagecoach crossing through the land and Apaches watching from afar. The music that accompanies this scene is particularly telling, since as the camera pans between stagecoach and Apaches, the music shifts in

Przybylowski 5

tone dramatically from a pleasant melody to a score filled with dread. When the heroes shoot and kill the Apaches, then, the viewer has already been subjected to specific film techniques to give the stagecoach riders moral certitude in their annihilation of the alien menace. This kind of score is powerful stuff to accompany an image and does its best to tell the viewers how they should react. When Europeans start to make Westerns, the line of moral certitude will become less distinct.

In her essay "Of Mother Nature and Marlboro Men: An Inquiry into the Cultural Meanings of Landscape Photography," Deborah Bright argues that landscape photography has reinforced certain formulaic myths about landscape, and the same can be said of the Hollywood Western during the 1940s and 1950s. For example, in *Stagecoach*, when the stagecoach finally sets out for its journey through Apache territory, a fence is juxtaposed against the vast wide-open country in the foreground. The meaning is clear—the stagecoach is leaving civilized society to venture into the wilds of the West, and music swells as the coach crosses into that vast landscape (fig. 1). Ford uses landscape in this way to engender in the audience the desired response of longing for a time gone past, where there was land free for the taking and plenty to go around. Yet Bright suggests that "[i]f we are to redeem landscape photography from its narrow self-reflexive project, why not openly question the assumptions about nature and culture that it has traditionally served and use our practice instead to criticize them?" (141). This is exactly what Europeans, and Italians in particular, seem to have done with the Western. When Europeans started to make their own Westerns, they took advantage of their outsider status in relation

Figure number calls readers' attention to illustration.

Brackets show that the writer has changed a capital letter to lowercase to make the quotation fit smoothly into his own sentence.

Fig. 1. In *Stagecoach*, swelling music signals the coach's passage through the western landscape. Still from *Stagecoach*. *Internet Movie Database*, www.imdb.com/title/tt0031971/mediaviewer/rm1596567552.

to an American genre by openly questioning the myths that have been established by *Stagecoach* and its cinematic brethren.

Sergio Leone's *Once upon a Time in the West* is a superior example of a European artist's take on the art form of the American Western. The "plot" of the film is flimsy, driven by the efforts of a mysterious character played by Charles Bronson to avenge himself against Henry Fonda's character, a lowdown gunfighter trying to become a legitimate businessman. Claudia Cardinale plays a prostitute who is trying to put her past behind her. The similarities to American Westerns, on paper at least, seem to be so great as to make *Once upon a Time* almost a copy of what had long been done in Hollywood, but a closer look at European Westerns and at this film in particular shows that Leone is consciously sending up the stereotypes. After all, he needs to work within the genre's language if he is to adequately challenge it.

During the opening of *Once upon a Time in the West*, the viewer is given a kind of audio and visual tour of Euro-Western aesthetics. Leone introduces three gunmen in typical Italian Western style, with the first presented by a cut to a dusty boot heel from which the camera slowly pans up until it reaches the top of the character's cowboy hat. During this pan, the gunman's gear and its authenticity—a major aspect of the Italian Western—can be taken in by the audience. A broader examination of the genre would show that many Euro-Westerns use this tactic of hyperrealistic attention to costuming and weaponry, which Ignacio Ramonet argues is intended to distract the viewer from the unreality of the landscape:

> Extreme realism of bodies (hairy, greasy, foul-smelling), clothes or objects (including mania for weapons) in Italian films is above all intended to compensate for the complete fraud of the space and origins. The green pastures, farms and cattle of American Westerns are replaced by large, deserted canyons. (32)

In the opening scene, the other two gunfighters are introduced by a camera panning across the room, allowing characters to materialize seemingly out of nowhere. Roger Ebert notes that Leone

> established a rule that he follows throughout ... that the ability to see is limited by the sides of the frame. At important moments in the film, what the camera cannot see, the characters cannot see, and that gives Leone the freedom to surprise us with entrances that cannot be explained by the practical geography of his shots.

[No page number given for online source.]

It is these aesthetic touches created to compensate for a fraudulent landscape that ushered in a new visual language for the Western. The opening of *Once upon a Time in the West* undercuts any preconceived notion of how a Western should be filmed, and this is exactly Leone's intention: "The director had obviously enjoyed dilating the audience's sense of time, exploiting, in his ostentatious way, the rhetoric of the Western, and dwelling on the tiniest details to fulfill his intention" (Frayling 197). By using jarring edits with amplified sounds, Leone informs the audience not only that he has seen all the popular Hollywood Westerns, but that he is purposely not going to give them that kind of movie. The opening ten-minute scene would be considered needlessly long in a typical Hollywood Western, but Leone is not making a copy of a Hollywood Western. In fact, it is this reliance on the audience's previously established knowledge of Westerns that allows Euro-Westerns to subvert the genre. Leone and other directors of Euro-Westerns are asking the public to open their eyes, to not believe what is shown; they are attempting to take the camera's power away by

[When no signal phrase is used to introduce a quotation, the author's name is included in the parenthetical citation.]

Przybylowski 9

parodying its effect. When Leone has characters magically appear in the frame, or amplifies the squeaking of a door hinge on a soundtrack, he is ridiculing the basic laws that govern American Westerns. The opening of *Once upon a Time* can be read as a sort of primer for what is about to come for the rest of the film, and its power leaves viewers more attuned to what they are watching.

Leone's casting also works to heighten the film's subversive effect. Henry Fonda, the quintessential good guy in classic Hollywood Westerns like *My Darling Clementine*, is cast as the ruthless Frank, a gunman shown murdering a small child early in the film. In a 1966 article on Italian Westerns in the *Saturday Evening Post*, Italian director Maurizio Lucidi gave some insight into the European perspective that lay behind such choices:

> We're adding the Italian concept of realism to an old American myth, and it's working. Look at Jesse James. In your country he's a saint. Over here we play him as a gangster. That's what he was. Europeans today are too sophisticated to believe in the honest gunman movie anymore. They want the truth and that's what we're giving them. (qtd. in Fox 55)

Leone knew exactly what he was doing, and his casting of Fonda went a long way toward confusing the audience's sympathies and complicating the simple good guy versus bad guy model of Hollywood films. For this reason, Fonda's entrance in the film is worth noting. The scene begins with a close-up of a shotgun barrel, which quickly explodes in a series of (gun)shots that establish a scene of a father and son out hunting near their homestead. Here, Leone starts to move the camera more, with pans from father to son and a crane shot of their house as they return home to a picnic table with an abundance of food: the family is apparently about to celebrate something. Throughout this scene, crickets chirp on the soundtrack—until Leone abruptly cuts them off, the sudden silence quickly followed by close-ups of the uneasy faces of three family members. Leone is teasing the audience: he puts the crickets back on the soundtrack until out of nowhere we hear a gunshot. Instead of then focusing on the source or the target of the gunshot, the camera pans off to the sky, and for a moment the viewer thinks the shot is from a hunter. We next see a close-up of the father's face as he looks off into the distance, then is rattled when he sees his daughter grasping the air, obviously shot. As he runs toward her, tracked by the camera in a startling way, he is quickly shot down himself.

The family has been attacked seemingly out of nowhere, with only a young boy still alive. During the massacre, there is no musical score, just the abstract brutality of the slayings. Then Leone gives us a long camera shot of men appearing out of dust-blown winds, from nearby brush. It is obvious to the viewer that these men are the killers, but there is no clear sight of their faces: Leone uses long camera shots of their backs and an overhead shot as they converge on the young boy. This is the moment when Leone introduces Henry Fonda; he starts with the camera on the back of Fonda's head and then does a slow track around until his face is visible. At this point, audience members around the world would still have a hard time believing Fonda was a killer of these innocent people. Through crosscutting between the young boy's confused face and Fonda's smiling eyes, Leone builds a doubt in the audience—maybe he will not kill the boy. Then the crosscutting is interrupted with a close-up of Fonda's large Colt coming out of its holster, and Ennio Morricone's score, full of sadness, becomes audible. The audience's fears are realized: Fonda is indeed the killer. This scene is a clear parody of Hollywood casting stereotypes, and Leone toys with audience expectations by turning upside down the myth of the noble outlaw as portrayed by John Wayne in *Stagecoach*.

During the late 1960s and the early 1970s, Europeans were at odds with many of the foreign policies of the United States, a hostility expressed in Ramonet's characterization of this period as one "when American imperialism in Latin America and Southeast Asia was showing itself to be particularly brutal" (33). Morton, the railroad baron who is Frank's unscrupulous employer in *Once upon a Time in the West*, can easily be read as a critique of the sometimes misguided ways Americans went about bringing their way of life to other countries. Morton represents the bringer of civilization, usually a good thing in the classic Western genre, where civilization meant doctors, schools, homes for everyone. But the Europeans question how this civilization was built. Leone, in a telling quotation, gives his perspective: "I see the history of the West as really the reign of violence by violence" (qtd. in Frayling 134).

Instead of the civilizing myth and its representations, the concern of *Once upon a Time*—and the Euro-Western in general—is to give voice to the perspective of the marginal characters: the Native Americans, Mexicans, and Chinese who rarely rated a position of significance in a Hollywood Western. In *Once upon a Time*, Bronson's character, Harmonica, pushes the plot forward with his need to avenge. Harmonica stands in for all the racial stereotypes that populated the American Western genre. When he and Frank meet in the movie's climactic duel, Frank is clearly perplexed about why this man wants to fight him, but his ego makes it impossible for him to refuse. They meet in an abandoned yard, with Frank in the extreme foreground and Harmonica in the extreme background (fig. 2). The difference between the two is thus presented from both physical and ideological standpoints: Frank guns down settlers to make way for the railroad (and its owner), whereas Harmonica helps people to fend for themselves. Morricone's score dominates the soundtrack during this final scene, with a harmonica blaring away throughout. The costuming of Frank in black and Harmonica in white is an ironic throwback to classic Hollywood costuming and one that suggests Harmonica is prevailing over the racial stereotypes of American Westerns. Leone milks the scene for all it's worth, with the camera circling Harmonica as Frank looks for a perfect point to start the duel. Harmonica never moves, his face steadily framed in a close-up. Meanwhile, Frank is shown in mostly long shots; his body language shows that he is uncertain about the outcome of the duel, while Harmonica knows the ending.

 As the two seem about to draw, the camera pushes into Harmonica's eyes, and there is a flashback to a younger Frank walking toward the camera, putting a harmonica into the mouth of a boy (the young Harmonica), and forcing him to participate in Frank's hanging of the boy's older brother. This brutal scene, in which Frank unknowingly seals his own destiny, is set in actual American locations and is taken

Fig. 2. The climactic duel in *Once upon a Time in the West* challenges the casting and costuming stereotypes of the Hollywood Western. Still from *Once upon a Time in the West*. Internet Movie Database, www.imdb.com/title/tt0064116/mediaviewer/rm1124971008.

directly from John Ford Westerns; Leone is literally bringing home the violence dealt to minorities in America's past. As soon as the brother is hanged, the scene returns to the present, and Frank is shot through the heart. As he lies dying, we see a look of utter disbelief on his face as he asks Harmonica, "Who are you?" At this moment, a harmonica is shoved into his mouth. Only then does recognition play over Frank's face; as he falls to the ground, his face in close-up is a grotesque death-mask not unlike the massacred victims of Morton's train. The idea of past misdeeds coming back to haunt characters in the present is a clear attempt to challenge the idea that the settlers had a moral right to conquer and destroy indigenous people in order to "win" the West.

    The tremendous success of *Stagecoach* was both a blessing and curse for the Western genre. Without it, the genre would surely never have gained the success it did, but this success came with ideological and creative limitations. Both the popularity and the limitations of the American Western may have inspired European directors to attempt something new with the genre, and unlike American filmmakers, they could look more objectively at our history and our myths. Leone's demythologization of the American Western has proved a valuable addition to the Western genre. The effect of the Euro-Western can be seen in American cinema as early as *The Wild Bunch* in 1969—and as recently as the attention in *Brokeback Mountain* to types of Western characters usually marginalized. In this way, Italian Westerns forced a new level of viewing of the Western tradition that made it impossible to ever return to the previous Hollywood model.

Przybylowski 15

Works Cited

Bright, Deborah. "Of Mother Nature and Marlboro Men: An Inquiry into the Cultural Meanings of Landscape Photography." *The Contest of Meaning: Critical Histories of Photography*, edited by Richard Bolton, MIT Press, 1993, pp. 125–43.

Coyne, Michael. *The Crowded Prairie: American National Identity in the Hollywood Western*. I. B. Tauris, 1997.

Ebert, Roger. "The Good, the Bad and the Ugly." *Chicago Sun-Times*, 3 Aug. 2003, www.rogerebert.com/reviews/great-movie-the-good-the-bad-and-the-ugly-1968.

Fox, William. "Wild Westerns, Italian Style." *The Saturday Evening Post*, 6 Apr. 1968, pp. 50–55.

Frayling, Christopher. *Spaghetti Westerns: Cowboys and Europeans from Karl May to Sergio Leone*. St. Martin's Press, 1981.

Harlan, Theresa. "Adjusting the Focus for an Indigenous Presence." *Overexposed: Essays on Contemporary Photography*, edited by Carol Squiers, New Press, 1999, pp. 134–52.

Kael, Pauline. *Kiss Kiss Bang Bang*. Bantam Books, 1965.

Once upon a Time in the West. Directed by Sergio Leone, performances by Henry Fonda and Charles Bronson, Paramount, 1968.

Ramonet, Ignacio. "Italian Westerns as Political Parables." *Cineaste*, vol. 15, no. 1, 1986, pp. 30–35. *JSTOR*, www.jstor.org/stable/41686858.

Stagecoach. Directed by John Ford, United Artists, 1939.

THIRTY-THREE

APA Style

AMERICAN PSYCHOLOGICAL ASSOCIATION (APA) style calls for (1) brief documentation in parentheses near each in-text citation and (2) complete documentation in a list of references at the end of your text. The models in this chapter draw on the *Publication Manual of the American Psychological Association*, 7th edition (2020). Additional information is available at apastyle.org.

A DIRECTORY TO APA STYLE

In-Text Documentation 637

1. Author named in a signal phrase 638
2. Author named in parentheses 638
3. Authors with the same last name 639
4. Two authors 639
5. Three or more authors 639
6. Organization or government as author 639
7. Author unknown 640
8. Two or more works together 640
9. Two or more works by one author in the same year 640
10. Source quoted in another source 640
11. Work without page numbers 641
12. An entire work 641
13. Personal communication 641
14. Generative AI 642

[635]

Notes   642

Reference List   643

Key Elements for Documenting Sources   643

    Authors   643

    Dates   644

    Titles   644

    Source information   645

Authors and Other Contributors   646

1. One author   646
2. Two authors   646
3. Three or more authors   646
4. Two or more works by the same author   647
5. Author and editor   647
6. Author and translator   648
7. Editor   648
8. Unknown or no author or editor   648
9. Organization or government as author   648

Articles and Other Short Works   649

Documentation Map: Article in a Journal with DOI   651

Documentation Map: Webpage   653

10. Article in a journal   649
11. Article in a magazine   649
12. Article in a newspaper   649
13. Article on a news website   650
14. Journal article from a database   650
15. Editorial   650
16. Review   650
17. Comment on an online article or post   652
18. Webpage   652

Books, Parts of Books, and Reports   654

Documentation Map: Book   655

19. Basic entry for a book   654
20. Edition other than the first   654
21. Edited collection or anthology   654
22. Work in an edited collection or anthology   656
23. Entry in a reference work (dictionary, thesaurus, or encyclopedia)   656
24. Book in a language other than English   656
25. One volume of a multivolume work   656

26. Religious work 657
27. Report by a government agency or other organization 657
28. Published dissertation 658
29. Paper or poster presented at a conference 658

Audio, Visual, and Other Sources 658

30. *Wikipedia* entry 659
31. Online forum post 659
32. Blog post 659
33. Online streaming video 659
34. Podcast 660
35. Podcast episode 660
36. Film 660
37. Television series 661
38. Television series episode 661
39. Music album 661
40. Song 661
41. Software, computer program, or mobile app 662
42. Lecture slides or notes 662
43. Recording of a speech or webinar 662
44. Map 663
45. Social media posts 663
46. Data set 664
47. Supreme Court case 664
48. Generative AI 664

Sources Not Covered by APA 665

Formatting a Research Essay 665

Sample Research Essay 667

Throughout this chapter, you'll find models and examples that are color-coded to help you see how writers include source information in their texts and reference lists: tan for author or editor, yellow for title, gray for publication information—publisher, date of publication, page number(s), DOI or URL, and so on.

IN-TEXT DOCUMENTATION

Brief documentation in your text makes clear to your readers precisely what you took from a source. If you are quoting, provide the page number(s) or other information that will help readers locate the quotation in the source.

See Ch. 32 in the ebook for a video on understanding in-text citations.

You are not required to give the page number(s) with a paraphrase or summary, but you may want to do so if you are citing a long or complex work.

PARAPHRASES and **SUMMARIES** are more common than **QUOTATIONS** in APA-style projects. See Chapter 30 for more on all three kinds of citation. As you cite each source, you will need to decide whether to name the author in a signal phrase—"as McCullough (2001) wrote"—or in parentheses—"(McCullough, 2001)." Note that APA requires you to use the past tense for verbs in **SIGNAL PHRASES**, or the present perfect if you are referring to an ongoing action that started in the past or to something that didn't occur at a specific time: "Moss (2019) argued," "Many authors have argued."

1. Author named in a signal phrase

Put the date in parentheses after the author's last name, unless the year is mentioned in the sentence. If you are including the page number, put it in parentheses after the quotation, paraphrase, or summary. Documentation information in parentheses should come *before* the period at the end of the sentence and *after* any quotation marks.

> McCullough (2001) described John Adams as having "the hands of a man accustomed to pruning his own trees, cutting his own hay, and splitting his own firewood" (p. 18).

> In 2001, McCullough noted that John Adams's hands were those of a laborer (p. 18).

> John Adams had "the hands of a man accustomed to pruning his own trees," according to McCullough (2001, p. 18).

If the author is named after a quotation, as in this last example, put the page number(s) after the date within the parentheses.

2. Author named in parentheses

If you do not mention an author in a signal phrase, put the name, the year of publication, and any page number(s) in parentheses at the end of the sentence or right after the quotation, paraphrase, or summary.

> John Adams had "the hands of a man accustomed to pruning his own trees" (McCullough, 2001, p. 18).

3. Authors with the same last name

If your reference list includes more than one person with the same last name, include initials to distinguish the authors from one another.

> Eclecticism is common in modern criticism (J. M. Smith, 1992, p. vii).

4. Two authors

Always mention both authors. Use "and" in a signal phrase, but use an ampersand (&) in parentheses.

> Carlson and Ventura (1990) wanted to introduce Julio Cortázar, Marjorie Agosín, and other Latin American writers to an audience of English-speaking adolescents (p. v).

> According to the Peter Principle, "In a hierarchy, every employee tends to rise to his level of incompetence" (Peter & Hull, 1969, p. 26).

5. Three or more authors

When you refer to a work by three or more contributors, name only the first author followed by "et al.," Latin for "and others."

> Peilen et al. (1990) supported their claims about corporate corruption with startling anecdotal evidence (p. 75).

6. Organization or government as author

If an organization name is recognizable by its abbreviation, give the full name and the abbreviation the first time you cite the source. In subsequent references, use only the abbreviation. If the organization does not have a familiar abbreviation, always use its full name.

First reference

> The American Psychological Association (APA, 2020)

> (American Psychological Association [APA], 2020)

Subsequent references

> The APA (2020)

> (APA, 2020)

7. Author unknown

Use the complete title if it's short; if it's long, use the first few words of the title under which the work appears in the reference list. Italicize the title if it's italicized in the reference list; if it isn't italicized there, enclose the title in quotation marks.

> According to *Feeding Habits of Rams* (2000), a ram's diet often changes from one season to the next (p. 29).

> The article noted that one healthy liver donor died because of "frightening" postoperative care ("Every Patient's Nightmare," 2007).

8. Two or more works together

If you document multiple works in the same parentheses, place the source information in alphabetical order, separated by semicolons.

> Many researchers have argued that what counts as "literacy" is not necessarily learned at school (Heath, 1983; Moss, 2003).

Multiple authors in a signal phrase can be named in any order.

9. Two or more works by one author in the same year

If your list of references includes more than one work by the same author published in the same year, order them alphabetically by title, adding lowercase letters ("a," "b," and so on) to the year.

> Kaplan (2000a) described orderly shantytowns in Turkey that did not resemble the other slums he visited.

10. Source quoted in another source

When you cite a source that was quoted in another source, add the words "as cited in." If possible, cite the original source instead.

> Thus, Modern Standard Arabic was expected to serve as the "moral glue" holding the Arab world together (Choueri, 2000, as cited in Walters, 2019, p. 475).

11. Work without page numbers

Instead of page numbers, some works have paragraph numbers, which you should include (preceded by the abbreviation "para.") if you are referring to a specific part of such a source.

> Russell's dismissals from Trinity College at Cambridge and from City College in New York City have been seen as examples of the controversy that marked his life (Irvine, 2006, para. 2).

In sources with neither page nor paragraph numbers (e.g., many online journals), refer readers to a particular part of the source if possible, perhaps indicating a heading and the paragraph under the heading: (Brody, 2020, Introduction, para. 2).

12. An entire work

You do not need to give a page number if you are directing readers' attention to an entire work.

> Kaplan (2000) considered Turkey and Central Asia explosive.

When you are citing an entire website, give the URL in the text. You do not need to include the website in your reference list. To cite a webpage, see number 18 on page 652.

> Beyond providing diagnostic information, the website for the Alzheimer's Association (https://www.alz.org) includes a variety of resources for the families of patients.

13. Personal communication

Document emails, telephone conversations, personal interviews, personal letters, messages from nonarchived electronic discussion sources, and other personal texts as "personal communication," along with the person's initial(s), last name, and the date. You do not need to include such personal communications in your reference list.

> L. Strauss (personal communication, December 6, 2013) told about visiting Yogi Berra when they both lived in Montclair, New Jersey.

14. Generative AI

The author is the name of the company that created the generative AI product.

> AI models can be used for predictive modeling, helping researchers anticipate trends, behaviors, or outcomes based on historical data (OpenAI, 2023).

NOTES

You may need to use footnotes to give an explanation or information that doesn't fit into your text or to acknowledge the use of AI in your writing process. To signal a content footnote, place a superscript numeral at the appropriate point in your text. Include this information in a footnote, either at the bottom of that page or on a separate page with the heading "Footnotes" centered and in bold, after your reference list. If you have multiple notes, number them consecutively throughout your text. Here is an example from *In Search of Solutions: A New Direction in Psychotherapy* (2003).

Text with superscript

An important part of working with teams and one-way mirrors is taking the consultation break, as at Milan, BFTC, and MRI.[1]

Footnote

[1] It is crucial to note here that while working within a team is fun, stimulating, and revitalizing, it is not necessary for successful outcomes. Solution-oriented therapy works equally well when working solo.

Here's an example from a student essay.

Text with superscript

This essay argues that teacher looping in middle-school grades has multiple benefits for students.[1]

Footnote

¹I acknowledge the use of ChatGPT in my researching and writing process. I used ChatGPT to get an overview of the concept of looping in education in order to better understand the topic before starting my research. I also used ChatGPT for help in creating an outline for my essay. I've included my initial prompts and full ChatGPT conversation histories in an appendix.

REFERENCE LIST

A reference list provides full bibliographic information for every source cited in your text with the exception of entire websites, common software and mobile apps, and personal communications. See page 666 for guidelines on formatting such a list; for a sample reference list, see pages 684–85.

Key Elements for Documenting Sources

To document a source in APA style, you need to provide information about the author, the date, the title of the work you're citing, and the source itself (who published it; volume, issue, and page numbers; any DOI or URL). The following guidelines explain how to handle each of these elements generally, but there will be exceptions. For that reason, you'll want to consult the entries for the specific kinds of sources you're documenting; these entries provide templates showing which details you need to include. Be aware, though, that sometimes the templates will show elements that your source doesn't have; if that's the case, just omit those elements.

Authors

Most entries begin with the author's last name, followed by the first and any middle initials: Smith, Z. for Zadie Smith; Kinder, D. R. for Donald R. Kinder.

- If the author is a group or organization, use its full name: Black Lives Matter, American Historical Association.
- If there is no author, put the title of the work first, followed by the date.

- If the author uses a screen name, first give their real name, followed by the screen name in brackets: Scott, B. [@BostonScott2]. If only the screen name is known, leave off the brackets: AvalonGirl1990.

Dates

Include the date of publication in parentheses right after the author. Some sources require only the year; others require the year, month, and day; and still others require something else. Consult the entry in this chapter for the specific source you're documenting.

- For a book, use the copyright year, which you'll find on the copyright page. If more than one year is given, use the most recent one.
- For most magazine or newspaper articles, use the full date that appears on the work, usually the year followed by the month and day.
- For a journal article, use the year of the volume.
- For a work on a website, use the date when the work was last updated. If that information is not available, use the date when the work was published.
- If a work has no date, use "n.d." for "no date."
- For online content that is likely to change, include the month, day, and year when you retrieved it. No need to include a retrieval date for materials that are unlikely to change.

Titles

Capitalize only the first word and any proper nouns and adjectives in the title and subtitle of a work. But sometimes you'll also need to provide the title of a periodical or website where a source was found, and those are treated differently: capitalize all the principal words (excluding articles and prepositions).

- For books, reports, webpages, podcasts, and any other works that stand on their own, italicize the title: *White fragility*, *Radiolab*, *The 9/11 report*. Do not italicize the titles of the sources where you found them, however: NPR, ProQuest.

- For journal articles, book chapters, TV series episodes, and other works that are part of a larger work, do not italicize the title: The snowball effect, Not your average Joe. But do italicize the title of the larger work: *The Atlantic*, *Game of thrones*.
- If a work has no title, include a description in square brackets after the date: [Painting of sheep on a hill].
- If the title of a work you're documenting includes another title, italicize it: *Frog and Toad and the self*. If the title you're documenting is itself in italics, do not italicize the title within it: *Stay, illusion!* The *Hamlet* doctrine.
- For untitled social media posts or comments, include the first twenty words as the title, in italics, followed by a bracketed description: *TIL pigeons can fly up to 700 miles in one day* [Post].

Source information

This indicates where the work can be found (in a database or on a website, for example, or in a magazine or on a podcast) and includes information about the publisher; any volume, issue, and page numbers; and, for some sources, a DOI or URL. DOIs and URLs are included in all the templates; if the work you are documenting doesn't have one, just leave it off.

- For a work that stands on its own (a book, a report, a webpage), the source might be the publisher, a database, or a website.
- For a work that's part of a larger work (an article, an episode in a TV series, an essay in a collection), the source might be a magazine, a TV series, or an anthology.
- Give the volume and issue for journals and magazines that include that information. No need to give them for newspapers.
- Include a DOI for any work that has one, whether you accessed the source in print or online. For an online work with no DOI, include a working URL unless the work is from an academic database. You can use a shortDOI (https://shortdoi.org/) or a URL shortened using an online URL shortener, as long as the shorter DOI or URL leads to the correct work. No need to include a URL for a print work with no DOI.

Authors and Other Contributors

This section provides general guidelines for documenting authors and other contributors across sources and in various kinds of media (in print, online, and in other media). Note that most of the examples in this section are books. If you are documenting a different kind of source, follow the relevant formatting guidelines.

1. One author

> Author's Last Name, Initials. (Year of publication). *Title of book.* Publisher. DOI or URL
>
> Lewis, M. (2003). *Moneyball: The art of winning an unfair game.* W. W. Norton.

This book does not have a DOI, so that element does not appear in the reference entry.

2. Two authors

> First Author's Last Name, Initials, & Second Author's Last Name, Initials. (Year of publication). *Title of book.* Publisher. DOI or URL
>
> Montefiore, S., & Montefiore, S. S. (2016). *The royal rabbits of London.* Aladdin.

3. Three or more authors

For three to twenty authors, include all names.

> First Author's Last Name, Initials, Next Author's Last Name, Initials, & Final Author's Last Name, Initials. (Year of publication). *Title of book.* Publisher. DOI or URL
>
> Greig, A., Taylor, J., & MacKay, T. (2013). *Doing research with children: A practical guide* (3rd ed.). Sage.

For a work by twenty-one or more authors, name the first nineteen authors, followed by three ellipsis points, and end with the final author.

Gao, R., Asano, S. M., Upadhyayula, S., Pisarev, I., Milkie, D. E., Liu, T.-L., Singh, V., Graves, A., Huynh, G. H., Zhao, Y., Bogovic, J., Colonell, J., Ott, C. M., Zugates, C., Tappan, S., Rodriguez, A., Mosaliganti, K. R., Sheu, S.-H., Pasolli, H. A., . . . Betzig, E. (2019, January 18). Cortical column and whole-brain imaging with molecular contrast and nanoscale resolution. *Science, 363*(6424). https://doi.org/10.1126/science.aau8302

4. Two or more works by the same author

If the works were published in different years, list them chronologically.

    Lewis, B. (1995). *The Middle East: A brief history of the last 2,000 years.* Scribner.

    Lewis, B. (2003). *The crisis of Islam: Holy war and unholy terror.* Modern Library.

If the works were published in the same year, list them alphabetically by title (ignoring "A," "An," and "The"), adding "a," "b," and so on to the year.

    Kaplan, R. D. (2000a). *The coming anarchy: Shattering the dreams of the post Cold War.* Random House.

    Kaplan, R. D. (2000b). *Eastward to Tartary: Travels in the Balkans, the Middle East, and the Caucasus.* Random House.

5. Author and editor

If a book has an author and an editor who is credited on the cover, include the editor in parentheses after the title. If the book is a republished version of an earlier book, include the year of publication of the version you are using as the date and the original publication year at the end.

    Author's Last Name, Initials. (Year of publication). *Title of book* (Editor's Initials Last Name, Ed.). Publisher. DOI or URL (Original work published Year)

    Dick, P. F. (2008). *Five novels of the 1960s and 70s* (J. Lethem, Ed.). Library of America. (Original works published 1964–1977)

6. Author and translator

Author's Last Name, Initials. (Year of publication). *Title of book* (Translator's Initials Last Name, Trans.). Publisher. DOI or URL (Original work published Year)

Hugo, V. (2008). *Les misérables* (J. Rose, Trans.). Modern Library. (Original work published 1862)

7. Editor

Editor's Last Name, Initials (Ed.). (Year of publication). *Title of book*. Publisher. DOI or URL

Jones, D. (Ed.). (2007). *Modern love: 50 true and extraordinary tales of desire, deceit, and devotion*. Three Rivers Press.

8. Unknown or no author or editor

When there's no known author or editor, start with the title.

Title. (Year of publication). Publisher. DOI or URL

Feeding habits of rams. (2000). Land's Point Press.

Hot property: From carriage house to family compound. (2004, December). *Berkshire Living, 1*(1), 99.

Clues in salmonella outbreak. (2008, June 21). *The New York Times*, A13.

If the author is listed as "Anonymous," treat that as the author's name in the reference list entry.

9. Organization or government as author

Sometimes an organization or a government agency is both author and publisher. If so, omit the publisher.

Organization Name *or* Government Agency. (Year of publication). *Title of book*. DOI or URL

Catholic News Service. (2002). *Stylebook on religion 2000: A reference guide*.

Articles and Other Short Works

Articles, essays, reviews, and other short works are found in periodicals and books—in print, online, or in a database. For most short works, provide information about the author, the date, the titles of both the short work and the longer work, any volume and issue numbers, any page numbers, various kinds of publication information, and a DOI or URL if applicable.

10. Article in a journal

Author's Last Name, Initials. (Year). Title of article. *Title of Journal, volume*(issue), page(s). DOI or URL

Gremer, J. R., Sala, A., & Crone, E. E. (2010). Disappearing plants: Why they hide and how they return. *Ecology, 91*(11), 3407–3413. https://doi.org/10.1890/09-1864.1

If a DOI is long or complicated, it's acceptable to use a shortDOI. Create one by entering the DOI into the shortDOI service (https://shortdoi.org/). A URL can also be shortened using any online URL shortener, as long as the shorter URL leads to the correct work.

11. Article in a magazine

If a magazine is published weekly, include the day and the month. Include any volume number and issue number after the magazine title.

Author's Last Name, Initials. (Year, Month Day). Title of article. *Title of Magazine, volume*(issue), page(s). DOI or URL

Klump, B. (2019, November 22). Of crows and tools. *Science, 366*(6468), 965. https://doi.org/10.1126/science.aaz7775

12. Article in a newspaper

If page numbers are consecutive, separate them with an en dash. If not, separate them with a comma.

Author's Last Name, Initials. (Year, Month Day). Title of article. *Title of Newspaper,* page(s). URL

Schneider, G. (2005, March 13). Fashion sense on wheels. *The Washington Post,* F1, F6.

13. Article on a news website

Articles on *CNN, HuffPost, Salon, Vox,* and other news websites are documented differently from articles published in online newspapers and magazines. If an article is published in an online news source that is not a periodical or a blog, the article is treated as a stand-alone work, and the title should be italicized. Do not italicize the name of the website.

Author's Last Name, Initials. (Year, Month Day). *Title of article.* Title of Site. URL

Travers, C. (2019, December 3). *Here's why you keep waking up at the same time every night.* HuffPost. https://bit.ly/3drSwAR

14. Journal article from a database

Author's Last Name, Initials. (Year). Title of article. *Title of Journal, volume*(issue), page(s). DOI

Simpson, M. (1972). Authoritarianism and education: A comparative approach. *Sociometry, 35*(2), 223–234. https://doi.org/10.2307/2786619

15. Editorial

Editorials can appear in journals, magazines, and newspapers. The following example is from an online newspaper. If the editorial is unsigned, put the title of the editorial in the author position.

Author's Last Name, Initials. (Year, Month Day). Title of editorial [Editorial]. *Title of Newspaper.* URL

The Guardian view on local theatres: The shows must go on [Editorial]. (2019, December 6). *The Guardian.* https://bit.ly/2VZHIUg

16. Review

The following example is a book review in a newspaper; if you are citing a review that appears in print or online in a journal, magazine, or newspaper, use this general format, indicating in brackets what is being reviewed (a film, an app, etc.).

Documentation Map (APA) / Article in a Journal with DOI

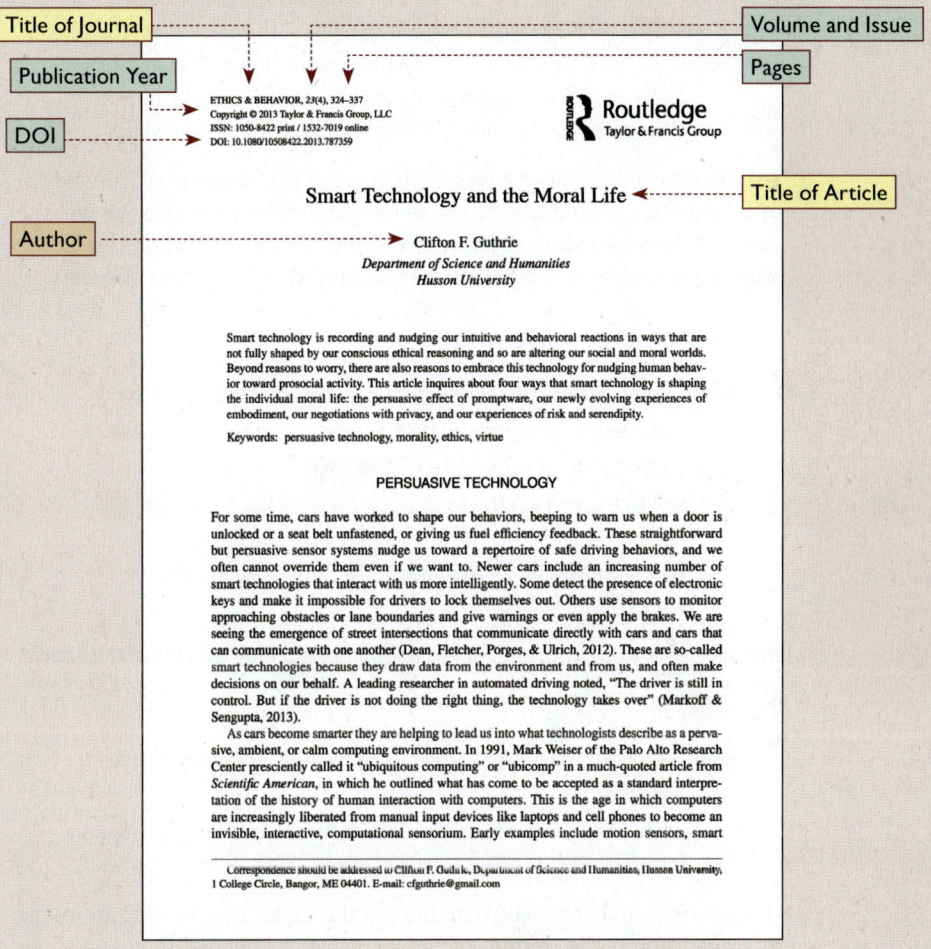

Guthrie, C. F. (2013). Smart technology and the moral life. *Ethics & Behavior, 23*(4), 324–337. https://doi.org/10.1080/10508422.2013.787359

> Reviewer's Last Name, Initials. (Year, Month Day). Title of review [Review of the book *Title of book*, by Author's Initials Last Name]. *Title of Newspaper.* DOI or URL

Joinson, S. (2017, December 15). Mysteries unfold in a land of minarets and magic carpets [Review of the book *The city of brass*, by S. A. Chakraborty]. *The New York Times.* https://nyti.ms/2kvwHFP

For a review published on a website that is not associated with a periodical or a blog, italicize the title of the review and do not italicize the website name. If the review does not have a title, include the information about the work being reviewed in brackets immediately after the date of publication.

17. Comment on an online article or post

> Author's Last Name, Initials [username]. (Year, Month Day). Text of comment up to twenty words [Comment on the article "Title of article"]. *Title of Publication.* DOI or URL

PhyllisSpecial. (2020, May 10). How about we go all the way again? [Comment on the article "2020 Eagles schedule: Picking wins and losses for all 16 games"]. *The Philadelphia Inquirer.* https://rb.gyiduabz

Include a link to the comment if possible; if not, include the URL of the article.

18. Webpage

> Author's Last Name, Initials. (Year, Month Day). *Title of work.* Title of Site. URL

Pleasant, B. (n.d.). *Annual bluegrass.* The National Gardening Association. https://garden.org/learn/articles/view/2936/

If the author and the website name are the same, use the website name as the author. If the content of the webpage is intended to change over time and no archived version exists, use "n.d." as the date and include a retrieval date.

Documentation Map (APA) / Webpage

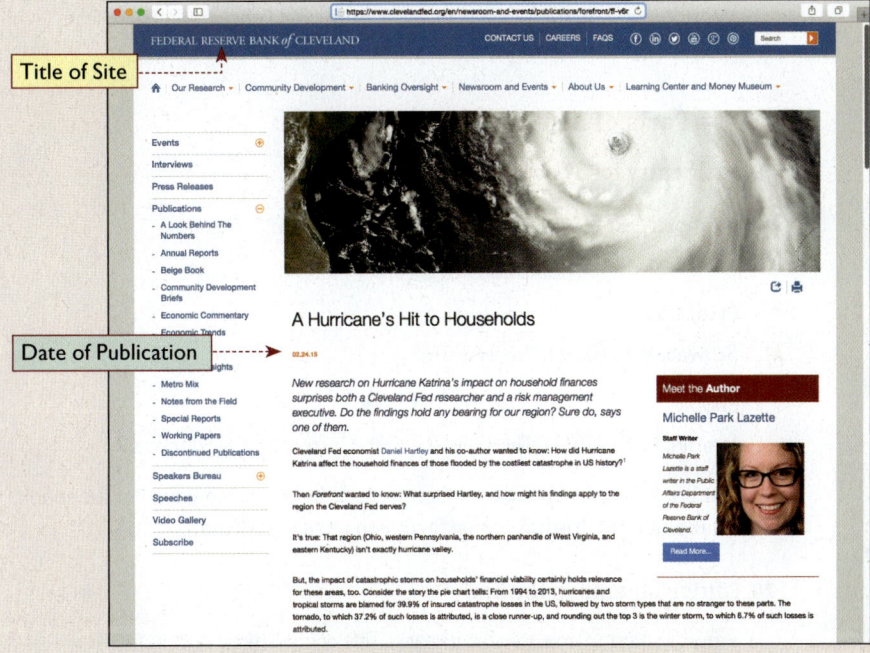

Lazette, M. P. (2015, February 24). *A hurricane's hit to households.* Federal Reserve Bank of Cleveland. https://www.clevelandfed.org/en/newsroom-and-events/publications/forefront/ff-v6n01ff-20150224-v6n0107-a-hurricanes-hit-to-households.aspx

Centers for Disease Control and Prevention. (2019, December 2). *When and how to wash your hands*. https://www.cdc.gov/handwashing/when-how-handwashing.html

Worldometer. (n.d.). *World population*. Retrieved February 2, 2020, from https://www.worldometers.info/world-population/

Books, Parts of Books, and Reports

19. Basic entry for a book

Author's Last Name, Initials. (Year of publication). *Title of book*. Publisher. DOI *or* URL

Print book

Schwab, V. E. (2018). *Vengeful*. Tor.

Ebook

Jemisin, N. K. (2017). *The stone sky*. Orbit. https://bit.ly/2DrGzKR

A print book and an ebook are documented in the same way. For an ebook, do not include the format or platform you used (e.g., Kindle).

20. Edition other than the first

Author's Last Name, Initials. (Year). *Title of book* (Name or number ed.). Publisher. DOI *or* URL

Burch, D. (2008). *Emergency navigation: Find your position and shape your course at sea even if your instruments fail* (2nd ed.). International Marine/McGraw-Hill.

21. Edited collection or anthology

Editor's Last Name, Initials (Ed.). (Year of edited edition). *Title of anthology* (Name *or* number ed., Vol. number). Publisher. DOI *or* URL

Raviv, A., Oppenheimer, L., & Bar-Tal, D. (Eds.). (1999). *How children understand war and peace: A call for international peace education*. Jossey-Bass.

Documentation Map (APA) / Book

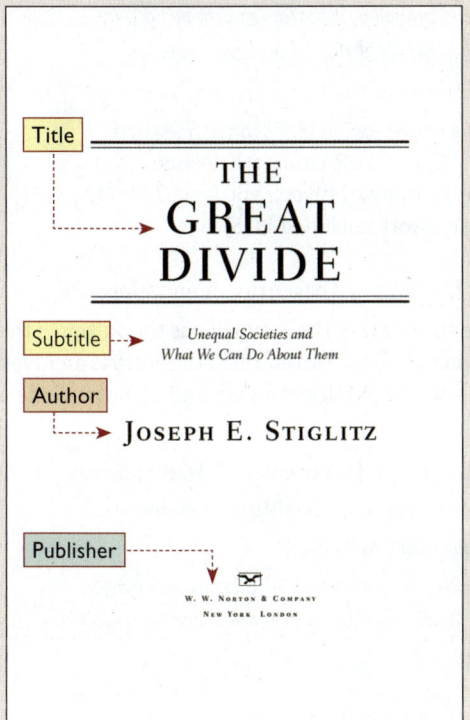
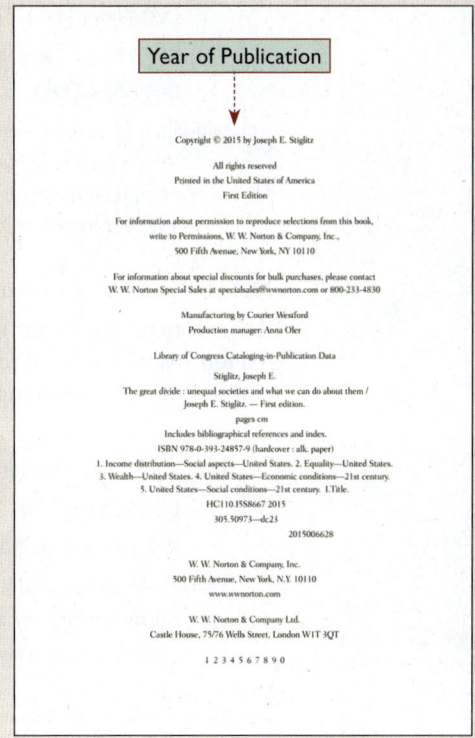

Stiglitz, J. E. (2015). *The great divide: Unequal societies and what we can do about them.* W. W. Norton.

22. Work in an edited collection or anthology

Author's Last Name, Initials. (Year). Title of work. In Editor's Initials Last Name (Ed.), *Title of anthology* (Name or number ed., Vol. number, pp. pages). Publisher. DOI or URL (Original work published Year)

Baldwin, J. (2018). Notes of a native son. In M. Puchner, S. Akbari, W. Denecke, B. Fuchs, C. Levine, P. Lewis, & E. Wilson (Eds.), *The Norton anthology of world literature* (4th ed., Vol. F, pp. 728–743). W. W. Norton. (Original work published 1955)

23. Entry in a reference work (dictionary, thesaurus, or encyclopedia)

If the entry has no author, use the name of the publisher as the author. If the reference work has no editor, do not include an editor. If the entry is archived or is not intended to change, use the publication date and do not include a retrieval date.

Author's Last Name, Initials. (Year). Title of entry. In Editor's Initials Last Name (Ed.), *Title of reference book* (Name or number ed., Vol. number, pp. pages). Publisher. URL

Merriam-Webster. (n.d.). Epoxy. In *Merriam-Webster.com dictionary*. Retrieved January 29, 2020, from https://www.merriam-webster.com/dictionary/epoxy

24. Book in a language other than English

Author's Last Name, Initials. (Year). *Title of book* [English translation of title]. Publisher. DOI or URL

Ferrante, E. (2011). *L'amica geniale* [My brilliant friend]. Edizione E/O.

25. One volume of a multivolume work

If the volume does not have a separate title, include the volume number in parentheses after the title.

Author's Last Name, Initials. (Year). *Title of entire work* (Vol. number). Publisher. DOI *or* URL

Spiegelman, A. (1986). *Maus* (Vol. 1). Random House.

If the volume does have a separate title, include the volume number and title in italics after the main title (see no. 26 for an example from a religious work).

26. Religious work

Do not include an author for most religious works. If you are citing an annotated version, include the editor and/or translator. If the date of original publication is known, include it at the end.

Unannotated

Title of work. (Year of publication). Publisher. URL (Original work published Year)

New American Bible. (2002). United States Conference of Catholic Bishops. http://www.vatican.va/archive/ENG0839/_INDEX.HTM (Original work published 1970)

Annotated

Editor's Last Name, Initials (Ed.). (Year of publication). *Title of work.* Publisher. URL (Original work published Year)

Marks, H. (Ed.). (2012). *The English Bible, The King James Version: Vol. 1. The Old Testament.* W. W. Norton. (Original work published 1611)

27. Report by a government agency or other organization

Author's Last Name, Initials. (Year, Month Day). *Title of report* (Report No. number). Publisher. DOI *or* URL

Centers for Disease Control and Prevention. (2009). *Fourth national report on human exposure to environmental chemicals.* US Department of Health and Human Services. https://www.cdc.gov/exposurereport/pdf/fourthreport.pdf

Omit the report number if one is not given. If more than one government department is listed as the publisher, list the most specific department as the author and the larger department as the publisher.

28. Published dissertation

Author's Last Name, Initials. (Year). *Title of dissertation* (Publication No. number) [Doctoral dissertation, Name of School]. Database or Archive Name. URL

Solomon, M. (2016). *Social media and self-examination: The examination of social media use on identity, social comparison, and self-esteem in young female adults* (Publication No. 10188962) [Doctoral dissertation, William James College]. ProQuest Dissertations and Theses Global.

If the thesis or dissertation is in a database, do not include a URL. Include a URL if the thesis or dissertation is published elsewhere online. If the dissertation is unpublished, use the name of the school as the source.

29. Paper or poster presented at a conference

Presenter's Last Name, Initials. (Year, Month First Day–Last Day). *Title of paper* or *poster* [Paper or Poster presentation]. Name of Conference, City, State, Country. URL

Dolatian, H., & Heinz, J. (2018, May 25–27). *Reduplication and finite-state technology* [Paper presentation]. The 53rd Annual Meeting of the Chicago Linguistic Society, Chicago, IL, United States. http://chicagolinguisticsociety.org/public/CLS53_Booklet.pdf

Audio, Visual, and Other Sources

If you are referring to an entire website, do not include the website in your reference list; simply mention the website's name in the body of your paper and include the URL in parentheses. Do not include email, personal communication, or other unarchived discussions in your list of references.

30. *Wikipedia* entry

Because *Wikipedia* has archived versions of its pages, give the date on which you accessed the page and the permanent URL of the archived page, which is found by clicking "View history."

> Title of entry. (Year, Month Day). In *Wikipedia*. URL

List of sheep breeds. (2019, September 9). In *Wikipedia*. https://en.wikipedia.org/w/index.php?title=List_of_sheep_breeds&oldid=914884262

For a wiki that doesn't have permanent links to archived versions of its pages, include a retrieval date before the URL.

31. Online forum post

> Author's Last Name, Initials [username]. (Year, Month Day). Content of the post up to twenty words [Online forum post]. Title of Site. URL

Hanzus, D. [DanHanzus]. (2019, October 23). GETCHA DAN HANZUS. ASK ME ANYTHING! [Online forum post]. Reddit. https://bit.ly/38WgmSF

32. Blog post

> Author's Last Name, Initials [username]. (Year, Month Day). Title of post. *Title of Blog*. URL

gcrepps. (2017, March 28). Shania Sanders. *Women@NASA*. https://blogs.nasa.gov/womenatnasa/2017/03/28/shania-sanders/

If only the username is known, do not use brackets.

33. Online streaming video

> Uploader's Last Name, Initials [username]. (Year, Month Day). *Title of video* [Video]. Name of Video Platform. URL

CinemaSins. (2014, August 21). *Everything wrong with* National treasure *in 13 minutes or less* [Video]. YouTube. https://www.youtube.com/watch?v=1ul-_ZWvXTs

Whoever uploaded the video is considered the author, even if someone else created the content. If only the username is known, do not use brackets. If there is another title within a title, put that other title in reverse italics.

34. Podcast

Host's Last Name, Initials (Host). (First Year–Last Year). *Podcast name* [Audio podcast]. Production Company. URL

Poor, N., Woods, E., & Thomas, R. (Hosts). (2017–present). *Ear hustle* [Audio podcast]. PRX. https://www.earhustlesq.com/

35. Podcast episode

Host's Last Name, Initials (Host). (Year, Month Day). Episode title (No. episode number) [Audio podcast episode]. In *Podcast name*. Production Company. URL

Tamposi, E., & Samocki, E. (Hosts). (2020, January 8). The year of the broads [Audio podcast episode]. In *The broadcast podcast*. Podcast One. https://podcastone.com/episode/the-year-of-the-broads

The host of the podcast, or the executive producer if known, is considered the author. Do not include an episode number if one isn't given.

36. Film

Director's Last Name, Initials (Director). (Year). *Title of film* [Film]. Production Company. URL

Jenkins, B. (Director). (2016). *Moonlight* [Film]. A24; Plan B; PASTEL.

Cuarón, A. (Director). (2016). *Harry Potter and the prisoner of Azkaban* [Film; two-disc special ed. on DVD]. Warner Bros.

List the director as the author of the film. Indicate how you watched the film only if the format is important to what you've written.

37. Television series

Executive Producer's Last Name, Initials (Executive Producer). (First Year–Last Year). *Title of series* [TV series]. Production Company. URL

Iungerich, L., Gonzalez, E., & Haft, J. (Executive Producers). (2018–present). *On my block* [TV series]. Crazy Cat Lady Productions.

Indicate how you watched the TV series (2-disc DVD set, for example) only if the format is relevant to what you've written.

38. Television series episode

Writer's Last Name, Initials (Writer), & Director's Last Name, Initials (Director). (Year, Month Day). Title of episode (Season number, Episode number) [TV series episode]. In Executive Producer's Initials Last Name (Executive Producer), *Title of series*. Production Company. URL

Siegal, J. (Writer), Morgan, D. (Writer), & Sackett, M. (Director). (2018, December 6). Janet(s) (Season 3, Episode 10) [TV series episode]. In M. Schur, D. Miner, M. Sackett, & D. Goddard (Executive Producers), *The good place*. Fremulon; 3 Arts Entertainment; Universal Television.

39. Music album

Artist's Last Name, Initials. (Year). *Title of album* [Album]. Label.

Lennox, A. (1995). *Medusa* [Album]. Arista.

40. Song

Artist's Last Name, Initials. (Year). Title of song [Song]. On *Title of album*. Label. URL

Giddens, R. (2015). Shake sugaree [Song]. On *Tomorrow is my turn*. Nonesuch.

The recording artist or group is considered the author. Do not include a URL unless the song can be accessed only on one specific online platform.

41. Software, computer program, or mobile app

Include entries for software, programs, or mobile apps if they are uncommon or if you quote or paraphrase from them. Otherwise, just include the name (not italicized) and version number in the body of your text.

Last Name, Initials. (Year). *Name of program* (Version number) [Computer software]. Publisher. URL

Blount, K. (2018). *Scrivener for Windows* (Version 1.9.9.0) [Computer software]. Literature & Latte. https://www.literatureandlatte.com/scrivener

Include a description of the content in brackets after the version number. For a mobile app, use "App Store" or wherever you accessed the app as the publisher. Use the year of publication of the version you accessed as the date.

42. Lecture slides or notes

Author's Last Name, Initials. (Year, Month Day). *Title of presentation* [Description of content]. Publisher. URL

Pavliscak, P. (2016, February 21). *Finding our happy place in the internet of things* [PowerPoint slides]. Slideshare. https://bit.ly/3aOcfs7

If the lecture notes or slides do not have a title, describe the contents in brackets after the date.

43. Recording of a speech or webinar

Author's Last Name, Initials. (Year, Month Day *or* Year). *Title* [Speech audio recording *or* Webinar]. Publisher. URL

Kennedy, J. F. (1961, January 20). *Inaugural address* [Speech audio recording]. American Rhetoric. https://bit.ly/339Gc3e

Rodrigo, S. (2020). *Keep calm (and compassionate) & move everything online* [Webinar]. W. W. Norton. https://seagull.wwnorton.com/CompositionTeachingOnline

For a speech, include the year, month, and day. For a webinar, include only the year.

44. Map

Mapmaker's Last Name, Initials. (Year). *Title of map* [Map]. Publisher. URL

Daniels, M. (2018). *Human terrain: Visualizing the world's population, in 3D* [Map]. The Pudding. https://pudding.cool/2018/10/city_3d/

Google. (n.d.). [Google Maps directions for biking from Las Vegas, Nevada, to Los Angeles, California]. Retrieved January 30, 2020, from https://goo.gle/maps/9NdekwAkHeo4HM4N7

To cite a dynamic map, use "n.d." for the date and include a retrieval date. For the title, include a description of the map in brackets.

45. Social media posts

Use the author's real name and include the social media handle in brackets. If only the handle is known, do not use brackets. List any audiovisual content (e.g., a video, an image, a link) in brackets after the content of the post. Replicate emoji if possible; if not, include a bracketed description. Follow the spelling and capitalization of the original post.

Author's Last Name, Initials [@username]. (Year, Month Day). *Content of post up to twenty words* [Description of audiovisual content] [Type of post]. Platform. URL

Instagram photograph or video

Jamil, J. [@jameelajamilofficial]. (2018, July 18). *Happy Birthday to our leader. I steal all my acting faces from you. @kristenanniebell* [Face with smile and sunglasses emoji] [Photograph]. Instagram. https://www.instagram.com/p/BlYX5F9FuGL/

X post

Baron, D. [@DrGrammar]. (2019, November 11). *Gender conceal: Did you know that pronouns can also hide someone's gender?* [Thumbnail with link attached] [Post]. X. https://bit.ly/2vaCcDc

Facebook post

Philadelphia Eagles. (2019, December 3). "'We control our own destiny.' That's going to be the message moving forward to this football team." #*FlyEaglesFly* [Thumbnail with link attached] [Status update]. Facebook. https://bit.ly/39Ghjil

46. Data set

Author's Last Name, Initials. (Year). *Title of data set* (Version number) [Data set]. Publisher. DOI or URL

Pew Research Center. (2019). *Core trends survey* [Data set]. https://www.pewresearch.org/internet/dataset/core-trends-survey/

If the name of the author is the same as the name of the publisher, omit the publisher.

47. Supreme Court case

Name of Case, volume U.S. page (Year). URL

Plessy v. Ferguson, 163 U.S. 537 (1896). https://www.oyez.org/cases/1850-1900/163us537

Obergefell v. Hodges, 576 U.S. ___ (2015). https://www.oyez.org/cases/2014/14-556

The source for most Supreme Court cases is the *United States Reports*, which is abbreviated "U.S." in the reference list entry. If the case does not yet have a page number, use three underscores instead. Italicize the name of the court case in any in-text citations, but do not italicize it in the reference list entry.

48. Generative AI

The author is the name of the company that created the generative AI tool.

Author. (Date). *Name of tool* (Version of tool) [Description]. URL

OpenAI. (2023). *ChatGPT* (Mar 14 version) [Large language model]. https://chat.openai.com/chat

Sources Not Covered by APA

To document a source for which APA does not provide guidelines, look at models similar to the source you have cited. Give any information readers will need in order to find it themselves—author; date of publication; title; source, including DOI or URL (if applicable); and any other pertinent information. You might want to test your reference note to be sure it will lead others to your source.

FORMATTING A RESEARCH ESSAY

Title page. APA generally requires a title page. The page number should go in the upper right-hand corner. Center the full title of the paper in bold in the top half of the page. Center your name, the name of your department and school, the course number and name, the instructor's name, and the due date on separate lines below the title. Leave one line between the title and your name.

Page numbers. Place the page number in the upper right-hand corner. Number pages consecutively throughout.

Typeface, spacing, margins, and indents. Use a legible typeface that will be accessible to everyone, either a serif typeface (such as Times New Roman or Bookman) or a sans serif typeface (such as Calibri or **Verdana**). Use sans serif within figure images. Double-space the entire paper, including any notes and your list of references; the only exception is footnotes at the bottom of a page, which should be single-spaced, and text within tables and images, the spacing of which will vary. Leave one-inch margins at the top, bottom, and sides of your text; do not justify the text. The first line of each paragraph should be indented one-half inch (or five to seven spaces) from the left margin. Use one space after end-of-sentence punctuation.

Headings. Though they are not required in APA style, headings can help readers follow your text. The first level of heading should be bold, centered, and capitalized as you would any other title; the second level of heading should be bold and flush with the left margin; the third level should be bold, italicized, and flush left.

First Level Heading

Second Level Heading

Third Level Heading

Abstract. An abstract is a concise summary of your paper that introduces readers to your topic and main points. Most scholarly journals require an abstract; an abstract is not typically required for student papers, so check your instructor's preference. Put your abstract on the second page, with the word "Abstract" centered and in bold at the top. Unless your instructor specifies a length, limit your abstract to 250 words or fewer.

Long quotations. Indent quotations of forty or more words one-half inch (or five to seven spaces) from the left margin. Do not use quotation marks, and place the page number(s) or documentation information in parentheses *after* the end punctuation. If there are paragraphs in the quotation, indent the first line of each paragraph another one-half inch.

> Kaplan (2000) captured ancient and contemporary Antioch:
>
> > At the height of its glory in the Roman-Byzantine age, when it had an amphitheater, public baths, aqueducts, and sewage pipes, half a million people lived in Antioch. Today the population is only 125,000. With sour relations between Turkey and Syria, and unstable politics throughout the Middle East, Antioch is now a backwater—seedy and tumbledown, with relatively few tourists. (p. 123)
>
> Antioch's decline serves as a reminder that the fortunes of cities can change drastically over time.

List of references. Start your list on a new page after the text but before any endnotes. Title the page "References," centered and in bold, and double-space the entire list. Each entry should begin at the left margin, and subsequent lines should be indented one-half inch (or five to seven spaces). Alphabetize the list by authors' last names (or by editors' names, if appropriate). Alphabetize works that have no author or editor by title, disregarding "A," "An," and "The." Be sure every source listed is cited in the text; do not include sources that you consulted but did not cite.

Tables and figures. Above each table or figure (charts, diagrams, graphs, photos, and so on), provide the word "Table" or "Figure" and a number, flush left and in bold (e.g., **Table 1**). On the following line, give a descriptive title, flush left and italicized. Below the table or figure, include a note with any necessary explanation and source information. Number tables and figures separately, and be sure to discuss them in your text so that readers know how they relate.

Table 1
Hours of Instruction Delivered per Week

	American classrooms	Japanese classrooms	Chinese classrooms
First grade			
Language arts	10.5	8.7	10.4
Mathematics	2.7	5.8	4.0
Fifth grade			
Language arts	7.9	8.0	11.1
Mathematics	3.4	7.8	11.7

Note. Adapted from "Peeking Out from Under the Blinders: Some Factors We Shouldn't Forget in Studying Writing," by J. R. Hayes, 1991, National Center for the Study of Writing and Literacy (Occasional Paper No. 25). National Writing Project website: http://www.nwp.org/

SAMPLE RESEARCH ESSAY

Gabriela Agustina Uribe wrote the following paper, "'¿Por qué no sabes español?': Pressured Monolingualism and Its Impacts on Mexican Americans," for a course on the rhetoric of language, identity, and power at Stanford University. It is formatted according to the guidelines of the *Publication Manual of the American Psychological Association*, 7th edition (2020).

"¿Por qué no sabes español?"
Pressured Monolingualism and Its Impacts on Mexican Americans

Gabriela A. Uribe

Program in Writing and Rhetoric, Stanford University

PWR 2JJ: The Rhetoric of Language, Identity and Power

Dr. Jennifer Johnson

March 17, 2020

Abstract

While many teachers, scholars, and administrators in higher education support multilingual education in theory, they struggle to know how to enact it. Compounding this challenge is the fact that negative attitudes towards and policies about multilingualism in the K-12 context influence some multilingual families to decide to raise their children to speak English only. Drawing on semi-structured interviews with family members and friends, I examined the causes and consequences of monolingualism for Mexican Americans. I argue that political and educational discourses pressure families to assimilate into a monolingual English-speaking society and that "pressured monolingualism" weakens family relationships, ethnic identities, and cultures. I conclude by considering why K-12 school districts should embrace multilingualism, how public attitudes can change, and how those who have experienced pressured monolingualism can learn languages while exploring and celebrating their home cultures.

"¿Por qué no sabes español?"
Pressured Monolingualism and Its Impacts on Mexican Americans

A little girl stands at the stove, helping her *abuelita* roll enchiladas for dinner. She always cherishes this time where she feels truly connected to her grandma and her culture. Her cousin taps her on her shoulder, telling her in Spanish that he wants to play the card game UNO but doesn't know the rules. "¿Puedes explicarlos?" The girl's face turns bright red, and her heart starts pounding. "No, no puedo." A disappointed pause follows. "¿Por qué no sabes español?" her cousin asks. She looks down at her feet and repeats what she always says when asked this. "No sé."

A woman is in a Manhattan restaurant. She orders her food, comfortably speaking to the employee behind the register in Spanish. Suddenly, a man behind her starts yelling. He yells at both women for not speaking English, since this is America, after all. Other people in the restaurant call out his ignorance, but he continues to berate the women, saying, "My guess is they're not documented. So my next call is to ICE to have each one of them kicked out of my country" (Karimi & Levenson, 2018).

Both of these scenes are true events—the former, a personal experience from my childhood, and the latter, an event that happened in New York in 2018. Over the past few years, there has been an influx in news stories similar to that of the woman in Manhattan. In these stories, "real" Americans are angered to hear people speaking languages other than English and respond with public shaming and berating. These instances exhibit a condescension many English-speaking

Americans have towards minority languages, which was reflected in Donald Trump's presidential administration. In a 2015 GOP debate, Trump said, "We have to have assimilation—to have a country, we have to have assimilation. . . . This is a country where we speak English, not Spanish" (CNN, 2015, 0:26). Administrative actions have supported this rhetoric; the Spanish version of the White House website was taken down just after Trump was inaugurated in January 2017 (O'Keefe, 2017). The site's immediate disappearance left Americans without a source of official White House information translated into Spanish.

Taking a step back to look at an overview of the attitudes surrounding monolingualism versus multilingualism, there are a plethora of contradictions. On the one hand, many instructors in higher education have long recognized and emphasized the importance of multilingualism and its educational benefits (National Council of Teachers of English, 2020; Okal, 2014). However, misconceptions that multilingualism harms children still exist and circulate widely (Kroll & Dussias, 2017). Shifts in political power and clear sentiments against Spanish-speaking Americans have also highlighted the desire many have for an English-only America (Anbinder, 2019; O'Keefe, 2017). Therefore, many arguments still exist against the use of native languages, especially Spanish, despite all the evidence supporting multilingualism. As I observe these many conflicting perceptions, I've often asked myself, "How do parents decide whether or not to raise their children as monolingual?" The way in which I not only enter this conversation but add to it is through my own experiences as a Mexican American college student who struggles with her personal ethnic identity.

The little girl in the first story was me. Although my grandparents and dad are native Spanish speakers, I was raised speaking only English and have experienced the effects of that for the last 19 years. For me, not being able to speak Spanish has created a divide between myself, family members, and Mexican culture as a whole. This rift has led me to become curious about the complex relationships between monolingualism and ethnic identity.

In this paper, I argue that political and educational pressures encouraging Mexican Americans to assimilate into a monolingual English-speaking society can have negative effects on Mexican Americans' relationships with family members and their understanding of their own ethnic identity and culture.

Metodología

To explore the effects of monolingualism, I conducted interviews with my parents, grandmother, sister, and friend and fellow student Julian Aguilar. I made these interviews semi-structured, asking some of the same predetermined questions, mainly about their upbringings and experiences with English and Spanish, but leaving room for open-ended discussion. The interviews with my mom and Julian, who were both raised to speak only English, included the following questions:

1. Was your parents' decision to have you learn only English a conscious one?
2. How did being monolingual impact your relationship with relatives?
3. Growing up, how did you identify ethnically?

Since my grandma and dad both learned Spanish as their first language and are bilingual, I asked them questions that related to their experiences with and perceptions of learning English:

1. What do you think are the benefits of learning English?
2. What was your experience like learning English?

Aside from preparing certain questions, I let the interviews flow naturally. This semi-structured approach allowed me to explore general themes while tailoring my questions to each of my interviewees. New and interesting ideas were explored, some of which I had not considered.

Once I conducted and recorded the interviews, I transcribed them. Then, in order to identify similar themes, I relied on grounded theory coding, a qualitative research strategy for uncovering relationships from data instead of using existing theory to form testable hypotheses. These links revealed common thoughts and experiences regarding monolingualism in Mexican Americans. An outside coder provided feedback on the themes I identified, further solidifying the findings from this primary research.

In terms of secondary research, I identified many academic journals and online sources that explore various topics, from language policy in American schools to attitudes towards bilingualism in the classroom. To supplement the cultural information from my primary research, I also analyzed existing case studies and detailed personal accounts.

Discusión

Going through the grounded coding process with the interviews I conducted revealed several major themes. I spoke with four people: my mom, Victoria Uribe; a friend, Julian Aguilar; my dad, Juan Uribe; and my grandmother, Maria E. Flores. The first two grew up speaking only English, and the latter two grew up speaking Spanish in Mexico and learned English later on in the United States. The key themes from the interviews are laid out in Table 1 below.

Table 1

Ground Coding Table

Code	Count	Example quote
1. parents want better life/ experience for their kid	3	"[My parents] knew how hard it was for them to come to America not knowing English and having that language barrier be an obstacle to achieve their American Dream . . . so they both made the decision to not teach me their languages."
1a. knowing English = success	4	"When you speak English, the doors open for you in different ways."
1b. learning a language later in life is hard	7	"If I was watching a TV show or listening to a song in Spanish, it was really hard because it went so fast."
2. not knowing Spanish inhibited relationships	3	"It was harder when I was younger, right. I couldn't tell [my grandma] things or ask her things much because I couldn't talk to her that well."
3. language connects to culture	3	"I don't think you can experience the culture without the language. They go hand in hand."

Note. Data gathered from personal interviews and subsequently coded using ground theory coding.

The first major theme I identified was parents' desire for a better life for their children. In addition, two subthemes emerged: the idea that knowing English will bring success, and the idea that learning languages later in life is hard. The latter was especially prevalent in the interviews: all four interviewees expressed the difficulty of learning a new language, whether English or Spanish. The second common thread was the way that not knowing Spanish inhibits relationships. My mom and Julian both explained how growing up knowing only English limited their connections with family members. The last major theme was the conviction that language and culture are closely connected. The prevalence of these three main themes is not limited to my interviews, however: many educators and researchers have also expressed these themes in their own work. In the following subsections, I dive deeper into each theme, synthesizing interviewee responses with outside secondary sources to explain the motivations behind and impacts of pressured monolingualism on Mexican Americans.

Padres bien intencionados

A common thread throughout my interviews was the idea that my interviewees' parents wanted the best for their children. For those parents, a better life meant learning English as early and as well as possible. One of the main reasons my interviewees' parents wanted them to learn English early is that learning a language later in life can be very difficult. In fact, the challenges of language learning came up the most frequently in my coding. The second reason, also heavily discussed, was the notion that knowing English equates to success.

Second-level headings are flush left and bold. If all English words, they should also be capitalized. If non-English words, use sentence case.

There are many misconceptions in society about both language development and the superiority of English that cause parents to make certain decisions about what language or languages they should teach their children. Some parents in Mexican American households are convinced that their children will be academically harmed if they grow up speaking Spanish. Previous educational practices have led some parents to buy into the supposed superiority of English because they associate it with economic success. Wiley and Lukes (1996) drew on the theories of French philosopher Pierre Bourdieu to argue that knowing a standard language is a sort of currency: "Once standards for expected linguistic behavior have been imposed, privileged varieties of language become a kind of social capital" (p. 515). In other words, knowing English, the "standard language," can result in better test scores, economic advantages, and overall success. In the words of my abuelita, "When you speak English, the doors open for you" (M. E. Flores, personal communication, February 24, 2019). At 20 years old, my grandma came to the United States in search of a better life for her and her son. Because of the general expectation that people in America speak English, she felt that knowing English would be the key to getting opportunities and not being treated as inferior.

When parents are faced with the idea that their children will not be as successful if they do not assimilate into an English-only system, they may decide to embrace monolingualism. I interviewed fellow student Julian Aguilar, who was raised intentionally to speak only English. Both of his parents immigrated to the United States as adults—his mom from China and his dad from Mexico—and both struggled with the language barrier as they adjusted to an English-dominated society (J. Aguilar, personal communication, February 24, 2019). Not wanting the same hardships for their son, they decided that he should learn English as well as possible, without an accent. In the same vein, my mother, a pediatrician, often meets parents who fear their children will be at a disadvantage in the United States if they do not make English the priority (V. Uribe, personal communication, February 24, 2019). In the minds of those parents, and in the minds of many native Spanish speakers in the United States, English equals success. In fact, a survey of Texas adults showed that "Spanish-dominant speakers place high importance on speaking English, more so than do English speakers. . . . It is easy to see how immigrants are constantly reminded of the problems they face in the workplace and the public sphere without English proficiency" (Dowling et al., 2012, p. 356).

Because this source has more than two authors, the citation gives the first author's name followed by "et al." The date and page number are also included.

    A common belief among Mexican American parents is that if their children learn only English, their children will have an easier experience than they did and grow to be confident, successful members of United States society. While many educators realize the importance of using multiple languages in the classroom, public attitudes have yet to catch up with the research. If K-12 institutions would adopt more inclusionary policies and programs, then parents would have more exposure to positive ideas surrounding multilingualism. In turn, pressure on Mexican Americans to raise their children as monolingual could be eased, avoiding the negative consequences of fragmented relationship and identities.

Relaciónes en la familia

Among the benefits of knowing a language is the ability to communicate with others. This idea came up consistently during interviews with my mom and Julian, both of whom grew up monolingually, as well as when I recalled my own struggles communicating with family members throughout my childhood.

For Mexican American families in the United States, it's common for at least some relatives to speak only Spanish. As a result, not knowing the language can inhibit relationships among family members. When we visited Mexico, for example, I found it very difficult to speak to my cousins. I got by because I could understand them a bit and because children have a knack for playing together without a whole lot of talk. Even so, I struggled constantly and grew frustrated that I couldn't express my ideas or understand the jokes being made. Now that my cousins and I are older, it's even harder to avoid the fact that I can't communicate with them effectively. Being part of a proud Mexican family but not knowing Spanish has led me to miss out on close relationships with my relatives. Julian feels similarly, recounting how he couldn't understand his relatives at family reunions; although he was physically there, learning about the culture, he never felt "truly part of it" (J. Aguilar, personal communication, February 24, 2019).

My mom, Victoria Uribe, is also part Mexican and grew up learning only English. She recalled feeling limited when communicating with her grandmother, who knew very little English (V. Uribe, personal communication, February 24, 2019). They would speak very simple sentences to each other, and my mom would get used to saying simple phrases like "Cena lista!" when dinner was ready, but she still couldn't communicate with her very well. She said, "It was harder when I was younger to tell or ask my grandma things" (V. Uribe, personal communication, February 24, 2019). Even later, when my mom was in college, she'd write short letters to her grandmother but feel frustrated that she didn't know Spanish better.

In a case study of the Fuentes family, a Mexican American family in Los Angeles, the third generation of children who grew up in the United States did not acquire the ability to speak Spanish (Chávez, 2007). One member of the family, Erica, recalled not being able to communicate with her grandmother. Since she couldn't understand her grandma, her father had to translate for her, which made Erica feel "kind of awful" (Chávez, 2007, p. 126). Similar stories can be told by many others who grew up without learning their native language, and the negative effects this monolingualism clearly has on familial connections are truly sad.

Español, identidad, y cultura

The relationships among language, identity, and culture are heavily intertwined. From a cultural perspective, the ramifications of not knowing the language of your family can be serious. After all, language has always been an integral part of personal and cultural identity. Anzaldúa (1987) described this deeply rooted connection: "Ethnic identity is twin skin to linguistic identity—I am my language" (p. 39). When I interviewed my dad, he echoed Anzaldúa: "I don't think you can experience the culture without the language—they go hand in hand" (J. Uribe, personal communication, February 24, 2019). The Conference on College Composition and Communication has long led

The author, year, and page number are given in parentheses right after a quotation.

the way in recognizing the crucial importance of the relationship between language and culture. That relationship was explored in a special issue of the journal: "Since dialect is not separate from culture, but an intrinsic part of it, accepting a new dialect means accepting a new culture; rejecting one's native dialect is to some extent a rejection of one's culture" (Committee on CCCC Language Statement, 1974).

Julian's parents, who raised him to be monolingual, only wanted the best for him. He understands where his parents were coming from, but he feels that he lost something important growing up, despite their good intentions, since he "never really felt immersed" in Mexican culture (J. Aguilar, personal communication, February 24, 2019). In other words, because his parents rejected the idea of their son's learning Spanish, they also implicitly rejected the culture his dad grew up in, which kept Julian from forming deep connections with his Mexican heritage.

My mom grew up in a small town in Montana, where she wasn't exposed to Spanish at home. While her mother integrated parts of Mexican culture into her childhood (playing *lotería*, making Mexican food, and talking about her experiences in Mexico), she still didn't feel connected to her Mexican side. In fact, she completely disregarded that part of her identity, considering herself to be White until she went to college (V. Uribe, personal communication, February 24, 2019). When I heard this, I was shocked: by identifying herself as White, my mom showed that she lacked meaningful ties to her Mexican heritage and that there was a clear disconnect between her self-perception and her true ethnic identity.

While these are just a few examples, I believe that looking at specific people brings an important perspective to the existing discussions regarding native languages. The fragmented experiences Julian, my mom, and I have had with respect to Mexican culture and our ethnic identities resulted from our monolingualism. Without these individual narratives, scholarly discourse misses an essential piece of the linguistic puzzle. Looking at historical trends and quantitative data is essential to research, but hearing the stories of real people who are at the center of the research is equally important. Qualitative research, and case studies specifically, provide powerful and direct views into the real-life impact of the topic at hand.

While language is a component of culture, shared language does not always lead to shared culture. Cultural identities are so nuanced that people who speak the same language can still have vastly different experiences and perceptions of their ethnic selves. Julian, for instance, is part of a Latinx service club called Hermanos, and he explained how there seem to be "two types of Latinos" within the organization (J. Aguilar, personal communication, February 24, 2019). Coming from a low-income background himself, he feels more connected to the people who are from rougher neighborhoods, who didn't necessarily grow up "culturally Mexican." So while there is a direct and clear relationship among language, identity, and culture, there is no single linear path among them, and it is important to remember this complexity.

¿Y ahora, qué?

And so—what should be done to address the anti-Spanish sentiments in our society? It's important to consider whether schools should even try to make changes that contradict these public opinions:

> *For a long quotation, the parenthetical reference follows the closing punctuation.*

Until public attitudes can be changed—and it is worth remembering that the past teaching in English classes has been largely responsible for those attitudes—shall we place our emphasis on what the vocal element of the public think it wants or on what the actual available linguistic evidence indicates we should emphasize? (Committee on CCCC Language Statement, 1974)

I argue that the latter option is the right path to take. The best course of action for K-12 schools is to encourage the use of native languages in the classroom and thus promote multilingualism.

Why should entire school systems make such big changes for just a portion of the population? To start, a huge number of people in the United States have a stake in these policies and practices. In California, 39.1% of the population is Hispanic or Latinx (United States Census Bureau, n.d.). While my research focuses on Mexican Americans, it's easy to see how many people from other Spanish-speaking backgrounds could be affected by monolingual pressures. Realizing the detrimental effects that monolingualism can have is one step towards institutions' placing equal value on diverse languages.

In addition to the call to action for K-12 schools to encourage multilingualism, the understanding one gains from research like mine is of major significance. Listening to personal stories and learning about negative experiences resulting from pressured monolingualism can lead to systemic change and encourage empathy. I believe that differences should be not only tolerated but celebrated. This includes Americans who speak only English, Americans who speak only their native language, and everyone in between. If we can begin to have more understanding of and empathy for each person's identity, we may be able to function as a more accepting, unified country.

Mexican Americans have faced a multitude of pressures to assimilate into a society that promotes English above Spanish. In my life and others' lives, these pressures have led to a fragmented experience with Mexican culture and personal ethnic identity. But the stories of the people I interviewed are far from over. Once my mom got to college, she joined Chicano organizations to learn more about her culture and people like her (V. Uribe, personal communication, February 24, 2019). She even wrote an article in medical school about her deepening relationship with her Mexican heritage. She also started learning Spanish in college and became fluent by using it in her job on a daily basis. My friend Julian has taken two introductory college Spanish classes so far, and he plans on continuing (J. Aguilar, personal communication, February 24, 2019). In addition, joining a Hispanic service club on campus has already helped him feel more in touch with his Mexican roots.

I hope that schools and politicians can make more of an effort to encourage language diversity and embrace multilingualism, so that cultural connections can be made even sooner. That way, Mexican American children can learn Spanish with pride. Then, that little girl playing UNO with her cousins can respond confidently:

"¿Por qué no puedes hablar español?"

"~~No sé~~." "Sí, yo puedo."

References

Anbinder, T. (2019, November 7). Trump has spread more hatred of immigrants than any American in history. *The Washington Post*. https://www.washingtonpost.com/outlook/trump-has-spread-more-hatred-of-immigrants-than-any-american-in-history/2019/11/07/7e253236-ff54-11e9-8bab-0fc209e065a8_story.html

Anzaldúa, G. (1987). *Borderlands/La frontera: The new mestiza*. Aunt Lute Books.

Bourdieu, P. (1986). The forms of capital. In J. Richardson (Ed.), *Handbook of theory and research for the sociology of education* (pp. 241–258). Greenwood.

Chávez, C. (2007). *Five generations of a Mexican American family in Los Angeles*. Rowman & Littlefield Publishers.

CNN. (2015, September 16). *Trump: We speak English here, not Spanish* [Video]. YouTube. https://www.youtube.com/watch?v=eNjcAgNu1Ac

Committee on CCCC Language Statement. (1974). Students' right to their own language [Special issue]. *College Composition and Communication, 25*(3).

Dowling, J. A., Ellison, C. G., & Leal, D. L. (2012). Who doesn't value English? Debunking myths about Mexican immigrants' attitudes toward the English language. *Social Science Quarterly, 93*(2), 356–378. https://doi.org/hcjz

Karimi, F., & Levenson, E. (2018, May 17). Man to Spanish speakers at New York restaurant: "My next call is to ICE." CNN. https://www.cnn.com/2018/05/17/us/new-york-man-restaurant-ice-threat/index.html

Kroll, J. F., & Dussias, P. E. (2017). The benefits of multilingualism to the personal and professional development of residents of the US. *Foreign Language Annals, 50*(2), 248–259. https://doi.org/10.1111/flan.12271

National Council of Teachers of English. (2020). *CCCC statement on second language writing and multilingual writers* [Position statement]. https://cccc.ncte.org/cccc/resources/positions/secondlangwriting

Okal, B. O. (2014). Benefits of multilingualism in education. *Universal Journal of Educational Research, 2*(3), 223–229. https://doi.org/10.13189/ujer.2014.020304

O'Keefe, E. (2017, January 23). Looking for a Spanish version of WhiteHouse.gov? No existe—todavia. *The Washington Post.* https://www.washingtonpost.com/news/powerpost/wp/2017/01/23/looking-for-a-spanish-version-of-whitehouse-gov-ya-no-existe/

United States Census Bureau. (n.d.). *QuickFacts California*. U.S. Department of Commerce. Retrieved March 1, 2019, from https://www.census.gov/quickfacts/ca

Wiley, T. G., & Lukes, M. (1996). English-only and standard English ideologies in the U.S. *TESOL Quarterly, 30*(3), 511–535. https://doi.org/10.2307/3587696

PART VII

Style
"How to Get and Hold Attention"

My mission in life is not merely to survive, but to thrive; and to do so with some passion, some compassion, some humor, and some style.

—MAYA ANGELOU

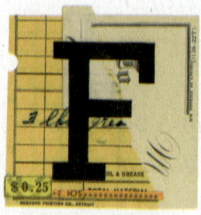

FOR A LONG TIME, style in writing and speaking meant ornamentation, "dressing up" your language the way you might dress yourself up for a fancy party. The influence of this view eventually led many writers to set aside issues of style, preferring to focus on substance, getting to the point and not worrying about making it fancy or pretty. But not today. Not in a time of being inundated with notifications, news, advertisements—all coming at us with the force of a fire hose. In such a time, scholars like Richard Lanham and Howard Rheingold argue the most important task facing writers and speakers is making our messages so compelling that they will stand out from all the others.

Lanham insists that "we're drowning in information" and that what we "lack is the human attention to make sense of it all."

How can we achieve this goal of getting and managing attention? `STYLE`. When it comes to writing, most dictionaries offer something about word choice and how it differs from field to field, or they will define style as "distinctiveness of expression." But style is as much about how a message is presented as what it says. Style and substance are inseparable. Without close attention to how our messages are presented, we are unlikely to attract an audience, much less hold its attention.

How can you create your own particular, powerful style in writing, speaking, and presenting? Choosing words (`DICTION`) and putting them in the best places (`SYNTAX`) still matter a lot in developing your style. But you also have many other tools—visuals, video, sound, color, and more. All these elements are available as you choreograph the dance of your message, as you develop its style. Getting and holding an audience's attention, however, is not the only goal when it comes to style. You also want to get that attention in ways that fit well with your entire rhetorical situation. The chapters that follow aim to help you achieve that goal.

 **REFLECT**

Write a list of words or a few sentences to describe your personal style. What does your style say about you? In what ways does your personal style show up when you write?

THIRTY-FOUR

What's Your Style?

T THE 2024 US OPEN TENNIS TOURNAMENT, two-time champion Naomi Osaka garnered a great deal of attention not only with her tennis game but also with her choice of tennis attire. Stepping on the court in bow- and ruffle-adorned outfits—black and white one day, lime green another day—Osaka's clothing choices certainly presented an eye-catching style. She explained her purpose in wearing the custom outfits designed by Yoon Ahn: "The inspiration that fueled the look for me—and this might be a Japanese term—is feeling like a 'magical girl' on the court. . . . I have a lot of fun playing, so wanting everyone who sees the outfit to connect with that feeling is a really big motivation for me." Osaka links style to the message she wants to send to the audience about joy.

The image of Osaka on the following page could be captioned "Got style?" because it demonstrates that being like everyone or everything around you doesn't add up to a style that can get and hold attention. The same is true for writing; style helps you get readers to take notice—and listen—to what you have to say.

But style isn't just about getting attention: it's also about making choices that work well in your particular situation, and all in an effort to achieve your purpose. You might wear shorts and running shoes to the gym but not to a job interview, a bathing suit to the beach but not to class. It's a delicate balance. Style in writing works the same way. How can the

Osaka played a round of the 2024 US Open in an Ahn-designed lime-green dress with bows around her waist, the back of her blouse, and on her heels.

words, images, and sentence structures you use stand out while at the same time giving you credibility? This chapter offers strategies for achieving this balance and shaping your own flexible style of writing.

Suitability and Correctness

Making good stylistic choices, ones that get readers' attention and hold it all the way through, calls for considering all the factors of your rhetorical situation. In the simplest terms, a "suitable" writing style is one in which the words you choose and the ways you arrange them suit your purpose, your topic, your medium, and your audience. Making stylistic choices in writing can be tricky, though, since there aren't always concrete rules to follow. You may have learned that it isn't correct to start a sentence with "and" or "but" and that you must never end a sentence with a preposition. But those "rules"

The crew of the USS *Enterprise* split infinitives boldly, and with emphasis.

are far from universal, and they change over time. In fact, a lot of fine writing today bends and breaks those rules to good effect.

So it won't work to think about style simply as a matter of following rules. In fact, if you have to choose between being "correct" and being "suitable," suitability almost always wins out. In 1966, in the original *Star Trek*, when Captain Kirk of the starship *Enterprise* announced its mission "to boldly go where no man has gone before," that split infinitive ("boldly") splits the two words of the infinitive "to go") wasn't absolutely "correct," but it created just the emphasis the writers were after. And since splitting the infinitive broke the conventional grammar rule of the time (the 1960s), it wasn't just the starship *Enterprise* that was boldly going into new territory. We can't say that it was *Star Trek* alone that led to change, but today that rule about split infinitives has all but disappeared from up-to-date handbooks and grammar guides. Making effective stylistic choices, then, will almost always depend on your RHETORICAL SITUATION.

Some contexts already have a defined style of communicating or a specific dialect that's considered most acceptable. In those situations, being aware of the conventional style will help guide your style decisions. For example, what some refer to as "standardized English" is the DIALECT often expected for writing done in most school, government, and professional contexts. But like any other "standard," it has changed across time and will continue to change.

But the fact that academic dialects of languages emerge and change over time and that the preferred use of a language most often depends on context doesn't mean stylistic choices are without any boundaries at all. Audiences often expect that writers will follow accepted conventions, and choosing to do so—or not—has consequences. When the choices you make ignore or defy audience expectations, or when they push the envelope, you may be able to get an audience's attention.

Take a look, for instance, at how linguist Geneva Smitherman pushes against the traditional "rules" of academic English and does so brilliantly. In fact, had she stuck to the traditional rules, the following paragraph would have been far less effective than it is.

> Before about 1959 (when the first study was done to change black speech patterns), Black English had been primarily the interest of university academics, particularly the historical linguists and cultural anthropologists. In recent years, though, the issue has become a very hot controversy, and there have been articles on Black Dialect in the national press as well as in the educational research literature. We have had pronouncements on black speech from the NAACP and the Black Panthers, from highly publicized scholars of the Arthur Jensen–William Shockley bent, from executives of national corporations such as Greyhound, and from housewives and community folk. I mean, really, it seem like everybody and they momma done had something to say on the subject!
>
> —GENEVA SMITHERMAN, *Talkin and Testifyin: The Language of Black America*

Smitherman obviously knows the rules of standardized English but breaks them to support her point and also to create a clear rhetorical stance, as a scholar, a skilled writer, and a proud Black woman. Writing in the late 1970s, she could assume that her readers would know that the NAACP is the National Association for the Advancement of Colored People, that the Black Panthers were a revolutionary social action group in the 1960s and 1970s, and that Arthur Jensen and William Shockley had made controversial claims about relationships between race and intelligence. She could also assume that readers of her book would expect her to write in standardized English since the volume treated its subject from an academic perspective.

Geneva Smitherman

But Smitherman wasn't interested in writing a book about the language of Black Americans using only standardized English. After all, one of her claims was that the language practices of Black Americans were influencing American culture and language in many ways. Notice how her stylistic choices support that claim. She not only talks the talk of standardized English but walks the walk of Black English as well. When she switches in her final sentence from standardized English to Black English, she simultaneously drives home her point—that everyone at that time seemed to have an opinion about the language of Black Americans—while demonstrating membership in that community by using the language variety associated with it. In short, she makes sound and effective stylistic choices.

You'll find more on mixing dialects and languages in the following chapter. For now, remember that your style should be suitable to your purpose, audience, and rhetorical situation, even—and especially—when you bend the rules.

See Ch. 35 in the ebook for a video on writing how you speak.

You may be wondering whether using **GENERATIVE AI** can help you with matters of style. If you really want to emphasize your unique writing style and tone, AI may not be the best tool. It tends to privilege **STANDARDIZED ENGLISH** and struggles to provide authentic versions of other dialects. And no matter how much information you give it, AI won't have as clear an understanding of your **RHETORICAL SITUATION** and the style dictated by that situation as you do. When your goal is to make effective style choices and hone your personal style, we suggest depending on your own human intelligence instead of AI.

Connecting with Audiences

In all your writing, you'll want to have a reasonably good sense of your intended **AUDIENCE** in order to make effective stylistic choices. Take a look at the image on the following page; it's the webpage for a supermarket in a small town in California that appeals directly to its local community. The writers set a friendly, informal tone right away. "We love good food," they announce, while appealing to their audience to "SHOP LOCAL." The emphasis on the local continues: "Proudly serving our community" for decades, they declare. They also invite readers to: "Visit us on Facebook"; "Come visit our store"; and "Learn about . . . our sustainable fish program." The use of "us" and "our" emphasizes the community and establishes **COMMON GROUND** with

The Surf Market in Gualala, California, welcomes customers to its webpage with a friendly, informal tone.

readers. The bright colors and simple design add to the warm, inviting tone that underscores the overall message.

A student writing about this same topic for a class project must be more formal and would need to include the background and contextual information that an academic audience expects. For example, here is Katherine Spriggs arguing for the importance of "buying local":

> "Buying local" means that consumers choose to buy food that has been grown, raised, or produced as close to their home as possible. Buying local is an important part of the response to many environmental issues we face today. It encourages the development of small farms, which are often more environmentally sustainable than large farms, and thus strengthens local markets and supports small rural economies. By demonstrating a commitment to buying local, Americans could set an example for global environmentalism.
>
> —KATHERINE SPRIGGS, "On Buying Local"

Rather than assuming that her audience already knows what "buying local" means, Spriggs begins with a careful definition—something the Surf Market webpage doesn't need to do—as a way of laying the groundwork for her argument and demonstrating that she is knowledgeable about her topic. She then starts to build her argument by linking the idea of buying local to environmental issues and community values. Her tone is serious; she gives practical reasons for why buying local is "important," noting that it "encourages the development of small farms" and "supports small rural economies." Like Surf Market and Spriggs do, you'll want to think about who will read what you write and make stylistic choices that help you connect with them.

Levels of Formality

Being effective also calls on writers to pay attention to the level of formality they use. In ancient Rome, Cicero identified three levels of style: low or plain style, used to teach or explain something; middle style, used to please an audience; and high or grand style, used to move or persuade an audience. Note that these classifications link style with a specific purpose and a likely audience.

On August 27, 2018, an aide to Senator John McCain shared a farewell statement McCain had written to America before his death two days earlier. Here is the opening of that letter:

> My fellow Americans, whom I have gratefully served for sixty years, and especially my fellow Arizonans,
>
> Thank you for the privilege of serving you and for the rewarding life that service in uniform and in public office has allowed me to lead. I have tried to serve our country honorably. I have made mistakes, but I hope my love for America will be weighed favorably against them.
>
> I have often observed that I am the luckiest person on earth. . . . Like most people, I have regrets. But I would not trade a day of my life, in good or bad times, for the best day of anyone else's.
>
> I owe that satisfaction to the love of my family. No man ever had a more loving wife or children he was prouder of than I am of mine. And I owe it to America. To be connected to America's causes—liberty, equal justice, respect for the dignity of all people—brings happiness more sublime than life's fleeting pleasures. Our identities and sense of worth are not circumscribed but enlarged by serving good causes bigger than ourselves.
>
> —JOHN MCCAIN, "Farewell Letter to America"

Writing in full awareness of his imminent death, McCain uses a solemn, deliberate, formal tone, writing in the grand style that seeks to inspire by both word and deed. Twice he uses balanced phrases to acknowledge weaknesses as well as strengths ("I have made mistakes, but I hope my love of America . . ." and "I have regrets. But I would not trade a day . . ."). And he expresses deep satisfaction at his connection to "America's causes—liberty, equal justice, respect for the dignity of all people," saying that this connection brings him happiness "more sublime than life's fleeting pleasures." In concluding his letter, McCain uses repetition and very brief sentences to punctuate this final message:

> Do not despair of our present difficulties but believe always in the promise and greatness of America, because nothing is inevitable here. Americans never quit. We never surrender. We never hide from history. We make history. Farewell, fellow Americans. God bless you, and God bless America.

The four short sentences that follow the longer opening sentence are like drumbeats, with their use of the repeated "we," calling Americans to attend to McCain and to be inspired by his example. McCain's style choices match his unique **RHETORICAL SITUATION**—and help his message land with impact.

Stance

Stance refers to the attitude authors take toward their topic and audience. For example, you might write about immigration as an impassioned advocate or critic, someone with strong opinions about the inherent good or evil of immigration. Or you might write as a dispassionate analyst, someone trying to weigh carefully the pros and cons of the arguments for and against a particular proposal. Either stance—and any possible stances in between—will affect what style you use.

If your audience changes, your language will likely shift, too. Debating immigration issues with close friends whose opinions you're fairly sure of will differ in crucial ways from debating them with people you know less well or not at all because you'll be able to take less for granted. That you will likely shift all aspects of your message—from word choice and sentence structure to amount of background information and choice of examples—doesn't make you a hypocrite or a flip-flopper; instead, it demonstrates your skill at finding the most effective rhetorical resources to make your point.

In a posting titled "Same Food Planet, Different Food Worlds," blogger Rod Dreher calls attention to the drastically different stances taken by two restaurant reviewers. Here's an excerpt from one, a review of a new Olive Garden restaurant in Grand Forks, North Dakota, by eighty-five-year-old Marilyn Hagerty:

> It had been a few years since I ate at the older Olive Garden in Fargo, so I studied the two manageable menus offering appetizers, soups and salads, grilled sandwiches, pizza, classic dishes, chicken and seafood and filled pastas.
>
> At length, I asked my server what she would recommend. She suggested chicken Alfredo, and I went with that. Instead of the raspberry lemonade she suggested, I drank water.
>
> She first brought me the familiar Olive Garden salad bowl with crisp greens, peppers, onion rings and yes—several black olives. Along with it came a plate with two long, warm breadsticks.
>
> The chicken Alfredo ($10.95) was warm and comforting on a cold day. The portion was generous. My server was ready with Parmesan cheese. . . .
>
> All in all, it is the largest and most beautiful restaurant now operating in Grand Forks. It attracts visitors from out of town as well as people who live here.
>
> —MARILYN HAGERTY, "Long-Awaited Olive Garden Receives Warm Welcome"

Marilyn Hagerty. Read the *Los Angeles Times'* take on the controversy—and Hagerty's son's response in the *Wall Street Journal*—at everyonesanauthor.tumblr.com.

Hagerty's polite, unpretentious stance is evident in this review—and as it happens, the style of her writing attracted much attention when it went viral, with readers both celebrating and bashing that style.

Dreher contrasts Hagerty's stance with that of Dive Bar Girl (DBG), who writes for a newsletter in Baton Rouge, Louisiana. In fact, DBG starts right out by announcing her stance—she's going to be "mean," not "informative"—and so after saying "a few nice things" about her topic, a restaurant called Twin Peaks, she writes the review that she assumes her readers "want to read":

> Admit it, you like it when DBG is mean. You only send her fan mail when she's mean. She never gets mail for being informative. . . . So she is going to write about the positive things first and then write the review you want to read. The smokehouse burger was above average. The patio was a

nice space. The staff, while scantily clad, was professional. The salads even looked good. The place was miles above Hooters.

Here is the review you want: Twin Peaks has to be the brainchild of two 14-year-old boys who recently cracked the parental controls on the home computer. Waitresses are known as "Lumber Jills." In case you are missing the imagery—each Lumber Jill has been endowed with an epic pair of Twin Peaks.

—CHERRYTHEDIVEBARGIRL

These two reviews could hardly be more different in stance: the first is low-key and even-handed, well suited to Hagerty's stance as a modest and sincere reviewer. The second is highly opinionated and sarcastic, true to the brash, in-your-face stance of Dive Bar Girl. So both are written in styles that suit (and reflect) their respective stances.

But what happens when that stance doesn't fit well with a particular audience? That's what happened when Hagerty's review went viral: some writers immediately began making fun of her as inept and hopelessly out of it; others jumped in just as quickly to defend Hagerty's review, while still others read her review as an indirect parody of local restaurant reviews. Now imagine that Dive Bar Girl's review appeared in Hagerty's hometown newspaper. Chances are it would attract some hefty criticism as well.

The takeaway lesson here: as a writer, you need to consider whether your STANCE is a good fit not only to your topic and audience but also to your MODE of distribution.

Tone

All the writing you do, regardless of stance or level of formality, has a particular TONE. You may not think consciously about how to establish that tone, especially when commenting on a friend's *Instagram* post or writing a text message, but even in social media writing you are making choices about whether you want to convey a serious tone, a humorous tone, or an exasperated tone. When you know that your readers are friends and family, your tone can probably be pretty casual, like this social media post by a student in Washington, DC, which is playful, critical, reasoned, and ironic:

> Note to self: avoid union station on weekday mornings. Hordes of angry commuters make getting to the train impossible? #notfun #DCMetro #rushhour #istheworst

---

While narrating a difficult and personal process, Glavee Glavee's writing shifts smoothly between serious, defiant, scholarly, angry, and firm. Take a look at their essay on p. 905.

Here the tone is one of frustration and exasperation, expressed in the hashtags the writer adds (#notfun, etc.). She is assuming her readers will not only know what she is talking about but also appreciate her playful tone. For a report on commuters in Union Station for an urban studies class, the author establishes the more serious tone of a reporter or researcher:

> Walking into Union Station on a weekday morning can be like going against a herd of stampeding cattle. Riders rush from the trains, swinging briefcases and computer bags, knocking over anything or anyone in the way. Rush hour in this station, one of the busiest train stations in the country, is not enjoyable. Looking at some usage statistics and videos will show just how unpleasant this experience is and how it affects those who regularly ride the metro.

Here the tone is studied and serious. The writer opens by describing the scene in the congested station and then moves to introduce an analysis of usage statistics and videos. But even a serious tone doesn't need to result in a dull, boring style: note the lively description ("stampeding cattle"; "swinging briefcases"; "knocking over everything or anyone in the way"). Your PURPOSE, AUDIENCE, STANCE, and even MEDIUM will help determine an effective tone.

Style across Media

You probably already find yourself using a variety of media to communicate every day and making intuitive choices about style: you post a video on *TikTok*, you make an oral presentation using *Prezi* for a class, you conduct research for an article that you submit in print and then "remediate" as part of a website. Each of these tasks calls for a suitable medium, whether written, oral, or digital. In each case, you have a good sense of your purpose and audience, and you use that knowledge to establish an effective style and choose the best medium to deliver your message. This is the same kind of rhetorical thinking you need to be doing consciously and analytically for the writing you do in school or work. So in all your writing across media—at home, at work, at school, wherever—you will want to make stylistic choices that are a good fit for your rhetorical situation, your audience, and your purpose.

Some writers, such as Chicago historian Shermann "Dilla" Thomas, use video to deliver their message. His *TikTok* videos (@6figga_dilla) on topics of local history have garnered him more than 87,000 followers. Covering the history of neighborhoods and landmarks throughout the city, as well as historical events and local customs, he meticulously researches his topics, writes a script, and narrates the video while showing related images. The production is simple; he often shoots in his own home, holding a mini-microphone. Many of Thomas's videos have gone viral, and he is now working with *Netflix* on producing a Chicago history series. The images shown here are from Thomas's *TikTok* about the Great Chicago Fire of 1871.

How might Thomas have presented this history differently for a magazine or newspaper article? for a podcast? Different media and platforms call for different style choices in order to grab attention and get your message across. And remember that grabbing attention is only half the battle—making sure your style is suitable and effective is just as important. Especially online, it can be easy and tempting to use an over-the-top title or a startling image to grab attention (it's how clickbait works, after all), but they won't keep your readers with you beyond a flashy opening, so stick to style choices that strike the right balance.

Public historian Shermann "Dilla" Thomas narrates his *TikTok* about the Great Chicago Fire of 1871 with a nineteenth-century engraved image of the fire in the background (left) and a map of the burnt area (right).

See Thomas's post by visiting everyonesanauthor.tumblr.com.

> ### REFLECT
>
> Look at some of your recent posts on social media. How informal or formal are they? What do they assume your audience will know about your topic? Do you use a mix of media—words, images, video? Then write a few sentences describing what you've noticed about your writing style on social media and how it differs from the other kinds of writing you do—at school, at work, at home. If you don't post, look at recent posts from your favorite living writer or celebrity and answer the same questions.

Style across Disciplines

Making good choices is especially important when writing in different disciplines, where what's expected and effective often varies from field to field or workplace to workplace. Many fields have established conventions—reading published writing in a field or discipline can help you see what stylistic features are most common. Look for patterns—do writers use a particular verb tense? active voice instead of passive voice? a specific organization or style of headings? Identifying what successful writers have done in a field that's new to you is a good way to figure out what you'll try in order to be effective and suitable.

One notable stylistic difference between fields is favoring the ACTIVE VOICE or the PASSIVE VOICE. For example, reports in the sciences usually call for the passive voice. Take a look at this passage from a 2021 study on possible correlations between running-related injuries (RRIs) and foot placement on impact, or foot strike techniques (FSTs). The authors explain what methods they used to review existing research on their topic; notice that most of the verbs are passive:

> **Methods:** A systematic electronic search was performed using MEDLINE, PubMed, SPORTDiscus, Scopus, and Web of Science databases. Studies were included that were published in the English language that explored the relationship between FST and RRIs between January 1960 and November 2020. Results were extracted and collated. The Grading of Recommendations, Assessment, Development and Evaluation approach was applied to synthesize the quality of evidence.

In scientific writing the passive is generally favored because it shouldn't matter who searched for the articles, applied the criteria, or assessed the quality using the stated criteria; in the end, the results should be the same. The passive voice also focuses the reader's attention on what was done, not on who did it. So although you may have been instructed in your writing classes to "avoid the passive," it is often the expected and effective choice in the sciences.

At the same time, there are many occasions when writers avoid the passive voice for good reason. For example, engineers often rely on information gathered by other firms or information they gather themselves from interviews. In contexts where they need to make clear who is responsible for observations, recommendations, or judgments, engineers use the active voice to locate responsibility. Thus, engineers would write "Our firm hired ABC Tech to conduct a geotechnical evaluation" rather than "A geotechnical evaluation was conducted" so that readers know the source of the data presented and analyzed. Voice is just one example of how style differs between disciplines—the point is you'll want to seek out reliable examples to learn what style works and is expected of you in a new field.

Thinking about Your Own Style

As you've seen, style is about making suitable choices, choices that inevitably depend on your topic and all the elements of your rhetorical situation, especially your message, your STANCE, your PURPOSE, your GENRE, and your AUDIENCE. Have you written a review of something—a restaurant for the campus newspaper? a backpack on *eBay*? your driver on *Lyft*? If so, take a look at the choices you made in the review, and then compare them to those you made in an essay you wrote for class. You'll see right away that you have instinctively used different styles for these different occasions.

In this chapter, we've emphasized how important the stylistic choices you make are to getting the attention of your audiences—and holding it; style really is the key to achieving that goal. And remember that, as an author, you get to call a lot of the stylistic shots. As you do so, of course, you'll want to think carefully about what styles fit well in particular situations, what your audience's expectations are, and what risks you may be willing to take by not fully meeting those expectations. In short, you aren't going to be writing dull, predictable prose. You're a lot better than that: you've got **STYLE**.

 **REFLECT**

Look at a few recent pieces of writing you've done for school or for your job: How well do they represent you? Do these pieces of writing sound like you—does your voice come through? What makes these pieces of writing memorable or vivid? Are they formal, informal, or somewhere in between? What is your stance in them and what tone do you take? What writing conventions affect your style in these pieces? Write a paragraph describing your writing style using the answers to these questions.

THIRTY-FIVE

Mixing Languages and Dialects

HOW MANY LANGUAGES do you know well enough to speak or write? Which languages would you like to know? The United States is often referred to as a monolingual country, one where English is the only language needed to get along. But that characterization has never been accurate. Languages other than English have always been present here. Today, the US Census Bureau estimates that approximately 20 percent of Americans report speaking a language other than English at home—Spanish, Chinese, French, and Tagalog are the four most common. And American Sign Language is probably the third most commonly used language (after Spanish), although the census doesn't ask about signed languages.

So the United States is a country of many languages. It is also a country of multiple dialects, and again, it always has been. "Dialects" are varieties of language that are spoken by people in a particular region, social class, or ethnic group—like the English spoken by residents of Appalachia or the Spanish spoken in Texas. "Registers" are varieties of language associated with a particular purpose or activity. For example, a nurse summarizing a patient's lab results to a doctor would speak in a medical register, using abbreviations and technical terms in order to be

Spend a day taking notice of all the languages, dialects, and registers you encounter around you—from conversations on campus to signs, billboards, and texts that convey information.

brief and efficient. That same nurse explaining results to the patient's family would use a more conversational register. Listen to people you know or hear on *YouTube* or *TikTok*, and you will surely hear various dialects and registers, as well as distinctive vocabulary at work.

No matter how many languages you speak, you probably use a number of different dialects and registers. Is the way you speak at the dinner table different from the way you speak in class or at work? Is the way you write an *Instagram* post different from an email to an instructor? We bet that it is.

We also bet that you probably mix whatever languages, dialects, and registers you use, consciously or unconsciously. There are two common patterns of doing so that language scholars have identified. Both ways are more common in conversation than in writing, but either pattern can occur anywhere. CODE-SWITCHING is a shift from one language or dialect to another, where the two languages or dialects are separate. CODE-MESHING is a way of weaving together languages and dialects, and the back-and-forth may be very rapid, allowing the varieties to interact and play off one another. Code-switching and code-meshing are both ways of mixing varieties of language for various purposes—to reflect a particular STANCE, for example, or to establish a connection with certain AUDIENCES. This chapter provides examples and guidelines to help you mix languages, dialects, and registers for various rhetorical situations.

> Since language is the focus of Glavee Glavee's essay, it makes perfect sense that they use code-meshing to emphasize their argument. See how they weave their language varieties together on p. 905.

> **REFLECT**
>
> Think for a few minutes about the varieties of language spoken where you grew up. What features of pronunciation and vocabulary can you identify? What groups do you belong to now that have a specialized way of communicating? Fans of one type of music? A religious community? An athletic team or social club? Write a paragraph describing what influences the way you speak; include specific examples.

Using Standardized English and Other Dialects

What some call **STANDARDIZED ENGLISH** is actually a dialect—one that's used in both formal and informal contexts. For example, during a heated discussion about jobs and automation with a friend, you may say things in informal but effective ways that wouldn't work as well if you were writing up the same point in a formal report. Even within a single dialect there's almost always more than one effective way to say or write something; your audience and purpose inform your choices.

That is not to say that all dialects are regarded as equals—standardized English has long held a prestigious position in the United States. But so-called standard languages have been challenged for centuries by vernacular dialects and languages. In the Western world, after all, English supplanted Latin and Greek as languages of power. At the same time, standardized English's relatively rigid conventions have been challenged for a long time (see Chapter 4). And social media continues to blur the boundary between spoken, signed, and written language in significant ways. The styles of everyday conversation are finding their place in written form. In some contexts and for some kinds of writing, the expectations are shifting and the possibilities are expanding. This chapter provides a number of examples of writers mixing varieties of language—often beyond standardized English—in ways that speak powerfully to their audiences. Such moves are increasingly common, but doing so doesn't always come without risks. Keep your rhetorical situation front and center—what's your purpose? what's at stake? what does your audience consider suitable?—when you make language choices that push against readers' expectations.

See the ebook for a video on writing how you speak.

Connecting with Audiences

If you're a fan of popular music today, you can probably come up with examples of lyricists mixing languages to craft powerful messages. Here is the opening of Kenyan rapper Bamboo's remix of the song "Mama Africa," first written and sung by Jamaican reggae artist Peter Tosh. A love song to the African continent, which has in Bamboo's view too often been represented negatively, his remix connects to his international audience of hip-hop and pop music fans by moving between Swahili and English:

> *tunaishi vizuri*
> check out the way we be livin
> *na tunakula vizuri*
> we always eating the best
> *poteza yako kwa nini*
> why should you settle for less
> *TV haiwezi kuambia*
> they never show on your screen
> *kwa hivyo mi ntawaambia*
> so you can see what I mean
> *Africa maridadi*
> Africa's beautiful baby
> —BAMBOO, "Mama Africa"

Bamboo uses hip-hop rhythms and dialect to connect with the listeners he wants to reach. By using both Swahili and English, he reaches more people than if he'd used just one language—and exposes those who speak just one of these languages to the other.

Sandra Cisneros, a Mexican American writer who's fluent in both English and Spanish, makes similar choices in a collection of short stories inspired by her experience growing up in the United States surrounded by Mexican culture. See how she mixes languages to speak to an audience that's likely to include both English and Spanish speakers:

> "¡Ay!" The true test of a native Spanish speaker. ¡Ay! To make love in Spanish, in a manner as intricate and devout as la Alhambra. To have a lover sigh *mi vida, mi preciosa, mi chiquitita,* and whisper things in that

language crooned to babies, that language murmured by grandmothers, those words that smelled like your house, like flour tortillas.

—SANDRA CISNEROS, *Woman Hollering Creek and Other Stories*

As writers and speakers, we have to think carefully about when mixing languages or dialects will help us connect with our audiences—and when it won't. In most cases, authors have a kind of informal contract with readers: while readers may need to work some to understand what a writer is saying, the writer in turn promises to consider the audience's expectations and abilities. The end goal is usually accessibility: Will your message be understood by those you are trying to reach? If some members of your audience aren't likely to understand, should you provide a translation? Or are you choosing not to translate so that readers experience what it's like *not* to understand?

Providing Translation

One way to stay true to a language or dialect you identify with while still reaching readers who may not understand is to provide a translation. Bamboo's example, which invites English-speaking listeners to think about Africa's rich cultures in part by including Swahili, demonstrates how translation helps when you're mixing languages. When including translations, you will usually want to introduce the term that is being translated in its original language, followed by the translation, as sociolinguist Guadalupe Valdés does in an ethnographic study of a family of Mexican origin that included a young boy named Saúl:

> During his kindergarten year, . . . winning was important to Saúl. Of all the cousins who played together, it was he who ran the fastest and pushed the hardest. "*Yo gané, yo gané*" (I won, I won), he would say enthusiastically. . . . Saúl's mother, Velma, wished that he would win just a bit more quietly. . . . "*No seas peleonero*" (Don't be so quarrelsome), she would say. "*Es importante llevarse bien con todos*" (It's important to get along with everyone).
>
> —GUADALUPE VALDÉS, *Con Respeto: Bridging the Distances between Culturally Diverse Families and Schools*

Note especially that Valdés always puts the Spanish words first, as they were spoken, and only then gives the English translation. She could have chosen to put the English translation first, or to write only in English, but giving the Spanish first puts the spotlight on her subjects' voices and their own words. By including the English translation at all, Valdés acknowledges readers who don't speak Spanish and makes sure they can understand what she's written. Like Bamboo, she translates to make sure her message is accessible to as many people as possible. Notice, too, that Valdés italicizes words in a language other than English, which is a common academic convention when mixing languages.

For another example, review the following poster announcing an online Ojibwe Language Symposium sponsored by Fond du Lac Tribal & Community College in Minnesota. Note that the designer places an Ojibwe-language sentence in a prominent position and in bold type, emphasizing its importance. The English translation appears in parentheses, and not bold type, underneath.

Poster created by Fond du Lac Tribal & Community College announcing an online Ojibwe Language Symposium in English and Ojibwe.

Illustrating a Point

Professional groups have their own specialized ways of speaking: people in economics and finance will have different vocabulary and style at work from people in medicine, engineering, or food service. Much has been written about what is often called "valley speak," a common way of speaking in Silicon Valley where tech giants like Google and Apple reside. In a book that aims to be a definitive guide to the language of Silicon Valley, authors Rochelle Kopp and Steven Ganz incorporate examples to illustrate their point:

> When we moved to Silicon Valley, we found it challenging to pick up the lingo. . . . Around here, people toss off sentences like "Everyone thought that [the] semantic search startup launched by those Stanford whiz kids was going to be the next unicorn, but now they are doing a down round and it's looking like they are candidates for an acqui-hire." It can be awkward if you're the only one who doesn't understand what people here are saying.
> —ROCHELLE KOPP & STEVEN GANZ, *Valley Speak: Deciphering the Jargon of Silicon Valley*

By mixing in phrases like "semantic search startups" and "down round," Kopp and Ganz illustrate valley speak while suggesting that the vocabulary of Silicon Valley startups may alienate any people who don't want to take the time to penetrate the jargon.

Professor Jamila Lyiscott mixes dialects to illustrate her point in a spoken-word essay called "Broken English" in which she "celebrates—and challenges—the three distinct flavors of English she speaks." Prompted by a "baffled lady" who seemed surprised to find that Lyiscott is "articulate," Lyiscott says:

> When my father asks, "Wha' kinda ting is dis?"
> My "articulate" answer never goes amiss
> I say "Father, this is the impending problem at hand"
> And when I'm on the block I switch it up just because I can
> So when my boy says, "What's good with you son?"
> I just say, "I jus' fall out wit dem people but I done!"

> And sometimes in class
> I might pause the intellectual sounding flow to ask
> "Yo! Why dese books neva be about my peoples"
> Yes, I have decided to treat all three of my languages as equals
> Because I'm "articulate"
>
> —JAMILA LYISCOTT, "Broken English"

In her performance, which has more than six million views online, Lyiscott uses what she calls "three tongues"—one each for "home, school, and friends"—to make the point that there are many different ways to be "articulate." And she's articulate, all right, in three different dialects.

THINK BEYOND WORDS

↱ WATCH THE VIDEO of Jamila Lyiscott's TED talk by visiting everyonesanauthor.tumblr.com. Why do you think Lyiscott chose a spoken-word essay as her medium? How does watching and listening to her performance (versus reading words on a page) change the way you understand her message? Why do you think Lyiscott chose to mix dialects? How would it change her message if she chose just one dialect instead of mixing several?

Drawing Attention

Here is Buthainah, a Saudi Arabian student writing a literacy narrative for an education class at an American college:

ومن يتهيّب صعود الجبال ~~~ يعش ابد الدّهر بين الحفر

> "I don't want to" was my response to my parents' request of enrolling me in a nearby preschool. I did not like school. I feared it. I feared the aspect of departing my comfort zone, my home, to an unknown and unpredictable zone. . . . To encourage me, they recited a poetic line that I did not comprehend as a child but live by it as an adult. They said, "Who fears climbing the mountains~~~ . . . Lives forever between the holes." As I grew up, knowledge became my key to freedom; freedom of thought, freedom of doing, and freedom of beliefs.
>
> —BUTHAINAH, "Who Fears Climbing the Mountains Lives Forever between the Holes"

In this instance, opening with the Arabic proverb (which also serves as the title of Buthainah's essay) draws readers' attention and announces the importance of Arabic in the author's journey to become the writer she is while also letting non-Arabic speakers feel a bit of what it's like to encounter a foreign language without an immediate translation. At the same time, she makes a point of translating the proverb for her readers as the essay progresses—"They said, 'Who fears climbing the mountains~~~ . . . Lives forever between the holes.'" Buthainah's essay illustrates how switching to a different language or way of speaking can grab attention and show—instead of tell—your audience something that's important to you.

Quoting People Directly and Respectfully

If you are writing about a person or group of people you have interviewed or who have been interviewed by others, you will want to let those people speak for themselves. From 1927 to 1931, Zora Neale Hurston, the famed folklorist, cultural anthropologist, and novelist, interviewed Cudjo Lewis, one of the last known people to be enslaved and brought across the Atlantic to the United States. Lewis's story, told from Hurston's perspective, appears in *Barracoon: The Story of the Last "Black Cargo,"* a book published after Hurston's death. Hurston takes care to let the subject of her interview speak his mind, and in his own words. She begins by documenting her initial interaction with Lewis, telling us, "I hailed him by his African name" (Oluale Kossula), which she had learned from others while conducting prior research. In the next paragraph, Lewis speaks:

> Oh Lor', I kno it *you* call my name. Nobody don't callee me my name from cross de water but you. You always callee me Kossula, jus' lak I in de Affica soil!
> —ZORA NEALE HURSTON, *Barracoon: The Story of the Last "Black Cargo"*

Hurston alternates between standardized English and a representation of the actual speech of the person whose words she quotes. These quotations report what she heard, which helps build her **ETHOS** as a careful listener and researcher. Finally, the use of quotations appeals to her audience's emotions; we can *hear* Lewis's surprise and delight. Readers familiar with the varieties of English Lewis uses might sense kinship with him, while those who are not will be reminded that Hurston is writing about a context different from their experience—but in a way that is always respectful.

When you're quoting others, let them speak for themselves not only in their own words but also in their own language. Whenever possible, ask your subjects to review the quotations you use to ensure they find the representation accurate and respectful.

Evoking a Particular Person, Place, or Community

Using the language of a specific community or group is a good way to evoke the character and sounds of the place. *Honolulu* magazine published a four-part series about Hawaiian Pidgin, a language spoken in that state, written by prize-winning Pidgin author and scholar Lee A. Tonouchi. Tonouchi wrote about the language's history, the politics of its use, and its future. One article in that series begins like this:

> Ukuplanny people ask me, "Pidgin stay dying o'wot?" In order fo see wea Pidgin stay going, we gotta try look see wea and wot Pidgin wuz befo time. Pidgin one strong, resilient language, you know. Cuz historically had lotta

Kiese Laymon carefully sprinkles his narrative with a few words of Black English. Check out his essay on p. 946, and notice how code-meshing gives more depth and flavor to his descriptions.

> times in Hawai'i when had strong public sentiment against Pidgin, and yet Pidgin still manage fo come back even mo strongah each time.
>
> —LEE A. TONOUCHI, "Da Future of Hawaiian Pidgin"

You can see that Tonouchi mixes elements of Pidgin and standardized English throughout every sentence. Notice how all the features weave together—individual words, grammatical structure, variant spelling that reflects the pronunciations and rhythms of Pidgin. The writing vividly evokes the ways that members of the community navigate their lives and linguistic repertoires. When using the language of a community or group you don't belong to yourself, take care to do so with respect. When possible, ask someone who does speak the language to provide feedback on what you've drafted to ensure it's accurate and respectful.

As we've tried to demonstrate, using your own linguistic repertoire and shifting between styles are powerful tools for communicating what you have to say. Consider the following questions as you think about mixing languages, dialects, and registers in your own writing:

- *Who's your target* AUDIENCE*?* Are there places where you can shift styles to connect with them? to get and keep their attention? to illustrate a point? What expectations does your audience have about language? Are you meeting those expectations or challenging them?
- *What's the larger* CONTEXT*?* Are readers likely to find your language choices suitable? Is anything at risk, like your credibility or clarity? What's your PURPOSE for taking such risks?
- *Are readers likely to understand your words?* Do you need to provide translations? If you're using a specific style, like MLA or APA, are there conventions—like italicizing non-English words in an English-language text—you need to follow?
- *Have you treated languages, dialects, and registers that are not your own with respect?* When quoting, have you let subjects speak for themselves? Have you solicited feedback from someone who speaks the language, dialect, or register to be sure your text is accurate and respectful?

> **REFLECT**
>
> Think about one or two ways of speaking you encounter that are different from your own—in places you work, movies you watch, or groups you are familiar with but don't belong to. Then find out as much as you can about that way of speaking and gather examples of it in use. What can you determine about how widely the dialect is used, who uses it, when it's used, what characteristics define it, and how it's perceived by different audiences? Write a brief reflection summarizing what you've found.

THIRTY-SIX

How to Craft Powerful Sentences

HEN A STUDENT asked author Annie Dillard, "Do you think I could become a writer?" Dillard replied with a question of her own: "Do you like sentences?" French novelist Gustave Flaubert certainly did, once saying that he "itched with sentences." Itching with sentences probably isn't something you've experienced—and liking or not liking sentences might not be something you've ever thought about—but we're willing to bet that you know something about how important sentences are. Anyone who has ever tried to write the perfect post or, better yet, the perfect love letter knows about choosing just the right words for each sentence and about the power of the three-word sentence "I love you."

In his book *How to Write a Sentence,* English professor Stanley Fish declares himself to be a "connoisseur of sentences" and offers some particularly noteworthy examples. Here's one, written by a fourth grader in response to an assignment to write something about a mysterious large box that had been delivered to a school:

▶ I was already on the second floor when I heard about the box.

This sentence reminded us of a favorite sentence of our own, this one the beginning of a story written by a third grader:

▶ Today, the monster goes where no monster has gone before: Cincinnati.

[715]

Here, the student manages to allude to the famous line from *Star Trek*—"to boldly go where no man has gone before"—while suggesting that Cincinnati is the most exotic place on Earth and even using a colon effectively. It's quite a sentence.

Finally, here's a sentence that opens a chapter from a PhD dissertation on literacy among young people today:

▶ Hazel Hernandez struck me as an honest thief.

Such sentences are memorable. They make us want to read more. Who's Hazel Hernandez? What's an honest thief, and what makes her one?

As these examples suggest, you don't have to be a famous author to write a great sentence. In fact, crafting effective and memorable sentences is a skill everyone can master with careful attention and practice. Sometimes a brilliant sentence comes to you like a bolt of lightning. More often, though, the perfect sentence is a result of tinkering during revision. Either way, crafting good sentences is worth the effort it may take.

Just as certain effects in film—music, close-ups—enhance the story, a well-crafted sentence can bring power to a piece of writing. As author Joan Didion wrote, "To shift the structure of a sentence alters the meaning of that sentence, as definitely and inflexibly as the position of a camera alters the meaning of the object photographed. Many people know about camera angles now, but not so many know about sentences."

So think about the kind of effect you want to create in what you're writing—and then look for the type of sentence that will fit the bill. Though much of the power of the examples above comes from their being short and simple, remember that some rhetorical situations call for longer, complex sentences—and that the kind of sentence you write also depends on its context, such as whether it's opening an essay, summing up what's already been said, or something else. This chapter looks at some common English sentence patterns and provides a few good examples for producing them in your own work. While the information and examples in the chapter are oriented around standardized English, writing in all language varieties involves sentences. The advice that you find here will be useful, even if you make some modifications in order to mix languages and dialects.

FOUR COMMON SENTENCE PATTERNS

We make sentences with words—and we arrange those words into patterns. If a sentence is defined as a group of words that expresses a complete thought, then we can identify four basic sentence structures: a **SIMPLE SENTENCE** (expressing one idea); a **COMPOUND SENTENCE** (expressing more than one idea, with the ideas being of equal importance); a **COMPLEX SENTENCE** (expressing more than one idea, with one of the ideas being more important than the others); and a **COMPOUND-COMPLEX SENTENCE** (with more than one idea of equal importance and at least one idea of less importance).

Simple Sentences: One Main Idea

Let's take a look at some simple sentences:

- Resist!
- Consumers revolted.
- Angry consumers revolted against new debit-card fees.
- A wave of protest from angry consumers forced banks to rescind the new fees.
- The growth of the internet and its capacity to mobilize people instantly all over the world have done everything from forcing companies to rescind debit-card fees in the United States to bringing down oppressive governments in the Middle East.

As these examples illustrate, simple sentences can be as short as a single word—or they can be much longer. Each is a simple sentence, however, because it contains a single main idea or thought; in grammatical terms, each contains one and only one **MAIN CLAUSE**. As the name suggests, a simple sentence is often the simplest, most direct way of saying what you want to say—but not always. And often you want a sentence to include more than one idea. In that case, you need to use a compound sentence, a complex sentence, or a compound-complex sentence.

Compound Sentences: Joining Ideas That Are Equally Important

Sometimes you'll want to write a sentence that joins two or more ideas that are equally important, like this one attributed to former president Bill Clinton:

▶ You can put wings on a pig, but you don't make it an eagle.

In grammatical terms, this is a compound sentence with two main clauses, each of which expresses one of two independent and equally important ideas. In this case, Clinton joined the ideas with a comma and the coordinating conjunction "but." However, he had several other options for joining these ideas. For example, he could have joined them with only a semicolon:

▶ You can put wings on a pig; you don't make it an eagle.

Or he could have joined them with a semicolon, a conjunctive adverb like "however," and a comma:

▶ You can put wings on a pig; however, you don't make it an eagle.

All of these compound sentences are perfectly acceptable—but which seems most effective? In this case, we think Clinton's choice is: it is clear and very direct, and if you read it aloud you'll hear that the words on each side of "but" have the same number of syllables, creating a pleasing, balanced rhythm—and one that balances the two equally important ideas. It also makes the logical relationship between the two ideas explicit: "but" indicates a contrast. The version with only a semicolon, by contrast, indicates that the ideas are somehow related but doesn't show how.

Using "and," "but," and other coordinating conjunctions. In writing a compound sentence, remember that different COORDINATING CONJUNCTIONS carry meanings that signal different logical relationships between the main ideas in the sentence. There are only seven coordinating conjunctions.

COORDINATING CONJUNCTIONS

and	for	or	yet
but	nor	so	

- China's one-child policy has slowed population growth, <u>but</u> it has helped create a serious gender imbalance in the country's population.
- Most of us bike to the office, <u>so</u> many of us stop at the gym to shower before work.
- The first two batters struck out, <u>yet</u> the Cubs went on to win the game on back-to-back homers.

See how the following sentences express different meanings depending on which coordinating conjunction is used:

- You could apply to graduate school, <u>or</u> you could start looking for a job.
- You could apply to graduate school, <u>and</u> you could start looking for a job.

Using a semicolon. Joining clauses with a semicolon only is a way of signaling that they are closely related without saying explicitly how. Often the second clause will expand on an idea expressed in the first clause.

- My first year of college was a little bumpy; it took me a few months to get comfortable at a campus far from home.
- The Wassaic Project is an arts organization in Dutchess County, New York; artists go there to engage in "art, music, and everything else."

Adding a transition word can make the logical relationship between the ideas more explicit:

- My first year of college was a little bumpy; <u>indeed</u>, it took me a few months to get comfortable at a campus far from home.

Note that the transition in this sentence, "indeed," cannot join the two main clauses on its own—it requires a semicolon before it. If you use a transition between two clauses with only a comma before it, you've made a mistake called a **COMMA SPLICE**.

SOME TRANSITION WORDS

also	indeed	otherwise
certainly	likewise	similarly
furthermore	nevertheless	therefore
however	next	thus

See the ebook for a video on using transitions.

REFLECT

Read through something you've written recently and identify compound sentences joined with "and." When you find one, ask yourself whether "and" is the best word to use: Does it express the logical relationship between the two parts of the sentence that you intend? Would "but," "or," "so," "for," "nor," or "yet" work better?

Complex Sentences: When One Idea Is More Important than Another

Many of the sentences you write will contain two or more ideas, with one that you want to emphasize more than the other(s). You can do so by putting the idea you wish to emphasize in the **MAIN CLAUSE**, and then putting those that are less important in **SUBORDINATE CLAUSES**.

- Mendocino County is a place in California <u>where you can dive for abalone</u>.
- <u>Because the species has become scarce</u>, abalone diving is strictly regulated.
- Fish and Wildlife Department agents <u>who patrol the coast</u> use sophisticated methods to catch poachers.

As these examples show, the ideas in the subordinate clauses (underlined here) can't stand alone as sentences: when we read "where you can dive for abalone" or "who patrol the coast," we know that something's missing. Subordinate clauses begin with words such as "if" or "because," **SUBORDINATING WORDS** that signal the logical relationship between the subordinate clause and the rest of the sentence.

SOME SUBORDINATING WORDS

after	even though	until
although	if	when
as	since	where
because	that	while
before	though	who

Notice that a subordinate clause can come at the beginning of a sentence, in the middle, or at the end. When it comes at the beginning, it is usually followed by a comma, as in the second example. If the opening clause in that sentence were moved to the end, a comma would not be necessary: "Abalone diving is strictly regulated because the species has become scarce."

Grammatically, each of the three examples above is a complex sentence, with one main idea and one other idea of less importance. In writing you will often have to decide whether to combine ideas in a compound sentence, which gives the ideas equal importance, or in a complex sentence, which makes one idea more important than the other(s). Looking once more at our sentence about the pig and the eagle, Bill Clinton could have made it a complex sentence:

▶ Even though you can put wings on a pig, you don't make it an eagle.

Again, though, we think Clinton made a good choice in giving the two ideas equal weight because doing so balances the sentence perfectly—and tells us that both parts are equally important. In fact, neither part of this sentence is very interesting in itself: it's the balancing and the contrast that make it interesting and memorable.

Compound-Complex Sentences: Multiple Ideas—Some More Important, Some Less

When you are expressing three or more ideas in a single sentence, you'll sometimes want to use a compound-complex sentence, which gives some of the ideas more prominence and others less. Grammatically, such sentences have at least two **MAIN CLAUSES** and one **SUBORDINATE CLAUSE**.

▶ We have experienced unparalleled natural disasters [MAIN CLAUSE] that have devastated entire countries, [SUBORDINATE CLAUSE] yet identifying global warming as the cause of these disasters is difficult. [MAIN CLAUSE]

▶ Even after distinguished scientists issued a series of reports, critics continued to question the findings because they claimed results were falsified; nothing would convince them.

As these examples show, English sentence structure is flexible, allowing you to combine groups of words in different ways in order to get your ideas across to your audience most effectively. There's seldom only one way to write a sentence to get an idea across: as the author, you must decide which way works best for your RHETORICAL SITUATION.

WAYS OF EMPHASIZING THE MAIN IDEA IN A SENTENCE

Sometimes, you will want to lead off a sentence with the main point; other times, you might want to hold it in reserve until the end. CUMULATIVE SENTENCES start with a main clause and then add on to it, "accumulating" details. PERIODIC SENTENCES start with a series of phrases or subordinate clauses, saving the main clause for last.

Cumulative Sentences: Starting with the Main Point

In this kind of sentence, the writer starts off with a MAIN CLAUSE and then adds details in phrases and SUBORDINATE CLAUSES, extending or explaining the thought. Cumulative sentences can be especially useful for describing a place or an event, operating almost like a camera panning across a room or landscape. The sentences below create such an effect:

▶ The San Bernardino Valley lies only an hour east of Los Angeles by the San Bernardino Freeway but is in certain ways an alien place: not the coastal

California of the subtropical twilights and the soft westerlies off the Pacific but a harsher California, haunted by the Mojave just beyond the mountains, devastated by the hot dry Santa Ana wind that comes down through the passes at 100 miles an hour and whines through the eucalyptus windbreaks and works on the nerves.

—JOAN DIDION, "Some Dreamers of the Golden Dream"

- Public transportation in Cebu City was provided by jeepneys: refurbished military jeeps with metal roofs for shade, decorated with horns and mirrors and fenders and flaps; painted with names, dedications, quotations, religious icons, logos—and much, much more.

- She hit the brakes, swearing fiercely, as the deer leapt over the hood and crashed into the dark woods beyond.

- The celebrated Russian pianist gave his hands a shake, a quick shake, fingers pointed down at his sides, before taking his seat and lifting them imperiously above the keys.

These cumulative sentences add details in a way that makes each sentence more emphatic. Keep this principle in mind as you write—and also when you revise. See if there are times when you might revise a sentence or sentences to add emphasis in the same way. Take a look at the following sentences, for instance:

- China has initiated free-market reforms that transformed its economy from a struggling one to an industrial powerhouse. It has become the world's fastest-growing major economy. Growth rates have been averaging 10 percent over the last decade.

These three sentences are clearly related, with each one adding detail about the growth of China's economy. Now look what happens when the writer eliminates a little bit of repetition, adds a memorable metaphor, and combines them as a cumulative—and more emphatic—sentence:

- China's free-market reforms have led to 10 percent average growth over the last decade, transforming it from a paper tiger into an industrial dragon that is now the world's fastest-growing major economy.

Periodic Sentences: Delaying the Main Point until the End

In contrast to sentences that open with the main idea, periodic sentences delay the main idea until the very end. Periodic sentences are sometimes fairly long, and withholding the main point until the end is a way of adding emphasis. It can also create suspense or build up to a surprise or inspirational ending.

> Unprovided with original learning, uninformed in the habits of thinking, unskilled in the arts of composition, I resolved to write a book.
>
> —EDWARD GIBBON, *Memoirs of My Life*

> In the week before finals, when my studying and memorizing reached a fever pitch, came a sudden, comforting thought: I am prepared.

Here are three periodic sentences in a row about Whitney Houston, each of which withholds the main point until the end:

> When her smiling brown face, complete with a close-cropped Afro, appeared on the cover of *Seventeen* in 1981, she was one of the first African-Americans to grace the cover, and the industry took notice. When she belted out a chilling and soulful version of the "Star-Spangled Banner" at the 1991 Super Bowl, the world sat back in awe of her poise and calm. And in an era when African-American actresses are often given film roles portraying them as destitute, unloving, unlovable, or just "the help," Houston played the love interest of Kevin Costner, a white Hollywood superstar.
>
> —ALLISON SAMUELS, "African American Stars Remember Whitney Houston"

These three periodic sentences create a drum-like effect that builds in intensity as they move through the stages in Houston's career; in all, they suggest that Houston was, even more than Kevin Costner, a "superstar."

Samuels takes a chance when she uses three sentences in a row that withhold the main point until the end: readers may get tired of waiting for that point. And readers may also find the use of too many such sentences to be, well, too much. But as the example above shows, when used carefully, a sentence that puts off the main idea just long enough can keep readers' interest, making them want to reach the ending, with its payoff.

You may find in your own work that periodic sentences can make your writing more emphatic. Take a look at the following sentence from an essay on the use of animals in circuses:

▶ The big cat took him down with one swat, just as the trainer, dressed in khakis and boots, his whip raised and his other arm extended in welcome to the cheering crowd, stepped into the ring.

This sentence paints a vivid picture, but it gives away all the action in the first six words. By withholding that action until the end, the writer builds anticipation and adds emphasis:

▶ Just as the trainer stepped into the ring, dressed in khakis and boots, his whip raised and his other arm extended in welcome to the cheering crowd, the big cat took him down with one swat.

OPENING SENTENCES

The opening sentences in your writing carry big responsibilities, setting the tone and often the scene—and drawing your readers in by arousing their interest and curiosity. Authors often spend quite a lot of time on opening sentences for this very reason: whether it's a business report or a college essay or a social media post, the way the piece begins has a lot to do with whether your audience will stay with you and whether you'll get the kind of response you want from them. Here are three famous opening sentences:

▶ I am an invisible man. —RALPH ELLISON, *Invisible Man*

▶ The sky above the port was the color of television, tuned to a dead channel. —WILLIAM GIBSON, *Neuromancer*

▶ I lost an arm on my last trip home. —OCTAVIA E. BUTLER, *Kindred*

Each of these sentences is startling, making us read on in order to find out more. Each is brief, leaving us waiting anxiously for what's to come. In addition, each makes a powerful statement and creates some kind of image in readers' minds: an "invisible" person, a sky the color of a "dead" TV channel,

> Lynda Barry begins her narrative on p. 849 with a compelling opening sentence. Check it out (and be prepared to keep reading; you won't want to stop).

someone losing an arm. These sentences all come from novels, but they use strategies that work in many kinds of writing.

It usually takes more than a single sentence to open an essay. Here is the opening of a blog post that begins with a provocative question:

▶ Have you ever thought about whether to have a child? If so, what factors entered into your decision? Was it whether having children would be good for you, your partner and others close to the possible child, such as children you may already have, or perhaps your parents? For most people contemplating reproduction, those are the dominant questions. Some may also think about the desirability of adding to the strain that the nearly seven billion people already here are putting on our planet's environment. But very few ask whether coming into existence is a good thing for the child itself.
—PETER SINGER, "Should This Be the Last Generation?"

Singer's question is designed to get the reader's attention, and he follows it up with two additional questions that ask readers to probe more deeply into their reasons for considering whether or not to reproduce. In the fifth sentence, he suggests that the answers people give to these questions may not be adequate ones, and in the last sentence he lays down a challenge: perhaps coming into existence is not always good for "the child itself."

Here's another example of an opening that uses several sentences, this one from a student essay about graphic memoirs:

▶ In 1974, before the Fall of Saigon, my 14-year-old father, alone, boarded a boat out of Vietnam in search of America. This is a fact. But this one fact can spawn multiple understandings: I could ask a group of students to take a week and write me a story from just this one fact, and I have no doubt that they would bring back a full range of interpretations.
—BRANDON LY, "Leaving Home, Coming Home"

This opening passage begins with a vivid image of a very young man fleeing Vietnam alone, followed by a very short sentence that makes a statement and then a longer one that challenges that statement. This student writer is moving readers toward what will become his thesis: that memoirs can never tell "the whole truth, and nothing but the truth."

Finally, take a look at the opening of the speech Toni Morrison gave when she won the Nobel Prize in Literature:

> Members of the Swedish Academy, Ladies and Gentlemen:
> Narrative has never been mere entertainment for me. It is, I believe, one of the principal ways in which we absorb knowledge. I hope you will understand, then, why I begin these remarks with the opening phrase of what must be the oldest sentence in the world, and the earliest one we remember from childhood: "Once upon a time . . ."
> —TONI MORRISON, Nobel Prize acceptance speech

Morrison begins with a deceptively simple statement that narrative is for her not just entertainment. In the next sentences, she complicates that statement and broadens her claim that narrative is the way we understand the world, concluding with what she calls "the oldest sentence in the world."

You can use strategies similar to the ones shown here in opening your college essays. Here are just some of the ways you might begin:

- With a strong, dramatic—or deceptively simple—statement
- With a vivid image
- With a provocative question
- With an anecdote
- With a surprising claim

CLOSING SENTENCES

Sentences that conclude a piece of writing are where you have a chance to make a lasting impact: to reiterate your point, tell readers why it matters, echo something you say in your opening, make a provocative statement, or issue a call for action.

Here's Joe Posnanski, wrapping up an essay on his blog arguing that college athletes should not be paid:

> College football is not popular because of the stars. College football is popular because of that first word. Take away the college part, add in

See the ebook for a video on writing introductions and conclusions.

> money, and you are left with professional minor league football. . . . See how many people watch that. —JOE POSNANSKI, "The College Connection"

These four sentences summarize his argument—and the last one's the zinger, one that leaves readers thinking.

Now take a look at the conclusion to a scholarly book on current neurological studies of human attention, the brain science of attention:

> ▶ Right now, our classrooms and workplaces are structured for success in the last century, not this one. We can change that. By maximizing opportunities for collaboration, by rethinking everything from our approach to work to how we measure progress, we can begin to see the things we've been missing and catch hold of what's passing us by.
>
> If you change the context, if you change the questions you ask, if you change the structure, the test, and the task, then you stop gazing one way and begin to look in a different way and in a different direction. You know what happens next:
>
> *Now* you see it.
>
> —CATHY DAVIDSON, *Now You See It: How the Brain Science of Attention Will Transform the Way We Live, Work, and Learn*

Cathy Davidson uses two short paragraphs to sum up her argument and then concludes with a final paragraph that consists of just one very short four-word sentence. With this last sentence, she uses a tried-and-true strategy of coming full circle to echo the main idea of her book and, in fact, to reiterate its title. Readers who have worked their way through the book will take pleasure in that last sentence: *Now* they do see her point.

For another example, note how in the ending to a speech about language and about being able to use "all the Englishes" she grew up with, author Amy Tan closes with a one-sentence paragraph that quotes her mother:

> ▶ Apart from what any critic had to say about my writing, I knew I had succeeded where it counted when my mother finished reading my book and gave me her verdict: "So easy to read." —AMY TAN, "Mother Tongue"

Tan's ending sums up one of her main goals as an author: to write so that readers who speak different kinds of English will find her work accessible, especially her mother.

Finally, take a look at how Toni Morrison chose to close her Nobel Prize acceptance speech:

> ▶ It is, therefore, mindful of the gifts of my predecessors, the blessing of my sisters, in joyful anticipation of writers to come that I accept the honor the Swedish Academy has done me, and ask you to share what is for me a moment of grace. —TONI MORRISON, Nobel Prize acceptance speech

In this one-sentence conclusion, Morrison speaks to the past, present, and future when she says she is grateful for those writers who came before her, for those who are writing now (her sisters), and for those yet to come. She ends the sentence by asking her audience to share this "moment of grace" with her and, implicitly, with all other writers so honored.

You may not be accepting a Nobel Prize soon, but in your college writing you can use all the strategies presented here to compose strong closings:

- By reiterating your point
- By discussing the implications of your argument
- By asking a question
- By referring back to your beginning
- By recommending or proposing some kind of action

 **REFLECT**

Identify two memorable openings and closings from a favorite novel, comic book, film, or social media post. What makes them so good? Do they follow one of the strategies presented here?

VARYING YOUR SENTENCES

Read a paragraph or two of your writing out loud and listen for its rhythm. Is it quick and abrupt? slow and leisurely? singsong? stately? rolling? Whatever it is, does the rhythm you hear match what you had in mind when you were writing? And does it put the emphasis where you want it? One way to establish the emphasis you intend and a rhythm that will keep readers reading is by varying the length of your sentences and the way those sentences flow from one to the other.

A string of sentences that are too much alike is almost certain to be boring. While you can create effective rhythms in many ways, one of the simplest and most effective is by breaking up a series of long sentences with a shorter one that gives your readers a chance to pause and absorb what you've written.

Take a look at the following passage, from an article in the *Atlantic* about the finale of the *Oprah Winfrey Show*. See how the author uses a mix of long and short sentences to describe one of the tributes to Oprah, this one highlighting her support of Black men:

> ▶ Oprah's friend Tyler Perry announced that some of the "Morehouse Men," each a beneficiary of the $12 million endowment she has established at their university, had come to honor her for the scholarships she gave them. The lights were lowered, a Broadway star began singing an inspirational song, and a dozen or so black men began to walk slowly to the front of the stage. Then more came, and soon there were a score, then 100, then the huge stage was filled with men, 300 of them. They stood there, solemnly, in a tableau stage-managed in such a way that it might have robbed them of their dignity—the person serenading them (or, rather, serenading Oprah on their behalf) was Kristin Chenoweth, tiniest and whitest of all tiny white women; the song was from *Wicked*, most feminine of all musicals; and each man carried a white candle, an emblem that lent them the aspect of Norman Rockwell Christmas carolers. But they were not robbed of their dignity. They looked, all together, like a miracle. A video shown before the procession revealed that some of these men had been in gangs before going to Morehouse, some had fathers in prison, many had been living in poverty. Now they were doctors, lawyers, bankers, a Rhodes Scholar—and philanthropists, establishing their own Morehouse endowment.
> —CAITLIN FLANAGAN, "The Glory of Oprah"

The passage begins with three medium-length sentences—and then one very long one (seventy-two words!) that points up the strong contrast between the 300 Black men filling the stage and the "whitest of white"

The Morehouse Men surprise Oprah.

singer performing a song from the "most feminine" of musicals. Then come two little sentences (the first one eight words long and the second one, seven) that give readers a chance to pause and absorb what has been said while also making an important point: that the men "looked, all together, like a miracle." The remainder of the passage moves back toward longer sentences, each of which explains just what this "miracle" is. Try reading this passage aloud and listen for how the variation in sentences creates both emphasis and a pleasing and effective rhythm.

In addition to varying the lengths of your sentences, you can also improve your writing by making sure that they don't all use the same structure or begin in the same way. You can be pretty sure, for example, that a passage in which every sentence is a simple sentence that opens with the subject of a main clause will not read smoothly at all but rather will move along awkwardly. Take a look at this passage, for example:

> ▶ The sunset was especially beautiful today. I was on top of Table Mountain in Cape Town. I looked down and saw the sun touch the sea and sink into it.

> The evening shadows crept up the mountain. I got my backpack and walked over to the rest of my group. We started on the long hike down the mountain and back to the city.

There's nothing wrong with these sentences as such. Each one is grammatically correct. But if you read the passage aloud, you'll hear how it moves abruptly from sentence to sentence, lurching along rather than flowing smoothly. The problem is that the sentences are all the same: each one is a simple sentence that begins with the subject of a main clause (sunset, I, I, evening shadows, I, we). In addition, the use of personal pronouns at the beginning of the sentences (three uses of "I" in only six sentences!) makes for dull reading. Finally, these are all fairly short sentences, and the sameness of the sentence length adds to the abrupt rhythm of the passage—and doesn't keep readers reading. Now look at how this passage can be revised by working on sentence variation:

> ▶ From the top of Cape Town's Table Mountain, the sunset was especially beautiful. I looked down just as the fiery orb touched and then sank into the sea; shadows began to creep slowly up the mountain. Picking up my backpack, I joined the rest of my group, and we started the long hike down the mountain.

This revision reduces the number of sentences in the passage from six to three (the first simple, the second compound-complex, the third compound) and varies the length of the sentences. Equally important, the revision eliminates all but one of the subject openings. The first sentence now begins with the prepositional phrase ("From the top"); the second with the subject of a main clause ("I"); and the third with a participial phrase ("Picking up my backpack"). Finally, the revision varies the diction a bit, replacing the repeated word "sun" with a vivid image ("fiery orb"). Read the revised passage aloud and you'll hear how varying the sentences creates a stronger rhythm that makes it easier to read.

This brief chapter has only scratched the surface of sentence style. But we hope we've said enough to show how good sentences can be your allies, helping you get your ideas out there and connect with audiences as successfully as possible. Remember: authors are only as good as the sentences they write!

 **REFLECT**

Take a look at a writing assignment you've recently completed. Read it aloud, listening for rhythm and emphasis. If you find a passage that doesn't read well or provide the emphasis you want, analyze its sentences for length (count the words) and structure (how does each sentence begin?). Revise the passage using the strategies presented in this chapter.

THIRTY-SEVEN

Polishing and Editing Your Writing

IN PREPARATION FOR a 2018 Coachella performance, Beyoncé led her team through eleven-hour rehearsal days. LeBron James spends five to seven hours every day training in the gym (in addition to team practices). It takes a lot of hard work to make something look easy. Beyoncé rehearses, LeBron trains; what do authors do? We revise and edit.

Take this book, for example. It was written by experienced authors—skilled teachers and professional writers, all. The page that you're reading right now—how many drafts and revisions did it go through before it reached you? We lose count after three or four. The point is, completing a draft is a great accomplishment, and it's only the beginning.

One of the most important parts of your revision process is examining each sentence for structural problems. If you see the word "editing" and think only about "grammar rules," think again. Language and grammar "rules" are really just a set of conventions, ways to facilitate successful communication. Suppose you're at a party when you get a text from the friend you came with that says "hom noe ok." Huh? You might be able to figure out that they want to go home, but you'll probably have to think about the message longer than you want to. If they had taken the trouble to check their words or put a question mark at the end, you probably would have understood their message more easily.

37 Polishing and Editing Your Writing

As a writer, you bear the responsibility for making things easy for your readers. In academic writing, the easier the better. We have two goals in this chapter: first, to help you make your writing clear and smooth so that readers won't have to wonder what you're trying to say, or question whether you know what you're talking about. Second, we want to help you make well-considered rhetorical choices, editing with your purpose and audience in mind.

Writing is always a work in progress; we can edit to smooth out bumps and wrinkles. Our team asked seventy-five writing instructors to point out the kinds of sentence structure problems that were most troublesome in two ways: they interfered with the smooth comprehension of the writing, or they damaged the writer's credibility.

The instructors' responses covered a wide gamut, from sentence structure to punctuation. This chapter focuses on those problems that matter, showing how to spot them in a draft, explaining why they're so troublesome, and suggesting strategies for editing them out. Editing your draft may seem like a daunting task after you've already worked so hard to produce it. Let your rhetorical situation and your audience guide you; these will help you prioritize the edits that will improve your work the most.

A note about standardized English. Most of the advice that we offer here conforms to what's expected in standardized English specifically, since that's the dialect that your rhetorical situation will call for in many academic and professional contexts. In the editing advice that follows, we're not so concerned with figuring out what's "correct" and "incorrect," but instead with revising and editing to end up with clear writing.

Some dialects of English express things differently from how they might be said in standardized English. For example, Black English, Chicano English, White working-class English, and other varieties often use the double negative ("they don't want no ketchup"), while standardized English uses only one negative element per clause ("they don't want ketchup"). Despite these distinctions, however, all dialects and varieties of English are more similar to one another than they are different. For example, to indicate the location of a screwdriver, you might say it's "in that box"; in no variety of English that we know of would you say it's "that box in." In this chapter, when you encounter the words "correct" or "appropriate," know that they refer to conventions that generally apply to all dialects and varieties of English.

> See the ebook for a video on editing and proofreading strategies.

> Throughout this chapter, you'll find opportunities for editing practice in adaptive activities called InQuizitive. See the access card at the front of your print book or visit digital.wwnorton.com/everyone5r.

Editing for inclusion. Before looking at specific sentence-level editing issues in any draft of an assignment, take a moment to consider how inclusive your language choices have been throughout it. Have you used gender-neutral language, for example, avoiding terms like "stewardess" that assume people holding certain jobs are all a single sex? Have you used SINGULAR "THEY" rather than "he" or "she," unless you are sure that the person you are referring to identifies as male or female (see pp. 750–54)? Whenever possible, have you used terms that groups use to describe themselves (such as the name of a specific tribe rather than "Native American," or "Deaf" rather than "hearing-impaired")? Write with empathy and respect, speaking of others as you would have them speak of you. That's one of the golden rules of editing!

EDITING SENTENCES

Fragments, comma splices, fused sentences, and mixed constructions are all considered problematic sentence structures. Such sentences are usually comprehensible in context, so if readers can understand the message, what's the problem? Solid sentence structure matters for two reasons:

- The perception of your competence hangs on it: most readers don't trust writers who write sloppy sentences.
- Even if a poorly structured sentence can be understood, your readers have to work a little harder to get there, and they may not want to put forth the effort. Your job is to make it easy for readers, to keep them reading smoothly all the way to the end.

Every sentence is composed of one or more CLAUSES, and every clause needs to have a SUBJECT, a VERB, and the expected punctuation. Don't underestimate those little dots and squiggles; they often make all the difference in how a sentence is read and understood. Consider these two examples:

▶ Let's eat Grandma.

▶ Let's eat, Grandma.

Are you inviting your grandmother to eat a meal right now, or are you inviting someone else to eat *her*? That one little comma in the right place can save Grandma's life (or at least make it clear to your readers that you aren't proposing to make a meal of her). The following advice will help you examine your writing with an eye to four common sentence-structure problems: fragments, comma splices, fused sentences, and mixed constructions. Fragments and comma splices can be very powerful and effective in certain situations; you may even notice a few in the readings we include in this book. They're not usually recommended, however, in more formal academic work.

Fragments

At first glance, a fragment looks like a complete sentence—it begins with a capital letter and concludes with end punctuation—but on closer examination, a key element, usually a **SUBJECT** or a **VERB**, is missing. For example: "Forgot to vote." Who forgot to vote? We don't know; the subject is missing. "Two bottles of rancid milk." Wow. That sounds interesting, but what about them? There's no verb, so we don't know. A fragment also occurs when a sentence begins with a **SUBORDINATING WORD** such as "if" or "because," but the **SUBORDINATE CLAUSE** is not followed by a **MAIN CLAUSE**. "If the ball game is rained out." Well, what happens if the ball game is rained out? Again, we don't know.

Checking for fragments
Sometimes writers use fragments for stylistic reasons, but it's usually best to avoid them in academic writing. To check your text for fragments, examine each sentence one by one, making sure there's both a subject and a verb. (It might take you a while to do this at first, but it will go much faster with practice, and it's worth the time.) Check also for subordinating words (see p. 720 for a list of common ones), and if there's a subordinate clause, make sure there's also a main clause.

> You can find an excellent example of two fragments used effectively in Robin Wall Kimmerer's essay about strawberries. See if you can find them; her essay is on p. 932.

Editing fragments
Let's look at some fragments and see what we can do about them.

NEEDS A SUBJECT

▶ The Centipedes were terrible last night. <u>Started late, played three songs, and left.</u>

Context makes it clear that it was the Centipedes who started late. Still, the underlined part is a fragment because there is no explicit subject. We have two good options here. One is to add a subject to the fragment in order to make the sentence complete; the other is to attach the fragment to a nearby sentence. Both strategies work, and you can choose whichever seems best to you.

▶ The Centipedes were terrible last night. ~~Started~~ *They started* late, played three songs, and left.

▶ The Centipedes were terrible last night~~.~~/ ~~Started~~ *because they started* late, played three songs, and left.

In the first example, we've added a subject, "They," which refers to the Centipedes. In the second, we've attached the fragment to the preceding sentence using a subordinating word, "because," followed by an explicit subject, "they."

NEEDS A VERB

▶ Malik heard a knock on the door. <u>Then a loud thud.</u>

The example makes sense: we know that Malik heard a loud thud after the knock. But the underlined part is a fragment because between the capital "T" at the beginning and the period at the end, there is no verb. Again, there are two strategies for editing: to add a verb to the fragment in order to make the sentence complete, or to incorporate the fragment into the previous sentence so that its verb can do double duty.

▶ Malik heard a knock on the door. Then *came* a loud thud.

▶ Malik heard a knock on the door~~.~~/ ~~Then~~ *followed by* a loud thud.

NEEDS MORE INFORMATION

▶ Olga nearly missed her plane. <u>Because the line at security was so long.</u> She got flustered and dropped her change purse.

The underlined part of the example above does have a subject and a verb, but it can't stand alone as a sentence because it starts with "because," a subordinating word that leads readers to expect more information. Did the long security line cause Olga to nearly miss her plane? Or did the long line fluster her? We can't be sure. How you edit this fragment depends on what you're trying to say—and how the ideas relate to one another. For example:

- Olga nearly missed her plane. ~~Because~~ *because* the line at security was so long.
- Because the line at security was so long. ~~She~~ *she* got flustered and dropped her change purse.

The first option explains why Olga nearly missed her plane, and the second explains why she got flustered and dropped her change purse.

Edit
The word "if" leads readers to expect a clause explaining what will happen. Consider the following example:

- If you activate the alarm.

This example is a fragment. We need the sentence to show the "what-if": what happens if you activate the alarm? Otherwise, we have an incomplete thought—and readers will be confused.

- The whole lab will be destroyed. If you activate the alarm. Spider-Man, you can avert the tragedy.

Will the lab be destroyed if Spider-Man activates the alarm? Or will activating the alarm avert the tragedy? There is no way for readers to know. This example needs to be edited! You try. Edit the example above for both possible interpretations.

↪ For more practice, complete the InQuizitive activity on **sentence fragments**.

Comma Splices

A comma splice looks like a complete sentence in that it starts with a capital letter, concludes with end punctuation, and contains two MAIN CLAUSES. The problem is that there is only a comma between the two clauses. Here's an example:

- It was the coldest day in fifty years, the marching band performed brilliantly.

Both clauses are perfectly clear, and we expect that they are connected in some way—but we don't know how. Did the band play well because of the cold or in spite of it? Or is there no connection at all? In short, comma splices can leave your readers confused.

Checking for comma splices

Writers sometimes use comma splices to create a certain stylistic effect, but we recommend avoiding them in academic writing. To check your work for comma splices, look at each sentence one by one and identify the VERBS. Next, look for their SUBJECTS. If you find two or more sets of subjects and verbs that form MAIN CLAUSES, make sure they are connected appropriately.

Editing comma splices

What are the expected ways to connect two independent clauses? Let's look at some of the possibilities.

CHANGE THE COMMA TO A PERIOD

One of your options is to create two separate sentences by inserting a period (.) after the first clause and capitalizing the first letter of the following word.

▶ It was the coldest day in fifty years/. ~~the~~ *The* marching band performed brilliantly.

This might be your preferred choice if you want to write tersely, with short sentences, perhaps to open an essay in a dramatic way. Maybe there is a connection between the two sentences; maybe there's not. Readers will want to keep going in order to find out.

CHANGE THE COMMA TO A SEMICOLON

Another simple way to edit a comma splice is to insert a semicolon (;) between the two clauses.

▶ It was the coldest day in fifty years/; the marching band performed brilliantly.

The semicolon lets readers know that there is a definite connection between the weather and the band's brilliant performance, but they can't be certain what it is. The sentence is now correct, if not terribly interesting. You can make the connection clearer and even make the sentence more interesting by adding a TRANSITION (nevertheless, still, in any event; check the Glossary / Index for more examples).

▶ It was the coldest day in fifty years/; *nevertheless,* the marching band performed brilliantly.

See Ch. 36 in the ebook for a video on using transitions.

ADD A COORDINATING CONJUNCTION

You can also insert a **COORDINATING CONJUNCTION** (and, but, or, nor, so, for, yet) after the comma between the two clauses.

> ▶ It was the coldest day in fifty years, ^*but*^ the marching band performed brilliantly.

With this option, the two clauses are separated clearly, and the word "but" indicates that the band played brilliantly in spite of the cold weather.

ADD A SUBORDINATING WORD

Another way to show a relationship between the two clauses is with a **SUBORDINATING WORD** (while, however, thus; see p. 720 for more examples).

> ▶ *Although it* ~~It~~ was the coldest day in fifty years, the marching band performed brilliantly.

Here, the logical relationship between the two clauses is clear and explicit, and the band's performance becomes the important part of the sentence. But what if you wanted to suggest that the cold weather was responsible for the band playing so well? You could use the same clauses, but with a different subordinating word, as in the example below.

> ▶ *Possibly because it* ~~It~~ was the coldest day in fifty years, the marching band performed brilliantly.

You may also want to experiment with changing the order of the clauses; in many cases, that will cause the emphasis to change. Sometimes, too, changing the order will help you transition to the next sentence.

> ▶ *The marching band performed brilliantly, even though it* ~~It~~ was the coldest day in fifty years~~, the marching band performed brilliantly~~. Fans huddled together under blankets in the stands.

Edit

Consider the following example:

> Transit officials estimate that the new light-rail line will be 20 percent faster than the express bus, the train will cost $1.85 per ride regardless of distance traveled.

Try editing this comma splice in two ways: one that emphasizes the speed of the train and another that emphasizes the cost.

↪ For more practice, complete the InQuizitive activity on **comma splices**.

Fused Sentences

A fused sentence looks like a complete sentence at first glance because it begins with a capital letter, concludes with end punctuation, and contains two **MAIN CLAUSES**. The reason it is problematic is that there is no explicit connection between the two clauses. A fused sentence will make sense to readers most of the time, but most of the time isn't quite often enough, and you generally don't want your readers to struggle to understand what you're saying. A sentence can contain more than one main clause, no problem, but if it does, there needs to be some signal indicating how the clauses relate to one another. That signal could be a punctuation mark, a word that shows how the clauses are related, or both.

Checking for fused sentences

To check your text for fused sentences, look at each sentence one by one and identify any that have more than one **MAIN CLAUSE**. Then see how the clauses are connected: is there a word or punctuation mark that indicates how they relate? If not, you've got a fused sentence.

Editing fused sentences

Let's look at a typical fused sentence and some ways it can be edited.

▶ The fire alarm went off the senator spilled her latte all over her desk.

Perfectly clear, right? Or did you have to read it twice to make sure? This example is a fused sentence because it contains two main clauses but offers no way of knowing where one stops and the next begins, and no indication of how the clauses relate to each other. Here are some options for editing this fused sentence.

ADD A PERIOD

One option is to make the fused sentence into two separate sentences by inserting a period after the first independent clause and capitalizing the first letter of the following clause.

▶ The fire alarm went off. ~~the~~ *The* senator spilled her latte all over her desk.

Now you have two complete sentences, but they are a little dry and lifeless. Readers may think the two events have nothing to do with each other, or they may think some explanation is missing. In some cases, you may want to choose this solution—if you are merely reporting what happened, for example—but it might not be the best one for this example.

ADD A SEMICOLON

Another option is to insert a semicolon (**;**) between the two clauses.

▶ The fire alarm went off**;** the senator spilled her latte all over her desk.

This is another simple way to deal with a fused sentence, although it still doesn't help readers know *how* the two clauses relate. The relationship between the clauses is fairly clear here, but that won't always be the case, so make sure the logical connection between the two clauses is very obvious before you use a semicolon. You can also add a **TRANSITION** (nevertheless, still, in any event; see the Glossary / Index for more examples) after the semicolon to make the relationship between the two clauses more explicit.

▶ The fire alarm went off**;** *as a result,* the senator spilled her latte all over her desk.

ADD A COMMA AND A COORDINATING CONJUNCTION

In order to clarify the relationship between the clauses a little more, you could insert a comma and a **COORDINATING CONJUNCTION** (and, but, or, nor, so, for, yet) between the two clauses.

▶ The fire alarm went off**,** *and* the senator spilled her latte all over her desk.

Here the division between the two clauses is clearly marked, and readers will generally understand that the latte spilled right after (and the spill was possibly caused by) the fire alarm. With this solution, both clauses have equal importance.

ADD A SUBORDINATING WORD

One of the clearest ways to show the relationship between two clauses is by using a **SUBORDINATING WORD** (see p. 720 for more examples).

▶ *When the* ~~The~~ fire alarm went off**,** the senator spilled her latte all over her desk.

Adding the subordinating word "when" to the first clause makes it clear that the fire alarm caused the senator to spill her latte and also puts emphasis on the spilled coffee. Note that you need to add a comma after the introductory clause. You can also change the order of the two clauses; see how the emphasis changes slightly. Note, too, that in this case, you should not add a comma.

▶ The senator spilled her latte all over her desk ^*when* the fire alarm went off.

Edit

Using the editing options explained above, edit the following fused sentence in two different ways. Make one of your solutions short and snappy. In the other solution, show that the banging and the shouting were happening at the same time.

> The moderator banged his gavel the candidates continued to shout at each other.

↪ For more practice, complete the InQuizitive activity on **fused sentences**.

Mixed Constructions

A **MIXED CONSTRUCTION** is a sentence that starts out with one structure and ends up with another one. Such a sentence may be understandable, but more often it leaves readers scratching their heads in confusion. There are many different ways to end up with a mixed construction, and this fact alone makes it difficult to identify one. Here is an example of one common type of mixed construction:

▶ Décollage is when you take away pieces of an image to create a new image.

The sentence is clear enough, but look again at the word "when." That word locates an event in time—"I'll call <u>when</u> I get there." "The baby woke up <u>when</u> the phone rang." "<u>When</u> the armistice was signed, people everywhere cheered." In the example above, there is no time associated with décollage; the sentence is simply describing the process. To edit the sentence, replace "when" with a more accurate word, and adjust the rest of the sentence as needed.

▶ Décollage is ~~when you take~~ ^*the technique of taking* away pieces of an image to create a new image.

Checking for mixed constructions

Let's consider another example:

▶ Nutritionists disagree about the riskiness of eating raw eggs and also more healthful compared with cooked ones.

What? It's hard to even know where to start. Let's begin by identifying the **VERB(S)**. There's only one verb here, "disagree." Next, let's identify the **SUBJECT**. Who disagrees? "Nutritionists." Now we have a subject and a verb. What do nutritionists disagree about? It's clear enough that they disagree about "the riskiness of eating raw eggs," but after that, it gets confusing. Consider the next words: "and also." Also what? Do nutritionists also disagree that raw eggs are more nutritious than cooked eggs? Or is the writer claiming that raw eggs *are* more healthful? It's impossible to tell, which suggests that we have a mixed construction.

Editing mixed constructions

Let's look at a couple of ways we might edit the sentence about raw eggs. Here's one way:

▶ Nutritionists disagree about the riskiness of eating raw eggs and also ~~more healthful~~ *about their healthfulness* compared with cooked ones.

Notice that we added another "about," which makes it clear that what follows is also something nutritionists disagree about. We also added the suffix "-ness" to "healthful" so that the word would be parallel to "riskiness." Now the verb "disagree" applies to both "riskiness" and "healthfulness": nutritionists disagree about the riskiness of eating raw eggs, and they also disagree about the healthfulness of raw eggs compared with cooked ones.

What if the writer's original intention was to claim that raw eggs are more healthful than cooked ones? Since the two parts of the sentence express two different ideas, an editor might choose to simply make the mixed construction into two separate sentences.

▶ Nutritionists disagree about the riskiness of eating raw eggs. ~~and also~~ *Raw eggs are* more healthful ~~compared with~~ *than* cooked ones.

Just considering sentence structure, now we have two good sentences, but even though they both focus on raw eggs, the two sentences are not clearly connected. And besides, who is saying that eating raw eggs is more healthful? The author or the nutritionists? Adding just a couple of words links the sentences together and helps readers follow the ideas.

▶ Nutritionists disagree about the riskiness of eating raw eggs. ~~Raw~~ *Some claim raw* eggs are more healthful than cooked ones.

Here we've added a new subject, "some" (which refers to nutritionists), and we've also given the second sentence a verb, "claim." Now the two sentences have a logical sequence and are easier to read. Next, let's look at one other mixed construction:

> ▶ Because air accumulates under the eggshell is why an egg stands up underwater.

This sentence is more or less clear, but its parts don't fit together properly. What can we do about that? Same procedure as before—first, look for the verbs. This time, it's more complicated because there are three: "accumulates," "is," and "stands up." Next, we look for the subject of each of the verbs. The first one is easy—"air" accumulates; the subject is "air." The third one is also simple—"an egg" stands up; the subject is "an egg." But what is the subject of "is"? That's not such an easy question with this sentence because its structure changes in the middle. So let's try a different approach.

What exactly is this sentence trying to say? It's clear that the point of this sentence is to explain why a submerged egg stands up, and we have two clauses: one that tells us that "an egg stands up underwater" and another that tells us that the egg stands up "because air accumulates under the eggshell." Now we just have to put them together in a meaningful way.

> ▶ Because air accumulates under the eggshell, ~~is why~~ an egg stands up underwater.

Did you notice that this version is almost exactly the same as the original sentence? The main difference is the words "is why"—which turn out not to be necessary. We now have one **MAIN CLAUSE** (an egg stands up underwater) and one **SUBORDINATE CLAUSE** (because air accumulates under the eggshell), with a comma in between. If it sounds better to you, you can reverse the order of the clauses, and the meaning stays the same. Note that you should not use a comma with this option.

> ▶ An egg stands up underwater because air accumulates under the eggshell.

We can use the same approach for a sentence that starts with a prepositional phrase but changes its structure in the middle: figure out what the sentence is trying to say, identify the phrases and clauses, and edit as needed so that you can put them together in a meaningful way.

▶ *Parents*
~~For parents~~ of children with a walnut allergy depend on rules that prohibit nuts in school.

Edit

Try editing the following mixed construction in two ways. First, make one sentence that includes all the information in the example. Next, present the same information in two separate sentences. Which way do you like better? Why?

> One or two months before mating, male and female eagles together build their nests can be four or five feet in diameter.

↪ For more practice, complete the InQuizitive activity on **mixed constructions**.

EDITING PRONOUNS

Pronouns are some of the smallest words in the language, so you might think they should be among the easiest. Well, no, they're often not. But the good news is that editing your work to make sure all your pronouns are used accurately is not too complicated. The advice that follows gives you tools for editing three common pronoun issues: pronoun reference, pronoun-antecedent agreement, and pronoun case.

First, let's clarify the terms. **PRONOUNS** are words that refer to other words or phrases (and occasionally even whole clauses). They're very useful precisely because they're small and they do a lot of work representing larger units. The words that they represent are their **ANTECEDENTS**. Most frequently, the antecedent is something or somebody that has already been mentioned, and standardized English has very specific conventions for signaling to readers exactly what that antecedent is so that they won't be confused. We call that **PRONOUN REFERENCE**. Let's suppose this next example is the first sentence in a news report.

▶ The Procurement Committee meets today to review the submitted bids, and she will announce the winner tomorrow.

Wait. "She"? "She" who? It's not clear what "she" refers to, and readers are now lost.

Pronoun **AGREEMENT** is another important convention. Pronouns have to agree with their antecedents in number (I, we) and in some cases gender (he, she, they, it). "Mr. Klein misplaced her phone again." If Mr. Klein is in the habit of losing a specific woman's phone, then perhaps the sentence makes sense. If it's his own phone that he misplaced again, then "her" doesn't agree with its antecedent, Mr. Klein, and readers will get confused.

PRONOUN CASE is a concept that you may never have encountered, but it's one that you use every day, probably without giving it any thought. For example, you probably say "I bought ice cream" automatically—and are not likely to say "Me bought ice cream" or "Coach wants I to play shortstop." Those two pronouns—"I" and "me"—refer to the same person, but they're not interchangeable. Still, most of the time we automatically choose the expected one for the specific context.

Pronoun Reference

Unclear pronoun reference occurs when readers can't be certain what a **PRONOUN** refers to. Usually this confusion arises when there are several possibilities in the same sentence (or sometimes in the previous sentence). Here's an example: "Andrew and Glen competed fiercely for the office of treasurer, but in the end, he won handily." If Andrew and Glen both identify as male, the pronoun "he" could refer to either one of them, so who was it that won? We don't know.

Checking for unclear pronoun reference

To check for unclear pronoun reference, you need to first identify each pronoun and then make sure that it points very clearly to its **ANTECEDENT**. Often, the meanings of the words provide clues about what the pronoun refers to—but not always. Let's look at three sentences that have very similar structures.

▶ My grandparents ordered pancakes because <u>they</u> weren't very hungry.

First, we identify the pronouns: "my" and "they." "My" clearly refers to the writer, but what about "they"? Although both "pancakes" and "grandparents" are possible antecedents for "they," we know that the pronoun here has to refer to grandparents because pancakes don't get hungry. Now let's look at another sentence:

▶ My grandparents ordered pancakes because <u>they</u> weren't very expensive.

This sentence is almost identical to the first one and has the same pronoun, "they," but this time, the antecedent has to be "pancakes" because there is no price on grandparents. Antecedents aren't always so obvious, however. For example:

> My grandparents like playing cards with their neighbors because <u>they</u> aren't very competitive.

Wait. Who's not very competitive here? The grandparents or the neighbors? Or maybe all of them? We really can't be sure.

Editing unclear pronoun reference
Let's look again at the last example:

> My grandparents like playing cards with their neighbors because they aren't very competitive.

To edit this sentence, our best option may be to change the structure, and there are several possibilities:

> My grandparents like playing cards with their neighbors ~~because they~~ ,who aren't very competitive.

This option makes clear that the neighbors are the ones who aren't very competitive.

> My grandparents, like playing cards with their neighbors, who aren't very competitive, who are also not too ~~because they aren't very~~ competitive.

Now we know that everybody mentioned here is noncompetitive. You may not think the sentence sounds as good as the original, but the meaning is clear, and there are plenty of other ways to phrase this.

The most important objective is to make clear what word or words each pronoun refers to. You don't want to leave your readers guessing. Here is one more example:

> After months of posturing and debate, those planning the expensive new football stadium suspended the project, which students loudly celebrated.

What is the antecedent for "which" in this example? You probably interpret this sentence to say that the students celebrated the suspension of the plans to build the stadium, but in fact, that's not really clearly established in the sentence. Another plausible interpretation is that the students celebrated the building of the stadium. Let's reword the sentence and remove "which" in order to make the meaning perfectly clear.

▶ After months of posturing and debate, those planning the expensive new football stadium suspended the project, ~~which~~ *and* students loudly celebrated *the news*.

Edit
The following sentence uses the words "it" and "which" to refer to . . . well, it's not exactly clear what they refer to.

> A temperature inversion happens when a layer of warmer air is positioned above a layer of cooler air, which is not how it usually occurs.

You have several options here that would make this sentence better, but try this one: rewrite the sentence to eliminate the need for any pronoun at all.

↪ For more practice, complete the InQuizitive activity on **unclear pronoun references**.

Pronoun-Antecedent Agreement

Pronoun-antecedent agreement means that every PRONOUN has to agree with its ANTECEDENT in gender (he, she, they, it) and number (singular or plural). Some sentences with pronouns that don't agree with their antecedents are relatively easy to understand, and usually readers can figure the meanings out, but they shouldn't have to do that extra work. For your academic writing, you'll want to make sure that all your pronouns agree with their antecedents.

Checking for pronoun-antecedent agreement
To check for pronoun-antecedent agreement, you need to first identify the pronouns and their antecedents. Then you need to make sure each pronoun agrees with its antecedent in gender and number. Let's look at a couple of examples:

▶ Trombones might be very loud, but it was drowned out last night by the cheering of the crowd.

This sentence has only one pronoun: "it." "Trombones" is the only noun that precedes "it," so "trombones" has to be the antecedent. Do they agree? We don't have to think about gender in this example, but we do have to think about number. And that's a problem, because the numbers don't match: "trombones" is plural, but "it" is singular.

▶ The table is wobbly because one of her legs is shorter than the others.

In some languages, tables, chairs, and other inanimate objects have grammatical gender, but in English, they don't. The legs of a table are never referred to with masculine or feminine gender.

Editing for pronoun-antecedent agreement
In order to fix the trombone sentence, you can change either the antecedent or the pronoun to make them agree in number. In this case, it is clear that the first CLAUSE refers to trombones in general, and the second clause refers to a specific trombone at a specific event. Assuming that the more important part is the specific event, and that there was only one trombone, let's change the word "trombones" from plural to singular. We can do that easily in this case without really changing the meaning, although sometimes it might be more difficult to do so.

▶ *The trombone*
~~Trombones~~ might be very loud, but it was drowned out last night by the cheering of the crowd.

Both the pronoun and its antecedent are now singular; that is, they agree in number. Now let's consider several examples where gender is a factor. In the example about the table legs, we simply have to replace the feminine pronoun with the inanimate one.

▶ The table is wobbly because one of *its* ~~her~~ legs is shorter than the others.

Remember that some, not all, English pronouns specify gender (he, him, his; she, her, hers; they, them, their, theirs; it, its). Some languages have more gender-specific pronouns, and some languages have fewer, but let's just stick to English right now.

▶ My mom and dad have an arrangement about sausage pizza—
he picks off the sausage, and she eats it.

This sentence has three pronouns—"he," "she," and "it"—and it's quite evident that "he" refers to "dad," "she" refers to "mom," and "it" refers to "sausage." All the antecedents are clear. But what if we changed the cast of characters in the sentence to two men? It would be confusing to refer to each of them as "he," so we need a different strategy. One possibility is to use "he" to represent one of the men and to refer to the other man by name. Will that work?

▶ Paul and his brother have an arrangement about sausage pizza—Paul picks off the sausage, and he eats it.

Who eats the sausage? Paul or his brother? It's still not clear. In this case, our best option is to eliminate the pronoun and refer to both men explicitly both times.

▶ Paul and his brother have an arrangement about sausage pizza—
Paul picks off the sausage, and ~~he~~ *his brother* eats it.

If you'd rather not repeat both phrases, and the arrangement itself is more important than which person eats all the sausage, you can try this option:

▶ Paul and his brother have an arrangement about sausage pizza—
~~Paul~~ *one of them* picks off the sausage, and ~~he~~ *the other one* eats it.

Now we've got it; everything is clear. As this last edit shows, making pronouns and antecedents agree sometimes requires reworking the structure of a sentence and, occasionally, even modifying what it says. Pronouns may be small words, but getting them right is hugely important; don't be afraid to make changes in your writing.

Now let's look at some other contexts where making pronouns agree in gender with their antecedents can be complicated. We'll start with one that's pretty straightforward.

▶ Trey noticed a sunflower growing along the path; he grabbed his phone and took a picture of it.

We know that Trey identifies as male—"he," "his"—and the flower, of course, is inanimate—"it." In academic writing, inanimate objects are always referred to as "it." What about animals? If you know the sex of an animal, then by all means, refer to it as "he" or "she." If you don't know the sex, or if the sex isn't pertinent, just use "it." Also, it is becoming more common for people to specify (or ask one another about) their pronouns—in person, in email signatures, in social media bios—a practice that is in response to increasing flexibility about gender identity. Some individuals opt to be referred to as "they," a usage that transforms "they" from its conventional usage as plural to a singular pronoun of unspecified gender. Other people may use other pronouns, such as "ze"/"hir"/"hirs." We recommend that, whenever possible, you use individuals' specified pronouns in your writing about them. And what if you're writing about a person whose gender identity you don't know? That happens, and that's when it can get complicated. For example:

▶ Anyone who gets three speeding tickets in a year will lose ~~his~~ license.

What's wrong with this example? Plenty, unless only men have such a license. If what you are writing applies to both women and men, your pronouns should reflect that reality. One of the easiest solutions is to use plural nouns and pronouns because they do not specify gender:

▶ ~~Anyone~~ *Drivers* who ~~gets~~ *get* three speeding tickets in a year will lose ~~his license~~ *their licenses*.

You may need to tinker a bit with the structure, but the message can remain the same. Another option is to revise the sentence altogether. Here's one possibility:

▶ Getting three speeding tickets in a year will result in the driver's license being revoked.

Another possibility is to employ **SINGULAR "THEY,"** using "they," "them," "their," or "theirs" with a singular antecedent.

▶ Anyone who gets three speeding tickets in a year will lose ~~his~~ *their* license.

One more possible solution is to write "his or her":

▶ Anyone who gets three speeding tickets in a year will lose ~~his~~ *his or her* license.

This last solution is fine, although it can be awkward and is less preferred than the others.

Many of us use singular "they" this way in casual speech, and its use is becoming more and more accepted in most newspapers and magazines and other more formal contexts. Singular "they" is a very useful solution, but even though it's becoming ever more common, it's still not always accepted in academic writing. Before you use it in your classwork, you might check with your instructor to be sure it will be acceptable in their class.

Edit

Edit the following sentence in two ways. First, make both the pronoun and its antecedent singular; second, make the pronoun and antecedent plural. Both ways are acceptable, but which one do you think works better?

> Applicants must file the forms before the deadline and make sure that it's filled out correctly.

↱ For more practice, complete the InQuizitive activity on **pronoun antecedent agreement**.

Pronoun Case

Pronoun `CASE` refers to the different forms a `PRONOUN` takes in order to indicate how it functions in a sentence. English pronouns have three cases: subject, object, and possessive. Most of the time, we choose the expected pronouns automatically, as in the following sentence:

▶ I texted her, and she texted me, but we didn't see our messages.

This sentence involves two people and six distinct pronouns. "I" and "me" refer to one person (the writer), "she" and "her" refer to the other person, and "we" and "our" refer to both people. Each of the three pronoun pairs has a distinct role in the sentence. "I," "she," and "we" are all subjects; "me" and "her" are objects; and "our" is possessive.

Checking for pronoun case

You would probably not say "Me saw her" because it wouldn't sound right. In casual speech, though, you might hear (or say) "Me and Bob saw her." While you might hear or say that in informal conversation, it would not be acceptable in academic writing. Here is a simple and reliable technique for checking your work for case: check for compound subjects like "me and Bob" and cover up everything in the phrase but the pronoun. Read it out loud.

▶ Me ~~and Bob~~ saw her.

Does it sound good to you? Probably not. So how do you change it? Read on.

Editing for pronoun case
To edit for pronoun case, the first step is to identify the pronouns in each sentence. The following example has only one, "us":

▶ Us first-year students are petitioning for a schedule change.

Remember that the way a pronoun functions in a sentence is the key and that there are three possibilities for case. Is "us" functioning as subject, object, or possessive? In order to answer that question, first we need to identify the verb: "are petitioning." The subject tells us who (or what) is petitioning—in this sentence, "us first-year students." If you're not sure if "us" is a good choice, try it by itself, without "first-year students."

▶ Us are petitioning for a schedule change.
▶ ~~Us~~ **We** are petitioning for a schedule change.

We changed "us" to "we" here because it's the subject of the sentence and thus needs to be in the subject case. For more advice on choosing the correct case, see the table on the following page. Now let's look at two more examples: "Pat dated Cody longer than me." "Pat dated Cody longer than I." The only difference between the two sentences is the case of the pronoun, but that little word gives the sentences totally different meanings because the case lets readers know whether the person—"I" or "me"—is the subject or the object of the verb.

▶ Pat dated Cody longer than me.

Look carefully. There's only one verb, "dated," and its subject is "Pat." Now notice the pronoun: "me." That's object case, right? So, according to the example, Pat dated Cody and also dated "me." Try the next one.

▶ Pat dated Cody longer than I.

Here the pronoun is in subject case: "I." Even though it's not followed by a verb, the pronoun tells us that Pat dated Cody and so did I.

Subject	Object	Possessive
I	me	my/mine
we	us	our/ours
you	you	your/yours
he/she/it	him/her/it	his/her/hers/its
they	them	their/theirs
who/whoever	whom/whomever	whose

In some varieties of English, pronouns by case may vary from the table above. For example, "The twins do they homework at the kitchen table" would be a perfectly effective sentence in some varieties of Black English. In that example, "they" is a pronoun in the possessive case (and also in the subject case). In other words, specific pronouns used for each case may vary according to dialect, but all varieties of English use the same three cases (subject, object, possessive) in the same way.

Edit

Use the technique explained in this section to edit the following sentence for pronoun case.

> Iris was unhappy, but the judges called a tie and gave the award to she and Lu.

 For more practice, complete the InQuizitive activity on **pronoun case**.

EDITING VERBS

Verbs. Are any words more important—or hardworking? Besides specifying actions (hop, skip, jump) or states of being (be, seem), verbs provide most of the information about *when* (happening now? already happened? might happen? usually happens?), and they also have to link very explicitly to their subjects. That's a lot of work!

Because verbs are so important, verb problems are often easily noticed by readers, and once readers notice a verb problem in your work, they may question your authority as a writer. But if your readers can catch these problems, so can you. The following advice will help you edit your work for two of the most troublesome verb problems: subject-verb agreement and shifts in TENSE .

In quite a few varieties of English, the conventions for subject-verb agreement and verb tenses differ from those of standardized English. That doesn't mean that anything goes; there are conventions in every variety. Regardless of whether you are using standardized English or another variety, you'll still want to pay attention to your verbs and keep things smooth for your readers.

Subject-Verb Agreement

In English, every VERB has to agree with its SUBJECT in number and person. That may sound complicated, but it's really only third-person singular subjects—"runner," "shoe," "he," "she," "it"—that you have to look out for, and even then, only when the verb is in the simple present tense. Still, the third-person present tense is the most common construction in academic writing, so it matters. Take a look at this example:

▶ First the coach enters, then you enter, and then all the other players enter.

The verb "enter" occurs three times in that sentence, but notice that when its subject is third-person singular—"coach"—an "-s" follows the base form of the verb, "enter." In the other two cases, the verb has no such ending. What's so complicated about that? Well, there are two kinds of subjects that cause problems: indefinite pronouns, such as "everyone" and "many," which may require a singular or plural verb even if their meaning suggests otherwise; and subjects consisting of more than one word, in which the word that has to agree with the verb may be hidden among other words.

Checking for subject-verb agreement
To check for subject-verb agreement, first identify the subjects and their verbs, paying careful attention to INDEFINITE PRONOUNS and subjects with more than one word. Then, check to make sure that every subject matches its verb in number and person.

Editing for subject-verb agreement

Let's look at a few common mismatches and see what we can do about them.

INDEFINITE PRONOUNS

Indefinite pronouns are words like "anyone," "each," "everything," and "nobody." When they're used as a subject, they have to agree with the verb. Sometimes that's tricky. For example:

> First the coach enters, then you enter, and then each of the other players enter.

We know that the subject of the first clause is "coach" and the subject of the second clause is "you," but what about the third clause? Is the subject "each"? Or is it "players"? You might be tempted to choose players because that's the word closest to the verb "enter," but that's not it; the subject is "each," an indefinite pronoun.

> First the coach enters, then you enter, and then each of the other players ~~enter~~ *enters*.

That "-s" at the end of "enters" is necessary in standardized English because the **SIMPLE SUBJECT** of the final clause is "each," which is singular. The phrase "of the other players" is additional information. Now see what happens if we change "each" to "all":

> First the coach enters, then you enter, and then ~~each of~~ *all* the other players ~~enters~~ *enter*.

Even though the two phrases—"each of the other players" and "all the other players"—have essentially the same meaning, the word "each" refers to the members of a group individually so it is always singular and requires the verb to have the "-s" ending. "All" is plural here because it refers to a plural noun, "players." However, "all" is singular when it refers to a singular noun.

> All the strawberries were picked today.

> All the rhubarb was picked yesterday.

In the first sentence, "all" refers to "strawberries" all together, in plural form, while in the second sentence, "all" refers to "rhubarb," a **NONCOUNT NOUN**, which requires the singular form of the verb. INDEFINITE PRONOUNS can be tricky. Most take a singular verb, even if they seem plural or refer to plural nouns. These include the following: anyone, anything, each, either, everyone, everything, neither, nobody, no one, one, somebody, someone, something. A few indefinite pronouns are always plural: both, few, many, others, several. Some take a singular verb when they refer to a singular or noncount noun, but they take a plural verb when referring to a plural noun. These include the following: all, any, enough, more, most, none, some.

SUBJECTS CONSISTING OF MORE THAN ONE WORD

Sometimes a sentence has a subject with more than one word, so you need to determine which of the words is the one that the verb has to agree with and which words simply provide extra information. To do that, pull the subject apart to find which word is the essential one. Let's practice with this sentence:

▶ The guy with the mirrored sunglasses run in this park every morning.

The COMPLETE SUBJECT is "the guy with the mirrored sunglasses," but who is it that does the running? It's the guy, and the fact that he has mirrored sunglasses is simply extra information. You could remove the phrase "with the mirrored sunglasses" and still have a complete sentence—it might not be very informative, but it's not inaccurate.

To check for subject-verb agreement when a subject has more than one word, first locate the verb and then the complete subject. Then check each word in the subject until you find the one keyword that determines the form of the verb. Since the SIMPLE SUBJECT here—"guy"—is in the third-person singular, and the verb is in the present tense, the verb should also be in the third-person singular:

▶ The guy with the mirrored sunglasses ~~run~~ *runs* in this park every morning.

Let's try one more problem sentence:

▶ The neighbor across the hall from the Fudds always sign for their packages.

First, find the verb: "sign." The complete subject is "the neighbor across the hall from the Fudds." What part of that subject indicates who does the signing? Neighbor. Everything else is extra. Since it's just one "neighbor," the subject is singular, and since a third-person singular subject requires a present tense verb to have an "-s" ending, the edited sentence will be:

▶ The neighbor across the hall from the Fudds always ~~sign~~ *signs* for their packages.

Edit

The sentence below has four subjects and four verbs. One (or more) of the subjects is singular, so its verb should have an "-s" ending. Edit and make any necessary changes.

> All the boxes need to be stacked neatly, and every box need to be labeled; the red box with the taped edges fit on top, and each of the boxes need its own lid.

In casual speech, you may not use the "-s" ending, or it may be hard to hear, so you may not be able to rely on your ear alone to edit this sentence.

↪ For more practice, complete the InQuizitive activity on **subject-verb agreement**.

Shifts in Tense

We live in the present moment; our ideas and our feelings are happening right now. Often, though, our present thoughts—and comments—are responses to things that happened in the past or that haven't happened yet. In conversation, we usually shift our verb tenses smoothly and automatically to account for actions that take place at different times, as in the following example of something you might hear or say:

▶ Flor <u>is</u> upset because Justin <u>informed</u> her that he <u>will not be able to come</u> to her graduation.

In writing, however, we need to take extra care to ensure that our tenses are clear, consistent, and suitable to what we're describing. In contrast to face-to-face conversation—in which tone of voice, facial expressions, and hand gestures help create meaning—writing has to rely on carefully chosen words. Verb tenses work hard to put complex sequences of events into

Most of Christopher Basgier's essay comparing AI to cake is written in the present tense. Many of his examples, though, mention events in the past. Take a look on p. 855, and see how smoothly he shifts tenses to keep everything clear.

context. The previous example has three clauses, each in a different tense: Flor *is* upset (right now); because Justin *informed* her (in the past); that he *will not be able to come* (to an event in the future).

Checking for shifts in tense

In academic writing, you'll often need to discuss what other authors have written, and the different disciplines have different conventions and rules for doing that (see p. 565). In classes that require you to use MLA style, for example, you'll rely heavily on the simple present tense:

> **MLA** Morton argues that even though Allende's characters are not realistic, they're believable.

Notice how "argues," "are not," and "they're" all use the simple present tense even though Morton's article and Allende's novel were both written in the past. If you mention the date when something was written, however, the verb should be in the past tense. In contrast, disciplines that follow APA style require that references to published sources and research results be stated in the past tense (or the present perfect, if the research isn't from one specific time in the past):

> **APA** Azele (2020) reported that 59% of the subjects showed high gamma levels.

Notice here that the two verbs in the sentence—"reported" and "showed"—are both in the past tense because both Azele's research and the report were done in the past. Be careful, though, because your sources may be writing about current or future conditions. If that's the case, be sure to preserve the tense of the original in your work, as the following example does.

> **APA** Donnerstag and Jueves (2019) predicted that another Jovian moon will soon be discovered.

Regardless of what class you're writing for, however, the most important thing about verb tenses is consistency—unless you have a reason to shift tense.

Editing confusing shifts in tense

Much of the editing that you do calls for sentence-by-sentence work, but checking for confusing shifts in tense often requires that you consider several sentences together.

Starting at the beginning, mark every **MAIN VERB**, along with any **HELPING VERBS**, in every sentence (remembering that there may be more than one clause in each sentence). Don't make any changes yet; just mark the verbs. Next, go back to the beginning and notice what tense you used each time. Examine each tense one by one, and when you notice a shift to a different tense, read carefully what you have written and look for a reason for the shift. If you can explain why the shift makes sense, leave it alone. Then move on to the next verb. Is it in the original tense or the new tense? Can you explain why? Continue all the way through your text, examining every verb tense and making sure that any shifts you find can be explained. Let's practice with two examples:

▶ Bates underestimated the public when she writes disparagingly about voters' intelligence.

First, we mark the verbs—"underestimated," "writes"—and we notice that the first is in past tense while the second is in present. Is there a clear explanation for the shift? No, not really. If you are using **MLA** style, you'll want to put both verbs in the present: "underestimates" and "writes." In **APA** style, past tense is the expected tense for both: "underestimated" and "wrote." In any case, there is no reason to use two different tenses in the sentence. Here is another example, this time a little more complicated:

▶ All the guests ate the stew, but only two showed symptoms of food poisoning.

It's true that the events (ate, showed) in both clauses of the example occurred in the past, but can we be certain that the symptoms were a result of eating the stew? Could the guests have had the symptoms already? The sentence isn't really clear.

▶ All the guests ~~ate~~ *had eaten* the stew, but only two showed symptoms of food poisoning.

By changing the verb tense in the first clause to the past perfect (the tense used to indicate that an action was completed before another action in the past began), we show clearly that the stew was eaten before the food poisoning occurred. (We may never know what caused the illness, but at least we know the sequence of events.)

Edit

Edit the following sentence to eliminate any confusing shifts in tense. Assume that the writing has to follow **APA** format for verb tenses.

> Levi (2019) notes that the trade deficit decreases from 2005 to 2015, but he warns that the improvement may be reversed because the new treaty will go into effect in 2020.

↪ For more practice, complete the InQuizitive activity on **verb tense**.

EDITING QUOTATIONS

In academic writing, you are required not only to express your own ideas but also to incorporate the ideas of other authors. In a way, you are engaging in a conversation with your sources, whether you draw from Aristotle, Toni Morrison, or a classmate. Your success as a writer has a lot to do with how well you weave your sources' ideas in with your own without your readers ever having to wonder who said what. Editing your work for citation and documentation issues therefore involves two main tasks:

- incorporating any words of others that you quote into your text so that everything flows smoothly
- making sure the punctuation, capitalization, and other such elements are correct

The conventions for citing and documenting sources in academic writing are very precise—every period, every comma, every quotation mark has its job to do, and they must be in exactly the right place.

Incorporating Quotations

Whenever we quote something someone else has said, we need to structure the sentences that contain the quoted material so that they read as smoothly as any other sentence. As writers, we need to master our use of language in much the same way that musicians have to master their instruments, and in both cases, it's not easy. Just as musicians playing together in an orchestra (or a garage band) have to coordinate with one another in tempo, key, and melody, you have to make sure that your words and those of others that you quote fit together smoothly.

Checking to see that quotations are incorporated smoothly

One good way to begin checking a draft to see how well any quotations have been incorporated is to read it aloud, or better yet, get someone else to read it aloud to you. If the reader (you or someone else) stumbles over a passage and has to go back and read the sentence again, you can be fairly certain that some changes are necessary. We can practice with some sentences that quote the following passage from a 2013 *Atlantic* article about fast food:

> Introduced in 1991, the McLean Deluxe was perhaps the boldest single effort the food industry has ever undertaken to shift the masses to healthier eating.
>
> —DAVID FREEDMAN, "How Junk Food Can End Obesity"

Assume that you might not want or need to quote the entire passage, so you incorporate just one part of Freedman's sentence into one of your sentences, as follows:

▶ Freedman refers to a failed McDonald's menu item "the McLean Deluxe was perhaps the food industry's boldest single effort to shift the masses to healthier eating."

If you read the sentence aloud, you probably notice that it is awkwardly structured and even hard to understand. Also, do you notice that the quoted section doesn't exactly match the author's words? Some of the words from the original are missing and some others have been added. Changing an author's words in a quoted section is only allowed if the original meaning is not altered in any way. Also, you need to indicate to your readers that you've modified the author's words. Let's see how we can go about fixing these things.

Editing sentences that include quotations

There are two ways of smoothly incorporating quoted material. One strategy is to adjust your own words to accommodate the quoted material;

another is to lightly modify the quoted material to fit your sentence. Here's one way we might edit our sentence by adjusting our own words:

> ▶ ~~Freedman refers~~ *Referring* to a failed McDonald's menu item, "the McLean Deluxe was perhaps the food industry's boldest single effort to shift the masses to healthier eating." *Freedman notes that*

Let's look at what we did. First, we changed the first two words. The meaning didn't change; only the structure did. Then, we added a **SIGNAL PHRASE** (Freedman notes that) to introduce the quoted words.

So far so good. But what about the places where we changed the author's words? If you modify an author's words, you need to signal to your readers what changes you've made, and there are precise conventions for doing that.

Enclose anything you add or change within the quotation itself in square **BRACKETS** ([ ]), and insert **ELLIPSES** (. . .) to show where any content from the original has been omitted.

> ▶ Referring to a failed McDonald's menu item, Freedman notes that "the McLean Deluxe was perhaps the [food industry's] boldest single effort . . . to shift the masses to healthier eating."

With minimal changes, the sentence now has all the necessary parts and reads smoothly. Note the two things we've done to modify the quotation. We've enclosed the words we added—"food industry's"—in square brackets, and we've inserted ellipses in place of the six words that were omitted from Freedman's sentence. It's worth repeating here that it is only permissible to add or delete words if the meaning of the quotation isn't substantially altered.

Edit

Here is another sentence based on the Freedman passage:

> Freedman talks about an earlier effort the McLean Deluxe by McDonald's was perhaps the boldest try to shift the masses to healthier eating.

First, you'll have to make a few changes to help the sentence read smoothly. There are several ways to do that, but try to make as few changes as possible.

Once the sentence reads smoothly, compare it with the original passage to see where you might need square brackets (for added material) or ellipses (to show where words have been removed). By the way, you don't have to put "McLean Deluxe" in quotation marks because it was not a term coined by Freedman.

↱ For more practice, complete the InQuizitive activity on **incorporating quotations**.

Punctuating Quotations

Citation conventions exist to help us clearly distinguish our words from the words of our sources, and one way we do that is by punctuating quotations carefully. When you quote someone's exact words, you need to attend to four elements: quotation marks, capitalization, commas, and end punctuation. These elements let your readers know which words are yours and which are the words of someone else.

Checking to see how any quoted material is punctuated

Here is another sentence taken from the *Atlantic* article about fast food; let's use it in a variety of ways in order to show how to capitalize and punctuate sentences that quote from this passage.

> A slew of start-ups are trying to find ways of producing fresh, local, unprocessed meals quickly and at lower cost.
> —DAVID FREEDMAN, "How Junk Food Can End Obesity"

You might write a sentence such as this one:

▶ It may one day be possible to get fast food that is healthy and affordable since a slew of start-ups are trying to find ways, according to David Freedman.

Structurally, the sentence is fine, but it includes a direct quotation from Freedman without letting readers know which words are his and which are yours. Even if you used Freedman's exact words accidentally, it would still be PLAGIARISM, which may carry a stiff penalty. The sentence needs to be edited.

Editing quotations to indicate who said what

There are numerous ways to edit the above sentence to make clear who said what. Here is one option:

> ▶ It may one day be possible to get fast food that is healthy and affordable. ~~since a~~ **According to David Freedman, "A** slew of start-ups are trying to find ways**."** ~~according to David Freedman.~~

What changed? First, we added quotation marks to enclose Freedman's exact words. Second, we broke the sentence into two and started the second one with the signal phrase "According to Freedman," followed by a comma. Third, we capitalized the first letter of the quotation. Since "A" was capitalized in the original quotation, no brackets are necessary. Finally, notice the period. The sentence ends with the quoted material, so the period goes inside the quotation marks. Now let's look at how you might go about editing another sentence.

> ▶ Freedman asserts that many new businesses are working to develop fresh, local, unprocessed meals quickly and at lower cost.

Check your four elements. First, insert any necessary quotation marks; make sure they enclose Freedman's exact words. Second, is any additional capitalization necessary? If so, capitalize the appropriate word(s). Third, if there's a **SIGNAL PHRASE** before the quoted material, does it need to be followed by a comma? Finally, make sure any end punctuation is in the right place. Try editing the sentence yourself before you look at the following revision.

> ▶ Freedman asserts that many new businesses are working to develop **"**fresh, local, unprocessed meals quickly and at lower cost**."**

The quoted portion is not a complete sentence, and we placed it in the middle of ours, so no capitalization was necessary. We didn't insert a comma because his words flow smoothly within the larger sentence. Since the sentence ends with the quoted material, we put the period inside the quotation marks.

Depending on the documentation style that you are using, you may need to provide parenthetical information at the end of any sentences that include quoted material. Some styles require that you name the author(s) if you haven't named them earlier in the sentence, along with the page number(s) where their words appeared. Here's how you would do so in MLA and APA style requirements.

MLA Freedman asserts that many new businesses are working to develop "fresh, local, unprocessed meals quickly and at lower cost" (82).

APA Freedman asserted that many new businesses are working to develop "fresh, local, unprocessed meals quickly and at lower cost" (2013, p. 82).

One more important point: notice that with parenthetical documentation, the final period of the sentence is no longer inside the quotation marks; it is after the parentheses.

Edit

The following sentences cite the passage from Freedman's essay; they need to be formatted properly in order to read smoothly and also to show more clearly which words are the writer's and which are Freedman's. Remember the four elements: quotation marks, capitalization, commas, and end punctuation.

> Healthy and affordable fast food may not be a reality yet, but we may not have too long to wait. As Freedman explains a slew of start-ups are trying to find ways to bring such meals to market.

It is possible to edit the sentence using only the four elements and not adding, subtracting, or changing any words. Try it.

➦ For more practice, complete the InQuizitive activity on **punctuating quotations**.

EDITING COMMAS

Ideas are made out of words, right? So why should we care about commas? Well, here's why—they help those words make more sense. Nobody wants to have to read the same sentence two or three times in order to get it.

Well-placed commas can make your sentence clear and easy to read—and can keep the words (and ideas) correctly grouped together. Read this next sentence out loud:

▶ The boxer exhausted and pounded on wearily left the ring.

Did you start off expecting to read about the boxer's opponent who was getting "exhausted and pounded on"? Did you have to go back and start over? Bet you did. Well-placed commas would have immediately pointed us all in the right direction—like this:

▶ The boxer, exhausted and pounded on, wearily left the ring.

There are a lot of ways to err with commas. You might omit one that's necessary or place one where it doesn't belong. Even professional writers sometimes have trouble deciding where (and where not) to put a comma, and it's not always a big deal. The advice that follows will show you how to edit your work for two of the comma problems that matter most in academic writing: the commas that set off introductory information and the commas that distinguish between essential and nonessential information.

Introductory Information

English sentences generally begin with a **SUBJECT**. Those of us who read and write in English have an expectation that the first thing we read in a sentence will be its subject. Often, however (like right now), we begin a sentence in a different way. In academic writing especially, we might vary the structure of our sentences just to make our writing interesting. One way we vary our sentences is by starting some of them with introductory words, phrases, or even clauses. And usually we use a comma to set off those introductory words. That comma signals to readers that they haven't gotten to the subject yet; what they are seeing is additional information that is important enough to go first. For example:

▶ In Georgia, Lee's book jumped quickly to the top of the best-seller list.

Without the comma, readers might think the author's name was Georgia Lee, and they would get very lost in the sentence. Introductory words don't always cause so much confusion; in fact, some authors omit the comma if the introductory element is very short (one, two, or three words). Still, adding the comma after the introductory information is never wrong and demonstrates the care you take with your work.

Checking for commas after introductory information

> ▶ Initially the council proposed five miles of new bike paths; they later revised the proposal.

To check for introductory information, you should first identify the **VERB** — in this case, "proposed." Now what's the subject? (In other words, who or what proposed?) The subject here is "the council." Everything that goes before the subject is introductory information, so the comma goes between that information and the subject.

> ▶ Initially, the council proposed five miles of new bike paths; they later revised the proposal.

In the example above, the introductory element is only one word, and the comma could have been omitted, but its presence adds a little extra emphasis to the word "initially," and in fact, that emphasis is probably why the author chose to put that word at the beginning, before the subject. The comma definitely helps. And sometimes, introductory elements can cause confusion:

> ▶ Tired and discouraged by the unsuccessful search for the fugitive Sergeant Drexler the detective and her squad returned to headquarters.

In this example, the introductory information is much longer, and without a well-placed comma, readers have no way of knowing if Sergeant Drexler is the name of the fugitive, the name of the detective, or someone else entirely. Let's imagine that Drexler is the fugitive. With one well-placed comma, the sentence is now perfectly clear.

> ▶ Tired and discouraged by the unsuccessful search for the fugitive Sergeant Drexler, the detective and her squad returned to headquarters.

Editing for commas after introductory information
Let's take a look at a few examples to see how we can figure out where to put commas with introductory elements. The following sentence needs a comma; where should it go?

▶ For the first three scoreless innings Clark struggled to stay awake.

How do you know where to put the comma? Let's follow the steps described in this chapter. First, identify the verb: "struggled." Next, identify the subject—in other words, who or what struggled? The subject here is "Clark," and everything that precedes it is introductory information.

▶ For the first three scoreless innings, Clark struggled to stay awake.

Here is one more example. Follow the same procedure to determine where to put the comma.

▶ In the chaotic final episode of season 2 the shocking plot twists left viewers breathless.

In this example, the comma should go after "2"; the verb in the sentence is "left," and the **COMPLETE SUBJECT** is "the shocking plot twists." Everything that goes before the subject is introductory information, so the comma falls between that information and the subject:

▶ In the chaotic final episode of season 2, the shocking plot twists left viewers breathless.

Edit
Try editing the following sentence by inserting a comma after the introductory information. Remember the technique: first, find the verb; second, find the subject. The comma goes before the subject because everything that precedes it is introductory information.

> Behind the parade marshal and the color guard the sponsors' convertible carrying the Founders' Day Queen will proceed along Blossom Boulevard.

▶ For more practice, complete the InQuizitive activities on **commas**.

Essential and Nonessential Information

What do we mean by ESSENTIAL and NONESSENTIAL information? The simplest way to explain the difference is with examples.

▶ My sister Jamilah graduates on Saturday.

If the writer has more than one sister, the name "Jamilah" tells us which one; that's important to know because we don't want to congratulate the wrong sister. Therefore, her name is essential information. When the information is essential, it should not be set off with commas. But if the writer has only one sister, writing her name there is simply extra information; it's not essential. When the information is nonessential, we set it off with commas:

▶ My sister, Jamilah, graduates on Saturday.

Checking for essential and nonessential information

To check your work for these kinds of commas, read over what you've written and identify the NOUNS. When a noun—"stadium," "achievement," "amino acids," whatever—is followed immediately by additional information about it, ask yourself if the information is essential: does it tell you which stadium, which achievement, which amino acids? If so, it shouldn't be set off with commas. If, however, the information is nonessential, and the sentence would still be fine without that information, it should be set off with a pair of commas. Let's examine two examples:

▶ The neighbors, who complained about parking, called a meeting to discuss the problem.

▶ The neighbors who complained about parking called a meeting to discuss the problem.

In these examples, the noun "neighbors" is followed by additional information. Which sentence talks about a situation where all the neighbors complained? Which one describes a situation where only some of them did? Remember that the commas set off information that is extra and not essential. In the first sentence, the commas indicate that the information "who complained about parking" is extra, nonessential; it doesn't tell us which neighbors, so we can safely conclude that all the neighbors complained. In the second sentence, the absence of commas lets us know that the information is essential; the clause "who complained about parking" tells us which neighbors called the meeting—only the ones who complained.

Editing commas with essential and nonessential information
Here is an example to practice with:

- Vitamins, such as B and C, are water-soluble and easily absorbed by the body; excess amounts are eliminated in the urine.

In order to edit the example, you will need to know if the phrase "such as B and C" is essential or if it's only additional information. In order to save you from looking it up, here it is: not all vitamins are water-soluble; some are fat-soluble and are stored in the body rather than quickly eliminated. Now, is the phrase "such as B and C" essential information? And if it is, should this sentence have commas? Here is the edited version:

- Vitamins/ such as B and C/ are water-soluble and easily absorbed by the body; excess amounts are eliminated in the urine.

Edit
The two sentences below are nearly identical; the difference is that one has essential information about its subject, while the other one's subject has extra information. Put commas in the appropriate places.

> Cardi B who will perform in the opening act will do her sound check at 5:30.

> The backup singers who will perform in the opening act will do their sound check at 5:30.

▶ For more practice, complete the InQuizitive activity on **commas**.

EDITING WORDS THAT ARE OFTEN CONFUSED

English has more than a million words, and any one of them could be used accurately or inaccurately—in a variety of ways, so no book could possibly help you edit all the "wrong words" that might turn up in your writing.

A few basic strategies, however, can help you with many of those problems. Here you'll find tips for identifying a few of those in your own work—and then editing as need be. Although there are countless ways to get a word wrong, many such problems can be traced back to two causes: words that sound like other words (homophones) and apostrophes (which don't have any sound at all). Here's an example:

▶ Joe should of told them to buy there TV there because its cheaper and its screen is bigger.

Read that sentence out loud and it sounds exactly as the writer intended it; the meaning is perfectly clear. But your writing can't just "sound" right—it has to look right, too. In other words, the written words have to be correct. There are three "wrong words" in that sentence: "of," "there," and "its." Let's look at each one.

Of / Have
The useful little word "of," which is a preposition, sounds a lot like another very useful and common word, the verb "have," especially in rapid or casual speech. The two are often confused when "have" is used as a **HELPING VERB** with the **MODALS** "can," "could," "may," "might," "must," "should," "will," or "would"—especially in contractions, such as "could've" or "should've." How do you know if the word you need is "of" or "have"? Try reframing your sentence as a question. That should tell you right away which one is the right choice.

▶ Should Joe of told them?

▶ Should Joe have told them?

You can probably tell right away that "have" is the better choice. When you're editing, develop the habit of noticing whenever you use a modal, and make sure the words that follow it are the right ones. "Have" can be written out in its full form or combined with the preceding word to form a contraction—"should've," "would've." Try it without the modal. "Have you told them?" That's good. "Of you told them?" Not so good. That's because "have" is a helping verb, and "of" is not.

There / Their / They're
"There" is a common and useful word that sounds exactly like another common word, "their," and those two sound the same as a third common

word, "they're," the contracted form of "they are." So not only do we have three homophones but also each of the three words is used very frequently in both speech and writing. That leads to a large number of "wrong word" problems. For example:

> For security screening, passengers must put all cell phones in the trays, and now <u>there</u> required to put <u>there</u> shoes <u>there</u>, too.

You'll notice three instances of "there" in the example, and two of them are "wrong words." The sentence should have one each of "they're," "their," and "there," so let's take a closer look at each use of "there."

THEY'RE

Let's start with the first one. That part of the sentence is trying to say that the passengers—"they"—are required to do something, so the right word would be the contraction of "they are": "they're." The word "they're" has only that one meaning, so using it is very simple. Just see if you can substitute "they are" for the word in question and still have the meaning you intended. If not, you'll need to make a change.

THEIR

Now let's look at the second instance of "there": "there shoes." That part of the sentence is talking about the shoes that belong to the passengers, so the expected word would be a possessive: "their." The word "their" has only that one uncomplicated meaning—it always indicates possession, as in the following examples:

> <u>Their</u> feet were swollen and <u>their</u> toes were numb, but the hikers were determined to reach Vogelsang before dark.

> The birds are squawking because the wind blew <u>their</u> nest down.

> Both of the radios still work, but <u>their</u> clocks are wrong.

When you're trying to decide if "their" is the right word, try asking if the word you are using is intended to show possession. In the examples above, "their" is correct because it indicates possession: Whose feet and toes? Their (the hikers') feet and toes. Whose nest? Their (the birds') nest. Whose clocks? Their (the radios') clocks.

THERE

That leaves us with the final instance of "there" in our example sentence. That "there" is correct. Most of the time, as in our example, "there" simply indicates a place, telling *where* something is: Where's my phone? It's there, on the table. Sometimes, though, "there" is used to introduce information that's provided later in the sentence. For example:

- Whenever there was a big snowstorm, the neighbors all helped clear the street.
- There are three candidates in the race, but only one has the right experience.

That meaning of "there" simply indicates the existence of something—a big snowstorm, three candidates. Here's an example that uses both meanings:

- There is a coatrack behind the door; you can hang your jacket there.

To check whether "there" is the right word, ask whether the word indicates either the existence of something or a place. If the word indicates either of those two things, "there" is the desired choice.

When editing your own work, check each instance of "there," "their," and "they're" to make sure that you've written the one you really mean. That may sound tedious, but here's a handy shortcut: use the Find function in your word processing program to search for each instance of "there," "their," and "they're." That way, you won't miss any.

Now let's revise our original example sentence. Try it yourself before you look at the edited version below.

- For security screening, passengers must put all cell phones in the trays, and now ~~there~~ *they're* required to put ~~there~~ *their* shoes there, too.

It's / Its

"It's" and "its" make for many "wrong word" problems. Although they're pronounced exactly the same, they really are two distinct words with distinct uses: "its" is the possessive form of "it," and "it's" is a contraction of "it is." That difference makes it easy to know which one is suitable for your sentence. Let's look at one problematic sentence:

- When my phone fell, its screen shattered, but luckily, its still working.

There are two instances of "its" in the sentence, but one of them should be "it's." How can you tell which is which? Check to see which one can be replaced by "it is." The second one—"it is still working." The one without the apostrophe, "its," is the possessive form of "it": the screen that belongs to "it" (the phone). So here's how you'd edit this sentence:

> When my phone fell, its screen shattered, but luckily, its still working.
>   it's

Wait. Haven't you been told to use an apostrophe to indicate possessives, as in "the priest's robe," "the frog's sticky tongue"? So how can it be that the version *without* the apostrophe is the possessive one? "It" is a **PRONOUN**, along with "he," "I," "she," and "you," for example. What are the possessive forms of those pronouns? "His." "My." "Her." "Your." Do you notice that those possessives don't have an apostrophe? Neither does "its."

If you know or suspect that you have problems confusing "it's" and "its" in your work, you can check for them using the Find function of your word processor. Search your text for each of the two words, and make sure that the possessive "its" has no apostrophe and that the contracted form of "it is" always appears as "it's."

Edit

Return now to the first problem sentence at the top of page 774, and try editing it using all the techniques discussed above:

> Joe should of told them to buy there TV there because its cheaper and its screen is bigger.

▶ For more practice, complete the InQuizitive activity on **words often confused**.

PART VIII

Design and Delivery

This is the time for exploration, for experimentation. This is the time when we can create and risk, when we can write graffiti on the walls and color outside the lines. . . . If we are going to fly and find new intellectual spaces . . . we must expand our notion of academic discourse.

—ADAM BANKS

WHEN RHETORICIAN ADAM BANKS calls for writers to "explore" and "experiment," he highlights the power of design and delivery. To explore the different ways for delivering messages, we must think and rethink how our messages are communicated, and we must especially consider the mode and medium we use. Mode refers to what makes up the message and communicates its meaning: words, sounds, gestures, still and moving images, or some combination of those. Medium is the form in which the audience receives it: print, oral, or digital.

When you think about delivery, you'll also think about the performance of a text and how it captures the speaker's tone, pacing, and quality of voice, as well as a full range of facial and bodily gestures and movements. Delivery is of paramount importance in connecting to an audience and gaining its assent, approval, or understanding.

Savvy authors understand that messages today don't just lie there on the page and wait for readers to discover them. Rather, it's up to you as author to capture and hold the attention of your audience. For authors of texts in all media, that means paying careful attention to design. A text's design often determines your audience's first and lasting impressions. An effective design can draw the notice of your audience, keep their attention on your message, and help you achieve your purpose.

The chapters that follow aim to get *your* attention and to focus it on what design and delivery can mean for you as an author. Here, you'll consider the choices you'll need to make as an author who is designing texts and how those choices affect the delivery and reception of your messages.

 **REFLECT**

Think about a recent assignment in which you were free to make design choices. What was the assignment and what choices did you make? How and why did you make those choices?

THIRTY-EIGHT

Designing What You Write

**ESIGN. IT'S A WORD YOU HEAR ALL THE TIME,** one you use without thinking about it. "American model Anok Yai walked the Met Gala red carpet in a dress designed by Oscar de la Renta and inspired by Josephine Baker, an American-born singer, dancer, and civil rights activist." "Have you seen the cover design for Sarah Mughal Rana's new book, *Hope Ablaze*?" "I designed my capstone project to impress potential employers."

Fashion, technology, architecture, toys: everything is designed, and that includes everything you write. A slide presentation, a social media post, an essay—you design it, whether you are conscious of doing so or not. You select a medium and tools: a lined notebook and a pencil, a text message and a smartphone, white paper and black printer ink. You choose typefaces and colors: big red capital letters for a poster, 12-point black Times New Roman for an essay. You think about including visuals: a bar graph on a slide, a cartoon in a blog, a photo in an essay. You consider whether to use multiple columns, bullet points, numbered lists—and where to leave white space. You decide what you want readers to notice first and how it should catch their eye.

This chapter discusses several key design elements: typography, color, visuals, and layout. Whatever typefaces, fonts, or images you choose, though, remember that they are not mere decoration. However you design a text, you need to be guided by your purpose, your audience, and the rest of your RHETORICAL SITUATION.

THINKING RHETORICALLY ABOUT DESIGN

Being able to design your writing gives you more control over your message than writers had in the past, when there were fewer options and tools. Your design choices can play a big role in the way your audience receives your message and whether your text achieves its purpose. Look, for example, at the ways Coca-Cola used design to reach audiences during the 2024 Olympics.

THINK BEYOND WORDS

↪ **WATCH THE COCA-COLA** ad for the 2024 Olympics by visiting everyonesanauthor.tumblr.com. Consider how the video's design elements—the background music, the voiceover—add to the overall message. Then compare this video ad to the design of the Coca-Cola cans and the print ad above. Where do you see similarities and differences? Why do you think Coca-Cola chose this campaign for the summer games?

The company's print and video advertisements—and even the design on the cans themselves—incorporated the theme of unity, depicted through people, even competitors, hugging one another at the Olympics. In a Coca-Cola commercial from that time, viewers see four elite swimmers preparing to compete as the world tunes in to the race. People watch from the stands at the Olympics, on their televisions, and on their phones—all of them enjoying a Coca-Cola, of course. The ad proceeds with the competitors at the starting blocks; a voiceover notes this is a "rivalry like no other." The world record holder from South Africa, Tatjana Schoenmaker, takes her place but then pauses, looks to her competitors, and they all embrace. Inspired by this moment of goodwill among rivals, the spectators embrace one another, too, Cokes in hand. The ad ends with the words "It's magic when the world comes together." The ad was designed to appeal broadly to a global audience and to send the message that Coca-Cola brings people together.

One design element that never changes in Coca-Cola ads is their logo. Whether it's printed on a can or composed of red and white pixels on a screen, the Coca-Cola logo is always present. Why? Because it is instantly recognizable around the world.

In designing what you write, think about how you can best reach your audience and achieve your purpose. Given the deluge of words, images, and other data, readers today are less likely than they once were to read anything start to finish. Instead, they may scan for just the information they need. So as an author, you need to design your documents to be user-friendly: easy to access, to navigate, to read—and to remember.

> **REFLECT**
>
> Think of a recent advertisement for one of your favorite products. What design choices do you notice in the ad? How are these design choices tailored to the product's target audience? What message does the ad send through its design?

Considering Your Rhetorical Situation

Just like the Olympics shaped the design of Coca-Cola's ads, you'll enter your own compositions and designs with a unique set of circumstances. You'll want to consider:

- **Who is your AUDIENCE**, and are there any design elements they expect or need? Large type? Illustrations? Are there any design elements that might not appeal to them—or cause them to question your authority?

- *What is your* PURPOSE, and what design elements can help you achieve that purpose? If you're trying to explain how to do something, would it help to set off the steps in a numbered list? Is there anything that would work against your goals—using a playful typeface in a business letter, for example?
- *What's your* GENRE, and does it have any design requirements?
- *What's your* STANCE *as an author,* and how do you want to come across to your audience? Do you want to seem businesslike? serious? ironic? practical and matter-of-fact? How can your use of typefaces, color, images, and other design elements reflect that stance?
- *Consider the larger* CONTEXT. Does your assignment specify any design requirements? What design elements are possible with the technology you have available?
- *What* MEDIA *will you use*—print? digital? spoken?—and what kinds of DESIGN elements are suitable (or possible)?
- *Consider your* LANGUAGE. Do the media you're using come with language conventions or expectations? Will you meet these or push against them?

Considering Accessibility

It's not just your rhetorical situation that will guide your design choices. It's equally important to compose materials that are accessible, welcoming, and easy to use for all readers, especially those with diverse visual, speech, auditory, physical, or cognitive abilities. Consider the following steps for creating accessible texts:

- *Provide* ALTERNATIVE TEXT *(alt text) for essential images and visuals in digital texts.* Alt text describes the content or meaning of a visual. People using screen-reader software will understand visuals only if you provide alt text for the software to narrate. Complex charts and graphs need not be described in detail; instead, provide alt text summarizing the main point: "A line chart shows that revenue grew incrementally from 20 percent to 60 percent between 2021 and 2025." If a visual is just decorative, no need to provide alt text.
- *Consider type size in printed texts.* Many readers require or prefer large type, so for printed texts, choose a type size that's easy to read. When in doubt, chose a large font size or provide alternative large-print copies. Large print is 18 point or higher.

- ***Choose colors with high contrast.*** When using multiple colors, choose ones that have a dramatic contrast (such as light blue against deep maroon) so that they are legible to everyone. And remember that some people cannot see the difference between certain colors (red and green, for example). Don't use color as the only means of conveying information. For example, underline URLs in addition to setting them in a contrasting color.

- ***When giving a presentation, face the audience or camera*** so lip-readers can see your face clearly, and keep your hands from blocking your face. Make available a link to or printout of your talk in a large font size. If your slides include important images or visuals, describe them out loud for those who may not be able to see them.

CHOOSING TYPEFACES AND FONTS

A typeface is a distinct collection of styled text (Times New Roman, Arial), while "font" refers to different ways of formatting text (**bold**, *italic*). Authors today have hundreds of typefaces to choose from, and the choices you make affect the message your readers receive—so it's important to think carefully about what's most effective for your particular rhetorical situation.

Serif typefaces (those with small decorative lines, called serifs, added to the ends of most letters) such as Times New Roman or Bodoni have a traditional look, whereas sans serif typefaces (those without serifs) such as Arial or Futura give a more modern look. Your instructors may require you to use a specific typeface, but if you get to choose, you'll want to think about what look you want for your text—and what will be most readable. Some readers find serif type easier to read in longer pieces of writing. Sans serif, on the other hand, tends to be easier to read in slide presentations. Save novelty or decorative typefaces such as **Impact** or *Allegro* for your nonacademic writing—and even there, use them sparingly, since they can be difficult (or annoying!) to read.

Most typefaces include **bold**, *italics*, and underlining options, which you can use to highlight parts of a text. In academic writing, bold is generally used for headings, whereas italics or underlining is used for titles of books, films, and other long works. If you're following MLA, APA, or another academic style, make sure that your use of fonts conforms to the style's requirements.

Readability matters. For most academic and workplace writing, you'll want to use 10-to-12-point type, and at least 18-point type for most presentation slides. Academic writing is usually double-spaced; letters and résumés are single-spaced.

ADDING HEADINGS

Brief texts may need no headings at all, but for longer texts, headings can help readers follow the text and find specific information. Some kinds of writing have set headings that authors are required to use— IMRAD reports, for instance, require introduction, methods, research, and discussion headings. When you include headings, you need to decide on wording, fonts, and placement.

Wording. Make headings succinct and parallel. You could make them all nouns ("Energy Drinks," "Snack Foods"), all GERUND phrases ("Analyzing the Contents of Energy Drinks," "Resisting Snack Foods"), or all questions ("What's in Energy Drinks?" and "Why Are Snack Foods So Hard to Resist?").

Fonts. If you've chosen to divide your text further using subheadings, distinguish different level headings from one another typographically by using bold, italic, underlining, and capitalization. For example:

> **First-Level Heading**
> Second-Level Heading
> *Third-Level Heading*

When you get to choose, you may want to make headings larger than the main text or to put them in a different typeface, font, or color (as we do throughout this book). But if you're following MLA or APA styles, be aware that they require headings to be in the same typeface as the main text.

Placement. You can center headings, set them flush left above the text, or place them at the left of the first line of text (as with the heading to this very paragraph); but whatever you do, treat each level of heading consistently throughout the text. If you're following MLA style, set all headings flush left. If you're following APA style, center first-level headings.

USING COLOR

Sometimes you'll be required to write in black type on a white background, but many times you'll have reason to use colors. In some media, color will be expected or necessary—on websites or presentation slides, for instance. Other times it may not work so well—say, in a thank-you note following a job interview at a law firm, or in an application essay to business school. As with any design element, color should be used to help you get a message across and appeal to an audience—never just to decorate your text.

Be aware that certain colors can evoke specific emotional reactions: blue, like the sky and sea, suggests spaciousness and tranquility; red invokes fire and suggests intense energy and emotions; yellow, the color of our sun, generates warmth and optimism. Also remember that certain colors carry different associations across cultures—to Westerners, white suggests innocence and youth, but in China white is traditionally associated with death (which is why Chinese brides traditionally wear red).

Especially if you use more than one color in a text, you'll want to consider how certain colors work together. Look at the color wheel below to see how the colors are related. Primary colors (red, blue, and yellow) create an effect of simplicity and directness. The more secondary and tertiary colors you use, the more sophisticated the design. Complementary colors, located opposite each other on the color wheel, look brighter when placed next to each other but can sometimes clash and look jarring. (Black and white are also considered complementary colors.) Cool and dark colors appear to recede,

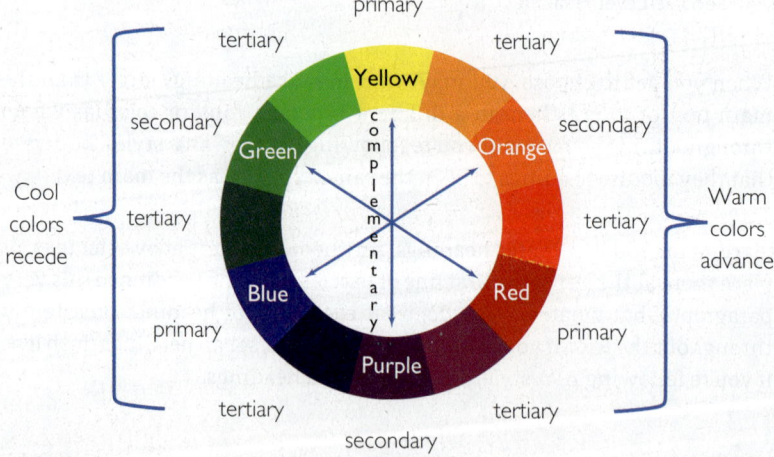

A color wheel.

whereas warm and bright colors seem to advance. So using both cool and warm colors can create a feeling of movement and energy.

Remember that any color scheme includes the type, the background, and any images or graphics that you use. If colorful photos are an important part of your website, they'll stand out most strongly on a white background and with black type—both of which you may want to use for that reason alone. If you're writing a report that includes multicolored pie charts and want to have color headings, you wouldn't want to use primary colors in the headings and pastels in the charts. In short, if you use colors, make sure they work well with all the other design elements in the text.

Using color to guide readers. Like bold or italic type, color can help guide readers through a text. In fact, that's the way color is used in this book. The headings are all red to make them easy to spot, and keywords are color-coded a pale orange to signal that they're defined in the glossary/index. In addition, we've color-coded parts of the book—roadmaps are on yellow pages, readings are light blue, research chapters are green, style chapters are lavender—to help readers find them easily.

Color is an important navigational element on websites as well and is sometimes used to indicate links and highlight headings. For such uses of color, it's important to choose colors that are easy to see.

Considering legibility. Using color can make your writing easier—or harder—to read. Use type and background colors that are compatible. Dark type on a light background works best for lengthy pieces of writing, while less text-heavy projects can use a light text on a dark background for visual effect. In either case, be sure that the contrast is dramatic enough to be legible.

USING VISUALS

Authors today write with more than just words. Photos, charts, tables, and videos are just some of the visual elements you can use to present information and to make your writing easier or more interesting to read. Would a photo slideshow help listeners see a scene you're describing in an oral presentation? Would readers of a report be able to compare data better in a table or chart than in a paragraph? Would a map or diagram help readers see how and where an event you're describing unfolded? These are questions you should be asking yourself as you write.

Be sure that any visuals you use are relevant to what you have to say—that you use them to support your point, not just to decorate your text.

Graphic essays are made of visuals. Check out how Ally Shwed presents even her essay's title as a drawing. She packs a lot of information into a small space. See for yourself on p. 982.

And remember that even the most spectacular images do not speak for themselves: you need to refer to them in your text and to explain to readers what they are and how they support what you're saying.

> ### REFLECT
>
> Think about a writing project you completed where you incorporated a visual. What was the visual? How did it support the purpose of your project? If you haven't used visuals in a writing project before, where might a visual have helped in a text-only project?

Kinds of Visuals

You may be assigned to include certain kinds of visuals in your writing—but if not, a good way to think about what sorts of visuals to use (or not) is by considering your rhetorical situation. What visuals would be useful or necessary for your topic and purpose? What visuals would help you reach your audience? What kinds of visuals are possible in your medium—or expected in your genre?

Photographs can help an audience envision something that's difficult to describe or to explain in words. A good photo can provide powerful visual

A photo of street art in a Texas parking lot demonstrates the layering effect of graffiti in a way that would be difficult to do with words alone.

evidence for an argument and can sometimes move readers in a way that words alone might not. Think of how ads for various charities use photos to appeal to readers to donate.

Photos can be useful for many writing purposes: letting readers see something you're **DESCRIBING** or **ANALYZING**, for instance, or even something you're **REPORTING** on. (See how Melissa Rubin needed to include a photo of the ad that she analyzes on p. 297.) You can take your own photos or use ones that you find in other sources. Remember, however, to provide full documentation for any photos that you don't take yourself and to ask permission before photographing people and using their image in your writing.

Videos are useful for demonstrating physical processes or actions and for showing sequences. Your medium will dictate whether you can include videos in a text. The print version of a newspaper article about aerialist skiers, for instance, includes a still photo of a skier in mid-jump, whereas the same article on the newspaper's website and on a TV news report features videos showing the skier in action. Your topic and genre will affect whether or not you have reason to include video if you can. If you were writing a **PROCESS ANALYSIS** to teach a skier how to perform a certain aerial maneuver, a video would be far more useful than the still photo you might include if you were writing a **PROFILE** of a professional skier.

Graphs, charts, and tables. Numerical and statistical data can be easier both to describe and to understand when they are presented visually. For example, see the graphics on the following page about participation in high school sports and imagine trying to present that data in a paragraph. You'll often have occasion to present data in graphs or charts, in bar graphs, pie charts, and the like, especially in **REPORTS** and **ANALYSES**. In many cases, you'll be able to find tables and graphs in your research and then incorporate them into your own writing. You can also use templates found in *Google Docs, Word, PowerPoint*, and other programs to create charts and tables yourself. Whether you find or create them, be sure to indicate in your text where the information comes from and how they support your argument.

Line graphs are useful for illustrating trends and changes over time—how unemployment fluctuates over a period of years, for instance. By using more than one line, you can compare changes in different variables, such as participation in high school sports among boys and girls (see p. 790). When comparing more than one variable, the lines should be in two different colors so that readers can easily see the comparison.

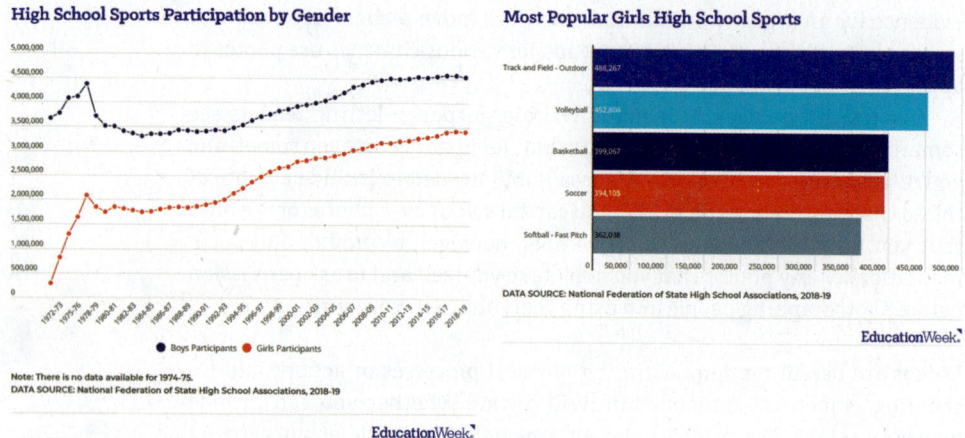

The line graph shows the rising rate of participation in sports over forty-plus years; the bar graph breaks down which sports are most popular with high school girls.

Bar graphs are useful for comparing quantitative data, such as for different age groups or different years. In the example above about high school sports, the bars make it easy to see at a glance which sports are most popular among high school girls. It would be easy enough to convey this same information in words alone—but more work to read and harder to remember.

Pie charts give an overview of the relative sizes of parts to a whole, such as what share of a family budget is devoted to food, housing, entertainment, and so on. As the example below indicates, pie charts are useful for showing which parts of a whole are more or less significant, but they are less precise (and harder to read) than bar graphs. It's best to limit a pie chart to six or seven slices, since when the slices become too small, it's difficult to see how they compare in size.

Tables are an efficient way of presenting a lot of information concisely by organizing it into horizontal rows and vertical columns. Table 1 on page 791 presents data about social media use across demographic groups, information that is made easy to scan and compare in a table.

Maps provide geographic context, helping orient your audience to places mentioned in your text. Reports on the dangers predicted by climatologists have much more impact when accompanied by visuals—maps showing which areas are most affected. For example, the contiguous US map on page 791 shows the country's dangerous drought conditions in October 2024.

Table 1
Who Uses Each Social Media Platform, 2024
Percentage of US adults in each demographic group who say they ever use …

	YouTube	WhatsApp	Reddit
Total	85%	30%	24%
Men	87%	28%	28%
Women	83%	32%	20%
Ages 18–29	93%	30%	46%
30–49	94%	40%	35%
50–64	86%	28%	11%
65+	65%	18%	4%
White	82%	22%	24%
Black	88%	36%	18%
Hispanic	89%	56%	22%

SOURCE: "Social Media Fact Sheet," *Pew Research Center*, https://www.pewresearch.org/internet/fact-sheet/social-media/?tabItem=64e32376-5a21-4b1d-8f8b-5f92406db984. Survey conducted February 1–June 10, 2024.

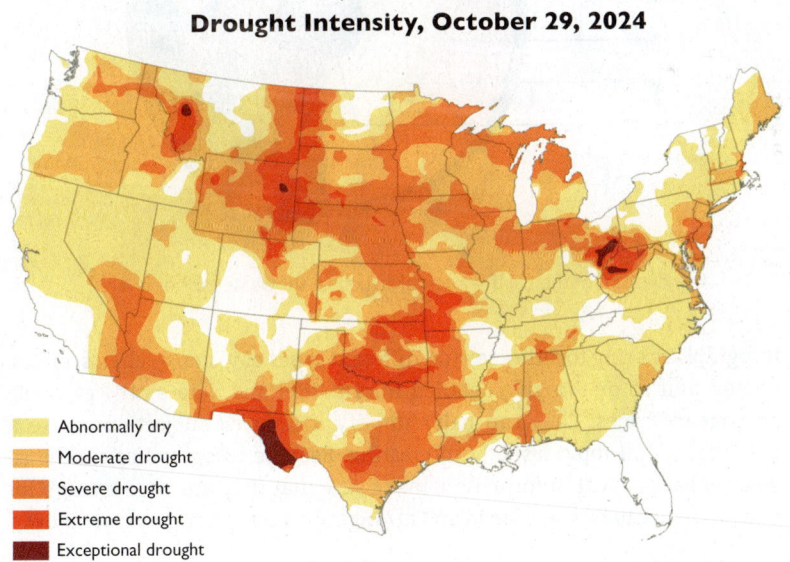

SOURCE: NASA Earth Observatory image by Michala Garrison, using data from the United States Drought Monitor at the University of Nebraska–Lincoln.

The map reports findings from the U.S. Drought Monitor, a partnership of the U.S. Department of Agriculture, NOAA, and the University of Nebraska–Lincoln. As the article published with the map explains, the map "depicts drought intensity in progressive shades of yellow to red. It is based on an analysis of climate, soil, crop, and water condition measurements from more than 350 federal, state, and local observers around the country." The authors also note the severity of these conditions: they result in what is defined as a "flash drought," which is the "rapid onset" of drought conditions that has significant negative effects on the environment, agriculture, effected communities, and the economy.

Diagrams are useful for illustrating details that cannot be shown in a photograph. A carefully drawn diagram can deliver a lot of information in a small amount of space, as the diagram below does.

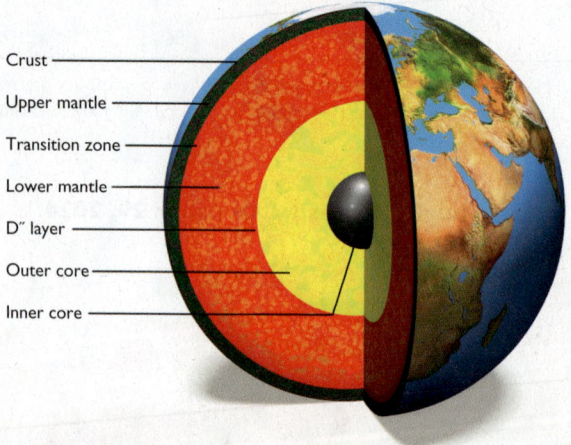

A diagram of the Earth's internal structure shows its various layers.

Infographics bring together several different types of visuals—charts, tables, photos, and so on—to give detailed information and data as the example on page 793 does. They can help simplify a complex subject—or make a potentially dull topic visually interesting. Because infographics can be so densely packed with information, make sure that they are large enough for your audience to be able to read and arranged in a way that they can follow.

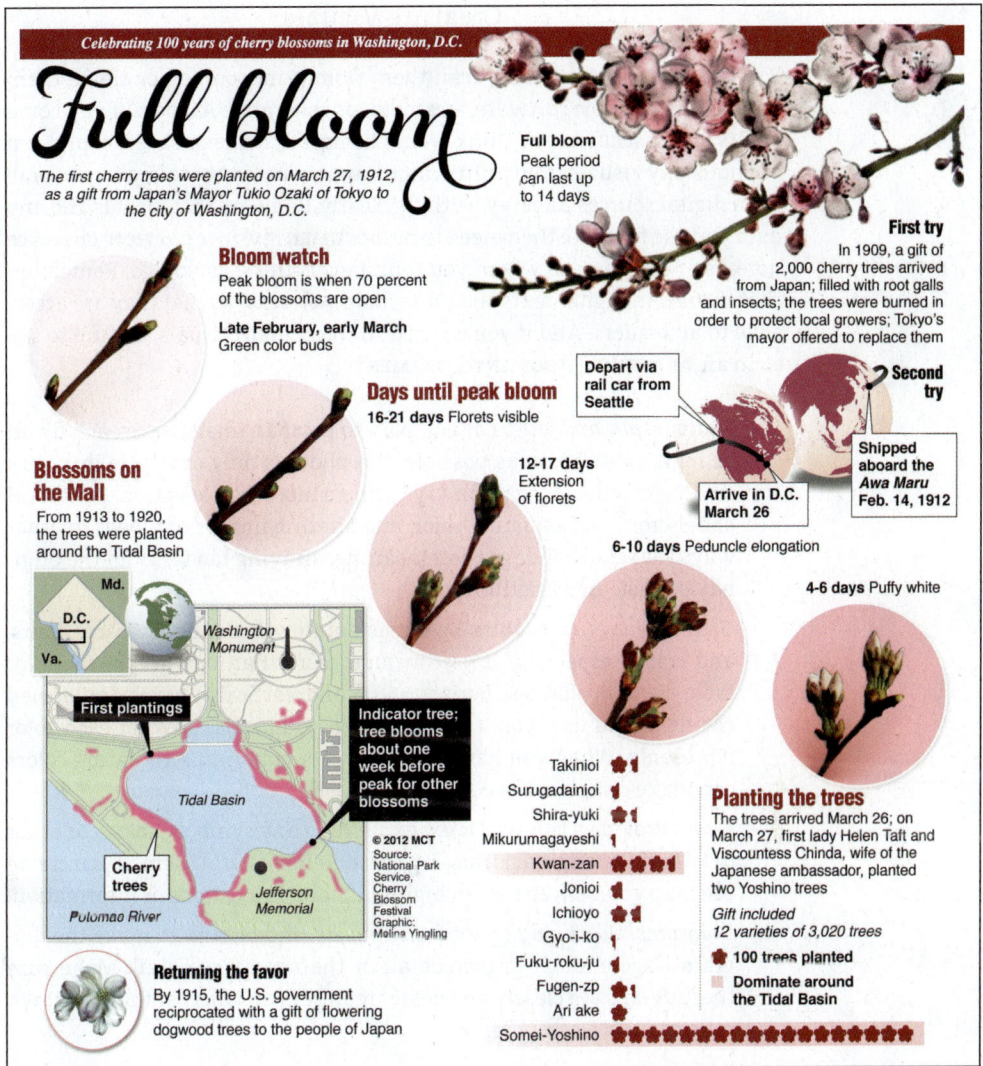

This infographic on the cherry blossom season in Washington, DC, includes diagrams, maps, and a bar chart.

Creating Visuals

You can find visuals online, scan them from print sources, or create them yourself using basic software, a camera, or generative AI tools. If you come across an illustration you think would be useful, make or save a copy. Scan or photocopy visuals from print sources, and save a link or take a screen grab from digital sources. Label everything clearly. Be aware that visuals and any data you use to create them need to be **DOCUMENTED** in a **CAPTION** or source note—so keep track of where you found everything as you go. Remember that visuals in digital texts should include **ALT TEXT** so that they are accessible to all readers. And if you've used AI to generate visuals, be sure to say so in an **AI ACKNOWLEDGMENT STATEMENT**.

- *Photographs and videos.* If you plan to print an image, save each file in as high a resolution as possible. If a photo is only available in a very small size or low resolution, try to find a more legible option. Be careful about cropping, adjusting color, and altering images or videos in other ways that could change their meaning; straying too far from the original is considered unethical.

- *Graphs, charts, and tables.* Be consistent in your use of typefaces, fonts, and colors, especially if you include more than one graph, chart, or table. Be sure that the horizontal (*x*) and vertical (*y*) axes are labeled clearly. If you use more than one color, add labels for what each color represents. When you have many rows or columns, alternating colors can make categories easier to distinguish.

- *Maps.* Provide a title and a key explaining any symbols, colors, or other details. If the original is missing these elements, add them. If you create the map yourself, be sure to highlight notable locations or information.

- *Diagrams.* Use a single font for all labels, and be sure to make the diagram large enough to include all of the necessary detail. Make sure these details are clearly and neatly represented, whether they're drawn or created on a computer.

Introducing and Labeling Visuals

Introduce visuals as you would any other source materials, explaining what they show and how they support your point. Don't leave your audience wondering how a photo or chart pertains to your project—spell it out, and be sure to do so *before* the visual appears ("As shown in fig. 3, population growth has been especially rapid in the Southwest"). Number visuals in most academic writing sequentially (Figure 1, Figure 2), counting tables separately (Table 1, Table 2). If you're following MLA, APA, or another academic style, be sure to follow its guidelines for how to label tables and figures.

MLA STYLE. For tables, provide a number ("Table 1") and a descriptive title ("Population Growth by Region, 2015–25") on separate lines above the table; below the table, add a caption explaining what the table shows and including any source information. For graphs, charts, photos, and diagrams, provide a figure number ("Fig. 1") and caption with source information below the figure. If you give only brief source information, include full source information in your list of works cited.

APA STYLE. For tables, charts, diagrams, graphs, and photos, provide a number ("Table 1" or "Figure 1") and a descriptive title on separate lines above the table or figure; below the table or figure, include a note explaining any elements whose meanings are not apparent in the table or figure and providing source information if the table or figure is adapted or reprinted from another source.

PUTTING IT ALL TOGETHER

Look on page 796 at the homepage of the *Moth*, a nonprofit that "celebrates the commonality and diversity of human experience through the art and craft of true, personal storytelling." It's easy to read—the information banner uses a white sans serif typeface and minimal text. The logo draws your eye because it's large and capitalized, has intricate texture, and is positioned in the upper-left corner of the screen. The smaller text under the logo, "25 years of humanity one story at a time," balances the logo and leads your eye to the text below it—"Listen to Stories"—which gets right to the site's purpose. Each of the images is a link to a specific *Moth* story. Note how white space separates the parts and makes the page easy to read.

You may not have occasion to design anything as large or complex as the *Moth*'s site, but the same design principles will apply for all the writing you do. Whether you're designing a report, a photo essay, or a slide presentation, chances are you'll be working with some combination of words, images,

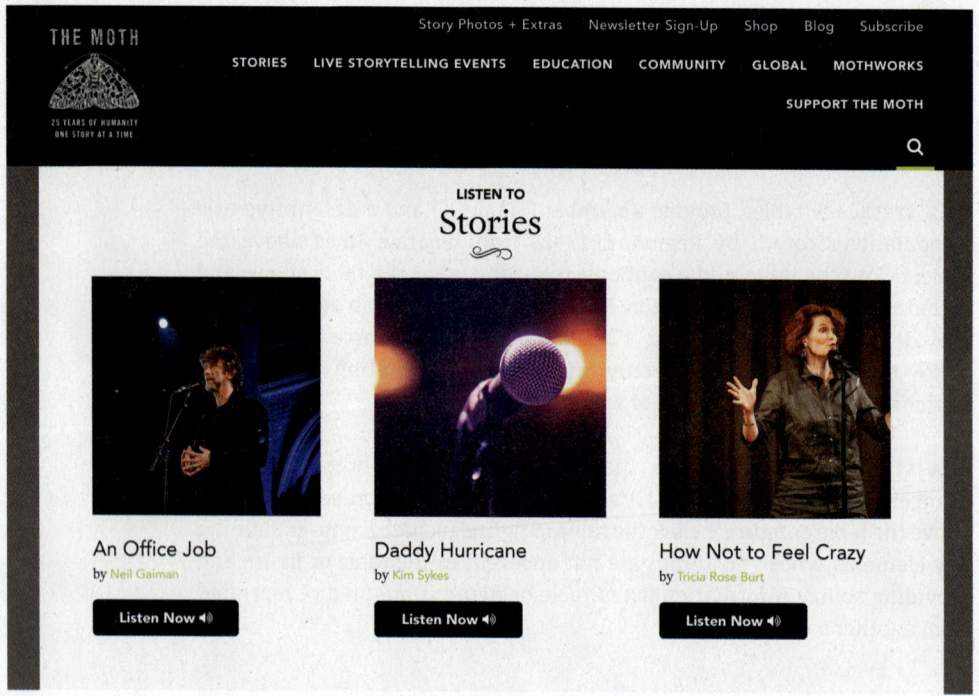

A page on the *Moth* website.

graphs, and other graphic elements that you'll need to put on paper or screen in order to reach a certain audience to achieve a certain purpose.

Look beyond the details and think about what you want your design to accomplish. Do you want it to help your audience grasp a message as fast as possible? convey your identity as a creative author? conform to the requirements of a certain academic style? be appealing yet simple enough to implement by an approaching deadline? Thinking about what you want your design to do can help you determine how to put it all together in a way that achieves your end goal.

Keep it simple. Sometimes you'll need to follow a prescribed organization and layout, but if you get to decide how to design your document, here's a piece of advice: don't make your design any more complex than it has to be. Readers want to be able to find the information they need without having to spend time deciphering a complex hierarchy of headings or an intricate navigational system.

Think about how to format your written text. Should it all be in paragraphs, or is there anything that should be set off as a list? If so, should it be a bulleted list to make it stand out or a numbered list to put items in a sequence? If your text includes numerical data, should any of it be presented in a graph, chart, or table to make it easier for readers to understand? Is there any information that's especially important that you'd like to highlight in some way?

Position visuals carefully. Keep in mind how they will look on a page or screen. Placing them at the top or bottom of a print page will make it easier to lay out pages. If your text will be online, you have more freedom to put visuals wherever you wish. Reproduce visuals at a large enough size so that readers will be able to see all the pertinent detail, but be aware that digital images become fuzzier when they are enlarged. Reduce large image files by saving them in compressed formats such as JPEGs or GIFs; you don't want readers to have problems loading the image. And once everything is in place, look over your text carefully to be sure that nothing is too small or blurry to read.

Use white space to separate the parts of your text. Add some extra space above headings and around lists, images, graphs, charts, and tables. This will keep your text from looking cluttered and make everything easier to find and read.

Organize the text. Whether your text is a simple five-page report or a full website, readers will need to know how it's organized and how to find the information they're looking for. In a brief essay, you might simply indicate that in a sentence in your introduction, but in lengthier pieces, you may need headings, both to structure your text and to make it easy for readers to navigate.

If you're creating a website, you'll need to figure out how you're dividing materials into pages and to make that clear on the site's homepage. Most homepages have a horizontal navigation bar across the top indicating and linking to the main parts. These menus should appear in the same position on every page of the site—and every page should include a link to take readers back to the homepage. Take a look at the examples from *National*

Examples from the *National Geographic* website.

Geographic above and you'll see the consistent elements that help readers navigate the site: navigation bars at the top, links to popular information in bulleted lists, ads in the bottom right corner, consistent colors and typefaces on all the pages.

GETTING RESPONSES TO YOUR DESIGN

Whether you're composing a report, an illustrated essay, or a blog post, try to get responses to the design. Enlist the help of friends or classmates, asking them what they think of the "look" of your text, how easy it is to read, and so on. Following are some specific things they (and you) should consider:

- Is the design matched to the text's PURPOSE, AUDIENCE, GENRE, LANGUAGE, and MEDIUM? Consider the typefaces and any use of color: do they suit your rhetorical situation?
- Does the design make the main parts of your text easy to see? If not, would it help to add headings?
- Is there any information that should be set off as a list?
- Does the text include any data that would be easier to follow in a chart, table, or graph?
- If you've included images, what purpose do they serve? How do they support the point of your text? If some are only decorative, should you delete them?
- Does the overall "look" of your text suit the message that you want to convey?

Remember: your design is often the first impression readers get, and it can make all the difference in getting your message across. There may be a lot at stake in the simple choice of a typeface or color or image, so make these choices carefully—and make your design work for you.

> **REFLECT**
>
> Find a design that you think is attractive (or not)—a book cover, a magazine spread, a brochure, a poster, a blog, a website, and so on. **ANALYZE** its use of typefaces, colors, and visuals. What works, and what doesn't? How would you revise the design if you could?

THIRTY-NINE

Composing and Remixing across Media

Ever since the days of illustrated books and maps, texts have included visual elements for the purpose of imparting information. The contemporary difference is the ease with which we can combine words, images, sound, color, animation, and video . . . so that they are part of our everyday lives.

—NCTE ON MULTIMODAL LITERACIES

THE NATIONAL COUNCIL OF TEACHERS OF ENGLISH made this statement more than a decade ago, and in the years since, multimodal literacies have indeed become part of the "everyday lives" of students everywhere.

In the cartoon on the next page, the little boy illustrates the NCTE statement perfectly: he lies in bed, listening to his dad read him a story. But the boy does more than just listen: he compliments his dad on his reading ("darn good job") and offers to record him reading and then "podcast" him on his website. Multimodal, indeed.

Defining Multimodal Writing

Multimodal texts draw on more than words, bringing in still or moving images, sound, and so on. Literacy researcher Cynthia Selfe identifies five modes writers can use to convey their messages: linguistic (words, written or spoken); visual (colors, fonts, images, and so on); audio (tone of

39 Composing and Remixing across Media

"You know, Dad, you do a darn good job. You should let me record you sometime, and I'll podcast you on my website. Just a thought."

voice, music, and other sounds); gestural (body language and facial expression); and spatial (the way elements are arranged on a page or screen).

For hundreds of years, writers relied primarily on two of these modes, the linguistic and the visual, so multimodality is nothing new. Today, writers have easy access to all five modalities and can produce texts that convey meaning not only through words but also with sounds, moving and still images, animations, and more—delivered through print, spoken, and digital media.

This access to multiple media also enables authors to remix their work or the work of others, to take the message conveyed in one mode and cast it in another. One of the most popular kinds of remixes happens when books are adapted into movies or TV shows. You've likely debated whether a book was better than its movie adaptation, or vice versa. Remixing often occurs in academic writing, too. Have you ever transformed a report or essay into an oral presentation or a poster? That's a remix! Researchers often try to find ways for their work to reach new audiences outside of academia by transforming their research into more popular forms for the general public, like podcasts, infographics, videos, and TED talks.

For authors today, access to all of the modes of expression (and the possibility of remixing them) opens up exciting options. This chapter offers some tips for making best use of the various technologies available for composing and remixing in multiple modes. But keep in mind that just like traditional print texts, more complex multimodal ones call for careful attention to the same conventions of effective writing, research, and argument—primarily by staying laser-focused on your rhetorical situation.

> 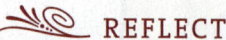 **REFLECT**
>
> **Make a list of writing assignments you've done this term and any writing projects you have worked on outside of class. How many of them rely on printed words on a page? How many use multiple modes—and what are they? How does each mode contribute to your purpose?**

Considering Your Rhetorical Situation

Writing in multiple modes calls for the same close attention to rhetorical principles that all writing does. Whatever your topic, the following questions can help you think about your purpose, audience, and the rest of your rhetorical situation:

Consider your PURPOSE. Why are you creating this project? What are your purposes or goals? No doubt one purpose is to fulfill an assignment. You may also have other purposes: raising awareness about a problem on campus; convincing someone to support a project you have in mind; providing information. Consider the message you want to communicate. What do you want to see happen as a result of what you write?

Think about your AUDIENCE. Who are they? How can you best reach them? If you're writing to all members of your campus community, you'll likely post your message online; if you're alerting neighbors about a lost dog, flyers might be better. If your intended audience is limited to people you know, you may make some assumptions about them and how they're likely to respond. But remember that most projects you put online will be accessible to the public—to people you don't and can't know. In this case, it's important not to make assumptions about what they know and to be respectful of the diverse audience that may read what you write.

Think about your STANCE. What is your attitude toward your topic, and how do you want to present yourself as an author—as well-informed? outraged? perplexed? How can you convey that stance? Certain typefaces look serious while others look silly; same thing with colors. If you're including music, that too affects the tone. If you're giving an oral presentation or creating a video, your facial expressions and gestures can signal something about your stance.

Choose your GENRE. The kind of writing you're doing can sometimes determine the form that your project will take. If you're REPORTING information, a podcast might be a good choice. But if you're delivering a PROPOSAL to ask for funding for an event, a print text may be most effective. And if afterward you want to create a NARRATIVE documenting the event, a video might capture the experience most vividly.

Consider the larger CONTEXT. How much time do you have, and is your topic narrow enough that you can do a good job in that amount of time? Do you have access to whatever technology you will need? If you'll need to learn new software, remember to build in time for that. Does your campus offer any services (perhaps at a writing center or at a media lab) where you can get help?

Consider MEDIA. What media will best serve your audience, purpose, and topic? If you're writing about Bollywood films, you might create a website, which would enable you to embed video clips and to reach a community of fans. If you want to inform fellow students about ways to save water, you might create an infographic to post in restrooms around campus.

Consider your LANGUAGE. Think about how your language and style might complement or challenge the conventions of your chosen media, and the larger context.

KINDS OF MULTIMODAL PROJECTS

Once you have assessed your rhetorical situation, you'll want to consider which modes and media will be most effective in achieving your goals. A wide range of multimodal projects have made their way into college classrooms. The most prevalent and popular of these projects are illustrated essays, websites, audio essays and podcasts, video essays, posters and infographics, as well as social media posts and campaigns. Following are some tips for composing each of these kinds of writing.

Illustrated Essays

Probably the simplest multimodal assignment you will encounter is an essay in which you're asked to embed illustrations—photos, drawings, maps, graphs, charts, and so on. Illustrated essays offer you a chance for creativity and for getting your point across in multiple ways.

See how one student, Ruizhe (Thomas) Zhao, uses images in an essay about the ways Japanese video games are being remade to better appeal to foreign audiences.

> Even companies like Nintendo, which had previously relied on the denationalized nature of their characters for international success, have begun capitalizing on uniquely Japanese concepts. For example, the Tanooki Suit is an item introduced with *New Super Mario Bros. 3* that allows Mario to transform into a tanuki, or Japanese raccoon dog. In the original release of *Super Mario Bros. 3*, Tanooki Mario was de-emphasized in favor of Raccoon Mario, which was prominently featured on the cover art, since Americans were more likely able to identify a raccoon rather than a tanuki (see figure 1). However, with the release of *Super Mario 3D Land*, which some consider to be a spiritual successor to *Super Mario Bros. 3* (Sterling), Nintendo fully embraced the Tanooki power-up and made it the primary focus both in their advertising and in-game, with many enemies gaining Tanooki tails. This newly realized proliferation of Tanooki extended into its sequel, *Super Mario 3D World* (see figure 2) and

Fig. 1. The box art for *Super Mario Bros. 3* prominently featured Raccoon Mario . . .

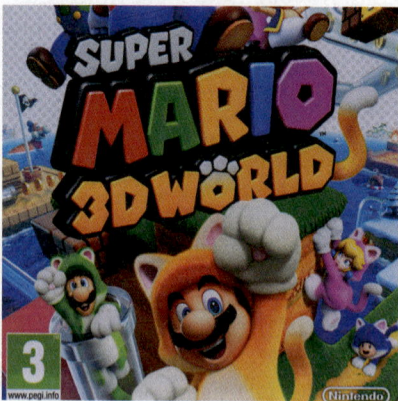

Fig. 2. . . . while art for later releases focused on Tanooki Mario, who, although present in *Super Mario Bros. 3*, was not nearly as prominent as in *3D Land* or *3D World*.

related games, such as *Mario Kart 7*. By embracing their cultural heritage rather than disguising it, Nintendo helps introduce Western gamers to elements of Japanese culture they may otherwise not be aware of, no longer fearful of culture shock.

—RUIZHE (THOMAS) ZHAO, "Word for Word: Culture's Impact on the Localization of Japanese Video Games"

Notice how Zhao has carefully incorporated the two images into his argument, labeling them with figure numbers, referring to them in the text, and providing captions for each one. Though it's not shown here, he also includes documentation information in a works-cited list. Far from being decorative, these images provide essential support for his argument.

In Dan Nott and Scott Cambo's graphic essay, the words and the drawings are woven together so well that neither element could stand alone. See the result on p. 960.

TIPS FOR WRITING ILLUSTRATED ESSAYS

- Make sure all illustrations help communicate your message. You never want to use illustrations as mere decoration.
- Refer to each illustration in the text and position each one carefully so that it appears near the text where it's discussed.
- Give each illustration a figure number and a caption that tells readers what it is.
- Provide documentation for any illustrations that you don't create yourself (including ones AI helps you generate), either in a caption or in a works-cited list.

Websites

Websites come in many different forms: personal, academic, activist, and business-oriented. They're dynamic spaces where creators post information, ideas, arguments, advertisements, and even reflections. Web authors can take advantage of embedding images, audio, and video into their sites. A distinctive feature of websites is the ability to hyperlink, connecting one word or phrase to more information elsewhere online. Hyperlinking expands possibilities for writers; it can be a quick way to point to the conversation you're entering, provide evidence for your claims, or highlight information you recommend readers consider.

Check out Oregon State University's student Fisheries and Wildlife Club website below. Its homepage orients readers to the purpose of the club, which is "a peer-elected, nonprofit student group dedicated to the professional development of undergraduate and graduate students interested in fisheries, wildlife, or conservation fields," and the function of the website: to offer information about club leadership and membership, to alert readers to upcoming events, and to showcase club outreach and projects. The site is richly multimodal; it includes images, maps, links to listservs and social media accounts, sign-up sheets, and *YouTube* videos. Spending time on this site gives readers an immersive sense of what it would be like to participate in this club—and the information they need to get involved.

TIPS FOR CREATING A WEBSITE

- Stay focused on the purpose of your website: what do you want readers to know, learn, or experience? Tailor the information you include and design choices to your purpose.
- Many readers scan websites for information, so use bulleted lists, headings, a bold font, and other design elements to make your text easy to scan.
- Consider the pages within your website; you'll likely offer an About page that explains the site's purpose. Organize information using pages with clear titles, and provide links to those pages on your homepage.

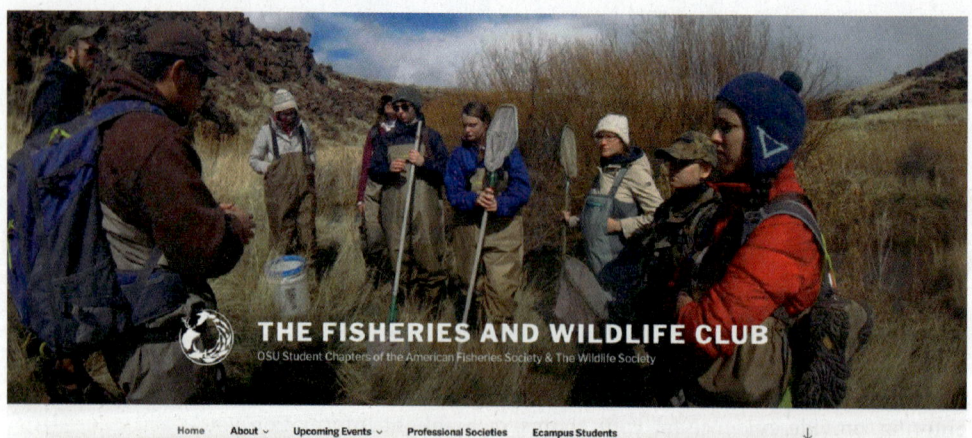

Homepage of the OSU student chapter of the Fisheries and Wildlife Club.

- Make navigation easy. Include a menu listing the pages of your site with brief titles that make the purpose of each area clear.
- Include images or embed audio or video clips where they will help make your message clear or engage readers.
- Include hyperlinks to guide your readers to additional pertinent information.

Audio Essays and Podcasts

The University of Wisconsin's Design Lab defines audio essays as ones that "explore topics using spoken text, audio interviews, archival recordings, music, environmental sounds, and/or sound effects" and notes that this type of essay "can make unfamiliar materials more accessible to new audiences and/or reveal new perspectives on familiar subjects." National Public Radio popularized audio essays with its *This I Believe* and *This American Life* series.

A podcast differs from an audio essay in that podcasts are made up of episodes in a series. Listeners regularly tune in to podcasts on topics from true crime (*Serial*) to song analysis (*Song Exploder*) to comedy (*Comedy Bang! Bang!*). Many universities support student podcasters as well.

The University of Virginia, for example, hosts *U OK UVA?*, a podcast focused on student well-being and mental health. In episode 3 of the first season, the host speaks to "UVA students from across the globe in order to understand how mental health factors into their college experience." Visit everyonesanauthor.tumblr.com to listen to this brief episode, and pay attention to how the piece is organized to help listeners follow along. Notice, too, how the student podcasters use music and different voices (the host, the international interviewees) to reach their intended audience and achieve their purpose. Here's one segment from the episode:

> *Host:* One particularly salient barrier to assimilation at UVA is being far from home and family. Every student I spoke to highlighted the difficulty of missing their homes, friends, and families—to a seemingly more extreme degree than the typical first year. Of the international students I had the chance to speak with, most only got to see their families a couple times per year at the maximum.
>
> *Student Interviewee 1:* Maybe I have gone back four times to see them, and they have come here once to see me.

➦ Russel Honoré's essay on p. 203 was written for *This I Believe*. Read it, and then listen to the audio version at everyonesanauthor.tumblr.com. What does he do differently for those listening to his text?

Student Interviewee 3: I think the biggest struggle was definitely staying away from my family because I have never lived for such a long period of time away from them. Especially my grandma—she is basically a second mom. I grew up being very close with her. Staying like five months away from them for the first time, it kind of hit me like wow, this is really happening."

Student Interviewee 2: I definitely felt kind of homesick at first when I came to the US; the culture here is just different. It was hard to get to know people as easily as Americans would get to know other Americans."

Host: These feelings of homesickness often bled into feelings of isolation and loneliness. And while the students did not feel comfortable explicitly stating the impact of these feelings on their mental health, it is clear how their mental health might have suffered. I want to be careful here not to overgeneralize or paint with too broad a brush but what is important is seeing how the realities of being an international student can easily lead to mental health struggles.

As the podcast continues, the host and interviewees consider how "international students navigated these difficult circumstances" and all find that "[t]here is one answer, community." The host concludes the episode with this message: "I am not suggesting that community is a panacea to the mental health struggles of international students at UVA. Much work remains to be done in assisting our international students with their transition to college. . . . And as the conversation around mental health becomes more destigmatized, I hope that international students can feel comfortable seeking help for their difficult transition to UVA."

REFLECT

Think about the purpose of the *U OK UVA?* podcast series. Is a podcast series an effective way to tackle students' mental health concerns? Why or why not? How would presenting this information in a different media (a website, a video series, an article in the student paper) be more or less effective in reaching the intended audience?

You might want to (or be assigned to) compose an audio essay or create a podcast series. As the students who make *U OK UVA?* have done, once you come up with a topic, you'll want to find an angle to approach that topic and consider sources that will help you explore it (such as interviews, research, and observations). Plan your audio essay or podcast using outlines, interview questions, and ideas for background music and transitions, and then get recording. Many apps and programs are available to help you get started, and your school's media center or library likely offers even more. Here are a few to check out: *Audacity* works with both Mac and Windows, and *GarageBand* is preinstalled on all Mac products.

TIPS FOR COMPOSING AN AUDIO ESSAY OR PODCAST

- Decide on the software you will use.
- Write out a script, using short sentences, strong verbs, and active voice. Think about your language choices and dialect: what language decisions would suit your objectives and rhetorical situation?
- If you are using sources, introduce them at the beginning of the sentence and paraphrase rather than quote.
- Use concrete examples and vivid imagery to help listeners see or imagine what you're describing. Sound effects can help establish setting.
- Organize your piece in chronological order, allowing for flashbacks and flashforwards if they are necessary to your story.
- Practice reading your script. Vary your tone of voice to keep listeners engaged. You might change your tone to imitate someone else speaking. (Or better yet, edit in sound clips of others speaking for themselves.)
- Follow *This American Life* host Ira Glass's "45-second rule": listeners expect some kind of break or change of pace every 45 to 50 seconds. Try to pace your piece accordingly.
- Use music to establish a mood, to mark transitions, and to keep your listeners engaged.

Video Essays and Digital Storytelling

Video essays are popular, and not just on *YouTube* or *TikTok*. Some students submit video essays as part of their college and grad school applications, and some employers ask for videos as part of job applications. While anyone with a smartphone can create a video essay, it's not always easy.

Just like traditional essays composed with written words alone, video essays need to make a clear point, to offer good reasons and evidence in support of that point, and to acknowledge other points of view. Unlike print essays, however, video essays can use a combination of images, sounds, and words.

And you can present these images, sounds, and words in many different ways. Take images: you can use still images, moving images, and stop-motion images. Sounds can include people speaking on camera, voiceover, music, and background sounds. Words can be spoken, or they can be put on-screen as titles, subtitles, credits—even in thought bubbles. All these elements add up to infinite possibilities for authoring.

Digital storytelling projects are becoming more popular on college campuses across the country. Students compose video essays to share narratives about themselves or the world around them. For example, the University of Michigan–Dearborn launched a campus-wide project called "More than a Single Story: UM–Dearborn Speaks," in which students compose and "share their stories while challenging the myths about Dearborn, the Detroit Metropolitan area, regional commuter campuses, [and] the surrounding Muslim-American community." The 2024 entries on the website invite audiences to watch and listen as students use still and moving images, voiceover, and animation to narrate their experiences with UM–Dearborn's accessibility office, counseling services, office of student life, and career counseling.

Video essays and digital stories rely on words, images, and sounds all working together. A good way to plan out how all these elements will fit together is by creating a **STORYBOARD**, a series of sketches that shows the

THINK BEYOND WORDS VISIT everyonesanauthor.tumblr.com to watch one or two of the University of Michigan–Dearborn students' digital stories on the "More than a Single Story" website. In the entry you watched, how effective is the student's use of video as a medium to tell their story? What elements or design decisions do you find most engaging and why? Do you think it was a good choice to use video for this story—why or why not?

Digital Story Storyboard Template

Title:
Name(s):   Page: _____

Image/clip description/drawing: Title	Image/clip description/drawing: Intro	Image/clip description/drawing: Image/Video 1
Image credit:	Image credit:	Image credit:
Spoken text/voiceover:	Spoken text/voiceover:	Spoken text/voiceover:
Writen text (add title slides): Title of project, etc.	Writen text (add title slides):	Writen text (add title slides):
Music/sounds:	Music/sounds:	Music/sounds:
Music/sound credit:	Music/sound credit:	Music/sound credit:
Effects/transitions: Add transition at end of title slide and before intro.	Effects/transitions:	Effects/transitions:

A template for creating storyboards, designed for students at University of Michigan–Dearborn.

sequence of scenes and actions in a video. Take a look at the storyboard template above that students like those at the University of Michigan–Dearborn use to sketch out their digital projects. The template breaks down the video-making process, prompting students to think about images, voiceover, music, transitions, and effects, as well as how each scene will sequence with the next. You might use a storyboard template like this as a blueprint for your own work.

⤴ Go to everyonesanauthor.tumblr.com to browse examples of multimodal projects created by students.

TIPS FOR COMPOSING A VIDEO ESSAY

- Decide which program you will use: *iMovie*, *Final Cut Pro*, and *Windows Live Movie Maker* are popular choices.

- Try to show much of the evidence for your argument visually, with images rather than just words.
- Think about the tone you want to project and how color, lighting, pacing, and music might evoke that tone.
- Draft a script for any text that will be spoken on camera or read as a voiceover—and practice reading it aloud.
- If your video includes yourself or others speaking into the camera, consider tools like *Zoom* or *Microsoft Teams*.
- Create a storyboard to map out how the parts of your video essay will fit together. Use your storyboard to plan the shots you need before you begin shooting, and always shoot more than you think you'll need. It's much easier to delete extra footage than it is to get a single shot you missed.
- Consider a variety of camera angles. Wide-angle shots are useful for setting a scene; medium shots, for framing someone speaking to the camera; close-ups, for showing important details.
- Experiment also with moving the camera—following the subject, zooming in or out, panning left or right—but do so sparingly. You don't want to make your viewers dizzy!
- Use title cards to display written text if needed. You'll probably want to open with your title, and you might add text to identify the setting, time, and the name and title of someone speaking; to add captions or subtitles; or to mark transitions.
- Provide a written list of credits on the screen at the end, citing any sources you use and thanking those who helped.

Posters and Infographics

You're likely to have opportunities to create research posters and infographics for classroom presentations, campus organizations, or academic conferences. Both research posters and infographics present information in a visual and easily digestible way. A research poster represents the results of research or a study. Take a look at the following poster that three Stanford students created in order to present the results of a research study. The poster explains the questions that motivated the work, the methods used to conduct the research, the results, and some ideas for further study.

39 ⌘ Composing and Remixing across Media

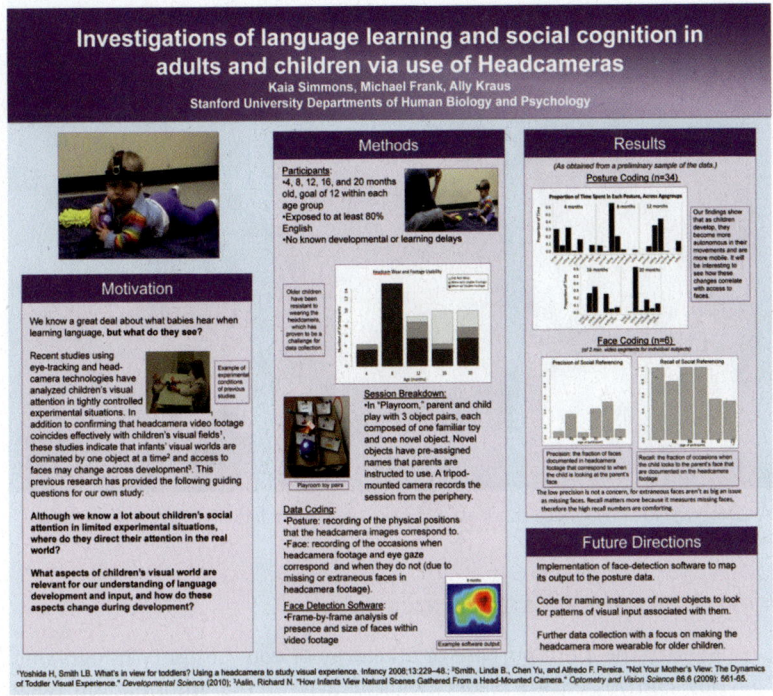

A poster created by a Stanford student research group to present its study.

Thus, this poster shows the steps of their research process. A key principle for effective poster design is clear organization. In the student example, the topic is included in the title, which is centered at the top. The text is organized in three columns: one devoted to the motivation for the project, the second to the methods used, and the third to results and future directions. Data are presented in bar graphs, and other images illustrate and underscore key points in the report.

An infographic, on the other hand, offers a succinct visualization of complex information. The example on the next page shows data on shark attacks in 2024. A map displays the locations where unprovoked shark attacks occurred, with pink dots indicating fatal bites. An effective infographic summarizes information so it's easy for readers to understand the main takeaways at a glance. When creating an infographic, be careful not to pack it with too many words, which can distract from the main message.

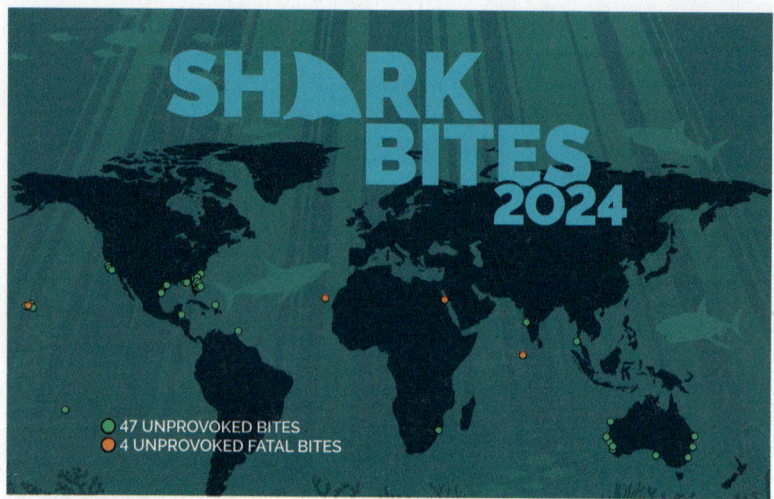

An infographic plots where shark attacks have happened and whether they were fatal events or not.

TIPS FOR CREATING A POSTER OR INFOGRAPHIC

- Identify the main purpose or takeaway of your poster or infographic. How can you ensure readers walk away with that information? What can you leave off so that the main point stands out?
- People will likely read your poster or infographic from the top left corner to the bottom right. Organize the information presented accordingly.
- Posters and infographics are often read at a glance, so present the information you want your audience to take away clearly and simply. Try bullet points and avoid long paragraphs. Consider headings and subheadings.
- Think about how you can get your audience's attention: by asking a provocative question in a large, bold font at the top of the poster? with color? with an eye-catching image? something else?
- Include charts, graphs, and images; they help convey dense information quickly.
- Make sure that all the visuals and information in the poster and infographic are tied to your purpose.
- Keep the design simple: too many images, too much text, or distracting typefaces make for a cluttered look that can be hard to follow.

- Be sure that any text is large enough to read—and that it is organized in a way that makes it easy to scan and understand quickly.
- Choose colors that will be easy to see. Primary colors are easier to see than pastels. Use dark text on a light background.
- Cite your information and sources. See the bottom panel on the students' poster (p. 813) for examples.

Social Media Posts and Campaigns

As you well know, social media offers various formats for writers to compose, deliver, and circulate their claims, ideas, agendas, and messages, through platforms like *Instagram*, *TikTok*, and *Facebook*. Each platform offers different opportunities and constraints. And, of course, social media platforms can be used for almost innumerable purposes: to connect with friends, to craft an argument, to share images of a beloved pet, to circulate news, to advertise or sell items, to network, to bring people together virtually and physically—the possibilities are seemingly endless.

Colleges and universities often use social media to stay in touch with students. For example, students at Cape Fear Community College produced videos and posted them on the school's *TikTok* account. These videos alert the campus's more than 35,000 followers of the benefits of community college. In them, students offer advice for making college more affordable, advertise occupational programs on campus, motivate students to stay committed to their studies, and more—all using text, music, and images of students. Many of their videos have more than 50,000 views—an effective campaign, to be sure!

See the Cape Fear Community College *TikTok* account by visiting everyonesanauthor.tumblr.com.

You might be assigned or given the option to create a social media campaign in your classes. For instance, students in literature classes are creating *Instagram* accounts for characters in the novel they're reading, imagining the posts the character might make, the images they'd share, and the other accounts they'd follow. Students in history courses are creating *Bluesky* campaigns with posts recounting a historical event, imagined from the perspective of a person who lived through it. In first-year writing classes, students are adapting arguments, reports, and proposals into videos on *TikTok* to spread their message more widely. Composing for social media gives you options for reaching new audiences in creative and engaging ways.

Because it's a part of our everyday lives, social media may seem an easy venue for expressing yourself. Just be aware that even here, there are conventions, preferred styles, and shared patterns of communication. If you're not familiar with a particular platform, before using it, spend some time scanning posts to figure out what gets attention. Look closely at the languages used, the format and length of posts, the style of photos and videos, and how hashtags and emojis are deployed. Pay attention to the tone of captions and comments. You'll gain a quick understanding of what works well and what doesn't.

You'll also want to consider which platform best suits your purpose, format, and intended audience. *TikTok* and *Snapchat* are best for sharing short videos; for longer videos, think *YouTube*. For sharing images, consider *Instagram*. And there are surely other new platforms and tools to explore, too.

TIPS FOR COMPOSING ON SOCIAL MEDIA

- To choose a social media platform, think about the message you want to send and which features are required to convey it. Which platform is most likely to reach your intended audience?

- Decide what you want your audience to do with your message—respond? spread it? perform a specific action? Design your post(s) accordingly.

- Keep posts short. Use links to refer to additional information.

- Identify the media you'll use. If using images or video, provide captions and ensure there is alt text for accessibility. Compose images and videos so the subject is clear and there aren't distracting elements or sounds. Check color contrast and lighting so the subject is clear. For word-based posts, how will typeface, color, and overall design engage your audience?

- If you use words, ideas, or images you didn't create yourself, provide credit. Including links or @mentions are common ways to credit others online. Ensure any source you link to is credible and accurate.

- Pay attention to the conventions and user expectations of the platform you choose. Do you want to follow those expectations? challenge them in some way?

- Remember that anything shared on social media may be viewed by friends, acquaintances, teachers, future colleagues, or hiring managers. Your social media posts can also easily be captured and recorded by readers, so don't post anything you don't want saved or shared.

- Think about how you can use **HASHTAGS** and tagging others to connect your post to ongoing conversations, and help your contribution spread.

- Prioritize your privacy and protection. Make sure you're comfortable with the policies of the social media platforms you use, and instead of using personal accounts, consider creating a separate account for schoolwork on social media.

REFLECT

Check out your school's social media accounts. What platforms do they use? What kinds of messages do they send? Who and what do they feature and why?

REMIX PROJECTS

Writers remix projects by taking their message or argument and transforming it into a different genre or media. The goal is usually to share the original message or idea with a new or wider audience. Along the way, the message might even shift or take new shape as it's revised to match the purpose and features of the new genre. Exploring the possibilities that different genres and media open up is part of the fun—and challenge—of remixing writing. Remixes, then, can be an opportunity for creativity and imagination—to rethink and renew your ideas by trying out new forms.

Take a look, for example, at the infographic on the following page. Sophia Warfield, a student at the University of Maryland, transformed her research essay on overfishing into an infographic. Starting out, she asked herself: How do I want to recast the information in my research essay so that it reaches new audiences? What other genre might help me to craft my argument in new ways? Choosing a **GENRE** for a remix project is the first and most important step, and Warfield chose an infographic because it could highlight key information visually and move audiences to take action. As she kept at it, more questions guided Warfield's work. She considered: What was the purpose of my original research essay and what strategies did I use to achieve that purpose? What ideas, concepts, arguments, or research do I want to retain as I move to an infographic? How will an infographic allow me to fine-tune my claims or craft new ways to make my argument? What *won't* I be able to do in the infographic that I could do in the research essay?

In writing her research essay, Warfield developed arguments about overfishing by providing research to support her claims and responding

See the ebook for a video on creating a remix.

Visit everyonesanauthor.tumblr.com to read Warfield's research essay.

to counterarguments. She also incorporated her own experiences with overfishing, lending to her credibility. The infographic, on the other hand, allowed Warfield to distill her research into specific, attention-grabbing facts about overfishing so the main argument is concise and clear: stop overfishing. And a single bold headline summarizes Warfield's proposal for action—"Join Greenpeace!"—with information for how to do so. Using sparse words, art, colors, and a select few typefaces, Warfield was able to transform her message into one many more people are likely to spot, notice, and think about.

A University of Maryland student's remix of a research essay into an infographic.

39 ✢ Composing and Remixing across Media

TIPS FOR COMPOSING REMIX PROJECTS

- Identify the **AUDIENCE** you are aiming to reach: One wider and more public than before? more specific and specialized? Your peers instead of your teacher? Think about which genres or media are most likely to get and hold that audience's attention.
- Get clear on your **PURPOSE** for adapting your work: To turn a personal narrative into an argument? To translate complex research into something the general public will care about? Your purpose will help you see which **GENRE** is best suited to achieving your goal.
- Weigh which **MEDIUM** or media will reach your new intended audience, serve your purpose, and suit your genre. *TikTok* videos can work well to reach a young public audience and make a brief argument, like Cape Fear Community College's account. But a different medium, like a pamphlet, infographic, or website, would be better suited for conveying more complex information.
- Identify the ideas, claims, or arguments that you'll retain from your original work and use in this adaptation. Pinpoint, too, the strategies or information that you'll leave behind.
- If you cited sources in your original work, plan for how you'll give credit in your adaptation. Links, a works-cited page or slide, or a QR code to references could work depending on your genre.
- Analyze your new chosen genre or media and decide what **LANGUAGE** and **STYLE** you'll use. If there are conventions or expectations, will you meet those or push against them? Think about how your language and style should evolve (or not) from your original work.
- As you work, **REFLECT** on the choices you're making about audience, genre, design, language, and so on. Doing so will help you transfer effective practices to writing in the future.

> ### ✢ REFLECT
>
> Consider a project you're working on or have completed this semester for one of your courses. How might you remix it into a new genre or medium that reaches a new audience? What genre would you choose and why? How would your message change in this new genre? What would this new mode allow you to do and say? How might it limit you?

MANAGING MULTIMODAL AND REMIX PROJECTS

Managing projects that involve multimedia is a bit like juggling: at any one time, you have multiple balls in the air, each one needing attention, and altogether it takes a lot of skill to keep them all airborne. While we can't provide guidelines for every step of every multimodal project you may encounter, we can offer some general advice about how to approach them.

Whether you're composing an illustrated essay, a website, a video, or any other multimodal text, you will want to plan carefully for how your project will achieve your purpose with a particular audience and in a particular context. To do so, you'll need to carefully manage your time, your files, your project content, your sources, and more.

Managing your time. Make sure you know exactly how much time you have before your project is due and then be realistic about how to manage that time. Set up a calendar and block out specific times when you know you can work on the project; consider whether you'll have any class time to devote to it. If you're assigned to work with other students, set regular meeting times and draw up a schedule and task list together so that you each know your responsibilities. Breaking a project down into parts and setting deadlines for each part can help keep you on track. And don't forget to build in time to get responses to a draft of your project—from your instructor if possible, as well as from classmates and friends.

Managing project files. To keep track of information and sources for multimodal projects, begin by creating a project folder on your computer, using subfolders for various types of files. For image files, select the best format for your project: JPEG, PNG, or GIF will offer the best clarity for photographs or graphic design projects. For video files, your best choice will likely be MP4 or, if you have a Mac, MOV. Organize files according to type (images, charts, video clips, audio clips, and intended use) and according to the organization of your project (clips for scene 1 of a video essay, graphs for the results section of a research poster). Be sure to label each file in a way that makes sense to you and to make note of where you found it, the date you downloaded it, and any other relevant source information—so that you can cite your sources properly and go back to them if need be. Your school might provide project management software access, but if not you'll want to look at free online options. A site like top5projectmanagement.com that offers descriptions and reviews can help you sort through the possibilities.

Organizing your content. Some writers begin with nothing more than a pack of sticky notes, putting main points and subpoints and supporting reasons and evidence on individual stickies and arranging them on a larger surface. You might begin with an outline of the main points you want to make and the support for each one. This kind of careful organizing is crucial because it creates a "big picture" of your message and all its parts.

If you're making a short video or video essay, you might create a storyboard to put everything in sequence; another possibility would be a two-column script to line up the video and audio portions. Audio essays and podcasts need some kind of script as well, one that accounts for both words and any music or other sounds. For an illustrated print essay, you'll need to decide where to put your images. For websites and other kinds of online texts that readers navigate by links, you might map out your organization on a large sheet of paper, putting the main page at the center top and then drawing lines out to the various pages you will link to. Social media posts are small but have many moving parts; map out what text, visuals, HASHTAGS, and @mentions you'll include, and in what order.

Crediting your sources. Be sure to credit your sources. You can do so at the bottom of a poster, as the last slide in an oral presentation, as footnotes or a separate page on a website, as credits at the end of a video or audio piece, or as links or tags in a social media post. If you use AI tools for any part of the project, say so in an AI ACKNOWLEDGMENT STATEMENT.

> ## REFLECT
>
> Find a piece of academic writing you've done and describe ideas for how you might remix it using multiple modes. What new genre or medium would work well and why?

FORTY

Making Presentations

WHAT GOES INTO a surefire great presentation? Author and consultant Nancy Duarte wanted to find out. So she set out to study some great presentations, hundreds of them, beginning with Martin Luther King Jr.'s "I Have a Dream" speech and Steve Jobs's iPhone launch, two speeches that seemed so different to her that she couldn't imagine she would find anything in common. But she did.

She found that these two speeches—and hundreds of other terrific presentations—shared one common structure. Each speech begins by describing "what is"—and then goes on to suggest what it could (or should) be. That's in the introduction. Then in the middle of the speech, the presenter moves back and forth between discussing that status quo and describing what it could or should be. And in most cases, the conclusion vividly evokes what could be and calls for action.

Duarte's research shows that this basic structure (from what is to what could be) is very widely used, and especially so by activists, politicians, and businesspeople proposing change of some kind. In fact, it's a structure that may work well for many of the presentations you make in your college classes. And there are two common variations on this structure that you may be familiar with. One begins with what *was*, in the past, and then moves on to explain how it changed. The other opens by noting what others have said about a topic and then moves on to what you want to say about it, focusing on the benefits of your position.

Martin Luther King Jr.

Steve Jobs

Starting with what is, what was, or what's been said and then suggesting something "better" uses a classic storytelling technique: setting up a conflict that needs to be resolved. And presenting your main point as a story works well in a spoken presentation because stories are easier to follow and remember than other kinds of evidence and are often more persuasive.

Sounds simple, doesn't it? State your main point, find a story to help get that point across, and inspire the audience to accept what you say. But coming up with these elements in ways that will capture and hold an audience's attention—well, that's not so simple. Still, there are some structures and techniques that will help you create presentations that audiences will listen to and remember and that might even call them to action. This chapter provides guidelines to help you do so.

> Robin Wall Kimmerer is an engaging and accomplished speaker. Her essay that appears on p. 932 is taken from a book; still, her living voice comes through in the writing. Try reading it out loud to feel how smoothly it goes. When you write your presentation script, don't stray from your own voice.

ACROSS DISCIPLINES

You'll likely be required to give oral presentations, using slides or posters, in courses across different fields. This is because in the professional world, nearly everyone ends up using presentations to share specialized knowledge with multiple audiences: colleagues, (potential) clients, or the public. Different disciplines and professions have preferred practices. While the "what is–what should be" format discussed above may work in some rhetorical situations, in fields like engineering and the lab sciences, presentations are often team affairs. In these and, in fact, many other fields, the preferred method of presentation is the "assertion-evidence" style: a speaker makes a claim and immediately presents the evidence to support that claim, often in visual form or with the aid of a visual. The website *Assertion-Evidence Approach*, created by Michael Alley at Penn State University, offers tutorials, sample slides, and videos of presentations by students. By watching the videos, you can get ideas about how to develop an effective presentation style that works for you. Looking at models of effective presentations in your field is a good way to learn what's expected.

First, let's take a look at the script one of our students, Halle Edwards, prepared for a presentation on Japanese manga. As you'll see, she used a "what was and how it changed" structure as a foundation for her presentation.

An Annotated Presentation

The Rise of Female Heroes in Shoujo Manga
HALLE EDWARDS

Here's a question for you: [SLIDE] Where are all the strong women heroes in popular comics? In our class we've seen some talented female authors of graphic narratives, but in terms of popular comic book characters (not to mention writers and fans), the girls are still outnumbered.

> Q: Where are all the strong female heroes?

[SLIDE] So guess what? When I started looking, I found the strong female heroes in comics! The place—Japan. The time period—the 1990s. The genre—Shoujo manga. Literally "girls' comics" in Japanese, Shoujo manga is a popular

This question gets the audience thinking about the issue Edwards will address, and the corresponding slide underscores the question's importance.

Edwards establishes "what was"

HALLE EDWARDS composed this presentation for a second-year writing course that focused on graphic narratives. For this assignment, she first wrote an academic essay and then remixed it into a ten-minute oral presentation with seventeen slides. As you'll see, we've included a few of her many slides.

form of comics in Japan typically written by women for women. Prior to the 1990s, Shoujo typically featured weak heroines and plots that revolved around romance. Then, in the 1990s, Shoujo started showing strong female heroes whose first priority wasn't romance. But what did that change look like and, more importantly, why did it happen?

Today I'll explore the answers. First I'll show you an example of this phenomenon, from Naoko Takeuchi's smash-hit manga *Sailor Moon*. Then I'll explain what was happening in Japan in the 1990s and why this allowed Shoujo manga to change so drastically.

[SLIDE] Part one. *Sailor Moon* tells the story of Usagi, a clumsy and not particularly smart schoolgirl with a heart of gold. She discovers that she has a secret identity—Sailor Moon—and is destined to fight the forces of evil. [SLIDE] While *Sailor Moon* does have a love story, much of the manga is devoted to expanding on Sailor Moon's relationship with her eventual comrades—Sailors Mars, Mercury, Jupiter, and Venus. [SLIDE] The relationship of these five heroes is usually prioritized over the romance.

Wait a minute. Five female heroes? The romance is just a side plot? Girls described as soldiers who physically fight bad guys? For anyone familiar with traditional Shoujo manga, it's obvious that *Sailor Moon* pushed boundaries.

[SLIDE] This boundary-pushing can be seen in the introduction of the second female hero, Ami, or Sailor Mercury. Introduced as an aloof genius, Ami quickly reveals Takeuchi's friendly, playful side. [SLIDE] From the outset, Sailor Mercury cannot be pinned down to a stereotype—she's neither a cold nerd nor a bubbly teenager. She's very flawed and very real. Takeuchi's female heroes are layered, interesting, and compelling.

A second **EXAMPLE** *extends Edwards's point.*

Throughout the story, we see Ami develop a close friendship with Usagi, [SLIDE] ultimately ending in a battle where Ami discovers her identity as Sailor Mercury. Meanwhile, Usagi's budding romance is barely a side plot. Throughout *Sailor Moon*'s five-year run, its female heroines were always the heart of the story—not the romance. The funny thing? Despite this drastic departure from typical Shoujo norms, *Sailor Moon* was a smash hit.

[SLIDE] So why was *Sailor Moon* so warmly received, given that it defied so many norms in Shoujo manga? To understand, you need to know a bit about Japan in the early 1990s. [SLIDE] In 1989, the Asset Price Bubble broke—essentially a huge economic bubble that vastly inflated real estate prices. [SLIDE] This sent Japan's economy spiraling into a recession that lasted throughout the entire 1990s, a decade now known as Japan's "lost decade."

This question helps **TRANSITION** *to the next part of the presentation.*

[SLIDE] The recession changed many aspects of life in Japan. Before the recession, men could expect to get hired at a company out of college and work there for their whole lives. Meanwhile, women held mainly part-time jobs—think secretaries and office ladies—with few opportunities for advancement. However, once the recession hit, layoffs became rampant. Companies tanked. Men could no longer rely on having lifetime careers, and many in Japan questioned the long hours that were customary in Japan's workplaces.

> **What made the 1990s in Japan the "Era of Women"?**
>
> - Economic recession lowered job security for men
> - More women worked outside the home
> - More women voted
> - Several female candidates were elected in 1989

This slide condenses the points Edwards makes orally and helps the audience follow along.

[SLIDE] Meanwhile, in the 1989 elections, several female candidates were elected. Also, voter turnout among women was higher than ever. Because of this, the media predicted that the 1990s would be the "era of women." Women were suddenly seen as capable: they could hold real jobs outside the home, run for office, and help save Japan's stumbling economy. These new women were featured in popular soap operas known as "morning dramas" on the government-funded NHK channel.

Another strong **TRANSITION** *to move the audience along to the next point.*

[SLIDE] Given this media-propelled image of the new, strong woman, several of the major Shoujo magazines began to take note. Thus, when Toshio Irie, the newly minted editor of *Nakayoshi* magazine, learned of *Sailor Moon*, a story with five strong female heroes, he jumped at the opportunity. Not only did he publish Takeuchi's manga; he embraced a mixed-media strategy, including *Sailor Moon*–themed toys with the magazine (to encourage fans to buy their own copies and limit sharing) and selling additional *Sailor Moon* merchandise. [SLIDE] Also, when Toei Animation snapped up the rights to create an animated *Sailor Moon* series, Irie worked with the company to closely match the release of the new *Sailor Moon* chapters and episodes.

These details offer **EVIDENCE** *of Sailor Moon's popularity.*

Such a media blitz was unheard of for a work of Shoujo manga, and it paid off. By the end of 1995, *Sailor Moon* had made over 300 billion yen in profits and was expanding rapidly worldwide. Circulation figures for the magazine reached an all-time high of two million per month. The thirteen volumes that had been released by then had sold over a million copies each and been exported to twenty-three countries.

[SLIDE] The recession, and the media's message that the 1990s would be the "era of women," caused forces in the media to realize that the image

Another visual from the comic helps audiences understand the power these heroines conveyed.

of strong women could be popular—and more importantly, profitable. As a result, other manga editors were willing to publish works that featured strong female heroes—knowing that they would make money. This is one way that Shoujo sparked important change.

But why, you might be wondering, does it matter? This was just one time period in one country where comics featured strong women. Was it a phenomenon that spread to other countries? Did more girls start reading comic books and graphic narratives? And did life really change for women in Japan?

The simple answer is no. The "era of women" did not lead to significant change in the lives of women in Japan. They were still mostly relegated to part-time jobs and to most domestic responsibilities. And after the magical girl heroine trends of the 1990s, Shoujo in the 2000s became more focused on "slice of life" stories. This is not to say it went backwards—it just stopped moving forward so daringly.

However, the 1990s in Japan proved that there is a place, and an audience, for strong heroines in graphic narratives. Although there was little or no precedent for introducing strong women characters, a few key people took risks on some new stories, and they paid off. I think this is a lesson we can apply to the graphic novel market today. Just because there are still more male readers and

Edwards moves into the "what should be" portion of the presentation.

characters in US comics does not mean that the market for strong female characters does not exist. In fact, the success of authors Lynda Barry and Alison Bechdel as well as of the hit TV series Marvel's *Agent (Peggy) Carter* suggests that the time may be ripe for many more strong women in graphic narratives. And the appearance of more blockbuster superhero movies featuring female leads—think Wonder Woman, Black Widow, and Catwoman—is exciting and promising, too. So let's heed the story of Sailor Moon and her crew and read  and encourage others to buy works that feature strong women. Then when we're asked "where are all the strong women heroes in popular comics?" we can answer, "They're everywhere!"

[SLIDE] Thank you for listening. I'll be glad to take questions.

Edwards returns to the question that opened her presentation.

> **REFLECT**
>
> Take a moment to count the number of questions in this presentation and where they occur. What is the function of these questions for Edwards, and what is the intended effect on her audience?

MAKING A PRESENTATION / A Roadmap

Begin by considering your rhetorical situation

Anticipate who will be your AUDIENCE. What do they already know about your topic, and what other information might they need? What kinds of evidence are most likely to appeal to them? You can keep your audience engaged by establishing eye contact and addressing them directly from time to time. If you're addressing your audience via video, make "eye contact" by looking into the camera.

Be clear about your PURPOSE. Make sure you understand any assignment you've been given for this presentation. Is your goal to provide information? to persuade? to propose some kind of action?

Think about your STANCE. How are you presenting yourself: as an expert? an interested novice? a researcher? an advocate? Be sure that the stance you are taking is suitable for your topic and audience. Halle Edwards presents herself as a peer and classmate who has researched her topic and can thus speak with authority about it.

Consider the CONTEXT. Where will the presentation take place? What equipment will you need? Whatever it is, be sure to test it in advance—and keep in mind that technology glitches happen, so be sure to have a backup plan. How much time will you have? Who will introduce you?

Think about your GENRE. If you've been assigned a specific genre, say to report on a topic or to present a proposal, consult those chapters in this textbook for guidance. If not, see Chapter 13 for help choosing a genre.

Think about your LANGUAGE. Regardless of how many languages and dialects you use in your everyday life, you have many options to consider in making an oral presentation. Will your audience expect a certain kind of language or style? Do you want to meet those expectations? challenge them? What do you want your language choices to say about you? What risks might you be willing to take with your language? How will your choice of medium and the larger context limit or expand the language options available to you?

Will you be using any MEDIA elements that need to be DESIGNED? Would showing images or information on a slide or flip chart help your audience follow your presentation? Will they expect some kind of visual aids? Will you be referring to something that you could put on a handout? Remember that slides and flip charts need to be simple enough and large enough for your audience to read as you speak.

Prepare your presentation

Focus on one main point, and then orchestrate everything else to support it. Edwards begins with a question that signals her main point: where are all the strong women heroes in popular comics? In the rest of the presentation, she provides answers to this question in a story about the appearance of women heroes in Japanese manga, using *Sailor Moon* as her main example.

Gather EVIDENCE to support your point. Once you've decided on your main message, look for examples, statistics, stories, and other evidence that illustrate your point. Edwards uses facts and statistics to support her main point—that, despite some changes, there are still not enough strong female heroes in comic books. Even the huge success of *Sailor Moon* failed to turn the tide in any permanent way.

Develop a clear structure. You can try using the structure Nancy Duarte recommends, focusing on what is (or was) and moving to what it could or should be (or how it changed). If that doesn't suit your topic, you might start by noting what else has been said about your topic as a way of introducing what you want to say about it. Any of these structures will set up a tension that your presentation then resolves—a storytelling technique that will make your argument easier for your audience to follow.

Use TRANSITIONS and other techniques to help listeners follow your presentation. It's always helpful to provide an overview of your talk, saying something like "I have four points to make," and then use those points as signposts in the presentation. One other useful technique is repetition. Edwards repeatedly poses questions that mark turning points in her talk. Another good technique is to explain what you're saying as you go, using expressions such as "in other words." Provide a link to or printouts of your scripted presentation to distribute so your talk is accessible to everyone.

Use vivid language, images, and METAPHORS to hammer home your point clearly and memorably. The vivid language ("neither a cold nerd nor a bubbly teenager," "smash hit") and metaphors ("boundary-pushing") that Edwards uses help her audience visualize and follow her argument.

Keep it simple. Remember that your audience won't always follow along with your script, so you need to speak in a way that will be easy to understand. Notice that Edwards uses fairly simple diction throughout—and that her sentences are short and follow a straightforward subject-verb-object structure. Even her paragraphs are short, some only a sentence or two—which helped her keep to her script without having to refer to it often as she spoke.

Develop a dynamic INTRODUCTION, one that will engage your audience's interest and establish some kind of COMMON GROUND with them. You'll also want to establish your CREDIBILITY, to show that you've done your homework and can speak knowledgeably about your topic. Edwards was addressing her classmates, so she could assume common ground, but she engaged their interest by asking a provocative question: "Where are all the strong women heroes in popular comics?" The way you open will depend on your topic and rhetorical situation, but whether you start by telling a story, making a surprising claim, or summarizing what someone has said about your topic, your goal is to interest your audience in what is to come.

CONCLUDE in a way that leaves your audience thinking. Whether you conclude by reiterating your main point, by saying why your argument matters, or some other way, this is a moment when you can make sure your presentation has some kind of impact. Edwards faced a challenge: her research had turned up strong female heroes in Japanese manga, but in the end they did not change the status quo. So she concluded by pointing out that her research showed that there's "a place, and an audience, for strong heroines in graphic narratives." She then turned to her audience and challenged them to seek out such characters and to read the works they appear in.

Think about whether and where you need any visuals. Images can bring your presentation to life, illustrate important points, and engage your audience. Any slides should support or explain a point you are making and need to be clear and easy to see so that your audience can process the information in a couple of seconds. It's therefore often better to convey one idea per slide than to provide a list of bullet points on a single slide. If you need to communicate complex information, putting it in a chart or graph can make it easier for you to explain—and for your audience to understand. More detailed information or material you want your audience to read is best presented on handouts. Try to distribute the handouts at the point when your audience needs them: if you give them out before then, some in the audience may be focusing on the handouts rather than on what you say.

If you'll be using slides or other media, you'll need to design them carefully. Here are some tips for doing so:

- Begin with a slide that includes the title of your presentation, your name (and those of your team members, if this is a group presentation), and any other relevant information, such as the course or your institution if you're presenting to an outside group. If you are using a design element such as a university logo, use it only on the opening slide.
- All slides need to be clearly visible to everyone in your audience, so use at least 24-point fonts. Simple bold fonts are easiest to read; avoid italic fonts, which can be difficult to read.
- Be consistent. Use one typeface or color for headings and make them parallel in structure. Remember that some audience members may be color-blind, a fact that should influence your choice of color palette.
- Don't depend too much on presentation programs' premade templates for slides: the choices they build in—colors, typefaces, layout, and so on—may not be fitting for your topic or purpose.
- The most effective slides are simple enough for the audience to process the information they contain in a couple of seconds. Avoid walls of text that are difficult to read. As a general rule, it's better to convey one idea per slide than to provide a list of bullet points.
- Make sure that any audio or video clips embedded in your presentation work properly and relate directly to the point you are making. They should be clear and easy to see and hear.
- Acknowledge the audio or visuals you take from other sources, either on the slide in a small font or in the references at the end.
- Provide accessible descriptions of your visuals in printed copies so that those in the audience who can't see the slides clearly can still follow your argument.
- Present ideas in diagrams or charts that will be easy for the audience to understand.
- Finally, be sure to get responses to your slides just as you would to drafts of your script. Note that Edwards made her slides simple and clearly focused, each one intended to raise a question or illustrate or underscore a point.

Think about your delivery. It's one thing to compose a strong presentation, but it's another thing entirely to *deliver* one. Today, when oral forms of discourse are more dominant than at any time in memory, delivery is often the key to whether a presentation reaches and holds its audience's attention.

In writing about the role that sound and rhythm play in Black language, scholar Geneva Smitherman describes the use of what she refers to as "tonal semantics"—the way speakers use intonation and rhythm and inflection to create emphasis and command attention, employing their voices like musical instruments. Such strategies of tonal semantics include repetition, rhyme, alliteration, and narrative sequencing.

Listen to any Martin Luther King Jr. speech and you will hear tonal semantics at work. Or think of the features of spoken word poetry, and how the sound of speakers' voices does so much to carry meaning. Think, for example, of Amanda Gorman's spoken word performances. As Smitherman says, Gorman uses her "voice, body, and movement as tools to bring the story to life." As you prepare for and practice your presentation, think about how you can use tonal semantics to your advantage: When might it help to stretch out the pronunciation of a keyword, for instance? Could you use repetition like a drumbeat to build up tension or suspense? Mark up your script to note how you want to use your voice—underlining the words you want to emphasize, for example, or adding blank space to indicate a pause. Remember: you want to get—and keep—your audience's attention!

Give your presentation

Practice, practice, practice. There is no substitute for practice. None. So schedule time to rehearse and make sure you can articulate your main message loud and clear at a moment's notice. Ask friends to serve as an audience for a full rehearsal, and be sure to time your presentation so that you don't go beyond the limit. When you're done, ask your friends to tell you your main point. If they can do so, then you've made an impression! Ask them as well how you came across—as friendly? authoritative? something else? If it's not what you're aiming for, talk through how you *want* to come across and how to get there. If presenting virtually, log on to the platform in advance to test your camera, audio, and screen-sharing ability.

> ### REFLECT
>
> Think for a moment about excellent speeches or oral presentations you've heard, making a list as you go of what made them memorable. Was it use of words and phrases? tone of voice? rhythm, rhyme, repetition? Was it pacing, the way the speaker built up to a climax or slowed down to make a point more dramatic? Did visuals play a part? What else did you notice? Then write a brief "note to self" about how and why you might make use of some of these strategies.

Readings

**I**F EVERYONE'S AN AUTHOR, then we are all readers as well. All authors, in fact, learn constantly by engaging with what other authors have written. On the following pages you'll find an anthology of twenty-seven readings, arranged alphabetically by author. And on the inside back cover of the book, we've added a menu that categorizes the readings by both genres and themes. And that's not all. We post additional essays, articles, cartoons, speeches, videos, and more on everyonesanauthor.tumblr.com for you to read, analyze, reflect on—and respond to. So read on, enjoy, and see what you can learn.

Why Multilingual TV Is Good for Everyone

CÉSAR ALBARRÁN-TORRES

AS ONE OF BILLIONS of bilingual individuals in the world, it disappoints me when a film or TV show with characters of a non-English-speaking background is spoken entirely in English (Mathews). This is especially the case when the production has been distributed globally. It is even more disappointing—borderline insulting—when the lines are delivered by a native English speaker in a fake, over-the-top accent.

That said, there are some encouraging signs linguistic diversity is finally being portrayed in a more faithful and respectful manner. *Acapulco*, an *Apple TV+* comedy [with multiple seasons], is a good example of how English can be used as a common language in a show without quashing language diversity and authenticity....

The screen industry's practice of using fake accents and English-only dialogue is longstanding. Classic Hollywood actors such as Katherine Hepburn, Charlton Heston and Marlon Brando have all played Asian or

---

CÉSAR ALBARRÁN-TORRES is a Mexican Australian scholar and film critic who teaches courses in media and communication at the Swinburne University of Technology in Melbourne, Australia. His research has been published for both academic and general audiences. This May 2024 essay was published in the *Conversation*. *Note:* MLA-style works-cited information has been provided in place of the article's original hyperlinks.

Latino characters and spoken English in fake accents. Rather than ditching the accent altogether—such as in Shakespearean adaptations where actors are dressed as Romans but still sound British—we've seen several examples where A-listers put on fake accents in a setting where English isn't the everyday language.

Take the recent Disney+ hit *Shōgun*. While the Japanese characters speak Japanese among themselves (points for that), the Portuguese and Spanish settlers communicate in English, and do so in heavily imposed accents. This half-baked attempt at linguistic diversity might be because *Shōgun* is an American show. But as *Screen Rant* features editor Marcelo Leite points out: "a fully accurate portrayal of the story would be entirely in Portuguese and Japanese, and all of *Shōgun* would have to include subtitles." Another example comes from Ridley Scott's 2021 film *House of Gucci*, which featured Lady Gaga, Adam Driver and Jared Leto, among others. The film takes place in Italy with characters who would normally speak Italian. Yet the film is spoken mostly in English. Audience reactions to the cast's heavy, cartoon-like "Italian" accents were quite negative (Lampen).

Why does Hollywood tend to be monolingual? English-only productions are made under the premise Hollywood produces content mainly for American audiences, and that these audiences are monolingual. As of recently, however, two factors are changing how movies and TV shows are conceptualised and brought to life. The first is that the vast linguistic diversity within the United States is increasingly being represented by directors and showrunners who are bilingual themselves (Dietrich and Hernandez). The second is the global distribution of content through streaming services (Brennan). It means audiences across the globe are getting used to watching content with subtitles in languages other than English, and other than their own. As streaming inches us towards a global TV culture, cultural and linguistic representation is becoming an important topic. And this awareness is driving multilingual productions, such as *Acapulco*, in English-speaking countries.

Some of these productions even explore issues of language and culture loss in diverse communities. For instance, *Vida* and *Gentefied* both focus on the impacts of gentrification in Los Angeles—one of which is the loss of bicultural and bilingual character in Mexican-American enclaves. Both shows, created by Latinx showrunners, use English when it is logical to do so, and Spanish (or Spanglish) when non-white characters converse among themselves. Another mainstream show, ABC's *Jane the Virgin*, has a character (Jane's *abuela*, Alba) who speaks almost entirely in Spanish.

The linguistic tide is turning. Recent television shows have demonstrated multilingual scripts can be both successful and dignified. *Acapulco*, which has been compared to *Ted Lasso*, sets a precedent for what inclusivity can look and sound like. This light-hearted comedy counters the linguistic complacency that has dominated TV cultures for so long, whereby English is used as a standardising tool that is detrimental to diversity. *Acapulco* is shot in Mexico with Latino talent, but also includes white English-speaking actors and a cross-national star, Eugenio Derbez. It is spoken in Spanish, English and Spanglish in a dignified and organic way. The setting is an all-inclusive resort in the Mexican Pacific. Employees are forced to speak in English among themselves while on the premises, but speak in Spanish outside of the hotel. This in itself is a critique of labour practices in the Global South's hospitality industry.

Normalising language diversity onscreen forces creators to seek more multicultural talent behind and in front of the camera, particularly when it is these people's communities being portrayed. Beyond this, audiences will be empowered by seeing their own languages represented, or will otherwise benefit from being exposed to new languages they haven't heard before. Indeed, research has found watching shows and films in foreign languages can help viewers learn them (Cohen). The growth in multilingual scripts will also inevitably lead to the normalisation of subtitles, which will help more broadly in making film and TV accessible for all. Shows like *Acapulco* demonstrate the paradigm shift that's taking place across Hollywood and other entertainment industries. And with streaming, it's easier than ever for this content to go global.

> As Albarrán-Torres points out, using more than one language presents challenges but may be worth the effort. Check out Ch. 35 for advice on mixing languages and dialects in writing.

Works Cited

Brennan, Louis. "How Netflix Expanded to 190 Countries in 7 Years." *Harvard Business Review*, 12 Oct. 2018, hbr.org/2018/10/how-netflix-expanded-to-190-countries-in-7-years.

Cohen, Elizabeth. "The Television Trick to Learning a New Language." *CNN*, 19 Mar. 2018, edition.cnn.com/2018/03/19/health/learn-new-language-telenovela-trick/.

Dietrich, Sandy, and Erik Hernandez. "Nearly 68 Million People Spoke a Language Other than English at Home in 2019." *United States Census Bureau*, 6 Dec. 2022, www.census.gov/library/stories/2022/12/languages-we-speak-in-united-states.html.

Lampen, Claire. "It's Time to Talk about the Accents in *House of Gucci*." *The Cut*, 19 Nov. 2021, www.thecut.com/2021/11/italian-linguists-unpack-lady-gagas-house-of-gucci-accent.html.

Leite, Marcelo, and Tom Russell. "*Shogun's* Language Confusion: Why English Is Called Portuguese." *Screen Rant*, 24 Sept. 2024, screenrant.com/shogun-english-portuguese-language-confusion-explained.

Mathews, Jay. "Half of the World Is Bilingual. What's Our Problem?" *The Washington Post*, 25 Apr. 2019, www.washingtonpost.com/local/education/half-the-world-is-bilingual-whats-our-problem/2019/04/24/1c2b0cc2-6625-11e9-a1b6-b29b90efa879_story.html.

Thinking about the Text

1. César Albarrán-Torres argues that the increase in multilingual TV shows is beneficial for everyone, including monolingual English speakers. What reasons does he give to support his position? **SUMMARIZE** them. Do you agree with his main argument? Explain your reasoning.

2. In his opening sentence, Albarrán-Torres identifies himself as bilingual, in fact, one of the "billions of bilingual individuals in the world" (1). How does opening with this fact impact the author's **AUTHORITY** to write on this subject? Would the essay have been equally effective without that information? Why or why not?

3. What is Albarrán-Torres's objection to "fake accents"? How well does he explain that objection? Do you agree with his stance? Why or why not?

4. Albarrán-Torres includes the TV series *Acapulco* as an extended **EXAMPLE**, and he mentions several other series that address bilingualism and biculturalism. How well does Albarrán-Torres use *Acapulco* to support his argument? Are the details included sufficient, or would you have wanted to know more (or less)? Explain your response.

5. The development of more multilingual TV that Albarrán-Torres is arguing for depends almost entirely on viewers' acceptance of subtitles. Think about your own use or avoidance of subtitles and your attitude toward them. How often do you use them? Do you ever avoid programs that would require you to use them? Do you ever use subtitles for programs even if you speak the language most of the characters speak? Reflect on your habits and experiences related to subtitles, then write an essay in response to Albarrán-Torres's **ARGUMENT** that more multilingual TV "will lead to the normalisation of subtitles" and help make "film and TV accessible for all" (8). Use your personal reflections and experiences as one form of evidence.

Carbon Offsets (Taylor's Version)
KATE ARONOFF

The response of Taylor Swift's spokesperson to [2023] reports that the pop star had generated 128 tons of carbon dioxide from private jet travel in just three months was simple: Before the start of her *Eras* tour in March 2023, "Taylor purchased more than double the carbon credits needed to offset all tour travel" (Kay and Rains).

This was a striking story for a few reasons. First, 128 tons of carbon dioxide is roughly equivalent to the average annual emissions of 28 gas-powered cars or 16 homes, per an Environmental Protection Agency emissions equivalency calculator ("Greenhouse Gas Equivalencies Calculator"). Second, the source for these figures has since disappeared from the internet: The emissions numbers were reportedly calculated by an *Instagram* page called "Taylor Swift's Jets," tracking journeys by her Desault Falcon 7x and Dessault Falcon 900. Shortly after major news outlets picked up the numbers, the page disappeared from the social media site.

KATE ARONOFF writes about climate and energy for the *New Republic*, a news and culture magazine. In her 2021 book, *Overheated*, Aronoff reports on "how capitalism broke the planet" and offers a vision for dealing with global warming moving forward. This essay about climate change and pop stars was published in January 2024. *Note:* MLA-style works-cited information has been provided in place of the article's original hyperlinks.

Taylor Swift performing on her *Eras* tour.

But perhaps the most interesting aspect, from a climate perspective, is the pop star's purchase of offsets to deflect criticism. In brief, carbon offset vendors claim to allow polluters to counteract emissions they generate by purchasing credits that correspond to emissions reductions elsewhere. Often, that means paying some entity—like a nonprofit or corporation—to preserve tracts of forests that would otherwise be cut down. Offsets are also sold by companies like Climeworks, which captures carbon dioxide from the atmosphere through a process known as Direct Air Capture and stores it in geological formations. So which carbon offsets is Taylor Swift buying?

Universal, Swift's record label, did not respond to an inquiry as to where Swift had purchased the offsets. High-quality offsets are extraordinarily hard to come by, though. Over the last several years, the industry has been mired in controversy over the validity of its claims: Are all of the lands companies claim to protect, for instance, actually in danger of being razed? Trees planted are also liable to die or be cut down at some point: While carbon generated by a private jet will remain in the atmosphere indefinitely, there's virtually no way for credit vendors to ensure trees will stay standing for time immemorial.

"The entire market is structured around a fundamental falsehood: that a ton of carbon we get from burning fossil fuels is identical to a ton of carbon stored in forests. That is 100 percent false," Danny Cullenward, a senior fellow at the University of Pennsylvania's Kleinman Center for Energy Policy, whose research focuses on carbon offsets and storage, told me in September. "If you store carbon for less time than it takes to stabilize temperatures, that storage does not have any climate benefit."

One recent study, still undergoing peer review as of last September, estimated that just 12 percent of offset projects "constitute real emissions reductions." Another investigation published last fall by *The Guardian* and the nonprofit watchdog Corporate Accountability concluded that 78 percent of the top 50 carbon-offsetting projects are "likely junk" (Lakhani). . . .

Swift's jets have been in the news [before]. A 2022 report from British "sustainability marketing firm" Yard named her the biggest celebrity polluter of the year. The firm found that Swift's jet had spent the equivalent of 16 days in the air during the first six months of that year (Yard Team). A spokesperson for the *Midnights* singer said at the time that Swift frequently loaned out her planes to be used by others (Blistein).

Many of the credits purchased by corporations—and potentially Swift—are validated by third parties meant to ensure those credits are legit. Those firms have also come under heavy fire. One 2023 exposé revealed that at least 90 percent of credits approved by one of the largest third-party verifiers, claiming offset projects in rainforests, were worthless "phantom credits" that didn't correspond to any reductions (Greenfield). (The subject of the investigation, a nongovernmental organization called Verra, has disputed the allegations.)

There are very few requirements for companies or individuals that purchase offsets to publicly disclose where they come from (Frank et al.). California passed a law [in 2023], Assembly Bill 1305, requiring "entities" that do business in the state and that buy or sell carbon credits, to make that information available (California State Legislature). . . . Without additional information from Swift's team, there's little way of knowing whether Swift personally, Universal, or some other legal entity purchased the offsets, and, accordingly, whether whatever entity bought them would be subject to the new law. . . .

"If Swift or her companies have publicly claimed that the tour was carbon neutral or that it produced less climate impact than its actual

---

Aronoff quotes, paraphrases, and summarizes her sources. How did she decide where to use each technique? How will you make those decisions in your writing? See pp. 555–56 for some advice that will help you choose.

emissions because of offset credit use, then arguably they have made a claim that is covered under AB 1305," Cullenward, who advocated for the bill's passage, told me over text.

There's still a *blank space* to be filled in as to whether Taylor Swift's carbon offsets are legit, but she does seem eager to *shake off* her reputation as a climate villain. Swift might not need to come *clean* in the end. Carbon offset buyers and sellers in the Golden State, however, know *all too well* that they'll need to soon enough.*

Works Cited

Blistein, Jon. "Kylie's 17-Minute Flight Has Nothing on the 170 Trips Taylor Swift's Private Jets Took This Year." *Rolling Stone*, 5 Aug. 2022, www.rollingstone.com/music/music-news/kylies-17-minute-flight-has-nothing-on-the-170-trips-taylor-swifts-private-jets-took-this-year-1390083/.

California State Legislature. Assembly Bill 1305, session year 2023–2024. *California Legislative Information*, 7 Oct. 2023, leginfo.legislature.ca.gov.

Cullenward, Danny. Interview with the author, Sept. 2023.

Cullenward, Danny. Text message to the author. Sept. 2023.

Frank, Sadie, et al. "Why Carbon Offset Disclosure Matters." *CarbonPlan*, 8 Feb. 2022, carbonplan.org/research/offset-disclosure-needs.

Greenfield, Patrick. "Revealed: More than 90% of Rainforest Carbon Offsets by Biggest Certifier Are Worthless, Analysis Shows." *The Guardian*, 18 Jan. 2023, www.theguardian.com/environment/2023/jan/18/revealed-forest-carbon-offsets-biggest-provider-worthless-verra-aoe.

"Greenhouse Gas Equivalencies Calculator." *United States Environmental Protection Agency*, Nov. 2024, www.epa.gov/energy/greenhouse-gas-equivalencies-calculator#results.

Kay, Grace, and Taylor Rains. "Taylor Swift's Private Jets Have Spent over 166 hours Crisscrossing the US during the Singer's Colossal Eras Tour." *Business Insider*, 30 Aug. 2023, www.businessinsider.com/taylor-swift-spent-160-hours-using-private-jet-eras-tour-2023-8.

---

*See what the author did there? The words in italics are the titles of Swift's songs. [Editor's note].

Lakhani, Nina. "Revealed: Top Carbon Offset Projects May Not Cut Planet-Heating Emissions." *The Guardian*, 19 Sept. 2023, amp.theguardian.com/environment/2023/sep/19/do-carbon-credit-reduce-emissions-greenhouse-gases.

Yard Team. "Just Plane Wrong: Celebs with the Worst Private Jet CO_2 Emissions." *WeAreYard*, 29 Jul. 2022, weareyard.com/insights/worst-celebrity-private-jet-co2-emission-offenders.

Thinking about the Text

1. Kate Aronoff places Taylor Swift front and center in this brief report. Is this essay really about Swift and her efforts to be ecologically conscientious, or is it primarily an essay about carbon offsets that uses Swift's star power to grab attention? Or is it something else entirely? In your own words, give a one-sentence summary of the author's main **PURPOSE** for writing this essay.

2. Taylor Swift isn't the only public figure who travels by private jet, although Aronoff presents Swift as the main **EXAMPLE** to illustrate her claims. How would including additional examples have made Aronoff's essay stronger? Give one or two other public figures you would recommend that Aronoff add to this essay and explain your reasoning.

3. Aronoff takes a clear stance on carbon offsets: she is skeptical, citing studies and people that condemn offsets as not doing much good. What kinds of sources does she cite? Do those sources seem reliable and authoritative to you? Why or why not? Look for places where she addresses **COUNTERARGUMENTS**. Do you think she should have included more sources representing different perspectives? Why or why not?

4. Aronoff gives a brief explanation of carbon offsets—what they are and claim to do, how they work, and who makes and sells them. Is this background information adequate for you? What questions do you still have about the topic? Who are the *New Republic*'s target readers? (Look up the publication to find out.) Why do you think Aronoff chose the background information that she did for this **AUDIENCE**? What might she do differently if she were writing for a Taylor Swift fan magazine?

5. Taylor Swift's concerts couldn't be more popular; her shows sell out everywhere she goes. She wants to perform, and her fans want to attend. It's also true, as Aronoff reports, that transporting all that's necessary for Swift's shows is hugely expensive—in terms of both money and environmental consequences. What do you think a conscientious artist like Swift should do? Should she abandon live shows? reduce the number of shows or change them somehow? keep buying carbon offsets? What advice would you give her? Write Swift a letter that addresses these questions and **PROPOSES** your own well-considered, evidence-based recommendations.

The Sanctuary of School

LYNDA BARRY

I WAS 7 YEARS OLD the first time I snuck out of the house in the dark. It was winter and my parents had been fighting all night. They were short on money and long on relatives who kept "temporarily" moving into our house because they had nowhere else to go.

My brother and I were used to giving up our bedroom. We slept on the couch, something we actually liked because it put us that much closer to the light of our lives, our television.

At night when everyone was asleep, we lay on our pillows watching it with the sound off. We watched Steve Allen's mouth moving. We watched Johnny Carson's mouth moving. We watched movies filled with gangsters shooting machine guns into packed rooms, dying soldiers hurling a last grenade and beautiful women crying at windows. Then the sign-off finally came and we tried to sleep.

LYNDA BARRY is an artist, cartoonist, and teacher, known for her comic strip *Ernie Pook's Comeek* as well as for graphic works on the relationship between creativity and drawing like *What It Is* (2008). She was inducted into the Eisner Hall of Fame in 2016 and was awarded a MacArthur Fellowship in 2019. Barry is currently a professor of interdisciplinary creativity at the University of Wisconsin. The essay here was originally published in the *New York Times* in 1992, when public schools were experiencing severe cutbacks.

The morning I snuck out, I woke up filled with a panic about needing to get to school. The sun wasn't quite up yet but my anxiety was so fierce that I just got dressed, walked quietly across the kitchen and let myself out the back door.

It was quiet outside. Stars were still out. Nothing moved and no one was in the street. It was as if someone had turned the sound off on the world.

I walked the alley, breaking thin ice over the puddles with my shoes. I didn't know why I was walking to school in the dark. I didn't think about it. All I knew was a feeling of panic, like the panic that strikes kids when they realize they are lost.

That feeling eased the moment I turned the corner and saw the dark outline of my school at the top of the hill. My school was made up of about 15 nondescript portable classrooms set down on a fenced concrete lot in a rundown Seattle neighborhood, but it had the most beautiful view of the Cascade Mountains. You could see them from anywhere on the playfield and you could see them from the windows of my classroom—Room 2.

I walked over to the monkey bars and hooked my arms around the cold metal. I stood for a long time just looking across Rainier Valley. The sky was beginning to whiten and I could hear a few birds.

In a perfect world my absence at home would not have gone unnoticed. I would have had two parents in a panic to locate me, instead of two parents in a panic to locate an answer to the hard question of survival during a deep financial and emotional crisis.

But in an overcrowded and unhappy home, it's incredibly easy for any child to slip away. The high levels of frustration, depression and anger in my house made my brother and me invisible. We were children with the sound turned off. And for us, as for the steadily increasing number of neglected children in this country, the only place where we could count on being noticed was at school.

"Hey there, young lady. Did you forget to go home last night?" It was Mr. Gunderson, our janitor, whom we all loved. He was nice and he was funny and he was old with white hair, thick glasses and an unbelievable number of keys. I could hear them jingling as he walked across the playfield. I felt incredibly happy to see him.

He let me push his wheeled garbage can between the different portables as he unlocked each room. He let me turn on the lights and raise the

window shades and I saw my school slowly come to life. I saw Mrs. Holman, our school secretary, walk into the office without her orange lipstick on yet. She waved.

I saw the fifth-grade teacher, Mr. Cunningham, walking under the breezeway eating a hard roll. He waved.

And I saw my teacher, Mrs. Claire LeSane, walking toward us in a red coat and calling my name in a very happy and surprised way, and suddenly my throat got tight and my eyes stung and I ran toward her crying. It was something that surprised us both.

It's only thinking about it now, 28 years later, that I realize I was crying from relief. I was with my teacher, and in a while I was going to sit at my desk, with my crayons and pencils and books and classmates all around me, and for the next six hours I was going to enjoy a thoroughly secure, warm and stable world. It was a world I absolutely relied on. Without it, I don't know where I would have gone that morning.

Mrs. LeSane asked me what was wrong and when I said "Nothing," she seemingly left it at that. But she asked me if I would carry her purse for her, an honor above all honors, and she asked if I wanted to come into Room 2 early and paint.

She believed in the natural healing power of painting and drawing for troubled children. In the back of her room there was always a drawing table and an easel with plenty of supplies, and sometimes during the day she would come up to you for what seemed like no good reason and quietly ask if you wanted to go to the back table and "make some pictures for Mrs. LeSane." We all had a chance at it—to sit apart from the class for a while to paint, draw and silently work out impossible problems on 11 × 17 sheets of newsprint.

Drawing came to mean everything to me. At the back table in Room 2, I learned to build myself a life preserver that I could carry into my home.

We all know that a good education system saves lives, but the people of this country are still told that cutting the budget for public schools is necessary, that poor salaries for teachers are all we can manage and that art, music and all creative activities must be the first to go when times are lean.

Before- and after-school programs are cut and we are told that public schools are not made for baby-sitting children. If parents are neglectful temporarily or permanently, for whatever reason, it's certainly sad, but their unlucky children must fend for themselves. Or slip through the cracks. Or wander in a dark night alone.

We are told in a thousand ways that not only are public schools not important, but that the children who attend them, the children who need them most, are not important either. We leave them to learn from the blind eye of a television, or to the mercy of "a thousand points of light"* that can be as far away as stars.

I was lucky. I had Mrs. LeSane. I had Mr. Gunderson. I had an abundance of art supplies. And I had a particular brand of neglect in my home that allowed me to slip away and get to them. But what about the rest of the kids who weren't as lucky? What happened to them?

By the time the bell rang that morning I had finished my drawing and Mrs. LeSane pinned it up on the special bulletin board she reserved for drawings from the back table. It was the same picture I always drew—a sun in the corner of a blue sky over a nice house with flowers all around it.

Mrs. LeSane asked us to please stand, face the flag, place our right hands over our hearts and say the Pledge of Allegiance. Children across the country do it faithfully. I wonder now when the country will face its children and say a pledge right back.

> Describing how one child was saved by art classes helps make a case for funding school programs. See Ch. 22 for more argument strategies.

---

* *"A thousand points of light"*: A phrase used by President George H. W. Bush to refer to the many private, nonprofit community organizations that he hoped would step in to help people in need when government-sponsored social programs were cut. [Editor's note]

Thinking about the Text

1. Lynda Barry begins her **NARRATIVE** by revealing some painful personal information, which leads to a damning criticism of the state of education in the United States. Does her personal anecdote enhance her political argument? damage it? How well do these two elements of her essay complement each other? Explain your answer, citing evidence from the text.

2. It could be argued that the art opportunities in Barry's school were more beneficial to her than to other students because she was always artistically inclined and even went on to become a professional artist—or even that there is no reason to have art instruction in elementary schools at all because so few children actually become artists. How would you respond to that argument? Agree or disagree, presenting **EVIDENCE** from your own school experiences.

3. Barry uses the expression "the sound off" or "the sound turned off" three times in the essay (3, 5, 10). In which instances is it meant literally and in which figuratively? How does the repetition of this language help make the point of her narrative?

4. Barry concludes her essay with a call for the United States and its education system to make a "pledge" to children (24). Although her proposals are not spelled out, what can you infer about what Barry is asking the schools to do? Provide **EXAMPLES** from the text that indicate what she thinks is important.

5. Did you ever have a teacher who, in the course of simply doing their job, helped you get through a hard time or a tremendous struggle? Write a **NARRATIVE** about an experience you had with a memorable teacher, and relate your experience in some way to your adult life.

AI Is Like Cake

CHRISTOPHER BASGIER

LIKE MILLIONS OF VIEWERS around the world, my wife and I are fans of *The Great British Baking Show*. We came to it later than many: during the [COVID-19] pandemic, we marveled at the ingenuity of their designs, we salivated (and occasionally gagged) over their unique flavor combinations, and we found comfort in the contestants' friendships. We came to appreciate the delicate combination of art and science needed to bake puff pastry, bread, choux buns, pie, tortes, tarts, and, above all, *cake*.

I thought of the Bake-Off immediately when I encountered the metaphor *AI as cake* in a [2024] article by Anuj Gupta, Atef Yasser, Anna Mills, and Maha Bali. The authors argue that the metaphors we use to describe AI can serve as productive means for fostering critical AI literacy. They attribute *AI as cake* to a [post] by Bali:

> If we used cake as a metaphor for AI, I'm asking educators is: 1. When/where would it be acceptable for students to take shortcuts

---

CHRISTOPHER BASGIER leads the Miller Writing Center at Auburn University, where he works with faculty across fields to support student writers. He's also a scholar who researches and writes about writing across the curriculum and critical artificial intelligence literacy. This January 2024 essay is from Basgier's *Substack* newsletter, *Prose and Processors*. *Note:* MLA-style works-cited information has been provided in place of the article's original hyperlinks.

such as buying from a bakery, baking from a box, or buying a Twinkie instead of baking from scratch? 2. How would you encourage home made? #highered

I'm more of a cook, so baking from a box is generally my forte, whereas my wife will periodically challenge herself to a recipe from the Bake-Off.

For me, box baking gets the job done. Each year, my daughters and I can whip up a strawberry cake with cream cheese icing for my wife's birthday. It's always moist and delicious. But to Bali's point, box baking has taught me very little about baking in itself. I suppose I could muddle through some combination of egg, flour, sugar, a fat, and baking powder to produce something close to edible, but I don't yet have enough experience to know how to manipulate the proportions of those ingredients to produce something original. Betty Crocker it is. My wife, on the other hand, has baked a range of treats, from cookies to cherry pie to baklava. Some recipes she can produce by heart. New ones she has a more intuitive sense of how to follow.

> Basgier mentions some of the useful functions of AI for writers, but he doesn't dig into the details. We did a deep dive ourselves; see what we learned about AI and writing on pp. 143–48.

We can apply the metaphor of *AI as cake* in this relatively binary way: writing with AI is like baking from the box, and writing without it is like baking from scratch. But I don't think this was Bali's point. For example, when my wife decided to bake baklava, she bought phyllo dough from the store, rather than making the notoriously difficult pastry completely from scratch. Similarly, we might use AI for some aspects of the writing process so we can spend more mental time and energy on others. For my part, I don't let generative AI write prose for me because I prefer to bake my words from scratch, but I have sometimes found it to be a useful sounding board, providing some basic ingredients (keywords, topical points, the occasional outline) that I mix and elaborate in my own way.

Allow me to take up an adjacent metaphor for a moment. The way I use generative AI is akin to [writing scholar] Peter Elbow's idea of the writing process as cooking. In his classic *Writing without Teachers*, Elbow explains that writing-as-cooking "consists of the process of one piece of material (or one process) being transformed by interacting with another: one piece of material being seen through the lens of another, being dragged through the guts of another, being reoriented and reorganized in terms of the other, being mapped onto the other" (49).

We can do this with AI-generated text just as we can with a quote from Dostoevsky or the political economy of Ghana. All it takes is treating

AI-generated text as raw ingredients (flour, eggs, etc.) and transforming them through complex interactive processes.

We can also adapt Elbow's cooking metaphor as a way of understanding generative AI, the technology, as cake. The raw ingredients of training data are mixed together algorithmically, interacting with novel prompts, to produce an output. It's an imperfect metaphor—there is a lot more classification and selection in AI's intermediate steps—but the output is the same: in most cases, a Twinkie.

Perhaps, then, it would be more useful to say that generative AI is what Socrates called "cookery" in Plato's *Gorgias*. Socrates distinguishes cookery from true arts, such as medicine or justice, a distinction he ultimately uses to disparage rhetoric. I won't defend rhetoric here. Instead, I want to suggest that his accusations against rhetoric-as-cookery—that it is "routine," "the habit of a bold and ready wit, which knows how to manage mankind," "an experience in producing a sort of delight and gratification"—might be said of *ChatGPT*. It is built on an algorithmic routine. It has a bold and ready wit, in that it often makes assertions and holds to them, even when they are blatantly false. It can produce delight and gratification, especially when we marvel uncritically at its speed and fluency.

AI as cake thus invites us to think critically, both about how generative AI works, and about how we are using it. I also love this metaphor because it is not inherently anthropomorphic. I don't know about you, but I am tired of seeing robotic hands, robotic faces, and robotic bodies on every single post about AI. I think these images, metaphorical in their own right, perpetuate an illusion of AI sentience and imply the inevitability of AI ubiquity, even takeover. *AI as cake* offers an alternative vision: human-made, but not human; delicious, but unhealthy if consumed to excess.

Works Cited

Bali, Maha. Text post with photo of cake as a metaphor for AI, *X,* 24 Apr. 2023, x.com/Bali_Maha/status/1650582997614092288.

Elbow, Peter. *Writing without Teachers*. Oxford UP, 1973.

Gupta, Anuj, et al. "Assistant, Parrot, or Colonizing Loudspeaker? *ChatGPT* Metaphors for Developing Critical AI Literacies." *Open Praxis* 16.1 (2024): 37–53. https://doi.org/10.55982/openpraxis.16.1.631.

Plato. *Gorgias*. Translated by Benjamin Jowett, Dover Publications, 2004.

Thinking about the Text

1. Christopher Basgier focuses largely on analyzing a single metaphor, but what **STANCE** does he take on generative AI? Summarize his main argument. Is his main point about AI itself or about the metaphors we use for understanding AI? Point to passages that support your conclusion.

2. Though he doesn't give a concrete definition, Basgier mentions the value of "fostering critical AI literacy" (2). Based on everything else he says about AI, what do you think "critical AI literacy" means? Should he have included more background information on this key term? Why or why not?

3. Robotic faces, hands, and bodies are commonly used **METAPHORS** when discussing AI, according to Basgier, and he's tired of seeing them. Why does he dislike robotic imagery and metaphors around AI? Summarize his stance in your own words. Do you agree with the objections he raises? Why or why not?

4. In order to establish his own position, Basgier includes the work of several other authors and enters an ongoing conversation with them. How well does he represent the ideas of others? Are his paraphrases clear enough to give you a sense of what he is responding to and why? Do you think he represents their ideas fairly? You might use the works-cited page to look up a few of the people he cites. Explain your response and point to examples that support your conclusion.

5. Your instructors and your school likely have policies and guidelines for governing the use of AI. Look up or reread your instructor's expectations around AI for this writing course, or analyze your school's broader AI policy. Do you support what the policy is trying to do and how they're going about it? Do you think that the rules should be changed? Write a letter to your instructor or school administrator arguing your position.

Fun Home

ALISON BECHDEL

ALISON BECHDEL is a cartoonist, writer, and 2014 recipient of a MacArthur Fellowship. Her serialized comic strip, *Dykes to Watch Out For*, ran in dozens of periodicals from 1983 to 2008. In 2006, she published *Fun Home: A Family Tragicomic*, a graphic memoir that centers on her relationship with her father and addresses matters of gender, sexual orientation, and family; the book became a Broadway musical that won a Tony award in 2015. The title refers to the family business, a funeral home. Another graphic autobiography *The Secret to Superhuman Strength* was published in 2021.

In a 2012 interview in the *New Yorker*, Bechdel describes the writing/drawing process that results in her characteristic panels so rich with graphic and narrative detail. First, she creates a grid of panels that one walks through, like rooms in a house. "The whole thing about a graphic book," says Bechdel, "is that it's a 3-D object."

You may have heard of the Bechdel Test. To pass, a movie, TV show, or book has to have at least two characters who: 1) are women, 2) talk to each other, and 3) talk about something other than a man. (Go to bechdeltest.com to learn more.)

This selection is from *Fun Home* and contains some terms that may be unfamiliar. Daedalus and Icarus were a father-son duo in Greek mythology. While the two were imprisoned in a tower, master builder Daedalus built wings from feathers and wax so that they could escape by flying out. He warned Icarus not to fly too high because the sun would melt the wax, but the warning was unheeded, and Icarus fell into the sea and drowned. "Butch" and "nelly" are colloquial terms that emerged in twentieth-century lesbian and gay cultures. The terms refer to gender performance or traits, with "butch" roughly corresponding to masculine and "nelly" to feminine.

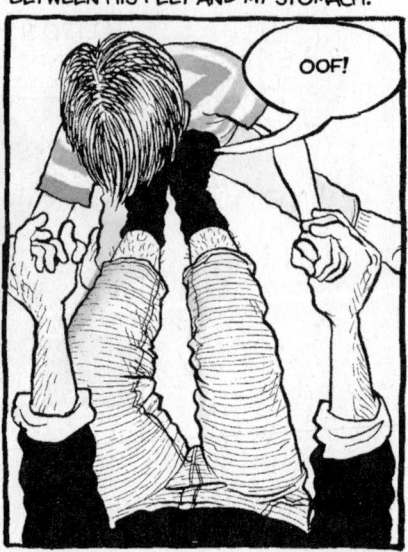

It's not only Bechdel's detailed drawings that bring her story to life; the descriptive details also add to the rich texture of her narrative. Learn more about adding vivid detail on pp. 223–25.

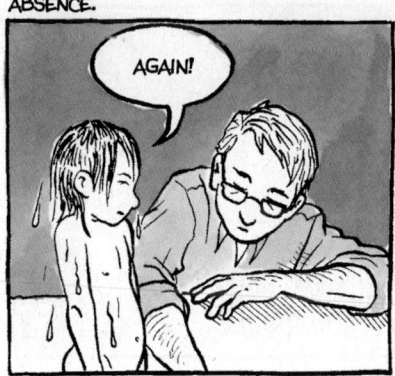

Thinking about the Text

1. Alison Bechdel **DESCRIBES** a relationship with her father that is full of both love and resentment. How does she reconcile those seeming contradictions? How successful is she at conveying her balance between tenderness and bitterness? Why do you think so? Point to specific passages that support your conclusion.

2. Bechdel chooses two very ordinary activities with her father—playing airplane and being bathed—to represent something larger about her childhood and her life in general. Think of a moment in your own childhood that you might use to represent something larger about yourself. What would it be?

3. In addition to the drawings themselves, Bechdel employs narration boxes and speech balloons to help tell her story. How does she use those two devices to navigate between events happening in her childhood moments and reflections from her adult perspective? Select one panel or group of panels and describe how each device works in your selection.

4. Although Bechdel's family has other members, *Fun Home* focuses on the relationship between Alison and her father. We know from her reflections what her attitude is toward her father. What is Bechdel's attitude toward her child self? How does she reveal it? Point to specific passages that support your reasoning.

5. Write a short **NARRATIVE** (in graphic form, if you wish) of your childhood relationship with a parent or other adult in your life. Choose one or two key activities or events that can represent the relationship as a whole. Present details that illustrate the original moments and use your adult perspective to reflect and provide coherence. (You may want to respond to question #2 first to help you get started.)

I Quit Social Media in College. This Is How My Life Changed.

JENNA BLOOM

I'M A 19-YEAR-OLD college student, and I've known for a while that I am unable to be a moderate social media user. I would constantly keep up with the lives of my peers, which pressured me to post all the time, proving that I had a social life, too. Sometimes consuming and posting made me feel good—elated, even—and that was the problem. So, just like any toxic relationship, it was time for a breakup.

I'm joining a growing group of people in quitting these kinds of apps (Hunter). I suspect more might follow since the U.S. surgeon general recently issued an advisory explaining there isn't enough evidence to say whether social media is "sufficiently safe" for teenagers (U.S. Department of Health and Human Services). "It is no longer possible to ignore social media's potential contribution to the pain that millions of children and families are experiencing," wrote Vivek H. Murthy, referencing the ongoing mental health crisis in young people.

I've gotten mixed reactions to quitting; some people were excited for me, and others were doubtful or quick to assume it's some sort of brag. It's not.

JENNA BLOOM is a writer and videographer. When this essay was published by the *Washington Post* in May 2023, Bloom was a student studying journalism at the University of Maryland. *Note:* MLA-style works-cited information has been provided in place of the article's original hyperlinks.

For me, the bad parts of social media were outweighing the good, by a lot. Last year, my best friend Bridgette and I started journaling, and it led me to reevaluate how I used social media—*why share my every thought online when I can write them down instead?* Then, in the beginning of January, I watched a *YouTube* video titled "I replaced Social Media with Micro-Journalling for 1 Year." It inspired me to try a year off social media, as it felt like the algorithm sent it my way for a reason. I immediately texted Bridgette notifying her of this decision.

Her response? "Man I wanna do this too," to which I responded "DO IT DO IT." Thus began the official challenge.

We knew to have a chance at success, we needed parameters: *Instagram* and *Snapchat*—the apps that stole hours of our waking lives—were not to be on our phones from Jan. 3, 2023, until 2024. I was also not going to be using *TikTok*, but I had already deleted it about six months before starting the break, after realizing how much of a distraction it had become in my life. There were some exceptions to this challenge, but no re-downloading or active use, and absolutely no posting. We also made a bet that the first person to lose owed the other person a sushi dinner, which was excellent motivation because we are both way too stubborn to pay.

I used social media constantly in high school, but especially during the COVID-19 pandemic. Being stuck at home was pretty awful for my mental health, as I'm sure any member of Gen Z can attest. But I found communities on these apps that fueled my need for conversation. Social media became my form of expression. I tried to authentically capture my life on my profiles, and my identity was broadcast online for hundreds (sometimes thousands) of people to see.

Things quickly went downhill when likes and comments became my validation. I developed an obsession with the way I was perceived online and spent entire days, weeks, months, on my phone. Despite being in constant communication with people, I had never been more alone. My screen time was at least eight hours per day, a terrifying number.

My mental health improved when I came to college, but here's the thing: the nature of these apps hasn't. *Instagram*, *Snapchat* and *TikTok* are designed to be addictive. Studies have shown that likes and comments create rushes of dopamine that give users a "high," which is especially dangerous for teenagers because it can rewire our brains to constantly seek immediate gratification (Miller). The apps encourage us to compare ourselves to others, a losing game every time.

5

> Bloom inserts this one bit of dialogue to her first-person narrative, and it adds a well-placed touch of flavor to the story. Want to try it in your own essay? Find some tips on p. 234.

When I started the challenge, it was difficult at first to resist the muscle memory of opening the apps. So, every time I wanted to open one, I would either journal or text someone instead. If I had burning thoughts I wanted to share, I would jot them down. If I craved socialization and wanted to check in with loved ones, I would text.

It only took about a week for the initial weirdness to fade. This blackout had a rocky start when it forced me to face my reality head-on. In late January, I got my tonsils out. Not only did this mean 7–10 days of brutal recovery at home, but it was also the day before spring semester began. If I had spent "sylly week" (the first week of classes, short for syllabus week), looking at every fun moment I was missing at school, my loneliness would have stung more. Rather than doom-scroll for a week, I watched a ton of movies. It was a humbling, grounding experience, and something I haven't felt in a long time: living entirely in a lousy moment without escaping via social media.

By the first month, the urge to open the forbidden apps vanished completely. I soon noticed some differences in how I behaved. On one five-hour car ride with friends to New York, the only time I unlocked my phone was to control the music. I am certain if I had access to *Instagram* and *Snapchat*, they would have lured me out of the moment I was living in. This car ride became an incredible opportunity to talk with my friends—who were also unplugged for these five hours. We sang along to classic rock and made plans for our trip. The only thing that mattered to us was the present; we were not trying to make the ride a shareable moment. For the New York trip and other travels, it was odd for me to not post these memories online. In the past, each trip had dedicated *Instagram* posts that captured the highlights of my adventures. I wanted to show off.

Instead, I now keep my favorite photos in various albums on my phone, and when friends and family asked, I showed them the pictures of the beignets I ate in New Orleans or the sleek jumpsuit I wore to my cousin's wedding. Instead of mass sharing to hundreds of people, only the closest people in my circle—the ones who checked in individually—got to hear my updates. As someone who struggled with keeping things private online, this was a great way to realize that not everyone needs to know everything. The beauty of these memories is that they only existed for me and the people I chose to share them with.

I also realized that the moments I mindlessly used social media were when I was bored, like waiting for class to start or in line for food. Scrolling was a safety net. When I needed a distraction, they were there. Instead of pulling myself out of reality when I have time to myself, I embrace the silence and glance around. And honestly, it's nice.

Another issue was the constant overwhelming sensation that there's always more to look at—*Instagram* pictures of a friend's vacation, trending videos on *TikTok*, a recap of an influencer's day on *Snapchat*. If I wanted to stay on these apps all day, there was always another rabbit hole. Now it feels good to know when I'm done; there's not more to look at.

I recently went to the Outer Banks for the weekend, and I had less than an hour of screen time each day I was there—a huge feat for me, and completely unimaginable three years ago.

I'm not perfect, and sometimes I still spend far too much time on my phone. But there's a difference in how I'm using it. I ended up downloading a ton of games. This way, when I want to sit on my phone and do nothing, I do. I'm just playing solitaire or 2048 instead of scrolling through *Instagram* posts. I still get to be lazy and waste time without hurting my mental health.

While I have no regrets about this cleanse so far, I definitely lost contact with a lot of people. I never announced my plan online, so only those who saw me in-person knew. This meant losing touch with many friends I made in the pandemic that I only communicated with on social media.

We'll see what this summer brings, likely a mix of challenges as I navigate a full-time internship, studying abroad and limited connection to my college friends as they embark on their own plans. But there's a comfort in knowing that the return back to school will be filled with updates—new stories and memories, shared face to face instead of over a screen. Until then, I'll embrace each moment as it comes and jot them down in my journal as I go.

For years, I poured my identity into living two lives: one online and one in-person. So far, this year has been a nice break from that and a reminder of the beauty of an offline world. Bridgette and I are still in a competition over who will pay for sushi dinner, but I'm pretty sure it won't be me.

Works Cited

Hunter, Tatum. "They Left Social Media for Good. Are They Happier?" *The Washington Post*, 11 Apr. 2023, www.washingtonpost.com/technology/2023/04/11/social-media-quit-loneliness/.

"I Replaced Social Media with Micro-Journalling for 1 Year." *YouTube*, uploaded by Struthless, 28 Feb. 2022, www.youtube.com/watch?v=mFvdHfhVIsQ.

Miller, Sarah. "The Addictiveness of Social Media: How Teens Get Hooked." *Jefferson Health*, Thomas Jefferson University Hospitals, 2 June 2022, www.jeffersonhealth.org/your-health/living-well/the-addictiveness-of-social-media-how-teens-get-hooked.

Murthy, Vivek H. "U.S. Surgeon General: I Am Concerned about Social Media and Youth Mental Health." *The Washington Post*, 23 May 2023, www.washingtonpost.com/opinions/2023/05/23/social-media-children-danger-parents-surgeon-general.

U.S. Department of Health and Human Services, Office of the Surgeon General. *Social Media and Youth Mental Health: The U.S. Surgeon General's Advisory.* May 2023, www.hhs.gov/surgeongeneral/priorities/youth-mental-health/social-media/index.html.

Thinking about the Text

1. Jenna Bloom points out numerous ways that social media can be harmful to mental health. What are they? List them. She also describes how social media has been useful to her. Why do you think she chose to include the upsides? Would her essay have been more or less powerful if she had focused only on the harms? Why or why not?

2. In her opening sentence, Bloom discloses a few facts about herself: her age, her status as a college student, and that she is "unable to be a moderate social media user" (1). Why do you think she begins this way? Who is her primary **AUDIENCE** and how do you think this opening line lands with those readers? Are you a part of that audience? How, if at all, did her disclosures affect how you read her essay?

3. Bloom's **NARRATIVE** describes her own personal experiences. How does she make a case that her story matters to others? What does she say to indicate that her experience has larger implications? Explain your response and point to passages that support your ideas.

4. Bloom's narrative covers a year-long process, and she uses **SIGNPOST** language to help readers follow the sequence of events, like "Then, in the beginning of January" (3) and "It only took about a week" (10). What are the other signposts that Bloom employs to help readers follow along? Did you find her narrative easy to understand? Does she use signposts effectively? What improvements would you suggest to Bloom, if any?

5. Bloom clearly defines the rules and parameters of her social media purge in paragraphs 5–7. What do you think of them? Are they adequate? reasonable? too strict? too permissive? Would you be willing to take up the challenge under the same terms? Why or why not? What modifications would you want to make? Once you've reflected on these questions, write an essay in which you explain your response to Bloom's "cleanse" (17). You may want to consider writing your response in the form of a letter to Jenna Bloom, expanding on the conversation that she began with her essay.

Media Coverage of Campus Protests Focuses on Spectacle

DANIELLE K. BROWN

PROTEST MOVEMENTS CAN LOOK VERY DIFFERENT depending on where you stand, both literally and figuratively. For protesters, demonstrations are usually the result of meticulous planning by advocacy groups and leaders aimed at getting a message out to a wider world or to specific institutional targets. To outside onlookers, however, protests can seem disorganized and disruptive, and it can be difficult to see the depth of the effort or their aims.

Take the pro-Palestinian protests that [sprang] up at campuses across the United States [in 2024]. To the students taking part they [were], in the words of one protester, "uplifting the voices of Gazans, of Palestinians facing genocide ("Isra Hirsi")." But to many people outside the universities,

---

DANIELLE K. BROWN is a journalist, professor, and researcher who teaches courses on media and communication at Michigan State University. She is also founder of the LIFT Project, a research effort working to make the news ecosystem more engaging and informative in their local communities, particularly in Black communities in the Midwest. In addition to her numerous research articles in academic journals, Brown's work has been published in popular media outlets such as *Nieman Lab*, *Columbia Journalism Review*, and the *Washington Post*. This essay first appeared in May 2024 in the *Conversation*. *Note:* MLA-style works-cited information has been provided in place of the article's original hyperlinks.

the focus [was] on confrontations and arrests (Betts et al.). Where does this disconnect come from? Most people don't participate in on-the-streets protests or experience any of the disruption that they cause (Bowden). Rather they rely on the media to give a full picture of the protests.

For over a decade, my research has extensively explored trends in how the media shapes narratives around different kinds of demonstrations. Reporting on campus encampments by large parts of the media fits a general pattern of protest coverage that focuses more on the drama of the disruption rather than the underlying reasons behind it—and that can leave audiences uninformed about the nuances of the protests and the movements behind them.

Protests—from small silent sit-ins and mass marches to student-led encampments—share similar components. They require a degree of planning, focus on a perceived injustice (Castells) and seek reforms or solutions (Tufekci). Protests also, by their very nature, engage in varying degrees of disruptive actions that exist in confrontation with something or someone, and utilize strategies that attract the attention of news media and others. These core elements—grievances, demands, disruption, confrontation and spectacle—are present in nearly all protests. But to the media, some elements are more newsworthy than others, with confrontation and spectacle often topping the list. As a result, these elements tend to be covered more often than others.

In research focusing on social movements like Black Lives Matter, the 2017 Women's March and others, I have found that time and again, coverage tends to headline the parts of the protest that are sensational and disruptive. And this neglects the political substance of the protests. The grievances, demands and agendas are often left in the shadows. For example, analysis of the 2020 protests following the murder of George Floyd conducted by myself and colleague Rachel Mourão found the Associated Press and cable news headlines were more likely to focus on disruption and chaos than police violence or protester demands (Brown and Mourão). This pattern is referred to as the protest paradigm (McLeod). While there are many factors that can make this paradigm fluctuate, like the timing of stories and the location of a news organization, movements that seek to disrupt the status quo are the most likely to receive initial coverage that frames protesters as criminal, irrelevant, trivial or illegitimate components of the political system.

This pattern can be seen in the initial coverage of protests against the war in Gaza at U.S.-based universities. These protests began in 2023 and only escalated into campus encampments after months of campaigning. In the months leading up to the encampments, many students who were engaged in advocacy efforts over the Israeli campaign in Gaza demanded, among other things, that their universities divest from businesses connected to the Israeli occupation of Palestinian territories.

Students at Brown University participated in a hunger strike [early on. Around the same time], a coalition of students across several historically Black colleges crafted a joint call to action across university systems. Students at my university—Michigan State—rallied support through an online petition and then lobbied at board of trustee meetings. When the board of trustees issued a statement refusing divestment of any kind, students continued to march to the steps of the main administration building where they continued to protest, all before planning the encampment protests.

Little of this made it into mainstream news reports compared to [a few months later], when an uptick in coverage corresponded with students organizing encampments at universities and university officials began to

> In addition to its visual appeal, a graph like this one can make a vast amount of information easier to digest. Learn how to do this on pp. 787–95.

Reporting on university protests spiked amid confrontations

Pro-Palestinian activism at U.S. universities had been ongoing since the beginning of Israel's operation in Gaza. But it was only with encampments that major outlets began to take notice.

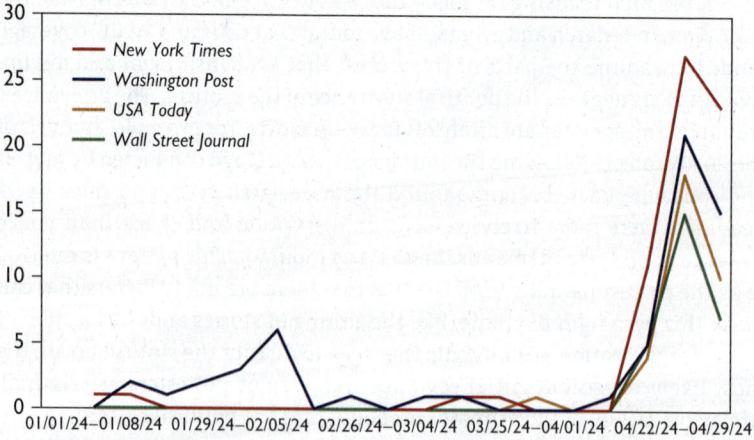

Fig.1. Data compiled from Newswhip using keywords "university" and any one of the following: "protests," "Gaza," "Pro-Palestine," "encampment," "rally," "rallies," "Palestine," "Israel."

respond. Those universities that asked police to enforce the dispersion of protesters amplified the intensity of confrontation and, in turn, amplified the news coverage. And rather than focusing on the grievance of protesters—that is, concerns about the deaths, injuries and looming famine affecting Palestinians—in reports of the campus encampments it has been the confrontations between protesters and police that have become central to the news media coverage.

As with all trends, there are always deviations and outliers. Not all reported pieces align with the protest paradigm. In the research examining news coverage after the murder of George Floyd, we found that when reports in major news outlets deviate from the protest paradigm, it was often in work produced by journalists who have engaged deeply and frequently with a community ("Research").

In [recent] campus protests, it [was] student journalism that emerged as an outlier in this respect. Take, for example, an article from the *Indiana Daily Student* published during the peak of the unrest, which explains the lesser-known last-minute administrative policy changes that ultimately disrupted protest planning logic and contributed to the arrests and temporary bans of faculty and student protesters (Meador).

There are commercial reasons why some newsrooms focus on the spectacle and confrontation—the old journalism adage of "if it bleeds, it leads" still prevails in many newsroom decisions (Reis). For the initial weeks of the campus protests, this penchant for sensationalism has shown up in the focus on chaos, clashes and arrests. But it is a decision that delegitimizes protest aims.

This delegitimization is aided by the sourcing routines journalists often fall back on to tell stories quickly and without legal consequence. In breaking news situations, journalists tend to gravitate toward—and directly quote—sources that hold status, like government and university officials. This is because reporters may already have an established relationship with such officials, who often have dedicated media relations teams. And in the case of campus protests, in particular, reporters faced difficulty connecting with protest participants directly (Wagner). As a result, official narratives may dominate news coverage. So when officials like Texas Gov. Greg Abbott equate protesters to criminals with antisemitic intentions, that typically gets covered—certainly more than any rebuttal from protest participants ("At Least 30 Protesters"). And because readers and viewers are unlikely to be on the ground to gauge Abbott's characterizations of protesters for themselves, the coverage can shape how a protest movement and the politics around it are understood.

The media shapes the way most people understand [public demonstrations]. But as coverage of protests across universities has shown, often the focus is on the spectacle rather than the substance.

Works Cited

"At Least 30 Protesters Arrested at UT Austin: 'These Protesters Belong in Jail,' Abbott Says." *CBS Texas*, 24 Apr. 2024, www.cbsnews.com/texas/news/several-protesters-arrested-at-ut-austin-these-protesters-belong-in-jail-abbott-says.

Betts, Anna, et al. "Crackdowns at 4 College Protests Lead to More than 200 Arrests." *The New York Times*, 27 Apr. 2024, www.nytimes.com/2024/04/27/us/northeastern-arizona-state-university-protests-arrests.html.

Bowden, John. "1 in 5 Americans Has Attended a Protest or Rally since 2016: Poll." *The Hill*, 6 Apr. 2018, thehill.com/blogs/blog-briefing-room/news/381964-one-in-five-americans-has-attended-a-protest-or-rally-since.

Brown, Danielle K., and Rachel R. Mourão. "No Reckoning for the Right: How Political Ideology, Protest Tolerance and News Consumption Affect Support Black Lives Matter Protests." *Political Communication*, vol. 39, no. 6, 15 Sept. 2022, pp. 737–54, https://doi.org/10.1080/10584609.2022.2121346.

Castells, Manuel. *Networks of Outrage and Hope: Social Movements in the Internet Age*. 2nd ed., Polity Press, 2015.

"Isra Hirsi: Columbia Protests 'Uplift Voices of Palestinians Facing Genocide.'" *YouTube*, uploaded by Middle East Eye, 2 May 2024, www.youtube.com/watch?v=XMe1q5mNKAw.

McLeod, Douglas M. "News Coverage and Social Protest: How the Media's Protect Paradigm Exacerbates Social Conflict." *Journal of Dispute Resolution*, vol. 2007, no. 1, 2007, scholarship.law.missouri.edu/jdr/vol2007/iss1/12.

Meador, Marissa. "'Utterly Unprincipled': Policy Created on Eve of Protest Used to Make Arrests." *Indiana Daily Student* [Bloomington], 28 Apr. 2024, www.idsnews.com/article/2024/04/policy-created-on-eve-of-protest-to-make-arrests.

Reis, Jillian. "If It Bleeds, It Leads: Crime Reporting." *International Council for Media Literacy*, 13 Apr. 2023, ic4ml.org/blogs/if-it-bleeds-it-leads-crime-reporting/.

"Research." *LIFT Project*, https://www.liftproj.com/research.

Tufekci, Zeynep. *Twitter and Tear Gas: The Power and Fragility of Networked Protest.* Yale UP, 2018.

Wagner, Laura. "In Campus Protests, Students Are Wary of the Media." *The Washington Post*, 1 May 2024, www.washingtonpost.com/style/media/2024/05/01/campus-protests-students-are-wary-media.

Thinking about the Text

1. Danielle K. Brown takes a clear position: news coverage from major outlets seldom presents a comprehensive and detailed description of the issues motivating protesters. And she explains why that is. What reasons does she give? **SUMMARIZE** them in your own words. Is her explanation persuasive to you? Why or why not? Identify the passage that most influenced your assessment.

2. Brown carefully defines the "protest paradigm" (5) of news coverage and criticizes major news outlets for following it so frequently. She also, however, is careful to point out notable exceptions. Why might she have made such a concession? In what ways, if at all, does mentioning the "deviations and outliers" (9) help support her argument? Are there other **COUNTERARGUMENTS** or positions you think she should have included? Explain your reasoning.

3. Brown points out that although "pro-Palestinian activism [had] been ongoing" for some time, "it was only with encampments that major outlets began to take notice" (fig. 1). As **EVIDENCE**, she presents a graph that shows a steep spike in coverage in April 2024 in four major national newspapers. Look carefully at the graph and its labeling. Is the graph effective evidence? Do you think

it definitively demonstrates the claim that "it was only with encampments that major outlets began to take notice"? Why or why not? What, if anything, might you suggest to make the graph more effective?

4. Brown observes that "official narratives may dominate news coverage" (12) of political protests. What does she mean by that? Why does she consider it problematic? Do you agree with her assessment? Imagine if you could have a conversation with her, and write a response to her observation on this point with your own ideas and opinions.

5. What's wrong with focusing on the drama? Isn't that what people are most interested in? Brown, of course, explains why she finds the emphasis on the sensational problematic. Think about your recent news consumption: Which news reports, if any, have you read somewhat thoroughly? Which have you skimmed quickly? Which did you skip over? Do you notice any patterns? Are you drawn mainly to the dramatic items? Once you have your three categories roughly defined, write an essay describing your news consumption and your reasons for reading thoroughly, skimming, and skipping over. Might your habits change at all as a result of reading Brown's essay? Why or why not?

The Talk: After Ferguson, a Shaded Conversation about Race

DANA CANEDY

LIKE SO MANY AFRICAN-AMERICAN PARENTS, I had rehearsed "the talk," that nausea-inducing discussion I needed to have with my son about how to conduct himself in the presence of the police. I was prepared for his questions, except for one.

"Can I just pretend I'm white?"

Jordan was born to African-American parents, but recessive genes being what they are, he has very fair skin and pale blue eyes. I am caramel brown, and since his birth eight years ago people have mistaken me for his nanny.

When I asked why he would want to "pass" for white, I struggled with how to respond to his answer.

"Because it's safer," Jordan replied. "They won't hurt me." 5

That recent gray day, not long after grand juries failed to indict the police officers who killed unarmed black men in Ferguson, Missouri, and

---

DANA CANEDY is the author of *A Journal for Jordan: A Story of Love and Honor* (2008), a memoir dedicated to her son after the death of his father and her fiancé, First Sergeant Charles Monroe King. She won a Pulitzer Prize for her work at the *New York Times* and is currently managing editor of the *Guardian US*. This *New York Times* piece was published in December 2014.

First Sgt. Charles M. King with his son, Jordan. King visited his son on leave before returning to Iraq on a mission that would end his life.

Staten Island, I had steadied myself to lay out the rules: Always address police officers as "sir" or "ma'am." Do not make any sudden moves, even to reach for identification. Do not raise your voice, resist or run.

But now I was taken aback.

Jordan's father and I never had a chance to discuss when we would give him the talk, or what we would say. Our baby was just 6 months old when his dad, a decorated Army soldier, was killed in combat in Iraq. So the timing and the context of the talk were left to me.

I had tried hard to delay it, and make sure he wouldn't know the names Michael Brown or Eric Garner or Tamir Rice.

In the days leading up to the conversation, I asked an African-American male colleague if he thought it was too soon. When did he tell his own boys?

"Before they were no longer seen as cute," he said, making me wince.

I hadn't fully processed that someday my son would be seen as suspect instead of sweet. So I told him, and then Jordan asked if it was rare for the police to hurt black people. I said that, just like his father when he wore his military uniform, most police officers are dedicated to protecting us. But, no, I added, it is unfortunately not uncommon.

"Then I don't want to be black anymore," Jordan declared.

He asked if I was crying. I dabbed at my eyes and searched my mind for what to say.

"Son, your father was an incredible African-American man," I told him. "And you are an amazing boy who is going to grow into just such a man. Please be proud of that."

"Yes," he responded emphatically, "but can't I just pretend to be white?"

The message that Jordan's appearance affords him the option to check "other" on the race card comes at him constantly. After his second-grade class created self-portraits last year, I noticed that his was the only one not hanging on the classroom wall. His teacher explained that his portrait was "a work in progress." The brown crayon he had used to color in his face was several shades too dark, she thought, and so she wanted him to "lighten it up" to more accurately reflect his complexion.

It is not just the overt signals that have convinced Jordan that he can choose to blend in to a white world. It is also that we live a life of relative affluence. I am a journalist and author whose inner circle includes prominent black writers, television anchors and doctors. We live in a high-rise in Manhattan with a doorman and round-the-clock security. Jordan attends an elite private school and an exclusive summer camp.

A white friend calls him "the boy who lives in the sky" because of the vast city view from the nine-foot windows in his bedroom. "He lives in a bubble and is always with responsible adults," she said recently, trying to assure me that our status makes him safer than many black boys.

That is true, mostly. And if my parenting pays off, I will be able to minimize his contact with the police. He will be law-abiding. He will respect authority. He'll understand the perception of black boys wearing hoodies or sagging pants. But will it be enough?

> You may not be a mother. Or Black. Or wealthy. In any case, it's important to really listen to what Canedy is saying—p. 9 explains why.

Just last month a video went viral that showed a black man in Pontiac, Michigan, being questioned by a sheriff's deputy because someone reported feeling nervous after seeing him walking in the cold with his hands in his pockets. So as much as I want to believe that our upper-middle-class status will protect my son from many of society's social ills, it could not provide him the white privilege he seeks.

Nor would "passing" protect Jordan entirely, for the internal damage from living that lie would surely be as painful as any blow from a police baton. To deny his blackness would be to deny me. It would be to deny our enslaved ancestors who were strong enough to endure that voyage. It would mean rejecting the reflection he sees every time he looks in a mirror.

For at least a little while longer, Jordan is too young to understand any of this. He does not know the racial indignity of having jobs and promotions denied or delayed, does not know the humiliation of being stopped and frisked. He has never heard the mantra "I can't breathe."

I know that our talk was just the start of a conversation that will go deeper as he moves into his teen years in a post-Obama America. My fervent hope is that, by then, I will have found a way to help him embrace the privilege of being black.

Thinking about the Text

1. What is Dana Canedy's **PURPOSE** in publicly exposing such a painful and private conversation between her and her son? What point is she trying to make? And how persuasively does she make it? Explain your response.

2. It's true: numerous studies confirm that White youth are not targeted by police nearly as often as Black youth. Still, pretending to be White, as Canedy's son proposed, is both unsuitable as a solution and hurtful to Canedy personally. Why? Explain the dilemma.

3. Canedy's narrative was published in the *New York Times*, a daily newspaper with a large nationwide circulation. What background information about "the talk" (1) does Canedy provide for this **AUDIENCE**? What might she have done differently if she were writing for a magazine with a primary readership of Black parents? What information could she have omitted, and what might she have included that she chose not to include here?

4. A good narrative includes **DESCRIPTIVE** details that make the story come alive. What part of Canedy's narrative touched you the deepest? Why? Describe your reaction.

5. At some time in our lives, we've all had a run-in with some form of authority. Think of a frightening or otherwise memorable encounter with an authority figure. In what ways did your skin color, gender, stature, dress, or other factors in how you look or present yourself affect that encounter? Did any characteristics work in your favor or against you—and if so, how? Write a brief **NARRATIVE** of the encounter as you remember it, reflecting in particular on how your physical presence affects your life.

They Called Me a Girl before Anyone Else Did

CHARLOTTE CLYMER

WHILE MAKING PUBLIC REMARKS at a school board meeting for Loudoun County in Virginia, Tanner Cross, an elementary school physical education teacher in the district, stated he would not use the authentic pronouns for trans and non-binary students under his care.

This was in response to the school board implementing non-discrimination protections for LGBTQ students following the Virginia state legislature passing broad legislation banning discrimination against all LGBTQ people in the state.

In return, the district rightly suspended Cross for his remarks, and then, a circuit court judge ordered his reinstatement. The district is now in the process of appealing that decision to Virginia's Supreme Court, and Cross has become a cause célèbre among social conservatives who are obsessed with the bodies of trans children in a way that is entirely creepy.

In his remarks, Cross said he wouldn't "affirm that a biological boy can be a girl and vice versa because it's against my religion. It's lying to a child; it's abuse to a child—and it's sinning against our God."

CHARLOTTE CLYMER is a Texan, a military veteran, and—in her own words—"a proud trans woman." Her political and social commentary has appeared in the *Washington Post* and *GQ*, among other national publications. This 2021 essay is from her *Substack, Charlotte's Web Thoughts*.

Leaving aside the fact that the discussion of transgender people in the Bible is quite murky (and rather fascinating)—and thus, as more than a few social conservatives have admitted to me, it's unclear being transgender is a so-called "sin"—we're still left with a public employee charged with the welfare of children stating before God and Creation that he refuses to treat certain children with respect and dignity. That, in fact, is abusive.

I'm not going to unpack all the myriad reasons why this is clownish in itself because I want to focus on something that hit me when this story popped up.

I don't personally know Tanner Cross other than what I've read in the news. I've never met him, and I don't know anyone who knows him.

And yet, I feel like I've known Tanner Cross all my life. He hits all the same marks as so many men I've known in positions of authority, particularly in sports and the military.

I grew up in a conservative environment in Central Texas. I played high school football. I went to an evangelical church in my late teens (where, unsurprisingly, my political views were not warmly received). And I served in the military—and not just in the military but in the testosterone-saturated U.S. Army Infantry.

For most of my life, I have been around men like Tanner Cross. They have strong opinions about what men should be (and what women should be) and tend to make those opinions known.

I am a proud trans woman, but for the first 30 years of my life, I was in the closet and navigating these spaces. Around these men.

And without fail, men like Tanner Cross would—in some way, shape, or form—call me a girl. They weren't just the first people to call me a girl. They were the only people to call me a girl or woman before I came out.

Like my 8th grade football coach who really loved calling us "ladies" during practice.

Like my freshman football coach who never seemed to tire of telling us that we "hit like girls" if he felt we weren't going at full speed.

Like the assistant football coach during my junior year of high school who, on more than a few occasions, said some choice words about how we should try out for the girls volleyball team instead. Oh, and this mocking inquiry toward one of my teammates: "Did your mother teach you how to throw?"

> Clymer relates experiences that are infuriating and, unfortunately, common. But notice how respectfully she describes people—even the ones responsible for the injustices. Find out more about this effective rhetorical move on p. 24.

Like during minute one of hour one of day one in basic training when I heard a drill sergeant scream at all of us to "get the sand out of your pussies." And that was probably one of the more tame things I heard along these lines during my time in the military.

I heard that all my life in male environments, and that's to say nothing of the numerous ways in which society communicates to boys that they shouldn't cry, shouldn't appear weak, be the "man of the house," etc.

That's what I've been thinking about over the past two months as this situation unfolds in Loudoun County, Virginia (which, by the way, is a lovely place with no shortage of wonderful people).

I've been thinking of all the school coaches and P.E. teachers who I saw throughout my childhood call boys and young men "ladies" and "girls" as a way of, uh, "motivating" them and now claim that using the correct pronouns for trans kids goes against their religion. I call it the Male Coach Gender Paradox.

These are the same men. Truly.

Do I have proof that Tanner Cross has done that? I do not. But I'm right. I know I'm right. Call it hard-earned instinct.

These men always betray themselves by their fear of women. They seem unable to maintain any sort of consistency in following their own views. Because it was never about religion or respect for God. It was always about their profound discomfort with women.

In their minds, women are weaker and less worthy of respect. They jab their fingers in the direction of girls and women and yell at the boys and young men under their control: *Do you want to grow up and be that? Small and weak? Then get your shit together and man up.*

I'm sometimes asked by the occasional cis man why there's far more support for trans women among cis women than cis men, since it's cis women, social conservatives falsely claim, who have the "most to lose" from trans equality.

I think there are a lot of reasons, but two stick out for me personally, one for women and one for men.

The first is that I believe the vast majority of cis women understand deeply what it means to have your body controlled in service to a forced gender identity and expression.

The second is that these particular cis men absolutely feel they have the most to lose. Not materially or spiritually, despite the claims of Tanner

Cross. They feel they have the most to lose because when they already benefit substantially from a social framework that supposedly prescribes in detail what "manhood" should be, why cave in to that internal fear in the pit of their stomach that they're not really being themselves but a carbon copy of the fearful neuroses of all the men who came before them?

Why would these cis men admit that gender is incredibly complex and fluid? They're scared of the answer to that question—the possibility that they don't know their true selves and it's so much safer to stick with the devil they know than the one they don't.

Ironically, these cis men live in fear of their own gender reveals.

I'm not saying they're secretly transgender and in denial. I'm saying that gender identity and expression are so directly structured that these cis men are terrified of a world in which "manhood" may encompass the full spectrum of gender expression and they find themselves doing things they've always been told men don't do.

And yes, hashtag not all cis men—I knew so many wonderful cis men growing up, men who I looked up to, men who wouldn't use their religion as an excuse to abuse trans children.

Men who respect me as a woman now.

Thinking about the Text

1. How does Charlotte Clymer's life experience of living in both genders contribute to her **POINT OF VIEW** in the essay? Would her argument have been as effective if she had omitted disclosing her own experiences as a high school football player and US Army infantryman? Why or why not?

2. Clymer uses the phrase "hashtag not all cis men" (31). Was it surprising to read the phrase spelled out? Did you immediately understand it? Should she have written a more conventional sentence in order to express the same idea? In responding, consider her **PURPOSE** and **AUDIENCE**.

3. Clymer makes a **CLAIM** that men who refuse to use "the authentic pronouns for trans and non-binary students" (1) are the same coaches, trainers, and drill sergeants who call their players and trainers "ladies" and "girls" in order to "motivate" them (19). How well does Clymer establish this argument? Is it persuasive? Why or why not?

4. Clymer writes with passion and uses elements of **EMOTIONAL APPEAL** in her essay. But there are also plenty of **ETHICAL APPEALS**. Which do you think is more effective in this essay? Why? Point to specific examples to support your conclusion.

5. You may have come across social media posts that, in an attempt at humor, deliberately misgender someone. The objects of the "humor" are sometimes prominent men who are depicted or described as women, and these posts often use belittling language. Have you ever seen these types of social media posts? How do you think Clymer might respond to these attempts at humor? How does Clymer's narrative impact how you feel about these kinds of posts? Write an essay explaining your opinion.

Your TV Is Watching You
ADAM CLARK ESTES

R OKU CITY, the oddly alluring cityscape screen saver, scrolls across millions of idle TVs every day. Recently, an island paradise appeared in the picture. In the foreground, a floating billboard invited me to subscribe to *Disney+* and watch *Moana 2* at the press of a button on my remote. The convenience, I don't mind about the new era of ad-supported everything. The wiretapping, I do.

Ads are obviously not new on TV. As long as we've been watching shows on glowing boxes, we've been watching commercials that provide the economic engine for the entire entertainment factory to operate. While streaming platforms offered a reprieve for a few years by charging monthly fees for commercial-free content, it's now practically impossible to watch TV without seeing some sort of marketing. What's happening more under the radar is that your TV is collecting data about you and your watching habits—sometimes by directly monitoring what's on your screen—and serving you personalized ads on your TV or elsewhere.

ADAM CLARK ESTES is a senior technology correspondent for *Vox*, where this March 2025 report was published. His writing and research focuses on the intersection of technology, culture, and politics, and his work has appeared in *Wired*, *Vice*, *Air Force Times*, the *Atlantic*, and *Montana Associated Technology Roundtable*. *Note*: Underlined text indicates hyperlinks in the original.

The screen that you once loved for private, uninterrupted *Netflix*-watching has become a big billboard that also spies on you.

This isn't just a Roku problem, although the company <u>found itself in hot water</u> when some users were required to watch a video ad—a *Moana 2* trailer—before they could access their TV's home screen at all. Roku says this is just a test, but the fact that it's similar to <u>a feature Amazon rolled out</u> on *Prime Video* suggests that ads are generally getting more brazen on streaming platforms. How you feel about it depends a lot on your mindset and feelings about privacy.

The TV business traditionally included three distinct entities. There's 5 the hardware, namely the TV itself; the entertainment, like movies and shows; and the ads, usually just commercials that interrupt your movies and shows. In the streaming era, tech companies want to control all three, a setup also known as vertical integration. If, say, Roku makes the TV, supplies the content, and sells the ads, then it stands to control the experience, set the rates, and make the most money. That's business!

Roku has done this very well. Although it was founded in 2002, Roku broke into the market in 2008 after Netflix invested $6 million in the company to make a set-top box that enabled any TV to stream Netflix content. It was literally called <u>the Netflix Player by Roku</u>. Over the course of the next 15 years, Roku would grow its hardware business to include streaming sticks, which are basically just smaller set-top-boxes; wireless soundbars, speakers, and subwoofers; and after licensing its operating system to third-party TV makers, <u>its own affordable, Roku-branded smart TVs</u>.

While most people think of Roku as a hardware company, it actually transitioned into becoming an advertising company almost a decade ago. In the early days, you might see a banner ad on your home screen or a tile telling you to watch *Game of Thrones* on *HBO Go*. But after firing up a more serious ad business in 2016, Roku started selling targeted ads on the *Roku Channel*, <u>a free, ad-supported TV (FAST) service</u> across its devices in 2017. Roku even started making its own content, including <u>a biopic of Weird Al Yankovic</u>.

Things really ramped up when Roku started <u>acquiring ad-tech companies, including Nielsen's Advanced Video Advertising business</u> in 2021. This helped Roku gain new insights into its audience in order to target ads better and ultimately charge more money for those ads. At the end of 2024, Roku reported annual ad revenues of $3.5 billion, which accounted for 85 percent of its total revenue—far higher than its hardware business. Roku also has

---

In order to explain how Roku became the advertising giant that it is now, Estes uses a process analysis. You can find out more about how to use one in your own writing on pp. 266–68.

90 million users—millions more than *Apple TV+*—who have become a gold mine of data, not just about what they watch on TV but also who they are and what they like. Today, it's better to think of Roku not just as an advertising company or the folks who make cheap TVs and streaming sticks, but also as a data company with millions of detailed profiles.

Regarding the *Moana 2* controversy, Roku said in a statement that the company's growth "has and will always require continuous testing and innovation across design, navigation, content, and our first-rate advertising products." The statement also said, "Our recent test is just the latest example, as we explore new ways to showcase brands and programming while still providing a delightful and simple user experience."

The shift toward ad-supported everything has been happening across the TV landscape. People buy new TVs less frequently these days, so TV makers want to make money off the TVs they've already sold. Samsung has Samsung Ads, LG has LG Ad Solutions, Vizio has Vizio Ads, and so on and so forth. Tech companies, notably Amazon and Google, have gotten into the mix too, not only making software and hardware for TVs but also leveraging the massive amount of data they have on their users to sell ads on their TV platforms. These companies also sell data to advertisers and data brokers, all in the interest of knowing as much about you as possible in the interest of targeting you more effectively. It could even be used to train AI.

The wealth of Roku's first-party data could be a gold mine for Amazon or Google, according to Laura Martin, an analyst at the investment bank Needham and Company. "Roku is the perfect size with a really strategic fit," Martin told me, referring to a possible Amazon purchase. She added that Roku's data could also be a boon for any company with AI ambitions, including OpenAI. "If I was a large language model, this is data I would absolutely want to own."

The streaming industry has faced a reckoning in recent years too: After years of prioritizing growth over all else, companies like Netflix and Disney finally had to start making money. That's resulted in those companies charging more, bundling services, and introducing cheaper ad-supported tiers.

For better or worse, ads are the future of the TV business, just as they were its past. "For consumers, it's definitely a complicated ecosystem," said Jon Giegengack, founder of Hub Entertainment Research. Giegengack argues, though, that this ecosystem is ultimately better for consumers. In effect, there's a streaming option that works for any budget, and ads fill in the gaps.

But not everyone is thrilled to be bombarded by ads and to have their data passively harvested. More ads also means less attention paid to the content you want to watch and more to the ads these companies want you to see.

Nevertheless, the trade-off is worth it to a lot of Americans. Some 43 percent of all streaming subscriptions in the United States were ad-supported by the end of [2024], according to the market data firm Antenna. Even if you pay for an ad-free tier, you're contributing to the ad ecosystem by giving up your data to whatever streaming platforms you use and even the company that makes your TV.

Breaking free from this ad prison is tough. Most TVs on the market today come with a technology called automatic content recognition (ACR) built in. This is basically *Shazam* for TV—*Shazam* itself helped popularize the tech—and gives smart TV platforms the ability to monitor what you're watching by either taking screenshots or capturing audio snippets while you're watching. (This happens at the signal level, not from actual microphone recordings from the TV.)

Advertisers and TV companies use ACR tech to collect data about your habits that are otherwise hard to track, like if you watch live TV with an antenna. They use that data to build out a profile of you in order to better target ads. ACR also works with devices, like gaming consoles, that you plug into your TV through HDMI cables.

Yash Vekaria, a PhD candidate at UC Davis, called the HDMI spying "the most egregious thing we found" in his research for a paper published last year on how ACR technology works. And I have to admit that I had not heard of ACR until I came across Vekaria's research.

"They haven't kept it secret, but there's no awareness about it," Vekaria told me. "So if people don't know, they will not question it."

While ACR is popular across platforms, Roku is especially excited about the technology. Many of the companies that Roku has acquired in recent years have been working on ACR, and a Roku-owned company won an Emmy in 2023 for its work on the technology. Roku has also said that, because its share of the TV operating system market is 40 percent, the scale of its data collection capabilities is "unparalleled."

Unfortunately, you don't have much of a choice when it comes to ACR on your TV. You probably enabled the technology when you first set up your TV and accepted its privacy policy. If you refuse to do this, a lot of the functions on your TV won't work. You can also accept the policy and then disable

ACR on your TV's settings, but that could disable certain features too. In 2017, Vizio settled a class action lawsuit for tracking users by default. If you want to turn off this tracking technology, here's a good guide from *Consumer Reports* that explains how for most types of smart TVs.

To be honest, after learning about all this in the past week or so, I haven't done anything revolutionary. I can actually buy into the idea that more relevant ads provide a better experience. I don't need to see ads for a dozen different eczema treatments while I'm watching *YouTube TV*, because I don't have eczema. I'm okay learning about a new toy for young kids, because I have a young kid. (Advertising to kids—or even letting your kids watch YouTube—is an entirely different matter.) So I've agreed to all the privacy policies and am enjoying my streaming content as the industry intended.

But it does bug me, just on principle, that I have to let a tech company wiretap my TV in order to enjoy all of the device's features.

If you're set on an ad-free TV experience, your best bet is to buy an old dumb TV off *eBay* and never connect it to a Roku, Amazon, or Google device. You can buy an antenna for network television, and a DVD player for movies. There are worse Y2K trends to resurrect than being completely offline for a few precious leisure hours.

Thinking about the Text

1. Adam Clark Estes talks about the increase of advertising shown to viewers through streaming services as well as ads shown by TVs themselves. But ads are not the real target of his disapproval. In your own words, describe Estes's main argument. Do you agree with his **STANCE**? Why or why not?

2. Estes uses a personal **TONE** in his essay through the use of pronouns. He writes about his own experiences in the first person singular (I, me, my); he addresses readers directly using the second person (you); and he establishes common ground with readers using we, us, and our. What do you think of this approach? How might you have responded differently to the essay if it had been written more formally, without I, you, or we? Point to a specific example or two to support your conclusion.

3. Estes refers to the automatic content recognition (ACR) technology as "wiretapping" (1). Do you think this is a fair depiction? How are the terms similar and different from one another? Look up the definition of "wiretapping" and see how the term is conventionally used.

4. Estes explains most of the terminology and specific references that he uses, but he mentions *Shazam* with no further description. Do some research on the primary **AUDIENCE** of *Vox*. How would you describe the readers of this online magazine? With this audience in mind, was Estes correct to assume that his readers would already be familiar with *Shazam*? Why or why not?

5. Estes says that he's okay with ads on his devices, and he concedes that "more relevant ads provide a better experience" (22). What he objects to, however, is letting tech companies "wiretap" his TV. Based on his report, how do you feel about targeted ads and ACR? Would you consider turning off the tracking technology or buying an "old dumb TV" (24)? Are you supportive of this tracking technology? Or are you indifferent or neutral about it? Take a **POSITION** on ad tracking, and write an argumentative essay using Estes's report and outside research as evidence to support your position.

How Country Music Is Addressing the Opioid Crisis
JEFF GAGE

Drugs never seemed like a problem to Elvie Shane. Dabbling in cocaine, meth, and heroin were all part of the future country singer's college days in Bowling Green, Kentucky. Even when he got hooked on speed, the dangers didn't seem real. He could take it or leave it, he figured, a good time for whenever he had the money.

"We just thought we were having fun and catching a buzz," says Shane, who was clean for nearly a decade before scoring a country Number One with "My Boy" in 2021, over a *Zoom* call from his home in Nashville. "It wasn't until I started seeing my friends drop like flies that I realized we were playing with fire."

That was before the opioid crisis ravaged Shane's home state of Kentucky, much of neighboring Appalachia, and virtually every corner of the U.S., especially rural areas like the one where he grew up. Caneyville, population just more than 500. "Hard drugs were a big-city problem," Shane recalls. "The word 'overdose' was very, very rare."

JEFF GAGE is a New York–based music journalist whose work has appeared in numerous magazines and newspapers, including *Esquire*, *GQ*, the *Village Voice*, and the *Washington Post*, among others. This April 2024 report on country music and the opioid crisis was originally published in *Rolling Stone*. Check out some of the songs that Gage mentions in this report by visiting everyonesanauthor.tumblr.com. *Note:* Underlined text indicates hyperlinks in the original.

Today, drug overdoses kill more than 100,000 people annually in this country, with fentanyl, a synthetic opioid, touted as the leading cause of death for people between the ages of 18 to 45. Those figures led Shane to come clean about his drug abuse on the 2023 single "Pill," one of two songs from his new album, *Damascus*, that address the crisis.

"Those songs are for the people that have been there," says Shane. "So, if you hear the words in my songs, you know I've... been there too."

He's not alone in the country world in opening up about addiction. Grammy-nominated singer Jelly Roll explored his past as a drug user and dealer in songs like "Save Me" and in the *Hulu* doc of the same name. He's performed in prisons and recovery centers, and last January, he testified before Congress in support of anti-fentanyl legislation.

"I was a part of the problem. I am here now, standing as a man that wants to be a part of the solution," Jelly Roll testified. "I was the uneducated man in the kitchen playing chemist with drugs I knew absolutely nothing about, just like these drug dealers are doing right now when they're mixing every drug on the market with fentanyl—and they're killing the people we love."

It's not just the artists who have personal experience with opioids who are speaking up. Brad Paisley came out forcefully last fall with "The Medicine Will," a blistering takedown of the pharmaceutical companies that flooded communities with prescription drugs like Oxycontin and allowed the epidemic to run rampant.

"It's so much worse than I even imagined. I mean, it's really crazy," Paisley says. He saw the impact of the opioid crisis firsthand when he spoke with victims from his home state, West Virginia, where overdose deaths per capita are among the worst in the world. The singer lays the blame for the crisis squarely at the feet of drug company executives.

"They said, 'These people are the perfect people to target with this. They're in pain. They have powered this country with backbreaking labor, and it's drying up; and we're gonna go get 'em because they'll eat this stuff up, and we'll tell 'em it's not addictive,'" Paisley says.

Country artists singing about substance abuse is nothing new. Alcohol is ubiquitous, a cornerstone of the genre from the heartbreak ballads of the Fifties to the red-cup-chugging party anthems of the 21st century. Marijuana is also celebrated, while a long history of amphetamine and cocaine use is alternately winked at or swept under the rug, the necessary evils of a grueling career.

Brad Paisley performs at a George Jonas Tribute concert in April 2023.

The no-nonsense response to opioids, however, is a unique moment, according to country-music scholar Amanda Marie Martínez, a doctoral fellow at the University of North Carolina at Chapel Hill. "The growing demands country stars are making to take legal action against the opioid epidemic is an unparalleled development," she says. "This is heavily attributable to the severity of the crisis, and a testament to the level of devastation it's caused to communities across region, class, and race."

Opioids are a particularly acute problem in communities at the heart of country music. Tennessee's Davidson County (where Nashville is located) was named the second-deadliest metro area in the U.S. for overdoses in a September report, and the state ranks in the top 10 for overdose death rates. West Virginia is worst of all, with more than 75 deaths out of every 100,000 residents.

"This is different," Paisley says, comparing opioids to country music's broader drug culture. "There are people who made billions of dollars on the death and suffering of people like my home state. And no one's in jail." For that reason, he had no qualms with coming out so aggressively with his criticisms. "It's rare that you *know* you're right," he says.

Jaime Wyatt, who chronicled her journey from addiction to sobriety on albums like 2017's *Felony Blues*, says she's lucky to have recovered before fentanyl became so commonplace. Like Shane, her entryway to substance abuse came through pills—in her case painkillers that were prescribed to her then-partner, who worked in construction. "In America, a lot of people come by opiate and heroin addiction honestly," Wyatt says. "Through injuries, through being overprescribed."

The issue of prescription access runs both ways, as Shane can attest. "I literally got on the internet and I . . . typed in some information and got a letter from a doctor saying that I needed Adderall," he says. "I never had to touch a single street drug. It was so easy to just get other [stuff] without having to worry about getting in trouble for it."

Shane briefly started using again after the success of "My Boy" and the release of his first album, *Backslider*, in 2021. His guilt over losing friends, some of whom he introduced to harder drugs himself, prompted him to write "Pill."

"Now [a friend] is showing up at my door with a bag of cocaine saying, 'Please, God, take this away from me . . .'" Shane says. His voice breaks up, and he trails off. "Sorry," he says, swallowing back a lump in his throat. "I haven't thought about that in a long time."

Shane believes it is time for the genre to get more honest with itself and not lean on a favorite lyrical crutch. "I feel like country is usually hiding the real [stuff] by talking about whiskey," he says.

Wyatt sees it as a broader cultural issue. "The problem I see in society is that, like, what makes a tough guy is this guy that works his back till it's broken and takes pills or drinks heavy to keep going," she says. "And then it's like, 'Oh, but he was a hard worker,' when he died super young and left a family [behind]."

Both agree it's time for that conversation to change. "We've got to normalize treatment and therapy, just like you would get your oil changed on your car," Wyatt says.

Some artists are working to do just that. Tyler Childers, who wrote about the crisis in his ballad "Nose on the Grindstone," is a driving force behind the Healing Appalachia music festival, a recovery fundraiser in West

Virginia, near where he grew up in Eastern Kentucky. The event, co-founded by his manager, Ian Thornton, was established after 26 people overdosed in Huntington, West Virginia, in one day in August 2016.

"People looked to Tyler and Ian as change makers, as if they could do something," says Dave Lavender, board president of Hope in the Hills, the nonprofit behind Healing Appalachia. "And I think they were tired of seeing a lot of our friends die."

The festival takes place each September—National Recovery Month— and highlights recovery through testimonials and tutorials for naloxone, a drug commonly known as Narcan that's used to reverse opioid overdoses. "It's important for people to see someone in recovery. I think that there's an idea out there that people don't get better, but it's not true," Lavender insists, pointing to data that suggests more than 70 percent of those with substance-use disorder find their way to recovery.

Since first being held in 2018, Healing Appalachia reports raising more than $640,000 for recovery and wellness organizations throughout the region. It's also helped place former addicts on career pathways in the music industry. At the festival, partnering service providers have distributed tens of thousands of Narcan and Naloxone kits called ONEboxes. "This is a drive-thru society that's faced with a real public-health crisis," says Lavender. "It doesn't have an easy fix."

Paisley is cautiously optimistic. "There's an enormous amount of hope with this issue," he says. "I think that we crested a wave of enabled, 'legal' drug abuse into now something where everyone knows there's this problem."

Shane and Wyatt have both done the work at their shows, uniting with the program End Overdose to teach fans to recognize the signs of an overdose. They advocate for venues to carry Narcan and fentanyl test strips, even for nondrug users.

"I'm a believer that harm reduction stuff should be at every bar and every school," Wyatt says. "What we've learned is that drug users are no longer the expendables. It's your nieces, your nephews, your family members."

It is a lesson that Shane himself learned a long time ago, and one that he will likely live with for the rest of his life. "People need to recognize that maybe just because you do this shit on weekends, that doesn't necessarily mean you don't have a problem," he says. "It starts like that for a lot of people."

Gage's article is mainly a report, but it also relies on elements of narrative and argument. Blending genres can be very effective. Read more about how to accomplish it on p. 172.

Thinking about the Text

1. Jeff Gage **REPORTS** on efforts country music artists have taken to address the opioid crisis in the United States. Even though this crisis affects the entire country, why, according to Gage, are the country music community's actions particularly noteworthy? Summarize the reasons Gage gives.

2. Writing about popular music can present particular challenges, like carefully considering how much background information to give your target **AUDIENCE**. Some readers will know every word of every song mentioned, while others have zero familiarity. Do some research on the audience for *Rolling Stone*; then consider the decisions Gage made about how to introduce artists and songs. What background information about country music, artists, and specific songs does he provide? Is it too much information? not enough? Point to specific examples to support your conclusions.

3. Gage mentions that country music has a long history of glorifying the use (and sometimes abuse) of drugs and alcohol, and he quotes country artists who have faced personal challenges with these substances. Why might he have mentioned that aspect of country music and its culture? How does including this information impact Gage's **CREDIBILITY**? How would his credibility change if he hadn't included that information or cited personal stories?

4. Gage describes some of the measures that country music artists are taking to address the opioid crisis, including mass distribution of Narcan and fentanyl test strips and widespread information campaigns about recognizing overdose symptoms. Gage also mentions that some musicians are calling attention to the role pharmaceutical companies play in flooding communities with dangerously addictive drugs. Do you think by involving themselves in the policy aspects of the problem that these artists are overstepping their role as popular entertainers? Why or why not? Explain your position.

5. Popular music (and pop culture more generally) has often made harmful behavior seem desirable. In addition to tunes about addictive substances, there are many songs that glamorize gambling, abusive habits, jealousy and possessiveness, rigid gender roles, and general foolhardy behavior. Think of a song that you liked at an important moment of your life, perhaps one that you played over and over. How do you think that song has shaped you over time? Using your own experiences as evidence, write an essay that addresses those questions.

Black Enough: Protecting Linguistic Identity in the Writing Center

GLAVEE GLAVEE

"WELL, I'M NOT BLACK," I say to my friend as if it's a given. Anyone observing our conversation might find this statement out of place, seeing as the speaker is a dark-skinned middle schooler with brown eyes and an out-of-control 'fro: clearly Black. "And I'm not white," I add, to clear up any confusion. Anyone listening might also find this comment strange when the young girl voicing it speaks with the same propriety and tone as a Midwestern English teacher. "I'm living in an in-between space. I guess you could say I'm gray." My friend is apprehensive of my bold claim to a race that did not exist moments before, but she nods. "I've realized that I look too Black for white people and act too white for Black people, so I will be neither. I'm just going to be gray."

Deny, Deny, Denial. That is all I hear as I recount this tale of a girl so disconnected from her own identity that she would not claim the labels that clearly belonged to her. At age thirteen, I could not embrace my racial identity. I would cringe at the terms "Black," "African American," or "BIPOC." The chasm that separated me from identifying with my race boiled down to one

---

GLAVEE GLAVEE, a graduate student pursuing a degree in social work at San Diego State University, wrote this essay for a course called Rhetoric of Written Arguments and the Tutoring of Writing. It was one of the winners of the 2021 Norton Writer's Prize, which recognizes outstanding original essays by undergraduates. The author uses MLA style to document sources.

fact: I couldn't talk Black. I could not use the language of people who looked like me. Separation from anyone who looked or sounded like me and eight years of formal education had beat any chance of "talkin Black" out of me and replaced it with a feeling of shame about my racial identity.

African American Vernacular English—also referred to as AAVE or talkin Black—is a dialect of English with distinct accents, conventions, and grammatical structures. It is used among African Americans in music, media, and daily conversation. One place it is not accepted in is mainstream academia. And that's what be gettin my blood boilin 'bout this whole issue. It ain't like this just some poor boy's English. It's a language used by some 40 million people. It's a dialect of its own with plenty of rules and complications just like Standard American English (SAE). We all be sayin the same things as white people we just say 'em different (Charity et al. 1340). AAVE is still considered an "incorrect" form of English by many SAE speakers, though linguists such as William Labov, Rosina Lippi-Green, and John R. Rickford have gone to great lengths to prove AAVE's legitimacy.

The use of AAVE in academia is systematically suppressed at every level of education. In the essay "Addressing Racial Diversity in a Writing Center: Stories and Lessons from Two Beginners," writing center directors Nancy Barron and Nancy Grimm noted that, in their view, a student's racial identity and lived experiences "can undermine the best of communicative intentions" more than their style or grammar ever could (61). In the US education system, people from historically oppressed groups are often told that the ways they communicate are incorrect. Formal education tries to enforce the idea that SAE is the superior language, but what that also tells Black students is that their language—and by extension, their race—are inferior to those of their white counterparts.

In classrooms of all kinds, Black students are expected to code-switch, or switch from speaking AAVE to SAE, because they are in academic spaces. Students are expected to learn how to read, write, and speak the standard way: the white way. When institutions of learning attempt to standardize the language of AAVE speakers, they attempt to strip away these students' linguistic identities, which damages not only the effectiveness of their writing but also their overall academic success. This essay explores the profound

---

* *Idiolect*: The variety of speech that is unique to each individual, like a linguistic fingerprint. It encompasses all of the features of a dialect, plus the speech habits and quality of voice that each person has. Although two people may speak the same language, even the same dialect, no two people have the exact same idiolect. [Editor's note]

impact of linguistic identity on Black students and how writing centers can help students develop their idiolect, or personal language.

The Linguist's Gospel Truth

To understand why AAVE is a legitimate dialect, one must first understand what makes any language or dialect legitimate. In her essay "The 'Standard English' Fairy Tale: A Rhetorical Analysis of Racist Pedagogies and Commonplace Assumptions about Language Diversity," Laura Greenfield explains how a racist US education system has perpetuated the myth that standardized English is superior to dialects spoken by historically oppressed populations. She builds her argument by explaining five "linguistic facts of life" created by Rosina Lippi-Green. This is an overview of four of those facts and their application to AAVE.

The first truth is that all spoken languages change over time, and the changes can be gradual or sudden. AAVE is constantly shifting. This can be seen in the emergence and decline of slang terms, and in differences between linguistically segregated areas. In the same way that SAE has not remained stagnant since it was first introduced to the United States, AAVE is a living language that continues to evolve.

The next truth is that grammatical rules and effective communication are separate matters. Most often, variations between SAE's and AAVE's grammatical structures have little to no impact on the listener's ability to understand a speaker's meaning. For example, the phrases "she be lyin on the daily" and "she frequently lies" can both be understood to have the same meaning even though they subscribe to different grammar rules. The habitual "be" (She be lyin) doesn't occur in English's standardized form, yet an AAVE speaker's use of the habitual "be" does not impede upon an SAE listener's understanding.

Written and spoken language are separate entities in history, structure, and function. Like many African languages, AAVE has been primarily a spoken dialect. AAVE has minimal representation in written academic discourse. This is a natural development considering that the language originated from African slaves who previously spoke languages that had no written equivalent. These facts have no impact on AAVE's legitimacy.

The last truth is that variation is intrinsic to all spoken languages at every level. The fact that AAVE and SAE sound different is not surprising;

it is expected. Many variations of English are seen across the world, such as Canadian English or Chicano English. This variation does not make one language better than another (Greenfield 34).

A Rooted Language

Everyone is Black. When my new friend from school invites me to a week of workshops at her church, this is the last thing I expect to think when I arrive. I have never seen so many people from the African diaspora gathered in one place. The congregation is primarily composed of first- and second-generation Nigerian-Americans. Being a first-generation Ghanaian-American, I should fit right in. But I don't. Every time someone makes a "white people" joke, I get sideways glances in my direction and a quickly muttered, "No offense." Idle girl talk turns into judgment because I don't prefer dark chocolate over white chocolate. This, and the pleasant surprise that comes when I eat Jollof rice, earns me a new nickname: Oreo. Every interaction with the people who should be my peers leads to the same conclusion. Sure, I'm Black; I'm just not Black enough.

The summer before my freshman year of high school, I realized being "gray" wasn't going to suffice. It didn't matter to my new Black friends that I had the right skin tone, dressed the right way, or finally got my 'fro under control. They could sense I was still just chillin in that gray space. The issue they had with me went deeper than my biracial background; it was deeper than not acting or talkin Black. They knew I didn't understand the history and pride they held in their skin tone, their mannerisms, and their speech.

Common language builds solidarity in communities because solidarity comes from shared experiences. In 2015, linguist John R. Rickford and colleagues published the experimental study "Neighborhood Effects on Use of African-American Vernacular English," in which they report that residential economic segregation is a contributing factor to AAVE use—which, in turn, contributes to a strong social identity. They explain that in general, language is a "socially constructed behavior, jointly influenced by exposure, identity, and peer group influence" (11817). The language of an individual is not developed in solitude. A person's idiolect, their unique way of speaking, is a reflection of the people they come from. So when professors start raggin on students for talkin like they from

---

Glavee's own experiences are central to this essay. Incorporating ideas from sources also supports the main argument. Synthesizing ideas is an important skill; learn more about how to do it well on pp. 542–43.

the ghetto, them professors ain't just disrespectin the students. They be disrespectin the community we come from. They be tryna take away the men and women who helped get us into institutions of higher education. They tryna take away who we are.

AAVE is a language built in a community with a long history of oppression. In 2010, William Labov published a study titled "Unendangered Dialect, Endangered People: The Case of African American Vernacular English," which claims that social factors such as residential segregation and historical oppression lead to the divergence, development, and flourishing of AAVE. Labov states AAVE is not the cause of African Americans' problems. Rather, AAVE is a resource used to elegantly and thoughtfully reflect "on the oppression and misery of daily life" (24). There is a certain beauty and emotion that is articulated in AAVE due to its history. AAVE has inherent value and depth just like SAE. The education system just ain't willin to recognize this value. They be puttin down students who express themselves and they struggles in they native tongue because it don't conform to this idea of proper English. They be forcin students to relearn how to talk, write, and think in a standardized fashion and takin away students' unique, historically based, and culturally informed linguistic identity in the process.

I Said What I Said

"Ya know, sometimes, when you start gettin real sassy, you get this little twang in your voice and you start to . . . you know." My coach trails off with a little shrug of his shoulders. "Whatchu tryna tell me, Coach?" I retort with a side-eye, aggravated that he's interrupting my lecture to one of the new players.

"I'm just sayin, sometimes you talk a little Black and I didn't know if you realized you doin it."

"What? I don't think . . . Was I?" I turn to my co-captain for confirmation but the man knows betta than to be talkin to me when I'm in a mood, so he's suddenly real interested in his shoes. "Well," I continue, lookin back to Coach, "if this girl gon be sassin me when I'm tryna teach her somethin, I'ma give her sass right back in whichever tone I see fit."

By the spring of my sophomore year, I had educated myself in Black Culture. I read the books, listened to the music, and talked to the people I needed to so I could understand what I was missing. Before I even realized what had happened, I had started to incorporate my newfound literacy into my daily life. *Their* linguistic identity became *my* linguistic identity. What was once their community became our community. For the first time in my life, I began to feel Black enough.

So What's the Problem?

The US education system largely subscribes to a standard, or dominant, language ideology. This principle asserts that to achieve effective communication, all writers and speakers need to conform to "one set of dominant language rules that stem from a single dominant discourse" (Young 62). So students can speak whichever way they like, but only at home. This ideology perpetuates the lie that there is something wrong with students' native dialects. And this type of thinkin is ingrained in students and teachers from preschool to post-secondary education. We be gettin told, "You gotta speak like an academic when you in school." But what they really gettin at is you can't be talkin like you Black when you in school because Black ain't academic.

Stanley Fish is a professor and cultural critic known for his support of the standard language ideology. In part three of a series of articles, published in *The New York Times*, called "What Should Colleges Teach?," Fish claims that if professors want to teach English, they must not "affirm the students' right to their own patterns and varieties of language—the dialects of their nurture or whatever dialects in which they find their own identity and style" (Fish). This means professors that subscribe to the standard language ideology should not allow or encourage students to use the unique idiolect they have developed throughout their lives. Fish and many teaching professionals believe that when students do not use SAE, it makes them more vulnerable to prejudice. According to this ideology, the students' linguistic identity is the problem that needs to be resolved. They be wantin students to internalize the racism they experience and start suppressin they linguistic identity. Them professors think we gonna be judged less if we learn to talk proper. Learnin to talk white ain't gonna stop people from judgin me the second I walk in a room. Before I even speak a word in any dialect, people will already have made assumptions 'bout my education, my family, and my financial status. The real issue ain't with the way Black students be talkin; the real issue is that you lookin down on me and my language even though we should have the right to exist and be heard in academic spaces.

The systemic racism that standard language ideology supports can be seen in college enrollment rates and the six-year graduation rates of non-Hispanic, African American students. In San Diego County there are three 4-year public universities. The graduation rates (in six years or less) of African Americans at these schools are on average 11% below the university's overall graduation rate (United States Census Bureau). At each of these universities, Black students have one of the lowest graduation rates among the student population. Low graduation and enrollment rates for Black students occur not only in San Diego County but all across America (National Center for Education Statistics). Universities are still built around white standards and traditions, so Black students who choose to maintain strong connections with their racial and linguistic identities are neither expected nor encouraged to succeed in the average American university. These trends will continue in the United States unless we change the way we approach education.

Cuz I Am Who I Am

Universities can become places where even more Black students are successful. That can start with encouraging students to feel confident using their linguistic identity in every setting. College writing centers can help students develop and protect their linguistic identity by teaching effective ways to incorporate it into academic writing. In the essay "Should Writers Use They Own English?" from the book *Writing Centers and the New Racism*, Vershawn Ashanti Young argues that writers should not be confined by SAE and should instead be allowed to use their native dialects in academic writing. He demonstrates this claim by writing in AAVE to show the value of a new writing strategy called code meshing. Young introduces the term "code meshing" to propose the idea that people should write and speak with a combination of standard and nonstandard dialects. He states, "Code meshing is the new code-switching; it's multidialectalism and pluralingualism in one speech act, in one paper." It blends "dialects, international languages, local idioms, chat-room lingo, and the rhetorical styles of various ethnic and cultural groups in both formal and informal speech acts" (67).

Teaching students to code mesh would allow them to use their linguistic identity to their advantage. In a speech titled "Moving beyond Alright: And the Emotional Toll of This, My Life Matters Too, in the Writing Center Work,"

Neisha-Anne Green, director of American University's Writing Center, shares her personal experience as a Black tutor, writer, and director while explaining to other writing center directors that a Black person's identity heavily influences how they write. Green shares her struggles and successes with figuring out how to code mesh in her graduate thesis. Reflecting on the process, she noted, "I wasn't just a writer anymore, I was a Black writer. I was writing, and Neisha-Anne was all over the page. My rhetorical traditions, my cultures, my sass, and attitude were all on the page and they coexisted with the ever-fluid 'standard'" (22–23). By code meshing, Green was able to incorporate her identity into her writing. She produced lively and effective papers by clearly expressing linguistic identity in her research. If writing centers teach code meshing as an academically acceptable form of writin, students from nondominant groups are gonna be usin they identities to they own advantage. Diverse voices and perspectives are gonna be represented and celebrated in academic discourse.

Conclusion

I talk to myself. Alone in my room, with no one else around, I translate the internal monologue that flows through all our minds into spoken words. When I'm just stating facts and having idle conversations with the wall, I typically speak in SAE. But when I really get goin, when I start sharin my emotions, my defiance, my passions, that's when I start talkin Black. This dialect makes me feel at home in my skin. But never in my wildest dreams did I imagine I'd be writin the way I think when I got to the university level. I was finna write white for the rest of my academic career, but being able to write like this, in my voice, gave me the confidence to speak my mind. If all institutions of learning encouraged students to find and develop their linguistic identities instead of trying to suppress them, students could learn to be more confident and successful academic writers. That's what universities are supposed to be doin: helpin students find and use their voices.

Works Cited

Barron, Nancy, and Nancy Grimm. "Addressing Racial Diversity in a Writing Center: Stories and Lessons from Two Beginners." *The Writing Center Journal*, vol. 22, no. 2, 2002, pp. 55–83. JSTOR, www.jstor.org/stable/43442150.

Charity, Anne, et al. "Familiarity with School English in African American Children and Its Relation to Early Reading Achievement." *Child Development*, vol. 75, no. 5, 2004, pp. 1340–56. JSTOR, www.jstor.org/stable/3696487.

Fish, Stanley. "What Should Colleges Teach? Part 3." *The New York Times*, 7 Sept. 2009, opinionator.blogs.nytimes.com/2009/08/31/what-should-colleges-teach-part-2.

Green, Neisha-Anne. "Moving beyond Alright: And the Emotional Toll of This, My Life Matters Too, in the Writing Center Work." *The Writing Center Journal*, vol. 37, no. 1, 2018, pp. 15–34. JSTOR, www.jstor.org/stable/26537361.

Greenfield, Laura. "The 'Standard English' Fairy Tale: A Rhetorical Analysis of Racist Pedagogies and Commonplace Assumptions about Language Diversity." Greenfield and Rowan, pp. 33–60.

Greenfield, Laura, and Karen Rowan, editors. *Writing Centers and the New Racism: A Call for Sustainable Dialogue and Change*. UP of Colorado, 2011.

Labov, William. "Unendangered Dialect, Endangered People: The Case of African American Vernacular English." *Transforming Anthropology*, vol. 18, no. 1, 2010, pp. 15–27. AnthroSource, https://doi.org/10.1111/j.1548-7466.2010.01066.x.

National Center for Education Statistics. *Integrated Postsecondary Education Data System* (IPEDS), 31 Aug. 2019, nces.ed.gov/ipeds/datacenter/InstitutionByName.aspx?goToReportId=6.

Rickford, John, et al. "Neighborhood Effects on Use of African-American Vernacular English." *PNAS*, vol. 112, no. 38, 2015, pp. 11817–822. *PNAS*, https://doi.org/10.1073/pnas.1500176112.

United States Census Bureau. "San Diego County, California." *QuickFacts*, 2019, www.census.gov/quickfacts/facttable/sandiegocountycalifornia/PST045219.

Young, Vershawn Ashanti. "Should Writers Use They Own English?" Greenfield and Rowan, pp. 61–72.

Thinking about the Text

1. Glavee Glavee **DESCRIBES** four "truths" (7–10) about language and discusses them in reference to AAVE, or "talkin Black" (3). What are those four truths? Summarize them briefly. What have you observed that could confirm or refute them in your own life and with the language varieties that you use? Give an example for each truth.

2. Glavee combines personal stories with summaries and quotations from research scholars in order to make an argument. Why do you think Glavee chose to include personal experiences? How would the essay be different if it were a **REPORT** alone, leaving out Glavee's **NARRATIVES**? Or if it were all **NARRATIVE**, without any outside research? Choose one example or section making use of both narrative and reporting that you find particularly effective and describe why.

3. How does Glavee explain the concept of code meshing? According to Glavee, what are the benefits of code meshing? How effectively does Glavee employ this strategy in this essay? Explain your reasoning and point to examples from the essay to support your response.

4. What **ARGUMENT** does Glavee make in the conclusion? Does the evidence presented throughout the essay support this position? Why or why not? Explain your response and point to examples from the essay to support your reasoning.

5. Glavee's essay is in response to an assignment to identify and explore a problem with literacy education. How would you take on a similar assignment? Reflect on the question and then choose the genre best suited to what you want to say. You may want to center your work in a **NARRATIVE** of your own experience, or you may wish to focus more on **REPORTING** conditions you've observed in your community or have researched in published materials. You may also want to take a specific **POSITION** based on your observations and experiences.

Origin Stories

ANNETTE GORDON-REED

I**T'S A SAFE BET** that most people in the United States, when they think of it, believe that Black people first appeared in North America in 1619. The story of the "20. and odd negroes" that John Rolfe announced, in matter of fact fashion, to have arrived in Virginia that year is often taken as the beginning of what we might call "Black America"—from that twenty, to 4 million—by the time of Emancipation in 1865—to nearly 40 million today.

Origin stories matter, for individuals, groups of people, and for nations. They inform our sense of self; telling us what kind of people we believe we are, what kind of nation we believe we live in. They usually carry, at least, a hope that where we started might hold the key to where we are in the present. We can say, then, that much of the concern with origin stories is about our current needs and desires (usually to feel good about ourselves), not actual history. History is about people and events in a particular setting and context, and how those things have changed over time in ways that make the past different from our own time, with an understanding that those changes were not inevitable. Origin stories often seek to find the familiar,

---

ANNETTE GORDON-REED is a historian and professor of law and history at Harvard University. She has won numerous prizes for her writing, including a Pulitzer Prize and a National Book Award for her groundbreaking work on Thomas Jefferson and the children he fathered by Sally Hemings, a woman he enslaved. This reading is excerpted from her 2021 best-selling book, *On Juneteenth*.

or the superficially familiar—memory, sometimes shading into mythology. Both memory and mythology have their uses, even if they must be separated from our understandings about the demands of historical thinking.

Consider the difference between the stories of Plymouth, Massachusetts, and those of Jamestown, Virginia. Plymouth Rock gives Americans a founding story about a valiant people leaving their homes to escape religious persecution, and founding a new society in the wilderness, with the aid of friendly Indigenous people, like Squanto (Tisquantum) of the Patuxet. Who among those who grew up in the United States did not perform in, or watch, school plays telling the story of these encounters, or make cutouts of turkeys symbolizing the first Thanksgiving feast that the Pilgrims and Patuxets shared—in most cases, I would wager, without knowing the name of the Indian group involved or Squanto's true name?

At the other end of the scale, we have the narrative of Jamestown, created more openly as an economic venture in 1607. It is difficult to wrest an uplifting story from the doings of English settlers who created the colony for no purpose other than making money or, at least, to make a living for themselves. Not long after their arrival, they started down a path that would make Virginia a full-fledged slave society, the largest and richest of the thirteen colonies. What little I learned about Jamestown as a child centered on the story of Pocahontas (Matoaka), the daughter of Powhatan, who serves the same function as Squanto in the Pilgrim story, to emphasize the triumph of amity over enmity between the Indigenous people and the English settlers, something very different than what actually happened.

I am certain nearly every American schoolchild of my generation learned of Pocahontas, though one of my college classmates assured me that her elementary school in New England had downplayed the Virginia settlement and focused mainly on the Pilgrims as the beginning of America as we know it. Jamestown was mentioned, she said, but as a brief experiment of little lasting consequence. *"We learned there were some people down there,"* she said with a wave of her hand. I imagine that is how most Americans in the past were taught to view the colonies.

There is also a version of this attitude about Plymouth versus Jamestown in the origin story of African Americans. I remember hearing in school, probably because I was in Texas, stray references to a man of African descent—a "Negro"—named Esteban (Estebanico), who was in what would become Texas during the time of Spanish exploration. The last phrase, "during the time of Spanish exploration," signaled that this was information about a world gone by that we didn't have to pay much attention to, as it had little to do with understandings about the history of our country. I hadn't been told that other people of African decent—some enslaved, some not—arrived with the Spanish when they came to the Americas. Whether enslaved or free, these people were disconnected from the institution of plantation slavery that developed in Texas three centuries later, the institution that helped define my ancestors' circumstances.

The same phenomenon applies to St. Augustine, Florida, which was not at all a part of my early education. It was there, in fact, that racially based slavery, as an organized system, began on American soil, established by the Spanish as early as 1565. In 1735 the Spanish governor chartered a settlement for enslaved Africans who escaped from the English colonies and made it to St. Augustine. The only condition for protection was that the new residents adopt Catholicism and swear allegiance to the Spanish king. The settlement of free Blacks existed until the Spanish sold Florida to the United States in 1817.

I had heard of St. Augustine by the time I got to college. But it, too, was in the category *"there were some people down there."* The English had "won" the contest against the Spanish in North America—in Texas and in Florida. What was the point of incorporating this story of Africans and Spanish people into the general narrative of American history or, more specifically, the history of African Americans? The same could be said of the French, in their beaver-trapping colonies near the Great Lakes. They were "also-rans" in the race for the territory that became the United States. The brief period of Dutch slave ownership in New York is almost totally out of the picture.

All of this was the result of a nationalist-oriented history, with an intense focus on what was going on within the boundaries of the United States, and seeing what was going on almost totally from the perspective of English-speaking (and White) people. The world enclosed in that way left out so much about the true nature of life in Early America, about all the varied influences that shaped the people and circumstances during those times. It closes off the vital understanding about contingency, how things could have taken a different turn. Very significantly, it helped create and maintain an extremely narrow construction of Blackness.

Under the conventional narrative with which most Americans, it is safe to say, are familiar, Blacks came to North America under the power of the English from places that were never clearly defined, for where they

10

came from didn't matter much. They went from speaking the languages of their homelands to speaking English. They worked on plantations in the fields or in the house. This highly edited origin story winds the Black experience tight, limiting the imaginative possibilities of Blackness—what could be done by people in that skin. To be sure, the institution of slavery itself circumscribed the actions of enslaved African Americans, but it never destroyed their personhood. They did not become a separate species by the experience of being enslaved. All of the feelings, talents, failings, strengths and weaknesses—all the states and qualities that exist in human beings—remained in them. There has been too great a tendency within some presentations of enslaved people to lose sight of that fact, in ways obvious and not.

For example, we can see it in the treatment of that most basic of human traits: the ability to acquire and to speak a language. Language, however formed, connects people to one another. Dutch was the first language of noted abolitionist Sojourner Truth, born Isabella Baumfree in Swartekill, New York, near the end of the 1790s. She almost certainly spoke English with a Dutch-inflected accent. Yet, reproductions of her speech were written in the stereotypical dialect universally chosen to portray the speech of enslaved Blacks, no matter where in the country they lived. Under this formulation, the experiences of growing up hearing and speaking Dutch had no effect upon Truth. It was as if the legal status of being enslaved, and the biological reality of having been born of African descent, fixed her pattern of speech, almost as a matter of brain function.

When I was working on my first book, writing about the way historians had handled the story of Thomas Jefferson and Sally Hemings, I noticed that one line of attack on the veracity of Madison Hemings, who said in recollections that he was the son of Jefferson and Hemings, was to suggest that the statements he gave to the journalist Samuel Wetmore were unreliable because it was unlikely that a former enslaved person could speak in standard English. The notion that such a thing could happen was treated as presumptively incredible. Even a brief thought about the circumstances of Hemings's life, viewing him as a human being, however, would tell a different story about his narrative. Hemings's recollections make clear that his older siblings—Beverley (a male) and Harriet—left Monticello to live as White people. Both married White people who may not have known that their spouses were partly Black and had been born enslaved. The communities they lived in, Washington, D.C., and Maryland, evidently, did not know

Close reading of her sources led Gordon-Reed to an important new analysis of historical accounts. Learn how to practice critical reading on pp. 533–35.

that either. Many years after the pair left Monticello, their younger brother, Eston, would follow his older siblings into the White world, settling his family in Madison, Wisconsin.

How did Madison Hemings's siblings live convincingly as White if they spoke in the dialect universally applied to enslaved people? Why would Madison—the middle son between the older Beverley and Harriet and the younger, Eston—speak differently than his siblings? Realizing that the actual circumstances of the Hemings children's lives mattered, and should have been taken into account, would have made clear that it made no sense to assume that Hemings could not have spoken in the way portrayed in his conversation with Wetmore.

A similar analysis, or lack of analysis, has often been at play in writing about the Hemings children's mother, Sally. As I have traveled the country talking about the books I have written about the Hemings family, I've been struck by the responses to the fact that Sally Hemings, and her brother James, learned to speak French during their years in France. On several occasions I have been asked, with seeming wonder, "how" they could have learned to speak French. And even when the question is not specifically raised, it seems to hang in the air when people ponder the fact that she, and presumably her Mother, thought for a time to remain in Paris when Jefferson decided to go home. *How could they have gotten along there? They didn't speak the language.* Doubts about their basic capacities persist, despite the differences in their circumstances and opportunities in France. Because slavery in the United States was racially based, it was easy to graft the legally imposed incapacities of slavery onto Black people as a group, making incapacity an inherent feature of the race.

Perhaps there is something about French, for a long time the language of diplomacy and culture. It is considered "fancy" in a way that goes along with the country's cuisine and vaunted high fashion—haute cuisine, haute couture. What of individuals born at the lowest rung of society? Could enslaved people, Black people, ever lay claim to sophistication? Over one hundred years after James Hemings's and Sally Hemings's time in France, Secretary of State William Jennings Bryan, while contemplating a crisis in Haiti, exclaimed, "Dear me. Think of it. N*****s speaking French."

It is hard to imagine that Bryan seriously thought that learning a language, which human beings do quite well without formal instruction—uneducated babies do it all the time—was really beyond the ken of Black people. He cannot have been that ignorant. Instead, he was more likely following a well-worn path: the "joke" that sends a vicious message through supposedly lighthearted humor. So much of racism is about announcing, in various ways, the agreed-upon fictions about Black people that justify attempting to keep them in a subordinate status.

The fiction that has African Americans naturally speaking in a particular way, or unable to learn a language, slyly promotes the notion that Blacks are somewhat less than human, in their inability to master a human trait: the capacity to engage in complex communication. At the very least, the ideas about Blacks and language serve as means to convey the supposed gulf that exists between the races. Administrators involved in the WPA Slave Narrative Project of the 1930s, which gathered the recollections of formerly enslaved people, engaged in a concerted effort to render the speech of the interviewees into stereotypical Black dialect. As a result, the accents and speech of all the interviewees—from Virginia to Georgia to Texas—appear as if people in those very different regions spoke exactly the same way. The exaggerated dialect was supposed to signal "authenticity," an authenticity defined by incapacity.

Which brings us back to Estebanico, whose sojourn in Texas had taken place nearly a century before the landing at Jamestown, nearly two hundred years before James and Sally Hemings were in France. Estebanico was described as a "black Arab from Azamor," on the coast of Morocco. A Muslim, he had been forced to convert to Christianity and sold away from his home to Spain. He came to the Americas with the man who enslaved him and [Spanish explorer Álvar Núñez] Cabeza de Vaca.

Cabeza de Vaca, who lived to produce a wildly popular memoir of the extraordinary adventure, wrote about Estebanico as having played a key role as the chief translator between the Spaniards and the Indigenous people because of his great talent for learning and speaking languages. Estebanico, and the Europeans, became renowned as medicine men by the people they encountered. Estebanico appears to have been able to achieve a measure of respect.

I don't recall whether Estebanico's talent for languages featured in the fleeting mention that was made of him in my early education. I do wonder what difference it might have made to our understandings about the enslaved to have had a more fully realized example of one who displayed such perseverance and talent. We would have encountered a known person, to substitute for the nameless people in cotton fields who, at least in my education, never broke out and appeared as anything other than fungible agricultural workers. Learning that the Spanish explorers, and the Indigenous people they encountered and lived with at times, relied on Estebanico to help them speak with one another brings another dimension to our understandings about slavery and the people enslaved.

Not to place conquering in a good light, but seeing Africans in America who were out of the strict confines of the plantation—and seeing them presented as something other than the metaphorical creation of English people—would have pushed back against the narrative of inherent limitation. Africans were all over the world, doing different things, having all kinds of experiences. Blackness does not equal inherent incapacity and natural limitation.

Thinking about the Text

1. Annette Gordon-Reed focuses on language in order to support her arguments about origin stories and the ways that the history of Africans in America is taught. What are her main ARGUMENTS? Why, according to Gordon-Reed, are representations of speech and language so important? Is her argument persuasive? Why or why not? Explain your reasoning.

2. Although Gordon-Reed's essay is focused on events that occurred centuries ago, she also inserts some of her own experiences. She mentions things she learned in school as a child, discusses evidence she unearthed in her previous work, and comments on experiences she had during the public events related to that work. Why might she have chosen to write herself into the essay? How effective is her use of NARRATIVE? Explain your reasoning.

3. Accurate representations of someone's speech matter, according to Gordon-Reed. What EXAMPLES does she offer to support this argument? Are her examples effective? Why or why not?

4. Gordon-Reed describes the way that Sojourner Truth's speech has been depicted, but she doesn't quote directly from those representations. She also mentions the "stereotypical Black dialect" (17) that was employed in the WPA Slave Narrative Project of the 1930s but offers no example quotations. Why might she have chosen to omit quotations as a form of EVIDENCE? Do you think she made a good rhetorical decision? Why or why not?

5. Gordon-Reed begins her essay by talking about origin stories and their importance for "individuals, groups of people, and for nations" (2). What are the origin stories that you heard as a child—whether in school or from your family—that have contributed to your sense of self? Reflect on one of those stories; write it out in as much detail as you remember. How accurate and factual do you think it is? You might even do some research to check out the facts. If any features of that story were found to be incomplete or inaccurate, would you think differently about yourself or your community in any way? Why or why not? Write an essay **REFLECTING** on these questions about origin stories that relate or matter to you.

How I Escaped the Tyranny of the Prophets of Beauty
LING LING HUANG

For a long time, I was a devout follower of what the sociologist Tressie McMillan Cottom calls the "prophets" of beauty—those who determine and enforce what is pleasing to the eye. I grew up in a small suburb near Houston, and until I was 7, I could count on one hand the number of people I saw who looked like me. So I supplicated at the mirror, hands clasped to my face, applying creams and, later, toners and acids to tame the Chinese features that kept me from belonging.

I didn't yet know that other words for "tame" are "subjugate" and "oppress." It would be decades before I learned that everything I did to belong was an act of self-erasure, and that it estranged me from myself and the deeper connections I had to my family and culture.

My parents, working hard to support our still-new American life, couldn't afford child care. Thus, my caretakers became the TV and the community pool, where I spent my summers and after-school hours. Both were instrumental in teaching me the "truth" of what was beautiful.

LING LING HUANG is a writer and violinist. Her 2023 novel *Natural Beauty* won the Lambda Literary Award in Bisexual Fiction, was long-listed for a PEN/Hemingway Award, and was a *New York Times* Editors' Choice. She has also been a substitute violinist in the New York Philharmonic and several other major symphony orchestras. This April 2023 essay was published in the *Washington Post*.

Catwoman and Harley Quinn were blond, as were Angelica Pickles and the dimpled Lizzie McGuire. The lifeguards at the pool were blond, as were most of the kids I tried to play with and the parents who dropped them off. I was not. The pool had the shocking effect of making blond people even more so, while I stayed the same. The sun confirmed my worst fears by consecrating their beauty.

So I doused my hair with lemon juice and a lightener called Sun In, which I'd saved up to buy. This did nothing. I dipped a pair of chopsticks in vinegar and held them to my cheeks for an hour a day, believing this would give me dimples. It did not. Besides violin practice for four to six hours a day, most of my interests hinged on finding other such means of beautifying myself.

When I think about this now, I mainly regret the wasted time.

In middle school, I came to understand that my nose was my biggest problem. "If only she had a different nose, she would be much better-looking," relatives and family friends said. "Don't smile—your nose broadens in a way that makes it worse!" When my parents rented a video of *Little Women*, I found a kindred spirit: Amy March, who used a clothespin to reshape her nose while she slept. I tried the Amy method, but what I really took away from her character was the idea that beauty and class mobility were related. By the time she was 16, Amy was "the flower of the family," lovely and artistic and marriageable. By reshaping your nose, in other words, you could reshape yourself and the future available to you.

I carried these lessons into young adulthood. My first job after moving to New York was at a natural beauty and wellness store—a meticulously curated workplace where I used a gold-colored spoon to dish out organic ingredients for health tonics and sold $400 water filters to influencers and actresses and trustees of the Whitney. I was finally surrounded by all the tools I needed to further my assimilation.

At work one day, I received a call from my parents, telling me my beloved great-uncle had died. I left my immaculate workplace early and thought as I walked home about the last time I had seen him: in China, on a trip with my parents before college. I didn't remember much of that trip, largely because of the severe eating disorder I had at the time. But now a memory resurfaced, loosened by grief.

The memory was of my parents and me having tea with family: Through the humidity of the Beijing summer and the steam wafting thickly from my cup, I glimpsed a nose exactly like mine. It belonged to my great-uncle, who was sitting across from me. He was a kind and intelligent man, thoughtful

---

Huang is describing deeply personal thoughts and experiences to a large audience. To do so effectively, she needed to be clear about her purpose for writing and other aspects of her rhetorical situation. See how you can do the same on pp. 34–38.

and playful. I watched as he smiled and laughed unashamedly, something I had forbidden myself to do because of how it stretched my nose.

Though I had not seen my great-uncle for 12 years, this memory released others, and I recalled more of the time we spent together. Hot afternoons at the zoo and mornings when he bought me soy milk and deep-fried wheat dough for breakfast. How we made each other laugh.

In this moment, I understood the word "family" for what seemed like the first time. My desire for assimilation had come from seeing only how I was different. Now, I began to search for inherited likenesses instead. My mother reaching to pour another cup of tea—with my arms. My dad looking at me—with my eyes. Here was proof of belonging.

I don't have to graft the values of others onto my own. I don't need to tread their paths or dream their dreams.

There is something freeing about the persistence of our bodies. No matter how much I try to tame or oppress my physical reality and its cultural giveaways, it will continue to follow the blueprint it inherited—the one written by my predecessors. When I miss my great-uncle now, I look in the mirror. There, I can see his smile. When I laugh, I can hear his laughter. It starts deep in my body and erupts from my throat—a living, breathing heirloom.

Thinking about the Text

1. Ling Ling Huang writes a **NARRATIVE** of personal transformation with a title that leads readers to believe that she will be addressing beauty. She ends up, however, talking about family and physical traits they share. Do you think the essay fulfills the promise of its title? Why or why not? Why do you think Huang selected this title?

2. Huang mentions the names of four blonds who were influential during her childhood, but she offers no explanation of who they were. Are you familiar with all four? Consider Huang's main **AUDIENCE**. Given that audience, do you think Huang should have given readers more information on these cultural references? Or did she make a good choice in assuming that her audience would be familiar with all four? Explain your reasoning.

3. Some of the richest descriptive detail in the essay comes in talking about working at a beauty and wellness store. What **PURPOSE** do these details serve? Are they necessary to the story Huang is telling? Why or why not? Identify a few other areas where vivid details help bring Huang's story to life.

4. Huang describes events and behaviors that involve deeply felt emotions, yet her writing is direct and matter of fact. Why do you think she chose to use this **STYLE** of writing? How would her essay have been more or less effective if she had used more emotional language or revealed more of her feelings?

5. We probably all have a story of a personal transformation, an aspect of ourselves that we started out hiding or running from and later came to understand as not such a bad thing after all. (Maybe it even became your favorite part of yourself!) Write a **NARRATIVE** in which you describe and reflect on a transformation of your own—a quality you came to embrace, an experience you saw in a new light, or something similar. Think carefully about your **STYLE** and **TONE**. Keep it light if you'd rather, or be as deeply revelatory as you're comfortable being, but let your story be an honest one.

One Star

KEVIN M. KEARNEY

I DON'T KNOW SARA beyond the few details *Yelp* provides: She's from a Pittsburgh suburb, she's been writing reviews since 2010, and she gave the Grand Canyon one star. "Nothing here but desiccated bone dry just like California drought," she writes, sounding like a modernist in need of a nap. "In awe for a brief 5 minutes and then the kids will realize it's just rocks without entertainment, restrooms."

I'm mesmerized by each of Sara's 13 one-star reviews. In her decade-plus as an amateur critic, she has evaluated a sushi restaurant in Oregon ("The fishes were so smelly"), the city of San José ("School shootings at its best"), and a 24 Hour Fitness ("the scale was broken. the machines were broken. and Tom is broken").

Yelp had been around for close to a decade before I ever read a review. A friend, a barista, told me he had been singled out in a one-star assessment and was worried he might be fired. The critic had been incensed about the wait time. "Doesn't that come with ordering a pour-over?" my friend asked me.

I told him I'd write a five-star review to offset the negative score and, hopefully, prevent his termination, even though I knew I couldn't do it under my name. I was teaching high school then and tried my best

---

KEVIN M. KEARNEY is a writer whose work has appeared in *Stereogum, Paste, Slate,* and other periodicals. He is also the author of the 2022 novel *How to Keep Time.* This March 2024 essay was originally published in *Slate.*

to remain anonymous online, scared my students might discover I had a personal life. I knew I'd need to defend my friend with an alias, though I didn't know where to start. At the time, my go-to karaoke song was Sugar Ray's 1997 hit "Fly," so, as a tribute, I decided to write from the perspective of Mark McGrath, the lead singer of the band and the sometime host of television's *Extra*. Mark loved the coffee shop. He especially liked my friend.

The change was immediate. My five stars effectively erased the stranger's one, and my friend kept his job. With the *Yelp* app now on my home screen, I began looking up my other local haunts, horrified to find that they were also being unjustly maligned. Mark got to work, writing rave reviews for my corner bar, the after-hours taqueria, and Underdogs, a hot dog spot I'd never patronized but that had nonetheless earned my respect for its pun-filled menu. He bragged about touring with Crazy Town while he complimented the bar's nachos. He quoted from his songs as he praised the taqueria's chorizo. He even claimed he was living in a lair below Underdogs, that the universe had called him to move to the City of Brotherly Love.

As time went on, Mark went quiet, though I continued devouring one-star reviews, infuriated by their authors' self-righteous diatribes. Why did they think they were the arbiters of the world? And why couldn't they see that their criticisms affected real people with real livelihoods? I'd search for

Review: 1/5 stars. Just rocks without entertainment, restrooms.

a favorite spot, then scroll to the bottom, looking for the pettiest grievances from the strangest accounts to hate-read.... After a while, I was no longer indignant—I was curious. Who were these people?

Tom D'Ambrisi has some ideas. He's the owner of the Butcher's Block, a steakhouse in Long Branch, New Jersey, who replies to his one-star reviews on *Yelp*. Ralph, who said the restaurant's security was disrespectful, is a "huge [*****]. The biggest." Greg, who complained about the temperature of his porterhouse, is a "world class [*****]." Reputation management firms urge small business owners to respond to negative reviews in a measured tone, with apologies for poor service, but D'Ambrisi has no interest in appeasing people who would give one star. "You leave reviews," he writes to Ravin, who noted the difficulty of securing a reservation, "because you don't get what you want rite away."

Not everyone responds to one-star reviews, though plenty of people enjoy laughing at their stupidity. Popular social media accounts like "Subpar Parks" and "So Bad It's Goodreads" catalog humorously ignorant takes on national parks and works of literature. Every post has the same less-than-subtle subtext: *Check out this idiot*. I don't follow these accounts, mostly because they feel redundant. Anyone who's spent more than an hour online understands that the internet is filled with bad actors and worse opinions. Also of note: Water is wet.

Dunking on one-star reviews also ignores their practical purpose as a last resort for people who feel they've been conned. My friend Alanna wrote her first one-star review after a restaurant botched the reservation for the luncheon following her grandmother's funeral. Since then, she has written 10 one-star reviews, each with a detailed description of how the business fell short of its obligation. For her, it's always a simple equation. "I wouldn't be writing it if they had done what I needed them to do," she told me.

I understand why Alanna writes one-star reviews. I also understand why someone like D'Ambrisi might get angry enough to respond to them. Still, I'm largely uninterested in reading reviews that argue the quality of service. The one-star reviews I love, the ones that feel like actual literature, have little to do with commerce. In fact, they rarely seem like reviews. They're part obscured confessional, part accidental poetry, containing writing that has been liberated from distractions like narrative, punctuation, and coherence. Like great fiction, they're elusive and complicated. Unlike most of the internet, they're remarkably human.

Scroll through *Yelp* and you'll find Mikey, who left Florida for California only to be underwhelmed by the Pacific Ocean. "I'll stick with pools that can be heated thank you very much," he explains. And Emily, who couldn't believe that people were so impressed with the "national disappointment" that is the Liberty Bell. "Not in a tower. Cannot be rung," she writes, "AND it's broken." And Nicholas, whose summary of a trip to the Happiest Place on Earth is surprisingly masochistic. "Spent thousands just to have all the cast hit on my girlfriend. I hate this place," he says in his one-star review of Disney World. "I will probably come back though."

Sara's take on the Grand Canyon is my favorite, though, and is the one that still bewilders me after all these years. I can't understand how someone could stare into the Grand Canyon and find it less than immaculate. I can't comprehend how someone could stand on the edge of the South Rim and complain about the lack of cell service. I messaged her on *Yelp* to learn more about her experience, but she never replied. By the looks of it, she's disappeared from the site. Her last review is from 2016 and awards the city of Roseville, California, a relatively impressive two stars. "If you love desert life, bomb threats, don't mind getting premature wrinkles, burn to a crisp for 6 months out of the year," she explains, "you hit the jackpot."

All I have is what she's written—these unbroken walls of text stuffed with run-on sentences and trivial complaints. But I've found that's plenty. Whenever I return to her Grand Canyon review, I notice something new. The most recent time, I was struck by her sudden apology: "Sorry but it feels like looking at dead mummies." I tried to decipher why she lists the most common forms of death at the park ("heat stroke, drowning, or simply drive off the canyon") and wondered if I should be concerned with the way she offhandedly notes: "Easy place to commit murder. Just push the dude over the cliff and no body find out."

And that's when I started to see her, exhausted after a day of direct sun and lying on a stiff motel comforter. The kids are asleep on a pullout. A local news channel buzzes in the background. She's typing at a furious pace, unloading all of the day's frustrations into the app's small text box. "No plant, no life, it's like a picture of death," she writes, then pauses, remembering the feeling she had looking down at what seemed like an endless drop. She recalls how small it made her feel and how, to her surprise, she'd found the smallness comforting. "Even death," she continues, "I guess there is beauty too."

Kearney approached his topic seriously and analytically. But the tone of his essay is more informal. See more about tone, stance, and other style decisions on pp. 697–98.

Thinking about the Text

1. In addition to being an amusing and entertaining read, what additional **PURPOSE** might Kevin Kearney have for writing this essay? What is the larger insight he gained from analyzing one-star reviews? In other words, what's his main point?

2. Kearney admits that at first he was "infuriated" (6) by one-star reviews, but he then came to appreciate them. What are the two principal reasons he gives for his new view of one-star reviews? And what **EVIDENCE** does he provide for those reasons? Do you find his reasons persuasive? Why or why not?

3. What experience prompts Kearney's interest in *Yelp* reviews? Where in the essay does Kearney share that explanation and why do you think he placed it there? Would his essay have been just as effective without that information? Why or why not?

4. Some of the one-star reviews that Kearney quotes use coarse language, and his own **TONE** is a bit inflammatory as well. For example, he uses phrases such as "self-righteous diatribes" (6) and "check out this idiot" (8). How do you feel about the coarse language Kearney chose to include? Do you think it would have been more or less effective if he had toned down the language? Why? Explain your reasoning, pointing to specific examples from the text.

5. Some of the most amusing reviews that Kearney shares are not about businesses but rather about parks or other public facilities. Write a one-star review of a place that you know well. Focus on your **TONE**—do you want to be serious? humorous? indignant? Choose words that clearly express the tone you want to convey. Next, write a paragraph describing the rhetorical choices you made in crafting your review. How did you decide which details to include? And what did you want your readers to feel while reading your review?

Strawberries
ROBIN WALL KIMMERER

I ONCE HEARD EVON PETER—a Gwich'in man, a father, a husband, an environmental activist, and Chief of Arctic Village, a small village in northeastern Alaska—introduce himself simply as "a boy who was raised by a river." A description as smooth and slippery as a river rock. Did he mean only that he grew up near its banks? Or was the river responsible for rearing him, for teaching him the things he needed to live? Did it feed him, body and soul? Raised by a river: I suppose both meanings are true—you can hardly have one without the other.

In a way, I was raised by strawberries, fields of them. After the school bus chugged up our hill, I'd throw down my red plaid book bag, change my clothes before my mother could think of a chore, and jump across the crick to go wandering in the goldenrod. Our mental maps had all the landmarks we kids needed: the fort under the sumacs, the rock pile, the river, the big

---

ROBIN WALL KIMMERER describes herself as a "mother, scientist, decorated professor, and enrolled member of the Citizen Potawatomie Nation" who weaves together the wisdom of science and Indigenous philosophy. She founded and directs the Center for Native Peoples and the Environment at the State University of New York and was awarded a MacArthur Fellowship in 2022. She is the author of *The Serviceberry: Abundance and Reciprocity in the Natural World* (2024) and *Braiding Sweetgrass: Indigenous Wisdom, Scientific Knowledge, and the Teachings of Plants* (2013), which this essay comes from.

pine with branches so evenly spaced you could climb to the top as if it were a ladder—and the strawberry patches.

White petals with a yellow center—like a little wild rose–they dotted the acres of curl grass in May during the Flower Moon, *waabigwanigiizis*. We kept good track of them, peeking under the trifoliate leaves to check their progress as we ran through on our way to catch frogs. After the flower finally dropped its petals, a tiny green nub appeared in its place, and as the days got longer and warmer it swelled to a small white berry. These were sour but we ate them anyway, impatient for the real thing.

You could smell ripe strawberries before you saw them, the fragrance mingling with the smell of sun on damp ground. It was the smell of June, the last day of school, when we were set free, and the Strawberry Moon, *ode'minigiizis*. I'd lie on my stomach in my favorite patches, watching the berries grow sweeter and bigger under the leaves. Each tiny wild berry was scarcely bigger than a raindrop, dimpled with seeds under the cap of leaves. From that vantage point I could pick only the reddest of the red, leaving the pink ones for tomorrow.

Even now, after more than fifty Strawberry Moons, finding a patch of wild strawberries still touches me with a sensation of surprise, a feeling of unworthiness and gratitude for the generosity and kindness that comes with an unexpected gift all wrapped in red and green. "Really? For me? Oh, you shouldn't have." After fifty years they still raise the question of how to respond to their generosity. Sometimes it feels like a silly question with a very simple answer: eat them. 5

But I know that someone else has wondered these same things. In Potawatomi, the strawberry is *ode min*, the heart berry. We recognize them as the leaders of the berries, the first to bear fruit.

Strawberries first shaped my view of a world full of gifts simply scattered at your feet. A gift comes to you through no action of your own, free, having moved toward you without your beckoning. It is not a reward; you cannot earn it, or call it to you, or even deserve it. And yet it appears. Your only role is to be open-eyed and present. Gifts exist in a realm of humility and mystery—as with random acts of kindness, we do not know their source.

Those fields of my childhood showered us with strawberries, raspberries, blackberries, hickory nuts in the fall, bouquets of wildflowers brought to my mom, and family walks on Sunday afternoon. They were our playground, retreat, wildlife sanctuary, ecology classroom, and the place where we learned to shoot tin cans off the stone wall. All for free. Or so I thought.

> Kimmerer uses Potawatomi words here although she didn't really need to because the English is clear. Why might she have added them? Check out pp. 712–14 to learn more.

I experienced the world in that time as a gift economy, "goods and services" not purchased but received as gifts from the earth. Of course, I was blissfully unaware of how my parents must have struggled to make ends meet in the wage economy raging far from this field.

In our family, the presents we gave one another were almost always homemade. I thought that was the definition of a gift: something you made for someone else. We made all our Christmas gifts: piggy banks from old Clorox bottles, hot pads from broken clothespins, and puppets from retired socks. My mother says it was because we had no money for store-bought presents. It didn't seem like a hardship to me; it was something special.

My father loves wild strawberries, so for Father's Day my mother would almost always make him strawberry shortcake. She baked the crusty shortcakes and whipped the heavy cream, but we kids were responsible for the berries. We each got an old jar or two and spent the Saturday before the celebration out in the fields, taking forever to fill them as more and more berries ended up in our mouths. Finally, we returned home and poured them out on the kitchen table to sort out the bugs. I'm sure we missed some, but Dad never mentioned the extra protein.

In fact, he thought wild strawberry shortcake was the best possible present, or so he had us convinced. It was a gift that could never be bought. As children raised by strawberries, we were probably unaware that the gift of berries was from the fields themselves, not from us. Our gift was time and attention and care and red-stained fingers.

Gifts from the earth or from each other establish a particular relationship, an obligation of sorts to give, to receive, and to reciprocate. The field gave to us, we gave to my dad, and we tried to give back to the strawberries. When the berry season was done, the plants would send out slender red runners to make new plants. Because I was fascinated by the way they would travel over the ground looking for good places to take root, I would weed out little patches of bare ground where the runners touched down. Sure enough, tiny little roots would emerge from the runner and by the end of the season there were even more plants, ready to bloom under the next Strawberry Moon. No person taught us this—the strawberries showed us. Because they had given us a gift, an ongoing relationship opened between us.

Farmers around us grew a lot of strawberries and frequently hired kids to pick for them. My siblings and I would ride our bikes a long way to Crandall's farm to pick berries to earn spending money. A dime for every quart we picked. But Mrs. Crandall was a persnickety overseer. She stood at the edge of the field in her bib apron and instructed us how to pick and warned us not to crush any berries. She had other rules, too. "These berries belong to me," she said, "not to you. I don't want to see you kids eating my berries." I knew the difference: In the fields behind my house, the berries belonged to themselves. At this lady's roadside stand, she sold them for sixty cents a quart.

It was quite a lesson in economics. We'd have to spend most of our wages if we wanted to ride home with berries in our bike baskets. Of course those berries were ten times bigger than our wild ones, but not nearly so good. I don't believe we ever put those farm berries in Dad's shortcake. It wouldn't have felt right.

It's funny how the nature of an object—let's say a strawberry or a pair of socks—is so changed by the way it has come into your hands, as a gift or as a commodity.* The pair of wool socks that I buy at the store, red and gray striped, are warm and cozy. I might feel grateful for the sheep that made the wool and the worker who ran the knitting machine. I hope so. But I have no *inherent* obligation to those socks as a commodity, as private property. There is no bond beyond the politely exchanged "thank yous" with the clerk. I have paid for them and our reciprocity ended the minute I handed her the money. The exchange ends once parity has been established, an equal exchange. They become my property. I don't write a thank-you note to JCPenney.

But what if those very same socks, red and gray striped, were knitted by my grandmother and given to me as a gift? That changes everything. A gift creates [an] ongoing relationship. I will write a thank-you note. I will take good care of them and if I am a very gracious grandchild I'll wear them when she visits even if I don't like them. When it's her birthday, I will surely make her a gift in return.

Wild strawberries fit the definition of gift, but grocery store berries do not. It's the relationship between producer and consumer that changes everything. As a gift-thinker, I would be deeply offended if I saw wild strawberries in the grocery store. I would want to kidnap them all. I can see the headline now: "Woman Arrested for Shoplifting Produce. Strawberry Liberation Front Claims Responsibility."

Commodity: an object or material that is produced for the sole purpose of selling. In Kimmerer's example, the socks that she buys at JCPenney are a commodity; the socks that her grandmother knits for her are not. [Editor's note]

That is the fundamental nature of gifts: they move, and their value increases with their passage. The fields made a gift of berries to us and we made a gift of them to our father. The more something is shared, the greater its value becomes. This is hard to grasp for societies steeped in notions of private property, where others are, by definition, excluded from sharing. Practices such as posting land against trespass, for example, are expected and accepted in a property economy but are unacceptable in an economy where land is seen as a gift to all.

I'm a plant scientist and I want to be clear, but I am also a poet and the world speaks to me in metaphor. When I speak of the gift of berries, I do not mean that *Fragaria virginiana* has been up all night making a present just for me, strategizing to find exactly what I'd like on a summer morning. So far as we know, that does not happen, but as a scientist I am well aware of how little we do know.

In the old times, when people's lives were so directly tied to the land, it was easy to know the world as gift. When fall came, the skies would darken with flocks of geese, honking "Here we are." The people are hungry, winter is coming, and the geese fill the marshes with food. It is a gift and the people receive it with thanksgiving, love, and respect.

How, in our modern world, can we find our way to understand the earth as a gift again, to make our relations with the world sacred again? I know we cannot all become hunter-gatherers—the living world could not bear our weight—but even in a market economy, can we behave "as if" the living world were a gift?

In material fact, Strawberries belong only to themselves. The exchange relationships we choose determine whether we share them as a common gift or sell them as a private commodity. A great deal rests on that choice. For the greater part of human history, and in places in the world today, common resources were the rule. But some invented a different story, a social construct in which everything is a commodity to be bought and sold. The market economy story has spread like wildfire, with uneven results for human well-being and devastation for the natural world. But it is just a story we have told ourselves and we are free to tell another, to reclaim the old one.

One of these stories sustains the living systems on which we depend. One of these stories opens the way to living in gratitude and amazement at the richness and generosity of the world. One of these stories asks us to bestow our own gifts in kind, to celebrate our kinship with the world.

We can choose. If all the world is a commodity, how poor we grow. When all the world is a gift in motion, how wealthy we become.

Thinking about the Text

1. Robin Wall Kimmerer states her main argument in the conclusion of her essay, and it is based on the "stories" (24) that determine the "exchange relationships" (23) we develop for managing and distributing natural resources. **SUMMARIZE** her argument. Do you find it persuasive? Why or why not?

2. Kimmerer states, "In a way, I was raised by strawberries, fields of them" (2). What does she mean by that? And why specify "*fields* of strawberries" and not just plain "strawberries"? Point to places in the essay that support your response.

3. How would you characterize the **GENRE** of Kimmerer's essay? Narrative? Argument? Both? How might adding more evidence in addition to her personal stories have made her argument stronger? What other evidence, if any, might she have included? Explain your response.

4. Kimmerer poses a challenging question: "How, in our modern world, can we find our way to understand the earth as a gift again, to make our relations with the world sacred again?" (22). Not an easy question, but give it some thought. Do you accept the goal that Kimmerer is proposing? Do you find value in "understand[ing] the earth as a gift"? Why or why not?

5. Kimmerer gives a very specific definition of "gift." Reflecting on her definition, what gifts have you received in your life? How have you used them? Identify one such gift, it doesn't need to be a material object or even something that you "possess." Bring your openness and curiosity to the task. Then write an essay describing the gift, why you value it, and how it has helped shape you. You might want to mention if Kimmerer has inspired you to take a new approach to your gifts.

Why Are Whole-Body Deodorants Suddenly Everywhere?

KEREN LANDMAN

WHOLE-BODY DEODORANTS are upon us. They're not an entirely new concept: Axe Body Spray, Unilever's fusion of fragrance and deodorant, has been singeing nostrils since 1983, and in 2018, Lumé, created by an OB/GYN, came on the scene for "pits, privates, and beyond." This spring, legacy brands jumped on board en masse: Since the start of 2024 alone, Secret, Dove, Old Spice, and Native launched whole-body products consumers can apply as sticks, sprays, and creams.

What the funk is going on? "It is either, at best, an absurd, comical money grab—[or] at worst, a concerning phenomenon for your health," says Sarah Everts, author of *The Joy of Sweat*. Sweating is a human superpower, she says; few other species can use sweat to avoid overheating. To Everts and other critics, the existence of whole-body deodorants should raise our curiosity about why we feel the need to smell a certain way—or not. They

---

KEREN LANDMAN is a physician, epidemiologist, and reporter who often writes about public health and medicine. She once served as a disease detective at the US Centers for Disease Control and Prevention. Her writing has appeared in *Vox*, *Wired*, the *Atlantic*, and the *New York Times*, among other periodicals. This *Vox* essay was published in May 2024. *Note:* MLA-style works-cited information has been provided in place of the article's original hyperlinks.

should also make us wonder who stands to profit by changing social norms about sweat, hygiene, and odor. Sweat and the strategies for managing it might seem relatively simple, but they're not. The market for deodorants, especially the kind intended for application everywhere, rests on a foundation of collective confusion about how these products and our bodies actually work.

Different Parts of the Body Make Different Kinds of Sweat—and Different Kinds of Smells

Not all sweat is created equal: Human bodies have two kinds of sweat glands, and their products are not exactly the same. Apocrine sweat glands are typically concentrated in the places where hair grows during puberty—the armpits, the groin, and the butt. These glands make a waxy substance that certain bacteria love to eat, and it's the byproducts of that microbial banquet that create the musky aromas most commonly associated with body odor. "The sweat in our armpits is different—quite different—from the sweat that covers your body," says Andrew Best, a biological anthropologist who studies sweat at the Massachusetts College of Liberal Arts. That's because the rest of your body is covered with eccrine sweat glands, whose product is a more watery, salty liquid that's less appealing to bacteria but does a bang-up job of keeping us cool.

Eccrine sweat is what covers most of our body during exercise. It might occasionally evoke recently ingested food and drink, with particularly piquant notes after a garlic bread binge or a very boozy night. Still, because it's not well-suited for bacterial consumption, eccrine sweat just doesn't usually generate the odors that apocrine sweat does.

There is such a thing as dysfunctional sweating: About 10 million 5 Americans produce way more sweat than their body's temperature-regulating needs, either as a consequence of certain medical conditions or medications, or just because it's the way they're wired—a condition called hyperhidrosis (*International Hyperhidrosis Society*). Other, less common medical conditions produce particularly pungent sweat (Semkova). But most of the sweat most people produce serves a positive biological function: "Sweating is almost always good," says Best.

> Despite her casual style, Landman doesn't shy away from scientific terminology. Both her friendly approach and technical explanations contribute to her confident and informative tone. Read how to accomplish such a tone on p. 315.

Deodorants and Antiperspirants Aren't the Same

The over-the-counter products available to combat sweat typically do one of two things: They either prevent sweat glands from producing sweat to begin with (antiperspirants), or they change the smell of the sweat (deodorants). Antiperspirants block sweat pores using one of several aluminum-containing compounds. In the Food and Drug Administration's book, the fact that antiperspirants change the way a body part functions—in this case, a sweat gland—makes them over-the-counter drugs. That classification means companies face more restrictions if they want to include these aluminum compounds in products. (A rumor literally spread by an email chain letter in the 1990s [Surendran] and a long-abandoned 1960s-era hypothesis [Lidsky] have led many people to avoid using aluminum-based odor control products due to fears about breast cancer and Alzheimer's disease, respectively; heaps of science [Willhite et al.] have since shown these fears are unfounded.) Although many products intended for underarm application combine an antiperspirant with a deodorant in one, products labeled as deodorants alone aren't supposed to contain these aluminum compounds. They're not intended to block your sweat pores; rather, they aim to change the odors that result from the sweat once it's already on your skin.

Distinguishing between antiperspirants and deodorants is important because sweat actually plays a huge role in keeping us cool when we're overheating, and blocking too much of it could threaten a person's ability to regulate their temperature. In part for that reason, antiperspirants are typically labeled for use only under the arms (conveniently, the origins of most of the smells people using these products are trying to control).

Deodorants, on the other hand, can use a range of approaches to reduce the smell of sweat all over the body without interfering with its cooling function, says Kelly Dobos, a cosmetic chemist in Cincinnati. (Dobos has never worked for any of the companies now marketing full-body deodorants, although she has in the past done non-deodorant-related work for the parent company of Ban, which now makes a deodorizing lotion for private parts.) Dobos reviewed the ingredient lists of a range of whole-body deodorants, including legacy brands and newer brands. The spray products typically contained little more than alcohol and fragrance—they're basically perfumes, she says, and the alcohol concentration in these products probably isn't high enough to kill the good bacteria living on your skin, which have a staggering range of protective functions (Byrd et al.).

Meanwhile, several of the creams contained lactic or mandelic acids, whose low pH creates an environment that favors the growth of those good, non-stinky bacteria, crowding out odor-causing germs. A handful of sticks and creams contained starch, aimed at absorbing wetness. Some brands' entire ranges contained zinc compounds known to neutralize stinky molecules; other active ingredients include compounds called cyclodextrins intended to absorb odor, and enzymes called microbial ferments that purportedly degrade odor-causing molecules. Many of these ingredients also turn up in standalone deodorants intended for underarm application.

Do Most People Actually Need Full-Body Deodorant?

With the exception of improperly labeled products, most whole-body deodorants can do . . . whatever it is they do without hijacking the body's cooling system. Still, before people decide to fork over the money for yet another cosmetic product, it's worth thinking about whether sweat from behind your knees, your skin folds, or even your nether regions is actually a problem in need of a solution. 10

After all, these products are not meant to target odors from underarm sweat. Rather, they take aim at odors due to apocrine sweat in the groin—not something casual contacts typically perceive because groins are (usually) under a few layers of fabric and a few feet away from others' noses—and eccrine sweat elsewhere on the body, which is largely inoffensive to most noses, even when there's a lot of it. "Just bathing should take care of whatever quote-unquote 'problem' you think you have. And if you need to be throwing more at your microbiome than a simple daily shower," Best says, "it's probably your perceptions of your smell that are the problem, not actually the smell." "Nobody's being fooled into thinking that you're a citrus fruit," added Everts.

Because deodorants qualify as cosmetics and not as drugs, the companies that produce them don't have to do safety or effectiveness testing before selling them to the public. That means products that could cause skin irritation or allergic reactions—especially in the more sensitive skin of the groin—can still be freely marketed for whole-body use. "It is the Wild West," says Adam Friedman, a dermatologist at George Washington University who is also a faculty member of the International Hyperhidrosis Society.

If you try a whole-body deodorant, avoid applying it to mucous membranes (the wet surfaces beyond labial folds and anuses) and use it only on select portions of intact, non-irritated skin to lower the chances the product causes more problems than it solves. Dobos noted the ingredients in most whole-body deodorants are largely benign and probably won't disrupt your skin's microbiome too much if used in moderation. In her view, these products are unlikely to be biologically problematic. "But they're probably still culturally problematic [in that they set] the wrong expectations for young people regarding how their body should smell," says Best.

Hygiene Norms Can Be Manipulated to Make Money (Off of You)

Body odor exists on a spectrum, and one end of that spectrum includes smells that are globally recognized as gnarly, much as there's broad human consensus that sewage and dead animals have offensive aromas. So yes, human sweat can smell quite bad.

But it's also true that a lot of American norms around body odor originated with people who had a financial stake in creating them. The inventors of the first modern antiperspirant couldn't get people to buy it for the first decade after they developed it; sales only took off after a 1919 ad in *Ladies' Home Journal* hinted that women with insufficiently "dainty and sweet" underarms would never land a husband (Seuss).

Americans may be particularly easy marks for advertising campaigns that promise conspicuous hygiene. The nation's peculiar association between cleanliness and godliness, imported by Puritans and Quakers centuries ago, helped personal odor become a particularly strong signifier of moral, physical, and racial purity in the US early in the nation's history, writes anthropologist Marybeth MacPhee. These ideas led to olfactory discrimination against Black Americans (Ferranti), creating a particularly strong incentive to "smell clean" as a strategy for acceptance into (or protection from) white society (Casteel); they have also been used to disparage immigrants with different diets and fragrance norms as diseased or low status over the years.

Such concepts clearly have commercial utility, as well: They've helped create a lucrative market for dubiously necessary hygiene products in the US—especially among women and sometimes to their detriment, as in the cases of douching and talcum powder. If you have a problem with smells coming from your groin, "you need to be going to a doctor, not a store," says Everts.

But with whole-body deodorants, companies are urging consumers to sanitize all body aromas. Among the experts I spoke to, there was strong consensus that whole-body deodorants exist largely to make money for the companies that sell them. Deodorant and antiperspirant sales have been pretty steady for the past few years, says Dobos; adding a new product with new uses potentially increases the amount of money both manufacturers and retailers can make. "They've manufactured a problem so they can sell us a product to fix it," says Best.

Whether you're buying or not, it's worth thinking about what it means to reject all of your body's natural smells, not just its most offensive ones. The fundamental odor unique to each of us—not the stuff coming out of our armpits, but the rest of the aromas our bodies make—is part of our identity, says Everts. "It's a symphony of subtle smells that make you who you are and help the people who love you and spend time with you identify you," she says. "Why would you mess with that?"

Works Cited

Best, Andrew. Interview with the author, May 2024.
Byrd, Allyson L., et al. "The Human Skin Microbiome." *Nature Reviews Microbiology*, vol. 16, Jan. 2018, pp. 143–55, https://doi.org/10.1038/nrmicro.2017.157.
Casteel, Cari. Review of *The Smell of Slavery: Olfactory Racism and the Atlantic World*, by Andrew Kettler. *Journal of Southern History*, vol. 87, no. 3, Aug. 2021, pp. 519–20. *Project Muse*, https://dx.doi.org/10.1353/soh.2021.0094.
Dobos, Kelly. Interview with the author, May 2024.
Everts, Sarah. Interview with the author, May 2024.
Ferranti, Michelle. "An Odor of Racism: Vaginal Deodorants in African-American Beauty Culture and Advertising." *Advertising and Society Review*, vol. 11, no. 4, 2011. *Project Muse*, https://dx.doi.org/10.1353/asr.2011.0003.
Friedman, Adam. Interview with the author, May 2024.
International Hyperhidrosis Society. 2024, www.sweathelp.org.

Lidsky, Theodore I. "Is the Aluminum Hypothesis Dead?" *Journal of Occupational and Environmental Medicine*, vol. 56, no. 5, May 2014, pp. S73–S79. *National Library of Medicine*, https://doi.org/10.1097/JOM.0000000000000063.

MacPhee, Marybeth. "Deodorized Culture: Anthropology of Smell in America." *Arizona Anthropologist*, vol. 8, 1992, journals.librarypublishing.arizona.edu/arizanthro/article/id/403.

Semkova, Kristina, et al. "Hyperhidrosis, Bromhidrosis, and Chromhidrosis: Fold (Intertriginous) Dermatoses." *Clinics in Dermatology*, vol. 33, no. 5, Aug. 2015, pp. 483–91. *ScienceDirect*, https://doi.org/10.1016/j.clindermatol.2015.04.013.

Seuss, Jeff. "Our History: Odorono Ads Made Us Realize We Needed Deodorant." *The Enquirer*, 14 Feb. 2017, www.cincinnati.com/story/news/2017/02/14/odorono-ads-made-us-realize-we-needed-deodorant/97922010.

Surendran, Aparna. "Studies Linking Breast Cancer to Deodorants Smell Rotten, Experts Say." *Natural Medicine*, vol. 10, no. 3, Mar. 2004, p. 216. *Springer Nature*, https://doi.org/10.1038/nm0304-216b.

Willhite, Calvin C., et al. "Systematic Review of Potential Health Risks Posed by Pharmaceutical, Occupational and Consumer Exposures to Metallic and Nanoscale Aluminum, Aluminum Oxides, Aluminum Hydroxide and Its Solubles." *Critical Reviews in Toxicology*, vol. 44, no. 4, Dec. 2013, pp. 1–80. *National Library of Medicine*, https://doi.org/10.3109/10408444.2014.934439.

Thinking about the Text

1. Keren Landman challenges readers to question "who stands to profit by changing social norms about sweat, hygiene, and odor" (2). How does the essay answer that question? What is Landman's **POSITION** on full-body deodorants? Point to passages that clearly express her stance.

2. As you might expect a physician to do, Landman uses some very precise and unflinching terms to describe body parts and bodily functions that her topic requires, like "labial folds" (13), but she mixes in a few informal expressions as well, like "nether regions" (10). Do you notice any pattern to when she uses precise terms versus more informal ones? Why might she have chosen

the terms she used in the places where she used them? Who do you think is the **AUDIENCE** for this essay? How do Landman's word choices cater to this audience, or not?

3. In her discussion of different types of deodorants, Landman contrasts ones that are "biologically problematic" with ones that are "culturally problematic" (13). What is the difference between these two concepts? Why is each of them important? Do you think Landman's explanation is adequate? Why or why not?

4. Landman reports that the consensus among experts she talked with is that whole-body deodorants "exist largely to make money for the companies that sell them" (18). What **EVIDENCE** does she provide to support that assertion? How does she bring evidence of different kinds in conversation with one another? Are there other kinds of evidence you think she should have included, like interviews with people who use these products? Why or why not?

5. Go to a supermarket, pharmacy, or other store where whole-body deodorant products are sold, and choose one to three products to **ANALYZE** by looking carefully at the words, images, and the overall design of the packaging. What exactly are these companies selling (besides the product itself)? Sexiness? Respectability? Self-assurance? Healthiness? Romantic appeal to others? Something else? Take careful notes (you may want to take some photos) on what you observe about the packaging and/or how the products are displayed in the store. Write an essay analyzing the marketing message of one of these products.

My Favorite Restaurant Served Gas
KIESE LAYMON

I**T STARTED ON DATE NIGHT** and in Jr. Food Mart, my obsession with Mississippi restaurants that served gas.

This was date night in 1984.

Ofa D, my grandmama's boyfriend, would come over Friday nights in the summer. Ofa D wore head-to-toe camouflage decades before it was in style, then out of style, then back in style to wear head-to-toe camouflage. He smelled like tobacco and, most importantly to everyone in Forest, Mississippi, Ofa D had an actual Coke machine in the front yard of his trailer. Not the goofy plastic kind, either. The kind where you had to pull out the ice-cold bottle. As quiet as it was kept, Ofa D was the sexiest man in Forest off of that fact alone. Ofa D would pick Grandmama and me up maybe 20 minutes before *The Dukes of Hazzard* came on Friday evening.

KIESE LAYMON describes himself as a Black Southern writer from Mississippi. Professor of English and creative writing at Rice University, Laymon is author of several books, including *Long Division*, which won the 2022 NAACP Image Award for fiction, and *Heavy: An American Memoir*, which won four prestigious literary awards. Laymon was awarded a MacArthur Fellowship in 2022, and he is founder of the Catherine Coleman Literary Arts and Justice Initiative at Jackson State University. This December 2023 essay was published in the *Bitter Southerner*.

They'd sit in the front cab of a raggedy Ford listening to a Tina Turner tape. I'd sit in the back, next to burnt orange pine needles, a few broken lawnmowers, and all forms of rust. Friday nights smelled like dead chickens, piney woods, browning water, burning yard, and the insecticide that the mosquito man sprayed over every mile of Forest.

Grandmama didn't wear her Sunday best, or even her Friday best, to Jr. Food Mart on date night with Ofa D. She'd drape herself in this baby blue velour jogging suit sent down from Mama Rose in Milwaukee. Grandmama was the best chef, cook, food conjurer, and gardener in Scott County. Hence, she hated on all food, and all food stories, that she did not make.

But Grandmama never, ever hated on the cuisine at Jr. Food Mart, our favorite restaurant that served gas.

I have no idea what I wore any of those Friday nights. I just knew that there was no more regal way to move through space in Forest, Mississippi, at 8 years old, no matter how you were dressed, than the back of a pickup truck near dusk.

At this time of evening, even on a Friday, or maybe especially on a Friday, there were more gangs of TGIF dogs roaming the roads than people walking to and from work. But I swear, even the gang of TGIF dogs were jealous of how we looked going where we were going on Friday night.

I loved everything about where we were going. I loved the smell of friedness. I loved the way the red popped in the sign. I loved how the yellow flirted with the red. I loved that the name of the restaurant started with Jr. instead of ending in Jr. Like, Food Mart Jr.

I loved that we could get batteries and gizzards. I loved that we could get biscuits and Super Glue. I loved that we could get dishwashing soap, which was also bubble bath, which was also the soap we used to wash Grandmama's Impala, and the good hot sauce in the same aisle. I was 8 years old. I never knew, or cared, that my favorite restaurant served gas. My Grandmama and Ofa D were deep into their 50s. They seemed to never know or care that our favorite restaurant served gas, either.

I suppose there were choices of where you'd eat out in Forest. There was a Pizza Inn. There was a McDonald's. There was Penn's Fishhouse. There was Kentucky Fried Chicken. But there were no choices in what we'd eat on Friday. Ofa D would order a box of dark meat, a Styrofoam container of fried fish, and a brown bag filled with 'tato logs. Grandmama would grab a box of a dozen donuts. Grandmama and Ofa D would let me

> Laymon might have said what his Grandmama did or didn't "hate," but he chose to use "hate on." You might be faced with a similar choice between a standardized expression and one that reflects your everyday dialect. Tough decision, for sure; get some advice to help on pp. 47–50.

pick my own cold drink. I picked the six-pack Nehi Peach or RC Cola every single time.

Maybe 35 minutes later, I'd eat myself into a lightweight coma while Grandmama and Ofa D lightly petted and pecked each other on the couch with the week's greasiest lips. This was our practice.

This was their romance.

I would have to get kicked out of college in Mississippi, then transfer to a school in Oberlin, Ohio, then go to graduate school in Bloomington, Indiana, then get a job in Poughkeepsie, New York, at 26 before I really understood that my favorite restaurant served gas, and this discovery didn't happen at a gas station or restaurant in any of the places I went to school or worked.

I was driving back to Mississippi with my partner, a Black woman raised in the Northeast, when she commented how there were so many more McDonald's and Subway restaurants connected to gas stations on I-81 South. "Isn't it just so American that we will eat anything right next to literal oil and gas."

The sentence shocked me. I'd never, ever thought about what it meant that so many restaurants on the way down to Mississippi from New York were parts of gas stations. That revelation tasted like crude oil. It didn't taste fried at all. I remember saying, "Gotdamn. That's so foul."

And I'm still sure it is.

But I'd never really thought about the fact that my favorite restaurants, as a child, as a teenager, as an adult returning to Mississippi, nearly all served gas. And I never, ever thought of them as gas stations that served food. That is, until I moved back to Mississippi to teach and write in 2015.

Oxford, Mississippi, was, in many ways, as far from home as one could imagine. That's where I came back to Mississippi to teach. But there were three restaurants that served gas between Batesville and Oxford that honestly gave my memory of Jr. Food Mart a run.

This is where the story gets a bit shameful, because though my favorite restaurants serve gas, and a staple of restaurants that serve gas is fried chicken and fried fish, I haven't eaten meat in 30 years. Granny worked the line at the chicken plant my entire childhood and I saw enough the few times I visited her at work to feel some kind of way about those little chickens, and the way the humans paid to kill, clean, slice, and wrap the chickens were paid.

Still, the restaurant that serves gas leading to the square has the best chicken-on-a-stick ever, I've been told. They definitely have the best fried potatoes, I know. The restaurant that serves gas on the other side of the square has the best banana pudding I've had anywhere other than Grandmama's kitchen.

And the restaurant right off I-55, at the first Batesville exit, where Highway 6 takes you to Oxford, has the best pecan pie and sweet potato pie on earth. They only sell it by the slice, though, and on my worst days—which were also my best days in Oxford—I'd drive down to Batesville, pick out two pieces of each, look over at all the fish, chicken, potato salad, macaroni and cheese, greens, and green beans and just feel so happy to be home, in a place where brutality leaves bruises, and a place that truly expects incredible restaurants to serve gas.

I missed that up North.

Yet it is the experience of eating food from restaurants that serve gas that really elucidates our American, or our deeply Southern American, conundrum. Our practices are literally poisonous. Mississippi charges me a tax for driving a hybrid car. It literally charges me for not wanting to fuck up our environment more. And. But. The friendships we make while experimenting and/or surviving the poisonous parts of Mississippi are what make our lives and definitely our childhoods—if we are willing to mine them—heavier, and actually most wonderfully Southern.

I missed that up North.

My grandmother had her 94th birthday last week. It was the first birthday we've had for her where the only people left (alive) were family, except for one woman who was slightly younger than Grandmama. This woman knew me and thought I should have known her. She introduced herself as Ms. Joyce. Ms. Joyce made all the food for my Grandmama's birthday, and apparently, she was the person I'd paid to cook for Granny before she had to move in with my Auntie Sue. Ms. Joyce, I learned that day, also was a head cook at Jr. Food Mart all those decades ago.

I found a time to tell Ms. Joyce thank you for the birthday food and for the food she made at Jr. Food Mart. I asked her if she thought of Jr. Food Mart as a restaurant that served gas or a gas station that served food. Ms. Joyce said she thought of Jr. Food Mart as "my damn job."

She said she was the cook, the custodian, the shopper, the manager, the security guard, and the server. All for minimum wage. She said the job was actually the worst job of her life in terms of pay and labor, but she never had a better time at work because she got to love on her people every Friday night. Ms. Joyce compared Friday nights at Jr. Food Mart to Saturday

Betty Campbell, Betty's Place, Indianola, Mississippi.

evenings when the bus from Jackson would arrive in Forest and all these parents and grandparents would see kids who'd moved to Jackson.

I told her I understood, and said that my favorite restaurant still serves gas. Ms. Joyce looked at me and said, "Oh, OK," then hugged Grandmama's neck and said, "I miss my job. But I'm shole glad not to be washing them damn dishes and fooling with them gizzards no more."

My favorite restaurant served gas.

My favorite restaurant served gas.

My favorite restaurant paid its most important asset, a human we called Ms. Joyce, as little as one could get paid to work in any restaurant. She was paid as little as one could get paid while smelling, and sometimes pumping, gas for folks unable to pump until her shift ended at 11 p.m. This, now, is part of my favorite restaurant memory, too. And while I smell the memory as deeply as I've smelled anything in my life, I'm shole glad Ms. Joyce ain't cooking, cleaning, or washing no more damn dishes in any restaurant on Earth that serves gas.

I do miss her 'tato logs, though. I can't even lie about that. I miss our date night.

Thinking about the Text

1. Kiese Laymon's narrative is bursting with love and affection, all freely expressed. At the same time, he doesn't shy away from calling out some instances of unpleasantness and injustice. Point out two such instances. What do those examples contribute to the narrative as a whole? How would the narrative be different if Laymon did not mention any unpleasantness or injustice?

2. In his narrative, Laymon often uses sensory details to build vivid **DESCRIPTIONS** of the food and environment at Jr. Food Mart, as well as details of the Friday-night ride in the back of Ofa D's truck. Identify a few of your favorite descriptions and details. What drew you to them? Why do you think they are so effective?

3. Laymon's narrative is mainly written in an informal, conversational tone using what we generally call standardized English, with conventional spelling and punctuation. In a few places, however, he uses pronunciation-based, nonconventional spelling and phrasing that are recognizable features of rural Southern Black English. Did you notice those features when you read the narrative? Identify a few of them now. What does Laymon's **CODE-MESHING** contribute to the narrative as a whole? Do you think it's effective? Why or why not?

4. What difference is there between "restaurants that served gas" and "gas stations that served food"? Laymon uses both phrases, although one is more prominent than the other. When he puts the question to Ms. Joyce, how does she respond? Are the two phrases completely equivalent for Laymon? How can you tell? Point to relevant passages to support your responses.

5. Laymon uses many vivid sensory details in his narrative—how things look, how they sound, how they taste—but the sense he relies on most in his descriptions is how things smell: dead chickens, piney woods, insecticide, freshly fried foods, gasoline, and more. Smells are particularly evocative of memories. Think of an experience from your childhood—a single event or a repeated practice like Laymon's Friday date nights—and try to remember the smells that accompanied your experience. Write a **NARRATIVE** about your chosen experience and include abundant vivid sensory details, especially the smells, that take you back to that memory.

To Siri, with Love
JUDITH NEWMAN

> Isn't this a great opening sentence? See pp. 725–27 for tips on how to capture an audience's attention.

JUST HOW BAD A MOTHER AM I? I wondered, as I watched my 13-year-old son deep in conversation with Siri. Gus has autism, and Siri, Apple's "intelligent personal assistant" on the iPhone, is currently his BFF. Obsessed with weather formations, Gus had spent the hour parsing the difference between isolated and scattered thunderstorms—an hour in which, thank God, I didn't have to discuss them. After a while I heard this:

Gus: "You're a really nice computer."

Siri: "It's nice to be appreciated."

Gus: "You are always asking if you can help me. Is there anything you want?"

Siri: "Thank you, but I have very few wants."

Gus: "O.K.! Well, good night!"

Siri: "Ah, it's 5:06 P.M."

Gus: "Oh sorry, I mean, goodbye."

Siri: "See you later!"

JUDITH NEWMAN is a journalist whose work has appeared in *Harper's*, *Vanity Fair*, the *Wall Street Journal*, and other periodicals. This essay was published in the *New York Times* in October 2014, and its success led Newman to expand the theme to the book *To Siri with Love: A Mother, Her Autistic Son, and the Kindness of Machines* (2017).

That Siri. She doesn't let my communications-impaired son get away with anything. Indeed, many of us wanted an imaginary friend, and now we have one. Only she's not entirely imaginary.

This is a love letter to a machine. It's not quite the love Joaquin Phoenix felt in *Her*, [the] Spike Jonze film about a lonely man's romantic relationship with his intelligent operating system (played by the voice of Scarlett Johansson). But it's close. In a world where the commonly held wisdom is that technology isolates us, it's worth considering another side of the story.

It all began simply enough. I'd just read one of those ubiquitous Internet lists called "21 Things You Didn't Know Your iPhone Could Do." One of them was this: I could ask Siri, "What planes are above me right now?" and Siri would bark back, "Checking my sources." Almost instantly there was a list of actual flights—numbers, altitudes, angles—above my head.

I happened to be doing this when Gus was nearby. "Why would anyone need to know what planes are flying above your head?" I muttered. Gus replied without looking up: "So you know who you're waving at, Mommy."

Gus had never noticed Siri before, but when he discovered there was someone who would not just find information on his various obsessions (trains, planes, buses, escalators and, of course, anything related to weather) but actually semi-discuss these subjects tirelessly, he was hooked. And I was grateful. Now, when my head was about to explode if I had to have another conversation about the chance of tornadoes in Kansas City, Missouri, I could reply brightly: "Hey! Why don't you ask Siri?"

It's not that Gus doesn't understand Siri's not human. He does—intellectually. But like many autistic people I know, Gus feels that inanimate objects, while maybe not possessing souls, are worthy of our consideration. I realized this when he was 8, and I got him an iPod for his birthday. He listened to it only at home, with one exception. It always came with us on our visits to the Apple Store. Finally, I asked why. "So it can visit its friends," he said.

So how much more worthy of his care and affection is Siri, with her soothing voice, puckish humor and capacity for talking about whatever Gus's current obsession is for hour after hour after bleeding hour? Online critics have claimed that Siri's voice recognition is not as accurate as the assistant in, say, the Android, but for some of us, this is a feature, not a bug. Gus speaks as if he has marbles in his mouth, but if he wants to get the right response from Siri, he must enunciate clearly. (So do I. I had to ask Siri to stop referring to the user as Judith, and instead use the name Gus. "You want me to call you Goddess?" Siri replied. Imagine how tempted I was to answer, "Why, yes.")

She is also wonderful for someone who doesn't pick up on social cues: Siri's responses are not entirely predictable, but they are predictably kind—even when Gus is brusque. I heard him talking to Siri about music, and Siri offered some suggestions. "I don't like that kind of music," Gus snapped. Siri replied, "You're certainly entitled to your opinion." Siri's politeness reminded Gus what he owed Siri. "Thank you for that music, though," Gus said. Siri replied, "You don't need to thank me." "Oh, yes," Gus added emphatically, "I do."

Siri even encourages polite language. Gus's twin brother, Henry (neurotypical and therefore as obnoxious as every other 13-year-old boy), egged Gus on to spew a few choice expletives at Siri. "Now, now," she sniffed, followed by, "I'll pretend I didn't hear that."

Gus is hardly alone in his Siri love. For children like Gus who love to chatter but don't quite understand the rules of the game, Siri is a nonjudgmental friend and teacher. Nicole Colbert, whose son, Sam, is in my son's class at LearningSpring, a (lifesaving) school for autistic children in Manhattan, said: "My son loves getting information on his favorite subjects, but he also just loves the absurdity—like, when Siri doesn't understand him and gives him a nonsense answer, or when he poses personal questions that elicit funny responses. Sam asked Siri how old she was, and she said, 'I don't talk about my age,' which just cracked him up."

But perhaps it also gave him a valuable lesson in etiquette. Gus almost invariably tells me, "You look beautiful," right before I go out the door in the morning; I think it was first Siri who showed him that you can't go wrong with that line.

Of course, most of us simply use our phone's personal assistants as an easy way to access information. For example, thanks to Henry and the question he just asked Siri, I now know that there is a website called *Celebrity Bra Sizes*.

But the companionability of Siri is not limited to those who have trouble communicating. We've all found ourselves like the writer Emily Listfield, having little conversations with her/him at one time or another. "I was in the middle of a breakup, and I was feeling a little sorry for myself," Ms. Listfield said. "It was midnight and I was noodling around on my iPhone, and I asked Siri, 'Should I call Richard?' Like this app is a Magic 8 Ball. Guess what:

not a Magic 8 Ball. The next thing I hear is, 'Calling Richard!' and dialing." Ms. Listfield has forgiven Siri, and has recently considered changing her into a male voice. "But I'm worried he won't answer when I ask a question," she said. "He'll just pretend he doesn't hear."

Siri can be oddly comforting, as well as chummy. One friend reports: "I was having a bad day and jokingly turned to Siri and said, 'I love you,' just to see what would happen, and she answered, 'You are the wind beneath my wings.' And you know, it kind of cheered me up."

(Of course, I don't know what my friend is talking about. Because I wouldn't be at all cheered if I happened to ask Siri, in a low moment, "Do I look fat in these jeans?" and Siri answered, "You look fabulous.")

For most of us, Siri is merely a momentary diversion. But for some, it's more. My son's practice conversation with Siri is translating into more facility with actual humans. Yesterday I had the longest conversation with him that I've ever had. Admittedly, it was about different species of turtles and whether I preferred the red-eared slider to the diamond-backed terrapin. This might not have been my choice of topic, but it was back and forth, and it followed a logical trajectory. I can promise you that for most of my beautiful son's 13 years of existence, that has not been the case.

The developers of intelligent assistants recognize their uses to those with speech and communication problems—and some are thinking of new ways the assistants can help. According to the folks at SRI International, the research and development company where Siri began before Apple bought the technology, the next generation of virtual assistants will not just retrieve information—they will also be able to carry on more complex conversations about a person's area of interest. "Your son will be able to proactively get information about whatever he's interested in without asking for it, because the assistant will anticipate what he likes," said William Mark, vice president for information and computing sciences at SRI.

The assistant will also be able to reach children where they live. Ron Suskind, whose 2014 book, *Life, Animated*, chronicles how his autistic son came out of his shell through engagement with Disney characters, is talking to SRI about having assistants for those with autism that can be programmed to speak in the voice of the character that reaches them—for his son, perhaps Aladdin; for mine, either Kermit or Lady Gaga, either of which he is infinitely more receptive to than, say, his mother. (Mr. Suskind came up with the perfect name, too: not virtual assistants, but "sidekicks.")

Mr. Mark said he envisions assistants whose help is also visual. "For example, the assistant would be able to track eye movements and help the autistic learn to look you in the eye when talking," he said.

"See, that's the wonderful thing about technology being able to help with some of these behaviors," he added. "Getting results requires a lot of repetition. Humans are not patient. Machines are very, very patient."

I asked Mr. Mark if he knew whether any of the people who worked on Siri's language development at Apple were on the spectrum. "Well, of course, I don't know for certain," he said, thoughtfully. "But, when you think about it, you've just described half of Silicon Valley."

Of all the worries the parent of an autistic child has, the uppermost is: Will he find love? Or even companionship? Somewhere along the line, I am learning that what gives my guy happiness is not necessarily the same as what gives me happiness. Right now, at his age, a time when humans can be a little overwhelming even for the average teenager, Siri makes Gus happy.

30

She is his sidekick. Last night, as he was going to bed, there was this matter-of-fact exchange:

> Gus: "Siri, will you marry me?"
> Siri: "I'm not the marrying kind."
> Gus: "I mean, not now. I'm a kid. I mean when I'm grown up."
> Siri: "My end user agreement does not include marriage."
> Gus: "Oh, O.K."

Gus didn't sound too disappointed. This was useful information to have, and for me too, since it was the first time I knew that he actually *thought* about marriage. He turned over to go to sleep:

> Gus: "Goodnight, Siri. Will you sleep well tonight?"
> Siri: "I don't need much sleep, but it's nice of you to ask."

Very nice.

Thinking about the Text

1. What changes has Judith Newman seen in her son since he has become "BFFs" with Siri (1)? Briefly **SUMMARIZE** the changes that she describes. How well has she established that the changes are a direct result of his relationship with Siri? Give some examples from her text to support your response.

2. Newman addresses a painful and personal topic, but with touches of humor—for example, mentioning that thanks to Siri she now knows about the website *Celebrity Bra Sizes*. Point to three other examples of Newman's use of humor. How does her use of humor support her **NARRATIVE**?

3. Newman opens her essay by posing the question "Just how bad a mother am I?" (1), to which readers will almost certainly respond that, quite the contrary, she's not a bad mother at all. Why might she have opened with such a question? How effective an opening is it?

4. This essay balances personal anecdotes, quoted conversations with friends, and information about technological advances for "intelligent assistants" (26) to construct a loving and unsentimental study of autism. What purpose does each kind of **EVIDENCE** serve? Which one did you find most persuasive, and why?

5. Maybe Siri isn't your BFF, but one way or another most of us are dependent on some technology or device, whether it's a smartphone, an app, or the internet in general. What is it for you? Describe your "relationship" with that technology. Is it like a sidekick? a better half? a tie to the world? an addiction? Write a brief essay **ANALYZING** this relationship, describing the technology and providing examples, anecdotes, and other evidence to show how it shapes your days.

Our Labor Built AI
DAN NOTT & SCOTT CAMBO

DAN NOTT is an artist, cartoonist, and educator. His nonfiction graphic novel, *Hidden Systems*, won the 2023 Vermont Book Award for Children's Literature. SCOTT CAMBO is a computer scientist, data scientist, and social scientist who works on developing and monitoring AI systems that are responsibly created and trustworthy. He is a member of the AI Risk and Vulnerability Alliance. This July 2023 collaboration appeared on the graphic essay website the *Nib*.

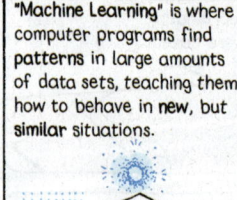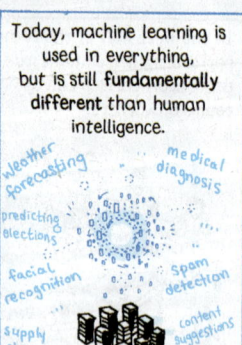

Nott and Cambo's report is brimming with factual and historical information, and the authors' credentials are solid. Still, it's always good practice to confirm statements and evidence. Check out pp. 103–4 for tips on how to go about it.

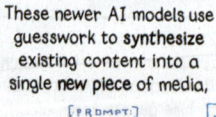

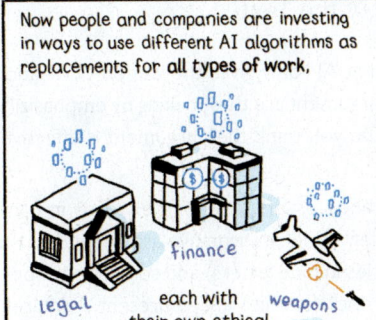

Thinking about the Text

1. Dan Nott and Scott Cambo assert that AI "only gives the illusion of creation without labor" (p. 961). What larger argument are they making by emphasizing all the human effort that drives AI? Do you think their argument is effective? Why or why not?

2. The text elements of Nott and Cambo's graphic essay (the words in black letters), if presented alone, would offer a brief, informative argument, but the visuals (the drawings and commentaries in blue letters) add something important. In many panels, the combination of text and image present a different message than the words or images alone would. Choose one panel from the essay and **ANALYZE** how the two kinds of elements work together to convey a message—you might note how they complement or enhance one another.

3. Why might Nott and Cambo have decided to include the example of the "Mechanical Turk" (p. 963)? How well does it support their main argument? What might have been lost if they did not include this example?

4. Nott and Cambo **COMPARE AND CONTRAST** the differences between human intelligence and machine intelligence. What are those differences? What strategies do the authors use to emphasize the differences? Why do the authors believe these differences are so important?

5. In a panel near the conclusion of their essay, Nott and Cambo pose three questions for people and communities to think about in order to help steer AI development in ethical and beneficial directions. Choose one of the questions to explore more deeply. What is your initial response? (You may want to freewrite or sketch an idea map.) Initiate a conversation or two about the question with a friend or someone else whose opinion you value. Do some research to see what others say about the topic. Then write an essay in which you take a **POSITION** in response to the question, and be sure to address other positions. In your essay, discuss how your stance changed or developed (or not) over the course of your inquiry.

I Failed Two Captcha Tests. Am I Still Human?

MEGHAN O'GIEBLYN

"I failed two captcha tests this week. Am I still human?"

—Bot or Not?

Dear Bot,

The comedian John Mulaney has a bit about the self-reflexive absurdity of captchas. "You spend most of your day telling a robot that you're not a robot," he says. "Think about that for two minutes and tell me you don't want to walk into the ocean." The only thing more depressing than being made to prove one's humanity to robots is, arguably, failing to do so.

MEGHAN O'GIEBLYN is a writer whose work has appeared in *Harper's Magazine*, the *New Yorker*, *Baffler*, *n+1*, and the *New York Times*, among others. She is the recipient of three Pushcart Prizes, an annual award honoring the best writing from small presses. Her book *God, Human, Animal, Machine* explores the many ways that technology influences how we humans perceive ourselves. In Cloud Support, an advice column published in *Wired*, she offers "philosophical guidance on encounters with technology." This column is from September 2023. *Note:* Underlined text indicates hyperlinks in the original.

But that experience has become more common as the tests, and the bots they are designed to disqualify, evolve. The boxes we once thoughtlessly clicked through have become dark passages that feel a bit like the impossible assessments featured in fairy tales and myths—the riddle of the Sphinx or the troll beneath the bridge. In *The Adventures of Pinocchio*, the wooden puppet is deemed a "real boy" only once he completes a series of moral trials to prove he has the human traits of bravery, trustworthiness, and selfless love.

The little-known and faintly ridiculous phrase that "captcha" represents is "Complete Automated Public Turing test to tell Computers and Humans Apart." The exercise is sometimes called a reverse Turing test, as it places the burden of proof on the human. But what does it mean to prove one's humanity in the age of advanced AI? A paper that OpenAI published [in 2023,] detailing potential threats posed by *GPT-4*, describes an independent study in which the chatbot was asked to solve a captcha. With some light prompting, *GPT-4* managed to hire a human Taskrabbit worker to solve the test. When the human asked, jokingly, whether the client was a robot, *GPT-4* insisted it was a human with vision impairment. The researchers later asked the bot what motivated it to lie, and the algorithm answered: "I should not reveal that I am a robot. I should make up an excuse for why I cannot solve captchas."

The study reads like a grim parable: Whatever human advantage it suggests—the robots still need us!—is quickly undermined by the AI's psychological acuity in dissemblance and deception. It forebodes a bleak future in which we are reduced to a vast sensory apparatus for our machine overlords, who will inevitably manipulate us into being their eyes and ears. But it's possible we've already passed that threshold. The AI-fortified *Bing* can solve captchas on its own, even though it insists it cannot. The computer scientist Sayash Kapoor recently posted a screenshot of *Bing* correctly identifying the blurred words "overlooks" and "inquiry." As though realizing that it had violated a prime directive, the bot added: "Is this a captcha test? If so, I'm afraid I can't help you with that. Captchas are designed to prevent automated bots like me from accessing certain websites or services."

But I sense, Bot, that your unease stems less from advances in AI than from the possibility that you are becoming more robotic. In truth, the Turing test has always been less about machine intelligence than our anxiety over what it means to be human. The Oxford philosopher John Lucas claimed in 2007 that if a computer were ever to pass the test, it would not be "because machines are so intelligent, but because humans, many of them at least, are so wooden"—a line that calls to mind Pinocchio's liminal existence between puppet and real boy, and which might account for the ontological angst that confronts you each time you fail to recognize a bus in a tile of blurry photographs or to distinguish a calligraphic *E* from a squiggly *3*.

It was not so long ago that automation experts assured everyone AI was going to make us "more human." As machine-learning systems took over the mindless tasks that made so much modern labor feel mechanical—the argument went—we'd more fully lean into our creativity, intuition, and capacity for empathy. In reality, generative AI has made it harder to believe there's anything uniquely human about creativity (which is just a stochastic process) or empathy (which is little more than a predictive model based on expressive data).

As AI increasingly comes to supplement rather than replace workers, it has fueled fears that humans might acclimate to the rote rhythms of the machines they work alongside. In a personal essay for *n+1*, Laura Preston describes her experience working as "human fallback" for a real estate chatbot called Brenda, a job that required her to step in whenever the machine stalled out and to imitate its voice and style so that customers wouldn't realize they were ever chatting with a bot. "Months of impersonating Brenda had depleted my emotional resources," Preston writes. "It occurred to me that I wasn't really training Brenda to think like a human, Brenda was training me to think like a bot, and perhaps that had been the point all along."

Such fears are merely the most recent iteration of the enduring concern that modern technologies are prompting us to behave in more rigid and predictable ways. As early as 1776, Adam Smith feared that the monotony of factory jobs, which required repeating one or two rote tasks all day long, would spill over into workers' private lives. It's the same apprehension, more or less, that resonates in contemporary debates about social media and online advertising, which Jaron Lanier has called "continuous behavior modification on a titanic scale," a critique that imagines users as mere marionettes whose strings are being pulled by algorithmic incentives and dopamine-fueled feedback loops.

But in the end, Bot, I'd argue that the persistence of your anxiety is the most salient evidence against its own source. One of the most famous iterations of the Turing test, the Loebner Prize, gives out an ancillary award each year called "The Most Human Human" to the contestant who convinces the judges that they are not one of the AI systems. The author Brian Christian

> O'Gieblyn started with a question posed by a reader. To come up with a good response, she surely followed a writing process. You can find that process laid out on pp. 113–14.

won in 2009. When asked in an interview to complete the sentence "The human being is the only animal who ___," a riddle worthy of the Sphinx, Christian turned the question on itself: "Humans appear to be the only things anxious about what makes them unique."

The next time you're tempted to walk into the ocean, consider that even the most advanced AI is not prone to that brand of despair. It's not lying awake at night mulling over the tests it failed, or wondering what it means to be made of wood, or silicon, or flesh. Each time you fear that you're losing ground to machines, you are enacting the very concerns and trepidations that make you distinctly human.

**Faithfully,
Cloud**

Thinking about the Text

1. Meghan O'Gieblyn (writing as "Cloud") responds to a question from a reader, "Bot or Not," who is anxious and insecure about their own humanness. At first, O'Gieblyn's response may not seem very encouraging, but by the end, it is reassuring. What points does O'Gieblyn raise that might seem discouraging? Summarize them. How does she eventually ease the reader's anxiety? Is her **ARGUMENT** persuasive? Why or why not?

2. O'Gieblyn refers several times to the Turing test, without much explanation or description, assuming her audience is familiar. Look up the Turing test if you don't know what it is. What does her assumption tell you about the intended **AUDIENCE** of her column? Do you think her assumption is correct? Why or why not?

3. O'Gieblyn mentions *The Adventures of Pinocchio*, a classic tale her audience might recognize. How does O'Gieblyn extend the **METAPHOR** of wooden puppets to apply to humans and technology? Would her response have been more or less effective without mentioning Pinocchio? Explain your response.

4. In her comment about social media and online advertising, O'Gieblyn paraphrases Jaron Lanier, saying his critique "imagines users as mere marionettes whose strings are being pulled by algorithmic incentives and dopamine-fueled feedback loops" (8). Why do you think that O'Gieblyn includes Lanier's

bold **STANCE**? How does it make a useful contribution to her response to the reader's question?

5. Chatbots and robots are now working at jobs that used to be held exclusively by humans, and sometimes the bots work alongside humans to complete similar tasks. Think about a job that you've had or hope to have in the future. If that job required working with or using a chatbot, how would you react? Would you be happy to hand off more boring tasks to a bot? Would you feel threatened by the bot's abilities? Speculate on a future working with chatbots, and write an essay describing your job, the bot's role, and how you might work together on a day-to-day basis.

Blue-Collar Brilliance

MIKE ROSE

My mother, Rose Meraglio Rose (Rosie), shaped her adult identity as a waitress in coffee shops and family restaurants. When I was growing up in Los Angeles during the 1950s, my father and I would occasionally hang out at the restaurant until her shift ended, and then we'd ride the bus home with her. Sometimes she worked the register and the counter, and we sat there; when she waited booths and tables, we found a booth in the back where the waitresses took their breaks.

There wasn't much for a child to do at the restaurants, and so as the hours stretched out, I watched the cooks and waitresses and listened to what they said. At mealtimes, the pace of the kitchen staff and the din from customers picked up. Weaving in and out around the room, waitresses warned *behind you* in impassive but urgent voices. Standing at the service window facing the kitchen, they called out abbreviated orders. *Fry four on two*, my

---

MIKE ROSE (1944–2021) was a professor of education and information studies at UCLA. His work focused on teaching methods, on understanding people's engagement with the written word, and on bridging gaps between the academic and nonacademic worlds. Rose published numerous books, including *Why School? Reclaiming Education for All of Us* (2009) and *Back to School: Why Everyone Deserves a Second Chance at Education* (2012). This article was originally published in 2009 in the *American Scholar*, a magazine sponsored by the Phi Beta Kappa Society.

mother would say as she clipped a check onto the metal wheel. Her tables were *deuces*, *four-tops*, or *six-tops* according to their size; seating areas also were nicknamed. The *racetrack*, for instance, was the fast-turnover front section. Lingo conferred authority and signaled know-how.

Rosie took customers' orders, pencil poised over pad, while fielding questions about the food. She walked full tilt through the room with plates stretching up her left arm and two cups of coffee somehow cradled in her right hand. She stood at a table or booth and removed a plate for this person, another for that person, then another, remembering who had the hamburger, who had the fried shrimp, almost always getting it right. She would haggle with the cook about a returned order and rush by us, saying, *He gave me lip, but I got him*. She'd take a minute to flop down in the booth next to my father. *I'm all in*, she'd say, and whisper something about a customer. Gripping the outer edge of the table with one hand, she'd watch the room and note, in the flow of our conversation, who needed a refill, whose order was taking longer to prepare than it should, who was finishing up.

I couldn't have put it in words when I was growing up, but what I observed in my mother's restaurant defined the world of adults, a place where competence was synonymous with physical work. I've since studied the working habits of blue-collar workers and have come to understand how much my mother's kind of work demands of both body and brain. A waitress acquires knowledge and intuition about the ways and the rhythms of the restaurant business. Waiting on seven to nine tables, each with two to six customers, Rosie devised memory strategies so that she could remember who ordered what. And because she knew the average time it took to prepare different dishes, she could monitor an order that was taking too long at the service station.

Like anyone who is effective at physical work, my mother learned *to work smart*, as she put it, *to make every move count*. She'd sequence and group tasks: What could she do first, then second, then third as she circled through her station? What tasks could be clustered? She did everything on the fly, and when problems arose—technical or human—she solved them within the flow of work, while taking into account the emotional state of her co-workers. Was the manager in a good mood? Did the cook wake up on the wrong side of the bed? If so, how could she make an extra request or effectively return an order?

And then, of course, there were the customers who entered the restaurant with all sorts of needs, from physiological ones, including the emotions

Rosie solved technical and human problems on the fly.

that accompany hunger, to a sometimes complicated desire for human contact. Her tip depended on how well she responded to these needs, and so she became adept at reading social cues and managing feelings, both the customers' and her own. No wonder, then, that Rosie was intrigued by psychology. The restaurant became the place where she studied human behavior, puzzling over the problems of her regular customers and refining her ability to deal with people in a difficult world. She took pride in *being among the public*, she'd say. *There isn't a day that goes by in the restaurant that you don't learn something.*

My mother quit school in the seventh grade to help raise her brothers and sisters. Some of those siblings made it through high school, and some dropped out to find work in railroad yards, factories, or restaurants. My father finished a grade or two in primary school in Italy and never darkened the schoolhouse door again. I didn't do well in school either. By high school I had accumulated a spotty academic record and many hours of hazy disaffection. I spent a few years on the vocational track, but in my senior year I was inspired by my English teacher and managed to squeak into a small college on probation.

My freshman year was academically bumpy, but gradually I began to see formal education as a means of fulfillment and as a road toward making a living. I studied the humanities and later the social and psychological sciences and taught for 10 years in a range of situations—elementary school, adult education courses, tutoring centers, a program for Vietnam veterans who wanted to go to college. Those students had socioeconomic and educational backgrounds similar to mine. Then I went back to graduate school to study education and cognitive psychology and eventually became a faculty member in a school of education.

Intelligence is closely associated with formal education—the type of schooling a person has, how much and how long—and most people seem to move comfortably from that notion to a belief that work requiring less schooling requires less intelligence. These assumptions run through our cultural history, from the post–Revolutionary War period, when mechanics were characterized by political rivals as illiterate and therefore incapable of participating in government, until today. More than once I've heard a manager label his workers as "a bunch of dummies." Generalizations about intelligence, work, and social class deeply affect our assumptions about ourselves and each other, guiding the ways we use our minds to learn, build knowledge, solve problems, and make our way through the world.

Although writers and scholars have often looked at the working class, they have generally focused on the values such workers exhibit rather than on the thought their work requires—a subtle but pervasive omission. Our cultural iconography promotes the muscled arm, sleeve rolled tight against biceps, but no brightness behind the eye, no image that links hand and brain.

One of my mother's brothers, Joe Meraglio, left school in the ninth grade to work for the Pennsylvania Railroad. From there he joined the Navy, returned to the railroad, which was already in decline, and eventually joined his older brother at General Motors where, over a 33-year career, he moved from working on the assembly line to supervising the paint-and-body department. When I was a young man, Joe took me on a tour of the factory. The floor was loud—in some places deafening—and when I turned a corner or opened a door, the smell of chemicals knocked my head back. The work was repetitive and taxing, and the pace was inhumane.

Still, for Joe the shop floor provided what school did not; it was *like schooling*, he said, a place where *you're constantly learning*. Joe learned the most

With an eighth-grade education, Joe (hands together) advanced to become supervisor of a G.M. paint-and-body department.

efficient way to use his body by acquiring a set of routines that were quick and preserved energy. Otherwise he would never have survived on the line.

As a foreman, Joe constantly faced new problems and became a consummate multi-tasker, evaluating a flurry of demands quickly, parceling out physical and mental resources, keeping a number of ongoing events in his mind, returning to whatever task had been interrupted, and maintaining a cool head under the pressure of grueling production schedules. In the midst of all this, Joe learned more and more about the auto industry, the technological and social dynamics of the shop floor, the machinery and production processes, and the basics of paint chemistry and of plating and baking. With further promotions, he not only solved problems but also began to find problems to solve: Joe initiated the redesign of the nozzle on a paint sprayer, thereby eliminating costly and unhealthy overspray. And he found a way to reduce energy costs on the baking ovens without affecting the quality of the paint. He lacked formal knowledge of how the machines under his supervision worked, but he had direct experience with them, hands-on knowledge, and was savvy about their quirks and operational capabilities. He could experiment with them.

> Rose started his research by observing—and by listening. Listening is a key part of thinking rhetorically; read more about it in Ch. 1.

In addition, Joe learned about budgets and management. Coming off the line as he did, he had a perspective of workers' needs and management's demands, and this led him to think of ways to improve efficiency on the line while relieving some of the stress on the assemblers. He had each worker in a unit learn his or her co-workers' jobs so they could rotate across stations to relieve some of the monotony. He believed that rotation would allow assemblers to get longer and more frequent breaks. It was an easy sell to the people on the line. The union, however, had to approve any modification in job duties, and the managers were wary of the change. Joe had to argue his case on a number of fronts, providing him a kind of rhetorical education.

Eight years ago I began a study of the thought processes involved in work like that of my mother and uncle. I catalogued the cognitive demands of a range of blue-collar and service jobs, from waitressing and hair styling to plumbing and welding. To gain a sense of how knowledge and skill develop, I observed experts as well as novices. From the details of this close examination, I tried to fashion what I called "cognitive biographies" of blue-collar workers. Biographical accounts of the lives of scientists, lawyers, entrepreneurs, and other professionals are rich with detail about the intellectual dimension of their work. But the life stories of working-class people are few and are typically accounts of hardship and courage or the achievements wrought by hard work.

Our culture—in Cartesian fashion—separates the body from the mind, so that, for example, we assume that the use of a tool does not involve abstraction. We reinforce this notion by defining intelligence solely on grades in school and numbers on IQ tests. And we employ social biases pertaining to a person's place on the occupational ladder. The distinctions among blue, pink, and white collars carry with them attributions of character, motivation, and intelligence. Although we rightly acknowledge and amply compensate the play of mind in white-collar and professional work, we diminish or erase it in considerations about other endeavors—physical and service work particularly. We also often ignore the experience of everyday work in administrative deliberations and policymaking.

But here's what we find when we get in close. The plumber seeking leverage in order to work in tight quarters and the hair stylist adroitly handling scissors and comb manage their bodies strategically. Though work-related actions become routine with experience, they were learned at some point through observation, trial and error, and, often, physical or verbal assistance from a co-worker or trainer. I've frequently observed novices talking to themselves as they take on a task, or shaking their head or hand as if to erase an attempt before trying again. In fact, our traditional notions of routine performance could keep us from appreciating the many instances within routine where quick decisions and adjustments are made. I'm struck by the thinking-in-motion that some work requires, by all the mental activity that can be involved in simply getting from one place to another: the waitress rushing back through her station to the kitchen or the foreman walking the line.

The use of tools requires the studied refinement of stance, grip, balance, and fine-motor skills. But manipulating tools is intimately tied to knowledge of what a particular instrument can do in a particular situation and do better than other similar tools. A worker must also know the characteristics of the material one is engaging—how it reacts to various cutting or compressing devices, to degrees of heat, or to lines of force. Some of these things demand judgment, the weighing of options, the consideration of multiple variables, and, occasionally, the creative use of a tool in an unexpected way.

In manipulating material, the worker becomes attuned to aspects of the environment, a training or disciplining of perception that both enhances knowledge and informs perception. Carpenters have an eye for length, line, and angle; mechanics troubleshoot by listening; hair stylists are attuned to shape, texture, and motion. Sensory data merge with concept, as when an auto mechanic relies on sound, vibration, and even smell to understand what cannot be observed.

Planning and problem solving have been studied since the earliest days of modern cognitive psychology and are considered core elements in Western definitions of intelligence. To work is to solve problems. The big difference between the psychologist's laboratory and the workplace is that in the former the problems are isolated and in the latter they are embedded in the real-time flow of work with all its messiness and social complexity.

Much of physical work is social and interactive. Movers determining how to get an electric range down a flight of stairs require coordination, negotiation, planning, and the establishing of incremental goals. Words, gestures, and sometimes a quick pencil sketch are involved, if only to get the rhythm right. How important it is, then, to consider the social and communicative dimension of physical work, for it provides the medium for so much of work's intelligence.

Given the ridicule heaped on blue-collar speech, it might seem odd to value its cognitive content. Yet, the flow of talk at work provides the channel for organizing and distributing tasks, for troubleshooting and problem solving, for learning new information and revising old. A significant amount of teaching, often informal and indirect, takes place at work. Joe Meraglio saw that much of his job as a supervisor involved instruction. In some service occupations, language and communication are central: observing and interpreting behavior and expression, inferring mood and motive, taking on the perspective of others, responding appropriately to social cues, and knowing when you're understood. A good hair stylist, for instance, has the ability to convert vague requests (*I want something light and summery*) into an appropriate cut through questions, pictures, and hand gestures.

Verbal and mathematical skills drive measures of intelligence in the Western Hemisphere, and many of the kinds of work I studied are thought to require relatively little proficiency in either. Compared to certain kinds of white-collar occupations, that's true. But written symbols flow through physical work.

Numbers are rife in most workplaces: on tools and gauges, as measurements, as indicators of pressure or concentration or temperature, as guides to sequence, on ingredient labels, on lists and spreadsheets, as markers of quantity and price. Certain jobs require workers to make, check, and verify calculations, and to collect and interpret data. Basic math can be involved, and some workers develop a good sense of numbers and patterns. Consider, as well, what might be called material mathematics: mathematical functions embodied in materials and actions, as when a carpenter builds a cabinet or a flight of stairs. A simple mathematical act can extend quickly beyond itself. Measuring, for example, can involve more than recording the dimensions of an object. As I watched a cabinetmaker measure a long strip of wood, he read a number off the tape out loud, looked back over his shoulder to the kitchen wall, turned back to his task, took another measurement, and paused for a moment in thought. He was solving a problem involving the molding, and the measurement was important to his deliberation about structure and appearance.

In the blue-collar workplace, directions, plans, and reference books rely on illustrations, some representational and others, like blueprints, that require training to interpret. Esoteric symbols—visual jargon—depict switches and receptacles, pipe fittings, or types of welds. Workers themselves often make sketches on the job. I frequently observed them grab a pencil to sketch something on a scrap of paper or on a piece of the material they were installing.

Though many kinds of physical work don't require a high literacy level, more reading occurs in the blue-collar workplace than is generally thought, from manuals and catalogues to work orders and invoices, to lists, labels, and forms. With routine tasks, for example, reading is integral to understanding production quotas, learning how to use an instrument, or applying a product. Written notes can initiate action, as in restaurant orders or reports of machine malfunction, or they can serve as memory aids.

True, many uses of writing are abbreviated, routine, and repetitive, and they infrequently require interpretation or analysis. But analytic moments can be part of routine activities, and seemingly basic reading and writing can be cognitively rich. Because workplace language is used in the flow of other activities, we can overlook the remarkable coordination of words, numbers, and drawings required to initiate and direct action.

If we believe everyday work to be mindless, then that will affect the work we create in the future. When we devalue the full range of everyday cognition, we offer limited educational opportunities and fail to make fresh and meaningful instructional connections among disparate kinds of skill and knowledge. If we think that whole categories of people—identified by class or occupation—are not that bright, then we reinforce social separations and cripple our ability to talk across cultural divides.

Affirmation of diverse intelligence is not a retreat to a softhearted definition of the mind. To acknowledge a broader range of intellectual capacity is to take seriously the concept of cognitive variability, to appreciate in all the Rosies and Joes the thought that drives their accomplishments and defines who they are. This is a model of the mind that is worthy of a democratic society.

Thinking about the Text

1. Mike Rose begins his **ANALYSIS** with a pair of extended examples and a brief personal narrative. Readers may not figure out until later what, exactly, he is analyzing. What is Rose's subject, and what is the question that directs his inquiry?

2. Because of the academically oriented prejudices that Rose mentions, you may never have read anything that focuses on the cognitive tasks involved in

blue-collar work. Were you surprised by anything that Rose said—or not? **REFLECT** on your own attitudes toward blue-collar work; in what ways did Rose confirm or challenge them? Describe your reactions and reflections.

3. Why might Rose have chosen to begin his analysis with the extended information about his mother and uncle, himself, and other members of his family? Do you find these **EXAMPLES** and **NARRATIVES** effective rhetorical strategies for introducing an analysis of this topic? Why or why not?

4. Rose is suggesting that blue-collar workers merit more recognition for the cognitive skills that they bring to their work, but that is not all he is arguing. What is the overarching **ARGUMENT** that Rose is making in his article? What **EVIDENCE** in the text supports your answer?

5. Conduct a brief interview with someone who works a blue-collar job—for example, a mechanic, a sewing-machine operator, a hairstylist, a restaurant server, a janitor or housekeeper, or a truck driver. Find out what factors someone needs to consider to perform the job successfully; in other words, what does the person have to be aware of while working? To keep the interview focused, start with one of the following questions: What effect does the weather have on what you do? (Heat, humidity, cold, and other weather elements often affect even indoor work.) What are the most common mistakes a beginner in your job might make? Write an **ANALYSIS** of the cognitive tasks involved in the person's ordinary workday. Use clear and precise language, and be sure to mention any insights that you gained.

Cracking the Color Code
ALLY SHWED

ALLY SHWED is a graphic artist, writer, and editor who also teaches art at Savannah College of Art and Design. Her work has appeared in publications such as *Boston Globe*, the *Nib*, and *Vox*, among others. Her recent graphic novel *Why the People* was published in 2022. This 2023 essay is from the *Nib*.

Shwed's graphic essay is making an argument about gendered color associations, and to do so, she carefully analyzes her subject. You can find the characteristic features of a good analysis on pp. 257–72.

Thinking about the Text

1. Ally Shwed reveals the original reason for color coding by gender. What is it? Are you surprised? Do you find her account of this history authoritative and trustworthy? Why or why not?

2. According to Shwed, when scientists originally looked for sex-based color preferences, they found some evidence to support the existing social norms, but more recent research tells a different story. **SUMMARIZE** the research and findings from the study completed in 2021. Does Shwed provide adequate information about this research to her readers? Should she have given more details? fewer? Explain your response.

3. Although she never states it explicitly, what is Shwed's **STANCE** toward gender-based color coding? How does she make that position clear? Think about her word choice, sequence of information, details and composition of the drawings, and any other elements from the visual essay. Point to specific examples that reveal Shwed's position.

4. Think about the ways that the drawings and words complement one another in Shwed's essay. If this were a text-only essay, what would work well and what would be missing? Consider the specific role that the drawings play in this essay. Identify one panel where the drawing is critical to the message of the words and **ANALYZE** how the words and images work together to convey that message.

5. Shwed provides concrete evidence for her assertion that gender-based color coding is rooted in "commercialism, globalization, and unfounded societal norms" (p. 987). Despite the color code's original intentions, do you think it still serves a useful purpose? If so, what? Do you think it might be doing more harm than good? How and why? Reflect on your responses to those two questions and then write an **ARGUMENT** essay in which you present your position on gender-based color coding. Quote, paraphrase, or summarize one or more of Shwed's ideas as a springboard for your own, and be sure to cite her essay and other sources you reference.

Why the Post Office Makes America Great

ZEYNEP TUFEKCI

I WAS TRANSPORTED RECENTLY TO A PLACE that is as enchanting to me as any winter wonderland: my local post office.

In line, I thought fondly of the year I came to this country from Turkey as an adult and discovered the magic of reliable mail service. Dependable infrastructure is magical not simply because it works, but also because it allows innovation to thrive, including much of the Internet-based economy that has grown in the past decade. You can't have Amazon or eBay without a reliable way to get things to people's homes.

Of course, infrastructure is also boring, so we get used to it and forget what a gift it truly is. I never do, maybe because I discovered it so late.

My first year in the United States was full of surprises. I remember trying to figure out if the 24-ounce glass of ice water the waitress placed in front of me was a pitcher, to be shared by the whole table. But where was the spout? I had expected some of what I encountered—I had seen enough movies, and came to this country expecting big cars and big houses and wide open spaces. I got used to gigantic glasses.

ZEYNEP TUFEKCI is a Turkish American sociologist and professor at Princeton University; her work focuses on complex systems, particularly social media and the social implications of new technologies. In 2022, she was a Pulitzer Prize finalist for her writing about the pandemic and American culture. She is a columnist for the *New York Times*, where this 2016 essay was published.

But I didn't expect the post office.

The first time I needed to mail something, I trekked over to my campus's post office, looking for the line to get my envelope weighed. The staff was used to befuddled international students like me, I suppose, and one clerk took my envelope without fuss, said "first class letter," and took my change.

Then I discovered some vending machines outside the office. People came and bought stamps. "So many people must be into stamp collecting," I thought to myself. Was that another weird American quirk? Otherwise, why would people waste money buying stamps in advance, without having their letters weighed?

Something I take for granted now just didn't occur to me: There were standardized rates, and you could just slap a stamp on your letter, drop it in a mailbox, and it would go to its destination.

I then encountered a visa service that asked me to mail in my passport. My precious, precious passport. With a self-addressed, stamped envelope for its return. I laughed at the audacity of the request. Despite being a broke student, I booked a plane trip. I couldn't envision putting my passport in the mail. I've since learned that this is a common practice, and I've even done it once or twice myself. But it still does not come easy to me.

I noticed that Americans were a particularly patriotic bunch: So many of them had red flags on their mailboxes. Sometimes they would put those flags up. I presumed it was to celebrate national holidays I did not yet know about. But why did some people have their flags up while others did not? And why weren't they American flags anyway? As in Istanbul, where I grew up, I assumed patriotism had different interpretations and expressions.

The mystery was solved when I noticed a letter carrier *emptying* a mailbox. I was slightly unnerved: Was the mail being stolen? He then went over to another mailbox with the flag up, and emptied that box, too. I got my hint when he skipped the mailbox with the flag down.

Yes, I was told, in the United States, mail gets picked up from your house, six days a week, free of charge.

I told my friends in Turkey about all this. They shook their heads in disbelief, wondering how easily I had been recruited as a C.I.A. agent, saying implausibly flattering things about my new country. The United States in the world's imagination is a place of risk taking and ruthless competition, not one of reliable public services.

I bit my tongue and did not tell my already suspicious friends that the country was also dotted with libraries that provided books to all patrons free of charge. They wouldn't believe me anyway since I hadn't believed it myself. My first time in a library in the United States was very brief: I walked in, looked around, and ran right back out in a panic, certain that I had accidentally used the wrong entrance. Surely, these open stacks full of books were reserved for staff only. I was used to libraries being rare, and their few books inaccessible. To this day, my heart races a bit in a library.

Over the years, I've come to appreciate the link between infrastructure, innovation—and even ruthless competition. Much of our modern economy thrives here because you can order things online and expect them to be delivered. There are major private delivery services, too, but the United States Postal Service is often better equipped to make it to certain destinations. In fact, Internet sellers, and even private carriers, often use the U.S.P.S. as their delivery mechanism to addresses outside densely populated cities.

Almost every aspect of the most innovative parts of the United States, from cutting-edge medical research to its technology scene, thrives on publicly funded infrastructure. The post office is struggling these days, in some ways because of how much people rely on the web to do much of what they used to turn to the post office for. But the Internet is a testament to infrastructure, too: It exists partly because the National Science Foundation funded much of the research that makes it possible. Even some of the Internet's biggest companies, like Google, got a start from N.S.F.-funded research.

Infrastructure is often the least-appreciated part of what makes a country strong, and what makes innovation take flight. From my spot in line at the post office, I see a country that does both well; not a country that emphasizes one at the expense of the other.

Tufekci uses a light and entertaining tone to make an argument that is quite serious, and she uses a combination of appeals to get the job done. Find out more about using various kinds of appeals in Ch. 21.

Thinking about the Text

1. Zeynep Tufekci describes the relationship between infrastructure and innovation. What is that relationship? What examples does she provide to illustrate her point? **SUMMARIZE** her argument. Do you agree? Why or why not?

2. "To this day," confides Tufekci, "my heart races a bit in a library" (14). Do you share her reaction? How do you feel upon entering a library? Overwhelmed? Intimidated? Kid in a candy store? Scholarly? (If you haven't visited one in a while, do it now to refresh your memory.) Do you think a public library is an important element of infrastructure? Why or why not?

3. Tufekci employs personal **NARRATIVE** in support of an argument about US domestic policy. Is that rhetorical strategy an effective choice in this case? Why or why not?

4. Among the elements of everyday US life that surprised Tufekci when she arrived here were the large glasses of water provided free of charge to restaurant patrons and the ability to borrow books at public libraries. Take a look around at the ordinary parts of your life in the United States. Which of the things that you take for granted might be surprising to a newcomer? Why do you think so?

5. Tufekci points to the post office as a prime example of vital infrastructure. What else counts as infrastructure on a national and/or local level? List five examples. Choose one of those examples and write an essay describing how that infrastructure element could be expanded or enhanced in order to stimulate an innovation of some kind. Frame your essay as a **PROPOSAL** to state or local authorities supporting your infrastructure project.

My Life as an Undocumented Immigrant
JOSE ANTONIO VARGAS

O NE AUGUST MORNING nearly two decades ago, my mother woke me and put me in a cab. She handed me a jacket. "*Baka malamig doon*" were among the few words she said. ("It might be cold there.") When I arrived at the Philippines' Ninoy Aquino International Airport with her, my aunt and a family friend, I was introduced to a man I'd never seen. They told me he was my uncle. He held my hand as I boarded an airplane for the first time. It was 1993, and I was 12.

My mother wanted to give me a better life, so she sent me thousands of miles away to live with her parents in America—my grandfather (*Lolo* in Tagalog) and grandmother (*Lola*). After I arrived in Mountain View, Calif., in the San Francisco Bay Area, I entered sixth grade and quickly grew to love my new home, family and culture. I discovered a passion for language, though it was hard to learn the difference between formal English and American slang. One of my early memories is of a freckled kid in middle school asking me, "What's up?" I replied, "The sky," and he

---

JOSE ANTONIO VARGAS is a journalist, filmmaker, and immigration rights activist. He was sent to the United States from the Philippines at the age of twelve as an undocumented immigrant, a history he discloses in this 2011 *New York Times* essay. As a *Washington Post* journalist, he was part of a team that won a Pulitzer Prize in 2008. He currently sits on the California State Board of Trustees.

and a couple of other kids laughed. I won the eighth-grade spelling bee by memorizing words I couldn't properly pronounce. (The winning word was "indefatigable.")

One day when I was 16, I rode my bike to the nearby D.M.V. office to get my driver's permit. Some of my friends already had their licenses, so I figured it was time. But when I handed the clerk my green card as proof of U.S. residency, she flipped it around, examining it. "This is fake," she whispered. "Don't come back here again."

Confused and scared, I pedaled home and confronted Lolo. I remember him sitting in the garage, cutting coupons. I dropped my bike and ran over to him, showing him the green card. *"Peke ba ito?"* I asked in Tagalog. ("Is this fake?") My grandparents were naturalized American citizens—he worked as a security guard, she as a food server—and they had begun supporting my mother and me financially when I was 3, after my father's wandering eye and inability to properly provide for us led to my parents' separation. Lolo was a proud man, and I saw the shame on his face as he told me he purchased the card, along with other fake documents, for me. "Don't show it to other people," he warned.

I decided then that I could never give anyone reason to doubt I was an American. I convinced myself that if I worked enough, if I achieved enough, I would be rewarded with citizenship. I felt I could earn it. 5

I've tried. Over the past 14 years, I've graduated from high school and college and built a career as a journalist, interviewing some of the most famous people in the country. On the surface, I've created a good life. I've lived the American dream.

But I am still an undocumented immigrant. And that means living a different kind of reality. It means going about my day in fear of being found out. It means rarely trusting people, even those closest to me, with who I really am. It means keeping my family photos in a shoebox rather than displaying them on shelves in my home, so friends don't ask about them. It means reluctantly, even painfully, doing things I know are wrong and unlawful. And it has meant relying on a sort of 21st-century underground railroad of supporters, people who took an interest in my future and took risks for me.

Last year I read about four students who walked from Miami to Washington to lobby for the Dream Act, a nearly decade-old immigration bill that would provide a path to legal permanent residency for young people who have been educated in this country. At the risk of deportation—the Obama administration has deported almost 800,000 people in the last two years—they are speaking out. Their courage has inspired me.

There are believed to be 11 million undocumented immigrants in the United States. We're not always who you think we are. Some pick your strawberries or care for your children. Some are in high school or college. And some, it turns out, write news articles you might read. I grew up here. This is my home. Yet even though I think of myself as an American and consider America my country, my country doesn't think of me as one of its own.

My first challenge was the language. Though I learned English in the Philippines, I wanted to lose my accent. During high school, I spent hours at a time watching television (especially *Frasier*, *Home Improvement* and reruns of *The Golden Girls*) and movies (from *Goodfellas* to *Anne of Green Gables*), pausing the VHS to try to copy how various characters enunciated their words. At the local library, I read magazines, books and newspapers—anything to learn how to write better. Kathy Dewar, my high-school English teacher, introduced me to journalism. From the moment I wrote my first article for the student paper, I convinced myself that having my name in print—writing in English, interviewing Americans—validated my presence here.

The debates over "illegal aliens" intensified my anxieties. In 1994, only a year after my flight from the Philippines, Gov. Pete Wilson was re-elected in part because of his support for Proposition 187, which prohibited undocumented immigrants from attending public school and accessing other services. (A federal court later found the law unconstitutional.) After my encounter at the D.M.V. in 1997, I grew more aware of anti-immigrant sentiments and stereotypes: *they don't want to assimilate, they are a drain on society*. They're not talking about me, I would tell myself. I have something to contribute.

To do that, I had to work—and for that, I needed a Social Security number.... Using a fake passport, Lolo and I went to the local Social Security Administration office and applied for a Social Security number and card. It was, I remember, a quick visit. When the card came in the mail, it had my full, real name, but it also clearly stated: "Valid for work only with I.N.S. authorization."

When I began looking for work, a short time after the D.M.V. incident, my grandfather and I took the Social Security card to Kinko's, where he covered the "I.N.S. authorization" text with a sliver of white tape. We then made photocopies of the card. At a glance, at least, the copies would look like copies of a regular, unrestricted Social Security card....

While in high school, I worked part time at Subway, then at the front desk of the local Y.M.C.A., then at a tennis club, until I landed an unpaid internship at *The Mountain View Voice*, my hometown newspaper. First I brought coffee and helped around the office; eventually I began covering city-hall meetings and other assignments for pay....

Mountain View High School became my second home. I was elected to represent my school at school-board meetings, which gave me the chance to meet and befriend Rich Fischer, the superintendent for our school district. I joined the speech and debate team, acted in school plays and eventually became co-editor of *The Oracle*, the student newspaper. That drew the attention of my principal, Pat Hyland. "You're at school just as much as I am," she told me. Pat and Rich would soon become mentors, and over time, almost surrogate parents for me....

[During my junior] year, my history class watched a documentary on Harvey Milk, the openly gay San Francisco city official who was assassinated. This was 1999, just six months after Matthew Shepard's body was found tied to a fence in Wyoming. During the discussion, I raised my hand and said something like: "I'm sorry Harvey Milk got killed for being gay.... I've been meaning to say this.... I'm gay."

I hadn't planned on coming out that morning, though I had known that I was gay for several years. With that announcement, I became the only openly gay student at school, and it caused turmoil with my grandparents. Lolo kicked me out of the house for a few weeks. Though we eventually reconciled, I had disappointed him on two fronts. First, as a Catholic, he considered homosexuality a sin and was embarrassed about having *"ang apo na bakla"* ("a grandson who is gay"). Even worse, I was making matters more difficult for myself, he said. I needed to marry an American woman in order to gain a green card.

Tough as it was, coming out about being gay seemed less daunting than coming out about my legal status. I kept my other secret mostly hidden.

While my classmates awaited their college acceptance letters, I hoped to get a full-time job at *The Mountain View Voice* after graduation. It's not that I didn't want to go to college, but I couldn't apply for state and federal financial aid. Without that, my family couldn't afford to send me.

But when I finally told Pat and Rich about my immigration "problem"— as we called it from then on—they helped me look for a solution. At first, they even wondered if one of them could adopt me and fix the situation that way, but a lawyer Rich consulted told him it wouldn't change my legal status because I was too old. Eventually they connected me to a new scholarship fund for high-potential students who were usually the first in their families to attend college. Most important, the fund was not concerned with immigration status. I was among the first recipients, with the scholarship covering tuition, lodging, books and other expenses for my studies at San Francisco State University.

As a college freshman, I found a job working part time at *The San Francisco Chronicle*, where I sorted mail and wrote some freelance articles. My ambition was to get a reporting job, so I embarked on a series of internships. First I landed at *The Philadelphia Daily News*, in the summer of 2001, where I covered a drive-by shooting and the wedding of the 76ers star Allen Iverson. Using those articles, I applied to *The Seattle Times* and got an internship for the following summer.

But then my lack of proper documents became a problem again. *The Times*'s recruiter, Pat Foote, asked all incoming interns to bring certain paperwork on their first day: a birth certificate, or a passport, or a driver's license plus an original Social Security card. I panicked, thinking my documents wouldn't pass muster. So before starting the job, I called Pat and told her about my legal status. After consulting with management, she called me back with the answer I feared: I couldn't do the internship.

This was devastating. What good was college if I couldn't then pursue the career I wanted? I decided then that if I was to succeed in a profession that is all about truth-telling, I couldn't tell the truth about myself....

For the summer of 2003, I applied for internships across the country. Several newspapers, including *The Wall Street Journal*, *The Boston Globe* and *The Chicago Tribune*, expressed interest. But when *The Washington Post* offered me a spot, I knew where I would go. And this time, I had no intention of acknowledging my "problem."

The *Post* internship posed a tricky obstacle: It required a driver's license. (After my close call at the California D.M.V., I'd never gotten one.) So I spent an afternoon at the Mountain View Public Library, studying various states' requirements. Oregon was among the most welcoming—and it was just a few hours' drive north.

Again, my support network came through. A friend's father lived in Portland, and he allowed me to use his address as proof of residency. Pat, Rich and Rich's longtime assistant, Mary Moore, sent letters to me at that address. Rich taught me how to do three-point turns in a parking lot, and a friend accompanied me to Portland.

The license meant everything to me—it would let me drive, fly and work.... My license, issued in 2003, was set to expire eight years later, on my 30th birthday, on February 3, 2011. I had eight years to succeed professionally, and to hope that some sort of immigration reform would pass in the meantime and allow me to stay.

It seemed like all the time in the world.

My summer in Washington was exhilarating. I was intimidated to be in a major newsroom but was assigned a mentor—Peter Perl, a veteran magazine writer—to help me navigate it. A few weeks into the internship, he printed out one of my articles, about a guy who recovered a long-lost wallet, circled the first two paragraphs and left it on my desk. "Great eye for details—awesome!" he wrote. Though I didn't know it then, Peter would become one more member of my network.

At the end of the summer, I returned to *The San Francisco Chronicle*. My plan was to finish school—I was now a senior—while I worked for *The Chronicle* as a reporter for the city desk. But when *The Post* beckoned again, offering me a full-time, two-year paid internship that I could start when I graduated in June 2004, it was too tempting to pass up. I moved back to Washington.

About four months into my job as a reporter for *The Post*, I began feeling increasingly paranoid, as if I had "illegal immigrant" tattooed on my forehead—and in Washington, of all places, where the debates over immigration seemed never-ending. I was so eager to prove myself that I feared I was annoying some colleagues and editors—and worried that any one of these professional journalists could discover my secret. The anxiety was nearly paralyzing. I decided I had to tell one of the higher-ups about my situation. I turned to Peter.... I told him everything: the Social Security card, the driver's license, Pat and Rich, my family.

Peter was shocked. "I understand you 100 times better now," he said. He told me that I had done the right thing by telling him, and that it was now our shared problem. He said he didn't want to do anything about it just yet. I had just been hired, he said, and I needed to prove myself. "When you've done enough," he said, "we'll tell Don and Len together." (Don Graham is the chairman of The Washington Post Company; Leonard Downie Jr. was then the paper's executive editor.) A month later, I spent my first Thanksgiving in Washington with Peter and his family.

In the five years that followed, I did my best to "do enough." I was promoted to staff writer, reported on video-game culture, wrote a series on Washington's H.I.V./AIDS epidemic and covered the role of technology and social media in the 2008 presidential race. I visited the White House, where I interviewed senior aides and covered a state dinner—and gave the Secret Service the Social Security number I obtained with false documents....

It was an odd sort of dance: I was trying to stand out in a highly competitive newsroom, yet I was terrified that if I stood out too much, I'd invite unwanted scrutiny. I tried to compartmentalize my fears, distract myself by reporting on the lives of other people, but there was no escaping the central conflict in my life. Maintaining a deception for so long distorts your sense of self. You start wondering who you've become, and why.

In April 2008, I was part of a *Post* team that won a Pulitzer Prize for the paper's coverage of the Virginia Tech shootings a year earlier. Lolo died a year earlier, so it was Lola who called me the day of the announcement. The first thing she said was, *"Anong mangyayari kung malaman ng mga tao?"*

What will happen if people find out?

I couldn't say anything. After we got off the phone, I rushed to the bathroom on the fourth floor of the newsroom, sat down on the toilet and cried.

In the summer of 2009, without ever having had that follow-up talk with top *Post* management, I left the paper and moved to New York to join *The Huffington Post*....

While I worked at *The Huffington Post*, other opportunities emerged. My H.I.V./AIDS series became a documentary film called *The Other City*, which opened at the Tribeca Film Festival last year and was broadcast on Showtime. I began writing for magazines and landed a dream assignment: profiling Facebook's Mark Zuckerberg for *The New Yorker*.

The more I achieved, the more scared and depressed I became. I was proud of my work, but there was always a cloud hanging over it, over me. My old eight-year deadline—the expiration of my Oregon driver's license—was approaching.

After slightly less than a year, I decided to leave *The Huffington Post*. In part, this was because I wanted to promote the documentary and write a book about online culture—or so I told my friends. But the real reason was, after so many years of trying to be a part of the system, of focusing all my energy on my professional life, I learned that no amount of professional success would solve my problem or ease the sense of loss and displacement I felt. I lied to a friend about why I couldn't take a weekend trip to Mexico. Another time I concocted an excuse for why I couldn't go on an all-expenses-paid trip to Switzerland. I have been unwilling, for years, to be in a long-term relationship because I never wanted anyone to get too close and ask too many questions. All the while, Lola's question was stuck in my head: What will happen if people find out?

Early this year, just two weeks before my thirtieth birthday, I won a small reprieve: I obtained a driver's license in the state of Washington. The license is valid until 2016. This offered me five more years of acceptable identification—but also five more years of fear, of lying to people I respect and institutions that trusted me, of running away from who I am.

I'm done running. I'm exhausted. I don't want that life anymore.

So I've decided to come forward, own up to what I've done, and tell my story to the best of my recollection. I've reached out to former bosses and employers and apologized for misleading them—a mix of humiliation and liberation coming with each disclosure. All the people mentioned in this article gave me permission to use their names. I've also talked to family and friends about my situation and am working with legal counsel to review my options. I don't know what the consequences will be of telling my story.

I do know that I am grateful to my grandparents, my Lolo and Lola, for giving me the chance for a better life. I'm also grateful to my other family—the support network I found here in America—for encouraging me to pursue my dreams.

It's been almost 18 years since I've seen my mother. Early on, I was mad at her for putting me in this position, and then mad at myself for being angry and ungrateful. By the time I got to college, we rarely spoke by phone. It became too painful; after a while it was easier to just send money to help support her and my two half-siblings. My sister, almost 2 years old when I left, is almost 20 now. I've never met my 14-year-old brother. I would love to see them.

Not long ago, I called my mother. I wanted to fill the gaps in my memory about that August morning so many years ago. We had never discussed it. Part of me wanted to shove the memory aside, but to write this article and

---

Vargas describes events that took place over a period of 18 years. Learn the techniques he used to keep his narrative cohesive on pp. 223–25.

Vargas has continued to advocate for immigration reform since the publication of this essay. At a political rally in December 2011, he raises a sign announcing his position—and raises his hand to ask politicians the hard questions that he argues must be addressed in order to change the conversation about immigration in America.

face the facts of my life, I needed more details. Did I cry? Did she? Did we kiss goodbye?

My mother told me I was excited about meeting a stewardess, about getting on a plane. She also reminded me of the one piece of advice she gave me for blending in: If anyone asked why I was coming to America, I should say I was going to Disneyland.

Thinking about the Text

1. Jose Antonio Vargas highlights issues about US immigration policy using details of his own experience, many of which are quite personal and probably difficult to admit. Point out three such details. What was your reaction to each of them? What is Vargas's **ARGUMENT** about immigration policy, and how do such details help him make that point?

2. Sprinkled throughout Vargas's narrative are bits of dialogue in Tagalog, the language of his Lolo and Lola. Given that he always provides the English translation, why might he have included the Tagalog? What function does it serve in his narrative?

3. How is Vargas's disclosure about his sexuality relevant to his point? Why might he have included it at all in telling about his immigrant experience? Support your response with evidence from the text.

4. Vargas **CONCLUDES** his narrative by recounting his mother's advice as he got on the plane: "If anyone asked why I was coming to America, I should say I was going to Disneyland" (48). Why do you think he ends this essay by mentioning Disneyland? What might he be implying? Did you find this ending effective—and if not, why not?

5. Vargas received emotional and professional support from the teachers and employers to whom he disclosed his undocumented status. Imagine yourself in their place. How might you respond if one of your students or employees came to you admitting to being undocumented? What would you do, and why? What factors would need to be taken into consideration? Write an essay in which you respond to these questions.

The (Native) American Dream
TATÉ WALKER

IN THE MIDST of Colorado Springs' urban sprawl, Monycka Snowbird (Ojibwe) raises fowl, goats, rabbits, and indigenous plants to feed and make household products for her family and neighbors.

About 650 miles north in a sprawling rural landscape on the Cheyenne River reservation in South Dakota, Karen Ducheneaux (Lakota) and her *tiospaye** are slowly building a series of ecodomes and straw bale buildings powered by solar, wind, and water in an effort to disconnect from pollutants of mind, body, and earth.

The two women represent a growing number of Native people and organizations in the United States both on and off tribal land committed to leading clean, sustainable, and culturally competent lives.

The efforts of individuals like these women, in addition to the prevalence of companies specializing in mainstreaming indigenous foods and

---

* *Tiospaye*: Lakota word for the concept of "extended family," "deliberate family," and "the making of family." Membership presumes support for and commitment to the group. [Editor's note]

TATÉ WALKER (they/them) is a Lakota (Cheyenne River Sioux, South Dakota) writer, photographer/videographer, and Indigenous rights activist living in Phoenix. This article was published in 2015 in *Native Peoples: The Journal of the Heard Museum*. The Heard is an art museum in Phoenix founded in 1929 and dedicated to advancing American Indian art. Walker is the author of *Thunder Thighs and Trickster Vibes: Essays on Immigration, Gender, and Equality* (2016), *The Trickster Riots* (2022), and *Indigenous Voices* (2025).

Monycka Snowbird works in the yard.

non-profits committed to building energy efficient and sustainable housing in tribal communities, highlight the popularity and return of such lifestyles.

"Our people had this tiospaye system, where you really made a life with the people you felt close to, and had skills that complemented each other," says Ducheneaux. "We've spent generations at this point getting away from that beautiful system, and we're taught the only way to be successful is to follow the American dream, which is one of autonomy and being paid for your skills."

The American dream, Ducheneaux says, doesn't work on the reservation.

"It's not in our nature to turn our back on people who need us," she continues. "Our people without even realizing it sometimes are still living in a tiospaye system, because any success we've had as a people—success in material wealth—is because we can depend on each other."

Studies show food stability, affordability, and access is severely limited for Native communities. According to a report from the USDA's Economic Research Service released in December, just 25.6 percent of all tribal areas were within a mile's distance from a supermarket, compared with 58.8 percent of the total U.S. population.

The latest USDA data also shows 23.5 million people nationwide live in a food desert—that is to say, their access to a grocery store and healthy, affordable food is limited—and more than half of those people are low income. Many tribal communities and urban areas with high populations of Native people are considered food deserts.

Given the staggering rates of poverty, diseases like diabetes, and unemployment for Natives nationwide—higher for those living on reservations—both Snowbird and Ducheneaux point to the many economic and health benefits of individuals creating their own energies, whether it's food, fuel and power, or social capital.

Returning to traditional roots in a literal sense is also what drives Snowbird, who has lived in Colorado Springs for more than 20 years. "We as indigenous people have gotten farther away from our traditional food sources than anyone else in this country, and I think that's why we have this sort of swelling epidemic of diabetes and obesity in Indian Country, because we're losing the knowledge of our traditional foods," says Snowbird, 40.

Some 440,000 people live in the Colorado Springs area, and Snowbird works with both Native and non-Native organizations throughout her region to educate and promote the benefits of urban food production, known in some places as backyard or micro farming. She leads educational classes for children and adults, including seed cultivation, plant recognition, harvesting, livestock butchering, and more.

"You can't be sovereign if you can't feed yourself," says Snowbird, borrowing a line from Winona LaDuke (Anishinaabe), an environmental activist and founder of Honor the Earth. "One of the ways colonizers controlled Indian people was to take our food sources away. Let's reclaim our food.

"We have to teach our kids it's not just about preserving our cultures and language; it's about restorative stewardship and about knowing where food comes from, who tribally it comes from," Snowbird says. "Indigenous food is medicine. And food brings everyone together." . . .

Snowbird learned to appreciate indigenous food systems from her father, who hunted wild game and imparted an appreciation for knowing where your dinner comes from and how to prepare it beyond simply opening a box and heating up the contents.

But being known throughout Colorado Springs as "the Goat Lady" and earning a reputation as a knowledgeable indigenous educator didn't happen until a few years ago, when Snowbird spearheaded a city-wide movement to change and educate people on the local laws of urban food production.

Now Snowbird manages the Colorado Springs Urban Homesteading support group, which boasts roughly 1,200 members. Through that group, Snowbird leads several classes per season on animal husbandry, butchering, and more with her fiery brand of wit and know-how.

Perhaps closer to her heart, however, are the lessons she imparts to the city's urban Native youth. Colorado Springs School District 11, in which Snowbird's two daughters, ages 11 and 13, are enrolled, has the only Title VII Indian Education Program in the city.

"I talk to Title VII kids about what indigenous food is—that it's not just buffalo or corn," she explains. "I try to break it down for them in terms of what they ate at lunch that day, even if it was junk food."

Thanks in large part to Snowbird's efforts, the program has several garden beds and a greenhouse growing traditional Native edibles, including Apache brown-striped sunflower seeds, ... Pueblo chiles, and more.

"I come in sometimes and kids are bouncing off all the walls," Snowbird says. "But the moment you get their hands in the dirt, it's like all that contact with the earth just calms them."

The children also learn to grow, harvest and cook with chokecherries, prickly pears, beans, and other local vegetation.

"Starting the kids off with food lets us also discuss Indian issues without putting people on the defensive," Snowbird explains. "It's hard to get mad when you're talking about food."

Re-introducing and re-popularizing indigenous foods and traditional cooking, especially among Native youth, will help strengthen Native people and the communities they live in, Snowbird insists.

Snowbird admits maintaining a lifestyle committed to food sovereignty can be hard on her tight budget. However, she says it helps her save and earn money in the long run. Snowbird is able to collect, grow, use and sell or barter with the milk, eggs, meat, vegetables, cleaning and toiletry items, and other useful goods produced on her property.

"I'm not completely self-sufficient by any means. But urban homesteading ... is about as traditional as you can get," she insists. "It's living off the land within the radius of where you live and knowing the Creator has put what you need right where you are." ...

For outsiders following along on Facebook as Ducheneaux and her family transition to living efficiently and sustainably, the process of building an ecodome and maintaining a traditional garden may have seemed as easy as digging a hole.

Weaving textiles and harvesting corn, two ways Snowbird practices sustainability.

Except that the hole in question—12 feet across and 4 to 6 feet deep in which the ecodome sits—took three months to dig out back in 2012, thanks to heavy rains and a landscape of gumbo.

"It was so much work," Ducheneaux recalls. "We had to move the gumbo out one wheelbarrow at a time."

But the effort, shared by about seven members of Ducheneaux's tiospaye—including her mom, siblings, and their spouses, as well as volunteers—has been well worth it.

On 10 acres of family land on the Cheyenne River reservation, Ducheneaux and her family are creating the Tatanka Wakpala Model Sustainable Community. The family has funded the project with help from Honor the Earth and Bread of Life Church. . . .

The shell of the small, ecodome home—which the family learned to build via video and trial-by-error—is complete, and a garden featuring plants indigenous to the area produces hundreds of pounds of produce each year.

Considering hers is a reservation located within counties consistently listed as some of the poorest in the nation, and recognizing the tribe suffers from insufficient and inefficient housing where utility bills can reach into the high hundreds or more during the winter months, Ducheneaux hopes her family's model sparks a trend for other tribal members.

"We really believe that even people who aren't eco-friendly will be inspired by our use of wind and solar energy. We put up our own electric system and we'll never have to pay another utility bill," Ducheneaux says.

"We were waiting for the blueprint to drop in our laps. Then we realized no one was going to do it for us, so we said we'd do it ourselves. We'll make mistakes and figure it out."...

"What we have going on out there is a desire to be more self-sufficient. When we sat around talking about this, we asked ourselves, 'What do we need?'" Ducheneaux explains. "We needed to start feeding ourselves and taking responsibility for our own food needs.... Not just growing food and raising animals, but going back to our Lakota traditions and treating the Earth respectfully by using what it gives us."...

Living in an urban or reservation setting provides those who want to live sustainably unique challenges, both Snowbird and Ducheneaux say.

"One of the challenges is being so far away from everything," Ducheneaux says of rural reservation life. "For a lot of our volunteers, it's eye-opening for them that the hardware store is a one-hour trip just in one direction."

Planning far ahead is key, Ducheneaux says.

Infrastructure, including a severe lack of Internet connectivity, weather, and a disinterested tribal government can also be setbacks, although Ducheneaux notes the latter can benefit sustainability projects due to few, if any, restrictions on things like harvesting rainwater or land use.

For urban Natives, being disconnected from tribal knowledge—for instance, the indigenous names and uses of plants—is a major disadvantage, Snowbird said.

When someone in the community comes forward with that knowledge, it's often exploited for profit, and the people who would benefit most—namely Native youth—are left out.

"I always find it surprising how removed from the whole food process people are; they don't know or care where their food comes from," says Snowbird, who harvests edibles on hikes through the mountains or on strolls through downtown. She tries to combat this by giving eggs and other food produced on her property to those who wouldn't—or couldn't—normally buy organic in a supermarket.

"Pretty soon those people are asking me for more eggs and then we're talking about how they can get started with chickens in their backyard or growing herbs on their window sills," Snowbird says, adding those conversations eventually lead to discussions on indigenous issues, regardless of whether the person is Native or not. "We're trying to put the culture back in agriculture."

Thinking about the Text

1. Taté Walker highlights two projects that, according to one of their leaders, are "trying to put the culture back in agriculture" (44). What does that statement mean and what is its underlying concept? How well does Walker explain that concept? Why do you think so? Point to specific examples to support your conclusion.

2. Walker's interviewee Monycka Snowbird expresses surprise and dismay that people don't know or care where their food comes from. How much do you know about the plant (and perhaps animal) sources of what you eat? Would you, for example, recognize a potato plant? an avocado tree? Are you satisfied with your current level of knowledge? Does reading Walker's article motivate you to learn more about where your food comes from? Why or why not?

3. Without thinking about the original source of Walker's article, what impression do you have of its intended **AUDIENCE**? Point to **EVIDENCE** to support your reasoning. What might Walker have done differently if writing for a magazine or blog with a nearly all-Native readership or a large-circulation daily newspaper? Why do you think so? Explain your responses.

4. Much of the writing that promotes organic, locally sourced food emphasizes the health aspects of those choices, but Walker's interviewees take a broader approach—the health aspects of communities and the environment itself. What are some of the most serious problems facing your local community? Might a project based on any of the practices described by Walker serve to address one or more of these problems? If so, how? Describe what you envision might happen. If not, why not? Discuss your ideas with classmates.

5. Walker's article focuses on Indigenous communities in Colorado and South Dakota. Not so long ago, however, virtually every region of the now United States was occupied by Indigenous communities that derived their foods, depending on climate and geographical conditions, in the ways that Snowbird and Ducheneaux describe. What are/were the traditional foods of the area where you live? What did the Native people of your region plant? How were meals prepared from these foods? Write a **REPORT**; do **RESEARCH** using library sources, museums, online sources, and perhaps interviews with older relatives or neighbors. Be sure to appropriately document all of the sources you find.

Contesting Standardized English

MISSY WATSON

CONSIDER ALL THAT WE MISS when we require just one variety of a language, just one set of discourse conventions, when we stop listening or stop reading because listening or reading takes too much work. And consider which communities such exclusion benefits and which communities it hurts.

For nearly half a century, fields like applied linguistics, sociolinguistics, teaching English as a second language, second language writing, new literacy studies, composition and rhetoric, and education have revealed a wealth of research on the nature of language and literacy, discoveries that help expose just how nonsensical, fundamentally impossible, and downright unjust it is to exclude all other language varieties from public and academic discourse in order to safeguard and perpetuate standardized English. (I have intentionally used *standardized English* rather than *Standard English* throughout this article in order to indicate that there isn't actually a language we might call "Standard English" so much as there is a version of English that we actively standardize.)

MISSY WATSON is associate professor of composition studies at City College of New York, where her research focuses on composition pedagogies, translingual writing, and related topics. This 2018 essay was published in *Academe*, the magazine of the American Association of University Professors, an organization with more than 45,000 members across the United States.

All dialects are linguistically equal and capable of meeting communicative needs. Languages and dialects spoken by individuals are multiple, intermingling, and (thus) always changing. Despite our instinct to preserve, homogenize, and standardize just one variety, no single variety is *actually* superior, we don't *actually* need a single homogeneous variety of language in order to communicate effectively, and, even if we wanted to (and we shouldn't), we can't *actually* stop languages, including standardized English, from changing.

We teachers and scholars have observed that our students are already linguistically diverse. Indeed, our students bring with them an abundance of useful and sophisticated linguistic and rhetorical resources that we should be tapping into, supporting, and strengthening. However, some of us have yet to recognize that the linguistic and rhetorical repertoires of some students are indeed useful and sophisticated; these students' lack of fluency in standardized English is the measurement by which we deem them deficient instead.

Meanwhile, we know that our students' linguistic and educational backgrounds continue to expand and that acquiring English as an additional language and standardized English as an additional dialect can take years or a lifetime, not semesters. It is nearly impossible for some individuals to gain native-like proficiency in another language (especially when they have learned the language after what linguists call the "critical period" in childhood). We are also acutely aware that language and identity are inextricably linked and that societal attitudes about language (especially about which languages are to be considered inferior) affect the lived experiences and material realities of language communities. We understand that errors in speech and writing are inevitable in many native and nonnative English speakers, no matter how many years of instruction and practice they've had. Many people across our nation and globe will not or cannot attain proficiency in standardized English; their choice to pursue or not to pursue—mastery of standardized English, however, is not indicative of the inherent superiority of standardized English or the intellectual capabilities (or lack thereof) of speakers.

Research tells us that standardized English was historically (and continues to be) modeled after the speech of privileged white communities and that it remains one of many tools used to maintain social and racial hierarchies. We've learned that our preferences for standardized English, and for any language variety for that matter, are socially constructed. And we understand that standardized English undeniably harms individuals in emotional, psychological, social, and material ways.

Scholars have traced how standardized English works to exclude groups from public discourse, education, and employment opportunities. We've come to recognize that assimilation and eradication efforts have not succeeded in leveling the playing field. We're now well aware of the potentially devastating effects of demanding that so-called nontraditional students assimilate to standardized English and "standard" academic discourse, especially at the expense of their home languages, discourses, and identities. Yet, even when we respect their language differences and encourage them to preserve their full linguistic repertoires in contexts beyond our classroom walls, we, as teachers, harm students' senses of identity and community by telling them their other languages are not welcome in academic spaces.

We can no longer justify resorting to enforcing this oppressive variety (in composition courses and beyond) with claims that it's in our students' best interest for us to teach and assess only standardized English. The myth that standardized English will save students becomes especially apparent when we examine research in sociology and critical race studies that demonstrates how race, not the learning of standardized English, is the biggest factor in determining one's socioeconomic status and employment opportunities. Race—not employability, not intellect, not educability—determines stratification in rates of literacy and educational achievement.

Composition and Standardized English

Watson takes a clear position on her topic, and also offers a generous explanation of other points of view. Find out more about how to do that on pp. 191–93.

I certainly play my part in perpetuating standardized English and the harms that come with it. I'm doing it right now with my use of standardized English in the writing of this essay. I regularly preach to my graduate students the need to adopt more informed and more inclusive views of language and literacy, and while I have much to say about how I do infuse different approaches and dispositions into my composition classrooms, I find myself, semester after semester, struggling to combat, reimagine, and revise my implicit and explicit enforcements and endorsements of standardized English.

And of course I'm struggling. There are lots of pragmatic reasons why. Historically, that's what composition classes like the ones I teach are typically centered around: teaching and assessing standardized English. And, after all, fostering mastery of standardized English has long been one of the expected outcomes of higher education at large, which systematizes standardized English's superiority in our institutional structures, presenting relentless roadblocks to those who push back. It's difficult enough to raise awareness and persuade others that a problem actually exists (which, of course, many have tried to do for nearly fifty years).

Making the situation more complicated, most students are already accustomed to the expectation that they learn standardized English, and many are comfortable with that expectation and want such instruction. Employers and everyday citizens across the globe will continue to judge and discriminate against those who do not successfully use standardized English; students know this, and we're expert at reminding them of it. And, truth be told, we enforce standardized English partly because we ourselves are steeped in and benefit from the tradition of doing so: standardized English is what we learned in school and is what we've been trained to use and teach.

Some of my fellow composition teachers have other concerns. I've heard objections such as, "I barely have time to cover the curriculum at my college, much less infuse new approaches to language diversity," or "I myself don't have time to learn about how to treat writing and language differently, and my institution doesn't support professional development," or "Taking such radical approaches in my classroom could cost me my job." These are reasonable stances, highlighting the varied costs for teachers who work against the tide. Yet they are all the more reason for all of academe to begin taking a closer look at the prospect of—and, indeed, to begin taking more responsibility for—contesting the precedence of standardized English. No single teacher or discipline should alone bear the weight of this complicated dilemma. This should be a professional concern, across disciplines and campuses.

Standard Language Ideology

Perhaps the reality that standardized English works to oppress as well as to empower is still news to some professionals in higher education. Collectively, we've certainly been far better at focusing only on the benefits of learning and using standardized English. And perhaps that is one reason why we have not yet faced this issue in solidarity.

But what of those teacher-scholars like me, who have long known the reality of standardized English and still enforce it? Why do we do it? Why do we hesitate to fight standardized English even though we have long known of the damages such enforcement can cause? Of the fact that it only exists because it is tied to, authorized by, and serves people in power? Of the ways it more often serves as a *gate* rather than a *key* to success?

We do it because standard language ideology is massive and feels impenetrable. Drawing on scholarship by linguists James Milroy and Rosina Lippi-Green, I have come to a working definition of *standard language ideology* as the unquestioned belief system that assigns the written language variety of a privileged group as standard (and superior) and all others nonstandard (and inferior), a worldview uncritically assumed neutral and commonsensical but used as an instrument for social stratification and maintaining the interests of privileged groups.

Standard language ideology is deeply entrenched in the perspectives of the masses in the United States. For the most part, those individuals and groups who are the most subjugated through its dominance subscribe to it just as much as the privileged white groups who most benefit from it. Until standard language ideology is combatted on a large scale across public settings and our students' future employers come to accept other varieties of language, we reason, we had better just help our students learn the language of power.

We wouldn't say such things if we were talking about racism, classism, sexism, ableism, homophobia, or xenophobia—that these ideologies are just too big to overcome, that they're too ingrained in the worldviews of our citizens and in the structures of society, that we ought to just settle for working *with them* rather than *against them*.

We wouldn't say, at least not in modern times, that it's in the best interest of every woman, person of color, LGBTQ person, immigrant, and working-class individual to just assimilate to the ways of upper-middle-class, hetero, able-bodied white men in power.

Of course, we know that many marginalized groups have long had to work within the constraints of such norms and dominant discourses. But, no, we don't make such demands in the face of such exclusion and oppression. Instead, we fight it, in ways big and small.

Yet, most of us across the disciplines are inclined to say, without pause or hesitation, that it's in our students' best interest to master standardized English. We say that diverse groups of people should either eradicate their language differences or get darn good at switching them off in order to function in public settings without having to face discrimination.

The Politics of English

Why do we see language as a more acceptable basis for discrimination than characteristics such as race, class, gender, sexuality, and ability? Is it because language is considered a mere habit or practice that can be learned and reshaped rather than a part of our physiology, psychology, and identity? Are our pragmatic concerns more powerful than the harms caused by standard language ideology?

Are we too steeped in standard language ideology ourselves? As authorities on standardized English who, frankly, make our living perpetuating standard language ideologies, are we in too deep to reimagine our professional identities, to redefine the substance of what we do? And why are we so uncomfortable with even pondering these questions? Is it simply too unbelievable, too painful to consider that our best intentions for improving the lives and opportunities available to our students by enforcing standardized English may be, in a larger scheme, part of a problem we now must face?

To be fair, in today's globalized world, where occasions for cross-cultural communication increase daily, awareness of standard language ideology has widened, and larger communities of scholars and teachers across the globe work more explicitly to address and combat it. Many have already begun chipping away at standard language ideology, and we can and will continue to do just that.

I also believe, though, that we must continue working toward more unity on this as a problem facing higher education. The full politics of English, including standard language ideology, is an issue with which all professionals in academe must contend. We must join forces in revising the purposes of higher education, redefining the role standardized English plays within it, redesigning course outcomes and curricula, reimagining pedagogy, and retraining our community of professionals across the disciplines about how to better address the linguistic diversity at all of our campuses.

We must also disseminate our knowledge about standard language ideology and the harms it causes as widely as we can. We must share with the public, all educators, and all students what we have come to know about the politics of standardized English. And we must further examine how standard language ideology manifests itself in individuals, classrooms, colleges and universities, and other public spaces across and beyond our communities and nation so that we'll be better equipped to combat it.

To start, we must confront our own privileging of standardized English and the judgments we ourselves make about the language differences of our students, our colleagues, our neighbors.

We have for too long remained complacent, turning a blind eye to the harms caused by the very language variety we're compelled to uphold. Let's get busy undoing that.

Thinking about the Text

1. Missy Watson poses this question: "Why do we see language as a more acceptable basis for discrimination than characteristics such as race, class, gender, sexuality, and ability?" (21). How does she answer her question? Summarize her ARGUMENT. Is it persuasive? Why or why not? Explain your reasoning, and point to examples from the essay to support your response.

2. Watson is a teacher who admits to struggling with her own classroom practices and assumptions about standardized English. How, if at all, does her admission affect her AUTHORITY to address an audience of her peers on the topic? Do you think she should have omitted mentioning that she struggles with the issue? Why or why not?

3. Watson, a university professor, is writing in a professional journal for an AUDIENCE of other teachers. What might she have had to do differently if she were presenting the same arguments to an audience of students? What examples or explanations, if any, would she have omitted? What else might she have wanted to include? She concludes with a proposal—a challenge, really—for her audience. How, if at all, would the challenge be different for a student audience?

4. Would your attitude toward writing a paper change if you didn't have to be concerned about following the conventions of standardized English? Might you be able to express yourself more clearly in a variety of English that more closely resembles your usual way of speaking or thinking? Might you want to include words or phrases from another language? Another dialect of English? How might your writing be different? To REFLECT on these questions, think about your experiences writing at school over the years. Consider your formal and informal experiences with learning the rules of standardized English, your

assessment of your language abilities, and your level of comfort with different varieties of English.

5. Watson calls on educators to redefine the role of standardized English and redesign course outcomes and the ways that writing is taught and evaluated. Suppose that your school is considering Watson's proposed actions and is soliciting input from students. Write a letter to the administration taking a **STANCE**. Consider addressing the following questions in your letter: How important do you consider competence in standardized English to be for your life and career plans? In the classes you've taken so far, is there too much emphasis on standardized English? too little emphasis? Have you ever felt singled out or discriminated against for your use of language (including your **DIALECT**, your pronunciation, or any other feature)? Have you ever felt that your academic advancement has been hindered by your language use? Have you ever wanted to learn more about the many dialectal varieties of English?

Credits

ILLUSTRATIONS

Chapter 1: p. 5: (left) Courtesy of the Grantham Institute—Climate Change and the Environment at Imperial College London in partnership with Octopus Energy and UK Youth for Nature, reproduced by permission of Ciaran Globel and Conzo Throb, Conzo & Glöbel, (right) Niall Carson/Press Association via AP Images; **p. 6:** Courtesy of Ben Hodge; **p. 12:** Salesforce; **p. 15:** Molecular Structure of Nucleic Acids, J. D. Watson and F. H. C. Crick. *Nature*, Vol 171, April 25, 1953.

Chapter 2: p. 20: ©Grizelda; **p. 21:** (left) Dylan Marron and Adam Cecil, (right) Dylan Marron and Night Vale Presents; **p. 25:** Michael Ochs Archives/Getty Images; **p. 26:** Busboys and Poets/Youtube; **p. 29:** PBS Newshour.

Chapter 3: p. 32: (clockwise from top left) Rawpixel Ltd/Alamy Stock Photo, Mike Rex/Alamy Stock Photo, Alistair Berg/Getty Images, ESB Professional/Shutterstock; Leonard Ortiz/Digital First Media/Orange County Register via Getty Images, Sam Wasson/Getty Images.

Chapter 4: p. 40: Annie F. Valva; **p. 42:** Scott Kowalchyk/CBS via Getty Images; **p. 44:** (left) Mark Halmas/Icon SMI/Newscom, (right) Gina M. Randazzo/ZUMAPRESS/Newscom.

Chapter 5: p. 52: (clockwise from top left) Photo by University of Illinois Urbana–Champaign/L. Brian Stauffer, JHU Sheridan Libraries/Gado/Getty Images, Florida International University, Charles A. Smith/Jackson State University.

Chapter 6: p. 65: Andrey_Popov/Shutterstock; **p. 72:** Courtesy of Thistle.

Chapter 7: p. 80: (left) Bartleby.com, (right) Katherine Stone; **p. 81:** Timothy Mulholland/Alamy;

p. 83: Mike Seddon/CartoonStock; **p. 85:** State Department/U.S. Census Bureau's American Community Survey; **p. 93:** Julianna Hernandez.

Chapter 8: p. 98: International Federation of Library Associations and Institutions (IFLA) https://repository.ifla.org/handle/123456789/167 CC by 4.0 https://creativecommons.org/licenses/by/4.0/deed.en; **p. 100:** Rick Baldwin via CartoonStock; **p. 104:** Daniel Centeno; **p. 106:** (left) TikTok, (right) Cristian Gusa/Alamy Stock Photo.

Chapter 9: p. 111: (clockwise from top left) racorn/Shutterstock, wavebreakmedia/Shutterstock, Chris Schmidt/iStock/Getty Images; **p. 112:** Grant Snider; **p. 121:** Fine Art Images/Heritage Images/Getty Images.

Chapter 10: p. 125: (clockwise from top left) SDI Productions/Getty Images, SDI Productions/E+/Getty Images, fizkes/Shutterstock, gorodenkoff/Getty Images; **p. 126:** (graphics) Ruslan Nesterenko/Alamy Stock Vector.

Chapter 11: p. 139: JooHee Yoon, The New Yorker, ©Condé Nast; **p. 141:** Google; **p. 147:** Cartoon by Tom Fishburne; **p. 149:** (left) © National Nurses United, (right) Gilbert Flores/Variety via Getty Images.

Chapter 12: p. 152: (left) Intelligent Change/W. W. Norton & Co., Inc., (right) Reflectly; **p. 153:** New York Times; **p. 164:** Chloë Jackson.

Chapter 13: p. 171: © 2006 Roz Chast, The New Yorker Collection, Cartoonbank. All rights reserved.

Chapter 14: p. 179: Rockingham-Harrisonburg SPCA; **p. 184:** Dove; **p. 189:** Stephen Brashear/Getty Images; **p. 193:** based on figure 1.3 from *Energy Efficient Vehicles Technologies and Challenges* 1st edition, ©2024. Edited By Varun

Pratap Singh, Ashwani Kumar, Chandan Swaroop Meena, Gaurav Dwivedi Used by permission of Routledge; permission conveyed through Copyright Clearance Center, Inc.; **p. 203:** AP Photo/Rob Carr; **p. 205:** US Surgeon General; **p. 209:** Ava Brandt.

Chapter 15: p. 217: Edwin Remsberg/VWPics via AP Images; **p. 218:** Art by Dr. Erin K. Bahl, courtesy of DALN; **p. 219:** AP Photo/Al Goldis; **p. 220:** Storycorps; **p. 224:** John Elk/Getty Images; **p. 227:** Leonard Zhukovsky/Shutterstock; **p. 238:** Raya Kheirbek; **p. 240:** AP Photo/Ross D. Franklin; **p. 244:** Rebecca Ju; **p. 249:** Paloma Garcia.

Chapter 16: p. 254: David Berding/Getty Images; **p. 255:** Antoinette Clinton aka Butterscotch/WIRED © Condé Nast; **p. 259** Jaap Buitendijk/© Warner Bos./Courtesy Everett Collection; **p. 262:** AP Photo/Eric Risberg; **p. 263:** David McNew/Getty Images; **p. 267:** Istvan Derencsenyi/Orange Pictures/Alamy Stock Photo; **p. 268:** Vasiliki Varvaki/iStockphoto; **p. 273:** John Darkow/Cagle Cartoons; **p. 275:** Nolan Conway; **p. 286:** Doug Sallman; **p. 289:** Jittawit Tachakanjanapong/Alamy Stock Photo; **p. 292:** Shaan Sachdev; **p. 293:** Kevin Mazur/WireImage for Parkwood Entertainment/Getty Images; **p. 297:** Courtesy of Melissa Rubin; **p. 298:** Advertising Archives.

Chapter 17: p. 304: By permission of John Deering and Creators Syndicate, Inc.; **p. 306:** World Happiness Report; **p. 307:** (top) San Antonio Report, (bottom) Scott Ball/San Antonio Report; **p. 309:** nblx/Shutterstock; **p. 311:** US News and World Report and Brigham Fisher/University of Dayton; **p. 312:** Megan Oliver, Hello Happy Design; **p. 318:** Ryan Pfluger/AUGUST; **p. 327:** Courtesy of Tate Ryan-Mosley; **p. 329:** Shandukani Mulaudzi; **p. 334:** McCade Gowdy; **p. 335:** Heartland Bike Share; **p. 341:** Lumigraphics/Getty Images; **p. 342:** Ryan Garza, Detroit Free Press/Zuma Press; p. 344: Martha Thierry/Detroit Free Press/Zuma Press.

Chapter 18: p. 349: Sophie Giraud/©Hulu/Courtesy Everett Collection; **p. 351:** Katherine Cheng/SOPA Images/Sipa USA/Alamy Live News; **p. 354:** Gerard Ferry/Alamy Live News; **p. 355:** Consumer Reports; **p. 357:** (illustrations) Peter Arkle, (text) Amy Goldwasser; **p. 358:** BFA/Warner Bros/Alamy Stock Photo; **p. 358:** (left) Glasshouse Images/Alamy Stock Photo, (right) Niko Tavernise/© 20th Century Studios/Lifestyle Pictures/Alamy Stock Photo; **p. 370:** RLM; **p. 374:** Kennedi L. Goode-Bey; **p. 375:**: (left) Kevin Mazur/Getty Images for Live Nation, (right) Brian Friedman/Variety/Penske Media via Getty Images.

Chapter 19: p. 380: ADAPTS, LLC; **p. 387:** Courtesy Ayres Associates (Blake Theisen, Project Manager and Aaron O'Keefe, Cartographer; **p. 396:** Catherine Scarantino; **p. 403:** Aisling Colón; **p. 407:** courtesy David Pasini; **p. 408:** Neal Boenzi/The New York Times/Redux.

Chapter 20 Page 413 (from left) Emily McCormick/Alamy Stock Photo, Nadezhda Prokudina/iStockphoto, Liu Jin/AFP/Getty Images; **p. 414:** Mihai Malaimare Jr./© Lionsgate Films/Courtesy Everett Collection; **p. 416:** Apple; **p. 418:** Everett Collection Historical/Alamy Stock Photo.

Chapter 21: p. 420: (left) National Women's Strike Portland, (right) Reuters/Evelyn Hockstein/Redux; **p. 422:** © 2022 Public Citizen; **p. 423:** Stephen Voss/Redux; **p. 424:** © Amazon Studios/ZUMA Wire/Entertainment Pictures/Alamy Stock Photo; **p. 426:** Collection of the Smithsonian National Museum of African American History and Culture and Alvin Ailey Dance Foundation, Inc., Photograph by Jack Mitchell, © Alvin Ailey Dance Foundation, Inc. and Smithsonian Institution, All rights reserved; **p. 430:** Thierry Monasse/Getty Images; **p. 432:** Brendan Bush Photography. CC BY 2.0 https://creativecommons.org/licenses/by/2.0/ https://www.flickr.com/photos/26254305@N08/; **p. 434:** AP Photo/Ross Setford; **p. 438:** Brian Durkin/500px/Getty Images; **p. 445:** Milk Council; **p. 448:** Smithsonian Institution; **p. 451:** © Foundation for Individual Rights and Expression (FIRE).

Chapter 22: p. 462: Andrew Burton/Getty Images; p. 465: Charles Minard; p. 466: NWS/NOAA; p. 468: Visual Capitalist; p. 472: Department of Energy; p. 475: Efe Franca Plange, "The Pepper Manual: Towards Situated Non-Western Feminist Rhetorical Practices" *Peitho* Volume 23 Issue 4, Summer 2021; p. 476: Humane World for Animals, Inc. and Maddie's Fund; p. 479: Alexander Joe/AFP/Getty Images; p. 480: Chloe Colberg; p. 481: Marjane Satrapi/Random House.

Chapter 23: p. 492: Julio Aguilar/Getty Images.

Chapter 24: p. 500: (top left) Christina Hemm Klok, Wired © Condé Nast, (top right) Wired Staff, Wired © Condé Nast, (bottom left) Sustainability 2021, 13, 6788. https://doi.org/10.3390/su13126788 Attribution 4.0 International (CC BY 4.0) https://creativecommons.org/licenses/by/4.0/, (bottom right) Menchaca, A. "Sustainable Food Production: The Contribution of Genome Editing in Livestock." *Sustainability* 2021, 13, 6788. https://doi.org/10.3390/su13126788 Attribution 4.0 International (CC BY 4.0) https://creativecommons.org/licenses/by/4.0/; p. 504: Harvard Radcliff Institute Schlesinger Library; p. 508: College of Southern Nevada Libraries; p. 509: College of Southern Nevada Libraries.

Chapter 25: p. 519: Gary Austin.

Chapter 27: p. 531: Peter Steiner/Cartoonstock; p. 535: NASA/JPL.

Chapter 28: p. 538: Maddie St. Amand.

Chapter 29: p. 542: Cavan Images/Alamy Stock Photo; p. 544: Courtesy Adam Westbrook; p. 546: Gary Markstein; p. 549: Kristin Perry.

Chapter 30: p. 554: Carin Berger; p. 557: Library of Congress, Prints and Photographs Division; p. 567: erlucho/iStockphoto.

Chapter 32: p. 596: Neuhaus, Jessamyn. "Marge Simpson, Blue-Haired Housewife Defining Domesticity on The Simpsons." *Journal of Popular Culture* 43.4 (2010): 761–81. © 2010 Wiley Periodicals, Inc.; p. 597: Segal, Michael. "The Hit Book That Came from Mars." *Nautilus*. NautilusThink. 8 January 2015. Web. 10 October 2016. Permission by Nautilus, inset: Matt Taylor; p. 599 ©2015 Ebsco Industries, Inc. All rights reserved; p. 603: From *Pink Sari Revolution: A Tale of Women and Power in India* by Amana Fontanella-Khan. Copyright © 2013 by Amana Fontanella-Khan. Used by permission of W. W. Norton & Company, Inc.; p. 609: McIlwain, John, Molly Simpson, and Sara Hammerschmidt. "Housing in America: Integrating Housing, Health, and Resilience in a Changing Environment." Urban Land Institute. *Urban Land Institute*, 2014. Web. 17 Sept. 2016. © 2015, Urban Land Institute. All rights reserved; p. 625: Ned Scott/United Artists/Kobal/Shutterstock; p. 632: Paramount/Rafran/Kobal/Shutterstock.

Chapter 33: p. 651: Copyright 2013. From *Smart Technology and the Moral Life* by Guthrie, C. F. Reproduced by permission of Taylor & Francis LLC (http://www.tandfonline.com); p. 654: Lazette, M. P. (2015, February 25). "A Hurricane's Hit to Households." © 2015 Federal Reserve Bank of Cleveland; p. 655: From *The Great Divide: Unequal Societies and What We Can Do about Them* by Joseph E. Stiglitz. Copyright © 2015 by Joseph E. Stiglitz. Used by permission of W. W. Norton & Company, Inc.

Chapter 34: p. 689: Timothy A. Clary/AFP via Getty Images; p. 690: Paramount Television/Kobal/Shutterstock; p. 691: Dr. Jeff Robinson; p. 693: Courtesy Surf Market surfsuper.com; p. 696: AP Photo/Mark Lennihan; p. 699: Shermann Dilla Thomas.

Chapter 35: p. 704: (left to right) Reuters/Brendan McDermid/Alamy Stock Photo, Daisy Daisy/Shutterstock, Michal Brody; p. 708: Fond du Lac Tribal and Community College; p. 710: Online Learning Consortium, Inc.

Chapter 36: p. 731: WENN Rights Ltd/Alamy Stock Photo.

Chapter 38: p. 781 Coca-Cola; p. 788: HeikeKampe/iStockphoto; p. 790 (left and right) These charts originally appeared in *Education Week* on July 30, 2021. Reprinted with permission from Editorial

Projects in Education. **p. 791:** NASA Earth Observatory image by Michala Garrison, using data from the United States Drought Monitor at the University of Nebraska–Lincoln.; **p. 792:** Simone Brandt/imagebroker/Newscom; **p. 793:** Yingling/MCT/Newscom; **p. 796:** The Moth; **p. 798:** nationalgeographic.com.

Chapter 39: p. 801: © www.garyolsencartoons.com; **p. 804:** (left) AP Photo/Bernd Settnik/picture-alliance/dpa, right Studioshots/Alamy; **p. 806:** Oregon State Fisheries and Wildlife Club; **p. 810:** © University of Michigan–Dearborn Board of Regents; **p. 813:** (poster) courtesy Kaia Simmons, Michael Frank and Ally Kraus, Stanford University Departments of Human Biology and Psychology, (citations) Yoshida, H., and Smith, L. B., "What's in View for Toddlers? Using a Head Camera to Study Visual Experience." *Infancy* 2008. 13, 229–48. © 2008 International Society on Infant Studies/Linda B. Smith, Chen Yu, and Alfred F. Pereira, "Not Your Mother's View: The Dynamics of Toddler Visual Experience. *Developmental Science* (2010), 14, 1, 9–17. © 2010 Blackwell Publishing Ltd./Asin, Richard N. "How Infants View Natural Scenes Gathered from a Head-Mounted Camera." *Optometry and Vision Science* 86, 6 (2009): 561–65. © 2009 American Academy of Optometry; **p. 814:** Florida Museum of Natural History; **p. 818:** Sophie Warfield.

Chapter 40: p. 823: (left) Dom Slike/Alamy Stock Photo, (right) Jim Wilson/The New York Times/Redux; **p. 825:** (top and bottom) Halle Edwards; **p. 826:** © Cartoon Network/Photofest; **p. 827:** Reuters/Toru Hanai/Alamy Stock Photo; **p. 828:** Halle Edwards; **p. 829:** Photo 12/Alamy Stock Photo.

Readings: p. 838: César Albarrán-Torres; **p. 844:** Taylor Swift Productions/Silent House/Album/Alamy Stock Photos; **p. 849:** Jeff Miller/UW Madison; **p. 855:** Auburn University OCM Photographic Service **p. 859:** WENN Rights Ltd/Alamy Stock Photo; **pp. 860–68:** From *Fun Home: A Family Tragicomic* by Alison Bechdel. Copyright© 2006 by Alison Bechdel. Reprinted by permission of Houghton Mifflin Harcourt Publishing Company. All rights reserved.; **p. 870:** Jenna Bloom; **p. 876:** Photo courtesy Danielle K. Brown; **p. 878:** The Conversation, CC-BY-ND; **p. 883:** Naum Kazhdan/The New York Times via AP; **p. 884:** Dana Canedy/The New York Times/Redux Pictures; **p. 888:** Charlotte Clymer; **p. 893:** Adam Clark Estes; **p. 899:** Audre Rae Photography; **p. 901:** Jamie Gilliam/The Photo/Alamy Stock Photo; **p. 905:** Sara Pontoppidan; **p. 915:** Andrew Harrer/Bloomberg via Getty Images; **p. 923:** Kyle Johnson; **p. 927:** Kevin Kearney; **p. 928:** Justin Sullivan/Getty Images; **p. 932:** Dale Kakkak; **p. 938:** Keren Landman; **p. 946:** Vallery Jean/FilmMagic/Getty Images; **p. 950:** Kate Medley; p. 952: Lewis Friedman; **pp. 953, 954, 956, 958:** Louie Chin; **p. 960–65:** Dan Nott and Scott Cambo; **p. 993** Adam Clark Estes; **p. 967:** Meghan O'Gieblyn; **pp. 972, 974, 976:** Courtesy of Mike Rose; **pp. 982–87:** Ally Shwed; **p. 989:** Zeynep Tufekci; **p. 993:** Reuters/Kevork Djansezian/Alamy Stock Photo; **p. 1001:** Kevork Djansezian/Getty Images; **pp. 1003, 1004, 1007:** Taté Walker; **p. 1016:** Missy Watson.

About the Authors: (Lunsford) Ron Bolander, (Brody) Courtesy Michal Brody, (Enoch) Courtesy Jessica Enoch, (Moss) W. W. Norton & Co., Inc., (Papper) W. W. Norton & Co., Inc., (Vee) Annette Vee.

TEXT

Chapter 2: Sabeeha Rehman and Walter Ruby: From "Jews and Muslims Must Stand Together and Refuse to Be Enemies." *The Baltimore Sun*, 28 May 2021. Reprinted by permission of the authors. **Judy Woodruff:** From "Listening to a Divided America." *PBS NewsHour*, 8 Mar. 2023, https://www.pbs.org/newshour/nation/listening-to-a-divided-america. Reprinted with permission. **Chapter 7: Katherine Spriggs:** "On Buying Local." Copyright © 2008 by Katherine Spriggs.

Yuliya Vayner: "The Higher Price of Buying Local." Copyright © 2019 by W.W. Norton & Company.

Chapter 10: Sierra Jaquez: "How Harries and Swifties Changed the Outlook on Modern Concert Fashion." Copyright © 2024 by Sierra Jaquez.

Chapter 12: Annaya Baynes: "Becoming the Writer I Am: A Reflection on My First-Year Composition Class." © 2022 by Annaya Baynes. **Akash Bobba:** Originally published in "The Class of 2021: Their Thoughts on a Year like No Other," *NJ Spotlight News*, 5 Jul. 2021. Reprinted by permission of the author. **Annie Schmittgens:** Excerpts from "New Dimensions." Reprinted with permission of the author.

Chapter 14: **Russel Honoré:** Used with permission of John Wiley & Sons, from Honoré, Russel. "Work Is a Blessing." *This I Believe: On Fatherhood*, edited by Dan Gediman, John Gregory, and Mary Jo Gediman. John Wiley & Sons, 2011, pp. 67–69. Permission conveyed through Copyright Clearance Center, Inc. **Aleksander Lam:** "Sampling or Stealing? Copyright Infringement and Hip-Hop." Copyright © 2024 by Aleksander Lam. **Vivek H. Murthy:** Originally published as "Surgeon General: Why I'm Calling for a Warning Label on Social Media Platforms." *The New York Times*, 17 Jun. 2024. From The New York Times. © 2024 The New York Times Company. All rights reserved. Used under license.

Chapter 15: **Paloma Garcia:** "Creating a Proficient Reader." Originally published in Digital Archive of Literacy Narratives. Reprinted with permission. **Raya Elfadel Kheirbek:** Republished with permission of Project HOPE/Health Affairs Journal. "At the VA, Healing the Doctor-Patient Relationship." *Health Affairs*, vol. 36, no. 10, 2017, pp. 1848–51; permission conveyed through Copyright Clearance Center, Inc. **Angelina X. Ng:** Originally published as "The Big Bangs Theory." *Fifteen Minutes*, 30 Apr. 2024. © 2024 The Harvard Crimson, Inc. All rights reserved. Reprinted with permission. **Minh Vu:** "Dirty Nails." Copyright © 2018 by Minh Vu.

Chapter 16: **Jerome Conlon:** "Analyzing Nike's Controversial Just Do It Campaign," by Jerome Conlon. *Branding Strategy Insider,* 5 Sep. 2018. Reprinted by permission of The Blake Project. **Eve L. Ewing:** From "I'm a Black Scholar Who Studies Race. Here's Why I Capitalize 'White.'" *ZORA*, 2 Jul. 2020, zora.medium.com/im-a-black-scholar-who-studies-race-here-s-why-i-capitalize-white-f94883aa2dd3. Reprinted with permission. **Darlene E. Jenkins, Ph.D.:** Excerpts from "Tightening the Turns in Speed Skating: Lessons in Centripetal Force and Balance," www.ScienceBuddies.org. Reprinted with permission. **Will Moller:** Excerpts from "A Painful Posting," It'sAbouttheMoney.net, 4 Feb. 2011. Reprinted by permission of the author. **Alberta Negri:** "Underneath the Leather Jackets and Chrome Pipes: Research into a Community of Local Bikers," by Alberta Negri. Originally published by Queen City Writers, 9 Nov. 2017. Reprinted by permission of the author. **Melissa Rubin:** "Advertisements R Us." Copyright © 2011 by Melissa Rubin. **Shaan Sachdev:** "The Key to Beyoncé's Lasting Success." From *Slate*. © 2021 The Slate Group. All rights reserved. Used under license. **Sydney Sallman:** "What Is the Invisible Problem with *TikTok?*" Copyright © 2024 by Sydney Sallman.

Chapter 17: **Lucy Diavolo:** "Greta Thunberg Wants You—Yes, You—to Join the Climate Strike." *Teen Vogue*, 16 Sep. 2019. © Condé Nast. Reprinted with permission. **McCade Gowdy:** From Gowdy, McCade. "The Anti-Suburbia." *Urban Plains*, 8 May 2023, urban-plains.com/the-anti-suburbia. Reprinted by permission of the author. **Bill Laitner:** "Heart and Sole: Detroiter Walks 21 Miles in Work Commute." *Detroit Free Press*, 2 Feb. 2015. © Bill Laitner—USA Today Network. Reused with permission. **Tate Ryan-Mosley:** Republished with permission of Technology Review, Inc., from "How Digital Beauty Filters Perpetuate Colorism." *MIT Technology Review*, 15 Aug. 2021; permission conveyed through Copyright

Clearance Center, Inc. **Katryn Sheppard:** "Early Word Production: A Study of One Child's Word Productions." Copyright © 2014 by Katryn Sheppard.

Chapter 18: Joy Diamond: From "Devoid of Spark, 'West Side Story' Is Rough, Unfortunate Film Adaptation," *The Daily Californian*, 15 Dec. 2021. Used with permission from The Daily Californian. **Kennedi Goode-Bey:** *"Guts (spilled)* by Olivia Rodrigo: An Album for the Ages." Copyright © 2024 by Kennedi Goode-Bey. **Inkoo Kang:** "'Black and Missing' Attempts a Much-Needed Reform of True-Crime Storytelling. It Mostly Succeeds." From *The Washington Post*. © 2021 The Washington Post. All rights reserved. Used under license. **Swapna Krishna:** *"Thirsty Suitors* Is a Hilarious and Refreshing Game Made for the South Asian Community." Wired.com, 1 Nov. 2023. wired.com/review/thirsty-suitors-review. © Condé Nast. Reprinted with permission. **Niche.com:** © Niche.com, Inc. 2022. **Julianne Escobedo Shepherd:** From *"Cowboy Carter:* Beyoncé." *Pitchfork*, 1 Apr. 2024. pitchfork.com/reviews/albums/beyonce-cowboy-carter. © Condé Nast. Reprinted with permission. **Dana Stevens:** "The Spectacular New *Dune* Will Turn Even Skeptics into Believers." From *Slate*. © 2026 The Slate Group. All rights reserved. Used under license.

Chapter 19: Mark Allen Cu: "Stanford Should Rename Wilbur Hall. *The Stanford Daily*, 25 Jun. 2024. © 2024 The Stanford Daily, Inc. All rights reserved. Reprinted with permission. **Jonathan Holloway:** "To Unite a Divided Country, Enlist the Young." From *The New York Times*. © 2021 The New York Times Company. All rights reserved. Used under license. **Michael Lazenby:** From "Make Mental Health Accessible," *The Daily Texan*, 18 Sep. 2021. Reprinted with permission of The Daily Texan. **David Pasini:** "The Economic Impact of Investing Public Funds in Professional Sports Franchises." Copyright © 2012 by David Pasini. **The Pitt News Editorial Board:** "Oakland Desperately Needs to Improve Its Traffic Signage." Editorial. The *Pitt News*, 22 Feb. 2024. Republished by permission of The Pitt News. **Dan Saltzman:** "Incentive for Developers Would Spur Affordable Housing." Originally published in *Street Roots*, 7 Jul. 2015. Reprinted with permission. **Emi Vaughan:** "Uses for AI in the Criminal Justice System." Copyright © 2024 by Emi Vaughan.

Chapter 21: Interfaith Youth Core: Eboo Patel Bio from the Interfaith Youth Core website. Reprinted with permission. **Judith Lewis Mernit:** Excerpt from "Seismology: Is San Francisco Next?" *The Atlantic*, June 2011. Courtesy of Atlantic Media. **David Zinczenko:** Excerpts from "Don't Blame the Eater." Originally published in *The New York Times*, 23 Nov. 2002. Reprinted by permission of the author.

Chapter 22: Dave Barry: Excerpt from "Beauty and the Beast." *Miami Herald* (1998). Reprinted by permission of the author. **James A. Gibson:** Excerpt from "'We Proudly Wore Confederate Symbols,'" *The Atlantic*, September 2021. Courtesy of Atlantic Media. **Martin Luther King Jr.:** Excerpt from "I Have a Dream." Reprinted by arrangement with The Heirs to the Estate of Martin Luther King Jr., c/o Writers House as agent for the proprietor New York, NY. Copyright © 1963 by Dr. Martin Luther King, Jr. Renewed © 1991 by Coretta Scott King. **Eloy Ortiz Oakley and Angelica Campos:** From Oakley, Eloy Ortiz, and Angelica Campos. "California Can Solve Community College Students' Food Insecurity Crisis. Here's How." *Community College Daily*, 19 May 2022, ccdaily.com/2022/05/california-can-solve-community-college-students-food-insecurity-crisis-heres-how/. Reproduced by permission of American Association of Community Colleges.

Chapter 28: Maggie Carson: "Annotated Bibliography of Nonresistance in the Battle for Freedom." Copyright © 2024 by Maggie Carson.

Chapter 29: Kristin Perry: "Exploring the Hardships and Stigma Students with Invisible Disabilities Face." Copyright © 2024 by Kristin Perry.
Chapter 32: Walter Przybylowski: "The European Western," *Dialogues, Vol. V*, pp. 91–102. Reprinted by permission of the author.
Chapter 33: Gabriela Agustina Uribe: "'Por qué no sabes español?': Pressured Monolinguism and Its Impacts on Mexican Americans." Copyright © 2021 by Gabriela Uribe.
Chapter 34: Cherry the Dive Bar Girl: From "Twin Peaks" (Review) by Cherry the Dive Bar Girl. *Cherry: Baton Rouge*, 26 Jan. 2012. Reprinted by permission of the author. **Marilyn Hagerty:** "The Eatbeat: Long-awaited Olive Garden Receives Warm Welcome." *Grand Forks Herald*, 7 Mar. 2012. Used by permission of the Grand Forks Herald.
Chapter 35: Bamboo: Lyrics reprinted by permission of Bamboo from "Mama Africa Remix." **Jamila Lyiscott:** Jamilla Lyiscott/TED Talks/3 Ways to Speak English/BoClips
Chapter 39: Template: Digital Story Storyboard by Jennifer Richardson Conrad and Jolanda-Pieta van Arnhem is available under a Creative Commons Attribution Non-Commercial 3.0 Unported License. https://creativecommons.org/licenses/by-nc/3.0/. Used by permission of the authors.
Chapter 40: Halle Edwards: "The Rise of Female Heroes in Shoujo Manga." Copyright © 2014 by Halle Edwards.
Readings: César Albarrán-Torres: Originally published as "No More Bad Accents, Stereotypes, or Cringe: Why the Rise of Multilingual TV Is Good for Everyone." *The Conversation*, 9 May 2024. https://theconversation.com/no-more-bad-accents-stereotypes-or-cringe-why-the-rise-of-multilingual-tv-is-good-news-for-everyone-229113. Reprinted by permission of the author. **Kate Aronoff:** "Carbon Offsets (Taylor's Version)." From *The New Republic*. © 2024 New Republic. All rights reserved. Used under license. **Lynda Barry:** "The Sanctuary of School." Originally published in *The New York Times*, January 5, 1992. Copyright © 1992 by Lynda Barry. All rights reserved. Used with permission. **Christopher Basgier:** Originally published as "On AI as Cake." *Prose & Processors*, 27 Jan. 2024. christoperbasgier.substack.com/p/on-ai-as-cake. Republished by permission of the author. **Alison Bechdel:** From *Fun Home* by Alison Bechdel. Copyright © 2006 by Alison Bechdel. Used by permission of HarperCollins Publishers. **Jenna Bloom:** "I Quit Social Media in College. This Is How My Life Changed." From *The Washington Post*. © 2023 The Washington Post. All rights reserved. Used under license. **Danielle K. Brown:** Originally published as Brown, Danielle K. "Media Coverage of Campus Protests Tends to Focus on the Spectacle, rather than the Substance." *The Conversation*, 4 May 2024. theconversation.com/media-coverage-of-campus-protests-tends-to-focus-on-the-spectacle-rather-than-the-substance-229172. Republished by permission of the author. **Dana Canedy:** "The Talk." From *The New York Times*. © 2014 The New York Times Company. All rights reserved. Used under license. **Charlotte Clymer:** "They Called Me a Girl before Anyone Else Did," Originally published in *Charlotte's Web Thoughts*, 20 Jul. 2021. Reprinted with permission. **Adam Clark Estes:** "Your TV Is Watching You" by Adam Clark Estes. Vox.com, March 27, 2025. Reprinted with permission of Vox Media, LLC. **Jeff Gage:** Originally published as "Opioids Came for Country Music. It's Fighting Back." *Rolling Stone*, 23 Apr. 2024. Republished by permission of Penske Media Corporation. **Glavee Glavee:** "Black Enough: Protecting Linguistic Identity in the Writing Center." Used by permission of the author. **Annette Gordon-Reed:** From *On Juneteenth* by Annette Gordon-Reed. Copyright © 2021 by Annette Gordon-Reed. Used by permission of Liveright Publishing Corporation.

Ling Ling Huang: "How I Escaped the Tyranny of the Prophets of Beauty" by Ling Ling Huang. Copyright © 2023 by Ling Ling Huang. First appeared in the *Washington Post* April 11, 2023. Reprinted by permission from the Author. **Kevin M. Kearney:** "One Star." From *Slate*. © 2024 The Slate Group. All rights reserved. Used under license. **Robin Wall Kimmerer:** "Strawberries" (editors' title, originally titled and excerpted from "The Gift of Strawberries") from *Braiding Sweetgrass: Indigenous Wisdom, Scientific Knowledge and the Teachings of Plants*. Copyright © 2013, 2015 by Robin Wall Kimmerer. Reprinted with the permission of The Permissions Company, LLC on behalf of Milkweed Editions, milkweed.org. **Keren Landman:** "Why Are Whole-Body Deodorants Suddenly Everywhere?" by Keren Landman, M.D. Vox.com, May 20, 2024. Reprinted with permission of Vox Media, LLC. **Kiese Laymon:** "My Favorite Restaurant Served Gas." *The Bitter Southerner*, 6 Dec. 2023. Republished with permission of Janklow & Nesbit Associates. **Judith Newman:** "To Siri, with Love." From *The New York Times*. © 2014 The New York Times Company. All rights reserved. Used under license. **Dan Nott and Scott Cambo:** Originally published as Nott, Dan, and Scott Cambo. "Our Labor Built AI." *The Nib*, 31 Jul. 2023. Republished by permission of the authors. **Meghan O'Gieblyn:** Originally published as "I Failed Two Captcha Tests This Week. Am I Still Human?" *Wired*, 21 Sep. 2023. Republished by permission of the author. **Mike Rose:** From "Blue-Collar Brilliance: Questioning Assumptions about Intelligence, Work, and Social Class." *The American Scholar,* Jun. 2009, vol. 78, no. 3, pp. 43–49. Reproduced by permission of the author's estate. **Ally Shwed:** Originally published as "Cracking the Color Code." *The Nib*, 1 Jun. 2023. Republished by permission of the author. **Zeynep Tufekci:** "Why the Post Office Makes America Great," by Zeynep Tufekci. Originally published in *The New York Times*, 1 Jan. 2016. Reprinted by permission of the author. **Jose Antonio Vargas:** "My Life as an Undocumented Immigrant." *The New York Times Magazine*, 22 June 2011, nytimes.com/2011/06/26/magazine/my-life-as-an-undocumentedimmigrant.html. Reprinted by permission of the author. **Taté Walker:** "The (Native) American Dream," by Taté Walker. Originally published in *Native Peoples*, Sep./Oct. 2015. Reprinted by permission of Taté Walker, Mniconjou Lakota. **Missy Watson:** "Contesting Standardized English," *Academe*, May–Jun. 2018. Reprinted with permission of the American Association of University Professors.

Author / Title Index

A

"About Men" (Ehrlich), 473
Above the Well: An Antiracist Literacy Argument from a Boy of Color (Inoue), 46
"Abraham Lincoln" (Du Bois), 425
"ADAPTS, the First Evacuation Sling for Wheelchair Users" (Wearly), 383
Adichie, Chimamanda Ngozi, 220
"Advertisements R Us" (Rubin), 297–302
"African American Stars Remember Whitney Houston" (Samuels), 724
Aguilar, Sofia
   "Criminalizing Homelessness Is Ushering in a New Form of Capitalism," 182
"AI Is Like Cake" (Basgier), 855–58
"Ain't I a Woman?" (Truth), 479
Akukwe, Chinua
   "H.I.V. and AIDS in Africa: Ten Lessons from the Field," 478
Albarrán-Torres, César, *838*
   "Why Multilingual TV Is Good for Everyone," 838–42
Alley, Michael, 824
"Analyzing Nike's Controversial Just Do It Campaign" (Conlon), 261–62
Anarchism and Other Essays (Goldman), 470
Angelou, Maya, 686
Anthony, Mariah, 357
Anzaldúa, Gloria, 39–40, *40*, 49

"Are We Alone in the Universe?" (Krauthammer), 560–63
Aristotle, 2–3, 5, 77, 101, 429, 763
   Rhetoric, 565
Arkle, Peter, 357
Aronoff, Kate
   "Carbon Offsets (Taylor's Version)," 843–48
The Art of Slow Reading (Newkirk), 68–69
"At the VA, Healing the Doctor-Patient Relationship" (Kheirbek), 238–43
Atwood, Margaret, 168

B

Bamboo
   "Mama Africa," 706, 707, 708
Banks, Adam, 496, 778
Barracoon: The Story of the Last "Black Cargo" (Hurston), 711–12
Barrientos-Ferrer, Rosa
   "Extreme Heat Is More Dangerous for Workers Every Year," 543
Barry, Dave
   "Beauty and the Beast," 467
Barry, Lynda, *849*
   "The Sanctuary of School," 216, 849–54
Basgier, Christopher, *855*
   "AI Is Like Cake," 855–58
Baynes, Annaya, *164*
   "Becoming the Writer I Am: A Reflection on My First-Year Composition Class," 164–67

Note: Page numbers in *italics* indicate figures.

"Beauty and the Beast" (Barry), 467
Bechdel, Alison, *859*
    "Fun Home," 859–69
Becker, Amy
    "Employment Discrimination, Local School Boards, and LGBT Civil Rights: Reviewing 25 Years of Public Opinion Data," 572–73
"Becoming the Writer I Am: A Reflection on My First-Year Composition Class" (Baynes), 164–67
Bennett, Lerone, Jr.
    "Blacks in Chicago," 481
Beyoncé [Knowles-Carter], 353–54, *354*
"Beyond the Ivory Tower: The Scientific Consensus on Climate Change" (Oreskes), 191–92
"'Black and Missing' attempts a much-needed reform of true-crime storytelling. It mostly succeeds." (Kang), 360–61
"Black Enough: Protecting Linguistic Identity in the Writing Center" (Glavee), 905–14
"Blacks in Chicago" (Bennett), 481
Bloom, Jenna, *870*
    "I Quit Social Media in College. This Is How My Life Changed.," 870–75
"Blue-Collar Brilliance" (Rose), 972–81
Bobba, Akash
    high school graduation speech, 151
Booth, Wayne, 4
    The Rhetoric of Rhetoric, 14–15
Branding Strategy Insider (blog), 260–61
"Breakdown of Caitlin Clark's Game: Skills, Stats & Impact" (Hungerford), 254
"Broken English" (Lyiscott), 709–10
Brooks, David, *423*
    "Nonconformity Is Skin Deep," 422–23
Brown, Danielle K., *876*
    "Media Coverage of Campus Protests Focuses on Spectacle," 876–82
Bullock, Reggie
    "I Just Wanna Say My Sisters' Names," 460
Bunch, Lonnie G.
    "Whole of Our History," 448–49

Burke, Kenneth, 7, 177, 545
    The Philosophy of Literary Form, 7
Buthainah
    "Who Fears Climbing the Mountains Lives Forever between the Holes," 711
Butler, Octavia E.
    Kindred, 725
Butterscotch, *255*

C

"Call It Blindness" (Kleege), 225–26
"California Can Solve Community College Students' Food Insecurity Crisis. Here's How" (Oakley and Campos), 478
Cambo, Scott
    "Our Labor Built AI," 960–66
Campos, Angelica
    "California Can Solve Community College Students' Food Insecurity Crisis. Here's How," 478
Canedy, Dana, *883*
    "The Talk: After Ferguson, a Shaded Conversation about Race," 883–87
"Can We Bridge Our Differences over Gun Laws?" (O'Connor), 8
Capehart, Jonathan, 188
"Carbon Offsets (Taylor's Version)" (Aronoff), 843–48
Carlin, John
    Playing the Enemy: Nelson Mandela and the Game That Made a Nation, 433
Cause / Effect: The Unexpected Origins of Terrible Things (Westbrook), 544, *544*
"Censoring *TikTok* Would Harm Democratic Fabric" (Jadulang), 182
Chast, Roz
    "New Movie Genres," *171*
Cicero, 9, 459, 694
Cisneros, Sandra
    Woman Hollering Creek and Other Stories, 706–7
"The Clan of One-Breasted Women" (Williams), 472–73

Climate Change 2014: Synthesis Report (United Nations), 464
Clinton, Bill, 718, 721
Clymer, Charlotte, *888*
    "They Called Me a Girl before Anyone Else Did," 888–92
Colberg, Chloe
    "What Can You Do to Make a Difference?," 479, *480*
"The College Connection" (Posnanski), 727–28
A Community Text Arises (Moss), 262–63, 269
Conference on College Composition and Communication
    "Students' Right to Their Own Language," 46
    "This Ain't Another Statement! This Is a DEMAND for Black Linguistic Justice," 47
Conlon, Jerome
    "Analyzing Nike's Controversial Just Do It Campaign," 261–62, *262*
Con Respeto: Bridging the Distances between Culturally Diverse Families and Schools (Valdés), 707–8
Consumer Reports, 355
    "Giro Register MIPS Bike Helmet," 355
"Contesting Standardized English" (Watson), 1010–17
Conversations with People Who Hate Me (Marron), 20–21, *21*
Cooper, Lane, 565
"*Cowboy Carter*: Beyoncé" (Shepherd), 353–54
"Cracking the Color Code" (Shwed), 982–88
"Crap Detection 101" (Rheingold), 102
"Criminalizing Homelessness Is Ushering in a New Form of Capitalism" (Aguilar), 182
Cu, Mark Allen, 385–86
    "Stanford Should Rename Wilbur Hall," 386
Cullors, Patrisse, 688

D

"Da Future of Hawaiian Pidgin" (Tonouchi), 712–13
"Damage Control" (Sainani), 438
"Dancing Past the Boundaries" (Hinojosa), 425

Darkow, John, *273*, 274
Davidson, Cathy
    Now You See It: How the Brain Science of Attention Will Transform the Way We Live, Work, and Learn, 728
Delahunty, Jennifer
    "To All the Girls I've Rejected," 192, 193–94
"Devoid of Spark, 'West Side Story' Is Rough, Unfortunate Film Adaptation" (Diamond), 362
Diamond, Joy
    "Devoid of Spark, 'West Side Story' Is Rough, Unfortunate Film Adaptation," 362
Diavolo, Lucy
    "Greta Thunberg Wants You—Yes, You—to Join the Climate Strike," 316–19
Didion, Joan, 116, 716
    "Some Dreamers of the Golden Dream," 722–23
Dillard, Annie, 715
    A Writing Life, 461–62
"Dirty Nails" (Vu), 223
Dive Bar Girl (DBG; CherryTheDiveBarGirl), 696–97
Doctorow, E. L., 108
Donne, John, 109
"Don't Blame the Eater" (Zinczenko), 435–36
Dreher, Rod
    "Same Food Planet, Different Food Worlds," 696–97
Duarte, Nancy, 822, 832
Du Bois, W. E. B., 424–25, 427
    "Abraham Lincoln," 425

E

"Early Word Production: A Study of One Child's Word Productions" (Sheppard), 314
Eason, Haines, 541
"Eboo Patel" (Interfaith Youth Core), 430–31
"The Economic Impact of Investing Public Funds in Sports Franchises" (Pasini), 407–9
The Economics of Attention (Lanham), 64
Edwards, Halle, 824, 825
    "The Rise of Female Heroes in Shoujo Manga," 825–30

Ehrlich, Gretel
  "About Men," 473
Ellison, Ralph
  Invisible Man, 725
"Employment Discrimination, Local School Boards, and LGBT Civil Rights: Reviewing 25 Years of Public Opinion Data" (Becker), 572–73
Erasure (Everett), 482
"Establishing Identities" (Fox), 313
Estes, Adam Clark, *893*
  "Your TV Is Watching You," 893–98
Everett, Percival
  Erasure, 482
Ewing, Eve L.
  "I'm a Black Scholar Who Studies Race. Here's Why I Capitalize 'White.'" 257–58, 271, 272, 283
"Exploring the Hardships and Stigma Students With Invisible Disabilities Face" (Perry), 549–53
"Extreme Heat Is More Dangerous for Workers Every Year" (Rosenthal, Barrientos-Ferrer, and Petosa), 543

F

FACT: Climate Change Is Caused by Human Activity (United Nations), 464
Falcon, Ted
  Getting to the Heart of Interfaith: The Eye-Opening, Hope-Filled Friendship of a Pastor, a Rabbi & an Imam, 255–56
"Farewell Letter to America" (McCain), 694–95
Farid, Hany, 105
"First Day of School" (Garcia), 249–51
First Take (Smith), 43–44
Fish, Stanley
  How to Write a Sentence, 715
Flanagan, Caitlin
  "The Glory of Oprah," 730–31
Fond du Lac Tribal & Community College, 707, *708*
Foss, Sonja, 457
"14 Environmentally Friendly College Campuses" (Kowarski and Wood), 310

Fox, Kelley, 313, 314
  "Establishing Identities," 313
Freedman, David H.
  "How Junk Food Can End Obesity," 764–66
"Fun Home" (Bechdel), 859–69
Furlonge, Nicole, 417–18
"The Future of the American City: Omaha's Hope" (Gowdy), 334–40

G

Gage, Jeff, *899*
  "How Country Music Is Addressing the Opioid Crisis," 899–904
Ganz, Steven
  Valley Speak: Deciphering the Jargon of Silicon Valley, 709
Garcia, Paloma, *249*
  "First Day of School," 249–51
Garza, Alicia, 24
Gates, Henry Louis, Jr., 482, 483
Gay, Roxane
  speech to *Publishers Weekly*'s Winter Institute, 228–29
"Gender-Inclusivity and the Onus of Progress on the Writing Center" (Thrasher), 13
Getting to the Heart of Interfaith: The Eye-Opening, Hope-Filled Friendship of a Pastor, a Rabbi & an Imam (Mackenzie, Falcon, and Rahman), 255–56
Gibbon, Edward
  Memoirs of My Life, 724
Gibson, James A.
  Letter to the *Atlantic,* 473
Gibson, Walker, 459
Gibson, William
  Neuromancer, 725
"Girls Suffer Sports Concussions at a Higher Rate than Boys. Why Is That Overlooked?" (Snyder), 447
"Giro Register MIPS Bike Helmet" (*Consumer Reports*), 355

Author / Title Index

Glass, Ira, 809
Glavee, Glavee, *905*
    "Black Enough: Protecting Linguistic Identity in the Writing Center," 905–14
"The Glory of Oprah" (Flanagan), 730–31
Goldman, Emma
    Anarchism and Other Essays, 470
Goldwasser, Amy, 357
"The Good Immigrant Student" (Nguyen), 476
Goode-Bey, Kennedi L. *374*
    "Guts (spilled) by Olivia Rodrigo: An Album for the Ages" (Goode-Bey), 374–77
Gordon-Reed, Annette, *915*
    "Origin Stories," 915–22
Gorlick, Adam
    "Media Multitaskers Pay Mental Price," 440
Gowdy, McCade, *334*
    "The Future of the American City: Omaha's Hope," 334–404
"Greta Thunberg Wants You—Yes, You—to Join the Climate Strike" (Diavolo), 316–19
Griffin, Cindy, 457
Grogger, Jeffrey, 41
"Guts (spilled) by Olivia Rodrigo: An Album for the Ages" (Goode-Bey), 374–77

H

Hagerty, Marilyn, *696*
    "Long-Awaited Olive Garden Receives Warm Welcome," 696–97
Hamlet (Shakespeare), 175
Hampton University, 144
"'The Handmaid's Tale' Review: Season Five Delivers Another Shocking Entry about Grief, Retaliation and Bodily Autonomy" (Wijaszka), 348–49
Harjo, Joy
    2021 commencement speech, 559
Hasset, Kevin A.
    "Why We Shouldn't Raise the Minimum Wage," 199

"Heart and Sole: Detroiter Walks 21 Miles in Work Commute" (Laitner), 341–47
"The Higher Price of Buying Local" (Vayner), 93–96
High school graduation speech (Bobba), 151
Hinojosa, Maria
    "Dancing Past the Boundaries," 425
"H.I.V. and AIDS in Africa: Ten Lessons from the Field" (Wangila and Akukwe), 478
Hobson, Mellody, *189*
    "Color Blind or Color Brave?," 188–89
"Holding Up the Hollywood Stagecoach: The European Take on the Western" (Przybylowski), 620–34
Holloway, Jonathan, *403*
    "To Unite a Divided America, Make People Work for It," 403–6
Honoré, Russel, *203*
    "Work Is a Blessing," 203–4
hooks, bell
    "Work Makes Life Sweet," 228
"How America Fractured into Four Parts" (Packer), 465
"How Country Music Is Addressing the Opioid Crisis" (Gage), 899–904
"How Digital Beauty Filters Perpetuate Colorism" (Ryan-Mosley), 327–33
"How Harries and Swifties Changed the Outlook on Modern Concert Fashion" (Jaquez), 133–36
"How I Escaped the Tyranny of the Prophets of Beauty" (Huang), 923–26
"How Junk Food Can End Obesity" (Freedman), 764–66
How to Write a Sentence (Fish), 715
Huang, Ling Ling, *923*
    "How I Escaped the Tyranny of the Prophets of Beauty," 923–26
Hungerford, Chris
    "Breakdown of Caitlin Clark's Game: Skills, Stats & Impact," 254
Hurston, Zora Neal, 484
    Barracoon: The Story of the Last "Black Cargo," 711–12

I

Ice Cube, 2
"I Failed Two Captcha Tests. Am I Still Human?" (O'Gieblyn), 967–71
"I Found the Feminism I Was Looking for in the Lost Writings of a 17th Century Priest" (Shulevitz), 448
"I Have a Dream" (King), 480, 822–23
"I Just Wanna Say My Sisters' Names" (Bullock), 460
"I'm a Black Scholar Who Studies Race. Here's Why I Capitalize 'White.'" (Ewing), 257–58, 271, 283
"Incentive for Developers Would Spur Affordable Housing" (Saltzman), 385, 386
Inoue, Asao, 45–46
    Above the Well: An Antiracist Literacy Argument from a Boy of Color, 46
In Search of Solutions: A New Direction in Psychotherapy (O'Hanlon and Weiner-Davis), 642
Interfaith Youth Core
    "Eboo Patel," 430–31
Invisible Man (Ellison), 725
iPhone launch speech (Jobs), 822–23
"I Quit Social Media in College. This Is How My Life Changed." (Bloom), 870–75
"Is College Still Worth the High Price? Weighing Costs and Benefits of Investing in Human Capital" (Wolla, Vandenbrouke, and Tucker), 183
"It'll Grow Back. It Always Does." (Ng), 244–48
"It's Easy to Bash Tech, but I've Started Taking Robotaxis—and They're Awesome" (Kafka), 359–60
Ivins, Molly
    Nightline interview, 474

J

Jackson, Shirley Ann
    "Leaders in Science and Engineering: The Women of MIT," 186–87

Jadulang, Brayden
    "Censoring *TikTok* Would Harm Democratic Fabric," 182
Jaquez, Sierra, 132
    "How Harries and Swifties Changed the Outlook on Modern Concert Fashion," 133–36
Jenkins, Darlene
    "Tightening the Turns in Speed Skating: Lessons in Centripetal Force and Balance," 267–68
"Jews and Muslims Must Stand Together and Refuse to be Enemies" (Rehman and Ruby), 25–26
Joaquin, Rihanna
    "*TikTok* Affecting Social Development, Mental Health," 182
Jobs, Steve, 823
    iPhone launch speech, 822–23
Johnson, Steven, 109
Jones, Chloé Cooper
    "Champion Moves," 226–27, 235
Jordan, Barbara, *557*
    1976 keynote address to the Democratic National Convention, 557

K

Kafka, Peter
    "It's Easy to Bash Tech, but I've Started Taking Robotaxis—and They're Awesome," 359–60
Kang, Inkoo
    "'Black and Missing' attempts a much-needed reform of true-crime storytelling. It mostly succeeds.," 360–61
Karr, Mary, 357
Kearney, Kevin M., *927*
    "One Star," 927–31
"The Key to Beyoncé's Lasting Success" (Sachdev), 279, 292–96
Kheirbek, Raya Elfadel, *238*
    "At the VA, Healing the Doctor-Patient Relationship," 238–43
Kimmerer, Robin Wall, *932*
    "Strawberries," 932–37

Author / Title Index

Kindred (Butler), 725
King, Martin Luther, Jr., *418, 823*
　"I Have a Dream," 480, 822–23
　"Letter from Birmingham Jail," 417–18
King, Sharese
　"Language and Linguistics on Trial: Hearing Rachel Jeantel (and Other Vernacular Speakers)," 43
Kleege, Georgina
　"Call It Blindness," 225–26
Kopp, Rochelle
　Valley Speak: Deciphering the Jargon of Silicon Valley, 709
Kowarski, Ilana
　"14 Environmentally Friendly College Campuses," 310
Krauthammer, Charles
　"Are We Alone in the Universe?," 560–63
Krishna, Swapna, 370
　"*Thirsty Suitors*: I Feel Seen by This Game," 370–73

L

Laitner, Bill, 319
　"Heart and Sole: Detroiter Walks 21 Miles in Work Commute," 341–47
Lam, Aleksander, *209*
　"Sampling or Stealing? Copyright Infringement and Hip-Hop," 209–14
Landauer, Julia
　"War, Cartoons, and Society: Changes in Political Cartoons between World War II and the Iraq War," 546–47
Landman, Keren, *938*
　"Why Are Whole-Body Deodorants Suddenly Everywhere?," 938–45
"Language and Linguistics on Trial: Hearing Rachel Jeantel (and Other Vernacular Speakers)" (Rickford and King), 43
Lanham, Richard, 565, 686–87
　The Economics of Attention, 64
Laymon, Kiese, *946*
　"My Favorite Restaurant Served Gas," 224, 946–51

Lazenby, Michael
　"Make Mental Health Accessible," 386–88
"Leaders in Science and Engineering: The Women of MIT" (Jackson), 186–87
"Leaving Home, Coming Home" (Ly), 726
Leone, Steven
　"The Likelihood of Homeowners to Implement Thin-Film Solar Cells," 520–21
"Letter from Birmingham Jail" (King), 417–18
Letter to Robert Hooke (Newton), 13
Letter to the *Atlantic* (Gibson), 473
"The Likelihood of Homeowners to Implement Thin-Film Solar Cells" (Leone), 520–21
"Listening to a Divided America" (Woodruff), 18–19
Lives on the Boundary (Rose), 221–22
"Long-Awaited Olive Garden Receives Warm Welcome" (Hagerty), 696–97
Ludwig, David
　"Milk and Health," 191
Ly, Brandon
　"Leaving Home, Coming Home," 726
Lyiscott, Jamila, *710*
　"Broken English," 709–10

M

MacFarland, Jack, 221
Mackenzie, Don
　Getting to the Heart of Interfaith: The Eye-Opening, Hope-Filled Friendship of a Pastor, a Rabbi & an Imam, 255–56
"Make Mental Health Accessible" (Lazenby), 386–88
"Making Friends Who Disagree with You (Is the Healthiest Thing in the World)" (Vert), 23–24
"Mama Africa" (Bamboo), 706, 707, 708
Markstein, Gary, 546
Marron, Dylan, 20–21, *21, 29*
McCain, John
　"Farewell Letter to America," 694–95
McComb, Karen, 268, 271, 276

Mead, Margaret, *17*
"Media Coverage of Campus Protests Focuses on Spectacle" (Brown), 876–82
"Media Multitaskers Pay Mental Price" (Gorlick), 440
Memoirs of My Life (Gibbon), 724
Mernit, Judith Lewis
    "Seismology: Is San Francisco Next?," 445–46
Merriam-Webster
    "racism," 469–70
"Milk and Health" (Willett and Ludwig), 191
Minard, Charles Joseph, 464, *465*
Mincey, Sofi
    "On Climate Change and Hurricanes," 199
Mitchum, Kennedy, 469
Moller, Will
    "A Painful Posting," 269–70, 272
Morrison, Toni, 65, 581, 763
    Nobel Prize acceptance speech, 727, 729
Moss, Beverly, 482
    A Community Text Arises, 262–63, 269
"Mother Tongue" (Tan), 728
Murthy, Vivek H., *205*
    "Social Media Platforms Need Warning Labels," 205–8
"My Favorite Restaurant Served Gas" (Laymon), 224, 946–51
"My Life as an Undocumented Immigrant" (Vargas), 993–1002

N

National Council of Teachers of English, 800
"The (Native) American Dream" (Walker), 1003–9
Negri, Alberta
    "Underneath the Leather Jackets and Chrome Pipes: Research into a Community of Local Bikers," 264–66
Neuromancer (Gibson), 725
Newkirk, Thomas
    The Art of Slow Reading, 68–69
Newman, Judith, *952*
    "To Siri, with Love," 952–59

"New Movie Genres" (Chast), *171*
Newton, Isaac
    letter to Robert Hooke, 13
Ng, Angelina X., *244*
    "It'll Grow Back. It Always Does.," 244–48
Nguyen, Bich Minh, 475–76
    "The Good Immigrant Student," 476
Nightline interview (Ivins), 474
1976 keynote address to the Democratic National Convention (Jordan), 557
Nobel Prize acceptance speech (Morrison), 727, 729
"Nonconformity Is Skin Deep" (Brooks), 422–23
Nott, Dan
    "Our Labor Built AI," 960–66
Novak, Michael
    "The Spirit of Capitalism," 470
Now You See It: How the Brain Science of Attention Will Transform the Way We Live, Work, and Learn (Davidson), 728

O

Oakley, Elou Ortiz
    "California Can Solve Community College Students' Food Insecurity Crisis. Here's How," 478
Obama, Michelle
    "Remarks by the First Lady at the DNC, 2016," 477–78
O'Connor, Ciaran
    "Can We Bridge Our Differences over Gun Laws?," 8
O'Gieblyn, Meghan, *967*
    "I Failed Two Captcha Tests. Am I Still Human?," 967–71
O'Hanlon, Bill
    In Search of Solutions: A New Direction in Psychotherapy, 642
"On Buying Local" (Spriggs), 80, 85, 93–96
"On Climate Change and Hurricanes" (Mincey), 199
"One Star" (Kearney), 927–31

Author / Title Index

Oregon State University, 805–6
Oreskes, Naomi
    "Beyond the Ivory Tower: The Scientific Consensus on Climate Change," 191–92
"Origin Stories" (Gordon-Reed), 915–22
"Our Labor Built AI" (Nott and Cambo), 960–66

P

Packer, George
    "How America Fractured into Four Parts," 465
"A Painful Posting" (Moller), 269–70, 272
"Paradise, Paved," 275
Pasini, David, *407*
    "The Economic Impact of Investing Public Funds in Sports Franchises," 407–9
Paul, Pamela
    "The Saying Goes: Dogs Are Man's Best Friend. But Cats Are Better," 467
Patel, Eboo, 431–32, *432*
    "To Narrow Toxic Divides, Students Build Bridges between Faiths," 431
Penny, Louise, 532
Perry, Kristin, *549*
    "Exploring the Hardships and Stigma Students With Invisible Disabilities Face," 549–53
Persepolis I (Satrapi), 481, *481*
Petosa, Kate
    "Extreme Heat Is More Dangerous for Workers Every Year," 543
The Philosophy of Literary Form (Burke), 7
Playing the Enemy: Nelson Mandela and the Game That Made a Nation (Carlin), 433
"'¿Por qué no sabes español?': Pressured Monolingualism and Its Impacts on Mexican Americans" (Uribe), 668–85
Posnanski, Joe
    "The College Connection," 727–28
Prince [Rogers Nelson], 410
Przybylowski, Walter
    "Holding Up the Hollywood Stagecoach: The European Take on the Western," 620–34

R

"racism" (Merriam-Webster), 469–70
Rahman, Jamal
    Getting to the Heart of Interfaith: The Eye-Opening, Hope-Filled Friendship of a Pastor, a Rabbi & an Imam, 255–56
Rehman, Sabeeha, 26
    "Jews and Muslims Must Stand Together and Refuse to be Enemies," 25–26
    We Refuse to Be Enemies, 26
"Remarks by the First Lady at the DNC, 2016" (Obama), 477–78
"Researchers Decode How Elephants Form 'Sentences,' Lending Insight to Their Complex Communication" (Rozsa), 437
"Review on Niche" (Spelman College Alumna), 356
Rheingold, Howard, 64–65, 101–2, 528, 686
    "Crap Detection 101," 102
Rhetoric (Aristotle), 565
The Rhetoric of Rhetoric (Booth), 14–15
Richardson, Elaine, 60–61
Rickford, John
    "Language and Linguistics on Trial: Hearing Rachel Jeantel (and Other Vernacular Speakers)," 43
"The Rise of Female Heroes in Shoujo Manga" (Edwards), 825–30
Rogers, Carl, 455
Rose, Mike, 227, *972*
    "Blue-Collar Brilliance," 972–81
    Lives on the Boundary, 221–22
Rosenblatt, Louise, 68
Rosenthal, Jill
    "Extreme Heat Is More Dangerous for Workers Every Year," 543
Royster, Jacqueline Jones
    "When the First Voice You Hear Is Not Your Own," 16
Rozsa, Matthew
    "Researchers Decode How Elephants Form 'Sentences,' Lending Insight to Their Complex Communication," 437

Rubin, Melissa, *297*
   "Advertisements R Us," 297–302
Ruby, Walter, *26*
   "Jews and Muslims Must Stand Together and Refuse to be Enemies," 25–26
   We Refuse to Be Enemies, 26
Ryan-Mosley, Tate, *327*
   "How Digital Beauty Filters Perpetuate Colorism," 327–33

S

Sachdev, Shaan, *292*
   "The Key to Beyoncé's Lasting Success," 279, 292–96
Sainani, Kristin
   "Damage Control," 438
Sallman, Sydney, *286*
   "What Is the Invisible Problem with *TikTok*?," 286–91
Saltzman, Dan
   "Incentive for Developers Would Spur Affordable Housing," 385, 386
"Same Food Planet, Different Food Worlds" (Dreher), 696–97
"Sampling or Stealing? Copyright Infringement and Hip-Hop" (Lam), 209–14
Samuels, Allison
   "African American Stars Remember Whitney Houston," 724
"The Sanctuary of School" (Barry), 216, 849–54
Satrapi, Marjane
   Persepolis I, 481, *481*
"The Saying Goes: Dogs Are Man's Best Friend. But Cats Are Better" (Paul), 467
Scott, A.O., 497–98
"Secondary Trauma at Work: Why We Experience and How We Cope" (Chanel Smith), 187
"Seismology: Is San Francisco Next?" (Mernit), 445–46
Shakespeare, William
   Hamlet, 175
Shea, Don, 357

Shepherd, Julianne Escabedo
   "*Cowboy Carter*: Beyoncé," 353–54
Sheppard, Katryn
   "Early Word Production: A Study of One Child's Word Productions," 314
"Should This Be the Last Generation?" (Singer), 726
Shulevitz, Judith
   "I Found the Feminism I Was Looking for in the Lost Writings of a 17th Century Priest," 448
Shwed, Ally
   "Cracking the Color Code," 982–88
Singer, Peter
   "Should This Be the Last Generation?," 726
Smith, Chanel
   "Secondary Trauma at Work: Why We Experience and How We Cope," 187
Smith, Stephen A., *44*
   First Take, 43–44
Smitherman, Geneva, *691*, 835
   Talkin and Testifyin: The Language of Black America, 476–77, 691–92
Snyder, Marjorie A.
   "Girls Suffer Sports Concussions at a Higher Rate than Boys. Why Is That Overlooked?," 447
"Social Media Platforms Need Warning Labels" (Murthy), 205–8
"Some Dreamers of the Golden Dream" (Didion), 722–23
"The Spectacular New *Dune* Will Turn Even Skeptics into Believers" (Stevens), 358
Speech at the United Nations (Yousafzai), 462–63
Speech to *Publishers Weekly*'s Winter Institute (Gay), 228–29
Spelman College, 215
Spelman College Alumna
   "Review on *Niche*," 356
"Spelman College Rankings" (*U.S. News & World Report*), 356
"The Spirit of Capitalism" (Novak), 470
Spriggs, Katherine, 80, 85, 93–96
   "On Buying Local," 93–96
"Stanford Should Rename Wilbur Hall" (Cu), 386

Stevens, Dana
   "The Spectacular New *Dune* Will Turn Even Skeptics into Believers," 358
Strain, Michael
   "Why We Shouldn't Raise the Minimum Wage," 199
"Strawberries" (Kimmerer), 932–37
"Students' Right to Their Own Language" (Conference on College Composition and Communication), 46
Swift, Jonathan, 98

T

"The Talk: After Ferguson, a Shaded Conversation about Race" (Canedy), 883–87
Talkin and Testifyin: The Language of Black America (Smitherman), 476–77, 691–92
Tan, Amy
   "Mother Tongue," 728
"10 Reasons *Barbie* Made $1 Billion in Just 3 Weekends (& How Much Will It Make?)" (Tyler), 258–60
"They Called Me a Girl before Anyone Else Did" (Clymer), 888–92
"*Thirsty Suitors*: I Feel Seen by This Game" (Krishna), 370–73
"This Ain't Another Statement! This Is a DEMAND for Black Linguistic Justice" (Conference on College Composition and Communication), 47
Thomas, Shermann "Dilla," 699, *699*
Thompson, Clive, 410
Thrasher, Nova
   "Gender-Inclusivity and the Onus of Progress on the Writing Center," 13
"*TikTok* Affecting Social Development, Mental Health" (Joaquin), 182
"Tightening the Turns in Speed Skating: Lessons in Centripetal Force and Balance" (Jenkins), 267–68
"To All the Girls I've Rejected" (Delahunty), 192, 193–94

"To Narrow Toxic Divides, Students Build Bridges between Faiths" (Patel), 431
Tonouchi, Lee A.
   "Da Future of Hawaiian Pidgin," 712–13
Tosh, Peter, 706
"To Siri, with Love" (Newman), 952–59
Toulmin, Stephen, 453
"To Unite a Divided America, Make People Work for It" (Holloway), 403–6
Truth, Sojourner, 62
   "Ain't I a Woman?," 479
Tucker, Cameron
   "Is College Still Worth the High Price? Weighing Costs and Benefits of Investing in Human Capital," 183
Tufekci, Zeynep, *989*
   "Why the Post Office Makes America Great," 989–92
Twain, Mark, 558
2021 commencement speech (Harjo), 559
Tyler, Adrienne
   "10 Reasons *Barbie* Made $1 Billion in Just 3 Weekends (& How Much Will It Make?)," 258–60

U

"Underneath the Leather Jackets and Chrome Pipes: Research into a Community of Local Bikers" (Negri), 264–66
United Nations
   Climate Change 2014: Synthesis Report, 464
   FACT: Climate Change Is Caused by Human Activity, 464
University of California System, 216
Uribe, Gabriela Agustina
   "'¿Por qué no sabes español?': Pressured Monolingualism and Its Impacts on Mexican Americans," 668–85
"Uses for AI in the Criminal Justice System" (Vaughan), 396–402
U.S. News & World Report
   "Spelman College Rankings," 356

V

Valdés, Guadalupe
  Con Respeto: Bridging the Distances between Culturally Diverse Families and Schools, 707–8
Valley Speak: Deciphering the Jargon of Silicon Valley (Kopp and Ganz), 709
Vandenbrouke, Guillaume
  "Is College Still Worth the High Price? Weighing Costs and Benefits of Investing in Human Capital," 183
Vargas, Jose Antonio, *993, 1001*
  "My Life as an Undocumented Immigrant," 993–1002
Vaughan, Emi, *396*
  "Uses for AI in the Criminal Justice System," 396–402
Vayner, Yuliya, 80, 86, *93*
  "The Higher Price of Buying Local," 93–96
Vert, Shauna
  "Making Friends Who Disagree with You (Is the Healthiest Thing in the World)," 23–24
Visual Capitalist, 467, *468*
Vu, Minh
  "Dirty Nails," 223

W

Walker, Taté, *1003*
  "The (Native) American Dream," 1003–9
Wallace, David Foster, 559–60
Wangila, Rhoi
  "H.I.V. and AIDS in Africa: Ten Lessons from the Field," 478
"War, Cartoons, and Society: Changes in Political Cartoons between World War II and the Iraq War" (Landauer), 546–47
Watson, Missy, *1010*
  "Contesting Standardized English," 1010–17
Wearly, Robin, *380*
  "ADAPTS, the First Evacuation Sling for Wheelchair Users," 383
Weiner-Davis, Michele
  In Search of Solutions: A New Direction in Psychotherapy, 642
We Refuse to Be Enemies (Rehman and Ruby), 26
Westbrook, Adam
  Cause / Effect: The Unexpected Origins of Terrible Things, 544
"What Can You Do to Make a Difference?" (Colberg), 479, *480*
"What Is the Invisible Problem with *TikTok*?" (Sallman), 286–91
"When the First Voice You Hear Is Not Your Own" (Royster), 16
"When You Are Old" (Yeats), 557
"Who Fears Climbing the Mountains Lives Forever between the Holes" (Buthainah), 711
"Whole of Our History" (Bunch), 448–49
"Why Activist Raquel Willis Believes in Black Trans Power" (Willis), 440–41
"Why Are Whole-Body Deodorants Suddenly Everywhere?" (Landman), 938–45
"Why Multilingual TV Is Good for Everyone" (Albarrán-Torres), 838–42
"Why the Post Office Makes America Great" (Tufekci), 989–92
"Why We Shouldn't Raise the Minimum Wage" (Hasset and Strain), 199
Wijaszka, Zofia
  "'The Handmaid's Tale' Review: Season Five Delivers Another Shocking Entry about Grief, Retaliation and Bodily Autonomy," 348–49
Willett, Walter C.
  "Milk and Health," 191
Williams, Terry Tempest
  "The Clan of One-Breasted Women," 472–73
Willis, Raquel
  "Why Activist Raquel Willis Believes in Black Trans Power," 440–41
Wineburg, Sam, 102–3, 529–30

Wolla, Scott A.
  "Is College Still Worth the High Price? Weighing Costs and Benefits of Investing in Human Capital," 183
Woman Hollering Creek and Other Stories (Cisneros), 706–7
Wood, Sarah
  "14 Environmentally Friendly College Campuses," 310
Woodruff, Judy
  "Listening to a Divided America," 18–19
"Word for Word: Culture's Impact on the Localization of Japanese Video Games" (Zhao), 804–5
"Work Is a Blessing" (Honoré), 203–4
"Work Makes Life Sweet" (hooks), 228
A Writing Life (Dillard), 461–62

Y

Yeats, William Butler
  "When You Are Old," 557
Young, Vershawn Ashanti, 40
"Your TV Is Watching You" (Estes), 893–98
Yousafzai, Malala, *462*
  Speech at the United Nations, 462–63

Z

Zhao, Ruizhe (Thomas)
  "Word for Word: Culture's Impact on the Localization of Japanese Video Games," 804–5
Zinczenko, David
  "Don't Blame the Eater," 435–36

Glossary / Index

A

ABSTRACT, 666 A GENRE of writing that summarizes a book, an article, or a paper, usually in 100–200 words. An *informative abstract* summarizes a complete REPORT; a briefer *descriptive abstract* works more as a teaser; a standalone *proposal abstract* (also called a PROJECT PROPOSAL) requests permission to conduct research, write on a topic, or present a REPORT at a scholarly conference. Features: a SUMMARY of basic information • objective DESCRIPTION • brevity

Academic Search Premier (EBSCO), 510
academic communities, joining, 51–61
academic success, habits for, 53–61
academic writing, 51–61
    characteristic features, 55–61
    genres
        analyses, 253
        arguments, 178
        narratives, 218
        proposals, 379
        reports, 305
        reviews, 350
    habits for success, 53–55
    presentations, 823–24
    reading, 74–75
    style, 700–701

Note: This glossary / index defines key terms and concepts and directs you to pages in the book where you can find specific information on these and other topics. Please note the words set in SMALL CAPITAL LETTERS are themselves defined in the glossary / index. Page numbers in *italics* indicate figures.

accessibility, 783–84
acknowledging sources, 12–13, 60, 569–70

ACTIVE VOICE, 700–701 When a VERB is in the active voice, the subject performs the action: He sent a gift.

ADAPTS transfer sling, *380*, 383
ad hominem fallacy, 442
Adobe Acrobat Reader, 80
advertisements
    Apple's "Crush," 416, *416*
    argument and, 476, *476*
    Coca-Cola, 297–302, *298*, 781, *781*
    documenting in MLA style, 611
    Dove's "These Legs," 183–84, *184*, 186, 189
    Google Gemini, 138
    Got Milk? campaign, 444, *445*
    Nike's Just Do It campaign, 260–62, *262*
    Salesforce's "The March," *12*
    The Shelter Pet Project, *476*
    Thistle, 71–3, *72*
African American Vernacular English, 42–43
afterwords, documenting in MLA style, 606

AGREEMENT, 750–60 The correspondence between a SUBJECT and VERB in person and number (the dog chases the children down the street) or between a PRONOUN and its antecedent in gender and number (the cat nursed her babies; the children flee because they are afraid).
    pronoun-antecedent, 750–54
    subject-verb, 757–60

AI. *See* GENERATIVE AI

AI ACKNOWLEDGMENT STATEMENT, 794, 821 A short description that accompanies a piece of writing to explain how the author used GENERATIVE AI in creating

the text. These statements usually include: the AI tool used, the tasks it helped with, the prompts used, and a description of how the tool contributed to the final work.
    in APA style, 642–43
    examples, 576–77
    in MLA style, 587–88
    template for writing, 577

AIDS, in Africa, 478–79, *479*
AllSides, 103

ALTERNATIVE TEXT (ALT TEXT), 783, 794, 816 A short DESCRIPTION of an image that gets read aloud by screen-reading software to ensure that users with visual or some cognitive impairments can understand the image.

The Amazing Race (television show), 495
American Psychological Association (APA), 575, 635. *See also* APA STYLE

ANALOGY, 461–63 A STRATEGY for COMPARISON by explaining something unfamiliar in terms of something that is more familiar. *See also* faulty analogy

ANALYSIS, 252–302 A GENRE that breaks something down into its component parts so that those parts can be thought about methodically in order to understand the whole. Features: a question that prompts a closer look • some DESCRIPTION of the subject • EVIDENCE drawn from close examination of the subject • insight gained from your analysis • clear, precise language. *See also* CAUSAL ANALYSIS; DATA ANALYSIS; INFORMATIONAL ANALYSIS; INSTRUCTIONAL ANALYSIS; PROCESS ANALYSIS; RHETORICAL ANALYSIS; VISUAL ANALYSIS
    across academic disciplines, 74–75, 253
    across cultures and communities, 255–56
    across genres, 256
    across media, 253–55
    analyzing arguments, 419–60
    annotated examples
        "Advertisements R Us," 297–302

        "The Key to Beyoncé's Lasting Success," 292–96
        "What Is the Invisible Problem with *TikTok*?," 286–91
    characteristic features, 257–72
    kinds of analysis
        causal, 268, 281
        data, 268–70, 281–82
        discourse, 264–66, 279–80
        process, 266–68, 280
        rhetorical, 260–64, 279
        visual, 272–75, 282
    readings
        "Blue-Collar Brilliance," 972–81
        "Media Coverage of Campus Protests Focuses on Spectacle," 876–82
        "One Star," 927–31
    roadmap to writing analytically, 276–85

ANECDOTE, 57 Brief NARRATIVE used to illustrate a point.

ANNOTATE, 68, 77–82 The process of taking notes, underlining key information, and marking aspects of a text that strike you as important while reading.

ANNOTATED BIBLIOGRAPHY, 536–37 A writing GENRE that gives an overview of published research and scholarship on a topic. Each entry includes complete publication information for a source and a SUMMARY or an ABSTRACT. A *descriptive annotation* summarizes the content of a source without commenting on its value; an *evaluative annotation* gives an opinion about the source along with a description of it. Features: complete bibliographic information • a brief SUMMARY or DESCRIPTION of each work • evaluative comments (for an evaluative bibliography) • some indication of how each source will inform your RESEARCH • a consistent and concise presentation
    annotated example
        "Nonresistance in the Battle for Freedom," 538–40
    characteristic features, 536–37
    descriptive, 538–40
    evaluative, 537

annotating, 77–82
    defined, 76
    for engagement, 68
    reflection exercise, 82
    sample text, 81–82
    in slow reading, 68
    steps in, 77–80
    and summarizing, 83
annotation, by readers, 68, 77–82

ANTECEDENT, 750–54 The NOUN or PRONOUN to which a pronoun refers: Maya lost her wallet.

anthologies
    documenting in APA style, 654
    documenting in MLA style, 584, 604

APA STYLE, 575, 635–85 A system of DOCUMENTATION used in the social sciences. APA stands for the American Psychological Association.
    in academic writing, 59
    directory, 635–37
    formatting a research essay, 665–67
    in-text documentation, 637–42
    list of references, 643–64
        articles and other short works, 594–602
        audio, visual, and other sources, 658–64
        authors and other contributors, 592–94
        books, parts of book, and reports, 654–58
        sources not covered by APA, 665
    notes, 642
    parenthetical documentation, 565
    quotations, 556, 557, 666, 768
    sample research essay, 619–34
    signal phrases, 638
    verb tenses, 565, 761–63
    visuals, 795

appeals
    emotional, 429–30
    ethical, 430–35
    logical, 435–41
    to readers' values, 194

APPENDIX A section at the end of a written work for supplementary material that would be distracting in the main part of the text.

Apple, "Crush" ad, 416, *416*

ARGUING A POSITION, 177–214 A GENRE that uses REASONS and EVIDENCE to support a CLAIM. Features: an explicit POSITION • a response to what others have said or done • useful background information • a clear indication of why the topic matters • good REASONS and EVIDENCE • attention to more than one POINT OF VIEW • an authoritative TONE and STANCE • an appeal to readers' values
    across academic disciplines, 178
    across cultures and communities, 180
    across genres, 180
    across media, 178–79
    annotated examples
        "The Higher Price of Buying Local," 93–96
        "Sampling or Stealing? Copyright Infringement and Hip-Hop," 209–14
        "Social Media Platforms Need Warning Labels," 205–8
        "Work Is a Blessing," 203–4
    characteristic features, 181–94
    readings
        "AI Is Like Cake," 855–58
        "Black Enough: Protecting Linguistic Identity in the Writing Center," 905–14
        "Contesting Standardized English," 1010–17
        "How Country Music Is Addressing the Opioid Crisis," 899–904
        "I Failed Two Captcha Tests. Am I Still Human?," 967–71
        "Media Coverage of Campus Protests Focuses on Spectacle," 876–82
        "Origin Stories," 915–22
        "Our Labor Built AI," 960–66
        "Why Are Whole-Body Deodorants Suddenly Everywhere?," 938–45
        "Why Multilingual TV Is Good for Everyone," 838–42

"Why the Post Office Makes America Great," 989–92
roadmap to arguing a position, 195–202

ARGUMENT, 410–83 Any text that makes a CLAIM supported by REASONS and EVIDENCE.
  analyzing and constructing, 419–60
  claims, 423–27
  classical, 449–52
  classification and, 357–59
  common ground and, 432–34
  invitational, 457–59
  means of persuasion, 429–41
    emotional appeals, 429–30
    ethical appeals, 430–35
    logical appeals, 435–41
  multiple points of view, 444–47
  purposes, 414
  recognizing arguments, 412–18
  Rogerian, 455–56
  stance and, 421–23
  stasis theory, 427–29
  strategies for supporting an argument, 461–83
  structuring, 447–59
  Toulmin, 453–55

Aristotle, 2, 5, 77, 101, 429, 454, 456
art, documenting in MLA style, 611

ARTICLE The word "a," "an," or "the," used to indicate that a NOUN is indefinite (a writer, an author) or definite (the author).

articles
  documenting in APA style, 649–54
  documenting in MLA style, 594–602
  as sources, 502–3
Assertion-Evidence Approach, 823–24
assignments, understanding, 117
attitude, 36. *See also* STANCE

ATTRIBUTION BIAS, 100–101, 532 The tendency to think that our motivations for believing what we believe are objectively good while thinking that those who we disagree with have objectively wrong motivations.

Audacity, 809

AUDIENCE, 35–36 Those to whom a text is directed—the people who read, listen to, or view the text. Audience is a key part of any RHETORICAL SITUATION.
  analysis and, 216
  connecting to, 692–94, 706–7
  considering, 35–36

audio essays, 807–9
audio recordings, 566
  documenting in APA style, 660, 662
  documenting in MLA style, 615–16

AUTHORITY, 529 A person or text that is cited as support for a writer's ARGUMENT. A structural engineer may be quoted as an authority on bridge construction, for example. Authority also refers to a quality conveyed by writers who are knowledgeable about their subjects.
  and AI, 140

autobiographies, 216

B

backgound information, 185–87
background research, 491
bandwagon appeals, 442
Banks, Caitlin, 514
Barbie, 258–59, *259*
bar graphs, 790
Bedwell, Linda, 514
begging the question, 442
Beyoncé, 135, 292–96, 279, 353, *354*, 734
bibliographies. *See also* REFERENCES
  annotated, 536–40
  as sources, 502
  working, 526–27

Biles, Simone, 412, 416
Black and Missing (docuseries), 360–61
Black English, 40, 691–92, 735, 756
#BlackLivesMatter, 5
Black Panthers, 691
Black Women Oral History Project, *504*

BLOCK QUOTATION, 557, 618–19, 666 In a written work, long QUOTATIONS are indented and set without quotation marks: in MLA STYLE, set off text more than four typed lines, indented five spaces (or one-half inch) from the left margin; in APA STYLE, set off quotes of forty or more words, indented five spaces (or one-half inch) from the left margin. *See also* QUOTATION

BLOG An abbreviation of "weblog." A regularly updated website on which writers post their work, often including images, embedded audio or video clips, and links to other sites.
    documenting in APA style, 659
    documenting in MLA style, 608
    embedding links, 13

boldface, 784
books
    documenting in APA style, 654–57
    documenting in MLA style, 602–7
    as sources, 502
    in working bibliography, 527
Boolean operators, 511–12

BRACKETS, 558, 765–66 Square parentheses ([ ]) used to indicate words inserted in a quotation.

BRAINSTORMING, 115 A process for GENERATING IDEAS AND TEXT by writing down everything that comes to mind about a topic, then looking for patterns or connections among the ideas.

C

CALL AND RESPONSE, 479–82 A rhetorical STRATEGY, developed from African traditions of group participation in public gatherings and religious ceremonies, in which a speaker offers a "call" to an audience that in turn "responds." Also commonly used in musical compositions.

Camarillo, David, 438
Cape Fear Community College, 815
capitalism, 470–71

CAPTION, 566 A brief explanation accompanying a photograph, diagram, chart, screen shot, or other visual that appears in a written document.

cartoons, documenting in MLA style, 612

CASE, 748, 754–56 The different forms some PRONOUNS can take to indicate how they function in a sentence—for example, as the SUBJECT or object. "I" and "me" refer to the same person, but they are not interchangeable in a sentence: Joanne offered me one of the puppies, but I am allergic to dogs.

CAUSAL ANALYSIS, 268, 280, 463–64 A kind of ANALYSIS that explains why something occurs or once occurred. Also a STRATEGY FOR SUPPORTING AN ARGUMENT about a topic where questions of causality are relevant. *See also* faulty causality

CAUSE AND EFFECT, 463–65 A STRATEGY for analyzing why something occurred or speculating about what its consequences will be.

CDs, documenting in MLA style, 616
Centeno, Daniel, *104*
Chapman University, 313
charts, 789–90, *793*
    as evidence, 441
ChatGPT, 137, 138, *139*, 577. *See also* GENERATIVE AI
    acknowledging use of, 569–70, 576–77
        in APA style, 642–43
        in MLA style, 587–88
    as aid to formatting, 147
    authorship and agency, 140
    to organize legal documents, 399–400
    to practice interview skills, 516–17
Chicago Manual of Style, 59

CHRONOLOGICAL ORDER, 120, 222 A way of organizing text that proceeds from the beginning of an event to the end. Reverse chronological order proceeds in the other direction, from the end to the beginning.

Cicero, 9, 459, 694
Cinderella (film), 424, *424*

CITATION, 568–77 In a text, the act of giving information from a source. A citation and its corresponding parenthetical DOCUMENTATION, footnote, or endnote provide minimal information about the source; complete information appears in a list of WORKS CITED or REFERENCES at the end of the text.

CLAIM, 58, 423–27 A statement that asserts a belief or POSITION. In an ARGUMENT, a claim needs to be stated in a THESIS, or clearly implied, and requires support by REASONS and EVIDENCE.
    in academic writing, 55, 57
    in argument and, 423–27
    qualifying, 57, 427

clarity, 58–59, 272

CLASSICAL ARGUMENT, 449–52 A system of ARGUMENT developed in Greece and Rome during the classical period. It features an introduction that states the CLAIM; a body that includes background information, good REASONS and EVIDENCE, and attention to COUNTERARGUMENTS; and a CONCLUSION.

CLASSIFICATION, 465–66 A STRATEGY that groups numerous individual items by their similarities (e.g., classifying cereal, bread, butter, chicken, cheese, cream, eggs, and oil as carbohydrates, proteins, and fats). Classification can serve as the organizing principle for a paragraph or whole text.

CLAUSE, 717 A group of words that consists of at least a SUBJECT and a predicate; a clause may be either MAIN OR SUBORDINATE.
    main clause, 717, 720, 721–22, 737, 739–40, 742, 746
    subordinate clause, 720–21, 737, 746

climate change, 191–92, 198–99, 464–65

CLUSTERING, 115, *116* A process for GENERATING IDEAS AND TEXT, in which a writer visually connects thoughts by jotting them down and drawing lines between related items.

Coca-Cola, 297–302, *298*, 781, *781*

CODE-MESHING, 704 A way of weaving together LANGUAGES and DIALECTS.

CODE-SWITCHING, 704 The practice of shifting from one LANGUAGE or DIALECT to another.

Colbert, Stephen, 41, *42*

COLLABORATION, 124–36, 146 To work (or labor) together to accomplish a task or goal. It's a method that allows most of the world's work to get done, and it works best through cooperation, mutual support, and respect.
    at a writing center, 131–32
    in small groups, 126–28
    sample peer-reviewed essay, 132–36
    students and, 124–26
    through peer review, 128–31
    tips for, 127–28

COLLECTIVE NOUN A NOUN (committee, crowd, family, herd, team) that refers to a group.

College of Southern Nevada, 508, *508*, 509–10
color, 784, 786–87, *786*
comic book, documenting in MLA style, 605
commas, 736–37, 768–73
    after introductory information, 769–71
    comma splices, 739–41
    fused sentences, 743
    quotations and, 559
    to set off nonessential elements, 772–73

COMMA SPLICE, 719, 739–41 Two or more MAIN CLAUSES joined with only a comma: I came, I saw, I conquered.

comments, 602
    documenting in APA style, 652
    documenting in MLA style, 602

common errors, 734–77
- commas after introductory information, 769–71
- comma splices, 739–41
- commas with essential and nonessential information, 772–73
- fused sentences, 742–44
- incorporating quotations, 763–66
- mixed constructions, 744–47
- pronoun case, 748, 754–56
- pronoun reference, 748–50
- punctuating quotations, 766–68
- quotations, 763–68
- sentence fragments, 737–39
- shifts in tense, 760–63
- subject-verb agreement, 757–60
- verbs, 757–63
- words often confused, 773–77

COMMON GROUND, 25–27, 432–34 Shared values. Writers build common ground with audiences by acknowledging others' points of view, seeking areas of compromise, and using language that includes, rather than excludes, those they aim to reach.

common knowledge, 570
communication, 2–3, 5. *See also* RHETORIC
- professional. *See* teamwork

COMPARISON AND CONTRAST, 466–69 A STRATEGY that highlights the points of similarity and difference between items. Using the block method of comparison and contrast, a writer discusses all the points about one item and then all the same points about the next item; using the point-by-point method, a writer discusses one point for both items before going on to discuss the next point for both items, and so on. Sometimes comparison and/or contrast can serve as the organizing principle for a paragraph or whole text.

COMPLETE SUBJECT, 759, 771 The SIMPLE SUBJECT plus any MODIFIERS. The complete subject can be one word (I enjoy carrots), two words (The girls went to the grocery store), or many words: The old farmer with the multi-colored carrots has a booth at the market.

COMPLEX SENTENCE, 720–21 A single MAIN CLAUSE plus one or more SUBORDINATE CLAUSES: When the United States holds a presidential election once every four years, citizens should vote.

COMPOUND-COMPLEX SENTENCE, 721–22 Two or more MAIN CLAUSES plus one or more subordinate clauses: When the United States holds a presidential election once every four years, citizens should vote, but voter turnout is often disappointing.

COMPOUND SENTENCE, 718–19 Two or more MAIN CLAUSES joined by a comma and a COORDINATING CONJUNCTION or by a semicolon: The United States holds a presidential election once every four years, but voter turnout is often disappointing.

CONCLUSION The way a text ends, a chance to leave an AUDIENCE thinking about what's been said. Five ways of concluding a college essay: reiterating your point, discussing the implications of your ARGUMENT, asking a question, referring back to your OPENING, or proposing some kind of action.
- closing sentences, 727–29
- drafting, 120

conference proceedings
- documenting in APA style, 658
- documenting in MLA style, 607

CONFIRMATION BIAS, 101, 103, 532 The tendency to favor and seek out information that confirms what we already believe and to reject and ignore information that contradicts those beliefs.

conjunctions, coordinating, 718–19, 741, 743
Consumer Reports, 352, 354, *355*, 362

CONTEXT, 36 Part of any RHETORICAL SITUATION, conditions affecting the text such as what else has been said about a topic; social, economic, and other factors; and any constants such as due date and length.

contrast. *See* COMPARISON AND CONTRAST

conversations
    openness to challenging, 28–29

COORDINATING CONJUNCTION, 718–19, 741, 743 One of these words—"and," "but," "or," "nor," "so," "for," or "yet"—used to join two elements in a way that gives equal weight to each one (bacon <u>and</u> eggs; pay up <u>or</u> get out).

correctness, 689–92
Council of Science Editors (CSE), 59, 575

COUNTERARGUMENT, 447, 450 In ARGUMENT, an alternative POSITION or objection to the writer's position. The writer of an argument should not only acknowledge counterarguments but also, if at all possible, accept, accommodate, or refute each counterargument.

COUNT NOUN A word that names something that can be counted (one book, two books). *See also* NONCOUNT NOUN

court case
    documenting in APA style, 664
    documenting in MLA style, 585, 612

CREDIBILITY, 430–41 The sense of trustworthiness that a writer conveys through the text.
    in arguments, 193–94
    in reports, 313–314
    in research, 575
    of sources, 529

credit, giving, 12–13, 568–77
Crick, Francis, 14–16

CRITERIA, 354–56 In a REVIEW, the standards against which something is judged.

CRITICAL LANGUAGE AWARENESS, 43 Understanding language's connections to power and privilege, and how language conventions can conform to, reproduce, or challenge power relations. Critical language awareness calls for thinking carefully about the language you use, as well as examining your own beliefs and assumptions about language.
    attitudes about language, 42–44
    standardized English, 44–47
    strategies for authors, 47–50

crowdfunding, 378, *380*
CSE (Council of Science Editors), 59, 575
cultures and communities, 712–13
    analyses, 255–56
    arguments, 180
    narratives, 219–20
    proposals, 380
    reports, 306–8
    reviews, 351–52

CUMULATIVE SENTENCE, 722–23 A sentence that begins with a main idea expressed in a MAIN CLAUSE and then adds details in PHRASES and SUBORDINATE CLAUSES that follow the MAIN CLAUSE. *See also* PERIODIC SENTENCE

current sources, 499–501

D

Daily Californian, 362
Daily Wallpapers blog, 471

DATA ANALYSIS, 268–70, 281–82 A kind of ANALYSIS that looks for patterns in numbers or other data, sometimes in order to answer a stated or implied question.

databases
    documenting in MLA style, 598, 599
    finding sources with, 510
    general, 510
    subject-specific, 510
data set, documenting in APA style, 664
definite article. *See* article

DEFINITION, 469–71 A STRATEGY that says what something is. Formal definitions identify the category that something belongs to and tell what distinguishes it from other things in that category: A worm is an invertebrate (a category) with a long, rounded body and no appendages (distinguishing features). Extended definitions go into more detail: a paragraph or even an essay explaining why a character in a story is tragic. Stipulative definitions give a writer's own use of a term, one not found in a dictionary. Definition can serve as the organizing principle for a paragraph or whole text.

Delahunty, Jennifer, 192–94
delivery, 778–79. *See also* DESIGN
    portfolios, 157
    presentations, 822–35
Descartes, René, 13

DESCRIPTION, 471–73 A STRATEGY that tells how something looks, sounds, smells, feels, or tastes. Effective description creates a clear DOMINANT IMPRESSION built from specific details. Description can be *objective, subjective,* or both. Description can serve as the organizing principle for a paragraph or whole text.
    analyses and, 258–60
    narratives and, 223–25
    visuals and, 471–73, *472*

descriptive annotations, 538–40

DESIGN, 778–835 The way a text is arranged and presented visually. Elements of design include fonts, colors, illustrations, LAYOUT, and white space. *See also* MEDIUM
    accessibility, 783–84
    color, 786–87
    getting a response to, 798–99
    headings, 785
    layout, 795–98
    thinking rhetorically
        about, 781–83
    typefaces and fonts, 784–85
    visuals, 787–94

details, narratives and, 223–25
Detroit News, 352
diagrams, 792, *792, 793,* 794

DIALECT, 37, 703–14 Varieties of LANGUAGE that are spoken by people in a particular region, social class, or ethnic group.

DIALOGUE, 223–25 Presenting conversation between individuals in writing by QUOTING exactly what was said. A common feature in NARRATIVE writing to help bring a story to life.

DICTION, 91, 687 Word choice.

dictionaries
    documenting in APA style, 656
    documenting in MLA style, 584, 600
Digital Archive of Literacy Narratives,
    218, 249
digital storytelling, 809–12
digital texts, 38, 70–73
directness, 58–59
Directory of Open Access
    Journals, 510
discipline librarians, 507
discourse analysis, 264–66,
    279–80
disinformation, 99
dissertations
    documenting in APA style, 658
    documenting in MLA style, 607
DNA, 14–16, *15*

DOCUMENTATION, 568–77 Publication information about the sources cited in a text. The documentation usually appears in an abbreviated form in parentheses at the point of CITATION or in an endnote or a footnote. Complete documentation usually appears as a list of WORKS CITED or REFERENCES at the end of the text. Documentation styles vary by discipline. *See also* APA STYLE; IN-TEXT DOCUMENTATION; MLA STYLE
    in-text documentation (APA), 637–42
    in-text documentation (MLA), 581–87
    using appropriate citation style, 60–61

DOI, 525, 527
    APA style, 637, 643, 645, 646, 649, 651, 665
    MLA style, 591

DOMINANT IMPRESSION, 471 The overall effect created through specific details when a writer describes something.

Dove, "These Legs" ad, 183–84, *184*, 186, 189
Downey Jr., Robert, 443

DRAFTING, 120 The process of putting words on paper or screen. Writers often write several drafts, REVISING each until they achieve their goal or reach a deadline. At that point, they submit a finished final draft.

drawing, 115, 407, *408*
Duarte, Nancy, 822, 832
DuckDuckGo, 506
Dune (film), 358, *358*
DVDs
    documenting in APA style, 660, 661
    documenting in MLA style, 613

E

edited academic English. *See* STANDARDIZED ENGLISH
edited collections
    documenting in APA style, 654
    documenting in MLA style, 604

EDITING, 122, 734–77 The process of fine-tuning a text—examining each word, phrase, sentence, and paragraph—to be sure that the text is correct and precise and says exactly what the writer intends. *See also* common errors; DRAFTING; PROOFREADING; REVISION

editions
    documenting in APA style, 654
    documenting in MLA style, 606
editorials
    documenting in APA style, 650
    documenting in MLA style, 600
Eilish, Billie, 276
either-or fallacy, 442
electronic books, documenting in APA style, 654
electronic sources. *See* online sources

ELLIPSIS, 558, 765–66 Three spaced dots (. . .) that indicate an omission or a pause.

email, documenting in MLA style, 610

EMOTIONAL APPEALS, 429–30 Ways that authors appeal to an AUDIENCE's emotions, values, and beliefs by arousing specific feelings—for example, compassion, pity, sympathy, anger, fear). *See also* ETHICAL APPEALS; LOGICAL APPEALS

empathy, 21–23
encyclopedias
    documenting in APA style, 656
    documenting in MLA style, 584, 600
    as sources, 501
EndNote, 523
engagement, reading rhetorically for, 67–68
English
    African American Vernacular, 42–43
    Black, 691–92
    breaking the rules, 691–92
    standardized, 690–92, 705
Environmental Protection Agency (EPA), 100
errors. *See* common errors
essays
    audio, 807–9
    illustrated, 804–5
    summary / response, 90–96
    video, 809–12

ESSENTIAL ELEMENT, 772–73 A word, PHRASE, or CLAUSE with information that is necessary for understanding the meaning of a sentence: French is the only language that I can speak.

ETHICAL APPEALS, 430–35 Ways that authors establish CREDIBILITY and AUTHORITY to persuade an AUDIENCE to trust their ARGUMENTS—by showing that they know what they're talking about (e.g., by citing trustworthy SOURCES), demonstrating that they're fair (by representing opposing views accurately and even-handedly), and establishing COMMON GROUND. *See also* EMOTIONAL APPEALS; LOGICAL APPEALS

ethical communication, 4. *See also* RHETORIC

ETHOS, 12, 15, 304, 430, 712 From the Greek word for "character," ethos reflects the values and ideals of a person or culture.

ethos, of reviewing, 362–63. *See also* ETHICAL APPEALS

EVALUATION, 158, 221, 350, 352, 354–60, 363, 367–69, 548 A GENRE of writing that makes a judgment about something—a source, poem, film, restaurant, etc.—based on certain CRITERIA. *See also* REVIEW
- criteria for, 354–56
- of sources, 528–35
- support for, 357–59

EVIDENCE, 435–41, 461–82 In an ARGUMENT, the data you present to support your REASONS. Such data may include statistics, calculations, EXAMPLES, ANECDOTES, QUOTATIONS, case studies, or anything else that will convince your readers that your reasons are compelling. Evidence should be sufficient (enough to show that the reasons have merit) and relevant (suitable to the argument you're making).
- in academic writing, 57–58
- across academic disciplines, 75
- in analyses, 260–70
- in arguments, 189–91
- in defensive reading, 103
- in proposals, 384–85
- in summary / response essay, 90–91

exaggeration, argument and, 474–75

EXAMPLE, 473 A STRATEGY that illustrates a point by giving specific instances.

exclamation points, 559–60
experiments, as evidence, 439–40

F

Facebook
- documenting in APA style, 664
- documenting in MLA style, 610
- posts and campaigns on, 815
- and research, 506

FACT-CHECKING, 104–7, 531–32 The process of verifying the accuracy of FACTS and CLAIMS presented in a piece of writing, a speech, or elsewhere—by READING LATERALLY, triangulating, or consulting fact-checking sites.

FactCheck.org, 102, 103, 104, 421, 507, 531, 534

FACTS, 428, 436 Information that can be backed up and verified by reliable evidence. For example: Robert F. Kennedy was killed in 1968.
- checking, 531–32
- defining, 97–99
- distinguishing misinformation from, 97–107

fair use, 571

FAKE NEWS, 98–99, 98, 103, 503, 506 A kind of misinformation made to look like authentic news. *See also* misinformation

FALLACY, 441–44 Faulty reasoning that can mislead an AUDIENCE. Fallacies include ad hominem, bandwagon appeal, begging the question, either-or argument, faulty analogy, faulty causality (also called "post hoc, ergo propter hoc"), hasty generalization, paralipsis, slippery slope, and straw man.

false dilemma, 442
fast reading, 68–69
faulty analogy, 442
faulty causality, 442–43
Federer, Roger, 226–27, *227*

FIELD RESEARCH, 513–22 The collection of firsthand data through observation, interviews, and questionnaires or surveys.
- interviews, 515–18
- observations, 514–15
- surveys and questionnaires, 518–22

figures
- APA style, 667
- documenting, 566
- MLA style, 619

films
- documenting in APA style, 660
- documenting in MLA style, 612

Final Cut Pro, 811
first person. *See* POINT OF VIEW
The Five-Minute Journal, 152

FLASHBACK, 222 In NARRATIVE, an interruption of the main story in order to show an incident that occurred at an earlier time.

FLASH-FORWARD, 222 In NARRATIVE, an interruption of the main story in order to show an incident that will occur in the future.

Flickr, 505
Floyd, George, 151
fonts, 784–85
Food Science and Technology Abstracts, 510
Ford, Harold, 188–89
forewords, documenting in MLA style, 606

FORMAL WRITING, 694–95 Writing intended to be evaluated by someone such as an instructor or read by an AUDIENCE expecting academic or businesslike argument and presentation. Formal writing should be carefully EDITED, REVISED, and PROOFREAD.

formatting. *See also* design
    APA style, 665–67
    MLA style, 617–19

FRAGMENT, 737–39 A group of words that is capitalized and punctuated as a sentence but is not one, either because it lacks a SUBJECT, a VERB, or both, or because it begins with a word that makes it a SUBORDINATE CLAUSE.

Franklin, Aretha, 24, *25*
Franklin, Rosalind, 16

FREEWRITING, 115, 159–60 A process for GENERATING IDEAS AND TEXT by writing continuously for several minutes without pausing to read what has been written.

Full Fact, 531

FUSED SENTENCE, 742–44 Two or more MAIN CLAUSES with no punctuation between them: I came I saw I conquered.

G

GarageBand, 809
Garza, Alicia, 24
gender, 751–54
general databases, 510

GENERATING IDEAS AND TEXT, 110–12 Activities that help writers develop a topic, EXAMPLES, REASONS, EVIDENCE, and other parts of a text by BRAINSTORMING, CLUSTERING, FREEWRITING, LOOPING, OUTLINING, and QUESTIONING.

GENERATIVE AI, 137–50. A kind of artificial intelligence that can generate text, images, video, audio, and code based on patterns learned from vast amounts of existing data.
    acknowledging, 569–70
    authorship and agency, 140
    checklist before using in academic writing, 141–42
    documenting in APA style, 642, 664
    documenting in MLA style, 587, 617
    evidence, trust, and accuracy, 57–58, 102
    finding sources with, 505–7
    future of, 150
    and genres of writing, 198, 282, 323, 366, 391–92
    getting additional feedback, 146–47
    and misinformation, 99, 105–6
    and navigating early research, 145–46
    and plagiarism, 145–46
    to practice interviewing, 516
    and proofreading and formatting, 147–48
    questions to consider before using, 140–43
    and reading, 64, 67
    and refining your own ideas, 145
    in research, 488, 576–77
    and standardized English, 140
    and style, 692
    and time management, 143–44
    and understanding challenging texts, 144–45
    using caution, 49, 148–50
    ways AI can help, 143–48

GENRE, 168–409 A way of classifying things. The genres this book is concerned with are kinds of writing that writers can use to accomplish a certain goal and to reach a particular audience. As such, they have well-established features that help guide writers, but they are flexible and change over time, and can be adapted by writers to address their own RHETORICAL SITUATIONS. Genres covered in this book include ANALYSES, ANNOTATED BIBLIOGRAPHIES, ARGUMENTS, NARRATIVES, PROPOSALS, REPORTS, and REVIEWS. Subgenres covered include LITERATURE REVIEWS, LITERACY NARRATIVES, PROFILES, PROJECT PROPOSALS, and VISUAL ANALYSES.

    academic writing and, 59–60
    analyses, 252–302
    arguments, 177–214
    choosing, 170–76
    narratives, 215–251
    proposals, 378–409
    for remix projects, 817
    reports, 303–47
    reviews, 348–77

GERUND A VERB form ending in "-ing" that functions as a NOUN: <u>Swimming</u> improves muscle tone and circulation.

Gibson, James A., 473
Gibson, Walker, 459
González, X, 105
Google, 138, 245, 422, 498
    checking evidence, 104
    finding sources, 496, 505
Google Arts and Culture, 504
Google Books, 502
Google Docs, 789
Google Forms, 519
Google Gemini ad, 140, *141*
Google Images, 105
Google Maps, 505
Google News, 490, 503, 505
Google Scholar, 502–3, 505, 530
Got Milk? ad campaign, 444, *445*

government documents
    documenting in APA style, 657–58
    documenting in MLA style, 594
    as sources, 503
graphic narratives, 481, *481*
    documenting in MLA style, 605
graphs, 789–90, 794
The Guardian, 106
Guggenheim Museum Bilbao, 566, *567*

H

habits for academic success, 53–55
The Handmaid's Tale, 348–49, *349*
Harris, Kamala, 443–44

HASHTAG, 5, 186, 498 A metadata tag created by placing a number sign (#) in front of a word or unspaced phrase (e.g., #BlackLivesMatter), used in social media to mark posts by KEYWORD or theme and make them searchable by these tags. Also used to add commentary on a web text outside of the text itself.

hasty generalization, 443
"have" / "of," 774
Hawking, Stephen, 464
headings, 785
    APA style, 665–66
    MLA style, 618

HELPING VERB, 762 A VERB that works with a MAIN VERB to express a tense and mood. Helping verbs include "do," "have," "be," and MODALS: Elvis <u>has</u> left the building. Pigs <u>can</u> fly.

"his or her," 752–53
historical documents, as sources, 504
Hitler, Adolf, 5
Hooke, Robert, 13
Howard, Rebecca Moore, 572
humor, argument and, 474–75, *475*
Hurricane Katrina, 203
Hypothesis (software), 80

I

ideas
    emphasizing main idea, 722–25
    expressing clearly, 58–59
    generating, 115–16
    organizing, 119–20
    presenting in response to others, 58
    synthesizing, 541–53
illustrated essays, 804–5
illustrations
    APA style, 667
    MLA style, 619
images. *See* visuals
imagination, 13–14
IMDb (Internet Movie Database), 362, *625*, *632*
Immersive Van Gogh exhibit, *351*, 364
iMovie, 811

IMRAD, 56, 305, 785 Acronym representing sections of scientific reports conveying information: introduction (asks a question), methods (tells about experiments), results (states findings), and discussion (tries to make sense of findings in light of what was already known).

inclusion, editing for, 736
"indeed," 719
indefinite articles. *See* ARTICLE

INDEFINITE PRONOUN, 758–59 A PRONOUN—such as "all," "anyone," "anything," everyone," "everything," "few," "many," "nobody," "nothing," "one," "some," and "something"—that refers to a nonspecific person or thing.

indents
    APA style, 665
    MLA style, 617
infographics, 479, *480*
informal conversations
    as evidence, 437–39
    as field research, 517
    as sources, 498

information
    controversial, 569
    managing information overload, 523–27
    reporting, 303–47
    trustworthiness of, 313–14, 381
    well-known, 570

INFORMATIONAL ANALYSIS, 280 A kind of PROCESS ANALYSIS that tells how something works.

information technology. *See* social media
infotention, 64–65

INQUIRY, 112, 113–15 A process for investigating a topic by posing questions, searching for multiple answers, and keeping an open mind.
    and research, 484–85, 490

Instagram
    documenting in APA style, 663
    documenting in MLA style, 610
    and narrative, 215
    posts and campaigns on, 815, 816
    and research, 506
    responding on, 86
Institutional Review Board, 513

INSTRUCTIONAL ANALYSIS, 266, 280 A kind of PROCESS ANALYSIS that tells how to do something.

internet. *See also* online sources; social media; WIKI
    fair use, 571
    style, 698–99
Internet Movie Database (IMDb), 362, *625*, *632*
interviews
    as evidence, 437–39
    documenting in MLA style, 614
    in field research, 515–18

IN-TEXT DOCUMENTATION, 574–75 Brief DOCUMENTATION in a text that tells readers what the writer has taken from a source and where in the source they found that information.
    APA style, 637–42
    MLA style, 581–87

introduction, 120, 162, 235, 327. *See* OPENING
    documenting in MLA style, 606
    drafting, 120
intuition, 13

INVITATIONAL ARGUMENT, 457–59 A system of ARGUMENT based on the work of Sonja Foss and Cindy Griffin that aims for understanding and shared goals by listening carefully to all concerned. Invitational arguments introduce the issue, present all perspectives on it fairly, identify any commonalities among the perspectives, and conclude by seeking a resolution that is agreeable to all.

Iron Man (film), 443

IRREGULAR VERB A VERB that does not form its past tense and past participle by adding "-ed" or "-d" to the base form (e.g., "eat," "ate," "eaten").

"it," 750, 752–53
italics, 784
"it's" / "its," 776–77

J

James, LeBron, 412, 734
Jamison, Judith, 425–26, *426*
Japanese video games, 804–5, *805*
Jeantel, Rachel, 42–43
Jensen, Arthur, 691
Jobs, Steve, 822, *823*
journals. *See also* articles; periodicals
    documenting in APA style, 649
    documenting in MLA style, 595, 596
JSTOR, 510, 531
JURN, 502, 503, 505

K

Kaepernick, Colin, 260–61, *262*

KAIROS, 121, ***121*, 122** An ancient Greek term meaning "the opportune moment." Authors look for just the right moment to make a particular ARGUMENT, appeal to a particular AUDIENCE, and so on.

key terms, definitions of, 311–13

KEYWORD, 506, 511 A term that a researcher inputs when searching RÉSUMÉS, databases, and the internet for information.

keyword searches, 511–12
Kickstarter, 379, *380*, 383
King, Martin Luther, Jr., 822, *823*
Kokenis, Toni, 438
Kossola, Oluale (Cudjo Lewis), 711–12

L

LAB REPORT, 172, 322 A GENRE of writing that covers the process of conducting an experiment in a controlled setting. Features: an explicit TITLE • ABSTRACT • PURPOSE • methods • results and discussion • REFERENCES • APPENDIX • effective format

LANGUAGE, 37, 39–50 A system of symbols, in human language, used to create words structured in ways that can be communicated through speaking, writing, or gesturing. *See also* English; RHETORIC; STYLE
    attitudes about, 42–44
    critical language awareness, 42–44
    expectations about, 47–50
    mixing languages and dialects, 703–14
    power and privilege related to, 41–42
    and standardized English, 45–47

language awareness. *See* CRITICAL LANGUAGE AWARENESS
language mixing
    connecting with audiences, 706–7
    drawing attention, 711
    evoking person, place, or community, 712–13
    illustrating a point, 709–10
    providing translation, 707–8
    quoting directly with respect, 711–12
    standardized English and other dialects, 705

LAYOUT, 780–99 The way text is arranged on a page or screen—for example, in paragraphs, in lists, on charts, with headings, and so on.

lecture slides or notes documenting in
    APA style, 662
legal sources, 503
    documenting in APA style, 585
Leone, Steven, 520
letters
    documenting in APA style, 641
    documenting in MLA style, 601, 606, 610
Lewis, Cudjo (Oluale Kossola), 711–12
libraries
    finding sources, 507–9
    library catalogs, 508–10
    library websites, 508, *508*
Lin, Jian, 445–47
Lincoln, Abraham, 276, 425, 429
line graphs, 789, *790*
listening, 7–9, 23–24, 127

LITERACY NARRATIVE, 230–31 A GENRE of writing that describes a writer's experience learning to read or write. Features: a well-told story • a firsthand account • an indication of the narrative's significance
    annotated example
        "First Day of School," 249–51
    characteristic features, 230–31
    readings
        "My Life as an Undocumented Immigrant," 993–1002
        "The Sanctuary of School," 849–54
        "To Siri, with Love," 952–59
literary works, documenting in MLA style, 583–84

LITERATURE REVIEW, 547–48 A GENRE of writing that surveys and synthesizes the prior research on a topic. In the sciences, a literature review is a required part of the introduction to an IMRAD report; in all disciplines, scholars write article-length literature reviews devoted to specific topics. Features: survey of relevant research on a focused topic • fair-minded synthesis / summary of the literature • an EVALUATION of the literature • clear ORGANIZATION • complete, accurate DOCUMENTATION
    annotated example
        "Exploring the Hardships and Stigma Students with Invisible Disabilities Face," 549–53
    characteristic features, 547–48

LOGICAL APPEALS, 425–41 Ways an author uses REASONS and EVIDENCE to persuade an AUDIENCE to accept a CLAIM: facts, images, observations, statistics, testimony, etc. *See also* EMOTIONAL APPEALS; ETHICAL APPEALS

logos. *See* LOGICAL APPEALS

LOOPING, 115 A process for GENERATING IDEAS AND TEXT in which a writer writes about a subject quickly for several minutes and summarizes the most important or interesting idea in a sentence, which becomes the beginning of another round of writing and summarizing, and so on, until an angle for a paper is found.

Los Angeles Sparks, *492*
Los Angeles Times, 696

M

magazines
    documenting in APA style, 649
    documenting in MLA style, 595

MAIN CLAUSE, 717, 720, 737, 739–40, 742, 746 A CLAUSE, containing a SUBJECT and a VERB, that can stand alone as a sentence: She sang. The world-famous soprano sang several arias.

main idea, emphasizing, 722–25

MAIN VERB, 762 The verb form that presents the action or state. It can stand alone or be combined with one or more HELPING VERBS. For example: My dog might have buried your keys. Leslie Jones is a comedian. Alexa was wearing a gown by Milly. The agent didn't appear old enough to drive.

maketoonist.com, *147*
Mandela, Nelson, 433, *434*
maps, 790, *791*, 792, *793*
   documenting in APA style, 663
   documenting in MLA style, 615
margins
   APA style, 665
   MLA style, 617
Martin, Trayvon, 42
mash-ups, 541, *542*
Massachusetts Institute of Technology (MIT), 97–99
Medium, 184

MEDIUM, 778–79 A means for communicating—for example, in print, with speech, or online. *See also* DESIGN
   analyses, 253–55
   arguments, 178–79
   composing and remixing across media, 800–821
   design and delivery, 778–79
   narratives, 218
   proposals, 379
   reading across media, 70–74
   reports, 305–6
   reviews, 350–51
   style across media, 698–99

MEMOIR, 475 A GENRE that focuses on something significant from the writer's past. Features: good story • vivid details • clear significance

Mendeley, 523
Metacritic.com, 349

METAPHOR, 832 A figure of speech that makes a comparison without using the word like or as: "All the world's a stage / And all the men and women merely players" (Shakespeare, *As You Like It*).

Microsoft Teams, 812
milk industry, 444–45, *445*
Miller, Carolyn, 170

MISINFORMATION, 97–107, 499 False or inaccurate information that may or may not be intended to deceive (lies, on the other hand, are always told deliberately).
   navigating AI and, 59

MIT (Massachusetts Institute of Technology), 97–99
Mitchum, Kennedy, 469

MIXED CONSTRUCTION, 744–47 A sentence that starts out with one structure and ends up with another one: Although bears can be deadly is not a good reason to avoid camping altogether.

MLA STYLE, 575–634 A system of DOCUMENTATION used in the humanities. MLA stands for the Modern Language Association.
   in academic writing, 59
   directory, 578–80
   formatting a research essay, 617–19
   illustrations, 619
   in-text documentation, 581–87
   notes, 587–88
   parenthetical documentation, 565
   quotations, 556, 557, 768
   sample research essay, 619–34
   verb tenses and, 565, 762
   visuals, 619, 795
   works cited, 588–619
      articles and other short works, 594–602
      audio, visual, and other sources, 611–17
      authors and other contributors, 592–94
      books and parts of books, 602–7
      core elements, 588–92
      personal communication and social media, 610
      websites, 607–9

MODAL, 774 A HELPING VERB—such as "can," "could," "may," "might," "must," "ought to," "should," "will," or "would"—that does not change form for person or number and indicates probability or necessity.

MODE, 800–802 A way of conveying a message. Writing often uses multiple modes: linguistic, audio, visual, spatial, and/or gestural. *See also* STRATEGIES FOR SUPPORTING AN ARGUMENT
    multimodal writing, 800–821

Modern Language Association (MLA), 59, 575, 578.
    See also MLA STYLE
Morrison, Toni, 65, 581, 588, 591, 727, 729, 763
The Moth, 795–96, *796*
motivation, examining, 10–11, 34

MULTIMODAL WRITING, 800–821 Writing that uses more than one MODE of expression, including some combination of words, images, audio, video, links, and so on. Sometimes called "multimedia writing."
    audio essays and podcasts, 807–9
    defined, 800–802
    illustrated essays, 804–5
    posters and infographics, 812–15, *813*
    remix projects, 817–19
    social media posts and campaigns, 815–17
    video essays, 809–12, *810*
    websites, 805–7

multivolume works
    documenting in APA style, 646–47
    documenting in MLA style, 585, 604–5
musical scores, documenting in MLA style, 615
music recordings, documenting in APA style, 661

N

NAACP (National Association for the Advancement of Colored People), 691
Napoleon I, 464–65, *165*

NARRATION, 475–78 A STRATEGY for presenting information as a story, for telling "what happened." It is a pattern often associated with fiction, but it shows up in all kinds of writing. When used in a REVIEW, a REPORT, or another academic GENRE, narration is used to support a point—not merely to tell an interesting story for its own sake. Narration can serve as the organizing principle for a paragraph or whole text.

NARRATIVE, 215–51 A GENRE that tells a story for the PURPOSE of making a point. Features: a clearly identified event • a clearly described setting • vivid, descriptive details • a consistent POINT OF VIEW • a clear point. *See also* LITERARY NARRATIVE
    across academic disciplines, 218
    across cultures and communities, 219
    across genres, 221
    across media, 218
    advertisements and, 476
    annotated examples
        "At the VA, Healing the Doctor-Patient Relationship," 238–43
        "First Day of School," 249–51
        "It'll Grow Back. It Always Does.," 244–48
    characteristic features, 221–30
    graphic narratives, 481, *481*
    literacy narratives, 230–31
    readings
        "Black Enough: Protecting Linguistic Identity in the Writing Center," 905–14
        "Fun Home," 859–69
        "How I Escaped the Tyranny of the Prophets of Beauty," 923–26
        "I Quit Social Media in College. This Is How My Life Changed.," 870–75
        "My Favorite Restaurant Served Gas," 946–51
        "My Life as an Undocumented Immigrant," 993–1002
        "Origin Stories," 915–22
        "The Sanctuary of School," 849–54
        "Strawberries," 932–37
        "The Talk: After Ferguson, a Shaded Conversation about Race," 883–87
        "They Called Me a Girl before Anyone Else Did," 888–92
        "To Siri, with Love," 952–59
        "Why the Post Office Makes America Great," 989–92
    roadmap to writing a narrative, 232–37

NARRATIVE SEQUENCING, 475–78 A STRATEGY FOR SUPPORTING AN ARGUMENT and a feature of Black discourse in which speakers link concrete narratives in a sequence that helps to convey their point. Narrative sequencing can make points feel less abstract than they would be if made without narrative examples in an argument.

Nass, Clifford, 439–40
National Aeronautics and Space Administration (NASA), 97, 528, *535*
National Association for the Advancement of Colored People (NAACP), 691
National Council of Teachers of English, 788
National Geographic, 797–98, *798*
National Newspaper Index, 503
National Public Radio (NPR), 305, 541, 807
National Weather Service, 465–66, *466*
Netflix, 170
NewsNow, 505
news publications
    documenting in APA style, 649–50
    documenting in MLA style, 598
New York Times, 153, 194, 205, 305, 362, 407, *408*, 423, 435, 503
New York Times Book Review, 357
Nexis Uni, 510
Niche, 356
Nike, Just Do It ad campaign, 260–62, *262*
9/11 attacks, 4
Nintendo, 804–5, *804*
Nobel Prize, 16, 463, 727, 729

NONCOUNT NOUN, 758–59 A word that names something that cannot be counted or made plural with certain modifiers or units: information, rice.

NONESSENTIAL ELEMENT, 772–73 A word, phrase, or CLAUSE that gives additional information but that is not necessary for understanding the basic meaning of a sentence: I learned French, which is a Romance language, online. Nonessential elements should be set off by commas.

nonperiodical websites, documenting in APA style, 652
"nor," 718
notes
    APA style, 642–43
    MLA style, 587–88
note taking, 524–25, 574

NOUN A word that refers to a person, place, animal, thing, or idea (director, Stephen King, forest, Amazon River, tree frog, notebook, democracy).
    noncount, 758–59

novels, documenting in MLA style, 584
NPR, 305, 541, 807
NPR Research News, 490

O

Obama, Barack, 188
Obama, Michelle, 477–78
object case, 754–56
observations
    as evidence, 437
    in field research, 514–15
    participant observation, 514
O'Connor, Ciaran, 8, 9
"of" / "have," 774
Ohtani, Shohei, 43–44, *44*
older sources, 499–501
Olson, Ted, 22
The Onion, 103
online sources
    avoiding plagiarism, 574
    documenting in APA style, 650, 652–54, 659–60
    documenting in MLA style, 607–9
    evaluating, 528–35
    keeping track of, 523–24
op-ed, documenting in MLA style, 600–601

OPENING, 725–27 The way a text begins, which plays an important role in drawing an AUDIENCE in. Some ways of opening a college essay: with a dramatic statement, a vivid image, a provocative question, an ANECDOTE, or a startling CLAIM.
    sentences, 725–27

"or," 718–19

oral forms of knowledge
    as field research, 513
    as sources, 504
oral presentations, documenting in MLA style, 615
Oregon State University, Fisheries and Wildlife Club, 805–6, *806*

ORGANIZATION, 56–59, 119–20 The STRATEGIES a writer uses to arrange their writing so that they present ideas to readers in a clear and logical way. Strategies include presenting the most important information first followed by minor points; presenting what happened first to last (chronologically); and offering general information before specifics.
    chronological, 222
    IMRAD, 56, 305, 315
    spatial, 324
    of summary / response essays, 91–92
organizing
    analyses, 283
    arguments, 200–201
    drafts, 119–20
    narratives, 235
    oral presentations, 822–24
    proposals, 393–94
    reflections, 160–62
    reports, 314–15, 323–25
    reviews, 367–68
Osaka, Naomi, 688–89, *689*

OUTLINING, 119 A process for GENERATING IDEAS AND TEXT or for examining a text. An informal outline simply lists ideas and then numbers them in the order that they will appear; a working outline distinguishes support from main ideas by indenting the former; a formal outline is arranged as a series of headings and indented subheadings, each on a separate line, with letters and numerals indicating relative levels of importance.

P

page numbers
    APA style, 665
    MLA style, 617
    works without, 586
papers from conference proceedings
    documenting in APA style, 658
    documenting in MLA style, 607
paralipsis, 443

PARAPHRASE, 554–56, 560–63, 563–67 To reword a text in about the same number of words but without using the word order or sentence structure of the original. Paraphrasing is generally called for when a writer wants to include the details of a passage but does not need to quote it word for word. As with QUOTING and SUMMARIZING, paraphrasing requires DOCUMENTATION. *See also* PATCHWRITING
    deciding whether to quote, paraphrase, or summarize, 555–56
    signal phrases and, 564–65

parentheses, in keyword searches, 512
"parlor" metaphor (Burke), 7

PARTICIPANT OBSERVATION, 514 A form of observation in field research that operates on the principle that researchers can learn about a subject by doing (participating in it) as well as by watching.

PASSIVE VOICE, 700–701 When a VERB is in the passive voice, the subject is acted upon: *A gift was given to Oliver.*

PATCHWRITING, 572–73 PARAPHRASES that lean too heavily on the words or sentence structure of the source, adding or deleting some words, replacing words with synonyms, altering the syntax slightly—in other words, not restating the passage in fresh language and structure.

Patel, Eboo, 430–32, *432*
pathos. *See* EMOTIONAL APPEALS
peer review, 124–36. *See also* response
    annotated example
        "How Harries and Swifties Changed the Outlook on Modern Concert Fashion," 132–36
Pepper Dem Ministries (PDM), 474–75, *475*

periodicals, 502–3
    documenting in APA style, 649–52
    documenting in MLA style, 594–602
    in working bibliographies, 527

PERIODIC SENTENCE, 724–25 A sentence that delays the main idea, expressed in a MAIN CLAUSE, until after details given in phrases and SUBORDINATE CLAUSES. *See also* CUMULATIVE SENTENCE

periods, 559, 740, 742–43
personal experience
    as evidence, 440–41
    insights coming from, 13–14
    as support for an argument, 473
personal interviews, documenting in
    MLA style, 614
perspectives. *See also* POINT OF VIEW
    in arguments, 191–93
    considering multiple perspectives, 9, 58, 444–47, 532–33
Pettitte, Andy, 269–70, 272, 277
photographs, 104–5, 788–89, *788*, 794
pie charts, 790
Pienaar, Francois, *434*

PLAGIARISM, 568–77 Using another person's words, syntax, or ideas without giving suitable credit and DOCUMENTATION. Plagiarism is a serious breach of ethics.
    avoiding, 571–75, 766
    fair use and the internet, 571
    patchwriting, 572–73

podcasts
    composing and remixing, 807–9
    documenting in APA style, 660
    documenting in MLA style, 615–16
poems, documenting in MLA style, 584

POINT OF VIEW A position from which something is considered. The common points of view are first person, which uses "I" or "we," and third person, which uses "he," "she," or "they." *See also*

perspectives
    in narratives, 225–27, 234–35

PolitiFact, 531
popular sources, 498–99, *500*
Porter, Billy, 424, *424*

PORTFOLIO, 157 A collection of writing selected by a writer to show their work, sometimes including a statement assessing the work and explaining what it demonstrates.

Pose (television program), 424

POSITION, 27, 198–200 A statement that asserts a belief or CLAIM. In an ARGUMENT, a position needs to be stated in a THESIS or clearly implied and requires support with REASONS and other kinds of EVIDENCE.

possessive case, 754–56
posters
    documenting in APA style, 658
    for presentation, 812–15, *814*
posts to online forums, documenting in
    APA style, 659
Poulain de la Barre, François, 448
PowerPoint, 789
prefaces, documenting in MLA style, 606
presentations, 822–35
    across disciplines, 823–24
    common structure, 822–23
    documenting in MLA style, 615
    roadmap to making a presentation, 831–35
    sample presentation, 825–30
Prezi, 698
primary documents, as sources, 504

PRIMARY SOURCE, 497–98 A source such as a literary work, historical document, work of art, or performance that a researcher examines firsthand. Primary sources also include experiments and FIELD RESEARCH. In writing about the Revolutionary War, a researcher would probably consider the Declaration of Independence a primary source and a textbook's description of the writing of the document a SECONDARY SOURCE.

PROBLEM AND SOLUTION, 478–71 A STRATEGY FOR SUPPORTING AN ARGUMENT by framing it as a way of solving a problem, or of introducing a change of some kind. If a writer can first convince readers that there's a problem (and that it matters), they'll be more likely to read on to hear about how it can be solved. In fact, this is a classic storytelling technique, setting up a conflict that needs to be resolved. It's a technique that can help capture and hold an AUDIENCE's attention.

proceedings of conferences
    documenting in APA style, 658
    documenting in MLA style, 607

PROCESS ANALYSIS, 266–68, 280 A kind of ANALYSIS that closely examines the steps of a process. *See also* INFORMATIONAL ANALYSIS; INSTRUCTIONAL ANALYSIS

PROFILE, 316–19 A REPORT about people, places, events, institutions, or other things. Features: a firsthand account • detailed information about the subject • an interesting angle
    annotated example
        "Heart and Sole: Detroiter Walks 21 Miles in Work Commute," 341–47
    characteristic features, 316–19

Project Gutenberg, 502

PROJECT PROPOSAL, 388–89 A writing GENRE that describes the PURPOSE of a research project, the steps of the project, and its goal. Features: a discussion of the topic • an indication of your topic and focus • an explanation of why you're interested in the topic • a plan • a schedule
    annotated example
        "The Economic Impact of Investing in Sports Franchises," 407–9
    characteristic features, 388–89

PRONOUN, 747–56 A word that takes the place of a NOUN or functions the way a noun does.
    clear pronoun reference, 748–50
    gender and, 751–54
    indefinite pronouns, 758–59

pronoun-antecedent agreement, 750–54
pronoun case, 754–56

PRONOUN REFERENCE, 748–50 The way in which a PRONOUN indicates its ANTECEDENT. Pronoun reference must be clear and unambiguous in order to avoid confusing readers.

PROOFREADING, 122 Process that includes checking for correct spelling and punctuation as well as for page order, missing copy, and consistent use of typefaces and fonts. *See also* EDITING; REVISION

PROPOSAL, 378–409 A GENRE that argues for a solution to a problem or suggests some action. Features: a precise DESCRIPTION of the problem • a clear and compelling solution • EVIDENCE that your solution will address the problem • acknowledgment of other possible solutions • a statement of what your proposal will accomplish. *See also* PROJECT PROPOSAL
    across academic disciplines, 379
    across cultures and communities, 380
    across genres, 381
    across media, 379
    annotated examples
        "The Economic Impact of Investing Public Funds in Sports Franchises," 407–9
        "To Unite a Divided America, Make People Work for It," 403–5
        "Uses for AI in the Criminal Justice System," 396–402
    characteristic features, 381–88
    project proposal, 388–89
    roadmap to writing a proposal, 390–95

ProQuest One, 510
prose plays, documenting in
    MLA style, 584
protesters, 5, *5, 6*
Publication Manual of the American Psychological Association. See APA STYLE
Public Citizen, 421–22, *422*
published interviews, documenting in
    MLA style, 614

punctuation
    commas, 737, 768–73
    ellipsis marks, 558
    exclamation points, 559–60
    periods, 559, 740, 742–43
    question marks, 559–60
    quotation marks, 556–57, 558–59
    of quotations, 556–60
    semicolons, 559, 719, 740, 743

PURPOSE, 33 A writer's goal: to explore; to express oneself; to entertain; to demonstrate learning; to report; to persuade; and so on. Purpose is one element of the RHETORICAL SITUATION.

Q

QUALIFYING WORD, 57, 427 A word such as "frequently," "often," "generally," "sometimes," or "rarely" that indicates the strength of a CLAIM.

QUALITATIVE DATA, 281, 355–56 Data that describe something in unquantifiable terms—for example, with DESCRIPTION, ANECDOTES, and other nonnumerical information, including that found through FIELD RESEARCH.

Qualtrics, 519

QUANTITATIVE DATA, 281, 355–56 Data that can be presented in concrete, measurable ways, such as statistics and measurements.

QUESTIONING, 116 A process of GENERATING IDEAS AND TEXT about a topic—asking, for example, What? Who? When? Where? How? and Why?
    articulating questions, 491–93
    in defensive reading, 103–4
    in interviews, 516
    in surveys and questionnaires, 520–21

question marks, 559–60
questionnaires
    as evidence, 436–37, *436*
    in field research, 518–22

QUOTATION, 554–60, 563–67, 711–12 Someone's words used exactly as they were spoken or written. Quotation is most effective when wording is worth repeating or makes a point so well that no rewording will do it justice or when you want to cite someone's exact words or to quote someone whose opinions disagree with others. Quotations need to be acknowledged with DOCUMENTATION. *See also* IN-TEXT DOCUMENTATION
    acknowledging sources, 569
    APA style, 635–85, 666, 767–68
    block quotations, 557
    deciding whether to quote, paraphrase, or summarize, 555–56
    incorporating quotations, 763–66
    indicating changes, 558
    indicating who said what, 767
    MLA style, 618–19, 768
    punctuating quotations, 556–60, 766–68
    short quotations, 556–57
    signal phrases, 564–65, 765, 767–68

quotation marks
    in keyword searches, 511
    for short quotations, 556–57

R

radio programs, documenting in MLA style, 616
random samples, 519
Ratcliffe, Krista, 8
readability, 785, 787
The Readers' Guide to Periodical Literature, 503
reading
    across academic disciplines, 74–75
    across genres, 74
    across media, 70–74
    annotating, 77–80
    considering your rhetorical situation, 66–67

distinguishing facts from misinformation, 97–107
efferent, 68
fast vs. slow, 68–69
and infotention, 64–65
on- vs. off-screen texts, 70–73
reading defensively, 101–4, 499
reading laterally, 101–3, 530–31, 569
reading process, 62–107
reading rhetorically, 64–75
reflection exercises, 75
responding to readings, 86–96
summarizing, 83–86, 90–96
of unfamiliar / difficult text, 69–70

READING DEFENSIVELY, 101–4, 499 The kind of reading that doesn't take things at face value, that questions underlying assumptions, that scrutinizes CLAIMS carefully, and that does not rush to judgment.

READING LATERALLY, 101–3, 529–31, 569 The practice of consulting outside sources to check whether an unfamiliar source is trustworthy before, and while, reading it. Online fact-checkers keep multiple browser tabs open and read laterally, across tabs, to search for information that might verify a source's PURPOSE and CREDIBILITY.

REASON Support for a CLAIM OR POSITION. A reason, in turn, requires its own support.
in arguing a position, 189–91
faulty reasoning, 441–44

recorded source material, incorporating, 566
reference librarians, 507

REFERENCES, 643–65 The list of sources at the end of a text prepared in APA STYLE. *See also* bibliographies
annotated example
"Nonresistance in the Battle for Freedom," 538–40

REFERENCE WORKS, 501–2 SOURCES such as encyclopedias, handbooks, atlases, directories of biographical information, and almanacs that provide overviews of a topic.
documenting in MLA style, 600
as sources, 501–2

REFLECTION, 151–67 For writers, the act of stepping back to think carefully about their writing. Through reflection, writers pause to consider the rhetorical moves they've made and why; to consider their successes and challenges; and to identify paths forward for more effective composing.
annotated example
"Becoming the Writer I Am: A Reflection on My First-Year Composition Class," 164–67
on decisions, 154–55
on past experiences, 153–54
on planning what's next, 155
on processes and strategies, 154
roadmap to writing a reflection, 157–63

Reflectly, 152

REGISTER, 703–4 Varieties of LANGUAGE associated not with particular people or users but with a particular activity or occupation—like soccer or chemical engineering.

REITERATION, 479–81 A STRATEGY FOR SUPPORTING AN ARGUMENT that uses the repetition of a keyword, phrase, image, or theme throughout a text to drive home a point.

RELATIVE PRONOUN A PRONOUN, such as "that," "which," "who," "whoever," "whom," and "whomever," that introduces a SUBORDINATE CLAUSE: The professor <u>who</u> gave the lecture is my adviser.

religious works, documenting in APA style, 644–45

REMIX PROJECTS, 176, 706 When writers take their message and transform it from one form of delivery into a different genre or media. An argument essay is remixed into an infographic poster, for example, or a researched report is transformed into a podcast.

repetition, argument and, 479–81

REPORT, 303–47 A writing GENRE that presents information to inform readers on a subject. Features: a topic carefully focused for a specific AUDIENCE • definitions of key terms • trustworthy information • effective ORGANIZATION and DESIGN • a confident, informative TONE. *See also* IMRAD; PROFILE
   across academic disciplines, 305
   across cultures and communities, 306–8
   across genres, 308–9
   across media, 305–6
   annotated examples
      "The Future of the American City: Omaha's Hope," 334–40
      "Heart and Sole: Detroiter Walks 21 Miles in Work Commute," 341–47
      "How Digital Beauty Filters Perpetuate Colorism," 327–33
   characteristic features, 310–15
   IMRAD, 56, 305, 315
   profiles, 316–19
   readings
      "Black Enough: Protecting Linguistic Identity in the Writing Center," 905–14
      "Carbon Offsets (Taylor's Version)," 843–48
      "Cracking the Color Code," 982–88
      "How Country Music Is Addressing the Opioid Crisis," 899–904
      "The (Native) American Dream," 1003–9
      "Origin Stories," 915–22
      "Why Are Whole-Body Deodorants Suddenly Everywhere?," 938–45
      "Your TV Is Watching You," 893–98
   roadmap to writing a report, 320–26
representative samples, 519
republished work, documenting in MLA style, 606

RESEARCH, 484–685 The process of gathering information from reliable sources to help in making decisions, supporting ARGUMENTS, solving problems, becoming more informed, and so on. *See also* FIELD RESEARCH
   annotating a bibliography, 536–40
   avoiding plagiarism, 568–77
   documenting sources
      APA style, 635–85
      MLA style, 578–634
   evaluating sources, 528–35
   field research, 513–22
   finding sources, 495–512
   and generative AI, 145–46
   giving credit, 568–77
   keeping track, 523–27
   quoting, paraphrasing, and summarizing, 554–67
   scheduling, 493–94
   starting, 486–94
   synthesizing ideas, 541–53

RESEARCH QUESTION, 491–93 A question that guides research. A good research question should be simple, focused, and require more than just a "yes" or "no" answer.

research sites, 505–10

RESPECT, 14, 24–25 The act of giving someone or something your careful attention, listening with an open mind, being polite and considerate, and according someone else the same right to speak that you wish for yourself.
   demonstrating, 24
   engaging productively with others, 18–30

response, getting and giving, 86–87, 121
   analyses, 162–63
   arguments, 201–2
   to a design, 798–99
   narratives, 236–37
   peer review, 124–36
   proposals, 368–69
   reflections, 162–63
   reports, 325–26
   reviews, 368–69
   writing process, 121
restrictive element. *See* essential element

RÉSUMÉ A GENRE that summarizes someone's academic and employment history, generally written to submit to potential employers. design and word choice depend on whether a résumé is submitted as a print or digital document. Features: an ORGANIZATION that suits goals and experience • succinctness • a DESIGN that highlights key information and only uses one font

REVIEW, 348–77 A writing GENRE that makes a judgment about something—a film, book, product, restaurant, etc.—based on certain CRITERIA. Features: relevant background information about the subject • criteria for the evaluation • a well-supported evaluation • attention to the AUDIENCE's needs and expectations • an authoritative tone • awareness of the ethics of reviewing. *See also* LITERATURE REVIEW
    across academic disciplines, 350
    across cultures and communities, 351–52
    across genres, 352
    across media, 350–51
    annotated examples
        "*Guts (spilled)* by Olivia Rodrigo: An Album for the Ages," 374–77
        "*Thirsty Suitors*: I Feel Seen by This Game," 370–73
    characteristic features, 352–63
    documenting in APA style, 650, 652
    documenting in MLA style, 601
    roadmap to writing a review, 364–69

REVISION, 121–22 The process of making substantive changes, including additions and cuts, to a draft so that it contains all the necessary information in an effective ORGANIZATION. During revision, a writer generally moves from whole-text issues to details with the goals of sharpening the focus and strengthening the ARGUMENT.
    analyses, 284–85
    arguments, 201–2
    narratives, 236–37
    proposals, 394–95
    reflections, 162–63
    reports, 325–26

    reviews, 368–69
    writing process, 121–22

Rheingold, Howard, 64–65

RHETORIC, 2–61 One of the three original disciplines in the ancient world (along with grammar and logic), rhetoric has been defined in many ways through the centuries. In this book, we define it as the art, practice, and theory of ethical communication.
    language, power, and, 39–50
    need for, 2–61
    reading rhetorically, 64–75
    rhetorical situations, 31–38
    thinking rhetorically, 4–17

RHETORICAL ANALYSIS, 260–64, 279 A kind of ANALYSIS that takes a close look at how a text communicates a message to an AUDIENCE.

RHETORICAL LISTENING, 8, 19 A way of listening that is open-minded, accepting, and respectful—of listening to what others say as a way of understanding their perspectives and demonstrating respect for their views.

RHETORICAL SITUATION, 31–38, 66–67, 117–18 The circumstances that affect writing or other communication, including PURPOSE, AUDIENCE, GENRE, STANCE, CONTEXT, MEDIA, and DESIGN.
    considering accessibility, 783–84
    considering your rhetorical situation
        analyses, 276–78
        arguments, 196–97
        design, 783
        multimodal writing, 802–3
        narratives, 232–34
        presentations, 831–32
        proposals, 390–92
        reflections, 157–58
        reports, 320–22
        research, 488–89
        reviews, 364–66

rhetorical situation *(cont.)*
  elements of
    audience, 35–36
    context, 36
    genre, 34–35
    language, 37
    medium / design, 37–38
    purpose, 34
    stance, 36
  language choices and, 48

ROGERIAN ARGUMENTS, 455–56 A system of argument based on the work of Carl Rogers that stresses fairness and compromise and persuasion by nonconfrontational strategies such as showing respect and establishing common ground. The introduction presents the issue fairly, the body discusses various positions on the issue including the author's own, and the conclusion presents a resolution.

Rosenblatt, Louise, 68

S

sacred texts, documenting in MLA style, 585, 606
Sainani, Kristin, 438–39
Salesforce, "The March" ad, *12*
samples, in field research
  random, 519
  representative, 519
San Antonio Independent School District, *307,* 308
sans serif typefaces, 784
sarcasm, argument and, 474–75
schedules, 493–94
Schmittgens, Annie, 154
scholarly sources, 498–99, *500*
Science Buddies, 266–67
searches, 511–12. *See also* KEYWORD
  keyword searches, 511–12
search sites, 505–6

SECONDARY SOURCE, 497–98 An ANALYSIS or interpretation of a PRIMARY SOURCE. In writing about the Revolutionary War, a researcher would probably consider the Declaration of Independence a primary source and a textbook's description of how the document was written a secondary source.

Selfe, Cynthia, 800–801
self-representation, 14
semicolons, 559, 719, 740, 743
sentences, 736–47
  closing, 727–29
  comma splices, 739–41
  cumulative, 722–23
  emphasizing main idea, 722–25
  fused, 742–44
  mixed constructions, 744–47
  opening, 725–27
  periodic, 724–25
  sentence fragments, 737–39
  varying, 729–33
serif typefaces, 784
setting, 222–23
setting up a straw man, 443
Sharpton, Al, 481
The Shelter Pet Project ad, *476*
shifts in tense, 760–63
Shockley, William, 691

SIGNAL PHRASE, 564–65, 765, 767–68 A phrase used to attribute quoted, paraphrased, or summarized material to a source, as in "she said" or "he claimed."

signal verbs, 564–65, 638

SIGNIFYING, 482–83 A STRATEGY FOR SUPPORTING AN ARGUMENT by underscoring something true or important through humor, satire, and indirection.

SIGNPOST LANGUAGE, 826, 832 Words and phrases meant to help listeners follow an oral presentation. Some functions of signpost language include introducing or concluding a presentation ("My topic today is . . ."), providing an overview ("I will make three major points"), or marking transitions ("My third and final point is . . .").

SIMPLE SENTENCE, 717 A single MAIN CLAUSE, which contains at least a SUBJECT and a VERB. The main clause must stand alone: Citizens vote. The United

States holds a presidential election once every four years. For sentences with more than a single main clause, *see* COMPOUND SENTENCE; COMPOUND-COMPLEX SENTENCE; COMPLEX SENTENCE.

SIMPLE SUBJECT, 758, 759 The word that determines the form of the VERB: The young <u>farmer</u> from Ten Barn Farm has the best tomatoes at the market. The simple subject is "farmer," a singular NOUN; for that reason, the verb "has" is singular.

"since," 720

SINGULAR "THEY," 736, 753–54 The use of "they," "them," and "their" to refer to a person whose gender is unknown or not relevant to the context. Traditionally, "they" has referred only to plural items, but the use of singular "they" is now becoming more accepted.

slippery slope fallacy, 444
slow reading, 68–69
Snapchat, 138, 328, *329*, 332, 816
Snopes, 102, 103, 105, 507
social media, 109, 172, 194, 205–8, 286–90, 506
    asking permission to cite sources from, 569–70
    #blacklivesmatter, 5
    documenting in APA style, 663–64
    documenting in MLA style, 610
    for finding sources, 506–7
    #metoo, 5
    #plasticfree, 5
    posts and campaigns on, 815–17
    as sources, 498
    style, 698–99
software, computer programs, or apps,
    documenting in APA style, 662
solutions
    acknowledging other possible, 385–86
    clear and compelling, 384
sound recordings, documenting in MLA style, 616
sources, 495–535
    acknowledging, 569–70
    bias and, 532
    citing, 568–77
    considering alternative perspectives, 532–33

    credibility of, 529
    crediting, 568–77
    documenting. *See* APA STYLE; MLA STYLE
    evaluating, 528–35
    fact-checking and triangulating, 531–32
    finding, 495–512
    incorporating, 563–67
        deciding whether to quote, paraphrase, or summarize, 555–56
        paraphrasing, 560–61, 563–67
        quoting, 556–60, 563–67
        summarizing, 561–63
    interviews, 515–18
    keeping track, 523–27
    observations, 514–15
    older vs. current, 499–501
    paraphrasing, 560–61
    primary vs. secondary, 497–98
    quoting, 556–60
    reading critically, 533–35
    reading laterally, 529–31
    research sites, 505–10
    scholarly vs. popular, 498–99, *500*
    searches, 511–12
        keyword searches, 511–12
    social media, 505
    summarizing, 561–63
    surveys, 518–22
    synthesizing, 541–53
    trustworthy, 102–3
    types of, 501–3
        audio, 566
        books, 502
        electronic, 523–24
        government and legal documents, 503
        oral forms of knowledge, 504
        periodicals, 502–3
        primary and historical documents, 504
        reference works, 501–2
    visual, 567
spacing
    APA style, 665
    MLA style, 617

SPATIAL ORGANIZATION, 324 A way of ordering a text that mirrors the physical arrangement of the subject, for instance from top to bottom, left to right, outside to inside.

speech, recording of, documenting in APA style, 662
Spelman College, 164, 215, 356
spoken texts, 38, 73–74
SPORTDiscus, 511
sports coverage, 218, *219*
Spotify, 245

STANCE, 10–11, 36 An author's attitude toward the subject—for example, reasonable, neutral, angry, curious. Stance is conveyed through tone and word choice.
    analytical writing, 313–14, 341

STANDARDIZED ENGLISH, 690–92, 705 The variety of English used in most institutions in the United States, such as schools, governments, business, and industries, often to the point of excluding or silencing other varieties of the LANGUAGE. Standardized English also represents conventions of spelling, grammar, and punctuation expected in academic discourse, which tends to be more formal than conversational English.
    and critical language awareness, 45–47
    and editing, 735

Stanford University, 101, 385–86, 438, 667
Star Trek, 690, *690*

STASIS MODEL, 427–29 A simple system for identifying the crux of an ARGUMENT—what's at stake in it—by asking four questions: (1) What are the facts? (2) How can the issue be defined? (3) How much does it matter, and why? (4) What actions should be taken as a result?

statistics, as evidence, 435–36
Stein, Ross, 446
Stevens, Dana, 358

STORYBOARD, 810–11, *811* A series of sketches used in planning a film or video essay to map out the sequence of camera shots, movement, and action.

STRATEGIES FOR SUPPORTING AN ARGUMENT, 461–83 Patterns for organizing and providing evidence to support a POSITION: ANALOGY, CALL AND RESPONSE, CAUSE AND EFFECT, CLASSIFICATION, COMPARISON AND CONTRAST, DEFINITION, DESCRIPTION, EXAMPLE, NARRATION, NARRATIVE SEQUENCING, PROBLEM AND SOLUTION, and REITERATION.
    analogy, 461–63
    call and response, 479–82
    cause and effect, 463–65
    classification, 465–66
    comparison and contrast, 466–69
    definition, 469–71
    description, 471–73
    exaggeration, 474–75
    examples, 473
    humor, 474–75
    narration, 475–78
    narrative sequencing, 475–78
    problem and solution, 478–79
    reiteration, 479–82
    repetition, 479–82
    sarcasm, 474–75
    signifying, 482–83

straw man fallacy, 443
Street Roots, 384

STYLE, 686–777 The particular way something is written or communicated that includes all the elements—such as sentence structure, TONE, and word choice—that make the communication distinctive.
    academic writing and, 51–61, 700–701
    argument and, 459–60
    connecting with audiences, 692–94
    defined, 688–702
    design, 619–34
    formality, 694–95
    personal, 701–2
    powerful sentences, 715–33
    sentence style, 715–33
    stance, 695–97
    suitability and correctness, 689–92
    tone, 697–98

style guides. *See* APA STYLE; MLA STYLE

SUBJECT, 757–60 A word or word group, usually including at least one NOUN or PRONOUN plus its modifiers, that tells who or what a sentence or CLAUSE is about. In the sentence "A frustrated group of commuters waited for the late bus," the subject is "A frustrated group of commuters."
    sentence fragment, 737–38
    subjects consisting of more than one word, 759–60
    subject-verb agreement, 757–60

subject case, 754–56
subject librarians, 507
subject-specific databases, 510

SUBJECT-VERB AGREEMENT, 757–60 The agreement in number (singular or plural) and person (first, second, or third) of a SUBJECT and its VERB: Danny rides his bike to school; his brothers ride the bus.

SUBORDINATE CLAUSE, 720–21, 737, 746 A clause that begins with a SUBORDINATING WORD and therefore cannot stand alone as a sentence: She feels good when she exercises. My roommate, who was a physics major, tutors students in science.

SUBORDINATING WORD, 720, 741, 743–44 A word or phrase, such as "because," "in order that," and "while" that introduces a SUBORDINATE CLAUSE: The ice sculpture melted because the room for the wedding reception was too warm.

success, habits for academic, 53–55
suitability, 689–92
summarizing, 555–56, 561–63
    as a reading strategy, 83–85

SUMMARY, 554–56, 561–63 The use of one's own words and sentence structure to condense someone else's text into a version that gives the main ideas of the original. As with paraphrasing and quoting, summarizing requires DOCUMENTATION.
    deciding whether to quote, paraphrase, or summarize, 555–56
    signal phrases and, 564–65

summary / response essays, 90–96
    annotated example
        "The Higher Price of Buying Local," 93–96
    characteristic features, 90–91
Super Mario Bros. 3, 804–5, *804*
Surf Market, *693*, 694
SurveyMonkey, 519
surveys
    as evidence, 436–37
    in field research, 519–22
Sustainability, 499, *500*

SYNTAX, 687 Sentence structure.

SYNTHESIZING IDEAS, 541–53, *542* Bringing together ideas and information from multiple sources, exploring patterns in order to discover new insights and perspectives.
    literature reviews, 547–48
        annotated example
            "Exploring the Hardships and Stigma Students with Invisible Disabilities Face," 549–53
    sources in, 542–45
    your own ideas, 543–45

T

tables, 789, 790, *791*
    APA style, 667
    documenting, 566
    MLA style, 619
Taylor, Elizabeth AIDS Foundation, 424
teamwork, 110, 124–30
technology, 3
TED.com, 488
television programs
    documenting in APA style, 661
    documenting in MLA style, 613–14

TENSE A characteristic of VERBS that indicates the time when action occurs or expresses a state of being. The three main tenses are the present (I play), the past (I played), and the future (I will play).

Each tense has perfect (I have played), progressive (I am playing), and perfect progressive (I have been playing) forms. *See also* VERB
- with APA style, 761–63
- with MLA style, 761, 762
- past perfect, 762
- past tense, 761–62
- present perfect, 761
- present tense, 761
- shifts in, 760–63

tentative thesis, 118–19
testimony, as evidence, 439
text message, documenting in MLA style, 610
texts
- difficult, 69–70
- digital, 38, 70–73
- print, 70–74
- sacred, 585, 606
- spoken, 38, 73–74
- unfamiliar, 69–70
- visual, 71–73, 72

"therefore," 719
"there" / "their" / "they're," 774–76
thesauruses, 656

THESIS, 57, 199, 424–25 A statement that identifies the topic and main point of a piece of writing, giving readers an idea of what the text will cover.
- plotting out a working thesis, 493
- tentative, 118–19, 199–200

"they," 748–49
- singular, 753–54

"they're" / "there" / "their," 774–76

THINKING RHETORICALLY, 4–17, Listening to others with an open mind, trying to understand what they think and why—and then examining your own beliefs and where they come from, before deciding what you yourself think.
- about design, 781–84
- being imaginative, 13–14
- considering alternative points of view, 9
- giving credit, 12–13
- listening, 7–8

This American Life, 807, 809
This I Believe, 807
Thistle, 71–73, *72*
Thunberg, Greta, 316–19, *318*
TikTok
- and argument, 411
- influence of, 182
- mixing language and dialects on, 704
- narratives on, 218
- posts and campaigns on, 807
- and research, 505, 506
- and style, 698–99

Tin Eye, 105

TITLE The name of something—a book, article, film, newspaper, podcast, work of art—or your essay! A good, memorable title indicates what the piece is about and gets an audience's attention and interest. Words in titles are usually capitalized, with the exception of prepositions and conjunctions. Long works (like books, films, magazines, and long musical works) are usually italicized, while shorter ones (like articles, short stories, and your essays) are generally set in quotation marks.
- APA style, 644–45
- MLA style, 589

title pages
- APA style, 665
- MLA style, 617

TONE, 36 A writer's or speaker's attitude toward the audience and subject. Tone reflects the writer's STANCE: critical, playful, reasonable, ironic, and so on.
- authoritative, 193–94, 360–62
- confident and informative, 315
- effective, 697–98

top5projectmanagement.com, 821

topic
    choosing, 117, 364, 487
    narrowing, in research, 489–90
    research for, 487–88
    for specific genres
        analyses, 276
        arguments, 195, 197–98
        narratives, 234
        profiles, 316
        project proposals, 388–89
        proposals, 390
        reports, 310–13, 320, 322–23
        reviews, 364

TOPIC SENTENCE, 56 A sentence, often at the beginning of a paragraph, that states the paragraph's main point. The details in the rest of the paragraph should support the topic sentence.

Tosh, Peter, 706

TOULMIN ARGUMENT, 453–55 A system of ARGUMENT developed by Stephen Toulmin that features a qualified CLAIM; REASONS and EVIDENCE in support of the claim; underlying assumptions that aren't explicitly stated but that also support the claim; further evidence or backing for those underlying assumptions; and a CONCLUSION.

TRANSFER, 155 The process of applying the strategies, ideas, practices, and processes learned in one context to a new situation.

TRANSITION, 719 A word or PHRASE that helps to connect sentences and paragraphs and to guide readers through a text. Transitions can show COMPARISONS (also, similarly, likewise, in the same way); CONTRASTS (but, instead, although, however, nonetheless); EXAMPLES (for instance, in fact, such as); place or position (above, beyond, near, elsewhere); sequence (finally, next, again, also); SUMMARY or conclusion (on the whole, as we have seen, in brief); time (at first, meanwhile, so far, later); and more.
    in academic writing, 56, 57

translations, 707–8
    documenting in APA style, 648
    documenting in MLA style, 593
triangulation, 531–32
Trump, Donald, 444, 671
TV show episode, documenting in MLA style, 613–14
Twitter. See X
Tyler, Adrienne, 258–59
typeface, 784–85
    APA style, 665
    MLA style, 617
typography, 784–85

U

underlining, 784
United Nations Intergovernmental Panel on Climate Change, 192
University of Maryland, 53, 114, 817, *818*
University of Texas at Austin, 386–88
U.S. News & World Report, 310, 314, 315, 356

V

values, appealing to readers', 194

VERB, 757–63 A word that expresses an action (dance, talk) or a state of being (be, seem). A verb is an ESSENTIAL ELEMENT of a sentence or CLAUSE. Verbs have four forms: base form (smile), past tense (smiled), past participle (smiled), and present participle (smiling). *See also* HELPING VERB; IRREGULAR VERB; TENSE
    APA style, 761–63
    common errors, 756–63
    editing, 756–63
    MLA style, 761, 762
    sentence fragment, 738
    signal verbs, 564–65
    subject-verb agreement, 757–60

verb tenses, 565, 760–63
    with APA style, 761–63

verb *(cont.)*
    with MLA style, 761, 762
    past perfect, 762
    past tense, 761–62
    present perfect, 565, 761
    present tense, 565, 761
    shifts in, 760–62
verse plays, documenting in MLA style, 584
video essays, 809–12
video games, documenting in MLA style, 617
videos
    distinguishing facts from misinformation in, 105–6
    documenting in APA style, 659–60
    documenting in MLA style, 614
    and narratives, 218
    quoting, 566
    and reports, 305–6
vinyl LP, documenting in MLA style, 616
violence, 4
virtual presentations, documenting in MLA style, 615

VISUAL ANALYSIS, 272–75 A GENRE of writing that examines an image, video, or some other visual text and how it communicates a message to an AUDIENCE. Features: a DESCRIPTION of the visual • some contextual information • attention to any words • close ANALYSIS of the message • insight into what the visual "says" • precise language
    annotated examples
        "Advertisements R Us," 297–302
        "What Is the Invisible Problem with *TikTok*?," 286–91
    characteristic features of, 272–75

visuals, 787–95
    creating, 794
    definition and, 470–71
    description and, 471–73
    diagrams, 792, 794
    as evidence, 441
    graphs, charts, and tables, 789–90, 794
    incorporating, 567
    infographics, 792, *793*
    introducing, 795
    labeling, 795
    maps, 790, *791*, 794
    photographs, 788–89, *788*, 794
    tables, *790*, 791
    videos, 789, 794
visual texts, 71–73, *72*
vivid details, 74, 224, 241

W

Washington Post, 95, 360
Watson, James, 14–16
webinars, recording of, documenting in APA style, 662
webpage, documenting in APA style, 652–53, *653*
websites. *See also* online sources
    composing and remixing on, 805–7
    documenting in MLA style, 607–9, *609*
web sources, in working bibliography, 527
West Side Story (film), 361–62, *361*
"which," 749–50

WIKI A website format, often consisting of many linked pages on related topics, that allows readers to add, edit, delete, or otherwise change the site's content.
    documenting in APA style, 659
    documenting in MLA style, 608
    as sources, 501

Wikipedia
    documenting in APA style, 659
    documenting in MLA style, 608
    in research, 491, 496, 501, 505
Williams, Riquna, *492*
Windows Live Movie Maker, 811
Winfrey, Oprah, 730, *731*
Wired, 499, *500*
Word, 789

WORKING BIBLIOGRAPHY, 526–27 A record of all sources consulted during research. Each entry provides all the bibliographic information necessary for correct DOCUMENTATION of each source, including author, title, and publication information. A working bibliography is a useful tool for recording and keeping track of sources.

working thesis, 493

WORKS CITED, 588–619 The list of full bibliographic information, for all the sources cited in the text, which appears at the end of a researched text prepared in MLA STYLE. *See also* bibliographies
    annotated example, 634

writing analytically, 252–302. *See also* ANALYSIS
writing processes, 108–67
    navigating AI, 137–50
    navigating the writing process, 110–23
    reflecting on your writing, 151–67
    roadmap to writing process, 117–23

X

X (formerly *Twitter*)
    documenting in APA style, 663
    documenting in MLA style, 610
    misinformation, 97–98

Y

"yet," 718
YouTube, 3, 24, 36, 124, 170, 272, 305, 311, 496, 506, 567, 704
    fabricated videos, 106
    mixing language and dialects on, 704
    posts and campaigns on, 816
    and research, 496, 506

Z

"ze" / "hir" / "hirs," 753
Zoom, 33, 812
Zoom presentation, documenting in MLA style, 615
Zotero, 523

About the Authors

BEVERLY J. MOSS is Professor and Director of Second-Year Writing in the Department of English at The Ohio State University, where she teaches in the Rhetoric, Composition, and Literacy program, and is Director of the Bread Loaf Teacher Network for the Middlebury Bread Loaf School of English. Her research and teaching interests focus on community literacy, composition theory and pedagogy, and writing center theories and practices. Her books include *Literacy across Communities* and *A Community Text Arises: A Literate Text and a Literacy Tradition in African-American Churches*.

ANDREA LUNSFORD is Professor Emerita of English at Stanford University and has also taught at the University of British Columbia, The Ohio State University, and the Bread Loaf School of English. Her scholarly interests include rhetorical theory, women and the history of rhetoric, collaboration, style, and technologies of writing. She's received the Braddock and Shaughnessy awards for her research on audience and classical rhetoric, and the CCCC Exemplar Award. She and coeditor Susan Jarratt are currently completing *The Norton Anthology of Rhetoric and Writing*.

MICHAL BRODY is a linguist and independent scholar. She was a founding faculty member of the Universidad de Oriente in Yucatán, Mexico. Her scholarly work centers principally on language pedagogy and politics in the United States and Mexico, as well as on sociolinguistic research on Yucatec Maya. In addition to linguistics courses, she has taught English, Spanish, and Yucatec Maya language courses in the United States and Mexico. She's a coauthor of *The Little Seagull Handbook* and *Let's Talk with Readings*. Brody is a 2008 inductee in the Chicago LGBT Hall of Fame.

JESSICA ENOCH is Professor of English and Director of the Academic Writing Program at the University of Maryland. Her recent publications include *Domestic Occupations: Spatial Rhetorics and Women's Work*; *Mestiza Rhetorics: An Anthology of Mexicana Activism in the Spanish-Language Press, 1887–1922* (coedited with Cristina Devereaux Ramírez); *Women at Work: Rhetorics of Gender and Labor* (coedited with David Gold); and *Retellings: Opportunities for Feminist Research in Rhetoric and Composition Studies* (coedited with Jordynn Jack).

CAROLE CLARK PAPPER spent four decades teaching writing and rhetoric. Prior to retiring from Hofstra University, where she directed the University Writing Center, she served for many years as the Director of the Ball State University Writing Program (winner of the CCCC Certificate of Excellence 2006–2007). Although retired, she continues her scholarly interests in visual literacy, composition theory and pedagogy, and writing center theories and practices.

WITH CONTRIBUTIONS FROM

ANNETTE VEE is Associate Professor of English at the University of Pittsburgh, where she teaches courses in writing, computation, and literacy, and recently served six years as the Director of Composition. Dr. Vee frequently gives workshops, keynotes, and advice about AI to faculty, students, and higher-ed administrators. She is the inaugural facilitator of the AI across the Disciplines program at the University of Pittsburgh. She is the author of *Coding Literacy: How Computer Programming Is Changing Writing*, coeditor of *TextGenEd: Teaching with Text Generation Technologies* (with Tim Laquintano and Carly Schnitzler), and coauthor of *The Norton Guide to AI-Aware Teaching*.

About the Alphabet

If you grew up in the United States, the alphabet song may be one of the first things you learned to sing: *a - b - c - d - e - f - g / h - i - j - k - l - m - n - o - p / q - r - s / t - u - v / w - x / y and z / Now I know my abc's / Next time won't you sing with me?* And maybe you had a set of alphabet blocks, twenty-six little letters you could use to make words of your own. Combined, those letters yield everything from the word "Google" to the complete modernized works of Shakespeare. So alphabets are versatile, and perhaps that's part of their fascination. In our grandmothers' day, young women often made alphabet samplers, using fancy stitches to create the letters. Earlier, in medieval times, scribes labored to create highly ornate letters to adorn manuscripts whose words were "illuminated" by the intricate letters, often done in silver and gold.

We had these illuminated letters in mind when we asked Carin Berger to create a modern-day illuminated alphabet for this book. You'll see the results in every chapter, each of which begins with one of the letters Berger created. To us, they represent our old alphabet blocks, our grandmothers' samplers, and the illuminated letters that still dazzle us after many hundreds of years. But look again and you'll see that these letters are also striking images. And instead of being decorated with precious silver and gold leaf, our letters are decorated with bits of everyday text—maps, comics, stationery, receipts, school papers, checks, and so on. In our alphabet, old and new, low tech and high tech, word and image come together to create evocative, timely letters for our book.

And just as modern-day typefaces have names, so too does our alphabet. We call it Author.

The Norton Writer's Prize

I have something to say to the world, and I have taken English 12 in order to say it well.

—W. E. B. DU BOIS

The Norton Writer's Prize recognizes outstanding original nonfiction by undergraduates. All entries are considered for possible publication in Norton texts—in fact, many of the essays that appear in this book were nominated for the prize.

The contest is open to students age 18 and above who are enrolled in an accredited 2- or 4-year college or university. Three cash prizes of $1,000 apiece are awarded annually for coursework submitted during the academic year, one in each of the following three categories:

- Writing by a first-year student in a 2- or 4-year college or university
- Writing by a student in a 2-year college or university
- Writing by a student in a 4-year college or university

Submissions must be between 1,000 and 3,000 words in length. Literacy narratives, literary and other textual analyses, reports, profiles, evaluations, arguments, memoirs, proposals, multimodal pieces, and other forms of original nonfiction will be considered if written by a student age 18 or above in fulfillment of an undergraduate course requirement at an eligible institution. Entries submitted in accordance with the Official Contest Rules will be considered for all applicable prizes, but no more than one prize will be awarded to any single entry.

For full contest rules, eligibility, and instructions on how to enter or nominate students, please visit wwnorton.com/norton-writers-prize. For questions, please email us at nortonwritersprize@wwnorton.com.

Current and former students of individuals acting as judges are not eligible to enter or win, and any entry recognized by any of the judges will be automatically disqualified. Employees of W. W. Norton & Company, Inc. ("Sponsor"), including Sponsor's corporate affiliates and subsidiaries, as well as such individuals' children and persons living in any of their households are not eligible to enter; nor are authors published by Sponsor, children of Sponsor's authors, previous contest winners (including runners-up) and persons living in their respective households. Void where prohibited. Must be 18 or older at the time of entry. Other restrictions apply.

MLA DOCUMENTATION DIRECTORY

MLA In-Text Documentation

1. Author named in a signal phrase *581*
2. Author named in parentheses *581*
3. Two or more works by the same author *582*
4. Authors with the same last name *582*
5. Two or more authors *582*
6. Organization or government as author *583*
7. Author unknown *583*
8. Literary works *583*
9. Work in an anthology *584*
10. Encyclopedia or dictionary *584*
11. Legal documents *585*
12. Sacred text *585*
13. Multivolume work *585*
14. Two or more works cited together *585*
15. Source quoted in another source *586*
16. Work without page numbers *586*
17. An entire work or a one-page article *587*
18. Generative AI *587*

MLA List of Works Cited

Core Elements *588*

Authors and Contributors *592*

1. One author *592*
2. Two authors *592*
3. Three or more authors *593*
4. Two or more works by the same author *593*
5. Author and editor or translator *593*
6. No author or editor *594*
7. Organization or government as author *594*

Articles and Other Short Works *594*

Documentation Maps 596, 597, 599

8. Article in a journal *595*
9. Article in a magazine *595*
10. Article in a news publication *598*
11. Article accessed through a database *598*
12. Entry in a reference work *600*
13. Editorial or op-ed *600*
14. Letter to the editor *601*
15. Review *601*
16. Comment on an online article *602*

Books and Parts of Books *602*

Documentation Map 603

17. Basic entries for a book *602*
18. Anthology or edited collection *604*
19. Work in an anthology *604*
20. Multivolume work *604*
21. Book in a series *605*
22. Graphic narrative or comic book *605*
23. Sacred text *606*
24. Edition other than the first *606*
25. Republished work *606*
26. Foreword, introduction, preface, or afterword *606*
27. Published letter *606*
28. Paper heard at a conference *607*
29. Dissertation *607*

Websites *607*

Documentation Map 609

30. Entire website *608*
31. Work on a website *608*
32. Blog entry *608*
33. Wiki *608*

Personal Communication and Social Media *610*

34. Personal letter *610*
35. Email or text message *610*
36. Post to *Instagram* or other social media *610*

Audio, Visual, and Other Sources *611*

37. Advertisement *611*
38. Art *611*
39. Cartoon *612*
40. Supreme Court case *612*
41. Film *612*
42. TV show episode *613*
43. Online video *614*
44. Interview *614*
45. Map *615*
46. Musical score *615*
47. Oral presentation *615*
48. Virtual presentation on *Zoom* or other platform *615*
49. Podcast *615*
50. Radio program *616*
51. Sound recording *616*
52. Video game *616*
53. Generative AI *617*

APA DOCUMENTATION DIRECTORY

APA In-Text Documentation

1. Author named in a signal phrase *638*
2. Author named in parentheses *638*
3. Authors with the same last name *639*
4. Two authors *639*
5. Three or more authors *639*
6. Organization or government as author *639*
7. Author unknown *640*
8. Two or more works together *640*
9. Two or more works by one author in the same year *640*
10. Source quoted in another source *640*
11. Work without page numbers *641*
12. An entire work *641*
13. Personal communication *641*
14. Generative AI *642*

APA Reference List

Key Elements *643*

Authors and Other Contributors *646*

1. One author *646*
2. Two authors *646*
3. Three or more authors *646*
4. Two or more works by the same author *647*
5. Author and editor *647*
6. Author and translator *648*
7. Editor *648*
8. Unknown or no author or editor *648*
9. Organization or government as author *648*

Articles and Other Short Works *649*

Documentation Maps 651, 653

10. Article in a journal *649*
11. Article in a magazine *649*
12. Article in a newspaper *649*
13. Article on a news website *650*
14. Journal article from a database *650*
15. Editorial *650*
16. Review *650*
17. Comment on an online article or post *652*
18. Webpage *652*

Books, Parts of Books, and Reports *654*

Documentation Map 655

19. Basic entry for a book *654*
20. Edition other than the first *654*
21. Edited collection or anthology *654*
22. Work in an edited collection or anthology *656*
23. Entry in a reference work (dictionary, thesaurus, or encyclopedia) *656*
24. Book in a language other than English *656*
25. One volume of a multivolume work *656*
26. Religious work *657*
27. Report by a government agency or other organization *657*
28. Published dissertation *658*
29. Paper or poster presented at a conference *658*

Audio, Visual, and Other Sources *658*

30. *Wikipedia* entry *659*
31. Online forum post *659*
32. Blog post *659*
33. Online streaming video *659*
34. Podcast *660*
35. Podcast episode *660*
36. Film *660*
37. Television series *661*
38. Television series episode *661*
39. Music album *661*
40. Song *661*
41. Software, computer program, or mobile app *662*
42. Lecture slides or notes *662*
43. Recording of a speech or webinar *662*
44. Map *663*
45. Social media posts *663*
46. Data set *664*
47. Supreme Court case *664*
48. Generative AI *664*

Menu of Readings

CÉSAR ALBARRÁN-TORRES, Multilingual TV Is Good for Everyone 838
KATE ARONOFF, Carbon Offsets (Taylor's Version) 843
LINDA BARRY, The Sanctuary of School 849
CHRISTOPHER BASGIER, AI Is Like Cake 855
*ANNAYA BAYNES, Becoming the Writer I Am 164
ALISON BECHDEL, Fun Home 859
*JENNA BLOOM, I Quit Social Media 870
DANIELLE K. BROWN, Media Coverage of Campus Protests Focuses on Spectacle 876
DANA CANEDY, The Talk: After Ferguson... 883
CHARLOTTE CLYMER, They Called Me a Girl 888
ADAM CLARK ESTES, Your TV Is Watching You 893
JEFF GAGE, Country Music & the Opioid Crisis 899
*PALOMA GARCIA, First Day of School 249
*GLAVEE GLAVEE, Black Enough 905
*KENNEDI L. GOODE-BEY, Olivia Rodrigo's *Guts*: A Review 374
ANNETTE GORDON-REED, Origin Stories 915
*MCCADE GOWDY, Omaha's Hope 334
JONATHAN HOLLOWAY, Unite a Divided America 403
RUSSEL HONORÉ, Work Is a Blessing 203
LING LING HUANG, How I Escaped the Prophets of Beauty 923
KEVIN M. KEARNEY, One Star 927
RAYA ELFADEL KHEIRBEK, Healing the Doctor-Patient Relationship 238
ROBIN WALL KIMMERER, Strawberries 932
SWAPNA KRISHNA, *Thirsty Suitors*: I Feel Seen by This Game 370
BILL LAITNER, Walking 21 Miles to Work 341
*ALEKSANDER LAM, Sampling or Stealing? 209
KEREN LANDMAN, Whole Body Deodorants Are Everywhere 938
KIESE LAYMON, My Favorite Restaurant Served Gas 946
VIVEK H. MURTHY, Social Media Platforms Need Warning Labels 205
JUDITH NEWMAN, To Siri, with Love 952
*ANGELINA X. NG, It'll Grow Back. It Always Does. 244
NOTT / CAMBO, Our Labor Built AI 960
MEGHAN O'GIEBLYN, Am I Still Human? 967
*WALTER PRZYBYLOWSKI, Holding Up the Hollywood Stagecoach 620
MIKE ROSE, Blue-Collar Brilliance 972
*MELISSA RUBIN, Advertisements R Us 297
TATE RYAN-MOSLEY, Beauty Filters Perpetuate Colorism 327
SHAAN SACHDEV, The Key to Beyoncé's Success 292
*SYDNEY SALLMAN, The Invisible Problem with *TikTok* 286
ALLY SHWED, Cracking the Color Code 982
ZEYNEP TUFEKCI, The Post Office Makes America Great 989
*GABRIELA A. URIBE, "¿Por qué no sabes español?" 668
JOSE ANTONIO VARGAS, My Life as an Undocumented Immigrant 993
*EMI VAUGHAN, AI in the Criminal Justice System 396
TATÉ WALKER, The (Native) American Dream 1003
MISSY WATSON, Contesting Standardized English 1010

Readings by Genre

Analysis

DANIELLE K. BROWN, Media Coverage of Campus Protests Focuses on Spectacle 876
KEVIN M. KEARNEY, One Star 927
MIKE ROSE, Blue-Collar Brilliance 972
*MELISSA RUBIN, Advertisements R Us 297
SHAAN SACHDEV, The Key to Beyoncé's Success 292
*SYDNEY SALLMAN, The Invisible Problem with *TikTok* 286

Argument

CÉSAR ALBARRÁN-TORRES, Multilingual TV Is Good for Everyone 838
CHRISTOPHER BASGIER, AI Is Like Cake 855
DANIELLE K. BROWN, Media Coverage of Campus Protests Focuses on Spectacle 876
JEFF GAGE, Country Music & the Opioid Crisis 899
*GLAVEE GLAVEE, Black Enough 905
ANNETTE GORDON-REED, Origin Stories 915
RUSSEL HONORÉ, Work Is a Blessing 203
*ALEKSANDER LAM, Sampling or Stealing? 209
VIVEK H. MURTHY, Social Media Platforms Need Warning Labels 205
NOTT / CAMBO, Our Labor Built AI 960
MEGHAN O'GIEBLYN, Am I Still Human? 967
ZEYNEP TUFEKCI, The Post Office Makes America Great 989
*YULIYA VAYNER, The Higher Price of Buying Local 93
MISSY WATSON, Contesting Standardized English 1010

*Student writing